Mainstream Mathematics for GCSE

Duncan Graham, BSc, BSc (Hons), MSc
and
Christine Graham, BEd (Hons)

MACMILLAN

First published 1996 by
MACMILLAN PRESS LTD
Houndmills, Basingstoke, Hampshire RG21 6XS
and London
Companies and representatives
throughout the world

ISBN 0–333–57878–3

A catalogue record for this book is available
from the British Library.
10   9   8   7   6   5   4   3   2   1
05   04   03   02   01   00   99   98   97   96

Printed in Hong Kong

Acknowledgements
The authors wish to thank the many students who have helped them in the
planning and writing of this textbook. Special thanks go to Nichola Klampfer
for transcribing many of the Units and to Richard Westman for transcribing
many of the Units and working through the numerous Exercises and
Examination questions, to check answers.

The authors and publishers would like to thank the following sources for the
use of illustrations: Casio Electronics Co. Ltd for the calculator photo on p.
278; ISL Worldwide for the World Cup 94 logo on p.353;
The author and publishers wish to thank the following for permission to use
copyright material: The Midland Examining Group, The Northern Examinations
and Assessment Board (incorporating Northern Examining Association and the
Joint Matriculation Board), Northern Ireland Schools Examination Council,
Southern Examining Group, University of London Examinations and
Assessment Council, and the Welsh Joint Education Committee for questions
from past examination papers.

Every effort has been made to trace all the copyright holders but if any have
been inadvertently overlooked the publishers will be pleased to make the
necessary arrangements at the first opportunity.

Contents

About this book

Mainstream Mathematics for GCSE has been written for use on a 2-year or a 1-year GCSE mathematics course. It was designed primarily as a textbook for 'mainstream' students intending to take Intermediate tier examinations but students on Higher tier courses will also find it useful.

The contents of this book are based on the revised National Curriculum documents published by SEAC in 1995 (following the Dearing Report). These documents provide the guidelines for GCSE examination from 1997 onwards.

The special format of this textbook has been planned carefully to make it easy to use by both teacher and student. Here are some key factors of its order and layout.

How the book is arranged

The work in this book has been arranged into **Units** and given simple 'topic' titles to make them easy to identify (see **Contents** list on p ii. The Units are grouped into two parts: **Part 1 : Making Sure; Part 2 : Moving On.**

In Part 1 the Units concentrate on 'making sure' of topics mainly in Levels 5 and 6 of the revised National Curriculum together with some earlier levels.

In Part 2 the Units 'move on' to Level 7 and 8 topics (with the most difficult Level 8 algebra being placed in the companion book *Extending Mainstream Mathematics*).

To reflect these differences between Parts 1 and 2, the order of the Units in the two parts does not follow the same pattern. Their styles of presentation are also distinctly different. (Descriptions of these are in the sections About Part 1 and About Part 2 below.)

Answers to selected questions in Exercises are on p 577–92 following Part 2. These give simple numerical and word answers but not drawings. A separate Answer Book contains answers to all the Exercises and answers to the Examination Questions in the book.

Finally there is an extensive **Index.**

How each Unit is organised

The structure of each Unit is basically the same.

Each Unit begins with its title and a **checklist of its objectives** to tell you what it is about. For example, this introduction is from a Unit in Part 2.
As well as giving you details of the topics covered in the Units, these lists are useful as progress checks as you work through the course. They can also help you to identify and organise revision topics and to prepare for the final examinations.

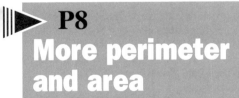

P8
More perimeter and area

This unit will help you to:
- calculate the perimeters and areas of parallelograms and trapeziums
- do length and area calculations for compound shapes

The checklist is followed by the **comprehensive text** arranged under clear side headings with **key words and phrases** in bold. In addition to the information and explanations there are numerous

worked examples, many of which are presented as **Questions** and **Answers**. Here is such an example from P17 Compound Measures.

Question

The oil in this can has a density of 0.72 g/cm^3.
A full can holds 1.5 litres.
What is the mass of this amount of oil?

Answer

Give density in g/cm^3, you need:
volume in cm^3 to get mass in g.
Volume of oil: 1.5 litres = 1.5 × 1000 cm^3
$$= 1500 \text{ cm}^3.$$

mass = density × volume
    = 0.72 × 1500
    = 1080 g
The oil in the can has a mass of 1080 g.

In a Question/Answer, the Question is usually an 'exam-type' question, and the Answer shows how the working can be set down clearly step-by-step. Comments in italics are designed to help students to understand the working. They do not have to be written down by them.

It is a good idea for students to try to answer these Questions as they do the work in a Unit. They may be convinced that they can simply 'think them through'. The real test of understanding is whether they can do the working on paper when the Answer is covered up. If any problems arise, then they can be sorted out at once.

The text is also interspaced with a variety of **things to do** related to the topics in the Unit. These include straightforward exercises to develop skills, knowledge and understanding, problem-solving exercises, discussion exercises, practical activities, games and investigations. **Using and Applying Mathematics** is integrated into the work in each Unit where appropriate.

At the end of most Units there is a selection of **actual GCSE Examination Questions**. Each of these has been chosen to familiarise students with typical questions set on the specific topics in the Unit. Students can try these questions immediately after completing the work in the Unit and/or later on in their course for consolidation and revision. Examples of complete Examination Papers are not provided because most teachers and students will prefer to use actual past papers set by their own Examining Group. Tests covering a range of topics can be made up by taking questions at random from several of the Examination Question sections.

About Part 1: Making Sure

The Units in Part 1 are designed to consolidate work most students will have met already. The amount of time a student spends on these Units will depend on his or her level of knowledge and understanding. Some students will need to revisit topics in detail, others will need only a brief review of topics when necessary.

To make topics easy to find, the Units are arranged into five groups under these headings:

Number	N Units
Algebra	A Units
Measures	M Units
Shape and Space	S Units
Handling Data	D Units

The text contains thorough notes and step-by-step explanations presented in very short sections. Each short section is followed by a carefully graded Exercise, related to the idea or ideas it contains. The questions are always about the work just before them in the text. This means that students can quickly look up the relevant information and worked examples if they are not sure what to do.

About Part 2: Moving On

In Part 2 the Units 'move on' to topics new to most students at this stage.

The order in which these Units are arranged forms a possible teaching programme. There is no need to follow the given order exactly. However this sequence of Units presents a balance of topics across different content areas and progresses through the levels of the National Curriculum.

You will find the following special features highlighted in Part 2 Units.

Memo
Measuring and drawing angles page 121

Memos remind the student of key information essential for the topic being studied. A Memo gives either the actual information needed or a page reference to show where to find the information in the book.

Summary

Summaries outline important information and ideas at key points in the development of a topic. They are useful for quick reference and as the basis of note-making by students.

 ## *Discussion Exercise*

Discussion Exercises provide ideas and questions for the student to think about and discuss. Ideally these should be done orally with other students and/or the teacher before the results of the discussions are written down. Students working on their own may need to write down their comments before meeting with their teacher to talk about them.

ACTIVITY

These Activities are usually practical tasks. They are often used to introduce new ideas, to reinforce understanding and to provide further practice in newly acquired skills. Some Activities are suitable for individual students to do, others are for use with small groups or the whole class.

 ## *Investigation*

The Investigations enhance and extend the work in the Units. They provide opportunities to explore ideas in more open-ended situations. The amount of guidance given and the level of difficulty vary. Trying these investigations will help students to prepare for doing GCSE Coursework. Some ideas may be suitable starting points for Coursework that will be examined.

Use of Calculators

A scientific calculator is needed for the work in this book and for use in GCSE Intermediate and Higher tier examinations. Ideally, students should own their own calculators. Teachers may wish to make sure that students' calculators are suitable for their courses.

Some units in this book focus specifically on the efficient use of calculators but this usage is reinforced throughout the text where

appropriate.

To highlight where work is done with and without a calculator, these symbols are used:

 shows where calculations are expected to be done with a calculator

 shows where calculations must be done without a calculator

Explanations and worked examples often include a sequence of keys to show one way to do the working. Some examples are:

From P1 Index Notation, p.241, showing how to key a negative power.

To find the value of 2^{-4},
we key in: 5 x^y 4 +/- =   0.0625

From p. 409, for a calcuation of the volume of a compound shape:

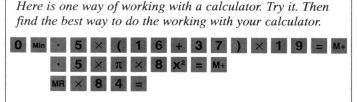

Here is one way of working with a calculator. Try it. Then find the best way to do the working with your calculator.

0 Min . 5 × (1 6 + 3 7) × 1 9 = M+
. 5 × π × 8 x² = M+
MR × 8 4 =

Watch the display for the step-by-step results as you go along.

These 'key codes' may need adapting for different makes and models of calculator. However, they are a good starting point for students trying to work out the 'best way' to do the working on their calculators.

Throughout the book, students are encouraged to be critical of 'calculator answers'. They are expected to check answers are reasonable by estimation and other methods and to give results to a suitable degree of accuracy. These points are also dealt with in detail in some Units.

Use of Computers

Most students using this book will have access to a computer at school or college or at home. They will also find easily obtainable software that links with the mathematics in their GCSE course. This software includes databases, spreadsheets, graph-drawing programs and statistical packages.

Ideas for computer-based activities and investigations are suggested in Units where these are thought to be particularly useful. No detailed instructions on the use of computers and software have been included because of the wide variety on the market. However, it is hoped that students will make effective use of the available software whenever it can enhance their mathematical learning.

PART 1
Making Sure

N1
Know your calculator

This unit will help you to:

■ use a calculator accurately and efficiently

■ use the basic keys to do calculations

■ check your calculator answers in various ways
  e.g. by deciding if your answer is sensible
       by estimating answers
       by using inverse operations

■ give sensible answers from the results on your
  calculator display.

In your **GCSE written examination** you will be expected to use a calculator. You will also use one in any **coursework** you do for assessment.

Most people can press buttons on a calculator. Your teacher and the examiner want to see more than this from you. Your calculator cannot think for you. It cannot understand 'problems'. You have to choose the right keys to do the right work.

Calculator work in this book

Look out for this **symbol** in this book.

It reminds you that a calculator has been used for the working in a question.

Sometimes you will find a key code also. For example, to work out 14×17

The key code is:

↑
Shows answer on display

This shows *one way* to do the working. It gives the keys to press in order. Try it if you have the keys it uses.

There may be *other ways* to do a calculation on your calculator. Always try to find the *best way*.

An examination question may ask you to show how you did a calculation on your calculator. Writing your own key codes is good practice for this.

Basic keys

There are several different makes and kinds of calculator. For your GCSE course you need a **scientific calculator** with **memory** and **brackets** keys. Ask your teacher to check that *your* calculator is suitable for *your* course.

Some keys 'look' the same on all models of calculator. For example:

Other keys may have different symbols on them on different models. For example,

power keys may be x^y y^x

Learn to use the keys on *your own calculator* correctly. Practise with the one you intend to use in the examination (or one like it). A 'borrowed one' may not be quite the same. The exam is not the time to find out about it!

All calculators have their own instruction booklet. Look up what to do in it if you need to.

Wherever possible in this book we have outlined how to use a calculator to do the appropriate working. Make sure that you use the keys and 'key codes' that work on your calculator in each case. Check that your calculator working always gives the *correct result*.

A scientific calculator will work out an expression such as $2 \times 8 + 3 \times 5$, correctly, if you simply key in the numbers and operations in the order they are written. For example:

Press: 2 × 8 + 3 × 5 =

Display: *31.*

▶ *Exercise* N1.1

Use your calculator to work out these. You should get the answers given in brackets if you have a scientific calculator.

1   $2 \times 34 + 7 \times 21$ (= 215)
2   $5 \times 43 - 3 \times 52$ (= 59)
3   $97 - 4 \times 13$ (= 45)
4   $7 \times 38 - 152$ (= 114)
5   $3 \times 27 + 4 \times 36 - 2 \times 83$ (= 59)
6   $198 - 2 \times 43 - 3 \times 27$ (= 31)
7   Rick had £5. He spent 75p on stamps, 96p on fruitgums and 67p on lemonade. How much was left? (= 262p or £2.62)
8

At the end of a week the mileometer on Sue's car reads 27 259. During the week Sue made journeys of 152 miles, 97 miles and 83 miles. What was the mileometer reading at the beginning of the week? (= 26 927)

Double function keys

To reduce the number of keys on a calculator, some keys have *more than one* function.

For example, this key ⌐%⌐ = has two functions. The symbol in green shows the 2nd function. The first function is as an 'equals' key. The second function is as a 'percentage' key.

To make a key perform its second function you have to press a key marked

SHIFT or **2nd F** or **INV** ← *for inverse*

INV is used on some calculators because the second function is often, but not always, the opposite of the first.

For example, this key **x²** has *'square'* and its opposite *'square root'* on the same key.

In general we have *not* shown 2nd function keys in key codes. Check that you know where and what they are on your calculator. Use them when you need to in the given key codes.

Clear keys

Some calculators have *only one clear key*. To clear the last entry (like rubbing out a mistake) you press it once. To clear the whole calculator (like switching off) you may have to press it twice.

Some calculators have *two clear keys*. One clears the last entry. The other clears the whole calculator.

Make sure you can use the clear keys correctly on *your* calculator. Always clear your calculator before starting a new calculation. In this book we use **C** to show this at the start of a key code.

Correcting mistakes

The safest way to correct a mistake is to start again. Clear your calculator, then enter the 'sum' again.

You can correct some keying-in mistakes easily – if you spot them as soon as you have made them! So watch what you are doing. Keep an eye on your calculator display.

Here are some common mistakes and how to correct them.

● **Wrong number**
Press the 'clear entry' key and enter the correct number.

For 27 + 54, Tom pressed **C 2 7 + 4 5** ← a mistake

To correct it, press **CE** ← *rubs out the last entry*

Enter the correct number **5 4 = 81.**
Take care to press 'clear entry' not 'all clear'.

● **Wrong instruction key**
Press the correct key at once and finish the 'sum'.

For 347 − 68, Chris pressed **C 3 4 7 ÷** ← *wrong key*

To correct it, press **−** ← *correct key*

and finish the 'sum' **6 8 =**
This gives the correct answer, 279. Try it.

▶ *Exercise* **N1.2**

1 For each of the following:
   ● work out the 'calculation to be done'
   ● copy 'our entry' on your calculator and correct it
   ● check that your answers to both calculations are the same.

   Calculation   Our entry
   to be done

(a) 598.4 ÷ 37.06 **5 9 8 • 4 ÷ 3 7 • 6**

(b) 43.79 + 15.82 **4 3 7**

(c) 6408.9 − 13.87 **6 4 0 8 • 9 − 3**

(d) 27.49 × 83.5 **2 7 • 9**

(e) 725.6 − 118.92 **7 2 5 • 6 − 1 1 •**

2 For each of the following:
   ● work out the 'calculation to be done'
   ● copy 'our entry' on your calculator and correct it
   ● check that your answers to both calculations are the same.

   Calculation   Our entry
   to be done

(a) 34.79 + 18.081 **3 4 • 7 9 ×**

(b) 78.8 × 46.3 **7 8 • 8 ÷**

(c) 136.94 ÷ 17.2 **1 3 6 • 9 4 −**

(d) 523.8 − 64.91 **5 2 3 • 8 ÷**

(e) 6407 × 23.5 **6 4 0 7 +**

Checking answers

Your calculator can make arithmetic quick and easy to do. But it is also easy to get **wrong answers**. You may enter the wrong numbers, press the wrong keys, forget to clear it, … .

You will get *fewer* 'wrong answers' if you **check your work**. So a quick check at the end of a calculation is well worth the short time spent on it.

Here are some checks you can do. Use them to help you to spot mistakes. Then you can correct any you find.

● **Think about the answer**
A wrong answer is often easy to spot if you think about it. Check that your answer makes sense! Does it seem right? The size of an answer is often obviously silly. It looks too big or too small. Your common sense tells you there is something wrong.

Suppose you plan to wallpaper your bedroom. You work out that it will take 800 rolls of paper. Is this sensible? Silly answers like this are written down in examinations. Don't leave your common sense outside the exam room.

● **Do a rough estimate**
A quick **estimate** or **approximation** can help you to spot mistakes. It gives you a rough idea of what the answer should be. Round off the numbers to make them easier (see Unit N3). Then use them to get an approximate answer (see Unit N3). Compare this estimate with your calculator answer. Make sure they are *about the same size*.

Question

Janet used a calculator to work out

$$\frac{37.5 \times 51.72}{12.5 \times 9.6} = 161.625$$

Without using your calculator show why her answer is not sensible.

continued

Answer

Round each number to 1 sf.

$37.5 \approx 40$ $51.72 \approx 50$
$12.5 \approx 10$ $9.6 \approx 10$

The calculation is roughly $\dfrac{40 \times 50}{10 \times 10} = \dfrac{2000}{100} = 20$

Janet's answer is far too big. So it is not sensible. I suspect that the display should show 16.1625. This is about the right size.

► Exercise N1.3

In these calculations, round each number to 1 significant figure, then say which answers are obviously wrong.
Do not use a calculator.

1   $9.37 \times 49.8 = 46.6626$
2   $21.89 \times 4.2 = 91.938$
3   $321 \div 98.2 = 32.68$
4   $7.3 \times 2.2 \times 0.9 = 144.54$
5   $24.7 \times 2.8^2 = 69.16$

6   $\dfrac{43.6 \times 39.2}{28.7 + 11.3} = 427.28$

7   $\dfrac{3.175 \times 12.48}{7.613} = 5.204$

8   $\dfrac{9.616 \times 12.16}{17.71} = 66.025$

● Do the calculation again

You can do the working again in the same way. But this is not always a good check. It is easy to make the same mistake again too.

Doing the calculation again in a **different way** is safer. Here are some ways to try. Remember to *write down your answer* while it is on the display and before you check it. (It's easy to forget!)

Addition

You can add numbers in *any order*. (The result is the *same*).
To check an addition, do it in a different order. The reverse order is easiest. You are less likely to miss a number this way.
Try this example: $36 + 124 + 57 =$
First add the numbers in this order:
Working:

 ← write it down!

Then add them in reverse order to check:
Check:

 ← same answer

Multiplication

You can also multiply numbers in any order (and get the same result). **To check a multiplication, do it in a different order.**
Try this example: $25 \times 94 =$
First multiply the numbers in this order:
Working: C 2 5 × 9 4 = *2350.* ← write it down

Then multiply them in reverse order to check:
Check: C 9 4 × 2 5 = *2350.* ← same answer

Subtraction

Changing the order in a subtraction gives a *different* result. So we need another way to check.

Addition and subtraction are **inverses** (opposites). You can **check a subtraction by doing an addition**. Add the number you took away to your answer. You should get the first number again.

For example, $7 - \mathbf{2} = 5$ and $5 + \mathbf{2} = 7$

On a calculator you need to use the answer you get on the display. So *do not clear it* before the check.

Try this subtraction and check:
Working: C 1 3 7 − 5 9 = *78.* ← Write down the answer

Check: + 5 9 = *137.* ← the first number
                         ↑
          the number you subtracted

Division

You get a *different* result if you switch the numbers in a division too. So this is no good as a check.
Multiplication and division are **inverses** (opposites).
You can **check a division by doing a multiplication**. Multiply your answer by the number you divided by. This should give the number you started with.

For example, $6 \div \mathbf{3} = 2$ and $2 \times \mathbf{3} = 6$.
Here is an example to try:
Working: C 1 1 2 8 ÷ 4 7 = *24.* ← write down the answer

Check: × 4 7 = *1128.* ← the number you started with
                    ↑
     the number you divided by

► Exercise N1.4

1   Check these addition questions by entering the numbers in a different order. Correct any answers which are wrong.
    (a) $63 + 107 + 94 = 264$
    (b) $214 + 137 + 62 = 314$
    (c) $3124 + 1006 + 16 = 4146$
    (d) $385 + 1023 + 570 = 1987$

2   Check these subtraction questions by doing an addition. Correct the ones that are wrong.
    (a) $237 - 65 = 172$
    (b) $1003 - 274 = 749$
    (c) $3178 - 1059 = 2199$
    (d) $524 - 78 = 446$

3   Check these multiplication questions by doing the multiplying in a different order. Correct any that are wrong.
    (a) $65 \times 18 = 1170$
    (b) $246 \times 28 = 6888$
    (c) $318 \times 247 = 78\,456$
    (d) $512 \times 23 = 11\,776$

4   Check these division questions by doing a multiplication. Correct any that are wrong.
    (a) $1792 \div 28 = 64$
    (b) $705 \div 15 = 47$
    (c) $2304 \div 36 = 46$
    (d) $2436 \div 42 = 85$

● **Use your knowledge of numbers**
You know a lot about numbers. You can use what you know to do some checks. Here are some examples for whole number calculations. You may think of others.

Look at the 'units' figure in the answer. Does it make sense?

For example, if you get $174\underline{2} \times 54\underline{3} = 945\ 90\underline{8}$
then you know there is a mistake
because $2 \times 3 = \underline{6}$ *not* $\underline{8}$.

All whole numbers are odd or even. You know that:

odd + odd = even	odd × odd = odd
even + even = even	even × even = even
odd + even = odd	odd × even = even

You can use this as a check. Are your numbers odd or even? What should they be?

For example, if you get $\quad 685 \quad + \quad 138 \quad = \quad 824$
$\qquad\qquad\qquad \uparrow \qquad\qquad \uparrow \qquad\qquad \uparrow$
$\qquad\qquad\quad$ odd $\quad + \quad$ even $\quad = \quad$ even
then you know there is a mistake
because odd + even = odd, *not* even.

Checks are shown in many examples in this book, but not all. To do so would take too much space. Try to remember to **do your own check** each time.

▶ *Exercise* **N1.5**

Without using your calculator, decide which of these calculations must be wrong.

1	$37 + 93 = 109$	**5**	$37 \times 24 = 889$
2	$25 \times 13 = 335$	**6**	$237 - 156 = 82$
3	$198 \div 16 = 9$	**7**	$1404 \div 54 = 26$
4	$106 + 327 = 434$	**8**	$362.8 - 273.8 = 88.8$

Giving answers

A calculator may give you an answer with lots of digits. (Most calculators have 8- or 10-digit displays). Usually you do not need or want all of these digits. It is not sensible and often incorrect to use them all.

It is a good idea to give your 'calculator answer' in your working. But you must *label it clearly*. You, and the examiner, can use it to check your work.

To answer a question, round your calculator answer to a **suitable degree of accuracy** (see Unit N3). An examination question may tell you what this is. Do what it says or you will lose marks. Often *you* will have to decide what is the suitable degree of accuracy to use. Look at the accuracy of the measurements or numbers in the problem to help you to decide. Make sure that you *state clearly in your answer* how you have rounded your result.

▶ *Exercise* **N1.6**

The answer that a calculator would give you is shown for each situation below. Use it to give a 'sensible answer' in each case.

1 Stanley poured 1 litre of lemonade into 17 glasses. Each glass held 58.82352941 mℓ.
2 Ruth cut 20 feet of string into 9 equal length pieces to tie up some parcels. Each piece was 2.222222222 feet long.
3 Ben cut a 500 gram cake into 6 equal pieces. Each piece weighed 83.33333333g.
4 Carly ran 100 metres in 12.6 seconds. On average, Carly ran 7.936507937 metres in 1 second.
5 One day last January, Mick recorded a temperature rise of 5°C in 3 hours. On average, the temperature rose 1.666666667°C each hour.

▶ # N2
Without a calculator

This unit will help you to:

■ use multiplication tables to do calculations in your head and with 'pencil and paper'

■ multiply and divide by 10, 100, 1000, ... in your head

■ multiply and divide by simple whole numbers in your head

■ multiply and divide a three-digit number by a two-digit number without using a calculator

■ use 'quick ways' to do some multiplications

■ use these 'non-calculator methods' to solve problems.

In everyday life (and in your mathematics examination) you will do difficult multiplications and divisions **with a calculator**. However, you have to be able to do some basic calculations **in your head** and with **pencil and paper**.

In your head

Tables

To do multiplication and division without a calculator you need to know the multiplication tables up to 9×9.

This **multiplication square** is one way to write down these 'times tables'.

To find 7×9, for example, look across the '7 row' and down the '9 column'. It gives the answer 63.

x	1	2	3	4	5	6	7	8	9
1	1	2	3	4	5	6	7	8	9
2	2	4	6	8	10	12	14	16	18
3	3	6	9	12	15	18	21	24	27
4	4	8	12	16	20	24	28	32	36
5	5	10	15	20	25	30	35	40	45
6	6	12	18	24	23	36	42	48	54
7	7	14	21	28	35	42	49	56	63
8	8	16	24	32	40	48	56	64	72
9	9	18	27	36	45	54	63	72	81

Some people learn their tables 'off by heart' as lists:

One times two is two. $1 \times 2 = 2$
Two times two is four. $2 \times 2 = 4$
Three times two is six. $3 \times 2 = 6$
And so on …

But you really need to be able to recall each 'fact' quickly on its own. Practise until you can do this.

Remember: you can multiply numbers in any order. This cuts down how many multiplication facts you have to learn.

For example,   if you know $7 \times 9 = 63$
              you also know $9 \times 7 = 63$.

ACTIVITY

Here are two activities to help you to practise your 'tables'. Write down your answers as quickly as you can. Check them with a calculator.

Multiplication squares
Copy and complete this 9×9 multiplication square.

Look carefully at the numbers along the top and down the side. They are not in order, 1 to 9.

Make up your own 9×9 multiplication squares for more practice.

Write the numbers 1 to 9 in different orders along the top and down the side.
Fill in the answer to each multiplication.

×	3	8	1	7	2	6	4	9	5
5									
9									
3									
6									
2									
8									
4									
1									
7									

Card practice
You need a pack of number cards. The pack should contain at least four of each of these number cards:

You can either number some cards yourself, or use a pack of ordinary cards, with Aces, face cards (J, Q, K) and 10s removed.

Shuffle your pack of cards. Deal out two cards, face up.

Multiply the two numbers.
Write down the answer.
Repeat this until you have used all the cards.

5 × 8 = 40

Knowing your multiplication tables also helps you to do **divisions**.

For example, look at $27 \div 9$.
You have to find 'how many 9s are in 27'.
From your tables, you know:
'three 9s are 27' i.e. $3 \times 9 = 27$
So $27 \div 9 = 3$ because $3 \times 9 = 27$.

Sometimes when one number is divided by another you get a **remainder**.

For example, look at $31 \div 6$.
31 is not in your '6 times table'.
But you know 'five 6s are 30' i.e. $5 \times 6 = 30$.
And $31 - 30 = 1$.
So $31 \div 6 = 5$ remainder 1.

► Exercise N2.1

Write down the answers only in this exercise. Do them as quickly as you can.

1 How many 4s are in:
   (a) 12   (c) 20   (e) 16?
   (b) 36   (d) 32

2 How many 7s are in:
   (a) 35   (c) 63   (e) 56?
   (b) 21   (d) 42

3 Find the missing numbers.
   (a) $? \times 2 = 14$ (c) $? \times 8 = 72$ (e) $? \times 9 = 63$
   (b) $? \times 6 = 24$ (d) $? \times 3 = 18$ (f) $? \times 5 = 40$

4 Work out.
   (a) $24 \div 3$ (e) $48 \div 6$ (i) $40 \div 8$
   (b) $35 \div 5$ (f) $56 \div 8$ (j) $54 \div 9$
   (c) $81 \div 9$ (g) $28 \div 7$ (k) $30 \div 5$
   (d) $18 \div 2$ (h) $24 \div 4$ (l) $49 \div 7$

5 Do these divisions. Each gives a remainder.
   (a) $37 \div 4$ (c) $29 \div 3$ (e) $58 \div 6$
   (b) $53 \div 7$ (d) $79 \div 9$ (f) $34 \div 5$

6 Find the remainder in each of these divisions.
   (a) $17 \div 5$ (c) $76 \div 8$ (e) $64 \div 7$
   (b) $33 \div 4$ (d) $85 \div 9$ (f) $39 \div 6$

ACTIVITY

Brains vs calculator

Compare your 'mental skills' and your 'calculator skills' by doing the multiplications below.

Time how long it takes you to do them 'in your head'.
Just write down the answers.

Now time how long it takes you to do them with a calculator. Don't cheat. Press all the keys you need for each multiplication.
As before, just write down the answers.

	(a)	(b)	(c)	(d)	(e)
1	4 × 5	5 × 5	2 × 3	7 × 2	8 × 7
2	3 × 3	5 × 2	6 × 5	2 × 8	7 × 3
3	3 × 4	4 × 2	6 × 9	5 × 4	2 × 5
4	2 × 4	7 × 6	5 × 8	2 × 8	9 × 4
5	6 × 3	3 × 8	2 × 9	7 × 7	5 × 7
6	9 × 4	4 × 3	8 × 5	7 × 9	9 × 6
7	2 × 7	6 × 6	7 × 4	8 × 3	9 × 7
8	8 × 6	5 × 9	8 × 5	7 × 8	8 × 8
9	7 × 5	6 × 4	9 × 3	8 × 4	9 × 9
10	9 × 5	9 × 8	8 × 9	5 × 6	6 × 7

Was your brain faster?

Now do the same with these divisions.

	(a)	(b)	(c)	(d)	(e)
1	6 ÷ 2	20 ÷ 5	9 ÷ 3	12 ÷ 4	24 ÷ 6
2	8 ÷ 4	36 ÷ 6	21 ÷ 7	10 ÷ 2	16 ÷ 8
3	6 ÷ 3	8 ÷ 2	18 ÷ 6	35 ÷ 7	27 ÷ 9
4	28 ÷ 4	24 ÷ 8	4 ÷ 2	27 ÷ 3	10 ÷ 5
5	16 ÷ 2	63 ÷ 7	45 ÷ 9	30 ÷ 5	36 ÷ 4
6	12 ÷ 3	30 ÷ 6	15 ÷ 5	56 ÷ 8	14 ÷ 7
7	16 ÷ 4	35 ÷ 5	40 ÷ 8	18 ÷ 2	36 ÷ 9
8	48 ÷ 6	32 ÷ 4	18 ÷ 9	64 ÷ 8	21 ÷ 3
9	49 ÷ 7	63 ÷ 9	72 ÷ 8	40 ÷ 5	12 ÷ 2
10	30 ÷ 6	20 ÷ 4	28 ÷ 7	15 ÷ 3	72 ÷ 9

Multiplying and dividing by 10, 100, 1000, …

$$37 \times 10 \ \ = \ \ 370$$
$$37 \times 100 \ = \ 3700$$
$$37 \times 1000 = 37000$$

$$37 \div 10 \ \ = \ \ 3.7$$
$$37 \div 100 \ = \ 0.37$$
$$37 \div 1000 = \ 0.037$$

Multiplying and dividing by 10, 100, 1000, … is easy. You simply have to change the **place values** of the figures. Look at the examples above. See how the place values of the figures (37) have been changed.

Sometimes a decimal point has to be put in (after the Units figure).
Any empty places up to the decimal point are filled with 0s (zeros). This keeps the place values of the figures correct.

It usually helps to think of the figures in 'place value columns' when you do these calculations. We have shown the columns in the examples below.

Remember:
Place values go 'up' as you move to the left in a number.

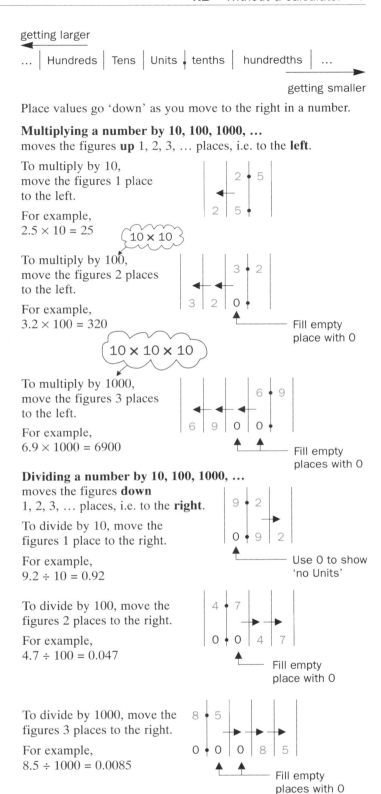

getting larger

| … | Hundreds | Tens | Units | tenths | hundredths | … |

getting smaller

Place values go 'down' as you move to the right in a number.

Multiplying a number by 10, 100, 1000, …
moves the figures **up** 1, 2, 3, … places, i.e. to the **left**.

To multiply by 10,
move the figures 1 place
to the left.

For example,
2.5 × 10 = 25

To multiply by 100,
move the figures 2 places
to the left.

For example,
3.2 × 100 = 320

Fill empty place with 0

To multiply by 1000,
move the figures 3 places
to the left.

For example,
6.9 × 1000 = 6900

Fill empty places with 0

Dividing a number by 10, 100, 1000, …
moves the figures **down** 1, 2, 3, … places, i.e. to the **right**.

To divide by 10, move the
figures 1 place to the right.

For example,
9.2 ÷ 10 = 0.92

Use 0 to show 'no Units'

To divide by 100, move the
figures 2 places to the right.

For example,
4.7 ÷ 100 = 0.047

Fill empty place with 0

To divide by 1000, move the
figures 3 places to the right.

For example,
8.5 ÷ 1000 = 0.0085

Fill empty places with 0

▶ *Exercise* **N2.2**

Do these in your head first. Then check them with your calculator.

1   Multiply each of these numbers by (i) 10, (ii) 100, (iii) 1000.
   (a) 8
   (b) 13
   (c) 7
   (d) 24
   (e) 19
   (f) 72
   (g) 154
   (h) 279
   (i) 360
   (j) 4216
   (k) 0.4
   (l) 2.6

(m) 0.07   (p) 0.008   (s) 0.01
(n) 22.9   (q) 127.4   (t) 527.96
(o) 58.2   (r) 19.36

2   Divide each of the numbers in question 1 by (i) 10, (ii) 100, (iii) 1000.

3   (a) 56×100 (e) 905×1000 (i) $27 \div 100$
    (b) $943 \div 10$ (f) $650 \div 100$ (j) 530×100
    (c) $78 \div 1000$ (g) 39×1000
    (d) 430×10 (h) $62 \div 1000$

4   (a) $6.4 \div 10$ (e) 0.8×1000 (i) 2.5×1000
    (b) $92.5 \div 1000$ (f) $5.9 \div 1000$ (j) 0.9×100
    (c) 0.17×100 (g) $67.8 \div 100$
    (d) 1.05×10 (h) $8.6 \div 100$

Multiplying simple multiples of 10, 100, 1000, ...

20, 30, 40, …, 90 are simple multiples of 10.
200, 300, 400, …, 900 are simple multiples of 100.
2000, 3000, 4000, …, 9000 are simple multiples of 1000.
And so on … .

Multiplications involving only two such simple numbers can also be done mentally.

To do multiplications like $7 \times 4 = 28$ in your head, you use your tables.

To do multiplications like $70 \times 400 = 28\,000$ in your head, you use two steps:

● Do the multiplication from your tables first.
● Then give this result its correct place value.

So to work out 70×400
you use $7 \times 4 = 28$
and $10 \times 100 = 1000$.

In these multiplications you can count 'trailing zeros' to check the place value is correct.

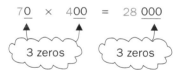

The zeros after the 7 and 4 in 70 and 400 'fix' their place values.
The 28 in the answer has the same number of zeros after it to give its correct place value.

Here are some other examples.

To work out 60×90,
you use $6 \times 9 = 54$
and $10 \times 10 = 100$.

To work out 3000×50,
you use $3 \times 5 = 15$
and $1000 \times 10 = 10\,000$.

Sometimes the 'table fact' itself gives a zero.
Take extra care when this happens.
Do not include this zero in your 'zero check'.

For example,
to work out 60×5000,
you use $6 \times 5 = 30$
and $10 \times 1000 = 10\,000$.

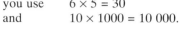

Look at the 'zero check':

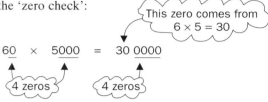

► *Exercise* N2.3

Do these in your head first.
Then check them with your calculator.

1   (a) 10×10
    (b) 10×100
    (c) 10×1000
    (d) $10 \times 10\,000$

2   (a) 100×10
    (b) 100×100
    (c) 100×1000
    (d) $100 \times 10\,000$

3   (a) 1000×10
    (b) 1000×100
    (c) 1000×1000
    (d) $1000 \times 10\,000$

4   (a) $10\,000 \times 10$
    (b) $10\,000 \times 100$
    (c) $10\,000 \times 1000$
    (d) $10\,000 \times 10\,000$

5   (a) 3×2
    (b) 30×20
    (c) 30×200
    (d) 300×200
    (e) 3000×20

6   (a) 7×6
    (b) 70×60
    (c) 700×60
    (d) 70×6000
    (e) 700×6000

7   (a) 9×8
    (b) 90×80
    (c) 900×80
    (d) 900×800
    (e) 90×8000

8   (a) 4×5
    (b) 40×50
    (c) 400×500
    (d) 400×50
    (e) 4000×500

9   (a) 80×60
    (b) 80×600
    (c) 8000×60
    (d) 800×600
    (e) 8000×6000

10 (a) 20×50
    (b) 200×500
    (c) 50×200
    (d) 500×2000
    (e) $20 \times 50\,000$

11 (a) 70×50
    (b) 60×6000
    (c) 8000×30
    (d) 2000×700
    (e) 3000×3000

ACTIVITY

Multiplication practice

Mental multiplication, like most skills, needs regular practice. Practise on your own or with another student.

Here is a simple way to generate lots of multiplications to do 'in your head'.

Make a pack of number cards.

Use these numbers on them at first ...

2, 3, 4, ..., 9
20, 30, 40, ..., 90
200, 300, 400, ..., 900
2000, 3000, 4000, ..., 9000.

Use larger numbers such as 20 000, 200 000, 2 000 000 later on if you like.

Shuffle the cards.

Turn over two cards ...

Multiply the numbers in your head ...

$40 \times 300 = 12\,000$

Write down the answer.

Repeat this until all the cards are used.

Check your answers with a calculator.

Dividing multiples of 10, 100, 1000, ...

Some multiples of 10, 100, 1000, ... are easy to divide by 2, 3, 4, ..., 9 in your head.
In these divisions you use just a single 'table fact'.
They also give whole number answers.

Look at these examples.

$60 \div 3 = 20$ $600 \div 3 = 200$ $6000 \div 3 = 2000$	6 tens $\div 3 = 2$ tens 6 hundreds $\div 3 = 2$ hundreds 6 thousands $\div 3 = 2$ thousands

See how each division uses $6 \div 3 = 2$.
This comes from your tables.
In each division, the place value of the 6 gives the place value of the 2 in the answer.

Here are some examples that use $32 \div 8 = 4$.

$320 \div 8 = 40$
$3200 \div 8 = 400$
$32000 \div 8 = 4000$

Sometimes the 'table fact' you use involves a zero.
Take extra care when this happens.
For example,
see how each division below uses $20 \div 4 = 5$.

$200 \div 4 = 50$
$2000 \div 4 = 500$
$20000 \div 4 = 5000$

You can also use the ideas shown above to do other divisions mentally.
They can help you to do some divisions by 20, 30, ..., 90
and by 200, 300, ..., 900
and by 2000, 3000, ..., 9000
and so on ...
You do each division in two main steps.

For example,
to divide by 20, you divide by 10 then by 2,
to divided by 200, you divide by 100, then by 2,
to divide by 2000, you divide by 1000, then by 2,
and so on ... .

Look at these examples.
$80\,000 \div 20 = 80\,00\!\!\not0 \div 2\!\!\not0 = 4000$
$6000 \div 200 = 60\!\!\not0\!\!\not0 \div 2\!\!\not0\!\!\not0 = 30$
$400\,000 \div 2000 = 400\,0\!\!\not0\!\!\not0 \div 2\!\!\not0\!\!\not0\!\!\not0 = 200$
See how you can change each to a division by 2.
Then you do that division as before.

Here are some other examples.
Look carefully at how each is changed to a division by a single digit.

$50\,000 \div 500 = 50\,0\!\!\not0\!\!\not0 \div 5\!\!\not0\!\!\not0 = 100$
$9000 \div 3000 = 9\!\!\not0\!\!\not0\!\!\not0 \div 3\!\!\not0\!\!\not0\!\!\not0 = 3$
$80\,000 \div 40 = 80\,00\!\!\not0 \div 4\!\!\not0 = 2000$

$2700 \div 90 = 270\!\!\not0 \div 9\!\!\not0 = 30$
$4200 \div 600 = 42\!\!\not0\!\!\not0 \div 6\!\!\not0\!\!\not0 = 7$
$810\,000 \div 9000 = 810\,0\!\!\not0\!\!\not0 \div 9\!\!\not0\!\!\not0\!\!\not0 = 90$

$30\,000 \div 6000 = 30\,0\!\!\not0\!\!\not0 \div 6\!\!\not0\!\!\not0\!\!\not0 = 5$
$2000 \div 50 = 200\!\!\not0 \div 5\!\!\not0 = 40$
$400\,000 \div 800 = 400\,0\!\!\not0\!\!\not0 \div 8\!\!\not0\!\!\not0 = 500$

►*Exercise* N2.4

Do these in your head first.
Then check them with your calculator.

1 (a) $800 \div 4$
(b) $6000 \div 3$
(c) $900\,000 \div 3$
(d) $70\,000 \div 7$
(e) $60 \div 2$

2 (a) $21\,000 \div 3$
(b) $5400 \div 9$
(c) $560 \div 7$
(d) $320\,000 \div 8$
(e) $1\,800\,000 \div 6$

3 (a) $20\,000 \div 4$
(b) $400 \div 5$
(c) $300\,000 \div 6$
(d) $1000 \div 5$
(e) $4\,000\,000 \div 8$

4 (a) $80 \div 20$
(b) $8000 \div 200$
(c) $800 \div 20$
(d) $80\,000 \div 2000$
(e) $800\,000 \div 200$

5 (a) $42\,000 \div 600$
(b) $420 \div 60$
(c) $4\,200\,000 \div 6000$
(d) $420\,000 \div 600$
(e) $42\,000 \div 6000$

6 (a) $300\,000 \div 5000$
(b) $30\,000 \div 50$
(c) $3000 \div 500$
(d) $3\,000\,000 \div 5000$
(e) $3000 \div 50$

7 (a) $90\,000 \div 30$
(b) $6000 \div 2000$
(c) $8000 \div 400$
(d) $9\,000\,000 \div 90$
(e) $60\,000 \div 300$

8 (a) $40\,000 \div 500$
(b) $2\,000\,000 \div 5000$
(c) $300\,000 \div 600$
(d) $10\,000 \div 20$
(e) $40\,000 \div 8000$

9 (a) $4800 \div 60$
(b) $280\,000 \div 700$
(c) $6\,300\,000 \div 90$
(d) $150\,000 \div 3000$
(e) $2\,500\,000 \div 50\,000$

10 (a) $450\,000 \div 5000$
(b) $6000 \div 200$
(c) $1\,200\,000 \div 60$
(d) $900\,000 \div 30\,000$
(e) $2000 \div 400$

Pencil and paper calculations

Multiplication of whole numbers

Many multiplications are too complicated to do all the working in your head. To do some of them, you can **split the working into steps** you can do 'in your head', then keep a record of each step with **pencil and paper**.

Splitting a whole number into its **place value parts** makes it easy to work with.

For example, 294 means 200 + 90 + 4.
To calculate 294 × 7,

you can work out:	200×7	=	1400
	90×7	=	630
	4×7	=	28
and add the results:	294×7	=	2058

For some multiplications, you may have to split both numbers into place value parts. For example,

to work out 63 × 518,
you split 63 into 60 + 3 and 518 into 500 + 10 + 8.

Then you multiply the parts together and add the results.
Here are three ways to keep a record of the working. Try all three ways. See how they compare with your usual way.

(a) On a grid

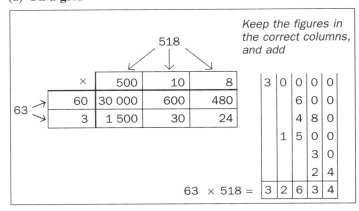

Keep the figures in the correct columns, and add

(b) Without a grid

Here is the same working without the grid. The calculations at the side show where each result comes from.

			5	1	8
		×		6	3
60×500	→	3	0	0	0	0
60×10	→		6	0	0
60×8	→		4	8	0
3×500	→	1	5	0	0
3×10	→		3	0
3×8	→		2	4
63×518	→	3	2	6	3	4

(c) The 'shortest' way

Mathematicians like to use short ways if they can. To make this working shorter they split it into fewer steps.

They use 60 × 518 instead of 60 × 500
                                                60 ×   10
                                                60 ×   8

They use 3 × 518 instead of   3 × 500
                                                3 ×   10
                                                3 ×   8

The working can be set out this way:

		518
		× 63
60×518	→	31080
3×518	→	1554
63×518	→	32634

Some people work out the units first, then the tens … .
Both ways give the same answer.

You can do 'long multiplications' any way you like, provided it always gives the *correct answer*.

In a written examination you have to show your working clearly. Choose the way you find easiest to do and explain. And practise using it successfully. Use your calculator to check your answers.

Remember the best way is the correct way that works best for you. It does not have to be the shortest.

Whichever way you use, don't forget to check your answer. Round the numbers and do the calculation in your head with these rounded numbers. Check that your estimate and answers are about the same size (see Unit N4).

For example, for 63 × 518

use $63 \approx 60$ and $518 \approx 500$.
These give $63 \times 518 \approx 60 \times 500 = 30\,000$

Comparing this estimate and our answer (32 634) shows they are about the *same size*.

▶ *Exercise* N2.5

Do these multiplications without using a calculator. Then use your calculator to check.

1 (a) 18×43
  (b) 29×57
  (c) 74×36
  (d) 65×91
  (e) 82×13
  (f) 66×47

2 (a) 19×632
  (b) 31×159
  (c) 307×56
  (d) 67×840
  (e) 463×64
  (f) 73×406

Some 'quick ways'

Most people have their own **'quick ways'** to so some multiplications. Here are a few to try:

● **To multiply by 5** (that is, 10 ÷ 2),
  multiply by 10, then divide by 2.

    For example, for 5 × 23
    work out   10 × 23 = 230
    then …   230 ÷ 2 = 115

● **To multiply by 50** (that is, by 100 ÷ 2),
  multiply by one hundred, then divide by 2.

    For example, for 50 × 612
    work out   100 × 612 = 61 200
    then …   61 200 ÷ 2 = 30 600

- **To multiply by 9** (that is, 10 – 1),
  multiply by 10, then subtract the number.

  For example, for 9×86
  work out $10 \times 86 = 860$
  then ... $-1 \times 86 = -86$
  $\overline{9 \times 86 = 774}$

- **To multiply by 99** (that is, 100 – 1),
  multiply by 100, then subtract the number.

  For example, for 99×317
  work out $100 \times 317 = 31\ 700$
  then ... $-1 \times 317 = -317$
  $\overline{99 \times 317 = 31\ 383}$

You may know other 'quick ways'. Pool your ideas with friends and family. Try out their 'short cuts'. See which ones are worth using. Remember they must *always give the correct answer*. Tricks that work only a few times will not do!

▶ *Exercise* N2.6

Use 'quick ways' to do these calculations. Then use your calculator to check.

1	24×5	**7**	9×24
2	5×138	**8**	137×9
3	276×5	**9**	576×9
4	17×50	**10**	99×18
5	50×50	**11**	146×99
6	50×830	**12**	354×99

Multiplication of decimals

You will do most **decimal 'long multiplications'** with a calculator. However you can do the working with pencil and paper if you are careful.

Ignore the decimal points in the numbers and do the working just like 'whole number multiplication'. Then put the decimal point in the answer to give it the correct place value. An easy way to do this is to count the total number of decimal places in the multiplication. There must be the same number of decimal places in your answer.

For example, for 0.76×90.2
work out 76×902

				9	0	2
			×		7	6
70×900	→	6	3	0	0	0
70×2	→			1	4	0
6×900	→		5	4	0	0
6×2	→				1	2
76×902	→	6	8	5	5	2

Put decimal point in correct
place. $0.76 \times 90.2 \quad = \quad 68.552$

Count decimal places to check.   3 dp   3 dp

Check: $0.76 \approx 0.8 \quad 90.2 \approx 90$
$0.76 \times 90.2 \approx 0.8 \times 90 = 72.0$

Comparing estimate : 72.0
and answer   : 68.552
shows they are *about the same size*.

Note: $\approx$ means 'is approximately equal to'

▶ *Exercise* N2.7

Do these multiplications without a calculator. Then use your calculator to check.

1	26×41.7	**5**	41×7.12
2	3.8×129	**6**	0.36×235
3	0.65×2.94	**7**	5.3×19.6
4	7.2×4.13	**8**	44.6×0.67

Division by whole numbers

One way to divide by a number is to use *repeated subtraction* of that number.

For example, to work out $790 \div 17$, you can find out 'how many 17s in 790?' by subtracting 17 over and over and over ... again. This works. But it is not very efficient.

It is quicker if you can subtract *multiples* of the number instead.

For example, to work out $790 \div 17$, try 10, 20, 30, ... 'lots' of 17 first, then try 1, 2, 3, ... 'lots' of 17 until you reach the answer.

Here is one way to record the working:

Too much

790		
− 680	←	40×17
110		
− 102	←	6×17
8		46×17

Try $50 \times 17 = 850$
$40 \times 17 = 680$
$5 \times 17 = 85$
$6 \times 17 = 102$

The result shows that there are 46 lots of 17 in 790 and 8 left over.
So $790 \div 17 = 46$ remainder 8

about the same size as 46

Check: $790 \approx 800 \quad\quad 17 \approx 20$
$790 \div 17 \approx 800 \div 20 = 40$

This way of recording the working shows clearly what you are subtracting each time. You can write down the multiples of 17 you try at the side. Or you may do them in your head. Whichever way you use in your examination, you must show the working clearly.

▶ *Exercise* N2.8

Do these divisions without using a calculator. Then use your calculator to check.

1	(a) $72 \div 24$	**2**	(a) $93 \div 11$
	(b) $80 \div 16$		(b) $92 \div 14$
	(c) $68 \div 17$		(c) $81 \div 26$
	(d) $58 \div 29$		(d) $95 \div 31$
	(e) $91 \div 13$		(e) $64 \div 15$
	(f) $96 \div 32$		(f) $88 \div 13$

3   (a) 164 ÷ 18   (d) 368 ÷ 29
   (b) 183 ÷ 12   (e) 581 ÷ 37
   (c) 257 ÷ 24   (f) 846 ÷ 52

Division by decimals

Every division by a decimal has a *'matching division'* by a whole number that gives the *same answer*. For example,

$$15 \div 0.3 = 50 \quad\longleftarrow$$
$$150 \div 3 \ = 50 \quad\longleftarrow \quad same\ answer$$

Dividing by a whole number is easier than dividing by a decimal. So we do this easier division instead.

To change any division by a decimal into the matching division by a whole number:

● Decide what you have to *multiply by* (10, 100, 1000 …) to change the decimal into a whole number.

● Then do the same to *both* numbers.

Now you can do the division by the whole number that you get.

For example, look at this division: 67.5 ÷ 2.8.
To change 2.8 to 28, you need to multiply by 10.
Multiply *both* numbers by 10 to get 675 ÷ 28.
Then do the long division:

675		
− 560	←	20 × 28
115		
− 112	←	4 × 28
3		24 × 28

10 × 28 = 280
20 × 28 = 560
30 × 28 = 840 ← *too many*

3 × 28 = 84
4 × 28 = 112 ← *nearly there*

This gives   675 ÷ 28 = 24 remainder 3 units
So   67.5 ÷ 2.8 = 24 remainder (3 units ÷ 10)

Check: 24 × 2.8 = 67.2
add remainder   = 0.3
                   = 67.5

► *Exercise* N2.9

Do these divisions without using a calculator. Then use your calculator to check.

1   24 ÷ 0.6   7   243 ÷ 0.27
2   7.2 ÷ 0.8   8   16 ÷ 0.32
3   10.8 ÷ 0.9   9   35.7 ÷ 0.51
4   284 ÷ 0.4   10   51.2 ÷ 6.4
5   1.47 ÷ 0.21   11   133 ÷ 9.5
6   9.8 ÷ 0.35   12   72 ÷ 7.2

Problem solving

In real life, and in most examinations, you are not usually given sums to do like this:

92 × 5		800 ÷ 0.2

You usually have to **solve problems**. You have to decide *what to do* and *how to do it*. It helps if you have a **general strategy**. Try these hints to help you to solve problems with arithmetic.

● Read, or listen to, the problem *carefully*.

● Find out what *question* you have to answer.

● Sort out the *facts* you are given.

● *Choose* the facts you need. You may *not* need all the facts you are given.

● *Plan* the calculation(s) you have to do to find the answer. You may need to add or subtract or multiply or divide. Sometimes you will have to work out several things.

● If the problem looks *difficult* because the numbers are awkward, think about what you would do if the numbers were easy. Then follow the *same plan* with the 'awkward numbers'.

● *Work out* the answer to the calculation(s). Make sure you have the correct unit(s) of measure if any.

● Decide the *solution to the problem* from your answer. Round your result if you need to.

● *Check* your solution if you can. Does it make sense? Is it about the right size? Does it actually solve the problem?

► *Exercise* N2.10

1   Try solving these problems in your head. Then use your calculator to check.
   (a) There are 40 eggs on a tray. How many eggs are there on 90 trays?
   (b) A fully loaded Boeing 747 jumbo jet carries 500 people. How many people could a fleet of 40 Boeing 747s carry?
   (c) A strip of wood 3000mm long is cut into 20 pieces of equal length. How long is each piece?
   (d) 40 people share equally a £2 million prize on the football pools. How much does each one get?
   (e) Julie's local telephone directory has 900 pages. How many pages will 700 copies of it contain altogether?
   (f) Roy's maths homework takes him 3000 seconds to do. How many minutes is this?

2   Use pencil and paper to solve these problems. Then use your calculator to check.
   (a) There are 36 biscuits in a packet. How many biscuits are there in 45 packets?
   (b) A pad of paper contains 256 sheets. How many sheets of paper are there in a dozen pads?
   (c) 108 balloons are shared equally among 27 children. How many balloons does each child get?
   (d) A '24 exposure' film can take 24 photographs. How many of these films do I need to buy to take 173 photographs?
   (e) On average, there are 376 words on each page of a book. The book has 95 pages. How many words does it contain?
   (f) Envelopes are packed in dozens. Rita needs envelopes for 210 letters she has to post. How many packs should she buy? How many envelopes will be left over?

N3
Decimal places and significant figures

This unit will help you to:

■ understand the idea of approximation

■ understand the difference between exact results and approximations

■ recognise decimal places

■ round numbers using decimal places

■ understand the meaning of significant figures

■ round numbers using significant figures

■ give sensible answers to calculations using these approximations.

Exact and approximate

You can count discrete things and give an **exact** number.

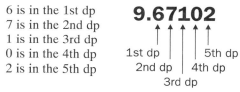

How many chairs? 3
How many legs? 12

Counting tells you 'how many' exactly.

Many numbers we use are approximations to the exact value. They are not exact. But they are about the right size. For example, these reports are about the same football match:

SHEFFIELD UNITED 2
LIVERPOOL 1
26,943 watch

27 000 SEE LIVERPOOL BEATEN

26 943 is the **exact** number of people counted at the match. 27 000 is an **approximation**. It gives you a good idea of the number at the match.

A measurement can *never* be exact. **All measurements are approximations**. This does not mean they are 'rough' or not measured carefully. They are **accurate to the stated level of accuracy**. For example,

The height of a baby is 52 cm (to the nearest cm).
The weight of a baby is 3 kg (to the nearest kg).

Measuring only tells you 'how much' to the stated level of accuracy.

You will often need to find approximate values during your GCSE course (and in everyday life). **Rounding values** is a common way to do this.

You have **rounded values to the nearest 1,10,100,** ... at an earlier level in your course. You should also be able to round values to a stated number of **decimal places or significant figures**.

 Discussion Exercise

Think of some other everyday situations in which numbers are used to describe things. Say whether these numbers are exact or approximate. For those numbers which are approximate, discuss suitable levels of accuracy.

Decimal places

The **decimal places (dp)** in a number come *after* the decimal point. For example, each of these numbers has 3 decimal places:

0.**792**   5.**001**   78.**060**   1254.**000**

To number the places (1st,2nd,3rd,...), start at the point and count to the right. For example, in this number

6 is in the 1st dp
7 is in the 2nd dp
1 is in the 3rd dp
0 is in the 4th dp
2 is in the 5th dp

9.67102

1st dp | 5th dp
2nd dp | 4th dp
3rd dp

A common way to approximate a decimal is to reduce the number of decimal places it has. The decimal is given **'correct to'** a stated number of decimal places.

For example,   0.371 =   0.4   (correct to 1 dp)
                16.054 = 16.05   (correct to 2 dp)
                9.1865 = 9.187   (correct to 3 dp)

The decimal 'ends' after the stated number of places. The *last figure* is rounded up or down in the way you have used for whole numbers.

To correct a decimal to a number of decimal places:

● Find the last decimal place you want.

● Then look at the figure in the next decimal place (to the right).

If this figure is *less than* 5, round *down*.
(Just forget the decimal places you do not want.)
If this figure is *5 or more*, round *up*.
(Add 1 to the figure in the last place you want.)

To correct a decimal to 1 dp, look at the 2nd dp,
                        to 2 dp, look at the 3rd dp,
                        to 3 dp, look at the 4th dp,
                        and so on.

Question

Give 29.3517 correct to (a) 1 dp (b) 2 dp (c) 3 dp

continued

Answer

(a) *To correct to 1 dp*

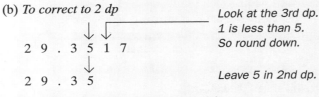

Look at the 2nd dp.
It is 5.
So round up.

Add 1 to 3 to give
4 in the 1st dp.

So 29.3517 = 29.4 (correct to 1 dp)

(b) *To correct to 2 dp*

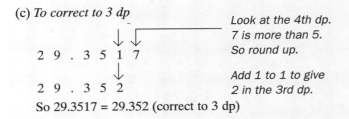

Look at the 3rd dp.
1 is less than 5.
So round down.

Leave 5 in 2nd dp.

So 29.3517 = 29.35 (correct to 2 dp)

(c) *To correct to 3 dp*

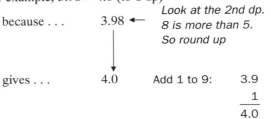

Look at the 4th dp.
7 is more than 5.
So round up.

Add 1 to 1 to give
2 in the 3rd dp.

So 29.3517 = 29.352 (correct to 3 dp)

To round up some numbers you add 1 to a 9.

1 + 9 = 10   You carry 1 up to the *next* place.
You have 0 in the *last* place.

For example, 3.98 = 4.0 (to 1 dp)

because . . .   3.98 ←   Look at the 2nd dp.
8 is more than 5.
So round up

gives . . .   4.0   Add 1 to 9:   3.9
$\frac{1}{4.0}$

Do *not* forget the 0.
Without it you do *not* have 1 dp.
Sometimes the result of 'adding 1' carries along several places. The rounded number will have more than one decimal place filled with 0s.
Here are some examples:

20.995   = 21.00 (to 2 dp)
1.6998   = 1.700 (to 3 dp)
0.29997 = 0.3000 (to 4 dp)
39.9996 = 40.000 (to 3 dp)

► Exercise N3.1

1   Write these numbers correct to 1 dp.
(a) 3.74   (e) 0.38
(b) 11.67   (f) 32.97
(c) 9.81   (g) 51.95
(d) 27.25   (h) 64.82

2   Correct each of these to (i) 1 dp (ii) 2 dp (iii) 3 dp.
(a) 15.42137   (d) 6.49229
(b) 5.82634   (e) 0.32145
(c) 9.52877   (f) 2.903075

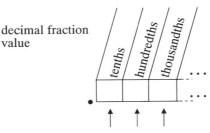

Different name, same approximation

Each decimal place has a **decimal fraction value**.

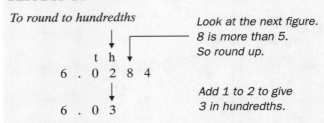

decimal fraction value

decimal places   1st 2nd 3rd · · ·

1st decimal place   →   tenths
2nd decimal place   →   hundredths
3rd decimal place   →   thousandths
and so on.

Rounding a decimal may be described in terms of 'decimal places' or 'decimal fractions'.

'to 1 dp' or 'to the nearest tenth or 0.1'
'to 2 dp' or 'to the nearest hundredth or 0.01'
'to 3 dp' or 'to the nearest thousandth or 0.001'
and so on.

You do the rounding in the same way.

Question

Round 6.0284 kg to the nearest hundredth of a kg.

Answer

To round to hundredths

Look at the next figure.
8 is more than 5.
So round up.

t   h
6 . 0 2 8 4

6 . 0 3   Add 1 to 2 to give
3 in hundredths.

So 6.0284 kg = 6.03 kg (to the nearest hundredth of a kg).

► Exercise N3.2

Round each of these measures to the nearest
(a) tenth of a unit,
(b) hundredth of a unit,
(c) thousandth of a unit.

1 7.4826 kg   4 17.3582 miles
2 10.07354 m   5 1.6745 hours
3 2.5493 km   6 0.02561 m

Quantities are often given in one unit of measure and the approximation in another.

Answers in £s are often given *'to the nearest penny'*. This is the same as rounding them *'to 2 dp'* because 1 penny = £0.01.

Answers in cm are often given *'to the nearest mm'*. This is the same as rounding them *'to 1 dp'* because 1 mm = 0.1 cm.

Answers in metres are often given *'to the nearest cm'*. This is the same as rounding them *'to 2 dp'* because 1 cm = 0.01 m.

Answers in litres can be given *'to the nearest ml'*. This is the same as rounding them *'to 3 dp'* because 1 ml = 0.001 litre.

Question

The answer to a calculation in kilometres is shown on this calculator display. Give this result in km correct to the nearest metre.

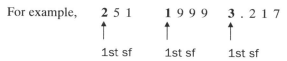

Answer

1000 m = 1 km   1 m = 0.001 km

To correct the result to the nearest metre, correct the number of km to 3 dp.

> Look at 4th dp
> 2 is less than 5.
> So round down.

$$1\ 6\ .\ 5\ 1\ 7\ 2\ .\ .\ .$$
$$\downarrow$$
$$1\ 6\ .\ 5\ 1\ 7$$

So the result is 16.517 km (to the nearest m).

► *Exercise* N3.3

1 Give 2.65138 km correct to the nearest m.
2 Give 3.47521 kg correct to the nearest g.
3 Give 1.694 m correct to the nearest cm.
4 Give 15.89237 kg correct to the nearest g.
5 Give 12.0795 m correct to the nearest mm.

Significant figures

A figure's place in a number is *important*. It tells you what the figure is worth.

$$3\ \mathbf{6}\ 2\ \mathbf{6}$$

6 hundreds   6 units

Each place has a *different value*.

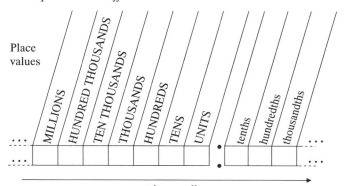

getting smaller

The place values get *smaller* as you go from left to right.

As you read a number from left to right, the first figure you come to that is *not zero* has the **highest place value**, so it is worth *most*. It is called the **most** or **first significant figure** (sf).

For example,   **2** 5 1   **1** 9 9 9   **3** . 2 1 7
          ↑   ↑   ↑
        1st sf   1st sf   1st sf

The same is true for numbers less than 1.

For example,   0 . 0 **1** 5 2   0 . 0 0 **4** 7   0 . 0 0 0 **3** 2
            ↑   ↑   ↑
          1st sf   1st sf   1st sf

To number significant figures (1st, 2nd, 3rd, ...) start at the *first significant figure* and count to the *right*.

For example, a length of 407 mm has three significant figures. It can be written in these ways using different units of length.

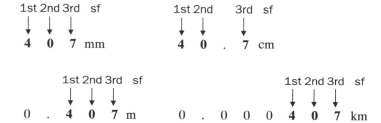

Each number has three significant figures.

   The 1st sf is 4
   The 2nd sf is 0
   The 3rd sf is 7

Note: Zeros *before* the 1st sf are not significant figures. A zero 'inside' a number, i.e. *after* the 1st sf counts as a significant figure.

► *Exercise* N3.4

1 Write down the first significant figure in each of these numbers
   (a) 23.19   (d) 0.628
   (b) 172.48   (e) 0.00517
   (c) 351   (f) 0.00219
2 Write down the second significant figure in each of these numbers
   (a) 149   (d) 0.387
   (b) 76.38   (e) 0.005061
   (c) 9.261   (f) 0.0008427

An easy way to approximate a number is to reduce how many significant figures it has. The number is given **'correct to'** a stated number of significant figures.
See the examples on the next page.

Here are some examples:

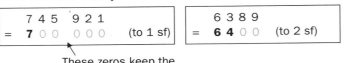

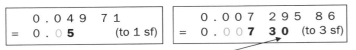

These zeros keep the place value of the 7 correct

This zero is needed to make 3 sf

To correct a number to a stated number of significant figures, you round it up or down in the usual way.

Find the *last* significant figure you want.
Then look at the next significant figure (to the *right*).
If this figure is *less than* 5, round *down*.
(Leave the last significant figure you want as it is).
If this figure is *5 or more*, round *up*.
(Add 1 to the last significant figure you want).

To correct a number to 1 sf, look at the 2nd sf,
to 2 sf, look at the 3rd sf,
to 3 sf, look at the 4th sf,
and so on.

 Make sure that you keep the *place value* of each figure *correct* in the number. You may need to fill some places with 0s to do this.
 Always check that your rounded number is of the *same order of size* as the original number. Writing the figures in the correct columns is one way to do this.

Question

(a) Give 14.083 correct to 3 significant figures.
(b) Correct 0.3651 to 2 significant figures.
(c) Round 0.009 317 to 1 significant figure.

Answer

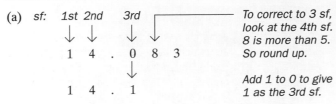

To correct to 3 sf, look at the 4th sf. 8 is more than 5. So round up.

Add 1 to 0 to give 1 as the 3rd sf.

So 14.083 = 14.1 (to 3 sf)

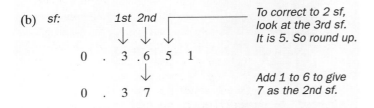

To correct to 2 sf, look at the 3rd sf. It is 5. So round up.

Add 1 to 6 to give 7 as the 2nd sf.

So 0.3651 = 0.37 (to 2 sf)

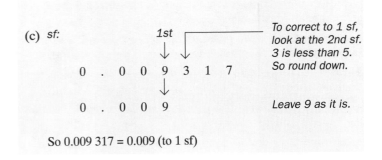

To correct to 1 sf, look at the 2nd sf. 3 is less than 5. So round down.

Leave 9 as it is.

So 0.009 317 = 0.009 (to 1 sf)

► Exercise N3.5

Correct each number to (a) 1 sf (b) 2 sf (c) 3 sf.
1 14.723   **5** 0.3215   **9** 0.036 81
2 5.8271   **6** 2385   **10** 0.009 5201
3 8.2504   **7** 0.061 49
4 163.85   **8** 0.008 471

Sometimes you have to fill in some 'places' with 0s to keep the place value of each figure correct.

Question

Correct the number 178 540 to
(a) 4 sf (b) 3 sf (c) 2 sf (d) 1 sf.

Answer

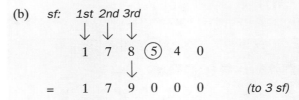

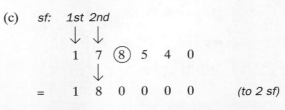

► *Exercise* N3.6

Correct each number to (a) 1 sf (b) 2 sf (c) 3 sf (d) 4 sf.

1 186 530   **3** 492 816   **5** 29 503 651
2 374 850   **4** 51 811 304   **6** 99 537 428

In some examples rounding makes a 0 that is *not 'inside'* the number into a significant figure. Make sure that you do not omit this zero.

Question

Give each of these numbers correct to 2 sf:
(a) 0.0395 (b) 0.997

Answer

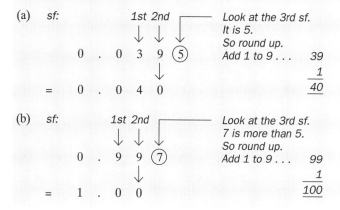

► *Exercise* N3.7

Give each of these numbers correct to 2 sf.

1 0.04831   **3** 0.003551   **5** 0.0995
2 0.06592   **4** 0.008964

Using approximations

An approximation is often used to make the size of a number easier to see and understand.

An examination question may tell you the approximation to use. Read it carefully. Do not confuse decimal places and significant figures.

Question

A book of 'interesting facts' gave these two lengths. Write each correct to two significant figures.

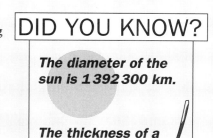

DID YOU KNOW?

The diameter of the sun is 1 392 300 km.

The thickness of a human hair is 0.0753 mm.

Answer

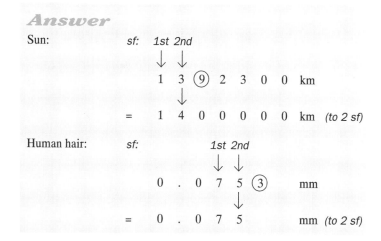

Sun: = 1 4 0 0 0 0 0 km *(to 2 sf)*

Human hair: = 0 . 0 7 5 mm *(to 2 sf)*

► *Exercise* N3.8

Write each number given in these 'interesting facts' to
(a) 1 sf (b) 2 sf.

1 The surface temperature of the sun is 5660 °C.
2 The star Sirius is 8.65 light years distant from Earth.
3 The Caspian Sea has an area of 143 550 square miles.
4 The solar probe Helios B reached a speed of 149 125 mph.
5 The mass of a panel pin is 0.000 107 kg.

Many calculations produce answers with a long string of figures. Sometimes these answers do not have a real or practical meaning. You have to round them to make them '**realistic**'.

For example, this answer in pounds has to be rounded to the nearest penny.

`148.7681`

£148.7681 = £148.77 (to the nearest penny).

A penny is our smallest unit of currency.

Always make sure that your answers make 'real sense'.

Often the answer you get is 'too accurate' for the problem it is supposed to solve. You are expected to round the answer to a **suitable degree of accuracy**. In an examination a mark (or marks) will be given for doing this.

The question may tell you what degree of accuracy to use. Do what it says or you will lose the mark(s).

Sometimes *you* have to decide what size of answer is sensible. Think about the problem. Use your common sense. The accuracy of an answer depends on the accuracy of the values used to produce it. Find the 'most accurate' of these values, i.e. the value with most decimal places or significant figures. Use this to help you to decide. In general, your answer should have *at most* one significant figure more than this value. Often it will have the same number of significant figures.

Always **record your calculator answer** in your working. **Label** it clearly.

Then **round it** to the chosen level of accuracy. If you have chosen this, you can say what you have done and why.

Question

The total weight of three identical parcels is 25.0 kg. What is the weight of each?

Answer

25.0 kg ÷ 3 = 8.333 ... kg (calculator)
            = 8.3 kg (to 1 dp)

Rounded to 1 dp because the weight is given to 1 dp.

► *Exercise* N3.9

Give the answer to each of these to a sensible degree of accuracy.

1   A 1 m length of ribbon is cut into three equal pieces. What is the length of each piece?
2   13 paperclips have a mass of 5 g. What is the mass of each paperclip?
3   1 litre of lemonade is poured into 15 cups. How much is in each cup?
4   3 lb of flour were used to make 26 buns. How much flour was used for each bun?
5   20 m of fabric were used to cover 12 chairs. How much was needed for each chair?

Examination Questions

1   Write 7.0586 correct to three significant figures.
                                      (Cambridge, 1990)

2   The measurements of this rectangular tile are 2.34 cm by 5.87 cm. What is the area of the shaded part of the tile correct to two significant figures?

                                      (SEG, 1988)

3   The diameter of a drill is $\frac{7}{16}$ of an inch.

   (a) What is the radius of the drill?
   (b) Write the diameter as a decimal, correct to 2 significant figures.
                                      (SEG, 1988)

4   The main span of the Humber Bridge is 1410 m long. Write this in kilometres correct to 1 decimal place.
                                      (ULEAC, 1989)

5   A petrol pump shows the price to be paid (in pounds and pence) and the quantity of petrol supplied (in litres, to two decimal places).
A garage charges 37.1p per litre for petrol. When I buy £15 worth of petrol, how many litres will be shown on the pump?

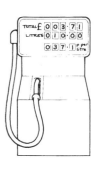

                                      (NEAB, 1989)

6   Hong Kong has the highest traffic density in the world. At the last survey there were 191 146 vehicles and 1091 km of road.
   (a) How many metres of road were there?
   Traffic density is measured in metres of road per vehicle.
   (b) Work out the traffic density in Hong Kong correct to 1 decimal place.
                                      (MEG, 1990)

7   (a) Express as decimals, correct to 5 decimal places,
       (i) $3\frac{1}{7}$ (ii) $\left(\frac{62}{35}\right)^2$
   (b) π = 3.14159 correct to 5 decimal places.
       Which of $3\frac{1}{7}$ and $\left(\frac{62}{35}\right)^2$ is the better approximation to this value of π and by how much is it different?
                                      (MEG, 1990)

8   Express the following fractions as decimals.
   (a) $\frac{5}{8}$
   (b) (i) $\frac{1}{13}$ to three significant figures
       (ii) $\frac{7}{9}$ to four decimal places
       (iii) $\frac{5}{11}$ to thirteen decimal places.   (NEAB, 1989)

9   The formula for calculating the density of an object is
       $$\text{density} = \frac{\text{mass}}{\text{volume}}$$
   A student measured the mass of an object as 142.7 grams, and its volume as 10.5 cm³.
   (a) Calculate the density of this object, giving your answer
       (i) correct to three decimal places,
       (ii) correct to three significant figures,
       (iii) correct to the nearest whole number.
   (b) Decide which of these three answers to part (a) would be the most appropriate for the student to select, giving a reason for your choice.
                                      (NEAB, 1989)

10 Aziz wants to make a plastic mug in the shape of a cylinder. The volume, V, of the mug must be 510 cubic centimetres and the height, h, 9.6 centimetres. Aziz has to work out the radius, r, in centimetres. He knows that r is given by the formula
       $$r = \sqrt{\frac{V}{\pi h}}$$
   (a) Taking π = 3.14, calculate the value of r, correct to 1 decimal place.
   (b) Explain clearly how Aziz could estimate the value of r, correct to 1 significant figure, if he did not have a calculator or mathematical tables.
                                      (MEG, 1989)

N4
Estimating answers

This unit will help you to:

■ use estimates for answers to simple 'real-life' problems

■ estimate the answer to a calculation involving whole numbers

■ use such an estimate to check that an answer is 'about the right size'.

An **estimate** of the answer to a calculation is often all you need in 'real-life' situations. It gives you a rough idea of what the actual answer should be.

Question

Tricia has saved £30 to buy some budget CDs. Each costs £4.99. Alice has saved £48 to buy some mid-priced CDs. Each costs £6.05.
Estimate how many CDs each girl can buy.
Explain your working.

Answer

Tricia: £4.99 is just less than £5.
There are 6 lots of £5 in £30.
So 6 CDs cost just less than £30.
Tricia can buy 6 CDs.

Alice: £6.05 is just more than £6.
There are 8 lots of £6 in £48.
So 8 CDs cost just more than £48.
Alice can buy only 7 CDs.

▶ *Exercise* N4.1

1 Estimate the total of each bill:

(a)

I. Carve Butcher

Steak	£6.87
Chops	£4.32
Lamb	£7.94
Stew	£2.43
Total	

(b)
Jack Fleecem Motor Repairs

Coil	£18.34
Plugs	£ 5.96
Battery	£25.58
Labour	£39.25
Total	

(c)
W. E. BOOZE OFF LICENCE

Beer	£ 8.21
Wine	£ 5.98
Spirits	£23.92
Total	

(d)
BOB'S CAFE

Sausage egg and chips	£1.95
Bacon and eggs	£1.15
Bread and butter	£0.80
2 teas	£0.40
Total	

2 Sara has £3.50 to spend on crisps for the party. A bag of crisps costs 24p. Estimate how many bags she can buy.

3 Peaches cost 18p each. Estimate how many you can buy for £2.

4 A carton holds 12 bottles of apple juice. There are 847 cartons in a warehouse. Approximately how many bottles are in the warehouse?

5 Rachel and Ben sold 146 raffle tickets every day for 16 days. Estimate the number of tickets they sold.

To estimate the answer to any calculation, first make the numbers easier (by rounding them) then use these easier numbers in the calculation.

Rounding all the numbers to 1 significant figure usually gives a calculation you can do in your head (see Unit N2).

The estimate may be larger or smaller than the actual answer. But it will give you an idea of its size.

Note: ≈ means **'is approximately equal to'**.

Question

(a) There are 54 rows of 29 chairs in a college hall.
Estimate the number of chairs in the hall. Then calculate the actual number.

(b) A college has 1003 students. On average there are 17 students in each class.
Estimate, then calculate, the number of classes.

Answer

(a) *Round each number to 1 sf* 54 ≈ 50   29 ≈ 30
Estimate: 54 × 29
                       ≈ 50 × 30 = 1500
Actual number: 54 × 29 = 1566

(b) *Round each number to 1 sf* 1003 ≈ 1000   17 ≈ 20
Estimate: 1003 ÷ 17
                       ≈ 1000 ÷ 20 = 50
Actual number: 1003 ÷ 17 = 59

▶ *Exercise* N4.2

1 Estimate the answers to these calculations. Then calculate the exact answer.

(a) 15 × 29   (d) 92 ÷ 31   (g) 97 × 3261
(b) 17 × 48   (e) 86 × 53   (h) 6091 ÷ 33
(c) 63 ÷ 19   (f) 278 ÷ 64

2 A shop sells oranges at 28p each. Approximately how much would it cost for a dozen?

3 437 cm of ribbon are left on a roll. It is cut into 23 equal length pieces. Roughly how long is each piece?

4 Pete travels, on average, 192 miles each working day. Estimate the distance he travels in 28 working days.

5 There are 2790 containers of washing up liquid in a warehouse. Roughly how many boxes are needed to pack them if each box holds 18 containers?

Some calculations involve *both* multiplication and division. You can estimate answers to these in the same way.
Round the numbers as before.
Then do the calculation step-by-step.
Here is an example:

To estimate the answer to
$$\frac{876 \times 41}{59}$$

you round each number:
$$\frac{900 \times 40}{60}$$

Do the multiplication first:
$$\frac{36\,000}{60} \longleftarrow \boxed{900 \times 40}$$

Then do the division:
$$600 \longleftarrow \boxed{36\,000 \div 60}$$

The estimate is 600.

Exercise N4.3

Estimate the answers to these. Show how you made each estimate.

1 $\dfrac{932 \times 81}{38}$

2 $\dfrac{88 \times 48}{297}$

3 $\dfrac{1409}{73 \times 11}$

4 $\dfrac{62 \times 420}{18 \times 29}$

5 $\dfrac{57 \times 42\,150}{18 \times 195}$

Estimates as checks

You can use an **estimate** to check that an answer is **'about the right size'**. An estimate helps you to spot an *incorrect* answer. It does *not* show that an answer is correct.

However, when using a calculator it is a good idea to estimate the answer to a calculation *first*, then you can check that your estimate and answer are a *reasonable match*. Other calculator checks are also given in Unit N1.

Question

A job is advertised at £275 per week. Two students work out the annual salary. Here are their results.

Estimate the annual salary.
Use your estimate to help you to comment on their results.

Answer

Round figures to 1 sf
Estimate:

52 weeks
$275 \approx 300 \qquad 52 \approx 50$
$£275 \times 52$
$\approx £300 \times 50 = £15\,000$

Jeff's answer £6875 is obviously wrong.
Tim's answer £14 300 is about the same size as £15 000.

Exercise N4.4

Which of these answers are obviously incorrect? Use estimates to spot them.

1 (a) $37 \times 21 = 777$ (d) $73 \times 106 = 7738$
(b) $53 \times 194 = 1028$ (e) $1300 \times 45 = 58\,500$
(c) $624 \times 37 = 28\,088$ (f) $82 \times 17 = 476$

2 The train travelled for 21 hours at an average speed of 47 mph. It travelled a distance of 98.7 miles.

3 Mrs Patel earns £8868 per year. That's £73.90 per month.

4 A textbook is 22 mm thick. I can store 45 textbooks on a 1m long shelf.

5 A parcel weighs 794 grams. 32 of these parcels weigh 2.54 kg altogether.

Examination Questions

1 Simon used his calculator to work out the value of 3.12×4.36. He wrote down the answer as 136.032.
(a) What simple check could Simon have used, without using his calculator, to show that his answer is incorrect?
(b) Write down the correct answer. (WJEC, 1994)

2 (a) For each of the following statements, write whether they are 'TRUE' or 'FALSE'.
(i) $873 + 416$ is about 1300
(ii) $1472 - 383$ is about 110.
(iii) $2780 \div 390$ is about 70.
(b) For each of the FALSE statements in part (a), write a more correct estimate of the answer to the calculation. (MEG, 1994)

3 Albert works out $612 \div 29$ on his calculator. He gets the answer 211.103448. *Without using a calculator* do a rough check to see if Albert's answer is correct. You must show all your working. (SEG, 1994)

4 In 1986, there were 2 004 500 accidents in the home in England. The table shows where these accidents occurred.

Place of Accident	Accidents (%)
Living Room	22
Kitchen	38
Bedroom	3
Hall	1
Bathroom	2
Garden	32
Unknown	2

(a) John estimated, without using a calculator, that there were approximately 800 000 accidents in the kitchen. Explain one way that he could have made this estimate.

(b) (i) Calculate the exact number of accidents that occurred in the kitchen.

(ii) Work out John's percentage error.

(NEAB, 1994)

5 The 42 members of a club buy 125 balls at £1.49 each. They share the cost equally between them. The treasurer uses his calculator to work out the cost to each member. He gets an answer of 44 pence.

Without using a calculator, use a rough estimate to check whether his answer is correct. You must show all your working.

(SEG, 1994)

6 (a) When buying his groceries in a supermarket, George estimates the maximum amount he will have to pay by rounding up the price of each article to the nearest 10p

(unless it is already a multiple of 10p). For example, an article costing £2.21 is rounded up to £2.30 and an article costing £1.58 is rounded up to £1.60.

On one particular occasion, he bought 12 articles and his estimate was £8.30.

What is the smallest possible total of the actual prices of the 12 articles? Show your working clearly.

(b) Alyson uses a similar method but she rounds the price of each article to the nearest 10p (up or down as necessary with 5p always being rounded up). For example, an article costing £2.21 is rounded down to £2.20 and an article costing £1.58 is rounded up to £1.60.

She bought 20 articles whose total price was £12.56. Calculate the greatest and least possible values of her estimate. Explain your method.

(MEG, 1994)

N5
Factors and multiples

This unit will help you to:

■ understand the idea of a factor

■ find the factors of a number

■ find the common factors of numbers

■ find the multiples of a number

■ understand the relationship between factors and multiples

■ find common multiples and the lowest common multiple of numbers

■ understand the idea of a prime number

■ check whether a number is prime or not

■ find prime factors.

Factors

A **factor** of a whole number is a whole number that divides *exactly* into it, giving a *whole number answer*.

For example,

8 is a factor of 24

24 ÷ 8 = 3 ← *whole number, nothing left over*

8 is not a factor of 30

30 ÷ 8 = 3 remainder 6 ← *something left over*

or 3.75 ←

1 is a factor of every number
because 1 divides exactly in to every number.

Every number is a factor of itself
because a number always divides exactly into itself.

So you always know these factors of any number.

 *Exercise* **N5.1**

In each case, use your calculator to check if the first number given is a factor of the second.

1 2, 104	**5** 9, 306	**9** 23, 943
2 3, 114	**6** 13, 223	**10** 17, 907
3 7, 197	**7** 15, 195	
4 8, 212	**8** 21, 650	

To find all the factors of a number, try *dividing it* by 1, 2, 3, ... in turn. A calculator makes this easy to do. Put the number in the *memory* and keep recalling it to do the divisions.

Write down those that divide exactly. That way you won't miss any!

Try this way to find the factors of 12.

Try 1: 12 ÷ 1 = 12 ✓	*Your calculator shows*
Try 2: 12 ÷ 2 = 6 ✓	*these answers.*
Try 3: 12 ÷ 3 = 4 ✓	
Try 4: 12 ÷ 4 = 3 ✓	
Try 5: 12 ÷ 5 = 2.4	
Try 6: 12 ÷ 6 = 2 ✓	
Try 7: 12 ÷ 7 = 1.714 2857	
Try 8: 12 ÷ 8 = 1.5	
Try 9: 12 ÷ 9 = 1.333 3333	
Try 10: 12 ÷ 10 = 1.2	
Try 11: 12 ÷ 11 = 1.091	
Try 12: 12 ÷ 12 = 1 ✓	

So the factors of 12 are 1, 2, 3, 4, 6 and 12.

This working is quick to do for a small number. But it would take a long time for a large number. Here are some useful **short-cuts**:

● Just *looking* at a whole number can show you whether it will divide exactly by 2 or 5 or 10.

last figure 0, 2, 4, 6, or 8 → factor 2
last figure 0 or 5 → factor 5
last figure 0 → factor 10

For example,   312**8** has a factor 2,
               629**0** has factors 2, 5 and 10,
               29**5** has a factor 5.

- An 'exact division' tells you about *two factors*:
  the number you divide by,
  and the answer you get.

Look at the factors of 12 again.

$12 \div 1 = 12 \rightarrow 1$ and 12 are factors
$12 \div 2 = 6 \rightarrow 2$ and 6 are factors
$12 \div 3 = 4 \rightarrow 3$ and 4 are factors.

But you can stop here. You have already found that 3 and 4 are factors! This saves a great deal of work.

▶ *Exercise* N5.2

Find all the factors of each of these numbers. Use a calculator to help you.

1	30	**3**	42	**5**	76	**7**	130
2	36	**4**	60	**6**	90	**8**	216

A **factor pair** of a number multiply together to give the number.

$40 = 1 \times 40$

$40 = 2 \times 20$

$40 = 4 \times 10$ *These are the factor pairs of 40.*

$40 = 5 \times 8$

Factor pairs make a pattern like this:

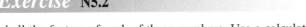

1   2   4   5   8   10   20   40

You can use them to check whether you have all the factors of a number.

Look at this factor pair pattern: 1   3   9

This is special because 9 is a square number and $3 \times 3 = 9$.

▶ *Exercise* N5.3

Write down all the factor pairs for each of these numbers.

1	4	**3**	13	**5**	52	**7**	88
2	10	**4**	35	**6**	72	**8**	130

Common factors

If two or more numbers have a factor *in common*, then the factor is called a **common factor**. The factor divides exactly into *each* number. For example,

2 is a factor of 6 since $6 \div 2 = 3$

2 is a factor of 8 since $8 \div 2 = 4$

So 2 is a common factor of 6 and 8.

1 is a factor of every number. So **1 is always a common factor**.

▶ *Exercise* N5.4

Find the common factors of

1	3 and 15	**4**	27 and 64	**7**	18 and 52
2	7 and 23	**5**	6 and 20	**8**	35 and 45
3	15 and 40	**6**	9 and 27		

Multiples

A **multiple of a whole number** is found by multiplying it by any whole number.

$4 \times 7 = 28$ So 28 is a multiple of 4 and
               28 is a multiple of 7.

Every number is a multiple of 1

because $1 \times$ 'number' = 'number'

Every number is a multiple of itself

because   'number' $\times 1$ = 'number'

The **multiples of 2, 5 and 10** are easy to spot.
Just look at the *last* figure (the *Units*).

Multiples of 2 (even numbers) end with 2 or 4 or 6 or 8 or 0.
Multiples of 5 end with 5 or 0.
Multiples of 10 end with 0.

Here are some examples:

$2 \times 1 = 2$	$5 \times 1 = 5$	$10 \times 1 = 10$
$2 \times 2 = 4$	$5 \times 2 = 10$	$10 \times 2 = 20$
$2 \times 3 = 6$	$5 \times 3 = 15$	$10 \times 3 = 30$
$2 \times 4 = 8$	$5 \times 4 = 20$	$10 \times 4 = 40$
$2 \times 5 = 10$	$5 \times 5 = 25$	$10 \times 5 = 50$
$2 \times 6 = 12$	$5 \times 6 = 30$	$10 \times 6 = 60$
$2 \times 7 = 14$	$5 \times 7 = 35$	$10 \times 7 = 70$
and so on.		

You can find the **multiples of a number** by multiplying it by 1, 2, 3, ... Knowing your *tables* can help you to do this.

You can also do this multiplying with a calculator. Put the number into memory and recall it for each multiplication. For example, to find the multiples of 19:

Press:

Display shows: m 19.   m 38.   m 57.   m 76. ...

Find some other multiples yourself this way.

Another simple way to find multiples is to just keep *adding on the number* over and over again (**repeated addition**). This is basically what multiplication is.

For example, to find the multiples of 6:

Press: C 6 + 6 + 6 + 6 + 6 + ...

Display shows: 6.   12.   18.   24.   30. ...

You enter the number and press ⊞, then enter the number and press ⊞ again, ... Each time you press ⊞, a multiple of the number is displayed.

Try this way yourself to find some other multiples.

Another way uses a **'constant function'**. This is like an automatic memory. It repeats an operation (+, −, ×, ÷) and a number for you.

Here are two ways to try. Find out which works on your calculator. Test them on an easy number like 2.

Enter the number.

Press **+** or Press **+** **+** Then keep pressing **=** .

Each time you press **=** , a multiple of the number comes on the display.

Press: **C** **2** **+** **=** **=** **=** **=**

Display shows: **4.** **6.** **8.** **10.**

or

Press: **C** **2** **+** **+** **=** **=** **=** **=**

Display shows: **4.** **6.** **8.** **10.**

Practise using the way that works on your calculator.

Multiples and factors are related.

$4 \times 3 = 12$ so 12 is a multiple of 4

$12 \div 4 = 3$ so 4 is a factor of 12

A number is a factor of all its multiples. So a multiple of a number can be divided exactly by that number. You can use this to test for multiples.

Question

Which of these numbers are multiples of 13?

39, 62, 221, 84, 397, 1625

Show your working clearly.

Answer

$39 \div 13 = 3$ ✓
$62 \div 13 = 4.769$ ✗
$221 \div 13 = 17$ ✓
$84 \div 13 = 6.462$ ✗
$397 \div 13 = 30.538$ ✗
$1625 \div 13 = 125$ ✓

39, 221 and 1625 are multiples of 13.

► *Exercise* N5.5

1 Which of these numbers are multiples of 7?
42, 65, 91, 105, 163.
2 Which of these numbers are multiples of 14?
78, 112, 184, 210, 234.
3 Which of these numbers are multiples of 17?
49, 68, 102, 157, 221.
4 Which of these numbers are multiples of 23?
92, 142, 184, 274, 529.
5 Which of these numbers are multiples of 47?
94, 238, 282, 423, 754.

Common multiples

If the multiples of *two or more* numbers have a multiple in common, then the number is called a **common multiple**. For example,

the multiples of 2 are   2,   4,   ⑥,   8,   10, ...
the multiples of 3 are   3,   ⑥,   9,   12, ...

So 6 is a common multiple of 2 and 3.

Lowest common multiple

Two or more integers may have *more than one* common multiple. The **lowest common multiple (LCM)** is the smallest multiple they have in common.

Question

Find the lowest common multiple of 15 and 18.

Answer

Multiples of 15:   15,   30,   45,   60,   75,   ⑨⓪,   105 ...
Multiples of 18:   18,   36,   54,   72,   ⑨⓪, ...
So the lowest common multiple of 15 and 18 is 90.

► *Exercise* N5.6

Find the lowest common multiple of each of these pairs of numbers.

1 24 and 8   4 15 and 12
2 12 and 20   5 18 and 30
3 10 and 16   6 16 and 24

Prime numbers

A **prime number** has *exactly two* factors. These are 1 and itself. For example, 3 is a prime number. Its *only* factors are 1 and 3. These are the *only* whole numbers that divide into it exactly.

$3 \div 1 = 3$ → factors 1 and 3
$3 \div 2 = 1.5$ → no factors

1 is not a prime number. It hasn't got enough factors.

$1 \div 1 = 1$ → factor 1

1 has one factor, not two.

6 is *not* a prime number. It has *two many* factors.

$6 \div 1 = 6$ → factors 1 and 6
$6 \div 2 = 3$ → factors 2 and 3

6 has four factors, not 'exactly two'.

Numbers like 6 that have *more than two* factors are called **composite numbers**. They make rectangular dot patterns. So they are also called **rectangular numbers** (see Unit A2).

It is useful to know the first ten prime numbers. These are:

2, 3, 5, 7, 11, 13, 17, 19, 23, 29.

2 is the only even prime number. All other primes are odd.

Prime or not prime

To find out if a number larger than 1 is prime, look for its **factors**. If you find a factor, other than 1 and itself, then the number cannot be prime.

You can test a number by dividing it by 1, 2, 3, 4, 5, ... But you do not need to.

Look for *'factor clues'* before you start dividing.

The only even prime number is 2. Numbers ending in 0, 2, 4, 6, 8 are even. So they cannot be prime ... you can reject them.

Numbers ending in 5 have a factor 5. So they cannot be prime ... you can reject them also.

That means that numbers ending in 1, 3, 7, or 9 may, or may not, be prime. You have to test them by dividing. But you only need to divide by the odd prime numbers 3, 7, 11, 13, ... (You have already 'tested' 2, 5 and all other even numbers by using the factor clues above.).

Question

For each of these numbers say whether it is prime or not prime:

(a) 2910   (b) 1375   (c) 247   (d) 283

Give a reason for each answer.

Answer

(a) 29$\underline{10}$ is not prime.
   1, 2910 and 2 are factors, that is, more than two factors.
(b) 137$\underline{5}$ is not prime:
   1, 1375 and 5 are factors, that is, more than 2 factors.
(c) 24$\underline{7}$ *may or may not be prime.*
   Test by dividing: 247 ÷ 3 = 82.3 ... → no factor
                          247 ÷ 7 = 35.2 ... → no factor
                          247 ÷ 11 = 22.4 ... → no factor
                          247 ÷ 13 = 19 ...   → factors
   So 247 is not prime.
   1, 247, 13, 19 are factors, that is, more than two factors.
(d) 28$\underline{3}$ *may or may not be prime.*
   Test by dividing: 283 ÷ 3 = 94.3 ... → no factor
                          283 ÷ 7 = 40.4 ... → no factor
                          283 ÷ 11 = 25.7 ... → no factor
                          283 ÷ 13 = 21.7 ... → no factor
                          283 ÷ 17 = 16.6 ... → no factor

   You can stop now
   The answer 16.6 ... is smaller than the number tested. This shows that numbers larger than this cannot be factors.
   283 is prime.
   It has exactly two factors, 1 and 283.

► *Exercise* N5.7

1   Which of these numbers cannot be prime?
   Explain your choices.
   (a) 108   (d) 151   (g) 284   (j) 1730
   (b) 117   (e) 149   (h) 776   (k) 2463
   (c) 145   (f) 356   (i) 912   (l) 9378

2   Give ten other numbers larger than 200 which cannot be prime.
3   For each number below, say whether it is 'prime' or 'not prime'. Give a reason for each answer.
   (a) 205   (d) 232   (g) 217   (j) 288
   (b) 211   (e) 201   (h) 296   (k) 253
   (c) 233   (f) 230   (i) 239   (l) 257

Prime factors

A **prime factor** is a factor that is a prime number. Prime numbers that divide exactly into a number are its prime factors. For example, the factors of 24 are

   1②,③, 4, 5, 6, 12 and 24.
   2 and 3 are also prime numbers.

So 2 and 3 are prime factors of 24.

► *Exercise* N5.8

1   Find the prime factors of each number from its list of factors.
   (a) the factors of 20 are 1, 2, 4, 5, 10, 20.
   (b) the factors of 81 are 1, 3, 9, 27, 81.
   (c) the factors of 66 are 1, 2, 3, 6, 11, 22, 33, 66.
   (d) the factors of 80 are 1, 2, 4, 5, 8, 10, 16, 20, 40, 80.
   (e) the factors of 68 are 1, 2, 4, 17, 34, 68.
2   Find the prime factors of:
   (a) 36   (e) 144   (i) 132
   (b) 92   (f) 64   (j) 156
   (c) 46   (g) 27
   (d) 75   (h) 100

Examination Questions

1   The numbers 1, 2, 3, 4, 6, 12 all divide exactly into 12. These numbers are called the factors of 12. Complete this list of factors of 20.
   1 ..., 4, ..., ..., 20   (ULEAC, 1989)

2   (a) Write down all the odd numbers between 20 and 30.
   (b) From your list of numbers, pick out and write down
      (i) all the multiples of 3,
      (ii) all the prime numbers,
      (iii) a square number.   (ULEAC, 1991)

3   This question is about the numbers
      21   22   23   24   25   26   27.
   From the list write down:
   (a) the smallest odd number,   (d) the even multiple of 3,
   (b) the only prime number,   (e) the factor of 81.
   (c) the only square number,   (ULEAC, 1991)

4   A computer prints out the following number pattern:
      3   6   10   15   21 ?
   (a) What is the next number in the pattern?
   (b) Which of the printed numbers is a multiple of 7?
   (c) Write down one even number from the printed list.
   (d) Three of the printed numbers when added together give an answer of 30. Write down the three numbers.
                                          (WJEC,1989)

5 Here is a sequence of numbers
50, 49, 47, 44, 40, 35, 29, ...
(a) Write down the next two numbers in the sequence.
(b) Which of these numbers are
(i) prime,
(ii) multiples of 4? (MEG, 1991)

6 It was suggested by Goldbach in 1742, but has never been proved, that all even numbers greater than 2 can be expressed as the sum of two prime numbers, for example $8 = 3 + 5$.
Express as the sum of two prime numbers
(a) 16,
(b) 96. (MEG, 1991)

7 (a) Any even number greater than 4 is the sum of two odd prime numbers.
For example $12 = 7 + 5$.
(i) Find the two prime numbers which add up to 8.
(ii) Find two prime numbers which add up to 38.
(b) Any number greater than 7 is the sum of three prime numbers. Find three prime numbers which add up to 24. (NISEAC, 1991)

8 Susan is trying to discover factors of 570, using a calculator. She has already discovered that the number 15 is a factor. To test whether the number 16 is a factor of 570, she does the calculation $570 \div 16$.
Her calculator shows:

35.625

(a) Is 16 a factor of 570?
Give a reason for your answer.
(b) Susan continues to look for factors. She tests the numbers 17, 18, onwards. What is the next factor she will find? (NEAB, 1989)

9 Find a number between 10 and 20 that is both a factor of 60 and also a multiple of 6. (MEG, 1989)

10 The factors of a number are those numbers that will divide into that number exactly.
(a) Complete this table.
(b) What is the next number after 9 that has an odd number of factors?
(c) What is the name given to the type of number that has an odd number of factors? (MEG, 1990)

Number	Factors	Number of Factors
2	1,2	2
3	1,3	2
4	1,2,4	3
5	1,5	2
6	1,2,3,6	4
7		
8		
9		
10		

11 A company car park has bays numbered from 1 to 50. The Managing Director organises an unusual plan for its use.
Employees are each given a parking number: they can use the bay with this number or any multiple of this number. For example, if your number is 15 you can use bay 15, 30 or 45.
(a) List the bays you can use if your number is 8.
(b) List the parking numbers of those who can use bay number 12.
(c) Which parking numbers allow you to use only one bay?
(d) If you had a choice, which parking number would you choose? Why?
(e) Which bay can be used by the most parking numbers? (MEG, 1990)

► **N6**
Squares, cubes and their roots

This unit will help you to:
■ understand and use the terms square, square root, cube and cube root
■ find squares, square roots, cubes and cube roots using a calculator and use them to solve simple problems
■ use trial and improvement to find square and cube roots.
■ give sensible answers from the results on your calculator display.

Squares

The **square** of any number is the number multiplied by itself.

For example, the square of 2.5 is $2.5 \times 2.5 = 6.25$.

The square of a *whole number* is called a **perfect square** or **square number**.
It makes a square pattern of dots.
For example, the square of 4 is $4 \times 4 = 16$.

• • • •
• • • • 16
• • • •
• • • •

a perfect square

A small figure ^{2} at the top of a number tells you to square it.
For example, $7^2 = 7 \times 7 = 49$
7^2 is usually read as 'seven squared' or 'the square of 7'.
The square of any number, n, is $n^2 = n \times n$.

It is useful to know and recognise the first ten square numbers.

$1^2 = 1$	$4^2 = 16$	$7^2 = 49$	$10^2 = 100$
$2^2 = 4$	$5^2 = 25$	$8^2 = 64$	
$3^2 = 9$	$6^2 = 36$	$9^2 = 81$	

You can use a calculator to work out squares.
Here are some ways to try. Test them on a square you know,
like $5^2 = 25$. Find out which work on your calculator.

- **Multiply the number by itself:**

- **Use the constant function:**

  Either  or

- **Use a 'square key':**
  The simplest is marked x^2

  You may not need the =

  Others look like this x^y or y^x
  These are called **power keys**.

  press 2 for a square

Choose the way you find easiest on your calculator. Practise
finding squares in this way.

Exercise N6.1

1   Find the missing numbers in these:
 (a) 25 is the square of ...   (c) 7 squared equals ...
 (b) ... is the square of 8   (d) ... squared equals 81

2   Find the missing numbers in these:
 (a) $4 \times 4 = 4^{...}$ (c) $... \times 10 = 10^2$
 (b) $2 \times ... = 2^2$ (d) $3 \times 3 = ...^2$

3   Use your calculator to work out these squares.
 (a) 12^2 (c) 20^2 (e) 6.1^2 (g) 9.2^2
 (b) 15^2 (d) 17^2 (f) 38^2 (h) 10.8^2

4   Use your calculator to work out these squares.
 (a) 0.5^2 (c) 0.9^2 (e) 0.21^2 (g) 0.86^2
 (b) 0.3^2 (d) 0.7^2 (f) 0.47^2 (h) 0.63^2
 Compare each answer with the number you squared.
 What do you notice?

Solving problems can involve using squares.
The area of a square is given by the length of
its side squared.

l

Area of square = l^2

Question

Jenny made a square-shaped patio. It was 2.6 m long.
What was its area?

Answer

Area of patio = $(2.6)^2$ m^2
        = 6.76 m^2

Exercise N6.2

1   Calculate the area of a square of side
 (a) 3 cm   (c) 35 mm   (e) 2.1 km
 (b) 4.5 cm   (d) 9 m   (f) 12.4 mm.

2   Tracy's parents wanted to buy a new carpet for the lounge
 which was in the shape of a letter L.
 Tracy could see that the
 floor could be divided
 into two squares as
 shown.
 Calculate:
 (a) the area of the larger
  square
 (b) the area of the smaller square
 (c) the total area of the floor.

4.9 m

4.9 m

2.6 m

2.6 m

Square roots

Look at this square dot pattern.
It has 25 dots in it.
There are 5 dots along each side.

 We say that 5 is the **'square root'**
 of 25.
 We write: $5 = \sqrt{25}$
 $\sqrt{}$ is the symbol for square root.

$\sqrt{25} = \sqrt{5 \times 5} = 5$

The 'square root of a number' multiplied by itself gives the number.

$\sqrt{n} \times \sqrt{n} = n$

For example, $\sqrt{81}$ means 'the number that gives 81 when you
       multiply it by itself'.

 $\sqrt{81} = 9$ because $9 \times 9 = 81$

The square root of a *square number* (or *perfect square*) is
always a *whole number*.
 It is worth knowing the first ten square numbers and their
square roots.

Square number	1	4	9	16	25	36	49	64	81	100
Square root	1	2	3	4	5	6	7	8	9	10

Most calculators have a **square root key** $\sqrt{}$ or $\sqrt{x}$

This key finds the square root of the number on the display. So
always enter the number *first*, then press the square root key.
Write down the result shown on the display. Then check it by
multiplying it by itself.
 You may have to round the square root you get to a number
of decimal places or significant figures.

Question

Work out $\sqrt{19.4}$ giving your answer correct to 2 significant
figures.

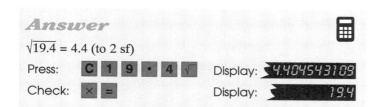

Answer

$\sqrt{19.4} = 4.4$ (to 2 sf)

Press: C 1 9 . 4 √   Display: 4.404543109

Check: × =   Display: 19.4

Note: To check your answer on the calculator, press × = after you have obtained your display answer. Sometimes the number you get may not be *exactly* the number you started with … but it should be very close to it. This happens when your display is too small to show all the digits in the square root.

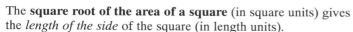

►*Exercise* N6.3

In this exercise, give each answer correct to 3 significant figures.

1 Calculate these square roots.
   (a) $\sqrt{5}$
   (b) square root of 6
   (c) $\sqrt{10}$
   (d) square root of 22
   (e) $\sqrt{2.8}$
   (f) $\sqrt{23.7}$
   (g) square root of 56
   (h) $\sqrt{36.1}$

2 Calculate these square roots.
   (a) $\sqrt{0.7}$
   (b) $\sqrt{0.2}$
   (c) $\sqrt{0.9}$
   (d) $\sqrt{0.041}$
   (e) $\sqrt{0.34}$
   (f) $\sqrt{0.06}$

   Compare each answer with the number whose square root you found. What do you notice?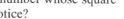

The **square root of the area of a square** (in square units) gives the *length of the side* of the square (in length units).

   Make sure that you give the correct unit of measure in your answer.

Remember: cm^2 will give a length in cm,
   m^2 will give a length in m,
   and so on.

Question

A chair has a square seat of area 850 cm^2. What is the length of each side of the square? Give your answer correct to the nearest mm.

Answer

$\sqrt{850} = 29.2$ (to 1 dp)   29.15475947

So the length of each side is 29.2 cm (to the nearest mm).

►*Exercise* N6.4

Each of the following is the area of a square. Calculate the lengths of the sides of each square. Give your answers correct to the stated degree of accuracy.

1 Area: 246 cm^2 Accuracy: to the nearest mm.
2 Area: 365 cm^2 Accuracy: to the nearest mm.

---

3 Area: 6.7 m^2 Accuracy: to the nearest cm.
4 Area: 8.4 m^2 Accuracy: to the nearest cm.
5 Area: 17.1 km^2 Accuracy: to 3 sf.
6 Area: 520 km^2 Accuracy: to 3 sf.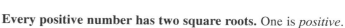

Every positive number has two square roots. One is *positive*. The other is *negative*.
For example, $3 \times 3 = 9$ so 3 is a square root of 9
   and $(^-3) \times (^-3) = 9$ so $(^-3)$ is also a square root of 9.

   The symbol $\sqrt{}$ means the 'square root of'.
   $\sqrt{9}$ means the positive square root of 9.
   $^-\sqrt{9}$ means the negative square root of 9.

The value given by a calculator is the positive square root of a number. You have to remember the negative sign $^-$ and negative root if you need it.

   A negative number does *not* have a square root that is a real number.

Try entering a negative number into your calculator and then press √ . Most calculators show $^-E^-$. The $^-E^-$ means error.

Cubes

The **cube of any number** is the number multiplied by itself and by itself again.
For example, the cube of 1.5 is $1.5 \times 1.5 \times 1.5 = 3.375$.
   A **perfect cube** or **cube number**
is the cube of a whole number.
It makes a 'cube pattern' of dots.
For example,
the cube of 2 is $2 \times 2 \times 2 = 8$

perfect cube

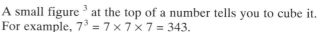

A small figure ^{3} at the top of a number tells you to cube it.
For example, $7^3 = 7 \times 7 \times 7 = 343$.

   7^3 is usually read as 'seven cubed' or 'the cube of 7'.

The cube of any number, n, is $n^3 = n \times n \times n$

It is useful to know and recognise some cube numbers:

   $1^3 = 1$ $3^3 = 27$ $5^3 = 125$
   $2^3 = 8$ $4^3 = 64$ $10^3 = 1000$

You can use your calculator to work out cubes.
You can use simple multiplication.
Or you can use the **constant function**.
But the quickest way is usually to use the **power key**:

   x^y or y^x

Enter the number, press the power key, then press 3 then = .
                                                        ↑
   For example, for 9^3 for a cube
   Press: C 9 x^y 3 = 729.

Practise finding cubes in this way.

►*Exercise* N6.5

Use the power key on your calculator to work out these cubes.

1 2^3 4 6^3 7 12^3 10 7.3^3
2 5^3 5 7^3 8 23^3 11 11.9^3
3 8^3 6 9^3 9 2.5^3 12 36.87^3

Volume is measured in cubic units.
The volume of a cube is given by the
length of its edge cubed.

Volume of cube = l^3

Question

A box for some chocolates is made as a cube with edge
11.5 cm long. What is its volume in cubic centimetres? Give
your answer to the nearest cm^3.

Answer

Volume of box = $(11.5)^3$ cm^3
= 1520.875 cm^3 (calculator)
= 1521 cm^3 (to the nearest cm^3).

► **Exercise** N6.6

Calculate the volume of each of these objects. Each object is a
cube. Give your answers to a sensible degree of accuracy.
1   A water tank with edge 1.3 m.
2   A box of sweets with edge 15 cm.
3   A box of tissues with edge 110 mm.
4   A box of tea with edge 7.6 cm.
5   A child's building brick with edge 137 mm.

Cube roots

A **cube number** (perfect cube) can be shown as a cube of dots.
The number of dots along each *edge* gives the **cube root** of the
cube number.

$\sqrt[3]{}$ means the **cube root of**.

For example, this dot pattern has 27
dots in it.
It has 3 dots along each edge.
We say that 3 is the cube root of 27.
We write $\sqrt[3]{27} = 3$.

Here are the first ten cube numbers and their cube roots.

Cube number	1	8	27	64	125	216	343	512	729	1000
Cube root	1	2	3	4	5	6	7	8	9	10

It is useful to know some of these, especially $\sqrt[3]{1000} = 10$.
The cube root of a *cube number* (*perfect cube*) is always a
whole number.

**The 'cube root of a number' multiplied by itself and by
itself again gives the number.**

$\sqrt[3]{n} \times \sqrt[3]{n} \times \sqrt[3]{n} = n$

You can use this to help you to find cube roots and to check
that a value is a cube root.
For example,

$\sqrt[3]{8}$ means 'the number that gives 8 when you multiply it by
itself and by itself again'.

$\sqrt[3]{8}$ = 2 because $2 \times 2 \times 2 = 8$.

To find the cube root of a number with a calculator you can use
the **cube root key** $\sqrt[3]{}$.
Just key in the number, then press the cube root key.
For example, to find the cube root of 120,

Press: **C 1 2 0** $\sqrt[3]{}$ **4.932424149**

Write down the number displayed. Then check by cubing it.

Press: x^y **3 =** **120.**

Practise finding cube roots with your calculator.

► **Exercise** N6.7

Use your calculator to work out the cube root of these numbers.
Check your answers by cubing them.

1	125	**4**	729	**7**	5.832
2	2744	**5**	216	**8**	29.791
3	15.625	**6**	0.125		

To solve problems you may need to find the cube roots of
numbers.

The **cube root of the volume of a cube** gives the *length of
the edge* of the cube. Check that you give the correct unit in the
answer. (Remember: cm^3 will give a length in cm; m^3 will give
a length in m, and so on.)

Question

A packing box in a warehouse is a cube with volume
70 m^3. What is the length of each edge of the cube? Give
your answer in metres correct to 2 decimal places.

Answer

$\sqrt[3]{70}$ = 4.12 (to 2 dp)

Edge of cube is 4.12 m (to 2 dp)

calculator

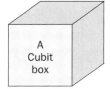

► **Exercise** N6.8

The company Cubit makes boxes in the
shape of cubes.
Here are the volumes of some Cubit boxes.
1   4736 cm^3
2   14 350 cm^3
3   4.1 m^3
4   19 683 mm^3
5   7.6 m^3
6   110 592 cm^3

A
Cubit
box

What is the edge length of each of these boxes? Give each
answer to a sensible degree of accuracy where necessary.

Square and cube roots by trial and improvement

Some questions may ask you to find a square or cube root by
trial and improvement. You *cannot* use the square root or
cube root key on your calculator. You must show how you got
your answer.

Here is a **basic strategy** to follow:

- Start with a sensible *'guess'* for what you want (square root or cube root). Use your knowledge of perfect squares and perfect cubes to help you. (See page 25 and page 27)

- For a square root, try: *'guess'* × *'guess'*.
  For a cube root, try: *'guess'* × *'guess'* × *'guess'*.
  See what result you get.

- If the result is the number whose square or cube root you want, then you have *found it!*
  If it isn't what you want, then use it to help you to make a better *'try'* next.

Use these guidelines to help you choose a better *'try'* each time:

- Compare the size of your result with what you want.

  If your result is *too big*, choose a *smaller 'try'* next.
  If your result is *too small,* choose a *larger 'try'* next.

- Look for *'opposite* results':

  result *too big* then result *too small,* or
  result *too small* then result *too big*.

When you get two *'opposite results'* like these, you know that the number you want is between the two numbers you tried.

Keep a neat **record** of your tries. Using a **number line** also helps you to choose what to try next.

Each time you try a number, mark it on the line. Use the result it gives (too big or too small) to shade the part of the number line you no longer need to try. This gives a useful *'picture'* of what you are doing.

Try 15:   15 × 15 × 15 = 3375.   *Too small*

The cube root is between 15 and 20.
Try whole numbers, starting with 16.

Try 16:   16 × 16 × 16 = 4096.   *Still too small.*
Try 17:   17 × 17 × 17 = 4913.   *That's it.*
So $\sqrt[3]{4913}$ = 17 because 17 × 17 × 17 = 4913.

► *Exercise* N6.9

Use trial and improvement to find these square roots and cube roots.

1 $\sqrt{529}$	**3** $\sqrt{2209}$	**5** $\sqrt[3]{2744}$
2 $\sqrt{729}$	**4** $\sqrt[3]{216}$	**6** $\sqrt[3]{226\,981}$

Sometimes you want only **approximate square roots or cube roots**.

Try whole numbers first. Find the *two consecutive whole numbers* your answer is between.

Then try *decimals* (to 1, 2, … decimal places) if you need to. Find the two consecutive numbers (for the approximation you want) that give *opposite results*. To decide which is 'nearer' to the answer you want, try the 'half-way value'. The result it gives shows you which number you want.

If the 'half-way value' is *too big*, you want the *smaller* number.
If the 'half-way value' is *too small*, you want the *larger* number.

Question

Find the cube root of 4913 by trial and improvement. Show your working clearly.

Answer

The cube root of 1000 is 10 because
10 × 10 × 10 = 1000.

4913 is larger than 1000.
So $\sqrt[3]{4913}$ is larger than $\sqrt[3]{1000}$ = 10.

Try numbers larger than 10.
Compare each result with 4913.

Try 20:   20 × 20 × 20 = 8000   Compare with 4913
                                        Too big
                                        Try a smaller number

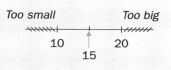

The cube root is between 10 and 20. Try half-way between, i.e. 15.

Question

Find $\sqrt{3}$ correct to 2 decimal places by trial and improvement. Show your working clearly.

Answer

The square root of 1 is 1 because 1 × 1 = 1.
The square root of 4 is 2 because 2 × 2 = 4.
3 is between 1 and 4.
So the square root of 3 is between 1 and 2.
Try half-way between, i.e. 1.5.

                                        Compare with 3

Try 1.5:   1.5 × 1.5 = 2.25.   *Too small.*
Try 1.6:   1.6 × 1.6 = 2.56.   *Still too small.*
Try 1.7:   1.7 × 1.7 = 2.89.   *Still too small.*   *opposite*
Try 1.8:   1.8 × 1.8 = 3.24.   *Too big.*   *results*

continued

The square root is between 1.7 and 1.8.
Try half-way between,
i.e. 1.75

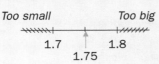

Try 1.75: $1.75 \times 1.75 = 3.0625$.   *Too big.*
Try 1.74: $1.74 \times 1.74 = 3.0276$.   *Still too big* ← *opposite*
Try 1.73: $1.73 \times 1.73 = 2.9929$.   *Too small.* ← *results*

The square root is between 1.73 and 1.74.
Try half-way between,
i.e. 1.735

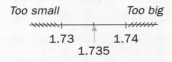

Try 1.735: $1.735 \times 1.735 = 3.010225$.   *Too big.*

Too small   Too big

1.73   1.735   1.74

The square root is between 1.73 and 1.735. It is on the
unshaded part of the number line.
This shows it is nearer to 1.73 than 1.74.

So $\sqrt{3}$ = 1.73 (to 2 dp).

► *Exercise* **N6.10**

Use trial and improvement to find the value of these correct to
2 decimal places. Show your working.

1   $\sqrt{5}$

2   cube root of 42

3   cube root of 1265

4   square root of 50

5   $\sqrt{160}$

6   cube root of 533.

◄

Examination Questions

1   You are given the following four digits which can be used
   once only in each answer.

   (a) Using all four digits, write down
       (i) the largest possible number,
       (ii) the smallest possible even number.
   (b) Using two of the digits, write down
       (i) a multiple of 5,
       (ii) a square number.
   (c) Using three of the digits, write down
       (i) a multiple of 4,
       (ii) a cube number.

(MEG, 1990)

2

Moving only along the given paths in the direction indicated
by the arrows, use the instructions below to find the
sequence which leads from the start to the finish.
   1 Start with a multiple of 7.
   2 Go to a prime number.
   3 Go to a cubic number.
   4 Finish with a square number.   (NISEAC, 1989)

3   In an investigation, Alison squares each digit in a number
   and adds the results. She calls this process 'squadding'.
   For example: $20 \rightarrow 2^2 + 0^2 = 4 + 0 = 4$
                $13 \rightarrow 1^2 + 3^2 = 1 + 9 = 10$
   If the number obtained after squadding is not a single digit,
   she repeats the process until a single digit is obtained. She
   calls this process 'super-squadding'.
   For example: $13 \rightarrow 1^2 + 3^2 = 1 + 9 = 10$
                $10 \rightarrow 1^2 + 0^2 = 1 + 0 = 1$
   She calls numbers like 13 which reduce to the number 1
   after super-squadding, 'nifty' numbers.
   (a) Perform the squadding operation on
       (i)   23,
       (ii) 24.
   (b) Which of the numbers in part (a) is a nifty number?
   (c) Show clearly why 37 is not a nifty number.
   (d) What is the first nifty number after 41?

(SEG, 1989)

4   (a) Calculate
       (i) $1 + 3$,
       (ii) $1 + 3 + 5$,
       (iii) $1 + 3 + 5 + 7$.
   (b) What do you notice about your answers to part (a)?
   (c) Calculate
       (i) $\frac{1}{2}[(1^3 + 3^3) + (1 + 3)]$,
       (ii) $\frac{1}{2}[(1^3 + 3^3 + 5^3) + (1 + 3 + 5)]$,
       (iii) $\frac{1}{2}[(1^3 + 3^3 + 5^3 + 7^3) + (1 + 3 + 5 + 7)]$.
   (d) What do you notice about your answers to part (c)?
   (e) Use your answers to part (b) and part (d) to suggest the
       value of
       (i)   the sum of the first 100 odd numbers,
       (ii)   the sum of the cubes of the first 100 odd numbers.

(MEG, 1989)

5   Charles says that $\sqrt{16 + 9}$ is less than $\sqrt{16} + \sqrt{9}$.
   Julie says he is wrong. Work out
   (a) $\sqrt{16 + 9}$, (b) $\sqrt{16} + \sqrt{9}$.
   Who is right?

(NEAB, 1989)

6 (a) The perimeter of a square is 64 cm. What is the area?
 (b) The area of a square is 64 cm². What is its perimeter?

(WJEC, 1989)

7 Write these numbers in order of size, smallest first.

$\sqrt{10}$ 3.14 $3\frac{1}{7}$

(ULEAC, 1989)

8 Each of these large cubes is made out of small cubes.

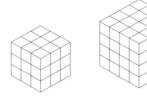

Complete this table:

Dimensions of large cube	Number of small cubes that are completely hidden inside the large cube, with no faces visible on the outside
$3 \times 3 \times 3$	$1^3 = 1$
$4 \times 4 \times 4$	$2^3 = 8$
$5 \times 5 \times 5$	$3^3 = \square$
$6 \times 6 \times 6$	$\square = \square$
$13 \times 13 \times 13$	$\square = \square$

How many small cubes are completely hidden in a $100 \times 100 \times 100$ cube?
Give a brief explanation for your answer.

(NEAB,1989)

9 (a) The values of 1^3 and 2^3 have been worked out in the table below. Complete the table to find the values of 3^3, 4^3 and 5^3.

$$1^3 = 1 \times 1 \times 1 = 1$$
$$2^3 = 2 \times 2 \times 2 = 8$$
$$3^3 = 3 \times 3 \times 3 = \ldots$$
$$4^3 = 4 \times 4 \times 4 = \ldots$$
$$5^3 = \ldots$$

 (b) (i) Use your answers to part (a) to complete the third line of the following pattern.

$$1^3 + 2^3 = 9 = 3^2$$
$$1^3 + 2^3 + 3^3 = 36 = 6^2$$
$$1^3 + 2^3 + 3^3 + 4^3 = \ldots = \ldots$$

  (ii) Write down the fourth line of this pattern.

 (c) A pupil continued with this pattern.
 For the sixth line he wrote:
$$1^3 + 2^3 + 3^3 + 4^3 + 5^3 + 6^3 = 784 = 28^2$$
 Is this line correct?
 Give a reason for your answer.

(NEAB,1991)

▶

N7
Directed numbers

This unit will help you to:

■ recognise directed numbers and use them in 'real-life' situations

■ compare and order directed numbers

■ use directed numbers in calculations (addition, subtraction and simple multiplications and division)

■ solve problems involving directed numbers.

Directed numbers show counting or measuring in two opposite directions. They are often used to show values *more or less than zero (0)*.

Some common 'everyday' examples of directed numbers are:
 temperatures more or less than 0°,
 heights above or below sea level,
 golf scores over and under par,
 bank balances in credit and overdrawn,
 locations N and S of the equator,
 AD and BC (after and before the birth of Christ).

In mathematics the words **positive** and **negative** and the signs $^+$ and $^-$ are used for directed numbers.

 Discussion Exercise

Think of some other situations which involve the use of directed numbers. Discuss your ideas with your group.

Positive and negative

This thermometer measures temperatures in degrees Celsius (°C)

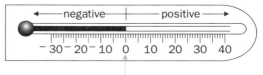

0 °C   (the freezing point of water)

Temperatures *more* than 0°C are *positive*.
Temperatures *less* than 0°C are *negative*.

In your classroom it should be about 20° more than zero. We can write this as ⁺20°C and say '*positive 20°*'. Normally we simply call it 20° without the sign.

A number without a sign is always positive ⁺.
In a freezer it should be about 20° less than zero. We write this as ⁻20° and say '*negative 20°*'. A negative number must have a ⁻ sign in front of it.

Many people and books do not put positive and negative signs at the 'top' of the number. They write them on the line like plus and minus signs, for example +3 and − 6, but they mean 'positive 3' and 'negative 6'. In this unit, positive and negative signs are written at the top of each number to help you to see the working.

 ## Investigation

Write down as many examples as you can think of which involve temperatures above and below zero. Write these as directed numbers with a positive or negative sign.

Comparing and ordering

The scale on a thermometer helps you to **compare** temperatures and put them in **order of size**.

As you move '*up*' the scale, the temperatures get *larger*.
As you move '*down*' the scale, the temperatures get *smaller*.

Question

Use the thermometer scale below to help you to answer these questions.
(a) Which is hotter, ⁻7°C or 3°C?
(b) Which is colder, ⁻1°C or ⁻10°C?
(c) Put these temperatures in order from the coldest to the hottest:

15°C,   ⁻12°C,   5°C,   ⁻2°C,   0°C

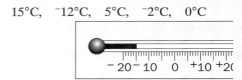

Answer

(a)   3°C is hotter than ⁻7°C

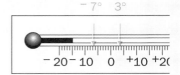

(b) ⁻10°C is colder than ⁻1°C

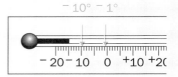

(c) The order is: ⁻12°C, ⁻2°C, 0°C, 5°C, 15°C.

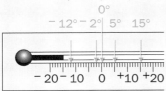

▶ *Exercise* **N7.1**

1   Compare these temperatures. Say which is hotter.
   (a) ⁻2°C or 4°C   (d) 0°C or ⁻5°C
   (b) ⁻8°C or 1°C   (e) ⁻21°C or ⁻25°C
   (c) ⁻6°C or ⁻9°C   (f) ⁻1°C or 1°C
2   Compare these temperatures. Say which is colder.
   (a) ⁻3°C or 0°C   (d) ⁻5°C or ⁻10°C
   (b) ⁻10°C or ⁻15°C   (e) 18°C or ⁻27°C
   (c) ⁻11°C or 12°C   (f) 10°C or 0°C
3   Put these temperatures in order. Start with the coldest.
   (a) 1°C, ⁻1°C, 0°C, ⁻6°C, 5°C
   (b) ⁻4°C, 9°C, ⁻10°C, ⁻1°C, 4°C
   (c) ⁻2°C, 4°C, 0°C, ⁻3°C, 10°C
   (d) 9°C, ⁻2°C, 3°C, ⁻1°C, ⁻7°C
   (e) 100°C, ⁻95°C, 43°C, ⁻70°C, ⁻11°C.

Number line

The scale on a thermometer is a simple **number line**.
   Drawing, or imagining, a number line can help you to compare any positive and negative numbers.

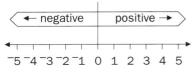

Number the line carefully.

Start at 0 and number '*above* 0' *positive*.
Start at 0 and number '*below* 0' *negative*.

> and <

You may need to use these symbols when comparing numbers.

> means 'is bigger than' or 'is greater than'
< means 'is smaller than' or 'is less than'.

Here are some examples of their use.

             5 > 3   3 < 5
      '5 is bigger than 3'   '3 is smaller than 5'

             2 > ⁻4   ⁻4 < 2
     '2 is bigger than ⁻4'   '⁻4 is smaller than 2'

            ⁻1 > ⁻2   ⁻2 < ⁻1
    '⁻1 is bigger than ⁻2'   '⁻2 is smaller than ⁻1'

Check these on the number line above.

Exercise N7.2

1 For each of these, say if it is right or wrong.
  (a) ⁻4 > 4   (e) 3 > ⁻4   (i) 7 < 5
  (b) ⁻6 < 5   (f) 0 < 1   (j) ⁻3 > ⁻9
  (c) 2 > ⁻2   (g) ⁻5 > ⁻2
  (d) 3 > 3   (h) ⁻3 < 0

2 Copy each pair of numbers. Put the correct symbol (> or <) between them.
  (a) 2, 1   (e) 2, ⁻3   (i) ⁻10, ⁻17
  (b) ⁻3, 4   (f) ⁻7, 7   (j) 8, ⁻9.
  (c) 1, 0   (g) 12, ⁻5
  (d) ⁻2, ⁻5   (h) ⁻13, 0

Temperature changes and differences

You can use a thermometer scale or a simple number line to work out **changes and differences** in temperature.

Question

Steven recorded the temperature every two hours.
(a) At 6 a.m. it was ⁻4°C. At 8 am it was ⁻1°C. By how much had the temperature risen?
(b) The temperature went up 5°C in the next two hours. What was the temperature at 10 am?
(c) At noon it was 5°C. At 2 pm it was ⁻2°C. By how many degrees had the temperature fallen?
(d) The temperature went down 4°C in the next two hours. What was the temperature at 4 pm?

Answer

(a) 3°C
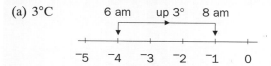

(b) 4°C
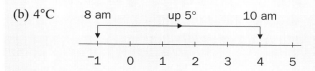

(c) 7°C
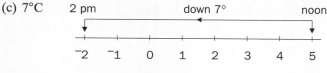

(d) ⁻6°C
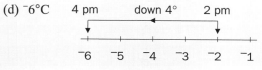

Exercise N7.3

1 The following table gives the starting and final temperatures for an air conditioned room. Copy and complete the table.

	Starting temperature °C	Final temperature °C	Change in °C	Direction up or down
	18	10	8	down
(a)	15	8		
(b)	3	12		
(c)	7		9	up
(d)	⁻2	6		
(e)		9	11	down
(f)	⁻7	⁻3		
(g)		⁻1	4	up
(h)		0	7	down

2 The weather forecast on television gives the temperature in different parts of the country at a particular time of day.
(a) On Monday it was 8°C in Birmingham and 12°C in Plymouth. How much warmer was Plymouth than Birmingham?
(b) On Tuesday, the temperature in Plymouth had fallen 5°C. What was the new temperature in Plymouth?
(c) On Tuesday, the temperature in Birmingham had fallen 9°C. What was the new temperature in Birmingham?
(d) On Wednesday, the temperature in Birmingham was 2°C. How much had the temperature risen since Tuesday?
(e) On Thursday, the temperature in Plymouth was 15°C colder than it was on Monday. What temperature was it on Thursday in Plymouth?

Addition and subtraction

Students are taught many different ways to add and subtract directed numbers. If you are sure that you understand and can use your method successfully, then use it. If you are not so sure, then here is a method for you to try.

To help you to do an addition or subtraction, think of directed numbers as temperatures with:

positive numbers as *hot* air,
negative numbers as *cold* air.

The first number is the starting temperature. Decide whether the addition or subtraction makes it go up or down. Use your common sense to work it out:

add hot air → it goes *up*
add cold air → it goes *down*
subtract hot air → it goes *down*
subtract cold air → it goes *up*

Work out how much it should change. Then find the final temperature. Use a number line (like a thermometer) to help you to do the working.

Here are some examples.
You can work out 5 + ⁻8 like this:

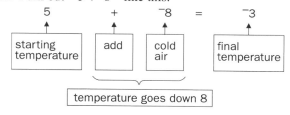

On a number line:

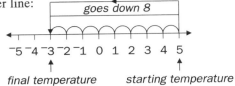

final temperature   starting temperature

You can work out ⁻2 – 3 = ⁻5 like this:

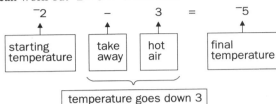

temperature goes down 3

On a number line:

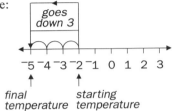

final temperature   starting temperature

You can work out ⁻1 – ⁻4 = 3 like this:

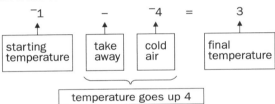

temperature goes up 4

On a number line:

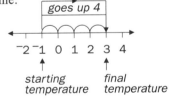

starting temperature   final temperature

Exercise N7.4

If you know and understand a method for adding and subtracting directed numbers, use it to answer these questions. If you are unsure of how to do this, try the hot/cold air idea to help you.

1	2 + ⁻3	**6**	2 – ⁻4	**11**	10 – ⁻11
2	⁻4 + 7	**7**	0 – ⁻8	**12**	⁻12 – 3
3	⁻5 – 4	**8**	⁻6 + ⁺2	**13**	0 – 5
4	6 – 7	**9**	8 – ⁻5	**14**	15 + ⁻8
5	⁻5 + 8	**10**	⁻4 – ⁻3	**15**	⁻11 – ⁻11

With practise you should be able to do these calculations without a number line. But do use one if it helps you to get the correct answer.

Always **check** whether your answer makes sense. Compare the size of the number you start with and your answer.

Adding a⁺ number makes a number larger.
For example,
    ⁻3 + 2 = ⁻1   ← larger than ⁻3

Adding a ⁻ number makes a number smaller.
For example,
    ⁻3 + ⁻2 = ⁻5   ← smaller than ⁻3

Subtracting a⁺ number makes a number smaller.
For example,
    ⁻3 – 2 = ⁻5   ← smaller than ⁻3

Subtracting a⁻ number makes a number larger.
For example,
    ⁻3 – ⁻2 = ⁻1   ← larger than ⁻3

It may help you to remember the following, too.

Subtracting a positive
or
adding its negative
} give the same answer.

For example,   2 – 7 = ⁻5
                2 + ⁻7 = ⁻5

Subtracting a negative
or
adding its positive
} give the same answer.

For example,   ⁻3 – ⁻2 = ⁻1
                ⁻3 + 2 = ⁻1

Exercise N7.5

Carry out these calculations without the help of a number line.

1	⁻3 + ⁻4	**5**	2 – ⁻4	**9**	3 + ⁻3
2	2 + ⁻5	**6**	⁻1 + ⁻6	**10**	⁻4 + 4
3	⁻1 – ⁻2	**7**	⁻5 – ⁻2		
4	4 + ⁻3	**8**	3 – ⁻3		

Multiplication and division

When **multiplying directed numbers**,

    if the signs are the *same*, the answer is *positive*,
    if the signs are *different*, then the answer is *negative*.

This gives:

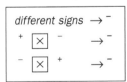

Here are some examples:

Both ⁺ →   2 × 5 = 10   → Answer ⁺
Both ⁻ →   ⁻3 × ⁻4 = ⁺12   → Answer ⁺
One ⁺, one ⁻ →   ⁺8 × ⁻6 = ⁻48   → Answer ⁻
One ⁻, one ⁺ →   ⁻2 × ⁺7 = ⁻14   → Answer ⁻

Exercise N7.6

Calculate:

1	⁻3 × 5	**4**	⁻3 × ⁻2	**7**	⁻6 × ⁻1	**10**	⁻8 × ⁻9
2	4 × ⁻3	**5**	⁻2 × 4	**8**	⁻2 × 3		
3	6 × ⁻1	**6**	3 × ⁻3	**9**	5 × ⁻7		

Sometimes you have to multiply more than two numbers. Multiply them 'two at a time'.

Question

Calculate

(a) $3 \times {}^-2 \times {}^-4$

(b) ${}^-1 \times {}^-2 \times 3 \times {}^-4 \times 5$

Answer

(a) *Put in twos*

$$\underbrace{3 \times {}^-2}\ \times {}^-4$$
$$= \quad {}^-6 \ \times {}^-4$$
$$= 24$$

(b) *Put in twos*

$$\underbrace{{}^-1 \times {}^-2} \times \underbrace{3 \times {}^-4} \times 5$$

Put in twos

$$= \quad {}^+2 \ \times \ \underbrace{{}^-12 \times 5}$$
$$\qquad {}^+2 \ \times \ {}^-60$$
$$= {}^-120$$

► *Exercise* N7.7

Calculate the answers to the following. (Remember to do them two at a time.)

1 ${}^-3 \times 4 \times 2$ **6** $7 \times {}^-6 \times 4 \times {}^-3$

2 $4 \times {}^-3 \times {}^-6$ **7** ${}^-4 \times {}^-3 \times 1 \times 2$

3 ${}^-2 \times {}^-3 \times 5$ **8** ${}^-6 \times {}^-12 \times 4 \times {}^-3$

4 ${}^-1 \times {}^-3 \times 2$ **9** $8 \times {}^-4 \times 3 \times {}^-6 \times 5$

5 $3 \times {}^-2 \times {}^-4 \times 2$ **10** ${}^-1 \times 0 \times {}^-11 \times 13 \times {}^-15$ ◄

Division of directed numbers follows the same pattern as multiplication. When dividing directed numbers,

if the signs are the *same*, the answer is *positive*,
if the signs are *different*, the answer is *negative*.

This gives:

same signs → $^+$	different signs → $^-$
$^+$ ÷ $^+$ → $^+$	$^+$ ÷ $^-$ → $^-$
$^-$ ÷ $^-$ → $^+$	$^-$ ÷ $^+$ → $^-$

Here are some examples:

Both $^+$ → ${}^+20 \div {}^+5 = {}^+4$ → Answer $^+$

Both $^-$ → ${}^-15 \div {}^-3 = {}^+5$ → Answer $^+$

One $^+$, one $^-$ → ${}^+18 \div {}^-6 = {}^-3$ → Answer $^-$

One $^-$, one $^+$ → ${}^-16 \div {}^+2 = {}^-8$ → Answer $^-$

► *Exercise* N7.8

Calculate:

1 ${}^+5 \div {}^-1$ **5** ${}^+18 \div {}^+9$ **9** ${}^-63 \div {}^-7$

2 ${}^-8 \div {}^-2$ **6** ${}^+24 \div {}^-3$ **10** $84 \div {}^-12$

3 ${}^-12 \div {}^+4$ **7** ${}^-10 \div {}^+5$

4 ${}^-20 \div {}^-5$ **8** ${}^+40 \div {}^-8$ ◄

Order of operations

When there is more than one operation ($+, -, \times, \div$) in a calculation, the **order** in which you do them is important.

Directed numbers obey the same 'order rules' as 'ordinary numbers'.

( ) Work out anything in brackets first.

$\times \div$ Do any other multiplication and division next (working from left to right).

$+ -$ Then do any other addition and subtraction (working from left to right).

Do the working step-by-step. Write the $^+$ and $^-$ signs clearly.

Question

Evaluate:

(a) $15 \div (6 - 9)$

(b) $7 - ({}^-5 + 2)(4 - {}^-6)$

Answer

(a) $15 \div (6 - 9)$

Inside brackets first $= 15 \div {}^-3$

Then division $= {}^-5$

(b) $7 - ({}^-5 + 2)(4 - {}^-6)$

Inside brackets first $= 7 - ({}^-3)({}^+10)$

Multiplication next $= 7 - {}^-30$

Then subtraction $= 37$

► *Exercise* N7.9

Calculate:

1 $(8 + {}^-4) \div {}^-2$ **6** $({}^-3 \times 2) + ({}^-4 + {}^-6)$

2 $({}^-3 + 1) - (4 + {}^-1)$ **7** $(5 - 3)({}^-6 - 4) + 2$

3 $8 - ({}^-5 + {}^-1)$ **8** ${}^-12 \times ({}^-3 + {}^-1)$

4 $16 \div (3 + {}^-5)$ **9** $(7 - 9)({}^-1 - 8) \div {}^-6$

5 $2(5 - 8) \times {}^-2$ **10** $28 \div [({}^-5 - 2)({}^-1 - 3)]$ ◄

Using a calculator

Your calculator should have a **change sign key**, such as $\boxed{^+/_-}$.
Pressing this key changes the sign of the number on the display.

To enter a negative number,
enter the figure(s) first, then press $\boxed{^+/_-}$.

For example, to enter $^-16$, press $\boxed{1}\,\boxed{6}\,\boxed{^+/_-}$.

The display should show $\boxed{16}$, then $\boxed{-16}$.

You can use a change sign key to do **calculations with directed numbers**. Always check that each number on the display has the sign you want before pressing an operation key ($+, -, \times, \div, =, \dots$).
Here are some examples.

To work out $^-6 + {}^-3 = {}^-9$

Press: $\boxed{C}\ \boxed{6}\ \boxed{^+/_-}\ \boxed{+}\ \boxed{3}\ \boxed{^+/_-}\ \boxed{=}$

Display shows: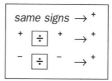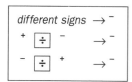

To work out $^-4 - 3 = {}^-7$

Press: $\boxed{C}\ \boxed{4}\ \boxed{^+/_-}\ \boxed{-}\ \boxed{3}\ \boxed{=}$

Display shows: $\boxed{-4}$ $\boxed{-7}$

To work out $5 \times {}^-8 = {}^-40$

Press:

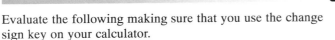

Display shows:

To work out ${}^-21 \div {}^-7 = 3$

Press:

Display shows:

You may find that, with practice, you can do these calculations faster in your head. When you are practising these skills you can use your calculator to check your answers.

► Exercise N7.10

Evaluate the following making sure that you use the change sign key on your calculator.

1 $6 + {}^-3$
2 $8 - {}^-4$
3 ${}^-3 + {}^-2$
4 $5 - {}^-3$
5 ${}^-3 \times 2$
6 $5 \times {}^-6$

7 ${}^-8 \times {}^-2$
8 $7 - {}^-3$
9 ${}^-16 \div 4$
10 ${}^-20 \div {}^-5$
11 $30 \div {}^-6$
12 ${}^-6 \times {}^-2 \times {}^-3$

Problem solving

To solve a problem, you have to decide what calculation to do. The words can give you clues. But you must think about the problem itself, then do what makes sense. A simple strategy for tackling number problems is given on page 12.

You may have to decide what the ⁻ sign means in a problem. In the next question a ⁻ sign shows an 'overdrawn' bank account.

Question

Mrs Jackson has an overdraft arrangement with her bank. This lets her spend more money than is in her account.

Work out the balance on her statement after each of these transactions. Use OD to show 'overdrawn'.
(a) Mrs Jackson has £250 in her account. She takes out £463.50.
(b) She withdraws £60 when her account is already £20 overdrawn.
(c) The balance is £120.85 OD before she pays in £78.99.

Answer

(a) $250 - 463.50 = {}^-213.50$ Balance: £213.50 OD
(b) ${}^-20 - 60 = {}^-80$ Balance : £80 OD
(c) ${}^-120.85 + 78.99 = {}^-41.86$ Balance: £41.86 OD

► Exercise N7.11

Mr Jones has a bank account which is sometimes overdrawn by arrangement with the bank manager. Express each of these situations using a positive sign for money in the bank and a negative sign for the amount overdrawn.

Example: a balance of £20 is ⁺£20 and overdrawn by £30 is ⁻£30.

1 Mr Jones has £200 in the bank.
2 He pays in £50. What is his new balance?
3 He buys a television for £325. What is his balance now?
4 He pays £40 into his account. What is his new balance?
5 He takes out some cash so that his balance becomes ⁻£85. How much cash did he take out?

Examination Questions

1 In an experiment a liquid cooled from 5°C to ⁻3°C in 12 minutes.
   (a) By how many degrees had the temperature fallen?
   (b) The temperature then fell a further 4°C.
      (i) What was the new temperature?
      (ii) If the temperature fell at the same rate, how long would this further cooling take?

(MEG, 1989)

2 This table gives the temperature in Sheffield during one week in January 1987.

Day	Sun	Mon	Tues	Wed	Thurs	Fri	Sat
Noon	⁻3°C	⁻2°C	1°C	⁻3°C	2°C	3°C	⁻2°C
Midnight	⁻8°C	⁻8°C	⁻6°C	⁻10°C	⁻6°C	⁻3°C	⁻5°C

(a) What is the lowest temperature in the table?
(b) On which day was there the biggest drop in temperature between noon and midnight?
(c) How much was this drop?
(d) What was the least rise in temperature between midnight one day and noon the following day?
(e) On the next Sunday the temperature was 8° higher at noon than at midnight the previous night. What was the temperature at noon?

(MEG, 1988)

3 In the book 'Charlie and the Amazing Glass Elevator' twenty years is taken off the age of a person for every tablet taken. It is possible to end up with a negative age.
   (a) Granddad Joe was 81 years when he took 3 tablets. Work out his new age.
   (b) Grandma Jane was 78 years when she took 4 tablets. Work out her new age.
   (c) When Charlie took one tablet his new age was –9 years. Work out Charlie's age before he took the tablet.

(ULEAC, 1991)

4  The water level in a reservoir is measured in metres on a scale as shown in the diagram on the left.
Readings were taken every four days during June last year. The readings were:
⁻2.2, ⁻1.5, ⁻0.5, 0.4, ⁻0.6, 0.2, ⁻1.1.
   (a) Write down the median of these readings.
   (b) Find the mean water level for the month.

(MEG, 1989)

5

Region by region Average Earnings in 1987				
	Office Workers		Shopfloor Workers	
Area	annual salary	compared to national average £6530 (%)	weekly wage	compared to national average £129.84 (%)
Grampian	£6500	– 0.46	£143.37	+ 10.42
West Midlands	£5918	– 9.37	£122.00	– 6.04
Leics/Northants	£6122	– 6.25	£120.35	– 7.31
E. Midlands (North)	£5724	– 12.34	£116.40	– 10.35
Staffordshire	£5784	– 11.42	£125.36	– 3.45
Central London	£8847	+ 35.48	£148.21	+ 14.15
Yorkshire/N-East	£6180	– 5.36	£132.50	+ 2.05
London Outer	£7683	+ 17.66	£142.21	+ 9.53
E. Midlands (South)	£6301	– 3.51	£130.77	+ 0.72
East Anglia	£6064	– 7.14	£123.00	– 5.27
Central Scotland	£6300	– 3.52		+ 1.60
Avon/Severn	£6105	– 6.51	£125.18	– 3.59

The table above compares the average earnings of workers in various areas of Britain with the national average in 1987.
(a) In which of these areas were office workers paid least?
(b) How much more, in £, was the weekly wage for shopfloor workers in Central London than the national average?
(c) In East Anglia, were office workers better paid than shopfloor workers? (Take 1 year as 52 weeks and show your working.)
(d) In which **two** areas was the salary for office workers nearest to the national average?
(e) For Central Scotland, the weekly wage for shopfloor workers is missing from the table. Calculate this weekly wage. (MEG, 1989)

6 A freezer is in a room where the temperature is 18°C. The temperature in the freezer is −24°C.
(a) Calculate the difference between these two temperatures.
(b) Calculate the temperature which is half-way between these two temperatures. (MEG, 1988)

7 The temperatures at noon in Montreal on the seven days of one week were as follows:

Sunday	− 5°C	Thursday	5°C
Monday	− 4°C	Friday	0°C
Tuesday	− 7°C	Saturday	− 4°C
Wednesday	1°C		

(a) Calculate the mean (average) of these temperatures.
(b) On which of these seven days was the noon temperature below the average for the week? (MEG, 1989)

8 In a general knowledge quiz, contestants were awarded +3 points for a correct answer, but − 2 points for an incorrect answer.
(a) What was the final score if a contestant answered
   (i) 5 questions correctly and 2 incorrectly,
   (ii) 2 questions correctly and 5 incorrectly?
(b) Three members of a team had final scores of − 2, +13 and − 7. What was the total team score?
(NISEAC, 1989)

9

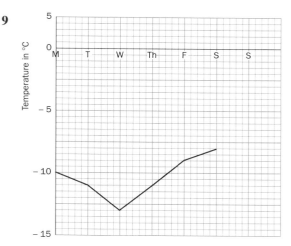

The graph shows the midday temperature in Toronto on each of six days in one week last year.
(a) What was the midday temperature on the Tuesday? Between Saturday and Sunday, the midday temperature dropped 7°C.
(b) Complete the graph to show the Sunday midday temperature. (ULEAC, 1989)

10 John has a credit balance of £12 on his bank account. He pays a bill of £22.50 at the local supermarket by cheque.
(a) What would be the balance on his account after this cheque had been passed for payment?
John now pays £15 into his bank account.
(b) What is the balance on his account now? (ULEAC, 1989)

11 Vicky calculates how much money she has in her bank account as follows.

Date		Amount in bank
January 1st		£50
January 14th	Withdrew £15	£35
January 21st	Withdrew £16.50	(A)
February 1st	Paid in £11	(B)
February 15th	Wrote cheque for £35	(C)

(a) How much money should Vicky enter at (A)?
(b) What amount should she enter at (B)?
(c) Vicky uses her calculator to find the answer to (C). The calculator displays − 5.5. Explain what this means.
(NEAB, 1988)

12 Pamela and Joanna are playing a game. They have 21 cards numbered ⁻10, ⁻9, ⁻8, ………⁻1, 0, 1, ……… 9, 10.
The cards are placed face down on the table in front of them. The rules of the game are:
(i) each girl picks up three cards,
(ii) her score is the sum of the numbers on the three cards,
(ii) the girl with the higher score wins.
(a) In the first game Pamela picked up ⁻10, ⁻4 and 6. What was her score?
(b) In the second game, Joanna picked up ⁻9, ⁻4 and 8. Pamela won this game by 2. The numbers on her first two cards were 5 and ⁻1. What number was on her third card?
(c) (i) What is the highest score possible when playing the game?
   (ii) In the third game Joanna had the highest possible score. Pamela had the lowest possible score. What was the difference in their scores? (MEG, 1991)

N8
Fractions, decimals and percentages

This unit will help you to:

■ recognise and understand the meaning of common fractions, decimals and percentages.

Types of fraction

A **fraction** is part of a whole one. Its size can be given in different ways.

Numbers like $\frac{1}{2}$ and $\frac{3}{4}$ are **common** or **vulgar fractions**. You write them as one number over another.

Numbers like 0.5 and 0.75 are **decimal fractions**. You write them with a decimal point.

Numbers like 50% and 75% are **percentages**. You write them with 'per cent' or %.

When we say simply 'fractions', we usually mean 'common fractions'. Decimal fractions are often just called decimals.

▶ *Exercise* **N8.1**

For each of the following write down whether it is a common fraction, a decimal fraction or a percentage.

1	$\frac{3}{10}$	**4**	0.25
2	0.7	**5**	$\frac{5}{8}$
3	60%	**6**	10%

Common fractions

When a whole one is divided into *equal* parts, each part can have *the same fraction name*.

Each part is 1 third.

The parts are not thirds.

The *top* and *bottom* numbers of a fraction tell you about its size.

$$\frac{\textbf{numerator}}{\textbf{denominator}}$$

The bottom number (de**nom**inator) gives the **name** of the fraction. It tells you how many equal parts are in the whole one.

The top number (**num**erator) tells you the **num**ber of these equal parts you are dealing with.

For example,

3 out of 5 equal parts are shaded.

So $\frac{3}{5}$ is shaded.

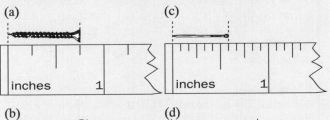

Question

Write down the length of each object as a fraction of an inch.

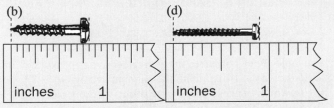

Answer

(a) $\frac{3}{4}$ inch *(3 out of 4 equal parts)*
(b) $\frac{13}{16}$ inch *(13 out of 16 equal parts)*
(c) $\frac{7}{12}$ inch *(7 out of 12 equal parts)*
(d) $\frac{9}{10}$ inch *(9 out of 10 equal parts)*

▶ *Exercise* **N8.2**

1 Write down the fraction shaded in each of these.

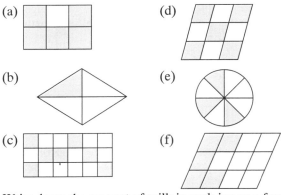

2 Write down the amount of milk in each jug as a fraction of a litre.

(a)　　　　(b)　　　　(c)　　　　(d)

Decimal fractions

In our number system, a figure's place in a number shows what it is worth.

It is a **deci**mal system. Each place value is based on **ten**.

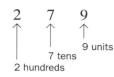

Tenths, hundredths, thousandths, ... are called **decimal fractions**. Their 'places' come *after* the decimal point.

Place values

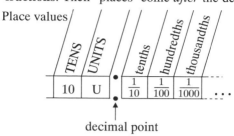

decimal point

A decimal point in a number separates the 'whole number part' from the 'fraction part'.

For example,

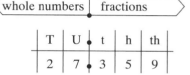

27.359 means

T	U	●	t	h	th
2	7	●	3	5	9

2 Tens 7 Units 3 tenths 5 hundredths 9 thousandths

We say:

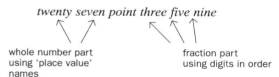

When there are *no* whole numbers we write a zero (0) in front of the decimal point.

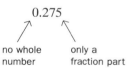

▶ *Exercise* **N8.3**

1 Write the following as decimal numbers. Use the decimal point.
 (a) 8 Hundreds   4 Tens   0 Units   3 tenths
 (b) 3 Tens   2 Units   5 tenths   4 hundredths
 (c) 0 Units   6 tenths   3 hundredths   7 thousandths
 (d) 9 Hundreds   2 Units   5 hundredths
 (e) 4 Thousands   6 Units   1 tenth
2 Write these numbers in words.
 (a) 6.29   (c) 0.47   (e) 0.006
 (b) 17.034   (d) 8.705

Percentages

Per cent % means 'per 100'
  or   'for every 100'
  or   'out of 100'

A **percentage** tells you 'an amount out of 100'
  or   'a number of hundredths'.

For example,
  28% means 28 out of 100 or $\frac{28}{100}$.

▶ *Exercise* **N8.4**

1 Write each of these percentages as a fraction with denominator 100.
 (a) 10%   (c) 75%   (e) 5%   (g) 54%
 (b) 50%   (d) 25%   (f) 28%   (h) 95%
2 Write each of these as a percentage.
 (a) 20 out of 100   (d) 8 out of 100
 (b) 30 out of 100   (e) 1 out of 100
 (c) 16 out of 100   (f) 100 out of 100
3 Twenty-three out of the first one hundred people to visit a new supermarket bought milk. What percentage of these shoppers bought milk?
4 On Saturday, 64 of the first 100 customers at a filling station bought unleaded petrol. What percentage of customers bought unleaded petrol?
5 In a crate of one hundred oranges, five were bad. What percentage of oranges were bad?

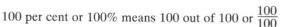

100 per cent or 100% means 100 out of 100 or $\frac{100}{100}$

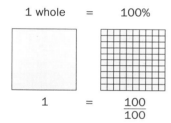

So 100% of something means 'all of it'.

All the percentage parts of something must add up to 100%. Sometimes you can use this to find a 'missing percentage'.

Question

People in Deemouth were asked:
'Do we need a new by-pass?'

(a) 70% of people asked were male. What percentage were female?
(b) 58% of those questioned said 'Yes', 23% said 'No' and the rest did not know. What percentage did not know?

Answer

(a) 100% − 70% = 30% were female.

(b) Yes: 58%
   No: + 23%
      ‾‾‾‾‾
        81%

Don't know: 100% − 81% = 19%.

▶ *Exercise* **N8.5**

1 The label on a cotton and polyester shirt states '60% cotton'. What percentage is polyester?

2   A packet of sausages states 'meat content 85%'. What percentage of the sausages are not meat?

3   At Wyfield School, 52% of the students are male. What percentage of the students are female?
   At lunchtime, 27% of the students have sandwiches, 38% have lunch in the refectory and the rest have no lunch or go home. What percentage of the students have no lunch or go home?

4   In a recent survey, 68% of the people asked said they would definitely vote at the next election and 21% were not sure. What percentage of people asked were definitely not going to vote at the next election?

5   Holiday makers flying from Bristol airport one Saturday were asked about their destination. 34% said Majorca, 26% said Crete, 24% said Corfu and 21% said Marbella. Explain why these figures should be treated with caution.

Examination Questions

1

   Figure A   Figure B   Figure C

   (a) What fraction of Figure A is shaded?
   (b) What fraction of Figure B is shaded?
   (c) What fraction of Figure C is shaded?

   (NISEAC, 1990)

2   Weather forecasters report cloud cover by the number of eighths of the sky which is covered by cloud.
   On a particular day cloud cover is given as five.
   (a) What fraction of the sky is covered with cloud?
   (b) What fraction of the sky is clear of cloud?

   (MEG, 1990)

3   Mr Smith has painted $\frac{3}{5}$ of the wall. What fraction of the wall is still to be painted?

   (ULEAC, 1990)

4      The diagram shows the percentages of City shops selling different products. What percentage of City shops are Food shops?

   (ULEAC, 1991)

5   This picture shows which foods provide the average adult with their total sugar intake. The percentage for soft drinks has been left out.

   (a) What percentage of the sugar intake comes from breakfast cereals?
   (b) What percentage of the sugar intake comes from soft drinks?

   (NEAB, 1988)

N9
Equivalent fractions

This unit will help you to:

■ understand the idea of equivalent fractions

■ find equivalent common fractions

■ simplify common fractions

■ change common fractions to decimals and vice versa

■ change common fractions to percentages and vice versa

■ change decimal fractions to percentages and vice versa

■ use equivalent fractions to compare and order fractions.

Equivalent fractions are different fraction names for the *same amount*. They have the same value but 'look' different.
   You can change a common fraction to another equivalent common fraction.
   You can also change

   fractions to decimals and percentages,
   decimals to fractions and percentages,
   percentages to fractions and decimals.

Equivalent common fractions

Amount shaded

$\frac{1}{2}$	$\frac{1}{2}$					$\frac{1}{2}$					
$\frac{2}{4}$	$\frac{1}{4}$			$\frac{1}{4}$			$\frac{1}{4}$			$\frac{1}{4}$		
$\frac{3}{6}$	$\frac{1}{6}$		$\frac{1}{6}$		$\frac{1}{6}$		$\frac{1}{6}$		$\frac{1}{6}$		$\frac{1}{6}$	
$\frac{4}{8}$	$\frac{1}{8}$	$\frac{1}{8}$	$\frac{1}{8}$	$\frac{1}{8}$	$\frac{1}{8}$	$\frac{1}{8}$	$\frac{1}{8}$	$\frac{1}{8}$			
$\frac{5}{10}$	$\frac{1}{10}$	$\frac{1}{10}$	$\frac{1}{10}$	$\frac{1}{10}$	$\frac{1}{10}$	$\frac{1}{10}$	$\frac{1}{10}$	$\frac{1}{10}$	$\frac{1}{10}$	$\frac{1}{10}$	
$\frac{6}{12}$	$\frac{1}{12}$	$\frac{1}{12}$	$\frac{1}{12}$	$\frac{1}{12}$	$\frac{1}{12}$	$\frac{1}{12}$	$\frac{1}{12}$	$\frac{1}{12}$	$\frac{1}{12}$	$\frac{1}{12}$	$\frac{1}{12}$

$\frac{1}{2}, \frac{2}{4}, \frac{3}{6}, \frac{4}{8}, \frac{5}{10}$, and $\frac{6}{12}$ of the strip (below left) is shaded.

But you can see that the *same amount* of each strip is shaded.

So $\frac{1}{2} = \frac{2}{4} = \frac{3}{6} = \frac{4}{8} = \frac{5}{10} = \frac{6}{12} = \ldots$ are all **equivalent fractions**.

▶ *Exercise* **N9.1**

Use the fraction strips (below left) to answer these questions.

1 Which of these are true and which are false?

(a) $\frac{1}{2} = \frac{2}{6}$ (d) $\frac{6}{8} = \frac{9}{12}$ (g) $\frac{4}{8} = \frac{1}{2}$

(b) $\frac{2}{8} = \frac{3}{12}$ (e) $\frac{7}{12} = \frac{1}{2}$ (h) $\frac{11}{12} = \frac{7}{8}$

(c) $\frac{1}{4} = \frac{2}{8}$ (f) $\frac{5}{6} = \frac{8}{12}$

2 Copy these and fill in the missing numbers.

(a) $\frac{2}{3} = \frac{?}{12}$ (d) $\frac{?}{8} = \frac{3}{4}$ (g) $\frac{5}{?} = \frac{4}{8}$

(b) $\frac{4}{6} = \frac{?}{12}$ (e) $\frac{3}{4} = \frac{9}{?}$ (h) $\frac{3}{?} = \frac{6}{8}$

(c) $\frac{3}{12} = \frac{?}{4}$ (f) $\frac{2}{?} = \frac{1}{4}$

Multiplying the top and bottom of a fraction by the *same number*, makes an equivalent fraction.

For example,

$$\overset{\times 2}{\underset{\times 2}{\frac{3}{4} = \frac{6}{8}}} \qquad \overset{\times 3}{\underset{\times 3}{\frac{2}{5} = \frac{6}{15}}} \qquad \overset{\times 5}{\underset{\times 5}{\frac{7}{10} = \frac{35}{50}}}$$

You can find an equivalent fraction for any fraction this way. Sometimes you know *one* of the numbers in the fraction you want. Use this to help you to find the 'multiplier' you need.

Question

Find the missing numbers in these fractions:

(a) $\frac{2}{3} = \frac{?}{12}$ (b) $\frac{4}{5} = \frac{24}{?}$

Answer

(a)

$$\overset{\times 4}{\underset{\times 4}{\frac{2}{3} = \frac{8}{12}}}$$

The multiplier is 4, because 3 × 4 = 12.

(b)

$$\overset{\times 6}{\underset{\times 6}{\frac{4}{5} = \frac{24}{30}}}$$

The multiplier is 6, because 4 × 6 = 24.

▶ *Exercise* **N9.2**

In each of these

(a) find the multiplier, then   (b) find the missing number.

1 $\frac{2}{3} = \frac{?}{12}$ 5 $\frac{18}{24} = \frac{?}{12}$ 9 $\frac{3}{?} = \frac{30}{70}$

2 $\frac{3}{4} = \frac{?}{16}$ 6 $\frac{6}{?} = \frac{2}{5}$ 10 $\frac{4}{7} = \frac{?}{35}$

3 $\frac{?}{18} = \frac{5}{6}$ 7 $\frac{7}{?} = \frac{21}{27}$ 11 $\frac{2}{5} = \frac{14}{?}$

4 $\frac{1}{3} = \frac{4}{?}$ 8 $\frac{4}{5} = \frac{20}{?}$ 12 $\frac{?}{20} = \frac{45}{60}$

To make a '**family**' or set of equivalent fractions, multiply the top and bottom of a fraction by 2, 3, 4, 5, … in turn. For example,

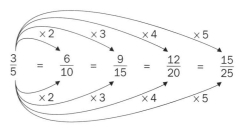

▶ *Exercise* **N9.3**

1 Write down the first five members of the family of equivalent fractions starting with

(a) $\frac{2}{3}$ (b) $\frac{3}{4}$ (c) $\frac{2}{5}$ (d) $\frac{5}{8}$

2 Write down the set of equivalent fractions made by multiplying $\frac{5}{6}$ by

(a) 2   (b) 3   (c) 5   (d) 7   (e) 10.

3 Copy and complete these to make sets of equivalent fractions.

(a) $\frac{3}{7} = \frac{?}{14} = \frac{9}{?} = \frac{12}{?} = \frac{?}{35}$ (c) $\frac{3}{10} = \frac{?}{20} = \frac{9}{?} = \frac{?}{40} = \frac{?}{50}$

(b) $\frac{5}{9} = \frac{10}{?} = \frac{?}{27} = \frac{?}{36} = \frac{25}{?}$

4 Does the first fraction given in each of these pairs belong to the equivalent fraction family of the second?

(a) $\frac{3}{4}, \frac{1}{4}$ (c) $\frac{18}{42}, \frac{3}{7}$ (e) $\frac{20}{30}, \frac{2}{3}$

(b) $\frac{13}{35}, \frac{2}{5}$ (d) $\frac{15}{36}, \frac{4}{9}$ (f) $\frac{27}{40}, \frac{7}{10}$

Dividing the top and bottom of a fraction by the *same number* makes an equivalent fraction too. For example,

$$\overset{\div 3}{\underset{\div 3}{\frac{3}{12} = \frac{1}{4}}} \qquad \overset{\div 2}{\underset{\div 2}{\frac{8}{10} = \frac{4}{5}}} \qquad \overset{\div 10}{\underset{\div 10}{\frac{40}{100} = \frac{4}{10}}}$$

This is often called **cancelling**.

Some people 'cancel' the figures like this when they divide.

$$\frac{\cancel{3}^{1}}{\cancel{12}_{4}} = \frac{1}{4} \qquad \frac{\cancel{8}^{4}}{\cancel{10}_{5}} = \frac{4}{5} \qquad \frac{\cancel{40}^{4}}{\cancel{100}_{10}} = \frac{4}{10}$$

You may know *one* of the numbers in the fraction you want. Use this to help you to find the number you have to divide by.

For example, to find the missing number in $\frac{40}{48} = \frac{?}{6}$

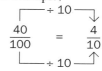

divide by 8

$$\overset{\div 8}{\underset{\div 8}{\frac{40}{48} = \frac{5}{6}}}$$

because 48 ÷ 8 = 6

► *Exercise* N9.4

1   Write down the fraction you get when you cancel by the given number.

(a) $\frac{6}{10}$ cancel by 2   (d) $\frac{12}{15}$ cancel by 3

(b) $\frac{9}{12}$ cancel by 3   (e) $\frac{27}{63}$ cancel by 9

(c) $\frac{8}{12}$ cancel by 4   (f) $\frac{20}{60}$ cancel by 20

2   In each of these
(i) find the divisor, then
(ii) find the missing number.

(a) $\frac{6}{12} = \frac{?}{2}$ (e) $\frac{50}{?} = \frac{5}{6}$ (i) $\frac{35}{63} = \frac{?}{9}$

(b) $\frac{12}{27} = \frac{4}{?}$ (f) $\frac{3}{?} = \frac{21}{28}$ (j) $\frac{30}{36} = \frac{5}{?}$

(c) $\frac{21}{24} = \frac{?}{8}$ (g) $\frac{5}{9} = \frac{25}{?}$ (k) $\frac{3}{4} = \frac{?}{20}$

(d) $\frac{?}{30} = \frac{3}{5}$ (h) $\frac{?}{6} = \frac{14}{42}$ (l) $\frac{?}{26} = \frac{4}{13}$ ◄

Cancelling is also called **simplifying** a fraction. The equivalent fraction has *simpler (smaller)* numbers in it.
   A fraction is in its **simplest form** when its top and bottom numbers are as small as possible. (1 will be the only whole number that divides exactly into both). For example, look at this cancelling:

$$\frac{60}{100} = \frac{6}{10} = \frac{3}{5}$$

You cannot cancel again.
So $\frac{3}{5}$ is the *simplest form* of $\frac{60}{100}$.

A quicker way to do this is to divide the top and bottom numbers by their **highest common factor** (**HCF**).
This is the *largest* whole number that divides exactly into both.

In this example, 20 is the HCF.

$$\frac{60}{100} = \frac{3}{5}$$

Don't worry if you can't spot the HCF. Doing it in 'steps' gives the same result.

'Simplest form' is sometimes called **'lowest terms'**.
So $\frac{60}{100}$ is $\frac{3}{5}$ when put in its *lowest terms*.

► *Exercise* N9.5

Write each of these fractions in simplest form.

1 $\frac{6}{10}$ 5 $\frac{32}{80}$ 9 $\frac{35}{75}$

2 $\frac{18}{24}$ 6 $\frac{4}{20}$ 10 $\frac{45}{80}$

3 $\frac{50}{100}$ 7 $\frac{18}{20}$ 11 $\frac{24}{30}$

4 $\frac{16}{40}$ 8 $\frac{75}{100}$ 12 $\frac{40}{65}$ ◄

Changing fractions to decimals

To change a fraction to a decimal, divide the top number by the bottom number. For example,

$$\frac{5}{8} = 5 \div 8 = 0.625$$

Some fractions give **terminating decimals**. Each division works out exactly and the decimal comes to an end (terminates).

► *Exercise* N9.6

Write each of these fractions as a decimal.

1 $\frac{3}{5}$ 3 $\frac{7}{8}$ 5 $\frac{13}{50}$ 7 $\frac{9}{12}$

2 $\frac{3}{8}$ 4 $\frac{7}{20}$ 6 $\frac{18}{25}$ 8 $\frac{20}{50}$ ◄

Not all fractions give terminating decimals. Some decimals continue without end. These are called **non-terminating decimals**. For example,

$\frac{1}{3} = 0.333\,333\,333 \ldots$ the 3s repeat for ever.

$\frac{3}{11} = 0.272\,727\,272\,7 \ldots$ the 27s repeat for ever.

$\frac{4}{7} = 0.571\,428\,571\,428 \ldots$ the 571 428s repeat for ever.

These fractions give **recurring** or **repeating decimals**. In a recurring decimal a digit or group of digits is repeated for ever.
   A short way to write these is

$\frac{1}{3} = 0.\dot{3}$

$\frac{3}{11} = 0.\dot{2}\dot{7}$

$\frac{4}{7} = 0.\dot{5}7142\dot{8}$

The dots show the repeating pattern.
A dot is placed over the *first* and *last* digit of the group of repeating digits.

► *Exercise* N9.7

1   Change these fractions to decimals.

(a) $\frac{1}{9}$ (d) $\frac{5}{11}$ (g) $\frac{14}{27}$

(b) $\frac{4}{9}$ (e) $\frac{6}{13}$ (h) $\frac{13}{37}$

(c) $\frac{1}{6}$ (f) $\frac{1}{12}$

2 Change these fractions to decimals.

(a) $\frac{1}{7}$ (c) $\frac{3}{7}$ (e) $\frac{5}{7}$

(b) $\frac{2}{7}$ (d) $\frac{4}{7}$ (f) $\frac{6}{7}$

What do you notice?

Changing fractions to percentages

A percentage is an amount 'out of 100'.
A fraction with 100 'on the bottom' is easy to change to a percentage. The 'top number' tells you the percentage.
For example, $\frac{95}{100} = 95\%$.

▶ *Exercise* N9.8

1 Write these fractions as percentages.

(a) $\frac{26}{100}$ (d) $\frac{17}{100}$ (g) $\frac{77}{100}$

(b) $\frac{45}{100}$ (e) $\frac{53}{100}$ (h) $\frac{94}{100}$

(c) $\frac{8}{100}$ (f) $\frac{67}{100}$

2 Copy and complete these.

(a) $\frac{7}{50} = \frac{?}{100} = ?\%$ (d) $\frac{9}{20} = \frac{?}{100} = ?\%$

(b) $\frac{7}{10} = \frac{?}{100} = ?\%$ (e) $\frac{37}{50} = \frac{?}{100} = ?\%$

(c) $\frac{6}{25} = \frac{?}{100} = ?\%$ (f) $\frac{17}{20} = \frac{?}{100} = ?\%$

Any fraction can be written as a percentage.
The whole is always 100%.
So you find the fraction of 100%.

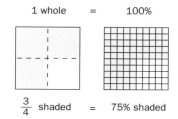

$$\frac{3}{4} \text{ shaded} = 75\% \text{ shaded}$$

For example, to change $\frac{3}{4}$ to a percentage
you work out $\frac{3}{4}$ of 100%
or $\frac{3}{4} \times 100\% = 75\%$.

You can work this out on a calculator. Divide the top of the fraction by the bottom. Then multiply by 100.

For example, since $\frac{3}{4} = 3 \div 4$

try: **C 3 ÷ 4 × 1 0 0 =** `75.`

So $\frac{3}{4} = 75\%$.

Some calculators do part of this work for you.
If you have a **%** key,

try this: **C 3 ÷ 4 %** `75.`

You should get 75 again. If you do not, then your calculator does not work in this way. Find out how your **%** key works.

▶ *Exercise* N9.9

Use your calculator to change these fractions to percentages.

1 $\frac{2}{5}$ **4** $\frac{3}{4}$ **7** $\frac{13}{20}$ **10** $\frac{6}{25}$

2 $\frac{1}{2}$ **5** $\frac{5}{20}$ **8** $\frac{17}{25}$ **11** $\frac{3}{16}$

3 $\frac{2}{7}$ **6** $\frac{3}{8}$ **9** $\frac{7}{8}$ **12** $\frac{23}{40}$

When the fraction gives a *non-terminating decimal*, you have to give the decimal correct to a stated number of **decimal places or significant figures** (see Unit N3).

Question

Change these to percentages correct to 1 dp.

(a) $\frac{2}{3}$ (b) $\frac{5}{11}$ (c) $\frac{7}{27}$

Answer

(a) $\frac{2}{3} = \frac{2}{3} \times 100\% = 66.666...\%$
           $= 66.7\%$ (to 1 dp)

(b) $\frac{5}{11} = \frac{5}{11} \times 100\% = 45.4545...\%$
           $= 45.5\%$ (to 1 dp)

(c) $\frac{7}{27} = \frac{7}{27} \times 100\% = 25.925\,92...\%$
           $= 25.9\%$ (to 1 dp)

▶ *Exercise* N9.10

Change these fractions to percentages. Give each percentage correct to 1 dp.

1 $\frac{5}{7}$ **4** $\frac{9}{13}$ **7** $\frac{4}{19}$ **10** $\frac{9}{11}$

2 $\frac{6}{11}$ **5** $\frac{7}{9}$ **8** $\frac{2}{21}$

3 $\frac{7}{17}$ **6** $\frac{1}{6}$ **9** $\frac{5}{27}$

Changing decimals to fractions

A decimal is a way to write a number of tenths, hundredths, thousandths...
Remember the place values after the decimal point.

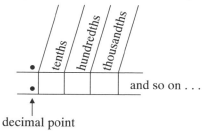

To write a decimal as a fraction, look at the decimal's *last digit*. Its *place value* tells you what kind of fraction it is, i.e. the *bottom number*. The *digits* tell you how many of that fraction you have, i.e. the *top* number.

For example, $0.\mathbf{9}$ $= 9$ tenths $= \frac{9}{10}$

$0.0\mathbf{7} = 7$ hundredths $= \frac{7}{100}$

$0.2\mathbf{1} = 21$ hundredths $= \frac{21}{100}$

$0.08\mathbf{3} = 83$ thousandths $= \frac{83}{1000}$

► *Exercise* N9.11

Write each of these decimals as a fraction. Do not cancel the fractions you get.

1 0.3	**4** 0.007	**7** 0.318	**10** 0.205
2 0.05	**5** 0.013	**8** 0.41	**11** 0.85
3 0.26	**6** 0.106	**9** 0.073	**12** 0.027

Changing decimals to percentages

To change a decimal to a percentage, multiply the decimal by 100. You may do this in your head. But you can do it on your calculator.

For example, $0.45 = 0.45 \times 100\% = 45\%$

► *Exercise* N9.12

Change each of these to a percentage.

1 0.3	**4** 0.37	**7** 0.24	**10** 0.68
2 0.76	**5** 0.01	**8** 0.035	**11** 0.065
3 0.08	**6** 0.005	**9** 0.75	**12** 0.305

Changing percentages to fractions

A percentage gives a number 'out of 100'.

For example,   1% means '1 out of 100' or $\frac{1}{100}$

29% means '29 out of 100' or $\frac{29}{100}$

So it is easy to give any percentage as a fraction with 100 on the bottom.

Sometimes you can **cancel** the fraction to a simpler form.

For example,   36% means $\frac{36}{100}$.

You can cancel by 4:

So $36\% = \frac{9}{25}$

$$\frac{36}{100} = \frac{9}{25}$$ (÷ 4)

It is useful to know these as you often need them:

$1\% = \frac{1}{100}$	$75\% = \frac{3}{4}$	$33\frac{1}{3}\% = \frac{1}{3}$
$5\% = \frac{1}{20}$	$50\% = \frac{1}{2}$	$66\frac{2}{3}\% = \frac{2}{3}$
$10\% = \frac{1}{10}$	$25\% = \frac{1}{4}$	
$20\% = \frac{1}{5}$	$12.5\% = \frac{1}{8}$	

► *Exercise* N9.13

Change each of these to a fraction. Cancel the fraction if you can.

1 17%	**4** 30%	**7** 80%	**10** 12%
2 20%	**5** 40%	**8** 95%	**11** 60%
3 5%	**6** 66%	**9** 2%	**12** 38%

Changing percentages to decimals

To change a percentage to a decimal, just divide the number by 100. You may do the working in your head, but you can use your calculator if you want to.

For example,   9% means $\frac{9}{100}$ or $9 \div 100 = 0.09$

It is useful to know these too:

1% = 0.01	75% = 0.75
5% = 0.05	25% = 0.25
10% = 0.1	12.5% = 0.125
50% = 0.5	

► *Exercise* N9.14

Change these percentages to decimals.

1 17%	**4** 65%	**7** 3%	**10** 73%
2 26%	**5** 80%	**8** 9%	**11** 48%
3 30%	**6** 99%	**9** 64%	**12** 88%

Comparing and ordering

Comparing fractions of the *same* thing or the *same* quantity is easy. You can just compare the fractions themselves.

For example, these 'cakes' are the same size. You can see that $\frac{1}{3}$ of this size cake is larger than $\frac{1}{4}$ of it.

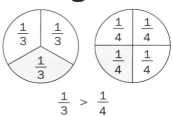

Sometimes we compare fractions of *different* things or *different* quantities. The size of each fraction depends on the sizes of the things or quantities. You *cannot* just compare the fractions.

For example, these 'cakes' are different sizes.
You can see that $\frac{1}{3}$ of one cake is smaller than $\frac{1}{4}$ of the other.

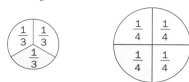

To compare fractions of *different* quantities you have to work out the amount for each fraction (see Unit N12).

In this unit we are comparing fractions of the *same* quantity in each case. We use the symbols > and < to show how the numbers compare in size.

> means 'is greater than' or 'is larger than'
< means 'is less than' or 'is smaller than'.

Common fractions

Fractions with the same denominator (bottom number) are simple to compare. They are the same kind of fraction.

For example, $\frac{2}{5}$, $\frac{3}{5}$, $\frac{1}{5}$, $\frac{4}{5}$ are all *fifths*.

You can put them in order, starting with the smallest:

$$\frac{1}{5} < \frac{2}{5} < \frac{3}{5} < \frac{4}{5}$$

► *Exercise* N9.15

1 For each pair of fractions, say which is bigger.

  (a) $\frac{2}{5}$, $\frac{5}{7}$ (d) $\frac{15}{32}$, $\frac{11}{32}$

  (b) $\frac{9}{10}$, $\frac{7}{10}$ (e) $\frac{7}{40}$, $\frac{6}{40}$

  (c) $\frac{16}{23}$, $\frac{11}{23}$

2 Put these fractions in order. Start with the biggest.
$$\frac{9}{11}, \frac{2}{11}, \frac{5}{11}, \frac{1}{11}, \frac{6}{11}$$

3 Put these fractions in order. Start with the smallest.
$$\frac{17}{20}, \frac{8}{20}, \frac{19}{20}, \frac{3}{20}, \frac{12}{20}, \frac{16}{20}$$

Fractions with different denominators are different kinds of fractions. To compare them, write them all as fractions with the *same denominator*. (This is often called the *common denominator*.) You use equivalent fractions to do this.

Sometimes you can use the largest denominator you have as the common denominator. It is easier if you can.

For example, look at $\frac{2}{3}$ and $\frac{7}{12}$.

You can use 12 as the common denominator, because **3 × 4 = 12**.

To change $\frac{2}{3}$ to $\frac{?}{12}$, multiply top and bottom by 4.

$$\overset{\times 4}{\frac{2}{3} = \frac{8}{12}}_{\times 4}$$

$\frac{7}{12}$ is smaller than $\frac{8}{12}$ i.e. $\frac{7}{12} < \frac{8}{12}$

So $\frac{7}{12}$ is smaller than $\frac{2}{3}$ i.e. $\frac{7}{12} < \frac{2}{3}$

Question

The sizes of 5 nuts in inches are:

$$\frac{7''}{16}, \frac{5''}{8}, \frac{1''}{2}, \frac{11''}{16}, \frac{3''}{4}$$

Put them in order of size, starting with the smallest.

Answer

Make 16 the common denominator.
Write all fractions as sixteenths.

$$\overset{\times 2}{\frac{5}{8} = \frac{10}{16}}_{\times 2} \qquad \overset{\times 8}{\frac{1}{2} = \frac{8}{16}}_{\times 8} \qquad \overset{\times 4}{\frac{3}{4} = \frac{12}{16}}_{\times 4}$$

Write the sixteenths in order.
Then put their equivalent fractions in order.

$$\frac{7''}{16}, \frac{8''}{16}, \frac{10''}{16}, \frac{11''}{16}, \frac{12''}{16}$$

$$\frac{7''}{16}, \frac{1''}{2}, \frac{5''}{8}, \frac{11''}{16}, \frac{3''}{4}$$

Sometimes you have to change *all* the fractions to equivalent fractions to compare them. To find their common denominator, you can multiply all the bottom numbers together.

For example, to put $\frac{1}{2}$, $\frac{2}{3}$ and $\frac{3}{5}$ in order of size,

you can use $2 \times 3 \times 5 = 30$ as common denominator.

$$\overset{\times 15}{\frac{1}{2} = \frac{15}{30}}_{\times 15} \qquad \overset{\times 10}{\frac{2}{3} = \frac{20}{30}}_{\times 10} \qquad \overset{\times 6}{\frac{3}{5} = \frac{18}{30}}_{\times 6}$$

Put the thirtieths in order: $\frac{20}{30} > \frac{18}{30} > \frac{15}{30}$

Rewrite as equivalent fractions: $\frac{2}{3} > \frac{3}{5} > \frac{1}{2}$

► *Exercise* N9.16

1 Write all these fractions as sixteenths, then put them in order starting with the largest.
$$\frac{5}{16}, \frac{1}{2}, \frac{13}{16}, \frac{1}{4}, \frac{3}{8}$$

2 Write all these fractions as tenths, then put them in order starting with the smallest.
$$\frac{9}{10}, \frac{2}{5}, \frac{1}{2}, \frac{7}{10}, \frac{3}{5}$$

3 Put these fractions in order. Start with the smallest. Change each fraction to twelfths first.
$$\frac{7}{12}, \frac{1}{6}, \frac{2}{3}, \frac{1}{2}, \frac{1}{4}, \frac{3}{4}, \frac{1}{3}$$

4 A machine produces tubes with these diameters.
$$\frac{1''}{5}, \frac{4''}{15}, \frac{1''}{2}, \frac{1''}{3}, \frac{1''}{10}, \frac{1''}{15}$$
Put these in order of size. Start with the largest.

5 Another machine produces tubes with these diameters.

$$\frac{7}{20}'' , \ \frac{1}{5}'' , \ \frac{7}{10}'' , \ \frac{1}{10}'' , \ \frac{4}{5}'' , \ \frac{1}{2}''$$

Put these in order of size. Start with the smallest.

To compare fractions you can also use the **lowest common multiple (LCM)** of the bottom numbers as the common denominator. This gives the **lowest common denominator**.

To work out the LCM of the denominators, you can:
- either list their multiples until you find it
- or use the product of their prime factors (see Unit N5).

Use the way you find easier.

Question

In a school survey about school uniform,

$\frac{4}{9}$ of the votes are 'for',

$\frac{5}{12}$ of the votes are 'against'.

Which gets the bigger fraction of the votes? Explain your answer.

Answer

Find the LCM of 9 and 12.

By listing multiples:
   multiples of 9: 9, 18, 27, ㉟, 45, …
   multiples of 12: 12, 24, ㉟,
Or by using products of primes:

$$\left.\begin{array}{l} 9 = \underline{3} \times 3 \\ 12 = \underline{2} \times \underline{2} \times 3 \end{array}\right\} \ \text{LCM: } 2 \times 2 \times 3 \times 3 = 36$$

Change both fractions to 36ths:

$$\frac{4}{9} \ \overset{\times 4}{\underset{\times 4}{=}} \ \frac{16}{36} \qquad \frac{5}{12} \ \overset{\times 3}{\underset{\times 3}{=}} \ \frac{15}{36}$$

'For' gets the bigger fraction.

$\frac{4}{9} \left(= \frac{16}{36} \right)$ is bigger than $\frac{5}{12} \left(= \frac{15}{36} \right)$

Exercise N9.17

1 For each set of fractions below
   (i) find the lowest common denominator,
   (ii) write each fraction using that denominator.

(a) $\frac{2}{3} , \frac{1}{6} , \frac{3}{4}$ (c) $\frac{3}{8} , \frac{5}{12} , \frac{1}{6}$ (e) $\frac{1}{10} , \frac{4}{15} , \frac{7}{20}$

(b) $\frac{1}{2} , \frac{3}{5} , \frac{2}{15}$ (d) $\frac{1}{3} , \frac{1}{7} , \frac{1}{6}$ (f) $\frac{1}{3} , \frac{3}{4} , \frac{5}{8}$

2 A consumer organisation asked a group of people to try out a new washing powder. One sixth of those who used it liked it very much, $\frac{4}{15}$ of the group only just preferred it to their usual powder and $\frac{2}{5}$ of the group disliked it. The rest of the group offered no opinion about it. Which was the largest category of people questioned?

Fractions are often changed to **decimals or percentages to compare** them. Most people find percentages easier to compare.

Question

Tina got most marks in DT (Design and Technology). But she cannot tell whether it is her best test result.
(a) Change each result to a percentage.
(b) Put Tina's subjects and marks in order, largest percentage first.

Tina: Test results			
Maths	$\frac{67}{100}$	DT	$\frac{70}{80}$
English	$\frac{66}{75}$	Art	$\frac{15}{20}$

Answer

(a) Maths: $\frac{67}{100} = 67\%$

    English: $\frac{66}{75} \times 100\% = 88\%$

    DT: $\frac{70}{80} \times 100\% = 87.5\%$

    Art: $\frac{15}{20} \times 100\% = 75\%$

Do the working on your calculator. Use your % *key if you can.*

For example, for $\frac{66}{75}$

try   C 6 6 ÷ 7 5 × 1 0 0 =

or   C 6 6 ÷ 7 5 %

(b) English (88%), DT (87.5%), Art (75%), Maths (67%).

Exercise N9.18

1 For each set of fractions below
   (i) change each fraction to a percentage,
   (ii) write them in order starting with the smallest.

(a) $\frac{2}{5} , \frac{1}{2} , \frac{2}{15}$ (d) $\frac{4}{5} , \frac{9}{10} , \frac{4}{15} , \frac{7}{20}$ (g) $\frac{7}{12} , \frac{6}{7} , \frac{5}{10} , \frac{3}{7}$

(b) $\frac{3}{8} , \frac{1}{4} , \frac{7}{10}$ (e) $\frac{71}{100} , \frac{7}{8} , \frac{31}{50} , \frac{11}{20}$ (h) $\frac{18}{30} , \frac{17}{20} , \frac{16}{17} , \frac{15}{16}$

(c) $\frac{1}{2} , \frac{5}{8} , \frac{3}{4}$ (f) $\frac{5}{6} , \frac{2}{3} , \frac{7}{9} , \frac{11}{15}$

2 Steve obtained these results in his tests last month:

Maths: $\frac{16}{20}$ English: $\frac{13}{15}$ History: $\frac{18}{25}$

French: $\frac{21}{40}$ Geography: $\frac{24}{30}$ Design Technology: $\frac{11}{25}$

(a) In which subject did Steve get his lowest percentage mark?
(b) In which subject did he get his best percentage mark?
(c) In which two subjects were his percentages equal in value?

3 Tina wanted to compare these test scores for herself and some friends:

Tina: $\frac{31}{50}$ Pete: $\frac{13}{20}$ Alison: $\frac{19}{50}$

Nick: $\frac{12}{25}$ Jim: $\frac{4}{5}$ Charlotte: $\frac{9}{10}$

(a) Change each test score to a percentage.
(b) Who has the highest percentage score?
(c) Who has the lowest percentage score?
(d) Write the scores in order, starting with the lowest percentage.

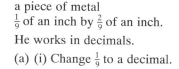

Examination Questions

1 A supermarket employs 18 women and 9 men. Find what fraction of the staff is women. Give your answer in its simplest form.

(SEG, 1990)

2 (a) Complete the following (an example has been done for you).

Example $\frac{5}{6} = \frac{25}{30}$

(i) $\frac{3}{5} = \frac{?}{30}$ (ii) $\frac{7}{10} = \frac{?}{30}$ (iii) $\frac{8}{15} = \frac{?}{30}$

(b) Which of the fractions $\frac{3}{5}, \frac{7}{10}, \frac{8}{15}$ is nearest to $\frac{1}{2}$?

(SEG, 1989)

3 George has a collection of drills whose sizes are marked in inches. The sizes he has are:

$\frac{3}{8}, \frac{1}{2}, \frac{1}{4}, \frac{5}{8}$ and $\frac{9}{16}$.

(a) Which of these drills is the largest size?
(b) The local store sells drills which start at $\frac{1}{4}$ inch and go up to $\frac{3}{4}$ inch in steps of $\frac{1}{16}$ inch.
(i) Which size is half-way between $\frac{3}{8}$ inch and $\frac{1}{2}$ inch?
(ii) How many drills would George need to buy to complete his set?

(MEG, 1988)

4 $\qquad \frac{2}{5}, \frac{3}{8}, \frac{4}{9}$

(a) Convert the three fractions shown above into decimals.
(b) Which of the three fractions is the smallest?

(MEG, 1989)

5 An engineer needs to cut a piece of metal $\frac{1}{9}$ of an inch by $\frac{2}{9}$ of an inch. He works in decimals.

(a) (i) Change $\frac{1}{9}$ to a decimal.
(ii) Change $\frac{2}{9}$ to a decimal.
(b) Write down a fraction which is equal to 0.888888888 ...

(SEG, 1991)

6 Write 12% as a decimal. (Cambridge, 1991)

7 The road sign on the left shows a 1 in 5 steep hill. It is being replaced by a sign which gives the slope as a percentage. What is the percentage figure? (NEAB, 1988)

8 A school has 840 pupils. $\frac{3}{10}$ of them live less than 1 mile from school.
45% of them live between 1 mile and 3 miles from school. The rest live more than 3 miles from school.
What percentage of the pupils live more than 3 miles from school? (ULEAC, 1988)

9 11 out of every 20 people in the World live in Asia (not counting the USSR).
(a) What fraction of the World's population lives in Asia?
(b) What is this fraction as a decimal?
(c) What percentage of the World's population lives in Asia? (WJEC, 1988)

10 Karen, Sally and Rebecca were each asked to estimate what fraction of the pupils in a school could swim.
Karen estimated $\frac{3}{5}$ of the pupils.
Sally estimated 0.75 of the pupils.
Rebecca estimated 80% of the pupils.
(a) Convert $\frac{3}{5}$ to a percentage.
(b) Convert 0.75 to a percentage.
When all the pupils were asked it was found that 77.4% of the pupils were able to swim.
(c) Which girl had the best estimate? (ULEAC, 1991)

N10
Decimals in order

This unit will help you to:
■ compare and order decimal fractions and decimals.

Comparing decimal fractions

In a decimal the *position* of the figures is important as well as their '*size*'. You have to take this into account when comparing decimals.

To help you to compare decimal fractions, write them in *columns* in a '*place value table*'. Then you can start at the decimal point and compare figures with the *same decimal place value*, tenths first, then hundredths, and so on …

For example, to compare 0.0936 and 0.17 look at them in this table.

Keep decimal points in line

Compare the figures in the 'tenths' column.
0 tenths is smaller than **1** tenth.
So 0.**0**936 is smaller than 0.**1**7, i.e. 0.0936 < 0.17.

0 is smaller than 1

Sorting decimal fractions in this way is like sorting words into alphabetical order. For example, **ANGLE** comes before **BEARING** because **A** comes before **B** in the alphabet.

When the figures in a column are the same, compare the figures in the *next* column (to the *right*). Keep comparing in this way until you can put the decimal fractions in order of size.

For example, to compare 0.5981 and 0.5927 look at them in this table. The figures in the tenths and hundredths columns are the same. Compare the figures in the thousandths column.
2 thousandths is smaller than **8** thousandths.
So 0.**5**9**2**7 is smaller than 0.**5**9**8**1, that is, 0.5927 < 0.5981.

same *same*   *2 is smaller than 8*

This is also like alphabetical sorting. For example, **ARC** and **AREA** both start **AR** … But **ARC** comes before **AREA** because **C** comes before **E** in the alphabet.

► *Exercise* **N10.1**

1   Compare each pair of decimal fractions.
    Say which is smaller in each case.
    (a) 0.735, 0.537
    (b) 0.0953, 0.162
    (c) 0.281, 0.2975
    (d) 0.03614, 0.11
    (e) 0.00614, 0.00613
    (f) 0.0101, 0.00867

2   Copy each pair of decimal fractions.
    Write the correct symbol, (> or <), between each pair.
    (a) 0.17   0.3   (d) 0.01342   0.0135
    (b) 0.2101   0.1947   (e) 0.0264   0.02604
    (c) 0.0237   0.024   (f) 0.00731   0.007309

Sorting and ordering decimal fractions

To sort a *list* of decimal fractions into order of size, compare them in the same way. Use their tenths first to compare them, then their hundredths, and so on … until you have them in order. Again think about how you sort words into alphabetical order to help you.

For example, follow these steps to write down these decimals in order, starting with the smallest:

0.309, 0.299, 0.0999, 0.3, 0.31

● Put them in a 'place value table':

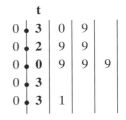

● Look at tenths first.
  0 tenths is the smallest → 0.**0**999 is the smallest.
  2 tenths is next   → 0.**2**99 is next.

● The others all have **3** tenths.
  Look at their hundredths …

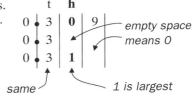

empty space means 0

same   *1 is largest*

1 hundredth is larger than **0** hundredths.
So 0.31 is the largest.

● The others have 0 hundredths.
  Look at their thousandths …

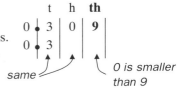

same   *0 is smaller than 9*

0 thousandths is smaller than **9** thousandths.
So 0.3 is smaller than 0.309.

● Now put them in order:
  Check down the columns to see they are correct.

  We can write this as:
  0.0999 < 0.299 < 0.3 < 0.309 < 0.31

  0.0999 │ smallest
  0.299
  0.3
  0.309
  0.31   ▼ largest

> # *Exercise* N10.2

1 Here is a list of decimals:
0.6, 0.27, 0.207, 0.06, 0.83, 0.9
(a) Which number is the largest and which is the smallest?
(b) Put this list into order of size using the symbol <
starting with the smallest.

2 Write the following decimals in order.
Start with the smallest.
(a) 0.131, 0.094, 0.13, 0.756
(b) 0.4072, 0.0742, 0.7042, 0.2047
(c) 0.6, 0.064, 0.397, 0.21
(d) 0.005, 0.0051, 0.0512, 0.4
(e) 0.0038, 0.0037, 0.00374, 0.003808

Whole numbers and decimal fractions

Many numbers have a whole number part *and* a decimal fraction part. To sort these into order of size, sort the whole number parts into the correct order first. Then use the decimal fractions to sort numbers with the same whole number part into order. A place value table also helps you to do this.

Question

Peter has off-cuts of wood of these lengths in his workshop:
1.95 m, 2.5 m, 1.91 m, 2.03 m, 0.69 m, 2.17 m
Write these lengths in order of size, longest first.

Answer

Place them in a place value table:

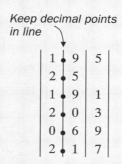

Keep decimal points in line

The order of size is:

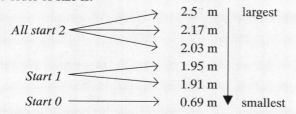

We can write this as:
2.5 m > 2.17 m > 2.03 m > 1.95 m > 1.91 m > 0.69 m

> # *Exercise* N10.3

1 Write these lengths in order of size. Start with the shortest.
3.2 m, 2.17 m, 3.02 m, 4.5 m, 4.35 m, 1.98 m.

2 Write these masses in order of size. Start with the heaviest.
4.2 kg, 3.15 kg, 4.02 kg, 2.14 kg, 2.85 kg, 0.93 kg.

3 (a) A plumber has cut some lengths of copper pipe measuring:
1.87 m, 1.64 m, 0.34 m, 2.08 m, 1.07 m, 2.31 m, 1.27 m.
He has to load them into his van starting with the longest. Which one should he put in first?
(b) Put the lengths of pipe into order using the symbol > starting with the longest.

Examination Questions

1 Write down the reading given by the pointer on the scale.

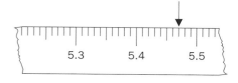

(MEG, 1988)

2 (a) What number is the printed arrow pointing to?
(b) Draw an arrow on the diagram pointing to the number 1.03.

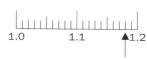

(SEG, 1989)

3 2.8   2.705   2.72
Write these numbers in order of increasing size.
(ULEAC, 1988)

4 Write these numbers in order of size, smallest first.
0.66   0.625   0.088   0.667   (NEAB, 1988)

5 0.299   0.309   0.0999   0.3   0.31
From these five numbers
(a) write down the smallest,
(b) write down the largest,
(c) take the first number in the list from the last number in the list.   (ULEAC, 1988)

6 36.499   36.609   36.069   36.71   36.0999   35.999
(a) Which of the six numbers above is the largest?
(b) List all of the numbers which are bigger than $36\frac{1}{2}$.
(ULEAC, 1988)

N11
Fractions and quantities

This unit will help you to:

■ write one quantity as a common or decimal fraction of another

■ give one quantity as a percentage of another

■ find a change in a quantity as a percentage.

One quantity as a fraction of another

A fraction is a way to show part of something.
It can be written as a common fraction, like $\frac{1}{2}$,
or a decimal fraction, like 0.5,
or a percentage, like 50%.   (see Unit N8)

You can write **one quantity as a fraction of another.**

For example, 37 pence is a fraction of £1 (= 100p).

You can write it as: $£\frac{37}{100}$ or £0.37 or 37% of £1.

This shows how the two quantities *compare* in size. The quantities involved must be of the *same* kind, i.e. both numbers, both lengths, both times, and so on ... Any units of measure must be the same too.

Using common fractions

You often get a 'mark' written as a fraction:

$$\frac{\text{your mark}}{\text{total number of possible marks}}$$

For example, a mark of 9 out of 10 is $\frac{9}{10}$.

You can use a fraction to describe part of any group of things in the same way.

$$\frac{\text{number in the part you 'want'}}{\text{total number}}$$

For example, 5 people took their driving test,

3 out of 5 passed. $\frac{3}{5}$ passed.

2 out of 5 failed. $\frac{2}{5}$ failed.

▶ *Exercise* **N11.1**

1   Sue bought a box of ten peaches. Two were bad.
    What fraction of the peaches were
    (a) bad   (b) good?

2   Mick bought eight gobstoppers. Three were red.
    What fraction of the gobstoppers were
    (a) red   (b) not red?

3   28 students out of a group of 30 passed the maths test.
    What fraction of the students
    (a) passed the test (b) did not pass the test?

4   Nine out of one hundred parts produced by a machine were faulty.
    What fraction of the parts produced were
    (a) faulty   (b) not faulty?

5   Mandy planted 200 bulbs in her garden. One hundred and seventy seven bulbs produced flowers.
    What fraction of the bulbs
    (a) produced flowers   (b) did not produce flowers?

Sometimes you are *given* the numbers you need for the fraction you want. Sometimes you have to *work them out*. So read the question carefully. It may even remind you to find the total number of things first.

We usually make fraction answers as simple as possible. So cancel if you can (see Unit N9). Questions often tell you to do this. You will lose marks if you don't.

Question

Give fractions in their simplest form.

A Year 11 group are allowed a choice of

Sport	Number of students
Soccer	10
Netball	14
Hockey	12

sports for their games lessons. The table lists their choices.
(a) How many students are in this group?
(b) What fraction chose soccer?
(b) What fraction did not choose hockey?

Answer

(a) *Total:* 10 + 14 + 12 = 36

(b) *Soccer:* 10 out of 36 = $\frac{10}{36}$ = $\frac{5}{18}$

(c) *'Not hockey'* is soccer and netball:

    10 + 14 = 24

    Not hockey: 24 out of 36 = $\frac{24}{36}$ = $\frac{2}{3}$

▶ *Exercise* **N11.2**

In this exercise, give all fractions in their simplest form.

1   In a tube of Marties, 7 are green, 8 are red, 3 are yellow and 2 are brown. What fraction of these Marties are
    (a) green   (b) red   (c) yellow   (d) brown?

2   In a full car park, 75 of the cars are British, 48 are French , 31 are Italian and 46 are German. What fraction of these cars are
    (a) British   (b) French   (c) Italian   (d) German?

3   In a flower bed in Ruth's garden, 12 of the flowers are red, 14 are yellow, 6 are white and 8 are pink. What fraction of these flowers are
    (a) red   (b) yellow   (c) white   (d) pink?

4 On Ted's bookshelf there are 6 books on cookery, 10 on music and 14 novels. What fraction of these books are
(a) on cookery (b) on music (c) novels?

5 In Carrie's cutlery drawer there are 10 knives, 8 forks and 6 spoons. What fraction of these items are
(a) knives (b) forks (c) spoons?

One quantity A as a fraction of another quantity B, is written as $\frac{A}{B}$. Then it is given in its simplest form.

Make sure that the quantities have the *same unit of measure*, if any. Change one if you need to.
   For example, in a money problem the amounts must be both in pounds or both in pence.
   Choose the unit you find easier to work with.

Question

John did 5 hours revision one Saturday. He spent 45 minutes of this time studying history.
(a) Give John's Saturday revision time in minutes.
(b) What fraction of this time was spent studying history? Give your answer in its simplest form.

Answer

(a) 5 hours = 5 × 60 minutes = 300 minutes
(b) *45 minutes out of 300 minutes* $= \frac{45}{300} = \frac{3}{20}$

Cancelling:
$$\frac{45}{300} = \frac{9}{60} = \frac{3}{20}$$
(÷5 and ÷3)

▶ *Exercise* **N11.3**

1 Express the first quantity as a fraction of the second. Then simplify the fraction if you can. Take care with the units.
(a) 5 cm, 50 cm   (g) 2 kg, 12 kg
(b) 10 m, 40 m   (h) 500 g, 2 kg
(c) 8 cm, 64 cm   (i) 2ℓ, 6ℓ
(d) 12 km, 60 km   (j) 750 mℓ, 2ℓ
(e) 6 mm, 3 cm   (k) 20 minutes, 1 hour
(f) 50 cm, 2 m   (l) 30 pence, £5

2 Trish spent £2.75 on vegetables. She paid with a £10 note. What fraction of the note was spent on vegetables?

3 Jim spent 2 hours gardening last Sunday. He spent 50 minutes cutting the grass, 25 minutes trimming the hedge and the rest of the time weeding. What fraction of this time did Jim spend
(a) cutting the grass (b) trimming the hedge (c) weeding?

4 Lisa bought a 2 lb bag of flour. She used 12 oz for a pizza, 10 oz for pancakes and the rest for bread rolls. What fraction of this flour was used to make
(a) pizza (b) pancakes (c) bread rolls?

5 Don bought a 2 m length of formica for a kitchen worktop. The worktop is 1 m 60 cm long.
(a) What length of formica was unused?
(b) What fraction of the formica was
   (i) used (ii) not used?

Using decimals

To give **a quantity as a decimal fraction of another**, write it as a common fraction first. Then change it to a decimal by dividing the 'top' by the 'bottom'.
   You may need to round the decimal to a number of decimal places or significant figures (see Unit N3).
   Times are often changed to decimal fractions of a minute, an hour, a day, as in the next example. Then they can be used in calculations with a calculator.

Question

(a) Write 9 hours as a decimal fraction of a day.
(b) Write 5 minutes as a decimal fraction of an hour. Give your answer correct to 3 decimal places.
(c) Write 2 days as a decimal fraction of a week correct to 2 significant figures.

Answer

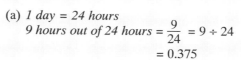

(a) *1 day = 24 hours*
   9 hours out of 24 hours $= \frac{9}{24} = 9 \div 24$
   $= 0.375$

(b) *1 hour = 60 minutes*
   5 minutes out of 60 minutes $= \frac{5}{60} = 5 \div 60$
   $= 0.083333333$ (calculator)
   $= 0.083$ (to 3 dp)

(c) *1 week = 7 days*
   2 days out of 7 days $= \frac{2}{7} = 2 \div 7$
   $= 0.285714285$ (calculator)
   $= 0.29$ (to 2 sf.)

▶ *Exercise* **N11.4**

In this exercise, give your answer to a sensible degree of accuracy where necessary.

1 Give the first quantity as a decimal fraction of the second.
(a) 5 cm, 20 cm   (f) 12 minutes, 40 minutes
(b) 2 kg, 10 kg   (g) 7 mm, 30 mm
(c) 60 mℓ, 100 mℓ   (h) 4 oz, 12 oz
(d) 4 cm², 16 cm²   (i) 7 feet, 16 feet
(e) 80 g, 400 g   (j) 3 yards, 11 yards

2 Give the first quantity as a decimal fraction of the second. Be careful with the units.
(a) 10 cm, 4 m   (e) 25 cm, 30 m
(b) 4 weeks, 2 years   (f) 300 mℓ, 2ℓ
(c) 50 g, 1 kg   (g) 12 days, 3 weeks
(d) 5 months, 2 years   (h) 8 mm, 5 cm

Using percentages

To find **one quantity as a percentage of another**, write the quantity as a fraction of the other first. Then change the fraction to a percentage. You can do this on a calculator.

Question

A gardener sowed 48 tomato seeds in the same conditions in a greenhouse. Only 39 of these seeds grew into plants. What percentage of the tomato seeds sown in the greenhouse grew into plants?

Answer

As a fraction: $\frac{39}{48}$

As a percentage: $\frac{39}{48} \times 100\% = 81.25\%$

So 81.25% of the sown seeds grew into plants.

Calculator work　C　3　9　÷　4　8　×　1　0　0　=

If your calculator has a **%** key, then try this:

C　3　9　÷　4　8　%

On some calculators this gives the same answer.

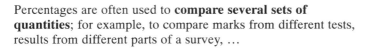

► Exercise N11.5

1　Express the first number as a percentage of the second.
　(a) 5, 20　　(e) 15, 120　　(i) 34, 200
　(b) 7, 35　　(f) 35, 700　　(j) 69, 300
　(c) 4, 80　　(g) 20, 50
　(d) 12, 60　　(h) 3, 20
2　In Exeter, 13 out of every 20 families own a car. What percentage of Exeter families are
　(a) car owners　(b) not car owners?
3　In Birmingham, 4 out of every 5 households have a telephone. What percentage of households in Birmingham
　(a) have a telephone　(b) do not have a telephone?
4　38 out of every 40 fish sold by Fast Fry are cod. What percentage of fish sold are
　(a) cod　(b) not cod?
5　21 out of 25 cars serviced by Ripoff Motors were found to be faulty. What percentage of cars serviced were found to be
　(a) faulty　(b) not faulty?

Percentages are often used to **compare several sets of quantities**; for example, to compare marks from different tests, results from different parts of a survey, …

Question

At the end of term Jane got 14 marks out of 20 in the mathematics test and 56 marks out of 70 in the science test. For which test did Jane get the higher percentage mark?

Answer

Mathematics: *As a fraction:* $\frac{14}{20}$

As a percentage: $\frac{14}{20} \times 100\% = 70\%$

C　1　4　÷　2　0　×　1　0　0　=

or try:

C　1　4　÷　2　0　%

Science:　　*As a fraction:* $\frac{56}{70}$

As a percentage: $\frac{56}{70} \times 100\% = 80\%$

C　5　6　÷　7　0　×　1　0　0　=

or try:

C　5　6　÷　7　0　%

So Jane got a higher percentage mark in the science test.

► Exercise N11.6

1　In a bag of 20 apples, 2 are bad. In another bag of 25 apples, 3 are bad. Which bag has the bigger percentage of bad apples?
2　Nicky scored 28 out of 40 in a Maths exam and 45 out of 60 in a Science exam. In which exam did Nicky get the higher percentage mark?
3　Strongford United have played 12 matches and won 9. Weakling Wanderers have played 10 matches and won 8. Which team has won the larger percentage of its matches?
4　In a bag of 25 mixed fruit sweets, 7 are blackcurrant. In another bag of 30 mixed fruit sweets, 8 are blackcurrant. Which bag has the larger percentage of blackcurrant sweets?
5　In Sid's allotment 17 out of 50 rows of vegetables contain potatoes. In Fred's allotment, 13 out of 40 rows of vegetables contain potatoes. Which allotment contains the greater percentage of potatoes?

When comparing quantities, any *units of measure* **must** be the *same*. If the quantities are given in different units, then change them to the same unit before doing the calculation.

Question

At the beginning of the year Winston's height was 1.24 metres. During the year he grew 6 cm. What was the percentage increase in Winston's height? Give your answer to the nearest 1%.

Answer

Write increase and original height in the same unit.

Increase: 6 cm ◄—————————————► same unit

Original height: 1.24 m = 124 cm
6 cm as a percentage of 124 cm is:
$\frac{6}{124} \times 100\% = 4.838\,709\,677$ (calculator)

$= 5\%$ (to the nearest 1%)

C　6　÷　1　2　4　×　1　0　0　=

or try:

C　6　÷　1　2　4　%

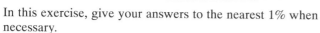 **Exercise** N11.7

In this exercise, give your answers to the nearest 1% when necessary.

1 Express the first quantity as a percentage of the second.
(a) 50 cm, 2 m
(b) 600 g, 6 kg
(c) 29 p, £2
(d) 15 m, 0.75 km
(e) 25 g, 0.5 kg
(f) 385 mℓ, 2ℓ

2 Mae weighed 13 stones. At Weightshifters she lost 2 stones 9 pounds. What was the percentage loss in Mae's weight?

3 When Sally planted a tree in her garden its height was 1 m 46 cm. During the year the tree grew 9 cm. What was the percentage increase in the tree's height?

4 Mark bought a 3 kg bag of flour. On the way home the bag split and he lost 235 g of flour. What percentage of the flour was lost?

5 At the beginning of the year Denise had £80 in a savings account. At the end of the year interest of £4.80 was added to the account. What was the percentage increase in her savings account?

You may have to work out an *actual change* in a quantity (increase or decrease) and then give it as a **percentage change**. Always work out the change as a percentage *of the quantity you started with*.

$$\text{Percentage change} = \frac{\text{Actual change}}{\text{Original quantity}} \times 100\%$$

 **Question**

A stand in the local football ground holds 14 500 people. Making it into an 'all seat' area will reduce its capacity to 9425.
(a) What is the reduction in capacity?
(b) By what percentage will the capacity be reduced?

 **Answer**

(a) 14 500 − 9425 = 5075
(b) $\frac{5075}{14\ 500} \times 100\% = 35\%$.

Percentage reduction is 35%.

You can do all of this working on a calculator.
The following way uses the memory and % *key. The answers you have to record in your working are shown on the display.*

Try this way on your calculator. See if it works.
Find the best way to do the working on your calculator.

Profit and loss are often given as percentages of the *cost price*. This makes it easier to compare the profit or loss made on different items.
Some people remember this formula:

$$\text{Percentage profit (or loss)} = \frac{\text{Profit (or loss)}}{\text{Cost price}} \times 100\%$$

But really you are just working out one amount (the profit or loss) as a percentage of another (the cost price). Make sure that the amounts are either *both* in pounds or *both* in pence. You may need to change one.

Question

(a) A greengrocer makes £15 profit on some oranges. They cost £60. What is the percentage profit?
(b) The same greengrocer paid £40 for some potatoes and sold them for £52.50. What percentage profit was made?
(c) On which item did the greengrocer make the better profit?

Answer

(a) $\frac{£15}{£60} \times 100\% = 25\%$ profit on oranges

(b) Profit: £52.50 − £40 = £12.50

Percentage profit: $\frac{£12.50}{£40} \times 100\%$
$= 31.25\%$ on potatoes

One way to do the working:

 ← profit

← percentage profit

Find the best way with your calculator.

(c) The better profit was on potatoes.

 Exercise N11.8

In this exercise, give your answers to the nearest 1% when necessary.

1 Calculate the percentage increase or decrease in each of these quantities.

	original quantity	new quantity
(a)	25 g	30 g
(b)	50 m	75 m
(c)	80 p	70 p
(d)	50 cm	44 cm
(e)	£60	£45
(f)	8 litres	7 litres

2 Calculate the percentage increase or decrease in each of theses quantities. Watch the units.

	original quantity	new quantity
(a)	£34	£37.60
(b)	28 m	29 m 14 cm
(c)	5 litres	5 litres 280 mℓ
(d)	2 kg	1 kg 600 g
(e)	7 lb 2 oz	6 lb 12 oz

3 The price of a Panasonic NV-R50 Camcorder is reduced in the sale from £700 to £649.99. What is the percentage reduction?

4 In 1993 Millstone School had 950 students on roll. In 1994 the number of students increased to 1026 students. What is the percentage increase in the number of students attending Millstone School?

5 Rod tried to pour a pint of milk into a plastic bottle. He spilt some of it and ended up with only 17 fl oz. What is the percentage loss in milk? (1 pint = 20 fl oz.)

6 The cost of a return journey by rail from Exeter to Norwich rose from £42 to £47.50. What is the percentage increase in this fare?

7 Over Christmas, Steve's weight increased from 10 st 8 lb to 11 st 2 lb. What was Steve's percentage weight gain?

8 At the beginning of a journey Pete checked the tyre pressures on his car were all $20\,kg/cm^2$. At the end of his journey the pressure in one tyre had fallen to $18\,kg/cm^2$. What was the percentage loss in pressure for this tyre?

9 Quicksale Motors bought a car for £5250 and quickly sold it for £7999. What was the percentage profit?

10 Gasfit Ltd paid £97 for a gas fire which it sold for £138.99. It paid £178 for a cooker which it had to dispose of in the sale for £149.99. Calculate the percentage profit on the fire and the percentage loss on the cooker.

Examination Questions

1 There are 20 pupils in a class. Five of them are left-handed.
(a) What fraction of the class is left-handed?
(b) Write this fraction as a decimal.
(c) What percentage of the class is left-handed?
(d) What percentage of the class is right-handed?
(WJEC, 1991)

2 Some of the nutritional contents of 100 grams of Bran Cereal are as follows:
 Fat 5.0 grams
 Protein 11.6 grams
 Fibre 21.5 grams
(a) What fraction of Bran Cereal is fat?
(b) A normal helping of Bran Cereal is 40 grams.
 (i) Express 40 grams as fraction of 100 grams. Give the fraction in its simplest form.
 (ii) How many grams of fibre does a normal helping of Bran Cereal contain? (MEG, 1988)

3 A farmer has 105 cows, 87 sheep and 15 pigs.
(a) What is the total number of animals?
(b) What fraction of the animals are sheep? Give your answer in its simplest form. (SEG, 1989)

4 Here is a recipe for making 12 cakes.

240 g	Flour
120 g	Fat
180 g	Sugar
2	Eggs

The total weight of the cakes is 600 g.
What percentage of this weight is fat?
(ULEAC, 1994)

5

Paper mills in this country produce different sorts of paper. The figures for 1988 are given in this table.

Type of paper	Production in thousands of tonnes
Newsprint	495
Printing and writing	1187
Corrugated cardboard	1085
Packing paper and board	547
Tissue and toilet paper	493
Industrial and special	325

(a) Find the total paper production in 1988.
(b) What percentage of the total is newsprint?
(MEG, 1991)

6 For an examination paper the marks for Section A must lie between 40 and 50 (inclusive). The marks for Section B must lie between 50 and 60 (inclusive).
The total must be 100.
One year the paper had 40 marks for Section A and 60 marks for Section B. The following year it had 50 for each section.
(a) What was the percentage increase in Section A marks?
(b) What was the percentage decrease in Section B marks?
(MEG, 1991)

7 All the students in a College were asked questions about 'Smoking'. Some of the results are given in the table.

	Have smoked	Have never smoked	Total
Males		132	237
Females	187	169	
Total		301	593

(a) Fill in the missing entries in the table.
(b) What percentage of females have never smoked?
(NEAB, 1991)

8 In 1989 Pugh the fireman was paid £15 450. In 1990 he had a payrise and was then paid £16 686. What was his percentage payrise? (SEG, 1991)

9

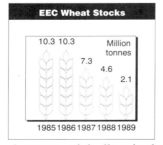

(a) What was the percentage fall in EEC Wheat Stocks from 1985 to 1989?
(b) In 1989 the Wheat Stock in the United Kingdom was 40 000 tonnes. What percentage of the EEC total was this?
(MEG, 1991)

10 A camera originally priced at £125 was sold for £99 as a 'special offer'. Calculate the percentage reduction from the original price. (MEG, 1991)

N12
Fractions of quantities

This unit will help you to:

■ Find a common fraction of a quantity with and without a calculator

■ compare fractions of quantities

■ calculate any percentages of a quantity with a calculator

■ find simple percentages of quantities without a calculator

■ increase and decrease a quantity by a percentage.

You will often want to find a fraction of a quantity. Here are some ways to do the working, with and without a calculator. Always make sure that your answer has the correct unit of measure if there is one.

Using common fractions

To find a fraction of something, share it out *equally* first. The *'bottom number'* of the fraction tells you how many 'equal shares'. Dividing the quantity by the 'bottom number' of the fraction gives '1 share'.

To find a **half** $\left(\frac{1}{2}\right)$, divide by **2**.

To find a **third** $\left(\frac{1}{3}\right)$, divide by **3**.

To find a **quarter** $\left(\frac{1}{4}\right)$, divide by **4**.

To find a **fifth** $\left(\frac{1}{5}\right)$, divide by **5**.

To find a **sixth** $\left(\frac{1}{6}\right)$, divide by **6**.

And so on …

You may want more than 1 of the equal shares. The *top* of the fraction tells you how many you want.

To find $\frac{2}{3}$ of something, find $\frac{1}{3}$ of it, then multiply by **2**.

To find $\frac{3}{4}$ of something, find $\frac{1}{4}$ of it, then multiply by **3**.

To find $\frac{7}{10}$ of something, find $\frac{1}{10}$ of it, then multiply by **7**.

And so on …

You can do the working with or without a calculator.

Question

(a) How many centimetres are there in 1.75 m?
(b) How many centimetres is $\frac{3}{5}$ of 1.75 m?

Answer

(a) 1 m　　= 100 cm
　　1.75 m = 175 cm

(b) $\frac{1}{5}$ of 175 cm = 175 ÷ 5 = 35 cm

　　$\frac{3}{5}$ of 175 cm = 3 × 35 cm = 105 cm.

▶ *Exercise* **N12.1**

1　Calculate

(a) (i) $\frac{1}{5}$ of 75 m

　　(ii) $\frac{2}{5}$ of 75 m

(b) (i) $\frac{1}{6}$ of £84

　　(ii) $\frac{5}{6}$ of £84

(c) (i) $\frac{1}{8}$ of 60 kg

　　(ii) $\frac{3}{8}$ of 60 kg

(d) (i) $\frac{1}{4}$ of 240 cm

　　(ii) $\frac{3}{4}$ of 240 cm

(e) (i) $\frac{1}{20}$ of 880 mℓ

　　(ii) $\frac{17}{20}$ of 880 mℓ.

2　(a) (i) How many grams in 2.4 kg?
　　　(ii) How many grams in $\frac{7}{8}$ of 2.4 kg?

　(b) (i) How many millilitres in 3.2ℓ?
　　　(ii) How many millilitres in $\frac{5}{8}$ of 3.2ℓ?

　(c) (i) How many millimetres in 9.9 cm?
　　　(ii) How many millimetres in $\frac{2}{3}$ of 9.9 cm?

　(d) (i) How many fluid ounces in 2 pints?
　　　(ii) How many fluid ounces in $\frac{4}{5}$ of 2 pints?

　(e) (i) How many pounds in 8 st 5 lb?
　　　(ii) How many pounds in $\frac{5}{9}$ of 8 st 5 lb?

The fraction in a question may not be for the value you want. Don't be caught out! Make sure you answer the *actual* question, not the one you think it should be. So read it carefully.

In the next question the fraction describes the number of girls. The question asks for the number of boys.

Question

Simon's school has 256 pupils. $\frac{5}{8}$ of them are girls. How many are boys?

Answer

　　$\frac{1}{8}$ of pupils = 256 ÷ 8 = 32

Girls: $\frac{5}{8}$ of pupils = 32 × 5 = 160

Number of boys = number of pupils − number of girls
　　　　　　　　= 256 − 160
　　　　　　　　= 96

▶ *Exercise* N12.2

1　A market stall has 900 apples for sale. Some are red and the rest are green. If $\frac{8}{15}$ of the apples are red, how many are green?

2　A box contains 150 biscuits, $\frac{1}{3}$ of them are chocolate biscuits. How many of them are not chocolate biscuits?

3　Mr Thompson has 450 books, $\frac{4}{9}$ of which are large print books. How many of them are not large print books?

4　There are 210 cars in a car park, $\frac{3}{7}$ of which are blue. How many cars are not blue?

5　There are 7200 trees in a park, $\frac{5}{12}$ of them are oak trees. How many are not oak trees?

You may want to **compare fractions of things**. The same fraction is not always the same amount. A bigger fraction is not always a bigger amount. It all depends on what they are fractions of! (see p44–45.)

You have to work out the amount each fraction gives. Then you can compare the amounts.

Question

Ann has £6. She buys a book with $\frac{1}{5}$ of it.
Tom has £7.50. He spends $\frac{1}{6}$ of it on a magazine.
Who spends more money? How much more?

Answer

Ann:　$\frac{1}{5}$ of £6 = £6 ÷ 5 = £1.20

Tom:　$\frac{1}{6}$ of £7.50 = £7.50 ÷ 6 = £1.25

£1.25 – £1.20 = £0.05 = 5p
Tom spends 5p more than Ann.

▶ *Exercise* N12.3

1　Which is the larger amount:

(a)　$\frac{2}{5}$ of £40　or　$\frac{3}{5}$ of £25?

(b)　$\frac{3}{7}$ of 49 kg　or　$\frac{3}{8}$ of 48 kg?

(c)　$\frac{2}{9}$ of 81ℓ　or　$\frac{2}{5}$ of 80ℓ?

(d)　$\frac{7}{12}$ of 60 m　or　$\frac{8}{11}$ of 40 m?

(e)　$\frac{3}{5}$ of 2.5 km　or　$\frac{3}{7}$ of 2.8 km?

(f)　$\frac{2}{3}$ of 3.9 kg　or　$\frac{3}{4}$ of 4.6 kg?

2　Tracey has £84. She went to the disco with friends and spent $\frac{1}{8}$ of it. Her brother David has £69 and spent $\frac{1}{6}$ of it at the cinema. Who spends more money? How much more?

3　Ann ate $\frac{2}{5}$ of a 300 g cake. Jill ate $\frac{2}{3}$ of a 150 g cake. Who ate more cake? How much more?

To find a fraction of something, you can change the fraction to a decimal (by dividing 'top' by ' bottom'). Then find that decimal fraction of the quantity. You can do all the working with a calculator.

Question

Find $\frac{5}{8}$ of £30.

Answer

$\frac{5}{8}$ of £30 = 5 ÷ 8 × £30

　　　　= 0.625 × £30

　　　　= £18.75　

▶ *Exercise* N12.4

For each of these questions, first change the fraction into a decimal and then carry out the calculation.

1　$\frac{2}{5}$ of £60

2　$\frac{3}{8}$ of 40 kg

3　$\frac{4}{15}$ of £75

4　$\frac{2}{3}$ of 1.5 m

5　$\frac{3}{10}$ of £8.50

6　$\frac{5}{12}$ of 3.6 kg.

Using percentages

There are several ways to find **percentages of quantities** *with a calculator*. Here are two ways to try. The first way works with any calculator.

Divide the percentage by 100 (to change it to a decimal). Then multiply by the amount.

You may not need this =.

For example, for 12% of 15

try　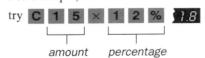

So 12% of 15 is 1.8.

If your calculator has a %, try this way. Enter the amount, multiply by the percentage you want, then press %.

For example, for 12% of 15

try

　　　　amount　　percentage

Not all % keys work in this way. If you do not get 1.8, find out how to use your % key.

Using a % key is often quicker than other ways. Make sure that you can use yours correctly.

▶ *Exercise* N12.5

Use your calculator for this exercise.

1　Find 12% of
　(a) 30　　(b) 45　　(c) 70

2　Find 15% of
　(a) 20　　(b) 45　　(c) 55

3　Find 26% of
　(a) 40　　(b) 65　　(c) 90

4　Find 38% of
　(a) 25　　(b) 65　　(c) 80

5　Find 74% of
　(a) 30　　(b) 85　　(c) 120

You often have to work out **percentages of money**. After a money calculation, look carefully at the number you get. Make sure you write it correctly as an amount of money. You may have to round your answer too.

Question

A college 'Fun Run' raises £2143.50 for charity. After a vote they decide to give

    20% to Dr Barnado's

    37.5% to Save the Children Fund

and 42.5% to the local Hospice.

How much money do they give to each charity?

Answer

Dr Barnado's: 20% of £2143.50 = £428.70
Calculator gives: 428.7 ← *'Add' 0 to make £s and pence*

Save the Children Fund: 37.5% of £2143.50 = £803.81
Calculator gives: 803.8125 ← *Round to nearest penny*

Local Hospice: 42.5% of £2143.50 = £910.99
Calculator gives: 910.9875 ← *Round to nearest penny.*

Here is one way to do the working. It uses a memory and ▨ *key. Try it if you can.*

Find the easiest way to do this working on your calculator.

You can find percentages of **other quantities** this way too.

Exercise N12.6

1 Use your calculator to find
  (a) 14% of £26   (d) 13% of 28 kg
  (b) 72% of £85   (e) 16% of 14 m
  (c) 31% of 15 ℓ   (f) 38% of 120 km

2 Sue earns £235 per week. From this she pays 18% for income tax, 6% superannuation and 5% into a savings scheme. Calculate (correct to the nearest penny)
  (a) the amount she pays each week for
    (i)   income tax
    (ii) superannuation
    (iii) savings.
  (b) How much money is left each week after these deductions?

You can work out some simple percentages of quantities *without a calculator*.

Here are some ways for you to try. You may find them useful in everyday life and in Aural Tests.

We all have our favourite methods. Find out which are easiest for you. Then practise using them. Check your answers with your calculator. You may find that working in your head is faster than your calculator.

- Look for percentages that are *simple fractions*.
  For example, $50\% = \frac{1}{2}$ $25\% = \frac{1}{4}$
  You can use the fractions instead of the percentages. They are usually easier.

- 10% is the same as $\frac{1}{10}$.
  To find 10% of a quantity, divide it by 10.

- 5% is half of 10%.
  To find 5% of a quantity, divide it by 10, then divide it by 2.

- 1% is the same as $\frac{1}{100}$.
  To find 1% of a quantity, divide it by 100.

- Use the *'penny in the pound'* method for money.
  1% of £1 (= 100 p) is 1p.
  So to find 1% of an amount of money, just work out '1p for every £'.
  For example, 1% of £27 is 27p
               1% of £16.42 is 16.42p.

You can find many percentages of money using this method.

Exercise N12.7

Do not use a calculator for this exercise.

1 Find
  (a) 25% of £40   (d) 1% of £300   (g) 10% of £165
  (b) 10% of £50   (e) 2% of £30   (h) 5% of £165
  (c) 5% of £40   (f) 75% of £80

2 VAT is currently $17\frac{1}{2}\%$.
Use $17\frac{1}{2}\% = 10\% + 5\% + 2\frac{1}{2}\%$ to work out the VAT on items which cost
  (a) £40   (b) £60   (c) £90.
Check your answers with a calculator.

Percentage changes

The **change** (increase or decrease) in a quantity is often described as a percentage; for example, profit and loss, price rises and discounts, …

To **increase a quantity by a percentage**, you can work out the actual increase and then add it to the original quantity to find the actual new quantity.

Question

In 1989 the population of Wyeton was 10 675. In 1990 it increased by 8%. What was Wyeton's population in 1990?

Answer

Increase: 8% of 10 675 →   854
1989 Population   → 10 675+
1990 Population   → <u>11 529</u>

continued

You can do this working in different ways on a calculator. Whichever way you use, your written working should be the same.

This way works on most calculators. Try it on yours.

Increase. Write it down ↓

1990 population ↗

You may not need the first ▣ . Try it without. But make sure that you get the correct answer!

If you have a ▣ key, then try this way:

C 1 0 6 7 5 × 8 % ▣ 854.

+ ▣ = 11529.
↗
You may not need this =.

If you get a different answer, then find out the easiest way to use your calculator for this work.

► Exercise N12.8

1   Increase each of these numbers by 15%.
    (a) 300   (c) 40   (e) 85
    (b) 120   (d) 500   (f) 108
2   Increase these amounts by 6%.
    (a) £20   (c) £48   (e) £13
    (b) £16   (d) £120   (f) £42
3   In 1993 the population of Wadebridge was 4850. In 1994 it increased by 2%. What was the population of Wadebridge in 1994?
4   Last year there were 480 sheep on Jim Laycocks's farm. This year his flock increased by $12\frac{1}{2}$%. How many sheep does he have this year?
5   Sally Middleton had £360 in a savings account before interest at $4\frac{1}{2}$% was added. How much did Sally then have in her account?
6   Find the VAT inclusive price of a television set when VAT at $17\frac{1}{2}$% is added to the basic price of £234.   ◄

To work out what 'something' is after a percentage decrease, work out the percentage, then subtract it from the 'something' you started with.

Question

Barjinder gets $12\frac{1}{2}$% staff discount. How much did he pay for this computer at his shop?

£996

Answer

Discount: $12\frac{1}{2}$% of £996 = £124.50
Amount paid: £996 – £124.50 = £871.50
So he paid £871.50 for the computer.

Find the easiest way to do this work on your calculator. Here are two ways for you to try.

Discount. Write it down ↓

Without a ▣ key:

With a ▣ key:

C 9 9 6 × 1 2 . 5 % 124.5

You may not need this =. ↗

► *Exercise* N12.9

In this exercise, give your answers correct to the nearest penny.
1   Stereo radio/cassette player. Normal price £39.99. 10% off.
    (a) Find the discount.
    (b) Find the sale price.
2   Dual bed. Normal price £224. 12% off.
    (a) Find the discount.
    (b) Find the sale price.
3   Plastiwhite windows. Summer sale 40% off.
    Normal price £1876.
    (a) Find the discount.
    (b) Find the sale price.
4   Wimbledon Sunglasses. Single vision £72.95.
    Pre-championship offer 5% off.
    (a) Find the discount.
    (b) Find the offer price.
5   Ultimate kitchen. Normal price £5699. Offer price less 8%.
    (a) Find the discount.
    (b) Find the offer price.   ◄

You can work out the **new quantity after an increase** as a percentage of the original quantity and then find the actual new quantity.

For example, if you start with a certain amount (100%) and increase it by x%, then you end up with $(100 + x)$% of the original amount.

You can use this way because they are all percentages of the original amount.
(Remember: your answer is the new quantity *after* the increase, *not* the increase itself.)

Question

Sarah earns £120 a week. She receives a pay rise of 7%. How much does she earn each week after the pay rise?

Answer

Sarah's wage is 100%
Sarah's new wage = 100% + 7% = 107%

New wage = 107% of £120
          = £128.40

or try

► Exercise N12.10

1 Peter earns £127.50 a week. He is given a pay rise of 4%. How much does he earn each week after the pay rise?
2 VAT at $17\frac{1}{2}$% is added to the basic price of some garden fencing costing £563.60. What is the actual cost of the fencing?
3 Due to inflation, Perkins Brothers increased the price of their goods by 6%. What is the new price of an article which used to be priced at £68?
4 A rail ticket, currently priced at £26, is due to rise by 9% in the new year. What will be the new price of the ticket?
5 A builder estimates that the cost of building a new house is £54 500. When completed, the actual cost was 3% higher than the estimate. What was the final cost?

The **new quantity after a decrease** can be worked out in a similar way but the decrease is **subtracted**.

For example, if you start with a certain amount (100%) and decrease it by x%, then you end up with $(100 - x)$% of the original amount.

(Remember: your answer is the new quantity *after* the decrease, *not* the decrease itself.)

Question

A car journey uses 12.5 litres of petrol. A new additive reduces consumption by 4%. How much of the new type of petrol would be needed for the same journey?

Answer

Original amount of petrol is 100%.
New amount is 100% − 4% = 96%.

96% of 12.5 litres = 12 litres.
So 12 litres of new petrol are needed.

or try

► Exercise N12.11

1 The price of oranges at the local supermarket has fallen by 5% this week. Last week an orange cost 40 p. What is the price this week?

2 A lorry, loaded with 425 kg of gravel has to shed 7% of its load for safety reasons. What weight is the lorry now carrying?
3 A company employing 250 people has to reduce the size of its workforce by 4%. How many people are now employed by the company?
4 Carmen is allowed a staff discount of $7\frac{1}{2}$% on items she buys at work. How much does Carmen actually pay for an item priced at £62?
5 The price of a microwave oven is reduced by $12\frac{1}{2}$% in the sale. What is the sale price if the marked price is £184?

If you know a *percentage change* and its *result*, that is, the new quantity, then you can find the **original quantity**. The new quantity will be:

$(100 + x)$% of the original after an *increase*
$(100 - x)$% of the original after a *decrease*.

You can use these to find 1% and then 100% (the whole) of the original.

Question

A wine merchant sells a case of wine for £72 and makes a profit of 20%. How much did he pay for the wine?

Answer

If the cost price is 100%,
then the selling price is 100% + 20% = 120%.
So 120% represents the selling price of £72.

120% is £72
÷ 120
1% is £$\frac{72}{120}$
× 100
100% is £$\frac{72}{120}$ × 100 = £60

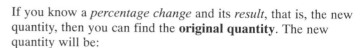

So the cost price of the wine was £60.

► Exercise N12.12

1 Calculate the original price of goods with these stated selling prices and profit margins.

	selling price	% profit
(a)	£42	5%
(b)	£80	25%
(c)	£40	60%
(d)	£60	20%
(e)	£56	12%

2 A shopkeeper sells trousers at £30 and shirts at £26. He makes a 25% profit on the trousers and a 30% profit on the shirts. How much did he pay for each item?

It is important to realise that an increase of *x*% is not 'cancelled' by a decrease of *x*%. This is because percentage change is always found as a *percentage of the original quantity*. The following example illustrates this.

Question

A dealer bought a car for £3000 and sold it at a profit of 25%. The buyer then had to sell it back to the dealer at a loss of 25%. How much did the buyer get for the car?

Answer

For the dealer:
Cost price = £3000
Selling price = (100% + 25%) of £3000
             = 125% of £3000
             = £3750

For the buyer:
Cost price = £3750
Selling price = (100% − 25%) of £3750
             = 75% of £3750
             = £2812.50

► *Exercise* N12.13

1   What is the result of increasing each of these numbers by 25% and then decreasing each new value by 25%?
    (a) 60   (c) 140   (e) 36
    (b) 80   (d) 40   (f) 72

2   A tennis club had 800 members at the beginning of 1993. During the year the membership increased by 20%. In 1994 the membership decreased by 20%. How many members did the club have at the end of 1994?

Examination Questions

1   A water tank is three-eighths full. 35 litres of water are needed to fill it up. What is the capacity of the tank?
    (NEAB, 1989)

2   Kadeem cut a circular apple pie into two halves. He then cut one of the halves into three equal pieces. He ate one of the smaller pieces.
    (a) What fraction of the whole pie did Kadeem eat?
    David ate the other two smaller pieces.
    (b) What fraction of the whole pie did David eat? (Give your answer in its simplest form).
    (MEG, 1990)

3   Eric makes a cake weighing $1\frac{1}{2}$kg.
    38% of this weight is flour.
    Calculate the total weight, in grams, of all the other ingredients.
    (MEG, 1990)

4   There were two bottles of copper sulphate solution on a shelf in a laboratory.
    The 3 litre bottle, A, was 55% full.
    The 2.5 litre bottle, B, was three-quarters full.
    The laboratory assistant was asked to fetch the bottle which contained the most copper sulphate solution. Which bottle should have been taken?
    (Explain in full how you get your answer).
    (NEAB, 1990)

5   A report in a local paper reads as follows.

RAIL FARES UP

Rail fares are to be increased.
The smallest price rise will be 11%.
In some cases fares will go up by as much as 21%.

(a) Peter's return fare to Leeds is £40.
    It is to go up by the smallest increase. By how much will his fare rise?
(b) (i) Angela's season ticket costs £1500.
        She expects it to go up by 21%. What does Angela expect her new season ticket to cost?
    (ii) When Angela buys her new season ticket she is charged £1825. Comment on the report in the local paper.
    (NEAB, 1989)

6   Value added tax (VAT) is 17.5%. What is the actual price a customer would have to pay for the television?

(NISEAC, 1991)

7   The marked price is £27.95.
    How much would you pay, to the nearest penny, at the 'special offer' price?

(ULEAC, 1988)

8   The normal price of the microwave in both shops is £260. Dilys buys the microwave at the Central Store at the sale price. Simon buys the microwave at the Super Market at the sale price. How much more than Simon does Dilys pay for her microwave?
    (WJEC, 1990)

9

VICAR SPEAKS OUT

'If we had raised 15% more, we would have achieved our target of £65 000 for the restoration of the church roof'.

How much did they actually raise? (WJEC, 1991)

10

DRIVE AWAY TODAY
THE CAR OF YOUR CHOICE
ONLY 20% DEPOSIT

Lisa buys the car of her choice. She pays a deposit of £820. What is the total cost of the car? (MEG, 1991)

11 The local store is holding a sale.

DISCOUNT STORES LTD.
CLOTHES SALE
20% OFF
ALL MARKED PRICES

(a) Find the sale price of a pullover marked at £14.70.
(b) Find the original marked price of a shirt that you buy in the sale for £8.40. (SEG, 1991)

12 A teacher ordered some new textbooks. She worked out the total cost from the prices in the bookseller's catalogue and this came to £590.
(a) The catalogue was an old one and prices had increased by 8%. Calculate the new total cost.
(b) The bookseller will allow a discount of $12\frac{1}{2}$% of the new total cost. How much will the books now cost? (MEG, 1989)

13

BUY YOUR NEW TV AT
BLOGGS
$17\frac{1}{2}$% OFF
A NEW COLOUR TV AT
£350 + V.A.T. ($17\frac{1}{2}$%)
LESS $17\frac{1}{2}$% DISCOUNT

Buy at
MacBargains
WE PAY THE V.A.T.
NEW COLOUR TV
£350
WE PAY THE $17\frac{1}{2}$% V.A.T.

Bloggs and MacBargains are offering the same type of colour TV.
(a) How much would you pay for a new colour TV set at
(i) Bloggs?
(ii) MacBargains?
(b) Is one cheaper than the other? If so, which one and by how much?

(NISEAC, 1991)

N13
Ratio

This unit will help you to:

■ understand and use the idea of a ratio

■ find and use equivalent ratios

■ understand and use the relationship between ratios, fractions and percentages

■ understand the idea of direct proportion

■ use direct proportion to solve problems.

A **ratio** *compares* things. The things may be numbers, lengths, masses, amounts of money, …

For example, in this picture there are 5 nuts and 3 bolts. We say that the ratio of *nuts to bolts* is *5 to 3*. We write the ratio as 5 : 3. The colon(:) means 'to'.

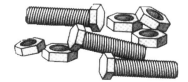

A ratio can also be written as a fraction.

So 5 : 3 can be written as $\frac{5}{3}$.

The *order* in which the ratio is given is important. The 'thing' that is given *first* in the comparison must be *first* in the ratio.

For example, the ratio of *nuts to bolts* is 5 : 3 or $\frac{5}{3}$, the ratio of *bolts to nuts* is 3 : 5 or $\frac{3}{5}$.

A ratio with a : sign can compare only numbers or 'like measures'.

For example, length with length,
mass with mass,
time with time, and so on …

It compares numbers of the same unit of measure.

For example, numbers of centimetres,
numbers of kilograms,
numbers of seconds, and so on …

So to compare two quantities in a ratio with a : sign, they must have the *same* unit of measure.

A ratio with a : sign has itself no units of measure. It just has numbers.

For example, the ratio of 4 kg to 1 kg
is written as 4 : 1

Any ratio written in the form n : 1 shows that the first quantity is 'n times' the second quantity.

► *Exercise* N13.1

1   Write each of the following as ratios with a : sign.
  (a) 2 m to 1 m   (d) 1 cm to 1000 cm
  (b) 3 kg to 1 kg   (e) 2 m^2 to 3 m^2
  (c) 1ℓ to 7ℓ (f) 5 gallons to 4 gallons

2   Write each of these ratios as fractions.
  (a) 5 kg to 8 kg   (d) 2 pints to 5 pints
  (b) 3 seconds to 7 seconds   (e) 5 pints to 2 pints
  (c) £4 to £9   (f) 9 sweets to 16 sweets

2   Write each of these ratios as fractions in their simplest form.
  (a) 2 seconds to 8 seconds   (d) 20 hours to 18 hours
  (b) 6 litres to 15 litres   (e) 30 days to 36 days
  (c) 8 cm^2 to 14 cm^2 (f) £22 to £33

3   In class 7A there are 18 boys and 12 girls. What is the ratio of boys to girls? Give your answer in its simplest form.

4   A car dealer has 40 saloon cars and 12 sports cars for sale. What is the ratio of
  (a) saloon cars to sports cars
  (b) sports cars to saloon cars?
  Give each answer as a fraction in its simplest form.

5   In Mr Pink's flowerbed there are 60 red roses and 25 white roses. What is the ratio of
  (a) red roses to white roses
  (b) white roses to red roses?
  Give each answer in its simplest form using the : sign.

Simplifying ratios

A ratio is usually given as simply as possible, that is, in its **simplest form** (just like a fraction).

For example, in this picture there are 9 sausages and 6 eggs, so the ratio of *sausages to eggs* is *9 : 6*.

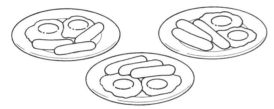

For every 3 sausages there are 2 eggs.
So the simplest form of 9 : 6 is 3 : 2.

You often need to simplify a given ratio. Simply *divide* each part by the *same number*. This is just like cancelling fractions (see p.41).

A ratio is in its simplest form when 1 is the only whole number that divides exactly into each part.

Question

(In this 'hand' of cards, what is the ratio of diamonds (♦) to clubs (♣)?. Give your answer in its simplest form.

Answer

There are 12 'diamonds' and 4 'clubs'.
Ratio of diamonds to clubs is

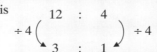

► *Exercise* N13.2

1   Write each of these as ratios with a : sign.
  Then write the ratios in simplest form.
  (a) £2 to £4   (d) 10 kg to 12 kg
  (b) 6 cm to 9 cm   (e) 25 yards to 10 yards
  (c) 15 gallons to 5 gallons   (f) 35 m to 49 m

To compare *quantities* in a ratio they must have the *same* unit. If they are not the same, then you must change them to the same unit. A ratio has *no* unit.

Question

In a charity swim, Bill swam 600 m and Sarah swam 2 km. What is the ratio of Bill's distance to Sarah's? Give the ratio in its simplest form.

Answer

Bill swam 600 m.
Sarah swam 2 km = 2 × 1000 m = 2000 m.
Ratio of bill's distance to Sarah's distance is

  600 m to 2000 m = 600 : 2000 = 3 : 10

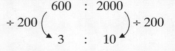

► *Exercise* N13.3

Write each ratio in this exercise in simplest form.
1   Write these ratios using the : sign.
  (a) 1 m to 60 cm   (d) 2 gallons to 6 pints
  (b) 40 cm to 2 m   (e) 2 kg to 750 g
  (c) 1 hour to 35 minutes   (f) 500 mℓ to 1ℓ

2   David has two pieces of wood. One is 3 m long and the other is 80 cm long. What is the ratio of
  (a) the longer to the shorter piece
  (b) the shorter to the longer piece?

3   Gary ran 2 km and Brian ran 800 m. What is the ratio of
  (a) Gary's distance to Brian's distance
  (b) Brian's distance to Gary's distance?

4   Write these ratios using the : sign.
  (a) 1.5 m to 60 cm   (d) 125 mℓ to 0.25 ℓ
  (b) 30 cm to 2.4 m   (e) £1.75 to 80 p
  (c) 2.5 kg to 450 g   (f) 125 g to 3.5 kg

5 A bottle of wine holds 750 mℓ. A wine box holds 2.5 litres of wine. What is the ratio of the capacity of
(a) the bottle to the box
(b) the box to the bottle?

In some problems the quantities you are given are not the numbers you use in the ratio. You may have to do a calculation first. Always read the question carefully.

Question

A special order of 600 flowers is for daffodils and tulips. There are 240 tulips in the order. What is the ratio of daffodils to tulips? Give your answer in its simplest form.

Answer

Number of daffodils = 600 − 240 = 360

Ratio of daffodils to tulips is 360 : 240 = 3 : 2

$$\div 120 \left(\begin{array}{ccc} 360 & : & 240 \\ 3 & : & 2 \end{array} \right) \div 120$$

▶ *Exercise* N13.4

In this exercise, write all ratios as simply as possible.
1 A shop has a large container of 500 red and green apples. If there are 150 red apples, what is the ratio of green to red apples?
2 Class 9C has 30 pupils of which 21 are girls. What is the ratio of girls to boys in class 9C?
3 A cake weighs 1200 g of which 480 g are fat. What is the ratio of fat to other ingredients in the cake?
4 Jim Makem made 140 telephone calls in the first quarter of this year of which 25 calls were long distance and the rest local. What is the ratio of long distance to local calls?
5 850 people attended a concert of which 600 travelled for 5 miles or less to get there. What is the ratio of people who travelled for 5 miles or less to people who travelled for more than 5 miles to attend the concert?

Equivalent ratios

Multiplying each part of a ratio by the *same* number also gives an equivalent ratio. This is just like making an equivalent fraction (see p.41).

Here are some examples equivalent to 5 : 3.

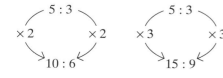

▶ *Exercise* N13.5

1 Write down the ratios equivalent to 5 : 8 when both parts of the ratio are multiplied by
(a) 2   (c) 7
(b) 5   (d) 8
2 Write down the ratios equivalent to 7 : 3 when each part of the ratio is multiplied by
(a) 3   (c) 9
(b) 4   (d) 12
3 Find five different ways of expressing the ratio 3 : 2. Each ratio you find must be equivalent to 3 : 2.
State clearly the multipliers you used each time.

You may need to write a ratio in another equivalent form to solve a problem. If it is in its simplest form, then multiply both parts by the same number to get the ratio you want. Find the multiplier from the numbers you know.

Question

The ages of a mother and daughter are in the ratio 8 : 3. If the mother is 40 years old, how old is the daughter?

Answer

Ratio of mother's age to daughter's age is

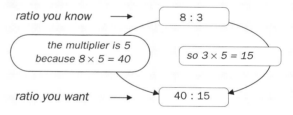

So if the mother is 40 years old, then the daughter is 15 years old.

▶ *Exercise* N13.6

1 Find the missing numbers in these.

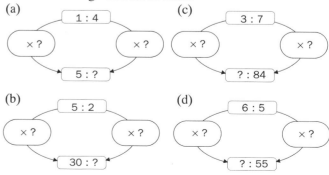

2 Tony and Liz won spot the ball. They shared their winnings in the ratio 3 : 4. Tony received the smaller share; he got £21. How much did Liz get?

3 Mick mixes brown and white flour in the ratio of 4 : 3 to make his bread. For Tuesday's batch he used 12 lb of brown flour. How much white flour did he use?

4 For Saturday's match the ratio of home supporters to away supporters was 7 : 2. 35 000 home supporters attended. How many away supporters were at Saturday's match?

5 Sid sawed a plank of wood into two pieces in the ratio 4 : 9. The longer piece was 180 cm long.
(a) How long was the shorter piece?
(b) How long was the plank?

Sometimes the given ratio is *not* in its simplest form. Change it to its simplest form first. Then solve the problem as before.

Question

A paint was made by mixing 9 tins of white paint with 6 tins of green paint. How many tins of white paint should be mixed with 4 tins of green paint to get the same colour?

Answer

Ratio of white paint to green paint is

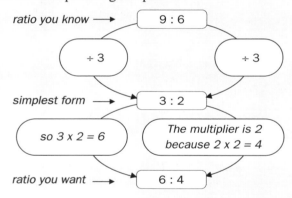

So 6 tins of white paint must be mixed with 4 tins of green paint.

▶ *Exercise* N13.7

1 Find the missing numbers in these equivalent ratios.

(e)
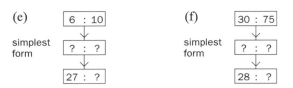

(f)

2 Find the missing numbers to make these colours of paint.

(a) Pink
| 10 white : | 6 red |
| 25 white : | ? red |

(c) Lemon
| 14 white : | 4 yellow |
| ? white : | 10 yellow |

(b) Sky
| 12 white : | 9 blue |
| 20 white : | ? blue |

(d) Sand
| 15 white : | 6 orange |
| ? white : | 14 orange |

3 Meg and Jim won £84 on the sweepstake. Meg got £48 and Jim got £36. Two weeks later they won again. When they shared their winnings in the same ratio as before, Jim's share was £45. How much did Meg get this time?

You can solve problems involving ratios with more than two parts in the same way.

Question

Concrete is made by mixing cement, sand and aggregate in different proportions by volume. A DIY book gives the following table for mixing different types of concrete.

Type of concrete	Ratio (by volume) cement : sand : aggregate
Foundations	1 : 3 : 6
General purpose	1 : 2 : 4

(a) Harry Smith makes some general purpose concrete to repair a garden wall. He uses 2 buckets of cement. How many buckets of (i) sand, (ii) aggregate should he use?

(b) Macdonalds are laying the foundations for Mr and Mrs Golby's new garage. They use 24 cubic feet of sand. How many cubic feet of (i) cement, (ii) aggregate should they use?

(c) Randalls require a new type of concrete for their new building. The builders use 6 lorry loads of cement, 15 lorry loads of sand and 27 lorry loads of aggregate. What is the ratio of cement to sand to aggregate for this new type of concrete? Give your answer in its simplest form.

Answer

(a)
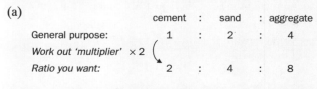

He should use: (i) 4 buckets of sand
(ii) 8 buckets of aggregate.

(b)

	cement	:	sand	:	aggregate
Foundations:	1	:	3	:	6
Work out 'multiplier'			$\downarrow$ ×8		
Ratio you want:	8	:	24	:	48

They should use: (i) 8 cubic feet of cement
(ii) 48 cubic feet of aggregate.

(c)

	cement	:	sand	:	aggregate
Simplify by dividing each part by 3	÷3 (	6	:	15	:	27
		2	:	5	:	9

Ratio of cement to sand to aggregate is 2 : 5 : 9.

► Exercise N13.8

1 Cheese Savouries are made by mixing butter, cheese, bran and flour in different proportions by weight. A book on cheese cookery gives the following ratios for these ingredients.

Cheese Savouries – Ratios (by weight)						
butter	:	cheese	:	bran	:	flour
3	:	4	:	1	:	2
				15 oz		
						10 lb
6 kg						
		200 g				

Copy and complete the table to show the missing weights.

2 This table gives the ratios of ingredients for making Hot Mulled Punch.

Hot Mulled Punch – Ratios (by volume)						
apple juice	:	ginger cordial	:	orange juice	:	grape juice
20	:	2	:	5	:	18
		10 fl.oz				
				500 mℓ		
						36 cups
800 mℓ						

Copy and complete the table to show the missing amounts for each mixing.

3 Gary makes Guy Fawkes Punch for Bonfire Night. He uses grenadine, egg white, orange juice, lemon juice and soda water in the ratios 2 : 3 : 50 : 5 : 15 respectively.
How much of each ingredient does he mix when he uses:
(a) 4 fl oz grenadine
(b) 450 mℓ lemon juice
(c) $1\frac{1}{2}$ cups of egg white
(d) 75 cℓ soda water
(e) 1 litre orange juice?

Ratios, fractions and percentages

A ratio $a : b$ can be written as a **common fraction** $\frac{a}{b}$.

If two quantities are in the ratio $a : b$ then the fraction $\frac{a}{b}$ also tells you how the **first quantity compares in size with the second.** Here are some examples:

Two lengths in the ratio 3 : 4 tells you that the first length is $\frac{3}{4}$ of the second.

Two masses in the ratio of 1 : 5 tells you that the first length is $\frac{1}{5}$ of the second.

Two areas in the ratio 6 : 1 tells you that the first area is $\frac{6}{1}$ i.e. 6 times the second.

Two volumes in the ratio of 7 : 5 tells you that the first volume is $\frac{7}{5}$ of the second.

► Exercise N13.9

For each of the following ratios, complete the sentence 'the first quantity is …of the second quantity'.
1 Two volumes in the ratio 3 : 5
2 Two areas in the ratio 2 : 7
3 Two masses in the ratio 5 : 4
4 Two lengths in the ratio 5 : 8
5 Two capacities in the ratio 3 : 1
6 Two temperatures in the ratio 1 : 6

To compare two or more ratios, you can rewrite them as common fractions with the same denominator. Use equivalent fractions to do this. (See p. 40.)

Question

Which is the larger ratio 3 : 7 or 4 : 9?

Answer

Write each ratio as a fraction
$3 : 7 \rightarrow \frac{3}{7}$ and $4 : 9 \rightarrow \frac{4}{9}$
then write them with a common denominator.

$$\frac{3}{7} = \frac{27}{63} \qquad \frac{4}{9} = \frac{28}{63}$$

(×9) (×7)

Compare fractions: $\frac{28}{63}$ is larger than $\frac{27}{63}$.

Rewrite as ratios: 4 : 9 is larger than 3 : 7.

▶ *Exercise* N13.10

For each of these pairs of ratios, work out which one is larger.

1 1 : 6   or   1 : 7
2 1 : 4   or   1 : 9
3 3 : 4   or   5 : 8
4 3 : 5   or   7 : 10

5 11 : 16   or   5 : 8
6 3 : 4   or   2 : 3
7 5 : 8   or   2 : 3
8 2 : 5   or   3 : 7

A ratio can also be rewritten as a **percentage**. Write it as a fraction first. Then change it to a percentage (see p.43).

Question

Which road sign warns you of the steeper hill? Explain your answer.

Answer

Write the ratio as a fraction.

$1 : 8 \rightarrow \frac{1}{8}$

Then write the fraction as a percentage.

$\frac{1}{8} = \frac{1}{8} \times 100\% = 12\frac{1}{2}\%$

$12\frac{1}{2}\%$ is steeper than 12%.

So 1 : 8 is steeper than 12%.

▶ *Exercise* N13.11

In each question below compare the ratio with the percentage. Say which is larger. Show your working.

1 1 : 2   and   55%
2 1 : 4   and   20%
3 2 : 5   and   28%

4 7 : 10   and   69%
5 3 : 8   and   38%
6 2 : 9   and   25%

Direct proportion

If two quantities vary but remain in the **same ratio**, they are said to be in **direct proportion**. They increase or decrease at the same rate. For example,

if one quantity is *doubled*, then the other is *doubled* too,
if one quantity is *trebled*, then the other is *trebled* too,
if one quantity is *halved*, then the other is *halved* too,
and so on...

Question

What is the cost of this River trip for:
(a) 2 adults
(b) 3 adults
(c) 10 adults
(d) 1 child?

RIVER TRIP
Adults: £1.50 each
Children: Half price

Answer

1 adult	→	£1.50	
(a) 2 adults	→	2 × £1.50	= £3.00
(b) 3 adults	→	3 × £1.50	= £4.50
(c) 10 adults	→	10 × £1.50	= £15.00
(d) 1 child	→	$\frac{1}{2}$ × £1.50	= £0.75

▶ *Exercise* N13.12

1 Pete is paid £6.50 per hour. How much does Pete earn when he works
   (a) 2 hours   (c) 8 hours
   (b) 3 hours   (d) a five-day week for 8 hours a day?
2 A loaf of bread costs 65 p. How much will I pay when I buy
   (a) 2 loaves   (b) 5 loaves   (c) 20 loaves for a party?
3 A lorry travels 8.4 miles on 1 litre of diesel. How far will the lorry travel on
   (a) 5 litres   (b) 12 litres   (c) 45 litres of diesel?
4 A force of 1 newton will extend a spring by 3.25 cm. How far will this spring by extended by a force of
   (a) 4 newtons   (b) 7 newtons   (c) 15 newtons?
5 The train fare for a single journey for an adult from Plymouth to London is £38. The child's fare is half this price. What is the cost of a single journey from Plymouth to London for
   (a) 2 adults   (c) 1 child   (e) 5 adults and
   (b) 3 adults   (d) 4 children   2 children?

To solve some direct proportion problems you may have to find the **'amount' for 1 unit of a quantity** first. This is sometimes called the **unitary method**.

Question

Ben's computer can print 1800 words in 5 minutes. Working at the same rate, how many words can it print in 7 minutes?

Answer

In 5 minutes it can print 1800 words.
In 1 minute it can print (1800 ÷ 5) words = 360 words.
In 7 minutes it can print (7 × 360) words = 2520 words.

▶ *Exercise* N13.13

1 For 6 hours work Lynne is paid £27. How much is she paid for 5 hours work?
2 7 biros cost £1.68. How much does a dozen biros cost?
3 A 3 kg container of dishwasher powder will do 75 washes. How many washes will a 5 kg container do?
4 8 peaches cost £1.80. How much will 10 peaches cost?
5 My car uses 4 litres of petrol when travelling 30 miles in town. How far will it travel in town on 10 litres of petrol?
6 A factory machine produces 600 washers every 3 minutes. How many washers will it produce in 8 minutes?

Recipes often give quantities for a number of people, for example, 4 or 6 people; or a number of things, for example, 10 or 20 buns. You may want a different number. So you have to alter the amounts.

To alter a recipe:
● divide by the number given to find the amount for one,
● multiply by the number needed.

Question

Alice has this recipe for 30 potato rolls. She needs 50 potato rolls for a Halloween party. How much of each ingredient will she need?

Potato Rolls
(makes 30)

450 g potatoes
675 g flour
150 mℓ milk
420 mℓ water
15 g yeast

Answer

	30 rolls	÷ 30 → 1 roll	× 50 → 50 rolls
potatoes:	450 g	÷ 30 → 15 g	× 50 → 750 g
flour:	675 g	÷ 30 → 22.5 g	× 50 → 1125 g
milk:	150 mℓ	÷ 30 → 5 mℓ	× 50 → 250 mℓ
water:	420 mℓ	÷ 30 → 14 mℓ	× 50 → 700 mℓ
yeast:	15 g	÷ 30 → 0.5 g	× 50 → 25 g

On your calculator you can divide by 30, then multiply by 50. Write down each part of the answer to show your working.

You can alter other mixtures, for example cement, metal alloys, etc this way too.

► Exercise N13.14

1 Tina uses these recipes for a Guy Fawkes party.

Tomato soup
for 6

450 g tomatoes
30 g butter
75 g long grain rice
1.5 ℓ stock

Soft Crust Baps
makes 10

150 mℓ hand hot milk
150 mℓ hand hot water
5 mℓ spoon of sugar
25 g fresh yeast *or*
10 g dried yeast
450 g strong plain flour
5 mℓ spoon of salt
50 g lard, cubed

Work out the amount of each ingredient Tina needs for each recipe for
(a) 1 person   (b) 16 people.

2 Work out the amount of each ingredient for each of these recipes when they are made for
(a) 6 people   (b) 10 people   (c) 21 people.

Steak and Kidney Casserole (serves 5)

900 g	stewing steak	50 g	beef dripping
450 g	ox kidney	825 mℓ	stock
50 g	plain flour	15 mℓ	Worcestershire sauce
125 g	onions		salt
100 g	mushrooms		pepper

Tipsy oranges (for 4)

100 g sugar
160 mℓ water
4 large oranges
20 mℓ orange liqueur

Rice salad (serves 15)

750 g long grain rice
900 g frozen mixed vegetables
60 g chopped walnuts
105 g sultanas
180 mℓ French dressing

Examination Questions

1 A forest of 600 trees is planted with pine trees and silver birch trees. There are 240 pine trees.
What is the ratio of pine trees to silver birch trees?
Give your answer in its simplest form.   (SEG, 1991)

2 Glider pilots use *glide ratio* to compare the performance of different gliders. It is the ratio of the horizontal distance travelled to the height lost.

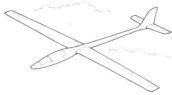

(a) A very basic glider has a glide ratio of 16 to 1.
It loses 500 m height. How far does it travel horizontally.
(b) A high performance glider has a glide ratio of 50 to 1.
It travels a horizontal distance of 5000 m.
How much height does it lose?   (MEG, 1990)

3 Sally is painting her house. She will give the paintwork 1 coat of undercoat paint and 2 coats of gloss paint.
(a) Write down the ratio of the amount of undercoat paint to the amount of gloss paint that she uses.
Sally buys 2 litres of undercoat paint.
(b) Work out the amount of gloss paint that she must buy.
Sally buys a 5 litre can of gloss paint. She uses the amount in part (b).
(c) Work out the amount of paint that she has left over, giving your answer in cm³.   (ULEAC, 1988)

4
MACARONI CHEESE

100 g	macaroni
60 g	cheese
25 g	cornflour
700 mℓ	milk
SERVES 4	

MACARONI CHEESE

… g	macaroni
… g	cheese
… g	cornflour
… mℓ	milk
SERVES 12	

(a) Fill in the gaps in the list of ingredients for macaroni cheese for 12 people.
(b) How much cheese would you need to serve 10 people?   (WJEC, 1989)

5   To make a basic potting compost the recommended 'recipe' is:

   7 litres loam
   3 litres peat
   2 litres sand
   small handful of chalk (0.1 litres).

   (a) When Worzell is making up a load of compost he uses 6 litres of peat. Work out how much of the other ingredients he uses.
   (b) Work out the total volume of the mixture.
   (ULEAC, 1991)

6   Carol is making a necklace of beads, using white and black beads in the ratio 2 : 3.
   She has 56 white beads.
   (a) How many black beads will she need?
   (b) How many beads will she use altogether?   (MEG, 1989)

7   Class 5P decides to raise money for charity.
   The teacher agrees to give £2 of her money for each £5 that the pupils raise.
   (a) How much must the teacher give when the class raises £60?
   (b) Give the ratio of teacher contribution to pupil contribution.   (ULEAC, 1991)

8   The number of pages in a magazine was increased from 48 to 80. If the price, which was previously 75p, is increased in the same ratio, what will the new price be?
   (MEG, 1989)

9   James is mixing some wallpaper paste. The instructions on the packet say

   Enough for 12 rolls of wallpaper.
   Mix all the contents with 8 pints of water.

   James does not want to make too much paste as he only has 3 rolls of wallpaper. How much water does he need to make enough paste for his needs?   (ULEAC, 1991)

10 Kerry agrees to help her father with some repairs to the brickwork of their house. She is given the job of making mortar by mixing sand and cement. In a Do-It-Yourself manual, she looked up the following information:

Type of mortar	Quantity of sand	Quantity of cement
For outside brickwork	4 parts	1 part
For inside brickwork	6 parts	1 part

   (a) Kerry makes some mortar for repairing an outside wall. She uses 2 buckets of cement. How many buckets of sand should she use?
   (b) Kerry then makes some mortar for repairs to the inside of the house. She uses 3 buckets of sand. How much cement should she add?
   (c) Kerry and her father build a garden wall using another type of mortar. Altogether they use 16 buckets of sand and 6 buckets of cement. What is the ratio of sand to cement for this type of mortar? Give your answer in its simplest form.
   (NEAB, 1989)

N14
Proportional division

This unit will help you to:

■ understand and use proportional division.

Proportional division is about sharing something in a *given ratio*. The ratio tells you how to do the sharing. For example, if cement and sand are mixed in the ratio of 1 : 2, then:

   1 shovel of cement and *2 shovels* of sand
      → *3 shovels* of concrete,
   1 bucket of cement and *2 buckets* of sand
      → *3 buckets* of concrete,
   1 tonne of cement and *2 tonnes* of sand
      → *3 tonnes* of concrete,
   1 part of cement and *2 parts* of sand
      → *3 parts* of concrete.

Dividing a quantity

To divide something in a given ratio, find:

(a) the total number of parts from the ratio,
   (for example, the ratio $a : b$ gives $(a + b)$ parts,
          the ratio $a : b : c$ gives $(a + b + c)$ parts,
          and so on …)
(b) what one part is,
(c) the amounts for the ratio.

The 'something' can be a number, an amount of money, a measurement, …

Question

A green paint is mixed from blue and yellow paint in the ratio 3 : 5. How much of each colour is needed to make 40 litres of this green paint?

Answer

The ratio 3 : 5 gives (3 + 5) = 8 parts.
40 litres of green paint are needed.

Green paint: 8 parts → 40 litres
1 part → (40 ÷ 8) litres = 5 litres
Blue paint: 3 parts → 3 × 5 litres = 15 litres
Yellow paint: 5 parts → 5 × 5 litres = 25 litres

Check 15 litres + 25 litres = 40 litres ✓

So 15 litres of blue paint and 25 litres of yellow paint are needed.

▶ *Exercise* **N14.1**

1 Divide each amount in the given ratio.
(a) £20 in the ratio 3 : 2
(b) £88 in the ratio 5 : 3
(c) £360 in the ratio 7 : 5
(d) 5 kg in the ratio 3 : 7
(e) 45 minutes in the ratio 7 : 2
(f) 330 mℓ in the ratio 9 : 2
(g) 35 m in the ratio 3 : 4
(h) 200 g in the ratio 9 : 11

2 Share these amounts between Tom and Sam.
(a) 6 pies so that Sam has twice as many as Tom.
(b) £54 so that Tom has 5 times as much as Sam.
(c) £1.25 so that Sam has four times as much as Tom.
(d) 300 mℓ of orange juice so that Tom has nine times as much as Sam.

3 This is a recipe for basic muesli. Adam Wholefoods sell basic muesli in these different sizes:
(a) 3 kg bag   (c) 18 kg sack
(b) 5 kg bag
What weight of each ingredient does each of these sizes contain?

> **Basic muesli**
>
> 1 part bran
> 4 parts rolled oats
> 2 parts rye flakes
> 3 parts sultanas

4 A lottery has £20, £10 and £5 prizes in the ratio 3 : 5 : 7. In May, 9750 of these prizes were won. How many of each were there?

5 Jackie is making 10 litres of Fizzy Fruit Cup for a disco party. She uses pineapple juice, grapefruit juice, passion fruit juice and lemonade in the ratios 6 : 1 : 3 : 15. How much of each liquid should she use? ◀

Sometimes the ratio in a proportional division problem is *not* in its simplest form. To do the working without a calculator, it is usually easier to simplify the ratio first.

Question

Three workers, Mr Allan, Miss Brown and Mrs Cork, hold 120, 200 and 40 shares respectively in their company. A total dividend of £1800 is paid to the three workers in the same ratio as their shares. How much does each worker receive? Do your working without a calculator.

Answer

The ratio of the shares is   120 : 200 : 40
                              ÷ 40 ↓ ÷ 40 ↓ ÷ 40 ↓
In its simplest form this is   3 : 5 : 1

This ratio gives (3 + 5 + 1) = 9 *parts*

Total dividend: 9 parts → £1800
                1 part → £1800 ÷ 9 = £200

Mr Allan's dividend: 3 parts → 3 × £200 = £600
Miss Brown's dividend: 5 parts → 5 × £200 = £1000
Mrs Cork's dividend: 1 part → £200
Check £600 + £1000 + £200 = £1800 ✓

▶ *Exercise* **N14.2**

1 Ann has 45p and Brenda has 75p. They spend all this money on a bag of 48 sweets and agree to share them in the same ratio as their money.
(a) Give this ratio in its simplest form.
(b) How many sweets should each girl get?

2 Jean and Sue start a business with their redundancy money. Jean invests £5500 in it. Sue invests £3500 in it.
(a) Give the ratio of their investments in its simplest form.
(b) Their first year profits are £10 800. They agree to share this in the same ratio as their investments. How much should each partner get?

3 Four brothers have 3000, 1500, 4500, and 6000 shares in the family firm. They sell them for £75 000. Divide this money between them in the ratio of their shares. How much should each brother get?

4 Brothers Bill and Ben have the same birthday. But Ben is two years older than Bill. Their Aunt Millie always sends them money for their birthday present. They have to share it in the same ratio as their ages.
(a) When Bill was 9 years old, Aunt Millie sent them £5 to share. How much did each boy get?
(b) Aunt Millie increased the amount she sent by £1 each year until Bill was 16. How much did each boy get each year? ◀

Examination Questions

1 Abbie and Steffi share £600.
Steffi receives three times as much as Abbie. Calculate how much of the money Steffi receives.

(SEG, 1990)

2 A copying machine uses a solution which is made by mixing a Toner and Dispersant. These have to be mixed: two parts Toner to one part Dispersant.
The machine uses 270 mℓ of the solution. How much Toner is used in this amount of solution?

(MEG, 1990)

3 On the label of this bottle it says, 'Mix 1 part blackcurrant with 3 parts water'. How much blackcurrant is needed to make 1 litre (1000 mℓ) of drink?

(MEG, 1988)

4 Bronze is made only of copper and tin in the ratio 9 : 2. How much copper would be needed to make 16.5 kilograms of bronze?

(MEG, 1990)

5 Hannah finds that the ratio of hits to misses when she throws darts at the bull's-eye is 7 to 3. Work out the number of times she will hit the bull's-eye if she throws 20 darts and the ratio remains the same.   (ULEAC, 1989)

6 When pupils learn to drive with the Shakespeare school of motoring it is found that the ratio of those who pass their driving test to those who fail is 5 : 2.

(a) In April, 20 pupils who have learnt at the school, pass. Work out how many you would expect to have failed.
(b) In May, 35 pupils who learnt at the school, take the test. Work out how many of these pupils you would expect to pass the test.   (ULEAC 1991)

7 Sand, cement and water are mixed in the following quantities to make 20 000000...kg of mortar.

Sand	12 kg
Cement	6 kg
Water	2 kg

(a) Express the ratio
    sand : cement : water
in its simplest form.
(b) How much cement would be needed to make 30 kilograms of mortar?   (MEG, 1991)

8 Arthur, Beryl and Colin formed a football pools syndicate. They agreed to share their winnings in the ratio of their weekly contributions. Each week Arthur paid 60p, Beryl paid 40p and Colin paid 35p. They won £54 000. How much did each one get?
   (NEAB, 1989)

9 Sophie and Helen are waitresses in a cafe. Sophie works 4 days each week and Helen 3 days. They share the tips in the ratio 4 to 3. The tips came to £21 one week.
(a) How much did Sophie get?

In the following week Helen got £6.30.
(b) How much did Sophie get in that week?
   (MEG, 1991)

10 Three sisters share a premium bond prize of £5 000. They share the money in the ratio of their ages. Andrea is 12, Beth is 13 and Christine is 15.
Calculate how much more Christine will receive than Andrea.
   (SEG, 1989)

N15
Scale

This unit will help you to:

- understand the idea of scale
- use scales to calculate 'real' and 'scale' lengths
- understand and use scales written in different forms, e.g. as a ratio, using lengths, …
- write scales in different forms
- find a scale from 'real' and 'scale' lengths.

Maps, drawings and models are often made 'to scale'. The **scale** compares *lengths*. It tells you how lengths on the map, drawing or model compare in size with the 'full size' real lengths.

These scale model kits all use the *same* scale, but it is written in different ways.

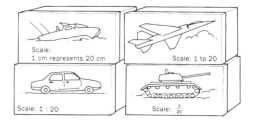

Each **scale** tells you that:

1 cm on the *model* stands for 20 cm on the *real thing*.
Lengths on the *real thing* are 20 × matching lengths on the *model*.
Lengths on the *model* are $\frac{1}{20}$ of matching lengths on the *real thing*.

▶ *Exercise* N15.1

Write each of these scales in three other ways. Use the pictures below left to help you.

1 1 cm represents 15 cm
2 1 to 24
3 $\frac{1}{10}$
4 1 : 75
5 A model is made to a scale of 1 to 30. What does this tell you about
(a) lengths of the real object,
(b) lengths on the model?

Finding lengths

You can use the scale of a map, drawing or model to **calculate lengths**. If you know the *real length*, you can find the matching 'scale length'. If you know a '*scale length*' you can find the matching *real length*.
Always check that your answer is sensible. Compare it with what you started with. Is it smaller or larger? Is this what you expected? If not, then look for a mistake in your working.

Question

A model farm is made using a scale of 1 : 24.
(a) The height of a model cow is 5 cm. What is the height of the real cow?
(b) A real horse is 168 cm long. How long is the model horse?

Answer

(a) Scale is 1 : 24.
Height of real cow = 24 × height of model cow
= 24 × 5 cm
= 120 cm
(b) Length of model horse = $\frac{1}{24}$ of length of real horse
= $\frac{1}{24}$ of 168 cm
= 168 cm ÷ 24
= 7 cm

► *Exercise* N15.2

1 A scale model is made using a scale of 1 : 40.
(a) What lengths on the real object correspond to these lengths on the scale model?
(i) 1 cm (ii) 3 cm (iii) 10 cm (iv) 16 cm
(b) What lengths on the scale model correspond to these lengths on the real object?
(i) 40 cm (ii) 80 cm (iii) 160 cm (iv) 100 cm.

2 A model racing car is made to a scale of 1 cm represents 30 cm. Copy and complete this table of model car lengths and real car lengths.

	Model car	Real car
scale →	1 cm	30 cm
(a) Length	14.5 cm	30 × 14.5 = 435 cm
(b) Wheelbase	9.0 cm	
(c) Height	3.5 cm	
(d) Diameter of front tyre	2.0 cm	
(e) Diameter of front wheel	1.0 cm	
(f) Diameter of rear tyre	2.5 cm	
(g) Diameter of rear wheel	1.1 cm	
(h) Length of rear aerofoil	1.5 cm	
(i) Height of rear aerofoil	2.6 cm	
(j) Number of wheels	4	

3 Dan Cook wanted to make a scale model of a real helicopter. The scale is 1 to 25. Copy and complete Dan's table for the real and model helicopter lengths.

	Real	Model
scale →	1 cm	$\frac{1}{25}$ cm
(a) Length	1500 cm	$\frac{1}{25}$ × 1500 cm = 60 cm
(b) Width	300 cm	
(c) Height	350 cm	
(d) Wheelbase	275 cm	
(e) Length of fuselage	1250 cm	
(f) Diameter of main rotor	1300 cm	
(g) Diameter of tail rotor	225 cm	
(h) Tail ground clearance	150 cm	
(i) Height of cabin door	125 cm	
(j) Width of cabin door	137.5 cm	

ACTIVITY

Look in magazines and your local shops and find details of some scale models. Write down the scale as a ratio and calculate the length of the real object. Check that your answers are sensible by estimating what the answer should be.

Look carefully at any **units of length** in a scale.

1 cm to 5 m	1 cm to 25 cm
↑ ↑	↑ ↑
different units	*same units*

Some scales are given with two *different* units. Others have the *same* unit. Make sure you use the correct unit in your working.

Question

The scale of this map is 1 cm to 75 km.
(a) Work out the distance between London and Manchester.
(b) Which place, A, B, or C, is about 300 km from London? Explain your answer.

Answer

(a) Distance on map = 3.4 cm
Actual distance = 3.4 × 75 km
= 255 km
(b) 75 km → 1 cm on map
300 km → 300 ÷ 75
= 4 cm on map
On map, town C is about 4 cm from London. So town C is about 300 km from London.

► *Exercise* N15.3

1 Use the map shown above to calculate the actual distances from
(a) Leeds to London (d) B to A
(b) Manchester to Leeds (e) C to B
(c) B to Manchester (f) A to C

2 A scale model of Concorde was built using a scale of 1 cm to 2 m. This table gives some details of the model and real Concorde. Copy and complete the table.

		Model	Real
	scale →	1 cm	2 m
(a)	Wing span	25 cm	
(b)	Length		62 m
(c)	Wheel track	3.8 cm	
(d)	Wheelbase		9 m
(e)	Height of doors		1.6 m
(f)	Width of doors	0.4 cm	
(g)	Length of cabin	39 cm	
(h)	Width of cabin	1.3 cm	
(i)	Height of baggage doors		1 m
(j)	Number of seats		144

Rewriting scales

To write a scale as a ratio such as 1 : n, the lengths must be in the same unit. Change one of them if you need to.

Question

Rewrite this scale as a ratio:
1 cm represents 5 m.

Answer

1 cm represents 5 m
1 cm represents 500 cm
The scale is 1 : 500.

▶ *Exercise* N15.4

Write these scales as ratios in the form 1 : n.
1   1 cm represents 10 m   4   1 mm to 4 cm
2   1 cm represents 3 m   5   1 cm to 2.5 m
3   1 m represents 5 km

Scales on maps are often written as a ratio 1 : n. Usually the number n is very large. Sometimes these are awkward to use. So we rewrite them as scales with different units.

Question

A map has a scale of 1 : 250 000.
Rewrite this as a scale in the form
    1 cm represents … km.

Remember:
1 km = 1000 m
      = 1000 × 100 cm
      = 100 000 cm

Answer

Scale 1 : 250 000
So 1 cm represents   250 000 cm
                    = (250 000 ÷ 100 000) km
                    = 2.5 km
Scale is 1 cm represents 2.5 km

▶ *Exercise* N15.5

Rewrite these map scales in the form 1 cm represents … km.
1   1 : 200 000   4   1 : 50 000
2   1 : 30 000   5   1 : 625 000
3   1 : 25 000

Finding scales

You can find a scale if you know a '*scale length*' and its matching *real length*.

You use them to work out the real length that '*1 unit of scale length*', (such as 1 cm, 1 mm) stands for.

To give the scale as a ratio, the two lengths must be in the same unit. Change one if you need to.

Question

In a model village, the church is 40 cm high. The height of the real church is 48 m. What is the scale of the model as a ratio?

Answer

Change real height to cm

    1 m = 100 cm
So 48 m = 4800 cm

'*scale length*'   →   '*real length*'
    40 cm   →   4800 cm
    1 cm   →   (4800 cm ÷ 40) = 120 cm
    1 cm   →   120 cm
Scale 1 : 120

▶ *Exercise* N15.6

1 Work out the scales for these models.

			Real	Model
(a)	Police helicopter	rotor span	8 m	25 cm
(b)	Phantom bomber	length	19.2 m	60 cm
(c)	Starfighter	length	16.8 m	35 cm
(d)	Flying boat	wingspan	31.68 m	44 cm
(e)	Ark Royal	length	237.6 m	33 cm

2 Work out the scales of these maps. Give your answers in the form 1 : n or n : 1 whichever is more suitable.

	Journey	Real distance	Map distance
(a)	Penybont to Knighton	22 km	44 cm
(b)	New St. Station to Great Barr	$6\frac{1}{2}$ miles	$19\frac{1}{2}$ inches
(c)	Exeter to Bristol	130 km	13 cm
(d)	Moreton to Swanmore	15 km	6 cm
(e)	Calder Hall to Sizewell	400 km	8 cm

Examination Questions

1 The map below is of part of the Peak District

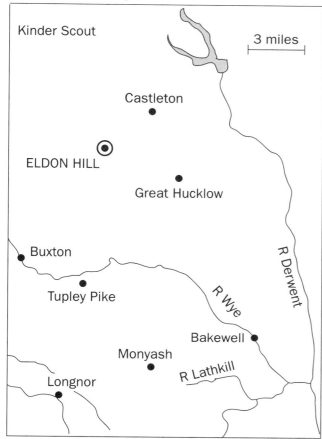

(a) Using the scale given on the map, state how many millimetres are used to represent 3 miles.

(b) On the map draw a straight line from Eldon Hill to Monyash. Calculate the distance in miles between these two places. Give your answer to the nearest mile.

(NEAB, 1988)

2 On a map with a scale of 1 : 1 000 000, the distance from London to Colchester is 6.3 cm. What is the real distance between the two towns in kilometres?

(ULEAC, 1989)

3 The scale on an Ordnance Survey map is 1 to 50 000.

(a) Work out the true distance between two places which are 1 centimetre apart on the map. Give your answer as a decimal fraction of a km.

(b) Work out how many centimetres on the map are equivalent to 1 km on the ground.

(ULEAC, 1991)

4 (a) A map has scale 1 to 20 000. What distance on the map would represent 1 km?

(b) Mary is preparing for her Duke of Edinburgh expedition. She has a different map with scale 1 to 50 000. The route she wants to use measures 30 cm on the map. How far will it be in kilometres if she walks this route?

(MEG, 1991)

5 The diagram shows the flag of the South Mainland Province. It is drawn to a scale of 1 to 40.

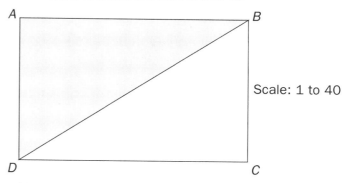

(a) Measure the length of BD on the diagram.

(b) What is the length of this diagonal on the actual flag?

(MEG, 1990)

6 On a scale model of a sports stadium the running track for the 100 metres is 10 centimetres long.

(a) Write 10 centimetres as a fraction of a metre.

(b) Work out the scale of the model to the real stadium.

The stadium has 20 000 seats.

(c) Write down the number of seats in the model.

(ULEAC, 1991)

7

The scale drawing shows a house with a garage. The actual height of the garage is 3 metres. Use your ruler to find the actual height, h metres, of the house. Give your answer correct to the nearest metre.

(MEG, 1990)

8 A $\frac{1}{80}$ scale model of the scene at a war-time invasion beach was made for a museum. Complete this table, giving answers in appropriate units.

	Actual scene	Model scene
Height of soldier	180 cm	
Length of tank		6.4 cm
Number of soldiers	400	

(NISEAC, 1990)

9 The model railway gauge called N-gauge is a scale of 1 : 160. The platform of a certain railway station is 85 m long. Calculate, correct to the nearest millimetre, the length of the model of the platform in N-gauge.

(NEAB, 1988)

A1
Basic algebra

This unit will help you to:

■ understand how letters stand for numbers in algebraic expressions
■ simplify algebraic expressions
■ substitute numbers for letters
■ form expressions using letters.

In **algebra** letters are used to stand for numbers. It is important that you know and understand the 'shorthand' used in algebra. For example,

a	means	$1 \times a$ or $1a$
$-a$	means	$-1 \times a$ or $-1a$
$3a$	means	$3 \times a$ or $(a + a + a)$
$\dfrac{a}{3}$	means	$a \div 3$ or $\frac{1}{3}$ of a
ab	means	$a \times b$
$2ab$	means	$2 \times a \times b$ or $(ab + ab)$
a^2	means	$a \times a$
a^3	means	$a \times a \times a$
$3a^2$	means	$3 \times a^2$ or $3 \times a \times a$ or $(a^2 + a^2 + a^2)$
$(3a)^2$	means	$3a \times 3a$ or $3 \times a \times 3 \times a$
$3ab^2$	means	$3 \times ab^2$ or $3 \times a \times b \times b$ or $(ab^2 + ab^2 + ab^2)$
$a^{\frac{1}{3}}$	means	$\sqrt[3]{a}$

▶ *Exercise* A1.1

1   Write out in full what these mean:
   (a) $7x$
   (b) $\dfrac{c}{5}$
   (c) y^4
   (d) $3p^2q$
   (e) $-4(3p)^2$
   (f) $c^{\frac{1}{2}}$
   (g) $(5ab)^2c$
   (h) $5(abc)^2$

2   Write these expressions as simply as possible.
   (a) $x \times x \times x \times x$
   (b) $x + x$
   (c) $\frac{1}{4}$ of s
   (d) $7 \times r^2$
   (e) $-2 \times p \times q$
   (f) $2q \times 2q \times 2q$
   (g) $2q \times q \times q$
   (h) $3r^2s + 3r^2s + 3r^2s$.

The **basic laws of arithmetic** are also true in algebra:

Examples	
Arithmetic	**In algebra**
Commutative laws	
$3 + 5 = 5 + 3$	$a + b = b + a$
$3 \times 5 = 5 \times 3$	$ab = ba$
$3 - 5 \neq 5 - 3$	$a - b \neq b - a$
$3 \div 5 \neq 5 \div 3$	$\dfrac{a}{b} \neq \dfrac{b}{a}$

Examples (continued)	
Arithmetic	**In algebra**
Associative laws	
$(3 + 5) + 2 = 3 + (5 + 2)$	$(a + b) + c = a + (b + c)$
$(3 \times 5) \times 2 = 3 \times (5 \times 2)$	$(ab)c = a(bc)$
$(3 - 5) - 2 \neq 3 - (5 - 2)$	$(a - b) - c \neq a - (b - c)$
$(3 \div 5) \div 2 \neq 3 \div (5 \div 2)$	$\dfrac{a}{b} \div c \neq a \div \dfrac{b}{c}$
Distributive laws	
$3 \times (5 + 2) = 3 \times 5 + 3 \times 2$	$a(b + c) = ab + ac$
$(3 + 5) \times 2 = 3 \times 2 + 5 \times 2$	$(a + b)c = ac + bc$

▶ *Exercise* A1.2

1   Check the commutative laws of algebra by using 6 and 2 instead of a and b respectively.

2   Check the associative laws of algebra by using 12, 6 and 2 instead of a, b and c respectively.

3   Check the distributive laws of algebra by using 2, 3 and 7 instead of a, b and c respectively.

4   Use other numbers of your own choice instead of a, b and c to further check the laws of algebra.
   Are the laws still true whatever numbers you use?

The **rules for signs** are also the same in arithmetic and algebra (see Unit N7).

Words to know

When letters are used to stand for *different* numbers, they are called **variables**.

Letters which have *fixed* values are called **constants**. All numbers are constants. For example,

   in $\frac{1}{3}\pi r^2 h$

r and h are variables (their values can change),
$\frac{1}{3}$ and π are constants (their values stay the same).

An **algebraic expression** is a calculation written using letters. So it is a collection of letters and symbols combined by at least one of the operations $+, -, \times, \div$. For example,

$$6x + 5 - y, \quad 2ab^3c^4, \quad \frac{x^2 - 1}{x + 2}$$

are all expressions.

Remember: $\times$ and $\div$ signs are not usually written in algebraic expressions but you know that

   ab means $a \times b$ and $\dfrac{a}{b}$ means $a \div b$.

The **terms** of an expression are linked by plus (+) or minus (−) signs. For example,

   the terms of $7x - 3y + 2$, are $7x$, $3y$ and 2.

A number on its own or a letter standing for a constant is called a **constant term**. For example,

   in $7x - 3y + 2$, the number 2 is a constant term.

A **term** can consist of a number, letters and powers of letters. For example,

the terms of $2xy + 3x^2 - 7x^2y^3$ are $2xy$, $3x^2$, $7x^2y^3$.

(Note: $2xy$, for instance, is only *one* term; x and y are not separate terms here.)

In a term the number always comes *first*. The letters are usually written in *alphabetical order*. For example, we write

$14xy^2z$ rather than y^214zx.

The number placed *in front of*, and thus *multiplying*, a letter or group of letters is called a **coefficient**. For example,

in $3x$, the x has a coefficient of 3.

In an expression, the + or − sign goes with the term which follows it. For example,

in $9x^2 - 4xy$, 9 is the coefficient of x^2, and
        −4 is the coefficient of xy.

Like terms contain the *same* 'algebraic quantity'. For example,

$7x$, $5x$ and $-x$ are like terms, but
$7x$, $5y$ and $-z$ are *not* like terms.

In like terms, the letters and the powers of each letter must be the same. For example,

$4b^2c$ and $-7b^2c$ are like terms, but
$4b^2c$ and $-7bc^2$ are *not* like terms
(b^2c and bc^2 are different!)

When looking for like terms, remember that the order of the letters in a term is *not* important. For example,

$ab^2c = acb^2 = b^2ac = b^2ca = cab^2 = cb^2a$.

Writing the letters in each term in alphabetical order may help you to spot like terms.

Answers are usually given in this way too. For example,

rewriting $3ab^2c$, $-5b^2ca$ and $6cab^2$
gives $3ab^2c$, $-5ab^2c$ and $6ab^2c$.

Now it is easy to see that these are like terms.

► *Exercise* **A1.3**

1 Write the letters in each of these pairs of terms in alphabetical order. Then say if they are 'like terms'.
   (a) $2ab$, $2ba$ (f) $2qp^2$, $7p^2q$
   (b) x^2y, y^2x (g) $9e^2gf$, $2g^2fe$
   (c) pqr, rqp (h) $-3x^2y^2$, $6y^2x^2$
   (d) $5dca$, $5cad$ (i) $-2r^3s^2$, $5s^2r^3$
   (e) $3rt^2s$, $3tr^2s$ (j) $2ps^2q$, $-9qp^2s$.
2 Say which of the following are true and which are false.
   (a) $3a^2b = 3ab^2$ (d) $7e^3f^2g = 7gf^3e^2$
   (b) $4p^2rq = 4qrp^2$ (e) $2abc = cba^2$
   (c) $-6xy^2z = 6zy^2x$ ◄

Simplification

Algebraic expressions can often be **simplified**. This makes them shorter and easier to read. The **four rules of addition, subtraction, multiplication and division** may be used to simplify expressions. Since the terms may be positive (+) or

negative (−), the **four rules of directed numbers** (see Unit N7) will apply.

Addition and subtraction

Only **like terms** can be **added** or **subtracted** to give a *single term*. This is often called **collecting like terms**. For example,

$5x + 3x + x = 9x$ (Remember: x means $1x$)
$7y - 2y = 5y$.

Unlike terms *cannot* be collected together and written as a single term. For example,

$3x - 7y$ and $5x + 3x^2 - 9x^4$ cannot be simplified.

Each is in its **simplest form**.

When collecting like terms, group together the positive (+) and negative (−) like terms. This makes them easier to work out. *Remember:* the + or − sign goes with the term that follows it.

Question

Simplify:
(a) $7x - 8x + 5x - x$
(b) $-3a^2 + 9a^2 - 11a^2 - 5a^2$
(c) $4bac + 11cab - 2bca$

Answer

(a) $7x - 8x + 5x - x$
Group + and − terms $= 7x + 5x - 8x - x$

Work them out $=\quad 12x \quad - 9x$
                        $= 3x$

(b) $-3a^2 + 9a^2 - 11a^2 - 5a^2$
Group + and − terms $= 9a^2 - 3a^2 - 11a^2 - 5a^2$

Work them out $= 9a^2 \quad\quad - 19a^2$
                        $= -10a^2$

(c) $4bac + 11cab - 2bca$
Rewrite letters in
alphabetical order $= 4abc + 11abc - 2abc$

Work them out $=\quad 15abc \quad - 2abc$
                        $= 13abc$

► *Exercise* **A1.4**

Simplify these expressions.
1 $a + a + a + a + a$ 8 $7x^2 - 3x^2 + 2x^2$
2 $3p + 5p$ 9 $5a - 2a - 6a + 8a$
3 $7m + 3m$ 10 $3pq - 6pq + 4pq$
4 $9r - 2r$ 11 $7xy^2 - 3xy^2 + 2xy^2$
5 $7x + 3x - 2x$ 12 $2ab^2 + 3b^2a - b^2a + 4ab^2$
6 $4p - p + 8p$ 13 $6r^2st + 3sr^2t - 5tsr^2$
7 $3q - 5q + q$ 14 $7xy^2z^3 + 5y^2xz^3 - 4z^3xy^2$ ◄

Expressions often contain **several sets of like terms**. Each set can be simplified *separately*. This is easier to do if you rewrite the expression with like terms next to each other.

Question

Simplify:
(a) $7x + 5 - 6y + 2x + 3y - y - 8$
(b) $3xy^2 + 2x^2y - 4y^2x + 6yx^2$

Answer

(a)
$$7x + 5 - 6y + 2x + 3y - y - 8$$

Group like terms $= 7x + 2x + 3y - 6y - y + 5 - 8$

Work them out $= \underbrace{9x} \quad \underbrace{- 4y} \quad \underbrace{- 3}$
$= 9x - 4y - 3$

(b)
$$3xy^2 + 2x^2y - 4y^2x + 6yx^2$$

Rewrite the letters in
alphabetical order $= 3xy^2 + 2x^2y - 4xy^2 + 6x^2y$
Group like terms $= 3xy^2 - 4xy^2 + 2x^2y + 6x^2y$

Work them out $= \underbrace{-xy^2} \quad \underbrace{+ 8x^2y}$
$= -xy^2 + 8x^2y$

▶ Exercise A1.5

Simplify these expressions.
1　$2p + 3q + p + 2q$
2　$5r + 2s - 3r + s$
3　$3m + 2n + 4m - n - m$
4　$3x + 3y + 3z - z - 2y$
5　$9p + 6q - 4p - 2q$
6　$6x + 4y - 5x - 5y$
7　$3xy - 4yz + 6xy - 3yz$
8　$3rs + 4sr - 2r^2$
9　$2ab^2 + 3a^2b - 5ab^2 + 6a^2b$
10　$3pq^2 - 5qp^2 + 2pq^2 - 4p^2q$

Multiplication and division

When **multiplying or dividing expressions**, it is easier if you group the numbers and the *same* letters together. Put the letters in alphabetical order. Always multiply or divide the *numbers* first. Then use **algebra shorthand** to simplify sets of the same letter.

Remember: A bracket may be used to show a multiplication. For example,

$a(bc)$ means $a \times (bc)$.

Question

Write these as simply as possible.
(a) $-4c \times 2a \times 3b$
(b) $2ab(-3bc)$
(c) $6mn^2 \times 5m^3n^4$
(d) $8a^3b^2 \div 4$

Answer

(a) $-4c \times 2a \times 3b = -4 \times 2 \times 3 \times a \times \underbrace{b \times c}$

$= \underbrace{-24} \quad \times \quad abc$
$= -24abc$

(b) $2ab(-3bc) = 2 \times -3 \times a \times \underbrace{b \times b} \times c$

$= \underbrace{-6} \quad \times a \times \underbrace{b^2} \times c$
$= -6ab^2c$

(c) $6mn^2 \times 5m^3n^4 = 6 \times 5 \times \underbrace{m \times m^3} \times \underbrace{n^2 \times n^4}$

$= \underbrace{30} \times \underbrace{m^4} \times \underbrace{n^6}$
$= 30m^4n^6$

(d) $8a^3b^2 \div 4 = \frac{8}{4}a^3b^2$
$= 2a^3b^2$

▶ Exercise A1.6

Write these expressions as simply as possible.
1　$2 \times 4p$
2　$3a \times 5b$
3　$12x \div 4$
4　$14p \div 7$
5　$p \times q \times 2r$
6　$4c \times 5d \times 2c$
7　$15pq \div 3$
8　$2ab \times 3ab^2$
9　$xy^2 \times 3x \times 5y$
10　$12a^2b^3 \div 4$
11　$5pqr \times 6pr^2$
12　$25x^2y \div 15$

Substitution

A **substitute** replaces something or someone. For example, in football a substitute replaces another player.

In algebra, **substitution** is replacing letters by numbers. This is used to find a **numerical value** for an expression.

When substituting numbers in an expression, it often helps to write out what the expression means.

Question

If $x = 2$ and $y = 5$, find the values of:
(a) $3x$
(b) x^3
(c) $4xy$
(d) $(4y)^2$
(e) $x + 6y$
(f) $4x^2 + 1$

Answer

(a) $3x = 3 \times x$
$= 3 \times 2$
$= 6$

(b) $x^3 = x \times x \times x$
$= 2 \times 2 \times 2$
$= 8$

(c) $4xy = 4 \times x \times y$
$= 4 \times 2 \times 5$
$= 40$

(d) $(4y)^2 = 4y \times 4y$
$= 4 \times y \times 4 \times y$
$= 4 \times 5 \times 4 \times 5$
$= 400$

(e) $x + 6y = x + (6 \times y)$
$= 2 + (6 \times 5)$
$= 2 + 30$
$= 32$

(f) $4x^2 + 1 = (4 \times x \times x) + 1$
$= (4 \times 2 \times 2) + 1$
$= 16 + 1$
$= 17$

In the examples in the last question we substituted **whole numbers** in expressions. You can substitute **decimals** in the same way. Use a calculator to do the working if you need to. For example, if $x = 1.7$ and $y = 4.2$,

$3x = 3 \times 1.7 = 5.1$
$x^3 = (1.7)^3 = 4.913$
$4xy = 4 \times 1.7 \times 4.2 = 28.56$
$(4y)^2 = (4 \times 4.2)^2 = 282.24$
$x + 6y = 1.7 + 6 \times 4.2 = 26.9$
$4x^2 + 1 = 4 \times 1.7^2 + 1 = 12.56$.

Check these yourself with your calculator.

▶ *Exercise* **A1.7**

1 Substitute $a = 4$ to find the values of:
  (a) $5a$ (g) $a \div 2$
  (b) $7a$ (h) $3a^2 \div 4$
  (c) $4a + 1$
  (d) $6a + 3$ (i) $\frac{a}{4} + 1$
  (e) $3a^2 - 1$
  (f) $8a - 2$ (j) $\frac{5a^2}{4} + 3$

2 If $p = 2$ and $q = 5$, find the value of:
  (a) $p + q$ (e) $3p^2 - q$
  (b) $q - p$ (f) $4q - 2p^2$
  (c) $2p + q$ (g) $q \div p$
  (d) $2q + p$ (h) $3q^2 \div 2p^2$

3 If $r = 5$, $s = 3$ and $t = 2$, find the value of:
  (a) rst (e) $r^2s + 6t^2 - s$
  (b) $r + s + t$ (f) $(st)^2 + 3rt$
  (c) $5r + 2s - t$ (g) $2rs^2 - 3t$
  (d) $4t^2 - s + r$ (h) $3(rs)^2 - 2(st)^2 + 5rt$

4 Substitute $x = 2.4$ to find the value of:
  (a) $4x$ (d) $5x^2 + 2$
  (b) $9x + 2$ (e) $(2x)^2 - 3$
  (c) $3x - 1$

5 If $m = 1.6$ and $n = 3.8$, find the value of:
  (a) $2m + n$ (d) $3n^2 - m$
  (b) $3n - m$ (e) $2m^2 - 3n + 1$
  (c) $5m + 6n$

Substituting in formulas

A **formula** is a short way of telling you how to work out something. It is an easy way to remember a result. Formulas are used in many different subjects and activities, not just in mathematics.

Some formulas are given 'in words'. For example,

    Area of a rectangle = length × width.

Some formulas are given using letters instead of words. You must know, or be told, what the letters stand for. For example, the formula

    $C = 35n + 50$

is used by a local newspaper to work out the cost, C pence, for an advert of n words.

    A formula makes it easy to work out a result. You *substitute numbers* you know in it. Then you do the working to find the value you want. Remember to give the *correct unit of measure* (if any) in your answer.

Question

A plumber works out the cost of doing a repair by using the formula

    $C = nr + t$

where C is the cost of the repair in £,
       n is the number of hours taken to complete the repair,
       r is the rate charged per hour in £, and
       t is the transport charge in £.

The plumber is called out to mend a burst pipe. The repair took 4 hours. The plumber charges £15 for transport and his rate per hour is £17.50.

What is the total cost of mending the pipe?

Answer

Values:	$n = 4$, $t = 15$, $r = 17.5$
Formula:	$C = nr + t$
Put in values:	$C = 4 \times 17.5 + 15$
Work it out:	$C = 85$

The cost of mending the pipe is £85.

▶ *Exercise* **A1.8**

1 A salesman's travelling expenses, £C, are worked out using the formula
    $C = \dfrac{28N}{100}$
where N is the number of miles travelled.
Calculate the expenses for journeys of
(a) 38 miles   (b) 50 miles   (c) 90 miles.

2 The cooking time, T minutes, for a joint of meat is given by the formula
    $T = 25 + 20W$
where W is the weight, in pounds, of the joint of meat.
Calculate the cooking time for joints weighing
(a) 5 lb   (b) $3\frac{1}{2}$ lb   (c) 9 lb   (d) $11\frac{1}{4}$ lb.

3 The number of seconds, t, taken by a stone to fall down a well of depth d metres is given by the formula
    $t = 0.45 \sqrt{d}$.
Calculate the time taken by a stone to fall down a well of depth:
(a) 16 m   (b) 18 m   (c) 20 m   (d) 34 m.
Give your answers to the nearest $\frac{1}{10}$ second.

4 The volume V cm^3 of this cone can be calculated using the formula
    $V = 1.05r^2h$
where r and h are both measured in cm.
    Use this formula to calculate the volume of a cone with
(a) $r = 5$, $h = 12$ (c) $r = 6$, $h = 10.6$
(b) $r = 4.5$, $h = 9$ (d) $r = 3.4$, $h = 7.2$
Give your answers to a sensible degree of accuracy.

Forming expressions

Statements in words are often written as algebraic expressions in mathematics. *Any* letter may be used to stand for the unknown number, but a *different letter* must be used for each *different unknown*. For example,

if *n* represents an unknown number, then:

3 more than the number → $n + 3$
7 less than the number → $n - 7$
5 times the number → $5n$
a quarter of the number → $\frac{1}{4}n$ or $\frac{n}{4}$
the number subtracted from $2 → 2 - n$
6 divided by the number → $\frac{6}{n}$
y more than the number → $n + y$
y less than the number → $n - y$
y times the number → ny or yn
the number divided by $y → \frac{n}{y}$
and so on…

Using a **flow diagram** is one way to form an expression. For example, this is the flow diagram for $2x + 3$

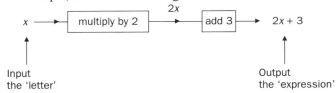

In these 'algebra' flow diagrams we usually use boxes for the instructions.

We always start an 'algebra flow diagram' with a letter. Then we build up the expression step-by-step. Each step must be done in the correct order. To check this we write the result of each step on the arrowed line after it.

For example, $2x$ is written after multiplying *x* by 2 in the above flow diagram.

For some flow diagrams you need to use brackets.

Question

Here are some instructions.

Think of a number. Multiply it by 8. Subtract 7. Multiply the result by 5. Add the number you first thought of.

Draw a flow diagram to form an expression for these instructions. Let *n* be the number you think of.

Answer

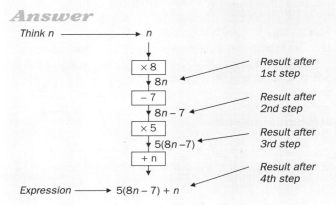

Some flow diagrams use square roots.
For example, here is the flow diagram to make the expression $\sqrt{5 - 3a}$.

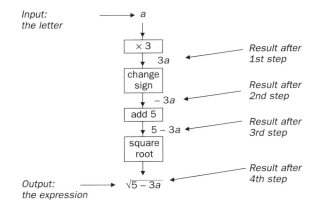

You often need to form expressions to make and solve equations. (see Unit A6.)

► *Exercise* **A1.9**

Draw flow diagrams to make these expressions.

1	$x + 5$	**8**	$4(2x + 3)$
2	$1 - 3c$	**9**	$\frac{4p - 1}{5}$
3	$2y - 1$		
4	$\frac{x}{7} + 3$	**10**	$\sqrt{3y^2 - 1}$
5	πr^2	**11**	$\frac{5}{x - 2}$
6	$\sqrt{x + 1}$		
7	$3p^2 - 5$	**12**	$7 - 6(x - 1)$

Examination Questions

1 (a) Simplify the expression $8a - 7b + c - 5a + 2c + b$.
  (b) What is the value of the expression when
  $a - 2b + c = 2$? (NISEAC, 1990)

2 When travelling on the London underground Carmen works out the length of time that her journey will take by the formula,
  $T = 3N + 5$.
  T is the length of time in minutes and N is the number of stops that the train will make. If the train will make a total of 7 stops work out the length that she expects the journey to take. (ULEAC, 1989)

3 A firm delivers coloured stones for garden paths. The cost £*C* is given by the formula
  $C = 3T + 3.5$
  where *T* is the number of tonnes bought.
  Use the formula to find the cost of 4 tonnes of stones.
  (NISEAC, 1991)

4 A coal merchant sells *B* bags of coal. The profit £*P* is calculated using the formula
  $P = 2B - 3J$
  where *J* is the number of delivery journeys made.
  (a) On 8th January the merchant sold fifty bags and made five delivery journeys. Calculate the profit.

(b) On 5th February the merchant sold forty bags and made no delivery journeys. Calculate the profit.

(NISEAC, 1990)

5 The area of shapes of this type is given by the formula

$$A = \tfrac{1}{2}(a + b) \times h$$

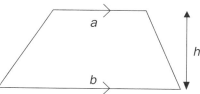

Work out the area of these two shapes of the same type. (All measurements in cm).
(i) $a = 10$ $b = 12$ $h = 5$
(ii) $a = 2.5$ $b = 3.5$ $h = 1.5$

(ULEAC, 1991)

6 Ecologists need to find the number of fish in a lake. One way to do this is to catch T fish. These are harmlessly tagged and allowed to go free. A little later N fish are caught. If R of these are found to be tagged, the total number of fish (P) can be calculated using the formula

$$P = \frac{T \times N}{R}.$$

Use the formula to solve this problem:
An ecologist catches 250 fish from a lake.

She tags and then releases them.
Two weeks later, in the same lake, she catches 160 fish.
She finds that 25 of them are tagged.
How many fish are there in the lake?

(MEG, 1991)

7 The stopping distance, d feet, of a car travelling at V miles per hour is given by the formula

$$d = V + \frac{V^2}{20}.$$

Calculate d when $V = 30$.

(SEG, 1990)

8 The purity of gold is measured in carats (K). The percentage of pure gold ($P\%$) in a ring is given by the formula

$$P = \frac{25 \times K}{6}.$$

(a) A gold ring is marked as being 18 carat gold. What percentage of the ring is pure gold?
(b) Someone offers to sell you a ring which is marked as 48 carat gold.
Would it be wise to buy it?
Explain your answer carefully.

(MEG, 1990)

A2
Shape patterns and numbers

This unit will help you to:

■ recognise and use shape patterns for numbers, including square, rectangular, triangular and cube numbers.

We study **patterns** in mathematics. We look for them. We describe them. We make them. We use them if we can.

The patterns are often in shapes, or in numbers, or in numbers associated with shapes.

Number shapes

For thousands of years whole numbers have been shown as patterns of dots. The Ancient Greeks gave shape names to some whole numbers. We still do this today.

Rectangle and line patterns

6 is shown as a *rectangular pattern of dots* on dice, dominoes and playing cards.

We call 6 a **rectangular number**.

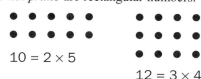

All whole numbers can be shown as a *line of dots*.

For example, 6 can be shown as ● ● ● ● ● ●

We do *not* call this a rectangular pattern.

Prime numbers (see Unit N5) do *not* make rectangular patterns. So, prime numbers are *not* rectangular numbers.

For example, 2, 3, 5 and 7 are prime numbers. They make line patterns but not rectangular patterns.

All whole numbers that are *not prime* are rectangular numbers.

For example, 10 and 12 are rectangular numbers.

$10 = 2 \times 5$

$12 = 3 \times 4$

▶ *Exercise* A2.1

1 By drawing patterns of dots say which of these numbers are rectangular numbers.
(a) 8   (c) 17   (e) 4   (g) 21   (i) 31
(b) 13   (d) 15   (f) 9   (h) 48   (j) 19

2 In a 'six set' of dominoes, the number of dots on each half ranges from 0 (blank) to 6. Dominoes with 6 dots on one half and not more than 6 dots on the other half are called 'six dot dominoes'. Here are all the 'six dot dominoes' in a 'six set':

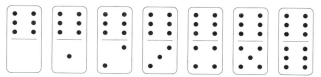

(a) Copy and complete the table on the following page.

Type of domino	6 dot	5 dot	4 dot	3 dot	2 dot	1 dot	blank
Total number of dots	63						0

(b) How many dominoes are there in a 'six set'?

(c) How many dominoes are there in a 'nine set'?

Square numbers

Some numbers, like 25, can be shown as a *square pattern of dots*.

We call them **square numbers**.

$25 = 5 \times 5 = 5^2$ said '5 squared'

These are the dot patterns for the first three square numbers.

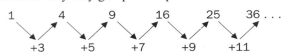

1st	2nd	3rd
1	4	9
$= 1 \times 1$	$= 2 \times 2$	$= 3 \times 3$
$= 1^2$	$= 2^2$	$= 3^2$

1 is counted as the first square number. It fits the pattern we use to work out square numbers.

It is useful to know the first ten square numbers.

1, 4, 9, 16, 25, 36, 49, 64, 81, 100

Look at the way they go up in 'steps' of odd numbers.

1   4   9   16   25   36 . . .

+3   +5   +7   +9   +11

Question

Square numbers can be built up like this:

1    $1 + 3 = 4$ $1 + 3 + 5 = 9$
     $= 2^2$ $= 3^2$

(a) Show how the next square number can be built up in the same way.

(b) Describe in your own words how the pattern is built up.

(c) Predict the sum of the first 100 odd numbers without doing the addition. Show your working clearly.

Answer

(a)

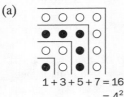

$1 + 3 + 5 + 7 = 16$
$= 4^2$

(b) 1st square number = 1st odd number
2nd square number = sum of first two odd numbers = 2^2
3rd square number = sum of first three odd numbers = 3^2
4th square number = sum of first four odd numbers = 4^2

(c) Sum of first 100 odd numbers = 100^2
$= 10\,000$

Exercise A2.2

1 By looking at patterns of dots, work out which of these numbers are square numbers.

(a) 24   (c) 48   (e) 64   (g) 10

(b) 36   (d) 16   (f) 50   (h) 81

2 Ken is making patterns of squares with matchsticks. The first two patterns are shown here.

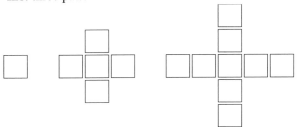

(a) Copy and complete this table.

Number of matches along a side	1	2	3	4	5	6
Number of small squares	1	4				
Number of matchsticks altogether	4					

(b) How many matchsticks will be needed to make the pattern with 36 small squares?

3 Ruth is making patterns using square tiles. Here are Ruth's first three patterns.

(a) Draw the next two patterns Ruth should make.

(b) Make a table to show the number of tiles needed to make each pattern.

4 Here is a square of side 2 cm. It is drawn on 1 cm dotty paper.

(a) How many dots are inside this square?

(b) How many dots are on the perimeter of the square?

(c) Draw some more squares on dotty paper and use them to copy and complete this table.

Length of side (cm)	1	2	3	4	5	6
Number of dots inside		1				
Number of dots on perimeter		8				
Total number of dots		9				

(d) Describe the patterns of numbers that appear in each row of your table.

Triangular numbers

Some numbers, like 15, make *triangular dot patterns*. We call them **triangular numbers**.

Here are the dot patterns for the first four triangular numbers.

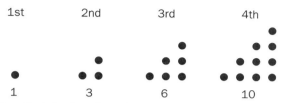

1st   2nd   3rd   4th

1   3   6   10

1 is called the 1st triangular number. It fits the way the pattern is built up.

Triangular numbers go up in 'steps' of 2, 3, 4, 5, …

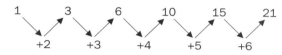

1   3   6   10   15   21

+2   +3   +4   +5   +6

These diagrams show how triangular numbers can be built up.

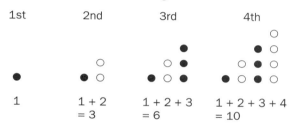

1st   2nd   3rd   4th

1   1 + 2 = 3   1 + 2 + 3 = 6   1 + 2 + 3 + 4 = 10

They show that:
1st triangular number = 1st whole number
2nd triangular number = sum of first two whole numbers
3rd triangular number = sum of first three whole numbers
and so on.

When you add *consecutive pairs* of triangular numbers, you form square numbers.

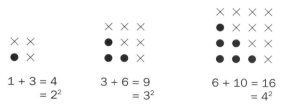

$1 + 3 = 4$ $3 + 6 = 9$ $6 + 10 = 16$
$= 2^2$ $= 3^2$ $= 4^2$

1st + 2nd triangular numbers → 2nd square number
2nd + 3rd triangular numbers → 3rd square number
3rd and 4th triangular numbers → 4th square number
and so on.

▶ *Exercise* A2.3

1   Draw dot patterns to show how
   (a) the 4th triangular number is made from the 3rd
   (b) the 5th triangular number is made from the 4th
   (c) the 6th triangular number is made from the 5th.
   Write down a sum of whole numbers for each of these triangular numbers.

Find the 10th triangular number without drawing a dot pattern. Show your working clearly.

2   You can make square numbers from two consecutive triangular numbers. Draw dot patterns to show how to make these numbers in this way:
   (a) the 5th square number
   (b) the 6th square number
   (c) the 7th square number.
   Which triangular numbers are used to make the 10th square number in this way?
   Predict first. Then draw the pattern to check.

3   This number pattern is made from square and triangular dot patterns.

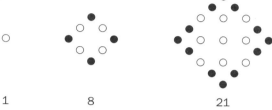

1   8   21

   (a) Explain how the third number has been made from a square number and four triangular numbers.
   (b) Draw diagrams to show the next two numbers in the pattern and write down their values.
   (c) Explain clearly how to make the sixth number in the pattern.

4   Shenfield College is setting out the seats for the annual chamber music concert. The first three rows have been set out like this:

   (a) How many seats are needed for the
     (i) 4th row, (ii) 5th row, (iii) 6th row?
   (b) Explain how to work out the number of seats needed for a row if you know the number of seats in the row before it.

5   This shape pattern has been made from matchsticks.

   (a) Draw the next two shapes in this pattern.
   (b) Copy and complete this table.

Number of triangles	Number of match-sticks used	Number of matches on the perimeter
1	3	3
2	5	
3		
4		
5		

   (c) How many matches are needed to make a shape with 10 triangles? How many matches will there be on the perimeter?
   (d) How many triangles are there in a shape with 50 matches on the perimeter?

Cube numbers

Cube numbers make *cubic dot patterns*.
Here are the dot patterns for the first three cube numbers.
Each is a 'cube' pattern of dots.

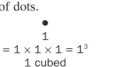 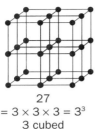

$$1$$
$$= 1 \times 1 \times 1 = 1^3$$
1 cubed

$$8$$
$$= 2 \times 2 \times 2 = 2^3$$
2 cubed

$$27$$
$$= 3 \times 3 \times 3 = 3^3$$
3 cubed

► *Exercise* **A2.4**

1 Work out the first ten cube numbers.
2 These two patterns have been made from cubes.

Pattern A

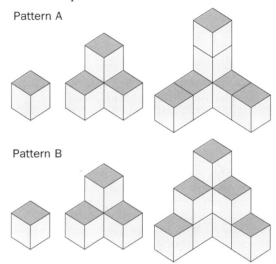

Pattern B

For each pattern:
(a) draw the next two shapes in the pattern
(b) copy and complete this table for the shapes in the pattern

Number of cubes high	1	2	3	4	5
Number of cubes used	1				

(c) predict the number of cubes needed to make the shape which is 9 cubes high.

Examination Questions

1

| 1 | 4 | 9 | 16 |

The figure shows a pattern of dots and numbers.
(a) Continue the pattern to show the next set of dots you would expect.
(b) Write the next number in the pattern after 16.
(ULEAC, 1991)

2 (a) Each pattern represents a triangular number.

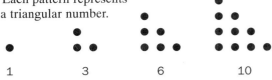

| 1 | 3 | 6 | 10 |

Draw the next two patterns and write the two triangular numbers under their patterns.
(b) Each pattern represents a square number.

$$1 + 3 = 4 \qquad 3 + 6 = 9 \qquad 6 + 10 = 16$$

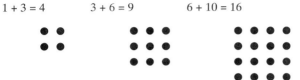

Which two triangular numbers when added together give the square number 36?
(c) How many dots will there be in each side of the pattern representing the square number 144?
(NEAB, 1990)

3

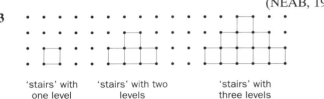

'stairs' with one level   'stairs' with two levels   'stairs' with three levels

A child is building sets of 'stairs' with some bricks.
The diagram shows the view of the 'stairs' that the child has built for 1, 2 and 3 levels.
(a) Draw the view for the 'stairs' with 4 levels.
(b) Complete the table.

Number of levels	Number of bricks
1	1
2	4
3	
4	

(c) How many bricks are needed to build a set of 'stairs' with 10 levels?
(ULEAC, 1988)

4

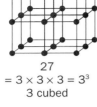

Pattern made of counters   1   2   3   4

(a) Draw the next pattern in the series.
(b) Complete the table.

Pattern Number	Number of counters in this pattern	Total number of counters used so far
1	1	1
2	3	4
3	5	9
4	7	...
5	...	...

(c) Write down the name of the type of numbers in the last column.

(ULEAC, 1991)

5 (a) Write down the next THREE numbers in EACH of the following number sequences:
   (i)   1, 4, 9, 16, …
   (ii) 0, 1, 3, 6, …

Here are some dot patterns:

First   Second   Third   Fourth
pattern pattern pattern   pattern

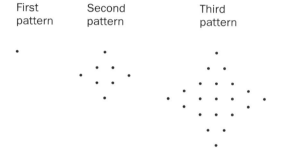

(b) (i)   Draw the FIFTH dot pattern.
   (ii) Write down the next THREE numbers in the number sequence
         1, 5, 12, 22, …

(c) Here is another dot pattern:

First   Second   Third
pattern   pattern   pattern

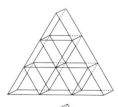

(i)   How many dots will there be in the FIFTH pattern?
(ii) Write down the next THREE numbers in the number sequence
      1, 8, 21, 40, …

(MEG, 1990)

6 An artist is working on a design for the cover of a mathematics newsletter. She produces this design which has three storeys.

She makes a model of the design using rectangular cards. The one storey model has one small triangle and needs three cards to build it.

one storey model

(a) The two storey model has four small triangles of the same size. Write down the number of cards needed to build it.
(b) Copy and complete the table.

two storey model

Number of storeys	Number of small triangles	Number of cards needed to build it
1	1	3
2	4	
3		
4		

(c) (i)   Describe the relationship between the number of storeys and the number of small triangles.
   (ii) Find how many storeys need to be built to have 64 small triangles.
(d) Comment on the pattern of numbers of cards needed to build the models.

(MEG, 1989)

7 Two short sticks of the same length and one long stick are used to form a right-angled triangle, Triangle 1, shown here.

Triangle 1

(a) Here are the next two triangles in a sequence.
   (i)   How many short sticks have been used to make Triangle 2?
   (ii) How many long sticks have been used in Triangle 3?

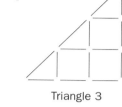
Triangle 2   Triangle 3

(b) Draw the next triangle in the sequence and write down the *total* number of sticks needed to make it.
(c) Use the answers you have obtained so far to complete this table:

Triangle	1	2	3	4
Long sticks				
Short sticks				
Total				

(d) Work out the total number of sticks required to make the next triangle in the sequence. (NEAB, 1990)

8 Kath investigates the maximum number of diagonals she can draw in these figures:

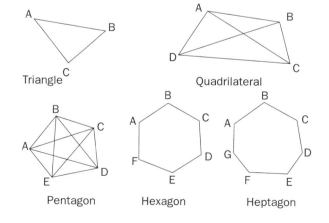

Triangle   Quadrilateral

Pentagon   Hexagon   Heptagon

She writes her results in a table.

Figure	Number of vertices	Number of diagonals
Triangle	3	0
Quadrilateral	4	2
Pentagon	5	5
Hexagon		
Heptagon		

(a) Copy Kath's table and fill in your results for the hexagon and heptagon.

(b) What is the maximum number of diagonals which could be drawn in a decagon (10 sided figure)?

(SEG, 1990)

9 Jenny O'Donnell is a fruit farmer. This year she has ordered 96 apple trees, which she wants to plant in a 'rectangular' pattern.

Here are two possible arrangements.

(i) Plant 1 row, with 96 trees in it.

(ii) Plant 3 rows, with 32 trees in each row.

(a) Write down all the other arrangements possible, given that Jenny does not want to plant more than 10 rows of trees.

(b) Last year, when the pear orchard was planted, there was only one possible 'rectangular' arrangement which had less than 10 rows.

Jenny remembers ordering between 32 and 40 trees. How many pear trees are there in the pear orchard?

(NEAB, 1990)

A3
Number sequences

This unit will help you to:

- recognise and continue a simple sequence of numbers
- use the method of differences to find the pattern in a sequence
- follow instructions to make a sequence
- find the rule used to generate a sequence.

A *pattern* of numbers given in a *definite order* is called a **sequence**. Some common sequences have special names. Here are some examples you should know.

Counting or whole numbers: 1, 2, 3, 4, 5, 6, …
Odd numbers: 1, 3, 5, 7, 9, 11, …
Even numbers: 2, 4, 6, 8, 10, 12, …
Square numbers: 1, 4, 9, 16, 25, 36, …
Cube numbers: 1, 8, 27, 64, 125, 216, …
Triangular numbers: 1, 3, 6, 10, 15, 21, …
Multiples
… such as multiples of 3: 3, 6, 9, 12, 15, 18, …
multiples of 10: 10, 20, 30, 40, 50, 60, …
Powers
… such as powers of 2: 1, 2, 4, 8, 16, 32, …
powers of 10: 1, 10, 100, 1000, 10 000, …
Fibonacci numbers: 1, 1, 2, 3, 5, 8, …
Prime numbers: 2, 3, 5, 7, 11, 13, …

Each number in a sequence is called a **term**.

Continuing sequences

A sequence can be described by **listing its first few terms**. For example,

5, 10, 15, 20, … ← These dots show that the sequence continues.

Sometimes you need to give the *next terms* in the sequence. First look for *patterns you know* such as numbers that are even, odd, square, cube, triangular, prime, multiples, …

You know about these patterns and how they are made. Use this to help you to continue the sequence. For example,

5, 10, 15, 20, … are 'multiples of 5'.
They are 1×5, 2×5, 3×5, 4×5, …

You can continue the sequence with 5×5, 6×5, 7×5, …
i.e. 25,   30,   35,   …

Question

Find the next three numbers in each sequence:
(a) 1, 8, 27, 64, …   (b) 1, 9, 25, 49, …

Answer

(a) *1, 8, 27, 64, …*
These are cube numbers 1^3, 2^3, 3^3, 4^3, …
so the sequence continues: 5^3, 6^3, 7^3, …
i.e.   125, 216, 343, …

(b) *First notice that 1, 9, 25, 49, are square numbers.*
But they are not the first four square numbers.
They are: 1^2, 3^2, 5^2, 7^2, …
Now you can see that they are odd numbers squared.
So the sequence continues, 9^2, 11^2, 13^2, …
i.e.   81, 121,169, …

Exercise A3.1

Find the next three numbers in each of these sequences. Look for sequences you know.

1 7, 14, 21, 28, …		**7** 11, 22, 33, 44, …
2 4, 16, 36, 64, …		**8** 1, 9, 36, 100, …
3 1, 27, 125, 343, …		**9** 3, 3, 6, 9, 15, …
4 1, 3, 9, 27, …		**10** −1, 0, −1, −1, −2, −3, …
5 8, 64, 216, 512, …		
6 4, 9, 25, 49, …		

If you do not know (or recognise) the pattern in a sequence, try to *work out how it is made*.

Look first to see if the numbers are getting bigger or smaller. Then work out how to get from one number to the next.

If the numbers are getting *bigger*, then something may be *added on* to each term or each term may be *multiplied* by something.

If the numbers are getting *smaller*, then something may be *subtracted* from each term or each term may be *divided* by something.

The 'something' may be the same number each time or form another number pattern.

Question

Find the next two numbers in each pattern. Show how you worked them out each time.
(a) 1, 4, 7, 10, ...
(b) 1, 3, 7, 13, ...
(c) 16, 8, 4, 2, ...
(d) 100, 99, 97, 94, ...
(e) 2, 20, 200, 2000, ...

Answer

(a) Add 3 each time.

(b) Add the even numbers 2, 4, 6, 8, 10, ...

(c) Divide by 2 each time.

(d) Subtract the counting numbers 1, 2, 3, 4, 5, ...

(e) Multiply by 10 each time.

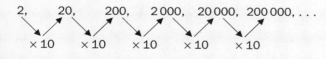

► **Exercise** A3.2

Find the next three numbers in each of these sequences. Show your working clearly.

1 2, 6, 10, 14, ...
2 200, 195, 190, 185, ...
3 1, 4, 16, 64, ...
4 729, 243, 81, 27, ...
5 2, 7, 17, 32, ...
6 5, 10, 30, 120, ...
7 5, 4, 1, −4, ...
8 100, 98, 94, 88, ...
9 7, 7, 14, 42, ...
10 20, 10, 5, 2.5, ...

◄

Looking at method of differences

Sometimes it is not obvious how to continue a sequence. When this happens, looking at **differences** usually helps.

Writing the differences in a table is a neat way to record your working. It often shows the pattern more clearly too. For example, look at the sequence and the 1st differences in this table:

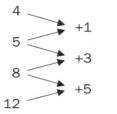

The differences are not the same. But there is a clear pattern, i.e. the odd numbers. It continues 7, 9, 11, . . .

You can *continue the 1st differences*, then use them to *continue the sequence* ...

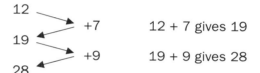

12 + 7 gives 19
19 + 9 gives 28

► *Exercise* A3.3

Use the method of differences to find the next three numbers in each of these sequences.

1 2, 3, 6, 11, ...
2 3, 5, 9, 15, ...
3 4, 7, 12, 19, ...
4 50, 49, 47, 44, ...
5 60, 58, 54, 48, ...
6 5, 9, 17, 29, ...
7 8, 13, 23, 38, ...
8 78, 75, 69, 60, ...

◄

When there is **no obvious pattern** in the 1st differences, work out the **2nd differences**. These are the differences between the 1st differences. For example, look at this difference table.

Terms	1st differences	2nd differences

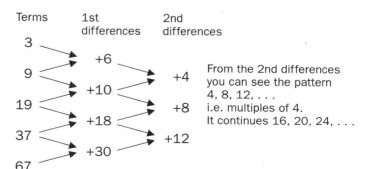

From the 2nd differences you can see the pattern 4, 8, 12, . . . i.e. multiples of 4. It continues 16, 20, 24, . . .

You can *continue the 2nd differences*, then use them to *continue the 1st differences*.

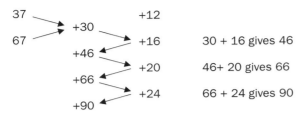

30 + 16 gives 46

46 + 20 gives 66

66 + 24 gives 90

Now you can use the *1st differences to continue the sequence*.

67 + 46 gives 113

113 + 66 gives 179

179 + 90 gives 269

The sequence is 3, 9, 19, 37, 67, 113, 179, 269, ...

The next two terms are 387 and 537. Check that you can work them out yourself.

Question

Use the method of differences to find the next term in this sequence:
    1, 15, 53, 127, 249, ...
Show your working clearly.

Answer

Terms	1st differences	2nd differences	
1			
	14		
15		24	*From the 2nd differences the pattern is 24, 36, 48, ...*
	38		*i.e. multiples of 12.*
53		36	*The next is 60.*
	74		
127		48	
	122		122 + 60 gives 182
249		60	
	182		249 + 182 gives 431
431			

The next term is 431.

▶ *Exercise* A3.4

Use the method of differences to find the next two terms in these sequences.
1 2, 11, 26, 47, ...
2 3, 12, 23, 37, 55, ...
3 1, 9, 18, 30, 47, ...
4 4, 7, 12, 19, 28, ...
5 2, 9, 20, 37, 62, ...
6 2, 6, 15, 34, 68, ...

This method of differences can be continued on the 3rd, 4th, ... differences if necessary. However, remember that although the method works for many sequences, it does *not* work for all of them.

Question

Find the 1st, 2nd and 3rd differences for the Fibonacci sequence:
    1, 1, 2, 3, 5, 8, 13, 21, 34, ...
Describe the result you obtain.

Answer

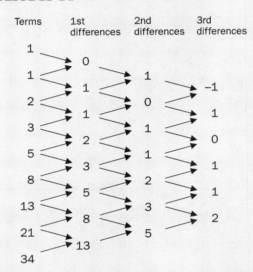

Each list of differences is itself a sequence of the 'Fibonacci type'. They obey the same rule. Each number after the first two is found by adding the two numbers before it.

▶ *Exercise* A3.5

Find the next three terms in each of these sequences. Which are 'Fibonacci type' sequences?
1 7, 26, 63, 124, 215, 339, ...
2 4, 6, 10, 16, 26, ...
3 1, 6, 14, 27, 49, 86, ...
4 3, 6, 9, 15, 24, 39, ...
5 5, 10, 15, 25, 40, 65, ...

Rules for sequences

A number sequence can be described by giving the **rule or pattern it follows**.

Often there is a rule that describes how to go **from one term to the next**. You have to be given the first term to start the sequence. When the rule involves several operations (+, −, ×, ÷, ...) take care to do them in the correct order. For example, instructions 'double then add 5' and 'add 5 then double' are not the same.

You may need to use your calculator to generate the terms.

Question

Ann worked out four sequences starting with the number 10.
Here are the rules she uses to go from one term to the next in
each sequence.

Sequence A: Add 7
Sequence B: Double and add 1
Sequence C: Add 2 and multiply by 3
Sequence D: Square

Write down the first four terms of each sequence.

Answer

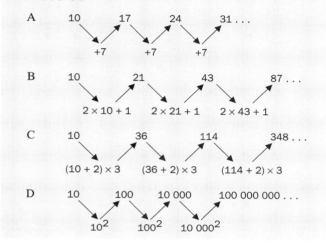

Answer

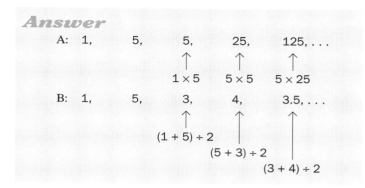

Exercise A3.6

Write down the first four terms of each of these sequences. Start
with the given number. Then go from one term to the next using
the rule.

1 Start: 2. Rule: Add 9.
2 Start: 5. Rule: Multiply by 4.
3 Start: 16. Rule: Subtract 3.
4 Start: 64. Rule: Divide by 2.
5 Start: 7. Rule: Multiply by 3 and add 1.
6 Start: 10. Rule: Subtract 2 and multiply by 3.
7 Start: 1. Rule: Add 2 then square.
8 Start: 1. Rule: Square then add 2.
9 Start: 2. Rule: Subtract 1 then double.
10 Start: 3. Rule: Double then subtract 1.

Sometimes the rule describes how to **combine terms** to get
another term.

Question

John works out two sequences A and B starting with the
numbers 1, 5.

To find each term in sequence A he multiplies the two
terms before it.

To find each term in sequence B he finds the average
(mean) of the two terms before it.

Write down the first five terms of each sequence.

Exercise A3.7

Write down the first five terms of the sequences made using
these rules.

1 Start with 1, 2. Rule: Each term is found by adding the two
terms before it and doubling.
2 Start with 2, 5. Rule: Each term is found by multiplying the
two terms before it and adding 1.
3 Start with 2, 1. Rule: Each term is found by multiplying the
two terms before it and doubling.
4 Start with 2, 4. Rule: Each term is found by adding the two
terms before it and squaring.
5 Start with 3, 5. Rule: Each term is found by finding the
difference between the two terms before it and squaring.

Given a sequence as a list of numbers, you can often **find the
rule** used to make it. Work out how to continue the sequence as
before. Then describe the rule in words.

Question

Describe in words how each term in these sequences is
formed from the term before it.
(a) 1, 4, 16, 64, …
(b) 10, 7, 4, 1, …

Answer

(a)

Each term is obtained by multiplying the term before it
by 4.

(b)

Each term is obtained by subtracting 3 from the term before it.

Exercise A3.8

Describe in words how each term in these sequences is formed
from the term before it.

1 2, 4, 6, 8, …
2 3, 7, 11, 15, …
3 2, 4, 8, 16, 32, …
4 50, 47, 44, 41, …
5 8, 4, 2, 1, $\frac{1}{2}$, …
6 3, 7, 15, 31, …

The first few terms of a sequence often do not give you enough information to identify the rule or pattern it follows. There may be *several possibilities*.

Question

A sequence starts 2, 3, 5, ...
Find three different ways to continue the sequence. Write down the next three terms and show clearly how you found them.

Answer

(a) 2, 3, 5, 7, 11, 13, ...
   The sequence of prime numbers. No 'rule', but this is a well-known sequence.

(b)

   The sequence starts at 2 then goes up by 1, 2, 3, 4, 5, ...

(c)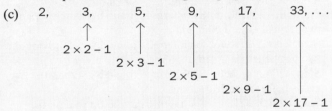

   The sequence starts at 2, then to find each term, double the term before it and subtract 1.

There are many other possibilities. Try to find some yourself.

► Exercise A3.9

Find three different ways to continue each of these sequences. Write down the next three terms in each sequence you make and show clearly how you found them.

1	2, 4, 8, ...	**4**	1, 2, 3, ...
2	2, 3, 6, ...	**5**	3, 7, 15, ...
3	5, 8, 12, ...		

◄

Examination Questions

1 (a) Write down the next three numbers in this sequence.
   3, 7, 11, 15, 19, ...
   (b) Explain how the sequence is formed.
   (c) Find the 50th number in the sequence.
   (NEAB, 1991)

2 Give the next two terms in each of the patterns
   (a) 1×2, 2×3, 3×4, 4×5, ...
   (b) 1, 3, 6, 10, ...
   (MEG, 1988)

3 Write down the next two numbers in the following sequences.
   (a) 41, 38, 35, ...
   (b) 64, 16, 4, ...
   (MEG, 1991)

4 (a) Complete this table:

$(1 \times 8) + 1 =$
$(12 \times 8) + 2 =$
$(123 \times 8) + 3 =$
$(1234 \times 8) + 4 =$
$(12345 \times 8) + 5 =$

(b) Use this pattern to write down the answer to
   $(123456789 \times 8) + 9 =$
   (NEAB, 1988)

5 (a) Complete lines 5 and 6 in the number pattern below.

Line 1	1	=	$1 = 1 \times 1$
Line 2	$1 + 3$	=	$4 = 2 \times 2$
Line 3	$1 + 3 + 5$	=	$9 = 3 \times 3$
Line 4	$1 + 3 + 5 + 7$	=	$16 = 4 \times 4$
Line 5	....	=	.... = ...
Line 6	....	=	.... = ...

In Line 4 the last number in the pattern is 7.
(b) What would be the last number in Line 10?
(c) What would all of the numbers in the pattern add up to in Line 12?
(d) Write down, in a few words, how you would describe to a friend a quick way of adding up the first 20 odd numbers.
   (SEG, 1989)

6 Look at the following number pattern.
   $1 + 3 \qquad\qquad = 4 = 2^2$
   $1 + 3 + 5 \qquad\quad = 9 = 3^2$
   $1 + 3 + 5 + 7 \quad\ = 16 = 4^2$
   $1 + 3 + 5 + 7 + 9 = a = b^2$
   (a) Calculate the value of a in the fourth line.
   (b) What number does b represent?
   (c) Write down the next line of the pattern.
   (d) Imagine that the pattern is continued. What will the seventh line of the pattern be?
   (NEAB, 1989)

7 Anita is doing an investigation. She makes a table of numbers:
   (a) Describe the pattern of the numbers in the first column.
   (b) Fill in the numbers in the next three rows of the table.
   (c) What would be the two numbers in the 20th row?
   (d) What would be the two numbers in the 1000th row?

3	4
6	7
9	10
12	13

   (SEG, 1989)

8 An amoeba divides in two every hour.

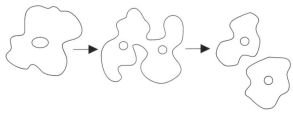

At 1 o'clock there is 1 amoeba.
At 2 o'clock there are 2 amoebae.
At 3 o'clock there are 4 amoebae.
At 4 o'clock there are 8 amoebae.
We assume that the amoebae do not die.
(a) Work out how many amoebae you will have at 5 o'clock.
(b) Work out how many amoebae you will have at 7 o'clock.
(c) Work out the time when you will have 256 amoebae.
(d) At the next 2 o'clock you have 8192 amoebae. Work out the time you had exactly half of these.

(ULEAC, 1991)

9 Look at the following pattern. There is a figure missing in the last line.

```
    1 × 1      = 1
   11 × 11     = 121
  111 × 111    = 12321
 1111 × 1111   = 1234321
11111 × 11111  = 1234*4321
```

(a) What figure should * be?
(b) Complete the answer for this line of the pattern
   111111 × 111111 =
(c) Write down the next complete line of the pattern.

(NEAB, 1988)

10 (a) Work out these multiplications, using your calculator.
   142857 × 1 = 142857
   142857 × 2 =
   142857 × 3 =
   142857 × 4 =
   142857 × 5 =
   142857 × 6 =
   Describe the pattern of numbers in your answers.
(b) Write down the next line in this sequence of multiplications.
   142857 × 14 = 1999998
   142857 × 21 = 2999997
   142857 × 28 = 3999996

(MEG, 1991)

A4
Coordinates

This unit will help you to:

■ use positive and negative coordinates to fix the position of a point

■ plot points given coordinates

■ recognise coordinate patterns.

Coordinates are an **ordered pair** of numbers. They give the **position** of a point using **axes** and an **origin**.

The coordinates of any point P are (x, y).

x-coordinate   *y*-coordinate

The first number is *always* 'across'. The 'across' axis is the **x-axis**. So the first number is called the **x-coordinate**.

The second number is *always* 'up or down'. The 'up and down' axis is the **y-axis**. So the second number is called the **y-coordinate**.

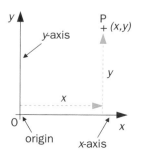

Exercise A4.1

1 Copy this sketch map on to a large grid. Label the places below on your map.

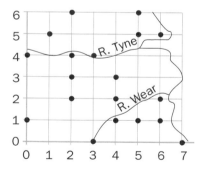

Consett (0,1)	Washington (4,2)	Prudhoe (0,4)
Seaham (6,1)	Peterlee (7,0)	Chester le Street
Felling (4,3)	Stanley (2,2)	(4,1)
Wallsend (5,5)	Throckley (1,5)	Durham (3,0)
Ponteland (2,6)	Sunderland (6,2)	Blaydon (2,4)
Tynemouth (6,5)	Whitley Bay (5,6)	Houghton le Spring
Newcastle (3,4)	Whickham (2,3)	(5,1)

2 Draw a sketch map of your own on a grid. Mark and name some places on your map. You can use real or imaginary places. Write down the coordinates of all your places.
   Swap maps with a classmate. Check each other's coordinates.

Negative coordinates

Coordinates can be **positive** or **negative** numbers. To find or plot these points you must have both positive and negative numbers on the axes.

On the *x*-axis:
values to the *right* of 0 are *positive* (+),
values to the *left* of 0 are *negative* (–).

On the *y*-axis:
values *above* 0 are positive (+),
values *below* 0 are negative (–).

As before, each pair of coordinates tells you how to get **from 0 to the point**.

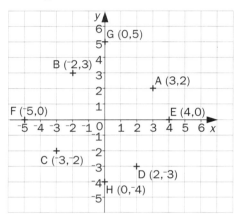

Check these points and their coordinates:

A (3,2)   … right 3, up 2
B (⁻2,3) … left 2, up 3
C (⁻3, ⁻2) … left 3, down 2
D (2, ⁻3) … right 2, down 3

Points on the axes have a zero (0) coordinate.

E (4,0) and F (⁻5,0) are on the *x*-axis (*y*-coordinate = 0)
G (0,5) and H (0,⁻4) are on the *y*-axis (*x*-coordinate = 0).

► *Exercise* A4.2

1 Each of these sets of ordered pairs will give you a picture. Draw two axes, number them from ⁻5 to 5. Plot the points, join them in order.
   (a) (⁻4,⁻2), (3,⁻2), (5,0), (2,0), (2,1), (1,1), (1,2), (0,2), (0,1), (⁻1,1), (⁻1,2), (⁻2,2), (⁻2,0), (⁻5,0), (⁻4,⁻2).
   (b) (⁻2,⁻4), (3,⁻4), (4,⁻3), (2,⁻1), (3,0), (4,0), (3,1), (1,⁻1), (3,⁻3), (5,⁻3), (0,⁻1), (⁻4,⁻1), (⁻2,⁻3), (⁻4,⁻3), (⁻2,⁻4).
   (c) (2,⁻3), (2,⁻4), (1,⁻4), (1,⁻3), (5,⁻3), (1,⁻1), (5,⁻1), (1,1), (4,1), (1,3), (3,3), (0,5), (⁻3,3), (⁻1,3), (⁻4,1), (⁻1,1), (⁻5,⁻1), (⁻1,⁻1), (⁻5,⁻3), (⁻1,⁻3), (⁻1,⁻4), (⁻2,⁻4), (⁻2,⁻5), (2,⁻5).
2 Each of these sets of ordered pairs will give you a well-known shape. Draw two axes and number them from ⁻7 to 7 for each set. Plot the points, join them in order to make a polygon. Name the shape you have drawn.
   (a) (⁻7,2), (⁻3,4), (1,⁻4), (⁻3,⁻6).
   (b) (2,⁻2), (⁻7,⁻5), (⁻5,2), (4,5).
   (c) (4,3), (7,1), (4,⁻1), (⁻3,1).
   (d) (⁻7,⁻3), (⁻4,0), (⁻1,⁻3), (⁻4,⁻6).
   (e) (4,3), (6,⁻1), (2,⁻3), (⁻4,⁻1).

Four quadrants

Crossing *x*- and *y*-axes divide the diagram into four parts. These parts are called **quadrants**.

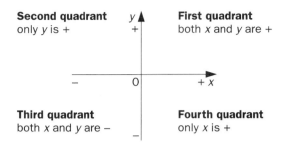

Second quadrant
only *y* is +

First quadrant
both *x* and *y* are +

Third quadrant
both *x* and *y* are –

Fourth quadrant
only *x* is +

These are useful checks when you are using coordinates.

► *Exercise* A4.3

In which quadrant will each of these points lie?
Say first, then plot to check.

1   (2,7)   6   (0,⁻5)
2   (⁻1,6)   7   (⁻3,⁻5)
3   (0,4)   8   (⁻2,4)
4   (5,⁻5)   9   (3,⁻8)
5   (2,⁻1)   10   (⁻5,⁻2)

Coordinate patterns

In a set of points there may be the same **relationship** (connection) between the *x*-coordinate and the *y*-coordinate for each point. If there is a **coordinate pattern**, then you can try to write a **rule** to show the pattern. Look for a rule that shows how to get the *y*-coordinate *from* the *x*-coordinate if you can.

For example, look at these points:

A(⁻3,⁻3), B(⁻1,⁻1), C(0,0), D(2,2), E(5,5),
  ↑ ↑   ↑ ↑   ↑ ↑   ↑ ↑   ↑ ↑
 equal   equal   equal   equal   equal

The *y*-coordinate is equal to the *x*-coordinate.

Using letters the rule is:

$y = x$.

Points with a coordinate pattern usually make a **pattern on the grid** too.

For example, points A, B, C, D and E lie in a *straight line* on the grid.

They make a **linear pattern**. If you draw the line through the points, then all the points on the line obey the coordinate rule:

$y = x$

Check some yourself. This rule is called the **equation of the line**.

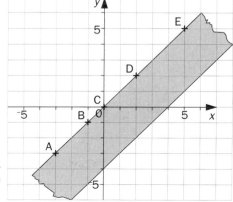

It is often easier to spot the coordinate pattern if you list the coordinates in a **table**.

For example, look at these coordinates:

(2,1), (2,0), (2,⁻3), (2,⁻2), (2,5).

The points all lie on the same straight line. This table lists their x and y values:

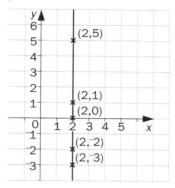

x	y
2	1
2	0
2	⁻3
2	⁻2
2	5

The x-coordinate is always 2. So $x = 2$ is the equation of the line they lie on.

Exercise A4.4

1   These points all lie on the same straight line.
   (0,3), (⁻1,3), (8,3), (⁻6,3), (2,3).
   Plot the points and draw in the line. Look for a coordinate pattern for this line. Give a rule to describe this pattern. Write down the coordinates of three more points on the line. Check they fit your rule.

Now repeat question **1** for each of these sets of points.

2   (⁻4,8), (6,8), (0,8), (⁻3,8), (⁻7,8)
3   (7,⁻7), (0,0), (⁻2,2), (3,⁻3), (⁻5,5)
4   (8,4), (⁻6,⁻3), (0,0), (4,2), (⁻10,⁻5)
5   (0,0), (1,2), (⁻2,⁻4), (⁻1,⁻2), (4,8)
6   (⁻1,⁻3), (0,0), (2,6), (1,3), (5,15)
7   (3,7), (⁻1,11), (10,0), (12,⁻2), (6,4)
8   (6,4), (0,⁻2), (2,0), (1,⁻1), (5,3)

Examination Questions

1   This grid shows a code. Each letter can be written by using its coordinates.

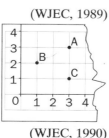

   (a) Decode this word:
       (1,2) (3,3) (4,2) (5,4) (6,6) (5,0)
   (b) Write the code for the word CUP.
   (c) The letters A E I O U are called vowels. Write a rule that fits the code for all the vowels.
                                           (WJEC, 1989)

2   This is part of Andrew's homework on coordinates. His paper has been torn.
   (a) Write down the coordinates of points A and B.
   (b) ABCD is a rhombus. Write down the coordinates of point D.

                                           (WJEC, 1990)

3   P is the point with coordinates (6,2) and Q is the point with coordinates (1,1).
   (a) Write down the coordinates of the point R.
   (b) (i) PQRS is a parallelogram. Copy the grid and mark and label the point S.
       (ii) Write down the coordinates of the point S.

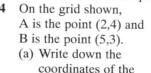

                                           (MEG, 1988)

4   On the grid shown, A is the point (2,4) and B is the point (5,3).
   (a) Write down the coordinates of the point C.
   (b) Find the area of the triangle ABC.
   (c) AC is a line of symmetry for the shape ABCD. Draw ABCD on a grid and write down the coordinates of D.   (NISEAC, 1988)

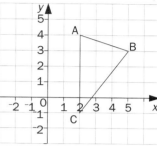

5   (a) On graph paper, mark and label the points
       A (2,4), B (⁻2,4), C (⁻2,⁻3).
       (Label both axes from ⁻4 to 4.)
   (b) Mark a point D so that ABCD is a rectangle.
   (c) Write down the coordinates of D.
                                           (MEG, 1989)

6   (a) (i) A (4,3), B (1,⁻4), C(⁻6,⁻4), D (⁻3,3). Mark and label these points on a grid.
       (Label each axis from ⁻8 to 6.)
       (ii) Draw the lines AB, BC, CD and DA. Write down the special name given to the quadrilateral ABCD.
   (b) Mark and label the point E (6,⁻8) on the grid. Draw the lines EA, EB and EC.
   (c) The points A, B, C, D and E represent five villages. The seven lines you have drawn represent roads. There are six possible routes that could be taken by a car when driving from village D to village E. (The car must not pass through any village more than once.)
       One route is D to C to B to E.
       Write down the other five routes.
                                           (MEG, 1988)

7   (a) Write down the coordinates of the points A, B, C and D.
   (b) What special type of quadrilateral is ABCD?
   (c) Copy the diagram and draw at least six more of these quadrilaterals , to form a tessellation.

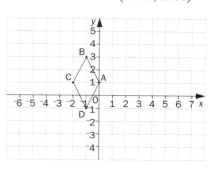

                                           (MEG, 1991)

8

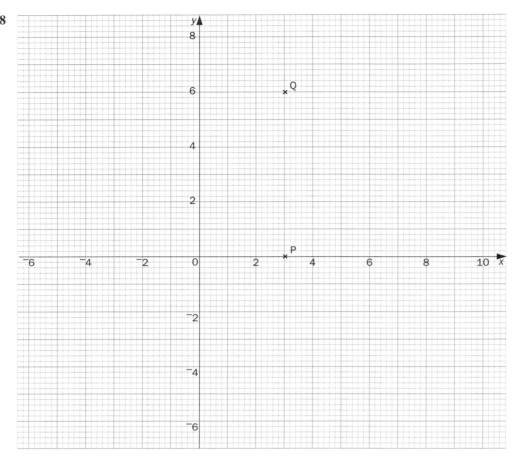

(a) Write down the coordinates of
   (i) P   (ii) Q.
(b) Plot and label the point R (7,6).
(c) Plot the point S so that PQRS is
   a rectangle.
(d) Write down the coordinates of
   the point where the diagonals of
   PQRS meet.
(e) Work out the area of rectangle
   PQRS.

(ULEAC, 1990)

A5
Line graphs from data

This unit will help you to:

■ read and interpret information given on a line
   graph

■ draw a line graph from a table of values

■ recognise misleading line graphs.

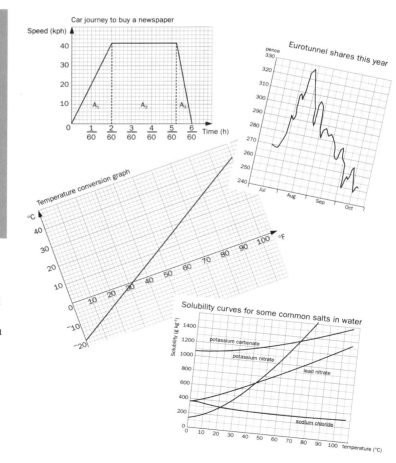

Looking at graphs

A **graph** gives a **picture of some information** (data). It is
usually easier and quicker to understand than lots of words and
numbers. It looks more interesting too.

But a graph isn't just a pretty picture. Looking at it can often
tell you more than simply looking at a list of facts and figures.

A graph can help you to:

● see any patterns or trends,

● spot any links or relationships between two sets of data,

● find and predict values not given in the data.

Reading graphs

A graph can give you a lot of information … if you know how to read it. Use these **key points** to help you.

- **Title**
  Read the title (and other information given) first. This tells you what the graph is about. That's important.
  What is each graph on page 92 about?

- **Axes**
  A *coordinate graph* has two axes. In mathematics these are often labelled x and y. But other letters and labels are usually used on 'practical graphs'.

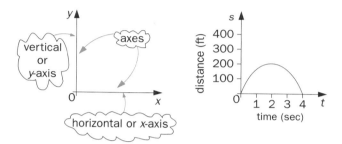

  Check the **labels** and any **units of measure** on the axes. These tell you what values are being shown on the graph.
  Look at the axes on page 92. What are they labelled?

- **Scales**
  Each axis has a scale (a number line) on it. Look carefully at the numbering. The square grid helps you to work out the scale. The simplest scale has 1 'space' for 1 unit. This is usually easy to spot.

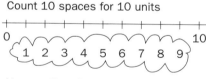

Count 10 spaces for 10 units

You can 'imagine' numbers in between

You may have *different* scales on the two axes. Then you need to work out what the scale is on *each axis*. You have to find out what each small space stands for. (Just like a number line or scale on a measuring instrument). Compare the number of small spaces with the amount it shows. Usually the numbers are easy. Graph paper with darker lines every 5 or 10 spaces makes it simpler too.

Each space may be a *whole number*.

For example,

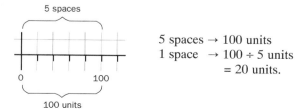

5 spaces → 100 units
1 space → 100 ÷ 5 units
        = 20 units.

Each space may be a *decimal or fraction*.

For example,

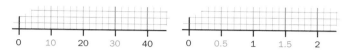

10 spaces → 1 unit
1 space   → 1 ÷ 10 units
         = 0.1 units.

You can put *extra marks and numbers* on the axes if it helps.

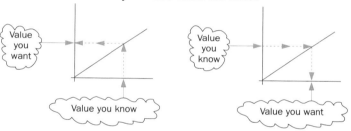

- **Values**
  On some graphs lines are drawn between plotted points. These line graphs can be straight or jagged or curved. Look for each kind of graph on page 92.
  To read values from a line graph:
  - find the 'value you know' on its axis,
  - move *up* (or *across*) the grid to the line,
  - move *across* (or *down*) the grid to the other axis,
  - read the 'value you want' from the scale.

  You can draw lines on the grid to help you.

Always use the *correct units of measurement*, if any, in your answers.

The **straight line graph** is the simplest kind of line graph. It shows a steady (constant) relationship between the two sets of values.

Conversion graphs (page D3 p 210) and travel graphs (P16 p362) are often straight line graphs. Look these up if you want to see these examples.

The next question is an example from science.

Question

The graph on the following page shows the results of a 'stretch test' on a spring. The length of the spring was measured when different masses were hung from it. Use the graph to answer these questions.
(a) How long was the spring before any masses were hung on it?
(b) What should be the length of the spring if these masses were hung on it?
  (i) 15 g (ii) 8 g
(c) What masses should give these lengths?
  (i) 12 cm (ii) 19 cm

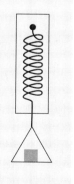

continued

Answer

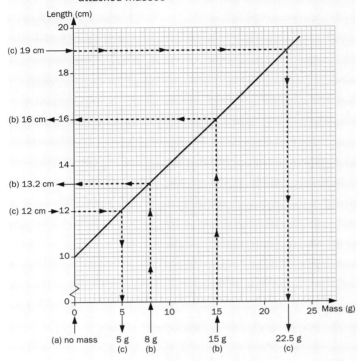

Graph showing the length of a spring for different attached masses

Work out the scale used on each axis.

Across → Mass:
10 'spaces' → 5 g
1 'space' → 5 g ÷ 10
= 0.5 g

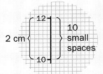

10 small spaces

5 g

Up ↑ Length:
10 'spaces' → 2 cm
1 'space' → 2 cm ÷ 10
= 0.2 cm

2 cm {
10 small spaces

Read values from the graph to answer the questions.
(a) *0 on Mass axis → 10 cm on Length axis.*
The spring was 10 cm long before any masses were hung on it.
(b) *Start on Mass axis each time.*
Read value from Length axis.

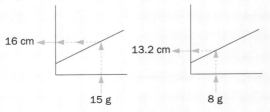

16 cm

15 g

13.2 cm

8 g

(i) 15 g mass gave a spring length of 16 cm.
(ii) 8 g mass gave a spring length of 13.2 cm.

(c) *Start on Length axis each time.*
Read values from Mass axis.

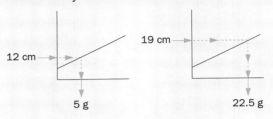

12 cm

5 g

19 cm

22.5 g

(i) 12 cm length was given by a 5 g mass.
(ii) 19 cm length was given by a 22.5 g mass.

The lines drawn on some line graphs have no *real* meaning. They are simply used to help you to see the 'shape' of the graph more easily. These lines are frequently, but not always, drawn dotted. This reminds you that you *cannot* use the lines to find 'in between' values. These graphs usually show *patterns* or *trends*.
Here is an example of a 'jagged-line' graph like this.

Question

Mr Clay has a maximum/minimum thermometer. He uses it to record the highest and lowest temperature in his greenhouse each day. The graph below shows one week's results.

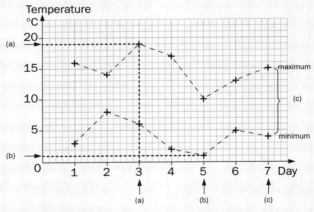

(a) When was the temperature highest?
What was the temperature?
(b) When was the temperature lowest?
What was the temperature?
(c) What was the temperature difference on day 7?

Answer

(a) *Look for the highest point on the graph.*
Read off values for Day and Temperature.
The temperature was highest on Day 3.
It was 19°C.
(b) *Look for the lowest point on the graph.*
Read off values for Day and Temperature.
The temperature was lowest on Day 5.
It was 1°C.

(c) *Read off the Temperatures for Day 7.*
Work out the difference.
$15° - 4° = 11°$
The temperature difference on Day 7 was 11°C.

▶ *Exercise* **A5.1**

1 Use the graph on page 94 showing the results of a stretch test on a spring to answer these questions.
  (a) What should be the length of the spring if these masses were hung on it?
      (i) 10 g   (ii) 13 g   (iii) 19 g   (iv) 24.5 g
  (b) What masses should give these lengths?
      (i) 18 cm   (ii) 11 cm   (iii) 17.2 cm   (iv) 12.4 cm
2 Use the graph on page 94 showing the maximum/minimum temperatures in Mr Clay's greenhouse.
  (a) What were the maximum and minimum temperatures on Day 6?
  (b) When was the minimum temperature 3°C?
  (c) When was the maximum temperature 17°C?
  (d) What was the smallest maximum temperature? On which day did this occur?
  (e) What was the greatest minimum temperature? On which day did this occur?
  (f) Which day had the greatest temperature difference? What was the difference in °C?
  (g) Which day had the smallest temperature difference? What was the difference in °C?
3 This graph shows the stopping distance, in feet, of a car travelling at various speeds, in mph, on both wet and dry roads.

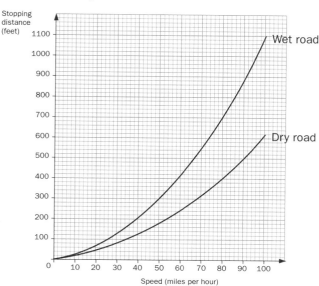

Stopping distance of a car

Use the graph to answer these questions.
  (a) Find the stopping distance on a dry road for a car travelling at
      (i) 90 mph   (ii) 60 mph   (iii) 30 mph.
  (b) Find the speed at which a car was travelling on a wet road when its stopping distance was
      (i) 300 feet   (ii) 720 feet   (iii) 60 feet.

(c) What is the difference between the stopping distances of a car travelling at 70 mph on the M1 motorway on a wet road and on a dry road?

Drawing a graph from data

An experiment, survey, project, exam paper, ... often gives you a table of data. You may need to draw a graph from that data. Use these **key points** to help you.

- **Pencil and ruler**
  Draw the graph in pencil first. Pencil is easy to rub out if you make a mistake or change your mind. You can write numbers, etc., in ink later, if you have time. Use a ruler for straight lines.

- **Squared paper**
  Use squared paper. It makes the graph easier to draw and read.

- **Title**
  Give the graph a title to explain what it is about.

- **Axes**
  You need *two axes* drawn at *right angles* to each other. Each axis must be *clearly labelled*. This may be done for you in an examination. If it is, then *check* the labels and units used. They should be the same as in the table.

  You may have to draw and label the axes yourself. Use the notes on 'Your own axes' on page 97 to help you to do this.

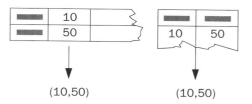

- **Scales**
  Each axis needs a scale (or number line) on it. Often this is given in an examination question. Make sure you know what *each small space* stands for. See 'Your own axes' about choosing your own scales.

- **Coordinates**
  Each pair of values in the table gives the coordinates for a point on the graph. Write down these coordinates if it helps.

▬	10
▬	50

▬	▬
10	50

(10,50)   (10,50)

- **Plot points**
  Use the coordinates to plot points. Mark each point neatly with a small cross **+**. Be as accurate as you can.

  Remember: Start at 0. Go across first.

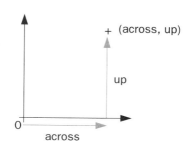

- **Draw lines**
  Decide whether it makes sense to
  join up the points or not. Draw
  straight lines with a ruler. Try
  to make curves as smooth as you can.

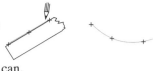

- **Use the graph**
  Now you can use the graph to find values not in the table.
  This is just 'reading the graph'.

Question

(a) Exbridge Motors hire out vans.
The cost depends on the distance
travelled. Some of their hire
charges are shown in this table:

Distance travelled (miles)	50	100	250	300	400
Hire charge (£)	30	60	150	180	240

On the grid below, plot 'Distance travelled' against 'Hire
charge' for these data. Draw a straight line graph through
your points. Label it clearly.

(b) Wyeton Vans also hire out vans.
This table gives some of their
charges. Draw a straight line graph
on the grid below to show their
charges. Label it clearly.

Distance (miles)	Charge (£)
100	90
300	150
500	210

(c) Answer these questions from your
graphs.
  (i) A motorist travels 430 miles in an Exbridge hire van.
  What is the hire charge?
  (ii) A firm pays £215 for a van hired from Exbridge
  Motors.
  How far did the van travel?
  (iii) For what distance do the two firms have the same
  charge?
  What is the charge?

Answer

Check axes

- *Labels:*
  Horizontal axis: 'Distance travelled (miles)'
  Vertical axis: 'Hire charge (£)'

- *Scales:*
  Distance axis: 10 spaces → 100 miles
  1 space → 100 miles ÷ 10
  = 10 miles

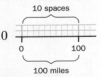

  Charge axis: 10 spaces → £50
  1 space → £50 ÷ 10
  = £5

(a) *Coordinates from the table:*
    Plot points
    Draw line and label it.
    (50,30)
    (100,60)
    (250,150)
    (300,180)
    (400,240)

(b) *Coordinates from the table:*
    Plot points
    Draw line and label it.
    (100,90)
    (300,150)
    (500,210)

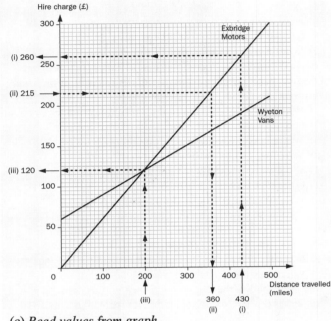

Graph of hire van charges against distance

(c) *Read values from graph.*
    (i)   430 miles → £260
          The hire charge is £260.
    (ii) £215 → 360 miles
          The van travelled 360 miles.
    (iii) *Look for the point where the lines cross*
          (200,120)
          The same charge is for a distance of 200 miles.
          The charge is £120.

The points you plot may not form a perfect straight line or
curve. But they may *suggest* a line.
  Look carefully at the points. Then try to draw the line that
fits them best. It will not go through all of them, just as many
as possible. About the same number of crosses will be above
and below it. Continue your line across most of the grid if you
can.

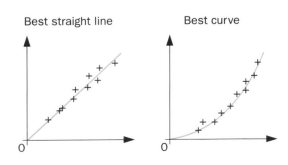

Best straight line   Best curve

Question

Colin poured a cup of tea. As it cooled
he noted the temperature of the tea every
5 minutes.

Here is his table of results:

Time (minutes)	0	5	10	15	20	25	30	35	40	45	50
Temperature (°C)	90	68	60	50	39	35	31	26	22	20	20

(a) Plot a graph to show Colin's results on the grid below.
(b) Use your graph to answer these questions:
   (i)   What was the temperature of the tea after 12 minutes?
   (ii) After how many minutes had the tea cooled to 32°C?
   (iii) What do you think was the temperature of the room?
   (iv) Briefly describe the pattern of cooling of the tea.

Answer

(a) *Draw graph.*
   Remember the key points:
   title, axes, scale, coordinates, points, line.
   Scale: Time axis: 1 space → 1 minute
   Temperature axis: 1 space → 2°C

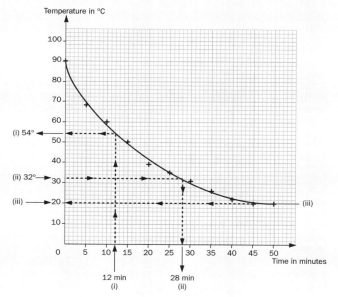

(b) *Read values from graph.*
   (i)   12 minutes → 54°C
         After 12 minutes the temperature was 54°C.
   (ii) 32°C → 28 minutes
         The tea was at 32°C after 28 minutes.
   (iii) The last few 'steady' temperatures were 20°C.
         I think that the room temperature was 20°C.
   (iv) The tea cools down quickly at first. Then it cools
         more gradually. It settles down to room temperature.

Your own axes

You may have to draw, label and number the axes yourself. Use
these points to help you.

- **Draw the two axes at right
  angles first.**
  Leave space to label and
  number them clearly.

  Draw them like this if all the
  values in the data are positive.

  You may have negative values …
  … on both axes,   or on one axis only.

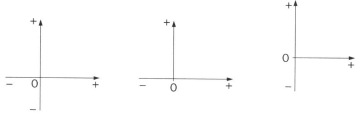

- **Label each axis carefully.**
  The headings in the table tell you the labels and units (if any)
  to use on each axis.
  First values in table   → horizontal axis (across)
  Second values in table → vertical axis (up)

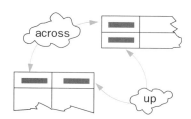

- **Mark a scale (number line) on each axis.**
  Look to see if a question *gives you the scale* to use.
  You will lose marks if you use your own scales instead.

Here are some **hints on choosing your own scales**.
Remember, they do not have to be the same on both axes.

1 Number each axis in
   equal steps. Use the
   'darker lines' on the
   graph paper. It's
   easier.

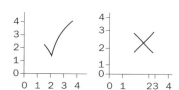

2 Make each 'small space' an *easy value to use*. It is usually
   easier if the numbers go up in 1s or 2s or 5s, 10s, 20s, 50s,
   100s, 200s, 500s, …

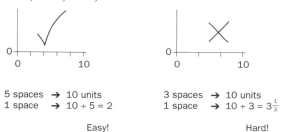

5 spaces → 10 units   3 spaces → 10 units
1 space → 10 ÷ 5 = 2   1 space → 10 ÷ 3 = 3⅓

                Easy!   Hard!

3 Look at the *largest* (and *smallest*) values needed for each axis. Make sure they fit on.

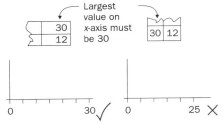

4 Try to make your graph fill most of your grid. The *bigger* the graph, the *more accurate* it can be.

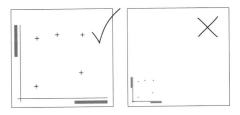

▶ *Exercise* **A5.2**

1 The table below shows record low temperatures each month in London.

Month	J	F	M	A	M	J	J	A	S	O	N	D
Temper-ature °C	⁻10	⁻9	⁻8	⁻2	⁻1	5	7	6	3	⁻4	⁻5	⁻7

(a) On graph paper draw a pair of axes like these:

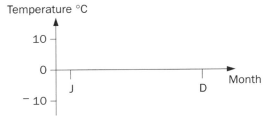

(b) Mark on your graph the points given in the table.
(c) Join the points you have plotted with dotted lines.

Use your graph to answer these questions:

(d) What was the lowest recorded temperature in London for the months of (i) March, (ii) September?
What is the difference between these temperatures in °C?
(e) What is the maximum record low temperature for one month in London?
In which month did this occur?
(f) In which month did London record its lowest temperature? What was the temperature in °C?
(g) Which month's minimum temperature is about half-way between the lowest recorded temperatures for July and November?
What is this temperature?

(h) Do points on the lines joining the points on your graph have any meaning? Give reasons for your answer.

2 This table shows how the electrical resistance of a wire changes with temperature.

Temperature in °C (T)	10	15	25	40	60
Resistance in ohms (R)	4.2	4.4	4.8	5.4	6.2

(a) On 2 mm graph paper draw a pair of axes like these. Use a scale of:
   2 cm represents 10°C on the T-axis,
   and 2 cm represents 0.2 ohms on the R-axis.

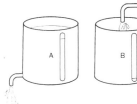

(b) Mark on your graph the five points from the table.
(c) Draw the straight line passing through the five plotted points.
Use your graph to find:
(d) the resistance of the wire when the temperature is:
   (i) 30°C, (ii) 45°C, (iii) 21°C, (iv) 58°C;
(e) the temperature of the wire when its resistance is:
   (i) 4.6 ohms, (ii) 5.2 ohms, (iii) 5.7 ohms.
By extending your graph backwards towards 0°C, estimate the resistance of the wire at 0°C.

3 Two identical cylindrical storage tanks are side by side in a factory. The capacity of each tank is 1000 litres.
   At 9 am one morning tank A is full of liquid and tank B is empty. A computer is programmed to turn two taps on simultaneously. One tap is set to empty tank A at a constant rate. The other tap is set to fill tank B at a constant rate. The two rates are *not* the same.

These two tables show how the amount of liquid changes with time in the two tanks.

Tank A

Time after 9 am, t (minutes)	0	50	100
Amount of liquid in tank, V (litres)	1000	500	0

Tank B

Time after 9 am, t (minutes)	0	60	100
Amount of liquid in tank, V (litres)	0	270	450

(a) Using a scale of 2 cm represents 20 minutes on the t-axis and 2 cm represents 100 litres on the V-axis clearly label and number the axes on a grid.
(b) On these axes plot the points for the values given in each table.
(c) Draw a straight line through each set of points and clearly label each line correctly with either 'Tank A' or Tank B'.
Use your graphs to answer the following questions. Mark your graphs clearly to show how you obtained each answer.

(d) (i) At what time do the two tanks contain the same amount of liquid?
How many litres of liquid is in each tank at this time?
(ii) At 10.25 am which tank contains more liquid? How much more?

Misleading graphs

Graphs do not always give a true picture. They can be misleading. Some graphs give a false impression by accident. But some are designed to deceive. They try to make you believe something that isn't true. So watch out. Don't be taken in.

Things to look out for are:

● No title – What's the graph about?
● No labels on axes – What does each axis measure? What units, if any, are used?
● Misleading labels on axes – Does the label actually tell you about that axis?
● No scale on axes – What size are the values?
● A 'strange' scale – Has it been numbered correctly? Is it too crowded or spread out?
● A scale not starting at zero – Has this distorted the picture?

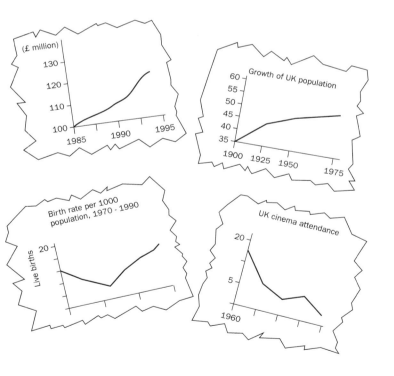

► *Exercise* **A5.3**

Look at the graphs shown above.
Say what is misleading about each graph.

There are usually plenty of misleading graphs in the media (TV, newspapers, magazines …) Make a 'rogue's gallery' of those you find. Point out what is wrong with them. ◄

1 The cost, £y, of hiring a car for x days is shown in the graph.

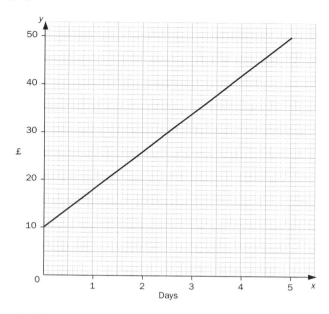

(a) Write down the cost of hiring a car for 2 days.
(b) Work out the number of days that a car could be hired for £34.
(c) A car is hired for 5 days. Work out the average cost of the car per day.

(ULEAC, 1989)

2 The graph shows the sales of a newly released compact disc over a period of 6 weeks.

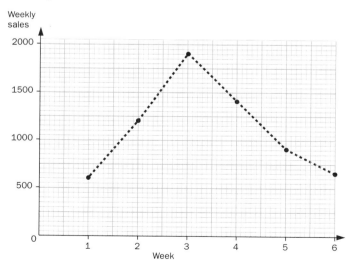

(a) How many discs were sold in the second week?
(b) After how may weeks did the total number of discs sold exceed 5000?
(c) How many discs were sold altogether during these 6 weeks?

(SEG, 1990)

3 A biologist studied how light affects leaf growth. This diagram shows the areas of two leaves during their growth.

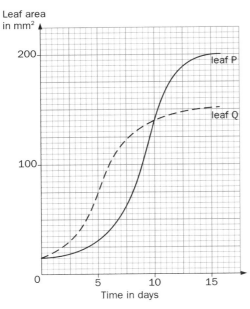

(a) Which leaf grew faster at first?
(b) Write down the area of the larger leaf after 15 days.
(c) After how many days did both leaves have the same area?

(MEG, 1990)

4 Meryl takes part in a medical experiment to show the danger of drivers drinking alcohol. She drinks some alcohol and blows into a breathalyser. Her alcohol level is 140 mg/mℓ. The doctors breathalyse her every hour. Here are her results:

Time	10.00	11.00	12.00	1.00	2.00	3.00
Result	140	132	124	116	108	100

(a) Plot these results on a graph.
(Mark the Time axis from 10.00 to 6.00.
Use a scale of 2 cm to 1 hour.
Mark the Alcohol Level axis from 60 to 140.
Use a scale of 1 cm to 10 mg/mℓ.)
(b) What is her alcohol level at 12.30?
(c) It is illegal, and very dangerous, for someone to drive if their alcohol level is above 80 mg/mℓ.
At what time will Meryl's alcohol level be 80 mg/mℓ?

(WJEC, 1989)

5 The percentage of male smokers in Britain for the years 1972 to 1986 are shown in the table.

1972	1974	1976	1978	1980	1982	1984	1986
52%	51%	46%	45%	42%	40%	37%	36%

(a) Estimate the percentage who smoked in 1975.
(b) Plot points to represent this information.
(c) Draw a straight line through the points for 1976 and 1986. Use it to estimate the percentage who will be smoking in 1992.

(d) Assuming that the line represents the percentages beyond 1992, estimate when the percentages will reach zero.

(MEG, 1989)

6 John threw a cricket ball. The table shows several positions of the ball.

Horizontal distance from John in metres (x)	0	5	10	15	20	25	30	35	40
Height above ground in metres (y)	1.7	4.6	6.8	8.1	8.7	8.4	7.4	5.6	3.0

(a) Plot these values on a graph and join your points with a smooth curve.
(Mark the *x*-axis from 0 to 40.
Use a scale of 2 cm to 5 units.
Mark the *y*-axis from 0 to 10.
Use a scale of 2 cm to 2 units.)
(b) Use your graph to answer the following:
(i) What is the greatest height reached by the ball?
(ii) How far horizontally is the ball from John when it is 5 m above the ground?
(iii) Estimate how far the ball is from John when it hits the ground.

(MEG, 1991)

7 (a) Give two criticisms of this graph.
(b) From the graph, estimate the number of building societies in 1980.

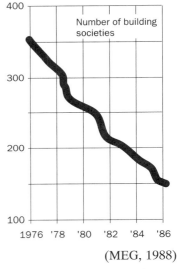

(MEG, 1988)

8 Write down TWO ways in which this graph is misleading.

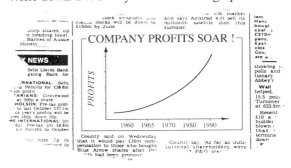

(SEG, 1991)

A6
Solving simple equations

This unit will help you to:

■ solve linear equations by a suitable method, e.g. inspections, trial and improvement, balancing flow diagrams.

Equations

An **equation** is a true statement containing an **equals sign** (=). It shows that two quantities (the *left-hand side* and the *right-hand side*) are equal. For example,

$$7 + 5 = 12 \quad \text{and} \quad 5 + 2 = 10 - 3$$

are *arithmetic* equations.

An **algebraic equation** contains letter(s) standing for unknown value(s). For example,

$$y = 7x + 1, \quad y = 2x^2, \quad x^3 - 8 = 0$$

are *algebraic* equations.

A **solution** of an equation is a number which, when put instead of the letter, *makes the equation true*. A solution of an equation is said to **satisfy** the equation.

To **check** a solution of an equation, substitute the value for the letter in the equation. The left-hand side and right-hand side should be equal in value. For example,

$x^3 - 8 = 0$ has the solution $x = 2$

Check:

LHS $\rightarrow x^3 - 8 = (2)^3 - 8 = 8 - 8 = 0$
RHS $\rightarrow 0$
LHS = RHS ✓

Linear equations

A **linear equation** has *no squares* or *higher powers* of the unknown(s). For example,

$$y = 7x + 1 \quad \text{and} \quad x - 9 = 10 \quad \text{are linear equations.}$$

The *simplest* type of linear equation has only *one* unknown, that is, only one letter. All the terms are 'letter terms in that unknown' and numbers. For example,

$x - 9 = 10$ is a linear equation in x,
$2y + 7 = 3y$ is a linear equation in y.

A linear equation with only *one* unknown has only *one* solution. For example,

$4 + x = 11$ has the solution $x = 7$ because $4 + 7 = 11$.

A simple linear equation can be solved by **inspection**, **trial and improvement**, **graph** or **balancing**.

An examination question may tell you which method to use. If it does, do not waste time doing it any other way. You cannot be given marks for the working, even if it is correct. If you can choose, use the *most accurate* and quickest way for you.

Always make sure that you show your working clearly. Check your answer by substituting it in the *original equation*.

Solving by inspection

Your knowledge of numbers helps you to spot some solutions quickly. Think about what the equation 'says' in words. Then work out which number fits it.

Here are some examples.

To solve	$x + 5 = 9$,
think	'What do I add to 5 to get 9?'
You know	$4 + 5 = 9$,
So	$x = 4$.

To solve	$8 - x = 6$,
think	'What do I subtract from 8 to get 6?'
You know	$8 - 2 = 6$,
so	$x = 2$.

To solve	$7x = 35$,
think	'What do I multiply by 7 to get 35?'
You know	$7 \times 5 = 35$,
so	$x = 5$.

To solve	$\frac{x}{4} = 3$
think	'What do I divide by 4 to get 3?'
You know	$12 \div 4 = 3$,
so	$x = 12$.

▶ *Exercise* **A6.1**

Solve these equations by inspection.

1	$x + 3 = 10$	**4**	$8 + x = 14$	**7**	$3x = 9$
2	$x - 5 = 3$	**5**	$13 - x = 2$	**8**	$5x = 15$
3	$\frac{x}{2} = 4$	**6**	$\frac{x}{4} = 2$	**9**	$\frac{x}{3} = 6$

Solving by trial and improvement

Solving a linear equation by **trial and improvement** is often easy to do. You can do the working quickly with a calculator. The **basic strategy** is always the same:

● Try a number instead of the letter in the equation. Look at the result it gives.
● If the result is what you want, then the number you tried is the solution.
● If the result is not what you want, then use it to help you to make a better 'try' next.

To help you choose a better number to try, use these guidelines.
● Compare the result with what you want.
  If your result was too big, choose a smaller 'try' next.
  If your result was too small, choose a larger 'try' next.

- Look for *opposite* results:
    Result *too big* then result *too small*, or
    result *too small* then result *too big*.
  When you get two opposite results like these, you know that
  a solution is between the two numbers you tried.

  Start with a *'sensible' guess* at the solution. Use the numbers
  in the equation to give you a clue. Keep a neat record of your
  tries. The answer below shows one way to do this in a table.
  Using a **number line** also helps you to choose what to try next.

  Each time you try a number, mark it on the line. Use the result
  it gives (*too big* or *too small*) to shade the part of the number
  line you no longer need to try. This gives a useful picture of
  what you are doing.

  Note: In the answers below a series of tables and number lines
  is drawn. These show the working step-by-step. In your answer
  you would fill in values in just one table and one number line.

Question

Solve $4x - 7 = 61$ by trial and improvement.
Show your 'tries' and results clearly.

Answer

Decide how to work out $4x - 7$ on your calculator first.

Try this: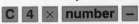

See if it works on your calculator.

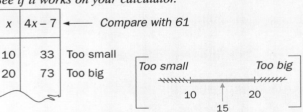

x is between 10 and 20.
Try 15, half-way between.

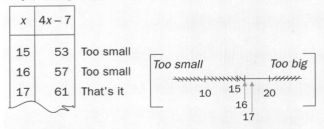

So $x = 17$ is the solution.

The solutions to some equations are not whole numbers. Find
their *whole number part first*. Then find their *tenths next*, then
any *hundredths*, and so on …

Question

Solve $6x + 5 = 28$ by trial and improvement. Give your
answer to 1 decimal place. Show your working clearly.

Answer

Try this key code on your calculator.

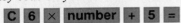

Find the best way to do the working on your calculator.

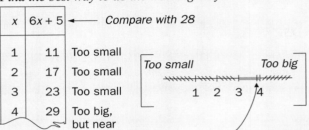

x is between 3 and 4 but nearer to 4, try 3.9

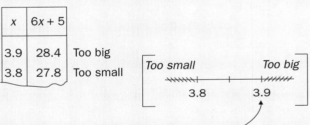

x is between 3.8 and 3.9, try 3.85

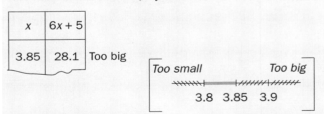

x is between 3.8 and 3.85 on the unshaded part of the line.
This shows it is nearer to 3.8 than 3.9.

So $x = 3.8$ (to 1 dp)

► *Exercise* A6.2

Solve these equations by 'trial and improvement'.
Show your 'tries' and results clearly.

1	$3x - 2 = 40$	**6**	$77 - 2x = 23$
2	$5x + 4 = 84$	**7**	$7x - 8 = 104$
3	$2x - 7 = 59$	**8**	$23 + 3x = 86$
4	$6x - 5 = 133$	**9**	$168 = 9x - 3$
5	$4 + 3x = 55$	**10**	$108 = 56 + 4x$

► *Exercise* A6.3

Solve these equations by trial and improvement. Give your
answers to 1 decimal place. Show how you obtained your
answers.

1	$3x + 2 = 13$	**4**	$5 + 3x = 12$
2	$6x - 7 = 10$	**5**	$7 + 9x = 20$
3	$7x + 9 = 17$	**6**	$12x - 5 = 18$

Solving by graph

You can solve a **linear equation** by drawing a **straight line graph**. The *x-coordinate* of the point where the line cuts the *x*-axis (i.e. $y = 0$) gives the *solution. Check* your answer by substituting the value into the original equation.

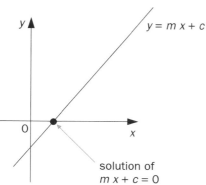

solution of $mx + c = 0$

Question

The diagram shows the graph of $y = 2x - 3$. Explain how to use the graph to solve the equation $2x - 3 = 0$.

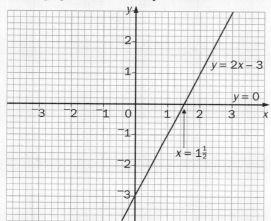

Answer

The graph of $y = 2x - 3$ *cuts the x-axis where* $y = 0$. *So the solution of the equation* $2x - 3 = 0$ *is the x-coordinate of the point where the line cuts the x-axis.*

The line cuts the *x*-axis where $x = 1\frac{1}{2}$.

So $x = 1\frac{1}{2}$ is the solution of $2x - 3 = 0$.

Check: $y = 2x - 3 = (2 \times 1\frac{1}{2}) - 3 = 3 - 3 = 0$ ✓

It is important to remember that solutions from graphs are often *only approximate*. Their accuracy depends on many factors: the scale on the *x*-axis, the accuracy of drawing, the size of the solution, ...

Solving by balancing

An equation is like a set of scales *in balance*.

The quantities on the left-hand side (LHS) balance and are *equal* to the quantities on the right-hand side (RHS). The equation, like the scales, will still balance if you do **exactly the same to each side**.

The balance will be unchanged if you:

(a) add the *same* quantity to *each side*,
(b) subtract the *same* quantity from *each side*,
(c) multiply *each side* by the *same* quantity,
(d) divide *each side* by the *same* quantity (not zero).

You can use these 'common sense' ideas of balancing to help you to solve equations.

When solving an equation you want all the 'letter terms' on one side of the equals sign and all the 'number terms' on the other.

i.e.   'letter terms' = 'number terms'

To obtain this you may need to get rid of some *unwanted* terms from each side of the equation. You must decide whether to add or subtract to get rid of these terms. The **inverses of + and −** help you to do this.

The inverse of + is −. So to get rid of a '+ term' use the matching '− term' For example,

to get rid of '+ 2', use '−2' because $+ 2 - 2 = 0$.

The inverse of − is +. So to get rid of a '− term' use the matching '+ term'. For example,

to get rid of '−5', use '+5' because $- 5 + 5 = 0$.

Remember: You must do the *same to each side* of the equation to keep it 'in balance'.
Always *check* your answer by *substitution*.

Question

Solve (a) $x + 8 = 13$ (b) $x - 7 = 3$

Answer

(a) *To get rid of +8,*
    use −8 on both sides

$$\begin{array}{r} x + 8 = 13 \\ -8 \quad -8 \\ \hline x \quad = 5 \end{array}$$

Check LHS: $x + 8 = 5 + 8 = 13$
RHS: 13   LHS = RHS ✓

(b) *To get rid of −7,*
    use +7 on both sides

$$\begin{array}{r} x - 7 = 3 \\ +7 \quad +7 \\ \hline x \quad = 10 \end{array}$$

Check LHS: $x - 7 = 10 - 7 = 3$
RHS: 3   LHS = RHS ✓

▶ *Exercise* **A6.4**

Solve each of these equations by balancing.

1 (a) $x + 3 = 10$
   (b) $x + 5 = 7$
   (c) $y + 9 = 12$
   (d) $p + 1 = 5$
   (e) $10 + r = 18$
   (f) $6 + s = 9$
   (g) $w + 15 = 20$
   (h) $13 + d = 13$

2 (a) $x - 4 = 8$
   (b) $y - 6 = 10$
   (c) $m - 1 = 9$
   (d) $a - 11 = 19$
   (e) $p - 17 = 25$
   (f) $r - 10 = 10$
   (g) $z - 13 = 18$
   (h) $q - 9 = 16$

3 (a) $7 + x = 20$
   (b) $31 = m + 12$
   (c) $n - 8 = 30$
   (d) $37 = m - 14$
   (e) $30 = n + 17$
   (f) $a - 12 = 24$
   (g) $35 = s - 19$
   (h) $16 = 15 + a$

When solving an equation you want to have the letter 'on its own'. *Remember: x means 1x.*

The 'letter term' may have a coefficient that is not 1. For example,

$3x$ has a coefficient of 3; it means $3 \times x$

$\frac{x}{2}$ has a coefficient of $\frac{1}{2}$; it means $x \div 2$.

You must decide whether to *multiply* or *divide* to make the coefficient equal to 1. The **inverses of** $\times$ **and** $\div$ help you to do this.

The inverse of $\times$ is $\div$. So to 'undo' a multiplication, use a matching division. For example,

to 'undo' $3 \times x$, use $\div 3$, because $3 \div 3 = 1$

The inverse of $\div$ is $\times$. So to 'undo' a division, use a matching multiplication. For example,

to 'undo' $\frac{x}{2}$, use $\times 2$ because $\frac{1}{2} \times 2 = 1$

Question

Solve (a) $4n = 10$ (b) $\frac{p}{7} = 5$

Answer

(a) *To 'undo'* $\times 4$*, use* $\div 4$

$$4n = 10$$

So divide each side by 4

$$\frac{4n}{4} = \frac{10}{4}$$

$$n = 2.5$$

Check LHS: $4 \times 2.5 = 10$
    RHS: 10   LHS = RHS ✓

(b) *To 'undo'* $\div 7$*, use* $\times 7$

$$\frac{p}{7} = 5$$

So multiply each side by 7

$$\frac{p}{7} \times 7 = 5 \times 7$$

$$p = 35$$

Check LHS: $\frac{p}{7} = \frac{35}{7} = 5$

    RHS: 5   LHS = RHS ✓

► Exercise A6.5

Solve each of these equations by balancing.

1 (a) $5n = 20$ (c) $7p = 21$ (e) $4w = 36$ (g) $9m = 63$
   (b) $6x = 48$ (d) $3r = 27$ (f) $8s = 40$ (h) $5q = 45$

2 (a) $\frac{x}{2} = 3$ (c) $\frac{a}{4} = 9$ (e) $\frac{m}{7} = 13$ (g) $\frac{c}{3} = 15$

   (b) $\frac{y}{3} = 5$ (d) $\frac{b}{2} = 12$ (f) $\frac{p}{10} = 1$ (h) $\frac{r}{6} = 4$

3 (a) $12m = 36$ (c) $20 = 8a$ (e) $\frac{s}{2} = 1.5$ (g) $9w = 13.5$

   (b) $\frac{y}{9} = 11$ (d) $4 = \frac{b}{8}$ (f) $42 = 12p$ (h) $4.5 = \frac{t}{6}$

Linear equations often involve **more than one operation**. For example,

$2x - 3 = 15$

involves multiplication ($2 \times x$) and subtraction (-3).

So *more than one inverse operation* is needed to solve such an equation. The *order* in which the operations are 'undone' is important.

Get rid of 'unwanted terms' by *adding or subtracting first*. Then get the letter 'on its own' by *multiplying or dividing*. Write out each step in full. This may help you to avoid making mistakes.

Question

Solve the equation $8x - 13 = 11$

Answer

To get rid of –13,
use +13 on both sides

$$\begin{array}{rr} 8x - 13 = & 11 \\ + 13 & + 13 \\ \hline 8x \quad = & 24 \end{array}$$

To 'undo' $\times 8$*, use* $\div 8$
Divide each side by 8

$$\frac{8x}{8} = \frac{24}{8}$$

$$x = 3$$

Check LHS: $8x - 13 = 8 \times 3 - 13$
          $= 24 - 13$
          $= 11$
    RHS: 11   LHS = RHS ✓

► Exercise A6.6

Solve each of these equations.

1 $2x + 9 = 13$ 6 $7b + 15 = 8$
2 $3y - 6 = 15$ 7 $6n - 19 = 5$
3 $20 = 4a + 8$ 8 $19 - 2p = 7$
4 $6r - 3 = 15$ 9 $7 = 21 - 4q$
5 $5x - 9 = 1$ 10 $21 = 13 - 4m$

Sometimes letters and numbers are on *both* sides of an equation. For example,

$4x + 5 = 14 + x$

In these examples, group all the 'letter terms' on one side of the equation first. Then solve the equation as before. Always check your solution.

Question

Solve $7x - 4 = 2x + 6$

Answer

To get rid of 2x,
use –2x on both sides

To get rid of –4,
use + 4 on both sides
To undo $\times 5$ *use* $\div 5$

$$\begin{array}{rr} 7x - 4 = & 2x + 6 \\ -2x & -2x \\ \hline 5x - 4 = & \quad 6 \\ + 4 & + 4 \\ \hline 5x \quad = & 10 \end{array}$$

Divide each side by 5

$$\frac{5x}{5} = \frac{10}{5}$$
$$x = 2$$

Check LHS: $7x - 4 = 7 \times 2 - 4 = 14 - 4 = 10$
RHS: $2x + 6 = 2 \times 2 + 6 = 4 + 6 = 10$

LHS = RHS✓

Usually we group all the 'letter terms' on the left-hand side . Sometimes it is easier to group them on the right-hand side. With practice you will be able to spot which side to choose. Often it is the side with the 'larger letter term'. This will give you a '+ letter term' which is easier to deal with.

Question

Solve the equation $5 - y = 6y - 9$

Answer

To get rid of $-y$,
 use $+y$ on both sides

$$5 - y = 6y - 9$$
$$ +y \quad +y$$

To get rid of -9,
 use $+9$ on both sides

$$5 = 7y - 9$$
$$+9 \qquad +9$$

To 'undo' $\times 7$, use $\div 7$

$$14 = 7y$$

Divide each side by 7

$$\frac{14}{7} = \frac{7y}{7}$$
$$2 = y$$

Check LHS: $5 - y = 5 - 2 = 3$
RHS: $6y - 9 = 6 \times 2 - 9 = 12 - 9 = 3$

LHS = RHS ✓

► *Exercise* **A6.7**

Solve these equations
1 $8x + 1 = 5x + 7$
2 $7y - 3 = 3y + 5$
3 $4c + 3 = c + 9$
4 $2n - 5 = n + 7$
5 $3r + 1 = 19 - 3r$
6 $5 - 6s = 10s - 11$
7 $4p + 7 = 2p + 15$
8 $9 - 3m = 1 - m$
9 $5d + 7 = d - 1$
10 $15 - 8z = 7 - 9z$ ◄

Equations with brackets

Brackets are used to group terms together. A number in front of the brackets multiplies everything inside the brackets.

For example,

$$3(x - 7) \quad \text{means} \quad 3 \times (x - 7)$$

In some equations with brackets, the number multiplying the brackets divides exactly into all the terms outside the brackets. Dividing throughout by this number first makes the equation easier to solve.

Question

Solve the equation $3(x - 7) = 15$

Answer

To 'undo' $\times 3$, use $\div 3$,
Divide each side by 3

$$3(x - 7) = 15$$
$$\frac{3(x - 7)}{3} = \frac{15}{3}$$
$$(x - 7) = 5$$

Remove brackets
$+7$ to both sides

$$x - 7 = 5$$
$$+7 \qquad +7$$
$$x = 12$$

Check LHS: $3(x - 7) = 3(12 - 7) = 3 \times 5 = 15$
RHS: 15

LHS = RHS✓

► *Exercise* **A6.8**

Solve these equations
1 $4(x + 3) = 20$
2 $3(r - 2) = 9$
3 $2(m - 5) = 14$
4 $5(y - 4) = 15$
5 $7(p + 3) = 49$
6 $9 = 2(r - 2)$
7 $12 = 3(2z + 3)$
8 $4(2m + 3) = 8$
9 $10 = 5(3s - 1)$
10 $9(5q + 2) = 18$ ◄

To solve some equations with brackets, you have to remove the brackets first. Collect any like terms together next. Then solve the equation and check your solution as usual.

Remember: To remove brackets, multiply each of the terms inside the brackets by the term outside the brackets.
For example,

$$5(2x + 3) = 5 \times 2x + 5 \times 3$$
$$= 10x + 15$$

Question

Solve $3(3p - 8) = 4(p - 1)$

Answer

Remove brackets
$-4p$ from both sides

$$3(3p - 8) = 4(p - 1)$$
$$9p - 24 = 4p - 4$$
$$-4p \qquad -4p$$
$$5p - 24 = -4$$

$+24$ to both sides

$$+24 \qquad +24$$
$$5p = 20$$

Divide each side by 5

$$p = 4$$

Check LHS: $3(3p - 8) = 3(3 \times 4 - 8) = 3 \times 4 = 12$
RHS: $4(p - 1) = 4(4 - 1)$
$= 4 \times 3$
$= 12$

LHS = RHS✓

Take care when there is a $-$ sign *outside* the bracket. When this happens the signs that were *inside* the brackets change when the brackets are removed.
For example,

$$-5(2x + 3) = (-5) \times 2x + (-5) \times 3$$
$$= -10x - 15$$

Question

Solve the equation $3(5v - 4) - 2(2v - 7) = 13$

Answer

Remove brackets

$$3(5v - 4) - 2(2v - 7) = 13$$

Remember $-2 \times -7 = +14$

$$15v - 12 - 4v + 14 = 13$$

Collect like terms

$$11v + 2 = 13$$

−2 from both sides

$$\begin{array}{r} -2 \quad -2 \\ \hline 11v = 11 \end{array}$$

Divide each side by 11

$$v = 1$$

Check LHS: $\quad 3(5v - 4) - 2(2v - 7)$
$\qquad = 3(5 - 4) - 2(2 - 7) = 3 + 10 = 13$
$\quad$ RHS: 13 $\quad$ LHS = RHS ✓

▶ *Exercise* A6.9

Solve these equations.

1. $5(2x - 3) = 2x + 1$
2. $3n + 17 = 2(4n + 1)$
3. $3(w + 5) - 14 = 25$
4. $16 = 5(3x - 1) - 9$
5. $9a - 2(a + 7) = 35$
6. $7x - 3 = 4(3 - 2x)$
7. $2(2n - 3) = 3 - 5n$
8. $1 + 8r = 5(3r - 4)$
9. $5b = 2(3 - 4b) + 20$
10. $16 - 3(2c - 4) = 3c + 1$
11. $4(4a + 1) = 3(5a + 6)$
12. $7(y + 1) = 4(2y - 1)$
13. $3(p - 4) + 2(p + 1) = 5$
14. $5(3x - 2) + 3(1 - 4x) = 2$
15. $2(r + 4) = r - 2$
16. $7(s - 4) = 3(2s - 2)$
17. $2(1 - 3b) - 3(2b - 5) = 17$
18. $3(2m + 1) = 4(3m - 1)$
19. $4(x - 1) - 2(x + 1) = 3$
20. $5(1 + 2z) = 4(3z + 1)$

Equations involving fractions

An equation involving a **fraction** is easier to solve when the fraction has been removed. You can do this by multiplying *every term* in the equation by the *denominator* of the fraction. Do not try to do too many steps at a time. *Check* your solution as before.

Question

Solve the equations (a) $\dfrac{2s}{3} = 7$ (b) $\dfrac{4w - 1}{7} = 3$.

Answer

(a)

$$\frac{2s}{3} = 7$$

Multiply each side by 3

$$3 \times \frac{2s}{3} = 3 \times 7$$

$$2s = 21$$

Divide each side by 2

$$\frac{2s}{2} = \frac{21}{2}$$

$$s = 10.5$$

Check LHS: $\dfrac{2s}{3} = \dfrac{2 \times 10.5}{3} = \dfrac{21}{3} = 7$
$\qquad$ RHS: 7 $\quad$ LHS = RHS ✓

(b)

$$\frac{4w - 1}{7} = 3$$

Use brackets

$$\frac{(4w - 1)}{7} = 3$$

Multiply both sides by 7

$$7 \times \frac{(4w - 1)}{7} = 7 \times 3$$

$$(4w - 1) = 21$$

+ 1 to both sides

$$\begin{array}{r} +1 \quad +1 \\ \hline 4w = 22 \end{array}$$

Divide each side by 4

$$\frac{4w}{4} = \frac{22}{4}$$

$$w = 5.5$$

Check LHS = RHS when $w = 5.5$

▶ *Exercise* A6.10

Solve these equations.

1. (a) $\dfrac{2x}{5} = 3$ (c) $\dfrac{5n}{2} = 20$

   (b) $\dfrac{4a}{3} = 10$ (d) $\dfrac{3p}{2} = 6$

2. (a) $\dfrac{x + 3}{2} = 4$ (c) $\dfrac{c - 1}{7} = 2$

   (b) $\dfrac{d - 2}{2} = 5$ (d) $\dfrac{2y - 1}{3} = 5$

3. (a) $3 = \dfrac{2n}{7}$ (c) $\dfrac{10m}{3} = 5$

   (b) $\dfrac{3r + 2}{7} = 2$ (d) $1 = \dfrac{2p - 5}{3}$

Solving by flow diagrams

Another way to solve an equation is to use a **flow diagram** and its **inverse diagram**. You can use this way to solve linear equations such as

$$5x - 4 = 31.$$

You draw a flow diagram to make the **expression**. Then you work out the *inverse of each step* for its inverse diagram.

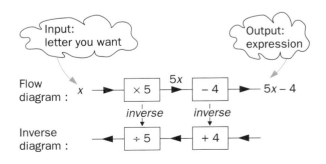

The equation gives: 'expression' = number.
The *expression* is the *output from the flow diagram*.
The *number* is the *input for the inverse diagram*.

Starting with this **input** you work through the inverse diagram step-by-step.

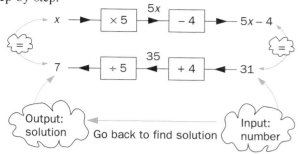

The **output** of the inverse diagram is the value of the letter. This is the **solution of the equation**.

So the solution of $5x - 4 = 31$ is $x = 7$.

Always check your solution by substituting it into the equation.

Check: if $x = 7$, $5x - 4 = 5 \times 7 - 4 = 31$ ✓

 Exercise **A6.11**

Use flow diagrams to solve these equations.

1 $a + 7 = 9$

2 $5x = 7.5$

3 $2p - 5 = 1$

4 $11 - 3y = 14$

5 $3(x - 4) = 10.5$

6 $9 - 3(7 - x) = 3$

7 $\dfrac{7x - 2}{13} = 2$

8 $\dfrac{9}{c} = 2$

9 $\sqrt{5m + 1} = 4$

10 $\dfrac{3}{x - 2} = 1$

Examination Questions

1 Solve the equation $8 + 3x = 20$. (NEAB, 1988)

2 Solve the equations
(a) $5z = 18$ (b) $8 + 3w = 14$ (MEG, 1988)

3 Solve the equation $3x + 4x = 5x + 6$. (MEG, 1990)

4 Solve the equations
(a) $4(x - 2) = 18$ (b) $5 - 3x = {}^{-}7$ (MEG, 1991)

5 Solve the equations
(a) $2x - 5 = 10$ (b) $3(1 - 2x) = 21$ (NEAB, 1989)

6 Solve these equations
(a) $2x = 5$ (b) $3y + 7 = 1$ (c) $2(9 - 5z) = 28$ (MEG, 1990)

7 Solve the equations
(a) $3(x + 2) = {}^{-}6$ (b) $\dfrac{2x}{5} = 5$ (WJEC, 1990)

8 Solve the equations
(a) $4 + 3x = 37$ (b) $\dfrac{x - 2}{5} = 9$ (NEAB, 1990)

9 Solve the equation
$\dfrac{1 - 3x}{5} = 2$ (NEAB, 1988)

10 Solve the equations
(a) $2x + 7 = 12$ (b) $7 - 2x = 19$ (MEG, 1988)

11 Solve the equations
(a) $3x + 4 = {}^{-}14$ (b) $5(3 - 2x) = 30$
(NEAB, 1989)

A7
Solving simple problems with algebra

This unit will help you to:

■ solve a problem by forming and solving an equation.

Algebra is often used to **solve problems** given in words and sentences. Here is a useful **strategy** to help you to solve such problems.

1 *Read* the information given *carefully*. Decide on what are the unknown quantities that you have to find. Use diagrams if they help to sort out the information.

2 *Choose a letter* to stand for one unknown quantity you have to find. Sometimes there is more than one unknown. Try to use the information given to write each unknown in terms of this letter. Some problems will have units of measurement such as metres or centimetres in them. Make sure that all the expressions are in the *same units*.

3 Use the information given to find *two equal expressions*. At least one must use the letter you have chosen. Write these expressions as an equation.

4 *Solve the equation* you have made. Use the solution to *answer the question*, in words.

5 *Check your answer*. Use the original information in the problem in your check. Do not simply check your answer in your equation! You may have made a mistake when you formed the equation.

Question

In 1978 a '2nd class stamp' cost x pence and a '1st class stamp' cost 2 pence more.
(a) Write down, in terms of x, the cost of a '1st class stamp' in 1978.
(b) In June 1978, Tim bought 20 stamps; 11 were 2nd class stamps and the rest were '1st class'.
Write down an expression in terms of x for the total cost of the stamps.
(c) The stamps cost Tim £1.58. Use this fact to write an equation in x. Solve the equation to find the value of x.
(d) What was the cost of
(i) a 2nd class stamp   (ii) a 1st class stamp?

Answer

(a) A 1st class stamp costs $(x + 2)$ pence.
(b) 11 2nd class stamps cost : $11x$ pence
9 1st class stamps cost : $9(x + 2)$ pence
Total cost: $11x + 9(x + 2) = 11x + 9x + 18$
$= (20x + 18)$ pence
(c) Total cost : £1.58 = 158 pence
So, $20x + 18 = 158$

Solution of this equation:

By balancing
$20x + 18 = 158$
$\quad\;\; - 18 \quad -18$
$\overline{\quad 20x \qquad = 140}$
$\div 20 \quad \dfrac{20x}{20} = \dfrac{140}{20}$
$x = 7$

By trial and improvement		
x	$20x + 18$	Compare with 158
10	218	Too big
5	118	Too small
6	138	Too small
7	158	That's it!
	$x = 7$	

(d) (i) 2nd class: 7 pence
(ii) 1st class: 9 pence
Check 2nd class: $11 \times 7 = 77$
1st class: $9 \times 9 = 81$
Total $\overline{158}$ pence ✓

▶ *Exercise* A7.1

1   A biro costs 55p more than a pencil. The cost of a pencil is x pence.
(a) Write down, in terms of x, the cost of:
(i) a biro   (ii) 5 pencils   (iii) 3 biros.
(b) Five pencils and three biros cost £4.05. Use this information to write down an equation in terms of x.
(c) Solve the equation to find x.
(d) What is the cost of
(i) a pencil   (ii) a biro?
2   Tom's mother was 24 years old when Tom was born. Now she is twice as old as Tom. Tom is now n years old.
(a) Write down the present age of Tom's mother, in terms of n, in two different ways.
(b) Write down an equation connecting the two ways you found in (a).
(c) Solve your equation to find n.

(d) What are the present ages of
(i) Tom   (ii) Tom's mother?
3   In Julie's purse there are x 5p coins, twice as many 10p coins and six 2p coins. She has no other coins. Altogether Julie has £1.37 in her purse. How many 5p and 10p coins does Julie have in her purse?
4   Giles is twice as old as Ben and Sue is 5 years older than Ben. Ben is aged x years.
(a) Write down Giles's age in terms of x.
(b) Write down Sue's age in terms of x.
(c) The sum of all three ages is 73 years. Write this statement down as an equation in x and simplify it.
(d) Solve the equation to find x.
(e) How old are Giles, Ben and Sue?
5   Wayne and Sarah deliver newspapers. In an average week, Wayne earns £x. Sarah earns £3 more.
(a) Write down Sarah's average weekly earnings in terms of x.
Sarah's older sister Pat also delivers newspapers. She earns as much as Wayne and Sarah's wages put together.
(b) Find an expression for Pat's average weekly earnings in terms of x.
(c) The average weekly earnings of all three people added together are £26.
Write down this information as an equation in x and simplify it.
(d) Solve the equation to find x.
(e) What is each person's average weekly earnings?

When making up an equation or formula you may be able to use a relationship or rule you know. For example,

the perimeter of a shape is the sum of the lengths of its sides,
the angles of a quadrilateral add up to 360°,
the area of a rectangle is its length × its width.

So look for relationships like these in the question.

Question

The length of a rectangular field is 25 metres more than its width. The perimeter of the field is 450 metres. What is the actual width and length of the field?

Answer

Let the width of the field be x metres.
The length is 25 metres more than the width.
So the length of the field is $(x + 25)$ metres.

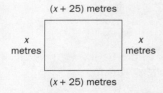

The perimeter of the field in metres is

$$(x + 25) + x + (x + 25) + x$$

But the actual perimeter is given as 450 metres, so

$$(x + 25) + x + (x + 25) + x = 450$$

Solve this equation to find *x*:

Remove brackets	$x + 25 + x + x + 25 + x = 450$
Collect like terms	$4x + 50 = 450$
Subtract 50 from	
each side	$4x + 50 - 50 = 450 - 50$
	$4x = 400$
Divide each side	$\dfrac{4x}{4} = \dfrac{400}{4}$
by 4	
	$x = 100$

The width of the field is 100 metres.
The length of the field is (100 + 25) metres = 125 metres.

Check: The perimeter of the field is
  100 m + 125 m + 100 m + 125 m = 450 m ✓

► *Exercise* **A7.2**

1 For each of these shapes
  (i)   write down an equation in *x*,
  (ii)   solve the equation to find *x*,
  (iii)   find the 'missing' dimensions.

(a) Square   (b) Equilateral triangle

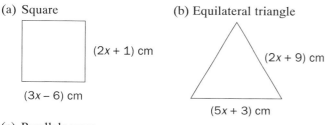

(c) Parallelogram

(d) Isosceles triangle

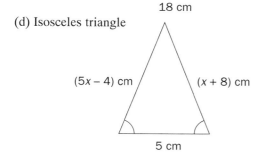

2 The perimeter of this isosceles triangle is 14 cm.
  (a) Write down an equation in *x*.
  (b) Solve the equation to find *x*.
  (c) What are the dimensions
      of the triangle?

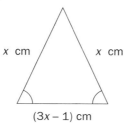

3 For each of these diagrams
  (i)   write down an equation in *x*,
  (ii)   solve the equation to find *x*,
  (iii)   find the size of each 'marked' angle.

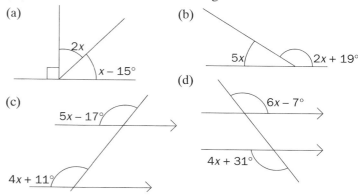

4 The width of a rectangular lawn is *x* metres. The length of the lawn is 3 metres longer than the width.
  (a) Write down an expression, in terms of *x*, for the length of the lawn.
  (b) The perimeter of the lawn is 36 metres. Write down an equation, in terms of *x*, and solve it to find the width of the lawn.
  (c) What is the length of the lawn?

5 The diagram shows a picture surrounded by a wooden frame, the width of the wood being *x* cm. Write down, in terms of *x*

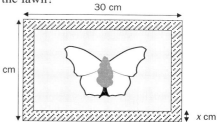

  (a) the length of the picture,
  (b) the width of the picture,
  (c) an expression for the perimeter of the picture and simplify it.
  The picture is known to have a perimeter equal to 80 cm.
  (d) Use this information to write down an equation in *x*.
  (e) Solve your equation to find the value of *x*. ◄

Sometimes you will have to work out a **relationship or rule** yourself from the information given. **Diagrams** are often helpful here too.

► *Exercise* **A7.3**

1 The diagram shows a number grid with a coloured box marked on it. This is called the '15 box'.

1	2	3	4
5	6	7	8
9	10	11	12
13	14	15	16
17	18	19	20
21	22	23	24
25	26	27	28
29	30	31	32
33	34	35	36

  (a) Find the total of the numbers in the '15 box'.

(b) Copy and complete this '26 box'.

Find the total of the numbers in it.

26	

(c) This is an '*n* box'.

n	

Copy and complete this '*n* box'.
Write the other three numbers in it in terms of *n*.

(d) Find and simplify an expression for the total of the numbers in the '*n* box'.

(e) An '*n* box' has a total of 126.
Write down an equation in *n*.
Solve the equation to find the value of *n*.

(f) Explain why the total of the four numbers in any 'box' cannot be (i) 73 (ii) 86.

2 Every year, the 'Ravers' and the 'Stompers' each give a concert in the School Hall. Tickets for each concert this year were the same prices; £4 and £6.

(a) Use the following information to complete the table below for the numbers of tickets sold.

	Number of £6 tickets sold	Number of £4 tickets sold
Ravers	*x*	
Stompers		

Eighty-two more £4 tickets were sold than £6 tickets for the Ravers concert.

Twice as many £6 tickets were sold for the Stompers than for the Ravers.

Seventeen fewer £4 tickets were sold for the Stompers concert than for the Ravers.

Altogether, 377 tickets were sold for the two concerts.

(b) Use the completed table to write down an equation in *x*.
(c) Solve the equation to find the value of *x*.
(d) How many £6 tickets were sold for each concert?
(e) How many £4 tickets were sold for each concert?

Examination Questions

1 Simon is aged *x* years. His sister Joanne is 3 years older.
(a) Write down Joanne's age in terms of *x*.
Their father is twice as old as Simon's and Joanne's ages added together.
(b) Find an expression for their father's age in terms of *x*.
(c) The sum of all three ages is 63 years.
Show that this last statement can be simplified to
$$6x + 9 = 63$$
(d) Solve this equation to find *x*.
(e) How old is their father?   (NEAB, 1990)

2 A clown is sharing some balloons between a number of children. He gives each child 5 balloons and finds that he has 31 balloons left.
(a) Assuming that there are *x* children, write down an expression in *x* for the total number of balloons.
(b) The clown continues to share out the balloons. When each child has 7 balloons, there are 5 left over.

(i) Write down an equation in *x*.
(ii) Solve your equation and find how many balloons the clown had altogether.
                                              (MEG, 1989)

3 In Weldon High School, pupils were allowed to go on the French trip or on the ski trip, but not on both.
(a) Use the following information to complete the table.
Last year, eight more pupils went on the ski trip than on the French trip.
This year, three times as many pupils as last year went on the French trip.
This year twice as many pupils as last year went on the ski trip.

	Number on French trip	Number on ski trip
Last year	*x*	
This year		

(b) 116 pupils altogether went on a trip this year. How many of these pupils went on
(i) the French trip (ii) the ski trip?   (NISEAC, 1990)

4 Triangle ABC is isosceles with
AB = AC.
Calculate the value of *x*.

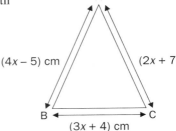

(ULEAC, 1991)

5

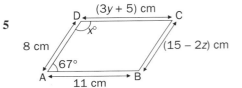

ABCD is a parallelogram.
(a) Calculate the value of *x*.
(b) (i) Write down an equation in *y*.
    (ii) Calculate the value of *y*.
(c) Calculate the value of *z*.   (MEG, 1991)

6

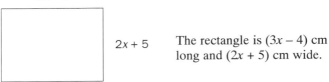

The rectangle is (3*x* − 4) cm long and (2*x* + 5) cm wide.

(a) If *x* = 12 find the perimeter of the rectangle in cm.
(b) If *x* = 10 find the area of the rectangle in cm².
(c) In terms of *x*, by how much is the length greater than the width?
(d) Find the value of *x* for which the figure is a square.
                                              (NISEAC, 1990)

M1
Changing metric units

This unit will help you to:

- identify a suitable metric unit for a measurement
- remember the relationships between the main units of length, mass and capacity
- change one metric unit to another.

We measure things using many different **units**.
We measure **length** in kilometres, metres …
We measure **mass** in kilograms, grams …
We measure **capacity** in litres, millilitres, …
and so on …

Sometimes we need to **change** or **convert one unit to another**.
 If you know the *relationship* between two units, you can change from one to the other.

Exercise M1.1

1 Which metric units would you measure these lengths in? Give the name and symbol for the unit.
   (a) length of a pen
   (b) thickness of an exercise book
   (c) height of a room
   (d) distance from London to Paris
   (e) length of your foot
   (f) length of a football pitch
   (g) length of the M1
   (h) thickness of a pencil

2 Which metric unit would you use to weigh these in? Give the name and symbol for the unit.
   (a) egg
   (b) yourself
   (c) sack of potatoes
   (d) bus
   (e) pencil
   (f) elephant
   (g) drawing pin
   (h) bag of sugar

3 Which metric units would you use to measure the capacity of these? Give the name and symbol for the unit.
   (a) petrol can
   (b) bottle of nail varnish
   (c) egg cup
   (d) bath
   (e) car's petrol tank
   (f) bottle of wine

4 Choose the most likely estimate for each of these:
   (a) the height of a house
      (i) 26 m (ii) 17 m (iii) 10 m (iv) 6 m
   (b) the length of a car
      (i) 14 m (ii) 9 m (iii) 7 m (iv) 4 m
   (c) a spoonful of medicine
      (i) 25 mℓ (ii) 5 mℓ (iii) 125 mℓ (iv) 5 cℓ
   (d) a cup of tea
      (i) 100 mℓ (ii) 500 mℓ (iii) 200 mℓ (iv) 50 mℓ
   (e) the mass of a person
      (i) 650 g (ii) 650 kg (iii) 6.5 kg (iv) 65 kg
   (f) the mass of an orange
      (i) 180 mg (ii) 180 g (iii) 180 kg (iv) 18 g

Thinking about changes

You need to use your common sense when changing units. Think about what you are doing. Use an easy example to help you. Here is one using pounds and pence.

Change a 1 pound coin to penny coins, and you get 100 penny coins. You end up with a *larger number* of coins, but the *same value*. A penny is smaller than a £. So the change was to a *smaller unit*. You get a *larger number* of that unit (100 instead of 1).

This happens whatever the units.

> **Change to a smaller unit → larger number of that unit.**

Now think about a change to a *larger unit*.

Change 100 penny coins to pounds and you get only 1 pound coin. You have a *smaller number* of coins, but the *same value*. A pound is larger than a penny. So the change was to a *larger unit*. You get a *smaller number* of that unit (1 instead of 100).

Again this is true, whatever the units.

> **Change to a larger unit → smaller number of that unit.**

Whichever way you use to change units, think about the change.

Ask yourself:

 Is it to a smaller or larger unit?
 Will I get a larger or smaller number of that unit?
 Does my answer make sense?

Exercise M1.2

Which is larger:
1 a gram or a kilogram
2 a millilitre or a litre
3 a centimetre or a kilometre
4 a tonne or a kilogram
5 a millimetre or a centimetre?

Metric units

Here are some of the **main metric units** you need to know.

Length:

1 kilometre = 1000 metres
1 metre = 100 centimetres = 1000 millimetres
1 centimetre = 10 millimetres

1 km = 1000 m
1 m = 100 cm = 1000 mm
1 cm = 10 mm

Mass:

1 kilogram = 1000 grams
1 tonne = 1000 kilograms

1 kg = 1000 g
1 t = 1000 kg

Capacity:

1 litre = 1000 millilitres
1 litre = 100 centilitres

1 ℓ = 1000 mℓ
1 ℓ = 100 cℓ

Learn these metric relationships.

Remember: the names give you clues:

kilo – thousand
centi – hundredth
milli –thousandth

In the metric system all units are linked by 10, 100, 1000, …
This makes changing metric units easy.

Write down the 'link' between the units. Draw an arrow to show the change you want. Then think about it. Get a 'mental picture' of the change.

Use some common sense. Is the change to a *smaller* or *larger unit*? Will you get a *larger* or *smaller number* of that unit? Do you multiply or divide? And by what?

Remember: When you **change units**, you are **not** changing the measurement. You only change the way you write or say it.

Here are some examples.

Try doing the working 'in your head'. Check them with a calculator if you want to.

To change cm to mm,
write the link cm → mm.

It gives 'multiply by 10'.

$$3 \text{ cm} = 3 \times 10 \text{ mm} = 30 \text{ mm}$$
$$7.5 \text{ cm} = 7.5 \times 10 \text{ mm} = 75 \text{ mm}$$
$$0.2 \text{ cm} = 0.2 \times 10 \text{ mm} = 2 \text{ mm}$$

$$\boxed{\times 10}$$
1 cm = 10 mm

Change to a smaller unit gives a larger number of them

To change mm to m,
write the link mm → m.

It gives 'divide by 1000'.

$$9000 \text{ mm} = (9000 \div 1000) \text{ m} = 9 \text{ m}$$
$$1250 \text{ mm} = (1250 \div 1000) \text{ m} = 1.25 \text{ m}$$
$$175 \text{ mm} = (175 \div 1000) \text{ m} = 0.175 \text{ m}$$
$$40 \text{ mm} = (40 \div 1000) \text{ m} = 0.040 \text{ m}$$
$$8 \text{ mm} = (8 \div 1000) \text{ m} = 0.008 \text{ m}$$

$$\boxed{\div 1000}$$
1000 mm = 1 m

Change to a larger unit gives a smaller number of them

To change kg into g,
write the link kg → g.

It gives 'multiply by 1000'.

$$13 \text{ kg} = 13 \times 1000 \text{ g} = 13\,000 \text{ g}$$
$$4.5 \text{ kg} = 4.5 \times 1000 \text{ g} = 4500 \text{ g}$$
$$0.18 \text{ kg} = 0.18 \times 1000 \text{ g} = 180 \text{ g}$$
$$0.007 \text{ kg} = 0.007 \times 1000 \text{ g} = 7 \text{ g}$$

$$\boxed{\times 1000}$$
1 kg = 1000 g

Change to a smaller unit gives a larger number of them

▶ *Exercise* M1.3

1 Copy and complete these:
(a) 5 km = … m
(b) 516 mm = … cm
(c) 4 m = … mm
(d) 429 m = … km
(e) 3000 mm = … m
(f) 6.31 km = … m
(g) 2 m = … cm
(h) 36 cm = … m
(i) 800 cm = … m
(j) 0.5 m = … mm
(k) 7000 m = … km
(l) 276 mm = … m
(m) 8.56 m = … cm
(n) 2.8 cm = … mm

2 Copy and complete these:
(a) 5 kg = … g
(b) 1.5 t = … kg
(c) 2.54 kg = … g
(d) 2 t = … kg
(e) 4.8 kg = … g
(f) 750 kg = … t

(g) 4000 g = … kg
(h) 3750 g = … kg
(i) 450 g = … kg
(j) 8500 kg = … t
(k) 6850 kg = … t
(l) 100 t = … kg

3 Copy and complete these:
(a) 5ℓ = … mℓ
(b) 1.5ℓ = … mℓ
(c) 5.65ℓ = … mℓ
(d) 8ℓ = … mℓ
(e) 6720 mℓ = … ℓ
(f) 150 mℓ = … ℓ
(g) 6000 mℓ = … ℓ
(h) 750 mℓ = … ℓ
(i) 2.75ℓ = … mℓ
(j) 5500 mℓ = … ℓ
(k) 4.5ℓ = … mℓ
(l) 5 mℓ = … ℓ

In a measurement calculation, all the measurements must be in the *same unit*. For example, for metric length calculations work all in metres, or all in centimetres, or all in millimetres, and so on …

So *change any units* if you need to. Make sure that you give the correct unit in your answer.

Questions often tell you which unit to give your answer in. Always use that unit or you will lose marks.

Question

(a) A factory has 4.75 tonnes of sugar to pack in 1 kg bags. How many bags will be filled?
(b) In one day the factory filled 1905 kilogram bags. How many tonnes of sugar did it use?

Answer

(a) *Write down the link:* t → kg.
Work out what to do:
multiply by 1000

$$\boxed{\times 1000}$$
1 t = 1000 kg

4.75 × 1000 = 4750 bags.

(b) *Write down the link:* kg → t.
Work out what to do:
divide by 1000

$$\boxed{\div 1000}$$
1000 kg = 1 t

1905 ÷ 1000 = 1.905 t.

▶ *Exercise* M1.4

1 Rick bought ten 600 mℓ bottles of mineral water. How many litres did he buy?
2 A jug holds 750 mℓ of milk.
  (a) How many litres will five jugs hold?
  (b) How many jugs can be filled from 3ℓ of milk?
3 A baker uses 350 g of cheese to make a cheesecake.
  (a) How many cheesecakes can he make with 7 kg of cheese?
  (b) One day he makes 50 cheesecakes. How many kilograms of cheese does he use?
4 A grocer packs and sells 400 g bags of coffee.
  (a) If she packs 24 bags in a case, how many kilograms of coffee is that?
  (b) How many bags can she fill from a 10 kg sack of coffee?
5 A drum holds 200 m of string. How many 125 cm lengths can be cut from this?

6 Joy had a 1 kg jar of sweets. She gave four children 175 g each. How many grams of sweets were left in the jar?

7 Stan bought a 5 kg bag of potatoes. He used three large potatoes, each weighing 320 g, for chips. How many kilograms of potatoes were left in the bag?

8 John had a full 1.5 litre bottle of mineral water. He filled four 200 mℓ glasses from it. How much water was left in the bottle? Give your answer in
(a) millilitres (b) litres.

9 Ben had plank of wood 3 m long. He cut off a piece, 157 cm long. What length of wood was left over? Give your answer in
(a) centimetres (b) metres.

10 (a) A factory dispatches its products in boxes which can hold a maximum weight of 3 kg. The total weight of production one day was 4.5 tonnes. How many boxes were needed?
(b) On a different day, 375 boxes were needed. What was the weight of production on that day?
(c) How many boxes are needed if the production one day is 5.1 tonnes?
(d) What weight of production would fill 614 boxes?

You can give metric measurements in a 'mixture' of units. For example, metric lengths can be given in

centimetres and millimetres,
metres and centimetres,
metres and millimetres,
and so on …

Usually we change them to *one unit only*. This makes them easier to use with a calculator.

Question

In 1987 the Women's World Record High Jump was 2 m 9 cm. Write this
(a) all in centimetres
(b) all in metres.

Answer

(a) *Change m to cm.*

Write the link: m → cm

Work out what to do:
'multiply by 100'.

```
        ┌─ × 100 ─┐
       1 m   =   100 cm

         ┌─ 2 m + 9 cm
× 100 ──┘
       = 200 cm + 9 cm
       = 209 cm
```

(b) *Change cm to m.*

Write the link: cm → m

Work out what to do:
'divide by 100'.

```
        ┌─ ÷ 100 ─┐
      100 cm  =   1 m

      2 m + 9 cm ─┐
                  └─ ÷ 100
       = 2 m + 0.09 m
       = 2.09 m
```

Exercise M1.5

1 Write these lengths in
(a) metres (b) centimetres.
(i) 3 m 25 cm (ii) 4 m 14 cm (iii) 10 m 6 cm
(iv) 7 m 2 cm

2 Write these lengths in
(a) centimetres (b) millimetres.
(i) 2 cm 7 mm (ii) 5 cm 2 mm (iii) 6 cm 0 mm
(iv) 4 cm 11 mm

3 Write these masses in
(a) kilograms (b) grams.
(i) 1 kg 800 g (ii) 2 kg 720 g (iii) 5 kg 78 g (iv) 3 kg 9 g

4 Write these capacities in
(a) litres (b) millilitres.
(i) 2ℓ 900 mℓ (ii) 3ℓ 250 mℓ (iii) 5ℓ 84 mℓ (iv) 1ℓ 8 mℓ

5 Write these capacities in
(a) litres (b) centilitres.
(i) 1ℓ 80 cℓ (ii) 2ℓ 67 cℓ (iii) 5ℓ 50 cℓ (iv) 3ℓ 7 cℓ

6 Write these masses in
(a) tonnes (b) kilograms.
(i) 1 t 960 kg (ii) 2 t 300 kg (iii) 3 t 72 kg (iv) 4 t 9 kg

7 A piece of wood is 2.6 m long. Andrea cut off pieces measuring 336 mm, 54.2 cm and 469 mm. What length of wood remained?

8 A 5 litre container is full of cider. Mick pours out 475 mℓ, 342 mℓ and 158 cℓ of cider. How much cider is left in the container?

9 A lift displays a notice saying 'maximum weight not to exceed 1 tonne'.
(a) What is the maximum number of people, each weighing 74 kg, that the lift can safely carry?
(b) If the lift carries that maximum number of people, what is the maximum weight of a suitcase one person could safely carry?

10 A car of length 4 m 37 cm is parked in a garage 5.64 m long. The space behind the car is 732 mm. How much space is there in front of the car? Give your answer in
(a) cm (b) mm.

Examination Questions

1 A measuring cup has a capacity of 100 millilitres. How many full cups are needed to fill a 1$\frac{1}{2}$ litre mixing bowl?
(ULEAC, 1990)

2 Small punnets are filled from the large box. How many punnets can be filled?

3kg box of strawberries

STRAWBERRIES 250g

250g punnet

(NISEAC, 1991)

3 Mrs Thornton needs 28 litres of wine for a party. She buys the wine in bottles. Each bottle holds 70 cl. How many bottles of wine does Mrs Thornton buy?
(NEAB, 1991)

4

(a) Traffic cones are to be placed at intervals of 20 metres along a section of motorway for 800 metres.
How many cones are required?

(b) On another section 2 kilometres long, cones are to be placed at intervals of 15 metres for 900 metres from the first cone and then at intervals of 10 metres for the remainder of the section.
How many cones are required?

(NISEAC, 1990)

5 (a) A bag contains 1 kg of onions. Each onion weighs about 90 g. Estimate the number of onions in the bag.

(b) Write in order of size, smallest first:
0.45 m, 40 cm, 375 mm

(SEG, 1989)

6 Here are the lengths of five pieces of wood.

A   5 cm
B   60 mm
C   0.07 m
D   0.005 m
E   0.5 m

(a) Which piece is the longest?
(b) Which piece is the shortest?

(ULEAC, 1991)

7 For a party, Elizabeth bought three bottles of fizzy drink. They contained 750 mℓ, 350 mℓ and 1.5 litres.
How much fizzy drink is there altogether, in litres?

(MEG, 1991)

8

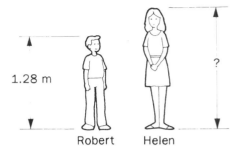

Robert is 1.28 m tall. He is 39 cm shorter than his sister Helen. How tall is Helen?

(WJEC, 1990)

▶ M2
More conversions

This unit will help you to:

- identify and use the main imperial units of length, mass and capacity in daily use
- give their rough metric equivalents
- change from one imperial unit to another
- change metric to imperial units and vice versa
- change one currency to another.

Imperial units

Metric units are supposed to be used for most standard measurements in this country now. But many people still use and 'think' in **imperial** units.

The following table gives the imperial units of length, mass and capacity that you are most likely to meet.

Length		
	1 mile	= 1760 yards
	1 yard	= 3 feet = 36 inches
	1 foot	= 12 inches
Mass	1 stone	= 14 pounds
	1 pound	= 16 ounces
Capacity	1 gallon	= 8 pints
	1 pint	= 20 fluid ounces

You may have to change from one imperial unit to another. You should be given the *'link'* between them in an examination question. Use it to work out what calculation to do. This is just like changing metric units but the numbers are not so simple. You may need to use your calculator. Here are some examples.

To change gallons to pints

use this 'link' …
It gives 'multiply by 8'.

$$\overset{\times 8}{1 \text{ gallon} \;=\; 8 \text{ pints}}$$

To change inches to yards

use this 'link' …
It gives 'divide by 36'.

$$\overset{\div 36}{36 \text{ inches} \;=\; 1 \text{ yard}}$$

Remember to think about what makes sense.

Changing to a smaller unit → larger number of them.

Changing to a larger unit → smaller number of them.

Question

(a) Roger weighs 13 stones 6 pounds. His American friend Hank weighs 200 pounds.
Who is heavier? By how many pounds? (1 st = 14 lb)

(b) Miss Baker's class is to make soup. She works out that altogether they need 146 fluid ounces of milk for it. How many pints of milk does she need to order?
(1 pint = 20 fluid ounces)

Answer

(a) *To change stones to lb, multiply by 14.*

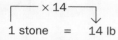

1 stone = 14 lb

13 stones = 13 × 14 lb = 182 lb

13 st 6 lb = (182 + 6) lb = 188 lb

Difference in weight: (200 − 188) lb = 12 lb

Hank (200 lb) is 12 lb heavier than Roger (188 lb).

(b) *To change fluid ounces to pints, divide by 20.*

20 fl oz = 1 pint

146 fl oz = (146 ÷ 20) pt = 7.3 pints.

She needs to order 8 pints of milk.

You may have to give imperial measures in a *mixture* of units. For example,

weights in pound and ounces, stones and pounds …
lengths in feet and inches, yards and feet, …

Question

Robert is 67 inches tall. How tall is he in feet and inches?
(1 foot = 12 inches)

Answer

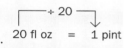

12 inches = 1 foot   1 foot = 12 inches

To change inches to feet, divide by 12.
This gives a whole number and, possibly, a fraction of a foot.

To change the fraction of a foot back to inches, multiply it by 12.

67 inches = 67 ÷ 12 feet
    = 5.583333333 feet
    = 5 feet + 0.583333333 × 12 inches
    = 5 feet 7 inches.

You can do this working with your calculator like this:

Change inches to feet:

Subtract whole number of feet: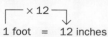

Change fraction of a foot back to inches:

► *Exercise* **M2.1**

1 Copy and complete these.
  (a) 2 gallons = … pints
  (b) 3 miles = … yards
  (c) 4 pints = … fluid ounces
  (d) 4 pounds = … ounces
  (e) 2 feet = … inches
  (f) 40 fluid ounces = … pints
  (g) 28 inches = … feet … inches
  (h) 165 pounds = … stones … pounds
  (i) 37 pints = … gallons … pints
  (j) 28 feet = … yards … feet

2 Answer these questions for each pair of amounts below.
  Which amount is larger? By how much is it larger?
  (a) 165 pounds; 11 stones 12 pounds
  (b) 43 feet; 15 yards 2 feet
  (c) 4 gallons 7 pints; 46 pints
  (d) 5195 yards; 3 miles 27 yards
  (e) 6 pints 13 fl oz; 131 fl oz.

Metric and imperial units

Usually we try to work in *either* metric units *or* imperial units. We try not to change from one to another. But sometimes we have to.

You should know roughly how the main units compare in size. Here are some useful comparisons.

Length (≈ means 'approximately equal to')

1 inch	≈ 25 mm or 2.5 cm
1 foot	≈ 30 cm
1 yard	≈ 90 cm … nearly 1 m
5 miles	≈ 8 km

1 cm	… not quite $\frac{1}{2}$ inch
1 m	… just over 1 yard
1 km	… just over $\frac{1}{2}$ mile
8 km	… about 5 miles

Mass

1 oz ≈ 30 g	
1 lb ≈ 450 g … nearly $\frac{1}{2}$ kg	

1 kg	≈ 2.2 lb … just over 2 lb
1 tonne ≈ 1 ton	

Capacity

1 pint	≈ 560 mℓ … just over $\frac{1}{2}$ litre
1 gallon ≈ 4.5 ℓ	

1 litre ≈ 1.75 pints

Exercise M2.2

Copy and complete these.

1	6 inches ≈ … cm	**6**	4 pints ≈ … ℓ
2	250 mm ≈ … inches	**7**	18 ℓ ≈ … gallons
3	80 km ≈ … miles	**8**	25 miles ≈ … km
4	3 oz ≈ … g	**9**	2250 g ≈ … lb
5	11 lb ≈ … kg	**10**	1680 mℓ ≈ … pints.

You might use these when shopping abroad.

If you want … 1 lb of apples, ask for '$\frac{1}{2}$ kg'

… $\frac{1}{2}$ lb of nuts, ask for '250 g'

… $\frac{1}{4}$ lb of sweets, ask for '125 g'

… a pint of milk, ask for '$\frac{1}{2}$ litre'

and so on …

Exercise M2.3

1 If you were in France, what would you ask for if you wanted:

(a)	5 lb of potatoes	(d)	1 pint of beer
(b)	3 lb of onions	(e)	1 oz of parsley
(c)	$\frac{1}{4}$ lb of chocolate	(f)	1 yard of ribbon?

2 When Francois visited Britain what did he ask for when he wanted:

(a)	60 cm of string	(d)	3 litres of beer
(b)	1 kg of carrots	(e)	$2\frac{1}{2}$ m of cable
(c)	$\frac{1}{4}$ kg of green beans	(f)	5 kg of potatoes?

An examination question may give you the link to use between an imperial and metric unit. If it does not, then *state* the approximate value you have used in your answer.

Question

David's scale and measuring jug are metric.

Use this table to change the recipe to metric too.

1 oz ≈ 30 g
1 pint ≈ 560 mℓ

> **SCONES**
> (makes 12)
> 8 oz flour
> $1\frac{1}{2}$ oz butter
> $\frac{1}{4}$ pint milk
> $1\frac{1}{2}$ tbs sugar
> pinch of salt

Answer

To change oz to g use 'multiply by 30'.

$$1 \text{ oz} \xrightarrow{\times 30} 30 \text{ g}$$

Flour: 8 oz ≈ 8 × 30 g   = 240 g
Butter: 1.5 oz ≈ 1.5 × 30 g = 45 g

To change pints to mℓ use 'multiply by 560'.

$$1 \text{ pint} \xrightarrow{\times 560} 560 \text{ ml}$$

Milk: $\frac{1}{4}$ pint ≈ $\frac{1}{4}$ × 560 mℓ   = 140 mℓ.

Exercise M2.4

Change these recipes to metric measures.

1
> **Coarse-cut orange marmalade**
> 3 lb Seville oranges
> 1 lemon
> $5\frac{1}{2}$ pt water
> 5 lb brown sugar

2
> **Creamy onion soup**
> $\frac{3}{4}$ lb onion
> $\frac{1}{4}$ lb potato
> 1 oz butter
> 1 pt milk
> $\frac{1}{2}$ pt vegetable stock
> 1 bay leaf
> salt and pepper

3
> **Choux pastry**
> $\frac{1}{4}$ pt water
> 2 oz butter
> $\frac{1}{4}$ lb flour
> 2 eggs

4
> **Italian pasta salad**
> 4 oz pasta rings
> 6 oz red peppers
> 2 oz black olives
> $\frac{1}{2}$ oz chopped parsley
> 2 fl oz French dressing
> 1 garlic clove
> salt and pepper

Currency conversion

Currency is money. Most countries use their own currency. In Britain we use pounds (£). This is called **sterling**.

When visiting a country, you usually need to pay for things using its own currency.

You can change money at banks, bureaux de change, some travel agents, some building societies, … Some places offer better **exchange rates** than others. But all charge you for making the change. This **commission** is usually a *percentage* of the amount of money changed.

Exchange rates can change every day. So they are usually listed daily in newspapers, banks, on television (ORACLE or CEEFAX), …

You will usually see two exchange rates for each currency. The '*Sell at*' rate and the '*Buy at*' rate.

Banks, etc. sell currency to you using the 'Sell at' rate. Here it is used to change £s to another currency. It tells you how much of a currency you get for £1 (*before* paying commission).

To change £s to another currency in this country, you multiply by the 'Sell at' rate.

Amount in other currency =
        amount in £s × 'Sell at' rate for that country

Question

Ken's family are going on a tour of Europe. They plan to visit France, Germany and Italy.

The chart shows the exchange rates on the day Ken changed some money.

Ken changed £40 into Francs, £150 into Deutschmarks (Marks), £275 into Lire.

TOURIST RATES

Country	Rate	Country	Rate
Australia (Dollars)	2.23	Ireland (Punts)	1.08
Austria (Schillings)	20.10	Italy (Lire)	2140.00
Belgium (Francs)	59.00	Japan (Yen)	243.00
Canada (Dollars)	2.02	Malta (Pounds)	0.55
Cyprus (Pounds)	0.81	New Zealand (Dollars)	2.95
Denmark (Kroner)	11.00	Norway (Kroner)	11.25
Holland (Guilders)	3.24	Portugal (Escudos)	253.00
Finland (Markka)	6.90	Spain (Pesetas)	178.00
France (Francs)	9.75	Sweden (Kronor)	10.59
Germany (Marks)	2.87	Switzerland (Francs)	2.46
Greece (Drachmas)	305.00	Turkey (Lire)	6000.00
Hong Kong (Dollars)	13.75	United States (Dollars)	1.75

Find out how much of each currency he got, before paying commission.

Answer

Francs:

Look in the table for: France (Francs) ... 9.75

40 × 9.75 Francs = 390 Francs

Deutschmarks:

Look in the table for: Germany (Marks) ... 2.87

150 × 2.87 Marks = 430.5 Marks

Lire:

Look in the table for: Italy (Lire) ... 2140.00

275 × 2140 Lire = 588 500 Lire

▶ *Exercise* M2.5

Use the above Tourist Rates table to answer the questions in this exercise.

1 Calculate how much of each of these currencies you would get if you exchange £120.

(a) French Francs (e) Danish Kroner
(b) Italian Lire (f) US Dollars
(c) Portuguese Escudos (g) German Marks
(d) Austrian Schillings (h) Hong Kong Dollars.

2 Calculate the cost of buying £25 worth of petrol in each of these countries.

Give your answers in foreign currency.

(a) France (e) Greece
(b) Belgium (f) Ireland
(c) Cyprus (g) New Zealand
(d) Finland (h) Switzerland

3 Plan a holiday in one of the listed countries. Estimate, in sterling, how much you might spend in that country.

Calculate how much of that country's money you would get when you exchange your sterling currency.

You may want to **compare prices** in other countries with ours in Britain.

To change another currency to £s (sterling), divide by the exchange rate you got. You may have to round your answer 'to the nearest penny'.

Question

Ken's mother likes to read a Sunday paper, wherever she is. Her paper costs 60p here. The table gives its price in other countries.

OVERSEAS PRICES

Country	Price	Country	Price
Austria	60 Sch	Italy	6,000 Lire
Belgium	120 BF	Luxembourg	100 Lfr
Canada	$C4.50	Madeira	600 Esc
Canaries	450 Ptas	Malta	70 Cents
Cyprus	£2.00	Morocco	40 Dirham
Denmark	26 Kr	Norway	26 Kr
Irish Rep	70p	Portugal	600 Esc
Finland	20 Fm	Spain	450 Ptas
France	20 FF	Sweden	26 Kr
Germany	6.50 DM	Switzerland	6 Sw. Fr
Gibraltar	£1.50	Tunisia	2.0 Td
Greece	500 Dr	USA (NY)	$4.50
Holland	7 G	USA (Other)	$5.00

Work out how much it will cost in pounds and pence in each country they will visit. (Use the exchange rates Ken got in the last question.)

Answer

France: 20 FF.

20 ÷ 9.75 = `2.051282051`

≈ £2.05

Germany: 6.50 DM

6.50 ÷ 2.87 = `2.264808362`

≈ £2.26

Italy: 6000 Lire

6000 ÷ 2140 = `2.803738318`

≈ £2.80

▶ *Exercise* M2.6

Use the Tourist Rates and Overseas Prices tables above to work out the cost of the 60p Sunday paper in

1 Austria   5 Finland
2 Greece   6 Denmark
3 Sweden   7 Malta
4 Holland   8 Canada.

Banks etc. **buy** foreign currency (but not coins) from you using the 'Buy at' rate. Here it is used to change another currency to £s. It tells you how much of that currency you have to give them to get £1 back (*before* paying commission).

The 'Buy at' rate is usually bigger than the 'Sell at' rate.

To change another currency to £s in this country, you divide by the 'Buy at' rate.

Amount in £s =

amount in other currency ÷ 'Buy at' rate for that currency

Question

After his holiday Ken had some foreign money left. He had 70 FF, 30 DM and 5000 Lire.

His bank bought it back from him. The table gives the exchange rates on that day.

TOURIST RATES

	Bank Buys	Bank Sells		Bank Buys	Bank Sells
Australia $	2.18	2.05	Italy Lire	2310	2175
Austria Sch	22.50	21.25	Japan Yen	240	224
Belgium Fr	67.30	63.40	Netherlands Gld	3.60	3.40
Canada $	1.965	1.845	Norway Kr	11.65	11.00
Denmark Kr	12.28	11.68	Portugal Esc	266.50	250.50
Finland Mkk	7.20	6.80	South Africa Rd	4.90	4.40
France FF	10.48	10.16	Spain Ptas	199	187
Germany DM	3.11	3.015	Sweden Kr	10.88	10.28
Greece Dr	275.75	257.75	Switzerland Fr	2.76	2.60
Hong Kong $	13.10	12.20	Turkey Lire	3915	3315
Ireland Pt	1.202	1.132	United States $	1.67	1.57

How much sterling (£s) should he get back for each amount before he pays commission?

Answer

Francs:
Look in 'Bank Buys' column for France FF ... 10.48

For 70 FF
70 ÷ 10.48 = `6.679389313`
≈ £6.68

DM:
Look in the 'Bank Buys' column for Germany DM ... 3.11
For 30 DM:
30 ÷ 3.11 = `9.646302251`
≈ £9.65

Lire:
Look in the 'Bank Buys' column for Italy Lire ... 2310
For 5000 Lire:
5000 ÷ 2310 = `2.164502165`
≈ £2.16

▶ *Exercise* M2.7

Calculate the amount of sterling you would receive if you exchanged the following amounts of foreign currency. (Use the 'Bank Buys' column in the above table and give each answer to the nearest penny.)

1   200 French Francs
2   150 German Marks
3   45 Irish Punts
4   10 000 Japanese Yen
5   130 Swiss Francs
6   50 Canadian Dollars
7   500 Danish Kroners
8   75 Australian Dollars

Examination Questions

1   According to a microwave oven instruction booklet, a leg of lamb should be cooked for 12 min/lb. Calculate the cooking time for a leg of lamb which weighs 1 lb 12 oz.
(ULEAC, 1991)

2   Mary loses 2 stones 5 lb whilst attending a weight-watchers' course, her weight is now 11 stones 12 lb. What was her original weight? (1 stone = 14 lb).
(NEAB, 1988)

3

	Petrol per litre		Exchange rates per £1 sterling
Austria (schillings)	10	Austria	21.15 schillings
France (francs)	5	France	10.14 francs
Greece (drachmas)	62	Greece	257.20 drachmas
Italy (lire)	1180	Italy	2159.00 lire
Spain (pesetas)	82	Spain	186.70 pesetas

In which country is petrol cheapest for the British tourist? (Show clearly your working.)   (NISEAC, 1991)

4   Paul and Pam are touring in France. They do not want to drive more than 280 miles in a day. Their map is in kilometres.
Pam knows that 5 miles is about 8 kilometres.

(a) What is 280 miles in kilometres?
(b) They want to stop at Avalon for lunch. A sign post says 'Avalon 108 km'. How far is this in miles?
(MEG, 1988)

5

Tyre pressures								
lb/sq in	20	22	24	26	28	30	32	34
kg/sq cm	1.41	1.55	1.69	1.83	1.97	2.11		2.39

(a) What pressure, in kg/sq cm is the same as 22 lb/sq in?
The figure in kg/sq cm equivalent to 32 lb/sq in has been missed out.
(b) What should the figure be?   (ULEAC, 1991)

6   Centrepoint Tower in Sydney is 304.8 metres high. Use your calculator to find its height in feet, taking 1 metre = 3.28084 feet.   (MEG, 1989)

7   The furlong is an old measure of distance. It is still used in horse races. 1 furlong is 220 yards, and 1 yard is 0.914 metres.

(a) How many metres long is a seven furlong horse race?
(b) Write your answer to (a) in kilometres correct to one decimal place.   (MEG, 1991)

8   Helen and Parveen are on holiday in West Germany. They buy one litre of milk in a supermarket, which costs them 1.09 DM. One pint of milk in Great Britain costs 28 p. In which country is milk more expensive? Show all relevant working.
(1 litre = 1.76 pints. Assume £1 = 3.15 DM).
(NEAB, 1989)

9 In 1988 the rate of exchange for Italy was £1 = 2200 lire.
   (a) Pam Thompson changed a £50 travellers' cheque whilst on holiday in Italy. How many lire could she have expected to receive?
   (b) During her visit to Venice she went for a ride in a gondola and paid the gondolier 77 000 lire. Calculate the equivalent cost of this ride in £.

   (SEG, 1989)

10 Gwyneth went to the bank to get her Greek money (drachmas) before going on holiday. The exchange rate was £1 = 248 drachmas.

   (a) How many drachmas should she get for £150?
   (b) (i) The bank, however, only gave 1000 drachma and 500 drachma notes. Gwyneth wanted at least £150 worth of drachmas and as little extra as possible. How many drachmas did she buy?
       (ii) The bank charged Gwyneth £3 for the exchange. How much, to the nearest penny, did she pay altogether for her holiday money?

   (WJEC, 1989)

M3
Perimeter and area

This unit will help you to:

■ find the perimeter of a shape
■ understand the idea of area
■ find area by counting squares
■ use the main metric and imperial units of area
■ calculate the perimeter and area of rectangles, squares and triangles
■ find edge lengths of rectangles from their areas
■ work out the relationships between the metric units of area.

The **perimeter of a plane shape** is the length of its boundary, that is, the distance around its edge. It is measured in **length units** such as metres (m), centimetres (cm), …

The **area of a plane shape** is the amount of surface it covers. Area is measured in square units such as **square metres** (m²), square centimetres (cm²), …

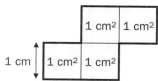

Perimeter of this shape = 10 cm
Area of this shape = 4 cm²

When calculating perimeters and areas, make sure that all the lengths are in the *same unit*. For example, you need …

all lengths in m to give perimeter in m,
all lengths in cm to give area in cm²,
and so on …

Change any units if you need to (see Unit M1).

Remember:

1 km = 1000 m	
1 m = 100 cm	
1 m = 1000 mm	
1 cm = 10 mm	

Exercise M3.1

Lenny made this floor plan of the college music annexe.

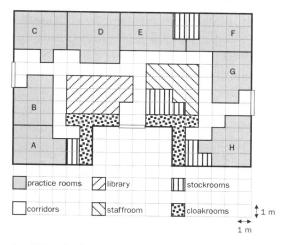

1 What is the outside perimeter of the music annexe?
2 Which room has the longest perimeter? Which room has the shortest perimeter? How long is each one?
3 Do any rooms have the same perimeter? If so, which? How long are they?
4 What is the floor area of each room on the plan?
5 What is the floor area of the corridors?
6 What is the total floor area of the music annexe?

There are **formulae** for calculating the **perimeters** and **areas** of common shapes. This unit contains the formulae for **rectangle**, **square** and **triangle**.

Rectangle

Perimeter of a rectangle

= 2 × length + 2 × width
= 2l + 2w

Area of a rectangle

= length × width
= lw

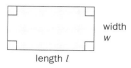

Question

A rectangular patio is 2 m long and 175 cm wide.
(a) Calculate its perimeter in centimetres.
(b) Calculate its area in square metres.

Answer

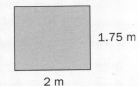

Length: 2 m = 200 cm
Width: 175 cm = 1.75 m

(a) Perimeter = 2 × length + 2 × width
    = 2 × 200 cm + 2 × 175 cm *(all lengths in cm)*
    = 400 cm + 350 cm
    = 750 cm

(b) Area = length × width
    = 2 m × 1.75 m   *(all lengths in m)*
    = 3.50 m^2

Square

A square is a special rectangle.
All its sides are the *same length*.

Perimeter of a square
    = 4 × length of one side
    = 4l

Area of a square = (length of one side)^2
    = l^2

Question

A square place mat is 185 mm long.
(a) Find its area in square centimetres.
(b) Find its perimeter in metres.

Answer

(a) 185 mm = 18.5 cm

    Area of square = length^2
        = 18.5^2 cm^2 = 342.25 cm^2

(b) 185 mm = 0.185 m

    Perimeter = 4 × 0.185 m = 0.74 m

▶ *Exercise* **M3.2**

1 Demontfort College have teams for tennis, netball, hockey, rugby, basketball and soccer. The following plans show the playing areas for each game. They are not drawn to the same scale.
   (a) At the start of training, each team runs once round the perimeter of its playing area. How far does each team run?

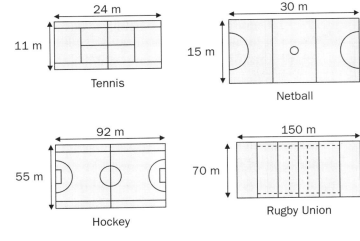

Tennis — 24 m, 11 m
Netball — 30 m, 15 m

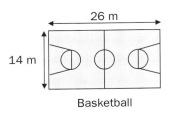

Hockey — 92 m, 55 m

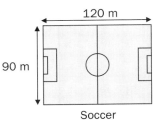

Rugby Union — 150 m, 70 m

Basketball — 26 m, 14 m
Soccer — 120 m, 90 m

   (b) Work out the size of each playing area in m^2.
       Put these areas in order of size. Start with the largest.
   (c) Many other games and sports have rectangular playing areas. Name as many as you can. Find their measurements in metres. Calculate their perimeters and areas.

2 A square table mat has sides of length 12.5 cm. Calculate
   (a) its perimeter in cm   (b) its area in cm^2.

3 A rectangular rug measures 5 m by 630 cm. The rug has a woven edging round its perimeter. Calculate
   (a) the length of its perimeter in cm   (b) its area in m^2.

4 A square coaster has sides of length 72 mm. Calculate
   (a) its perimeter in mm   (b) its area in cm^2

5 A rectangular field measures 2800 m by 1.2 km. Calculate
   (a) its perimeter in m   (b) its area in km^2.   ◀

If you know the perimeter or area of a **rectangle** and one of its sides, then you can **find the lengths of all of its sides**.

   Choose the correct formula: perimeter or area.
   Put in what you know.
   Then solve the equation you get.

Remember: Make sure the units 'match' first.
            Change any if you need to.
            Give the correct unit in the answer.

Question

Pat and Carol have rectangular lawns in their gardens.
(a) In Pat's garden the lawn is 4.5 m wide.
    It has a perimeter of 24 m. How long is it?
(b) In Carol's garden the lawn is 11 m long.
    Its area is 40 m^2. How wide is it?

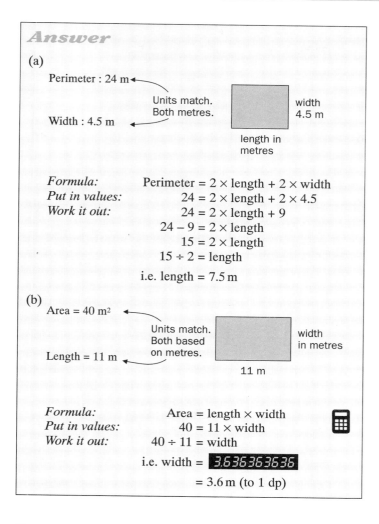

Answer

(a)

Perimeter : 24 m ←

Units match.
Both metres.

Width : 4.5 m ←

width
4.5 m

length in
metres

Formula:	Perimeter = 2 × length + 2 × width
Put in values:	24 = 2 × length + 2 × 4.5
Work it out:	24 = 2 × length + 9
	24 − 9 = 2 × length
	15 = 2 × length
	15 ÷ 2 = length
	i.e. length = 7.5 m

(b)

Area = 40 m² ←

Units match.
Both based
on metres.

width
in metres

Length = 11 m ←

11 m

Formula:	Area = length × width
Put in values:	40 = 11 × width
Work it out:	40 ÷ 11 = width
	i.e. width = `3.636363636`
	= 3.6 m (to 1 dp)

You can also work out the **length of the side of a square** from its perimeter or area.

Question

Terry is repairing two square-topped tables. He sticks 3.4 metres of plastic strip round the perimeter of the top of a coffee table. He uses 2.25 m² of formica to cover the top of a kitchen table.

How long is each table?

Answer

Coffee table

Formula:	Perimeter = 4 × length	length in metres
Put in value:	3.4 = 4 × length	
Work it out:	3.4 ÷ 4 = length	
	i.e. length = 0.85 m	

Kitchen table

Formula:	Area = (length)²
Put in value:	2.25 = (length)²
Work it out:	$\sqrt{2.25}$ = length
	i.e. length = 1.5 m

▶ *Exercise* **M3.3**

1 A rectangular birthday card has an area of 234 cm². It is 13 cm wide. What is its length?

2 A postage stamp is 23 mm long and has a perimeter of 84 mm. How wide is it?

3 A square-shaped bathroom tile has an area of 121 cm². What are its dimensions?

4 A rectangular rug, 2 m long, covers an area of 2.5 m². What is (a) its width   (b) its perimeter?

5 A rectangular field is 85 m wide and covers an area of 8000 m². Calculate its length correct to 1 dp. What is the perimeter of the field?

6 The perimeter of a rectangular table cloth is 30 feet. Its length is 8 feet 6 inches. Calculate its width in feet and inches. What is its area in square feet?

7 The perimeter of a rectangular shaped grill pan is 1.24 m. Its width is 27.2 cm. Calculate (a) its length in cm   (b) its area in cm² correct to the nearest 1 cm².

8 The area of a rectangular shaped school playground is 800 square yards. The length of the playground is 33 yards. Calculate (a) its width (b) its perimeter, each correct to the nearest foot.

Relationships between mm², cm², m² and km²

Here are the main relationships between the metric units of area, mm², cm², m² and km².

There is no need to remember these. But you may need to work them out.

1 cm² = 100 mm²
1 m² = 10 000 cm²
= 1 000 000 mm²
1 km² = 1 000 000 m²

To see why 1 cm² = 100 mm², look at these squares and their areas.

1 cm

1 cm

10 mm

10 mm

Area = 1 cm × 1 cm = 1 cm²   Area = 10 mm × 10 mm = 100 mm²

Since 1 cm = 10 mm, the sides of these squares are the same length. So the squares have the same area.
This gives 1 cm² = 100 mm².

You can work out the other relationships in this way too.

▶ *Exercise* **M3.4**

1 This diagram shows two squares, A and B.

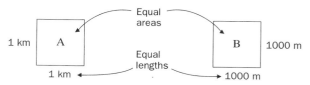

Equal areas

1 km   A

1 km

Equal lengths

B   1000 m

1000 m

Work out the area of square A in km²
Work out the area of square B in m².
How many m² in 1 km²? Explain your answer.

2 1 m = 100 cm. Work out how many cm^2 there are in 1 m^2.
3 1 m = 1000 mm. Work out how many mm^2 there are in 1 m^2.
4 Change 5 km^2 to square metres.
5 Change 8 m^2 to square centimetres.
6 Change 10 cm^2 to square millimetres.

Triangle

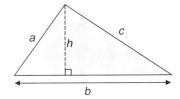

Perimeter of a triangle = sum of lengths of sides
$$= a + b + c$$

Area of triangle = $\frac{1}{2} \times$ base $\times$ perpendicular height
$$= \frac{1}{2} bh$$

To obtain this formula for the area of a triangle, think of the triangle as *half a rectangle*.

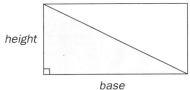
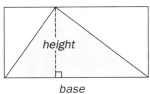

Area of this rectangle = base $\times$ height
Area of triangle = $\frac{1}{2} \times$ base $\times$ height.

Any side can be the base. The height is always at right angles to the base.

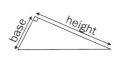
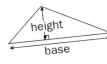
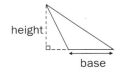
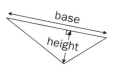

Question

Calculate the perimeter (in cm) and area (in cm^2) of this triangle.

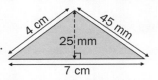

Answer

Change all units to cm.
To change mm to cm, divide by 10.

45 mm = 4.5 cm   25 mm = 2.5 cm

Perimeter = sum of lengths of sides
$$= 4 \text{ cm} + 7 \text{ cm} + 4.5 \text{ cm}$$
$$= 15.5 \text{ cm}$$

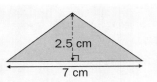

Base: 7 cm
Height: 2.5 cm

Area of triangle = $\frac{1}{2} \times$ base $\times$ height
$$= \frac{1}{2} \times 7 \times 2.5 \text{ cm}^2$$
$$= 8.75 \text{ cm}^2$$

▶ *Exercise* M3.5

1 Calculate the perimeters (in m) and the areas (in m^2) of each of these triangles.

(a)   (c)

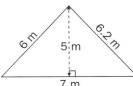

(b)   (d)

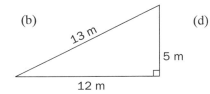
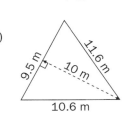

2 Calculate the perimeters (in mm) and the areas (in cm^2) of these triangles.

(a)   (c)

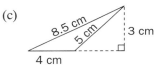

(b)   (d)

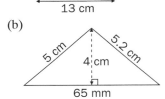
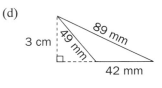

Examination Questions

1 A 60 m length of cling film on a roll is 30 cm wide.
Find the area of cling film on the roll *in m^2*.

(ULEAC, 1990)

2 (a) The square and the rectangular tile shown are equal in area. What is the length of one side of the square tile?

(b) Square tiles of side 20 cm and rectangular tiles 10 cm by 20 cm are used to tile a kitchen floor, part of which is shown.

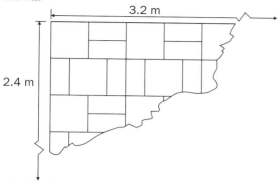

3.2 m

2.4 m

The kitchen floor measures 2.4 m by 3.2 m. How many of each type of tile are needed to tile the floor?

(SEG, 1989)

3

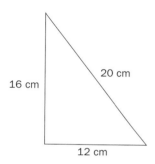

16 cm 20 cm 12 cm

A piece of wire is in the shape of a right-angled triangle with sides 12 cm, 16 cm and 20 cm.
It is then bent into the shape of a square.
How much bigger is the area of the square than the area of the triangle?

(WJEC, 1990)

4 Tracey wants to make a simple bookshelf with two triangular ends, a rectangular base and a rectangular back. The lengths are marked in centimetres. The thickness of the wood has been ignored.

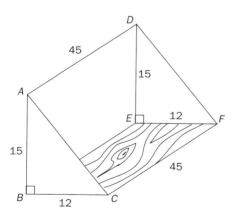

(a) What is the area of the base BCFE?
(b) What is the area of the back ADEB?
(c) What is the area of the end ABC?
(d) What is the total area of wood used?

(MEG, 1989)

5

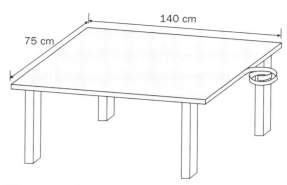

140 cm

75 cm

The rectangular table top above is to have a formica strip stuck to all its edges.
(a) What length of formica strip will be used? (Give the answer in metres.)
(b) The top of the table is covered with a sheet of formica. What area of formica is used? (Give the answer in square metres.)

(NISEAC, 1991)

6

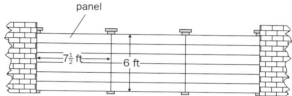

panel

$7\frac{1}{2}$ ft 6 ft

The diagram shows a fence made up of three panels between two brick walls. Each panel measures $7\frac{1}{2}$ ft by 6 ft.
Calculate
(a) the length of the fence
(b) the cost of the posts needed to put up the fence if each post costs £2.75
(c) the total area of the three panels.
(d) One litre of wood preservative covers 100 ft². How many litres are necessary to give two coats to *both* sides of the panels?

(NISEAC, 1991)

7

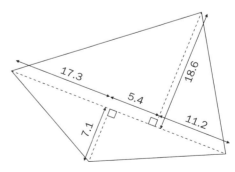

17.3 5.4 18.6 7.1 11.2

This is a sketch of Brian's garden.
The measurements are in metres.
(a) Calculate the area of the garden.
(b) Brian is going to sow grass seed over the whole garden. He uses 45 g of seed for each square metre. He can buy seed in 2 kg bags.
How many bags should he buy?

(MEG, 1988)

8 The figure shows a surveyor's sketch of an open piece of land ABCDE. All the measurements are in metres. The angles marked at F, G and H are right angles.
Calculate:
(a) the length, in metres, of BD
(b) the area of BCD in square metres, to the nearest square metre
(c) the area of ABDE in square metres, to the nearest metre
(d) the total area of ABCDE in square metres, to the nearest square metre
(e) the total area of ABCDE in hectares, to two decimal places. (1 hectare = 10 000 square metres).

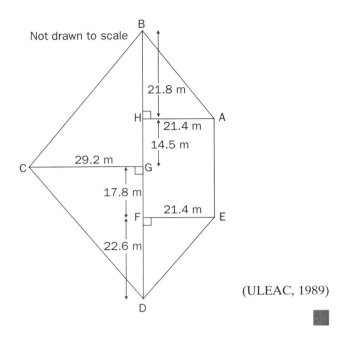

Not drawn to scale

(ULEAC, 1989)

M4
The circle

This unit will help you to:

■ find the circumference and area of a circle

■ understand the meaning of π and its approximate values

■ calculate the radius and diameter of a circle from its circumference or area.

Circumference

The *perimeter* of a circle is called its **circumference**.

The value of (**circumference ÷ diameter**) is the *same* for all circles. Its value cannot be stated exactly. But the Greek letter π (said 'pi') is used to stand for it.

circumference ÷ diameter = π

This relationship gives a formula for the circumference of a circle.

circumference = π × diameter
$$C = \pi d$$

or

circumference = π × 2 × radius
$$C = 2\pi r$$

In calculations you must use an *approximate value for* π.

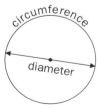

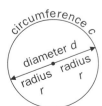

diameter = 2 × radius
d = 2r

You can use π = 3 for very approximate calculations. Usually you will be given the value of π to use.

When using decimals, π is often given as 3.14 or 3.142. When using fractions, π is given as $3\frac{1}{7}$ or $\frac{22}{7}$.

Your calculator may have a π key. You can just press this key instead of entering the approximate value yourself.

Your π key may give the value of π correct to six or more decimal places. So always check whether you may use this key to answer a 'circle question'.

Question

A circular cushion cover is to be trimmed with braid around its edge. The diameter of the cover is 40 cm. Calculate the length of braid required in metres. (Use π = 3.14)

Answer

Diameter: 40 cm = 0.4 m

Circumference = π × diameter
= 3.14 × 0.4 m
= 1.256 m

Length of braid required is 1.26 m (to the nearest cm).

Note: The answer is rounded to the nearest cm because this is a sensible degree of accuracy for lengths of items such as braid.

▶ *Exercise* **M4.1**

In this exercise use 3.142 as a value for π or use the π key on your calculator.
Give your answers to a sensible degree of accuracy if none is suggested in the question.

1 Calculate the circumference of each of these in
(a) mm (b) cm.
Give each answer correct to the nearest millimetre.

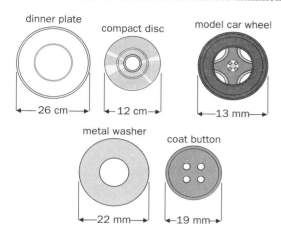

dinner plate

compact disc

model car wheel

←—26 cm—→ ←12 cm→ ←——13 mm——→

metal washer

coat button

←——22 mm——→ ←19 mm→

2 Measure the diameter of each of these coins in millimetres.

Use your measurements to calculate the circumference of
each coin in (a) mm (b) cm.

3 Calculate the circumferences of circles with these
dimensions
(a) radius 7 m   (c) diameter 3.8 cm
(b) radius 2.5 m   (d) diameter 9.6 cm

4 The diameter of a bicycle wheel is 60 cm. How far (in
metres) will the bicycle move when the wheels make one
complete turn?

5 The radius of a circular cricket field is 50 metres.
What is the distance round the boundary?

Area

Area of a circle = π × (radius)²
$$= \pi r^2$$

Here is a way to obtain this formula.

Cut a circle into 16 equal sectors.

radius

r

radius

½ circumference

Put them together like this:

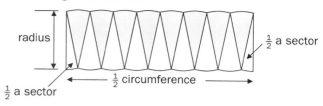

radius

½ a sector

½ a sector

½ circumference

The shape you make is *almost* a rectangle. (Cutting the circle
into more sectors makes it even more like a rectangle).

Its length = ½ circumference = ½ × 2πr = πr
Its width = radius = r

Area of rectangle = length × width = πr × r = πr²
So the area of the circle = πr²

If you know the radius of a circle, then you can use this formula
to find its area.

Sometimes you will be given the diameter instead of the radius.
Remember: radius = ½ diameter.

▶ *Exercise* M4.2

In this exercise use 3.142 as a value for π or use the π key on
your calculator. Give your answers to a sensible degree of
accuracy if none is suggested in the question.

1 Calculate the area of each of these in
(a) mm² (b) cm².

clock face

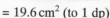

←——23 cm——→

wine glass
coaster

←96 mm→

Red Cross badge

35 mm

saucer

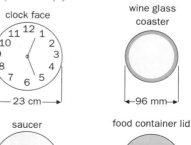

←——14 cm——→

food container lid

BISCUITS

←112 mm→

2 Use the measurements you made in question **2** of Exercise M4.1 to find the area of a circular face for each coin shown.

3 Calculate the areas of circles with these dimensions
(a) radius 2 m   (d) radius 12.7 cm
(b) radius 9 m   (e) diameter 28.2 cm.
(c) diameter 3.5 m

4 A circular table top is covered in formica. The radius of the top is 42 cm. What is the area of the formica used in
(a) cm²   (b) m²?

5 A circular garden pond has a diameter of 2.2 m. Calculate the area of the water surface in
(a) m²   (b) cm².

You can also work out the radius and diameter of a circle from its circumference or area.

Simply put the value you know in the correct formula:

$$C = 2\pi r$$
$$C = \pi d \quad \text{or} \quad A = \pi r^2$$

Then solve the equation you get.

Question

A flower pot has a circular top rim of length 42 cm and a circular base area of 180 cm². Calculate
(a) the radius of the top
(b) the diameter of the base.

Answer

(a) Top: circumference 42 cm
        radius r

Formula: $C = 2\pi r$
Put C = 42: $42 = 2\pi r$

Divide both sides by 2π: $\dfrac{42}{2\pi} = r$

So $r =$ **6.68450761** (using $\boxed{\pi}$ key)
        = 6.7 cm (to nearest mm)

(b) Base: area 180 cm²
        radius r

Formula: $A = \pi r^2$
Put A = 180: $180 = \pi r^2$

Divide both sides by π: $\dfrac{180}{\pi} = r^2$

Take square root: $\sqrt{\dfrac{180}{\pi}} = r$

So $r =$ **7.569397566** (using $\boxed{\pi}$ key)
        = 7.6 cm (to nearest mm)

▶ *Exercise* M4.3

In this exercise, use $\pi = 3.142$ or use the $\boxed{\pi}$ key on your calculator. Give your answers to a sensible degree of accuracy.

1 A hat has a circular rim trimmed with braid. The length of the braid is 138 cm. What is the radius of the hat?

2 A circular metal band around a cooker's ring measures 66 cm. What is the diameter of the ring?

3 The area of the circular base of a frying pan is 270 cm². What is the diameter of the base?

4 A circular rug has an area of 12.5 m². Calculate the radius of the rug.

5 A circular flower bed occupies an area of 55 m². What is its diameter?

6 A jar of marmalade has a circular metal lid whose circumference is 21 cm. What is the radius of the lid?

Examination Questions

1 A circus ring is a circle with diameter 15 metres. Calculate the distance round the edge of the ring. (Take π to be 3.14 and give your answer correct to the nearest metre.)

(WJEC, 1991)

2 The wheels on Diana's bicycle have a diameter of 70 cm.
(a) Calculate the circumference, in metres, of one wheel.
(b) Calculate the number of complete revolutions made by one wheel when Diana cycles 100 m.

(ULEAC, 1988)

3 The largest Big Wheel in the world is in Kobe, Japan. It has a circumference of 200 m.
What is its diameter?

(MEG, 1991)

4

The circular adjustable bangle above has a radius of 3 cm.
(a) Calculate its circumference. (You may take $\pi = 3.14$.)
(b) It is adjusted and its circumference is reduced by 2 cm. Find its new radius.

(NISEAC, 1990)

5 In this question take π as 3.14 or use the π button on your calculator.

When a paper clip is opened out, it looks like this.

(a) What is the total length of the straight parts of the paper clip?
(b) What is the total length of the curved parts of the paper clip?
(c) What is the total length of wire in the paper clip?
(d) A factory produces 20 million of these paper clips each year. How many kilometres of wire does the factory use each year? **Show clearly how you get your answer.**

(WJEC, 1990)

6 Sean is making a cake. The recipe he is using is for a square tin of side 15 cm. He only has circular tins. Work out the diameter of a circular tin that will hold the cake and make it the same depth.

(MEG, 1990)

7

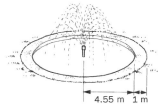

4.55 m   1 m

A circular pond has a radius of 4.55 m.
(a) Taking π to be 3.14, calculate (correct to two significant figures),
   (i) the circumference of the pond,
   (ii) the area of the pond.
(b) The pond is surrounded by a concrete path 1 m wide. Calculate the area of the surface of the path (correct to two significant figures).

(MEG, 1989)

8 Rachel has a cylindrical waste paper bin which is 30 centimetres high and 25 centimetres in diameter.

To make it easier to clean she is going to line the inside with stick-on plastic.

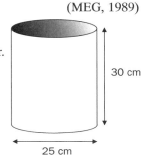

30 cm

25 cm

She wants to use one piece for the bottom

and one piece for the inside wall.

She has a rectangular sheet of plastic which measures 1 metre by 40 centimetres.
Use a diagram to help you work out whether this sheet of plastic is big enough to provide the two pieces which she needs to line the bin.
Explain your answer clearly.

(SCE, 1990)

9 In a large garden there is a circular flower bed which has a diameter of 12 metres.
(a) Calculate the area of the flower bed. (Give your answer correct to the nearest square metre.)
On a packet of fertiliser which is used on the bed, it says '500 g of fertiliser will cover approximately 31.5 m² of soil'.
(b) Calculate the approximate mass of fertiliser needed for this flower bed. (Give your answer in kg correct to 1 decimal place.)
The flower bed is to be enclosed with flexible fencing which can be bought in 2 metre lengths.
(c) Calculate the number of lengths of fencing that should be bought.

(ULEAC, 1991)

M5
More areas

This unit will help you to:

■ work out the areas of shapes made from squares, rectangles, triangles and circles.

Compound shapes

Many *complicated* shapes can be split into *simple* shapes such as rectangles, triangles, circles, …This helps you to find their areas.
   To find the total area, work out the area of each simple shape and add them together. Often you can split up the shape in different ways. For example,

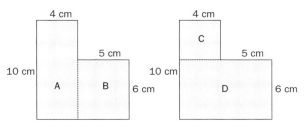

Choose the easiest way.
   Split it into the simplest shapes you can. Look for a way where you know all the lengths you need to work out the areas. For example, choose the first way shown on the left.

Area A: $4 \times 10 = 40\,\text{cm}^2$
Area B: $5 \times 6 = 30\,\text{cm}^2$
Total area A + B = $70\,\text{cm}^2$

Sometimes you have to work out some lengths. For example,

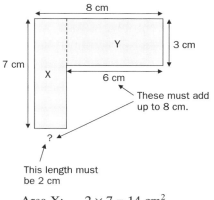

Area X: $2 \times 7 = 14\,\text{cm}^2$
Area Y: $6 \times 3 = 18\,\text{cm}^2$
Total area X + Y = $32\,\text{cm}^2$

> ### Exercise M5.1

Calculate the areas of these shapes.

1

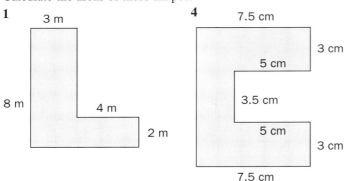

2

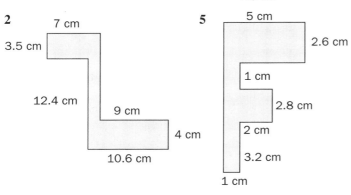

3

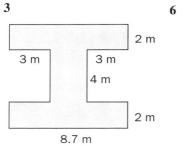

8.7 m

4

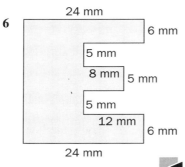

5

6

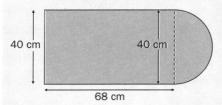

◀

Question

The sketch shows the shape of a formica work surface (not drawn to scale). The surface is made from a rectangle of sides 40 cm and 68 cm and half a circle of diameter 40 cm.

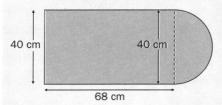

40 cm   40 cm

68 cm

Answer

Calculate the area of the work surface. (Take π to be 3.14.)

Area of the work surface
  = area of rectangle + area inside half a circle

Area of rectangle = length × width
           = 68 cm × 40 cm = 2720 cm^2

Diameter of circle = 40 cm

Radius of circle = $\frac{1}{2}$ of 40 cm = 20 cm

Area inside a circle = πr^2

Area inside half a circle = $\frac{1}{2}\pi r^2$
            = $\frac{1}{2}$ × 3.14 × 20^2 cm^2
            = 628 cm^2

Area of the work surface = 2720 cm^2 + 628 cm^2
            = 3348 cm^2

Here is one way to do this on a calculator. Try it. Then see if there is a better way to do it on your calculator.

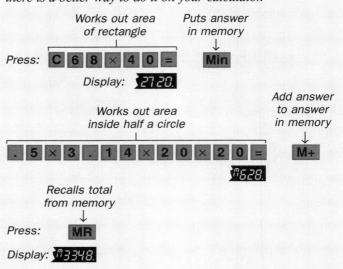

> ### Exercise M5.2

Calculate the areas of these shapes. (All curved lines are semicircles).

1

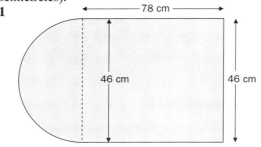

2

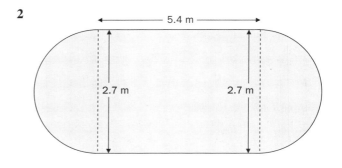

3

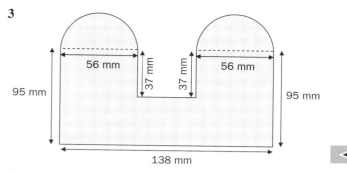

Some areas look like shapes with *hole(s)* cut out of them. To find this kind of area, work out:

area of whole shape – area of hole(s)

Question

The sketch shows a triangular metal plate with sides of 4.5 cm, 6 cm and 7.5 cm. It has three small circular holes cut out of it for fixing bolts. The radius of each circle is 4 mm. (The diagram is not drawn to scale).

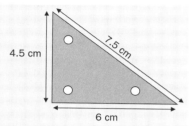

Calculate the remaining area of the metal plate to the nearest square centimetre. (Use $\pi = 3.14$.)

Answer

Area of metal in plate
= area of whole triangle – area of 3 circular holes

Area of circle = πr^2
= $3.14 \times 0.4^2 \text{ cm}^2$ *(4 mm = 0.4 cm)*

Area of 3 circular holes = $3 \times 3.14 \times 0.4^2 \text{ cm}^2$
= 1.5072 cm^2

Area of whole triangle = $\frac{1}{2} \times$ base $\times$ height
= $\frac{1}{2} \times 6 \text{ cm} \times 4.5 \text{ cm}$
= 13.5 cm^2

Area of metal in plate = $13.5 \text{ cm}^2 - 1.5072 \text{ cm}^2$
= 12 cm^2 (to the nearest cm²)

You can use the memory on a calculator to do this. Try this way if you can.

Works out area of 3 holes   *Puts answer in memory*

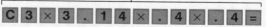

Display: **1.5072**

Works out area of whole triangle   *Subtracts answer recalled from memory*

Display: **13.5**   **11.9928**

There may be another way to do this on your calculator. Experiment to find out if there is. Choose the best way to do this on your calculator.

Exercise M5.3

1 Calculate the areas of these shaded shapes.
(a)

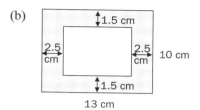

(b)

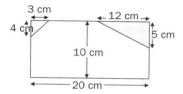

2 The shaded pieces are cut away from a rectangular piece of card 20 cm by 10 cm. Find the area of the shape that is left.

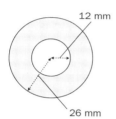

3 This washer has been made by cutting a circular hole of radius 12 mm from a circular disc of radius 26 mm. What is the area of the washer?

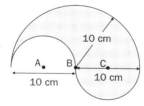

4 This metal cam is used on a machine. A, B and C are the centres of the semicircles shown. Calculate the area of the cam.

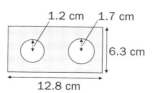

5 The diagram shows a rectangular cover plate. It has two circular holes cut out of it of radius 1.2 cm and 1.7 cm for two drive shafts to pass through. Calculate the area of this cover plate.

Examination Questions

1   The diagram shows a rectangular
lawn 9 m by 7 m. The lawn has
a path 1 m wide round it.
(a) What is the area of the lawn?
(b) What is the area of the path?

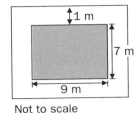

Not to scale

(MEG, 1991)

2   The diagram represents a Hockey Pitch ABCD measuring
100 yards by 60 yards. Each semicircular striking area has
centre G and radius sixteen yards.

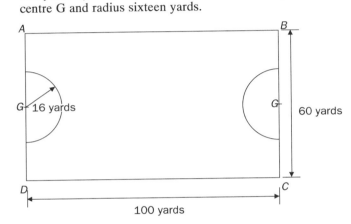

The groundsman marks ALL the lines with white chalk.
(a) Calculate the total length of all the lines, including the
    two semicircular striking areas.
At the end of the hockey season the groundsman decides to
reseed the two semicircular striking areas.
(b) Calculate the area to be reseeded.
    Take $\pi = 3.142$ or use the π key on your calculator.

(SEG, 1990)

3   (a) Calculate $3.14\,(5^2 - 2^2)$.
(In parts (b) and (c) take π to be 3.14 or use the π button on
your calculator.)
(b) Calculate the area of a circular piece of metal of radius
    5 mm.
(c) A circle of radius 2 mm is removed
    from the centre of a circular piece
    of metal of radius 5 mm to make a
    washer as shown here.
    Calculate the area of the metal
    removed.
(d) Calculate the shaded area of the
    washer in the diagram.

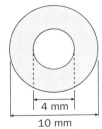

(SEG, 1989)

4   The diagram shows the plan of a concrete drive that Mr
Fraser intends to lay in his garden. ABC and CDE are
perpendicular straight lines and both DEFG
and ABHJ are rectangles. The arc HPG is part of a
circle, of radius 1 m, with centre at O.

AJ = EF = 3 m
AB = 6 m
BC = CD = 4 m
DE = 16 m
OB = OD = 4 m

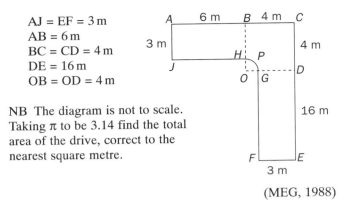

NB The diagram is not to scale.
Taking π to be 3.14 find the total
area of the drive, correct to the
nearest square metre.

(MEG, 1988)

5   The diagram shows a metal plate with four quadrants of a
circle cut away at the corners.

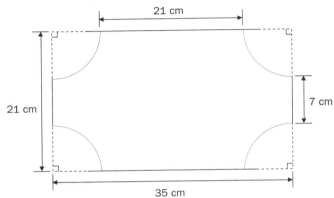

Calculate:
(i)   the radius of the circle of which the quadrants are a part
(ii) the total area cut away
(iii) the area of metal plate remaining.
(Use $A = \pi r^2$ and take $\pi = 3.14$.)

(NISEAC, 1988)

6   Ads-U-Like, an advertising display company, have designed
display stands for jewels and rings. The stands are made of
circular discs each 3 cm deep. The top and side of each
stand are covered with felt.
(a) For a disc with radius
    15 cm, calculate
    (i) the area of the top
    (ii) the area of the side.
(b) Two discs, one with
    radius 15 cm and the
    other with radius 25 cm,
    are stuck together to
    make another stand.
    The smaller disc is
    glued centrally over the
    larger disc as shown. The tops and sides are then
    covered with felt. What area of felt is used for this
    stand?

(MEG, 1991)

M6 Volume

This unit will help you to:

- understand the idea of volume
- find volume by counting cubes
- use the main metric and imperial units of volume
- calculate the volume of cubes and cuboids
- work out and use the main relationships between the common metric units of volume
- know and use the relationship between the main metric units of capacity and volume.

A calculator is a cuboid with these measurements. Calculate its volume in cubic centimetres. Give your answer to the nearest cm^3.

7 mm   6.5 cm   11.2 cm

Answer

Give all lengths in cm.
Length: 11.2 cm   width: 6.5 cm   height: 7 mm = 0.7 cm
Volume of cuboid = length × width × height
$$= 11.2 \times 6.5 \times 0.7 \ cm^3$$
$$= 50.96 \ cm^3$$
Volume of calculator = 51 cm^3 (to nearest cm^3)

The **volume** of a solid shape is the amount of space it occupies.

Volume is measured in **cubic units** such as cubic metres (m^3), cubic centimetres(cm^3) …

For example, each cube in this solid is a 1 centimetre cube. The solid is made from 10 cubes. So the volume of the solid is 10 cubic centimetres, i.e. $10 \ cm^3$.

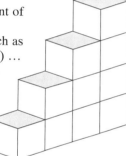

Volume formulae

There are **formulae** for calculating the **volumes** of common solids. This unit gives the volume formulae for **cuboids** and **cubes**.

When calculating volumes, make sure that all the measurements used are in *'matching' units*. For example,

lengths in m to give volume in m^3 $m \times m \times m \rightarrow m^3$
lengths in cm to give volume in cm^3 $cm \times cm \times cm \rightarrow cm^3$

If the measurements are in *'different' units*, then change them to 'matching' units before doing the calculation. See Unit M1.

Cuboid and cube

Volume of a cuboid
= length × width × height
= *lwh*

height *h*   width *w*   length *l*

A cube is a cuboid with all edges the same length.

Volume of a cube
= (length of one edge)^3
= l^3

l   *l*   *l*

▶ *Exercise* M6.1

1 This matchbox measures 19 mm by 53 mm by 37 mm. Calculate its volume in (a) mm^3 (b) cm^3.

19 mm   53 mm   37 mm

2 This box of cocktail sticks measures 10 mm by 15 mm by 5 cm. Calculate its volume in (a) mm^3 (b) cm^3.

5 cm   15 mm   10 mm

3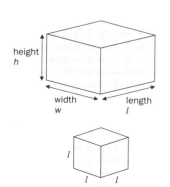

85 mm   85 mm   85 mm

This box of tissues is a cube. Its edges are each 85 mm long. Calculate its volume in cm^3.

4 Calculate the volume of this packing case.

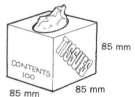

2 m   2.3 m   1.5 m

5 A room has a rectangular shaped floor measuring 5.3 m by 6.2 m. Its height is 420 cm. Calculate its volume.

Relationships between mm^3, cm^3, m^3, km^3

This table gives the main relationships between the common metric units of volume. You do not need to remember these, but you may need to work them out.

$1 \ cm^3 = 100 \ mm^3$
$1 \ m^3 = 1\,000\,000 \ cm^3$
$= 1\,000\,000\,000 \ mm^3$
$1 \ km^3 = 1\,000\,000\,000 \ m^3$

To see why 1 cm³ = 1000 mm³, look at these cubes and their volumes.

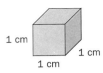   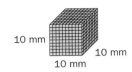

Volume
= 1 cm × 1 cm × 1 cm
= 1 cm³

Volume
= 10 mm × 10 mm × 10 mm
= 1000 mm³

Since 1 cm = 10 mm, the edges of these cubes are the same length. So the cubes have the same volume. This gives

1 cm³ = 1000 mm³.

You can work out the other relationships in the same way.

Each relationship gives the *link between two units*. This can be used to change from one unit to the other.

Decide which relationship you have to use. Write it down with the unit you want on the right hand side. Use the link between the units to work out whether to multiply or divide and by what.

For example, to change from cm³ to mm³ or from mm³ to cm³, you use 1 cm³ = 1000 mm³.

$$\overset{\times 1000}{\underset{1\ \text{cm}^3\quad = 1000\ \text{mm}^3}{\frown}}$$

To change cm³ to mm³, *multiply* by 1000.

5 cm³   = 5 × 1000 mm³   = 5000 mm³
1.2 cm³ = 1.2 × 1000 mm³ = 1200 mm³
0.7 cm³ = 0.7 × 1000 mm³ = 700 mm³

$$\overset{\div 1000}{\underset{1000\ \text{mm}^3 =\quad 1\ \text{cm}^3}{\frown}}$$

To change mm³ to cm³, *divide* by 1000.

9000 mm³ = (9000 ÷ 1000) cm³ = 9 cm³
1050 mm³ = (1050 ÷ 1000) cm³ = 1.05 cm³
460 mm³ = (460 ÷ 1000) cm³ = 0.46 cm³

▶ *Exercise* M6.2

1 This diagram shows two cubes, A and B.

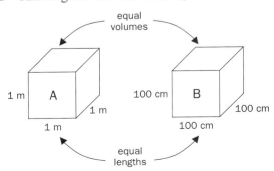

Work out the volume of cube A in m³.
Work out the volume of cube B in cm³.
How many cm³ in 1 m³? Explain your answer.

2 1 m = 1000 mm. Work out how many mm³ in 1 m³.
3 1 km = 1000 m. Work out how many m³ in 1 km³.
4 (a) Change 4 cm³ to cubic millimetres.
   (b) Change 750 mm³ to cubic centimetres.
   (c) Change 0.8 m³ to cubic centimetres.
   (d) Change 5175 cm³ to cubic metres.
   (e) Change 0.006 m³ to cubic millimetres.
   (f) Change 276 100 mm³ to cubic metres.
   (g) Change 0.000 007 km³ to cubic metres.
   (h) Change 2 000 000 m³ to cubic kilometres.
5 Change these volumes to cm³.
   (a) 0.25 m³   (c) 67.5 mm³
   (b) 450 mm³   (d) 0.0079 m³
6 Change these volumes to mm³.
   (a) 0.35 m³   (c) 4.1 cm³
   (b) 0.62 cm³   (d) 0.0008 m³
7 Change these volumes to m³.
   (a) 980 cm³   (c) 8951 mm³
   (b) 0.0002 km³   (d) 0.0125 km³

Volume and capacity

Capacity is the amount that something can hold. It is the measure of how much 'space' is inside something.

To measure the capacity of a container we use **liquid measures**.

The main metric units of capacity you will use are the **litre** (ℓ), **centilitre** (cℓ) and **millilitre** (mℓ).

1 litre = 100 centilitres
1 litre = 1000 millilitres

Capacity is sometimes referred to as 'liquid volume'. Units of capacity and volume are related.

Compare the capacity and volume of these cubes to see the relationship.

The 'inside edges' of this container are 1 cm.

The 'outside edges' of this cube are 1 cm.

    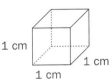

This container holds 1mℓ of liquid. Its capacity is 1mℓ.

This solid occupies 1cm³ of space. Its volume is 1cm³.

The container and solid are the **same size**.

1 millilitre = 1 cubic centimetre
1 mℓ = 1 cm³

1 litre = 1000 cubic centimetres
1 ℓ = 1000 cm³

This relationship can be used to change *capacities to volumes* and *volumes to capacities*.

To change litres to cm³, multiply by 1000.
To change cm³ to litres, divide by 1000.

Question

How many litres of orange drink are needed to fill completely this container?

Answer

Volume of cuboid = 45 cm × 35 cm × 30 cm
= 47 250 cm³
1000 cm³ = 1 litre
So capacity = (47 250 ÷ 1000) litres
= 47.25 litres

► Exercise M6.3

1 Change these to cubic centimetres.
(a) 7 mℓ   (c) 9 litres
(b) 590 mℓ   (d) 0.3 litres

2 Change these to litres.
(a) 4000 cm³   (c) 709 cm³
(b) 1502 cm³   (d) 6 cm³

3 Change these to millilitres.
(a) 5 cm³   (c) 275 cm³
(b) 93 cm³   (d) 6000 cm³

4 A large jug has a volume of 2150 cm³. How many litres of water can it hold when full?

5 This carton of juice measures 8 cm by 8 cm by 15 cm. Is it large enough to hold 1 litre of juice? Explain your answer.

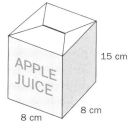

6 What is the volume of this tank in cubic centimetres? How many litres of water can it hold?

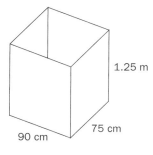

Examination Questions

1 This cubical box is full of coffee.
(a) Work out its volume.
(b) A firm uses a machine to put coffee into jars from the box. It puts 700 cm³ into each jar. How many jars will it fill?

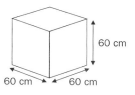

(MEG, 1990)

2 A firm makes dice 1 cm by 1 cm by 1 cm.
(a) The dice are packed in boxes. Each box holds 24 dice. Each box is 6 cm long. Complete the following table to show the different possible dimensions of the box.

length (cm)	height (cm)	breadth (cm)
6		
6		

(b) The firm is thinking of changing the shape of its boxes and using cube-shaped boxes. How many dice would a box 4 cm by 4 cm by 4 cm hold?
(c) Another cube-shaped box holds 27 dice. What are the dimensions of the box?

(WJEC, 1990)

3 Packets of biscuits have dimensions 10 cm by 6 cm by 4 cm. They are packed into cartons with dimensions 44 cm by 20 cm by 18 cm. No space is wasted.

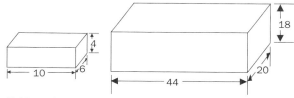

Not to scale

How many packets does one carton contain?

(SEG, 1990)

4 A firm that sells dog food decided to change the size of its tins.
The new tins are 16 cm tall and have a diameter of 8 cm. They are to be packed upright in cardboard boxes that are 64 cm long, 48 cm wide and 32 cm high.

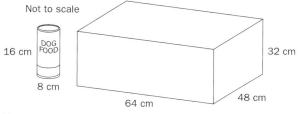

Not to scale

(a) How many layers of tins can be packed into the box?
(b) How many tins will fit along the length of the box?
(c) How many tins will fit along the width of the box?
(d) How many tins will the box hold?

(ULEAC, 1989)

5

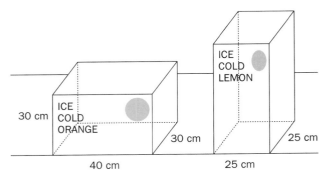

30 cm

ICE COLD ORANGE

30 cm

40 cm

ICE COLD LEMON

25 cm

25 cm

Birtles Snack Bar sells Ice Cold Orange and Ice Cold Lemon drinks.
The drinks are kept in containers as shown.

(a) What volume of orange is needed to fill completely the container of ice cold orange
 (i) in cm^3 (ii) in litres?

The container for ice cold lemon holds 25 litres when completely full.

Its base is square measuring 25 cm by 25 cm.

(b) (i) Work out the height of the lemon container.
  (ii) Work out the number of 20 cℓ glasses that can be filled from the full container of lemon.

(ULEAC, 1989)

6   A petrol can measures 29 cm by 17 cm by 11 cm.
 (a) Calculate the volume of the can in cm^3.
 (b) How many litres of petrol will the can hold when full? Give your answer to the nearest whole number.

(NEAB, 1989)

S1
Angles

This unit will help you to:

■ understand and use terms such as angle, degree, acute, obtuse, reflex ...

■ measure and draw angles to the nearest degree.

An **angle** is the *amount of turn*. In a diagram, an angle is shown by two lines (the **arms**) meeting at a point (the **vertex**).

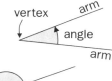

Angles are measured in **degrees** (°). **1 full turn** is 360 degrees (360°).

A $\frac{1}{2}$ turn is 180 degrees (180°). It is also called a **straight angle**.

A $\frac{1}{4}$ turn is 90 degrees (90°). It is also called a **right angle**.

An **acute** angle is less than 90°.
An **obtuse** angle is between 90° and 180°.
A **reflex** angle is between 180° and 360°.

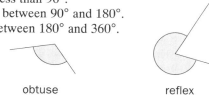

acute   obtuse   reflex

Measuring and drawing angles

You use a **protractor** to measure and draw angles. It is marked in degrees and has two scales.

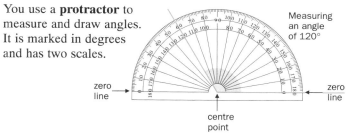

Measuring an angle of 120°

zero line   zero line

centre point

The two main types of protractor are shown here: a *semi-circular* one and a *circular* one. Both are used in a similar way.

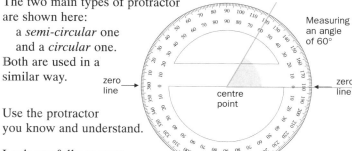

Measuring an angle of 60°

zero line   zero line

centre point

Use the protractor you know and understand.

Look carefully at your protractor. Make sure you can find these key parts:

centre point, zero line, clockwise scale, anticlockwise scale.

To **measure an angle**, follow these steps:

● Look at the angle. Roughly *estimate* its size. Decide whether it is less than 90°, between 90° and 180°, larger than 180°.

● Place the protractor on the angle, its *centre on the 'point'* of the angle (vertex), its *zero line along a line* (arm) of the angle.

● *Find the 0° on top of this arm* of the angle. Go round its scale until you reach the other arm. Count round the numbers on this scale as you go: 0°, 10°, 20°, ... then any extra degrees, 1°, 2°, ...

● Write down the *number of degrees* altogether.

● Compare your measurement with the estimate. *Check* it makes sense.

This angle measures 12°.
Check it with your protractor.

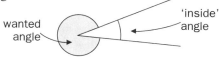

To **measure reflex angles** with a *circular* protractor, follow the steps given above. Using a *semi-circular* protractor, take these steps.

● Measure the *'inside'* angle at the vertex.

● Work out the size of: **360° – 'inside' angle.** This gives the angle you want.

wanted angle   'inside' angle

▶ *Exercise* **S1.1**

1 For each marked angle:
   ● say whether it is acute, obtuse or reflex
   ● estimate its size to the nearest 10°
   ● measure its size to the nearest degree.

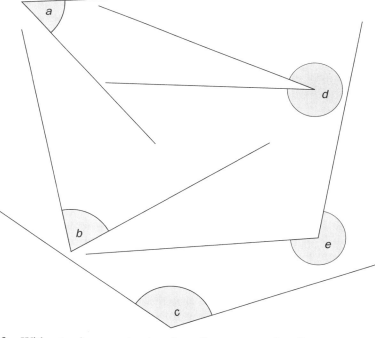

2 Without using a protractor, draw five acute angles, five obtuse angles and five reflex angles. Measure each angle to the nearest degree. Swap drawings with another student in your group. Check each other's angle measurements.

To draw an angle of a given size you need a ruler and sharp pencil as well as a protractor. Take these steps.

- Use a ruler to draw a *straight line*. This is one arm of the angle. Mark a *point* on it where you want the angle point (vertex) to be. Leave plenty of room for the angle.
- Put the *centre point* of the protractor *on the marked point*. Line up its zero line *on top of the line* you drew.
- Keep the protractor still. Find 0° *on top of the line you drew*. Count round its scale *from 0°* to the size you want. Put a dot next to it.
- Remove the protractor. Draw a straight line *through the point and dot*. This is the other arm of the angle.
- *Check* your angle looks about the right size.

Try to produce a neat, clean drawing. Untidy, messy work is difficult to understand. It is also likely to lose marks.

To draw reflex angles with a *circular* protractor, simply follow the steps given above. If you use a *semi-circular* protractor, take these steps.

- Work out the size of: 360° – reflex angle.

- Draw this smaller angle.

The 'other angle' at the point is the one you want.

ACTIVITY

Draw these angles. Label each with its size.
1 (a) 40° (b) 120° (c) 290° (d) 310°
2 (a) 45° (b) 135° (c) 265° (d) 345°
3 (a) 78° (b) 112° (c) 216° (d) 332°

Swap drawings with another student in your group. Check each other's angles.

To identify an angle, we may use:
- *a lower case letter* inside the angle
or ● *a capital letter* at the vertex of the angle
or ● *three capital letters* (the first letter is on one arm of the angle, the middle letter is at the vertex, the third letter is on the other arm).

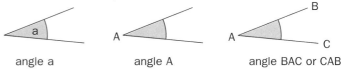

angle a   angle A   angle BAC or CAB

∠ and ^ are symbols for the word 'angle'.
For angle BAC, we write ∠BAC or BÂC.

Remember: If there is more than one angle at a point you must use three capital letters for each angle.

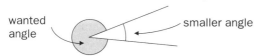

S2
Calculating angles

This unit will help you to:

■ know, use and explain angle facts related to
  – full, half and quarter turns
  – crossing lines
  – parallel lines.

Related angles

A full turn is 360°.
So **angles in a full turn add up to 360°**.

We also say:
Angles at a point add up to 360°.

120° + 105° + 45° + 90° = 360°

A straight angle is 180°.
So **angles in a straight angle add up to 180°**.

We also say:
Angles on a straight line add up to 180°.

21° + 115° + 44° = 180°

A right angle is 90°. So **angles in a right angle add up to 90°**.

Remember: **perpendicular** lines are at right angles to each other.

55° + 35° = 90°

We often use these facts to find 'missing angles' in diagrams.

Question

Calculate the size of each lettered angle in these diagrams.
Show your working clearly.
State the 'angle fact' you used in each case.

(a)   (b)

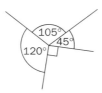

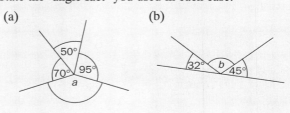

(c)

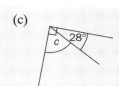

(d)

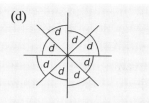

Answer

(a) a = $360° - 70° - 50° - 95°$
　　 = $145°$　　　　(Angles at a point add up to 360°.)

(b) b = $180° - 32° - 45°$
　　 = $103°$　　　　(Angles on a straight line add up to 180°.)

(c) c = $90° - 28°$
　　 = $62°$　　　　(Angles in a right angle add up to 90°.)

(d) $8d$ = $360°$
　　 d = $360° ÷ 8$ = $45°$　　(Angles at a point add up to 360°.)

► *Exercise* S2.1

Calculate the size of each lettered angle in these diagrams.
Show your working clearly.
State the 'angle fact' you used in each case.
Note: *The angles are not drawn accurately.*

1

2

3

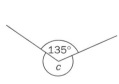

4

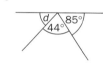

5

6

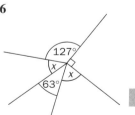

Vertically opposite angles

When two straight lines cross, they make four angles.
Opposite angles are equal.

We call them '**vertically opposite**' because they have the same **vertex**.

Marking (or imagining) an X shape can help you to spot opposite angles. It has been marked in green in the diagram above.

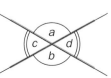

$a = b$ and $c = d$

When you know one angle in an X shape, you can find the other three.

Question

Find the size of angles a, b, and c in this diagram. Give a reason for each answer.

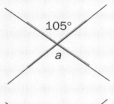

Answer

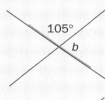

$a = 105°$
(Vertically opposite angles)

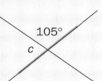

$b = 180° - 105° = 75°$
(Angles on a straight line add up to 180°.)

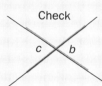

$c = 180° - 105° = 75°$
(Angles on a straight line add up to 180°.)

Check

$b = c = 75°$
(Vertically opposite angles)

This is just one way to work out the angles. It uses the given angle each time, just in case we made a mistake in the calculated angles. The final check is useful.

► *Exercise* S2.2

Find the size of all the lettered angles in these diagrams.
Give a reason for each answer.

1

3

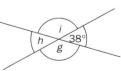

2

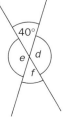

4

Angles and parallels

Parallel lines are always the *same distance apart*. They never meet, even if you make them longer. On diagrams we mark parallel lines with matching arrows.

A straight line which cuts parallel lines is called a **transversal**. Some of the angles it makes with the parallels are equal. They have special names.

Alternate angles

Alternate angles are formed when a transversal cuts parallel lines. (They are on *alternate* sides of the transversal and *between* the parallel lines.) These **alternate angles are equal**.

A pair of equal alternate angles is marked on each diagram below.

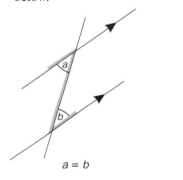

a = b   *x = y*

Marking (or imagining) a ⟋ or ⟍ shape can help you to spot alternate angles. They have been marked in green in the diagrams above to help you.

Find the size of the lettered angles in this diagram. Give a reason for each answer.

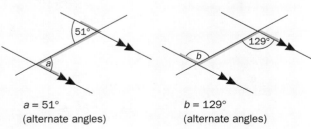

a = 51°
(alternate angles)

b = 129°
(alternate angles)

Find the size of the lettered angles in these diagrams.

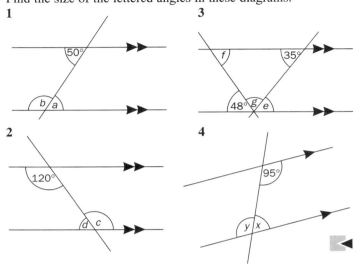

1

2

3

4

Corresponding angles

Corresponding angles are also formed when a transversal cuts parallel lines. (They are in *corresponding* or *matching* positions *between* the parallel lines and the transversal.)
These **corresponding angles are equal**.

A pair of equal corresponding angles is marked on each diagram below.

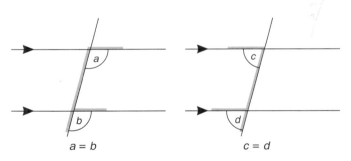

a = b   *c = d*

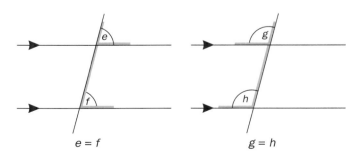

e = f   *g = h*

Marking (or imagining) an F or ꟻ shape can help you to spot corresponding angles. They have been marked in green in the diagrams above to help you.

Question

Find the size of the lettered angles in this diagram. Give a reason for your answer

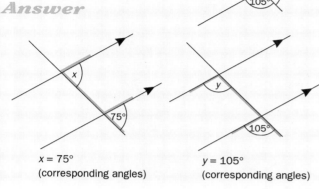

Answer

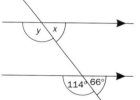

$x = 75°$
(corresponding angles)

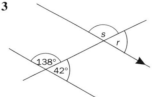

$y = 105°$
(corresponding angles)

► *Exercise* **S2.4**

Calculate the size of each lettered angle in these diagrams. Give a reason for each answer.

1

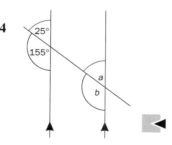

3

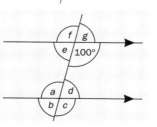

2

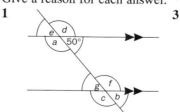

4

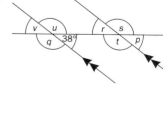

In this diagram a transversal cuts a pair of parallel lines. If you know one angle, then you can work out all the others. Equal angles are marked on the diagram.

Question

Calculate the size of the lettered angles in this diagram. Give a reason for each answer.

Answer

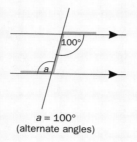

$a = 100°$
(alternate angles)

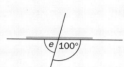

$c = 100°$
(corresponding angles)

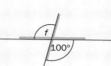

$f = 100°$
(vertically opposite angles)

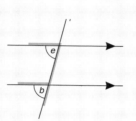

$e = 80°$
(straight angle, $100° + e = 180°$)

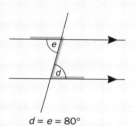

$b = 80°$
(corresponding angles)

$d = e = 80°$
(alternate angles)

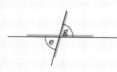

$g = e = 80°$
(vertically opposite angles)

This is one way to work out all the lettered angles. There are others.

► *Exercise* **S2.5**

Find the size of the lettered angles in these diagrams. Give a reason for each answer.

1

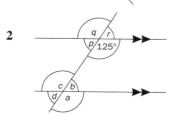

2

3

S3
Angles and shapes

This unit will help you to:

- name and identify polygons
- know the angle sum of a triangle and quadrilateral
- find the angle sum of any polygon
- calculate the size of each angle of a regular polygon
- know the sum of the exterior angles of a polygon
- know simple facts about angles in semicircles and between a tangent and radius
- solve problems using these angle facts, giving reasons for your answers.

Types of quadrilateral are given in Unit S5.

To identify polygons, we often use *captial letters* at their vertices.

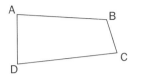

ABCD	ADCB
BCDA	DCBA
CDAB	CBAD
DABC	BADC

There are several correct 'labels' for a polygon. To give a correct 'label' obey these rules:

- Use each 'corner letter', but use it only once.
- Give the letters in the correct order.
  (Start at any vertex. Go round the polygon in one direction only. Do not go across the polygon.)

Polygons

A **polygon** is a flat shape with *straight sides*.

A *3-sided* polygon is a **triangle**.
A *4-sided* polygon is a **quadrilateral**.
A *5-sided* polygon is a **pentagon**.
A *6-sided* polygon is a **hexagon**.
A *7-sided* polygon is a **heptagon**.
An *8-sided* polygon is a **octagon**.
A *9-sided* polygon is a **nonagon**.
A *10-sided* polygon is a **decagon**.

Remember: a circle is *not* a polygon.

A **rectangular polygon** has *all* its sides *equal* and *all* its angles *equal*.

Types of triangle:

equilateral	isosceles	scalene
60° 60° 60°		
3 equal sides 3 equal angles (60°)	2 equal sides 2 equal angles	no equal sides no equal angles
acute-angled	**right-angled**	**obtuse-angled**
Each angle is acute (less than 90°)	One angle is a right angle (90°)	One angle is obtuse

Angles and polygons

Interior angles

The angles of a polygon are its **interior angles**. They are *inside* the polygon. Each interior angle is *at a vertex* and *between two sides* of the polygon.

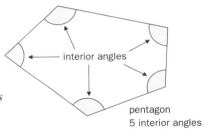

interior angles

pentagon
5 interior angles

A polygon's name tells you the number of interior angles it has.

Remember: tri → 3, quad → 4, pent → 5,
hex → 6, hept → 7, oct → 8

Angle sum of a polygon

The sum of the interior angles of a polygon is often called its **angle sum**.

You should *know* the angle sum of a triangle and a quadrilateral.

The angles of a triangle add up to 180°.

The angles of a quadrilateral add up to 360°.

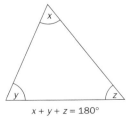

$x + y + z = 180°$

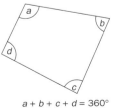

$a + b + c + d = 360°$

We can use these angle sums to find unknown angles in triangles and quadrilaterals.

Question

Work out the size of angle *a* in this quadrilateral.

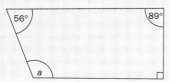

Answer

Add the three angles you know: 56° + 89° + 90° = 235°
Then subtract this total from 360°:

$$a = 360° - 235° = 125°$$

With a calculator, it is often easier to enter 360 first, then subtract the three angles you know:

`3 6 0 – 5 6 – 8 9 – 9 0 = ` `125.`

Don't forget to press `=` *at the end.*

Question

Find the angle sum of an octagon. Show all your working.

all diagonals from just one corner

Answer

This octagon has been split into 6 triangles.

Angle sum of 1 triangle = 180°.

Angle sum of 6 triangles = 6 × 180° = 1080°
So the angles of the octagon add up to 1080°.

ACTIVITY

1 On a large sheet of paper, draw a large decagon (10 sides).
   (a) Divide your decagon into triangles as shown above. Count the number of triangles and calculate the total of all of their angles.
   (b) Measure the interior angles of your decagon and add up your measurements. Compare your result with your answer from part (a).
       Are they the same? How good was your measuring?
2 Repeat the activity for some other polygons.

► *Exercise* S3.1

1 Work out the size of the angles marked with letters in these triangles.

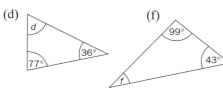

2 Work out the size of the angles marked with letters in these quadrilaterals.

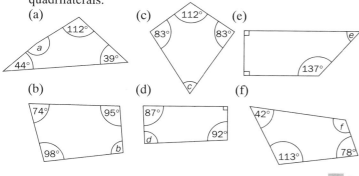

You can find the angle sum of **any polygon**. Here is one way to do it. Split the polygon into triangles by drawing all the diagonals from *just one* vertex (corner). Count the number of triangles made. Then use the angle sum of a triangle.

► *Exercise* S3.2

For each of these polygons
   (a) find the angle sum,
   (b) calculate the size of the angles marked with letters.

1

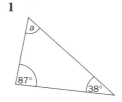

2

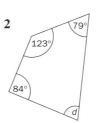

3

4

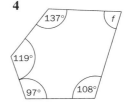

5

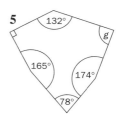

6

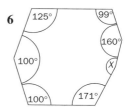

In a **regular polygon**, all the angles are the *same size*. So you can work out the size of each angle. Just divide the angle sum by the number of equal angles.

Question

Find the size of each angle in a regular octagon.

Answer

The angle sum of a regular octagon is 1080°.

A regular octagon has 8 equal angles.

Each angle is $\frac{1080°}{8} = 135°$.

▶ Exercise S3.3

1 Find the size of each interior angle of a regular
   (a) triangle   (c) pentagon (angle sum = 540°)
   (b) quadrilateral   (d) hexagon (angle sum = 720°)
2 The angle sum of a certain regular polygon is 3240°. The
   size of each interior angle of this polygon is 162°.
   How many sides does it have?

You can work out a **formula to find the angle sum of any polygon**. When you split a polygon into triangles by drawing all the diagonals from just one vertex, the number of triangles you get is 2 less than the number of sides of the polygon.
   An *n*-sided polygon → (*n* − 2) triangles

The sum of the angles in each triangle is 180°.
This gives the formula:

Angle sum of an *n*-sided polygon = (*n* − 2) × 180°
$$= (n − 2) × 2 \text{ right angles}$$
$$= (2n − 4) \text{ right angles}$$

If the polygon is **regular**, then each of the *n* angles is equal.
So to find the size of each angle, divide the angle sum by *n*.

Question

What is the size of an interior angle of a 12-sided regular polygon? The angle sum of an *n*-sided polygon is (2*n* − 4) right angles.

Answer

The polygon has 12 sides, so n = 12.

The angle sum of the polygon = (2*n* − 4) right angles
$$= (2 × 12 − 4) \text{ right angles}$$
$$= (24 − 4) \text{ right angles}$$
$$= 20 \text{ right angles or } 20 × 90°$$
$$= 1800°$$

Since the polygon is regular, it has 12 equal angles.
Each angle is 1800° ÷ 12 = 150°.

▶ Exercise S3.4

Use the formula above to calculate the size of an interior angle of a regular polygon with
(a) 5 sides (b) 6 sides (c) 8 sides (d) 9 sides (e) 10 sides.

Exterior angles

The **exterior angles** of a polygon are *outside* the polygon. An exterior angle is formed when a side of the polygon is made longer (produced).

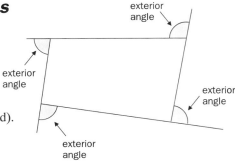

If you make each side of the polygon longer in turn, then you get all the exterior angles of the polygon. **An exterior angle and its interior angle always make a straight angle.** So they add up to 180°.

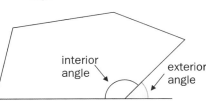

interior angle + exterior angle = 180°

ACTIVITY

1 Draw a polygon with 6 sides large enough to measure its angles. Draw its exterior angles by extending each side in order.
   Measure its exterior angles with a protractor. Add their sizes. What do you find?
2 Repeat activity **1** for a polygon with
   (a) 3 sides (b) 5 sides (c) 7 sides (d) 8 sides (e) 10 sides.
   What do you find?

Sum of the exterior angles of a polygon

The exterior angles of any polygon add up to 360°.
For example,
for this polygon:
a + b + c + d + e = 360°

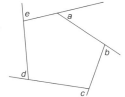

An *n*-sided **regular polygon** has *n* equal angles.
So each of its exterior angles is (360° ÷ *n*).
To find the size of each exterior angle of a regular polygon, divide 360° by the 'number of sides'.

Question

What is the size of each exterior angle of a regular octagon?

Answer

The exterior angles of an octagon add up to 360°.
A regular octagon has 8 equal angles.
Each exterior angle is 360° ÷ 8 = 45°.

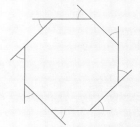

Exercise S3.5

1 What is the size of each exterior angle of a regular
 (a) quadrilateral (b) hexagon (c) decagon.
2 Each exterior angle of a regular polygon is equal to 15°.
 How many sides does it have?
3 Each exterior angle of a regular polygon is equal to
 10°. How many sides does it have?

Angles and circles

A **chord** is a straight line joining *any two*
points on a circle.
A **diameter** is a special chord. It passes through
the *centre* of the circle. A diameter is the longest
chord for a circle.

A **tangent** is a straight line which *touches* a circle at *one point*
only. This point is called the **point of contact**. If a tangent is
made longer, it still will not cut the circle.

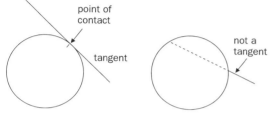

ACTIVITY

1 Draw an accurate diagram of a circle. Show the following
 clearly on your diagram and label them.
 (a) diameter (b) tangent (c) chord
2 What name is given to the longest chord which can be
 drawn on any circle?
3 Draw two chords of equal length on your circle. Measure
 the distance from the centre of each chord to the centre of
 the circle. What do you notice? Will this always happen?
4 Draw a line from the centre of your circle to the point
 where the tangent and circle meet. Measure the angle
 between this line and the tangent. What do you notice?
 Will this always happen?

Simple circle theorems

Angle in a semicircle theorem:

An angle in a semicircle is a right angle.

Theorem

The **converse** of this theorem is also useful. (The converse of a
theorem is the theorem put the other way round. For example,
the converse of 'a polygon with three sides has three angles' is
'a polygon with three angles has three sides'. Not all theorems
have converses which are true.)

Converse of Angle in a semicircle theorem:
If a circle passes through the vertices of a right-
angled triangle, then the hypotenuse of the
triangle is a diameter of the circle.

Converse

Question

Which angles are right angles in this
circle? Mark them on the diagram.
C is the centre of the circle.

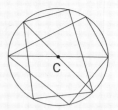

Answer

Each marked right angle is an angle in
a semicircle.

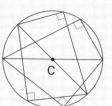

Exercise S3.6

Which angles are right angles in these circles?

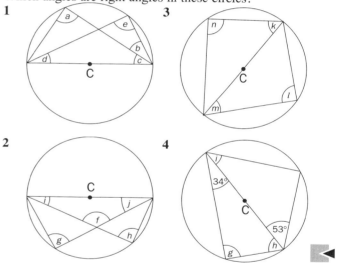

Tangent-radius theorem:

**A tangent to a circle is perpendicular
to the radius at the point of contact.**

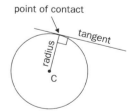

You can use these theorems to help you calculate the sizes of
other angles in a circle diagram.

Question

This diagram shows a circle, centre O,
and a tangent PQ to the circle. T is
the point of contact of the radius TO
and the tangent PQ. Calculate the
sizes of angles *a*, *b* and *c*.

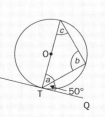

continued

Answer

OT is a radius and PQ is a tangent.
The angle between OT and PQ is angle OTQ.
So angle OTQ = 90° (tangent-radius theorem).

Angle *a* = 90° − 50° = 40°
Angle *b* = 90° *(angle in a semicircle)*
Angles a, b and c are the angles of a triangle.
Angle *a* + angle *b* = 40° + 90° = 130°.
So angle *c* = 180° − 130° *(angles of a triangle add up to 180°)*
         = 50°.

- **right angles**
  – perpendicular lines
  – marked right angles
  – in special quadrilaterals (Unit S5)
  – in circles
- **angle sums**
  – of a triangle (180°)
  – of a quadrilateral (360°)
  – of other polygons.

Use pencil to mark what you know, and what you find, on a diagram. This can help you to decide what to do.

 ## *Exercise* **S3.7**

Calculate the sizes of the lettered angles in these diagrams. In each case O is the centre of the circle and AT is a tangent.

1

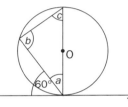

4

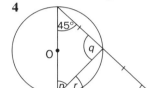

2

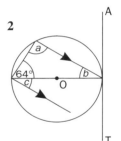

5

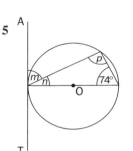

3

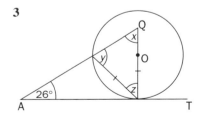

6

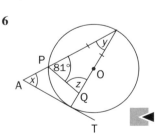

Calculating angles

To calculate the sizes of angles in a diagram you will often use *more than one* angle fact.

Look for:
- **related angles** making 90°, 180°, 360° (Unit S2)
- **equal angles**
  – vertically opposite (Unit S2)
  – with parallel lines (Unit S2)
  – in isosceles and equilateral triangles
  – in special quadrilaterals (Unit S5)
  – in regular polygons
  – due to symmetry (Unit S6)

Examination Questions

1 Work out the sizes of the angles labelled *a* and *b* in the diagram.

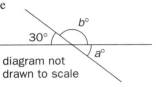

diagram not drawn to scale

(ULEAC, 1989)

2 Anne designs a badge for her youth club. The largest angle at the centre is 120°. The other three are each of size *x*°. Find the value of *x*.

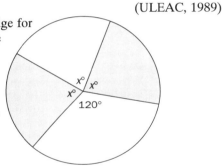

Not to scale

(MEG, 1990)

3

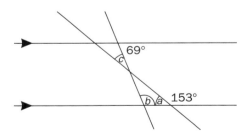

In the diagram above calculate the angles *a*, *b* and *c*.

(NISEAC, 1988)

4 The side view of a picnic bench is shown.

BC = AD
E is the mid-point of DC
AB is parallel to DC
∠BAE = 40°,
∠ADE = 60°

Work out the size of the angles marked *a* and *b*.

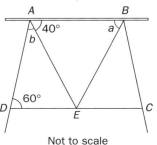

Not to scale

(MEG, 1991)

5 ABCDE represents a swimming pool with all its sides of equal length. A rope joins A to C and is parallel to ED. Given that ∠ BAC = 36° calculate:

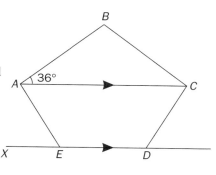

(a) ∠ ABC
(b) ∠ CAE
(c) ∠ AEX.

(SEG, 1988)

6

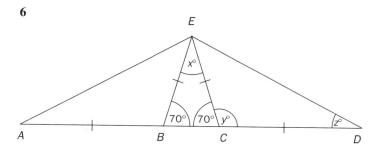

Not to scale

The diagram represents the beams used in the roof of a house. ABCD is a straight line and the lengths of AB, BE, EC and CD are all equal.
Calculate the sizes of the angles marked $x°$, $y°$ and $z°$.

(MEG, 1988)

7 Three mathematical shapes are drawn below.

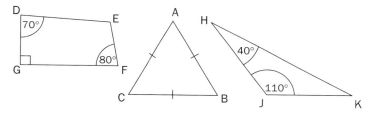

(a) Calculate the size of
   (i) angle E   (ii) angle C   (iii) angle K.
(b) The shapes are put together so that corners F, C, and J meet at point P, as shown in the diagram below.

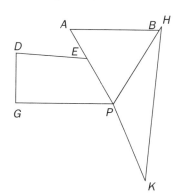

(i) Calculate the size of the obtuse angle GPK.
(ii) Explain why APK is **not** a straight line.

(NEAB, 1990)

8

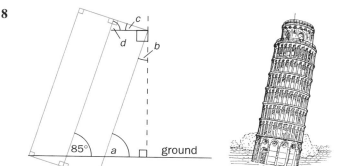

This sketch shows a cross-section through the leaning tower of Pisa. The angle the centre line makes with the ground is 85°. The sketch is not to scale.
Work out the angles a, b, c and d marked on the sketch.

(MEG, 1991)

9 This is a copy of a decoration. It is not drawn accurately.
Work out the value of
(a) angle p
(b) angle q.

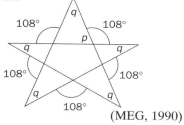

(MEG, 1990)

10

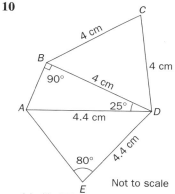

Not to scale

(a) (i) What type of triangle is BCD?
   (ii) What is the size of the angle BCD?
(b) Calculate the size of the angle DAB
(c) Calculate the size of angle BAE.

(SEG, 1991)

11 Three regular polygons are placed together as shown.
Calculate the size of the angle marked a.

(MEG, 1991)

12

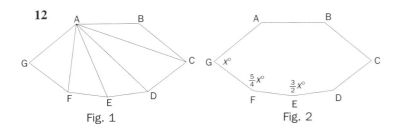

Fig. 1   Fig. 2

(a) Using Fig. 1, calculate the sum of the angles of the polygon ABCDEFG.
(b) If, in Fig. 2, angle GAB = angle ABC = angle DEF and angle FGA = angle BCD and angle EFG = angle CDE, calculate x.

(NISEAC, 1988)

13 (a) ABCDE is a regular polygon centre O.
  (i)   Calculate angle AOB.
  (ii) Calculate angle OAB.
  (iii) Calculate the size of an interior angle of a regular pentagon.

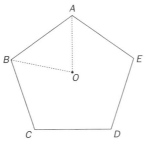

(b)

It is possible to make tessellations using equilateral triangles, squares or regular hexagons as shown in the diagrams above.
  Explain why it is not possible to make a tessellation using only regular pentagons.

(NEAB, 1989)

14 In the diagram below, ABCDE represents a regular pentagon.
Calculate
(a) angle BCD
(b) angle CBD
(c) angle BDE.

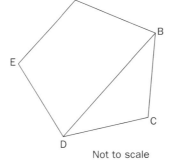

Not to scale

(Cambridge, 1991)

15

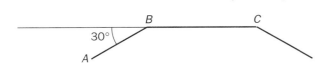

AB and BC are adjacent sides of a regular polygon. The exterior angle of this polygon is 30°. How many sides has this regular polygon?

(NEAB, 1990)

16 AB and BC are adjacent sides of a regular 12-sided polygon.
Calculate the size of angle ABC.

(ULEAC, 1990)

17 (a) Find the values of x and y.

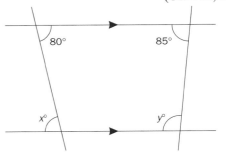

(b) AB is a diameter
AD = BD
∠CAB = 50°
Find the angles:
(i)   ∠ACB
(ii) ∠CBA
(iii) ∠ADB
(iv) ∠DAB

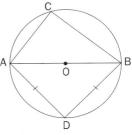

(c) The interior angle of a regular polygon is 3 times as big as the exterior angle. How many sides has the regular polygon?

(NISEAC, 1991)

18 AT and BT are tangents to the circle centre O.
(a) Angle ATB = 38°.
    Calculate angle AOB.
(b) Another circle is drawn with OT as its diameter. Explain why it passes through A and B.

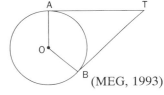

(MEG, 1993)

19 The diagram shows a circle, centre O. The diameter AB is produced to T, and TC is a tangent to the circle.
Calculate
(a) angle OCB
(b) angle CBT
(c) angle CTA.

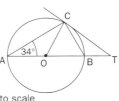

Not to scale

(MEG, 1993)

20 A, B and C are three points on a circle with centre O. TA and TB are tangents to the circle, and TOC is a straight line.
(a) Describe completely the transformation which maps triangle CAT on to triangle CBT.
(b) Angle AOT = 56°.
    (i)   Calculate angle AOC.
    (ii) Calculate angle ACO.
    (iii) Calculate angle ATB.

Not to scale

(MEG, 1993)

S4
Symmetry

This unit will help you to:

■ understand and use line and rotational symmetry

■ identify the symmetries of shapes.

Line symmetry

A shape with **line symmetry** looks *balanced*. You can divide it into *two matching halves*. The dividing line is called a **line of symmetry**. It is also called an **axis of symmetry**.

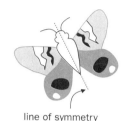
line of symmetry

If a shape can be *folded* so that one half fits *exactly* on top of the other, then the **fold line** is a line of symmetry.

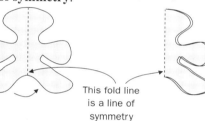
This fold line is a line of symmetry

If a *mirror* is placed along a line of symmetry, then the *half shape* and its reflection look like the full shape.

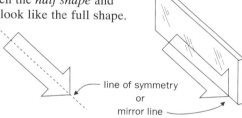
line of symmetry or mirror line

So a line of symmetry is often called a **mirror line**. Line symmetry is also called **mirror** or **reflection symmetry**.

Some shapes have *more than one* line of symmetry. Each dotted line on these shapes is a line of symmetry.

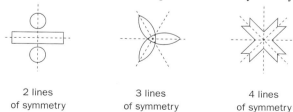

2 lines of symmetry   3 lines of symmetry   4 lines of symmetry

Some shapes do *not* have any lines of symmetry. Here are some examples.

► *Exercise* S4.1

How many lines of symmetry does each of these shapes have? Draw sketches to show where these lines are. Use a mirror to check if you are not sure.

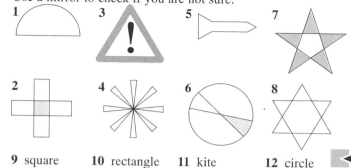

9 square   10 rectangle   11 kite   12 circle

Given part of a shape and its lines of symmetry, you may be asked to **complete the shape**. Make sure that you match *points, lines, shading, …*

Deal with one line of symmetry at a time. It is easier!

For example, look at the pattern on this tile.

Given the part of the pattern shown in black and the dotted lines of symmetry, you can draw the whole pattern.

You can build up the pattern step-by-step using each line of symmetry in turn. Try it.

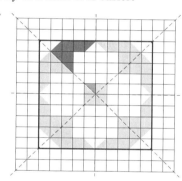

► *Exercise* S4.2

1   Copy and complete these drawings so that, in each case, the dotted line is a line of symmetry.

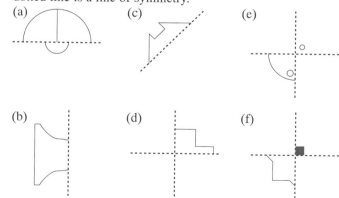

(a)   (c)   (e)

(b)   (d)   (f)

2   Terry drew six patterns on a square grid for some tiles. Here are descriptions of their lines of symmetry:
(a) 1 horizontal line only   (d) exactly 2 lines
(b) 1 vertical line only   (e) 2 sloping lines
(c) 1 sloping line only   (f) more than 2 lines.
Draw patterns of your own to fit these descriptions.

Rotational symmetry

A shape with **rotational symmetry** looks like its '*starting position*' several times during a rotation of 1 full turn. The 'number of times' tells you the **order of rotational symmetry**.

This road sign looks like its 'starting position' 3 times during a rotation of 1 full turn. It has rotational symmetry of order 3.

To check this, trace the shape and mark the top as shown. Rotate your tracing on top of the shape for one full turn about its centre. Count the number of times it fits exactly on top of the shape.

Some shapes look the same after they have been rotated half a turn (180°). We say that these shapes have **half-turn symmetry** or **point symmetry**. They have rotational symmetry of *order 2*.

Some shapes only look the same after being rotated the full turn (360°). They do *not* have rotational symmetry. We say they are of *order 1*.

Question

Which of these road signs does not have rotational symmetry? Give the orders of rotational symmetry of the other signs.

(a)   (b)   (c)   (d)   (e)

    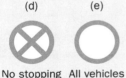

STOP sign ahead   Road clear   Hump bridge   No stopping (clearway)   All vehicles prohibited

Answer

Sign (c) does not have rotational symmetry.
Sign (a) : order 3
Sign (b) : order 2
Sign (d) : order 4
Sign (e) : order 'infinity' – *too many 'times' to count*.

You can check each answer by tracing the shape and rotating it.

► Exercise S4.3

1   Trace each of these shapes. Mark the top each time. Work out the order of rotational symmetry.

(a)   (b)   (c)

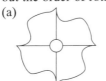

2   Which of these shapes have rotational symmetry? If a shape has rotational symmetry, give its order.

(a)   (c)   (e)

(b)   (d)   (f)

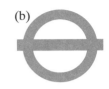 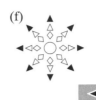

Line and rotational symmetry

Some shapes have *both* line *and* rotational symmetry.

 This shape has 5 lines of symmetry. It also has rotational symmetry of order 5.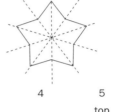

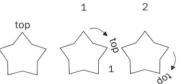 

► Exercise S4.4

1   Describe the symmetry of each of these letters.

A B C D E F G H I J K L M
N O P Q R S T U V X Y Z

Which of these letters have both line and rotational symmetry?

2   Which of these shapes have both line and rotational symmetry?

(a)   (c)   (e)

(b)   (d)   (f)

 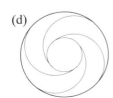

Give the number of lines of symmetry and the order of rotational symmetry for each shape.

Examination Questions

1 The symbol shown below is the logo used by a well-known car manufacturer.
(a) Make a sketch of this logo.
(b) On your sketch show clearly ALL lines of symmetry this logo has.

(SEG, 1990)

2 The design on a wall tile is a shaded pattern. The pattern has a horizontal and vertical line of symmetry.
(a) Complete the shading in the diagram to show all the pattern on the tile.
(b) What fraction of the tile is unshaded?

(NEAB, 1991)

3 Complete these drawings so that, in each case, the dotted line is a line of symmetry.
(a)   (b)   (c)

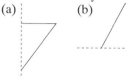 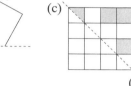

(MEG, 1990)

4 Complete the shading in the diagram so that the broken lines AB and CD are lines of symmetry.

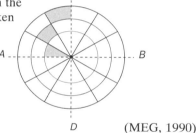

(MEG, 1990)

5 (a) Describe completely the symmetry of the pattern of shaded squares in the crossword puzzle opposite.
Helen is compiling a crossword puzzle. She wants the pattern of the shaded squares to have the same type of symmetry as the pattern in part (a) about the centre square *which is unshaded*.

(b) (You are advised to complete all this part of the question in pencil).
   (i) Complete the shading on the crossword puzzle.
   (ii) Complete the numbering of the squares in the puzzle.

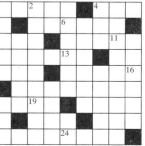

(NEAB, 1988)

6 A double glazing company uses the name

All of these letters have rotational and/or line symmetry. Complete the table to show the symmetries of each letter.

Symmetry type	Letters
Line symmetry only	
Rotational symmetry only	
Both line and rotational symmetry	

(SEG, 1991)

7 (a) The square tile ABCD is symmetrical in the lines AOC and BOD. Using reflections in the lines AOC and BOD, complete the whole pattern on the tile.
(b) What is the order of rotational symmetry about O of the tile?

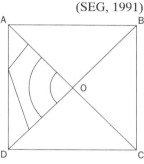

(ULEAC, 1990)

8

I	V	IX
II	VI	X
III	VII	XI
IV	VIII	XII

Set A   Set B   Set C

Set A consists of 4 road signs symbols, set B represents 4 dominoes and set C is made up of a rhombus, an isosceles triangle, a parallelogram and a square.
(a) Draw all the lines of symmetry on the symbols IV, VI and IX.
(b) There is one road sign in set A, one domino in set B and one geometrical shape in set C that have precisely ONE line of symmetry.
Write down the roman numerals that are alongside them.
(c) In this part of the question, study ONLY the rotational symmetries of the symbols I to XII.
   (i) Which dominoes have exactly the same rotational symmetry as road sign II?
   (ii) Which geometrical shape has exactly the same rotational symmetry as domino VII?
(d) Which ONE of the symbols II to XII has exactly the same line and rotational symmetries as symbol I?

(WJEC, 1989)

S5
Quadrilaterals

This unit will help you to:

■ recognise different types of quadrilaterals
■ know and use the properties of quadrilaterals
■ classify quadrilaterals using their properties.

A **quadrilateral** is a polygon with *4 sides*. It has *4 angles* and *4 vertices*.

A quadrilateral has two **diagonals**. They join *opposite* vertices of the quadrilateral.

diagonals

The angles of a quadrilateral add up to 360°.
$a + b + c + d = 360°$

Quadrilaterals make **tessellations,** i.e. tiling patterns without 'gaps'. (See Unit S10).

Special quadrilaterals

Some quadrilaterals have special names. Each special name has a special **property** related to it.

Special quadrilateral	Special property
trapezium	Only one pair of opposite sides parallel
parallelogram	Both pairs of opposite sides parallel
rhombus	All sides equal in length
rectangle	All angles equal (to 90°)
square	All sides equal in length and all angles equal (to 90°)
kite	Two pairs of adjacent sides equal

▶ *Exercise* **S5.1**

1 Hidden in this puzzle are six different quadrilaterals drawn on a 25-dot grid. Find each one, name it and describe it using the capital letters.

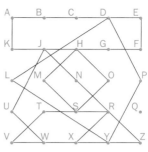

2 This quadrilateral is drawn on a 9-dot grid. Draw as many different quadrilaterals as you can on a 9-dot grid. If a quadrilateral has a special name, write it beside the shape. Name each shape using the capital letters.

3 (a) Draw a quadrilateral on dotty paper. Do not make it a special one.

Mark the mid-points of each side.
Join the mid-points in order to make a polygon.
What special shape have you drawn?

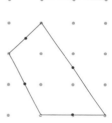

(b) Try doing this with some other quadrilaterals (not special ones).
What kind of shape do you get each time?
Try to draw an 'ordinary quadrilateral' so that when you join the mid-points you do not get this kind of shape. What do you find?

(c) Try this mid-point experiment with these special quadrilaterals:
rectangles, squares, rhombuses, parallelograms, kites and trapeziums.
Write about your findings.

Most of these special quadrilaterals have other special properties.

Parallelogram:

Opposite sides parallel

Opposite sides equal

Opposite angles equal

Diagonals bisect each other

Rhombus:

Opposite sides parallel

All sides equal

Opposite angles equal

Diagonals bisect each other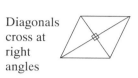

Diagonals bisect corner angles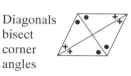

Diagonals cross at right angles

Rectangle:

All angles equal to 90°

Opposite sides equal

Opposite sides parallel

Diagonals equal in length and bisect each other

Square:

All angles equal to 90°

All sides equal

Opposite sides parallel

Diagonals equal in length and bisect each other

Diagonals cross at right angles

Diagonals bisect corner angles

45°

Kite:

Adjacent sides equal

One pair of opposite angles equal

Diagonals cross at right angles

Only one diagonal is bisected

Only one pair of opposite angles is bisected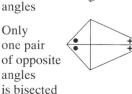

▶ *Exercise* S5.2

You can summarise the properties of quadrilaterals in a table like this. The properties of a kite are shown below.

Copy and complete the table yourself for the rest of the special quadrilaterals.

Properties	Kite
Only one pair of opposite sides parallel	✗
Both pairs of opposite sides parallel	✗
Two pairs of adjacent sides equal	✓
Both pairs of opposite sides equal	✗
All sides equal	✗
One pair of opposite angles equal	✓
Both pairs of opposite angles equal	✗
All angles equal (to 90°)	✗
One diagonal bisected by the other	✓
Diagonals bisect each other	✗
Diagonals equal in length	✗
Diagonals cross at right angles	✓
One pair of opposite angles bisected by a diagonal	✓
Both pairs of opposite angles bisected by a diagonal	✗

Quadrilaterals can be sorted into two main sets:
those which are parallelograms and those which are not.

Parallelograms

Not parallelograms

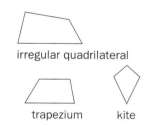

parallelogram   rhombus

square   rectangle

These quadrilaterals have all the properties of a parallelogram. The rhombus, rectangle and square have 'extra' properties.

irregular quadrilateral

trapezium   kite

▶ *Exercise* S5.3

Each description given below fits one or more quadrilaterals. Name as many as you can.

1 It has all angles equal.
2 Its diagonals cross at right angles.
3 It has two pairs of opposite sides parallel.
4 It has no equal length sides.
5 Its diagonals bisect each other.
6 It has all sides equal in length.
7 It has one pair of opposite angles equal.
8 Its diagonals are equal in length.

You can often use the properties of quadrilaterals to find lengths and angles.

Question

ABCD is a rhombus.
∠A = 34°, AB = 25 cm, BD = 14 cm and AC = 48 cm.
Its diagonals cross at O.

Draw a sketch diagram of ABCD. Work out the size of as many lengths and angles on it as you can. Give reasons for your answers.

Answer

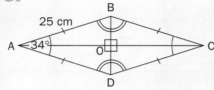

$AB = BC = CD = DA = 25$ cm   (equal sides of a rhombus)

$DO = OB = \frac{1}{2}DB = \frac{1}{2}$ of 14 cm = 7 cm } (diagonals bisect
$AO = OC = \frac{1}{2}AC = \frac{1}{2}$ of 48 cm = 24 cm } each other)

$\angle AOB = \angle BOC = \angle COD = \angle DOA = 90°$
                (diagonals cross at right angles)

$\angle BCD = \angle BAD = 34°$ (opposite angles are equal)

$\angle ABC = \angle ADC = \frac{1}{2}(360° - 2 \times 34°) = 146°$
                (angle sum is 360°, opposite angles are equal)

$\angle BAC = \angle CAD = \angle BCA = \angle ACD = \frac{1}{2}$ of 34° =17° }
$\angle ABD = \angle DBC = \angle CDB = \angle BDA = \frac{1}{2}$ of 146° =73° }
                (diagonals bisect angles)

► *Exercise* S5.4

Use angle and side properties of the shapes below to find
(a) the size of the lettered angles
(b) as many lengths as you can.
In each case give reasons for your answers.

1
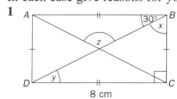

2
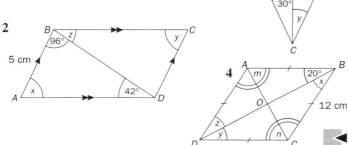

3
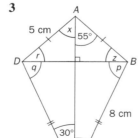

Examination Questions

1 On the grid below are 4 quadrilaterals. One diagonal has been drawn in each shape.

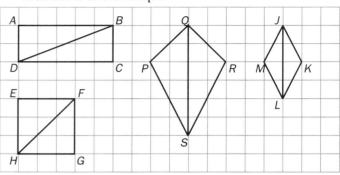

(a) What is the special name given to the quadrilateral PQRS?
(b) What is the special name given to the triangle ABD?
(c) In which shapes does the diagonal divide the quadrilateral into two isosceles triangles?
(d) In the shape JKLM, angle JML is 126°. Calculate, showing your method, the size of angle MJK.

(NEAB, 1989)

2 Below are five statements about the diagonals of a rectangle. The statement which is not **always** true is
A they bisect each other
B they cross at right angles
C they are equal in length
D each bisects the area of the rectangle
E they divide the rectangle into four triangles of equal area.

(ULEAC, 1989)

3 In the diagram AB is parallel to DC.
(a) Calculate the value of
 (i) x
 (ii) y.
(b) Write down a possible pair of values of s and t.

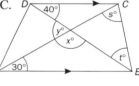

(NEAB, 1989)

4
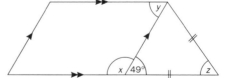

Use the diagram above to calculate the value of
(a) x   (b) y   (c) z.

(NEAB, 1990)

5 OABC is a parallelogram. OAD is a straight line. Work out the size of the angles marked x, y and z in the diagram.

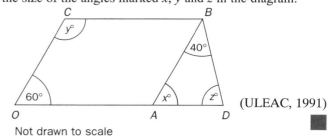

Not drawn to scale

(ULEAC, 1991)

S6
Symmetry and shapes

This unit will help you to:

■ identify the symmetries of triangles, quadrilaterals and other polygons

■ solve problems using the symmetry properties of polygons

■ identify planes of symmetry.

Triangles

Here are the symmetries of some named triangles.

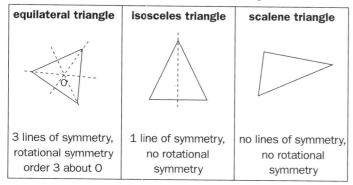

equilateral triangle	isosceles triangle	scalene triangle
3 lines of symmetry, rotational symmetry order 3 about O	1 line of symmetry, no rotational symmetry	no lines of symmetry, no rotational symmetry

Check these symmetries yourself with some triangles.

Quadrilaterals

Some quadrilaterals are symmetrical. Here are the symmetries of the quadrilaterals you have studied.

Square
4 lines of symmetry
Rotational symmetry of *order 4*.

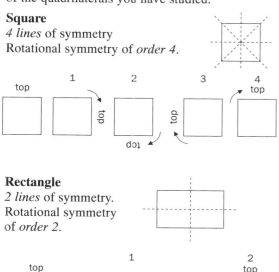

Rectangle
2 lines of symmetry.
Rotational symmetry of *order 2*.

Rhombus
2 lines of symmetry.
Rotational symmetry of *order 2*.

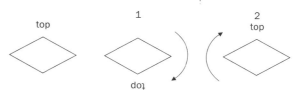

Parallelogram
No lines of symmetry.
Rotational symmetry of *order 2*.

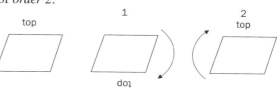

Kite
1 line of symmetry.
No rotational symmetry (i.e. *order 1*).

Trapezium
No lines of symmetry.
No rotational symmetry (i.e. *order 1*).

Isosceles trapezium
(opposite non-parallel sides equal in length)
1 line of symmetry.
No rotational symmetry (i.e. *order 1*).

Irregular quadrilateral
No lines of symmetry
No rotational symmetry (i.e. *order 1*)

▶ *Exercise* **S6.1**

1 Each description below fits one or more quadrilateral. Name as many as you can.
   (a) It has rotational symmetry of order 2.
   (b) It has 2 lines of symmetry.
   (c) It has no rotational symmetry.
   (d) It is the most symmetrical.
   (e) It has rotational symmetry only.
   (f) It has a single line of symmetry only.

2 (a) Copy this Venn diagram.

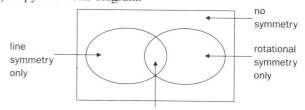

   (b) Write the name of each of these quadrilaterals in its correct place on your diagram:
       square, rectangle, rhombus, parallelogram, trapezium, isosceles trapezium, kite, irregular quadrilateral.

Regular polygons

A **regular** polygon has *all* its angles the same size and *all* its sides the same length.

| regular triangle (equilateral triangle) | regular quadrilateral (square) | regular pentagon | regular hexagon |

All regular polygons have *both line and rotational symmetry*. The *number of lines* of symmetry and the *order* of rotational symmetry is the same as the *number of sides*.

Question

Describe and draw diagrams to show the symmetry of a regular hexagon.

Answer

A regular hexagon has 6 lines of symmetry.

It has rotational symmetry of order 6.

   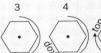

▶ *Exercise* S6.2

Describe and draw diagrams to show the symmetry of these regular shapes.

1 Regular pentagon.

2 Regular octagon.

3 Regular decagon.

4 Regular dodecagon.

Using symmetry in calculations

A line of symmetry 'cuts' a shape into *two 'matching' halves*.

matching halves

There are 'matching lengths' and 'matching angles' on *opposite* sides of the line. These matching parts must be equal.

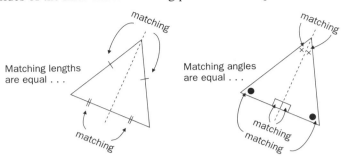

Matching lengths are equal . . .   Matching angles are equal . . .

This property of symmetrical shapes can help you to work out the size of some lengths and angles.

Question

The dotted line BX is a line of symmetry of triangle ABC.
(a) Work out and write down the sizes of as many angles and lengths as you can in this diagram.
(b) What kind of triangle is ABC?

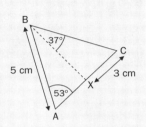

Answer

(a) *Mark equal lengths and angles on the diagram in pencil.*
AB = BC = 5 cm
CX = XA = 3 cm
AC = 3 cm + 3 cm = 6 cm
∠C = ∠A = 53°
∠ABX = ∠XBC = 37°
∠ABC = 37° + 37° = 74°
∠AXB = ∠BXC = 90°
(b) Isosceles triangle.

▶ *Exercise* S6.3

In each diagram below, the dotted line is a line of symmetry.
Use symmetry and other properties you know to find
(a) the size of the lettered angles
(b) as many lengths as you can.
In each case give reasons for your answers.

1

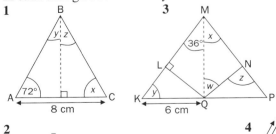

2

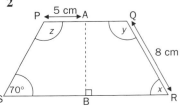

3

4

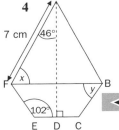

Plane symmetry

A **plane of symmetry** divides a solid into *two matching halves*. Each half is the exact *mirror image* of the other.

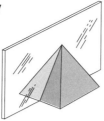

To find the planes of symmetry of a solid such as this cuboid, try to imagine it being cut into matching halves …

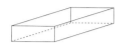

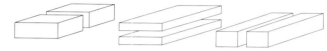

Then you can draw where the planes of symmetry are:

This cuboid has 3 planes of symmetry.

▶ *Exercise* S6.4

1   Each of these diagrams shows a solid and one of its planes of symmetry.
How many planes of symmetry does each solid have altogether? Show their positions on separate diagrams.

(a) Square based pyramid.   (c) Cube

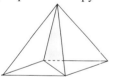
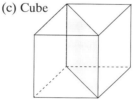

(b) Equilateral triangular prism   (d) Truncated square based pyramid.

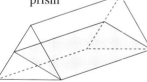
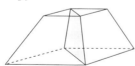

2   How many planes of symmetry does each of these solids have? Show their positions on separate diagrams.

(a)   (b)   (c)

1   The shapes drawn below are some that young children 'post' through the top of the box.
A teacher has the idea that the easiest shape to post is the one with the most lines of symmetry.
Draw as many lines of symmetry as you can on each of the shapes.
Under each shape write the number of lines of symmetry.

(MEG, 1989)

2

Fill in the table.

Triangle	Type	Number of lines of symmetry	Order of rotational symmetry
LMN			
	Isosceles		
	Right-angled		
	Scalene		

(NISEAC, 1990)

3   This is a sketch of a wooden roof frame. It is not drawn to scale. The dotted line is a line of symmetry.

Calculate the angles which are marked *a*, *b* and *c*.

(MEG, 1990)

4   Write down the number of planes of symmetry for each of these shapes.

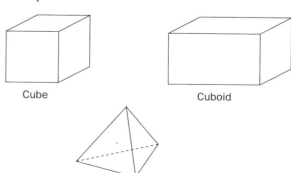

Cube   Cuboid

Regular tetrahedron   (ULEAC, 1994)

5

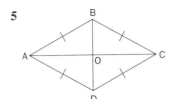

kite	bisect
rhombus	sixty
square	ninety
equal	right
opposite	one hundred
parallel	and eighty
perpendicular	

Fill in the blank spaces, choosing the most appropriate words from the list above (you may use words more than once).

(a) This quadrilateral is called a ....
(b) Opposite sides are .... and.........
(c) The diagonals of this shape .... one another at .... degrees
(d) Opposite pairs of angles are ....
(e) This shape fits its own outline when rotated through .... degrees about O.

(NISEAC, 1989)

6 (a) On a square grid, draw a quadrilateral which has exactly one line of symmetry. Show the line of symmetry of the quadrilateral.

(b) (i) On another square grid, draw a quadrilateral which has exactly two lines of symmetry. Show the lines of symmetry of the quadrilateral.

(ii) What is the order of rotational symmetry of the quadrilateral you have drawn in part (b) (i)?

(MEG, 1994)

7 A building block is in the shape of a cuboid which has dimensions 2 cm × 5 cm × 6 cm.

How many planes of symmetry has the block?

(SEG, 1989)

S7
Drawing shapes

This unit will help you to:

■ use basic drawing instruments to draw accurate diagrams

■ construct triangles and other polygons given the necessary measurements

■ make scale drawings to solve problems.

Many plane shapes can be drawn reasonably accurately with a sharp pencil, a ruler, a pair of compasses, a protractor and a set square.

You may use these drawings to make nets of 3D shapes, to solve practical problems in navigation, surveying, engineering, general design work, to make patterns, and so on …

You will find examples of some of these applications in this unit.

You should be able to use drawing instruments accurately already.

You need to be able to:
● draw and measure lengths *to the nearest mm*
● draw and measure angles *to the nearest degree*
● use compasses to draw circles and arcs *of a given radius*
● use compasses to mark lines *of a given length*
● use a set square and ruler to draw *parallel lines*.

You will use these techniques in the drawings in this unit. However, you may need to practise your drawing skills first to obtain the required accuracy. Drawing patterns is a good way to do this practice.

Some general drawing tips:
● Make sure that you have the *equipment* you need.
● Use drawing instruments that are in *good condition*.
● Work on a *flat surface*.
● Use *pencil*. It is easy to rub out if you make a mistake. Make sure it is a sharp pencil.
● Draw a *rough sketch* first ('freehand' if you like). Label it with the information you know.
● Draw the final diagram *neatly* and as *accurately* as possible.
● Leave all your 'construction lines' on your final drawing. *Do not rub them out.* You may get marks for them.
● *Label* your final drawing clearly.

Triangles

The way you draw a triangle depends on what you know about it. You can draw a triangle if you know:
● 3 sides, or
● 2 sides and the angle between them, or
● 1 side and 2 angles.
An example of each of these follows.

Three sides

You can draw a triangle if you know the lengths of its three sides. Use a ruler and compasses to mark the lengths.
For example, to draw triangle ABC with sides

AB = 8 cm, BC = 5 cm and AC = 7 cm,

follow these steps:

1 Make a rough sketch.
Label it with what you know.

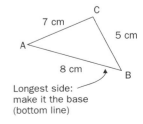

Longest side: make it the base (bottom line)

2 Draw a line longer than 8 cm (the longest side) with a ruler.

Leave plenty of room for the rest of the triangle

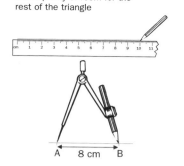

3 Open your compasses to 8 cm (length of AB). Use them to mark AB = 8 cm on the line.

4 Open your compasses to 7 cm (length of AC). Place the compass point on A. Draw an arc above the line.

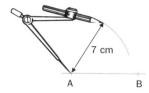

5 Open your compasses to 5 cm (length of BC). Place the compass point on B. Draw an arc to cut the arc you drew from A. Label point C.

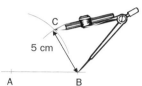

6 Join AC and BC with a ruler. Triangle ABC is now drawn.

Draw triangle ABC yourself. Measure the angles of your triangle.
They should be: ∠A = 38°, ∠B = 60°, ∠C = 82°
How good is your drawing?

An **equilateral triangle** is very easy to draw. All three sides are the same length. So keep your compasses set at this length for the drawing. For example, to draw an equilateral triangle with each side 5 cm, set your compasses to 5 cm.

Draw this equilateral triangle yourself.
To check your drawing, measure the angles.
Each angle should be 60°.

Exercise S7.1

Draw accurately these triangles.
1 Triangle ABC: AB = 7 cm, AC = 5 cm, BC = 3 cm
2 Triangle PQR: PQ = 4 cm, PR = 6.5 cm, QR = 2.5 cm
3 Triangle KLM: LM = 8 cm, KL = 5.6 cm, KM = 6 cm
4 Triangle RST: TR = 9.3 cm, RS = 4.7 cm, ST = 7.2 cm
5 Equilateral triangle XYZ: each side 7.5 cm.

Two sides and included angle

You can draw a triangle if you know the lengths of two sides and the size of the angle between them (the included angle).

First draw one side (usually the longer).
Next draw the angle and mark off the length of the other side.
Then you can complete the triangle.

For example, to draw triangle PQR with
   PQ = 7 cm, PR = 6 cm and angle P = 50°,
follow these steps:

1 Draw a rough sketch. Label it with what you know.

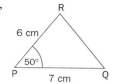

2 Draw a base line longer than 7 cm (the longer side) with a ruler.
3 Use your compasses to mark the length PQ = 7 cm on the line.
4 Use a protractor to draw an angle of 50° at P. Make sure you use the correct scale!

5 Use your compasses to mark the length PR = 6 cm along this line from P.

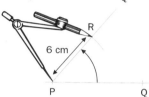

6 Join RQ with a ruler. Triangle PQR is now drawn.

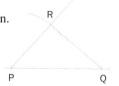

Draw triangle PQR yourself.
The other measurements should be:
RQ = 5.6 cm, ∠ Q = 56°, ∠ R = 74°.
How good is your drawing?

Exercise S7.2

Draw accurately each of these triangles
1 Triangle TUV: TU = 9 cm, TV = 7.5 cm, angle T = 30°
2 Triangle CDE: CD = 8.6 cm, DE = 5.9 cm, angle D = 45°
3 Triangle LMN: LM = 6.2 cm, MN = 3.7 cm, angle M = 70°
4 Triangle EFG: EF = 10 cm, FG = 9.4 cm, angle F = 55°

One side and two angles

You can draw a triangle if you know the length of one side and the size of two angles.

First draw the side.
Then draw the angles you know at the ends of this line with a protractor. This should complete the triangle.

For example, to draw triangle LMN with
   LM = 8.5 cm, angle L = 65° and angle M = 35°
follow these steps:

1 Draw a rough sketch. Label it with what you know.

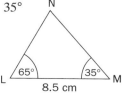

2   Draw a base line longer than 8.5 cm (the side you know) with a ruler.

3   Use your compasses to mark the length LM = 8.5 cm on this line.

4   Use a protractor to draw an angle of 65° at L. Make sure you use the correct scale!

5   Use a protractor to draw an angle of 35° at M. Make sure you use the correct scale!

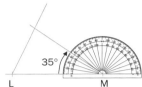

6   The two lines cross at N. Triangle LMN is drawn.

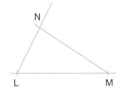

Draw triangle LMN yourself.
The other measurements should be:
∠ N = 80°, MN = 7.8 cm, LN = 5 cm.
How good is your drawing?

Sometimes the two angles you know are not at the ends of the given line. When this happens you have to work out the size of the third angle. You use 'the angle sum of a triangle is 180°.'
For example, in this triangle:
the angles you know are: 30° + 45° = 75°

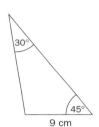

The third angle is: 180° − 75° = 105°.
Now you can draw the triangle as before.
Try it.

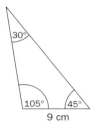

► *Exercise* **S7.3**

1   Draw accurately these triangles.
   (a) Triangle ABC: AB = 7.2 cm, angle A = 40°, angle B = 35°
   (b) Triangle RST: RS = 8.3 cm, angle R = 60°, angle S = 45°
   (c) Triangle XYZ: YZ = 9.8 cm, angle Y = 35°, angle Z = 115°
2   Draw accurately these triangles. You will have to calculate the size of the third angle first.
   (a) Triangle JKL: JL = 6.7 cm, angle K = 65°, angle J = 58°
   (b) Triangle UVW: UV = 10.4 cm, angle U = 108°, angle W = 26°
   (c) Triangle PQR: QR = 9 cm, angle P = 28°, angle Q = 36°

Other polygons

When drawing other polygons, for example, quadrilaterals, pentagons, etc., you will need to draw and measure lines and angles too. But each shape may need different 'steps' to draw it.

Use these points to help you to draw polygons:
(a) Draw a *rough sketch*. Label it with the information you are given.
(b) If it helps, mark the sketch with other *things you know* about the polygon, for example,

   a regular polygon has all its sides and angles equal,
   a parallelogram has opposite sides and angles equal,
   the angles of quadrilaterals add up to 360°,
   and so on …

(c) Use your sketch to help you to *decide the order* in which you are going to draw the sides and angles. There may be more than one 'good order'. Choose the one you find easiest.
(d) Write down the steps you have chosen in order to remind you.

For example, here is one way to draw a quadrilateral ABCD with AB = 9.5 cm, BC = 10.5 cm, CD = 12 cm, angle B = 100°, angle C = 80°.

Rough sketch with 'steps' marked on it.

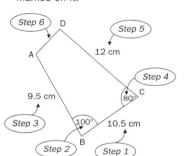

Order of steps:

1   Draw and measure BC = 10.5 cm (use ruler and compasses).
2   Draw angle B = 100° (use protractor and ruler).
3   Mark length BA = 9.5 cm (use a ruler and compasses).
4   Draw angle C = 80° (use protractor and ruler).
5   Mark length CD = 12 cm (use ruler and compasses).
6   Join AD (use ruler).

Now follow these steps and draw the quadrilateral. Choose another order for yourself. Check that it gives the same quadrilateral.

► *Exercise* **S7.4**

1   Draw accurately, a quadrilateral ABCD with AB = 9.5 cm, AD = 4.5 cm, BC = 4 cm, angle A = 53° and angle B = 67°. Measure and write down the length of DC.
   What special name is given to this type of quadrilateral?
2   Draw accurately, a rhombus PQRS with PQ = 5 cm and angle Q = 120°.
3   Draw accurately, a parallelogram ABCD with AB = 8 cm, AD = 5.6 cm and the diagonal BD = 7.5 cm.
   Measure the length of the other diagonal AC correct to the nearest millimetre. Measure the size of the obtuse angle to the nearest degree.
4   Draw accurately, an isosceles trapezium CDEF with CD = 9 cm, CF = 7 cm and the diagonal DF = 13 cm.
   Measure the size of the obtuse angle C to the nearest degree. Measure the length of the side EF to the nearest millimetre.

5 Draw accurately, a kite IJKL with IJ = 50 mm, JK = 80 mm and the diagonal IK = 110 mm.
   Measure the length of the other diagonal to the nearest millimetre. Measure the size of the smallest angle of the kite to the nearest degree.

6 Draw accurately, a pentagon ABCDE with AB = 6 cm, angle A = 105°, angle B = 100°, BC = 5 cm, angle C = 110°, CD = 4 cm and angle D = 110°.
   Measure and write down the lengths of the two sides AE and DE. Check that angle E measures 115°.

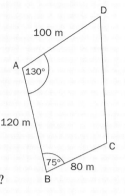

Scale drawing

Drawing '**to scale**' is a useful skill. Only a few people become architects, surveyors, designers, navigators, ... But lots of people plan a new kitchen or bathroom, furnish a room, design a garden layout, ... A scale drawing helps you to do jobs like these.

To do good scale drawings you will need to practise. Use these notes to help you.

1 *Start with a sketch.*
   You may draw a sketch 'freehand', but make sure it is easy to read. Do your best to show the shape and position of things on it. Mark in the lengths and angles you know. Give the units of measurement, such as metres (m) and degrees (°) clearly. Label it carefully.

2 *Find a suitable scale.*
   A question may give you the scale to use. Use this scale or you will lose marks!
   If you have to choose your own scale, keep these points in mind.
   • A 'suitable scale' is usually simple to use.
      For example, a scale of '1 cm to 10 m' is usually easier to use than '1 cm to 9 m'. To see why, use each scale to change 40 m to 'scale size'.
      Pick a scale with a number like 1, 2, 5, 10, ... in it if you can. These numbers are easy to divide by.
   • Very small drawings do not give very accurate answers. So try to make your drawing the largest that fits sensibly on your paper. Test 'your scale' on the largest lengths on your sketch to check.
      Write your chosen scale on your drawing.

3 *Work out the scale lengths you need using your scale* (see Unit N15).
   Take care with the units.
   It is a good idea to put your scale lengths in a table or on a sketch. This helps to organise your work. You can check quickly that you have all the lengths you want.
   Remember: The angles will be the same.

4 *Make the actual scale drawing using the scale lengths.*
   Follow the tips on p156. Keep your drawing as clean and neat as you can. A neat drawing looks better than a messy one. It is also easier to mark! Label it clearly.

You can use scale drawings to solve problems about angles and lengths.

Remember: The angles are the *same* as 'full-size'.
You have to *change* the lengths to 'full-size' using the scale to give 'real' answers.

Question

The sketch ABCD is of a field.
(a) Using a scale of 1 cm represents 20 m make an accurate scale drawing of the field.
(b) What size are the angles at the other corners of the field?
(c) A fence is to be put along CD. Find its length in metres.
(d) Peter walks straight across the field from A to C. Ken walks round the edge, A to B to C. How much further does Ken walk?

Answer

(a) *Change each length to 'scale size'.*

	Full size	Scale size	
Scale	20 m	1 cm	
AD	100 m	5 cm	← 100 ÷ 20 = 5
AB	120 m	6 cm	← 120 ÷ 20 = 6
BC	80 m	4 cm	← 80 ÷ 20 = 4

Write the scale clearly.   Scale: 1 cm represents 20 m.

Make the accurate drawing.
Use 'scale-size' lengths.
Remember: angles stay the same.

Measure AB = 6 cm first.
Then the angles (130° and 75°).
Mark off AD = 5 cm and BC = 4 cm next.
Join CD.

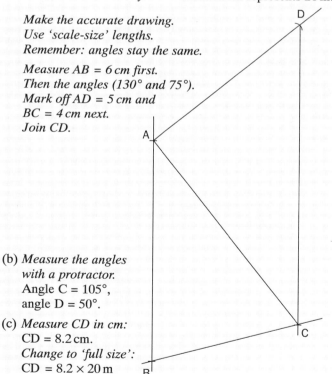

(b) *Measure the angles with a protractor.*
    Angle C = 105°, angle D = 50°.

(c) *Measure CD in cm:*
    CD = 8.2 cm.
    Change to 'full size':
    CD = 8.2 × 20 m
       = 164 m.

(d) Peter's walk: AC = 6.3 cm
    Change to 'full size': AC = 6.3 cm × 20 m = 126 m.

    Ken's walk: AB + BC = 120 m + 80 m = 200 m.

    Difference: 200 m − 126 m = 74 m.

    Ken walks 74 m further.

Exercise S7.5

1 This sketch shows a ladder PQ leaning against a wall.

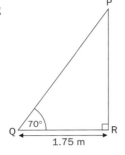

(a) Using a scale of 1 cm to represent 0.5 m, make an accurate scale drawing to show this.

Use your drawing to find

(b) the length of the actual ladder

(c) the actual distance PR the ladder reaches up the wall.

2 This sketch shows a triangular garden.

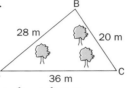

(a) Use a scale of 1 cm to 4 m to make an accurate scale drawing of the garden. Label the corners of the garden.

(b) Measure and write down the size of each angle of the triangle you have drawn.

(c) A straight path is to be made across the garden from A to the mid-point of BC. Draw the path on your triangle. Use it to find the actual length of the real path across the garden.

3 This is a sketch of the end of a lean-to garden shed.

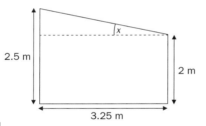

(a) Make an accurate drawing of the end of the shed. Use a scale of 1 cm to represent 0.5 m.

Use your drawing to find

(b) the length of the sloping edge of the roof in metres correct to 1 decimal place

(c) x, the angle the sloping edge of the roof makes with the horizontal.

4 Pat is making a model boat. This is a sketch of the sail on the real boat.

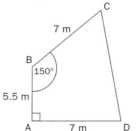

(a) Using a scale of 1 cm to represent 1 m, draw an accurate scale drawing of the sail.

(b) Measure CD on your drawing. Use your measurement to find the length, in metres, of this side of the 'real' sail.

Examination Questions

1 (a) Draw a triangle which has sides of length 6 centimetres, 8 centimetres and 10 centimetres.

(b) (i) On your diagram mark, with an X, the largest angle.

(ii) Measure and write down the size of the largest angle.

(c) A similar triangle has its longest side of length 60 centimetres. Work out the length of its shortest side.

(ULEAC, 1991)

2 ABCD is a quadrilateral whose four sides each have length 6 cm.

Angle ABC = 120°.

(a) Complete an accurate diagram of ABCD.

(b) What is the mathematical name for quadrilateral ABCD?

(SEG, 1991)

3 Town A is 4.5 km away from Town B.

Town B is 6.3 km away from Town C.

Town C is 6.9 km away from Town A.

(a) Using a scale of 2 cm = 1 km construct a diagram which indicates the positions of the three towns.

Town D lies inside the triangle ABC on the bisector of the angle ACB and is 4.4 km from Town A.

(b) Show the position of Town D on your diagram, using only ruler and compasses. Do not rub out any construction lines.

(NISEAC, 1991)

4 The diagram shows the base of a lighthouse, L, surrounded by three large rocks at A, B and C at the same level as L.

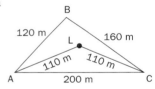

The distance AB is 120 m, the distance BC is 160 m and the distance AC is 200 m.

The lighthouse is 110 m from rock A and 110 m from rock C.

(a) Make an accurate scale drawing of the diagram. Use a scale of 1 cm to represent 20 m.

(b) From your diagram, find the actual distance of the lighthouse from rock B, in metres.

(NEAB, 1991)

5 Reuben wants to find the height of the tree in his back garden. He borrows a clinometer to measure the angle to the top of the tree.

His measurements are shown on the sketch below.

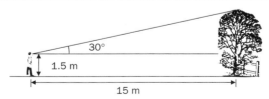

Use a scale of 1 cm to represent 1 m.

Draw a scale drawing to find the height of Reuben's tree.

(ULEAC, 1989)

S8
Bearings

This unit will help you to:

- recognise, describe and draw a direction given as a bearing
- find a bearing from one point to another
- calculate a bearing from angles
- fix the position of a point using two bearings or a bearing and distance
- use bearings to solve problems.

A **bearing** gives a direction in terms of an *angle*.
There are two kinds of bearings:
  compass bearings and **three figure bearings**.

Compass bearings

The four main compass directions are **North**, **South**, **East** and **West**.
They are called the **cardinal points**.
The directions *half-way* between the cardinal points are also marked on the diagram below.

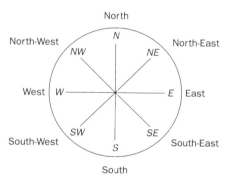

A compass bearing is based on the four main compass points. Its angle is measured from North or South, (whichever is nearer), turning towards East or West. It is an acute angle.

For example, N 50° E means 'from N measure 50° towards E'
  S 40° W means 'from S measure 40° towards W'

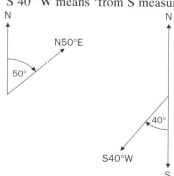

Sometimes you have to work out the angle for the compass direction.
  For example, in this diagram the angle between AP and the N-line through A is
90° − 48° = 42°.
So P is N 42° W of A.

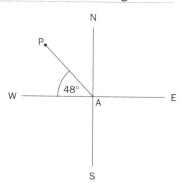

▶ *Exercise* **S8.1**

1 In what compass direction is the arrow pointing in each diagram?

(a)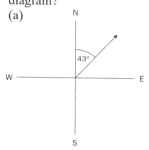

(c)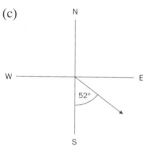

(b)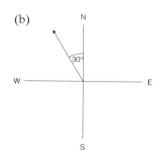

(d)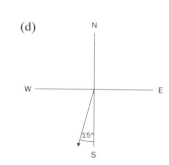

2 What is the compass direction of P from A in each diagram?

(a)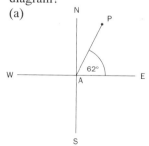

(c)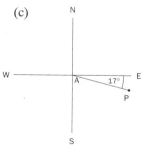

(b)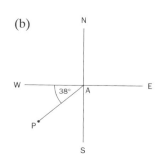

(d)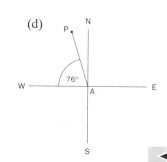

Three-figure bearings

When we talk about bearings nowadays, we mean '**three-figure bearings**'. By and large they have replaced compass bearings.

A three-figure bearing is always:

- an *angle* measured in *degrees*
- *measured from north*, turning *clockwise*
- given using *three figures*, from 000° to 360°.

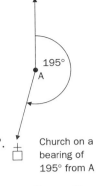

Church on a bearing of 195° from A

You use *extra zeros* to make the number up to three figures if you need to.

For example, 9° gives a bearing of 009°, 99° gives a bearing of 099°.

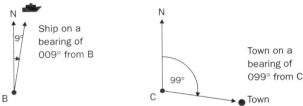

Ship on a bearing of 009° from B

Town on a bearing of 099° from C

A bearing gives the direction *from one point to another*. The word 'from' is important. It tells you *where* the angle for the bearing is measured.

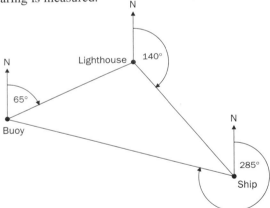

In this diagram:

the bearing of the Lighthouse from the Buoy is 065°,
the bearing of the Ship from the Lighthouse is 140°,
the bearing of the Buoy from the Ship is 285°.
Measure the angles with your protractor to check.

This is an **8-point compass**. These directions are still widely used. You may need to give them as bearings and vice versa. Both versions are shown on the diagram.

See how SW and 225° are the *same direction*.
Check that you can work out the others too.

The angle between any two of the '8-points' that are 'next to each other' is 45°.

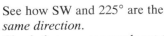

1 The diagram below shows directions from Birmingham (B) to some places in the UK. Give each direction as a bearing. (The scale is marked every 5° to help you.)

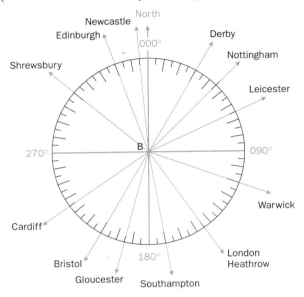

2 Here are some bearings from Birmingham.

Cheltenham 189°	Liverpool 317°
Coventry 108°	Norwich 081°
Exeter 214°	Sheffield 017°
Glasgow 332°	Stratford 136°

X marks the position of Birmingham on the diagram.
(a) Match each bearing to a direction marked with a letter.
(b) Estimate the bearings of the other lettered directions.

Finding bearings on maps and scale diagrams

A bearing is an *angle*. To measure or draw its size accurately you can use a *protractor*. Use a 360° protractor if you can. It is easier.

Memo
Measuring and drawing angles page 135

To find a bearing from a point P, take these steps.
- Place the protractor so that: – its 0° line is on the N-line through P – its centre is on P.
- Go round the scale clockwise ⟳ from 0°. Read off the direction you want.

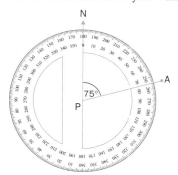

A is on a bearing of 075° from P.

To measure or draw a bearing at a point, you need an **N-line at that point.**

You may have to draw it yourself. Make sure you draw it *parallel* to the marked N-line. Use the grid lines or a set-square and ruler to help you.

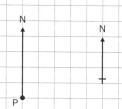

On most maps and drawings the N-line points up the page. But it doesn't always do so. Always check where it is.

Exercise S8.3

1 This diagram is based on the plan at the viewpoint at Foel Eyr in Wales.

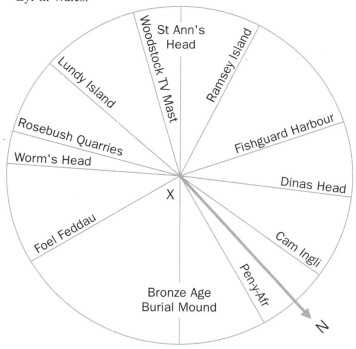

Measure the bearing of each landmark from point X at the centre of the plan.

2 These bearings give directions from a viewpoint near Stoke-on-Trent.

Longton 155°	Wolstanton Church 255°
Hanchurch Water Tower 205°	Baddeley Edge 058°
Sutton Common Tower 015°	Tunstall Church 321°
Mow Cop Castle 345°	Meaford Power Station 177°

Draw an accurate diagram to show these bearings. Mark the position of the viewpoint with the letter S.

3 This map shows some airfields in Britain.

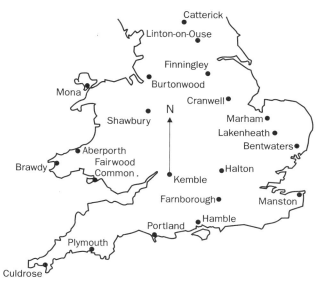

(a) Trace the N-line and the points showing each airfield. Find the bearing for each airfield from Kemble.
(b) Planes fly between these airfields. Find the bearing for each of these direct flights.
  (i) From Hamble to Manston
  (ii) From Portland to Brawdy
  (iii) From Mona to Cranwell
  (iv) From Linton to Shawbury
  (v) From Farnborough to Lakenheath

4 Draw diagrams to show these bearings.
Draw the N-line straight 'up' your page in each case.
(a) A is on a bearing of 130° from B.
(b) The bearing from C to D is 027°.
(c) The bearing from P to X is 215°.
(d) Y is on a bearing of 342° from L.

Calculating bearings

Not all diagrams are drawn accurately. Some diagrams are simply *sketches*. So you *cannot measure* angles to find bearings from them.

A sketch may show the direction you want. But you may have to calculate an angle to find its bearing.

Draw your own sketch for each bearing if it helps. Then use the angle facts you know to find the angles you want.

Memo

Calculating angles page 136

Question

The sketch shows a crossroads at C. *It is not drawn to scale.* Towcaster is due N of the crossroads. The Packham-Towcaster road is straight. The Wonfield to Ferton road is straight.

What is the bearing of each place from the crossroads? Show your working clearly.

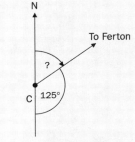

Answer

Towcaster: Due N of C.
Bearing: 000°

Ferton: 180°−125° = 55°
Bearing: 055°

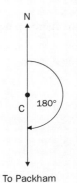
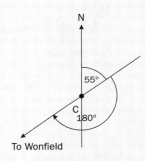

Packham: Due S of C
Bearing: 180°

Wonfield: 55° + 180° = 235°
Bearing: 235°

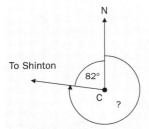

Shinton: 360°− 82° = 278°
Bearing: 278°

►Exercise S8.4

1 These diagrams show the directions of some airfields from Kemble (K). *They are not drawn to scale.* Write each direction as a bearing.

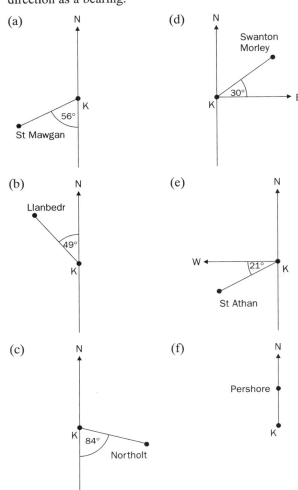

2 *This diagram is not drawn to scale.*

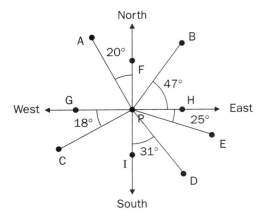

Find the bearing of each lettered point (A – I) from P.

Back bearings

You may know the bearing from one place A to another place B. The bearing 'back again', from B to A, is often called its **back bearing**.

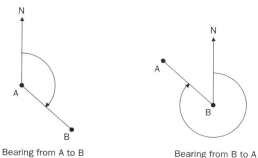

| Bearing from A to B | Bearing from B to A |

The two bearings are not the same. But they are related.

To find the back bearing from the original bearing you add or subtract 180°.

You can see this on a sketch of the bearings.

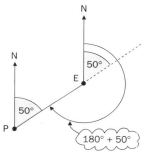

From Plymouth (P) to Exeter (E), the bearing is 050°.

50° + 180° = 230°

From Exeter (E) to Plymouth (P), the bearing is 230°.

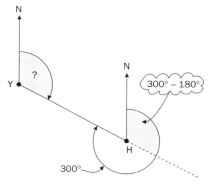

From Hull (H) to York (Y) the bearing is 300°.

300° − 180° = 120°

From York (Y) to Hull (H) the bearing is 120°.

Remember: The bearing must be from 000°, in the clockwise direction towards 360°.

▶ *Exercise* S8.5

1 In each of the diagrams following, give
   (i) the bearing of P from A,
   (ii) the bearing of A from P.

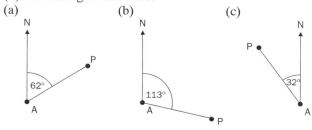

(d) 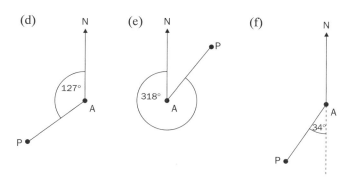 (e) (f)

2 The bearings of several ships from an oil rig O are given below.
   Axle: 325°   Defiant: 304°
   Baker: 095°   Esquire: 223°
   Congress: 189°   Federal: 132°
   Find the bearing of the oil rig from each ship.

Finding places

You are likely to use bearings to **solve problems** that involve navigating or surveying. You usually need to know *at least two* facts to find somewhere 'precisely'. You can use **two bearings or a bearing and a distance**.

Remember: A bearing gives the direction *from one point to another*. The word '*from*' is important. It tells you from where the angle is measured.

Two bearings

You can find where a place is if you know its **bearings from two other places**.

To mark its position on a scale diagram, take these steps.
● Draw N-lines at the two places. (Remember these are parallel lines.)
● Use the bearings to draw a line from each place. The point where the two lines cross is the place you want.
● Mark and label clearly the point you want.
On this scale diagram, C is on a bearing of 070° from A and 310° from B.

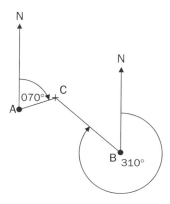

It is a good idea to draw a sketch before you do the accurate drawing. It reminds you which angles to measure.

In an exam your sketch also shows the examiner what you have tried to do … just in case you make a mistake.

► *Exercise* S8.6

1   The map shows the positions of two lighthouses A and B on the coast. Trace this map and mark the position of a lifeboat which is on a bearing of 060° from A and 285° from B.

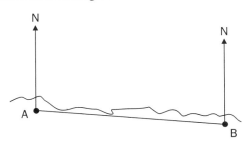

2

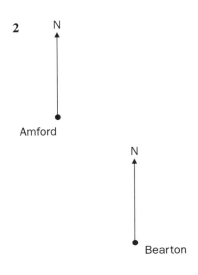

The positions of two towns are shown on this map. The position of a third town Crompton is on a bearing of 118° from Amford and 075° from Bearton.
Trace this map and mark on it the position of Crompton.

3   Queenston lies due east of Pinley on this map.

Rusley lies on a bearing of 134° from Pinley and 232° from Queenston.
Trace the map and mark the position of Rusley.

4   An oil rig, Oscar (O), is 10 miles due north of another oil rig, Roger (R).
At 12 noon, a ship (S) was seen on a bearing of 135° from O and 023° from R.
At the same time, a yacht (Y) was seen on a bearing of 225° from O and 346° from R.
   (a) Draw a diagram to show the positions of O, R, S and Y at 12 noon.
   (b) Find the bearing of the yacht from the ship at that time.

Bearing and distance

The **bearing and distance of a point from another point** fixes its position. You can mark it on a map or scale drawing.

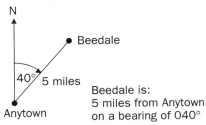

Beedale is:
5 miles from Anytown on a bearing of 040°

To use a bearing and distance to find a point, take these steps.
● Make a rough sketch.
● Draw an N-line at the point you are measuring *from*.
● Measure the bearing angle *at this point*, *clockwise* from N.
● Draw the '*direction line*' on this bearing.
● Use the *scale* to work out the length on your drawing.
● Measure the '*scale length*' from the point along your '*direction line*'.
● Mark and *label* the point.

Question

Marham is 86 km from RAF Cranwell on a bearing of 115°. Show the position of Marham accurately on the diagram below. Use a scale of 1 cm to 20 km.

Answer

● *Sketch:*

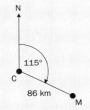

● *Work out scale length:*

$$\overset{\div 20}{20\,km \rightarrow 1\,cm \text{ on diagram}}$$

20 km → 1 cm on diagram
86 km → 86 ÷ 20
       = 4.3 cm

● *Make accurate drawing. Measure CM = 4.3 cm.*

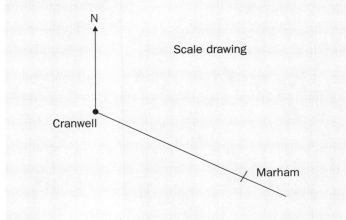

Scale drawing

◄

Always use an easy scale if you can.
A scale may be given in a question.
Use this scale or you will lose marks.

Memo
Scale
Unit N15

Exercise S8.7

For each pair of points, draw a rough sketch and scale drawing
to show their positions. Use the scale given in each case.

1 B is 7.5 km from A on a bearing of 150°.
   Scale: 1 cm to 1 km.
2 C is 120 km from D on a bearing of 065°.
   Scale: 1 cm to 20 km.
3 F is 45 km from E on a bearing of 280°
   Scale: 1 cm to 10 km.
4 H is 58 km from G on a bearing of 217°
   Scale: 1 cm to 10 km.
5 L is 24.5 km from K on a bearing of 173°.
   Scale: 1 cm to 5 km.

To solve a 'bearings problem' you may need to find the
position of *several* points.
Plan what to do on your rough sketch first.
Build up the scale drawing 'point by point'.

Question

An orienteering club set this exercise for new members.
From check-point A, walk 300 m on a bearing of 070° to
check-point B.
From check-point B, walk 400 m on a bearing of 135° to
check-point C.
From check-point C, walk on a bearing of 225° to checkpoint D, due south of B.
(a) Draw an accurate plan of this route.
    Use a scale of 1 cm to 100 m.
(b) Use your drawing to find the direct distance and bearing
    from D to A.

Answer

(a) ● *Sketch:*

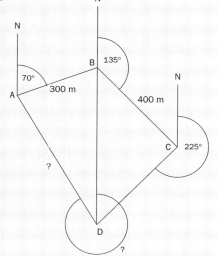

● *Working:*

From scale: $\ulcorner \div 100 \urcorner$
100 m → 1 cm

AB: 300 m → 300 ÷ 100 = 3 cm
BC: 400 m → 400 ÷ 100 = 4 cm

● *Drawing:*
From A, draw 070° direction line. Measure AB = 3 cm.
From B, draw 135° direction line. Measure BC = 4 cm.
From C, draw 225° direction line.
Draw line due South from B.
The last two lines cross at D.

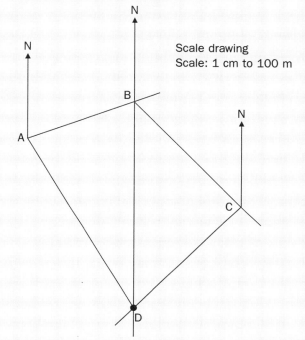

Scale drawing
Scale: 1 cm to 100 m

(b) ● *Join DA. Measure DA in cm.*
    Use scale to change to 'full-size' in m.
    On drawing: DA = 5.4 cm
    Actual distance : DA = 5.4 × 100 = 540 m
    ● *Measure angle for bearing at D: 329°*
    From D to A is a distance of 540 m
    on a bearing of 329°.

Exercise S8.8

Solve these problems by making scale drawings.

1 A yacht sails from Wyemouth on a bearing of 305°. After
   sailing for 5 miles it changes direction. It then sails for
   6 miles on a bearing of 190°. How far is the yacht from
   Wyemouth? On what bearing must the yacht sail to go
   straight back to Wyemouth?
   (Use a scale of 1 cm to 1 mile.)
2 A plane flies from Home Airfield on a bearing of 215° for
   65 km. It then flies on a bearing of 345° for a distance of
   95 km. How far is the plane now from Home Airfield?
   The pilot wants to fly straight back to Home Airfield. On
   what bearing should he fly?
   (Use a scale of 1 cm to 10 km.)

3 A fishing boat sails from Lowestoft for 8 km on a bearing of 060°. After fishing in this spot for a few hours, the boat sails to a point 7 km away on a bearing of 120°. There are no fish in this spot, so the captain turns the boat again and sails for 4 km on a bearing of 235°.
How far is the ship from Lowestoft now?
On what bearing must the ship sail to return to Lowestoft?
(Use a scale of 1 cm to 1 km.)

4 Richard walks 350 m from A to B on a bearing of 090°. He then walks from B to C, a distance of 210 m on a bearing of 200°. Finally he walks 150 m from C to D on a bearing of 050°. How far is Richard from his starting point now?
On what bearing must he walk to return to his starting point by the shortest route?
(Use a scale of 1 cm to 50 m.)

5 A and B are checkpoints on an orienteering course.
A is 1.8 km from the start (S) on a bearing of 323°.
B is on a bearing of 106° from A and 1.65 km from A.
The orienteering course goes from S to A to B, then straight back to S.
How long is the course altogether?
What is the bearing of B from S?
(Use a scale of 10 cm to 1 km.)

Examination Questions

1 (a) Measure the marked angle in the diagram below and state its value.
(b) Hence write down the bearing of Penrith from Keswick.

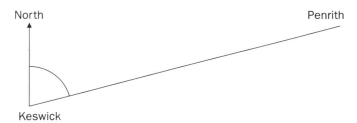

(NEAB, 1988)

2 The scale diagram shows the position of Norwich (N) and two towns on the coast of East Anglia, Sheringham (S) and Lowestoft (L).
(a) Measure and write down the values of
(i) x
(ii) y.
(b) What is the bearing of Sheringham from Norwich?

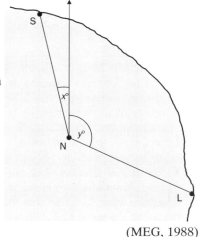

(MEG, 1988)

3 A boat leaves a port P and sails south east until it reaches a lighthouse L.
The boat then sails away from the lighthouse on a bearing of 240° until it reaches a harbour H.
The harbour is due south of the port.
(a) Sketch the path of the boat.
(b) What is the bearing of the lighthouse from the harbour?
(c) Find the size of the angle PLH.

(NISEAC, 1991)

4 The diagram show two ports. Bigh is due north of Allow. A ship is on a bearing 050° from Allow and 145° from Bigh. Mark the position of the ship on an accurate copy of the diagram.

(WJEC, 1989)

5 A ship is observed at a point P, 8 kilometres from a coast-guard station on a bearing of 040°, as shown on this scale diagram.
Fifteen minutes later the ship is at a point Q, 4 kilometres from the coastguard station on a bearing of 020°.

(a) Draw accurately on a tracing of the diagram the position of Q and join PQ.
(b) Use your diagram to find
(i) the speed of the ship in kilometres per hour
(ii) the bearing on which the ship is sailing.

(MEG, 1991)

6 A ship travels 25 km due north from a point A and then 35 km on a bearing of 045°. It then travels 60 km on a bearing of 285° to a point B.
(a) On a fresh page draw an accurate plan of this journey. Start with A in the centre of the page and two thirds of the way down. (Use a scale of 1 cm to represent 5 km.)
(b) Find, from your plan
(i) the distance in km from A to B
(ii) the bearing of A from B.   (SEG, 1990)

7 A helicopter takes off from base and flies for 18 kilometres on a bearing of 260°. It then turns and flies for 25 kilometres on a bearing of 155°. Make an accurate scale drawing of the journey using a scale 1 cm = 2 km.
(a) What bearing must be followed to return to base?
(b) How far is it from base?

(NISEAC, 1989)

8 Monifieth and St. Andrews are two coastguard stations.
Monifieth is 60 kilometres due north of St. Andrews.
(a) What is the scale of the diagram?
(b) A ship sends out an SOS.
The ship's bearing from St. Andrews is 045°.
The ship's bearing from Monifieth is 120°.
Mark the position of the ship on an accurate copy of the
diagram.
(c) The lifeboat from St. Andrews can travel at
12 kilometres per hour.
The lifeboat from Monifieth can travel at
8 kilometres per hour.
Which lifeboat should they launch?
Show all your working to support your answer.

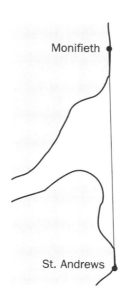

(WJEC, 1990)

S9
3-d from 2-d

This unit will help you to:

■ recognise and name simple solids

■ identify faces, edges and vertices of solids

■ make oblique and isometric drawings of simple 3-d shapes

■ recognise, identify and draw the plan, front and side elevations of simple solids.

Names

Three-dimensional (3-d) shapes are usually called **solids**.
Here are the main ones you should know.

Cube	Cuboid	Cylinder	Triangular prism

Cone   Square-based pyramid   Tetrahedron   Sphere

You should be able to recognise these shapes in your everyday
surroundings, in photos or in line drawings.
Hollow 3-d shapes like these are still called *solids* in
mathematics.

▶ *Exercise* S9.1

1 Look at this picture. Give each 3-d shape its mathematical
name.

2 Each of these objects is a simple solid. Give each its
mathematical name.
(a) tennis ball   (d) cola can
(b) tip of a sharp pencil   (e) ordinary dice
(c) CD box   (f) wedge of cheese

Faces, edges and vertices

A **face** is a surface of a solid.
It may be flat or curved.

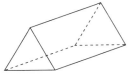

Cylinder
1 curved face and
2 flat faces

A solid with *all polygon faces* is called a **polyhedron**.
All its faces are flat.
(Plural of polyhedron is polyhedra.)

A triangular prism is a polyhedron.
2 triangular flat faces and
3 rectangular flat faces

An **edge** is the line where two faces meet.
It may be straight or curved.

Tetrahedron has:
6 straight edges

A point where edges meet is called a **vertex**.
(Plural of vertex is vertices.)

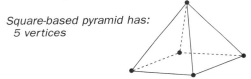

Square-based pyramid has:
5 vertices

All solids have faces. But not all solids have edges and vertices. The faces, edges and vertices of a solid can be used to identify it.

▶ *Exercise* S9.2

1 Look at examples of these solids.
    cube, cuboid, cylinder, triangular prism, cone,
    square-based pyramid, tetrahedron, sphere.
    Answer these questions for each.
    (a) (i) How many flat faces has it?
        (ii) How many curved faces has it?
    (b) (i) How many straight edges has it?
        (ii) How many curved edges has it?
    (c) How many vertices has it?
2 (a) Which solids named in question **1** are polyhedra?
    (b) Copy and complete this table for these polyhedra.

Name of poyhedron	Number of faces (F)	Number of vertices (V)	Number of edges (E)

There is a simple relationship between the number of *faces, vertices* and *edges* for polyhedra. Find it from the values in your table.

Check your rule works for these polyhedra.

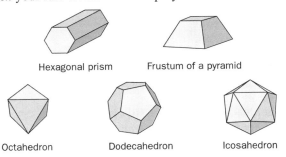

Hexagonal prism   Frustum of a pyramid

Octahedron   Dodecahedron   Icosahedron

The formula linking F, V and E is known as **Euler's Theorem**.
Euler was a Swiss mathematician who lived from 1707 to 1783.

Drawing 3-d shapes

There are several ways of drawing a 2-d picture of a 3-d shape.
Here is a cuboid drawn in four different ways.

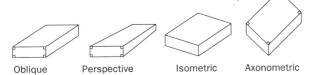

Oblique   Perspective   Isometric   Axonometric

Oblique and **isometric** drawings are the two simplest types to make. Here are some hints to help you to do these.

Practise each method on a grid of lines or dots first. Then try to do the drawings on plain paper.

Oblique drawings

In an oblique drawing of a solid, one face is seen 'straight on'.
This face is drawn the same shape as the face on the solid.

Use a **square grid** to help you to make oblique drawings.

Square grid
graph paper

Square grid
dotty paper

To make an oblique drawing of a cuboid, take these steps.
● Draw the '*front face*' (a rectangle).
● Then draw the '*opposite face*' the same size. Place it 'behind' but slightly to one side of the 'front face'.
● Join '*matching corners*' of the two faces.

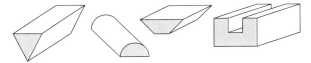

This gives a 'skeleton' picture of the cuboid. You can see all the edges.

In most cuboids, some edges are hidden. In drawings you can either make hidden edges dotted or rub them out.

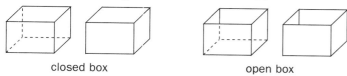

closed box   open box

To make an *oblique* drawing of a *cuboid*, you draw a *rectangle* for the front face. Drawing a *different* shape for the front face gives a *different* solid.

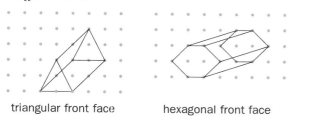

triangular front face   hexagonal front face

► *Exercise* S9.3

1 (a) Copy these oblique drawings of cuboids.

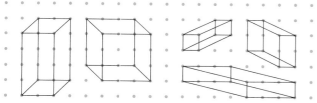

Which looks like a cube? Why?
(b) Copy the drawings again, rub out lines to make them look like open boxes.

2 Draw some different cuboids with these front faces.

Try placing the 'opposite face' in different positions. See what effect this has on your drawings.

3 Make different oblique drawings of solids with these front faces.

Isometric drawings

Isometric means 'of equal measure'. In an isometric drawing, parallel edges which are *equal on the solid* are shown as *equal on the drawing*.

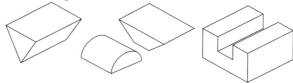

Parallel edges on the solid are *parallel on the drawing*.
Vertical edges on the solid are *vertical on the drawing*.
Horizontal edges on the solid are shown *sloping at 30° to the horizontal on the drawing*.

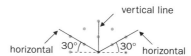

vertical line

horizontal 30° 30° horizontal

Angles on the solid look distorted on the drawing. Faces are not the correct shape.

This shows a square. It has 4 equal sides and opposite sides are parallel. But angles are not right angles.

This shows a rectangle. Opposite sides are equal and parallel. But angles are not right angles.

Use an **isometric grid** to help you to make isometric drawings. Make sure you put the grid as shown below.

Isometric grid graph paper   Isometric grid dotty paper

To make an isometric drawing of a cuboid, take these steps:

● Draw a 'top face' first. It is in fact a rectangle. But it looks like this … on the drawing. Equal parallel edges are equal lengths. But angles are distorted.

● Draw 'vertical' lines down from each 'corner point'. They are equal and parallel.

● Join matching 'bottom' corners.

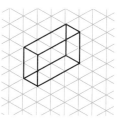

Isometric drawings are often used to show solids made from cubes.

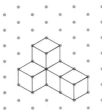

This solid is made from 5 cubes

► *Exercise* S9.4

1 (a) Copy these isometric drawings of cuboids.

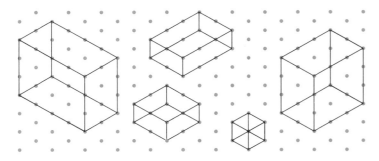

Which looks like a cube. Why?

(b) Copy the drawings again. Rub out lines to make them look like open boxes.

2 Draw some different cuboids with these top faces.

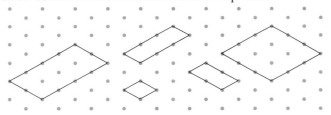

3 You can fit 'centimetre cubes' together to make other solids.

(a) There is only one 'two-cube solid'. Here is an isometric drawing of it. Make a different isometric drawing of it.

(b) There are two different 'three-cube solids'. Here are isometric drawings of them.

Make a different isometric drawing of each solid.

(c) There are eight different 'four-cube solids'. Work out what each looks like. (Use cubes if it helps.) Make two different isometric drawings of each solid.

(d) See how many different 'five-cube solids' you can make and draw.

Nets

A **net** is a *flat shape* that can be folded to make a solid.

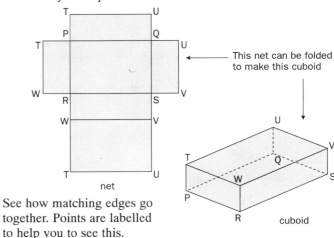

← This net can be folded to make this cuboid

See how matching edges go together. Points are labelled to help you to see this.

You can usually draw more than one net of a solid. There are 11 different nets of a cube! Here is just one of them.

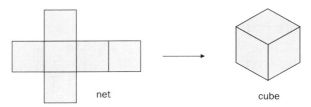

ACTIVITY

1 Trace the net of the cuboid shown above. Mark with the same colour, edges that go together.

2 Draw two different nets for the cuboid shown above. Trace the faces to help you.
Imagine folding up each net. Mark with the same colour edges that go together.

3 Draw as many different nets of a cube as you can. See if you can find the 11 different nets.
Cut each net out of squared paper. Check it folds up into a cube.
Check the nets are all different. Make sure you cannot turn them or flip them over to give the same shape.
For example, these nets are not different:

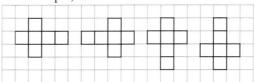

4 Look at this sketch of a cube open at the top.
If you cut along the edges marked ▬, you get a net in this shape.

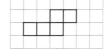

Now look at these sketches.

(a)   (b)   (c)   (d)

(e)   (f)   (g)

Imagine cutting along the edges marked ──
Sketch the net you should get.
Cut each net out of squared paper. Fold them to check your answers.

Many solids have simple nets.
Here are some nets for some well-known solids.

Tetrahedron
(or triangular-based pyramid)

 solid

 net

Regular tetrahedron
(equilateral triangle faces)

 solid

 net

Square-based pyramid

 solid

 net

Triangular prism

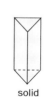 solid

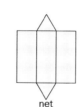 net

Hexagonal prism

 solid

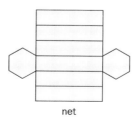 net

The 'look' of a shape can often show you whether it is a net of a solid. It can tell you which solid also.
Here are some clues to look for.
Look at the faces: Has it got the correct number for the solid you want? Are they the correct shape and size?

Look at the edges: Will matching edges go together?
Imaging folding it: Think of one face as the base. Which are the sides? Which is the top? Will it make the solid you want? Finally you can check your idea by drawing the shape. Then cut it out and try to fold it.
When making models from nets, we usually draw flaps on some edges. These are not part of the net. They simply make it easier to stick the net together.

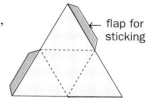 ← flap for sticking

► *Exercise* **S9.5**

1 Trace the nets shown in the left-hand column.
  Imagine folding up each net. Mark with the same colour, edges that will go together. Draw flaps on edges where needed to make the model.

2 Draw at least one different net for each of the solids shown in the left-hand column.
  Imagine making each net into a 3-d model. Draw flaps on edges where needed. Mark with the same colour flaps and edges that go together.

3 Name the solids made from these nets.

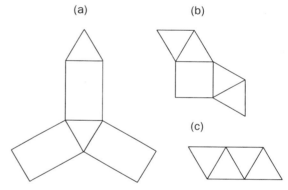

(a) (b)

(c)

4 Draw full-size nets for these cuboids.
  Write the lengths on all edges of your nets.

(a)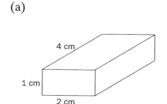

(b)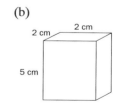

(c) a cuboid 5 cm long, 3 cm wide and 4 cm high.

5 Draw full-size nets for these solids.
  (a) A regular tetrahedron with each edge 4 cm long.
  (b) A square-based pyramid with each edge 3 cm long.
  (c) A triangular prism 6 cm long. Its triangular faces have sides 3 cm, 4 cm and 5 cm long.

Different points of view

3-d shapes look different from different points of view. But you can usually recognise what they are.

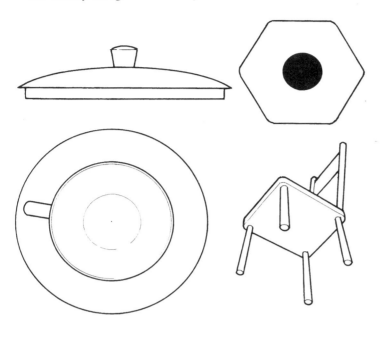

Exercise S9.6

Look at the pictures above.
Name the objects shown.

Drawings of 3-d shapes are often made from different points of view.
To show what the shape is like we use three views.

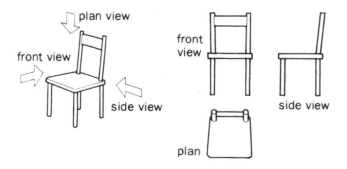

The view from *directly above* is called the **plan**.
The view from *directly in front* is called the **front view** or **front elevation**.
A view *directly from one side* is called a **side view** or **side elevation**.

Here is an isometric drawing of a 3-d shape.

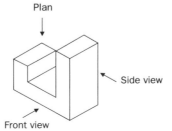

Three views of this solid are shown below.

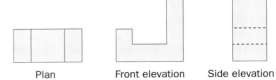

Plan   Front elevation   Side elevation

Solid lines show edges you can see from each viewpoint.
Dotted lines show 'hidden edges'.
To help you to see how to draw each view, look at the diagrams below. The edges and faces 'used' are highlighted.

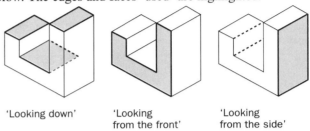

'Looking down'   'Looking from the front'   'Looking from the side'

Exercise S9.7

1 Here are some sketches of solids. Imagine what you would see if you looked at each solid in the directions of the arrows.

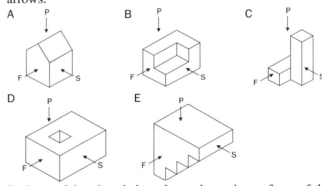

Each set of drawings below shows three views of one of the shapes.
Match each solid with its views. Say which view is which.

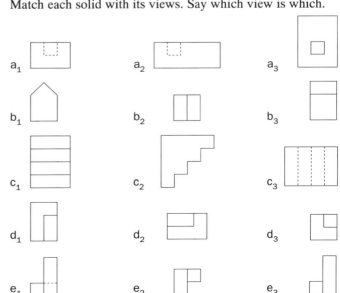

2 The diagrams below are sketches, plans and elevations of six solids.
Match each sketch to its plan and elevations.
Draw the four diagrams together.
Name the solid.
Mark which view is which.

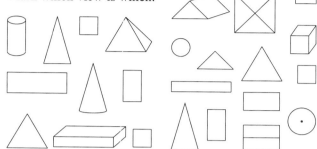

3 Draw views of each solid from the marked viewpoints.

(a)

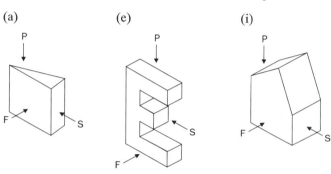

(e)

(i)

(b)

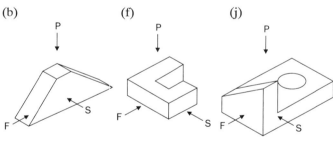

(f)

(j)

(c)

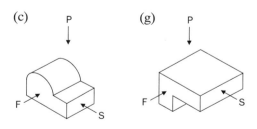

(g)

(d)

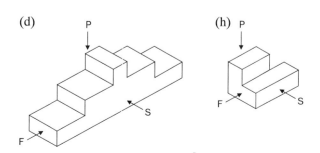

(h)

Examination Questions

1 The diagram shows part of the net of a prism. One face is missing.
(a) Complete the net accurately.
(b) State a possible use for this type of prism.

(MEG, 1988)

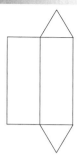

2 On the right is a drawing of a solid model built out of cubes.
(a) How many cubes would be needed to make this solid?

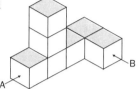

(b) If you look at the solid from A you would see this:

On a square grid draw a similar diagram to show what you would see if you looked at the solid from B.

(NEAB, 1990)

3

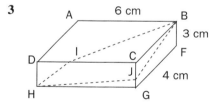

This sketch is not to scale.
It shows a box ABCDEFGH, 6 cm by 4 cm by 3 cm.
There is a piece of string HIB stretched from H to B over the edge DC so that HIB is as short as possible.
Another piece of string, HJB, is stretched from H to B over edge CG so that it is also as short as possible.
(a) Draw a half-size net of the box.
(b) How long is the string HJB?
(c) How long is DI?

(WJEC, 1990)

4 The diagram below represents a square-based pyramid.
Draw an accurate, full-sized net for this pyramid.

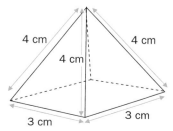

(NEAB, 1989)

5 A sweet is packed in a box which is a square-based pyramid. A sketch of the net of the box is shown below.

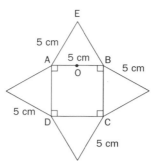

(a) Draw a diagram to form a full-size net of the box.
(b) Measure and write down the distance EO giving your answer to the nearest mm.
(c) Change your answer to (b) to centimetres.
Using your answer to (c):
(d) Work out the area of the triangle ABE. Give your answer to the nearest square centimetre.
(e) Work out an estimate for the complete area of the net. Give your answer to the nearest square centimetre.

(ULEAC, 1989)

6 The picture shows a stack of cubes. No cube is stuck to another.

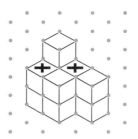

(a) What is the smallest number of cubes in the stack?
(b) The cubes marked with a cross are taken away. On spotty paper, draw the stack now.

(MEG, 1989)

S10
Moving shapes

This unit will help you to:

- understand the idea of a transformation

- draw and identify translations, rotations and reflections of points and plane shapes.

Looking at moves

A shape can be moved in three basic ways.
You can **slide it**, **turn it** or **flip it over**.

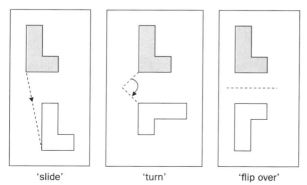

'slide'   'turn'   'flip over'

In mathematics these moves are called **translation**, **rotation** and **reflection**.

Transformations

A **transformation** is a *change*.
Translation, *rotation* and *reflection* are transformations.
Each *changes the position* of an object.
   Enlargement is also a transformation. It *changes the size* of an object. There is more about this in Unit S11, p 190.

Names and labels

The names **'object'** and **'image'** are often used in work on transformations.
The '*object*' is the original shape.

The transformation changes it into its '*image*'.
An object and its image are often labelled in a special 'matching way'.

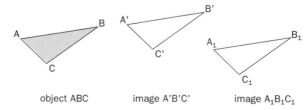

object ABC   image A'B'C'   image $A_1B_1C_1$

The *same letters* are used for *matching points*. But each letter on the image has a dash ' on it, or the same number on it.

Sometimes the word **'map'** is used instead of 'move' or 'transform' in these transformations. This is because a transformation is a special mapping.

Translation

A translation is sometimes called a *slide* or *shift*. It moves a shape in a straight line. The shape does not turn or flip over.

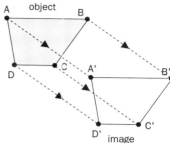

In a translation every point moves the *same distance* and in the *same direction*.

To describe a translation you must give the distance and direction moved.

A translation on a grid is easy to describe.
We split the move into two parts:
- horizontal (across ↔), and
- vertical (up or down ↕)

For the distance, count the number of 'steps' on the grid.
For the direction, use words or signs.

$$\begin{array}{cc} & + \uparrow \text{ up} \\ \text{left} \quad \text{right} & \\ \xleftarrow{\hspace{1cm}} \xrightarrow{\hspace{1cm}} & \\ - \quad + & - \downarrow \text{ down} \end{array}$$

The two moves may be written in a bracket like this:

$$\binom{\text{horizontal move}}{\text{vertical move}}$$

For example,

$\binom{2}{3}$ means right 2 up 3

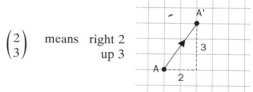

$\binom{3}{-2}$ means right 3 down 2

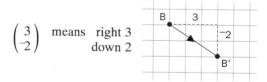

$\binom{-4}{1}$ means left 4 up 1

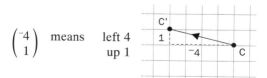

$\binom{-4}{-2}$ means left 4 down 2

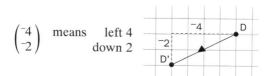

1

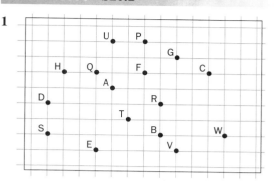

Describe the translation for each of these moves.
(a) from F to C   (f) from H to S
(b) from P to G   (g) from E to B
(c) from A to U   (h) from V to R
(d) from D to Q   (i) from B to Q
(e) from A to T   (j) from W to V

2 Copy these axes and points.

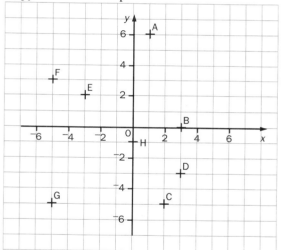

(a) Map each named point to its image by the given translation. Label each image clearly.
Translate A, 4 right 7 down to A_1
Translate B, 3 left 5 up to B_1
Translate C, 2 right 6 up to C_1
Translate D, 5 left 3 down to D_1
Translate E, 6 down to E_1
Translate F, 7 right to F_1
Translate G, 5 up to G_1
Translate H, 3 left to H_1
(b) Write down the coordinates of each point and its image. What do you notice?

3 Draw *x*- and *y*-axes and number them from ⁻10 to 10.
(a) Find the image of the origin (0,0) after each of these translations. Label each image clearly.

$$\binom{4}{6}, \binom{-7}{2}, \binom{0}{8}, \binom{5}{-3}, \binom{0}{-7}, \binom{3}{0}, \binom{-9}{-4}, \binom{-6}{0}$$

(b) Write down the coordinates of each image. What do you notice?

You may have to **translate a shape on a grid**. Each point on the shape moves the same distance and in the same direction. Translate each corner point in turn.
Then join them up in the correct order to make the image.

For example,
the diagrams below show how to translate triangle ABC by $\binom{2}{3}$.
You move each corner point 2 right, 3 up.

$$A \to A', \quad B \to B', \quad C \to C'$$

Then join A', B', C' to make triangle A'B'C'.

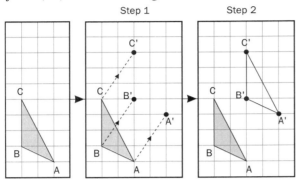

You may be asked to **'describe fully' a translation**. Each point on the shape moves in the same way. So you only need to work out how one point moves.

For example,
the shaded shape is translated to a new position in this diagram.

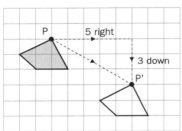

Look at the point P.
It has moved 5 right, 3 down to point P'.

You can describe the translation as $\binom{5}{-3}$

▶ *Exercise* **S10.2**

1   Draw this shape on a square grid. Draw and label the images of this shape after these translations.

(a) $\binom{2}{3}$ (e) $\binom{0}{-7}$

(b) $\binom{5}{0}$ (f) $\binom{0}{8}$

(c) $\binom{4}{-3}$ (g) $\binom{-7}{0}$

(d) $\binom{-2}{-3}$ (h) $\binom{-4}{5}$

2   Draw each shape on a square grid. Draw the image of each shape after the given translation. Write the description of each translation with each diagram.

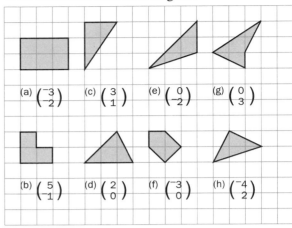

(a) $\binom{-3}{-2}$ (c) $\binom{3}{1}$ (e) $\binom{0}{-2}$ (g) $\binom{0}{3}$

(b) $\binom{5}{-1}$ (d) $\binom{2}{0}$ (f) $\binom{-3}{0}$ (h) $\binom{-4}{2}$

3   Describe the translations which map the shaded shape on to each lettered shape.

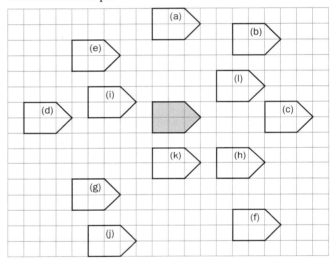

4

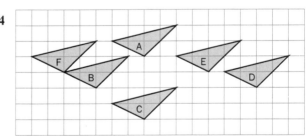

Each triangle above is labelled with a letter.
Describe the translations which map
(a) A on to C   (g) F on to B
(b) C on to A   (h) B on to F

(c) B on to D   (i) D on to A
(d) D on to B   (j) A on to D

(e) C on to E
(f) E on to C

Compare each 'pair' of translations.
What do you notice?

Rotation

A rotation is a turn. In a rotation an object *turns about a fixed point*. This point is called the **centre of rotation**.

To describe a rotation, we give three facts:
- the position of the centre
- the direction of the turn
- the amount of the turn.

The direction of the turn is ↺ or ↻.

↺ turns are anticlockwise or +

↻ turns are clockwise or −.

The amount of turn is given as a fraction of a turn, or an angle in degrees.

This rotation is about centre P, clockwise, through 135°

The most common rotations involve angles of 90°, 180°, 270°. Here is an example of each. The shaded shape is the object and P is the centre of rotation in each case.

+90° (anticlockwise $\frac{1}{4}$ turn)   −90° (clockwise $\frac{1}{4}$ turn)

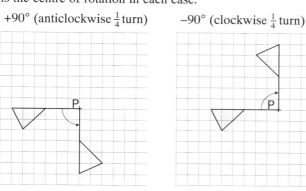

+180° (anticlockwise $\frac{1}{2}$ turn)   −180° (clockwise $\frac{1}{2}$ turn)

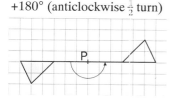 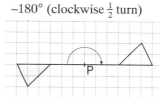

+270° (anticlockwise $\frac{3}{4}$ turn)   −270° (clockwise $\frac{3}{4}$ turn)

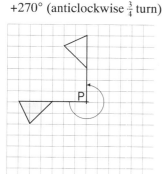 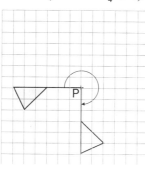

Drawing rotations

Here are two ways to draw rotations.

By tracing
Tracing paper can help you to rotate shapes.

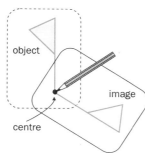

Take these steps:
- Trace the shape and centre of rotation.
- Place a sharp point (pencil, pen, compasses) on the traced centre and actual centre.
- Turn the traced shape around by the angle you want.
- Mark the position of the image on the paper below.

The simplest turns are 90°, 180° and 270°.

When the shape is on a grid, the grid lines help you to make these turns.
On your tracing, mark the centre with a cross along the grid lines like this …

As you turn the tracing, watch for the positions when the cross fits exactly over the grid lines again.

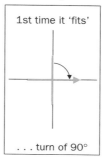  

1st time it 'fits'	2nd time it 'fits'	3rd time it 'fits'
… turn of 90°	… turn of 180°	… turn of 270°

Sometimes you need to use a protractor to measure the angle of turn.

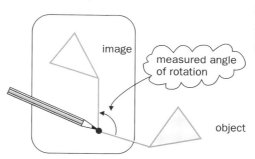

Memo

Measuring angles page 135

Join the centre of rotation to a point on the object.
Trace this line when you trace the shape and centre.
Draw the angle you want at the centre on your paper. Measure it from your 'drawn line'.
Turn your tracing about the centre until your traced line and your 'angle line' match.
Then draw the image as before.

Using grid lines
You can use grid lines to help you to rotate a point about a centre.

Draw or imagine 'steps across' and 'steps up or down' from the point to the centre.
Turn this 'L-shape' through the angle you want to find the image.

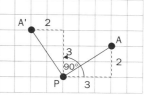

A rotation of +90° about P moves A to A'

To rotate a shape about a centre, rotate each 'corner point' in turn. Join the image points in the correct order to make the image.

For example,
the diagrams below show how to rotate the shaded shape about the centre +, through ⁻90° (i.e. 90° clockwise).

Step 1	Step 2	Step 3	Step 4

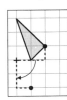

▶ *Exercise* S10.3

1 (a) Copy each flag on to a square grid. Rotate each shape through ⁺90° about the named centre point (A,B,C,D,E).

   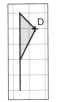 

   (b) Repeat part (a) using a rotation of ⁺180°.
   (c) Repeat part (a) using a rotation of ⁻90°.

2 Draw diagrams to show the following rotations on rectangle ABCD. Clearly label the image A′ B′ C′ D′ in each case.
   (a) 180° about A
   (b) 90° clockwise about C
   (c) 90° anticlockwise about C
   (d) 270° clockwise about D
   (e) 180° about 0
   (f) 270° anticlockwise about 0.

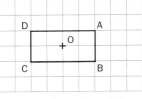

3 Find the image of each shape after the stated rotation. C is the centre of rotation in each case.

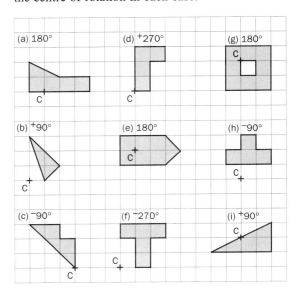

4 Draw and number *x*- and *y*-axes from ⁻8 to 8.
   Show the position of point P(4,3) after each of these rotations.
   Give the coordinates of each new point.
   (a) 180° about (0,0)   (d) ⁻90° about (⁻3,0)
   (b) ⁺90° about (1,4)   (e) ⁺270° about (0,4)
   (c) ⁻90° about (⁻6,5)   (f) ⁻270° about (7,0)

5 Trace each shape. Find the image of each shape after the given rotation. X is the centre of rotation.

(a) ⁺120°
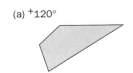

(b) ⁺45°   (c) ⁻45°
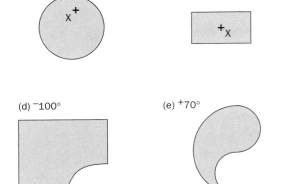

(d) ⁻100°   (e) ⁺70°
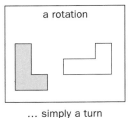 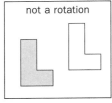 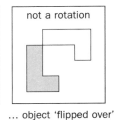

Describing rotations

To **recognise a rotation**, look for an image made by simply turning the object.
The object must not be 'flipped over'.

a rotation	not a rotation	not a rotation
… simply a turn	… no turn	… object 'flipped over'

To **describe the rotation,** you must find its *direction, angle* and *centre of rotation.*

Finding direction and angle of rotation

To see the angle of rotation, look at the angle between one line on an object and its image.
Decide on its direction ↺ or ↻
Find its size. (Measure it with a protractor if you need to.)

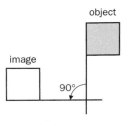

Anticlockwise, ¼ turn or +90°.

Sometimes you have to make the lines longer until they cross.

Note: The point where the lines cross is *not* usually the centre of rotation.

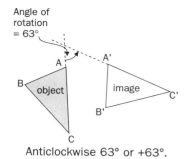

Anticlockwise 63° or +63°.

Finding the centre of rotation

'By eye'

In a rotation the **centre** is a *fixed point*. It does *not* move. Always look first for a point on the object that has not moved in the rotation. If you find one, it must be the centre.

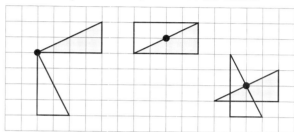

The point ● is the centre in each of these rotations.

For rotations of 90°, 180°, 270° on a grid, the centre is often easy to spot and check.
Compare the positions of the object and image.
Describe where you think the centre is.
Then test your point with a tracing of the object.

By drawing

For some rotations you may have to find the centre by drawing.

Join two 'matching points' on the object and image.
Then draw the perpendicular bisector of this line.
Do the same for two other 'matching points'.
The centre of rotation is where the two perpendicular bisectors cross.

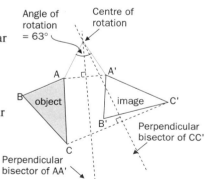

► *Exercise* **S10.4**

1 The unshaded triangles on the following diagram are images of the shaded triangle.
  (a) Which image(s) are not the result of a rotation?
  (b) For each rotation, give its centre, angle and direction.
     (The lettered points are the centres used.)
     Check your answers by tracing and turning the shaded triangle.

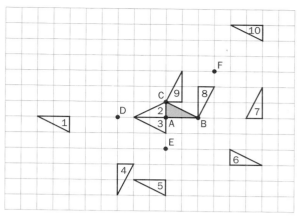

2 The lettered triangles below are images of the green triangle. Describe the rotation that has taken place in each case (i.e. give its centre, direction and angle of rotation).

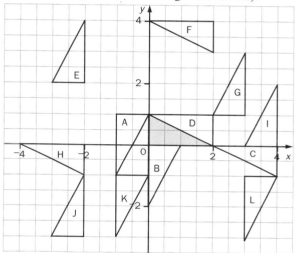

3 Each green shape has been rotated to a new position. Describe fully each rotation.

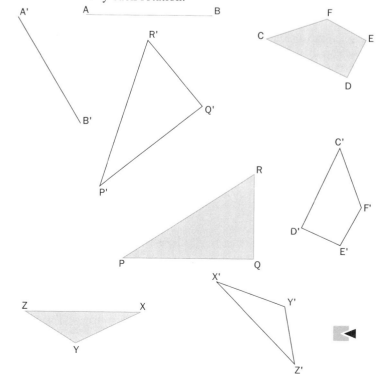

Reflection

Another way to move a shape is to *flip it over*.
This transformation is called a **reflection**.
It gives an image that looks like the reflection of the object in a mirror.

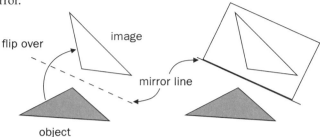

The dotted line above shows where to stand a mirror to get the image. (You can try this to check.)

Each point and its mirror image are the *same distance* from the mirror line.

Points on *one side* of the mirror line are reflected to the *other side*, (just like a *double-sided* mirror).

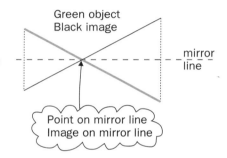

Green object
Black image

mirror line

Point on mirror line
Image on mirror line

Drawing mirror images

You may need to reflect a shape in a mirror line.

Using tracing paper

You can draw a mirror image on plain paper or on a grid using tracing paper.

Take these steps:

- Trace the shape and mirror line carefully. Mark the ends of the mirror line clearly.
- Flip the tracing over.
- Put your traced mirror line exactly on top of the actual mirror line. Make sure you match end-points.
- Press your pencil point on each corner point of the traced shape.
- Take away the tracing.
- Join up the dots in the correct order for the image.

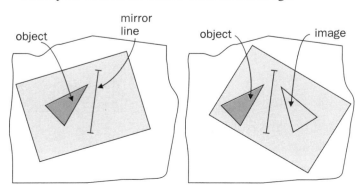

mirror line

object

object   image

Trace each diagram and reflect the shape in the dotted line.

1

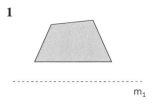

m_1

6

m_6

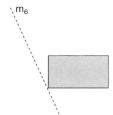

2

m_2

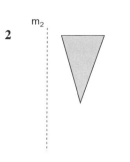

7

m_7

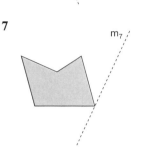

3

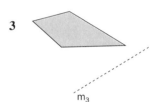

m_3

8

m_8

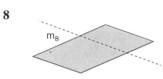

4

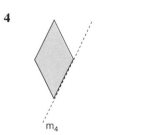

m_4

9

m_9

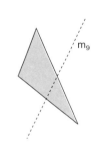

5

m_5

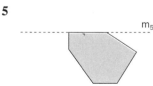

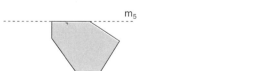

Using a grid

When the mirror line is on a grid line, it is easy to reflect a point. You can simply *count squares from the mirror line*.

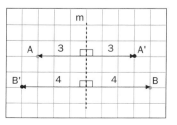

m

A   3   3   A'

B'   4   4   B

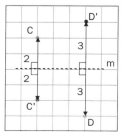

D'

C   3

2
2   m

3

C'

D

When the mirror line is at 45° to the grid lines, you can *count across squares diagonally.*
Turn your paper round so that the line 'looks' vertical if it helps.

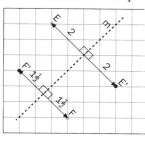 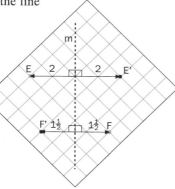

To reflect a shape, reflect each main point in turn. Then join them up in the correct order to make the image.

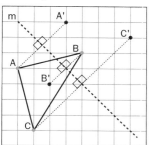 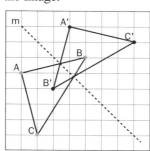

Remember:
The mirror line is like a 'double-sided' mirror.
A point on one side is reflected on to the other.

 Exercise S10.6

1 Copy the points and dotted mirror line in each diagram on to a grid.
Reflect the points in the mirror line in each case.
Label the images clearly. For example, label the image of A as A'.
Check your answers by tracing.

(a)

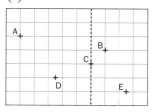

(b)

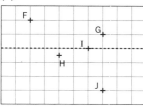

(c)

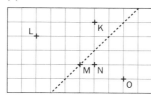

(d)

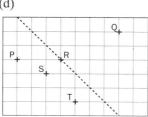

2 Copy each diagram on to a grid.
Reflect each shape in the dotted line using the grid.
Check your answers by tracing.

(a)

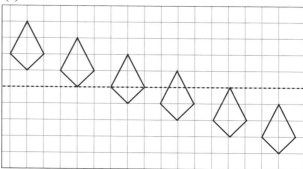

(b)

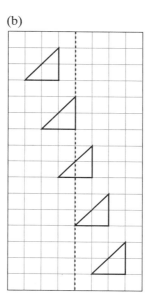

(c)

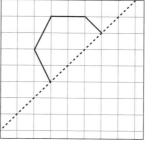

(d)

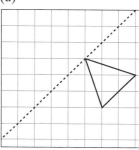

(e)

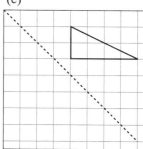

(f)

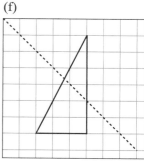

The position of a mirror line on a coordinate grid is often given using its *equation*.

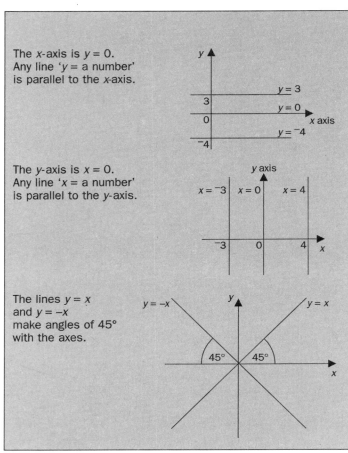

The *x*-axis is $y = 0$.
Any line 'y = a number' is parallel to the *x*-axis.

The *y*-axis is $x = 0$.
Any line 'x = a number' is parallel to the *y*-axis.

The lines $y = x$ and $y = -x$ make angles of 45° with the axes.

Question

(a) On the grid below, plot the point A(4,2).
   Reflect A in the *x*-axis. Label its image A_1.
   Reflect A in the *y*-axis. Label its image A_2.
   Reflect A in the line $y = x$. Label its image A_3.
   Reflect A in the line $y = -x$. Label its image A_4.
(b) Write down the coordinates of these image points.

Answer

(a)

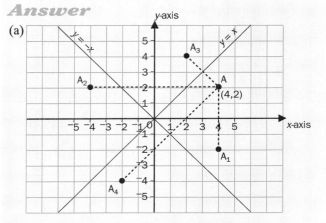

(b) $A_1(4,^-2)$, $A_2(^-4,2)$, $A_3(2,4)$, $A_4(^-2,^-4)$.

► *Exercise* S10.7

1 For each part of this question, draw a new diagram.
   Use axes numbered from $^-8$ to 8.
   Plot and label the points A(1,2), B(2,0), C(3,$^-$4), D(0,$^-$3), E($^-$3,$^-$2), F($^-$1,3).
   Label the image points clearly.
   (a) Reflect the points A–F in the *x*-axis.
   (b) Reflect the points A–F in the *y*-axis.
   (c) Reflect the points A–F in the line $x = 1$.
   (d) Reflect the points A–F in the line $y = ^-2$.
   (e) Reflect the points A–F in the line $y = x$.
   (f) Reflect the points A–F in the line $y = ^-x$.

2 Draw and label *x*- and *y*-axes from $^-8$ to 8.
   Plot and draw the triangle with corner points (0,2), ($^-$3,2) and ($^-$3,3). Shade in this triangle.
   Draw the mirror images of this triangle after reflection in each of the following mirror lines. Label each image clearly.
   (a) *x*-axis   (d) the line $x = ^-3$
   (b) *y*-axis   (e) the line $y = x$
   (c) the line $y = 3$ (f) the line $y = ^-x$.

3 Draw and label *x*- and *y*-axes from $^-8$ to 8.
   Plot the points A(3,7), B(4,7), C(4,4), D(3,4).
   Draw and shade in the rectangle ABCD.
   Reflect rectangle ABCD in each of these mirror lines.
   Label each image clearly.
   (a) the line $y = x$ (d) the *y*-axis
   (b) the line $y = ^-x$ (e) the line $x = ^-1$
   (c) the *x*-axis   (f) the line $y = 2$

Looking for mirror images

To **recognise the mirror image** of an object, look for an image that fits these two facts:
● The mirror image is the *same shape and size* as the object.
● The object looks as if it has been *picked up and flipped over* to give the image.

► *Exercise* S10.8

1 Which of the unshaded shapes are mirror images of the shaded shape?
   What is 'wrong' with each of the others?

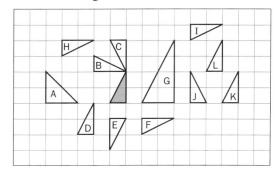

2 Which triangle is the mirror image of
(a) triangle A in line m_2
(b) triangle A in line m_3
(c) triangle D in line m_4
(d) triangle F in line m_4
(e) triangle H in line m_1
(f) triangle G in line m_2
(g) triangle E in line m_3
(h) triangle C in line m_1?

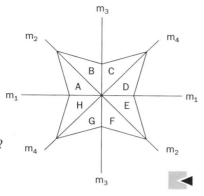

Finding mirror lines

To **describe a reflection** you must give the position of its mirror line.

The mirror line is half-way between each point and its mirror image.
This fact helps you to find its position.

Here are two ways to do this.

Tracing and folding
Trace the object and image carefully.
Fold the tracing paper so that one shape *fits exactly on top* of the other.
The fold line is the mirror line.

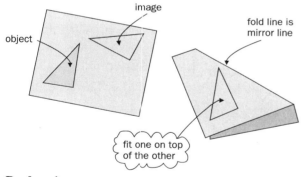

By drawing
Mark 'half-way' between two 'matching points' on the object and image.
Do the same for another pair of 'matching points'.
Draw a line through the 'half-way' marks.
This is the mirror line.

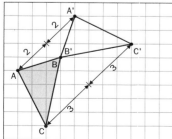
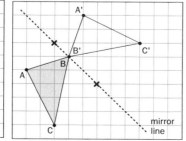

Sometimes the object and image *touch* or *cross* at a point.
This point must be on the mirror line.

The diagrams below show reflections.
Copy each diagram on to a grid.
Draw the mirror line in each case.
Check by tracing and folding.

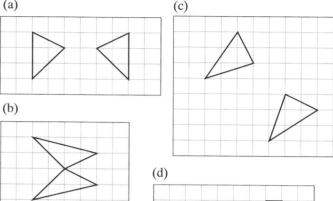

Tessellations

A **tessellation** is a pattern of shapes on a flat surface.
The shapes fit together *without gaps or overlaps*.
The pattern they make is *repeated regularly*.
It could go on forever if it were continued.

These pictures show some examples of tessellations.

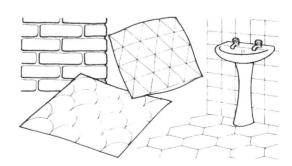

In some tessellations all the shapes are **congruent**, i.e. the same shape and size.
The shapes may be polygons or have curved edges.

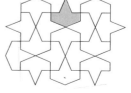

This 'polygon tessellation' is an ancient Arab design.

This 'curved shape' tessellation looks like overlapping fish scales.

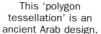

Congruent triangles of any shape tessellate.
Here are some examples.

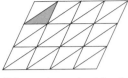 

Using an isosceles triangle   Using a right-angled triangle

Congruent quadrilaterals of any shape tessellate.
Here are some examples.

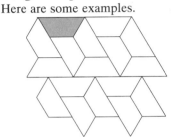 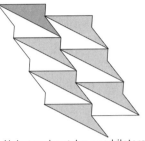

Using a trapezium   Using an irregular quadrilateral

Not *all* congruent shapes tessellate.
Circles, for example, do not tessellate.
However you arrange them, gaps are left between them.

 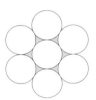

At every point where polygons meet in a tessellation, **the sum of the angles is 360°**.
Look at this example:

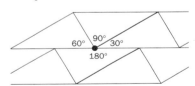

60° + 90° + 30° + 180° = 360°

Exploring the angles of a polygon can often show you whether it tessellates or not.

Look at regular polygons, for example.
Only three regular polygons tessellate 'on their own'.

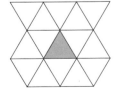 

To see why these polygons tessellate, look at the size of their angles.
Each regular polygon has all its angles equal.
A whole number of each 'angle' in these regular polygons makes 360°.
So these polygons fit together *exactly* round a point.

equilateral triangle: angles of 60°	square: angles of 90°	regular hexagon: angles of 120°
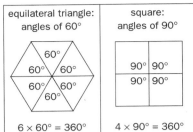		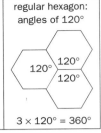
6 × 60° = 360°	4 × 90° = 360°	3 × 120° = 360°

Other regular polygons do not tessellate.
Their angles cannot be placed together to make exactly 360°.

For example, each angle in a regular pentagon is 108°.

3 × 108° = 324°

Three of these angles make less than 360°.

4 × 108° = 432°.

Four of these angles make more than 360°.
So regular pentagons cannot tessellate.

Tessellations can also be made from *two or more* basic shapes.

For example, regular hexagons and equilateral triangles make this tessellation. Look at the angles at each point marked •.

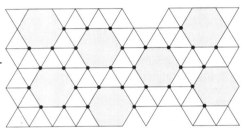

These angles come from one hexagon and four triangles.

They add up to 360°.

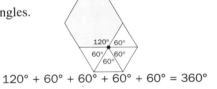

120° + 60° + 60° + 60° + 60° = 360°

If a shape tessellates, you can make the tessellation by moving the shape around.
You may *slide it* or *turn it* or *flip it over* or combine several of these moves.

Here are some examples.
Use the shading to help you to see how the black shape has been moved.

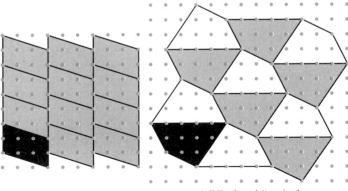

'sliding' only   'sliding' and 'turning'

To draw a tessellation, it often helps to trace the shape or to use a template or stencil of it.

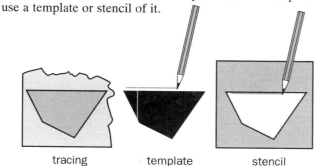

tracing   template   stencil

These devices make it easy to move the shape around.

You can also use a grid of dots or lines to help you to plan each move.

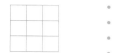

One way to create a new tessellating shape is to alter a shape you know tessellates.

Here is one way to do this with a square.

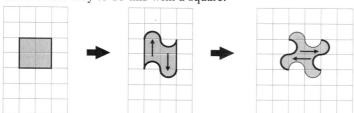

new shape   new tessellation

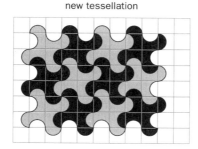

Here is a way to alter an equilateral triangle.

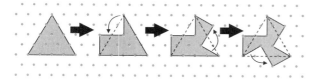

new shape   new tessellation

   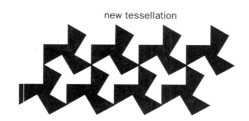

With some imagination, you can make tessellating pictures.

The artist Escher used this method to produce many interesting tessellations.

► *Exercise* S10.10

1 Which of these shapes tessellate?
Draw the tessellations to illustrate your answers.

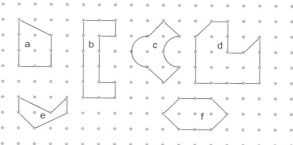

2 Each of these shapes tessellates.

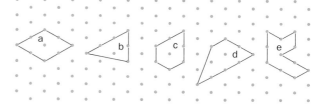

(a) Which can you tessellate by only sliding the shape?
(b) Describe how you have to move each of the other shapes to draw its tessellation.
Illustrate your answers clearly with drawings.

3 Draw two different triangles and two different quadrilaterals. Draw a tessellation with each of your shapes.

4 (a) This shape is called a **pentomino**.
It is made of five squares.
Draw at least two different tessellations with this pentomino.
Use shading or colouring to show how you move the shape to make each tessellation.

(b) There are 12 different shapes of pentomino. Here are the other 11 shapes.

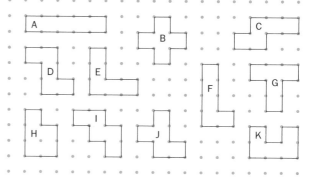

Which pentominoes tessellate on their own?
For each shape that does, show how it tessellates.
(c) Which pentominoes can you tessellate on their own by simply sliding the shape?
How do you have to move each of the others?

5   The diagram below shows ten regular polygons. Which of these regular polygons tessellate? Explain why each of the others do not tessellate.

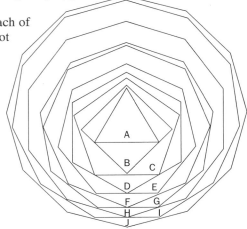

A Triangle
B Square
C Pentagon
D Hexagon
E Heptagon
F Octagon
G Nonagon
H Decagon
I Undecagon
J Dodecagon

6   Squares and equilateral triangles fit together exactly round a point. The diagram shows one way to do this.

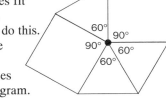

(a) Draw diagrams to show the other possible ways. Check the sizes of the angles round the point in each diagram.
(b) Draw tessellations using squares and equilateral triangles together. Trace the regular polygons in question **5** to help you.

7   Draw tessellations using these combinations of regular polygons. Trace the polygons in question **5** to help you.
(a) regular hexagons and equilateral triangles
(b) regular octagons and squares
(c) regular dodecagons and equilateral triangles
(d) regular hexagons, squares and equilateral triangles
(e) squares, regular hexagons and dodecagons.

8   Use the methods shown on p 187 to create a new tessellating shape from each of these shapes:
(a) a square   (d) a regular hexagon
(b) an equilateral triangle   (e) any other shape you know
(c) a parallelogram   tessellates.
Show how each of your new shapes tessellates.

Examination Questions

1   This pattern is taken from a paper tablemat found in Meg's cafe. State which of the shapes A, B, C or D is the odd one out, giving your reasons.

D   A   B   C   D   A

(MEG, 1990)

2   A wallpaper pattern is designed using a template. The template consists of a partly shaded circle. Part of the pattern is shown below.

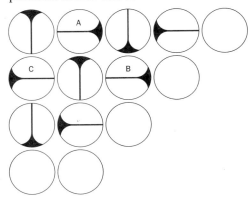

(a) What single transformation takes
(i) circle A onto circle B,
(ii) circle B onto circle C?
(b) Copy the pattern and continue it by completing the blank circles on the diagram.

(SEG, 1989)

3   A wall tile is placed on a wall. The next three tiles are placed so that the pattern on the tile is reflected in the lines PQ and RS. Copy and complete the diagram to show the pattern on all 4 tiles.
(SEG, 1990)

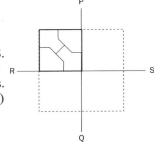

4   Copy the diagram accurately on to squared paper and draw the mirror image of the shaded shape in the mirror line marked.
(NEAB, 1989)

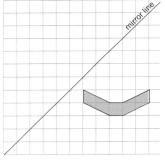

5   *The Sky at Night.*
If you watch the sky on a clear night, the stars appear to rotate anticlockwise about the Pole Star. The 360° rotation takes 24 hours.
The diagram shows the Pole Star (P) and the constellation of stars called Triangulum (T) at 8 pm.
Trace the diagram and draw the position of T at 2 am.

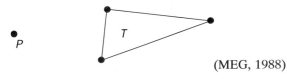

(MEG, 1988)

6

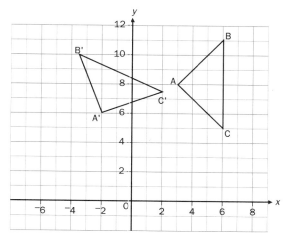

The drawing shows the triangle ABC and its image A'B'C' after an anticlockwise rotation. Copy the diagram on to squared paper.
(a) Join BB' and CC'.
    Using a pair of compasses construct the perpendicular bisectors of BB' and CC'. Make your arcs sufficiently large and clear so that the method you have used is obvious.
(b) Write down the x- and y- coordinates of the centre of rotation.
(c) Use your protractor to measure the angle of rotation.

(NEAB, 1990)

7

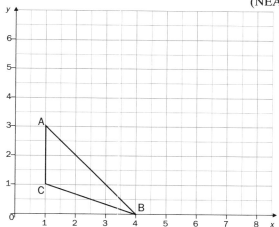

Copy the diagram on to a grid.
(a) Plot on the grid the points D(3,6), E(6,3), F(3,4) and join the points together.
(b) Describe the type of transformation that maps ABC to DEF.

(ULEAC, 1988)

8 Describe fully **three** different single transformations which will each map the square A to the square B on the grid opposite.

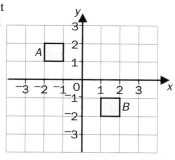

(NEAB, 1991)

9 Copy the diagram on to squared paper.

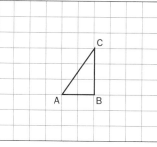

(a) In the diagram, rotate triangle ABC anti-clockwise through 90° about A. Label the image T.
(b) In the diagram, rotate triangle ABC anti-clockwise through 90° about C. Label the image S.
(c) Describe fully the single transformation which will map T on to S.

(MEG, 1989)

10 The diagram shows part of a tessellation of a quadrilateral.

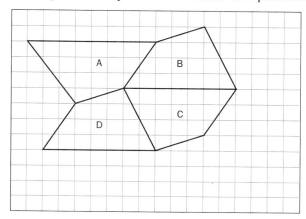

(a) (i) Describe completely the single transformation which maps A on to C.
    (ii) What type of transformation maps D on to C?
(b) Copy, and continue the tessellation by drawing three more of these quadrilaterals on the diagram.

(SEG, 1991)

11

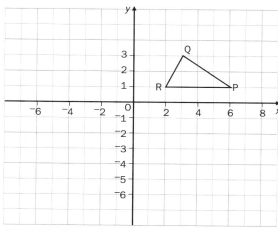

Copy this diagram on to a grid.
Shape PQR is translated seven left and six down.
Draw its image on the grid.

(ULEAC, 1990)

12 (a) On a grid, copy the diagram and draw the image of the shaded shape after a reflection in the y-axis. Label the image A.

(b) On the same grid, draw the image of the shaded shape after a quarter turn clockwise about the origin O(0,0). Label this image B.

(c) Describe fully the *single* transformation which maps A onto B.

(ULEAC, 1991)

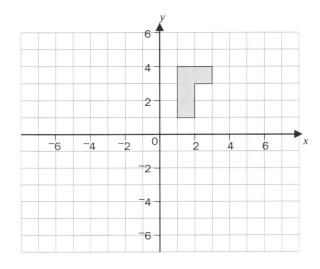

S11
Enlargement

This unit will help you to:

■ understand the idea of enlargement

■ enlarge shapes by a positive whole number scale factor

■ use a centre of enlargement to enlarge a shape

■ find the scale factor and centre of an enlargement.

Enlargement is a *transformation,* i.e. a *change* (see p 176).
Enlarging something *changes its size.*
Its *shape* and *angles* stay the *same.*
When something is enlarged, each length is *multiplied by the same number.*
This number is the **scale factor** of the enlargement.

length on enlargement = scale factor × original length

This slide has been enlarged to make the photo below. Each length on it has been made *2 times* as long. So *2 is the scale factor* of the enlargement.

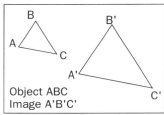

Names and labels

We often use the names '**object**' and '**image**' in work on enlargements.
The 'object' is the original shape.
The enlargement changes it into its 'image'.
In the previous example:

the slide is the 'object'
the photo is the 'image'.

An object and its image are often labelled in a special 'matching way'.

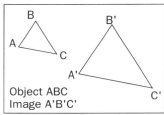

Object ABC
Image A'B'C'

Object XYZ
Image $X_1Y_1Z_1$

The same letters are used for matching points. But each letter on the image has a dash ' or the same number on it.

In the diagrams above, for example,

A and A' are matching points
A is on the object
A' is on the image

X and X_1 are matching points
X is on the object
X_1 is on the image

Drawing enlargements

Using a grid or dotty paper
Shapes are often drawn on a grid or dotty paper. This makes them easier to enlarge.

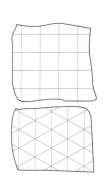

Use the lines or dots to find the lengths if you can. This is more accurate than measuring with a ruler.

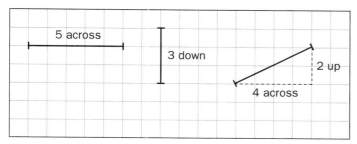

Count 'steps across' and/or 'steps up or down' for each line on the shape. (Write them down as a reminder.)
Multiply each number of 'steps' by the scale factor to enlarge it.
Then use these new 'steps' to draw the enlargement.

Question

This is the basic design for a model aircraft wing.
Enlarge the shape on the grid below. Use a scale factor of 3.

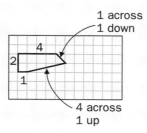

1 across
1 down
4 across
1 up

Answer

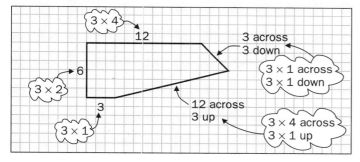

► *Exercise* **S11.1**

Copy and enlarge each given shape on $\frac{1}{2}$ cm squared paper. Use the scale factor given in each case.

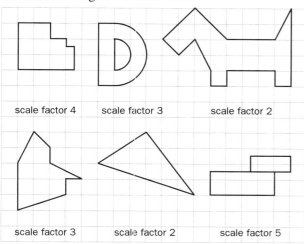

scale factor 4   scale factor 3   scale factor 2

scale factor 3   scale factor 2   scale factor 5

Using a centre of enlargement

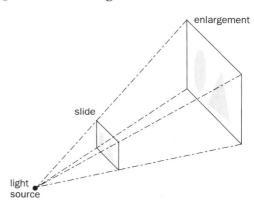

enlargement

slide

light
source

This is often called the **'ray method' of enlargement**. The *centre of enlargement* is like a light source. Lines from this point, like *rays of light*, produce the image.

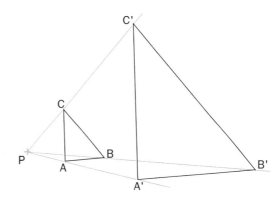

In this enlargement, P is the centre of enlargement.
The scale factor of enlargement is 3.

Lengths on shapes

The length of each line on the object is multiplied by this scale factor.

$A'B' = 3 \times AB$
$B'C' = 3 \times BC$
$C'A' = 3 \times CA$

Distances from P

The distance from centre P to each object point is also multiplied by the same scale factor.

$PA' = 3 \times PA$
$PB' = 3 \times PB$
$PC' = 3 \times PC$

Check these lengths and distances yourself on the diagram.

To enlarge a shape using a centre of enlargement, take these steps.

- Draw a line (a ray) *from the centre* of enlargement *through a corner point* of the shape.
  Measure *from the centre* to this corner point.
  Multiply this distance by the scale factor.
  Mark off the new distance *from the centre* along the ray.
- Repeat the above steps for each corner point of the shape.
- Join up the new points in the correct order to draw the enlargement.

The diagrams below show step-by-step how to enlarge triangle XYZ using centre P and scale factor 2.

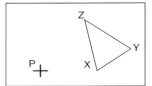

● Find the position of X'.

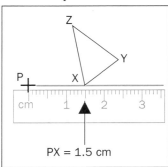

PX = 1.5 cm

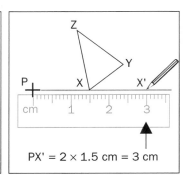

PX' = 2 × 1.5 cm = 3 cm

● Find the positions of Y' and Z'.

PY = 2.5 cm
PY' = 2 × 2.5 = 5 cm

PZ = 2 cm
PZ' = 2 × 2 = 4 cm

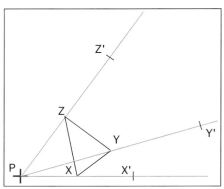

● Draw triangle X'Y'Z'.
This is the required enlargement of triangle XYZ.

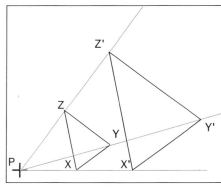

The centre of enlargement may be *outside* the shape, *inside* the shape or *on its edge*.

Enlargement of XYZ, using 0 as centre and scale factor 2

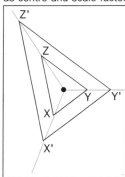

Enlargement of XYZ, using X as centre and scale factor 2

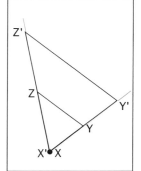

► *Exercise* **S11.2**

Trace triangle ABC. Enlarge ABC using the given scale factors and centres of enlargement.

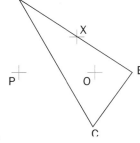

1   Centre: P. Scale factors: 2, 3 and 5.
2   Centre: A. Scale factors: 2 and 4.
3   Centre: B. Scale factors: 3 and 5.
4   Centre: C. Scale factors: 2 and 3.
5   Centre: O. Scale factors: 2, 3 and 4.
6   Centre: any other point inside the triangle. Scale factors: 2, 4 and 5.
7   Centre: X, the mid-point of AB. Scale factors: 2, 3 and 4.

Compare your images of ABC. What effect does using a different centre have?

You can also **draw an enlargement by the ray method on a grid** or dotty paper.
To find each 'image point':
● Count 'steps' *from the centre* of enlargement to a point on the object.
● Multiply the number of steps by the scale factor.
● Use these new steps to go *from the centre* to the 'image point'.

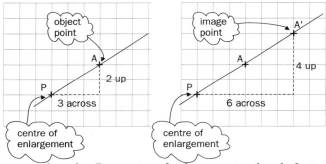

For example, using P as centre of enlargement and scale factor 2

from P to A is 3 across 2 up
from P to A' is 6 across 4 up

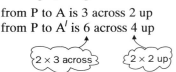

► *Exercise* **S11.3**

1   Copy each line AB and point P on to squared paper. Enlarge each line AB to A'B' from centre of enlargement P. Use the given scale factor in each case.

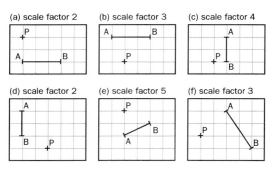

(a) scale factor 2   (b) scale factor 3   (c) scale factor 4
(d) scale factor 2   (e) scale factor 5   (f) scale factor 3

2 Copy each shape and enlarge it by the given scale factor.
Use point P as centre of enlargement.

(a) scale factor 4 (b) scale factor 2 (c) scale factor 3

3 Enlarge each shape in question **2** using point A as centre of enlargement and the given scale factor.

Coordinates are often used to give the position of the centre of enlargements and the vertices (corner points) of shapes.
Plot and label the points carefully.
Join points in the correct order to make the shape(s) you want.

Question

The vertices of triangle ABC are A(4,2), B(6,4) and C(3,6).
Draw the triangle ABC on the grid below.
Enlarge it using scale factor 3 and the centre of enlargement P(1,2).
Label the image triangle A$'$B$'$C$'$. Give the coordinates of its vertices.

Answer

• *Plot points and draw triangle ABC.*
• *Draw rays from P through A, B and C.*
• *Find image points A$'$, B$'$, and C$'$ using*

$$PA' = 3 \times PA, \quad PB' = 3 \times PB, \quad PC' = 3 \times PC$$

From P to A: 3 across   From P to A$'$: 3 × 3 = 9 across
From P to B: 5 across   From P to B$'$: 3 × 5 = 15 across
                2 up   3 × 2 = 6 up
From P to C: 2 across   From P to C$'$ 3 × 2 = 6 across
                4 up   3 × 4 = 12 up

• *Join points to draw triangle A$'$B$'$C$'$*

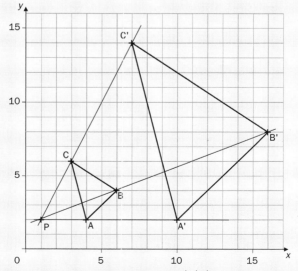

Coordinates of the vertices of A$'$B$'$C$'$ are:
A$'$(10,2), B$'$(16,8), C$'$(7,14)

Exercise **S11.4**

1 Triangle ABC has vertices at A(4,2), B(6,4) and C(3,6).
Draw each of these enlargements of ABC on separate diagrams.
Give the coordinates of the vertices of each image.
(a) Centre of enlargement (0,0). Scale factor 3.
(b) Centre of enlargement (4,2). Scale factor 2.
(c) Centre of enlargement (5,3). Scale factor 5.
(d) Centre of enlargement (4,4). Scale factor 4.
(e) Centre of enlargement (7,6). Scale factor 3.

2 Rectangle WXYZ has vertices at W(4,3), X(8,3), Y(8,5) and Z(4,5).
Draw these enlargements of WXYZ on separate diagrams.
Give the coordinates of the vertices of each image.
(a) Centre of enlargement (0,0). Scale factor 2.
(b) Centre of enlargement (6,4). Scale factor 3.
(c) Centre of enlargement (6,7). Scale factor 4.
(d) Centre of enlargement (8,5). Scale factor 2.
(e) Centre of enlargement (7,3). Scale factor 3.

3 Draw the four object shapes given below on the same axes.
(Use axes numbered from ⁻10 to 10.) Enlarge each shape using (0,0) as the centre of enlargement and scale factor 2.
Give the coordinates of the vertices of each image.
(a) Triangle ABC: A(3,2), B(3,5), C(1,5)
(b) Rectangle DEFG: D(⁻2, ⁻1), E(⁻2,⁻3), F(⁻5,⁻3), G(⁻5,⁻1)
(c) Pentagon OPQRS: O(0,0), P(2,0), Q(4,⁻2), R(4,⁻3), S(0,⁻4)
(d) Hexagon TUVWXY: T(⁻2,2), U(⁻1,2), V(⁻1,1), W(⁻3,1), X(⁻3,2), Y(⁻2,3)
Compare the coordinates of matching object and image points.
What do you notice?
Explain why this happens.

Finding the scale factor

The scale factor of an enlargement shows 'how many times larger' each length on the original shape has been made.

If each length is made 2 times as long, the scale factor is 2.
If each length is made 3 times as long, the scale factor is 3.
And so on …

To find this scale factor, you can compare any length on the image with what it is on the original shape.

$$\text{Scale factor} = \frac{\text{length on image}}{\text{matching original length}}$$

Make sure the lengths are in the same unit.
In this enlargement, for example,
ABC is the original shape,
A$'$B$'$C$'$ is the image.
Matching lengths AB and A$'$B$'$ are the easiest to measure here.

$$\text{Scale factor} = \frac{A'B'}{AB}$$
$$= \frac{4.5}{1.5}$$
$$= 3$$

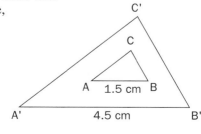

This enlargement is on a grid. For two 'matching lengths' here, simply *count* 'steps' on the grid.

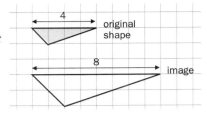

Scale factor = $\dfrac{\text{length on image}}{\text{matching original length}}$

$= \dfrac{8}{4}$ Both in 'steps' across

$= 2$

► *Exercise* S11.5

Find the scale factor of the enlargement in each diagram below. In each case, the shaded shape is the object.

1

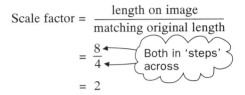

(a)

(b)

(c)

(d)

2

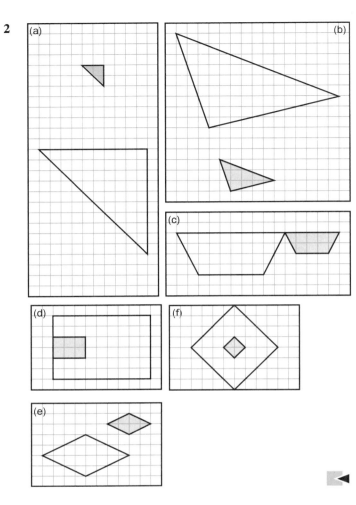

(a)   (b)

(c)

(d)   (f)

(e)

Finding centres of enlargements

To find the centre of an enlargement, draw straight lines through 'matching points' on the original shape and the image. The point where the lines cross is the centre of enlargement.

For example, to find the centre O for this enlargement…

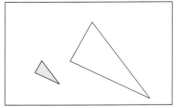

… draw these lines

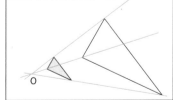

Always draw *three* lines if you can. Two lines give the point you want. The third line acts as a check.

Remember: The centre may be outside the original shape
            or inside it or on its edge.

► *Exercise* S11.6

1   Trace each object and image in question **1**, Exercise S11.5. Find the centre of enlargement in each case. Label it P.

2   Copy each object and image in question **2**, Exercise S11.5, on to a square grid. Find the centre of each enlargement. Label it clearly.

3 Each shaded shape is enlarged in the diagram below.
Describe each enlargement. (Give its scale factor and the coordinates of the centre of enlargement.)

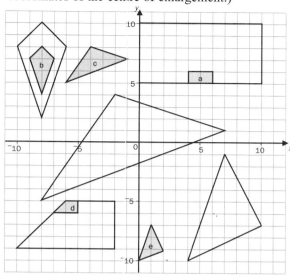

Examination Questions

1 On a $\frac{1}{2}$ cm square grid make a scale drawing of the car, with the lengths doubled.

(SEG, 1990)

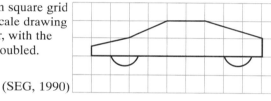

2 The diagram opposite shows the back of a doll's sweater. All the lengths are half the full size. Draw on squared paper the back of the full size sweater.

(WJEC, 1988)

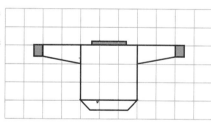

3

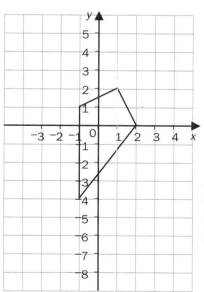

On a grid draw the image of the kite after an enlargement with scale factor +2 centre (0,0).

(NISEAC, 1990)

4

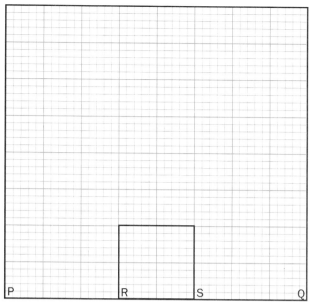

The square drawn on PQ is of side 8 cm and the square drawn on RS is of side 2 cm.
(a) Mark the centre of an enlargement which maps the smaller square on to the larger.
(b) State the scale factor of this enlargement.

(NISEAC, 1988)

5 Using a scale factor of 2, draw an enlargement of the triangle ABC.

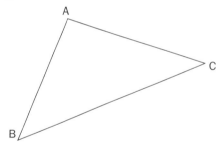

(NEAB, 1991)

6 Triangle EFG is an enlargement of triangle ABC.
(a) What is the scale factor of this enlargement?
(b) Write down the coordinates of the centre of enlargement.

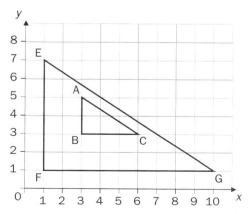

(MEG, 1991)

D1
Collecting and displaying data

This unit will help you to:

■ understand and use a variety of ways to collect and sort data

■ design and use observation sheets

■ interpret information given in the form of a pictogram or bar chart

■ draw pictograms and bar charts from data

■ recognise misleading pictograms and bar charts.

Data are **information** such as facts and figures. They are also called **statistics**. These facts are all statistics.

... 98% fat free, only 100 calories,

...the increase was 11.3%, or an average rise of £5.85 a week ...

...two-thirds of the new homes are for rent ...

... made a net loss of £141 million the previous year ...

... has spent 23 of her 79 years in the same house ...

... 65% of the 15-17 age group preferred pizza ...

... this year's collection totalled 152 tons, 17 tons more than last year ...

Statistics is also the name given to the *study of data*.
It involves:
1 collecting data
2 sorting data
3 displaying data in diagrams
4 analysing the results
5 coming to conclusions.

Collecting and sorting data

You can collect data in several ways. Here are some of the main ones.

- By asking questions …
  either 'in person' or with a written questionnaire.

- By observing things …
  and recording what happens.

- By doing an experiment …
  trying something, counting, measuring, …

- By finding someone else's data …
  given in books, newspapers, magazines, examination questions, …

JAN 1995 AMOUNT SPENT PER VISIT TO LOCAL STORE	
London	£10.58
S. England	£9.41
Anglia	£8.95
Scotland & Borders	£7.95
Wales & West	£7.85
Midlands	£7.84
S. West	£7.64
Lancs.	£7.32
Yorkshire	£6.50
Tyne Tees	

In your written examination you will be given any data you need. In an assignment you may have to collect data yourself.

When you first look at some data, all you may see is a jumble. You need to **sort the data** in some way. This means putting the data 'in order' so that it can be used.

Small amounts of data are easy to sort into a list. You can put them in **numerical** or **alphabetical order**.

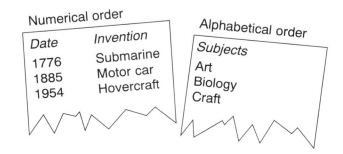

Numerical order

Date	Invention
1776	Submarine
1885	Motor car
1954	Hovercraft

Alphabetical order

Subjects
Art
Biology
Craft

Question

Did you know …?
These are the ten most spoken languages and the number of people who speak them.

German **119 million**
Chinese **700 million**
Spanish **240 million**
English **400 million**
Japanese **116 million**
Russian **265 million** Arabic **146 million**
Bengali **144 million**
Hindustani **230 million**
Portuguese **145 million**

(a) Write these languages in alphabetical order.
(b) Write the data in numerical order, 'most spoken language' first.

Answer

(a) alphabetical order
Arabic
Bengali
Chinese
English
German
Hindustani
Japanese
Portuguese
Russian
Spanish

(b) numerical order
1 Chinese 700 m
2 English 400 m
3 Russian 265 m
4 Spanish 240 m
5 Hindustani 230 m
6 Arabic 146 m
7 Portuguese 145 m
8 Bengali 144 m
9 German 119 m
10 Japanese 116 m

Data can often be sorted into a table. **Tallying** is an easy way to do this. Use these notes to help you to make a tally table.

- Table
  Draw a table with three columns. In the first column list all the possibilities you are counting, such as colours: blue, brown, green, …

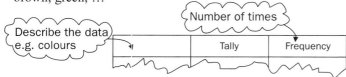

- Tally
  Work carefully through the data item by item. Make a tally mark | for each item – in the correct place! Group the tallies in fives ⌶⌶⌶⌶. This makes them easy to count.
  For example, instead of | | | | | | | | | | | | | | | | | | | | |
  you get ⌶⌶⌶⌶ ⌶⌶⌶⌶ ⌶⌶⌶⌶ ⌶⌶⌶⌶ |
  Faintly ring or cross out each item after you tally it. This helps you to avoid missing items or tallying them again.

- Total
  Add up the tallies for each thing.
  Write each total in the frequency column.
  As a check, add up all the frequencies.
  The total should be the same as the total number of items.
  If it is not, then you have to do the tallying again.

- Title
  Give it a short title, Say clearly what the data are about.

Question

In a survey, 50 people were asked about the number of people in their families. Here are the numbers they gave in their replies.

② ④ ③ ③ ⑤ ① ② ② ③ ④
① ② ② ② ③ ② ④ ③ ① ②
② ④ ② ③ ③ ④ ④ ⑤ ④ ③
③ ② ① ⑥ ④ ⑤ ⑥ ① ② ②
① ④ ③ ② ③ ⑦ ② ④ ④ ③

Complete the tally table below to show these results.

Answer

Ring each number after you tally it.
Add up the tallies to get each frequency.
Add up the frequencies to get the total.

Survey of number of people in families

Family size	Tally	Frequency
1	⌶⌶⌶⌶		6
2	⌶⌶⌶⌶ ⌶⌶⌶⌶ ⌶⌶⌶⌶	15
3	⌶⌶⌶⌶ ⌶⌶⌶⌶ ||	12
4	⌶⌶⌶⌶ ⌶⌶⌶⌶		11
5					3
6				2
7			1
	Total	50

Check: 50 in the survey.
50 is the total. ✓

A tally table shows frequencies (how many things occur). So it is also called a **frequency table**.

These frequency tables came from the last example.

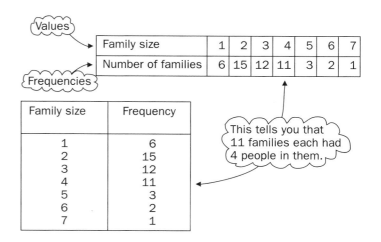

Family size	1	2	3	4	5	6	7
Number of families	6	15	12	11	3	2	1

Family size	Frequency
1	6
2	15
3	12
4	11
5	3
6	2
7	1

This tells you that 11 families each had 4 people in them.

Notice in a frequency table:
- The tally marks are usually left out.
- The data can go down or across the page.
- The 'items' come first in the table.
- The word 'frequency' may not appear – it may just say 'number' or 'number of …'.

When the items are numbers, make sure that you do not mix them up with the frequencies.

► *Exercise* **D1.1**

1 30 children were asked to name their favourite ice-cream.
(a) Copy and complete this tally table showing their choices.

Flavour	Tally	Frequency
Chocolate chip	ⅢⅠⅠ	6
Strawberry	ⅢⅠⅠⅠ	
Plain	ⅠⅠⅠⅠ	
Raspberry		9
Banana		4
	Total	

(b) Which was the most popular flavour?
(c) How many more children liked raspberry than liked strawberry?

2 Melanie is investigating the frequency of vowels in passages of English. She decided to examine this passage she read in a book.

> The majority of visitors who come to Norwich like to see the Cathedral. The aim of this book is to explain some of the many things you will see.

(a) Copy and complete this tally chart for the frequency of vowels in the passage.

Vowel	Tally	Frequency
a		
e		
i		
o		
u		
	Total	

(b) Which is the most frequent vowel in the passage?

3 The number of tracks on each of a pop group's fifteen record albums is

9, 8, 11, 10, 10, 12, 9, 11, 8, 8, 12, 9, 10, 12, 11.

Copy and complete this frequency table.

Number of tracks	8	9	10	11	12
Frequency					

4 Jamie counted the contents of 50 boxes of matches to check the claim made on the box. This is what he found:

39, 41, 40, 41, 38, 41, 39, 40, 39, 38,
41, 40, 42, 39, 41, 40, 40, 38, 42, 40,
40, 38, 41, 41, 39, 40, 39, 41, 40, 39,
42, 40, 40, 39, 41, 38, 40, 41, 41, 40,
39, 41, 41, 38, 40, 42, 41, 39, 40, 40.

Show this information in a tally chart. Is the claim on the box justified? Explain your answer.

Experiments and surveys

Two important ways to collect data are by experiment and by survey.

In an **experiment** we set up a situation and measure the effects, if any, that result from changes in that situation. This is a standard technique you will have used in science.

In a **survey** we collect data from situations that occur 'naturally'. We do not try to change the situation at all.

Here are some important questions to think about when doing an experiment or survey. Use them to help you to sort out your ideas.

- *What do you want to find out?* Why?
- *What data* will you need to collect? How will you decide?
- Which is the best way to *collect* the data? Why? Do you need any equipment?
- *How much* data will you need to collect? How will you decide?
- How *accurate* will your data have to be? Why? Can you *check* your data?
- How will you *record* your data? Why is this the best way?
- How will you *display* your data? Why?
- What *patterns*, if any, do your data show? What do they tell you?
- What *conclusions/predictions* can you make from your data? Can you *test* your conclusions/predictions?
- Are your results the ones you *expected*. Why?
- What kind of *report* will you present to describe what you did, your results, conclusions, etc.? Who is the report for?
- What *other questions* could you explore based on the results if you had time?

Observation sheets

Some data may be simply counted or collected as a list.

For example, the number of boys and girls in this playgroup is easy to count.

In many situations you need a *more organised* way to *record* your observations.

Plan carefully what you want to do. Design an **observation sheet** or **data collection sheet** before you start collecting data.

A **tally table** is often a neat way to record the data. Think carefully about the possible results you wish to record and note them on your sheet. Also, make a note of other important factors such as place, time of day, … which may affect your observations.

For example, this observation sheet is from a traffic survey.

CAR SURVEY

Date .... **Time** from ....

to ....

Location .... **Observer** ....

Number of passengers	Tally	Frequency
1		
2		
3		
4		
more than 4		

► *Exercise* **D1.2**

For each of the observation sheets below
(a) say how the sheet could be improved,
(b) redraw the sheet with your improvements included,
(c) suggest a real purpose for collecting the data.

1

Transport survey

Date ....

Vehicle	Number
car	
bike	
bus	
lorry	
van	

2

Dining room survey

Customer	Drink chosen

3

Crisps

Flavour	Price
plain	
cheese & onion	
smokey bacon	
salt & vinegar	
other	

4

TV viewing

Channel	Hours
BBC1	
BBC2	
ITV	
Ch 4	

◄

Displaying data

Diagrams are often used to display data. Most people find diagrams simpler to understand than a table. They are also more attractive and interesting to look at. A diagram can show data clearly without lots of words or figures. This helps you to spot any patterns and compare things easily.

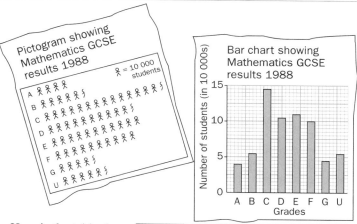

Here is the table the above diagrams come from.
To answer questions such as:

'Which grade did most students get?'
'Which grade did fewest students get?'

you have to look very carefully at the table. You only need to glance at either of the diagrams. Try it.

First Year GCSE Results

Mathematics GCSE Results 1988

Grade	Number of students
A	38 569
B	54 912
C	143 817
D	104 595
E	109 171
F	101 980
G	47 067
U	53 605
Total	653 716

Pictograms and **bar charts** are two common ways to display data. Notes about each of them follow.

Pictograms

A **pictogram** uses *simple pictures* or *symbols* to show data. It gives you a quick impression of the information.

Comparing data in a pictogram is easy. Just compare how many pictures each item has.

When you look at a pictogram, always read the title and key carefully. The **title** tells you what the pictogram is about. The **key** shows you what each little picture stands for.

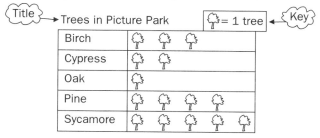

Each picture may stand for 1 piece of data.

Each 🌳 stands for 1 tree in this pictogram.
You can see:

the most common tree is sycamore (most 🌳)

the least common tree is oak (fewest 🌳)

You can count the number of each tree:
Birch 3, Cypress 2, Oak 1, Pine 4, Sycamore 5

Different pictures may be used for different kinds of data.

Types of tree in Picture Park

Deciduous	🌳🌳🌳🌳🌳🌳🌳🌳
Evergreen	🌲🌲🌲🌲🌲🌲

A different tree shape is used for each type of tree in this pictogram.
You can see more deciduous trees than evergreens. You can count 3 more.

Each picture may stand for *more than 1* piece of data. The key tells you the number. Count the pictures to find out how many times that number you have. *Part of a picture* stands for part (a fraction) of that number.

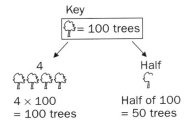

Key

🌳 = 100 trees

4
🌳🌳🌳🌳
4 × 100
= 100 trees

Half
🌲
Half of 100
= 50 trees

Question

The pictogram shows the number of sunny days during August at six seaside places. Answer the following questions about these data.

Aberystwyth	✖✖✖✖
Blackpool	✖✖✖ٔ
Brighton	✖✖✖✖
Exmouth	✖✖✖✖✖✖
Great Yarmouth	✖✖✖✖ ′
Oban	✖✖✖✦

Key:
✖ stands for 4 sunny days

(a) Which place had most sunny days? How many?
(b) Which place had fewest sunny days? How many?
(c) Which places had the same number of sunny days?
(d) What was the mean number of sunny days for these six places?

Answer

Use the key:

✖ 4 days   ٔ 2 days   ′ 1 day   ✦ 3 days
              ½ of 4 days   ¼ of 4 days   ¾ of 4 days

(a) *Look for 'most' pictures for 'most sunny days'.*
   Exmouth has 'most'.

   six ✖ ⟶ 6 × 4 = 24 days
   Exmouth had most sunny days. It had 24.

(b) *Look for 'fewest' pictures for 'fewest sunny days'.*
   Blackpool has 'fewest'.

   three ✖ ⟶ 3 × 4 = 12 days ٔ ⟶ 2 days
   Blackpool had fewest sunny days. It had 14.   14

(c) *Look for the same number of pictures.*
   Aberystwyth and Brighton had the same number of sunny days.

(d) *Find the number of sunny days for each place first.*
   Aberystwyth: 4 × 4 = 16
   Blackpool: 14
   Brighton: 16
   Exmouth: 24
   Yarmouth: (4 × 4) + 1 = 17
   Oban: (3 × 4) + 3 = 15
                              ———
                               102

   Mean = $\dfrac{\text{total of values}}{\text{number of values}} = \dfrac{102}{6} = 17$

A pictogram is one of the most eye-catching ways to show data. Watch out for them on television, in newspapers, magazines, books, … They are often used in advertisements and on posters.

Drawing pictograms

When drawing any diagram, remember:

- Draw it in pencil first.
  This makes it easier to correct mistakes and alter things. You can use ink, colour, shading, … later, if you have time.
- Be as neat and accurate as you can. Use drawing instruments (ruler, compasses, protractor, stencil, …)
- Give it a suitable title to show what your diagram is about.

Here are some hints to help you to draw a pictogram.

- Symbol
  Choose a simple picture or symbol that is easy to draw. Try to make it 'look like' the data in some way.
- Key
  Say clearly what each picture stands for. For large numbers make 1 picture stand for more than 1 piece of data. Choose an easy number to work with.
- Working
  Work out how many pictures you need for each part of the data. Divide each figure in the data by the number each picture stands for.
- Drawing
  Draw on squared paper. This helps you to keep the pictures in line. Try to draw each full picture the same size. Space them evenly. Estimate fractions of a picture if you need to.

Question

Alison works for a travel agent. She does a survey about 'Weekend Breaks'. The table gives some of her results. Show these data as a pictogram.

Place	Number of people
city	150
country	225
seaside	90
unknown	5

Use 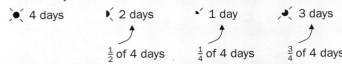 to stand for 50 people.

Answer

Work out how many pictures to draw.

1 picture → 50 people.

city: 150 ÷ 50 = 3   country: 225 ÷ 50 = 4.5
seaside: 90 ÷ 50 = 1.8   unknown: 5 ÷ 50 = 0.1

Draw the pictogram.

Pictogram about where people went for a Weekend Break.

City	🏢 🏢 🏢		
Country	🏢 🏢 🏢 🏢 🏢		
Seaside	🏢 🏢		
Unknown	▪		

Pictograms have two main disadvantages:

● They can take a long time to draw well.
● They are not always a very accurate way to show data. The data are often simplified before drawing. Figures are rounded. Fractions of pictures are estimated.

Misleading pictograms

Some pictograms are designed to mislead you.
You need to keep your wits about you when looking at them.

Look at this pictogram. The pictures are different sizes. They are not spaced equally. Comparing the data at a glance is not easy. Perhaps that is what is intended.

Makes of car in the town centre

Austin	🚗 🚗 🚗 🚗 🚗
Ford	🚗 🚗 🚗
Honda	🚗 🚗 🚗 🚗 🚗
Volvo	🚗 🚗 🚗
Saab	🚗 🚐

Pictograms are often used to show an increase or decrease. The change in the picture's size should show the change in the data. Often it does not.

Look at the words of this advertisement. Now compare the pictures. Lengths on the 1990 picture are 2 times those on the 1980 picture. But the area of the 1990 picture is 4 times that of the other. So the increase looks larger than it is.

In 1990 we built twice as many houses as 10 years ago

1980   1990

Here is a fairer way to show the increase. The change does not look so dramatic now.

In 1990 we built twice as many houses as 10 years ago

1980   1990

Look out for misleading pictograms in books, newspapers, … Make a 'rogue's gallery' showing what is wrong with them.

▶ **Exercise D1.3**

1 Jackie did a survey of colours of cars parked at the sports club. She displayed her data in a pictogram.

Colours of car in a car park	
colour	frequency
red	10
blue	2
green	15
black	5
orange	12
total	44

Colours of car in a car park	🚗 = 5 cars
colour	cars
red	🚗 🚗
blue	🚗
green	
black	
orange	

Jackie drew a 🚗 for every 5 cars she counted of each colour. Copy and complete Jackie's pictogram.

2 This pictogram represents the income received by a charity in 1993.

Donations 🪙 🪙 🪙 🪙 🪙

Interest 🪙 🪙 🪙

Legacies 🪙 🪙 🪙

The amount received from Donations was £5 million.

(a) Write, in figures, the amount represented by 🪙 in the pictogram.
(b) Write, in figures, the amount received from each source in 1993.
(c) In 1994, the amount received from Donations increased by £$\frac{1}{2}$ million, the amount received from Interest increased by £$\frac{1}{4}$ million, the amount received from Legacies fell by £$1\frac{1}{2}$ million.
Draw a pictogram for 1994. Use the symbol □ to represent £1 million.

3 Mr and Mrs Rizzi have opened a pizza parlour. Their lunchtime sales for the first two weeks are given in this frequency table.

Day	Frequency
Monday 11 February	40
Tuesday 12 February	68
Wednesday 13 February	42
Thursday 14 February	48
Friday 15 February	54
Monday 18 February	25
Tuesday 19 February	59
Wednesday 20 February	56
Thursday 21 February	45
Friday 22 February	55

Using ● to stand for 8 pizzas, draw a pictogram showing the lunchtime sales for the first fortnight.

Bar charts

A bar chart uses bars, side by side, to display data.
The bars can go up or across the page.
The length of a bar stands for the size of the data it shows.
This makes the data easy to compare. Just compare the lengths of the bars.

Reading bar charts

You may have to read some information from a bar chart. Here are some points to remember:

● Title
  Make sure that you know what the bar chart is about.
  Read the title and given information carefully to find out.
  Lots of people forget to do this!
● Axes
  Check the labels on the axes.
  One axis gives the labels for the bars.
  The other axis is a 'number line' (like a ruler). Its label tells you what the numbers are about.
● Scale
  Look carefully at the scale on the number line.
  It helps you to work out the 'size' for each bar.
  Work out what each 'small space' stands for if you need to.

A bar chart can show frequencies (numbers of things).

This bar chart shows the votes for favourite sports by Year 11.
The length of each bar gives the number of votes for each sport.

It clearly shows that:

soccer got most votes,
golf got fewest votes,
netball and rugby got
  the same, …

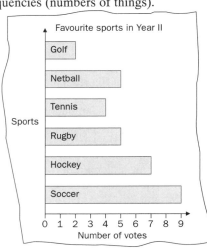

A bar chart can show amounts of something.

This bar chart gives the highest mountain in Scotland, England, Northern Ireland and Wales.

You can see that:

they are all
  below 1500 metres,
Scafell Pike is just
  below 1000 metres,
Snowdon is just
  above 1000 metres, …

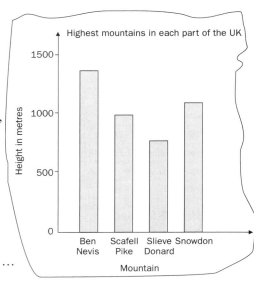

A 'vertical' bar chart is also called a column graph. Sometimes just lines are drawn instead of bars. Then it is usually called a line chart.

On some bar charts the scale is very easy. Each 'small space' stands for 1 unit. Here are some examples:

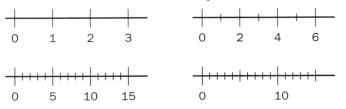

Some scales are not so easy.
Each small space may stand for more than 1 or a fraction. Here are some examples:

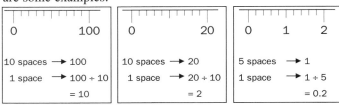

Question

The bar chart shows the amount of energy used by a man in one hour for various activities.

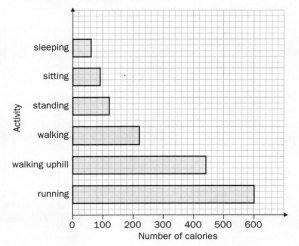

How many calories does each activity use?

Answer

Check axes
Labels: across: Number of calories
*   up: Activity*
Scale: 'calorie axis'

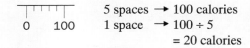

5 spaces → 100 calories
1 space → 100 ÷ 5
        = 20 calories

Work out each bar length.

running:	600 calories	standing:	120 calories
walking uphill:	440 calories	sitting:	90 calories
walking:	220 calories	sleeping:	60 calories

Drawing bar charts

An examination question may ask you to draw a bar chart. You may want to draw one from your own data. Here are some notes to help you.

- **Equipment**
  Use a ruler and sharp pencil.
  Draw on squared paper (graph paper). This makes the diagram easier to draw and read.

- **Axes**
  Draw two axes at right angles to each other.
  Decide whether the bars will go up or across the page.
  Label each axis clearly. Describe the data.

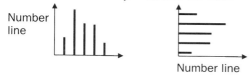

Number line

Number line

- **Scale**
  Work out an easy scale for the number line.
  Make each 'small space' an easy value to use.
  Try to make the diagram fill a sensible amount of the paper.
  Check that the largest value fits on the paper.
  Number the axis in equal steps.

Memo
Choosing your own scales p97

- **Drawing**
  Draw each bar the correct length for the data it shows.
  Make all the bars the same width.
  Leave equal spaces between them.
  Label each bar clearly.

- **Title**
  Give it a title to describe the data.

In some examination questions some of the drawing is done for you. You may find that the axes are drawn, labelled and numbered. Check the label on each axis. Check the scale on the number line.

Question

The table gives the number of calories per 25 g for various fruits.

On the following graph paper, draw a bar chart to show these data.

Fruit	Number of calories
apple	8.75
lemon	3.5
peach	8
pear	7.25
rhubarb	1.75

Answer

Check axes:
  Across: *Names of fruits*
  Up: *Number of calories.*

Scale on calorie axis:

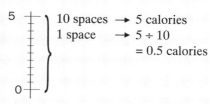

10 spaces → 5 calories
1 space → 5 ÷ 10
= 0.5 calories

Mark the number line every calorie (2 spaces) to help you to read values.

Draw bars to show the numbers.

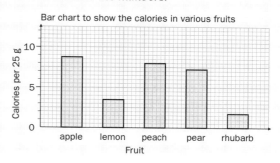

Bar chart to show the calories in various fruits

Sometimes you want to **compare data** in two or more bar charts. For instance, bar charts showing matching results for different sexes or different years or different subjects.

Looking at each diagram on its own is not a very easy way to compare them. The bar charts can be combined onto one diagram. The bars in each group are put next to each other. This makes them very simple to compare.

Question

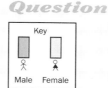

Key
Male Female

The bar chart shows how long men and women could expect to live, on average, in six countries.

Use it to answer the questions on the following page.

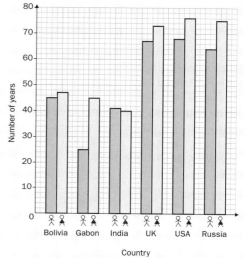

Male and female life expectancy

continued

(a) Who had the highest life expectancy?
How many years?
(b) Who had the lowest life expectancy?
How many years?
(c) In general can males or females expect to live longer?
Explain your answer.
In which country was this not so?
(d) What is the difference in the figures for the UK?
(e) In which country is there most difference between the figures?
How many years?

Answer

Check axes:
Labels: across: Country
*   up: Number of years.*

Scale: Years axis: 10 ┤┬ 5 spaces → 10 years
                             ├ 1 space → 10 ÷ 5
                          0 ┤┘   = 2 years

(a) *Look for longest bar. Read value from scale.*
'USA female' had the highest life expectancy.
76 years.
(b) *Look for shortest bar. Read value from scale.*
'Gabon male' had the lowest life expectancy.
25 years.
(c) The bar chart shows longer 'bars' for 'female' for most countries.
So, in general, this shows females can expect to live longer.
This is not so in India.
The two bars (for male and female) are about the same length.
(d) For the UK: Female : 73
                Male: 67
                Difference: 73 − 67 = 6 years.
(e) There is most difference between the figures for Gabon.
                Female: 45
                Male: 25
                Difference: 45 − 25 = 20 years.

A bar chart is a popular way to display data. Many people think that it is the easiest of the diagrams to understand. It can often be read quite accurately.

A bar chart shows clearly how each piece of the data compares with the others. You can see at a glance which of two bars is longer. However, a bar chart does not show how each piece of data compares with the whole data.

Exercise D1.4

1–4   Draw bar charts to show the data in each question in Exercise D1.1 on p 198.

Misleading bar charts

Like line graphs, bar charts can be misleading. So take a good look at them.

Memo
Misleading
graphs p 99

- Check the number line.
  What scale and units are used?
- Check the start of the scale.
  Does it start at zero (0)?
- Check the scale.
  Is it distorted - too squashed up or spread out?
- Check the width of the bars.
  Are they the same?

Exercise D1.5

Each advert below wants to show:

Say how they are misleading.

OUR BRAN GIVES YOU LOTS MORE FIBRE!

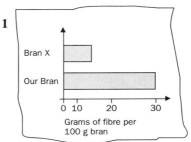

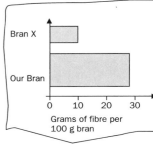

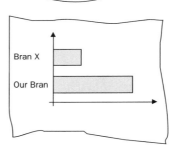

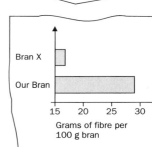

Look for other misleading bar charts in the media (TV, newspapers, magazines, …), in books, …

Collect some examples of these.
Say how they are misleading.

Examination Questions

1   Athletics competition results: USA medals

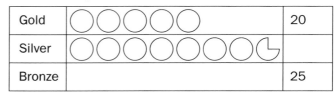

(a) How many actual medals does one complete circle in the chart represent?
(b) How many silver medals were won?
(c) Draw in the circles for the bronze medals.

(NEAB, 1990)

2

Key ▢ represents 50p	
Majorca	▢ ▢ ▢ ▯
Cyprus	▢ ▢ ▢ ▢ ▯
Portugal	▢ ▢ ▯
Gran Canaria	▢ ▯

The pictograph represents the average price of a bottle of wine in the places named.

(a) In which of the countries is wine cheapest?

(b) What is the average price of a bottle of wine in Portugal?

The average price of a bottle of wine in Egypt is £1.25.

(c) Complete the pictogram to show this information.

(ULEAC, 1990)

3 A pictograph in a newspaper uses a clock face to represent time. Two examples are shown below.

🕐 represents 1 minute   🕐 represents 25 seconds

(a) Draw a clock face to show how 45 seconds would be represented.

(b) The pictograph below shows how the world record for running the mile changed between 1868 and 1979.

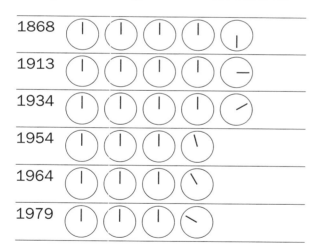

1868	🕐 🕐 🕐 🕐 🕐
1913	🕐 🕐 🕐 🕐 🕐
1934	🕐 🕐 🕐 🕐 🕐
1954	🕐 🕐 🕐 🕐
1964	🕐 🕐 🕐 🕐
1979	🕐 🕐 🕐 🕐

Roger Bannister became the first man to run a mile in less than four minutes. In which year did this occur?

(c) In 1964 the record time for the mile was 3 minutes 54.1 seconds.
In 1979 Sebastian Coe broke this record by 5 seconds. What was his record time?

(NEAB, 1990)

4 (a) Write in the totals in this tally table.

Type of shop	Tally	Total
Clothing	卌 ‖	
Electrical	‖‖	
Stationery	‖	
Shoe	卌 ‖	
Toy	卌	

(b) Draw a fully labelled bar chart of the results obtained.

(ULEAC, 1991)

5 The bar chart shows the profit/loss in thousands of pounds for the Aengael Toy Shop during the period September 1988 to April 1989 inclusive.

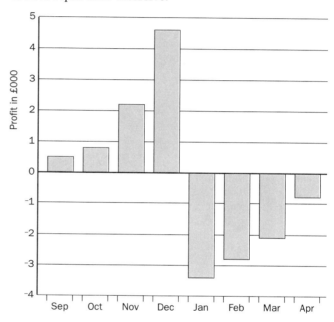

(a) Showing how you arrive at your answer, estimate the total profit during this period.

(b) Explain what the bar chart shows is happening to Aengael's profits during this period.

(NEAB, 1990)

6 Criticise the diagram below which shows the amounts borrowed, in millions of pounds, by Special Metal Panel plc, over a 5-year period.

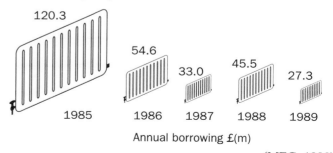

120.3	54.6	33.0	45.5	27.3
1985	1986	1987	1988	1989

Annual borrowing £(m)

(MEG, 1990)

D2
Pie charts

This unit will help you to:

■ understand and interpret data given in a pie chart

■ draw pie charts to display data.

A **pie chart** is a *circular* diagram used to display data. It shows how the data are divided into *groups*, so it looks like a pie cut into slices.

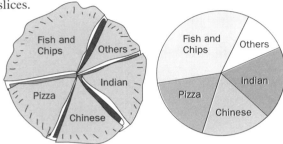

Favourite take-away foods   Favourite take-away foods

Pie charts used in the media (on television, in newspapers …) are often drawn as pictures of pies or other circular objects relevant to the data. You can display the data in the same way by using just a circle.

Interpreting pie charts

A pie chart can make it easy to compare groups in the data.

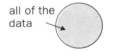 all of the data

 part of the data

The *whole 'pie'* stands for the *whole amount* of data being dealt with. Each *slice* stands for a named *part* of the data. Its size shows the size of that part of the data.

You can often tell at a glance which is the biggest/smallest slice of the pie, i.e. the biggest/smallest group in the data.

For example, the pie chart above shows clearly that:

● the most popular take-away food in the survey was Fish and Chips

● Pizza, Chinese and Indian take-aways were equally popular.

The main advantage of a pie chart is that you can see each *part* of the data as a *fraction* of the whole data.

Sometimes the sizes of these fractions are easy to estimate 'by eye'.

For example, you can see from this pie chart that:

● about $\frac{1}{2}$ of Year 11 came to school by bus

● about $\frac{1}{4}$ walked

● roughly the same, about $\frac{1}{8}$, came by car or by bike.

How Year II came to school

When you know the amount shown by the whole pie, you can work out how much is shown by each slice. Just find each fraction of the whole amount.

For example, in the travel survey about Year 11, there are 120 students.

$\frac{1}{2}$ of 120 = 60   So 60 came by bus.

$\frac{1}{4}$ of 120 = 30   So 30 walked.

$\frac{1}{8}$ of 120 = 15   So 15 came by car and 15 came by bike.

▶ *Exercise* D2.1

1   Sharon did a survey of hair colour of 240 students in Year 9. This pie chart shows her findings.

Hair colours of 240 Year 9 students

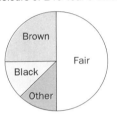

Estimate the number of students in each category.

2   This pie chart shows the proportions of students choosing each main course on today's menu.

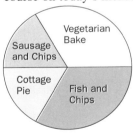

Today's Main Courses
Sausage & Chips
Fish & Chips
Vegetarian Bake
Cottage Pie

Altogether, 480 students were questioned about their choice.

Estimate the number of students choosing each dish.

Often you cannot find the fractions just by looking at the pie chart. But you can *work out* the size of each fraction from the angle at the centre of the circle for each slice.

There are 360° at the centre of a circle.

So 360° show all of the data.
1° shows $\frac{1}{360}$ of the data, and so on …

The fraction for each slice is given by:

$$\frac{\text{number of degrees at centre}}{360}$$

In an examination you may be *given* the angle at the centre, or you may have to *measure* it or you may have to *work it out*.

Question

This pie chart shows what is in Sureway Bran cereal.
(a) Calculate the angle for Fat on the diagram.
(b) An average 'serving' of this cereal weighs 45 g. How much fat is in this?

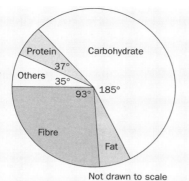

Not drawn to scale

Answer

(a) $360° - 185° - 93° - 37° - 35° = 10°$
(b) $\frac{10}{360}$ of 45 g = 1.25 g.

Pie charts often have *percentages* marked on them. You can use these to work out how much each slice shows. For example, the total surface area of the Earth is about 510 million km^2. From the pie chart, the land surface is 29% of this, that is, about 148 million km^2.

The Earth's surface

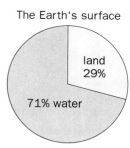

The *whole pie* shows *100%* of the data. So the percentages should add up to 100%. Sometimes the total is a little more or less than this. Often this is because the numbers have been rounded before the pie chart was drawn.

► *Exercise* **D2.3**

1 This pie chart shows the favourite sports of 260 students at Picton College.
(a) What percentage of students named netball as their favourite sport?
(b) Calculate the number of students naming each sport shown as their favourite.

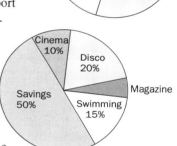

2 June is paid £30 per week for her part time work at Slomans. This pie chart shows what she does with her money each week.
(a) What percentage of her money is spent on a magazine each week? How much is this?
(b) Calculate the amount of money June saves each week.
(c) How much does June spend each week on
(i) Disco (ii) Cinema (iii) Swimming.

► *Exercise* **D2.2**

1 The 108 students in Year 10 at Fulford School were asked to name their favourite subject.
This pie chart shows their choices.
(a) Measure the angles at the centre of the pie chart.
(b) Work out the number of students choosing each named subject.

Year 10's favourite subjects

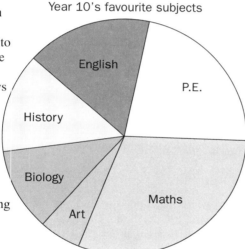

2 For each of these pie charts:
(a) calculate the size of the missing angle
(b) work out what each slice stands for.

(i) Dinner arrangements (360 pupils)

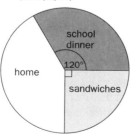

(ii) Traffic survey (90 vehicles)

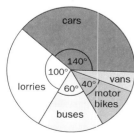

(iii) Year II's favourite sports (180 pupils)

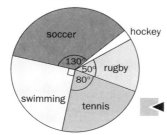

Drawing pie charts

The two main steps in drawing a pie chart are:
• *calculating* the angle for each slice
• *drawing* the slices on a circle diagram.

To find the angle for each slice in a pie chart, do the working step-by-step, like this:

1 Find the *total amount* to be shown on the pie chart. Add up the *frequencies* to find it if you need to.
2 *Divide* 360° (the angle at the centre of the circle) *by this total*.
This gives the angle for each item.

$$\text{angle for 1 item} = \frac{360°}{\text{Total number of items}}$$

3 *Multiply* the number of items (i.e., the frequency) for each group by the angle for 1 item. This gives the size of the angle for each slice.

Angle for a slice = frequency × angle for 1 item

You can do all this working with a calculator, but it is a good idea to put the results in a table.

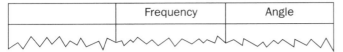

	Frequency	Angle

Check that the angles add up to 360°.

Remember: when angles are rounded to the nearest degree, the total may not be exactly 360°. Take this rounding error into account if you need to.

► *Exercise* **D2.4**

1   Tina decided to draw a pie chart to show a day in her life. She worked out that:

$$24 \text{ hours} \rightarrow 360°$$
$$1 \text{ hour} \rightarrow \frac{360°}{24} = 15°$$

activity	number of hours	number of degrees
lessons	5	5 × 15° = 75°
meals	1	
homework	3	
TV	2	
travel	1	
sleep	8	
others	4	
totals	24	360°

Copy and complete Tina's table showing the number of degrees needed for each activity.

2   Ron calculated the number of hours (to the nearest half hour) he spent watching different types of TV programmes over a 12-hour period. He decided to draw a pie chart to show his findings.

Types of TV programmes

type	hours	angle
film	4	
sport	3	
play	2	
documentary	$1\frac{1}{2}$	
educational	1	
news	$\frac{1}{2}$	
totals	12	360°

(a) Calculate the angle which represents 1 hour.
(b) Copy and complete Ron's table showing the number of degrees needed for each type of programme.

3   60 people were asked about their favourite breakfast drink. This table shows how they replied.

Favourite breakfast drink

drink	number
coffee	20
fruit juice	15
tea	10
milk	7
water	3
none	5
total	60

Work out the angle needed to show these results in a pie chart.

4   180 Year 9 students were asked to name their favourite school day. This table shows their replies.
Work out the angle needed to show these results in a pie chart.

Year 9's favourite school day

day	number
Monday	36
Tuesday	42
Wednesday	15
Thursday	20
Friday	55
don't know	12
total	180

To draw the slices for a pie chart on a diagram, you need: a sharp pencil, a ruler, a pair of compasses and a protractor.

Here are some hints to help you with the drawing.

1   *Draw a circle* with a pair of compasses. Make the radius as large as possible. (In some exam questions it may be drawn for you).
2   *Draw a radius* as a starting line.
3   Use a protractor to *draw the angle of each slice* at the centre of the circle. Make sure the centre of the protractor is at the centre of the circle. Measure the *first angle* from the *starting line*, then measure the *next angle* from the *new line*, and so on.
Measure the size of each angle very carefully. Any mistakes will mean that the slices will not fit into the circle. Draw the *smallest* angle *first,* then the next smallest, and so on … so that the *largest* angle is drawn *last.* This can help to reduce the effect of any errors.
4   *Label* each slice carefully. In an examination you may want to label the size of each angle also. If it is difficult to fit the full name of each group on each slice, label each with a letter and use a key to say what each stands for. In course-work you can shade the slices in different colours to make them easier to see. Do not spend valuable time doing this in your written exam.
5   Give the pie chart a suitable *title*.

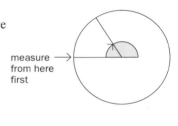

Starting line →

measure → from here first

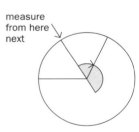

measure from here next

Question

This table gives some data from a newspaper survey. People were asked to choose which one of the listed Sunday papers they preferred to read. Draw a pie chart to show the findings.

Newspaper Survey

Sunday Times	75
News of the World	150
Sunday Mirror	100
Observer	50
Sunday Telegraph	25

Answer

Total number of people = 75 + 150 + 100 + 50 + 25
                       = 400

Angle for each person = 360° ÷ 400 = 0.9°

Paper	Frequency	Angle (degrees)
Sunday Times	75	75 × 0.9 = 67.5
News of the World	150	150 × 0.9 = 135
Sunday Mirror	100	100 × 0.9 = 90
Observer	50	50 × 0.9 = 45
Sunday Telegraph	25	25 × 0.9 = 22.5
Totals	400	360

Pie chart showing
which Sunday paper
some people
preferred to read.

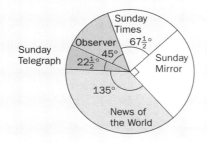

Exercise D2.5

Questions 1–4

Draw pie charts to show the data in Exercise D2.4.

5   A shopkeeper sells chocolate bars in four different sizes:
Extra large, Large, Medium, Small. One week his sales
figures were as follows:

   Extra large 35   Medium 50
   Large   70   Small   25

Draw a pie chart to represent these data.

6   A school has 900 pupils who come from 5 different towns.
The number coming from each town is shown below.

Town	Number of pupils
Barnville	320
Exford	280
Moreham	160
Newtown	90
Sidbury	50

Represent these data by drawing a pie chart.

Examination Questions

1   The pie charts are used to compare how two classes of 30
children travelled to school on a particular day. One of the
pie charts is for a class of 5-year olds and the other is for a
class of 15-year olds.
Which of these
pie charts do you
consider is for the
class of five-year
olds? Give a reason
for your answer.
   (SEG, 1990)

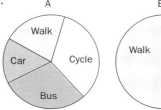
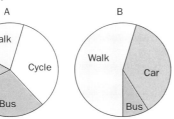

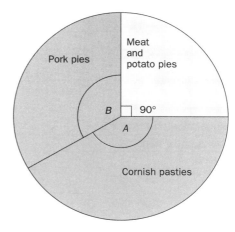

2   The pie chart above represents the sales for a small
butcher's shop in a given week. The butcher sold 66 meat
and potato pies in that week.
(a) What was the total number of pies and pasties sold
during the week?
(b) Measure and write down the size of angle A and the size
of angle B.
(c) How many pork pies were sold during the week?
   (NEAB, 1990)

3   Tim spent $2\frac{1}{2}$ hours doing homework
one evening. The pie chart shows
how he shared the time between
the three subjects.
Calculate how many minutes Tim
spent on his Maths homework.

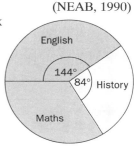

Not to scale

   (WJEC, 1991)

4

During photocopying, the pie chart shown above has been
partly blotted out. It represents the budget of a Passenger
Transport Authority for 1989.
(a) Measure accurately the two angles not given in the table
below. Write each answer as a whole number of
degrees.
(b) Using the information on the pie chart, calculate the
total expenditure for the year.

(c) Calculate the expenditure on each of the following:
Pensions and Financing
Rail Support.

Item	Angle	Amount
Subsidised Bus Services	90°	£18 million
Concessionary Fares	120°	£24 million
Administration and Marketing	30°	£6 million
Pensions and Financing		
Rail Support		
Total	360°	

(ULEAC, 1989)

5 The pie chart shows how a manufacturing firm used its income in 1990.

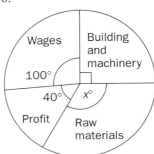

This diagram is NOT accurately drawn

(a) Calculate the value of *x*.
The firm made a profit of £5 million in 1990.
(b) Calculate the wage bill for the year.

(ULEAC, 1991)

6 The following table shows the percentage of sales for various makes of home computer in 1986.

(a) Show this information on a clearly labelled pie chart.
(b) If Amstrad and Sinclair had combined what would their percentage share of the sales have been?

Make	Percentage of market
Amstrad	38
Acorn	10
Sinclair	25
Commodore	10
Atari	15
Others	2

(MEG, 1989)

7 Listening figures for BBC Radio are:
Radio 1   8 million
Radio 2   5 million
Radio 3 $\frac{1}{2}$ million
Radio 4 $4\frac{1}{2}$ million
Represent this information in a pie chart, showing clearly how you have calculated the angles.

(MEG, 1989)

8 A School allocates its weekly timetable to pupils in the fifth year in the following way.

English	6 periods
Mathematics	5 periods
Science	8 periods
Games	5 periods
Options	16 periods

No pupil has a private-study (or free) period.
(a) How many periods are there in the week?
(b) Calculate the percentage of time allocated to Mathematics each week.
(c) Represent the above information in a pie chart, using a circle with a radius of 5 cm. Label each sector clearly.

(SEG, 1990)

▷ **D3**
Conversion graphs

This unit will help you to:

■ understand, interpret and use conversion graphs
■ draw a graph to convert one unit to another.

A **conversion** is a change from one thing to another. A **conversion graph** is used to change one unit of measure to another. It is usually a *straight line* graph.

Conversion graphs are usually used to change metric to imperial units (and vice versa) and from one currency to another.

Reading conversion graphs

Reading a conversion graph is like reading any line graph. Read what the graph is about and the labels on the axes first. Work out what the scale is on each axis. Then read off the values you want.

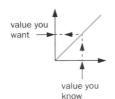
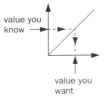

Draw *guidelines* on the graph if it helps (or if the question asks you to show what you did).

Readings from the graph can be **scaled up** (by multiplying by 10, 100, ...) or **scaled down** (by dividing by 10, 100, ...) to give a wider range of values. Examples of this are given in the answers to the following question.

Question

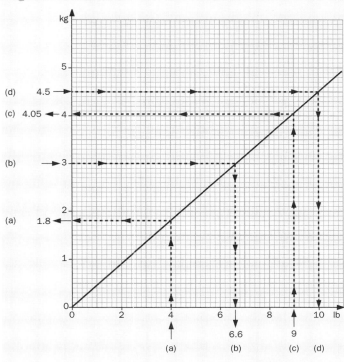

This conversion graph converts pounds (lb) and kilograms (kg). Use it to answer these questions. Show clearly how you obtained each value.
(a) Sue's empty suitcase weighs 4 lb.
   What is its weight in kilograms?
(b) Sue's baby sister weighs 3 kg.
   What does she weigh in pounds (lb)?
(c) Sue's brother weighs 90 lb.
   How much does he weigh in kilograms?
(d) Sue's handbag weighs 0.45 kg.
   How heavy is it in pounds (lb)?

Answer

Work out scales
   lb axis: 10 'small spaces'   →   2 lb
              1 'small space'   →   2 ÷ 10 = 0.2 lb
   kg axis: 10 'small spaces'   →   1 kg
              1 'small space'   →   1 ÷ 10 = 0.1 kg

(a) From graph: 4 lb → 1.8 kg
(b) From graph: 3 kg → 6.6 lb
(c) *To change 90 lb to kg,*
   change 9 lb and scale up (× 10).

   From graph:
   $\times 10 \left(\begin{array}{c} 9 \text{ lb} \longrightarrow 4.05 \text{ kg} \\ 90 \text{ lb} \longrightarrow 40.5 \text{ kg} \end{array} \right) \times 10$

(d) *To change 0.45 kg to lb,*
   change 4.5 kg and scale down (÷ 10).

   From graph:
   $\div 10 \left(\begin{array}{c} 4.5 \text{ kg} \longrightarrow 10 \text{ lb} \\ 0.45 \text{ kg} \longrightarrow 1 \text{ lb} \end{array} \right) \div 10$

Exercise **D3.1**

1   Use the conversion graph in the question opposite to do these.
   (a) Change these weights in pounds to kilograms:
      (i) 8 lb   (ii) 60 lb   (iii) 2.2 lb   (iv) 0.5 lb
   (b) Change these weights in kilograms to pounds:
      (i) 2 kg   (ii) 32 kg   (iii) 0.9 kg   (iv) 0.25 kg

2   When Simon went on holiday to France he used this graph to convert pounds (£) to French Francs (FF).

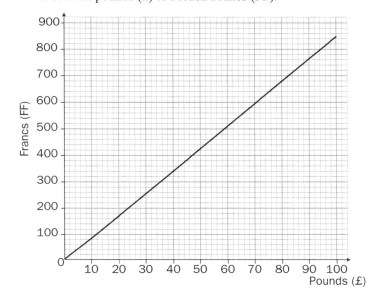

Use the graph to answer these questions.
   (a) How many French Francs would Simon get when he exchanged:
      (i) £100   (ii) £30   (iii) £75   (iv) £65?
      What rate of exchange has been used by Simon to draw this graph? Explain how you worked this out.
   (b) When Simon returned from holiday he wanted to exchange his unused French Francs for sterling (£). How much sterling would he receive if he exchanged
      (i) 400 FF   (ii) 500 FF   (iii) 750 FF   (iv) 230 FF
      Give each answer to the nearest £1.

Drawing conversion graphs

To draw a conversion graph you have to know a *link* between the two units. Usually you are given an **exchange rate** or **conversion factor**.

   For a *straight line graph*, you use this relationship to work out the coordinates of *three points* to plot. (You only need two, but the third is a check.)

   Choose easy values (such as 0 and whole numbers) to work with. Make sure the points fit on the grid but not too close together.

   Plot the points and draw a straight line through them.

   When you have drawn the graph you can use it to find values as before.

Question

Sharon changed her holiday money to dollars ($).
  She got 1.7 dollars to the £.
  On the axes below, draw a graph to change pounds (£) and dollars ($) using this exchange rate. Use your graph to answer the following questions.
  Put marks on your graph to show any readings made from it.
(a) How many dollars are equivalent to £7?
(b) A skirt Sharon likes costs $38. How much is this in £s?
(c) She spots a necklace costing $2200. What is its price in £s?

Answer

£ axis goes from 0–25 on the grid below.
Work out three pairs of values to fit this range.
Use £1 = $1.7.
Table of values:

£	0	10	20
$	0	17	34

$$10 \times 1.7 \qquad 20 \times 1.7$$

Work out scales:
  £ axis: 10 'small spaces' → £5
         1 'small space' → 5 ÷ 10 = £0.50
  $ axis: 10 'small spaces' → $10
         1 'small space' → 10 ÷ 10 = $1

Plot points and draw line.

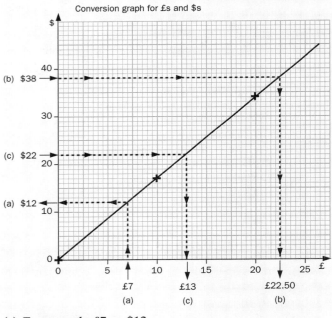

Conversion graph for £s and $s

(a) From graph: £7 → $12
(b) From graph: $38 → £22.50
(c) From graph: $22 → £13

  Scale up × 100

$$\times 100 \left(\begin{array}{c} \$22 \rightarrow £13 \\ \$2200 \rightarrow £1300 \end{array} \right) \times 100$$

► *Exercise* **D3.2**

1 When Nicky visited Holland she used this table of values to draw a graph to convert pounds (£) to Guilders (Fl).

Pounds (£)	0	10	100
Guilders (Fl)	0	27.5	275

(a) Draw Nicky's conversion graph on 2 mm graph paper. Use this scale:
    £ axis – 1 cm represents £10
    Fl axis – 1 cm represents 10 Fl.
(b) Use your graph to change these to Guilders.
    (i) £20   (ii) £70   (iii) £88   (iv) £55
(c) Use your graph to change these to pounds.
    (i) 100 Fl   (ii) 220 Fl   (iii) 50 Fl   (iv) 132 Fl

2 Use this table of values to draw a conversion graph for miles and kilometres.

miles (M)	0	50	75
kilometres (km)	0	80	120

Use this scale:
    M axis – 1 cm represents 10 miles
    km axis – 2 cm represents 10 kilometres
(a) Use your graph to change these distances in miles to kilometres.
    (i) 30 miles   (ii) 10 miles   (iii) 70 miles   (iv) 45 miles
(b) What distance in miles is equivalent to
    (i) 25 km   (ii) 100 km   (iii) 64 km   (iv) 9.6 km?

Examination Questions

1

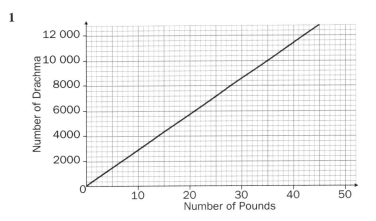

The graph shows how to convert between pounds (£) and Greek Drachma (D).
(a) Carol has saved £40 for her holiday and changes this into Drachma. How many Drachma will she get?
(b) While on holiday Carol spends 10 000 Drachma and changes the remainder back into pounds. How many pounds will she get?

(MEG, 1994)

2

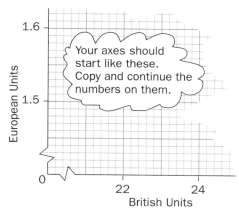

TYRE PRESSURES
The conversion table below is used by British car owners when travelling in Europe.

British Units	22	24	26	28	30	32	34
European Units	1.55	1.69	1.83	1.97	2.11	2.25	2.39

(a) Plot these figures as points on graph paper.

Your axes should start like these. Copy and continue the numbers on them.

(b) Join the points with a straight line.
(c) Mr Unsworth's car should have tyre pressures at 27 British Units. What is this pressure in European Units?
(d) Mr Unsworth's caravan should have tyre pressures of 36 British Units. What is this pressure in European Units?

(MEG, 1990)

3 Jill wants to compare the petrol prices of different garages. Jill decides to draw a conversion graph from £ per gallon to pence per litre.
She assumes that £2 per gallon is 40p per litre.
(a) On a grid like this mark this estimate.

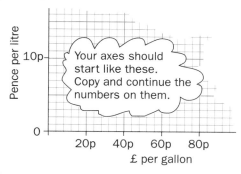

Your axes should start like these. Copy and continue the numbers on them.

(b) Join your plotted point to (0,0) to complete the conversion graph.
(c) Use your graph to find out how many
    (i) £ per gallon is 2p per litre
    (ii) pence per litre is £1.76 per gallon.

(ULEAC, 1989)

4

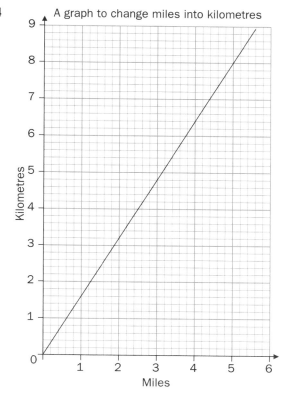

A graph to change miles into kilometres

(a) Change 4 miles into kilometres.
(b) Change 5.6 kilometres into miles.
(c) A runner who completes a marathon runs 26.2 miles. How many kilometres is this?

(SEG, 1988)

5 One kilogram is approximately equal to 2.2 pounds.
(a) Complete the table, and on a grid like that below draw a straight line graph to change kilograms to pounds.

Kilograms (kg)	2	4	6	8	10
Pounds (lb)	4.4				22

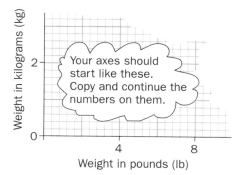

Your axes should start like these. Copy and continue the numbers on them.

(b) Use the graph to change
    (i) 18 lb to kg
    (ii) 4.2 kg to lb

One ton is equal to 2240 pounds.
One tonne is equal to 1000 kilograms.

(c) By how many pounds is one ton greater than one tonne?

(SEG, 1988)

D4
Averages and range

This unit will help you to:

■ understand the idea and use of an average
■ find the mean, median and mode for ungrouped data
■ calculate the total of the values in some data from its average
■ recognise the misuse of averages
■ decide which is the best average to use for data
■ calculate the range of data.

Looking at averages

An **average** is chosen to *represent* some data.
It gives you an impression of the data without having to look at all of it.

There are several different types of 'average'. The most common ones are:

● the **mean** – the *'equal shares'* average,
● the **median** – the *'middle value'*,
● the **mode** – what occurs *'most often'*.

Look at the averages on this page. What kind of data do they represent? What type of average do you think each is?

Comparing averages

Averages are often used to *compare* data.
You can compare groups by comparing their averages.

Athletes	Average height	Average weight
sprinters	182.9cm	68.2kg
jumpers	182.8cm	73.1kg
weight throwers	185.4cm	102.3kg
swimmers	179.3cm	72.1kg
divers	172.1cm	65.5kg
gymnasts	167.4cm	61.5kg
basketball players	189.1cm	79.7kg

You can see from the previous table, for example, that on average the basketball players are tallest, the gymnasts are lightest.

You can compare something with the average of the group it comes from.

For example, you can compare Megan's marks with her year group's average mark.

Subject	Megan's mark	Year group average	
Art	80	80	Average
English	70	71	Below average
French	57	48	Above average

Mean

Asked to 'find the average', most people work out the mean. Its full name is the **arithmetic mean**. This is the average you get when you share out some values equally.

For example
Keith, Amy and Terry work in a cafe.
At the end of each day they average
out their tips.
They put them together.
Then share them equally.
Each gets the same amount: £5.
This is the mean or average.

You cannot find the mean of things like colours, car makes, … You must have *numbers* or *measurements* such as lengths, masses, …

To work out the mean of some values, add up all the values to find the 'total of the values'. Then divide by how many values you have.

$$\text{Mean} = \frac{\text{total of the values}}{\text{number of values}}$$

When the values are measurements, make sure the units are all the same. Change any you need to. Check that you have the correct unit, such as cm, kg, … in your answer.

Question

Sanjeev measured the rainfall each day for one week. His results, in millimetres, are given below.

Mon	Tues	Wed	Thurs	Fri	Sat	Sun
0.8	1.3	0.9	1.2	1.4	1.1	1.7

Calculate the mean daily rainfall that week.

Answer

$$\text{Mean} = \frac{\text{total of the values}}{\text{number of values}} = \frac{8.4}{7}\text{mm}$$

$$= 1.2\text{mm}$$

Take extra care when finding the mean of 'times'.
Times are often given using two units, such as hours and minutes. You cannot simply enter them into your calculator like decimals. Deal with each unit on its own. You will have to change from one unit to another too.

Question

Shalid and four of his friends are in their school's Under 17 5-a-side football team.
Here are their ages:

Shalid	Greg	Paul	Tom	Darren
15y 6m	16y 2m	16y	14y 11m	15y 9m

What is their mean age?

Answer

To find the total of the ages:
Add months first.
Change to years and months.
Then add years.

Shalid	15 y	6 m
Greg	16 y	2 m
Paul	16 y	0 m
Tom	14 y	11 m
Darren	15 y	9 m
Total	78 y	4 m

2

28 m
= 2 y 4 m

$$\text{Mean age} = \frac{\text{total of the ages}}{\text{number of boys}} = \frac{78y\ 4m}{5}$$

$$= 15y\ 8m$$

To do the division:

Divide years by 5 first: 78y ÷ 5 = 15y r 3y

Change remainder to months: 3y 4m = 40m

Divide these months by 5: 40m ÷ 5 = 8m

A mean *may not* be one of the values used to find it. For example, in Shalid's 5-a-side football team, no-one is actually 15 years 8 months old. They are all either older or younger than the mean age.

Sometimes the mean is a value that does not exist. For example, the average number of children in a family is 2.4. Do you know a family with this number of children? It is not a 'real value'. But it is still useful.

You may have to find the mean of a lot of values or the mean of some large values. A calculator makes the working easy to do …if you are careful. Make sure that you use *all* the values. Tick each one as you enter it if it helps. You can check your answer quickly too. Try adding the values in a different way before dividing.

Exercise D4.1

1 Work out the means of the following items:
(a) 80p, £2.75, £1.20, 45p.
(b) 5 g, 7 g, 8 g, 5 g, 9 g, 2 g.
(c) 8 m, 4 m, 10 m, 8 m, 13 m, 12 m, 8 m.
(d) 15 kg, 30 kg, 75 kg, 55 kg, 35 kg.
(e) £3.25, £4, £2.60, £5.20, £5.40, £3, £5.25.

2 Mr and Mrs O'Neil pay an electricity bill every quarter (3 months). Last year their bills were:
£106.08, £86.82, £61.56 and £96.34.
What was their average (mean) quarterly bill?

3 The table shows the temperatures in Birmingham during a week in April last year.
Calculate the average daily temperature.

Day	Temperature
Sun	9°C
Mon	15°C
Tues	12°C
Wed	12°C
Thu	15°C
Fri	12°C
Sat	16°C

4 The price of a melon at eight different supermarkets and shops was:
£1.40, £1.48, £1.50, £1.45, £1.45, £1.40, £1.50 and £1.45.
Calculate the mean price of a melon.

5 The rainfall in Sparkton village was measured each day for one week. These are the results.

Day	M	T	W	T	F	Sa	Su
Rainfall (mm)	4.5	9.6	1.5	2.6	5.5	1.0	2.6

Calculate the average daily rainfall.

Totals from means

If you know the mean and the number of values used to find it, then you can find the total of the values.

Total of values = Number of values × Mean

Question

Tom has to do six practical tests in science.
(a) Grade A is given for a mean of 75 or over for the six tests. What is the smallest total mark that gets an A?
(b) Tom wants a grade A. After five tests his mean mark is 71. What is the smallest mark he must get for the last test?

Answer

(a) Smallest total number of marks for an A
= number of tests × smallest mean for an A
= 6 × 75
= 450

(b) Tom's total number of marks so far
= number of tests × mean
= 5 × 71
= 355
Mark needed = 450 − 355 = 95.

Exercise D4.2

1 Ken's mean (average) mark for his first five GCSE mock exams was 60. For his sixth exam, Ken got 84. What was Ken's mean mark for all six exams?

2   Julie wants to walk 97 miles along the Pennine Way in 9 days. On the first five days she walks 13, 11, 8, 12 and 9 miles.
  (a) How far must she walk in the remaining four days?
  (b) What is the average number of miles she must walk on each of the remaining four days?

3   The weights of five women, measured in kilograms, are
      51, 56, 54, 59, 53.
  (a) Calculate their average weight.
  (b) Another woman joins the group. As a result the average weight of the six women is 56 kg. What is the weight of the sixth woman?

4   Calculate the number of entries in the Exeter telephone book which has 806 pages and an average of 360 entries on each page. Give your answer to the nearest thousand.

5   Sudston Town Football Team play 21 home matches each season. The total attendance at the first 20 matches was 187 940.
  (a) Calculate the average attendance for these 20 matches.
  (b) The average attendance for all 21 matches was 9480. What was the attendance at the final match?

Median

The *middle value* is another average.
There are as many values above it as below it.
It is also called the **median**.

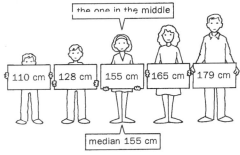

To find this average, put the values in *order of size* first.
Then you can pick out the middle value.
This is easy to do for a small number of values. It can take a long time for a lot of values.

Question

Here are the first round scores in a golf tournament:
  73, 79, 78, 80, 79, 74, 72, 76, 79, 77, 76.
What is the median mark?

Answer

Put scores in order of size.
Find the middle one.

  72, 73, 74, 76, 76, 77, 78, 79, 79, 79, 80.
                    ↑
                 middle

The median mark is 77.

An *even number of values* has not got 'one in the middle'. Two values share the middle place.
The 'middle' is half-way between those two.
To find it, *add the two middle values, then divide by 2.*

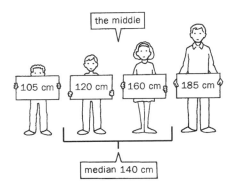

Question

Ten bags of potatoes were weighed to check their contents. Their masses in kilograms were:
  9.5, 9.9, 9.3, 9.8, 9.3, 9.2, 9.5, 9.6, 9.1, 9.3.

What is their median mass?

Answer

Put masses in order of size.
Find the two middle values.
Add them. Then divide by 2.

  9.1, 9.2, 9.3, 9.3, 9.3, 9.5, 9.5, 9.6, 9.8, 9.9
             9.3 + 9.5 = 18.8
             18.8 ÷ 2 = 9.4

The median mass is 9.4 kg.

Only numbers and measurements can have a middle value (median). Other things such as names, cars, colours, ... cannot be put in order of size. So they cannot have a middle (median) value.

► *Exercise* D4.3

1   For each set of items
      (i) arrange them in order of size,
      (ii) write down the median.
  (a) 12 cm, 14 cm, 11 cm, 6 cm, 15 cm
  (b) 15 kg, 4 kg, 8 kg, 13 kg, 9 kg, 12 kg, 14 kg
  (c) 24 s, 15 s, 22 s, 19 s, 14 s, 18 s, 20 s
  (d) 47, 37, 68, 54, 37, 43, 67, 36, 41
  (e) 7 m, 9 m, 3 m, 5 m, 15 m, 10 m, 13 m, 7 m, 13 m, 12 m, 5 m

2 Find the median for each set of values:
(a) 11 kg, 8 kg, 13 kg, 9 kg, 9 kg, 14 kg
(b) £8, £6, £9, £2, £3, £10, £6, £7
(c) 6 h, 10 h, 7 h, $5\frac{1}{2}$h, 11 h, $8\frac{1}{2}$h, 8 h, 5 h
(d) 164 cm, 184 cm, 179 cm, 187 cm, 172 cm
(e) 9, $6\frac{1}{2}$, 7, 10, $8\frac{1}{2}$, 7, 6, $6\frac{1}{2}$
(f) 13 m, 19 m, 21 m, 15 m, 12 m, 14 m, 21 m, 18 m
(g) 6.7, 9.2, 2.4, 10.1, 5.8, 8.5, 12.3, 3.4, 5.2
(h) 10.2, 5.8, 4.4, 9.3, 11.6, 8.7, 6.9, 7.5

3 When Lynne went on holiday, she recorded the mid-day temperature in °C on each of the ten days she spent at the seaside. Her results were as follows:
27, 29, 31, 23, 20, 28, 27, 24, 25, 26.
What was the median temperature?

Mode

What occurs 'most often' is another kind of average.

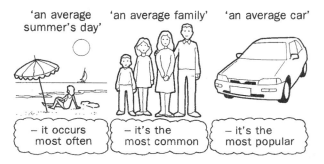

'an average summer's day' – it occurs most often

'an average family' – it's the most common

'an average car' – it's the most popular

This average is called the **mode**.
It tells you what is most common, most popular, most fashionable, …
Mode is the French word for fashion.

You can use this average for any sort of data. The data can be numbers, measurements, names, days, colours, …

Shops and manufacturers often use the mode. It helps them to decide what to order or make.

The mode is easy to spot from a table or diagram. Look for the item shown with the greatest frequency.

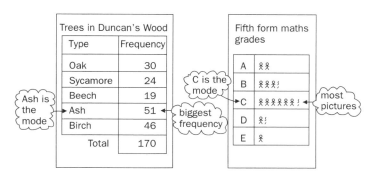

Trees in Duncan's Wood

Type	Frequency
Oak	30
Sycamore	24
Beech	19
Ash	51
Birch	46
Total	170

Ash is the mode
biggest frequency

Fifth form maths grades

A	👥👥
B	👥👥👥
C	👥👥👥👥👥
D	👥
E	👤

C is the mode
most pictures

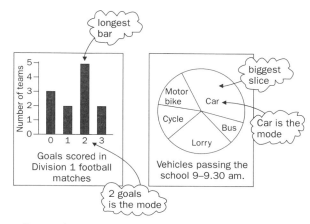

longest bar

Number of teams
Goals scored in Division 1 football matches

biggest slice

Motor bike   Car
Cycle
Lorry   Bus

Car is the mode

Vehicles passing the school 9–9.30 am.

2 goals is the mode

Normally you have to *count* the number of times each item occurs. (Making a tally table is a simple way to do this.) Then you can pick out the mode.

Remember: the mode is the actual item, not the number of times it occurs.

Data can have *more than one* mode.
Several different things may occur 'most often'.
For example,
darts and soccer both got the most votes in this survey:

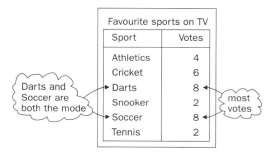

Favourite sports on TV

Sport	Votes
Athletics	4
Cricket	6
Darts	8
Snooker	2
Soccer	8
Tennis	2

Darts and Soccer are both the mode
most votes

Some data do not have a mode. All the data may be different …

I'm 29, the baby is 1
I'm 35
I'm 7

… or there may be an equal number of each item.

I'm 15   I'm 15   I'm 15
I'm 16   I'm 16   I'm 16

▶ *Exercise* **D4.4**

1 Write down the mode of each set. Doing a tally chart may help.
(a) 2, 5, 8, 4, 3, 4, 7, 6, 2, 4
(b) £3.50, £2, £5.50, £2.25, £5.50, £3.50, £5.50
(c) 14 cm, 17 cm, 9 cm, 8 cm, 13 cm, 9 cm, 15 cm
(d) 12 kg, 15 kg, 11 kg, 15 kg, 14 kg, 15 kg, 12 kg
(e) 1, 2, 3, 4, 5, 1, 2, 3, 4, 1, 2, 3, 1, 2, 1

2 Write down the mode of each set of quantities.
  (a) 5 p, 7 p, 10 p, 9 p, 9 p
  (b) 18, 14, 19, 12, 17, 13, 19
  (c) 4 m, 7 m, 6 m, 11 m, 8 m, 5 m, 9 m, 6 m
  (d) 9.9 kg, 10.4 kg, 10.0 kg, 10.1 kg, 9.8 kg, 10.4 kg
  (e) £3.53, £3.01, £3.07, £3.75, £3.01, £3.86, £3.01, £3.56

3

size	tally
6	5
$6\frac{1}{2}$	17
7	21
$7\frac{1}{2}$	16
8	15
9	11
10	2

Paul works in a shoe shop on a Saturday.
The manager wants to make a special purchase of
'Creepers'. He asked Paul to do a tally of sizes
of men's shoes sold that day.
Which size shoes will he order most of?

Misleading averages

The mean, median and mode of the same data can be very
different. but each can be called the average. This can be
misleading.

Look at these statements. All three are correct.
Each comes from the same data. But each is a different average.

SALARIES AT BLOGGS

Position	Number	Salary
Chairman	1	£150 000
Managing Director	1	£120 000
Directors	4	£100 000
Executives	4	£75 000
Foreman	10	£15 000
Skilled workers	60	£10 000
Semi-skilled	80	£7 500
Unskilled	130	£6 000
Office assistants	10	£5 000

The union leader gives the **mode** : £6000.
But only a *few* of the staff (10) get less than this.

The chairman gives the **mean**: £10 500.
But *most* of the staff (280) get less than this.
The staff splits into two groups:
  the management with high salaries (mean £97 000)
  the others with lower salaries (mean £7517).
A few high salaries increase the overall mean.

The newspaper gives the **median**: £7500.
This seems to be the fairest average in this case.

Look out for misleading averages like these in newspapers.

Which average?

You may have to decide which average to use for some data.
The average you choose depends on ...
• the data you have
• whether you have sorted it into a table or diagram already
• how much time you have
• what you want to use it for
and so on ...

Each average has its advantages and disadvantages.
These notes give some of them. They may help you to make up
your mind about which average to use.

Mean

Advantages	Disadvantages
Easy to work out with a calculator.	Can only be used for numbers or measurements.
Uses all the data.	Not always one of the values.
What most people think of as the average.	A few very large or small numbers can affect its size.

Median

Advantages	Disadvantages
Easy to find when the values are in order.	Can only be used for numbers or measurements.
Is one of the values if you have an odd number of values.	A lot of values can take a long time to put in order.
	May not be one of the values if you have an even number of values.

Mode

Advantages	Disadvantages
Can be found for any kind of data.	Not very useful for small amounts of data.
Simple to find – you count, not calculate.	May be more than one item.
Always one of the items in the data.	Does not exist if there is an equal number of each item.
Quick and easy to find from a frequency table, bar chart, pictogram, pie chart.	

Some examination questions just ask for the 'average' without
saying which one. When the data are numbers or
measurements, they usually want the mean. Say clearly that this
is what you have found.

Range

An *average* gives you one impression of some data.
How *spread out* the values are gives you another.
The **range** is the simplest **measure of spread**.
It is the difference between the largest and smallest values in
the data.

  range = largest value − smallest value

For example, look at these noon temperatures in April.

			APRIL		
S		13°	14°	10°	14°
M		13°	14°	8°	18°
T	8°	13°	15°	11°	19°
W	9°	13°	17°	12°	25°
T	7°	13°	16°	16°	
F	10°	11°	12°	14°	
S	6°	12°	11°	17°	

The average is 13°C.
But the temperatures are spread from 6°C to 25°C.

The range is
25°C – 6°C = 19° C.

Each ● on the diagram below stands for one of the temperatures in this table.
See how the temperatures are spread out from 6°C to 25 °C.

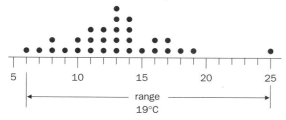

Two lots of data may have the same average but be very different. Their ranges can sometimes help you to compare them. They show you roughly how much the values vary.

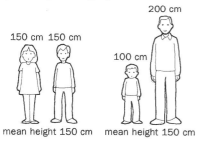

150 cm   150 cm

200 cm

100 cm

mean height 150 cm   mean height 150 cm

Question

Janice and Ann compare their maths homework marks.

Janice: 20, 16, 10, 3, 12, 10, 11, 14, 5, 19.
Ann: 13, 12, 11, 13, 13, 11, 12, 12, 11, 12.

(a) The two girls have the same mean mark. What is it?
(b) Work out the range for each girl's marks.
(c) Ann thinks that her homework marks are better than Janice's. Explain why.

Answer

(a) Mean mark = $\dfrac{\text{total of the marks}}{\text{number of marks}}$

$= \dfrac{120}{10} = 12$

(b) Janice: range of marks = 20 − 3 = 17
    Ann: range of marks = 13 − 11 = 2

(c) Janice's marks are more up and down. They have a bigger spread (range).
Ann's marks vary less. They are nearly all the same.

▶ *Exercise* D4.5

Use your answers to Exercise D4.3 to answer these questions.
1 Calculate the range of values given in each part of question **1**.
2 Calculate the range of values given in each part of question **2**.
3 What was the range of the temperatures Lynne recorded in question **3**?
4 The number of goals scored in each of eleven Football League matches on the first Saturday of last season was
    1, 2, 4, 0, 0, 6, 3, 2, 1, 0, 5.
    What was the range?
5 Two dice are thrown together and the numbers obtained are multiplied together. What is the range of possible scores? ◀

Examination Questions

1 As part of a statistics survey, the heights of all the pupils in a first-year class were measured. Three of the measurements were recorded as follows:

Pupil	Height
A	1.26 m
B	1.3 m
C	1.09 m

(a) Which of these three pupils is the tallest?
(b) Calculate the average height of the three pupils, giving your answer to the nearest cm.
(c) The average height for the whole class was 1.54 m. What does this tell you about the pupils A, B and C?
(NEAB, 1990)

2 Before landing on the moon, thousands of pictures were taken of its surface. These were to give an idea of the size of small craters. One picture showed craters with these diameters.
All measurements are in metres.
    1.1 1.2 1.6 1.0 2.4
    2.5 1.1 4.1 1.0 4.5
    3.6 1.4 1.3 1.5 1.5
(a) Calculate the mean diameter of these 15 craters.
(b) How many craters had a diameter greater than the mean?
(MEG, 1990)

3 When Kylie went on work experience to the local junior school, she decided to find the average height of a class of eleven-year-olds. Their heights, in metres, were
    1.20 1.25 1.21 1.40 1.30 1.25 1.36 1.43 1.25
    1.34 1.15 1.20 1.18 1.25 1.40 1.30 1.25 1.50
    1.26 1.54 1.30
(a) Work out the mean height.
(b) Which height occurred most often?
(c) Find the middle value of the heights.
(ULEAC, 1991)

4 The table shows the distances (in miles) Laura drives by car during the first three days of her five-day working week.

Mon	Tues	Wed	Thurs	Fri
140	133	183		

(a) Calculate Laura's mean (average) daily mileage for the first three days of this week.

(b) On Thursday Laura drives two-thirds as far as she did on Wednesday.
How far does she drive on Thursday?

(c) By the end of Friday, Laura's mean daily mileage for the five days is exactly 150 miles. How far did she drive on Friday?

(NEAB, 1991)

5 A street entertainer's takings for the week from Monday up to Friday lunchtime are £182.
How much must he earn on Friday afternoon to bring his average takings for a day's work up to £40?

(MEG, 1989)

6 The heights of 5 children, measured in cm, are given below.

120	112	136	129	128

(a) Calculate the mean height of these children.

(b) What is the range of the heights of these children?

(SEG, 1990)

7 The ages of four friends are 13 years 4 months, 12 years 10 months, 13 years 5 months and 14 years 1 month.
Find their average age.

(WJEC, 1990)

8 Claire conducted a survey on the hourly rates of pay at 10 local stores. The rates were:
£3.90, £3.80, £3.50, £3.70, £3.50, £3.20, £3.90, £3.80, £3.50, £3.70
Find:
(a) the modal rate
(b) the median rate
(c) the mean rate
(d) the range.

(SEG, 1990)

9 West Midlands Police recorded the speeds of 9 coaches at a particular point on the M6 motorway. The speeds recorded are in miles per hour to the nearest whole number.
58, 67, 54, 61, 74, 55, 59, 67, 58.
(a) What is the range of these speeds?
(b) Write down the median speed.

The police then recorded the speed of a tenth coach.
The mean speed of the ten coaches was 62 miles per hour.

(c) Calculate the speed of the tenth coach.

(SEG, 1989)

10 A company produced this diagram to illustrate their profits over a five-year period. Make two criticisms of the diagram.

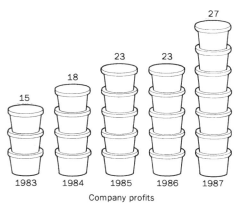

Company profits

(MEG, 1991)

11 After showing his manager a graph of his sales for the first six months of the year, a salesman suggested that he ought to have an increase in salary.

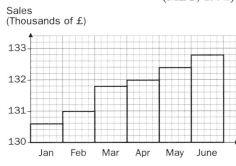

Suggest a reason, or reasons, why the manager refused the request on the evidence shown.

(NEAB, 1994)

12 Briefly explain why the following diagrams are misleading.

(i)
COMPANY SALES

(ii)
COMPANY PROFITS FOR 1981, 1982, 1983

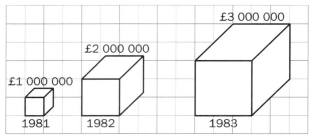

(WJEC, 1994)

D5
Simple probability

This unit will help you to:

- understand the basic idea of probability
- understand and use the probability scale from 0 to 1 and from 0% to 100%
- list all the possible outcomes for an activity and the favourable outcomes for an event
- calculate probability for equally likely outcomes
- understand the use of the word 'random'
- calculate the probability of an event 'not happening' from the probability of it 'happening'.

Probability is about *how likely* something is to happen. We often use the word **chance** for probability.

Some things *always happen*. We say they are **certain** to happen. For example, if you draw a triangle it has three angles. That's a certainty!

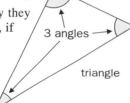

3 angles

triangle

Some things will *never happen*. We say they are **impossible**. For example, if you throw an ordinary dice you will never get a 7. That's impossible.

Some things are not certain, but not impossible either. They *may or may not happen*. For example, if you toss a coin it may land heads, or it may not.

We often judge chances in our daily lives. We use our common sense and what we 'know' to help us to decide what the chances are.

We usually use words to describe how likely something is.

'It's almost certain to rain today.'

'There's no chance of rain today.'

'There's a 50-50 chance of rain today.'

► *Exercise* **D5.1**

1 Here are some words we commonly use for 'chance'. Put these words in order, starting with the word that shows the 'smallest chance'.

> *evens   probably   fifty-fifty   dead-cert   no chance*
> *possibly   likely   poor chance   sure   no way*
> *very unlikely   certain   highly likely   good chance*

2 The prize in the raffle at the summer fete is a CD player.

Describe Belinda's chance of winning the prize if she buys:
(a) 1 ticket
(b) all the tickets
(c) a few tickets
(d) most of the tickets
(e) half the tickets
(f) no tickets.

Probability scale

In mathematics when we talk about the probability of 'something' happening, we call the 'something' an **event**. Probability is a *measure of how likely* an event is to happen. We use a number, not words, to describe its size.

We can give a probability a number from 0 to 1.

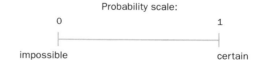

Probability scale:

0   1

impossible   certain

On this **probability scale**:

an event that is **impossible** is given a **probability of 0**,
an event that is **certain** is given a **probability of 1**.

For example,
the probability that you get a 7 on an ordinary dice is 0, the probability that a triangle you draw will have three angles is 1.

All other probabilities on this scale are *between 0 and 1*. They must be *less than 1*.
We write them as proper fractions or decimal fractions.

Remember:
In a proper fraction, the top number is smaller than the bottom. A decimal fraction starts 0. …

To **compare probabilities**, we compare the sizes of the fractions.

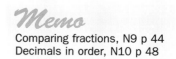

Memo

Comparing fractions, N9 p 44
Decimals in order, N10 p 48

The *less likely* an event is to happen, the *smaller* the fraction. The *more likely* an event is to happen, the *larger* the fraction.

For example, the college team coach estimates the team's chances of winning its matches this year.

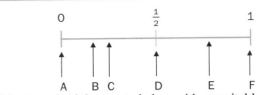

St. Peter's	0.1
Heathdale	0.95
Rumford	0.5

He thinks they are *most unlikely* to beat St. Peters.
  The probability, 0.1, is *very small*.
He thinks they are *almost certain* to beat Heathdale.
  The probability, 0.95, is very large (nearly 1).
He thinks they have a *50-50 chance* of beating Rumford.
  The probability is 0.5.

You can show these probabilities on a number line like this:

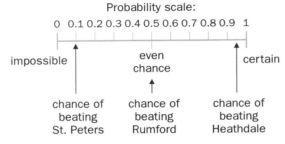

Probability scale:

0 0.1 0.2 0.3 0.4 0.5 0.6 0.7 0.8 0.9 1

impossible   even   certain
                   chance

chance of   chance of   chance of
beating   beating   beating
St. Peters   Rumford   Heathdale

Probabilities can also be given as **percentages**.
(A percentage is simply another way to write a fraction).

Percentage probability scale:

0%   100%

impossible   certain

This probability scale goes from **0%** for an **impossibility** to **100%** for a **certainty**.
All other probabilities on this scale must be *between 0% and 100%*. They must be *less than 100%*.
For example, the weather forecaster estimates the probability of rain on Bank Holiday weekend.

....AND A 75% CHANCE OF RAIN ON SATURDAY, 50% CHANCE ON SUNDAY BUT ONLY A 5% CHANCE ON MONDAY

She thinks it is *very likely* to rain on Saturday.
  The probability, 75%, is large.
She thinks there is an *even chance* of rain on Sunday.
  The probability is 50%.
She thinks there is *very little chance* of rain on Monday.
  The probability, 5%, is *very small*.

You can also show these probabilities on a 'percentage' number line.

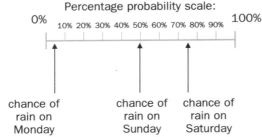

Percentage probability scale:

0%   100%
   10% 20% 30% 40% 50% 60% 70% 80% 90%

chance of   chance of   chance of
rain on   rain on   rain on
Monday   Sunday   Saturday

▶ *Exercise* **D5.2**

1

0   ½   1

A   B C   D   E   F

Match each of the events below with a capital letter marked on the probability scale above.
(a) A letter picked with a pin from the alphabet will be a consonant.
(b) A football captain will win the toss of a coin.
(c) A square will have four sides.
(d) You will live to be 200 years old.
(e) A card taken without looking from a pack of cards will be a 'diamond'.
(f) Throwing a fair dice will give you a six.

2 Copy this percentage probability line.

0%   50%   100%

On your copy, write A, B, C, D, E, F, and G to show, approximately, your estimates of the probabilities for these events.
A: It will get dark tonight.
B: It will snow in Devon in June.
C: There will be snow somewhere in Britain next winter.
D: Tomorrow will be Sunday if today is Saturday.
E: A drawing pin will land 'point up' if it drops on the floor.
F: A coin will land 'tails' if it is tossed.
G: The first player to leave the football field will be wearing number 5.

3 The police have named four accident blackspots in the centre of Fentown. If a motorist has an accident in Fentown the probability that it occurred at Highcliff roundabout is 0.24, at Monument Square is 0.13, in Renton Avenue is 0.22, at Molton Street junction is 0.31.
(a) At which blackspot is it
    (i) most likely that the accident occurred
    (ii) least likely that the accident occurred?
(b) Arrange the blackspots in order of accident likelihood. Start with the least likely blackspot.

4 When Rita goes birdwatching at her local river estuary, the probability that the first bird she spots is an avocet is 8%, a redshank is 27%, a blackheaded gull is 34%, a snipe is 0.9% and an oystercatcher is 12%.
(a) Which bird is Rita
    (i) most likely to spot first (ii) least likely to spot first?
(b) Arrange the birds in order of rarity. Start with the most rare first.

5 There is a hot-drinks machine in the sixth-form common room at Seldon College. A survey found that the probability that a student buying a drink from this machine would choose:
    soup is $\frac{1}{20}$, coffee is $\frac{2}{5}$, tea is $\frac{3}{10}$, and chocolate is $\frac{1}{4}$.
(a) Which drink bought from this machine is
    (i) most likely to be chosen
    (ii) least likely to be chosen?
(b) Arrange the drinks in order of popularity.

Listing outcomes

In probability we look at the likelihood of a particular event occurring.

For any 'activity' you can usually list all the possible **'outcomes'**.

Outcomes which give the 'event' *you are interested in* are called **favourable outcomes** for that event.

For example, consider 'getting an even number' when you throw a dice.

The activity is: 'throw a dice'.
All possible outcomes are: 1, 2, 3, 4, 5, 6.
The event you are interested in is: 'get an even number'.
The favourable outcomes are: 2, 4, 6.

You may be interested in different events resulting from the same activity.
For example, here are some other 'events' for the activity 'throw a dice'.

Event A: get a one.
Favourable outcome: 1.

Event B: get a multiple of 3.
Favourable outcomes: 3, 6.

Event C: get a prime number.
Favourable outcomes: 2, 3, 5.

▶ *Exercise* **D5.3**

Look at each activity in turn.
List all the possible outcomes for the activity.
List the favourable outcomes for each named event.

1 Activity: throw a dice.
  Event D: get a two.
  Event E: get an odd number.
  Event F: get a number bigger than 4.

2 Activity: take a coin from this purse.

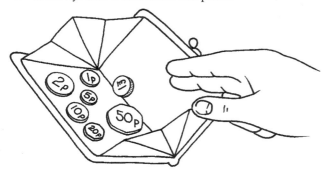

  Event A: get a £1 coin.
  Event B: get a 'silver coin'.
  Event C: get a coin worth less than 50p.

3 Activity: take a letter from the word PROBABILITY.
  Event A: get an R.
  Event B: get a vowel.
  Event C: get a consonant.

4 Activity : take a card from this 'hand'.
  Event A: get a 7.
  Event B: get a diamond.
  Event C: get a picture card.

Calculating probabilities

Outcomes which have an *equal chance* of happening are called **equally likely outcomes.**

For example, when you throw a fair dice, each outcome (1, 2, 3, 4, 5, 6) is equally likely to occur.

When all the outcomes of an activity are equally likely, you can calculate the probability of an event happening.

Probability of an event
$$= \frac{\text{Number of favourable outcomes for that event}}{\text{Total number of possible outcomes}}$$

This is sometimes called the **probability fraction**.

To calculate the probability for an event, you may need to list all the outcomes and the favourable outcomes first.
Then you can count how many there are.
The activity is usually one you have met before or one that is easy to imagine.

Question

Nick throws an ordinary dice. Write down the probability that he gets:
(a) a five   (d) more than two
(b) an even number (e) less than ten.
(c) a seven
Give each probability as a fraction in its simplest form.

Answer

Possible outcomes: 1, 2, 3, 4, 5, 6
Total number of possible outcomes = 6

(a) Event: 'get a 5'.
    Favourable outcomes: 5
    Number of favourable outcomes = 1

    Probability of getting a 5 $= \frac{1}{6}$

(b) Event: 'get an even number'
    Favourable outcomes: 2, 4, 6
    Number of favourable outcomes = 3

    Probability of getting an even number $= \frac{3}{6} = \frac{1}{2}$

continued

(c) Event: 'get a seven'.
No favourable outcomes (none of the numbers is 7).
So this event is impossible.

Probability of getting a seven = 0

(d) Event: 'get more than two'
Favourable outcomes: 3, 4, 5, 6
Number of favourable outcomes = 4

Probability of getting more than two = $\frac{4}{6} = \frac{2}{3}$

(e) Event: 'get less than ten'
All outcomes are favourable (all the numbers are less than ten).
So this event is certain to happen.

Probability of getting less than 10 = $\frac{6}{6}$ = 1.

▶ *Exercise* **D5.4**

In this exercise, give all fractions in their lowest terms.

Questions **1–4**
Calculate the probability for each named event in questions **1–4** in Exercise D5.3, when the outcomes are equally likely.

5 An octahedral (8-faced) dice has the numbers 1 to 8 painted on its faces. When thrown, it has an equal chance of landing on any one of its faces. Write down the probability that with one throw of the dice I get: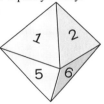

(a) a six   (d) a number less than six
(b) an odd number (e) a number more than six.
(c) a prime number

6 This spinner is made from a regular pentagon. When I spin it once what is the probability that I get:
(a) the letter C
(b) a vowel
(c) a consonant
(d) the letter H?

7 This unsharpened pencil is a regular hexagonal prism. The name HB Pencil is written on only one face. Write down the probability that when the pencil is rolled, it stops with the name on the top face.

8 When the pointer is spun it has an equal chance of landing on any one of the numbers on the disc. When Ruth spins the pointer once, what is the probability that the spinner lands on:
(a) 1
(b) 6
(c) an even number
(d) an odd number
(e) a prime number
(f) a number greater than 4?

For some activities the outcomes are listed for you. You can count the outcomes you need to find the probability you want.

Question

Each letter of the word MATHEMATICS is written on a separate piece of paper and put in a bag. Jenny closes her eyes and takes one piece of paper out of the bag.
What is the probability that she takes a paper with
(a) an M on it
(b) a vowel on it?

Answer

Activity: taking a piece of paper from the bag.
Each piece of paper is equally likely to be taken because Jenny closes her eyes before taking one.

Total number of possible outcomes $\underline{\text{MATHEMATICS}}$
  = total number of pieces of   11 letters
    paper in the bag
  = 11

(a) Event: get an M   MATHEMATICS (✓ ✓)
Number of favourable outcomes
  = number of papers with M on them
  = 2

Probability of getting an M = $\frac{2}{11}$

(b) Event: get a vowel   MATHEMATICS (✓ ✓ ✓ ✓)
Number of favourable outcomes
  = number of papers with a vowel on them
  = 4

Probability of getting a vowel = $\frac{4}{11}$

In some situations you do not need to list or count outcomes to find a probability. The information either tells you the numbers you want or you can work them out.

Question

A box of chocolate contains
  10 plain chocolates
  6 milk chocolates
  4 white chocolates
Rosemary takes a chocolate out of the box without looking.
What is the probability that it is
(a) a milk chocolate
(b) a milk or plain chocolate?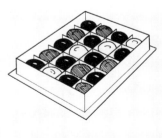

Answer

Activity: taking a chocolate from the box.
Each chocolate is equally likely to be taken because Rosemary takes one without looking.
Total number of possible outcomes
  = total number of chocolates
  = 10 + 6 + 4
  = 20

(a) Event: take a milk chocolate.

Number of favourable outcomes

= number of milk chocolates in the box

= 6

Probability of taking a milk chocolate $= \frac{6}{20} = \frac{3}{10}$

(b) Event: take a milk or plain chocolate

Number of favourable outcomes

= number of chocolates in box that are milk or plain

= 6 + 10

= 16

Probability of taking a milk or plain chocolate $= \frac{16}{20} = \frac{4}{5}$

In the last two worked examples, Jenny and Rosemary took an item '**without looking**'. This meant that they *could not affect* the result. So each outcome was *equally likely*.

Taking something '**at random**' also means that every item has an equal chance of being taken.

So for any 'random' activity, the outcomes are equally likely. This means that you can calculate probabilities as before when the activity is described as 'random'.

Question

Tom had a full pack of 52 cards. But he lost the queen of hearts.

Tom deals a card at random from his incomplete pack. What is the probability that it is a queen?

Answer

Activity: deal a card from Tom's pack of 51 cards.
Each card is equally likely to be dealt because it is done 'at random'.

Total number of possible outcomes

= number of cards in Tom's pack

= 52 − 1

= 51

Event: deal a queen

Number of favourable outcomes

= number of queens in Tom's pack

= 3

Probability of dealing a queen from Tom's pack

$= \frac{3}{51}$ ← Cancel by 3

$= \frac{1}{17}$

1 These dominoes are placed face down on a table.

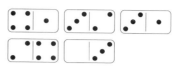

Without looking, Julie picks up a domino. What is the probability that Julie will pick up a domino with
(a) a blank on it
(b) a 3 on it
(c) an even number on it? (Zero is an even number.)

2 Six counters in a bag are numbered
    3   4   7   9   10   11
One counter is drawn at random from the bag. Calculate the probability that the number drawn is
(a) an even number   (c) a multiple of 3
(b) a prime number   (d) a square number.

3 A box contains six toffees, seven chocolates and eight mint creams. Robert takes a sweet at random from the box. Write down the probability that he takes
(a) a toffee   (b) a chocolate   (c) a mint cream.

4 The letters of the word BANANA are each written on a piece of paper and put into a bag. Without looking, Tony takes one piece of paper out of the bag. What is the probability that Tony takes a piece of paper with
(a) a B on it   (b) an A on it   (c) a consonant on it?

5 A student is chosen at random from a group which contains 18 boys and 11 girls. What is the probability that this student is
(a) a boy   (b) a girl?

6 240 tickets have been sold for the Summer Fete Raffle. What is the probability that I win first prize if I bought
(a) one ticket   (b) 7 tickets?

7 In a game of Bingo, the numbers 1 to 90 are written on 90 discs and placed in a drum. What is the probability that the first number, chosen at random
(a) is 69   (b) ends in a zero   (c) is a multiple of 9?

8 Kamal bought a bag of fruitgums. There were 8 black, 6 green, 9 red, 5 yellow and 6 orange.
Kamal takes one gum from the bag without looking. What is the probability that the gum is
(a) red   (b) yellow or black?

9 An ordinary pack of 52 cards has 4 suits of 13 cards each. Brian takes a card at random from this pack. Find, as a fraction in its simplest form, the probability that the card is:
(a) the 'two of diamonds'
(b) an ace
(c) a red card or a black card
(d) a heart
(e) a king, queen or jack.

10 Rod picks a card at random from a full pack. What is the probability that the card is
(a) a heart or a club
(b) a king or an ace?

Probability 'shorthand'

We often use a shorthand way to write a description of a probability.

P(A) means 'the probability of event A'.

For example,
P(head) means 'the probability of getting a head'.
P(prime) means 'the probability of getting a prime number'.
P(not 3) means 'the probability of getting a number that is not 3'.
P(2 or 5) means 'the probability of getting a 2 or a 5'.

'Happen' and 'not happen'

In any activity either a particular result *happens* or it does *not happen*.

These two events must account for all the possible outcomes. It is certain that one or the other will occur.

1 is the probability of something that is certain.

So **the probability of a result happening added to the probability of it not happening must be 1**.

Think about tossing a coin.
You can either get 'a head' or 'not a head'.
These two events account for all possible outcomes.

All possible outcomes:

'head'   'not a head'

$P(\text{head}) = \frac{1}{2}$

$P(\text{not a head}) = \frac{1}{2}$

$\frac{1}{2} + \frac{1}{2} = 1$

$P(\text{head}) + P(\text{not a head}) = 1$

Think about throwing a dice.
You can either get 'a multiple of 3' or 'not a multiple of 3'.
These two events account for all possible outcomes.

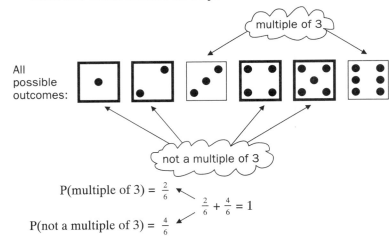

multiple of 3

All possible outcomes:

not a multiple of 3

$P(\text{multiple of 3}) = \frac{2}{6}$

$P(\text{not a multiple of 3}) = \frac{4}{6}$

$\frac{2}{6} + \frac{4}{6} = 1$

$P(\text{multiple of 3}) + P(\text{not a multiple of 3}) = 1$

In any activity, events 'A' and 'not A' account for all possible outcomes.

It is certain that one or the other will occur.

The probability of a certainty is 1.

This gives

$P(A) + P(\text{not } A) = 1$

You can use this fact to find the probability of a result not happening.

Work out the probability it will happen. Then subtract this probability from 1.

$P(\text{not } A) = 1 - P(A)$

Question

A hundred tickets were sold in a Christmas raffle for a turkey. Jamie bought 5 of these tickets.

What is the probability that
(a) Jamie wins the turkey
(b) Jamie does not win the turkey?
Give your answers as fractions in their simplest form.

Answer

(a) $P(\text{win}) = \frac{5}{100} = \frac{1}{20}$

The probability that Jamie wins the turkey is $\frac{1}{20}$

(b) $P(\text{not win}) = 1 - P(\text{win})$

$= 1 - \frac{1}{20}$

$= \frac{20}{20} - \frac{1}{20}$

$= \frac{19}{20}$

The probability that Jamie does not win the turkey is $\frac{19}{20}$

► *Exercise* **D5.6**

1 500 tickets were sold for a raffle. Alex bought 10 tickets. What is the probability that Alex
(a) wins first prize   (b) does not win first prize?

2 There are 150 cars in the Central Car Park. Eighty-five of the cars are British. What is the probability that the first car to leave the car park is
(a) British   (b) not British?

3 Sam has 14 socks in a drawer. Four of the socks are blue and three are white. Calculate the probability that the first sock taken at random from the drawer is
(a) blue   (c) white
(b) not blue   (d) not white.

4 A set of temporary traffic lights show green for 2 minutes, amber for 10 seconds and red for 50 seconds. What is the probability that the next motorist to arrive at the lights finds them
(a) on green   (c) not on red
(b) not on green (d) not on amber?

5 A crate contains 12 bottles of fruit juice. Four are apple, five are orange and three are lime. Dan is dying of thirst and takes a bottle at random from the crate. Calculate the probability that Dan takes a bottle containing
(a) apple juice
(b) not orange juice
(c) not lime juice
(d) not orange or apple juice.

Examination Questions

1 Look at this probability scale.

```
0            0.5           1
├──────┬──────┼──────┬──────┤
       ↑      ↑      ↑
       A      B      C
```

The arrows indicate the probabilities of three events A, B and C.
Put the letters A, B and C in the correct boxes in the table below.

Letter	Event
	At least one pupil will be absent from your school next week
	It will not get dark tonight
	A pupil chosen at random in a school containing 200 boys and 210 girls will be a boy

Event D is 'Tomorrow will be Thursday given that today is Wednesday'.
Event E is 'Four pupils in a class have their birthdays on the same date'
Put arrows on the probability scale to indicate the probabilities of D and E. Label the arrows D and E.

(WJEC, 1994)

2 A tube contains 10 Smarties: 5 are yellow, 3 are brown and 2 are green.
You pick a Smartie from the tube at random.
Write A, B and C on the 0 to 1 scale below to show approximately your estimates of these probabilities.

```
0            ½            1
├──────┬──────┼──────┬──────┤
```

A. The probability you pick a yellow Smartie.
B. The probability you pick a red Smartie.
C. The probability you pick a green Smartie.

(MEG, 1994)

3 The Ocean Hotel has rooms numbered from 500 to 517 on the fifth floor. Mr and Mrs Jones are given one of these rooms at random. What is the probability that the room given is numbered 511?

(SEG, 1990)

4 A fair dice has its six faces numbered 1, 2, 3, 4, 5, 6.
The dice is thrown and the score noted.
(a) What is the probability that the score is 3?
(b) What is the probability that the score is an odd number?
(c) What is the probability that the score is a number less than 7?
(d) What is the probability that the score is 7?

(SEG, 1989)

5 One card is selected at random from the hand shown in the diagram. Find the probability that the card selected is
(a) a picture card
(b) a diamond
(c) a FIVE.

(MEG, 1990)

6 Amy is playing dominoes. She has to pick up a domino from the pile. These dominoes are face down. Here are the dominoes which are in the pile. Remember Amy cannot see which domino is which.

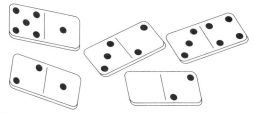

What is the probability that Amy will pick up a domino with a two on it?

(MEG, 1988)

7

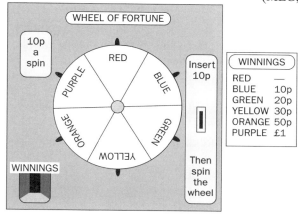

When a 'Wheel of fortune' in an amusement arcade is spun, the probability that it stops at a certain colour is given in the table.

Colour	Red	Blue	Green	Yellow	Orange	Purple
Probability	0.68	0.17	0.11	0.02	0.015	0.005

Joan inserts 10p and spins the wheel once.
What is the probability that
(i) the wheel stops at GREEN
(ii) the wheel stops at the most likely colour
(iii) the wheel stops at the least likely colour
(iv) Joan wins 60p
(v) Joan wins the largest prize available?

(NISEAC, 1991)

8 The table shows weekly car hire rates at some popular holiday destinations. Sheena decides to choose her holiday destination by picking one of the names from a hat. What is the probability that she will pick a destination with the cheapest weekly car hire rate?

```
THIS SUMMER'S LOWEST
CAR HIRE RATES
AND WE GUARANTEE IT!

★ Fully inclusive rates    MALAGA      £79
                           GIBRALTAR   £79
                           GERONA      £88
                           ALICANTE    £97
                           ALMERIA     £98
                           BALEARICS   £89
                           CANARIES    £79
★ Widest choice of         MALTA       £79
  rental locations         PORTUGAL    £84
                           GREECE      £159
                           CYPRUS      £125
```

(ULEAC, 1990)

9 (a) A bag contains eight toffees and five chocolates.
Andrew takes a sweet from the bag.
Write down the probability that he picks a toffee.

(b) Andrew eats the toffee and Robert now takes a sweet
from the same bag.
What is the probability that Robert will pick a
chocolate?

(WJEC, 1988)

10 Javed and Callum go on a camping weekend together. They
take two cans of soup, three cans of beans and two cans of
meat. The cans are all exactly the same size and shape.
After they had used one can of soup, it rained heavily and
the labels came off all the other cans. When they open the
next can, what is the probability that it contains

(a) beans

(b) soup?

(MEG, 1989)

11 A raffle is held at a disco and 150 raffle tickets are sold.
Sarah has bought ten tickets.

(a) Write down, in its simplest form, the probability that
Sarah will win first prize.

A disc jockey at the disco has twenty tapes, thirteen of
which belong to Sarah.

(b) What is the probability that the first tape he plays does
NOT belong to Sarah?

(SEG, 1990)

12 Trays of bulbs each contained 4 bulbs for pink hyacinths,
3 bulbs for blue hyacinths and 5 bulbs for white hyacinths.
A gardener selected one bulb at random from a tray to plant
in a bowl.
What is the probability that the hyacinth would be

(a) pink

(b) not white?

(NISEAC, 1989)

13 Ramondeep has a bag containing 12 beads. There are 5 red
beads, 3 green beads and rest are black. A bead is to be
chosen at random from the bag.
What is the probability, as a fraction, that

(a) the bead will be red

(b) the bead will not be green.

(c) the bead will be white?

(ULEAC, 1991)

14 John has bought five of the 500
tickets in a raffle. To win the
prize you must be present
when the tickets are
drawn, so John goes
along. Three tickets are
drawn. In each case
no-one is there to claim
the prize.

What is the probability that one of John's tickets will be
drawn next?

(MEG, 1988)

▶ **D6**

Combined outcomes

This unit will help you to:

■ find all the possible combined outcomes of
several activities by making a list, table or tree
diagram

■ calculate probabilities for these combined
outcomes.

Finding combined outcomes

In some probability problems we look at the **combined
outcomes** of several activities. The activities are often 'games'
such as …

● spinning a spinner and taking a card,

● throwing two dice,

● tossing a coin three times,
and so on …

To find all the possible combined outcomes you can make a
list, a table or a tree diagram. Try to 'imagine' the outcomes.
Then use a shorthand way to write them down.

Look at this example:
Nicky tosses a 1p coin and a 10p coin. Each coin can land
either heads or tails.
The combined outcomes are easy to 'imagine'.

You can write them in a
list like this.
Use H for heads
and T for tails

1 p coin	10 p coin
H	H
H	T
T	H
T	T

You can make a **table** like this.

		10p coin	
		H	T
1p coin	H	HH	HT
	T	TH	TT

*H on 1p coin
T on 10p coin*

You write the outcomes for one activity, i.e. tossing the 1p coin,
down the side.
You write the outcomes for the other activity, i.e. tossing the
10p coin, along the top.
Then you write the combined outcome in each square.

You can make a **tree diagram** like this …

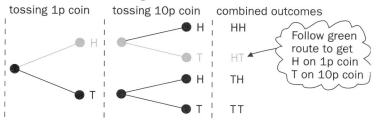

tossing 1p coin   tossing 10p coin   combined outcomes

Follow green route to get H on 1p coin T on 10p coin

You show each activity, i.e. tossing a 1p coin and tossing a 10p coin, by a 'stage' in the diagram. At each stage you draw *branches from a point* to show the *outcomes* for that activity. You write the outcomes at the *end of the branch*. Each route from left to right along the branches leads to a *combined outcome*. You write the combined outcome at the end of the route.

When the activities have only a few outcomes, listing all the possible combined outcomes may be easy. But you must make sure you list them *all*.

In most examples making a tree diagram or a table is safer. This helps you to be systematic. It makes sure you don't miss any of the combined outcomes.

► *Exercise* **D6.1**

1 A counter and a dice are used in a game. The counter has two faces, one marked 1, the other 2. The dice is an ordinary one. The counter and dice are thrown together. The numbers obtained are added together.
Copy and complete this table to show all the possible outcomes.

Number on dice

Number on counter	1	2	3	4	5	6
1	2					
2						7

2 Everyone entering the College All-Round Sports Championship must compete in one indoor, one outdoor (team) and one outdoor(individual) activity.
The choices are:
 Indoor: Badminton(B); Swimming (S).
 Outdoor (team): Football (F); Cricket (C); Hockey (H).
 Outdoor (individual): Tennis (T); Running (R).
Copy and complete this tree diagram to show all possible outcomes for the choices of three sports.

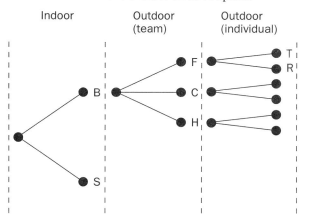

Indoor   Outdoor (team)   Outdoor (individual)   combined outcome

BFT

3 Pete arranges two piles of playing cards face downwards. One pile contains the 2, 3 and 4 of clubs only. The other pile contains the 2, 3 and 4 of diamonds only. Copy and complete this table to show all possible outcomes when one card is taken at random from each pile.

Card from 1st pile (clubs)	Card from 2nd pile (diamonds)
2	2

4 Two ordinary dice, one black, the other green, are thrown together. This table shows all possible outcomes.

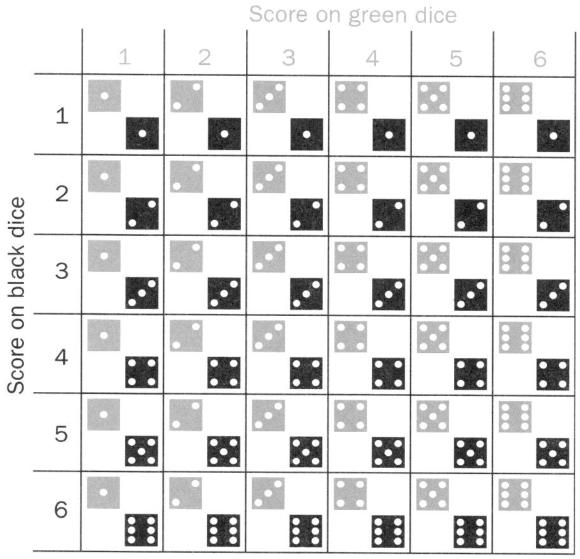

Score on green dice

Score on black dice

(a) Meg plays a game in which the two numbers obtained are added together.
Copy and complete this table showing all possible totals.

+	1	2	3	4	5	6
1	2					
2						
3				7		
4						
5						
6	8					

Score on green dice (column headers)
Score on black dice (row headers)

(b) Sam plays a game in which the two scores are multiplied together. Make a similar table showing all possible outcomes for this game.

(c) Rick plays a game which uses the difference between the two scores.
Make a table showing all possible outcomes for this game if all the differences are given as positive numbers or zero.

5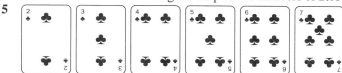

These six playing cards are shuffled and laid face down on a table. Simon picks three cards at random from this pile.
Copy and complete this list to show all possible outcomes for the three cards taken.
Note: The outcome 2 3 4 is the same as the outcomes 3 2 4, 4 2 3, … and so on.

2 3 4
2 3 5

6 In each class at Millington High School, two students are elected as representatives to the school council.

In class 11A, three boys (Al, Ben and Colin) and two girls (Sally and Tracey) have been nominated by other students.

(a) Draw a tree diagram showing all possible outcomes when two students are elected from these five, if one boy and one girl must be elected.

(b) List all the possible ways in which two students can be elected from the five students nominated, if no restrictions apply.

Calculating probabilities

Memo

To calculate probabilities when we have *equally likely outcomes* for a single activity we use:

Probability of an event

$$= \frac{\text{Number of favourable outcomes for that event}}{\text{total number of possible outcomes}}$$

When *combined outcomes are equally likely* we can calculate probabilities in the same way.

Use a list, table or tree diagram to find all the possible combined outcomes first. Then you can pick out the favourable outcomes for each event.

For two activities, a *table* is often the easiest way to list outcomes.

Question

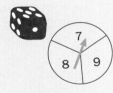

In a fair game, Pamela throws an ordinary dice and spins this pointer. The two scores are added together.

(a) Make a table to show all the possible total scores.

(b) Find the probability that the total score is
  (i)   9
  (ii) less than 11
  (iii) at least 12
  (iv) more than 6
  (v)   at most 9

Answer

(a) All the possible total scores are given in this table.

The game is fair, so each of these outcomes is equally likely.

Total number of possible outcomes
= total number of squares in the table
= 18

	Score from pointer		
+	7	8	9
1	8	9	10
2	9	10	11
3	10	11	12
4	11	12	13
5	12	13	14
6	13	14	15

(Score from dice)

(b) (i) Event: get a total of 9.
Number of favourable outcomes
= number of 9s in the totals in the table
= 2
$P(9) = \frac{2}{18}$ or $\frac{1}{9}$

(ii) Event: get a total less than 11.
Totals less than 11 in the table are 8, 9, and 10.
Number of favourable outcomes
= number of 8s, 9s, and 10s in the totals in the table
= 6
$P(\text{less than } 11) = \frac{6}{18}$ or $\frac{1}{3}$

(iii) Event: get a total of at least 12.
Totals of at least 12 in the table are 12, 13, 14, 15.
Number of favourable outcomes
= number of 12s, 13s, 14s, and 15s in the totals in the table
= 9
$P(\text{at least } 12) = \frac{9}{18} = \frac{1}{2}$

(iv) Event: get a total more than 6.
All totals in the table are more than 6.
Number of favourable outcomes = 18
$P(\text{more than } 6) = \frac{18}{18}$ or 1, i.e. a certainty!

(v) Event: get a total of at most 9.
Totals of 'at most 9' in the table are 9 and 8.
Number of favourable outcomes
= number of 9s and 8s in the totals in the table
= 3
$P(\text{at most } 9) = \frac{3}{18}$ or $\frac{1}{6}$

For two or more activities you can use a *tree diagram* to list outcomes.

Question

Gordon has these items of school uniform in his wardrobe:
  3 shirts:
    one blue, one grey, one white
  2 pairs of trousers:
    one pair blue, one pair grey
  2 pairs of socks:
    one pair grey, one pair white.
Gordon takes a shirt, a pair of trousers and a pair of socks at random from these items.

(a) Draw a tree diagram to show the colours of all possible outcomes.

(b) Find the probability that he gets:
  (i)   a grey shirt, blue trousers, grey socks
  (ii) items that are all the same colour
  (iii) three differently coloured items
  (iv) exactly two blue items
  (v)   at least one white item
  (vi) no white items.

Answer

(a) This tree diagram shows the colours of all possible combined outcomes. It gives them in this order: shirt, trousers, socks.
B – blue item, G – grey item, W – white item

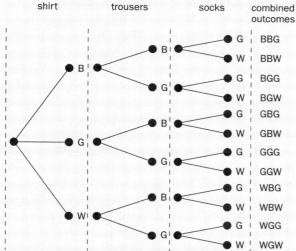

| shirt | trousers | socks | combined outcomes |

Total number of possible outcomes = 12. Gordon takes items at random. So each outcome is equally likely.

(b) (i) Event: get a grey shirt, blue trousers, grey socks.
Favourable outcomes: GBG
Number of favourable outcomes = 1

$$P(\text{Grey shirt, blue trousers, grey socks}) = \frac{1}{12}$$

(ii) Event: get items that are all the same colour.
Favourable outcomes: GGG
Number of favourable outcomes = 1

$$P(\text{same colour}) = \frac{1}{12}$$

(iii) Event: get three different colours.
Favourable outcomes: BGW, GBW, WBG
Number of favourable outcomes = 3

$$P(\text{three different colours}) = \frac{3}{12} \text{ or } \frac{1}{4}$$

(iv) Event: get exactly two blue items.
Favourable outcomes: BBG, BBW
Number of favourable outcomes = 2

$$P(\text{exactly two blue items}) = \frac{2}{12} \text{ or } \frac{1}{6}$$

(v) Event: get at least one white item.
Favourable outcomes: BBW, BGW, GBW, GGW, WBG, WBW, WGG, WGW
Number of favourable outcomes = 8

$$P(\text{at least one white item}) = \frac{8}{12} \text{ or } \frac{2}{3}$$

(vi) Event: get no white items
Gordon must get either no white items
or at least one white item.
This accounts for all possible outcomes.
So P(no white items) = 1 – P(at least one white item)

$$= 1 - \frac{2}{3}$$

$$= \frac{1}{3}$$

▶ *Exercise* D6.2

The questions in this exercise use the answers to questions **1–6** in Exercise D6.1.

1 Look at your answer to question **1** of Exercise D6.1.
  (a) How many possible outcomes are there altogether?
  (b) How many outcomes give a total of 5?
  (c) With one throw of the counter and dice, what is the probability of getting a total
     (i) of 5   (ii) of 1   (iii) which is an even number
     (iv) greater than 6?

2 Look at your answer to question **2** of Exercise D6.1.
  (a) How many possible outcomes are there altogether?
  (b) What is the probability that a competitor, selected at random, will have chosen to compete at
     (i) Badminton   (ii) Football
     (iii) Swimming and Tennis
     (iv) Cricket and Running
     (v) Swimming, Hockey and Running?

3 Look at your answer to question **3** of Exercise D6.1.
  (a) How many possible outcomes are there altogether?
     Calculate the probability that when Pete takes one card at random from each pile he gets
  (b) the two of clubs
  (c) the four of diamonds
  (d) two threes
  (e) a double, i.e. two cards showing the same number
  (f) a total of more than six, when the numbers on the two cards are added.

4 Look at your answer to question **4** of Exercise D6.1.
  (a) Calculate the probability that with the throw of the two dice, Meg gets
     (i) a total of 7   (ii) a total of 2
     (iii) a total greater than 9   (iv) a total less than 4
     (v) a total which is a multiple of 5
     (vi) a total which is a prime number.
  (b) Calculate the probability that with a single throw of the two dice, Sam gets
     (i) a score of 20
     (ii) a score less than 16
     (iii) a score greater than 100
     (iv) a score which is a square number
     (v) a score which is a prime number.
  (c) Calculate the probability that when Rick throws the two dice once, he gets
     (i) a score of zero
     (ii) a score of six
     (iii) a score less than 3
     (iv) a score greater than 4
     (v) a score which is a prime number.

5 Look at your answer to question **5** of Exercise D6.1.
  Calculate the probability that when Simon takes three cards at random he gets
  (a) the two of clubs   (b) the five of clubs
  (c) a total of the three cards equal to 12
  (d) a total of the three cards greater than 13.
  (e) a total of the three cards less than 10.

6 Look at your answer to question **6** of Exercise D6.1.

(a) If one boy and one girl from class 11A must be elected to the school council, what is the probability that
(i) Sally is elected   (ii) Ben is elected
(iii) Tracey and Colin are both elected?

(b) If no restrictions apply, what is the probability that
(i) both girls are elected   (ii) two boys are elected?

Examination Questions

1 Copy the table below and fill in all the possible choices of two different items. The first line has been done for you. (You will not need every line.)

CHOICES
Bacon and Sausage

MENU
EGG, BEANS, BACON, SAUSAGE
ANY TWO DIFFERENT
ITEMS.... £1·99

(MEG, 1990)

2 Wayne, Derek, Rachel, Sarah and Alison entered a competition. The first prize was a weekend in Amsterdam for two people. To their surprise they won and agreed to draw lots to decide who went to Amsterdam.

By listing all the possible combinations, or otherwise, find the probability that the lucky pair consisted of one boy and one girl.   (NEAB, 1989)

3 A supermarket runs a prize draw. Each customer is given a card with two whole numbers printed on it. Each number is chosen at random from the list 1, 2, 3, 4, 5, 6, 7, 8, 9 The customer adds her two numbers to find her total. Certain totals win a prize.

First number	Second number
9	5
5	9

(a) Copy and complete the table to show all the pairs of numbers which give a total of 14.

(b) Explain why a total of 14 is more likely than a total of 15.
(SEG, 1990)

4 Fair dice are made in the shape of regular tetrahedra, each of which has four faces. Two of these dice, one red and one blue, have their faces numbered from 1 to 4. In a game they are thrown and the numbers on their bases are added together to find the score.

What is the probability of
(a) scoring 8
(b) scoring 3
(c) scoring a double
(d) the number on the base of the blue die being larger than the number on the base of the red die?
(ULEAC, 1988)

5 In a game of monopoly, Anne throws two dice and adds the numbers together to obtain her score. The table shows the different ways each score can be obtained.

		Number on first die				
	1	2	3	4	5	6
1	2	3	4	5	6	7
2	3	4	5	6	7	8
3	4	5	6	7	8	9
4	5	6	7	8	9	10
5	6	7	8	9	10	11
6	7	8	9	10	11	12

(Number on second die labels the rows)

(a) How many different ways can Anne obtain a score?

(b) (i) Which score occurs most?
(ii) What is the largest score Anne could obtain?

(c) (i) What is the probability that Anne scores 5?
(ii) What is the probability that Anne scores more than 10?
(SEG, 1988)

6 Vijay and Baljit are playing a game with two fair five-sided spinners, one red and one blue. The blue spinner is numbered 5, 6, 7, 8, 9, and the red spinner is numbered 1, 2, 3, 4, 5. The final score is calculated by multiplying the two spinner scores together.

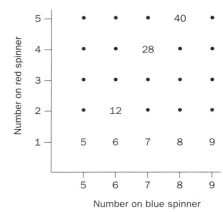

(a) Copy and complete this grid, which shows all the possible final scores.

Number on red spinner (vertical axis)
Number on blue spinner (horizontal axis)

Values shown on grid: at red 5: 40; at red 4: 28; at red 2: 12; bottom row labels 5, 6, 7, 8, 9.

(b) Find the probability that the final score is a square number.

(c) Find the probability that the final score is less than 30.
(MEG, 1989)

7 A spinner has the shape of a regular octagon. The eight edges of the spinner are numbered +5, −3, +3, −1, +1, +1, −5, +3.
When it is spun, the spinner is equally likely to finish on any of its eight edges and the number on this edge gives the score.

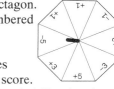

(a) The spinner is spun once. Find the probability that the score obtained is
(i) +3   (ii) a negative number.

(b) The spinner is spun twice. Find the probability that the total of the two scores is +10.

(c) The spinner is spun twice and the total score is −2. What could the scores have been for the first spin and the second spin? Write down all the possibilities.

(d) The spinner is spun five times. Explain why it is not possible to have a total score of +8.
(MEG, 1991)

8

A set of dominoes contains 28 pieces. Each domino can be represented by the pair (x,y) where x and y can each take the number values from 0 to 6.

x is larger than y, or equal to y.

For example, the dominoes above can be represented by the pairs $(3,1)$, $(2,0)$ and $(4,4)$.

(a) Complete the list of all the 28 pairs of numbers which represent a set of dominoes.

(6,6), (6,5), (6,4), (6,3), (6,2), (6,1), (6,0)
(5,5), (5,4), (5,3), (5,2), (5,1), (5,0)
.
.
.
.
(0,0)

(b) Write down
  (i) the number of dominoes for which either $x = 3$ or $y = 3$ or both
  (ii) the highest total $(x + y)$ on a domino.

(c) A domino is to be drawn at random from the set. What will be the probability that
  (i) it bears the number 6 (as x or as y)?
  (ii) it is a double (that is, $x = y$).

(d) A new set of dominoes is to be made containing all pairs of whole numbers from 0 to 10 (instead of 6). How many pieces will be needed in the set? Show your working clearly.

(ULEAC, 1989)

9 A fair spinner has the numbers 1, 2, 3, 4 and 5 on it. This spinner is spun and, at the same time, a coin is tossed. What is the probability of getting an odd number and a head?

(ULEAC, 1991)

PART 2
Moving on

P1
Index notation

This unit will help you to:

■ understand the meaning of index notation in arithmetic and algebra for whole number indices

■ use index notation with positive whole number indices in multiplication and division.

Powerful multiplications

Look at these multiplications and the numbers they give.

$$5 \times 5 = 25$$
$$5 \times 5 \times 5 = 125$$
$$5 \times 5 \times 5 \times 5 = 625$$
$$5 \times 5 \times 5 \times 5 \times 5 = 3125$$

Each multiplication uses only the number 5.
The numbers they give are called '**powers of 5**'.

We often use a 'shorthand' to write repeated multiplications of the same number.

5^2 is short for 5×5
5^3 is short for $5 \times 5 \times 5$
5^4 is short for $5 \times 5 \times 5 \times 5$
5^5 is short for $5 \times 5 \times 5 \times 5 \times 5$.

This shorthand is called **index notation** or **index form**.
You can use it for *powers* of any number.

Here is a power of 3 in **index form**.
The small raised ^{5} is the **index**.
The 3 at the bottom is the **base**.

3^5 — index
— base

The *base* 3 tells you it is a *power of 3*.
The *index* 5 tells you it is the *5th power of 3*.

The index shows you how many of the base number to multiply together.

$$3^5 = 3 \times 3 \times 3 \times 3 \times 3$$

You can say 3^5 as 'three to the five'
or 'three to the power five'
or 'three raised to the power five'.

Indices is the plural of the word index.
For example, in the numbers 5^4 and 3^5
the small ^{4} and ^{5} are the indices.

The **1st power** of a number is *always itself*.

$$1^1 = 1, \ 2^1 = 2, \ 3^1 = 3, \ 4^1 = 4, \ \dots$$

The **2nd** and **3rd powers** of a number have special names.
We call them '**squares**' and '**cubes**'.

7^2 is the 2nd power of 7.
7^2 is usually read as 'seven squared'
    or 'the square of seven'.
The *2nd power* of any number is that number *squared*.

$$\boxed{7^2 = 7 \times 7}$$

7^3 is the 3rd power of 7.
7^3 is usually read as 'seven cubed'
    or 'the cube of seven'.
The *3rd power* of any number is that number *cubed*.

$$\boxed{7^3 = 7 \times 7 \times 7}$$

Summary

The repeated multiplication of the same number (called the **base**) can be written in **index notation (index form)**. The **index** (the small raised figure) shows how many of the base number are in the multiplication. The result is called a **power** of the base number.

e.g. $2 \times 2 \times 2 \times 2 = 2^+$ is the 4th power of 2

The 1st power of a number is itself, e.g. $2^1 = 2$
The 2nd power is a square,   e.g. $2^2 = 2 \times 2$
The 3rd power is a cube,   e.g. $2^3 = 2 \times 2 \times 2$

▶ *Exercise* P1.1

1 Give these in index form.
  (a) 3×3 (e) $6 \times 6 \times 6 \times 6 \times 6$
  (b) $2 \times 2 \times 2 \times 2$ (f) $5 \times 5 \times 5 \times 5 \times 5 \times 5 \times 5$
  (c) $8 \times 8 \times 8$ (g) $10 \times 10 \times 10 \times 10 \times 10 \times 10$
  (d) 7×7 (h) $9 \times 9 \times 9 \times 9 \times 9 \times 9$

2 Write each number in full as a multiplication and work out its value.
  (a) 10^8 (c) 7^6 (e) 5^3 (g) 6^7
  (b) 2^{10} (d) 4^8 (f) 3^9 (h) 8^4

3 Write these in index notation and in full as multiplications.
  (a) 5th power of 7   (e) four to the power six
  (b) 9th power of 4   (f) nine to the power five
  (c) 4th power of 10   (g) six to the power four
  (d) 7th power of 2   (h) five to the power ten

4 Write these in index notation and in full as multiplications.
  (a) 6 cubed   (c) square of 10   (e) 9 cubed
  (b) 4 squared   (d) cube of 8   (f) 5 squared

Indices in algebra

Index notation is used in the same way in **algebra**.

For example, a^5 is the '*5th power of a*'.
    a is the base.
    5 is the index.

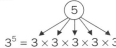

$$a^5 = a \times a \times a \times a \times a$$

a^5 is also read as '*a* raised to the power of five'
    or '*a* to the power five'
    or '*a* to the five'.

The 1st power of any value is itself.

$$a^1 = a, \qquad b^1 = b, \qquad c^1 = c, \qquad d^1 = d, \ \dots$$

For a^2, we say '*a* squared'. $a^2 = a \times a$
For a^3, we say '*a* cubed'. $a^3 = a \times a \times a$

In index notation, the index only applies to the number or letter it is written beside.

In $3a^2$, only the a is 'squared'.
$3a^2 = 3 \times a^2 = 3 \times a \times a$

In $5b^4$, only the b is ' to the power 4'.
$5b^4 = 5 \times b^4 = 5 \times b \times b \times b \times b$

In $2pq^3$, only the q is 'cubed'.
$2pq^3 = 2 \times p \times q^3 = 2 \times p \times q \times q \times q$

In $7x^2y^5$, only x is 'squared', only y is 'to the power 5'.
$7x^2y^5 = 7 \times x^2y^5 = 7 \times x \times x \times y \times y \times y \times y \times y$

▶ *Exercise* P1.2

1 Write these out in full as multiplications.
(a) a^3 (c) y^5 (e) n^8 (g) u^2
(b) x^6 (d) m^4 (f) p^7 (h) v^9

2 Write these in index form:
(a) $x \times x \times x \times x$
(b) $n \times n \times n \times n$
(c) $p \times p \times p \times p \times p \times p$
(d) $m \times m$
(e) $a \times a \times a \times a \times a$
(f) $s \times s \times s \times s \times s \times s \times s$
(g) $b \times b$
(h) $r \times r \times r \times r \times r \times r \times r \times r$

3 Write these in index form and in full.
(a) 'the fourth power of x' (e) 'n to the power 7'
(b) 'y to the five' (f) 'm squared'
(c) 'the square of p' (g) 'y cubed'
(d) 'r to the six' (h) 'the sixth power of a'

4 Write these out in full as multiplications.
(a) $2x^3$ (d) $5n^2m$ (g) $8r^4s^3$
(b) $4p^6$ (e) $6a^2b^3$ (h) $9abc^3$
(c) $3xy^2$ (f) $4u^2v^5$ (i) $10u^2vw^5$

5 Write these in index form.
(a) $4 \times a \times a \times a$
(b) $7 \times b \times b$
(c) $3 \times u \times u \times v \times v$
(d) $4 \times m \times m \times n \times n \times n$
(e) $7 \times x \times x \times x \times y$
(f) $2 \times p \times p \times q \times q \times q \times q$
(g) $8 \times r \times s \times s \times s \times s \times s$
(h) $6 \times b \times c \times b \times c \times b$
(i) $12 \times p \times q \times q \times p \times q$
(j) $20 \times m \times n \times n \times n \times m \times n$

Powers with a calculator

You can find the value of a number in index form in several ways with a calculator. Here are some to try.

• Use simple multiplication
You have already used simple multiplication to find powers.
6^4 means $6 \times 6 \times 6 \times 6$
To find 6^4 on your calculator,

press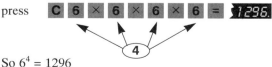

So $6^4 = 1296$

• Use a constant multiplier
Most scientific calculators have a **constant function**. You can use this to repeat a function, such as ×, and a number without entering them again and again …

To find 2nd, 3rd, 4th,… powers of a number, set up the number as a *constant multiplier*, then each press of = gives a higher power of it.

On some calculators, pressing × × makes the number on the display a constant multiplier. Then each press of = gives a power of that number.
To use this to work out 6^4,

you press

The K on the display shows that the constant function is set up.

Some calculators have an **automatic constant**.
You only need to press × *once* to set it up.

Other calculators have a **constant key** K.
To use this for powers,
you press ×, enter the base number and press K.
Then you press = over and over again, for each higher power.

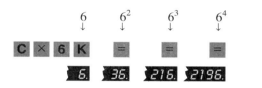

Find out how the constant multiplier works on your calculator. Look it up in your calculator booklet if you need to.

• Use a power key
The power key on most calculators is x^y or y^x.
Find this key on your calculator.
This key is very easy to use.
Enter the base number first, press the power key, enter the index and then press =.

For 6^4,
you press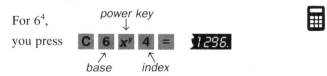

▶ *Exercise* P1.3

1 Use your constant multiplier to find these values.
(a) 9^3 (c) 7^4 (e) 10^7 (g) 8^7
(b) 6^6 (d) 15^5 (f) 3^8 (h) 12^4

2 Use the power key on your calculator to find these values.
(a) 2^9 (c) 3^{11} (e) 4^5 (g) 9^4
(b) 8^6 (d) 5^8 (f) 6^{10} (h) 24^3

3 Which do you think is larger?
(a) 2^3 or 3^2 (c) 3^4 or 4^3 (e) 8^5 or 5^8
(b) 10^2 or 2^{10} (d) 1^7 or 7^1 (f) 6^9 or 9^6
Now find out with your calculator.

4 Work out the value of:
(a) $2^5 \times 5^3$ (d) $10^4 \div 2^2$ (g) $9^6 \div 3^2$
(b) $10^6 \times 4^1$ (e) $8^2 \div 4^3$ (h) $2^7 \times 7^0$
(c) $7^2 \times 3^4$ (f) $6^3 \div 3^3$ (i) $10^4 \div 9^0$

Investigation

Unit digits

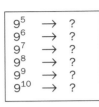

$9^1 = \quad\quad\underline{9}$
$9^2 = \quad\quad 8\underline{1}$
$9^3 = \quad\; 56\underline{9}$
$9^4 = 656\underline{1}$

Here are some powers of 9.
Look at each unit digit.
Describe the pattern
they make.

$9^5 \rightarrow ?$
$9^6 \rightarrow ?$
$9^7 \rightarrow ?$
$9^8 \rightarrow ?$
$9^9 \rightarrow ?$
$9^{10} \rightarrow ?$

Predict the unit digits
of these powers of 9.

Check your ideas
with your calculator.

Look for a link between the *index* and the *unit digit* in these
examples. Comment on what you find.

Investigate the unit digits of powers of *other* numbers.

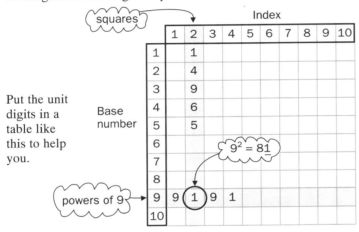

Put the unit
digits in a
table like
this to help
you.

Here are some ideas to explore. Think of some others yourself.

● Comment on the patterns made by the unit digits of …

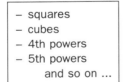

– squares
– cubes
– 4th powers
– 5th powers
    and so on …

– powers of 2
– powers of 3
– powers of 4
– powers of 5
    and so on …

● Use the patterns to predict the unit digits of these numbers.
2^{16}, 3^{11}, 4^{19}, 5^{14}, 6^{18}, 7^{12}, 8^{13}, 9^{15}, 10^{17}
2^{100}, 3^{59}, 4^{26}, 5^{98}, 6^{41}, 7^{35}, 8^{62}, 9^{72}, 10^{1000}
Describe how you found them.
● What happens to the unit digits for powers of
11, 12, 13, 14, …?
● Look at these numbers:

| 541 | | 528 | | 573 | | 646 | | 849 |
| 450 | | 787 | | 484 | | 635 | | 782 |

Which cannot be squares? Which cannot be 4th powers?

Which cannot be powers of 3? Which cannot be powers of 5?

Explain your answers.

What power?

1024 is a power of 4. $1024 = 4^?$

To find out 'what power of 4',
you can multiply 4 by itself over and over again…
until you reach 1024.
You can do this by simple multiplication.
Keep a record of each 4.

Press

$4^1 \quad 4^2 \quad 4^3 \quad 4^4 \quad 4^5$

So $1024 = 4^5$
To check, use your power key:

▶ *Exercise* P1.4

Find the answers to these by simple multiplication.
1   What power of 3 is 243? $243 = 3^?$
2   What power of 2 is 64? $64 = 2^?$
3   What power of 7 is 2401? $2401 = 7^?$
4   Express 10 000 000 as a power of 10.
5   Express 729 as a power of 9.
6   Express 1 953 125 as a power of 5.

128 is a power of 2. $128 = 2^?$

You can use a constant multiplier on a calculator to find out
'what power of 2'.
   Here is one way:

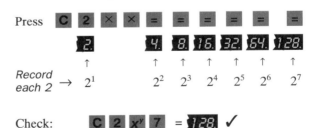

Press

*Record
each 2* $\rightarrow$ 2^1 $2^2 \; 2^3 \; 2^4 \; 2^5 \; 2^6 \; 2^7$

Check:

▶ *Exercise* P1.5

Use the constant multiplier on your calculator to answer these.
1   What power of 6 is 216?
2   What power of 8 is 512?
3   What power of 10 is 100 000?
4   Express 625 as a power of 5.
5   Express 248 832 as a power of 12.
6   Express 8000 as a power of 20.

👁 *Investigation*

Different powers

64 is a power of 2
and a power of 4
and a power of 8

$$64 = 2^6$$
$$64 = 4^3$$
$$64 = 8^2$$

Which numbers between 1 and 100 can be given as a power in more than one way?

Show each of the different ways.

Investigate the different ways numbers can be written as powers in index form.

Explore some numbers.
Here are some more examples to try.
Try some of your own.

343 59 049
1 000 000
390 625 81
4096

Organise your work systematically.
Look for patterns and relationships.
Describe any you find.
Try to find a rule.
See if it works for other numbers.
Comment on what you find.

Combining powers

Do these on your calculator.
Give each answer as an *ordinary number* and in *index form*.

$$2^2 \times 2^3 = \ldots\ldots = 2^?$$
$$5^2 \times 5^3 = \ldots\ldots = 5^?$$
$$9^2 \times 9^3 = \ldots\ldots = 9^?$$

Compare each multiplication with its answer in index form.
What do you find?
Predict the answers to these in index form.

$$4^2 \times 4^2 = 4^?$$
$$7^2 \times 7^2 = 7^?$$
$$10^2 \times 10^2 = 10^?$$

Then *check* your answers with your calculator.

Suggest a rule for multiplying powers of the same number in index form.

Test your rule on these multiplications.

$$3^4 \times 3^4 = 3^?$$ $$2^7 \times 2^5 = 2^?$$
$$7^1 \times 7^9 = 7^?$$ $$10^2 \times 10^5 = 10^?$$

Try it on some examples of your own.
Does it work?
If it doesn't, adapt it and test it again.

Now investigate division with powers like these:

$$7^3 \div 7^2 = 7^?$$ $$10^8 \div 10^3 = 10^?$$
$$2^7 \div 2^4 = 2^?$$ $$3^{10} \div 3^5 = 3^?$$

Find and test a rule for these.
Describe what you discover.

Write down the conclusions you have reached about multiplication and division with powers of the same number.

Multiplication

Multiplying powers of the *same base* is easy if they are in *index form*.

You may have already found a quick way to do this (in the Investigation 'Combining powers'). To get an answer in the *same base*, you just **add the indices**.

In this example, the base is 2.

$$2^3 \times 2^4 = 2^{3+4} = 2^7$$

Check this on your calculator.

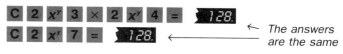

← The answers are the same

You can use the same 'short way' in algebra too.
In this example, the base is '*a*'.

$$a^3 \times a^4 = a^{3+4} = a^7$$

To see why this works, you can write the powers out in full as multiplications.

$$a^3 = a \times a \times a \quad \text{and} \quad a^4 = a \times a \times a \times a$$

So $a^3 \times a^4 = \boxed{a \times a \times a} \times \boxed{a \times a \times a \times a}$

$$= a^7$$

In some multiplications you have powers of the same base, and some other numbers.

Look at this example:

It means this:

To simplify it,
group the numbers together
and the powers of *a* together:

Now multiply:

simplify:

$$2a^4 \times 3a^5$$
$$= 2 \times a^4 \times 3 \times a^5$$
$$= \boxed{2 \times 3} \times \boxed{a^4 \times a^5}$$
$$= 6 \times a^9$$
$$= 6a^9$$

▶ *Exercise* **P1.6**

1. Work out these multiplications the 'short way'. Leave your answers in index form.
   (a) $2^3 \times 2^5$ (d) $5^4 \times 5^3$ (g) 8×8^6
   (b) $3^2 \times 3^4$ (e) $7^4 \times 7^2$ (h) $3^7 \times 3^6$
   (c) $3^3 \times 3$ (f) $6^5 \times 6^3$ (i) $9^4 \times 9^7$
   Check your answers with a calculator.

2. Use the 'short way' to simplify these.
   Then write them out in full to check them.
   (a) $a^2 \times a^5$ (d) $y^7 \times y^3$ (g) $x^2 \times x^8$
   (b) $b^4 \times b^2$ (e) $a^4 \times a^5$ (h) $n^3 \times n^6$
   (c) $x^6 \times x$ (f) $p^3 \times p^2$ (i) $m \times m^5$

3. Simplify these.
   (a) $2x \times 3x^2$ (d) $y^5 \times 6y$ (g) $3p^2 \times 6p^4$
   (b) $3x^4 \times 2x^3$ (e) $4p^3 \times 3p^2$ (h) $5x^2 \times x^6$
   (c) $4b^2 \times 2b^5$ (f) $2q^5 \times 3q^5$ (i) $9a^7 \times 7a^9$

Division

Index form helps with division too.

When the numbers are in the *same base* you can easily get an answer *in that base*. You just **subtract the indices**.

In this example, the base is 5.

$$5^8 \div 5^2 = 5^{8-2} = 5^6$$

Check the answer with your calculator.

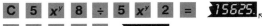

The same 'short way'works in algebra.

In this example, the base is y.

$$y^8 \div y^2 = y^{8-2} = y^6$$

You can show why this works like this:

$$y^8 \div y^2$$

Write the division as a fraction:

$$= \frac{y^8}{y^2}$$

Write the powers as multiplications:

$$= \frac{y \times y \times y \times y \times y \times y \times y \times y}{y \times y}$$

Cancel:

$$= \frac{\overset{1}{\cancel{y}} \times \overset{1}{\cancel{y}} \times y \times y \times y \times y \times y \times y}{\underset{1}{\cancel{y}} \times \underset{1}{\cancel{y}}}$$

Write in index form:

$$= y^6$$

Some divisions have simple numbers and values in index form. Writing these divisions as fractions makes them easier to simplify.

Here is an example.

To simplify this:

$$8x^4 \div 2x^3$$

Write as a fraction:

$$= \frac{8x^4}{2x^3}$$

Now divide:

$$= 4x^{4-3}$$

Then simplify:

$$= 4x^1$$

$$= 4x$$

To the power 0

Look at this division: $7^4 \div 7^4$

You know that a number divided by itself is 1.

$$7^4 \div 7^4 = 1$$

But you can also work it out like this:

$$7^4 \div 7^4 = 7^{4-4} = 7^0$$

The two answers must be the same.
So this shows: $7^0 = 1$

In fact, any number to the power 0 is 1.

$$2^0 = 1, \quad 3^0 = 1, \quad 4^0 = 1, \quad \ldots$$

This is also true in algebra.

$$a^0 = 1, \quad b^0 = 1, \quad c^0 = 1, \quad \ldots$$

You may find this useful when you simplify divisions.

▶ *Exercise* P1.7

1 Work out these divisions the 'short way'.
   Leave your answers in index form.
   (a) $3^6 \div 3^2$ (d) $2^9 \div 2^7$ (g) $9^6 \div 9^4$
   (b) $5^9 \div 5^3$ (e) $6^7 \div 6^5$ (h) $8^3 \div 8$
   (c) $4^8 \div 4$ (f) $7^4 \div 7^3$ (i) $10^8 \div 10^6$
   Check your answers with your caluclator.

2 Work out these the 'short way'.
   (a) $a^4 \div a^2$ (c) $x^5 \div x^3$ (e) $n^7 \div n^4$
   (b) $b^3 \div b$ (d) $p^6 \div p^2$ (f) $y^5 \div y^2$
   Now show why each division works out this way.

3 Simplify these. Leave your answers in index form.
   (a) $x^7 \div x^2$ (d) $n^5 \div n$ (g) $y^8 \div y^5$
   (b) $p^5 \div p^4$ (e) $m^8 \div m^3$ (h) $k^7 \div k^2$
   (c) $a^6 \div a^3$ (f) $c^6 \div c^5$ (i) $w^9 \div w^6$

4 Simplify these expressions.
   (a) $3a^3 \div a^2$ (d) $9p^7 \div 3p^2$ (g) $6s^3 \div s$
   (b) $6b^5 \div 2b^4$ (e) $8t^9 \div 4t^4$ (h) $8m^6 \div 2m^2$
   (c) $4m^6 \div 2m^3$ (f) $5b^3 \div 5b^2$ (i) $7x^4 \div 2x^3$

5 Simplify each of these expressions.
   (a) $x^8 \div x^8$ (d) $9a^2 \div 3a^2$ (g) $4k^3 \div 2k^3$
   (b) $b^4 \div b^4$ (e) $8c^3 \div 2c^3$ (h) $5r^7 \div 2r^7$
   (c) $p^2 \div p^2$ (f) $7x^6 \div 2x^6$ (i) $3n^4 \div 4n^4$

Summary

- To multiply powers of the same base in index form, add the indices.

$$a^m \times a^n = a^{m+n}$$

- To divide powers of the same base in index form, subtract the indices.

$$a^m \div a^n = a^{m-n}$$

▶ *Exercise* P1.8

Simplify, leaving your answers in index form.

1 $5^2 \times 5^4$ 11 $x^2 \times 3x^5$
2 $7^6 \div 7^2$ 12 $2y^3 \div y^3$
3 $x^4 \times x^3$ 13 $8p^5 \div 2p^3$
4 $m^8 \div m^3$ 14 $2d^2 \times 5d^3$
5 $2n^5 \div n^2$ 15 $12u^6 \div 3u^3$
6 $7m^5 \times m^6$ 16 $10m^7 \div 5m^6$
7 $p^3 \div p^3$ 17 $15n^7 \div 3n$
8 $6x^7 \div 2x$ 18 $7a^3 \times 2a^2$
9 $5r^2 \times 3r$ 19 $20p^4 \div 5p^4$
10 $5u^6 \div 4u^6$ 20 $9n^3 \times 2n^5$

Negative indices

Indices can also be **negative**.
A number with a negative index has a special meaning.
It is equal to '*1 over*' the same number with the *matching positive index*.

For example,

$$2^{-4} = \frac{1}{2^4} \qquad a^{-n} = \frac{1}{a^n}$$

You can use a *calculator* to show this relationship for numbers.
You can use the change sign key to enter the negative index.
It gives the answer as a decimal.

To find the value of 2^{-4},

we key in:  `0.0625`

To find the value of $\frac{1}{2^4}$

we key in:  `0.0625`

Both ways give the same answer.

So $2^{-4} = \frac{1}{2^4}$

You can also use *patterns* to show this relationship.

Look at the pattern
as you go down
this list of powers of 2.

The powers are divided by 2.
The indices go down by 1.

32	=	2^5
16	=	2^4
8	=	2^3
4	=	2^2
2	=	2^1
1	=	2^0
$\frac{1}{2}$	=	2^{-1}
$\frac{1}{4}$	=	2^{-2}
$\frac{1}{8}$	=	2^{-3}
$\frac{1}{16}$	=	2^{-4}
$\frac{1}{32}$	=	2^{-5}

From this pattern you can see that:

$2^{-4} = \frac{1}{16}$ and $2^4 = 16$.

So $2^{-4} = \frac{1}{2^4}$.

Discussion Exercise

- Look at the pattern of powers of 2 above.
  What does it show about these powers?

  $2^{-5}, \quad 2^{-3}, \quad 2^{-2}, \quad 2^{-1}, \quad 2^0$

  Discuss.

- Give the answer to $2^3 \div 2^7$ in index form.
  Work it out in two ways:
  (a) by the 'short way',
  (b) by writing the powers as repeated multiplications.
  What do your answers show?
  Discuss.

Exercise P1.9

1 Use your calculator to find the values of these.
  (a) 2^{-5} (c) 4^{-3} (e) 3^{-4} (g) 12^0 (i) 10^{-2}
  (b) 10^{-1} (d) 5^{-2} (f) 6^{-2} (h) 9^{-2} (j) 1^{-8}

2 Write each of these using a positive index.
  (a) 4^{-2} (c) 8^{-3} (e) 10^{-4} (g) x^{-5} (i) b^{-8}
  (b) 6^{-1} (d) 2^{-6} (f) a^{-7} (h) y^{-2} (j) c^{-1}

3 Rewrite each of these using a negative index.
  (a) $\frac{1}{10^2}$ (c) $\frac{1}{3^5}$ (e) $\frac{1}{9}$ (g) $\frac{1}{a^4}$ (i) $\frac{1}{c^6}$
  (b) $\frac{1}{4^7}$ (d) $\frac{1}{2^9}$ (f) $\frac{1}{x^3}$ (h) $\frac{1}{y}$ (j) $\frac{1}{b^8}$

4 Which has the larger value?
  (a) 4^3 or 4^{-3} (c) 6^{-1} or 6^1 (e) 3^{-2} or 3^{-5}
  (b) 7^{-1} or 7^0 (d) 10^4 or 10^0 (f) 5^{-2} or 5^1

Investigation

You can do multiplications and divisions involving numbers with negative indices.
Do they obey the same rules of indices?
Investigate.

As part of your investigation, test your ideas on number calculations like these:

$5^4 \times 5^{-2} = 5^?$ $3^5 \div 3^{-2} = 3^?$
$3^{-5} \times 3 = 3^?$ $2^{-2} \div 2^3 = 2^?$
$2^{-4} \times 2^{-2} = 2^?$ $10^{-7} \div 10^{-5} = 10^?$

Check your answers with your calculator.
Also test your ideas by simplifying expressions like these:

$a^3 \times a^{-4} = a^?$ $c^4 \div c^{-1} = c^?$
$x^{-1} \times x^3 = x^?$ $d^{-5} \div d^2 = d^?$
$b^{-2} \times b^{-5} = b^?$ $n^{-3} \div n^{-4} = n^?$

Check your answers by writing the powers as repeated multiplications and simplifying.

Report on what you find.

P2
Functions and graphs

This unit will help you to:

■ use input values to find outputs from simple functions

■ plot (input, output) values for a function as points on a grid

■ draw the graph of a simple function through its (input, output) points

■ recognise that graphs of functions may be straight lines or curves

■ draw the graph of a simple function from its equation and read values from it.

Memo

Looking back at functions

You can think of a **function** as a machine that *processes numbers*.

When numbers are put into it, it *acts* on them and other numbers are produced.

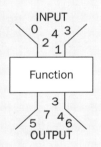

The numbers that are *put in* are called INPUTS.
The numbers that *come out* are called OUTPUTS.

A function does *exactly the same* to each input number.

It outputs *only one number* for each number put in.

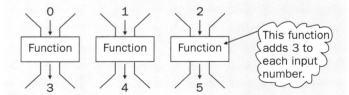

This function adds 3 to each input number.

Two *different* input numbers may give the *same* output.

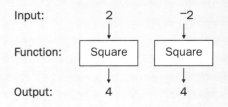

Input:	2	−2
Function:	Square	Square
Output:	4	4

You can make a **table of inputs** and the matching **outputs** for a function.

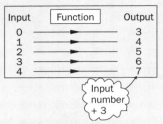

The function in this table is 'add 3'.
Each output number is its 'input number + 3'
If we call the input x, then the output is $x + 3$.
We can write this rule in symbols as

$$x \longrightarrow x + 3$$

We read this as

'x maps to $x + 3$'
or 'x goes to $x + 3$'

We say that '$x + 3$' is a **function of x**.

Discussion Exercise

1   Each function below is stated in words.
    Make an input-output table for each function.
    Find the outputs for the given inputs.
    Give the rule for each function in symbols.
    (a) Function: 'add 8'. Input: 0, 1, 2, 3, 4, x.
    (b) Function: 'subtract 2'. Input: 2, 5, 7, 0, 1, x.
    (c) Function: 'multiply by 4'. Input: 2, 0, 5, 3, 1, x.
    (d) Function: 'divide by 2'. Input: 4, 6, 0, 1, 2, x.
    (e) Function: 'double then add 3'. Input: 1, 5, 0, 4, 3, x.
    (f) Function: 'subtract from 8'. Input: 3, 0, 1, 2, −5, x.
    (g) Function: 'multiply by 3 then subtract from 10'.
        Input: 1, 0, 3 −1, −2, x.

2   The rules for these functions are given in symbols.
    Discuss what each means.
    Work out the outputs for the given input numbers.
    Make an input-output table in each case.
    (a) Function: $x \rightarrow x + 5$. Input: −2, −1, 0, 1, 2.
    (b) Function: $x \rightarrow x − 1$. Input: −3, −2, 1, 0, 1, 2.
    (c) Function: $x \rightarrow 3x$. Input: −1, 0, 1, 2, 3, 4.
    (d) Function: $x \rightarrow 7 − x$. Input: −2, −1, 0, 1, 2, 3.
    (e) Function: $x \rightarrow 2x − 1$. Input: −4, −2, −1, 0, 3.

You can often work out each output 'in your head'.
You can also use a calculator to help you.

For some functions you have to key in the instructions *step-by-step*.

For $x \rightarrow 1 − 2x$,
you key in | 1 | − | 2 | × | **input number** | = |

Some functions have a *single calculator key*.

For $x \rightarrow x^2$,
you simply key in | **input number** | x^2 |

Exercise P2.1

For each function below, find the outputs for the given *x* values.
Use your calculator to help you.

1   Function: $x \rightarrow 10 - x$. Input: 0, 1, 2, 3, 4, 5.
2   Function: $x \rightarrow 5x$. Input: −3, −2, −1, 0, 1, 2, 3.
3   Function: $x \rightarrow 3x + 2$. Input: −1, 0, 1, 2, 3, 4.
4   Function: $x \rightarrow 3 - 2x$. Input: −2, −1, 0, 1, 2.
5   Function: $x \rightarrow 5 - 3x$. Input: −3, −2, −1, 0, 1, 2.

Graphs of functions

You can write matching *input* and *output* numbers for a
function as **ordered pairs**.

Input	→ Output	Ordered pairs
x	→ *x* + 3	
0	→ 3	(0,3)
1	→ 4	(1,4)
2	→ 5	(2,5)
3	→ 6	(3,6)
4	→ 7	(4,7)

You can **plot these coordinates** as points on *x*- and *y*-axes.

These points for $x \rightarrow x + 3$
make a *pattern*.

They all lie on the *same
straight line*.

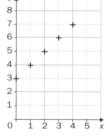

You can draw the line
through the points.

This line gives a *picture*
of the function.
It is called the **graph
of the function.**

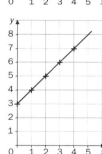

Each point on this line obeys the function rule

$$x \rightarrow x + 3$$

Each *x-coordinate* is an *input*.
Its matching *y-coordinate* is its *output x* + 3.
So at every point on the line $y = x + 3$.
We say the **equation of the line** is $y = x + 3$.
This equation shows **y is a function of x**.

Exercise P2.2

1   (a) For the function $x \rightarrow x + 3$ make an input-output table
        for these values of *x*:

        −5, −4, −3, −2, −1, 0, 1, 2, 3, 4, 5

(b) List the ordered pairs from
    the table.
(c) Draw *x*- and *y*-axes on
    squared paper.
    Number the *x*-axis
    from −5 to 5.
    Number the *y*-axis
    from −5 to 10.
    Use a scale of
    1 cm to 1 unit.
    Plot the points you have
    listed in (b).
    Draw a straight line that
    goes through all eleven
    points.
    Label the line with its equation,

    $$y = x + 3$$

(d) Write down the coordinates of five other points on this
    line.
    Check that each point obeys the function rule

    $$x \rightarrow x + 3$$

2   (a) For the function $x \rightarrow 2x + 1$, make an input-output table
        for these values of *x*:

        −3, −2, −1, 0, 1, 2, 3

(b) List the ordered pairs from your table.
(c) Draw *x*- and *y*-axes.
    Number the *x*-axis from −5 to 5.
    Number the *y*-axis from −10 to 12.
(d) Plot the points from part (b).
    Draw the graph of $y = 2x + 1$.
    Label the line with its equation.
(e) From your graph, find the values of *y* when:

    $$x = 4.5, \ x = 2.5, \ x = -1.5, \ x = -3.5$$

To draw the graph of a function, you may be given the
equation of the line.

Question

(a) Copy and complete
    this table of values
    for $y = 5 - x$.

x	−4	−2	0	2	4	5
y						

(b) Draw a graph of $y = 5 - x$ for values of *x* from −4 to 5.
(c) From your graph, find the value of *y* when $x = 3.5$, $x = -3$.
(d) From your graph, find the values of *x* when $y = 4.5$, $y = 6$.

Answer

(a) *Table of values:*

x	−4	−2	0	2	4	5
y	9	7	5	3	1	0

(b) *Plot points:*

(−4,9), (−2,7), (0,5), (2,3), (4,1), (5,0)

Draw line.

Label line with equation.

continued

Graph of $y = 5 - x$.

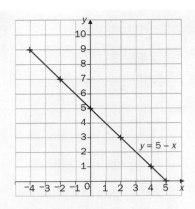

(c) *Find x-value.*
   Read off y-value.

   $x = 3.5 \rightarrow y = 1.5$
   $x = -3 \rightarrow y = 8$

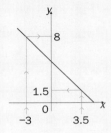

(d) *Find y-value.*
   Read off x-value.

   $y = 4.5 \rightarrow x = 0.5$
   $y = 6 \rightarrow x = -1$

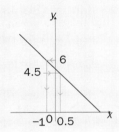

▶ *Exercise* P2.3

For each question in this exercise:
(a) Copy and complete this table of values for the given equation.

x	–4	–2	0	2	4	5
y						

(b) Draw a graph of the equation for values of x from –4 to 5.
(c) Use the graph to find the stated values.

1 Equation: $y = x + 4$
   (i) Find y when: $x = -3$, $x = 3.5$.
   (ii) Find x when: $y = 7$, $y = 4.5$.
2 Equation: $y = x - 3$
   (i) Find y when: $x = -2.5$, $x = 1.5$.
   (ii) Find x when: $y = -6$, $y = 0$.
3 Equation: $y = 1 - 2x$
   (i) Find y when: $x = 1$, $x = -2.5$.
   (ii) Find x when: $y = 6$, $y = -8$.
4 Equation: $y = 2x$
   (i) Find y when: $x = 4.5$, $x = -3.5$
   (ii) Find x when: $y = 6$, $y = -6$.
5 Equation: $y = 3x + 2$
   (i) Find y when: $x = 1$, $x = -3.5$.
   (ii) Find x when: $y = 0.5$, $y = -7$.

▶ *Exercise* P2.4

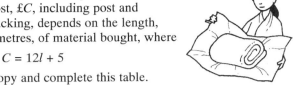

1 Mrs Patel buys material from a mail order company. The total cost, £C, including post and packing, depends on the length, l metres, of material bought, where

   $C = 12l + 5$

   Copy and complete this table.

l (metres)	1	2	3	4	5	
C (£)						

   Draw a graph of C against l on axes like these.
   (a) How much did it cost Mrs Patel when she bought $4\frac{1}{2}$ metres of material?
   (b) One week Mrs Patel paid £44 for material. How much did she buy?

2 When a stone is thrown down a well at 2 m/s, its speed, v m/s, at a time, t seconds, is given by the formula

   $v = 2 + 10t$

   Copy and complete this table.

t (s)	0	1	2	3	4
v(m/s)					

   Draw a graph of v against t on axes like these.
   (a) At what speed will the stone be travelling after $3\frac{1}{2}$ seconds?
   (b) For how long had the stone been travelling when its speed was 30 m/s?

3 The population, P, of a Pacific island, and the time, t years, since 1950 are connected by the formula

   $P = 2800 - 50t$

   Copy and complete this table.

t (years) since 1950	0	10	20	30	40
P (population)					

   Draw a graph of P against t on axes like these.
   (a) What was the population of the island in 1985?
   (b) In which year was the population of the island equal to half that in 1950?

4 The number of kilometres, K, approximately equal to the number of miles, M, is given by the formula

   $K = \frac{8}{5} M$

   Copy and complete this table.

M	0	10	20	30	40	50
K						

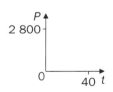

   Draw a graph of K against M on axes like these.
   (a) How many kilometres are equivalent to 35 miles?
   (b) Meika drove to a village 72 km from Amsterdam. How many miles is this?

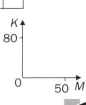

Curves

Not all functions have *straight line graphs*. Many are **curves**.

The graph of the function $x \rightarrow x^2$ is a *curve*.
Its equation is $y = x^2$.
To draw this graph, we take these steps:
- Make a table of *matching values* of x and y.

x	–3	–2	–1	0	1	2	3
y	9	4	1	0	1	4	9

We have used x-values from –3 to 3.
Each y-value is the *square* of its x-value, i.e. $y = x^2$.
Remember: when a negative number is squared, the result is
positive. For example, $(^-3)^2 = ^-3 \times ^-3 = ^+9$

- Write down the (x,y) coordinates from the table.
  $(-3,9)$, $(-2,4)$, $(-1,1)$, $(0,0)$, $(1,1)$, $(2,4)$, $(3,9)$.

- Draw x-and y-axes on
  squared paper.
  Label and number them.

- Plot the points with
  their coordinates taken from
  the table.
  These points do *not* lie on
  a straight line.

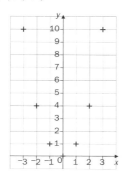

- Draw a smooth curve through
  the plotted points.
  Label the curve with
  its equation.

  The shape of this curve
  has a special name.
  It is called a **parabola**.

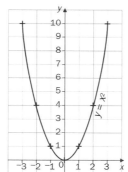

Drawing a smooth curve through a few points is not easy at first.
But, with practice, you should be able to do so.
   In the following Activity, you start by plotting lots of points
to draw the graph of $y = x^2$.
Then you try using fewer points to produce a reasonable curve.

ACTIVITY

Graph of $y = x^2$

Make a table of matching values
of x and y for $y = x^2$.

Take x values every 0.1 of a unit
from $^-3$ to 3.

Use the x^2 key on your calculator
to find each value of y.

 $\rightarrow y$

x	$\rightarrow$	x^2

x	y
–3	9
–2.9	8.41
–2.8	7.84
–2.7	7.29
⋮	
2.7	
2.8	
2.9	
3.0	

Now draw three diagrams showing the graph of $y = x^2$.
Follow the instructions for each diagram given below.

Graph 1.
- Draw x- and y-axes
  on 2 mm graph
  paper.
  Number the x-axis
  from –3 to 3.
  Number the y-axis
  from 0 to 9.
  Use the scale:
  2 cm = 1 unit.

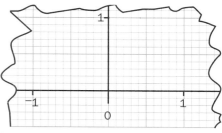

- Plot the sixty-one points from the table as accurately as
  you can.
- Draw a smooth curve through your points. Label it $y = x^2$.

Graph 2.
- Write down the ordered pairs from your table which have
  x values of:
     –3, –2.5, –2, –1.5 –1, –0.5, 0, 0.5, 1, 1.5, 2, 2.5, 3.
- Plot these coordinates on x- and y-axes. Use the same scale
  as before.
- Draw the graph of $y = x^2$ through these thirteen points.

Graph 3.
- Plot the points with x values –3, –2, –1, 0, 1, 2, 3.
  Use the same scale as before.
  Draw a smooth curve through these seven points.

 ### Discussion Exercise

- Describe the shape of the graph of $y = x^2$.
  What special features does it have?
  Does it have any symmetry?
  At what point on the graph is the y-value smallest?
  What happens to the curve at this point?
  Discuss the descriptions given by students in your group.
- Compare your three graphs of $y = x^2$ from the last Activity.
  The first drawing should give a good picture of the curve.
  How good are the other two?
  Try reading off y-values for x-values between –3 and 3.
  Check with your table.
  Where are they most inaccurate?
  Where was it most difficult to draw the curve?
  Where would it help to put in extra points?
  Discuss.

Summary

The graph of $y = x^2$ is a curve.
This curve is a special shape.
It is called a **parabola**.

This graph is symmetrical
about the y-axis.
It 'turns' at the origin, (0,0).
At this 'turning point',
y has its smallest or
minimum value.

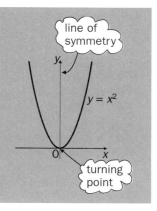

The graphs of other equations are also parabolas.
The next exercise gives you some practice in drawing some of them.
Here are some **hints to help you to draw curved graphs**.

- Do not try to use too few points.
  The *more points* you plot, the *easier it is to see* the shape of the graph. Using 'consecutive values of *x*' helps to show the pattern.

- Questions often give some *x*-values to use for points.
  Plot the points you get from these values first.
  Look at the 'shape' they show *before* trying to draw the curve through them.

- If any point you plot is obviously *not* on the 'curve' you expect, then *check it*. You may have made a mistake plotting the point or working out the value of *y*.

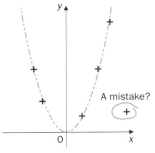

A mistake?

- If you are not sure what happens to the curve *in between two points*, plot an extra point to find out.

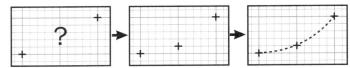

  You can plot as many extra points as you want.
  Remember: for each point, *choose a suitable x-value* and *work out the matching y-value*.

- Draw a *smooth curve* through your plotted points.

  Use a *sharp pencil*.
  Draw *lightly* at first.

  Work with your wrist 'inside' the curve.

  Turn your graph paper round if you need to.
  Try rotating the paper, using the heel of your hand as the pivot.

▶ *Exercise* P2.5

1 (a) Copy and complete this table of values for $y = \frac{1}{2}x^2$

x	−3	−2	−1	0	1	2	3
y							

   (b) Write down the (x,y) coordinates from the table.
   (c) Plot the points with these coordinates.
       Use a scale of 2 cm ≡ 1 unit.
   (d) Choose *x*-values for some extra points.
       Work out their *y*-values.
       Plot the points they give.
   (e) Draw a smooth curve through your points.
       Label it $y = \frac{1}{2}x^2$.

(f) From your graph, read off the *y*-values for these *x*-values:
   2.4, 1.7, 0.9, −2.9.
   Give each value to 1 decimal place.

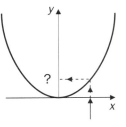

(g) From your graph, read off the *two x-values* for each of these *y*-values:
   4, 0.7, 1.8, 3.5.
   Give each value to 1 decimal place.

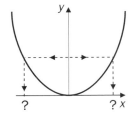

2

x	−2	−1	0	1	2	3	4
y							

(a) Copy and complete this table for each of the following equations.
   (i) $y = x^2 + 1$ (iii) $y = -x^2$
   (ii) $y = x^2 - 2$ (iv) $y = 10 - x^2$
(b) Draw the graph of each equation.
(c) From each graph, read off the *y*-values for *x* = 2.4 and *x* = −1.8.
   Give each value to 1 decimal place.
(d) From graphs (i) and (ii), read off the *x*-value(s) for *y* = 9.
(e) From graphs (iii) and (iv), read off the *x*-value(s) for *y* = −9.

3 The formula for the volume of this tank is

   $$V = 5l^2$$

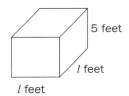

5 feet

l feet

l feet

(a) Copy and complete this table for $V = 5l^2$

l	0.25	0.5	0.75	1	1.25	1.5	1.75	2
V								

(b) Use this table of values to draw a graph of $V = 5l^2$.
   Use these scales:
   l-axis: 4 cm to 1 unit.
   V-axis: 1 cm to 1 unit.

(c) From your graph, find the volume of the tank when
   (i) *l* = 0.4   (ii) *l* = 1.6   (iii) *l* = 1.1
   Give each value correct to 1 dp.
(d) From your graph, find the value of *l* that gives
   (i) *V* = 3.2   (ii) *V* = 10   (iii) *V* = 17.5
   Give each value to 1 dp.

Examination Questions

1 $y = 10 + 3x$

   (i)   What is the value of y when $x = 10$?

   (ii)   Complete this table for values of x and y.

x		5	10
y	10		100

   (iii)   Use these values of x and y to draw the graph of
   $y = 10 + 3x$.
   (Number x-axis from 0–30. Scale: 5 cm to 10 units.
   Number y-axis from 0–100. Scale: 2 cm to 10 units.)

   (MEG, 1994)

2   I belong to a Bridge Club. The membership fee is £12 per year and every time I play bridge I pay £1.50.

   (a)   How much does it cost me altogether to play bridge
   (i)   10 times a year
   (ii)   40 times a year?

   (b)   Explain why the total cost £C of playing bridge n times per year is given by $C = 1.5n + 12$

   (c)   Draw the graph of $C = 1.5n + 12$.

   Non-members pay £3 every time they play bridge.

   (d)   On the same grid draw the graph of $C = 3n$.

   (e)   How many times a year can a non-member play bridge before it becomes cheaper to join the Bridge Club?

   (NEAB, 1991)

3   Below is a partly completed table for the function $y = 2x^2$.

x	–3	–2	–1	0	1	2	3
y		8		0		8	

   (a)   Complete the table by filling in the missing values of y.

   (b)   Plot these points and join them to form a smooth curve.

   (c)   Using the same axes draw the line $y = 10$.

   (d)   Write down the values of x where the line crosses the curve.

   (SEG, 1991)

4   A manufacturer has to make small rectangular tiles of different areas to cover various surfaces exactly.
   In each case, the length of the tile has to be three times the breadth.

   (a)   If the breadth of the tile is x cm, show that the area of the tile, A cm^2, is given by the expression $A = 3x^2$.

   The manufacturer makes out a table and draws a graph, to read off various sizes of tile.

x	0	0.5	1	1.5	2	2.5	3
$A = 3x^2$				6.75		18.75	

   (b)   Copy and complete the table above.

   (c)   Plot these values of x and A and complete the graph.

   (d)   From the graph, find
   (i)   the area of a tile of breadth 2.8 cm.
   (ii)   the breadth of a tile of area 11 cm^2.

   (NISEAC, 1988)

P3
More enlargement

This unit will help you to:

■   understand that a mathematical enlargement may make an object larger or smaller

■   recognise mathematical enlargements

■   know that a scale factor larger than 1 makes an object larger

■   understand that a scale factor which is a proper fraction makes an object smaller, i.e., it gives a reduction

■   draw reductions by using a grid and/or a centre of enlargement

■   find the scale factor and centre of enlargement for a reduction

■   use scale factors that are mixed numbers or improper fractions.

A change in size

Memo

In mathematics an **enlargement** *changes the size of* an object.
All the lengths change in the same way.
Angles and 'shape' stay the same.

Normally 'enlarging' means making something *larger*.

A 'model eye' is an enlargement of a real eye.

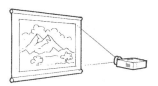

A projector enlarges the picture on a slide.

Changing the size of an object may make it *smaller*.

A scale model of a car
is the same shape as
the real car, but smaller.

This page has been
reduced on a
photocopier.

Making an object *smaller* in this way is often called a
reduction.
All its lengths are *reduced* in the same way.
Its angles and 'shape' *stay* the same.
A reduction of this kind fits the description of a mathematical
enlargement.
**In mathematics we use the word 'enlargement' for an
enlargement or a reduction.**

 ### Discussion Exercise

Consider the examples given below.
Which are *larger* than the original object?
Which are *smaller*?
Which are *mathematical enlargements*?
Discuss.

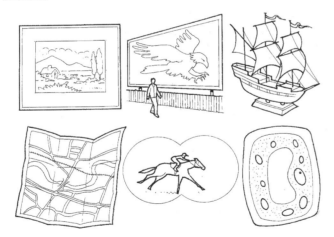

Suggest some other examples of mathematical enlargements
you see at home, in your work, outside school or college, …
Say whether they are smaller or larger than the original in
each case.
Discuss your ideas.

Looking at scale factors

 Memo

When an object is enlarged, each length is multiplied *by the
same number*.
This number is the **scale factor** of the enlargement.
Length on image = scale factor × length on object

Multiplying a length by a number larger than 1 makes it larger.
So using a *scale factor larger than* 1 must make an object *larger*.

In this diagram, for example,
the shaded object has been
enlarged by *scale factor 2*.
The *image is larger* than
the object.
Each length on the image is *twice*
(*2 times*) as long as the matching length
on the object.

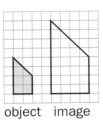

object   image

Multiplying a length by a proper fraction, such as $\frac{1}{2}$, 0.75, …
makes it smaller. So using a *scale factor that is a proper
fraction* must make an object *smaller*.
It gives a *reduction*.

In this diagram, for instance,
the shaded object has been
enlarged by a *scale factor of $\frac{1}{2}$.*
The *image is smaller* than the object.
Each length on the image is *half ($\frac{1}{2}$)*
of the matching length on the object.

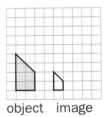

object   image

Summary

In mathematics an enlargement can make an object larger
or smaller.
Scale factor larger than 1 → image larger than object.
Scale factor a proper fraction → image smaller than object.

Drawing reductions

You have enlarged shapes by a
whole number scale factor. You
can use the same methods to draw
enlargements with other scale
factors.

Memo

Drawing enlargements
p 190

   To draw a reduction you use a scale factor that is a proper
fraction.
Each length on the image is this fraction of the matching
length on the object.

Length on image = fraction of length on object.

Memo

To find $\frac{1}{2}$ of something, divide it by 2.

To find $\frac{1}{3}$ of something, divide it by 3.

To find $\frac{1}{4}$ of something, divide it by 4.

To find $\frac{1}{5}$ of something, divide it by 5.

And so on.

To find $\frac{2}{3}$ of something, find $\frac{1}{3}$ of it then multiply by 2.

To find $\frac{3}{4}$ of something, find $\frac{1}{4}$ of it then multiply by 3.

And so on.

You can use a grid and/or a centre of enlargement to draw enlargements.

Using a grid

Memo

When you enlarge an object on a grid, use the grid lines to find lengths.
Count 'steps across' and/or 'steps up or down' to get the length of each line on the object.
Multiply these steps by the scale factor to draw the image.

Question

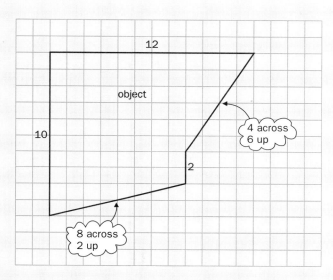

Enlarge the given shape by scale factor $\frac{1}{2}$ on the grid below.

Answer

Count 'steps' for each line on the object.
Write them down as a reminder.
Multiply each number of steps by $\frac{1}{2}$.
Draw the image with these reduced steps.

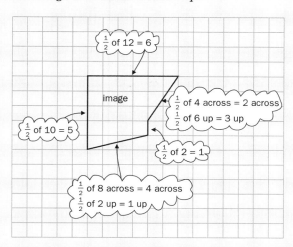

ACTIVITY

1 Copy this shape on to a $\frac{1}{2}$ cm square grid.

Draw enlargements of your diagram using these scale factors.

(a) $\frac{1}{2}$ (c) $\frac{1}{6}$ (e) $\frac{5}{6}$

(b) $\frac{1}{3}$ (d) $\frac{2}{3}$

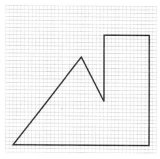

2 Copy this shape on to a $\frac{1}{2}$ cm square grid.

Enlarge your diagram by these scale factors.

(a) $\frac{1}{2}$ (c) $\frac{3}{4}$ (e) $\frac{7}{8}$

(b) $\frac{1}{4}$ (d) $\frac{3}{8}$

3 Draw a large shape on a square grid.
Try reducing it by different scale factors.
Design a pattern suitable for printing on paper, fabric, etc. based on your shape and its reductions.

Using a centre of enlargement

Memo

An enlargement may be described by a scale factor and centre of enlargement.
The *scale factor* makes the image the size we want.
The *centre* fixes where the image is drawn. This point may be outside, inside or on the edge of the object.

To draw an enlargement with a **centre of enlargement**, you can use the **ray method**.
Take these steps.

1 Draw straight lines (rays) from the centre through each main point on the object.

2 Find the distance from the centre to an object point along a ray.
Multiply this distance by the scale factor.
Measure the enlarged distance from the centre along the same ray.
Mark the image point.

A — object point
A' — image point
P — centre
$PA' = \text{fraction} \times PA$

3 Repeat step 2 for each object point.
Write down the distances if it helps.

4 Join the image points in the correct order to draw the image.

Question

On the answer sheet below, draw the image of triangle ABC after an enlargement with scale factor $\frac{1}{3}$ and centre P. Label the image A′B′C′.

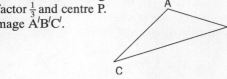

Answer

Draw 'rays' from P through points A, B and C.
Find and mark the position of the 'image points' on each ray.
Remember to measure from P each time.

On ray PA: PA = 6 cm
    PA′ = $\frac{1}{3}$ × PA = $\frac{1}{3}$ of 6 cm = 2 cm
On ray PB: PB = 7.5 cm
    PB′ = $\frac{1}{3}$ × PB = $\frac{1}{3}$ of 7.5 cm = 2.5 cm
On ray PC: PC = 4.5 cm
    PC′ = $\frac{1}{3}$ × PC = $\frac{1}{3}$ of 4.5 cm = 1.5 cm.

Join points to make image A′B′C′.

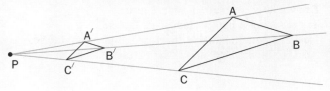

Discussion Exercise

In the enlargement shown above, the image is nearer to the centre than the object.

Why did this happen? Discuss.

In what kind of enlargements do you expect this will happen? Explain your answer.

► Exercise P3.1

1   Trace the diagram given below.
    Draw three enlargements of triangle DEF, each with scale factor $\frac{1}{2}$.
    (a) Use P as the centre of enlargement.
    (b) Use X as centre of enlargement.
    (c) Use D as centre of enlargement.
    Draw a separate diagram for each enlargement.

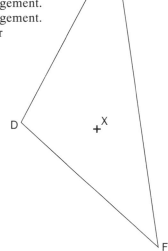

2   Make a full-size drawing of rectangle PQRS on plain paper. Draw two enlargements of your rectangle, each with scale factor $\frac{1}{3}$.
    (a) Use R as centre of enlargement.
    (b) Use C (the centre of the rectangle) as centre of enlargement.

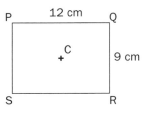

Enlargements by the ray method are often drawn on a grid. You can use the grid lines to help you to find distances from the centre of enlargement.

To draw the object you may be given the coordinates of its vertices (corner points) as in the next example.

Make sure you plot and label the points carefully. Label image points with matching letters as you find them.

Question

The vertices of a triangle are A(0,4), B(12,0), C(16,16). Plot these points and draw triangle ABC on the given axes. Draw two enlargements of triangle ABC, each using P(8,4) as centre of enlargement.
(a) Use scale factor $\frac{1}{4}$. Label the image $A_1B_1C_1$.
(b) Use scale factor $\frac{3}{4}$. Label the image $A_2B_2C_2$.
Write down the coordinates of the vertices of each image.

Answer

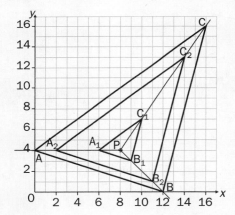

Object distances	Image distances	
	Scale factor $\frac{1}{4}$	Scale factor $\frac{3}{4}$
PA : 8 left	PA_1 : 2 left	PA_2 : 6 left
PB : 4 right 4 down	PB_1 : 1 right 1 down	PB_2 : 3 right 3 down
PC : 8 right 12 up	PC_1 : 2 right 3 up	PC_2 : 6 right 9 up

(a) A_1(6,4), B_1(9,3), C_1(10,7).
(b) A_2(2,4), B_2(11,1), C_2(14,13).

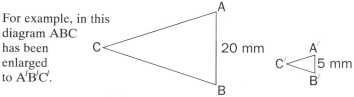

► *Exercise* P3.2

1 On separate diagrams, draw four enlargements of ABCD, each with scale factor $\frac{1}{2}$.
Use these centres of enlargement:
(a) P(10,1) (b) O(0,0)
(c) A(2,11) (d) X(6,7).
Give the coordinates of the vertices of each image.

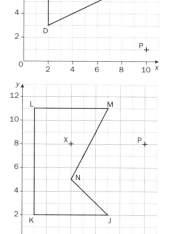

2 On separate diagrams, draw four enlargements of JKLMN, each with scale factor $\frac{1}{3}$.
Use these centres of enlargement:
(a) P(10,8) (b) K(1,2)
(c) X(4,8) (d) Q(13,11)
Give the coordinates of the vertices of each image.

3 Draw each of the following polygons on separate diagrams. Then enlarge each one using the given centre and scale factor. Give the coordinates of the vertices of each image.
(a) A(4,16) B(7,7) C(10,16)
   Centre: (1,1) Scale factor $\frac{1}{3}$.
(b) D(1,2) E(5,0) F(7,2) G(3,10)
   Centre: (9,8) Scale factor $\frac{1}{2}$.
(c) H(5,0) I(5,5) J(0,5) K(–5,0)
   Centre: (0,0) Scale factor $\frac{1}{5}$.
(d) L(4,0) M(4,4) N(0,4) P(0,8) Q(–4,8) R(–4,0)
   Centre: (0,–4) Scale factor $\frac{1}{4}$.
(e) S(–3,3) T(3,3) U(3,–3)
   Centre: (–9,–3) Scale factor $\frac{1}{6}$.

Finding a scale factor

Memo

In an enlargement, each length of an object is multiplied by the scale factor.
   Scale factor × length on object = length on image.
To find the scale factor of an enlargement, you can divide *any* length on the image by the matching length on the object.

$$\text{Scale factor} = \frac{\text{length on image}}{\text{matching length on object}}$$

The lengths must be in the same unit.
Use the two 'easiest' matching lengths if you can.
Check that your answer is *sensible* for the given image.

Image smaller than object
   → scale factor is a proper fraction.

For example, in this diagram ABC has been enlarged to A'B'C'.

Matching lengths A'B' on image and AB on object are easiest to measure.

$$\text{Scale factor} = \frac{\text{A'B'}}{\text{AB}} = \frac{5 \text{ mm}}{20 \text{ mm}} = \frac{1}{4}.$$

The image is smaller than the object, so the fraction $\frac{1}{4}$ makes sense for this scale factor.

Memo

You can also use distances from the centre of an enlargement to find the scale factor.

Scale factor = $\dfrac{\textbf{distance of an 'image point' from centre}}{\textbf{distance of matching 'object point' from centre}}$

On some diagrams, these distances are easier to find than matching lengths on the image and object.

For example, P is the centre of enlargement on this diagram.

Matching distances PA' and PA are easiest to find.

$$\text{Scale factor} = \frac{\text{PA'}}{\text{PA}} = \frac{6}{9} = \frac{2}{3}.$$

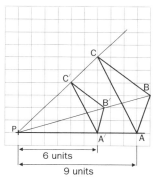

Finding a centre of enlargement

Memo

The centre of an enlargement and a matching object point and image point must lie on a straight line.

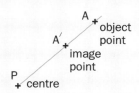

To find a centre of enlargement, draw straight lines through matching points on the object and image.
Make the lines long enough to cross.
The point where the lines cross is the centre of enlargement.

For example, for this enlargement, draw lines through
A and A',
B and B',
C and C',
D and D'.
They cross at P.
P is the centre of enlargement.

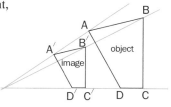

Exercise P3.3

1 In the diagram below, the green shape is an enlargement of the grey shape.
   Find:
   (a) the coordinates of the centre of enlargement
   (b) the scale factor of the enlargement.

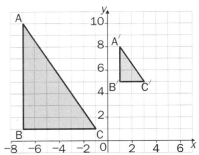

2 Plot the given points to draw each polygon and its image. Draw each pair of polygons on a separate diagram.
   Find the centre and scale factor of each enlargement.
   (a) A(9,3) B(9,7) C(3,5)
        $A'(5,2)$ $B'(5,4)$ $C'(2,3)$
   (b) D(5,1) E(9,5) F(5,9) G(1,5)
        $D'(2,1)$ $E'(3,2)$ $F'(2,3)$ $G'(1,2)$
   (c) H(8,8) I(20,8) J(20,11) K(17,11) L(14,17) M(8,17)
        $H'(4,4)$ $I'(8,4)$ $J'(8,5)$ $K'(7,5)$ $L'(6,7)$ $M'(4,7)$
   (d) N(3,0) P(3,3) Q(6,6) R(6,9) S(−6,9) T(−6,−6)
        U(−3,−6) V(−3,0)
        $N'(1,0)$ $P'(1,1)$ $Q'(2,2)$ $R'(2,3)$ $S'(−2,3)$ $T'(−2,−2)$
        $U'(−1,−2)$ $V'(−1,0)$
   (e) W(0,12) X(4,0) Y(−4,−4)
        $W'(0,6)$ $X'(1,3)$ $Y'(−1,2)$

Other scale factors

A scale factor need not be a *whole number* or *proper fraction*. It may be a *mixed number*, such as $1\frac{1}{2}$ or 1.5 or an *improper fraction*, such as $\frac{3}{2}$.

Any scale factor greater than 1 makes a shape larger.

   scale factor greater than 1 → image larger than object.

Here is an example.

Enlargement with scale factor $1\frac{1}{2}$, centre P.
ABCD is the object.
$A'B'C'D'$ is the image.

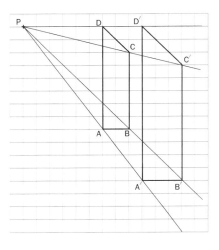

Each length on the image is $1\frac{1}{2}$ times the matching length on the object.

| $A'B' = 1\frac{1}{2} \times AB$ | $B'C' = 1\frac{1}{2} \times BC$ |
| $C'D' = 1\frac{1}{2} \times CD$ | $D'A' = 1\frac{1}{2} \times DA$ |

The distance from the centre P to a point on the image is $1\frac{1}{2}$ times the distance from P to the matching point on the object.

| $PA' = 1\frac{1}{2} \times PA$ | $PB' = 1\frac{1}{2} \times PB$ |
| $PC' = 1\frac{1}{2} \times PC$ | $PD' = 1\frac{1}{2} \times PD$ |

Check these matching lengths and distances yourself.

Exercise P3.4

1 On separate diagrams, draw four enlargements of ABCDEFG, each with scale factor $1\frac{1}{4}$.
   Use these centres of enlargement:
   (a) P(4,4)   (b) O(0,0)   (c) A(8,8)   (d) E(10,20).
   Give the coordinates of the vertices of each image.

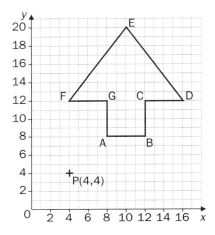

2 Repeat Question **1** of Exercise P3.2 p 251 but this time use a scale factor $1\frac{1}{2}$.
3 Repeat Question **2** of Exercise P3.2 p 251 but this time use a scale factor $1\frac{1}{3}$.
4 Repeat Question **3** of Exercise P3.2 p 251 but this time use these scale factors
   (a) $1\frac{1}{3}$ (b) $1\frac{1}{2}$ (c) $1\frac{1}{5}$ (d) $1\frac{1}{4}$ (e) $1\frac{1}{6}$.
5 In this diagram the green shape is an enlargement of the grey shape.
   Find
   (a) the coordinates of the centre of enlargement
   (b) the scale factor of the enlargement.

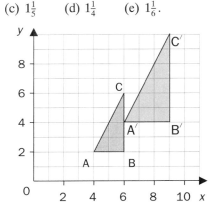

6 Plot the given points to draw each polygon and its image.
Draw each pair of polygons on a separate diagram.
Find the centre and scale factor of each enlargement.
   (a) A(2,5) B(4,5) C(6,3) D(4,3)
        A′(2,11) B′(7,11) C′(12,6) D′(7,6)
   (b) E(2,5) F(5,8) G(8,8) H(11,5)
        E′(1,6) F′(5,10) G′(8,10) H′(13,6)
   (c) I(2,8) J(6,4) K(−2,−4) L(−6,0)
        I′(2,9) J′(7,4) K′(−3,−6) L′(−8,−1)
   (d) M(2,3) N(6,1) P(6,5) Q(4,3)
        M′(2,5) N′(8,2) P′(8,8) Q′(5,5)

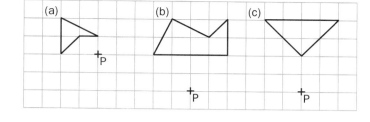

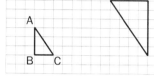

👁 *Investigation*

Upside-down enlargements

The larger triangle is an enlargement of triangle ABC. But it is upside-down.

1 Copy this diagram on to ½ cm squared paper.
Compare the sides of triangle ABC and the enlargement.
How many times longer are the sides of the enlargement?
Which sides of the larger triangle match AB, BC and CA?
Which points on the larger triangle match A, B and C?
Label them A′, B′ and C′ on your diagram.
Draw a straight line through each pair of matching points on your diagram.
The point where they cross is the centre of enlargement.
Label this point P.
Where is P in relation to the two triangles?
Compare the distances
   PA and PA′
   PB and PB′
   PC and PC′.
What do you notice about their sizes and direction?

*Remember:
You can use 'steps' on the grid instead of measuring lengths.*

      We usually use negative signs to show measuring in an opposite direction.
Suggest a scale factor for this enlargement.
2 Copy triangle ABC and point P on to another diagram.
Draw three upside-down enlargements of ABC with centre P.
Make lines ½ as long, 1½ times as long, 3 times as long.
Suggest a scale factor for each enlargement.
3 Draw these upside-down enlargements of triangle ABC on separate diagrams.
   (a) Centre A, sides 2 times as long.
   (b) Centre B, sides 3 times as long.
   (c) Centre C, sides 2½ times as long.
Suggest a scale factor for each enlargement.
4 Draw upside-down enlargements for each of these shapes.
Use point P as centre of enlargement in each case.
Make sides 2 times as long.

5 Draw these enlargements of triangle XYZ on separate diagrams.
   (a) Centre P, scale factor −2,
   (b) Centre X, scale factor −½,
   (c) Centre Y, scale factor −½,
   (d) Centre Z, scale factor −2,
   (e) Centre O, scale factor −3.

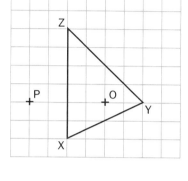

6 Draw these enlargements of rectangle DEFG on separate diagrams.
   (a) Centre O, scale factor −2,
   (b) Centre E, scale factor −½,
   (c) Centre G, scale factor −2 ½,
   (d) Centre P, scale factor −3,
   (e) Centre X, scale factor −1½.

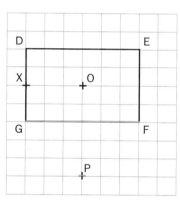

👁

Examination Questions

1

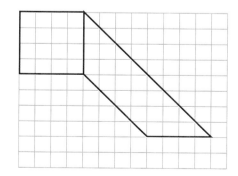

On a grid draw a reduction of this shape. Use a scale factor of ¼.

(MEG, 1988)

2 Emma has started to enlarge the shape ABC …
She has labelled the part she has enlarged A'B'C' …
(a) What scale factor is she using?
(b) Copy the diagram and complete the enlargement using that scale factor.

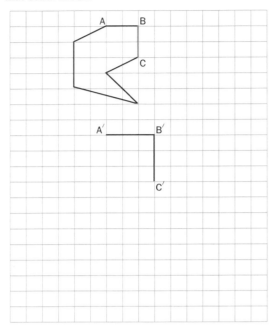

(MEG, 1989)

3 An irregular pentagon has vertices (–8,8), (–6,2), (–6,–4), (–12,–4) and (–12,2).
Plot the points and draw the pentagon. Also draw its enlargement by a scale factor of $\frac{3}{2}$ using the origin as the centre of enlargement.

(NICCEA, 1989)

4 Triangle B is an enlargement of triangle A.

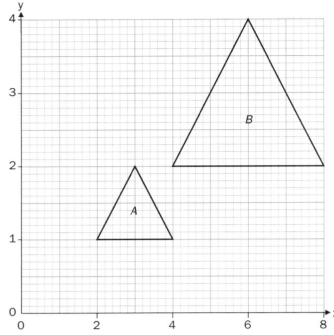

(a) State the coordinates of the centre of enlargement.
(b) Calculate the scale factor of enlargement.
(c) On graph paper enlarge triangle A by a scale factor of $\frac{1}{2}$, using the point (0,1) as the centre of enlargement.

(SEG, 1989)

5 Ultra-micro cameras can reduce lengths using a scale factor of $\frac{1}{150}$. What size would a single page of this book appear in a picture taken by such a camera? Give your answer in millimetres correct to 1 decimal place.

(MEG, 1989)

▷ P4

Sequences and *n*th terms

This unit will help you to:

■ understand that an expression for the *n*th term gives a 'rule' for a sequence

■ find the value of a term in a sequence given its *n*th term

■ find a number's position in a sequence given an expression for the *n*th term of the sequence

■ use notation, such as u_n, for the *n*th term of a sequence

■ find an expression for the *n*th term of a sequence from its first few terms.

Patterns in order

Look at this number pattern

1st line:	$1^2 - 1 = (1 + 1)(1 - 1)$
2nd line:	$2^2 - 1 = (2 + 1)(2 - 1)$
3rd line:	$3^2 - 1 = (3 + 1)(3 - 1)$

You can easily write down its next few lines:

4th line:	$4^2 - 1 = (4 + 1)(4 - 1)$
5th line:	$5^2 - 1 = (5 + 1)(5 - 1)$
6th line:	$6^2 - 1 = (6 + 1)(6 - 1)$

The 10th line is easy to write too …

10th line: $10^2 - 1 = (10 + 1)(10 - 1)$

And the 100th line …

100th line: $100^2 - 1 = (100 + 1)(100 - 1)$

and any other line …
The pattern goes on *forever* in the same way.

You can write a **general rule** to give the pattern.

Compare the 'line number' and the number in the pattern on that line.

  1st line: $1^2 - 1 = (1 + 1)(1 - 1)$
  2nd line: $2^2 - 1 = (2 + 1)(2 - 1)$
  3rd line: $3^2 - 1 = (3 + 1)(3 - 1)$

and so on…

In each case, you find the numbers are:

  (line number)^2 – 1 = (line number + 1)(line number – 1)

This gives a rule for the pattern.

If you use *n* for the line number, then the rule is:

  *n*th line: $n^2 - 1 = (n + 1)(n - 1)$.

It is always a good idea to **test** a rule to check it works. Try putting different numbers instead of the letter. Then make sure you get the result you expect each time.

If *n* = 5, the rule gives:

  5th line: $5^2 - 1 = (5 + 1)(5 - 1)$ ✓

If *n* = 10, the rule gives:

  10th line: $10^2 - 1 = (10 + 1)(10 - 1)$ ✓

▶ *Exercise* **P4.1**

For each number pattern
(i)   write down the next three lines
(ii) write down the 10th and 100th lines
(iii) give a general rule for the pattern for any line number *n*.

1   1st line: $1^2 + 1 = 1(1 + 1)$
     2nd line: $2^2 + 2 = 2(2 + 1)$
     3rd line: $3^2 + 3 = 3(3 + 1)$

2   1st line: $1^2 - 1 = 1(1 - 1)$
     2nd line: $2^2 - 2 = 2(2 - 1)$
     3rd line: $3^2 - 3 = 3(3 - 1)$

3   1st line: $2 \times 1^2 + 1 = 1(2 \times 1 + 1)$
     2nd line: $2 \times 2^2 + 2 = 2(2 \times 2 + 1)$
     3rd line: $2 \times 3^2 + 3 = 3(2 \times 3 + 1)$

4   1st line: $3 \times 1^2 - 1 = 1(3 \times 1 - 1)$
     2nd line: $3 \times 2^2 - 2 = 2(3 \times 2 - 1)$
     3rd line: $3 \times 3^2 - 3 = 3(3 \times 3 - 1)$

5   1st line: $2 \times 1^2 + 1 - 1 = (2 \times 1 - 1)(1 + 1)$
     2nd line: $2 \times 2^2 + 2 - 1 = (2 \times 2 - 1)(2 + 1)$
     3rd line: $2 \times 3^2 + 3 - 1 = (2 \times 3 - 1)(3 + 1)$

◀

Numbers in order

A list of numbers in a *definite order* is a **sequence**.
Each number in the sequence is called a **term.**

  The terms in a number sequence often fit a *pattern*. Knowing this pattern means you can **generate** (make) the sequence.
  The pattern for many sequences can be given as a rule for going from one term to another.

Here is a rule for generating a sequence:

  Start at 2.
  Add 2 to the last number to get the next.

It 'makes' this sequence …

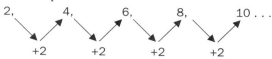

This rule is easy to use. But it has disadvantages.
Imagine you want the 100th term of this sequence.

  To find the 100th term, you have to know the 99th.
  To find the 99th term, you have to know the 98th.
  To find the 98th term, you have to know the 97th.
  And so on …

To find each term of the sequence, you have to know the term *before* it.

So to find the 100th term with this rule, you have to find 100 terms. This would take some time! (Try it if you like).

  A **rule** that links each term to its 'place' in the order would be more useful.

2, 4, 6, 8, … is a well known number sequence.
They are the even numbers.
There is a simple link between each even number and its 'place' in the sequence.

1st term: 2   → '1 pair' or 2×1

2nd term: 4   → '2 pairs' or 2×2

3rd term: 6   → '3 pairs' or 2×3

4th term: 8   → '4 pairs' or 2×4

and so on…

Each number is $2 \times$ its 'place number'.
So the *n*th even number = $2 \times n = 2n$.
The expression $2n$ gives a **rule for the *n*th term** in the sequence.

It gives it in terms of *n*.
We can use this rule to find any even number from its 'place' in the sequence.

  25th even number = $2 \times 25 = 50$
  100th even number = $2 \times 100 = 200$
  112th even number = $2 \times 112 = 224$ and so on …

Summary

The **general term** in a sequence is usually called its '*n*th term'. It is the number in the *n*th place in the order.
You can work out the numbers in a sequence from its '*n*th term rule'.
This *rule gives the link* between each term and its place in the order.
To list the first few terms …
  put *n* = 1 to get the 1st term,
  put *n* = 2 to get the 2nd term,
  put *n* = 3 to get the 3rd term,   and so on …

continued

To find a term in a particular 'place' …
   put n = 'place number' you want.
For example,
   put $n = 15$, to find the 15th term,
   put $n = 100$, to find the 100th term, and so on …

Question

Sequence A: nth term $2n + 5$
Sequence B: nth term $n^2 - 1$
Write down the first four terms and the 20th term of
sequences A and B. Show your working clearly.

Answer

A: nth term: $2n + 5$
   Put $n = 1 \rightarrow 2 \times 1 + 5 = 2 + 5 = 7$
   Put $n = 2 \rightarrow 2 \times 2 + 5 = 4 + 5 = 9$
   Put $n = 3 \rightarrow 2 \times 3 + 5 = 6 + 5 = 11$
   Put $n = 4 \rightarrow 2 \times 4 + 5 = 8 + 5 = 13$
   Put $n = 20 \rightarrow 2 \times 20 + 5 = 40 + 5 = 45$

B: nth term: $n^2 - 1$
   Put $n = 1 \rightarrow 1^2 - 1 = 1 - 1 = 0$
   Put $n = 2 \rightarrow 2^2 - 1 = 4 - 1 = 3$
   Put $n = 3 \rightarrow 3^2 - 1 = 9 - 1 = 8$
   Put $n = 4 \rightarrow 4^2 - 1 = 16 - 1 = 15$
   Put $n = 20 \rightarrow 20^2 - 1 = 400 - 1 = 399$

▶ *Exercise* **P4.2**

1 Here are the nth terms of some sequences.
   (a) $n + 1$ (b) $n - 1$ (c) $2n + 5$
   (d) $3n - 1$ (e) $2 - 3n$ (f) $6n - 5$
   (g) $\dfrac{n}{2}$ (h) $\dfrac{n + 1}{3}$ (i) $\dfrac{5}{n}$
   (j) $\dfrac{n}{2}(n + 1)$ (k) $(2n - 1)(n + 3)$ (l) $\dfrac{6}{n(n + 2)}$
   Write down the first five terms and the 20th term of
   each sequence.

2 (a) nth term: $2n + 1$
       Find the first three terms and the 25th term.
   (b) nth term: $7n + 3$
       Find the first four terms and the 12th term.
   (c) nth term: $9 - 5n$
       Find the first five terms and the 10th term.
   (d) nth term: $n(5 - n)$
       Find the first four terms and the 26th term.
   (e) nth term: $(n + 1)(3n - 1)$
       Find the first three terms and the 9th term.
   (f) nth term: $\dfrac{n(n - 1)}{2}$
       Find the first six terms and the 50th term.
   (g) nth term: $\dfrac{2n(3n + 1)}{3}$
       Find the first three terms and the 15th term.

If you know a *number* in a sequence *and the rule* for its nth
term, you can **work out its place** in the sequence.
Put the expression for the nth term equal to the number.
Then solve the equation you get to find the value of n.
You can use any method to solve
the equation. In the next example
we use the balance method.

Memo
Solving equations
p 103

Question

64 is a term in a sequence where the nth term is $5n + 4$.
Find its position in the sequence.

Answer

Put nth term equal to 64	$5n + 4 = 64$
Subtract 4 from both sides	$\dfrac{-4 = -4}{5n \quad = 60}$
Divide both sides by 5	$n \quad = 60 \div 5$
	$= 12$

So 64 is the 12th term in the sequence.

Check: Put $n = 12$ in $5n + 4$
               $= 5 \times 12 + 4 = 60 + 4 = 64$ ✓

▶ *Exercise* **P4.3**

1 The nth term of a sequence is $6n - 7$.
   Find the position of 53 in this sequence.
2 36 is a term of the sequence whose nth term is $3n + 12$.
   Which term is it?
3 -42 is a term in a sequence whose nth term is $8 - 5n$.
   Find its position in the sequence.
4 Which term of the sequence with nth term $7n + 3$ is the
   number 164?
5 Which term of the sequence with nth term $\dfrac{3}{2}(4n - 5)$ is
   equal to 28.5?

Sequence notation

A special shorthand is sometimes used for the terms in a
sequence.
The sequence is given a letter.
Then each term can be 'named' using this letter and a number.
When we use the letter u for a sequence,

   its 1st term is called u_1,
   its 2nd term is called u_2,
   its 3rd term is called u_3,
   its 4th term is called u_4,
   and so on …

The 'place number' of each term is written as a small number.
It is put after the letter and just below it. (A number written in
this way is called a **suffix**.)

In general, the *n*th term is called u_n.
The value of *n* tells you the position of the term in the sequence.
For example,

u_{10} means the 10th term,
u_{21} means the 21st term,
u_{100} means the 100th term.

The rule for the *n*th term of the sequence may be given as a formula:

$$u_n = \ldots$$

For example, if we use the letter *u* for this sequence:

2, 4, 6, 8, 10, …

we have $u_1 = 2$, $u_2 = 4$, $u_3 = 6$, $u_4 = 8$, $u_5 = 10$, …
This is the sequence of even numbers.
So the rule for its *n*th term is 2*n*.
We can write this as the formula:

$$u_n = 2n.$$

Question

$u_n = 6n - 7$ is the formula for the *n*th term of a sequence.
(a) Write down the first four terms of the sequence.
(b) Find the value of u_{25}. Which term is this?
(c) If $u_n = 53$, find the value of *n*.
What does this tell you about the number 53?

Answer

(a) *u_1, u_2, u_3, u_4 stand for the first four terms.*
Put n = 1, n = 2, n = 3, n = 4 in the formula $u_n = 6n - 7$
to find them.
$u_n = 6n - 7$
$u_1 = 6 \times 1 - 7 = 6 - 7 = -1$
$u_2 = 6 \times 2 - 7 = 12 - 7 = 5$
$u_3 = 6 \times 3 - 7 = 18 - 7 = 11$
$u_4 = 6 \times 4 - 7 = 24 - 7 = 17$
The first four terms are −1, 5, 11, 17.

(b) *To find u_{25}, put n = 25 in $u_n = 6n - 7$.*
$u_{25} = 6 \times 25 - 7 = 150 - 7 = 143$
$u_{25} = 143$ is the 25th term in the sequence.

(c) *Put $u_n = 53$ in $u_n = 6n - 7$*
To find n, solve the equation you get.
Here is the working using the balance method.

Formula	u_n	= 6*n*	− 7
Put u_n = 53	53	= 6*n*	− 7
Add 7 to both sides	+7		+7
	60	= 6*n*	
Divide both sides by 6	10	= *n*	

So *n* = 10.
This gives $u_{10} = 53$.
So 53 is the 10th term in the sequence.

In this book we usually use *u* for a sequence. Sometimes other letters, such as *T, t, s*, are used instead.
Using these letters, T_n, t_n and s_n all stand for the *n*th term.

▶ *Exercise* **P4.4**

1 $u_n = 2n + 3$ is the *n*th term of a sequence. Use it to find:
(a) the 12th term
(b) the fifth term
(c) u_{15}.
2 $u_n = -3n$ is the *n*th term of a sequence. Use it to find:
(a) u_7
(b) the eighth term
(c) the 20th term.
3 $u_n = 7 - 5n$ is the *n*th term of a sequence. Use it to find:
(a) the 9th term
(b) u_{30}
(c) the sixteenth term.
4 $u_n = 3n^2 - 4$ is the *n*th term of a sequence. Use it to find:
(a) the seventh term
(b) the 10th term
(c) u_{13}.
5 $u_n = 5n^2 - 4n + 3$ is the *n*th term of a sequence.
Use it to find:
(a) u_6
(b) the eleventh term
(c) the 17th term.

◯ Discussion Exercise

Exploring rules and sequences
3*n* is the *n*th term of a sequence.

1st term	2nd term	3rd term	4th term
$3 \times 1 = 3$	$3 \times 2 = 6$	$3 \times 3 = 9$	$3 \times 4 = 12$

Its first four terms are 3, 6, 9, 12, …

You can use the *rule* to continue the sequence:

5th term	6th term	7th term
$3 \times 5 = 15$	$3 \times 6 = 18$	$3 \times 7 = 21$

Or you can use the '*difference method*':

Terms: 3,   6,   9,   12,   15,   18,   21 . .

Differences: +3   +3   +3   +3   +3   +3
The terms go 'up' in 3s. The difference in each case is +3.
Compare this number with the rule for the *n*th term.
What do you notice?

• Copy and complete this table.

Rule for *n*th term	First four terms				Difference between terms
	1st	2nd	3rd	4th	
3*n* 3*n* + 1	3	6	9	12	+3
2*n* 2*n* + 1					
−3*n* −3*n* + 1					
−2*n* −2*n* + 1					

Compare the 'rule' and 'difference between terms' for each sequence. Discuss what you find.

Compare the rules and terms for each pair of sequences in your table.
Look for a pattern.
Discuss what it shows.

- Here are the rules for some other sequences.
  Find the first four terms of each sequence.
  Work out the difference between terms in each case.
  Put your results in a table as before.
  Look for patterns and relationships in them.
  Discuss your findings.

$$10n$$
$$10n + 1$$
$$10n + 7$$
$$10n - 1$$
$$10n - 12$$

- Look at these rules for nth terms:

$$\boxed{3n - 1} \quad \boxed{2n + 5} \quad \boxed{-3n + 2} \quad \boxed{-2n - 4}$$
$$\boxed{4n} \quad \boxed{4n + 3} \quad \boxed{5n} \quad \boxed{5n - 2} \quad \boxed{-6n} \quad \boxed{-6n + 1}$$

Without actually finding its terms, say what you know about each sequence. List as many facts about it as you can.
Discuss the ideas of the students in your group. Find out how they made each prediction.
Write down the first five terms of each sequence.
Check your group's predictions.
Which ideas were correct?
Discuss what they tell you.

- Discuss how looking at differences between terms can help you to find the nth term of a sequence.
  Use your method to find the rule for some sequences of your own.
  Discuss how you worked out each rule.
  Test your rules to make sure they work.

Finding the *n*th term

You may need to find the rule for the nth term of a sequence from a list of its first few terms.
Some sequences with special names have simple nth terms.
Here are some you have met.

Counting numbers: 1, 2, 3, 4, 5,…, **n**
Even numbers: 2, 4, 6, 8, 10, … , **2n**
Other multiples,
such as multiples of 3: 3, 6, 9, 12, 15, …, **3n**
      multiples of 5: 5, 10, 15, 20, 25, …, **5n**
      multiples of 10: 10, 20, 30, 40, 50, …, **10n**
Square numbers: 1, 4, 9, 16, 25, … **n²** n^2
Cube numbers: 1, 8, 27, 64, 125, …, **n³** n^3

It is useful to be able to recognise these. But don't worry if you can't. You can always work out their nth terms if you need to.
   The nth term of a sequence gives you the *link* between each term and its place value.
Always look for a simple link first.
Here are some hints to help you spot it.

- Write each term *under* its place number.
  This makes them easier to compare.
  Place number: 1   2   3   4 …
  Given terms: ?   ?   ?   ?

- *Compare* each term with its place number.
  See if 'doing the same thing' to each place number gives its term. Look for a pattern.

Look for simple links such as:

   given term = place number + 'something'
   given term = place number − 'something'
   given term = 'something' − place number
   given term = 'something' × place number
   given term = place number ÷ 'something'
   and so on …

- Work out any link you find *'in words'* first.
  Replace 'place number' in your link by the letter n.
  Then write the rule in terms of n:
             nth term = …

- Always *test* the nth term you find.
  Put $n = 1, 2, 3, …$ in turn. Check you get the given terms.
  Work out the next few terms from the 'pattern' of the sequence and from your nth term.
  Check that both ways give the same values.
  If they don't, look for a mistake in your working.

Question

Find an expression for the nth term of each of these sequences.
Write each nth term as $u_n = …$
(a) 6, 7, 8, 9, …
(b) 1, 0, −1, −2, …
(c) 9, 18, 27, 36, …

Answer

(a) Place number: 1   2   3   4
    Given terms: 6   7   8   9

Look for
the pattern: $\boxed{1 + 5} \quad \boxed{2 + 5} \quad \boxed{3 + 5} \quad \boxed{4 + 5}$

In each case,
   given term = its place number + 5
For the nth term, this is n + 5.
So $u_n = n + 5$.
Check: Continue the sequence:

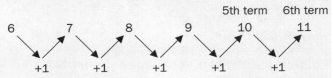

5th term is 10. $u_5 = 5 + 5 = 10$ ✓
6th term is 11. $u_6 = 6 + 5 = 11$ ✓

(b) Place number: 1   2   3   4
    Given terms: 1   0   −1   −2

Look for
the pattern: $\boxed{2 - 1} \quad \boxed{2 - 2} \quad \boxed{2 - 3} \quad \boxed{2 - 4}$

In each case,
   given term = 2 − its place number
For the nth term, this is 2 − n.
So $u_n = 2 - n$

Check: Continue the sequence:

5th term is –3. $u_5 = 2 - 5 = -3$ ✓
6th term is –4. $u_6 = 2 - 6 = -4$ ✓

(c) Place number: 1   2   3   4
     Given terms: 9   18 27 36

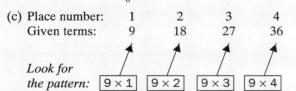

Look for the pattern: $\boxed{9 \times 1}$ $\boxed{9 \times 2}$ $\boxed{9 \times 3}$ $\boxed{9 \times 4}$

In each case,
    given term = 9 × its place number.
For the *n*th term, this is $9 \times n = 9n$
So $u_n = 9n$.

Check: Continue the sequence.

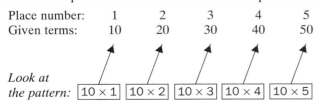

5th term is 45. $u_5 = 9 \times 5 = 45$ ✓
6th term is 54. $u_6 = 9 \times 6 = 54$ ✓

► *Exercise* P4.5

Find an expression for the *n*th term of each of these sequences.
1 3, 4, 5, 6, 7, …
2 4, 8, 12, 16, 20, …
3 1, 4, 9, 16, 25, …
4 –1, –2, –3, –4, –5, …
5 –5, –4, –3, –2, –1, …
6 9, 8, 7, 6, 5, …
7 –2, –1, 0, 1, 2, …
8 0.1, 0.2, 0.3, 0.4, 0.5, …
9 –3, –6, –9, –12, –15, …
10 $\frac{1}{2}$, 1, $1\frac{1}{2}$, 2, $2\frac{1}{2}$, … ◄

Looking at differences

In some sequences the link between each term and its place number is not obvious. You have to look for more clues to help you to find it.
    To continue a sequence we often look at the **differences** between terms. This difference method can also help us to find some rules for *n*th terms.
Here is a sequence you have met before:

    10, 20, 30, 40, 50, …

There is a simple link between each term and its place number.

Place number: 1   2   3   4   5
Given terms: 10 20 30 40 50

Look at the pattern: $\boxed{10 \times 1}$ $\boxed{10 \times 2}$ $\boxed{10 \times 3}$ $\boxed{10 \times 4}$ $\boxed{10 \times 5}$

In each case, given term = 10 × its place number.
So the rule for its *n*th term is 10*n*.

Looking at differences also shows a pattern.

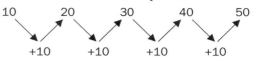

The difference between terms is always 10.
So there is an obvious connection between this number (10) and its *n*th term (10*n*).

    *n*th term = difference × *n*

'Exploring rules and sequences' on p. 257 investigates this relationship.
Look at your results from this activity to remind yourself about it.

Any sequence that goes up in equal steps of 10 also has 10*n* in its *n*th term.
Here is such a sequence:

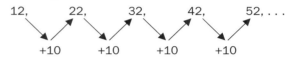

Its *n*th term contains 10*n*.
To find the rest of the *n*th term, we compare each term in this sequence with the terms of 10*n*.

Place number: 1   2   3   4   5
Terms of 10*n*: 10 20 30 40 50
Given terms: 12 22 32 42 52

Look at the pattern: $\boxed{10 + 2}$ $\boxed{20 + 2}$ $\boxed{30 + 2}$ $\boxed{40 + 2}$ $\boxed{50 + 2}$

You can see in each case that:
    given term = matching term of 10*n* + 2
So the rule for the *n*th term for this sequence is 10*n* + 2.
Check this also works for the next few terms.

☊ *Discussion Exercise*

● Find the rule for the *n*th term of each of these sequences. In each case, the rule contains 10*n*.

    7,   17,   27,   37,   47, …
    19,   29,   39,   49,   59, …
    60,   70,   80,   90,   100, …
    –15,   –5,   5,   15,   25, …

Discuss how you found the rest of the *n*th term for each sequence.
Continue each pattern by using differences.
Check your rule works in each case.

● Each of these sequences goes down in equal steps of 2. So the difference between terms is –2.

    –2,   –4,   –6,   –8,   –10, …
    8,   6,   4,   2,   0, …
    –3,   –5,   –7,   –9,   –11, …

Discuss how to find the *n*th term of each of these sequences. Test the *n*th rule you find in each case.

Summary

Some sequences are made by adding or subtracting the same number each time. The difference between each term and the next gives this number.

The nth term of such a sequence involves $\boxed{\text{difference}} \times n$

When terms go up in size, the difference is positive.
For example: 1, 5, 9, 13, ... goes up by 4 each time.
Its nth term contains $4n$.
It is $4n - 3$.

When terms go down in size, the difference is negative.
For example: 46, 42, 38, 34, ... goes down by 4 each time.
The nth term contains $-4n$.
It is $50 - 4n$.

To find the nth term of such sequences, take these steps.

- Work out the differences between terms.
  Make sure they are the same each time.

- Make a table to show:
  Place number ...
  Terms from rule (difference $\times n$) ...
  Given terms ...

  Write each term under its place number

- Compare terms in each place. Look for the pattern.
  You should find in each case:
  given term = 'other term' + something
  or given term = 'other term' − something

- Work out what the link is in words first.
  Then use it to write the nth term in terms of n.

- Test your rule to check it works.

Exercise P4.6

1 For each sequence below:
  (i) Write down the next three terms.
     Show how you worked them out.
  (ii) Find a rule for the nth term in terms of n.
     Check your rule with the three terms you have found.
     (a) 4, 8, 12, 16, ...   (d) 7, 12, 17, 22, ...
     (b) 1, 3, 5, 7, ...   (e) 3, 0, −3, −6, ...
     (c) 1, −1, −3, −5, ...

2 Find the nth term for each of these sequences.
  Write each rule as $u_n = ...$
     (a) 1, 6, 11, 16, ...   (d) 0, −1, −2, −3, ...
     (b) 3, 1, −1, −3, ...   (e) −5, −3, −1, 1, ...
     (c) 8, 14, 20, 26, ...

3 A sequence starts at 6 and each term is found by adding 3 to the previous term. Find an expression for the nth term.

4 A sequence starts with 4 and each term is found by subtracting 6 from the previous term. Find an expression for the nth term.

Fractions

The numbers in a sequence may be fractions.
To find the nth term of such a sequence, treat it as two separate sequences.

  Look at the top numbers (numerators) on their own. Find the nth term of this sequence.

Look at the bottom numbers (denominators) on their own. Find the nth term of this sequence.

Put the two nth terms together ... $\dfrac{\text{top number}}{\text{bottom number}}$

Question

Find the rule for the nth term of this sequence:

$$\frac{2}{1}, \frac{3}{4}, \frac{4}{9}, \frac{5}{16}, \cdots$$

Answer

- *Look at the sequence of top numbers.*

Place (n):	1	2	3	4
Top numbers:	2	3	4	5
Look for the pattern:	$1 + 1$	$2 + 1$	$3 + 1$	$4 + 1$

The nth term of the top numbers is $n + 1$.

- *Look at the sequence of bottom numbers.*

Place (n):	1	2	3	4
Bottom numbers:	1	4	9	16
Look for the pattern:	1^2	2^2	3^2	4^2

The nth term of the bottom numbers is n^2.

- *Put the nth terms together:* $\dfrac{\text{top number}}{\text{bottom number}}$

The nth term of the sequence is $\dfrac{n + 1}{n^2}$

Exercise P4.7

For each sequence, work out:
(a) the next two terms   (b) the rule for the nth term.

1 $\dfrac{1}{2}, \dfrac{1}{4}, \dfrac{1}{6}, \dfrac{1}{8}, \cdots$

2 $\dfrac{1}{2}, \dfrac{2}{3}, \dfrac{3}{4}, \dfrac{4}{5}, \cdots$

3 $\dfrac{3}{5}, \dfrac{4}{6}, \dfrac{5}{7}, \dfrac{6}{8}, \cdots$

4 $\dfrac{1}{5}, \dfrac{3}{10}, \dfrac{5}{15}, \dfrac{7}{20}, \cdots$

5 $\dfrac{1}{3}, \dfrac{4}{5}, \dfrac{9}{7}, \dfrac{16}{9}, \cdots$

6 $0, \dfrac{1}{2}, \dfrac{2}{3}, \dfrac{3}{4}, \cdots$

7 $\dfrac{2}{5}, \dfrac{4}{7}, \dfrac{8}{9}, \dfrac{16}{11}, \cdots$

8 $\dfrac{1}{7}, \dfrac{3}{14}, \dfrac{5}{21}, \dfrac{7}{28}, \cdots$

Discussion Exercise

Look at this fraction sequence:

$$\frac{1}{1}, \frac{3}{4}, \frac{2}{3}, \frac{5}{8}, \frac{3}{5}, \cdots$$

The top numbers and bottom numbers do not seem to form a sequence.
Discuss possible rules for its nth term.
Find the nth terms of each of these sequences.

1 $\dfrac{2}{3}, \dfrac{4}{9}, \dfrac{1}{2}, \dfrac{8}{15}, \dfrac{5}{9}, \cdots$

2 $1, \dfrac{2}{3}, \dfrac{1}{2}, \dfrac{2}{5}, \cdots$

3 $2, 1\dfrac{1}{2}, 1\dfrac{1}{3}, 1\dfrac{1}{4}, 1\dfrac{1}{5}, \cdots$

4 $1\dfrac{1}{2}, 1, \dfrac{3}{4}, \dfrac{3}{5}, \dfrac{1}{2}, \cdots$

5 $1, \dfrac{4}{5}, \dfrac{11}{15}, \dfrac{7}{10}, \dfrac{17}{25}, \cdots$

6 $\dfrac{1}{4}, \dfrac{1}{2}, \dfrac{9}{16}, \dfrac{4}{5}, \dfrac{25}{64}, \cdots$

Looking at second differences

This is a well known sequence:

1, 4, 9, 16, 25, ...

These numbers are the **square numbers**.
The rule for the nth term of this sequence is n^2.

1st term	2nd term	3rd term	4th term	5th term
$1^2 = 1$	$2^2 = 4$	$3^2 = 9$	$4^2 = 16$	$5^2 = 25$

Look at the table of differences for this sequence:

Terms:

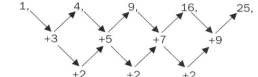

1st differences:

2nd differences:

The **1st differences** are not all the same.
But they do form a pattern: 3, 5, 7, 9,...
The **2nd differences** are all the same.
They are all +2.

 Discussion Exercise

- These nth terms of sequences involve n^2:

$$\boxed{n^2 + 1} \quad \boxed{n^2 - 1} \quad \boxed{n^2 + 10} \quad \boxed{n^2 - 5}$$

Find the first five terms of each sequence.
Write down tables of 1st and 2nd differences for these terms.
What do you find?
What happens in the table of 1st and 2nd differences if ...

the nth term is $n^2 + n$?
the nth term is $n^2 - n$?
the nth term is $n^2 + n + 1$?
the nth term is $n^2 - n - 1$?
and so on ...

Discuss your results.

- These nth terms of sequences also involve n^2:

$$\boxed{-n^2} \quad \boxed{2n^2} \quad \boxed{\tfrac{1}{2}n^2} \quad \boxed{-2n^2} \quad \boxed{-\tfrac{1}{2}n^2}$$

Investigate what their tables of 1st and 2nd differences show.
What happens if the nth term involves other terms such
as n, $2n$, $-n$, $+1$, $+2$,...?
Discuss your findings.

- Discuss how you can use a table of 1st and 2nd differences
to help you to find the nth term of a sequence.
Test your ideas on some sequences such as these:

5, 8, 13, 20, 29, ...
5, 20, 45, 80, 125, ...
0, 2, 6, 12, 20, ...
1, 7, 17, 31, 49, ...

See if you can predict a rule for each.
Discuss your ideas with the rest of your group.

Summary

The nth term of a sequence may involve n^2.

To spot such a sequence,
write out a difference table.

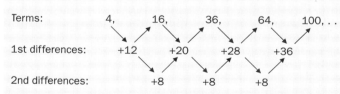

Terms:	
1st differences:	
2nd differences:	

When the 2nd differences are all the same, the nth term
involves n^2.

2nd differences all 2 $\rightarrow n^2$ in rule
2nd differences all 1 $\rightarrow \tfrac{1}{2}n^2$ in rule
2nd differences all 4 $\rightarrow 2n^2$ in rule
2nd differences all 6 $\rightarrow 3n^2$ in rule
and so on ...

Here are some hints to help you to find the rest of the rule.

- Write down the first few terms of the n^2 rule you have
found from the difference table.

- Compare these terms and the given terms.
Write each term under its place number to help you to
do this. Look for the pattern.
You should find:

given term = other term + something
or given term = other term – something

The 'something' may be the *same number* in each case, or
it may be a *number sequence*.
Work out the rest of the rule from the numbers.

- Test your rule with some values of n.
Check it gives the correct term each time.

Question

Find the rule for the nth term of the following sequence.
In each case the rule contains a power of n.
(a) 4, 16, 36, 64, 100, ...
(b) –1, 2, 7, 14, 23, ...
(c) 3, 10, 21, 36, 55, ...

Answer

(a) *Difference table:*

Terms:

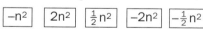

1st differences:

2nd differences:

The 2nd differences are all +8.
So the sequence is based on $4n^2$

Terms of n^2: 1 4 9 16 25
Terms of $4n^2$: 4 16 36 64 100

This is the given sequence.
So its nth term is $4n^2$.

continued

(b) *Difference table:*

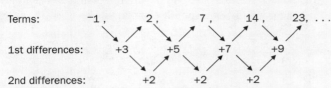

The 2nd differences are all +2.
So the sequence is based on n^2.
Compare terms of n^2 and the given sequence:

Place number:	1	2	3	4	5
Terms of n^2:	1	4	9	16	25
Given terms:	−1	2	7	14	23

*Look for
the Pattern:* | 1 − 2 | | 4 − 2 | | 9 − 2 | | 16 − 2 | | 25 − 2 |

In each case:

given term = | matching term of n^2 | − 2

So the rule for the *n*th term is $n^2 - 2$

(c) Difference table:

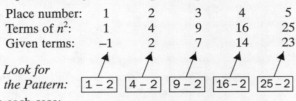

The 2nd differences are all +4
So the sequence is based on $2n^2$.
Compare terms of $2n^2$ and the given sequence:

Place number:	1	2	3	4	5
Terms of $2n^2$:	2	8	18	32	50
Given terms:	3	10	21	36	55

*Look for
the pattern:* | 2 + 1 | | 8 + 2 | | 18 + 3 | | 32 + 4 | | 50 + 5 |

The numbers added to the $2n^2$ terms are 1, 2, 3, 4, 5.
These are the 'place numbers'.
In each case:

given number =

| matching term of $2n^2$ | + | place number |

So the rule for the *n*th term is $2n^2 + n$.

► *Exercise* **P4.8**

Find the *n*th term of each of these sequences.
Write each rule as $u_n = \ldots$

1   2, 5, 10, 17, …
2   1, 7, 17, 31, …
3   −2, 1, 6, 13, …
4   −3, 0, 5, 12, …
5   2, 6, 12, 20, …

6   0, 2, 6, 12, …
7   3, 12, 27, 48, …
8   7, 13, 23, 37, …
9   5, 35, 85, 155, …
10 3, 15, 35, 63, …

Problem solving and investigations

You may obtain a **sequence of numbers** from an investigation,
a problem, a project, a practical situation, an exam question, …
    By finding a **pattern** in the sequence, you can work out *other*
terms in it. Then you can use these to **predict** other results in
the original situations.
    One way to do this is to find a **rule for the *n*th term** of the
sequence. This can be used to give any term you want in the
sequence. It will also give the position in the sequence of any
'result' you have.

► *Exercise* **P4.9**

1   The diagrams below show the first three 'dot patterns' in
    two sequences.
    Sequence 1:

    Sequence 2:

    For each sequence:
    (a) Draw the fourth pattern.
    (b) Calculate the number of dots in
        (i)   the fourth pattern
        (ii) the tenth pattern
        (iii) the *n*th pattern.

2   The diagrams below show the first three 'cube patterns' in
    some sequences.
    Sequence 1:   Sequence 2:

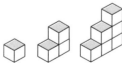

    For each sequence calculate the number of cubes in
    (a) the fourth pattern
    (b) the fifth pattern
    (c) the twelfth pattern
    (d) the *n*th pattern.

3   Sue uses small green and white tiles to make these shapes.
    They form part of a sequence.
    (a) How many white tiles
        are needed to make   1st   2nd   3rd
        (i)   the fourth shape   shape   shape   shape
        (ii) the fifth shape
        (iii) the fifteenth
              shape
        (iv) the *n*th shape?

(b) Scot has 120 white tiles. Sue uses all Scot's tiles to make another shape in the sequence. Which shape is this?

4 The diagram shows a sequence of shapes made from equilateral triangles. Each triangle is made from matchsticks.

(a) Copy and complete the following table:

Number of triangles	1	2	3	4	5	10
Number of matchsticks used						

(b) Find a formula giving the number of matchsticks used to make a shape with n triangles.
(c) How many triangles can you make using 751 matchsticks?
(d) If you had 840 matchsticks to make triangles and shapes like these, explain whether you would use them all or whether you would have some left over.

5 Greensleeves Garden Centre delivered 40 young apple trees to Sally Swire's allotment. Sally carried them, one at a time, from the delivery point to the holes she had already dug to plant them.

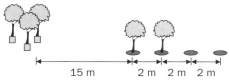

15 m   2 m   2 m   2 m

The first hole is 15 m from the delivery point and the other holes are at 2 m intervals along the same straight line.
(a) How far does Sally have to walk from the delivery point and back when she plants
  (i) the first tree   (iv) the tenth tree
  (ii) the second tree   (v) the fortieth tree
  (iii) the third tree   (vi) the nth tree?
(b) Which tree did Sally plant when she walked from the delivery point back to that point and covered a distance of
  (i) 110 metres   (ii) 158 metres?
(c) Explain why Sally never walks an even number of metres from the delivery point to any hole she dug.

6 Roger and Don started a part-time business together. The business made a loss of £2300 during the first year, £1400 during the second year and £500 during the third year. Roger and Don continued to improve the performance of the business at the same rate for the next twenty years.
(a) During which year did the business first make a profit?
(b) What profit did the business make during the
  (i) 10th year   (iii) 20th year
  (ii) 15th year   (iv) nth year ($n \leq 20$)?

7 The temperature in the lowest reaches of the Earth's atmosphere decreases by about 1.7°C for each 1000 feet of altitude. One day, climbers at their base camp on Everest recorded the temperature at 8°C.
(a) What temperature will the climbers record when they have climbed
  (i) 1000 ft   (iii) 5000 ft
  (ii) 2000 ft   (iv) 20 000 ft

  (v) 29 000 ft   (vi) n thousand feet ($n \leq 29$)?
(b) How far above base camp were the climbers when they recorded the atmospheric temperature as
  (i) −17.5°C   (ii) −29.4°C?

8 A car accelerates from rest at a French motorway service station. The distance it travels, in metres, during each of the first four seconds of its journey is shown in this table.

Time (s)	1	2	3	4
Distance (m)	2	3	5	8

Assuming that the car continues to accelerate in the same way:
(a) How far would you expect the car to travel in the fifth and sixth seconds?
(b) Work out a rule to give the distance travelled by the car in the nth second.
(c) During a particular second the car travelled 38 m. At the end of this second, for how long had it been travelling since it left the service station?

9 In the contract for Samantha Greig's new job her salary in the first year is given as £7500. The contract also states that her salary will be increased by £800 each year.
(a) What is Samantha's salary in her
  (i) third year at work
  (ii) seventh year at work
  (iii) nth year at work?
(b) In which year was Samantha's salary equal to £17 100?

👁 *Investigation*

Each year, the St. Nicholas College Reunion Society meet for their annual dinner. At the end of the evening, every member at the dinner shakes hands once and only once with every other member there.

  Investigate the number of handshakes made when different numbers of members attend the dinner. 👁

Examination Questions

1 Carol and Javed did an investigation together, in which they had to count the number of intersections in a series of diagrams. They got these results:

  3, 8, 15, 24

Their teacher asked them, for homework, to see if they could find a pattern in their results. The next day the pupils returned with this:

Carol   Javed

diagram	number	pattern
1	3	1×3
2	8	2×4
3	15	3×5
4	24	4×6
5		

diagram	number	pattern
1	3	$1^2 + 2 \times 1$
2	8	$2^2 + 2 \times 2$
3	15	$3^2 + 2 \times 3$
4	24	$4^2 + 2 \times 4$
5		

(a) Their teacher asked each pupil to continue their pattern for diagram 5. Write down what you would expect them to write in their tables.

(b) Their teacher then asked each pupil to write down a formula for the number of intersections in diagram *n*. Write down the two formulas that the pupils would have given.

(c) Show that these two formulas are equivalent to one another.

(MEG, 1988)

2 A pattern of blocks is laid out as follows.

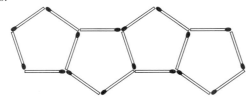

1st row	....	1 block
2nd row	....	4 blocks
3rd row	....	7 blocks
4th row	....	10 blocks

(a) How many blocks will there be on the 5th row?
(b) How many blocks will there be on the *n*th row?
(c) Which row has 28 blocks on it?

(NEAB, 1989)

3 Alison is making a chain of pentagons from matches, like this:

(a) How many matches will she need to make a chain of 6 pentagons?
(b) Explain how you can work out how many matches are needed to make a chain of *n* pentagons. (You may wish to give your answer as a formula.)

(NEAB, 1990)

4 Darren is laying tiles. He notices that, if he lays one red tile, he needs 8 white tiles to surround it completely. If he lays 2 red tiles end to end, he needs 10 white tiles to surround them. (See the diagram below.)

(a) How many white tiles will Darren need to surround
   (i) 4 red tiles end to end
   (ii) 7 red tiles end to end?
(b) Darren has 100 white tiles. How many red tiles laid end to end can be surrounded by these 100 white tiles?
(c) Darren has *m* red tiles. How many white tiles will he need to complete a similar pattern?

(NEAB, 1991)

5 A firm used a simple formula to calculate the redundancy money to be paid to its employees. The following redundancy payments were made.

Name	Number of years worked (N)	Redundancy money (£R)
Joseph	1	£700
Michael	2	£900
Paul	3	£1100
Neil	4	
John	5	£1500
Alison	9	£2300
James	10	£2500
Brian	35	

(a) Write down how much redundancy money Neil would receive, having worked at the firm for 4 years.
(b) Write down the formula connecting the amount of redundancy money, £R, and N, the number of years worked.
(c) Calculate how much redundancy money Brian would receive, having worked at the firm for 35 years.

(NEAB, 1990)

6 A computer has been programmed to generate a sequence of numbers. The first six numbers that it produces are

9, 16, 23, 30, 37, 44.

(a) Write down the next two numbers of the sequence that will appear.
(b) Work out the 60th number to appear.
(c) Write down an expression for the *r*th term of the sequence.
(d) How many terms of the sequence will the computer have produced when the first number over 2000 appears?

(NEAB, 1988)

7 (a) The first five terms of a sequence are

$T_1 = 1, T_2 = 3, T_3 = 6, T_4 = 10, T_5 = 15.$

Write down T_6, T_7, T_8, T_9.

(b) (i) Work out

$T_1 + T_2, T_2 + T_3, T_3 + T_4.$

(ii) Describe the pattern of your answers to (b) (i) and investigate whether it continues for $T_4 + T_5$.

(c) (i) Work out $T_1^2 + T_2^2, T_2^2 + T_3^2$.
   (ii) Compare your answers to (c) (i) with the sequence in (a). What can you say about $T_3^2 + T_4^2$?

(MEG, 1990)

P5
Scatter graphs

This unit will help you to:

■ draw scatter graphs from data
■ understand the idea of correlation
■ describe correlation shown on a scatter graph
■ draw line of 'best fit' on a scatter graph
■ use your line of best fit to estimate values.

Drawing scatter graphs

Dan looks at weather reports from seaside resorts for a project.
This table comes from Saturday's paper.

BRITISH READINGS AROUND THE COAST			
	Temperature °C	Sunshine hours	Rainfall mm
Tynemouth	8	6.0	1
Skegness	5	3.5	3
Eastbourne	7	4.7	1
Cromer	6	3.7	6
Lowestoft	8	4.6	9
Margate	7	3.1	14
Folkestone	8	5.9	0
Bognor	7	5.1	2
Ryde	7	3.5	11
Ventnor	4	2.5	19
Weymouth	8	5.3	7
Penzance	6	2.9	8
Newquay	5	2.1	11
Hunstanton	4	1.9	16
Anglesey	5	1.9	18

Dan thinks there should be a link between temperature and sunshine.
He cannot tell if this is true by simply looking at the figures.
He draws a graph to give a picture of the temperature and sunshine data. It is shown in the next column.
Look carefully at the graph.

The label on the horizontal axis is 'Temperature (in °C)'
The label on the vertical axis is 'Sunshine (in hours)'.
Each point plotted on the graph shows the temperature and sunshine for a resort in the table.
Here are some examples:

Point T (8,6.0) is for Tynemouth.
It shows a temperature of 8°C and sunshine of 6.0 hours.

Point S (5,3.5) is for Skegness.
It shows a temperature of 5°C and sunshine of 3.5 hours.

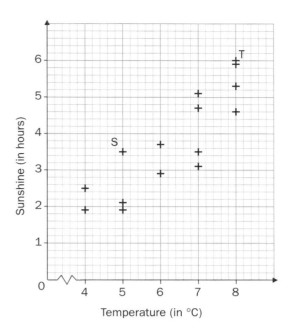

This type of graph is called a **scatter graph**.
The plotted points are *scattered* across the graph.
Scatter graphs are also called **scatter diagrams** and **scattergrams.**

Discussion Exercise

1 (a) Look at the temperature and sunshine for each resort in the table. List the coordinates they give for Dan's scatter graph.
(b) Look at Dan's scatter graph.
What does the ⌇ mean on the temperature axis?
Look at the scale on each axis.
What does each 'small space' stand for in each case?
(c) Draw Dan's scatter graph on 2 mm graph paper.
Use the given scales.
Label each point on your graph with the first letter of the resort's name.
(d) Dan says his graph shows:
'Towns that have higher temperatures get more sunshine.'
Do you agree?
Discuss.

2 (a) Draw a scatter graph of sunshine against rainfall for Dan's data.
(b) Look at the picture of these data given by your graph.
Does it suggest any link between these two variables?
If so, what do you think it is?
Discuss.

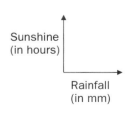

3 Draw a scatter graph of temperature against rainfall for Dan's data.
Discuss what the picture shows about these two variables.

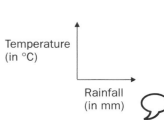

Summary

A **scatter graph** gives a picture of *two variables at the same time*. We use it to see if there is a **relationship** between two sets of data.
A scatter graph has two axes, one for each variable.
Each *ordered pair of values* in the data is plotted as a *point* on the graph.

Exercise P5.1

1   The table below lists the marks obtained by ten students in tests in science and mathematics;

Student	A	B	C	D	E	F	G	H	I	J
Science	50	43	56	57	68	66	65	70	62	71
Mathematics	61	57	56	58	52	49	48	45	52	44

(a) Do you think that the students who did well in science also did well in mathematics?

(b) Draw a scatter graph to show the data in the table. Use 2 mm graph paper and the scales shown on these axes.

(c) Does the picture shown by your scatter graph support your prediction in (a)? Explain your answer.

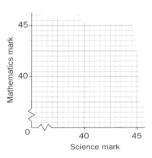

2   A technician investigated the purity of water supplied by the local Water Board over a 10-day period. The table opposite shows the levels of alkalinity and hardness, each measured in milligrams per litre (mg/ℓ).

Alkalinity (mg/ℓ)	Hardness (mg/ℓ)
33.9	51.1
29.2	45.1
22.9	41.4
26.3	46.1
31.9	48.1
32.0	50.1
29.5	46.4
26.2	45.1
28.1	45.4
27.3	43.1

(a) The technician thinks that the more alkaline the water, the harder it will be. What do you think?

(b) Draw a scatter graph to show the data in the technician's table. Use 2 mm graph paper and the scales shown on these axes.

(c) Does your scatter graph show what you expected? Comment on any relationship it suggests.

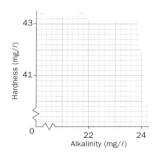

3   Ten contestants in a Masterbrain competition answered questions on both general and specialised knowledge. Their scores are shown in the table in the next column.

Contestant	RT	BM	AP	PM	CL	DJ	PS	GT	JF	AM
General knowledge	18	28	38	14	21	36	15	17	24	38
Specialised knowledge	29	38	32	16	33	42	41	28	20	23

(a) Do you think that contestants who did well in specialised knowledge also did well in general knowledge?

(b) Draw a scatter graph to show the data in the table. Use 2 mm graph paper and the scales shown on these axes.

(c) Does the picture shown by your scatter graph support your answer to (a)? Is there evidence to suggest a relationship between the two variables? If so, what is it?

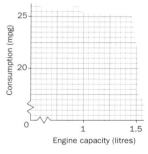

4   The table below gives the engine capacity in litres for various second-hand cars. It also gives the fuel consumption in miles per gallon (mpg) for the same steady speed of 30 mph.

Car	Engine capacity (litres)	Consumption (mpg)
Montego 1.3L	1.3	48.3
Montego 2.0L	2.0	40.4
Mercedes 500SE	5.0	21.0
Mercedes 420SE	4.2	21.7
Mercedes 300SE	3.0	27.2
Granada 2.9L	2.9	29.8
Rover 825i	2.5	29.5
Sierra 1.8L	1.8	37.9
Maestro 1.6L	1.6	43.3
Mini City	1.0	50.5

(a) Do you think there is a relationship between a car's engine capacity and fuel consumption? If you do, say what it might be.

(b) Draw a scatter graph to show the data in the table. Use 2 mm graph paper and the scales shown on these axes.

(c) What relationship, if any, does your scatter graph show? Were your ideas in (a) correct?

5   The table at the top of the next column shows the latitude and mean temperature for 15 towns last year.

(a) Each town's latitude is a measure of how far north of the equator it is.
Would you expect there to be a relationship between latitude and mean temperature?
Would you expect places with greater latitudes to have higher mean temperatures?

Town	Latitude	Mean temperature (°C)
A	60	4
B	53	10
C	52	11.5
D	44	12
E	60	6
F	45	12.5
G	50	9
H	60	4.5
I	39	17
J	56	8
K	40	16.5
L	53	8.5
M	49	11.5
N	52	11
O	42	18.5

(b) Draw a scatter graph to show the latitude and mean temperature for these 15 towns. Use 2 mm graph paper and the scales shown on these axes.

(c) Does your scatter graph suggest there is a relationship between the two variables? Comment on what it shows. Were your predictions correct?

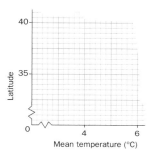

Repeated points

Jenny is a keen tennis player. She likes to serve lots of aces. Her teacher wants her to serve fewer double faults.

Jenny thinks there is this link between the two. Her teacher does not agree.

Jenny collects some data to try to support her idea.

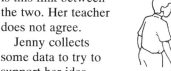

PLAYERS WHO SERVE MORE ACES, SERVE FEWER DOUBLE FAULTS

These results come from that day's matches.

	Aces	Double faults
Zara	2	2
Joan	2	5
Susan	2	5
Tracy	2	5
Helen	2	5
Parveen	3	8
Wendy	4	7
Ann	1	3

	Aces	Double faults
Betty	2	4
Sheila	0	0
Julie	4	7
Chris	3	8
Dot	4	9
Ellen	5	10
Judy	0	1
Fay	4	7

Jenny draws and labels axes like these.

But there is a problem.

Four players (Joan, Susan, Tracey and Helen) each have 2 aces and 5 double faults.

She cannot plot four points for these data on her axes. She can plot only one point.

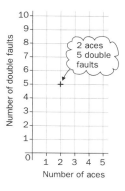

Jenny's data are numbers not measurements. To show these data, she can draw and label axes like these.

On these axes, *numbers are put in 'spaces' not on lines.*

So Jenny can plot four points for these data.

Each pair of numbers is marked as a point in a square. The point can be put anywhere in the square.

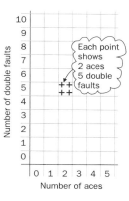

► *Exercise* P5.2

Use 1 cm or 2 cm graph paper for the graphs in these questions. Do *not* use 1mm or 2mm or 5mm graph paper.

1 Draw a scatter graph of Jenny's data. Do you think it supports her idea? Does it show that players who serve more aces, serve fewer double faults? Describe what you think it shows.

2 Steve thinks there is a link between the number of goals scored by the home team and the away team in soccer matches.

These results come from 40 games played in the Football League on one Saturday.

(Note: the home team's goals are always given first.)

0 – 0	2 – 1	1 – 0	4 – 2	2 – 1	2 – 2	3 – 0	3 – 3
0 – 3	4 – 3	3 – 2	3 – 3	1 – 0	3 – 1	1 – 3	2 – 4
0 – 2	3 – 0	1 – 1	1 – 3	3 – 3	2 – 0	1 – 1	3 – 0
0 – 4	3 – 4	2 – 1	1 – 0	3 – 2	0 – 2	1 – 0	3 – 2
1 – 0	4 – 1	0 – 3	2 – 1	0 – 3	2 – 0	4 – 3	4 – 0

(a) Draw and label axes like these. Draw a scatter graph of these football results on your axes.

(b) Describe what your graph shows. Do you think Steve is correct?

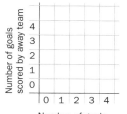

3   An external examiner grades students' work in two
practical tests.
The grades given to each student are listed below.
The first letter is the grade for Test 1.
The second letter is the grade for Test 2.

BD	CC	DA	BC	BE	BD	DB
DC	CB	DB	CD	CC	CB	CC
CC	AD	CB	BD	DC	DB	EB
EB	BD	DB	.EB	DA	EA	BC
BC	DB	CD	CC	DC	BD	DB

(a) Would you expect a student who does well in Test 1
to do well in Test 2?

(b) Draw a scatter graph
for these data. Use axes
like these.

(c) Comment on what
your graph shows.
Does it confirm what
you said in (a)?

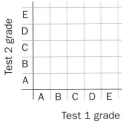

Test 2 grade

A B C D E
Test 1 grade

4   Aziz did a probability experiment
with black and green dice.
He threw the two dice 72 times.
His results are given below.
The first number is the score from
the black dice.
The second number is the score from the green dice.

4,1	1,1	6,2	6,6	3,1	5,1	3,6	4,1
2,6	2,5	1,6	3,5	5,5	3,2	1,4	5,5
2,1	1,3	3,2	5,3	3,2	5,3	4,2	1,6
3,5	2,1	3,6	1,5	3,3	2,5	5,6	4,3
6,5	5,1	4,5	5,4	4,1	6,6	5,4	3,4
2,3	3,4	6,2	3,4	5,1	3,1	5,4	2,3
3,3	1,3	4,4	1,5	2,2	5,1	3,6	2,6
1,1	6,3	3,1	1,1	5,3	6,2	6,5	6,1
6,2	2,2	2,2	5,6	4,1	1,4	5,3	5,2

(a) Would you expect there to be a relationship between the
scores on the two dice?
Explain your answer.

(b) Draw a scatter graph to
show Aziz's data.
Use axes like these.

(c) What does your graph
show? Does it support
your answer to (a)?

Score on green dice

6
5
4
3
2
1

1 2 3 4 5 6
Score on black dice

Correlation

Dan's weather report on page 265 gives three scatter graphs.
They are shown at the top of the next column.
Each graph helps us to see the relationship, if any, between two
variables.
We use the word **'correlation'** to describe the *relationship
between variables.*

Dan's Sunshine/Temperature graph shows **positive correlation.**

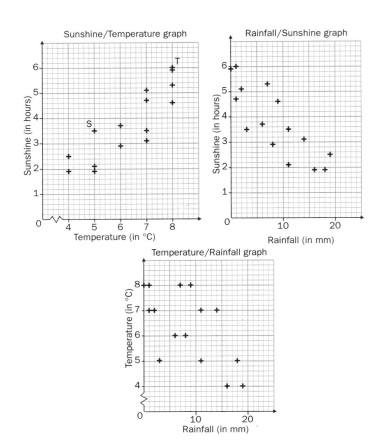

His Sunshine/Rainfall graph shows **negative correlation.**
His Temperature/Rainfall graph show **no correlation.**

Discussion Exercise

1   The sentences below are about the scatter graphs
drawn from Dan's weather data.
The missing words are:

  'sunshine', 'temperature', 'rainfall',
  'positive', 'negative', 'no'.

Discuss which words fit in the spaces. There is more than
one way to complete some of the sentences.

(a) The points on the ..../......... graph make a *definite
pattern*.
This graph shows .... correlation.

(b) The points on the ..../......... graph do *not* seem to
make a pattern.
This graph shows .... correlation.

(c) Larger .... values on the horizontal axis tend to go
with smaller .... values on the vertical axis.
This happens on the graph that shows ....
correlation.

(d) Smaller·........values on the horizontal axis tend to go
with smaller .... values on the vertical axis.
This happens on the graph that shows ....
correlation.

(e) Smaller .... values on the horizontal axis tend to go with larger .... values on the vertical axis.
This happens on the graph that shows .... correlation.

(f) Larger .... values on the horizontal axis tend to go with larger .... values on the vertical axis.
This happens on the graph that shows .... correlation.

(g) A 'band' of points slopes downwards across the ..../........ graph.
This graph shows ....correlation.

(h) A 'band' of points slopes upwards across the ..../........ graph.
This graph shows .... correlation.

(i) As the .... values increase in size, the .... values also tend to increase in size.
This happens on the graph that shows .... correlation.

(j) As the ....values increase in size, the .... values tend to decrease in size.
This happens on the graph that shows .... correlation.

2 Based on your discussion, list the features of a scatter graph that shows:
   (a) positive correlation
   (b) negative correlation
   (c) no correlation.
   Discuss your three lists.

Exercise P5.3

Look at the scatter graphs you drew in Exercises P5.1 and P5.2 on p 266 – p 268.
Describe each scatter graph.
Say whether it shows positive correlation, negative correlation or no correlation.

Summary

The points on a scatter graph may make a definite pattern.
This pattern suggests that the two variables are related.
We say there is a *correlation between them*.
The correlation may be positive or negative.

Positive correlation   positive correlation
The pattern on the scatter graph
will look something like this.
A 'band' of points slopes *upwards*
across the graph.
As one variable *increases* the other
variable tends to *increase* also.

Negative correlation   negative correlation
The pattern on the scatter graph will
look something like this.
A 'band' of points slopes *downwards*
across the graph.
As one variable *increases* the other
variable tends to *decrease*.

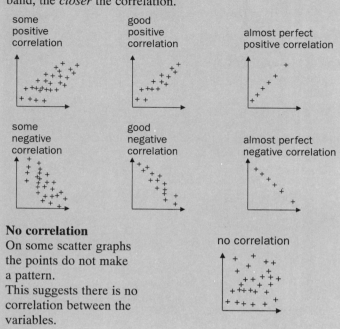

The width of a 'band' of points on a scatter graph shows how closely the variables are related. The *narrower* the band, the *closer* the correlation.

some positive correlation

good positive correlation

almost perfect positive correlation

some negative correlation

good negative correlation

almost perfect negative correlation

No correlation
On some scatter graphs the points do not make a pattern.
This suggests there is no correlation between the variables.

no correlation

Discussion Exercise

Discuss each of the following pairs of variables. Say whether you think there is likely to be positive correlation, negative correlation or no correlation between the variables. Give reasons for your answers. Sketch the kind of scatter graph you would expect in each case.

- Number of hours spent watching TV and time spent doing assignment work.
- Number of pages and weight of a newspaper.
- Number of letters in first name and surname.
- Age and house number of a person.
- Daily rainfall at a seaside resort and the number of people on the beach each day.
- Maths exam mark and time to run 100 m for students from one year group.
- Level of pollution in a river and the number of fish in that river.
- Height and shoe size of a group of primary school children.
- Number of people in a household and the amount of water used by the household.

Think of some other pairs of variables that are likely to have positive or negative or no correlation.
Discuss your ideas with other students in your group.
Do you agree about them?

Line of best fit

Kate measured the diameter
and circumference of
ten circles.
These are her data.

Diameter d (mm)	Circumference c (mm)
48	150
9	30
30	90
20	125
37	120
15	50
25	80
7	20
44	140
35	110

The scatter graph for Kate's data is shown below.

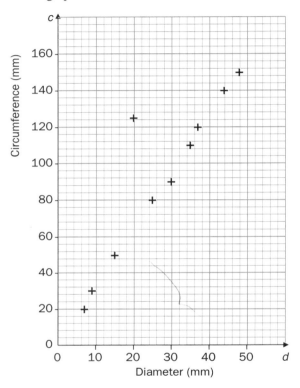

The points on the scatter graph *nearly all* lie in a straight line,
sloping upwards. This shows *almost perfect* positive correlation
between the two variables c and d.
To show this correlation even more clearly, we can draw a **line
of best fit.**

 ## Discussion Exercise

Draw a scatter graph for Kate's data.
Use 2 mm graph paper and the scales
shown on these axes.
On your graph draw the straight line
that you think 'fits' the points best.
Which points does your line go through?
Which points are just above your line?
Which points are just below your line?
Is any point nowhere near your line?
Discuss.

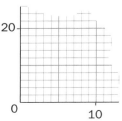

Look at the lines drawn by other students in your group.
Are they all the same?
Do some 'fit' the points better than others?
Discuss.

The points on a scatter diagram do not usually lie so close to a
straight line. However, when there is *correlation* between the
variables, the points lie mainly in a *band* across the graph.
Drawing the line that seems to fit the points best shows the
'trend' in the data.
This line is called the **line of best fit.**

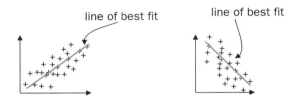

 ## Discussion Exercise

Four lines (labelled a, b, c, and d) have been drawn on
Dan's Sunshine/Temperature graph below.

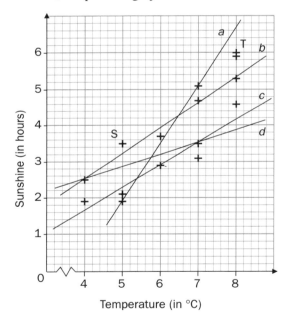

Which do you think 'fits' the data best?
Give reasons for your choice.
What do you think is 'wrong' with each of the others?
Discuss.

Drawing lines of best fit

One way to judge *where* to draw a line of best fit is simply *by
eye.* Place a ruler (a transparent one is best) across the band of
points. Move it until one of its edges fits the points best. Then
you can draw the line.
Here are some guidelines to help you to get the 'best fit'.
Try to make the line:
- match the *slope* shown by the plotted points
- have as many plotted points as possible *on* or *close to it*

- have about the same number of plotted points *above* it as *below* it
- have the points as *evenly balanced* about the line as possible.

To help you draw the line, you can also plot the *mean point* of the data. Take these steps.

- Find the mean of *each set* of data. These values are the coordinates of the mean point.
- Use a cross and circle ⊕ to plot the mean point. (This shows that it is not one of the original points on the scatter graph.)
- Draw the line of best fit so that it goes through this mean point.

For example, from Dan's sunshine/temperature data:

mean temperature $= \dfrac{95}{15} = 6.3$ (to 1 dp)

mean sunshine $= \dfrac{56.7}{15} = 3.8$ (to 1 dp)

You can plot the mean point (6.3,3.8) on the graph. Then draw the line of best fit.

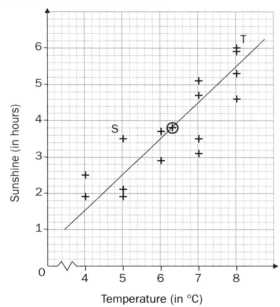

Sometimes an odd point obviously lies outside the main band of points. Its values often come from a mistake in the data. So you can usually ignore this point. Do not consider it when drawing the line of best fit. Do not include its value when calculating the mean point.

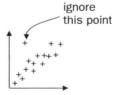

ignore this point

Some of the scatter graphs you drew in Exercise P5.1, p. 266 showed correlation between the variables.
Draw a line of best fit on each of these. ◀

Estimating values

The line of best fit shows the relationship between the two variables on the scatter graph. You can use the line to **predict an estimate** of one variable given the matching value of the other.
This is just like reading any other line graph.

Memo
Reading line graphs
p 93

For example, we can use the scatter graph below to estimate values for sunshine and temperature.

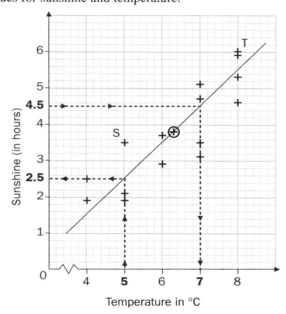

The temperature in Blackpool one day was 5°C.
An estimate of that day's sunshine in Blackpool is 2.5 hours.

Exmouth had 4.5 hours of sunshine on the same day.
An estimate of that day's temperature in Exmouth is 7°C.

These estimates are shown by the dotted lines on the graph above.

The accuracy of the estimate depends on how close the correlation is between the variables.
The closer the correlation, the more accurate the estimate.

narrow band of points

reasonable estimates

wide band of points

very approximate estimates

▶ *Exercise* **P5.4**

1 Plot the mean point (6.3,3.8) on your scatter graph of temperature and sunshine. Use it to draw the line of best fit on your scatter graph.
2 (a) Calculate the mean for the rainfall in Dan's data. (See p. 265.) What is the mean for the sunshine data?
   (b) Use these values for the means to plot the mean point on your scatter graph of sunshine against rainfall. Draw the line of best fit on this scatter graph.

► Exercise P5.5

To answer questions **1–5**, use the lines of best fit on the scatter graphs you have drawn in this unit.

1 Use your scatter graph of sunshine and rainfall.
  (a) Estimate the hours of sunshine for coastal resorts with these amounts of rainfall.
    (i)   10 mm
    (ii) 15 mm
    (iii) 23 mm
  (b) Estimate the number of millimetres of rain which fell in coastal resorts which had these hours of sunshine.
    (i)   2.4 hours
    (ii) 3 hours
    (iii) 4.6 hours

2 Use your scatter graph of science and mathematics marks.
  (a) Estimate the mathematics marks for students whose science marks are
    (i)   55
    (ii) 60
    (iii) 68.
  (b) Estimate the science marks for students whose mathematics marks are
    (i)   50
    (ii) 60
    (iii) 44.

3 Use your scatter graph of hardness and alkalinity of water.
  (a) Estimate the hardness of water which has a measured alkalinity of
    (i)   25 mg/ℓ
    (ii) 30 mg/ℓ
    (iii) 33 mg/ℓ.
  (b) Estimate the alkalinity of water which has a measured hardness of
    (i)   42 mg/ℓ
    (ii) 48 mg/ℓ
    (iii) 50 mg/ℓ.

4 Use your scatter graph of engine capacity and fuel consumption.
  (a) Estimate the fuel consumption for a car travelling at 30 mph with an engine capacity of
    (i)   4ℓ
    (ii) 1.5ℓ
    (iii) 2.4ℓ.
  (b) Estimate the engine capacity for a car travelling at 30 mph with a measured fuel consumption of
    (i) 45 mpg
    (ii) 30 mpg
    (iii) 27 mpg.

5 Use your scatter graph of mean temperature and latitude.
  (a) Estimate the latitude of a town with a mean temperature of
    (i)   14°C
    (ii) 7°C
    (iii) 15.6°C.
  (b) Estimate the mean temperature in °C of a town situated at a latitude of
    (i)   50
    (ii) 58
    (iii) 38.

6 The heights and weights of ten men, described as being of the same body frame, are given in this table.

Height (cm)	168	178	183	158	162	189	152	191	172	175
Weight (kg)	65	77	78	58	63	82	57	86	69	74

(a) Draw a scatter diagram to show these data. Use 2 mm graph paper and the scales shown on these axes.
(b) Draw a line of best fit.
(c) Use your scatter diagram to estimate
  (i) the height of a man weighing 73 kg
  (ii) the weight of a man 188 cm tall.

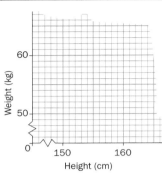

7 A group of students were entered for a music exam. Their mock and final exam marks are shown in this table.

Student	CM	PF	RL	MM	AT	RB	TA	LF	PS	WB	PW	AK
Mock exam	49	25	71	56	33	19	38	66	34	39	36	ill
Final exam	55	33	95	76	38	19	45	80	48	58	abs	67

(a) Draw a scatter diagram to show these exam marks. Use 2 mm graph paper and the scales shown on these axes.
(b) On the scatter diagram, draw a line of best fit.
(c) Philip was absent for the final exam but scored 36 marks in his mock exam. Estimate the mark he might have obtained in his final exam.
(d) Another student, Andrea, scored 67 marks in her final exam but did not take the mock exam due to illness. Estimate the mark she might have been awarded in her mock exam.
(e) Comment on the mock and final exam marks for this group of ten students.

👁 Investigation

Body measurements

Here are some standard body measurements.

  A height
  B armspan
  C handspan
  D foot length
  E wrist to elbow
  F circumference of head
  G circumference of wrist

Which pairs of measurements do you think are related?

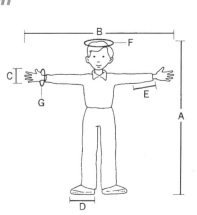

Ask the students in your class/year group for these data about themselves.
Use the data to investigate pairs of measurements for possible relationships. Draw a scatter graph for each pair.
Describe the correlation, if any, that they show.
Draw a line of best fit where appropriate.

Write a report on your work.
Comment on your results.
Were they what you expected?
What happens if you look at data from male and female students separately?

Car data

Consumer magazines publish these data about cars each year.

length
width
engine size
top speed
fuel consumption
fuel tank capacity
boot capacity
monthly running costs
monthly insurance costs
monthly depreciation

CAR FACTS	Rover 800
Model	2.0i
length (m)	4.88
width (m)	1.96
boot (litres)	505/895
tank (litres)	68
service (miles)	12000
mpg	32
insurance group	11
monthly cost (£)	220
depreciation	mid
top speed (mph)	126
accel (sec)	9.6

Which pairs of these variables do you think are related?
Predict the correlation, if any, between them.

Test your predictions by collecting data and drawing scatter graphs.
Write about what you discover.

Sports data

Data about many sports are published in newspapers, magazines, books, …
Your school/college will have records of its own sports data.

Investigate possible relationships between pairs of variables in some of these sports data.
Here are some ideas for investigations.
Think of others yourself if you want to.

Soccer: Points in league and number of games won/drawn/lost.
Goals for and against.
Cricket: Runs scored by each batsman in two innings.
Wickets taken by each bowler in two innings.
Tennis: Games won and lost in a match.
Tie-breaks and sets in a match.
Athletics: Times in 100 m and 200 m by the same runner.
Long jump and high jump distances by the same jumper.

Write a clear report of your investigations and results.

Examination Questions

1 For each pair of variables named, state whether they are *positively correlated*, *negatively correlated* or *uncorrelated*.

(a) The heights and weights of adult males.
(b) The weights and artistic abilities of 16-year-old girls.
(c) The height of a tree and its age.
(d) The volume of air remaining in a tyre and the time from when the tyre valve was opened.

(WJEC, 1994)

2 A teacher thinks that the nearer her pupils sit to the front of the class, the higher their test results will be. The scatter diagrams show the results for her second and fourth year classes.

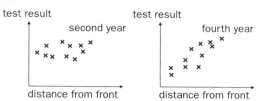

For each class, say whether the teacher's ideas are right or wrong. If she is wrong, describe what conclusions you could come to about that class.

(MEG, 1994)

3 This table shows the points scored and the fouls committed by players in a county basketball team over a season.

Player	Number of Points	Number of Fouls
Bogert	1	0
Bone	0	0
Campbell	2	0
Healey	6	6
Matthews	48	28
Hewitt	20	15
Naylor	71	30
Bennett	2	4
Perry	38	24
Evans	37	18

(a) Plot these figures on a graph.
(Use these scales: 2 cm to 10 points
2 cm to 10 fouls.)
(b) What conclusion can you make from your scatter diagram?

(MEG, 1988)

4 The table below contains the results for 10 pupils in end of term tests in Geography and Mathematics.

Pupil	Mathematics	Geography
A	20	60
B	30	60
C	55	40
D	80	45
E	20	65
F	35	50
G	55	50
H	70	50
I	50	60
J	45	45

(a) Plot these results to form a scatter diagram.
(Use this scale: 1 cm to 10 marks.)
Another pupil was absent for the Geography test but obtained 60 for the Mathematics test.

(b) Use the scatter diagrams to give an estimated Geography result.

(MEG, 1994)

5 Wesley travelled each day from Sheffield to various local towns making deliveries of computer equipment. He kept a record of the times and distances travelled as shown below.

Name: Wesley Roberts			
Date	Destination	Time(minutes)	Distance (km)
2/11/88	Chesterfield	25	18
5/11/88	Rotherham	20	10
7/11/88	Doncaster	45	32
15/11/88	Leeds	70	55
16/11/88	Derby	65	48
17/11/88	Barnsley	25	22
25/11/88	Manchester	70	60
26/11/88	Worksop	50	35
28/11/88	Huddersfield	55	44
30/11/88	Buxton	50	42

(a) On a grid, plot points in a scatter diagram to represent the various times and distances.
(Use these scales: 2 cm to 10 minutes
                    2 cm to 10 km.)

(b) Draw in a straight line of best fit.
(c) Calculate the gradient of this line and explain its significance.

(NEAB, 1989)

6 The manufacturers of a new car have conducted trials to measure its fuel consumption, y, in miles per gallon (mpg) for different speeds, x, in miles per hour (mph) of motorway travel.
The results are shown below.

Speed, x (mph)	30	40	45	50	55	60	67	70
Fuel consumption, y (mpg)	60	54	52	51	45	42	36	38

(a) On a grid, plot a scatter diagram to show how fuel consumption is influenced by speed.
(b) Draw a line of best fit through the data.
(c) Use your line of best fit to estimate the fuel consumption for this car when it is driven at a speed of 35 mph.

(WJEC, 1994)

P6
Accuracy in measurement

This unit will help you to:

- ■ recognise that measurement is approximate

- ■ choose an appropriate degree of accuracy for a measurement

- ■ recognise the degree of accuracy that can be obtained from a measuring instrument

- ■ choose a suitable instrument for a measurement task

- ■ recognise that a measurement expressed to a given unit has a possible error of half a unit

- ■ give the maximum possible error in a stated measurement

- ■ use a stated measurement to find the limits for the true measurement and its range of possible values.

Degrees of accuracy

All measurements are **approximate**.
This does not mean that they are not measured carefully.
It means they are *not 'exact'*. They are accurate, to a certain **degree of accuracy.**
For example,
a length may be measured to the nearest millimetre,
                              or to the nearest centimetre,
                              or to the nearest metre,
                              or to the nearest kilometre,
                              and so on …
The degree of accuracy used depends on *what* is being measured and *why*.

 Discussion Exercise

1 These pictures show the plan and end view of a Swimming Champion's medal.

Pam and Jo have to design a box for it.

Each girl measures the length, width and thickness of the medal.

Pam takes the measurements in centimetres.
She gives them *'to the nearest centimetre'*.
Jo takes the measurement in millimetres.
She gives them *'to the nearest millimetre'*.
What measurements would each girl write down?
Find out by measuring the diagrams.
Which measurements are most appropriate for designing the box?
Discuss.

2 Name a suitable unit and sensible degree of accuracy for each of the following measurements. Discuss your ideas with your group.
(a) The distance from London to Edinburgh.
(b) The weight of a double decker bus.
(c) The amount of milk left in a bottle.
(d) The time taken to travel from Birmingham to Bristol.
(e) The speed of an Intercity 125 train.
(f) The height of a boy.
(g) The thickness of a pane of glass.
(h) A dose of cough medicine.
(i) The width of a garden.
(j) The weight of a letter for posting.
(k) The capacity of the petrol tank of a car.
(l) The time to run 100 metres.
(m) The weight of a new-born baby.
(n) The temperature of a patient in hospital.
(o) The angle of elevation of the top of a building.

3 Suggest some things that would be measured to each of these degrees of accuracy.
Discuss your group's ideas.
(a) To the nearest km.
(b) To the nearest cubic metre.
(c) To the nearest 0.1 second.
(d) To the nearest day.
(e) To the nearest 100 m.
(f) To the nearest 50 g.
(g) To the nearest square yard.
(h) To the nearest 5 minutes.
(i) To the nearest minute.
(j) To the nearest 0.1°C.

Measuring instruments

The degree of accuracy of a measurement also depends upon *what you measure with*.
There are many instruments for measuring length, for example. Here are some of them.

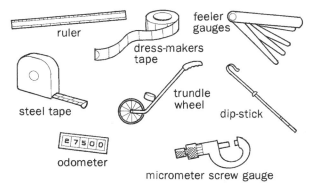

ruler, dress-makers tape, feeler gauges, steel tape, trundle wheel, dip-stick, odometer, micrometer screw gauge

In your mathematics lessons, you usually measure 'short' lengths with a ruler.

With a ruler like this you can measure *'to the nearest centimetre'*.

With a ruler like this, you can measure *'to the nearest millimetre'*.

Discussion Exercise

Discuss the instruments for measuring length shown in the pictures.

Which is most accurate? How accurate do you think it is?
Which is least accurate? How accurate do you think it is?

What sort of measuring jobs would each be used for?
Who would use them in their work?
In what situations would it be appropriate to use each?
Discuss your ideas with your group.

To what degree of accuracy would you expect to measure with each?
Discuss.

To judge the accuracy of a measuring instrument, you look at its **'scale'**.
You work out what each **'mark'** on the scale stands for.

For example, on this stop-watch, each mark stands for 1 second.

You can use it to measure times *'to the nearest second'*.

Discussion Exercise

1 These measuring instruments are for measuring liquids.

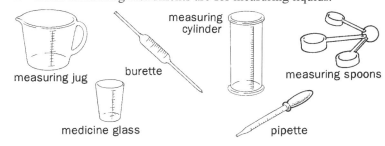

measuring jug, burette, measuring cylinder, measuring spoons, medicine glass, pipette

(a) Which would be used in a science lab?
(b) Which would be used at home?
(c) Describe a measuring job each is most suitable for.
(d) Which of these measuring instruments is most accurate? How accurate?
(e) Which do you think is least accurate? How accurate?
(f) Which would you use to measure these amounts?
100 mℓ, 25 mℓ, 500 mℓ, 5 mℓ, 140 mℓ.
Explain your answers.

2 These measuring instruments are for measuring time.

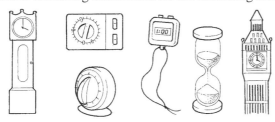

Discuss the accuracy of each measuring instrument.
Suggest a situation in which it would be sensible to use each.

3 To measure your weight you
could use bathroom scales.
To what degree of accuracy can
you weigh things with them?

Make a list of other weighing
instruments. What things could
be weighed with each?
In what situations would it be appropriate to use each of
them? How accurate is each? Discuss.

4 Look at these pictures of measuring instruments.

What is each used to measure? To what degree of accuracy
do you think each will measure? In what situations
are they likely to be used? Discuss.

'To the nearest unit'

Discussion Exercise

1

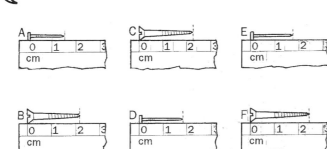

Some nails and screws are being measured in these pictures.
Use the pictures to answer these questions. (Do not use your
own ruler.)

Which is shortest? Which is longest?
Put them in order of length, shortest first.

Give the length of each 'to the nearest centimetre'.

How did you decide which is the 'nearest' centimetre for
each length? Discuss.
What do you notice about your results?

2 Which lengths given below are *2 cm, to the nearest cm*?
(a) 2.7 cm   (d) 2.5 cm   (g) 2.09 cm   (j) 1.09 cm
(b) 3.2 cm   (e) 1.45 cm   (h) 1.82 cm
(c) 1.8 cm   (f) 1.67 cm   (i) 3.01 cm
How did you decide?
Discuss.

Give some other lengths which are *2 cm, to the nearest cm*.
Discuss the lengths given by your group.

All lengths that *round up* to 2 cm, to the nearest cm are
longer than 1 cm. Explain why.
What is the *shortest* length that rounds up to *2 cm, to the
nearest cm*?
Discuss.
All lengths that *round down* to 2 cm, to the nearest cm are
less than 3 cm. Explain why.
What is the *smallest value* they are all less than?
Discuss.

3 Which of these lengths are *9 m, to the nearest metre*?
Discuss.
(a) 9.1 m   (d) 8.7 m   (g) 9.09 m   (j) 9.499 m
(b) 8.2 m   (e) 9.5 m   (h) 8.56 m
(c) 9.4 m   (f) 8.5 m   (i) 9.49 m
List some other lengths which are *9 m, to the nearest metre*.
Explain how you chose these lengths.

All lengths that *round up* to 9 m, to the nearest metre are
longer than 8 m. Explain why.
What is the *shortest* length that rounds up to *9 m, to the
nearest metre*?
Discuss.

All lengths that *round down* to 9 m, to the nearest metre are
less than 10 m. Explain why.
What is the *smallest* value they are all less than?
Discuss.

To measure something '**to the nearest unit**', you need a scale
marked *every unit*.
For example,
to measure lengths '*to the nearest centimetre*', you used a scale
marked *every centimetre*.

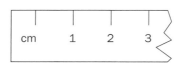

To give a measurement 'to the nearest unit' you have to
decide which 'unit mark' it is *nearest* to. These boundaries
between 'rounding up' and 'rounding down' are *halfway*
between each pair of 'unit marks'.

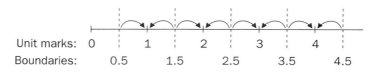

| Unit marks: | 0 | | 1 | | 2 | | 3 | | 4 | |
| Boundaries: | | 0.5 | | 1.5 | | 2.5 | | 3.5 | | 4.5 |

Half of 1 is $\frac{1}{2}$ or 0.5.
So the *halfway marks* are *0.5 less* than the nearest 'unit mark'
and *0.5 more* than the nearest 'unit mark'.

The nails and screws in the last exercise are all different lengths. But each measures '2 cm, to the nearest cm'.

The true measurement can be up to 0.5 cm *less than* 2 cm up to 0.5 cm *more than* 2 cm.

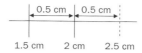

We say that 0.5 cm is the **maximum possible error** in this length.
Here the word 'error' does not mean 'a mistake'.
It is the *difference* between the *stated* measurement and the *true* measurement.
This maximum possible error tells us that the *stated measurement* could be up to 0.5 cm too small
or 0.5 cm too large.

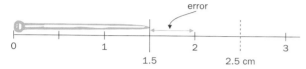

The *true length* could be *as small as 1.5 cm*.
This is the smallest length that rounds up to 2 cm.

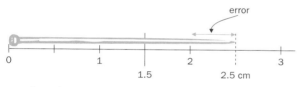

The *true length* could be *up to 2.5 cm long*.
It must be less than 2.5 cm because 2.5 cm rounds up to 3 cm. But it can be almost 2.5 cm long, e.g., 2.49999 … cm long.

We say that …
   1.5 cm is the **lower limit**
   for the true length
and 2.5 cm is the **upper limit**
   for the true length.

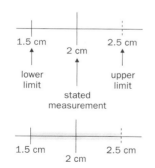

Lower limit: $2 - 0.5 = 1.5$ cm.

Upper limit: $2 + 0.5 = 2.5$ cm.

The true length lies in this shaded **range** of values.

The range of possible values for the true length is:

$$1.5 \text{ cm} \leq \text{true length} < 2.5 \text{ cm}$$

(i.e., the true length is *greater than or equal* to 1.5 cm
   but is *less than* 2.5 cm).

Summary

A measurement may be given as *M*, to the nearest unit.

- The maximum possible error in the measurement is half (0.5) of that unit.

- The true measurement may be less than or more than *M*. The limits of its possible values are:

   half (0.5) of the unit less than *M*
   half (0.5) of the unit more than *M*.

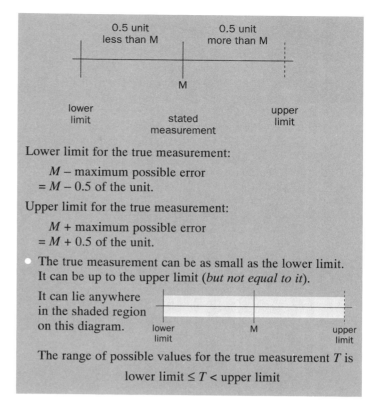

Lower limit for the true measurement:
   M – maximum possible error
   = *M* – 0.5 of the unit.

Upper limit for the true measurement:
   M + maximum possible error
   = *M* + 0.5 of the unit.

- The true measurement can be as small as the lower limit. It can be up to the upper limit (*but not equal to it*).

It can lie anywhere in the shaded region on this diagram.

The range of possible values for the true measurement *T* is

   lower limit $\leq T <$ upper limit

Limits and range

These ideas of **errors** and **limits** apply to *all measurements,* not just length.
To work out the maximum possible error and limits, you look at the stated measurement and how accurately it is given.

For example, at Croft's Dog Show, Bonzo's weight is given as 37 kg to the nearest kg.

Bonzo's weight is measured 'to the nearest kg'. It has a maximum possible error of 'half a kg' = 0.5 kg.

Bonzo's true weight may be less than or more than 37 kg.

The limits of its possible values are:
   0.5 kg less than 37 kg
and 0.5 kg more than 37 kg.

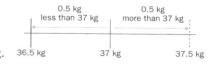

Lower limit for the true weight: $37 - 0.5 = 36.5$ kg.
Upper limit for the true weight: $37 + 0.5 = 37.5$ kg.

Bonzo's true weight can be as small as 36.5 kg. It can be up to 37.5 kg (but not equal to it).

It can lie anywhere in this shaded range of values.

The range of possible values for Bonzo's true weight, *W*, is

$$36.5 \text{ kg} \leq W < 37.5 \text{ kg}.$$

▶ *Exercise* P6.1

For each stated measurement in this Exercise, give
(a) the maximum possible error in the measurement
(b) the lower and upper limits for the true measurement
(c) the range of possible values for the true measurement.
1   Ronnie weighs 68 kg, to the nearest kilogram.
2   A length of cable measures 12 m, to the nearest metre.
3   The smallest angle in a triangle measures 17°, to the nearest degree.
4   It took Julie 9 minutes, to the nearest minute, to walk to school today.

5   The temperature of the tennis court reached 31°C, to the nearest degree Celsius.
6   The area of the envelope is 242 cm², to the nearest square centimetre.
7   The capacity of the swimming pool is 891 cubic feet, to the nearest cubic foot.
8   The volume of sand delivered was 10 cubic metres, to the nearest cubic metre.
9   The mass of breakfast cereal in a bowl is 30 g, to the nearest gram.
10   The bottle contains 75 *cl* of wine, to the nearest centilitre.

▶ P7
Calculator brackets and memory

This unit will help you to:

■ understand that each part of a calculation must be done in the correct order

■ know the correct order of operations (algebraic logic)

■ use the bracket keys on a calculator to do calculations in arithmetic and algebra

■ use brackets to change the order of operations

■ insert brackets to do calculations with a calculator in the correct order

■ know and use the basic memory facilities on a calculator

■ use the memory on a calculator to do calculations efficiently.

Calculator keys you know

This picture shows a scientific calculator. Its keys are like the keys shown in this book. You have met many of these keys already.

◯ *Discussion Exercise*

Look at the keys in the picture on the left.
Make a list of the keys you know how to use.
Discuss briefly how to use them.

Look at the keys on *your* calculator.
Compare its keys with the keys on your list.
Which keys look the same? Tick these keys on your list.

Are there any keys on your list not ticked?
If there are, think about what they are used for.
Which keys do you press on your calculator
to do the same things?

▶ *Exercise* P7.1

Below are some key questions about your calculator. Write each answer as a complete sentence. Make sure that the sentence says clearly what the answer is about. Give an example with a key code if you can.
For example, here is a good answer to question **3**(a).

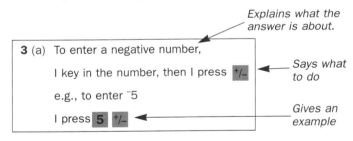

1   What make and model is your calculator?
2   How many digits can your calculator display at most?
3   Which key(s) do you press to do these?
   (a) Enter a negative number, for example, ⁻5.
   (b) Enter π.
   (c) Square a number, for example, 19^2.
   (d) Cube a number, for example, 24^3.
   (e) Raise a number to the power 4, for example, 7^4.
   (f) Find the square root of a number, for example, $\sqrt{961}$.
   (g) Find the cube root of a number, for example, $\sqrt[3]{512}$.
   (h) Change a fraction to a decimal, for example, $\frac{7}{8}$.
   (i) Change a fraction to a percentage, for example, $\frac{5}{12}$.
   (j) Find a percentage of a number, for example 12% of 60.

4 Some keys have more than one function.
  (a) How do you make a key perform its second function?
  (b) For which functions do you have to do this?
5 How do you do these?
  (a) Clear just the last entry.
  (b) Clear all the working done so far.
6 How can you correct these errors?
  (a) Wrong number keyed in.
  (b) Wrong operation keyed in.
7 How do you set up the constant facility?
8 Which other keys do you know how to use on your calculator? Explain how to use these keys.

Order in calculations

Calculations often have several parts. It is important to do them in the **correct order**. Some parts must be done before others. The laws of mathematics tell you the order in which to do them.

Order of operations

BIDMAS

B Anything inside **Brackets** first.

I **Indices** (powers or roots) next.

D
M } **Division** and **Multiplication** next (work from left to right).

A
S } **Addition** and **Subtraction** last (work from left to right).

This order of operations is called **algebraic logic**.

Your scientific calculator should use algebraic logic. When you key in a string of commands, it should do them in this order automatically.
Try this calculation on your calculator to check.

Using algebraic logic, the correct working is like this:

    2 + 3 × 4
  = 2 + 12   ◀——— Multiplying first
  =   14   ◀——— Adding next

Watch the display closely when you key in the calculation.

If the display shows 14 when you press **=** , your calculator uses algebraic logic. It reorders the sum for you. Then it does it in the correct order.

If you get 20 when you press **=** , your calculator does *not* use algebraic logic. It simply works from left to right through the calculation. To do the working correctly *you* have to put it in the correct order yourself.

For the work on your GCSE course you need a calculator with algebraic logic. Make sure that you have one.

Brackets on your calculator

Your calculator should have **bracket keys**

(or **[(..** to *open* the bracket,

) or **..)]** to *close* the bracket.

These may be called **parentheses keys** in your calculator handbook. Parentheses is another word for brackets.
  Find the brackets keys on your calculator. In this book we simply use **(** and **)** for them in key codes.
Make sure you use the correct keys on your calculator.

When you press your bracket key, a bracket symbol and number may appear on the display.

 (*pressed once*

The number shows how many sets of brackets you have opened. This is useful when you have brackets inside brackets.

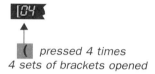

 (*pressed 4 times*
4 sets of brackets opened

Here is a calculation with brackets.

You do the working inside the brackets first ... then the division ...

      18 ÷ (2 + 4)
                ↓
  =   18 ÷   6
           ↓
  =   3

On most scientific calculators you simply key it in as given. Then you press **=** at the end.

The calculator should work it out in the correct order automatically.
Watch the display carefully.

When you press **)** , it works out (2 + 4)   *6.*
and displays the result.

When you press **=** , it works out 18 ÷ 6   *3.*
and displays the final answer.

Try it on your calculator.
If you do not get these results, check with your teacher.

Look at this calculation: 3(7 − 2) = 15.
A number is written in front of the bracket *without* an operation sign.

          3(7 − 2) means 3 × (7 − 2)

To key it into most calculators you have to press **×** in the correct place.

You press **×** after the number, but before the bracket.

Try this on your calculator.
What happens if you don't press **×** ?
Remember: *watch the display*.
Use it to help you to spot mistakes as you key in.

We often leave out the '× sign' between pairs of brackets too.
  $(9 - 4)(2 + 6)$ means $(9 - 4) \times (2 + 6)$

Remember to press ⊠ when you key it in.
Try it on your calculator.
What happens if you don't press ⊠ ?

► *Exercise* P7.2

1 Use the bracket keys on your calculator to do these.
  Then do them without your calculator to check.
  (a) $7(8 + 5)$ (e) $(8 + 12) \div (2 + 3)$ (i) $48 \div (7 + 5)$
  (b) $3(5 - 2)$ (f) $(23 - 5) \div (4 + 2)$ (j) $(38 + 16) \div 9$
  (c) $(7 + 4)5$ (g) $(15 + 7) \div (13 - 2)$
  (d) $6 + (7 - 2)$ (h) $(47 - 5) \div (15 + 6)$

2 Do these on your calculator. Then find an approximate
  answer to check. (Round each number to 1 significant
  figure).
  (a) $39.4 - (41.72 - 18.93)$
  (b) $7(19.4 - 8.7)$
  (c) $35(21.3 + 14.5)$
  (d) $(13.24 + 9.3)(8.7 + 3.3)$
  (e) $24.3 \div (11.4 - 8.7)$
  (f) $(17.2 - 11.2)(21.68 + 8.9)$
  (g) $(6.9 + 23.1)(62.47 + 13.68)$
  (h) $(4.58 + 12.9) \div 3.8$
  (i) $(31.7 + 9.42) \div (15.76 - 10.76)$
  (j) $151.7 - 6(28.74 - 14.28)$

3 Use your calculator to find the value of the following.
  Write down the full calculator display for each answer.
  Then correct it to 3 sf when necessary.
  (a) $12.6(15.4 + 17.9)$
  (b) $(26.8 + 19.6) \div 8.4$
  (c) $27.94 + (19.8 - 4.83)$
  (d) $(42.91 - 16.7) \div 11.4$
  (e) $(38.7 - 9.15) \div (7.23 - 3.17)$
  (f) $31.6 + 5.4(16.34 - 11.87)$
  (g) $(6.9 + 13.8)(14.72 - 7.4)$
  (h) $47.7 \div (12.4 + 9.36)$
  (i) $69.51 - 8(2.41 - 1.99)$
  (j) $76.3 \div (8.25 + 15.7)$

4 Evaluate the following.
  Write down each answer as shown on your calculator
  display. Round each answer sensibly.
  (a) $(2.3)^2 + (3.1)^2$
  (b) $(6.8)^2 - (2.4)^2$
  (c) $7.3 - \sqrt{4.7}$
  (d) $(2.8 + 4.3 \times 7.2)^2$
  (e) $(16.4 - 2 \times 6.93)^2$
  (f) $(\sqrt{11.6 - 7.41})^2$
  (g) $(38.7 - \sqrt{16.7})^2$
  (h) $\sqrt{17.2(8.6 + 3.14)}$
  (i) $(56.2 \div (11.01 + 0.86))^2$
  (j) $9.43 - \sqrt{(4.3 + 2.7)} - 0.87$

Changing order with brackets

To **change the order** in a calculation you can use brackets.
Anything put *inside brackets* is *worked out first*.

Look at this calculation, for example.

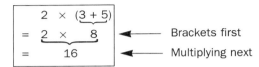

Multiplying first
Adding next

Our rule gives the answer 11.
Using brackets can **change the priority**.
This gives a *different order* and a *different answer*.

$$
\begin{array}{c}
2 \times (3 + 5) \\
= 2 \times 8 \\
= 16
\end{array}
$$

Brackets first
Multiplying next

To do some calculations in the order you want, you may need
to **insert brackets**.

When using a calculator remember the order in which it works:
● *Plan* what to do before you key it in.
  Think about what working has to be done. Decide the *correct
  order* to do it in. Insert extra brackets if you need to.
● Write down a *key code* if it helps.
  Check it does what you want with easy numbers. Watch the
  display to see what is happening.
● Use an *estimate* as a check.

◉ *Investigation*

Start with the numbers 3, 4 and 5.
Write down as many different calculations as you can with
these numbers.
You can use
  $+, -\times, \div$, brackets, fractions, squares and square roots.
Find the answers with your calculator.
Write down key codes for your working. Check they give the
answers you expect.
Discuss your results with your group.

What happens if ...
  ●you use different numbers
  ●you use more than three numbers?
Investigate.   ◉

Fractions, divisions and brackets

$\frac{3}{4}$ is one way to write '3 divided by 4'.

To work it out on a calculator,   ▦

you key in   3 ÷ 4 =

This works out: top number ÷ bottom number

Look at this fraction: $\dfrac{16}{3 + 5}$

It shows a division in the same way.
The top number is 16.
The bottom number is the answer to $\boxed{3 + 5}$.

So to work out $\dfrac{16}{3 + 5}$,

first you do: $\boxed{3 + 5}$

then work out: '16 divided by the answer you get'.

This gives: $16 \div 8 = 2$.

The 'fraction line' in $\dfrac{16}{3+5}$ acts like brackets.

It tells *you* to work out $\boxed{3+5}$ first.

To give a calculator the same instructions, you have to use brackets.
Put the working on the bottom into brackets:

$$\frac{16}{3+5} = \frac{16}{(3+5)}$$

Now you have the correct order to key it in:

$$\frac{16}{(3+5)} \text{ means } 16 \div (3+5)$$

This gives the correct answer: **2.**
Remember to watch the display carefully. Look for:

● the result when you press $\boxed{)}$ ... **8.**

● the answer when you press $\boxed{=}$ ... **2.**

Sometimes you will want to write these results in your working:

$$\frac{16}{(3+5)} = \frac{16}{8} = 2 \quad \text{— from display}$$

Here is another example:

$$\frac{22.7 + 23.6 \times 4.8}{41.84}$$

Put the working on 'top' into brackets:

$$\frac{(22.7 + 23.6 \times 4.8)}{41.84}$$

Then you can key in:

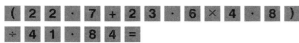

This gives the answer: **3.25**

Watch the display closely.
You can use the results to write down this working.

from display

$$\frac{(22.7 + 23.6 \times 4.8)}{41.84} = \frac{135.98}{41.84} = 3.25$$

As usual it is a good idea to estimate an answer to check.

Memo
Significant figures
p 15

Rounding each number to one significant figure gives a reasonable estimate.

$$\frac{(22.7 + 23.6 \times 4.8)}{41.84} \approx \frac{20 + 20 \times 5}{40} = \frac{120}{40} = 3$$

This estimate (3) and the calculator answer (3.25) are about the same size. So the answer is a sensible size.

Summary

A 'fraction line' is often used to show division.

$$\frac{\boxed{\text{top}}}{\boxed{\text{bottom}}} \text{ means } \boxed{\text{top}} \div \boxed{\text{bottom}}$$

Before doing the division:

● put any working on the 'top' into a bracket.

● put any working on the bottom into a bracket.

To key it into a calculator, use the brackets and $\boxed{\div}$.
The calculator will deal with the brackets first.
Remember to press $\boxed{=}$ to get the final answer.

Always check that the size of your answer is sensible. Round each number in the calculation to 1 significant figure and work out an estimate of the answer.

Question

Use your calculator to find the value of $\dfrac{52.6 + 13}{18.25 - 7.9}$.

(a) Write down the answer shown on your calculator display.
(b) Round this answer to 3 significant figures.

Answer

Put in brackets: $\dfrac{(52.6 + 13)}{(18.25 - 7.9)}$

Key in:

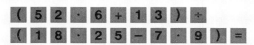

(a) 6.338164251
(b) 6.34 (to 3 sf)
Check: Round each number to 1 sf.

$$\frac{(50 + 10)}{(20 - 10)} = \frac{60}{10} = 6 \quad \begin{array}{l}\text{About the same size as calculator answer.}\\ \text{So the answer is a sensible size.}\end{array}$$

▶ *Exercise* **P7.3**

Use the brackets on your calculator to do this exercise.

1 Find the value of each fraction with your calculator.
   Do the working without a calculator to check.

   (a) $\dfrac{18}{2+4}$ (d) $\dfrac{43-8}{7}$ (g) $\dfrac{22+29}{22-5}$

   (b) $\dfrac{15}{7-2}$ (e) $\dfrac{17+19}{7+5}$ (h) $\dfrac{7 \times 4 + 8}{4 \times 9}$

   (c) $\dfrac{19+8}{9}$ (f) $\dfrac{60}{5 \times 3}$ (i) $\dfrac{36 + 9 \times 3}{44 - 5 \times 7}$

2 Evaluate these fractions with a calculator first. Then find their values without a calculator to check.

   (a) $\dfrac{8(17-5)}{3}$ (b) $\dfrac{9(5+3)}{12}$ (c) $\dfrac{6 \times 8 + 5 \times 10}{9+5}$

(d) $\dfrac{30 + 8(7 - 4)}{17 - 8}$ (f) $\dfrac{12 + 3 \times 7}{23 - 4 \times 3}$ (h) $\dfrac{28 + 6 \times 3}{3 + 4(9 - 4)}$

(e) $\dfrac{5 \times 6 - 2 \times 7}{5 + 3}$ (g) $\dfrac{7(6 + 3) - 11}{8 + 5}$ (i) $\dfrac{8(6 + 7) - 11}{14 + 17}$

3 Use your calculator to find the values of the following. Write down the full calculator display for each answer. Then correct it to 3 sf when necessary.

(a) $\dfrac{6.4 + 3.7}{2.1}$ (e) $\dfrac{2 \times 4.8 + 3 \times 5.41}{7.6 + 1.82}$

(b) $\dfrac{8.7}{9.3 - 2}$ (f) $\dfrac{6.4(11.91 - 4.4)}{3.7}$

(c) $\dfrac{11.8 - 3.24}{5.9}$ (g) $\dfrac{2.8 + 3.64 \times 2.1}{0.9 + 2 \times 4.01}$

(d) $\dfrac{7.04 + 8.3}{4.31 + 0.26}$ (h) $\dfrac{6.15(4.3 + 5.27) + 10.4}{13.6 - 2 \times 3.06}$

4 Evaluate the following. Write down each answer as shown on your calculator display. Round each answer sensibly.

(a) $\dfrac{\sqrt{9.32}}{2.7 + 4.6}$ (d) $\dfrac{7.9 + 12.3}{(4.8)^2}$ (g) $\sqrt{\dfrac{7.4 + 6.71}{9.4 - 5.8}}$

(b) $\dfrac{(3.7)^2}{2.8 + 4.1}$ (e) $\dfrac{\sqrt{14.23}}{8.6 - 3.72}$ (h) $\dfrac{17.71}{\sqrt{(2.7)^2 + (3.1)^2}}$

(c) $\dfrac{9.02 - 4.4}{\sqrt{3.75}}$ (f) $\sqrt{\dfrac{14}{3.2 + 5.1}}$

Substitution in algebra

Substitution p 76

Replacing letters by numbers is called **substitution**. This gives a *numerical value* for an expression. We also call it **evaluating the expression.**

To evaluate an expression with a calculator you may need to use the brackets keys.
Take these steps:
- Write down the expression.
- Replace the letters by the numbers given.
- Plan how to do the calculation.
- Insert any extra brackets if you need to.
- Key in the calculation.
- Use an estimate to check.

▶ *Exercise* **P7.4**

1 Substitute $p = 45$, $q = 9$ and $r = 18$ in the following:
(a) $p - (q - r)$ (f) $(p + q) \div (r - q)$
(b) $(p - r)q$ (g) $(p + q)(p - q)$
(c) $r(p + q)$ (h) $p^2 + (q + r)^2$
(d) $(p + q) \div r$ (i) $q^2 + (p - r)^2$
(e) $(p - r) \div q$ (j) $(p - q)^2 + r^2$

2 Given that $a = 16.27$, $b = 5.41$ and $c = 3.86$, evaluate the following expressions correct to 3 sf.
(a) $a(b + c)$ (b) $a(b - c)$

(c) $a + (b - c)^2$ (g) $(a - c)^2 \div b$
(d) $a - (b - c)^2$ (h) $\sqrt{(a^2 + b^2) \div c}$
(e) $(a + b) \div c$ (i) $(a + c)^2 - b$
(f) $\sqrt{b(a - c)}$ (j) $\sqrt{a(b + c)} - \sqrt{a(b - c)}$

3 Given that $p = 7.3$, $q = 5.2$ and $r = 3.9$, evaluate the following expressions correct to 3 sf.

(a) $\dfrac{15}{p + q}$ (d) $\dfrac{3p}{q + r}$ (g) $\dfrac{p^2 + q^2}{2r}$

(b) $\dfrac{7 + q}{r}$ (e) $\dfrac{p - q}{q + r}$ (h) $\dfrac{3(2p - q)}{q}$

(c) $\dfrac{p - q}{r}$ (f) $\dfrac{q^2}{p - r}$ (i) $\sqrt{\dfrac{p}{q + r}}$

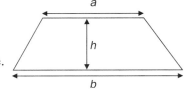

Formulas and brackets

Some formulas have brackets in them. To evaluate the formula with a calculator, key in the brackets as in the formula. Insert *extra brackets* in the working if you need to.

▶ *Exercise* **P7.5**

1 A DIY knife blade has the shape of a trapezium. The formula
$A = \frac{1}{2}(a + b)h$
gives the area of the blade.

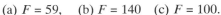

Calculate the area when:
(a) $a = 32$ mm, $b = 63$ mm and $h = 21$ mm
(b) $a = 2.8$ cm, $b = 5.9$ cm and $h = 1.8$ cm.

2 The formula $V = \pi l(R^2 - r^2)$ gives the volume of metal in this pipe.
Calculate the volume of metal in a pipe in which:
(a) $R = 12$ mm, $r = 10$ mm and $l = 250$ mm
(b) $R = 5.7$ cm, $r = 4.9$ cm and $l = 97.5$ cm.

3 The surface area S of a child's plastic toy is given by the formula $S = \pi r(2r + l)$.
Calculate the value of S when:
(a) $r = 67$ mm and $l = 112$ mm,
(b) $r = 5.4$ cm and $l = 9.8$ cm.

4 The formula for converting °F to °C is given by $C = \frac{5}{9}(F - 32)$.
Calculate the value of C when:
(a) $F = 59$,   (b) $F = 140$ (c) $F = 100$.

5 The formula $s = \frac{1}{2}(u + v)t$ is used in physics for an object travelling with constant acceleration in a straight line.
s is the distance travelled in metres.
u is the initial velocity in metres per second.
v is the final velocity in metres per second.
t is the time for which the object travels in seconds.
Work out the value of s when:
(a) $u = 7$, $v = 9$, $t = 2$
(b) $u = 20$, $v = 26$, $t = 3$
(c) $u = 34$, $v = 49$, $t = 7$.

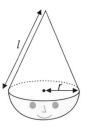

6 The formula $s = \dfrac{v^2 - u^2}{2a}$ is used in physics for an object travelling with constant acceleration in a straight line.

s is the distance travelled in metres.
u is the initial velocity in metres per second.
v is the final velocity in metres per second.
a is the acceleration in metres per second per second.

Work out the value of s when
(a) $u = 2$, $v = 7$, $a = 5$
(b) $u = 20$, $v = 30$, $a = 10$
(c) $u = 7.4$, $v = 14.8$, $a = 2.7$.

7 Two masses, M and m are connected by a string which passes over a fixed pulley.

(a) The acceleration a (m/s^2) of the masses is given by the formula

$$a = \frac{(M - m)\, g}{M + m}$$

where M and m are given in kg and g is the acceleration due to gravity in m/s^2.

Find a when:
(i) $M = 1.8$ kg, $m = 0.7$ kg and $g = 9.8$ m/s^2
(ii) $M = 2.3$ kg, $m = 0.9$ kg and $g = 9.8$ m/s^2

(b) The formula $T = \dfrac{2Mmg}{M + m}$ gives the tension T newtons in the string connecting the masses M and m.

Calculate the tension T when:
(i) $M = 3.4$ kg, $m = 1.6$ kg and $g = 9.8$ m/s^2
(ii) $M = 1.3$ kg, $m = 0.6$ kg and $g = 9.8$ m/s^2

The calculator memory

Your calculator has a **memory** where you can *store* a number during a calculation.

In your 'human memory', you can store *several numbers* at the same time.

In your calculator memory, you can store *only one number* at a time. This means you have to plan how to use it efficiently.

Basic operations

Most scientific calculators have the same basic memory operations. The keys used for them may vary from calculator to calculator. Make sure you know what the memory keys on *your* calculator look like.

Here is an outline of **six basic memory operations**. The keys shown in green are the ones used in key codes in this book.

- **To store a number in the memory**, you may press:

When a number is stored in the memory, a letter ^{m} usually appears in the top left hand corner of the display. This is a useful reminder.

Only the number shown on the *calculator display* can enter the memory.

To store a number, such as 9, we key in:

Puts 9 on the display   Stores 9 in the memory

To store the result of a calculation, such as $15 \div 3$, we key in …

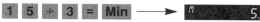

We *must* press ⊜ *before* Min .
This puts the result of the calculation on display, before storing it in the memory.

If we key in:

we get 3 in the memory, not the result of the calculation.

When a number is put in the memory, it *replaces* what is there. Any number already in the memory is 'lost'.

When you clear the display, the number in the memory is not affected.
The ^{m} reminds you it is still there.

- **To recall the number from memory**, you may press:

MR or RCL or RM

The calculator *reads* the number in the memory and *shows* it on the display. The number is *not 'removed'* from the memory. It is simply 'copied' on to the display. Any number already on the display is 'lost'.

You may want to recall the number from memory to use it in a calculation. To do this, simply press the 'recall memory' key where you would key in the number in the working.

Here are some examples.
To multiply 8 and the 'number in memory', we key in:

8 × MR =

To divide 8 by the 'number in memory', we key in:

8 ÷ MR =

To divide the 'number in memory' by 8, we key in:

MR ÷ 8 =

- **To clear the memory**, you may press:

MC or CM

This clears the memory *without clearing the display*.

On some calculators you may have to clear the display and put 0 in the memory.

When the memory is cleared, the *ⁿ* on the display should disappear.

Many calculators have a *'long-term memory'*. They keep the number stored in the memory even when the calculator is switched off.
So when you switch on your calculator, there may be a number still in the memory. It is a good idea to clear the memory before you start a new calculation.

To check the memory is clear, you can press the 'recall memory' key. A zero should appear on the display.

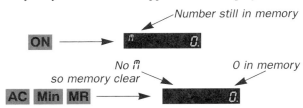

- **To exchange the number on the display and the number in the memory,** you may press:

$$x \longleftrightarrow M \quad \text{or} \quad \boxed{EXC}$$

You can use this to 'look at' the number in the memory, without losing the number on the display permanently.

- **To add a number to the contents of the memory,** you may press:

$$\boxed{M+} \quad \text{or} \quad \boxed{SUM}$$

This adds the number shown on the display to the number already in the memory.
For example,

adds 8 to the number in the memory and puts the total in the memory. You can recall the total from the memory to check.
If 0 is in the memory,

8 M+ puts 8 in the memory because 0 + 8 = 8

If 2 is in the memory,

8 M+ puts 10 in the memory because 2 + 8 = 10.

Always check whether the memory is empty or not when using this key.

- **To subtract a number from the contents of the memory,** you may press:

$$\boxed{M-} \quad \text{or} \quad \boxed{+/-}\ \boxed{SUM}$$

This subtracts the number shown on the display from the number already in the memory.
For example,

subtracts 5 from the number in the memory and leaves the answer in the memory.

You can recall the answer left in the memory to check.
If 0 is in the memory,

5 M– leaves –5 in the memory because 0 – 5 = –5

If 7 is in the memory,

5 M– leaves 2 in the memory because 7 – 5 = 2

MR ⟶ [*ⁿ*   2.]

Always check whether the memory is empty or not when you use this key.

ACTIVITY

Try these activities to explore the memory keys on your calculator.
Make sure you know what happens when you use them.

1   Read the instructions given below.
Write down the keys you would use on your calculator for each instruction.
Predict what will be on the display and in the memory after each step.
Then check your predictions with your calculator.
(Remember: To 'see' what is in the memory at each step, press the 'memory exchange key'. Then press it again to return the numbers to where they were).

(a) Clear memory.
(b) Put 4 into memory.
(c) Clear display.
(d) Recall the number from memory.
(e) Add 9 to memory.
(f) Recall the number from memory.
(g) Subtract 3 from memory.
(h) Recall the number from memory.
(i) Multiply 2 by the number in memory.
(j) Divide the number in memory by 5.
(k) Divide 40 by the number in memory.
(l) Replace the number in memory with that on the display.
(m) Clear the display.
(n) Clear the memory.
(o) Check that the memory is clear.

Now replace the numbers in the instructions with some of your own.
Work through the instructions with these numbers. Predict the numbers on the display and in the memory. Then use your calculator to check.
Make sure you get the results you expect.

2   Invent a list of instructions of your own like question **1**.
Make sure you know what is on the display and in the memory after each step.
Swap instructions with another student in your group.
Check each other's results.

3   Here are some key codes for your calculator.
For each key code:
- predict what is on the display and in the memory after each green key is pressed
- write down the 'matching' key code for your calculator
- use your calculator to check your predictions.

(a) `0` `Min` `5` `M+` `M+` `MR`

(b) `1` `0` `M+` `M+` `M+` `MR`

(c) `4` `0` `Min` `2` `M–` `M–` `M–` `MR`

(d) `0` `Min` `8` `÷` `2` `=` `Min`

(e) `0` `Min` `1` `2` `÷` `4` `M+`

(f) `0` `Min` `9` `M+` `4` `M+` `7` `M+` `2` `M–` `MR`

(g) `3` `Min` `6` `M+` `2` `M+` `MR`

(h) `3` `×` `5` `=` `Min` `2` `×` `4` `=` `M–` `MR`

(i) `5` `Min` `2` `0` `÷` `MR` `=` `MR` `=`

(j) `4` `+` `6` `=` `Min` `1` `2` `+` `8` `=` `÷` `MR` `=`

(k) `1` `0` `Min` `5` `M+` `M–`

(l) `2` `0` `Min` `4` `M–` `M+`

4 Write down at least five key codes using the memory keys on your calculator. Say what is on the display and in the memory after each key is pressed.

Using the memory

The calculator memory can help you to do many calculations *more efficiently*.

You will find key codes showing ways to use the memory in examples in this book. Always try these with the memory keys on your calculator. Then see whether you can find a 'better' way to do the working with your calculator. If you find a better way, make a note of it with a copy of the example. This means you can use it as a reminder in your later work and revision.

The memory is very useful in these three situations:
- when you have to use the same number repeatedly
- when you want to 'remember' the answer to a calculation to use it later
- when you want to keep a 'running total'.

Using a number repeatedly

Separate calculations

In some work with a calculator you use the *same* number *more than once*.

For example, to find the factors of 3920 you can key in:

`3` `9` `2` `0` `÷` `2` `=`

`3` `9` `2` `0` `÷` `3` `=`

`3` `9` `2` `0` `÷` `4` `=` and so on.

Keying in the same number again and again is tedious. Using the memory is more efficient. You can put the number into the memory. Then simply recall it each time you want to use it.

So to test 3920 for factors, put 3920 into the memory:

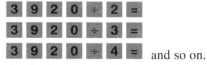

Then recall it each time you test a number:

and so on …

Discussion Exercise

Use your calculator to find the factors of 3920. Try it with and without using the calculator memory.
Discuss the advantages/disadvantages of both ways.

Exercise P7.6

Use your calculator memory to do the questions in this exercise.

1 Give the answers shown on your calculator display.
(a) Add 374.82 to each of these numbers:

251, 176, 476.8, 5214, 962.18

(b) Subtract 23.76 from each of these numbers:

125, 77, 314.9, 191.04, 8.35

(c) Multiply each number by 27.3:

5, 11, 18.6, 152, 213.7

(d) Divide each number by 235:

476, 592, 783.8, 18.1, 149.7

2 Work out the first ten multiples of each number.
(a) 17 (b) 41 (c) 53 (d) 79

3 Find all the factors of each number.
(a) 462 (b) 280 (c) 3003 (d) 2100

4 Sean's top-selling carpet costs £13.49 per square metre. How much do these amounts of carpet cost?
(a) 7 m² (b) 8.5 m² (c) 21.4 m² (d) 46.7 m²

5 When Sally went on holiday to France the rate of exchange was 8.74 francs (FF) to the pound. Here are the prices of some things she bought.

| 25FF | 39FF | 52FF | 78FF |

| 42FF | 5FF | 10FF | 136FF |

Change each price to its equivalent in sterling (£).

6 1 yard ≈ 0.914 metres.
Use this fact to do these conversions.
(a) Change these to metres.

5 yards, 14 yards, 22 yards, 56.5 yards.

(b) Change these to yards.

7 m, 23 m, 51 m, 76 m, 100 m.

7 Jane gets 15% discount at work. Last month she bought items with these marked prices.

| £6 | £7.50 | £5.99 | £15.88 |

| £8 | £12.30 | £11.49 | £26.99 |

Work out how much Jane paid for each item.
(*Hint:* Each item costs Jane 100% −15% = 85% of the marked price. 85% = 0.85)

8 Work out the final bill when VAT at 17.5% is added to these amounts.
(a) £76.52 (c) £58.27 (e) £103.00
(b) £89.34 (d) £93.68 (f) £131.19

Within one calculation

The *same number* may also appear *more than once* in a calculation. You can put the repeated number into memory. Then you simply recall it when you need it in the calculation.

For example,

when you substitute $n = 15$ into $3n^2 - 4n + 7$, you get this calculation:

$$3 \times 15^2 - 4 \times 15 + 7$$

Here is one way to do the working with a calculator. 15 is put into memory first.

Then we use **MR** each time 15 appears in the calculation.

| **1** **5** **Min** | **3** **×** **MR** **x^2** | **−** **4** **×** **MR** **+** **7** **=** | **622.** |

Puts 15 into 3×15^2 4×15
memory

Always plan the best way to do the working with your calculator. Here is a useful strategy to use.
- Do the calculation with a *simple* number first *without* a calculator.
- Think about the steps you take.
- Work out the key code for these steps.
- Test the key code with your simple number. Check it gives the same result as before.

Writing down your key code is a good idea. This is a useful reminder of what to do. It is easy to forget the steps, especially if you are nervous in an examination.

▶ *Exercise* P7.7

Find the value of each expression for the given values of x. Make use of your calculator memory to do the working. Write down the key code you use for each expression.

1 $x^2 - 2x + 3$
  (a) $x = 14$ (b) $x = 5.4$ (c) $x = 0.9$
2 $2x^2 + 3x - 1$
  (a) $x = 17$ (b) $x = 4.6$ (c) $x = 5.26$
3 $7 - 2x - x^2$
  (a) $x = 13$ (b) $x = 2.1$ (c) $x = 0.8$
4 $1 + 4x - 5x^2$
  (a) $x = 12$ (b) $x = 0.6$ (c) $x = 0.25$
5 $4x(3x + 7)$
  (a) $x = 15$ (b) $x = 3.2$ (c) $x = 0.9$
6 $-x(2x^2 - 5)$
  (a) $x = 11$ (b) $x = 3.5$ (c) $x = 4.7$
7 $(3x - 1)(5 - 2x)$
  (a) $x = 15$ (b) $x = 2.6$ (c) $x = 0.4$
8 $3x^2 - \dfrac{2}{x} + 5$
  (a) $x = 18$ (b) $x = 0.2$ (c) $x = 10.25$
9 $x^3 + 4x^2 - 3$
  (a) $x = 14$ (b) $x = 4.4$ (c) $x = 1.2$

👁 *Investigation*

Use your calculator memory to help you to explore these number patterns.
1 Continue each pattern.
   Comment on what you find.

(a) $101 \times 44 =$
   $101 \times 444 =$
   $101 \times 4444 =$
   $101 \times 44444 =$
   ...

(b) $141 \times 11 =$
   $141 \times 111 =$
   $141 \times 1111 =$
   $141 \times 11111 =$
   ...

(c) $143 \times 1 \times 7 =$
   $143 \times 2 \times 7 =$
   $143 \times 3 \times 7 =$
   $143 \times 4 \times 7 =$
   ...

(d) $101^1 =$
   $101^2 =$
   $101^3 =$
   $101^4 =$
   ...

2 (a) Write down the first seven multiples of 142 857. Notice anything?
   (b) Use your calculator to write down the next two multiples of 142 857.
       What do you notice now?
   (c) Try to write down the next five multiples of 142 857 without using your calculator. Then check your answers.
   (d) Now replace 142 857 by 7 in the calculator's memory. Use it to write down

   $$\frac{1}{7} \qquad \frac{2}{7} \qquad \frac{3}{7}, \ldots$$

   What do you notice this time?

3 Multiply any three consecutive numbers together e.g., $4 \times 5 \times 6$. Is the answer divisible by 24? Repeat with other sets of three consecutive numbers until you can say why some answers are divisible by 24 and others are not. (Putting 24 into memory makes the checking easier to do.)   👁

Storing an answer

The memory on a calculator is also useful when you are doing calculations with *several parts*. You can work out the answer to one part. Store it in the memory. Then recall it when you want to use it.

When using the memory in this way, you have to plan the working carefully.

Look at the example below.

$$\frac{395 + 162}{571 \div 91}$$

To do this calculation you need to take these steps.

- Work out the bottom part first.
  Store the answer in the memory.

  | **5** **7** **1** **÷** **9** **1** **=** **Min** |

  The result **6.274725275** is shown on the display when you press **=** .

- Work out the top part next.

  | **3** **9** **5** **+** **1** **6** **2** **=** |

  The result **557.** is displayed when you press **=** .

- Divide this result by the number in the memory.

  | **÷** **MR** **=** |

  The display shows **ᵐ88.76882662**

  This gives 89 to the nearest whole number.

- Use an estimate as a check as usual.

  $395 \approx 400 \quad 162 \approx 200 \quad 571 \approx 600 \quad 91 \approx 100$

$$\frac{395 + 162}{571 \div 91} \approx \frac{400 + 200}{600 \div 100}$$

$$= \frac{600}{6}$$

$$= 100$$

The answer (89) and the estimate (100) are about the same size. So the answer is a sensible size.

Exercise P7.8

Use the memory on your calculator to find the answers to the calculations in Exercise P 7.3 on p 281.

ℚ Discussion Exercise

What are the advantages of using the memory to do calculations with several parts?
What are the disadvantages?
Discuss.

When is it easier to use brackets instead of the memory?
When is it easier to use the memory?
Discuss.

Keeping a 'running total'

You can use the ⊞ key to **add up a list of numbers**. The *display* shows the 'running total', each time you press ⊞.
For example,

Adding a *few* numbers in this way is no problem. Adding a *long list* of numbers like this is not so simple. It is easy to lose track of where you are in the list.

You can also use M+ or SUM to add up a list of numbers. This method keeps the 'running total' in the *memory*, not on the display. The *last number* you entered is always shown clearly *on the display* each time you press M+ or SUM.
To display the final total, you press MR at the end.
For example,

By keeping the running total in the memory, it is easy to see where you are in the list. You just look at the number on the display.

It is also easy to correct mistakes. If you spot an incorrect number on the display, simply use M−, after M+. This subtracts the mistake on the display from the total in the memory.

When you use this method, always clear the memory first to make sure it is 'empty'. We used 0 Min to do this in the example above.

(Remember: M+ adds the number on the display to the number in the memory.)

Exercise P7.9

Use the memory in your calculator to do these.

1 Check the totals on these supermarket bills.

(a)	(b)	(c)
0.59	0.50	1.29
2.47	0.59	0.25
0.69	0.60	1.24
1.41	0.48	1.45
1.89	0.52	0.52
7.05	0.79	0.99
	0.56	1.19
	1.51	0.79
	5.55	0.65
		0.67
		0.83
		1.23
		0.89
		0.91
		12.90

2 Find the total distance travelled by a sales manager over the past ten days. His daily mileages are:

127, 164, 234, 169, 223, 87, 368, 188, 201, 156.

3 Calculate the mean average of these sets of values:
(a) £57, £76, £52, £65, £89, £48.50, £37.40.
(b) 17 cm, 11.9 cm, 21 cm, 16.5 cm, 65 cm, 47 cm, 70 cm.
(c) 54 kg, 58 kg, 54.9 kg, 52.3 kg, 55.1 kg, 54.3 kg, 52.4 kg, 55.9 kg, 58.5 kg.

4 Calculate the total of these numbers:

$4.1^2, 5.8^2, 7.3^2, 2.6^2, 4.8^2, 3.7^2, 9.2^2, 8.1^2, 6.6^2$.

5 What is the total cost of:
3 tins of paint at £5.64 each
12 rolls of paper at £7.28 each
4 packets of paste at £1.47 each?

6 Find all the factors of 28 except 28 itself.
Each time you find a factor, add it to the contents of the memory.
When you have found all the factors (except 28) recall the contents of the memory. What do you notice?
Any number which is equal to the sum of all its factors (except the number itself) is called a 'perfect' number.
Try to find some more 'perfect' numbers.

Examination Questions

1 $D = 1000 - 1.28 \times 16^2$
Use the formula to find the value of D.
(ULEAC, 1994)

2 (a) Use your calculator to find the value of
$$\frac{730 \times 8.45 \times 7}{83 \times 9}$$
and write down the full calculator display.
(b) Express your answer correct to one place of decimals.
(NEAB, 1988)

3 Use your calculator to find $\sqrt{\dfrac{2.43 \times 56.7}{1.118}}$
Give your answer correct to 3 significant figures.
(MEG, 1991)

4 (a) Use your calculator to find $\dfrac{5.31 \times \sqrt{7.61}}{25.2 + 6.7}$

(Write down all the figures in the display.)

(b) Round off your answer to part (a) to three significant figures.

(MEG, 1994)

5 (a) Calculate the exact value of $\dfrac{\sqrt{5.0176}}{1.4 \times 0.8^2}$.

(b) Find how many terms of the series $1 + \frac{1}{2} + \frac{1}{3} + \frac{1}{4} + \frac{1}{5} + \dots$ must be taken for the sum to exceed 2.8.

(MEG, 1988)

6 (a) Use your calculator to find the value of

$\dfrac{5.48 \times \sqrt{8.9}}{21.8 + 7.9}$.

(b) Give your answer to (a) correct to one decimal place.

(c) Jack, who did not have a calculator, worked out the result approximately by considering the numbers corrected to the nearest whole number. Write down the answer Jack would get. Show how you would work out the answer by this method.

(NEAB, 1994)

P8
More perimeter and area

This unit will help you to:

■ calculate the perimeters and areas of parallelograms and trapeziums

■ do length and area calculations for compound shapes

■ recognise and use units for areas of land

■ find lengths given the area of a parallelogram or trapezium.

Looking back at perimeter and area

Memo

The **perimeter** of a shape is the *total distance* around its edge. It is measured in length units such as mm, cm, m, ...
Area is the *amount of surface* a shape covers. It is measured in square units, such as cm², m², ...

Parallelograms

Memo

A **parallelogram** is a special quadrilateral (4-sided shape). Both pairs of opposite sides are parallel and equal.

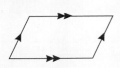

Rectangles, rhombuses and **squares** are all special parallelograms.

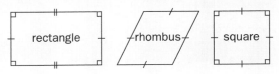

ACTIVITY

Parallelogram areas

● Draw parallelograms A, B, C and D on cm squared paper. Cut them out carefully.

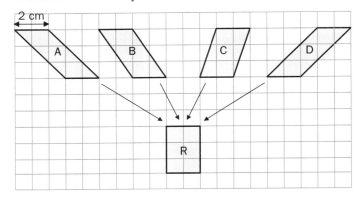

Cut up your parallelogram A so that the pieces make the rectangle shape, R. (Do not use more than two cuts. Use straight cuts only.) Stick your rectangle on to paper and mark the 'cut lines' clearly.

Now do the same with your parallelograms B, C and D.

● Shapes A, B, C, D and R must have the *same area*.
Explain why.
What is this area?
How did you find it?

● What *other* measurements are the *same* in all of these shapes?
Draw a different parallelogram with these measurements.
Find its area by counting squares.
Is it what you expected?

● Think about your work in this activity.
Discuss your findings.
Suggest ways to complete this sentence:
'It looks as if the area of a parallelogram is …'

● Test your ideas. See if they are true for other parallelograms.

▶ *Exercise* P8.1

1 (a) Compare parallelograms A, B, C and D in the next diagram. What have they got in common?

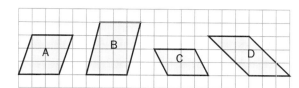

(b) What have parallelograms E, F, G and H got in common?

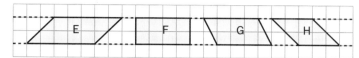

(c) *Predict* the answers to these questions for each set of parallelograms shown above.
Which have the same area?
Which has the largest area?
Which has the smallest area?
Explain how you made each prediction.
Check your answers by counting squares.

2 Draw three different parallelograms to fit each set of facts. Use squared paper.
(a) One side 5 cm, area 10 cm^2.
(b) Area 18 cm^2, one pair of parallel sides 3 cm apart.
Compare the three parallelograms in each set.
List all the measurements they have in common.
What do you notice?

3 (a) These parallelograms each have sides of length 3 cm and 5 cm. Say what you can about their areas.

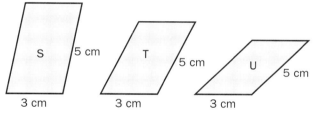

(b) Draw some different parallelograms with sides of 3 cm and 5 cm. Use squared paper to find their areas.
Comment on what you find.

4 Predict the area of each parallelogram below. Explain how you found it in each case. Then count squares to check.

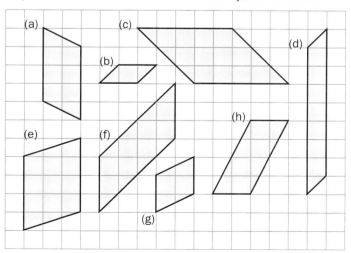

Finding a formula for area

A **formula** makes it easier to calculate an area.
There is a simple formula for the area of a parallelogram.
Here are two ways to work out what it is. Try them.

Discussion Exercise

Change the shape
One way to find the area of a parallelogram is to change it into a rectangle. You did this in the activity 'Parallelogram areas' on p 288.
   With some parallelograms, you can simply 'cut off' a triangle at one side and move it to the other side like this …

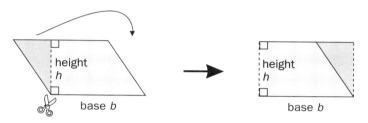

With other parallelograms, you have to cut and move *two* triangles like this…

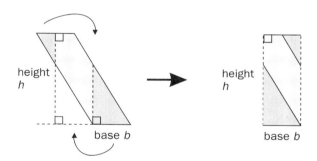

Think about the diagrams shown above.
Discuss what they show.
As part of your discussion complete the sentences given below. These lead to the formula you want.
The missing words and letters are given in this box.

base	height	parallelogram	rectangle
	right	same	*b* *h*

Start with any parallelogram with base …… and height ……. .
The height is at …… angles to the …… and its opposite side.

Change the parallelogram into a …… .
These two shapes have the same …… and height.

The rectangle has been made from the …… .
Their areas must be the …… .

Area of the rectangle = base × …… = ……*h*
Area of the parallelogram = …… × …… = ……

Two triangles

Another way to find the area of a parallelogram is to divide it into two triangles.

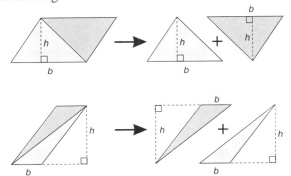

Discuss the diagrams shown above.

Develop a formula for the area of a parallelogram from them. As part of your discussion, complete the following sentences. The missing words and symbols are given below.

angles	base	diagonal	equal	height	
opposite	right	triangles	b	h	$\frac{1}{2}$

Start with any parallelogram with ......b and ......h.
The height is at .... to the base and its ......side.

Draw in a ....
This splits the parallelogram into two ....

Opposite sides of a parallelogram are ...... and parallel.
So each triangle has the same base ......
     and the same height ....

Area of each triangle = $\frac{1}{2} \times$ base $\times$ ...... = $\frac{1}{2}$ ...... h

Area of parallelogram = 2 × Area of the triangle
       = 2 × (...... × ...... × height)
       = ... × ......
       = b......

Summary

Area of parallelogram = **base × height.**

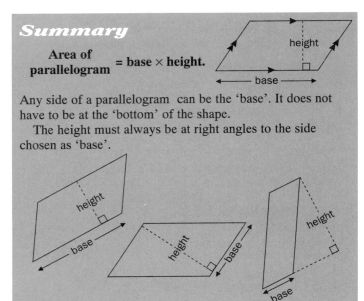

Any side of a parallelogram can be the 'base'. It does not have to be at the 'bottom' of the shape.
 The height must always be at right angles to the side chosen as 'base'.

To draw a 'height' *accurately* on a diagram, you can use a **set square**.

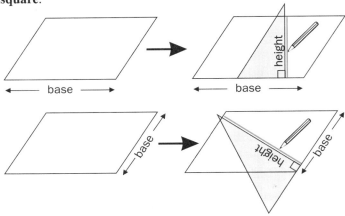

A parallelogram has four sides.
But opposite sides are equal and parallel.
So there are *two* possible values for its 'base'.
Each 'base value' has a *matching* 'height value'.

This means there are *two possible ways* to calculate the area of a parallelogram. The way you use depends on the 'base' and 'height' you know.

Question

Two accurate drawings of the same parallelogram PQRS are given below.
Find the area of the parallelogram in mm². Do this in two different ways.
Method 1: Use PQ as base.
Method 2: Use PS as base.
Measure all lengths to the nearest mm.

Answer

Method 1:
Draw 'height' RT at right angles to PQ. Measure base PQ and height RT.
base: PQ = 55 mm
height: RT = 20 mm
Area = base × height
   = 55 × 20
   = 1100 mm²

Method 2:
Draw 'height' QU at right angles to PS. Measure base PS and height QU.
base: PS = 22 mm
height: QU = 50 mm
Area = base × height
   = 22 × 50
   = 1100 mm²

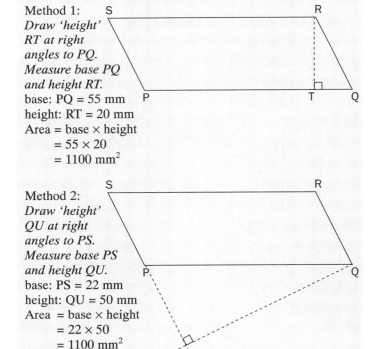

Memo

Perimeter

To find the perimeter of a parallelogram, add up the lengths of its sides. Opposite sides are equal. So perimeter is given by:

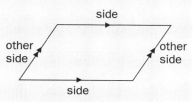

| 'side' + 'other side' + 'side' + 'other side'. |

or | 2 × 'side' + 2 × 'other side' |

or | 2 ('side' + 'other side') |

Here are some points to remember when calculating perimeters and areas:
- Identify the lengths you plan to use first. Then you can ignore any others.
- Make sure all lengths are in the same unit. Check it gives the unit you want in the answer. Change the units if you need to.
- Give the correct unit of measure in your answer.

Memo

1cm	=	10 mm
1m	=	1000 mm
1m	=	100 cm
1km	=	1000 m

Question

This diagram shows a parallelogram. It is not drawn accurately.
Calculate:
(a) its perimeter in millimetres
(b) its area in square centimetres to the nearest square centimetre.

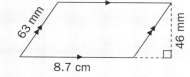

Answer

(a) *For perimeter in mm, all sides must be in mm.*
Side: 8.7 cm = (8.7 × 10) mm = 87 mm
Other side: 63 mm
Perimeter = (2 × 87) + (2 × 63) = 300 mm

(b) *For area in cm², base and height must be in cm.*
Base: 8.7 cm
Height: 46 mm = (46 ÷ 10) cm = 4.6 cm
Area = base × height = 8.7 × 4.6
$$= 40.02$$
$$= 40 \text{ cm}^2 \text{ (to the nearest cm}^2)$$

► Exercise P8.2

The parallelograms below are drawn accurately. Trace them carefully. For each parallelogram, calculate as accurately as you can:
(a) its perimeter
(b) its area in two different ways.
Measure the lengths you need to the nearest mm.
The two ways of calculating the area may not give exactly the same value in each case.
Explain why.

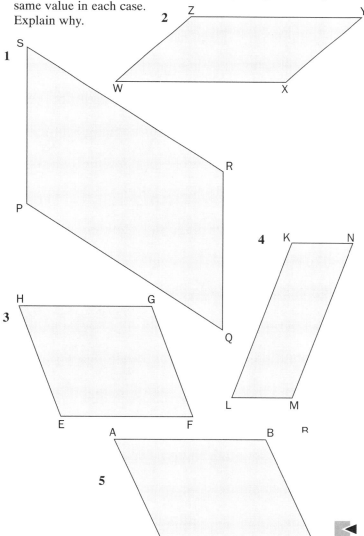

► Exercise P8.3

Calculate (a) the perimeter and (b) the area of each of these parallelograms.

1

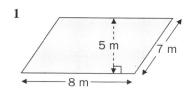

3

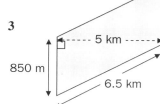

2

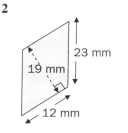

4

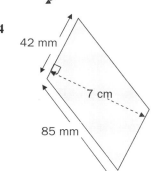

5

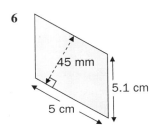

←— 2.5 m —→
2 m
85 cm

7

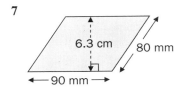

6.3 cm
80 mm
←— 90 mm —→

6

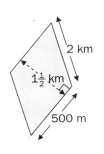

45 mm
5 cm
5.1 cm

8

2 km
$1\frac{1}{2}$ km
500 m

●Trapeziums

Memo

A **trapezium** is a quadrilateral with only one pair of sides parallel.

These are trapeziums:

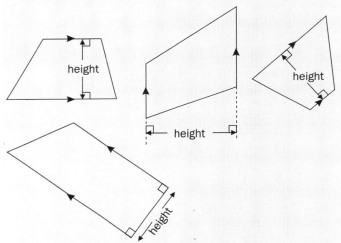

The distance between the parallel sides is called the height.
The height is at right angles to the parallel sides.

Area of a trapezium

There are several ways to find a formula for the area of a trapezium.
Here are some to try.

Discussion Exercise

Two together

Start with a trapezium.   Add an identical trapezium like this.

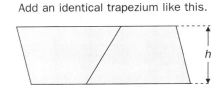

Think about the two diagrams you have just seen.
Discuss what they show.

As part of your discussion complete the following sentences.
They lead to the formula for the area of the trapezium.
The missing words and symbols are given in this box.

angles	area	base	height	parallel
	parallelogram	trapezium	size	
	$a + b$	h	$\frac{1}{2}$ 2 $\times$	

Start with any ....
Call the length of its ...... sides *a* and *b* and its height ....
The height is at right ...... to the parallel sides.

Put a congruent ...... with it.
It is the same shape and ....
Fit the two trapeziums together to make a ....

(a + b) is the ...... of the parallelogram.
...... is its height.
Area of this parallelogram = base $\times$ ......
                          = (......) $\times$ h

The parallelogram is made of ... trapeziums of the same area.
Area of trapezium = $\frac{1}{2}$ ...... of parallelogram.
                  = $\frac{1}{2}$ $\times$ (a + b) ....

Change the shape

Start with a trapezium.   Cut it up like this.

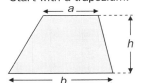 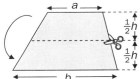

Make it into this shape.

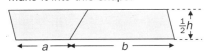

Two triangles

Start with a trapezium.   Draw in a diagonal.

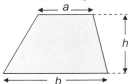 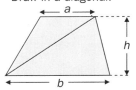

Make it into two triangles.

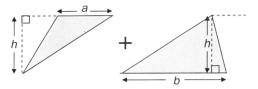

Each method shown in **Change the shape** and **Two triangles** leads to this formula:

Area of trapezium = $\frac{1}{2}(a + b)h$

Explain how in each case.
Discuss your ideas with your group.

The formula you have found uses the letters *a*, *b* and *h*. Without using these letters, explain what the formula tells you to do.
Discuss the explanations given by your group.
Which give the clearest instructions for working out the area of a trapezium?

Calculating perimeter and area of a trapezium

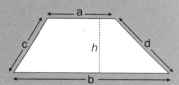

Summary

For a trapezium:
Perimeter = sum of lengths of four sides
Area = $\frac{1}{2}$ × (sum of parallel sides) × height

The height is the perpendicular distance between the parallel sides.
For this trapezium:
Perimeter = $a + b + c + d$
Area = $\frac{1}{2}(a + b)h$
All lengths must be in the same unit.
Change any if you need to.

Question

Measure lengths in this trapezium to the nearest millimetre. Use your measurements to calculate:
(a) its perimeter
(b) its area.

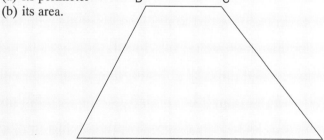

Answer

(a) Sides of trapezium:
   AB = 65 mm, BC = 45 mm, CD = 20 mm, DA = 40 mm
   All lengths in mm → perimeter in mm.
   Perimeter = 65 + 45 + 20 + 40 = 170 mm
(b) Parallel sides:
   AB = 65 mm, CD = 20 mm
   Height: distance between AB and CD = 36 mm.
   All lengths in mm → area in mm²

   Area of trapezium = $\frac{1}{2}$ × (sum of parallel sides) × height
   = $\frac{1}{2}$ × (65 + 20) × 36
   = $\frac{1}{2}$ × 85 × 36 = 1530 mm²

You can use the *brackets* on your calculator to work out the area of a trapezium.
For example, in the working in the last example,

for $\frac{1}{2}$ × (65 + 20) × 36

key in: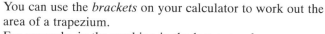

Look at the display for the answer to (65 + 20)
and for the final answer.
Write the results clearly in your working.

▶ *Exercise* P8.4

Use a ruler to measure lengths in each trapezium to the nearest millimetre. Use your measurements to calculate:
(a) the perimeter of each trapezium
(b) the area of each trapezium.

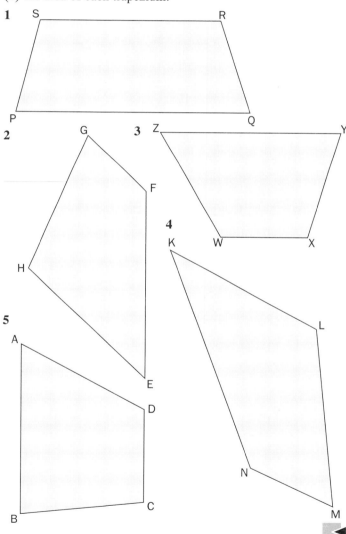

All the lengths you use in a calculation must be in the *same* unit.
Remember:
Always check the units of the lengths you plan to use.
Change any if you need to.
Make sure the unit you choose to work in gives the unit you want in the answer.

Question

This diagram shows the end wall of a roof space. Its shape is a trapezium.

(a) What is its perimeter in centimetres?

(b) What is its area in square metres?

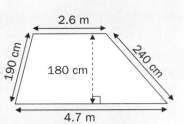

Answer

(a) *For perimeter in cm, the lengths of sides must be in cm.*

Parallel sides: 4.7 m = 4.7 × 100 cm = 470 cm

2.6 m = 2.6 × 100 cm = 260 cm

Other sides: 190 cm and 240 cm

Perimeter = 470 + 240 + 260 + 190 = 1160 cm

(b) *For area in m², lengths must be in m.*

Parallel sides: 2.6 m and 4.7 m

Height: 180 cm = 180 ÷ 100 = 1.8 m

Area of trapezium = $\frac{1}{2}$ × (sum of parallel sides) × height

= $\frac{1}{2}$ × (2.6 + 4.7) × 1.8

= $\frac{1}{2}$ × 7.3 × 1.8

= 6.57 m²

▶ *Exercise* P8.5

Calculate (a) the perimeter and (b) the area of each of these trapeziums.

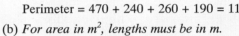

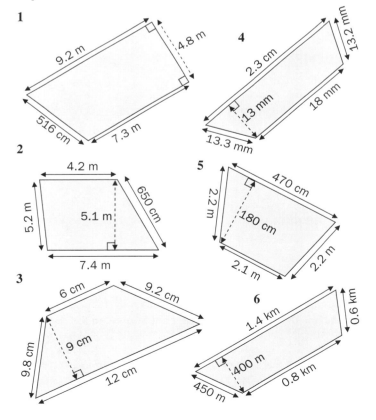

7

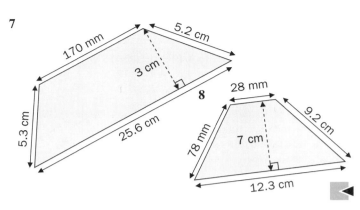

8

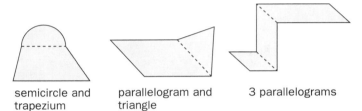

Compound shapes

You have found the perimeters and areas of squares, rectangles, triangles, circles, parallelograms and trapeziums.

Many *complicated shapes* can be *split* into these simple shapes. This helps you to find their perimeters and area.

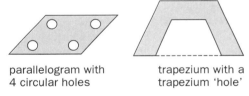

semicircle and trapezium

parallelogram and triangle

3 parallelograms

Add up the lengths round the edge to find the perimeter. Work out the area of each simple shape and add them together to find the total area.

Other shapes look like a simple shape with a hole or holes cut out of it.

parallelogram with 4 circular holes

trapezium with a trapezium 'hole'

To find this kind of area, work out:

Area of whole shape – Area of hole(s)

When you find the perimeters and areas of these compound shapes, always plan the working carefully.

Think about the most efficient way to use your calculator. Use the memory and bracket facilities if it helps. Keep a neat record of your results as you go along.

▶ *Exercise* P8.6

1 The diagram below shows a design for a wooden headboard for a bed. The centre section is a rectangle. The two outer sections are parallelograms with the same dimensions.

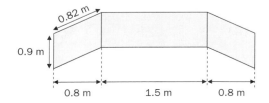

(a) Calculate the area of the headboard in square metres.

(b) Beading is to be attached around the edge of the headboard. How much beading is required?

2

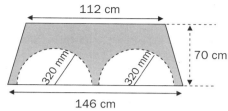

112 cm
70 cm
320 mm
320 mm
146 cm

The diagram shows the windscreen of a car. The two windscreen wiperblades each clean a semicircular area of the screen. Calculate the shaded area of the windscreen which is not cleaned by the two wiperblades.

3

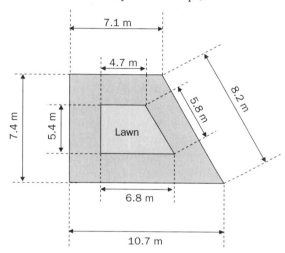

7.1 m
4.7 m
8.2 m
5.8 m
7.4 m
5.4 m
Lawn
6.8 m
10.7 m

This diagram shows the plan view of a lawn surrounded by a paved border.

(a) Calculate the area of the paved border.

(b) Brick edging is to be placed around the inner and outer perimeter of the paved border. Calculate the length of edging needed.

4   Brian is redecorating the stairs and landing in his house. This diagram shows the wall he wants to wallpaper.

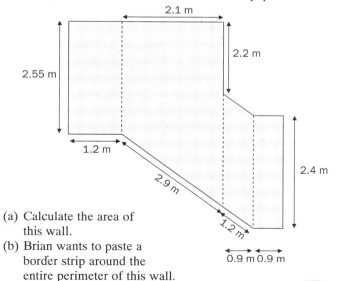

2.1 m
2.2 m
2.55 m
1.2 m
2.9 m
2.4 m
1.2 m
0.9 m   0.9 m

(a) Calculate the area of this wall.

(b) Brian wants to paste a border strip around the entire perimeter of this wall. How much will he need?

More area units

Area is usually measured in square units.

Metric	
square millimetre	mm^2
square centimetre	cm^2
square metre	m^2
square kilometre	km^2

Imperial	
square inch	in^2
square foot	ft^2
square yard	yd^2
square mile	mile^2

Other units are also used to measure areas of land, such as fields, farms, parks, ...

The special metric units for land area are the **are (a)** and **hectare (ha)**.

A square of side 10 m has an area of 1 are.

1 are = 100 square metres.

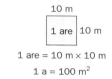

10 m
1 are   10 m
1 are = 10 m × 10 m
1 a = 100 m^2

The tennis court used for a singles match covers about 2 ares ... 1 are on each side of the net.

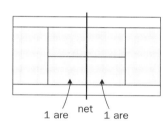

1 are   net   1 are

1 hectare = 100 ares

hect- means 100.

A square of side 100 m has an area of 1 hectare.

1 hectare = 10 000 square metres

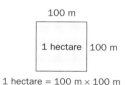

100 m
1 hectare   100 m
1 hectare = 100 m × 100 m
1 ha = 10 000 m^2

The playing area for a rugby union match is about 1 hectare.

Square metres are often used for some *small land areas* such as gardens, building plots, ...

Question

A soccer pitch for an international match is 100.5 m long and 73.1 m wide.

Find its area, to the nearest m^2,

(a) in square metres

(b) in ares

(c) in hectares.

continued

Answer

(a) Area of pitch = 100.5 m × 73.1 m

$\qquad\qquad\qquad$ = 7346.55 m^2

$\qquad\qquad\qquad$ = 7347 m^2 (to the nearest m^2)

(b) $\qquad$ 100 m^2 = 1 are

$\qquad$ Area of pitch = 7347 m^2 $= \dfrac{7347}{100}$ ares

$\qquad\qquad\qquad\qquad$ = 73.47 ares

(c) $\quad$ 10 000 m^2 = 1 hectare

$\qquad$ Area of pitch = 7347 m^2 $= \dfrac{7347}{10\,000}$ hectares

$\qquad\qquad\qquad\qquad$ = 0.7347 hectares

Square kilometres are usually used for *very large land areas*, such as cities, countries, ...

Question

The smallest country in the world is the Vatican City State. Its area is 0.44 km^2.
(a) Work out how many hectares there are in 1 km^2.
(b) Find the area of the Vatican City State in hectares.

Answer

(a) 1 km = 1000 m

$\quad$ So a square of side 1 km and a square of side 1000 m are equal in area.

$\qquad$ 1 km $\qquad\qquad\qquad\qquad$ 1000 m

$\qquad$ | A | 1 km $\qquad\qquad$ | B | 1000 m

Area A = 1 km × 1 km $\qquad$ Area B = 1000 m × 1000 m

$\qquad$ = 1 km^2 $\qquad\qquad\qquad\qquad$ = 1 000 000 m^2

$\qquad$ Area A $\;=\;$ Area B

$\qquad$ 1 km^2 = 1 000 000 m^2

$\qquad$ 1 km

$\qquad$ | 1 km^2 = 100 ha | 1 km

But 10 000m^2 = 1 hectare

$\qquad$ 1 km^2 = 100 ha

So 1 km$^2 = \dfrac{1\,000\,000}{10\,000}$ hectares

$\qquad\qquad$ = 100 hectares

There are 100 hectares in 1 km^2.

(b) Area of Vatican City State

$\qquad\qquad$ = 0.44 km^2

$\qquad\qquad$ = 0.44 × 100 hectares

$\qquad\qquad$ = 44 hectares

The special imperial unit for land areas is the **acre**.

$\quad$ The acre is a medieval land measure. In the Middle Ages the land was worked in strips. An acre was a strip that could be ploughed in a day.

It was 10 chains (220 yards) long and 1 chain (22 yards) wide.

$\qquad\qquad\qquad$ 10 chains

1 chain $\qquad\qquad\qquad\qquad\qquad\qquad$ 22 yards

$\qquad\qquad\qquad$ 220 yards

$\qquad$ 1 acre = 4840 square yards
$\qquad$ 640 acres = 1 square mile

An acre is smaller than a hectare.

1 hectare ≈ 2.5 acres

$\qquad\qquad$ | 1 hectare |

$\qquad\qquad$ | 1 acre |

Question

A rectangular field is 308 yards long and 165 yards wide. Find the area of this field:
(a) in square yards
(b) in acres
(c) in hectares
(Use 1 acre = 4840 yd^2 and 1 ha = 2.5 acres)

Answer

(a) Area of field = 308 yd × 165 yd

$\qquad\qquad\qquad$ = 50820 yd^2

(b) $\qquad$ 4840 yd^2 = 1 acre

$\qquad$ Area of field = 50820 yd$^2 = \dfrac{50\,820}{4840}$ acres

$\qquad\qquad\qquad\qquad$ = 10.5 acres

(c) $\qquad$ 2.5 acres = 1 ha

$\qquad$ Area of field = 50820 yd$^2 = \dfrac{10.5}{2.5}$ ha

$\qquad\qquad\qquad\qquad$ = 4.2 ha

▶ *Exercise* P8.7

1 Give the most suitable metric and imperial unit for the area of each of the following
$\quad$ (a) Your local park $\qquad$ (d) Wales
$\quad$ (b) The English Channel $\quad$ (e) Wembley Stadium
$\quad$ (c) A basketball court $\qquad$ (f) A supermarket

2 Change each of these areas to ares and to hectares.
$\quad$ (a) 75 250 m^2 $\qquad\qquad$ (c) 6900 m^2
$\quad$ (b) 4.2 km^2 $\qquad\qquad\;$ (d) 0.35 km^2

3 Change each of these areas to m^2 and to km^2
$\quad$ (a) 95 ares $\qquad\qquad$ (c) 6092 ares
$\quad$ (b) 180 ha $\qquad\qquad\;$ (d) 5000 ha

4 How many acres in each of these areas?
$\quad$ (a) 9000 yd^2 $\qquad\qquad$ (c) 3560 yd^2
$\quad$ (b) 4 miles^2 $\qquad\qquad$ (d) 0.75 miles^2

5 Change each of these to square yards and to square miles.
$\quad$ (a) 3 acres $\qquad\qquad$ (c) 29 acres
$\quad$ (b) 580 acres $\qquad\qquad$ (d) 700 acres

6 Roughly how many hectares in each of these?
$\quad$ (a) 145 acres $\qquad\qquad$ (c) 4000 yd^2
$\quad$ (b) 9 acres $\qquad\qquad$ (d) 0.5 miles^2

7 Approximately how many acres in each of these?
(a) 7 ha   (b) 45 ares
(c) 6.5 ha   (d) 72 ares

8 Calculate the area of these plots of land.
Give each in ares and in hectares.
Roughly how many acres is each?

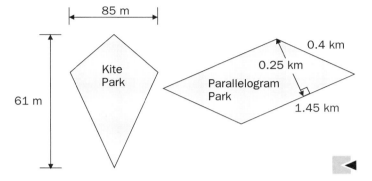

Offset surveys

The area of a plot of land can be found from the results of an
offset survey.
The following example shows the method used.

Helen and Damien did
an offset survey of a
local field.
They pegged a string from
one end of the field to the
other, roughly down the
middle. Then they measured
the shortest distance from
this **base line** to each corner. These are called the **offsets**.
   They also measured how far each offset was along the
base line.
This sketch plan of the field shows their results.

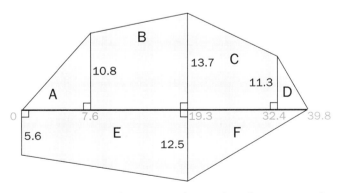

All measurements are in metres. The numbers in green are the
distances from O along the base line to each offset.
   The other numbers are offset distances, at right angles to the
base line.
The six regions of the field are lettered A to F.

 Discussion Exercise

• Discuss how to calculate the area of each region A to F
  on the plan above.

Make sure you answer these questions during your
discussion:
What shape is each region?
Which area formulas will be used?
Which lengths must you know for each area calculation?

• Calculate:
(a) the area of each region A to F in m^2
(b) the total area of the field, to the nearest m^2
(c) the area of the field in ares, correct to 3 sf.
Record your working neatly.
Make sure you show clearly what you have done.
Look at the ways other students in your group have set down
their working. Discuss their good and bad features.
Decide on the best way to show the working in an
examination.

• Discuss how to do this working efficiently
with a calculator.
Use its bracket and memory facilities to help you.
Try doing the working on your calculator.
Make a note of the most efficient method you find.

▶ *Exercise* **P8.8**

Two offset survey plans of fields are given below.
All measurements are in metres. Calculate the area of each field
in square metres.
Also give each area in a suitable 'land area' unit correct to
3 significant figures.

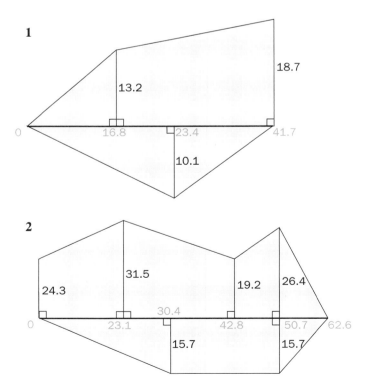

ACTIVITY

Do an offset survey of a suitable plot of land near your school or college.
Work with at least one other student.

Make a plan of the plot of land from your results. Draw the plan to scale.

Calculate the area of the plot of land from your plan. Give its size in square metres and in a special 'land area' unit.

Find the shape and area of your plot of land from a large scale Ordnance Survey map. Comment on what you find.

Finding lengths

Using parallelogram areas

There are two lengths in the formula:

> Area of parallelogram = base × height

If you know the area and one of these lengths, you can find the other length.

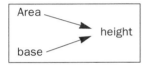 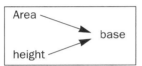

Question

ABCD is a sketch of a parallelogram whose area is 36 cm².
BC = 78 mm
CD = 52 mm
Calculate the length marked *l*.
Give your answer in centimetres.
Round it to the nearest millimetre.

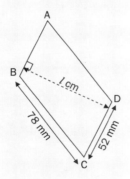

Answer

- *Draw diagram:*

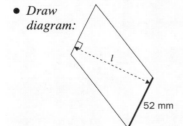

- *Find matching units:*

  area: 36 cm²

  base: 52 mm = 5.2 cm

  height: *l* cm

- *Formula:* Area of parallelogram = base × height
- *Values:* $36 = 5.2 \times l$
- *Working:* $36 \div 5.2 = l$

  `6.923076923`

- *Answer:* $l = 6.9$ cm (to nearest mm)
- *Check:* Area ≈ 5 × 7 = 35 ✓ About the same size as 36, the given area.

The last example shows how to *solve* such problems *step-by-step*.
Here are some notes about the key steps.

- Identify the base and height for the area you know. Mark them on a *diagram*. Use colour if it helps. 'Forget' any other lengths. You don't need them.
- Make sure the measurement have '*matching units*' for the unit you want.
  Remember:

      mm² and mm → mm
      cm² and cm → cm
      m² and m   → m
      and so on …

  Change units if you need to.
- Write down the *formula* for the area.
- Put in the *values* you know.
- Do the *working* to solve the equation you get.
- *Answer* the question.
  Don't forget the unit of length.
  Round your result sensibly if necessary.
- *Check* your answer is about the right size.

► *Exercise* **P8.9**

Each diagram below shows the sketch of a parallelogram. Use the information to calculate the length marked with a letter. Give your answers correct to the nearest millimetre.

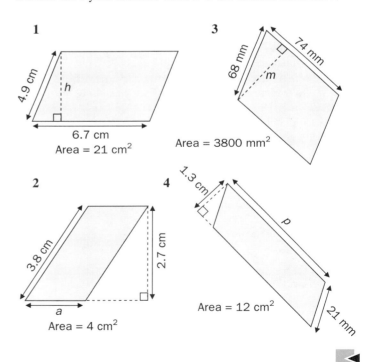

Using trapezium areas

There are three lengths in the trapezium formula:

> Area = ½ × sum of parallel sides × height

or   Area = ½ (*a* + *b*)*h*

If you know the area and any two of these lengths, you can find the third length.

The example below lists the key steps taken. Make sure you understand them.

Remember:
Always identify the parallel sides (*a* and *b*) and the height (*h*) of the trapezium first. Then you can 'forget' any other lengths.

Question

The area of this trapezium is 1080 mm². Calculate the height *h*.

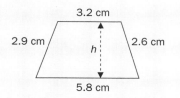

Answer

- *Draw diagram:*

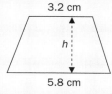

- *Find matching units:*
  area: 1080 mm²
  parallel sides:
  3.2 cm = 32 mm
  5.8 cm = 58 mm
  height: *h* mm

- *Formula:*   Area = ½ × (sum of parallel sides) × height
- *Values:* $1080 = \frac{1}{2} \times (32 + 58) \times h$
- *Working:* $1080 = \frac{1}{2} \times (90) \times h$
  $1080 = 45 \times h$
  $1080 \div 45 = h$

- *Answer:*   *h* = 24 mm
- *Check:*   Area ≈ ½ (30 + 60) × 20 = 900 ✓
  About the same size as 1080, the given area.

Here is an efficient way to do the working on a calculator. It uses the memory.

Display: **90.**   **45.**

`1` `0` `8` `0` `÷` `MR` `=`
Display: **24.**

Try it on your calculator.
Watch the answers it gives on the display.

► *Exercise* **P8.10**

1

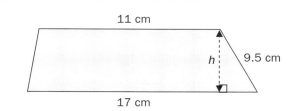

The area of this trapezium is 112 cm². Find *h*.

2 This diagram shows the cross-section of a swimming pool. Its area is 40.8 m².

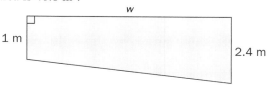

Calculate *w*, the width of the pool.

3 This diagram shows a metal support bracket. Calculate *p*, given that its area is 83.2 cm².

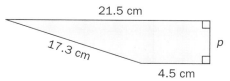

4 The area of a trapezium shaped flower bed is 37.8 m². The two parallel sides measure 3.7 m and 5.3 m. Calculate the distance between these sides.   ◄

Examination Questions

1 The diagram shows a parallelogram.

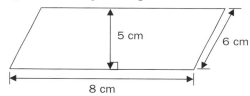

Calculate
(a) the perimeter of the parallelogram.
(b) the area of the parallelogram.

(NEAB, 1991)

2 A table top is made in the shape of a trapezium, as shown here.

Find the area of this table top.

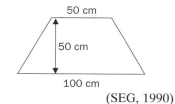

(SEG, 1990)

3 The diagram shows part of a basketball court. The shaded area is known as 'the key'. The key consists of a trapezium and a semi-circle. The dimensions are shown on the diagram which is *not drawn to scale*.

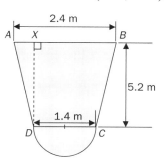

(a) Calculate
  (i) the length AX
  (ii) the area of the triangle AXD
  (iii) the area of the trapezium ABCD.
(b) Calculate
  (i) the area of the semi-circle to 2 decimal places
  (ii) the total shaded area.   *(continued)*

(iii) Calculate the distance around the curved part of the key from C to D.
(Take π to be $\frac{22}{7}$ or use the π button on your calculator.)

(SEG, 1989)

4   The diagram shows the end view of a greenhouse.

B is 2.5 m above ED.
AB = BC.
AE = CD = 2 m.
ED = 3 m.

Last winter, 40 cm of snow settled on the roof.

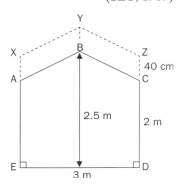

(a) Calculate the area, in m^2, of
   (i) the end of the greenhouse, ABCDE
   (ii) the end, XYZDE, *including* the layer of snow.
(b) Hence find the area of the snow section, XYZCBA.
(c) Explain why the answer to (b) should equal the width of the greenhouse multiplied by the depth of snow.

(ULEAC, 1988)

5   (a) Calculate the area of the parallelogram ABCD in the diagram.
(b) Use your answer to (a) to find the value of *x*.

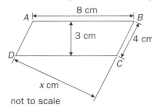

(MEG, 1991)

P9

Frequency distributions and diagrams

This unit will help you to:

- recognise and identify discrete and continuous data

- make and use frequency distribution tables and frequency diagrams from discrete data

- make and use frequency tables and frequency diagrams for grouped discrete data

- group continuous data into class intervals

- identify the boundaries, width and mid-points of class intervals expressed in different ways

- draw and use frequency diagrams for grouped continuous data

- draw frequency polygons for grouped data

- use frequency polygons to compare frequency distributions.

Discrete and continuous data

Zoe and Nicky collected data about their class.
Zoe collected only **discrete data**.
Her data were:

> number of children in family
> shoe size
> number of rooms in house
> marks scored in French test.

Discrete data have only certain *distinct* values. Each is an **exact value.**

For example,
the number of children may be 0, 1, 2, … but not $\frac{1}{2}$, $1\frac{1}{2}$, –2, … because you cannot have these number of children.

Discrete data are often *whole* numbers and are found *by counting*.
Sometimes they also include some fractions.

For example,
shoe sizes may be 4, $4\frac{1}{2}$, 5, $5\frac{1}{2}$, …
Only whole and $\frac{1}{2}$ sizes exist, other fractions do not.
So $4\frac{3}{4}$, 6.2, … have no meaning.

The *possible values* in discrete data go up in *'jumps'*.
They can be shown as *separate points* on a number line.

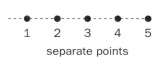

Nicky collected only **continuous data**.
Her data were:

> foot length
> time taken to travel to college
> weight of books in college bag
> amount of water drunk in a day.

Continuous data can be **any values within a certain range**.
These values are usually found *by measuring*. They are given to a suitable *degree of accuracy*. They cannot be given 'exactly'.

For example,
the foot lengths in Nicky's survey took values in the range of 19 cm to 27 cm.
Nicky's own foot length is *about* 21 cm. It may be given as 21 cm (to the nearest cm) or 20.7 cm (to the nearest mm).

The *possible values* in continuous data go up *continuously*.
They can be shown as a *continuous number line*.
Each point on the line is a possible value.

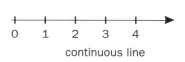

Discussion Exercise

1 Give some possible values Zoe could get in her survey of
 (a) rooms in houses
 (b) marks in French test.
 Give some values Zoe could not get.
 Explain your answers.
2 Suggest a possible range of values Nicky could get in her survey of
 (a) travel times
 (b) weights of books
 (c) water drunk.
 To what degree of accuracy would it be sensible to give these data? Discuss.
3 Are these data discrete or continuous?
 Discuss your answers.
 (a) Number of goals scored by a player in a season
 (b) Time taken to bake cakes
 (c) Shirt sizes
 (d) Population of the countries in the UK
 (e) Weight of newspapers
 (f) Temperature of an oven
 (g) Number of chocolates in boxes
 (h) Area of lawns on a housing estate
 (i) Capacity of buses
 (j) Height of trees
 (k) Volume of cornflakes packets
 (l) Number of lampposts on roads
 (m) Money paid for part time jobs
 (n) Capacity of freezers
 (o) Car lengths
 (p) Number of chairs in classrooms.
4 Give at least two examples of your own of discrete data.
 Suggest possible values for each example.
 Discuss your ideas with your group.
5 Give at least two examples of your own of continuous data.
 Suggest a possible range of values and a sensible degree of accuracy for the data in your examples.
 Compare your examples with those of others in your group.

Frequency distributions for discrete data

Frequency table

A shopping centre did a survey of users of their car park.
The number of people arriving in each car in the first 15 minutes are listed below.

1	2	2	3	4	4	1	2	1
3	3	1	2	4	2	2	4	2
2	3	3	3	2	1	5	2	3
2	3	3	1	1	3	5	3	2
1	3	2	4	5	2	3	1	2

Data in this form are called **raw data.** They have not yet been organised in any way.
These raw data are *discrete*. There are five *different* data values. In order of size, they are: 1, 2, 3, 4, 5.
Each data value occurs more than once. The number of times each value occurs is called its **frequency**.

To find the frequency for each data value you can make a **tally table**.

Memo
Tally tables
p 197

Here is the tally table for the car park data.

Number of people	Tally	Frequency
1	ЖЖ IIII	9
2	ЖЖ ЖЖ ЖЖ	15
3	ЖЖ ЖЖ III	13
4	ЖЖ	5
5	III	3
Total		45

Total number of cars in the survey

This is a **frequency distribution table**. It shows the frequency for *each* data value. It helps you to see how the data are *distributed* (spread).

A frequency distribution table is usually given *without* the tallies. It is often called simply a **frequency table**.
The word 'frequency' may not appear in the table.
Always make sure that you identify which numbers are the 'values' and which are the frequencies.

The table can have values going down or across the page.

Values   Frequency

Number of people	Number of cars
1	9
2	15
3	13
4	5
5	3
Total	45

Values →

Number of people	1	2	3	4	5
Number of cars	9	15	13	5	3

← Frequency

Frequency diagram

This bar graph is a **frequency diagram**. It displays the data from the car park survey.

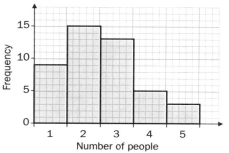

Look at the frequency diagram on p 301.

'Frequency' is on the *vertical* axis. The *height* of each bar shows a *frequency*. It shows how frequently each 'number of people' appears in the data.

The *horizontal* axis gives the *number of people* in each car in the survey. All the possible different numbers are listed, i.e., 1, 2, 3, 4, 5. They are in numerical order. So there are no gaps between bars. Each number is marked in the '*space*' for its bar.

The frequency diagram gives an instant impression of the data from the survey.

You can see that:

● Roughly half the cars had only 1 or 2 people in them.
● Very few cars were full.
● Most cars had just the driver and one passenger in them.

Summary

A frequency diagram is often used to give a picture of a frequency distribution. It shows the frequency with which each value occurs in the data.

A frequency diagram is a bar graph. It has frequency on the vertical axis. The horizontal axis is labelled with a description of the data.

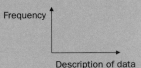

The data are numerical values, i.e., numbers or measurements.

The height of each bar represents a frequency of data. The bars are drawn next to each other, without gaps (unless there is a frequency of zero).

Remember:
Not all bar graphs are frequency diagrams. A frequency diagram must show frequencies. The data must be numerical, not items such as colours, names, and so on.

► *Exercise* P9.1

1 A dentist made a survey of the number of fillings in the teeth of some Year 8 children. Here are the results.

```
1  1  2  0  0  3  1  1  2
2  2  1  1  0  4  1  0  2
3  1  2  1  3  0  1  2  1
4  0  1  2  2  0  1  2  2
0  1  2  2  3  3  0  1  4
```

(a) How many children did the dentist survey?
(b) Make a frequency table to show the dentist's findings.
(c) Draw a frequency diagram to illustrate these data.
(d) What comments might the dentist have made about these children's teeth?

2 In a survey during a road safety campaign a number of drivers were asked to say how many accidents they had had in the last five years. The following list shows the results.

```
1  1  3  3  3  0  2  0  1  2
0  3  0  4  2  3  0  3  1  3
3  4  0  0  6  3  5  0  1  0
3  1  0  7  4  3  3  0  2  3
1  3  3  2  5  0  3  0  6  3
1  0  3  5  0  1  4  2  3  4
```

(a) How many drivers took part in the survey?
(b) Make a frequency table for these data.
(c) Draw a frequency diagram to illustrate the survey findings.
(d) Discuss the findings of the survey. Comment on any features the frequency diagram shows.

3 A population survey was carried out on the two villages of Ranstone and Snaresbrook. The tables below show the number of residents in each house in each of the two villages.

Ranstone:

Number of residents	1	2	3	4	5	6
Number of houses	5	24	14	20	3	4

Snaresbrook:

Number of residents	1	2	3	4	5
Number of houses	26	15	3	5	1

(a) On separate diagrams draw two frequency diagrams to illustrate the information gathered in the survey.
(b) Use your two frequency diagrams to comment on any differences you notice between the two distributions.

Grouping discrete data

Frequency table

A class of students took a science test. It is marked out of 100. Each mark is a whole number. Here are the test results for the class.

```
40  12  75  69  73  60
78  89  68  88  29  82
56  61   5  43  66  54
21  84  83  62  85  35
76  95  91  36  65  80
```

These raw data need to be organised in some way. One way is to put the marks in order of size. Then you can find the frequency of each mark by tallying.

Mark	Frequency	Mark	Frequency	Mark	Frequency
5	|	60	|	78	|
12	|	61	|	80	|
21	|	62	|	82	|
29	|	65	|	83	|
35	|	66	|	84	|
36	|	68	|	85	|
40	|	69	|	88	|
43	|	73	|	89	|
54	|	75	|	91	|
56	|	76	|	95	|

This gives a frequency table but it is not very useful. There are 30 different marks in the data. So the frequency for each mark is 1.

To obtain a clearer picture of the distribution, you can *group* the marks within **class intervals.**

The possible test marks range from 1–100.

Here are five class intervals you can use for them.

1–20,   21–40,   41–60,   61–80,   81–100.

The way the intervals are described is important. The marks are *discrete data*. They are whole numbers. So there are *no* marks in *between* these classes.

1 – 20 , 21 – 40 , 41 – 60 , 61 . . . . and so on

next mark   next mark   next mark

Each mark in the data belongs to *only one* interval.
It is no use using intervals such as 1–10, 10–20, 20–30, …
Marks such as 10, 20, 30, … would be in two intervals.
   The first class interval, 1 to 20, covers *20 possible marks*.
We say 20 marks is its **class width**.
   The class intervals given above all have the *same* width.
To sort the science test marks into these class intervals you can use a tally table as before.

Mark Class interval	Tally	Frequency
1– 20	II	2
21– 40	IIII	5
41– 60	IIII	4
61– 80	IIII IIII I	11
81–100	IIII III	8
Total		30

This is called a **grouped frequency distribution table**. It shows how the marks are *distributed* across the range 1–100. The frequencies give the number of times a mark in the data is in *each class interval*.

Frequency diagram

The frequency diagram below shows the grouped frequency distribution for the science test marks.

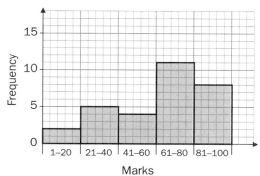

The *height* of each bar shows the *frequency for its class interval*.
The *base* of each bar is labelled with its *class interval*.
There are no values between class intervals. So there are *no gaps* between the bars.
   The class intervals are of *equal width*. So the bars are the *same width*.

If you use class intervals of another width, you get a different frequency diagram. The next exercise investigates what some of these look like.

Note:
In this book *all the class intervals* used for a distribution will be of *equal* width.

▶ *Exercise* P9.2

1   These four class intervals can also be used for the science test marks:

    1–25,   26–50,   51–75,   76–100.

  (a) What is the width of each class interval?
  (b) Copy and complete this frequency distribution table.

Mark Class interval	Tally	Frequency
1– 25		
26– 50		
51– 75		
76–100		
Total		

2   The first class interval for the science test data can also be 1–10.
  (a) What is the class width for this class interval?
  (b) How many class intervals of this width do you need for these data? What are the other class intervals?
  (c) Make a frequency table for the data using the class intervals from (b).

3 (a) The possible marks in the science test range from 1–100. You can group these marks into 20 equal width class intervals. What are these class intervals?
  (b) Use the class intervals from (a) to make a grouped frequency table for the science test data.

4   Draw a grouped frequency diagram from each frequency table in questions **1–3**.

◯ *Discussion Exercise*

- Compare the four grouped frequency diagrams showing the science test marks.
  Each frequency diagram uses a class interval of a different width.
  How many class intervals are used on each diagram?
  Which frequency diagram shows most detail?
  Which shows least detail?
- All four frequency diagrams give a picture of the data.
  Which do you think gives the best overall picture?
  Which do you think gives the worst?
  Give reasons for your answers.
  Discuss your ideas with other students in your group.
- The science teacher wants to draw *one* frequency diagram for an end of year report on the class. Which would you advise her to draw? Why? What comments, based on the diagram, could she make in her report?
- Other subject teachers also have to give a report on the class. Here are the highest and lowest marks given in each of their tests.

	Lowest mark	Highest mark
English	1	50
Mathematics	4	120
History	20	60
Geography	15	75
French	40	200

What would be suitable class intervals for a grouped frequency distribution for each subject's data?
Give reasons for your choices.

Discuss the class intervals suggested by the students in your group.
Which do you think are the best in each case?
Explain why.

Summary

Data may be *grouped into class intervals* in a frequency distribution. This is usually done when:
- each data value occurs only a few times

and/or ● the range of values is large.

The grouped frequency distribution shows the number of values in each class interval. Data may be grouped into different class intervals. It is easier to use equal class intervals. All the examples in this book have equal class intervals.

In an examination question you may be given the class intervals to use. Sometimes you have to choose them yourself.
Use these guidelines to help you:
- Do not use too many or too few groups. This can make it difficult to spot whether any patterns exist. Usually between 5 and 15 class intervals will give a reasonable 'picture' of the data.
- Make all the class intervals the same width.
- Describe each class interval carefully. Make sure there is no doubt about the class interval in which each value is placed.

► *Exercise* P9.3

1 A group of students at Sinclair High School took part in a sponsored swim at the local pool. The number of lengths completed by each student is shown below.

```
11  19  13  28   4   8  17  22  10
 5  22   6  17  20  23   8  11  21
27   9  18  20  16  12  11  13  24
13  19  22  16  25   3  12  15  18
15  29  23  18  16  29  14  25  17
```

(a) How many students took part in the swim?
(b) Copy and complete this grouped frequency distribution table for these data.

Number of completed lengths	Tally	Frequency
1– 5		
6–10		
11–15		
16–20		
21–25		
26–30		
Total		

(c) Draw a frequency diagram to illustrate these data.

2 The first 50 people to leave the newly opened Rosco Supermarket were each asked how much money they had spent. This list shows the amount, in pounds, spent by each customer.

```
21.76  35.28  59.21  15.67  42.11
30.10  29.14  43.91  52.43  28.77
40.22  31.61   8.92  37.22  20.16
20.94  40.91  34.71  44.62  38.71
45.69  22.14  54.67  25.62  39.15
26.19  50.80  32.35  23.60  43.08
46.02  34.17  13.70  36.96  26.24
42.34  41.76  46.81  24.87  67.29
41.04  33.64  36.07  58.15  11.21
18.23  45.45   5.06  44.68  35.28
```

(a) Copy and complete this grouped frequency table.
(b) Draw a frequency diagram to illustrate these data.

Amount spent (£)	Frequency
0.01–10.00	
10.01–20.00	
20.01–30.00	
30.01–40.00	
40.01–50.00	
50.01–60.00	
60.01–70.00	
Total	

Grouped continuous data

Frequency table

James travels to college by train.

He keeps a record of how late the train is each day for a term.
To get an overall picture of his data, he groups the times into 5-minute intervals.

This frequency table shows his grouped data.
t stands for 'time'.

Class interval (*t* minutes)	Frequency
$0 \leq t < 5$	19
$5 \leq t < 10$	16
$10 \leq t < 15$	6
$15 \leq t < 20$	9
$20 \leq t < 25$	7
$25 \leq t < 30$	3

Times are **continuous data**. Look carefully at how the class intervals are described.

$0 \leq t < 5$ means *t* is 0 or more, but less than 5.
$5 \leq t < 10$ means *t* is 5 or more, but less than 10
$10 \leq t < 15$ means *t* is 10 or more, but less than 15
and so on …

The class intervals make it clear to which group each time belongs.

The first class interval, $0 \le t < 5$, has a frequency of 19.
This means that 19 trains were less than 5 minutes late.
(This includes trains that were *not* late, i.e., 0 minutes late.)

The next class interval, $5 \le t < 10$, has a frequency of 16.
This means that 16 trains were 5 or more minutes late, but less than 10 minutes late.
And so on …

The class intervals show where the class boundaries are.

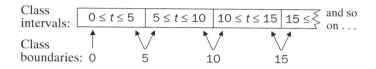

For the class interval $0 \le t < 5$,
the lower class boundary is 0,
the upper class boundary is 5.
The class width is $5 - 0 = 5$ minutes.

For the class interval $5 \le t < 10$,
the lower class boundary is 5,
the upper class boundary is 10.
The class width is $10 - 5 = 5$ minutes.
And so on …

Each class interval has the same width, i.e., 5 minutes.

Frequency diagram

You can draw this frequency diagram from James' frequency table on p 304.

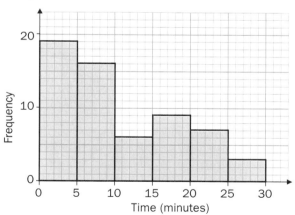

The times are continuous data. So the horizontal axis is a **continuous number line**. It covers *all* the possible times in the data.
The horizontal scale is numbered with the *class boundaries*.
The edges of each bar are *on* its class boundaries.
The class intervals are the *same* width. So the bars are the *same* width.

Describing class intervals

The class intervals used for James' data may be described in different ways.
Each way gives the *same* class boundaries and class width

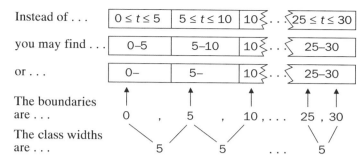

Note:
In the class intervals 0–5, 5–10, 10– , … the values of 5, 10, appear in *two* class intervals. This may cause confusion, so use another way to give the intervals if you can.

In the class intervals 0– ,5–, … 25–30, only the last class interval gives a lower and upper value.

Discussion Exercise

1 Below are some class intervals for continuous data.
What are the boundaries for each class?
What is the class width for each class interval.

(a) Class interval (l mm)	(b) Class interval (m grams)	(c) Class interval (A cm^2)
$20 \le l < 30$	20– 50	0–
$30 \le l < 40$	50– 75	100–
$40 \le l < 50$	75–100	200–
$50 \le l < 60$	100–125	300–
$60 \le l < 70$	125–150	400–500

Give the class intervals in each case in two different ways.

2 Here is another way to give class intervals for continuous data.
What do these class intervals mean?
What are the boundaries and width of each class? Discuss.
Suggest other ways to write the same class intervals.
Discuss your ideas.

Class interval (t seconds)
$65 < t \le 70$
$70 < t \le 75$
$75 < t \le 80$
$80 < t \le 85$
$85 < t \le 90$

Exercise P9.4

1 A market gardener checks the weights (in grams) of a number of tomatoes for grading purposes. Here are her results.

Weight (g)	60–65	65–70	70–75	75–80	80–85
Frequency	9	20	29	15	7

(a) How many tomatoes did the market gardener check?
(b) What are the boundaries and width of each class interval?
(c) Draw a frequency diagram for these data.
(d) Comment on the distribution of weights of the tomatoes checked.

2 Dennis Pyke spent two months travelling around Europe last summer. Each day, at noon, he recorded the temperature in whole degrees Celsius and wrote it in his diary. The temperatures are shown on the next page.

```
26  12  24  42  16  18  30  24  36   8
34  24  20  16  24  16  18  26  10  32
24  12  26  12  12  20  24  18  14  22
24  14  34  24  20  12  20  24  20  26
32  12  16  42  26  22  24  20  16  18
18  30  24  36   8  26  18  24  10  16
```

(a) Make a grouped frequency distribution table for these temperatures.
Use the class intervals 5–, 10–, 15–, …, 40–45.
(b) State the class boundaries and class width of each interval.
(c) Draw a frequency diagram of this distribution.
(d) Comment on any features you notice about this distribution of temperatures.

3 Sue Riley is a keen botanist. She measured the lengths, in whole millimetres, of 30 leaves on her basil plant. This list gives her findings.

```
41  64  60  73  75  79  56  91  70  61
65  77  82  55  96  81  67  45  75  86
59  87  33  52  70  75  78  64  76  62
```

(a) Make a grouped frequency distribution table for these measurements. Use the class intervals:
$30 \leq l < 40$, $40 \leq l < 50$, …, $90 \leq l < 100$, (l mm)
(b) What are the boundaries and width of each class?
(c) Draw a frequency diagram to illustrate Sue's findings.
(d) Suggest some comments Sue might make when discussing her findings.

4 The students in class 10B were asked to say how many whole numbers of minutes it took them to travel to college that day. Here are their replies:

```
 6  13  15  19  22  12  16  24
10  14  14  20  23   9  21   8
18  16  25  17  22  30   4  12
15  11  20  19   6  20  18  15
```

(a) Make a frequency table for these times. Use the class intervals:
$0 < t \leq 5$, $5 < t \leq 10$, …, $25 < t \leq 30$, (t minutes).
(b) State the boundaries and width of each class interval.
(c) Draw a frequency diagram for these data.
(d) Comment on the distribution of travelling times for the students in class 10B.

Measurements given 'to the nearest …'

Pilgrim School has a weather station.
Data are recorded every Friday at 10 am.
Temperatures are measured to the nearest degree Celsius.
    The results for last year are shown in this grouped frequency table.
The temperatures are grouped in $5°$ intervals. T stands for temperature.

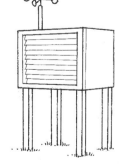

Class intervals Temperature (T °C)	Frequency
1– 5	5
6–10	13
11–15	14
16–20	12
21–25	6
26–30	2

Temperatures are continuous data. But the class intervals seem to have 'gaps' between the values.

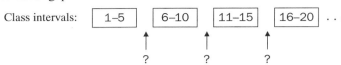

Class intervals:

The temperatures are measured '*to the nearest degree*'. This means that temperatures 'in between' whole degrees are *rounded up* or *down*.
'Half-way or more' between
    → round up
'Less than half-way' between
    → round down.

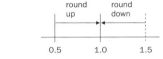

Temperatures from 0.5° to just under 1.5° are called 1°.
Temperatures from 1.5° to just under 2.5° are called 2°.
Temperatures from 2.5° to just under 3.5° are called 3°.
Temperatures from 3.5° to just under 4.5° are called 4°.
Temperatures from 4.5° to just under 5.5° are called 5°.

So the class interval 1–5 covers the temperatures:

from 0.5° to just under 5.5°,
i.e., $0.5 \leq T < 5.5$

The boundaries of *this class* are 0.5 and 5.5.
The boundaries of *each class* can be found from the stated intervals.

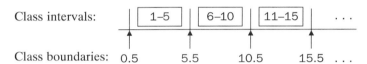

Class intervals:

Class boundaries: 0.5   5.5   10.5   15.5 …

Each boundary between two classes is *half-way* between the *upper value* stated in one class interval and the *lower value* stated in the next.
See how the class boundaries show what each class interval means.

Class interval
1– 5	means	$0.5 \leq T < 5.5$
6–10	means	$5.5 \leq T < 10.5$
11–15	means	$10.5 \leq T < 15.5$
16–20	means	$15.5 \leq T < 20.5$
21–25	means	$20.5 \leq T < 25.5$
26–30	means	$25.5 \leq T < 30.5$

The *width* of each class interval is also given by its boundaries. It is the *difference* between the *upper* and *lower boundary*.

For the class 1–5, the width is $5.5 - 0.5 = 5$
For the class 6–10, the width is $10.5 - 5.5 = 5$
For the class 11–15, the width is $15.5 - 10.5 = 5$
And so on …

All the class intervals have the same width. It is 5°C.

Frequency diagram

The class boundaries *separate one class from another*. On a frequency diagram of the distribution, the *edges* of each bar must be *on* its class boundaries.
    Following are two frequency diagrams drawn for the temperature distribution from Pilgrim School's data.
Look carefully at the numbering on the horizontal axes.

In this frequency diagram, the horizontal axis is marked with the *class boundaries*.
This makes it easy to draw.

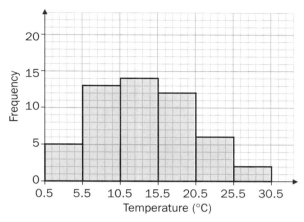

In the next frequency diagram, the horizontal axis is an *'ordinary' number line*.
See how the *edge*s of the bars are placed *on* the class boundaries using this scale.

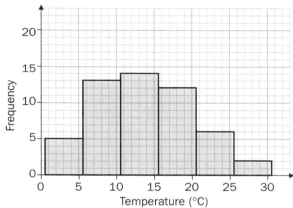

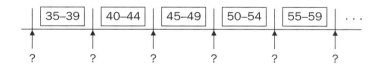

◯ *Discussion Exercise*

Below are some class intervals for continuous data. The measurements have all been made 'to the nearest ...'.
Find the 'missing' class boundaries for each class.
Work out the class width for each class interval.
Discuss how you found your answers.

1

| 35–39 | 40–44 | 45–49 | 50–54 | 55–59 | . . . |

2

| 1.0–1.9 | 2.0–2.9 | 3.0–3.9 | 4.0–4.9 | . . . |

3

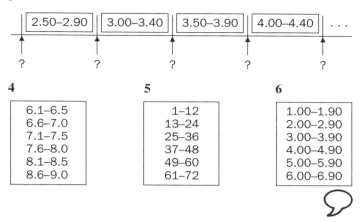

4

| 6.1–6.5 |
| 6.6–7.0 |
| 7.1–7.5 |
| 7.6–8.0 |
| 8.1–8.5 |
| 8.6–9.0 |

5

| 1–12 |
| 13–24 |
| 25–36 |
| 37–48 |
| 49–60 |
| 61–72 |

6

| 1.00–1.90 |
| 2.00–2.90 |
| 3.00–3.90 |
| 4.00–4.90 |
| 5.00–5.90 |
| 6.00–6.90 |

◯

Age distributions

Always look carefully at class intervals in age distributions. They often look as if they are given 'to the nearest year'. But ages are usually given in 'completed years'.

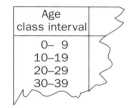

Age class interval
0– 9
10–19
20–29
30–39

For example, we say someone is 19 years old *from* his or her 19th birthday *until just before* their 20th birthday. So in this table, someone who is 19 years 364 days old is included in the 10–19 class interval.
This means that for ages, A years,

0– 9 means $0 \le A < 10$, i.e., from 0 to just under 10,
10–19 means $10 \le A < 20$, i.e., from 10 to just under 20,
and so on ...

This gives us the class boundaries for each age group.
For example,
for ages:

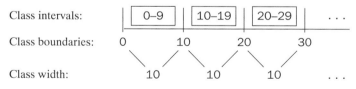

▶ *Exercise* **P9.5**

1 For a home economics investigation Kamal weighed each egg, to the nearest gram, in a batch delivered to the school kitchen.
This table shows his results.

(a) How many eggs did Kamal weigh?

(b) Draw a frequency diagram to illustrate Kamal's data.

(c) Comment on this distribution of weights of eggs.

Mass (grams)	Number of eggs
40–44	3
45–49	13
50–54	22
55–59	27
60–64	29
65–69	24
70–74	7

2 In a Simplon Factor competition, each contestant has to complete a set task in as short a time as possible.
This list gives the time, to the nearest second, taken by each contestant to complete the task.

```
31  44  27  46  25
12  58  35  32  46
22  15  23  41  38
36  25  45  17  40
50  32  36  57  39
```

(a) Make a frequency table for these data. Group the data into class intervals of:
1–10, 11–20, 21–30, 31–40, 41–50, 51–60 (seconds).
(b) Draw a frequency diagram from your frequency table.
(c) Comment on this distribution of times taken by the contestants to complete the task.

3 A theme park did a survey of ages of their visitors. The data in this frequency table is for the first hour on Sunday.

Age (in years)	0–9	10–19	20–29	30–39	40–49
Frequency	42	25	33	21	8

(a) Draw a frequency diagram to illustrate these data.
(b) Comment on any features your diagram shows about the age distribution of the visitors.

Frequency polygons

A frequency diagram is a frequency graph. It is a *bar* graph. This frequency diagram comes from a survey of students' bus fares to college.

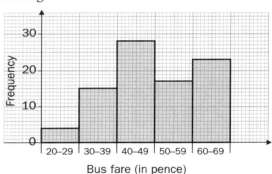

A **frequency polygon** is also a frequency graph. It is a *line* graph.
The polygon is made from the lines of the graph and the horizontal axis.
This frequency polygon is from the same student survey.

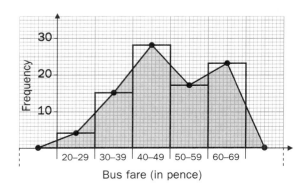

To draw a frequency polygon you can use the bars of a frequency diagram.
Mark the *mid-points* of the top line of each bar.
Then join the points in order, from left to right, with *straight lines*.

To make the lines into a polygon, you join the *ends* to the *horizontal axis*. Imagine there is an extra class interval at each end of the 'real classes'. These classes have zero (0) frequency. So the tops of their 'bars' are on the horizontal axis. Mark the mid-points of these imaginary bars. Join each point to the line graph.

► *Exercise* **P9.6**

Draw a frequency polygon on each frequency diagram you have drawn. They are from Exercises P9.2, P9.3, P9.4 and P9.5.

Discussion Exercise

1 The frequency polygon for the bus fares survey is drawn below without the bars.

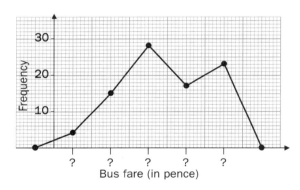

The numbers are missing from the scale on the horizontal axis.
What would you write for each '?' on the scale?
Discuss how to find these numbers.
What are the coordinates of each 'corner point' of the polygon?
Explain your answers.

Here is the frequency table for the bus fare survey data.

Bus fare (in pence)	20–29	30–39	40–49	50–59	60–69
Frequency	4	15	28	17	23

How can you draw the frequency polygon for these data without drawing the bars first?
Discuss.

2 Look at the frequency table for each frequency polygon you have drawn. (They are in Exercises P9.2, P9.3, P9.4 and P9.5).
Decide how to find the coordinates of the corner points of each polygon from its frequency table.
Discuss your ideas with other students in your group.

Summary

Drawing frequency polygons

You can draw a frequency polygon without drawing a bar graph first. You plot the points where the mid-point of the tops of the bars should be.
Here are the steps to take.

- The mid-point of each bar is at the mid-point of its class interval. Find these mid-point values from the class intervals in the tables.

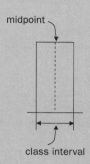

- Draw the axes as before. Frequency is on the vertical axis. Number it with a suitable scale. Label the horizontal axis with a description of the data. Mark the mid-point values on the scale.

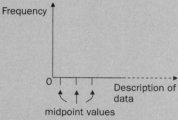

- Plot the mid-points against frequency for each class. Plot the mid-point of an extra 'imaginary' class at each end against frequency zero (0).
- Join all the plotted points, in order from left to right, with straight lines.
This gives the frequency polygon.

Finding mid-points
Take care to find the mid-point of each class interval correctly. Think carefully about the data and how the intervals are given.

For discrete data:
Find the smallest and largest possible values that each class can contain.

 mid-point of class interval
 $= \frac{1}{2}$ ('smallest possible value' + 'largest possible value')

e.g. The class interval 15–19 is for runs in cricket
 The 'smallest possible value' is 15.
 The 'largest possible value' is 19.
 The mid-point $= \frac{1}{2}(15 + 19)$
      $= 17$ runs

For continuous data:
Find the class boundaries for each class interval.

 mid-point of class interval
 $= \frac{1}{2}$ (lower class boundary + upper class boundary)

The class boundaries depend on how the data are recorded.

When data are recorded to the 'complete unit', the boundaries are often easy to see.
e.g. The class interval $10 \le t < 20$ is for times in 'complete minutes'.

The lower class boundary is 10.
The upper class boundary is 20.
The mid-point $= \frac{1}{2}(10 + 20)$
     $= 15$ minutes

When data are recorded '*to the nearest unit*', you have to work out the boundaries.
e.g. The class interval 60–69 kg is for masses measured to the nearest kg.
 The lower class boundary is 59.5
 The upper class boundary is 69.5
 The mid-point $= \frac{1}{2}(59.5 + 69.5)$
     $= 64.5$ kg

When data are *ages* remember they are recorded in a special way.
e.g. The class interval 15–19 is for ages in years.
 15–19 means 15 years to just under 20 years.
 The lower class boundary is 15.
 The upper class boundary is 20.
 The mid-point $= \frac{1}{2}(15 + 20)$
     $= 17.5$ years.

▶ *Exercise* **P9.7**

1   This frequency table gives the marks obtained by a number of Year 11 students at Monkton Comprehensive in an algebra test.

class interval	10–19	20–29	30–39	40–49	50–59	60–69
Frequency	3	9	21	19	12	2

  (a) Write down all the possible values that the first class interval can contain.
  (b) What is the class width and mid-point of the first class interval?
  (c) What are the mid-points of all the class intervals?
  (d) Draw a frequency polygon for these data.

2   Forty members of the Abbeyvale Youth Club were asked how many hours they spent watching television last week. Their replies in hours, to the nearest hour, are shown in this frequency table.

Time in hours	1–5	6–10	11–15	16–20	21–25	26–30
Frequency	3	8	12	9	6	2

  (a) Write down the class boundaries, class width and mid-point of the first class interval.
  (b) What are the mid-points of all the class intervals?
  (c) Draw a frequency polygon for these data.

3   Sanjit did a survey of the ages of cars parked at Cheapo Food Mart.
This frequency table shows his results.

Age in years	0–2	3–5	6–8	9–11	12–14	15–17
No. of cars	3	15	31	38	20	7

Draw a frequency polygon for Sanjit's data.

4 The heights, measured to the nearest centimetre, of 75 female students picked at random from Year 10 at Didmouth College are shown in this frequency distribution table.

Height (h) in cm	Frequency
$135 \le h < 140$	2
$140 \le h < 145$	5
$145 \le h < 150$	10
$150 \le h < 155$	17
$155 \le h < 160$	19
$160 \le h < 165$	15
$165 \le h < 170$	4
$170 \le h < 175$	2
$175 \le h < 180$	1

Draw a frequency polygon to illustrate these data.

Comparing frequency polygons

We often want to **compare frequency distributions** of the same kind of data.

For example, a teacher wants to describe the progress made by the students on her course. She compared the marks they got in tests at its start and end.

To **compare distributions** with the **same total frequency**, you can look at their frequency polygons. The shape of each graph gives a picture of how the data are distributed.

You can draw frequency polygons clearly *on the same diagram*. This makes their shapes easy to compare.

Question

A market gardener tests two new varieties of fast growing plants for hedges. They are called 'Thick and Fast' and 'Tall Screen'.
He grows 50 plants of each variety.

Their heights are measured to the nearest centimetre. The results below are from his final measurements at the end of the test period.

Class interval Height in cm	'Thick and Fast' Frequency	'Tall Screen' Frequency
30–34	6	1
35–39	5	2
40–44	9	2
45–49	14	5
50–54	8	11
55–59	4	12
60–64	3	10
65–69	1	7
Total	50	50

(a) Write down the class boundaries, class width and mid-point of the first class interval.
(b) What are the mid-points of all the class intervals?
(c) On the same diagram, draw a frequency polygon for each variety of plant.
(d) Use the frequency polygons to compare the two varieties.

Answer

(a) Class interval: 30–34 (Heights measured 'to the nearest cm'.)
    Class boundaries: 29.5 cm and 34.5 cm.
    Class width: 34.5 – 29.5 = 5 cm
    Mid-point: $\frac{1}{2}(29.5 + 34.5) = \frac{1}{2}(64) = 32$ cm.
(b) Class mid-points in cm:
    32, 37, 42, 47, 52, 57, 62, 67.
(c) *Plot mid-points against frequency for each distribution. Draw frequency polygons.*

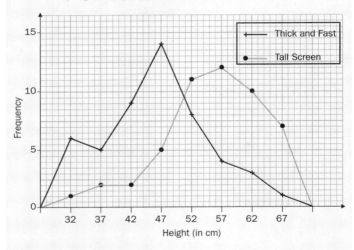

(d) *Compare the shape and position of the green and black lines of the two frequency polygons. Here are some comments you can make about them.*

The green and black lines 'start' and 'end' at the same points. So the range of heights of the two varieties is the same.

The black polygon has a bigger peak than the green polygon, but it is at a lower height value. So the group that contained most Thick and Fast plants had more plants in it than the group that contained most Tall Screen plants, but the heights were smaller.

In the right-hand half of the diagram (where the plants are taller), the green line is above the black line. So, in general, there are more 'tall' Tall Screen plants than 'tall' Thick and Fast plants.

In the left-hand half of the diagram (where the plants are shorter), the green line is below the black line. In general there are fewer 'short' Tall Screen plants than 'short' Thick and Fast plants.

It looks as if Tall Screen is the fastest growing variety in general. The Tall Screen plants were generally taller. There were fewer 'short' plants and more 'tall' plants.

► *Exercise* **P9.8**

Draw the frequency polygons for questions 1–4 in this Exercise on the diagrams you have already drawn for questions 1–4 in Exercise P9.7 p 309.

1 The Year 11 students at Monkton Comprehensive who did an algebra test also did an arithmetic test. This frequency table shows the distributions of marks in arithmetic.

Class interval	10–19	20–29	30–39	40–49	50–59	60–69
Frequency	1	4	11	26	17	7

(a) Draw a frequency polygon for these data.
(b) Comment on the students' performance in the two tests.

2 Forty members of Nenton Youth Club were asked how many hours they spent watching television last week. Their replies, in hours to the nearest hour, are given in this frequency table.

Time in hours	1–5	6–10	11–15	16–20	21–25	26–30
Frequency	9	19	7	3	2	0

(a) Draw a frequency polygon for this distribution.
(b) Comment on the television viewing habits of the members of Abbeyvale and Nenton Youth Clubs, based on these findings.

3 Sanjit did a survey of the ages of the cars parked at Upmark Delifood. This frequency table shows his findings.

Age in years	0–2	3–5	6–8	9–11	12–14	15–17
No. of cars	34	48	27	5	2	0

(a) Draw a frequency polygon for Sanjit's data.
(b) Comment on what the two frequency polygons show about the data Sanjit collected.

4 The heights, measured to the nearest centimetre, of 75 male students picked at random from the same year group at Didmouth College are shown in this table.

Height (h) in cm	Frequency
$135 \leq h < 140$	0
$140 \leq h < 145$	1
$145 \leq h < 150$	7
$150 \leq h < 155$	11
$155 \leq h < 160$	15
$160 \leq h < 165$	18
$165 \leq h < 170$	15
$170 \leq h < 175$	6
$175 \leq h < 180$	2

(a) Draw a frequency polygon to represent these data.
(b) Comment on the two graphs you have drawn for male and female students.

5 A teacher wanted to compare two reading books for use with her class. One of the ways she did this was to count the number of words per sentence in the first 100 sentences of each book. Here are her findings for the two books.

Book A

```
 2  11   1  25   1   7  26  14   9  23
13   7  15  30   2   4  16   5   1   7
21   1  18  23  10  15   9  21  25  10
 4   6  11  14   1   7   2  16  19   6
 7  10   1   8   9  24   8   6  21   3
 2  11  12   4  29   4  35  20  27   9
38  12   3  10  26  12  22  31  10  32
 9  22  22  18   2   6  37   8   6  21
11   6   7  28   9  17   7  12   6   8
 7  27  16  13   8  13   3  12   6  13
```

Book B

```
26  11   7  30  17   1  16  31  24  13
 9  26  17  34   6  18  11  11   2   6
 7  29  25  32   3  20  13  32   8  17
22   1  27  38  33  12   6  37  21  14
11  30  26  12  31   8  11  15  28  19
16   2  37  25  28  12  14   6   8  22
31   7  26  18   6  37  21  12  13   9
12  32  23  12  10   7  22   6  35   7
16  11  39  14  21  12   1  36  16  29
27  17  15  20  10  36  29  13   7  12
```

(a) Make a grouped frequency distribution table for each set of data.
Use the class intervals 1–5, 6–10, ..., 36–40.
(b) On the same diagram, draw a frequency polygon for each distribution.
(c) Use the frequency polygons to compare the two books.
(d) What do you think are the advantages and disadvantages of comparing books in this way?

6 Lisa and Ben did a project on the length of the pebbles on Beer beach. They measured the length, in centimetres to the nearest millimetre, of two sets of pebbles. One set was located at the eastern end of the beach, the other at the western end. Here are their results.

Eastern end:
```
5.5  4.3  3.1  5.2  6.0  4.1  4.4  3.7
4.6  5.1  6.0  4.2  3.8  4.7  5.6  6.3
6.9  4.2  3.6  5.0  6.7  5.5  6.2  4.5  4.6
```

Western end:
```
6.5  7.3  7.9  9.2  9.8  6.9  7.0  8.5
9.0  7.2  6.4  8.8  8.3  9.4  6.7  8.0
7.4  9.5  6.7  7.1  8.7  9.3  6.2  7.6  7.3
```

(a) Make a grouped frequency distribution table for the length of pebbles at the western end of the beach.
Use the class intervals:
3.0–3.4, 3.5–3.9, 4.0–4.4, ..., 6.5–6.9.
(b) Make a grouped frequency distribution table for the length of pebbles at the eastern end of the beach.
Use the class intervals:
6.0–6.4, 6.5–6.9, 7.0–7.4, ..., 9.5–9.9.
(c) On the same diagram, draw a frequency polygon for each distribution.
(d) Use the frequency polygons to compare the two distributions.
(e) Discuss the pebble size at the eastern and western ends of Beer beach, based on these data.

Examination Questions

1 The village of Deep Snoring has 45 inhabitants. Their ages (in completed years) are as follows:

32, 30, 6, 2, 0, 64, 71, 55, 59, 45, 14, 12, 22, 24, 19, 47, 43, 16, 15, 37, 51, 53, 17, 11, 18, 36, 61, 57, 56, 51, 46, 50, 24, 31, 36, 40, 58, 51, 68, 70, 72, 69, 33, 31, 6.

(a) Copy and complete the following table.
(b) Draw a frequency diagram to illustrate this information.

Age (in completed years)	Tally marks	Frequency
0– 9		
10–19		
20–29		
30–39		
40–49		
50–59		
60–69		
70–79		
	Total =	45

(NEAB, 1988)

2 In the Fourth Year at Broomswood School, 150 pupils took a mathematics test. The following results were obtained.

Marks in test	Number of pupils
1 – 20	16
21 – 40	35
41 – 60	60
61 – 80	24
81 – 100	15

(a) Draw a frequency diagram to illustrate this information.
(b) If the pass mark is 41, how many pupils passed?
(c) A pie chart is to be drawn to illustrate this information. What size should the angle be of the sector which represents pupils marks 41–60?

(ULEAC, 1988)

3 The weights (in kg correct to the nearest tenth) of a group of thirty dogs were recorded as follows:

15.4 14.8 15.8 14.3 14.6 15.0
16.2 13.9 15.2 15.1 16.0 15.2
14.4 15.4 15.7 16.2 14.9 14.7
15.5 14.6 14.4 15.9 14.1 14.3
14.6 13.7 15.5 14.3 14.7 15.1

(a) Complete the frequency table below.

Weight	Tally	Number of dogs
13.5 to 13.9	II	2
14.0 to 14.4	ⅢⅠ I	6
14.5 to 14.9	ⅢⅠ II	7
15.0 to 15.4		
15.5 to 15.9		
16.0 to 16.4		

(b) On graph paper, draw a frequency diagram to illustrate this information.

(WJEC, 1994)

4 45 children, working in groups, were asked to time each other's estimates of the length of a minute. Their estimates, correct to the nearest second, are given below.

53 47 77 63 59 54 62 65 71 77 42 68 67 51 72
57 73 48 61 46 51 50 63 68 54 50 65 53 78 69
44 56 77 58 55 79 66 58 67 52 48 70 49 71 73

(a) Copy and complete the table below.

Time in seconds	Tally	Frequency
40–44		
45–49		
50–54		
55–59		
60–64		
65–69		
70–74		
75–79		

(b) Using your results from part (a), display the information in a frequency diagram.

(NEAB, 1989)

P10
Average speed

This unit will help you to:

- recognise a unit of speed
- understand the idea of average speed
- calculate average speeds from distances and times
- work with times given in different units
- calculate distances from speeds and times
- calculate times from speeds and distances
- change one unit of speed to another.

How fast?

Speed is a measure of **how fast** something moves. It gives the distance moved in a unit of time.

This escalator moves 2 metres every second. We say its speed is '2 metres per second'.
We can write it as: 2 metres/second
or 2m/s
or 2 ms^{-1}

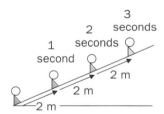

Metres per second is the SI unit of speed.
You may have used it in science.
Other common units of speed are:
    miles per hour (mph)
and kilometres per hour (km/h)
Most speedometers have both mph and km/h scales marked on them.

Speed limits in the UK and the USA are in mph.

Speed limits in other parts of Europe are in km/h.

Other units of speed, such as 'kilometres per second' or 'inches per year' are also used. But these are not as common.

 The speed of light is about 300 000 km/s.

 The speed of erosion is about 6 inches/year.

A unit of *speed* always links a *distance* with a *unit of time*.

 ### Discussion Exercise

- Which of these are units of speed?
  Explain what is wrong with each of the others.

  miles per year   mm/day   grams per second

  cm/litre   pence/hour   yards/minute

  metres per week   £s per month   mm/cm³

  pence per kg   feet per second   words per hour

- Think of some other possible units of speed.
  Write down at least five of them.
- Think about all the units of speed you know.
  In what situations would each be used?
  Discuss.
- Look at examples of speeds in newspapers, magazines, books, …
  What kind of 'moves' are they describing?
  What units of speed do they use?
  Discuss.

Average speed

Some things move at a **steady speed**. They go the *same distance in every second*.

Moving at a steady speed is not easy to do. When most things move, their speed *varies*. We usually use **average speed** to describe how they move.

Alex drives from Cardiff to Bristol. She travels the 45 miles in 1 hour. We say her average speed is
    45 miles per hour
  or 45 mph.
Her actual speed changes during the journey.
She went faster than 45 mph at times. She went slower than 45 mph at other times. Sometimes she stopped.
However if she had driven at 45 mph all the way, she would do the journey in the same time.

Simon drives 150 miles from Bristol to Brighton. It takes him 5 hours.

In 5 hours Simon travels 150 miles.
In 1 hour Simon travels 30 miles, on average.
We say his average speed is 30 miles per hour or 30 mph.
This means that if Simon had driven at 30 mph all the way, he would drive that distance (150 miles) in that time (5 hours).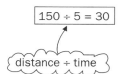

The average speed in mph can be found by dividing the distance in miles by the time in hours.

150 ÷ 5 = 30
distance ÷ time

You can write this as a formula:

| **Average speed = distance travelled ÷ time taken** |
| **or Average speed = $\dfrac{\text{distance travelled}}{\text{time taken}}$** |

The unit of speed depends on the distance and time units used.

Distance in **miles**, time in **hours**, give speed in **miles per hour**.

Distance in **metres**, time in **seconds**, give speed in **metres per second**.
For example, if Jamie runs 100 metres in 12.5 seconds, his average speed is 100 ÷ 12.5 = 8 m/s.

Distance in **kilometres**, time in **hours**, give speed in **kilometres per hour**.
For example, if a plane flies 5535 km to New York in 9 hours, its average speed is 5535 ÷ 9 = 615 km/h.

Remember:
Look carefully at the **units** of *distance* and *time* you use.
State clearly the **unit** of *speed* they give.

You often need to **round** the answer you get. Questions sometimes tell you what to do. Don't ignore this. You will lose marks if you do.
Round your answer sensibly if you need to.

Memo
Rounding answers
N3 p 13–17

▶ *Exercise* P10.1

Calculate the average speed of each of the following. State the unit of speed clearly in each answer. When you need to round an answer, give it correct to 1 decimal place.

1 189 miles in 3 hours.
2 4 seconds to travel 104 metres.
3 117 millimetres in 13 seconds.
4 4.5 hours to go 166.5 km.
5 A train goes 158 miles in 2 hours.
6 A bird flying for 1.5 hours covers 120 km.
7 An athlete runs 400m in 50 seconds.
8 A coach takes 3.5 hours to go 280 km in France.
9 A rowing boat moves 275 yards up river in 5 minutes.
10 In 3 seconds a football goes 156 feet.
11 The QE2 took 125 hours to travel 3080 miles to New York.
12 In 1938 the steam locomotive Mallard covered a distance of 253 miles in 2 hours.
13 Phileas Fogg travelled 'around the world' in 80 days, the distance being 25 000 miles.
14 When chasing an antelope, Charlie the cheetah covered a distance of 138 metres in 5 seconds.
15 When the ball left Demon Bowler Falcon's hand, it took 0.35 seconds to travel the 66 feet to the wicket.
16 Sammy the snail travelled 1000 mm in 900 seconds.
17 The first man-powered air crossing of the English Channel was made by Bryan Allen in Gossamer Albatross in 1979. He covered 20.5 miles in 2.5 hours.
18 On a recent flight, Concorde travelled 5500 km in 3 hours.
19 Tommy, the giant tortoise, travelled 100 metres in 22 minutes.
20 The racehorse Speedy Flyer ran 1320 yards in 73 seconds.

Changing units

Before finding an average speed, check the *units you want*. Compare them with the distance and time *units you have*. Change any units if you need to.

Memo

Metric units of length:

1 km	=	1000 m
1 m	=	100 cm
	=	1000 mm
1 cm	=	10 mm

Units of time:

60 seconds	= 1 minute	1 year	= 12 months
60 minutes	= 1 hour	1 year	= 365 days
24 hours	= 1 day	1 leap year	= 366 days
7 days	= 1 week		
52 weeks	= 1 year		

Always read questions carefully. They sometimes say which unit of speed to use.
Make sure you do what they ask. (You lose marks if you don't!) When the choice is *yours*, try to use the *most sensible unit* for the situation.

Question

Jeannie Longo cycled 20 km in a record time of 25 minutes 59.883 seconds at the Mexico City Games. What was her average speed in m/s? Round your answer to 2 decimal places.

Answer

● *Check units: for speed in m/s,*
     you need distance in metres, time in seconds.

● *Change units:*
    1km = 1000 m. So to change km to m, multiply by 1000.
    Distance: 20 km = 20 × 1000 m = 20 000 m.

    1 min = 60 s. So to change min to s, multiply by 60.
    Time: 25 min 59.883 s
         = 25 × 60 + 59.883 s = 1559.883 s

● *Write Formula:* Average speed = $\dfrac{\text{Distance}}{\text{Time}}$

● *Put in values:*   = $\dfrac{20\,000\text{m}}{1559.883\text{s}}$ ⟵ give m/s

                          = `12.82147443`

● *Round answer:*   = 12.82 m/s (to 2 dp)
   Remember unit.

   Here is an efficient way to do this working with a calculator.
   Change time to seconds first and put it into memory.

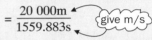

   Then work out average speed. Recall time from memory.

   Find the best way to do the working with your calculator. Whichever way you use, always show your working clearly.

▶ *Exercise* P10.2

1 Change these to kilometres:
   (a) 3000 m   (c) 27 800 m
   (b) 5500 m   (d) 785 m
2 Change these to metres:
   (a) 4 km   (c) 450 cm
   (b) 3.8 km   (d) 66 cm
3 Change these to seconds:
   (a) 5 minutes   (c) 2 hours 20 minutes
   (b) 2 hours
4 Change these to hours:
   (a) 5 days   (c) 2 weeks
   (b) 6 days 5 hours (d) 1 week 3 days

5 Find the average speed of each of these in km/h:
  (a) A coach journey of 1500 km in 2 days.
  (b) A canal boat journey of 56 km in half a day.
  (c) A $4\frac{1}{2}$ day cruise of 640 km.
  (d) A space probe travelled 9 million kilometres in a week.
  (e) A train journey from Moscow to Vladivostok, a distance of 10 200 km in 9 days 9 hours.

6 Find the average speed of each of these in m/s.
  Give each answer correct to 2 decimal places.
  (a) A car which travelled 5 km in 6 minutes.
  (b) A runner who ran 1.5 km in 3 minutes 32 seconds.
  (c) A cyclist who travelled 3 km in 5 minutes 48 seconds.
  (d) A deer which ran 1100 m in $1\frac{1}{2}$ minutes.
  (e) A mole which burrows 90 cm in 5 minutes.

Times and decimals

To calculate a speed as '… per hour', the time must be in *hours*.
Often a time is not a *whole number* of hours. Some times such as $\frac{1}{2}$ hour, 25 minutes, 55 seconds, …, are *part* of an hour.

Calculators normally work in decimals. So we usually **change any fractions of an hour into decimals** to key them into a calculator.

We often talk about 'half', 'quarter' and 'three-quarters' of an hour. These simple fractions are easy to change.

Remember: | $\frac{1}{2}$ = 0.5 | $\frac{1}{4}$ = 0.25 | $\frac{3}{4}$ = 0.75 |

To change minutes into hours, divide by 60.

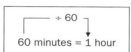

For example,

12 minutes = $\frac{12}{60}$ h = 0.2 h   (12 ÷ 60)

39 minutes = $\frac{39}{60}$ h = 0.65h   (39 ÷ 60)

49 minutes = $\frac{49}{60}$ h = 0.81666 …h   (49 ÷ 60)

 Discussion Exercise

• Consider whole numbers of minutes.
  Which are exact decimal fractions of an hour?
  Look for a pattern. Discuss.
  What kind of decimals are the others? Discuss.

  Minutes are often given as multiples of 5:

    5, 10, 15, 20, …

  What decimal fractions of an hour are these?
  Is there a pattern?
  Discuss.

• Discuss ways to change times such as 3 hours 25 minutes into 'hours' with your calculator.

  Decide on the best way for your calculator.
  Practise using this way.

Some speed questions ask you to **change a time to a decimal** and **round it to a given degree of accuracy**.
When you use the time in the calculation, it is more accurate to *work with the 'unrounded value'*. Always do this unless the question says otherwise.
Store the 'unrounded value' in your calculator memory using Min . Then recall it using MR when you need it.

Remember:
Before clearing any result from your calculator display, make sure you do not need it again later. If in doubt, store it in the memory or write it down.

Question

It is 205 miles by rail from Plymouth to Birmingham. The fast moving train takes 4 hours 38 minutes to do the journey.

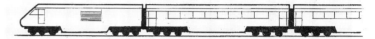

(a) Give this time in hours, correct to 2 decimal places.
(b) What is the train's average speed in mph?
    Give your answer to 1 decimal place.

Answer

(a) *Time:* 4 h 38 minutes = $4 + \dfrac{38}{60}$ hours

 4 ÷ 3 8 ÷ 6 0 = Min `4.633333333`

              = 4.63 hours (to 2 dp)

(b) Average speed = Distance ÷ Time   *Recalls time in hours from memory*

              = 205 ÷ MR

              = `44.24460432`

              = 44.2 mph (to 1 dp)

Seconds can also be changed into decimal fractions of an hour.
To change seconds to minutes, divide by 60.
To change these minutes to hours, divide by 60 again.
For example,
    54 seconds = 0.9 minutes = 0.015 hour

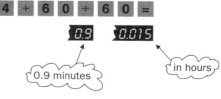

 5 4 ÷ 6 0 ÷ 6 0 =

        `0.9`   `0.015`

 0.9 minutes   *in hours*

 Discussion Exercise

Investigate the results of changing these to hours:

• seconds, such as 36 seconds.
• minutes and seconds, such as 2 min 5 seconds
• hours, minutes and seconds, such as
  1 h 17 min 2 seconds.

Discuss where times such as these occur.

► *Exercise* P10.3

1   Calculate the average speed for these journeys by road.
    Give each answer correct to the nearest 1 mph.
    (a) Birmingham to Norwich – 161 miles in $3\frac{1}{2}$ hours
    (b) Nottingham to Leeds – 73 miles in $1\frac{3}{4}$ hours
    (c) Oxford to Lincoln – 126 miles in $3\frac{1}{4}$ hours
    (d) York to Cardiff – 241 miles in $5\frac{3}{4}$ hours
    (e) Newcastle to Middlesborough – 37 miles in $\frac{3}{4}$ hour

2   Work out the average speeds of these train journeys in mph.
    (a) Birmingham to Exeter – 159 miles in 2 hours 56 minutes
    (b) London to York – 213 miles in 2 hours 38 minutes
    (c) Edinburgh to Birmingham –
        304 miles in 5 hours 49 minutes
    (d) Exeter to Plymouth – 48 miles in 53 minutes
    (e) Coventry to London Euston –
        99 miles in 1 hour 5 minutes.

Calculating distance

Diane drove up the motorway
to Carlisle.
Her average speed was 50 mph.
This means that, on average,
she went 50 miles in each
hour.
So, on average:

    in 1 hour she went 50 miles,

    in 2 hours she went 100 miles,   50 × 2

    in 3 hours she went 150 miles,   50 × 3

    in 4 hours she went 200 miles,   50 × 4

    and so on …   speed × time

The *longer the time*, the *greater the distance*.
The distance travelled in miles can be found by multiplying the
speed in mph and the time in hours. This gives the formula:

> **distance = average speed × time**

As usual, the units of measure in the formula must 'match'.
Look at the pattern of units.

If speed is in mph (**miles**/*hour*), time must be in *hours*.
The result is distance in **miles**.

> **miles**/*hour* × *hours* → **miles**

If speed is in **km**/*hour*, time must be in *hours*.
The result is distance in **km**.

> **km**/*hour* × *hours* → **km**

For example,
if Colin cycles at 20 km/h for 3 hours,
the distance he goes is 20 × 3 = 60 km.

If speed is in **metres**/*second*, time must be in *seconds*.
The result is distance in **metres**.

> **metres**/*second* × *seconds* → **metres**

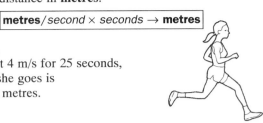

For example,
if Lisa runs at 4 m/s for 25 seconds,
the distance she goes is
4 × 25 = 100 metres.

► *Exercise* P10.4

Find the distance travelled for each of the following:
1   Viv jogs at 11 km/h for 2 hours.
2   Damon drives his Williams at 228 km/h for $1\frac{3}{4}$ hours.
3   Susie swims at 1.4 m/s for 30 seconds.
4   James cycles at 7.5 m/s for $\frac{1}{2}$ hour.
5   Leslie skis at 119 feet/second for 35 seconds.
6   A coach travels at 37 mph for $1\frac{1}{2}$ hours.

Look carefully at the **unit of speed** you plan to use in

> Distance = Average speed × Time

The speed shows:
    • the unit of time you must use
    • the unit of distance you will get.

If you have to **change the unit of time**, *do it first*. You can
store the result in your calculator memory if you need to. Then
you can recall it later to do the calculation.
    Don't forget to give the unit of distance in your answer.
Round your answer sensibly if necessary. If you have to **change
the distance to a difference unit**, *do this at the end*.

Question

A non-stop flight from
Los Angeles to Sydney
took 14 hours 50 minutes.
The plane flew at an
average speed of
504.75 mph.
How far did it fly?
Give your answer to the nearest mile.

Answer

• *Check units: Speed in mph, so time must be in hours
                        and distance will be in miles.*
• *Facts:*   Speed: 504.75 mph
                  Time: 14 h 50 minutes   *change to hours*
                  = $14\frac{50}{60}$ hours

                                            store result in memory

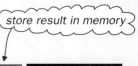

1 4 + 5 0 ÷ 6 0 = Min `14.83333333`

- *Formula:* Distance = Speed × Time
- *Put in values:* = 504.75 × 14 $\frac{50}{60}$
- *Work it out:* = 7487.125
- *Round result:* = 7487 miles

  (to the nearest mile)

$$\boxed{5}\ \boxed{0}\ \boxed{4}\ \boxed{\cdot}\ \boxed{7}\ \boxed{5}\ \boxed{\times}\ \boxed{MR}\ \boxed{=}$$

Recalls time from memory

- *Answer:* The plane flew 7487 miles (to the nearest mile).

▶ Exercise P10.5

1 Maxine is a sales manager. She drives all over the country for her job. She estimates she can average

  60 mph on motorways
  45 mph on A roads (main roads)
  32 mph on B roads (in the country)
  24 mph in town centres.

Calculate the distances she expects to travel for each of these journeys:
(a) on a motorway for
   (i) 2 hours   (iii) $\frac{3}{4}$ hour
   (ii) 4 hours 20 minutes   (iv) 3 hours 25 minutes,
(b) on a main road for
   (i) 1 hour   (iii) $2\frac{1}{4}$ hours
   (ii) 40 minutes   (iv) 1 hour 50 minutes
(c) on a 'B' road for,
   (i) 2 hours   (iii) $1\frac{1}{2}$ hours
   (ii) 55 minutes   (iv) 2 hours 10 minutes,
(d) in town for
   (i) 40 minutes   (iii) 15 minutes
   (ii) $1\frac{1}{2}$ hours   (iv) 1 hour 40 minutes.

2 A migrating bird flies at about 16 m/s.
How many kilometres does it fly in
(a) 30 s   (c) 2 h 40 minutes
(b) $7\frac{1}{2}$ minutes   (d) half a day?

3 Light travels at about 300 000 kilometres per second.
How far does it travel in
(a) 2.7 s   (c) 7 milliseconds (= 0.007s)
(b) 1 minute   (d) 25 milliseconds?

4 A car is travelling at 70 km/h.
How many metres does it cover in
(a) $\frac{1}{4}$ hour   (c) 0.6 minutes
(b) 5 minutes   (d) 25 s?

Calculating times

Robin goes on a sponsored walk.
His average walking speed is 4 mph.
So, on average, he walks
4 miles in each hour.

This means that, on average,
he walks 4 miles in 1 hour,

  8 miles in 2 hours,   ← *8 ÷ 4*
  12 miles in 3 hours,   ← *12 ÷ 4*
  16 miles in 4 hours,   ← *16 ÷ 4*
  and so on …   ← *distance ÷ speed*

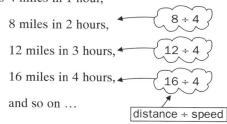

The time in hours can be found by dividing the distance in miles by the speed in mph.

You can write this as a formula:

$$\text{time} = \frac{\text{distance}}{\text{average speed}}$$

or **time = distance ÷ average speed**

Again, the *units of measure* must match in this formula. Always check the pattern of units.

If speed is in mph (**miles**/*hour*), distance must be in **miles**. The result is time in *hours*.

$$\boxed{\textbf{miles} \div \textbf{miles}/\textit{hour} \rightarrow \textit{hours}}$$

If speed is in **km**/*hour*, distance must be in **km**. The result is time in *hours*.

$$\boxed{\textbf{km} \div \textbf{km}/\textit{hour} \rightarrow \textit{hours}}$$

For example,
If a ferry sails 35 km
at an average speed of 10 km/h,
the time it takes is
35 ÷ 10 = 3.5 or $3\frac{1}{2}$ hours.

If speed is in **metres**/*second*, distance must be in **metres**. The result is time in *seconds*.

$$\boxed{\textbf{metres} \div \textbf{metres}/\textit{second} \rightarrow \textit{seconds}}$$

For example,
If Winston runs 400 m
at an average speed of 8 m/s,
the time he takes is
400 ÷ 8 = 50 seconds.

▶ Exercise P10.6

Find the times taken to do these journeys at the given average speeds.
1 Chris driving 385 miles on the motorway at 55 mph.
2 Emily walking 12 km at 6 km/h.
3 A train travelling 231 miles at 66 miles per hour.
4 A plane flying 1300 miles at 520 mph.
5 Sam running 200 metres at 5 m/s.

Always check the **units involved in a problem** before using the formula.

> Time = Distance ÷ Average Speed

Look at the unit of speed to find:
  • the unit of distance you must use,
  • the unit of time you will get.

If the distance you have is *not* in the unit you want, change it before you use the formula.

You can leave the result on your calculator display. Then it is ready for the calculation.

Remember to give the correct unit of time in your answer. Round it to a sensible value if you need to.

Question

Sam is training for a marathon. The course is 42.195 km long. Sam hopes to keep up an average speed of 2.5 m/s. What does he hope his time for the run will be? Give it to the nearest minute.

Answer

• *Check units:* Speed in m/s, so distance must be in metres and time will be in seconds.
• *Facts:*   Speed: 2.5 m/s
                Distance: 42.195 km
                = (42.195 × 1000) m = 42 195 m
• *Formula:*   Time = Distance ÷ Average Speed
• *Put in values:*   = 42 195 ÷ 2.5
• *Work it out:*   = 16878 seconds
                          = (16878 ÷ 60) minutes
• *Change s to min:*   = 281.3 minutes
• *Round as stated:*   = 281 min (to nearest minute)
• *Change to hours
  and minutes:*   = 4 hours 41 minutes
                              (to the nearest minute)

• *Answer:* Sam hopes his time will be 4 hours 41 minutes (to the nearest minute).

You may get a *decimal fraction of an hour* in your answer. Usually you will have to change it to *minutes* or *hours and minutes*.

Remember: To change hours
             to minutes, multiply by 60.

> 1 hour = 60 minutes

Question

The Jones family are on holiday in Spain. They plan to drive the 265 km from Madrid to Granada at an average speed of 80 km/h. How long do they expect the journey to take? Give your answer to the nearest 5 minutes.

Answer

• *Check units:* Speed in km/h, so distance must be in km and time will be in hours.

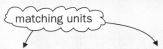

matching units

• *Facts:*   Speed: 80 km/h   Distance: 265 km
• *Formula:*   Time = Distance ÷ Average Speed
• *Put in values:*   = 265 ÷ 80
• *Work it out:*   = 3.3125 hours
                         = 3 hours + (0.3125 × 60) minutes
• *Change fraction of
  an hour to minutes:*   = 3 hours 18.75 minutes
• *Round:*   = 3 hours 20 minutes
                             (to the nearest 5 minutes)
• *Answer:* They expect the journey to take 3 hours 20 minutes (to the nearest 5 minutes).

Here is one way to do the working with a calculator.
Work out average speed: 2 6 5 ÷ 8 0 = 3.3125

Subtract whole number of hours: − 3 = 0.3125

Change fraction of an hour to minutes: × 6 0 = 18.75

Remember: Do not round any result until you reach the final answer.

Change other decimal fractions of times in questions to the most suitable unit or units where necessary.
Always check what the question asks you to do.

▶ *Exercise* P10.7

1 The answer on these calculators are times in hours.
   (a) 0.25   (d) 3.7
   (b) 1.266666666   (e) 4.85
   (c) 2.583333333   (f) 7.061666666

   Give times less than 1 hour in minutes.
   Give other times in hours and minutes.
   Round each to the nearest minute.

2 The answers on these calculators are times in seconds.
   Change them to minutes and seconds
   or hours, minutes and seconds as necessary.
   Then give each answer correct to the nearest minute.
   (a) 243.   (c) 1482.   (e) 12733.
   (b) 527.   (d) 9651.   (f) 17394.

3 Calculate the times taken to do these journeys at the given average speeds. Give each answer correct to the nearest minute.
   (a) Ernie walking 14 km at 5.5 km/h.
   (b) Mae jogging 11 miles at 6.5 mph.
   (c) A lorry travelling 352 miles at 47 mph.
   (d) A tortoise travelling 2.3 m at 0.004 m/s.
   (e) Ruth swimming 1500 m at 0.94 m/s.

Here is a 'mixed exercise'. Read the questions carefully. Some ask for speeds, some ask for times, some ask for distances.

► *Exercise* **P10.8**

1

```
Birmingham
  85  Bristol
 107   45  Cardiff
 157   81  119  Exeter       Distances in miles
 115  216  236  288  Leeds
  98  178  200  250   72  Liverpool
  88  167  188  239   43   34  Manchester
 199  125  164   45  328  294  281  Plymouth
 118  119  307  170  196  210  199  215  London
```

For each of the following journeys
(i) write down the distance, in miles, between the two named cities
(ii) work out the average speed in mph correct to the nearest mph.
(a) Birmingham to Leeds in $2\frac{1}{4}$ hours.
(b) Cardiff to Liverpool in $3\frac{1}{4}$ hours.
(c) Exeter to Plymouth in $\frac{3}{4}$ hour.
(d) London to Bristol in $2\frac{3}{4}$ hours.
(e) Manchester to Plymouth in $5\frac{1}{2}$ hours.

2 Anna caught the 0800 train from London and travelled to Newcastle at an average speed of 76 mph. The journey was 270 miles. What time did Anna arrive in Newcastle?

3 Tony plans a motorcycling trip in France.
He expects to average
   95 km/h on the autoroute   48 km/h on country roads
   35 km/h in towns   19 km/h in the centre of Paris.
Calculate the distances he expects to travel for each of these journeys:
(a) on an autoroute for
   (i) 4 hours   (iii) 2 hours 40 minutes
   (ii) $1\frac{1}{2}$ hours   (iv) 3 hours 25 minutes
(b) on a country road for
   (i) 2 hours   (iii) 45 minutes
   (ii) $2\frac{3}{4}$ hours   (iv) 1 hour 35 minutes
(c) in town for
   (i) $\frac{1}{2}$ hour   (iii) 1 hour 10 minutes
   (ii) 40 minutes   (iv) 2 hours 25 minutes
(d) in the centre of Paris for
   (i) 40 minutes   (iii) 1 hour 25 minutes
   (ii) $\frac{3}{4}$ hour   (iv) 1 hour 50 minutes.
One day, Tony made a journey consisting of:
   1 hour 4 minutes on an autoroute,
   2 hours 5 minutes on country roads and
   50 minutes in town.
Estimate the total distance Tony travelled.

4 Steve ran for his House on Sports Day. Here are his times:

Event	100 m	200 m	400 m	800 m	1000 m	1500 m
Time	12 s	26 s	65 s	2 min 25 s	3 min 45 s	5 min 50 s

Work out Steve's average speed in metres per second for each race. Give your answers correct to 1 decimal place.

5 A light aircraft left Exeter and flew to Edinburgh, a distance of 446 miles. It travelled at an average speed of 165 mph.
(a) Calculate the journey time in hours and minutes, correct to the nearest minute.
(b) The aircraft left Exeter at 11.15 am. At what time did it reach Edinburgh?

6 The distance from the Sun to Earth is 93 000 000 miles. Light travels at about 186 000 miles per second. How long does it take light from the Sun to reach the Earth? Give your answer in minutes and seconds.

7 The speed of the tape in a VHS video recorder is 2.43 cm/s.
(a) The 'E number' on a tape tells you the time in minutes available for recording.
   How long, in metres, is each of these tapes? Give your answers correct to 1 decimal place.

| E 180 | E 240 | E 210 |

(b) How many metres of tape will be used to record each of these programmes? Give your answers to the nearest centimetre.

1.25–1.30	Tom and Jerry
5.35–6.00	Neighbours
7.20–8.30	Athletics
3.55–4.30	Day in the Life. . .
8.15–10.25	King Kong

8 Helen and Darren cycled from Cherbourg to Caen, a distance of 120 km, at an average speed of 7 m/s. How long did it take them? Give your answer in hours and minutes to the nearest minute.

9 Here are some long-distance walking records for women. Calculate the average speed for each in kilometres per hour.

Distance	Time		
	h	min	sec
15 km		49	44.0
20 km	1	06	55.5
25 km	1	29	30
30 km	1	47	06
50 km	3	36	58

10 Sound travels at approximately 1100 feet per second in air. How long will it be before you hear a clap of thunder 2 miles away? (1 mile = 5280 feet.)   ◄

Whole journeys

Journeys are often made up of several parts or stages.
To find the average speed for the whole journey, you need the **total distance** and the **total time**.

Average speed = total distance ÷ total time

Question

Peter drives from London to Leeds up the M1. In 2 hours he travels 104 miles. Then he stops at a service station for a $\frac{1}{2}$ hour break. He drives the next 92 miles in $1\frac{1}{2}$ hours. What is his average speed for the journey?

continued

Answer

Total distance = 104 + 92 = 196 miles
Total time = $2 + \frac{1}{2} + 1\frac{1}{2}$ = 4 hours
Average speed = total distance ÷ total time
= 196 ÷ 4
= 49 mph

A calculator makes it easy to add 'awkward times'.
Here is one way to do this.
- Clear the memory first.
- Change each time to a decimal.
- Add each decimal time into the memory (use M+).
- Then recall the total for the calculation (use MR).

For example,
to add 2 h 35 min, 48 min and 3 h 40 min.
Press 0 Min to clear memory, `0.`

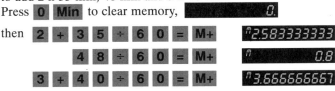

then
`2 + 3 5 ÷ 6 0 = M+`   `ᴹ 2.583333333`
`4 8 ÷ 6 0 = M+`   `ᴹ 0.8`
`3 + 4 0 ÷ 6 0 = M+`   `ᴹ 3.666666667`

To recall *total time*, press: `MR`   `ᴹ 7.05`

Question

Lynn's train journey
from Doncaster to
Swansea had three
stages.

Intercity train from Doncaster to Birmingham:
   85 miles in 2 hours 35 minutes
Change at Birmingham:
   a 48-minute wait
Sprintertrain from Birmingham to Swansea:
   133 miles in 3 hours 40 minutes.
Calculate the average speed for her journey.

Answer

Total distance = 85 + 133 = 218 miles
Total time = 2 h 35 min + 48 min + 3 h 40 min

> Work this out first and put into memory. See key codes above.

Average speed = total distance ÷ total time
= 218 ÷ MR

> Recall time from memory.

= `ᴹ 30.92198582`
= 31 mph (to nearest mph)

In some situations you know the average speeds for *parts of the journey*. Use each average speed to calculate the unknown distance or time.
Then work out | total distance ÷ total time |
to find the average speed for the *whole journey*.

Question

Fergal drives the
71 miles from Belfast
to Londonderry at an
average speed of 50 mph.
Then he drives for
$1\frac{1}{4}$ hours at 25 mph
to Omagh.
Find his average speed for the journey.

Answer

Distance:
1st part: Belfast → Londonderry: 71 miles
2nd part: Londonderry → Omagh:
   Distance = speed × time = 25 × 1.25 = 31.25 miles
Total distance = 71 + 31.25 = 102.25 miles.
Time:
1st part: Belfast → Londonderry:
   Time = distance ÷ speed = 71 ÷ 50 = 1.42 hours
2nd part: Londonderry → Omagh: 1.25 hours
Total time = 1.42 hours + 1.25 hours = 2.67 hours.

Average speed = total distance ÷ total time

= 102.25 ÷ 2.67

= `38.29588015`

= 38 mph (to the nearest mph).

Discussion Exercise

There are many ways to do the above working with a calculator.
Try some different ways with your calculator.
Use memory and/or brackets if it helps.
Write down 'key codes' for each of your methods.

Discuss the methods used by students in your group.
Which are easiest? Which are shortest? Which are most efficient? Discuss why.

Choose the 'best way' for you and your calculator.
Make a note of its key code for future reference.

► Exercise P10.9

1   Calculate the average speed for each of these journeys.
   Give each answer to a sensible degree of accuracy.
   (a) 96 km in 2 h then 36 km in 1 h
   (b) 52 miles in $1\frac{1}{4}$ h then 23 miles in $\frac{3}{4}$ h
   (c) 36 miles in 45 minutes then 8 miles in 10 minutes
   (d) 75 km in 55 minutes then 57 km in 40 minutes
   (e) 48 metres in 7 seconds then 77 metres in 12 seconds.

2 Carol and Imogen are on a cycling holiday in Spain. They plan a journey of 48 km which they wish to complete in $2\frac{1}{2}$ hours. They ride at an average speed of 20 km/h for 50 minutes, then stop for 15 minutes at a shop. At what average speed must they cycle for the rest of the journey?

3 Paul plans to drive 150 miles to see his girlfriend Gwen at an average speed of 50 mph.
He drives for the first half hour at 35 mph, the next hour at 60 mph and then for 40 minutes at 54 mph.
What average speed must he try to achieve for the remainder of his journey?

4 This table shows the distances, in miles, between some towns in the North of England.

Mr Peel is a sales representative for a Sheffield company.
One week he made the following four journeys.

					Hull
59	Leeds				
87	**63**	Middlesborough			
121	**91**	**37**	Newcastle		
68	**34**	**106**	**136**	Sheffield	
38	**24**	**49**	**83**	**60**	York

Monday: Sheffield to Hull.
    First 28 miles in 40 minutes,
    next 10 miles in 17 minutes,
    remainder of journey in 20 minutes.
Tuesday: Sheffield to Newcastle.
    First 50 miles in 65 minutes,
    next 70 miles in 84 minutes,
    break for coffee $\frac{1}{2}$ hour,
    remainder of journey in 27 minutes.
Wednesday: Newcastle to York.
    First 34 miles in 47 minutes,
    next 42 miles in 39 minutes,
    final stage of journey in $\frac{1}{2}$ hour.
Thursday: Sheffield to Middlesborough.
    First 45 miles in 58 minutes,
    next 30 miles in $\frac{3}{4}$ hour,
    break for coffee 25 minutes,
    final stage of journey in 47 minutes.
Use the mileage chart to work out Mr Peel's average speed for each of his four journeys that week.

Changing units of speed

A unit of speed links a 'distance unit' and a 'time unit'.
In some changes of unit, such as mp**h** ↔ km/**h**, you only have to change the 'distance unit'. The 'time unit' stays the same.

Here are some other examples.

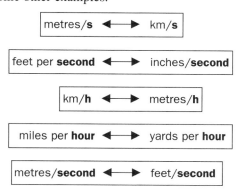

You are expected to know the 'table' for changing metric units of length.
For example,

    1 km   = 1000 metres
So 1 km/h = 1000 metres/hour

    7.5 km = 7.5×1000 metres = 7500 m
    7.5 km/h = 7.5×1000 metres/h = 7500 m/h

Always make a 'common sense check' on the size of your answer.

    Change to a larger unit → fewer of that unit
    Change to a smaller unit → more of that unit.

For example,
    km/h → metres/h is a change to a smaller unit.
So you should get more of that unit.
    7.4 km/h = 7500 metres/h
    7500 is more than 7.5.
    So this answer 'makes sense'.

When imperial units are involved, you are usually given the relationship to use to change the unit.

Question

Windspeed is measured on the Beaufort Scale from 1 to 12.
(a) 61 mph is Force 10 (whole gale). What is it in km/h? (5 miles ≈ 8 kilometres)
(b) 45 km/h is Force 6 (strong breeze). What is it in mph?

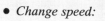

Answer

(a) • *Change miles to km:*
      5 miles ≈ 8 km
      1 mile ≈ $\frac{8}{5}$ km
      61 miles ≈ $61 \times \frac{8}{5}$ km
             = 97.6 km

  • *Change speed:*   61 mph = 98 km/h
                   (to nearest km/h)

  • *Check:* mph → km/h
      Change to smaller unit → more of them. ✓
      98 is more than 61. So answer makes sense.

(b) • *Change km to miles:*
      8 km ≈ 5 miles
      1 km ≈ $\frac{5}{8}$ mile
      45 km ≈ $45 \times \frac{5}{8}$ mile
            = 28.125 miles

  • *Change speed:*   45 km/h = 28 mph
                   (to nearest mph)

  • *Check:* km/h → mph
      Change to larger unit → fewer of them. ✓
      28 is less than 45. So answer makes sense.

Here are some useful imperial conversions.
Use them in the Exercises in this unit.

imperial units

1 mile	= 1760 yards (yd)
1 yard (yd)	= 3 feet (ft)
1 foot (ft)	= 12 inches (in)

imperial ↔ metric

5 miles	≈	8 km
1 yard	≈	1 metre
1 foot	≈	30 cm
1 inch	≈	2.5 cm

 Discussion Exercise

Which is faster, 1 m/s or 1 km/s?
Say what you think first. Then give both in either m/s or km/s
to find out.
Discuss what you find.

Now do the same with these pairs of speed units.

1 cm/year or 1 m/year

1 mph or 1 km/h

1 foot/s or 1 inch/s

1 mile/min or 1 yd/min

1 metre/h or 1 km/h

1 cm/s or 1 mm/s

1 yard/min or 1 m/min

1 cm/s or 1 inch/s

1 knot or 1 mph

1 foot/day or 1 m/day

When changing some speed units, the distance unit stays the
same.
For example, **miles** per hour ↔ **miles** per minute
                metres/second ↔ **metres**/hour.
Use your common sense to decide what to do. Think about how
the change in the time unit changes the speed.

Here are some examples.

Think about this change: miles/*hour* ——→ miles/*minute*

A minute is shorter than an hour. So common sense says you
must get 'fewer miles/minute'.

For example, to change 75 mph to miles/minute,
            divide by 60 because 60 minutes = 1 hour.

    75 mph = 75 ÷ 60 miles per minute
           = 1.25 miles per minute

Check: mph → miles/minute
            Change to a shorter time → fewer units. ✓
            1.25 is less than 75. So this answer makes sense.

Now think about this change:

metres/*second* ——→ metres/*hour*

An hour is longer than a second. So common sense says you
must get more 'metres per hour'.
Multiplying by 60 changes m/s to metres/minute.
Multiplying by 60 again changes it to metres/hour.

For example,
    5 m/s = 5 × 60 × 60 metres/hour
          = 18 000 metres/hour
Check: m/s → m/h
            Change to a longer time → more units. ✓
            18 000 is more than 5. So this answer makes sense.

 Discussion Exercise

Compare 1 km/h and 1 km/s.
Which do you think is faster?
Write both in either km/h or km/s to find out.
Discuss your results.

Now compare these pairs of speeds in the same way.

1 cm/hour and 1 cm/min

1 mile/s and 1 mile/h

1 inch/h and 1 inch/day

1 mm/min and 1 mm/s

1 cm/year and 1 cm/day

1 ft/s and 1 ft/min

1 m/day and 1 m/hour

1 mile/min and 1 mph

1 cm/h and 1 cm/s

1 yard/day and 1 yard/year

To change some speed units, such as km/h ↔ m/s, you have to
change *both* distance and time units.
Change one unit first and then the other.
Do each change step-by-step.
Don't try to do more than one step at a time.

Discussion Exercise

Top race speeds

Horse:
19 m/s

Man:
43 km/h

- Compare these top race speeds. Which do you think is faster?
  To find out you have to give both speeds in the same unit.
- These steps change km/h to m/s.
  Discuss what each step does.
  Use them to change 43 km/h.
  Which was faster, man or horse?

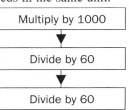

Multiply by 1000

Divide by 60

Divide by 60

- How can you change m/s to km/h?
  List the steps needed. Discuss.
  Use them to change 19 m/s to km/h.

Top speed fliers

Swift:
106 mph

Peregrine falcon
97 metres/s

Compare these speeds
Which do you think is faster?
Discuss how to change
        mph to metres/second
        and metres/second to mph.
(Use 5 miles ≈ 8 km.)

Exercise P10.10

Where necessary, give your answers to a sensible degree of accuracy.

1 Change these speeds to miles per hour.
  (a) 80 km/h   (c) 60 km/h   (e) 375 km/h
  (b) 36 km/h   (d) 100 km/h   (f) 1200 km/h

2 Change these speeds to kilometres per hour.
  (a) 70 mph   (c) 100 mph   (e) 700 mph
  (b) 45 mph   (d) 240 mph   (f) 1000 mph

3 Change these speeds to metres per second.
  (a) 15 cm/s   (c) 250 mm/s   (e) 65 mm/s
  (b) 68 cm/s   (d) 867 mm/s   (f) 7 mm/s

4 Change these speeds to metres per second.
  (a) 36 km/h   (c) 70 km/h   (e) 120 km/h
  (b) 90 km/h   (d) 85 km/h   (f) 350 km/h

5 Change these speeds to kilometres per hour.
  (a) 20 m/s   (c) 7 m/s   (e) 106 m/s
  (b) 35 m/s   (d) 85 m/s   (f) 230 m/s

6 Change these speeds to feet per second.
  (a) 30 mph   (c) 58 mph   (e) 123 mph
  (b) 2 mph   (d) 90 mph   (f) 250 mph

Examination Questions

1 Andrew cycles from his home to work every day. His average time for the journey is 20 minutes. He lives approximately 4 miles from work. Estimate his average cycling speed in miles per hour for the journey.
(SEG, 1991)

2 In the Kalibo 10 km race one of the competitors starts at 11.48 and finishes at 13.03.
  (a) How long does this competitor take to run the race?
  (b) What is this competitor's average speed?
(NISEAC, 1990)

3 John and Laura went on holiday. They kept a careful record of the times and the distances that they travelled.
On the first day they started at 0930, stopped for lunch for one hour, and arrived at their destination at 1630.
  (a) Work out the length of time that they were travelling.
They travelled at an average speed of 60 mph.
  (b) Work out the distance that they travelled.
(ULEAC, 1989)

4 From junction 10 to junction 13 on the M25 is $10\frac{1}{2}$ miles.
  (a) Due to roadworks, Graham travels this distance at an average speed of 15 miles per hour. How long does it take him?
  (b) Normally, he travels this distance at 70 miles per hour. How much extra time has he taken because of the roadworks?
(MEG, 1990)

5 The speed of the tape in a video-tape recorder is 23.4 mm/sec.
How many metres of tape would be used to record a programme lasting 25 minutes?
(NISEAC, 1991)

6 Karen ran $1\frac{1}{2}$ miles in 10 minutes.
  (a) Calculate her average speed in miles per hour.
  (b) What distance would Karen cover if she ran at the same average speed for 15 minutes?
(SEG, 1989)

7 In 1985, the athlete Said Aouitta of Morocco broke the world 1500 metres record. His run was timed at 3 minutes 29.46 seconds. If he ran at the same average speed for 5 kilometres what would his time be?
(Cambridge, 1990)

8 During a very severe storm, the wind speed in Scotland was recorded as 105 miles per hour.
  (a) Calculate this wind speed in kilometres per hour.
The speed limit in Austrian towns is 60 kilometres per hour.
  (b) Calculate this speed in miles per hour.
    (Take 5 miles as being equivalent to 8 kilometres.)
(SEG, 1990)

9

Imran and Knotty travel from Stourport to Loughton to play hockey. On the way there they travel via Oxford and they take 3 hours to travel the distance of 135 miles.
(a) Work out their average speed for this journey.
For the return journey they travel along the M1 and M6 and return via Birmingham. They travel at the same average speed as before but the journey is 153 miles by this route.
(b) Work out the length of time for the return journey.
(ULEAC, 1991)

10 Mr Beneton, on a camping holiday in Europe, travels from St. Malo to Houlgate at an average speed of 60 km/h for 2 hours. He then travels from Houlgate to Cherbourg, a distance of 84 kilometres, at an average speed of 70 km/h. Calculate the average speed of the whole journey from St. Malo to Cherbourg.
(Cambridge, 1990)

P11
Solving polynomial equations

This unit will help you to:

■ solve a range of equations involving squares and cubes by 'trial and improvement' methods.

Solving problems

Karen works at Cubox. She designs boxes for them.
Each design has a specification like this.
It gives a list of features the box must have.

> **Customer** : Plastibox
> **Specification** : Design A
> • cuboid
> • square base
>   (less than 20 cm long)
> • height 5 cm
> • volume 320 cm^3

From this specification she draws a sketch

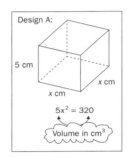

Design A:

5 cm

x cm

x cm

$5x^2 = 320$

Volume in cm^3

Then she makes an equation that fits the features.

 Discussion Exercise

What does x stand for in Karen's equation?
Explain why the volume is $5x^2$.

To find the dimensions for Design A, Karen has to solve the equation $5x^2 = 320$.

To solve this equation Karen uses her calculator and 'trial and improvement'. She chooses a number for x. She works out $5x^2$ with it. Then she compares the result with 320.

> *Memo*
> Solving equations by trial and improvement
> p 101–102

x has to be 'less than 20cm' (see the specification). So Karen starts with a sensible guess 'less than 20'. The table and number line below show her tries and results.

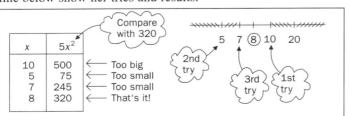

x	$5x^2$	
10	500	← Too big
5	75	← Too small
7	245	← Too small
8	320	← That's it!

Compare with 320

5   7 (8) 10   20

2nd try   1st try
            3rd try

$x = 8$ solves the equation $5x^2 = 320$

So the square base must be 8 cm long.
The box for Design A measures 5 cm by 8 cm by 8 cm.

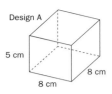

Design A

5 cm

8 cm

8 cm

▶ *Exercise* P11.1

Here are the sketches and equations for some other boxes for Plastibox. Explain how each equation is obtained.

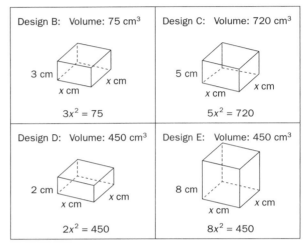

Design B: Volume: 75 cm^3	Design C: Volume: 720 cm^3
3 cm x cm x cm $3x^2 = 75$	5 cm x cm x cm $5x^2 = 720$
Design D: Volume: 450 cm^3	Design E: Volume: 450 cm^3
2 cm x cm x cm $2x^2 = 450$	8 cm x cm x cm $8x^2 = 450$

Find the dimensions of each box by trial and improvement.
Show your working clearly.

Harder problems

This specification for a box is more complicated:

> **Customer** : Imperial Box Co.
> **Specification** : Design I
> ● open topped box
> ● cuboid
> ● square base
>   (less than 20" long)
> ● height $\frac{1}{4}$ inch
> ● surface area
>   20 square inches

Karen draws two sketches to help her to make an equation.

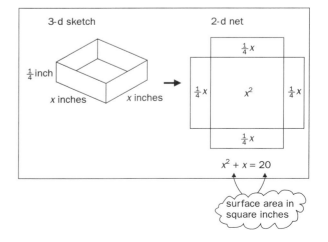

3-d sketch

$\frac{1}{4}$ inch

x inches   x inches

2-d net

$\frac{1}{4}x$

$\frac{1}{4}x$ x^2 $\frac{1}{4}x$

$\frac{1}{4}x$

$x^2 + x = 20$

surface area in square inches

Discussion Exercise

Explain why Karen uses $x^2 + x = 20$ for the surface area.
Look for clues in the specifications and her sketches.

Karen finds a solution to $x^2 + x = 20$ by trial and improvement.
She 'plans' how to work out $x^2 + x$ on her calculator first:

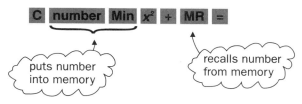

Then she tries numbers as before:

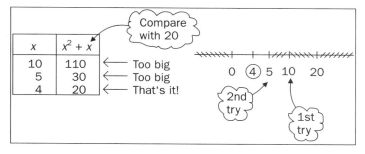

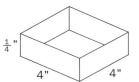

$x = 4$ is a solution to $x^2 + x = 20$.
So Design I measures
$\frac{1}{4}$" by 4" by 4".

Discussion Exercise

Try Karen's key code for $x^2 + x$ with your calculator.
See if it works.
Look for other ways to try numbers in $x^2 + x$ with your
calculator. Write a key code for each.
Which way do you prefer? Why?

► *Exercise* P11.2

These 3-d sketches and equations are for some other boxes for
the Imperial Box Company.

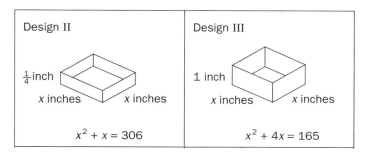

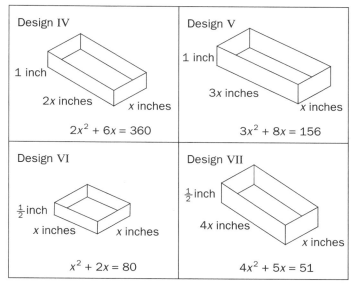

Find the dimensions of each box by trial and improvement.
Write down the key code you use for each.
Show your working clearly.

Approximate solutions

Here is another design problem Karen has to solve.

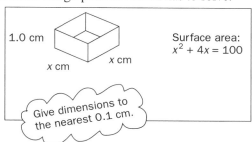

To find a value of x 'to the nearest 0.1 cm', Karen tries
whole numbers first …

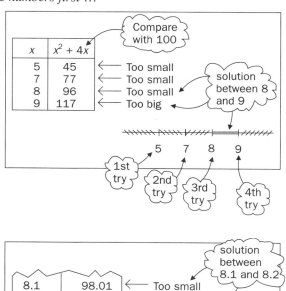

Then she tries *decimals with 1 dp* between 8 and 9:
Finally she decides which number (8.1 or 8.2) is nearest to the solution. To do this, she compares the results they give (98.01 and 100.04) with the result she wants (100).

100.04 is nearest to 100.
So $x = 8.2$ is nearest to the solution.
This gives:

$$x = 8.2 \text{ (to 1 dp)}$$

So the dimensions of the box are:
1.0 cm by 8.2 cm by 8.2 cm.

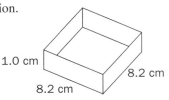

1.0 cm

8.2 cm

8.2 cm

► *Exercise* **P11.3**

Find a solution to each of these equations correct to 1 decimal place. Show your working clearly.

1   $x^2 + x = 13$ 6 $2x^2 - x = 60$
2   $x^2 - x = 5$ 7 $3x^2 - 2x = 100$
3   $x^2 + 3x = 2$ 8 $4x^2 + 5x = 8$
4   $x^2 - 4x = 7$ 9 $x(x + 1) = 25$
5   $2x^2 + x = 24$ 10 $x(x - 2) = 60$

Summary

Trial and improvement
You can find solutions to a range of equations by trial and improvement.
The basic strategy is always the same:
● Try a number instead of the letter in the equation.
  Look at the result it gives.
● If the result is what you want, then the number you tried is a solution.
  If the result is not what you want, then use it to help you to make a better 'try' next.

To help you choose a 'better' number to try, use these guidelines.
● Compare the result with what you want.
  If your result was *too big*, choose a '*smaller try*' next.
  If your result was *too small*, choose a '*larger try*' next.
● Look for opposite results:

     result *too big* then result *too small* or
     result *too small* then result *too big*.

  When you get two 'opposite' results like these, you know that a solution is between the two numbers you tried.

Always keep a neat record of your tries.
Use a table and/or a number line to do this.

Approximate solutions
For many equations you want only approximate solutions.
Try whole numbers first.
Then try decimals (to 1, 2, ... decimal places) if you need to.

Find the two consecutive numbers that give the approximation you want and that give 'opposite results'.
Then decide which is nearer to the solution.

Questions often tell you the approximation to use:
   'to the nearest whole number,
   'to 1, 2, ... decimal places,
   'to 1, 2, ... significant figures', ...
Always do what they ask – or you will lose marks.
Take care not to mix up 'decimal places' and 'significant figures'.

Calculator planning
You will use a calculator to solve most problems by trial and improvement.
Before trying any numbers ...
● Think about what you have to work out.
● Plan the best way to do the working with your calculator.
● Write down a 'key code' for your plan.
  This is a useful reminder especially if you're nervous in an exam.
● Test your 'key code' with a simple number.
  And check you get the same result without a calculator.

Question
The equation $x^2 - 6x = 45$ has a positive solution less than 20.
Find the value of this solution:
(a) correct to two significant figures
(b) correct to two decimal places.

Answer
Here is a key code for $x^2 - 6x$:

C **number** **Min** x^2 **−** **6** **×** **MR** **=**

Choose the best 'key code' for your calculator.

(a) *Solution correct to two significant figures:*

   We want a positive solution less than 20, so try whole numbers between 0 and 20.

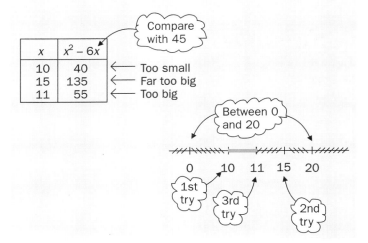

The solution is between 10 and 11.
Each of these consecutive numbers has 2 significant figures.
So decide which is nearer:

$x = 11$ gives $x^2 - 6x = 55$
$x = 10$ gives $\underbrace{x^2 - 6x = 40}$

This is nearest to $x^2 - 6x = 45$.
So $x = 10$ is nearest to the solution.
The solution is $x = 10$, correct to 2 significant figures.

(b) *Solution correct to two decimal places:*
We know the solution is between 10 and 11.
Try decimals with 1 dp between 10 and 11.

x	$x^2 - 6x$	
10.5	47.25	← Too big
10.3	44.29	← Too small
10.4	45.76	← Too big

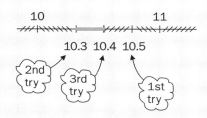

x is between 10.3 and 10.4.
Try decimals with 2 dp between 10.3 and 10.4

x	$x^2 - 6x$	
10.35	45.0225	← Too big
10.34	44.8756	← Too small

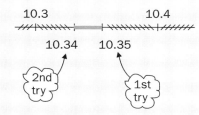

x is between 10.34 and 10.35
Each of these consecutive numbers has 2 dp.
So decide which is nearer:

Try $x = 10.345$
  $x^2 - 6x = 44.949025$ ← Too small

x is between 10.345 and 10.35.

So the solution is 10.35 (to 2 dp).

► *Exercise* **P11.4**

1 Find an approximate solution (correct to two significant figures) to each equation.
  (a) $x^2 + x = 10$ (c) $2x^2 - 5x = 10$
  (b) $x^2 - x = 7$ (d) $2x^2 + 3x = 15$

2 Find an approximate solution (correct to two decimal places) to each equation in question **1**.

3 Find a positive whole number solution to each of these equations.
  (a) $x^3 + x = 130$ (c) $x^3 + 8x = 801$
  (b) $x^3 - 3x = 52$ (d) $x^3 - x^2 - x = 15$

4 Find an approximate solution (correct to two significant figures) to each of these equations.
  (a) $x^3 + x^2 = 5$ (c) $x^3 - x = 20$
  (b) $x^3 - x^2 = 10$ (d) $x^3 + x^2 + x = 100$

5 Find an approximate solution (correct to two decimal places) to each equation in question **4**.

'Equals zero'

Many equations are given as 'something' = 0

To find solutions to these by trial and improvement, you compare 'trial results' with 0.
This is easy to do. Just look at their 'signs'.
  '– sign' → result *smaller* than 0.
  '*no sign*' → result *bigger* than 0.

Question

A solution to $x^2 - 8x + 9 = 0$ is between 0 and 5. Find its value correct to one decimal place.

Answer

Here is a key code for $x^2 - 8x + 9$:

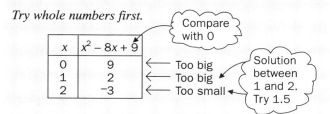

Use the best code for your calculator.

Try whole numbers first.

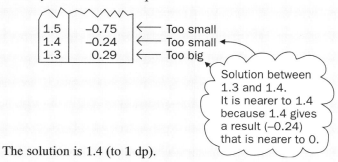

x	$x^2 - 8x + 9$	
0	9	← Too big
1	2	← Too big
2	−3	← Too small

Then try decimals with 1 dp.

1.5	−0.75	← Too small
1.4	−0.24	← Too small
1.3	0.29	← Too big

Solution between 1.3 and 1.4. It is nearer to 1.4 because 1.4 gives a result (−0.24) that is nearer to 0.

The solution is 1.4 (to 1 dp).

▶ *Exercise* **P11.5**

1 (a) Copy and complete this table
   of values of $x^2 - 4x - 50$ for
   whole number values of x
   from 0 to 10.

x	$x^2 - 4x - 50$
0	
1	

   (b) Between which pair of consecutive whole numbers does
   a solution of the equation $x^2 - 4x - 50 = 0$ lie?
   (c) Find this solution correct to two decimal places.

2 (a) Between which pair of consecutive whole numbers does
   a solution of $x^2 - 8x - 40 = 0$ lie?
   (b) Find an approximate value for this solution,
   correct to two decimal places.

3 Find an approximate solution to each equation. Give your
   answers correct to two decimal places.
   (a) $x^2 + x - 15 = 0$ (c) $2x^2 - 5x - 10 = 0$
   (b) $x^2 + 3x - 60 = 0$ (d) $x^3 + 8x - 270 = 0$

4 (a) Try whole number values of x from 0 to 8 in
   $x^2 - 7x + 8$.
   What do you notice about your results?
   (b How many solutions has $x^2 - 7x + 8 = 0$ between 0
   and 8? How can you tell?
   (c) Find each solution correct to two decimal places.

5 Each of these equations has more than one solution between
   0 and 10. Find approximate values for all of these solutions.
   Give your answers correct to one decimal place.
   (a) $x^2 - 4x + 2 = 0$ (c) $6x^2 - 11x + 5 = 0$
   (b) $x^2 - 6x + 3 = 0$ (d) $2x^2 - 4x + 1 = 0$.

More problem solving

Many problems lead to equations that you can solve by trial and
improvement. You will find examples of these in other Units.
But here are some for you to practise solving.

▶ *Exercise* **P11.6**

Use a 'trial and improvement' method to solve these problems.
Show your working clearly.

1 Sarah invested £240 in British
   Telecom shares. The cost, x pence,
   of each share is given by
   $$x^2 - 10x - 3000 = 0.$$
   Find the value of x.

   SHARE DEALING

2 Plastic-tray makes trays from sheets
   of plastic. The formula
   $$A = x^2 + 80x$$
   gives the area, A square millimetres, of plastic sheet used
   for a tray with a square base, x millimetres, long. The
   design for one tray uses 2500 mm^2 of plastic sheet.
   How long (to the nearest millimetre) is the base of this tray?

3 Van-design builds vans to customers' specifications. The
   width, x metres, and the volume, V cubic metres, of each
   van must satisfy the formula
   $$V = 3x^2 + 2x.$$
   A customer orders a van with a volume of 8 m^3.
   Find its width in metres (correct to 2 decimal places).

4 A tennis player hits a ball vertically
   upwards. After t seconds the ball is
   d metres above the ground.
   Use the formula
   $$d = 1 + 15t - 5t^2$$
   to find the first time the ball is 10 metres
   above the ground. Give the time correct to
   the nearest tenth of a second.

5 The speed, v miles per hour, of a car that can stop in a
   distance of 150 metres is given by the equation
   $$v^2 + 20v = 9000.$$
   Find this speed correct to the nearest mile per hour.

◉ *Investigation*

Spreadsheets

A computer spreadsheet can be used to solve equations by trial
and improvement.
Instead of calculating the result of each trial yourself you can
set up the spreadsheet so that the computer does it for you.
Investigate how to do this using the spreadsheet program on
your school or college computer.
Test your 'findings' on some of the equations in this unit.
Make up some equations of your own to solve.
Find out how to make a 'decimal search' for a solution with
your spreadsheet.
Write a report to describe what you have found out.   ◉

Examination Questions

1 (a) Susan wants to find, correct to one decimal place, a
   solution of the equation
   $$2x^2 = 5.$$
   She tries by guessing values of x that might satisfy the
   equation.
   First she tries $x = 1.2$ and gets the result 2.88 for $2x^2$.
   Then she tries $x = 1.9$ and gets the result 7.22 for $2x^2$.
   By trying other values of x and showing your working
   clearly, find a solution of the equation correct to one
   decimal place.
   (b) Susan now has to find, correct to one decimal place, the
   solution of the equation
   $$x^2 + x = 1.$$
   By trying values of x and showing your working clearly,
   find a solution to Susan's equation.
   (NEAB, 1994)

2 Nisha wishes to solve the equation
   $$x^2 + x = 14$$
   using trial and improvement.
   Continue Nisha's working until you know the value of x
   correct to one decimal place. Write down this answer.
   Try $x = 3.1$ $3.1^2 + 3.1 = 12.71$ which is too small.
   Try $x = 3.5$ $3.5^2 + 3.5 = 15.75$ which is too large.
   Try $x = 3.2$ $3.2^2 + 3.2 = \ldots\ldots$ which is $\ldots\ldots$
   (SEG, 1994)

3 (a) If $x = 2$ find the value of $x^2 + x$.
(b) If $x = 3$ find the value of $x^2 + x$.
(c) Estimate a solution of the equation $x^2 + x = 10$.
(d) Use a 'trial and improvement' method to improve on this estimate, giving your answer correct to 1 decimal place.

(MEG, 1994)

4 The equation

$$x(x + 1) = 10$$

has a solution between 2 and 3. Using decimal search or otherwise, find this value of x, giving your final answer correct to 2 decimal places.
Show your working clearly.

(MEG, 1994)

5 An open container in the shape of a cuboid has a square base of side x cm and a height of 2 cm (see opposite).
(i) Explain why the area of the face OABC is $2x$ cm²?

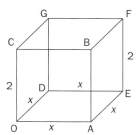

(ii) Show that the total surface area of the container is given by the formula $(x^2 + 8x)$ cm².
(iii) If the surface area is actually 27 cm², show that x must be greater than 2 and less than 3.
(iv) Estimate, correct to 1 decimal place, the side of the square base so that the surface area is 27 cm². You must show your working.

(MEG, 1994)

P12
Averages from frequency distributions

This unit will help you to:

■ find the mean, median, mode and range of ungrouped data from a frequency table

■ find the modal class and median class interval of grouped data from a frequency table

■ calculate an estimate of the mean from a grouped frequency distribution table

■ estimate the range of values in a grouped frequency table

■ use the above statistics to comment on the data in frequency distributions.

Mean, median, mode and range

You have found the mean, median, mode and range of raw data.
The **mean**, **median** and **mode** are **averages**. An average is a *single value* used to *represent* the data.
The **range** gives an idea of *how spread out* the data are.

 Memo

D4 Averages and range
p 214

Memo

mean = $\dfrac{\text{total of values}}{\text{number of values}}$

median: the 'middle value' when the data are in order of size.

mode: the value that occurs most often.

range = largest value − smallest value.

These statistics are also used to describe data given in frequency distributions.

Ungrouped frequency distribution

In an ungrouped frequency distribution, each *data value* is given *in order*.
The **frequency** shows *how often* each data value occurs.

Zelda did a survey of the families living in Newton Terrace. This frequency table shows the number of children in each of the families.

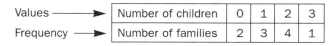

Number of children	0	1	2	3
Number of families	2	3	4	1

Values ──→ (Number of children)
Frequency ──→ (Number of families)

The 'values' in this frequency distribution are the number of children in each family.
The 'frequencies' are the number of families.

Zelda finds the range, mode, median and mean to describe these data in her survey report.

Range

For the range, you find the *largest* and *smallest* values in the table.
Largest value is 3.   Smallest value is 0.
Range is $3 - 0 = 3$ children.

Mode

For the mode, you look for the value that occurs *most often*.
This is the value with the *greatest frequency*.
The greatest frequency in the table is 4.
4 families each had 2 children.
The mode of the data is 2 children.
Remember: the mode is the *value*, not the frequency.

Median

One way to find the median is to list all the values in order of
size. Then you look for the '*middle* value'.
Here is the list of values for these data:

0, 0, 1, 1, | 1, 2, | 2, 2, 2, 3

two middle values.

There is an *even* number of values.
So there are *two* 'middle values'. Here they are 1 and 2.
The median is the mean of the two 'middle values'.
The median number of children is $\frac{1}{2}(1 + 2)$

$$= 1.5 \text{ children}$$

You can also find the median *directly from the table*.
The values in the table are already in order of size. You can *count
along the frequencies* to find where the middle value(s) lies.

For Zelda's data, adding the frequencies gives
    $2 + 3 + 4 + 1 = 10$
There are 10 values in the data.
Half of 10 is 5.
So the median is half-way between the 5th and 6th values.
Count along the frequencies to find these values.

Value	Number of children	0	1	2	3
Frequency	Number of families	2	3	4	1

2 values to here
2+3 = 5 values to here
6th value must be in here

The 5th value must be 1
The 6th value must be 2
The median is $\frac{1}{2}(1 + 2) = 1.5$ children.

Mean

To find the mean of the values in the data, you add up all the
values, then divide by the number of values.
In this frequency distribution,

the mean $= \dfrac{\text{total number of children}}{\text{number of families}}$

total of values

number of values

To find the mean, you can list the values from the table:

0, 0, 1, 1, 1, 2, 2, 2, 2, 3

The total number of children is:

$0 + 0 + 1 + 1 + 1 + 2 + 2 + 2 + 2 + 3 = 14$

The total number of families is 10.

The mean number of children per family is $\dfrac{14}{10} = 1.4$

You can also find the mean from the table, *without* listing
each value.
To find the *total of the values* you must take the frequency of
each value into account.
Look at the numbers of children in the table.
To find the *total number of children*, we multiply each 'number
of children' by its frequency, then add these numbers.

frequency × value

0 occurs 2 times $2 \times 0 = 0$
1 occurs 3 times $3 \times 1 = 3$
2 occurs 4 times $4 \times 2 = 8$
3 occurs 1 time $1 \times 3 = 3$
                    Total $\overline{14}$

Look at the numbers of families in the table.
To find the total number of families, we add these frequencies.

$2 + 3 + 4 + 1 = 10$
You can write the working table like this.

Value No. of children	Frequency No. of families	Frequency × value
0	2	$2 \times 0 = 0$
1	3	$3 \times 1 = 3$
2	4	$4 \times 2 = 8$
3	1	$1 \times 3 = 3$
Total	10	14

total of frequencies = number of values

total of 'frequencies × values' = total of the values

These totals give the same result as before:

Mean $= \dfrac{\text{total of 'frequency} \times \text{value'}}{\text{total of frequencies}}$

$= \dfrac{14}{10}$

$= 1.4$ children per family

Summary

You can find the **mean**, **median** and **mode** of an *ungrouped*
frequency distribution directly **from the frequency table**.
It is easier and quicker than using the raw data.

mean $= \dfrac{\text{total of 'frequency} \times \text{value'}}{\text{total of frequencies}}$

median: count down the frequencies to find the middle
        value(s)

mode: value with the greatest frequency.

Question

A motoring magazine
did a survey of prices
at petrol stations in
the U.K.
This table gives the
results for unleaded
petrol.

Price per litre (in pence)	Frequency
49.9	3
50.9	8
51.9	6
52.9	9
53.9	15
54.9	7
55.9	2

For this frequency distribution, find
(a) the number of petrol stations in the survey
(b) the range of prices
(c) the mode
(d) the median
(e) the mean.

Answer

(a) *Add the frequencies:*
3 + 8 + 6 + 9 + 15 + 7 + 2 = 50
50 petrol stations were in the survey.
(b) *Find the largest and smallest values in the table.*
Largest value: 55.9
Smallest value: 49.9
Range = Largest value – smallest value
$$= 55.9 - 49.9$$
$$= 6$$
The range of prices is 6 pence per litre.
(c) *Look for the value with the greatest frequency.*
The greatest frequency is 15.
The value that occurs 15 times is 53.9.
The mode is 53.9 pence per litre.
(d) The total of frequencies is 50.
Half of 50 is 25.
The median is half-way between the 25th and 26th values.
Count down the frequencies to find this position.

Value	Frequency	
49.9	3	3 values to here
50.9	8	3 + 8 = 11 values to here
51.9	6	11 + 6 = 17 values to here
52.9	9	17 + 9 = 26 values to here

The 25th and 26th values must both be 52.9.
The median is 52.9 pence per litre.

• *To find the total number of values, put the working in an extra column in the table like this.*

Price per litre (in pence)	Frequency No. of families	Frequency × value
49.9	3	3 × 49.9 = 149.7
50.9	8	8 × 50.9 = 407.2
51.9	6	6 × 51.9 = 311.4
52.9	9	9 × 52.9 = 476.1
53.9	15	15 × 53.9 = 808.5
54.9	7	7 × 54.9 = 384.3
55.9	2	2 × 55.9 = 111.8
Total	50	2649.0

total of frequencies = number of values

total of 'frequency × value' = total of the values

$$\text{mean} = \frac{\text{total of 'frequency} \times \text{value'}}{\text{total of frequencies}}$$
$$= \frac{2649.0}{50}$$
$$= 52.98$$
$$= 53.0 \text{ (to 1 dp)}$$
The mean is 53.0 pence per litre (to 1 dp).

You will usually do the working out for the mean on a calculator.
Try to use the memory to find the total of the values if you can.
Key in **frequency** × **value** = **M+**
for each multiplication in the table.
Each time you press **=** the answer to the multiplication comes on the display. Write each answer in the table. Pressing **M+** adds the answer to the memory.
To get the total of the values, press **MR**, the 'memory recall' key, at the end.
You can use a calculator in the usual way to add up the frequencies and work out the mean.

Discussion Exercise

Use the above method to calculate the mean in the last example. Investigate ways to do this working on your calculator. Which way(s) are most efficient and easiest to use?
Compare your methods with those of other students in your group. Remember, their calculators may not be the same as yours.
Find the best way to do the working on your calculator. Make sure you can record your working clearly. You will need to do this in your examination.

► *Exercise* P12.1

For each frequency distribution in this Exercise, find these statistics:
the mean, the median, the mode, the range.

1 This table shows the marks (out of 10) obtained by a number of students in an English test.

Mark	0	1	2	3	4	5	6	7	8	9	10
Frequency	0	2	3	3	5	12	20	25	17	10	3

How many students took the test?

2 In a survey, a number of drivers were asked how many accidents they had had in the last five years. Their answers are given in this frequency table.

Number of accidents	0	1	2	3	4	5	6
Frequency	17	13	21	4	2	2	1

How many drivers took part in the survey?

3 When Ranjit made a survey of the number of students in each class at Stanmoor Community College, this is what he found:

Number of students in class	27	28	29	30	31	32
Frequency	5	7	9	8	10	12

How many classes are there in the College?

4 A consumer organisation did a shopping survey. This table shows the prices charged for the same size tin and make of tomato soup.

Price (in pence)	52	53	54	55	56	57	58
Frequency	4	3	5	4	0	7	2

How many shops were surveyed?

5 The number of letters in each word in the first two paragraphs of a newspaper article gave these results.

Wordlength (letters)	1	2	3	4	5	6	7	8	9	10
Frequency	8	51	47	27	23	16	15	8	3	2

How many letters did the first two paragraphs contain?

6 The Carryfast Coach Company runs daily minibus excursions from Preston to Blackpool. The numbers of passengers carried each day during last year's holiday season are given in this table:

Number of passengers	15	16	17	18	19	20
Frequency	9	11	14	22	19	17

How many day's figures are included in the table?

 Discussion Exercise

Discuss the results of each survey outlined in Exercise P12.1. Include in your comments the averages you found. Write a short report on each survey's findings.

 *Exercise* **P12.2**

1 A flower grower is experimenting with a new variety of pot plant. He did a survey of the number of flowers on each plant in the greenhouse. The information obtained is shown in the table below.

Number of flowers per plant	0	1	2	3	4	5	6	7
Number of plants	3	10	60	55	52	40	23	7

(a) How many plants were inspected in the survey?
(b) Find the range, mode, median and mean of these data.
(c) Comment on what the statistics from (b) tell the grower.

2 A supermarket does a basket survey at its 'express checkout' till. The results are as follows:

Number of items per basket	1	2	3	4	5	6	7	8
Number of baskets	15	0	1	4	12	20	4	3

(a) How many baskets were checked in the survey?
(b) Find the range, mode, median and mean of the distribution.
(c) Comment on the results of the supermarket survey.

For questions **3–5**, find the range, mode, median and mean of the distributions in Exercise P9.1 p 302.
Use *frequency tables* to find these statistics *not* raw data.
Comment on what they tell you about the data in each case.

Grouped frequency distributions

In a grouped frequency distribution, the values are grouped in *class intervals*. The frequencies show the number of values in each class interval. If you do not have the raw data, you *do not know the actual values* in each class interval. So you *cannot find* the *actual* range, mode, median and mean of the distribution. However, you can make *reasonable estimates* of these statistics.

Grouped discrete data

The grouped data in the following example are **discrete**. This example shows you how to find the **modal class** and **median class** and **estimates** for the **range** and **mean**.

Bathway Student Drama Club meets every Wednesday during term-time. This frequency table is about attendances at club meetings last year. The club committee comments on these data in its annual report.

Number of students	Frequency
0– 9	1
10–19	2
20–29	11
30–39	9
40–49	14
50–59	3

Here are some of the statistics it includes in the report.

Total number of meetings.
Each frequency gives a number of meetings. To find the total number of meetings, simply add the frequencies:

$1 + 2 + 11 + 9 + 14 + 3 = 40$

There were 40 meetings of the club last year.

Range of attendances
You do not know the *actual* values in the data. So you cannot find the actual largest and smallest values.
The values in these data are discrete. So each class interval gives the largest and smallest possible value in that class.
The last class interval is 50–59.
The largest possible value in that class is 59.

The first class interval is 0–9.
The smallest possible value in that class is 0.

Largest possible value – smallest possible value = 59 – 0
= 59.
59 students is an **estimate of the range** of attendances.

Mode
You cannot say which value has the greatest frequency. So you cannot give a value for the mode.
The greatest frequency in the table is 14.
The class interval 40–49 has this frequency.
40–49 students is called the **modal class** or **modal group**.

Median
You cannot find the median value directly from this table.
You can find the *class interval that contains the median*.
Count down the frequencies to find the position of the middle value(s).
There are 40 values in the distribution.
Half of 40 is 20.
So the median is half-way between the 20th and 21st values.

Class intervals	Frequency	
0– 9	1	1 value to here
10–19	2	1 + 2 = 3 values to here
20–29	11	3 + 11 = 14 values to here
30–39	9	14 + 9 = 23 values to here

The 15th–23rd values are in the class interval 30–39.
So the 20th and 21st values are in this class.
30–39 students is called the **median class**.

Mean

To calculate the mean of these data you need to find the *total number of attendances* at the meetings.
Without knowing the number attending each meeting, you cannot find this total exactly. However you can make a reasonable estimate for it.
To find an estimate for the total number of values, you take the **mid-point of each interval** to represent that class. Then you assume that each item in the class has this mid-point value.
Take care when finding mid-point values.
These data are discrete.
So there are *two ways* to find the mid-point of each class.
You can list all the possible values in each class.
Then you can find the mid-point.

For example,
for the first class interval 0–9,
all the possible discrete values are:

$$0 \quad 1 \quad 2 \quad 3 \quad 4 \quad 5 \quad 6 \quad 7 \quad 8 \quad 9$$
$$\uparrow$$
$$\text{mid-point}$$

The mid-point is halfway between 4 and 5, i.e. 4.5.

You can also use the class interval to work out the mid-point.

mid-point of class interval
$= \frac{1}{2}$ (smallest possible value + largest possible value)

For example,
for the class interval 0–9,
the mid-point is $\frac{1}{2}(0+9) = 4.5$.

You can find the mid-points of all the class intervals in either way. They are:

4.5, 14.5, 24.5, 34.5, 44.5 and 54.5

Working out 'frequency × mid-point value' for each class gives an estimate of the total of the values in that class.
Then adding them together gives an estimate of the total of all the values.
As before, a table is an easy way to set down the working.

Class interval	Frequency	Midpoint	Frequency × midpoint
0– 9	1	4.5	1 × 4.5 = 4.5
10–19	2	14.5	2 × 14.5 = 29.0
20–29	11	24.5	11 × 24.5 = 269.5
30–39	9	34.5	9 × 34.5 = 310.5
40–49	14	44.5	14 × 44.5 = 623.0
50–59	3	54.5	3 × 54.5 = 163.5
	40		1400

Total of frequencies   Total of frequency × midpoint

Estimated mean $= \dfrac{\text{total of 'frequency} \times \text{mid-point'}}{\text{total of frequencies}}$

$$= \frac{1400}{40}$$

$$= 35$$

An estimate for the mean number of students at each meeting is 35.

Summary

You can find the following statistics from a grouped frequency distribution table.
Modal class or group: the class with the greatest frequency.
Median class or group: the class that contains the median (middle value). Count down the frequencies to find the position of the middle value(s).
Estimate of the mean:

$$\frac{\text{total of 'frequency} \times \text{mid-point'}}{\text{total of frequencies}}$$

Estimate of the range:
$$\binom{\text{upper boundary}}{\text{of highest class}} - \binom{\text{lower boundary}}{\text{of lowest class}}$$

▶ *Exercise* P12.3

1 This table gives the runs scored by the batsmen in a cricket competition.

Number of runs	0–9	10–19	20–29	30–39	40–49
Number of batsmen	6	14	9	5	2

Find these statistics for the data:
(a) the number of batsmen taking part
(b) an estimate of the range
(c) the modal group
(d) the median group
(e) an estimate of the mean.
Make some comments about the data based on these statistics.

2 A college did a survey of the cars in the visitors' car park at 12 noon each day during the spring term.
The results are as follows:

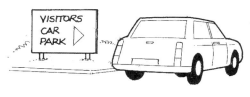

Number of cars	10–14	15–19	20–24	25–29	30–34	35–39	40–44	45–49
Number of days	1	1	2	8	19	14	4	1

Find:
(a) the mid-point of the 10–14 class interval
(b) an estimate of the mean number of cars per day
(c) the modal class
(d) the median class interval
(e) an estimate of the range.

Based on your answers, comment on the use of the visitors' car park.

3 (a) The raw data for a class's science test results are given on p 302. Find the mean, median and mode of the results from these data.

(b) On page 335 these results are sorted into class intervals 1–20, 21–40, ..., 81–100.
Find the modal class, median class and estimates of the mean and range of the data from this grouped frequency table. Compare your results with the answers from (a). Comment on what you find.

(c) In Exercise P9.2, page 303, you grouped the science test results into other class intervals. They were:

(i)   1–25, 26–50, ..., 76–100;
(ii) 1–10, 11–20, ..., 91–100;
(iii) 1–5, 6–10, ..., 96–100.

Find the modal class, median class and estimates of the mean and range from each grouped frequency table. Compare your results with those from (a) and (b). Comment on your findings.

(d) Based on the statistics you have found, comment on the performance of the students in this test.

For Questions **4** and **5**, find the modal group, median class and estimates of the mean and range of the distributions in Exercise P9.3, page 304. Use your grouped frequency tables to find these statistics.
Write a few sentences about what the statistics show about the data in each case. ◀

Grouped continuous data

You can also find the following statistics for grouped continuous data:

> modal class
> median class
> estimate of the mean
> estimate of the range.

To find an estimate of the mean you use the mid-point values as before. Take care to find these correctly from the class boundaries.

Memo

Mid-point values
p 309

For continuous data:

mid-point of class interval
$= \frac{1}{2}$(lower class boundary + upper class boundary).

Question

The police set up a speed camera on a road with a 30 mph limit. The camera records vehicle speeds to the nearest mph. The following frequency table is about speeds recorded in a trial run of the camera.

(a) What is the modal class for these data?

(b) How many speeds were recorded?

(c) In which class does the median of the data lie?

(d) Give an estimate of the range of speeds recorded.

(e) Write down the mid-points of the class intervals in the table.

(f) Calculate an estimate for the mean speed.

Speed mph	Frequency
16–20	1
21–25	13
26–30	22
31–35	23
36–40	2
41–45	4
46–50	5

Answer

(a) The greatest frequency is 23.
The class interval with this frequency is 31–35.

31–35 mph is the modal group.

(b) The total of the frequencies gives the number of speeds.

1 + 13 + 22 + 23 + 2 + 4 + 5 = 70

70 speeds were recorded.

(c) There are 70 speeds altogether.
Half of 70 is 35.
So the median is between the 35th and 36th speed, listed in order.
Count down the frequencies in the table to find the class interval that contains these speeds.

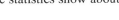

Speed mph	Frequency	
16–20	1	.... 1 value to here
21–25	13	.... 1+13 = 14 values to here
26–30	22	.... 14+22 = 36 values to here

The 35th and 36th values are in the class interval 26–30.
26–30 mph is the median class interval. The median lies in this class.

(d) The speeds are recorded to the nearest mph.
This means that class boundaries are not stated in the table.
For the first class, 16–20,
the lower class boundary is 15.5 mph (i.e. half way between 15 and 16).
For the last class, 46–50,
the upper class boundary is 50.5 mph (i.e. half way between 50 and 51).
An estimate for the range = 50.5 – 15.5
                                             = 35 mph

(e) For the first class, 16–20,
the class boundaries are 15.5 and 20.5.
The mid-point is $\frac{1}{2}$(15.5 + 20.5) = $\frac{1}{2}$(36)
                                             = 18 mph.
The mid-points of all the intervals are:

   18,   23,   28,   33,   38,   43,   48.

(f) *To find an estimate for the total of the values,*
work out 'frequency × mid-point' for each class interval.

Frequency	mid-point	Frequency x mid-point
1	18	1 x 18 = 18
13	23	13 x 23 = 299
22	28	22 x 28 = 616
23	33	23 x 33 = 759
2	38	2 x 38 = 76
4	43	4 x 43 = 172
5	48	5 x 48 = 240
Total: 70		Total: 2180

Estimate for the mean = $\dfrac{2180}{70}$

= 31.14285714

An estimate for the mean speed is 31 mph
(to the nearest mph).

Exercise P12.4

1 Packers at Santana's mail
order company are paid 'time
and a half' for each complete
hour of overtime worked.
The number of hours overtime
worked by them in the fortnight
before Christmas are given in
this table.
Find:

Hours overtime	Number of packers
1–	4
6–	2
11–	17
16–	11
21–	9
26–30	13

(a) the mid-point of each class interval
(b) an estimate of the mean hours overtime
(c) the modal class
(d) the median class interval
(e) an estimate of the range.
Use the statistics you have found to comment on these data.

2 The heights of the
boys in a Year Group
were measured to the
nearest centimetre.
This table shows a
grouped frequency
distribution of the
results.
Find:

Height (to the nearest cm)	Frequency
150–154	2
155–159	6
160–164	15
165–169	14
170–174	13
175–179	7
180–184	3

(a) the mid-point of
each class interval
(b) an estimate of the mean height
(c) the modal group
(d) the median class interval
(e) an estimate of the range.
Write a few sentences about the heights of the boys in this
Year Group, based on these statistics.

3 A health centre nurse noted the ages of women at an ante-
natal clinic one day.
The table shows her results grouped into class intervals.
Find:
(a) the mid-point of each class interval

(b) an estimate of the mean age
(c) the modal group
(d) the median class interval
(e) an estimate of the range.
Write some comments
about the age distribution
of the women at the clinic,
based on these statistics.

Age in years	Number of women
16–20	4
21–25	23
26–30	20
31–35	11
36–40	6
41–45	1

For Questions **4–10**, find estimates of the mean and range,
the modal group and the median class interval of the
distributions in Exercise P9.4, page 305 and Exercise P9.5,
page 307.
Use your grouped frequency distributions to find these
statistics.
Briefly comment on what your answers show about the
data in each question.

Comparing frequency distributions

You can compare frequency
distributions by comparing their
frequency diagrams and **polygons**.

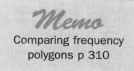

Memo

Comparing frequency
polygons p 310

You can also compare them by comparing their **averages** and
ranges.

 Discussion Exercise

Frequency polygons
are used to compare
the heights of two
varieties of hedging
plants in the Question/
Answer on page 310.
Use the grouped
frequency distributions
to find estimates for the

mean height and the range, the modal group and median class
interval for each variety.
Comment on what these results show about the two varieties.

Compare the information given by these statistics with
the picture given by the frequency polygons.
Discuss.

Exercise P12.5

In Exercise P9.8 on page 311, each question compares the
frequency polygons of two distributions.
Find estimates for the mean and the range, the modal group and
median class interval for the two grouped frequency
distributions in each case.
Comment on what these statistics show about the two
distributions in each question.
Compare your comments with those made earlier from the
frequency polygons.

Examination Questions

1 Joe works on the quality control at a large firm. She has to find the number of wrong items there are in each furniture kit.
   The following list gives the numbers of wrong items in 20 kits.

   1, 2, 0, 0, 0,
   4, 3, 2, 1, 1,
   0, 0, 2, 5, 4,
   3, 0, 1, 0, 2.

   (a) Copy and complete the following tally and frequency table.

Number of wrong items	Tally	Frequency
0	....	....
1	....	....
2	....	....
3	....	....
4	....	....
5	....	....

   (b) Draw a bar chart to represent the data.
   (c) Write down the mode of the data.
   (d) Work out the mean of the data.

   (ULEAC, 1989)

2 In a study of how daisies were growing in a lawn, Rachel marked out part of it in 30 cm squares. She counted the numbers of daisies in each square and these are shown on the diagram.

5	6	7	4	5
6	8	8	6	6
7	9	7	8	5
4	6	6	5	8
7	4	6	5	6

   (a) Copy and complete this frequency table:

Number of daisies	4	5	6	7	8	9
Number of squares	3		4			

   (b) Calculate the mean number of daisies per square.
   (c) The complete lawn measures 4.6 m by 5.8 m. Assuming daisies are growing in a similar way all over it, estimate the number of daisies in the lawn.

   (MEG, 1990)

3 A scientist wishes to test a new type of marrow. He grows 40 plants, and records how many marrows each plant produces. The results are shown in the table.

Number of marrows per plant	Number plants
0	10
1	0
2	0
3	3
4	2
5	4
6	9
7	10
8	2

   (a) (i) Calculate the total number of marrows on all 40 plants.
       (ii) Calculate the mean number of marrows per plant.
   (b) Find the median number of marrows per plant.
   (c) The scientist wishes to record the average number of marrows per plant. State two advantages of using the median rather than the mean in this situation.

   (SEG, 1990)

4 The stated limits of the monthly salaries (to the nearest £100) of managers and directors in an international business company, together with the numbers earning those salaries, are as shown in the table below.

Stated limits	Mid-point	Frequency	Mid-point × frequency
£2000–2900	£2450	39	£95 550
3000–3900		35	
4000–4900		29	
5000–5900		17	
6000–6900		8	
7000–7900		2	
Total			

   (a) What are the true limits of those in the category £2000–£2900?
   (b) Complete the column showing mid-points of the salary groupings.
   (c) How many managers and directors are there?
   (d) Complete the fourth column to help you to estimate the mean of the grouped salaries, to the nearest £10.

   (NEAB, 1988)

5 The table shows the numbers of people attending a church in a 50-week period.

Number of people	Mid-point of interval	Frequency
0– 19	9.5	0
20– 39	29.5	3
40– 59	49.5	10
60– 79	69.5	10
80– 99	89.5	17
100–119	109.5	8
120–139	129.5	2

   (a) Draw a frequency polygon, on a grid, to illustrate the data. Use the mid-points of the intervals. (Mark the 'number of people' axis from 0 to 140. Use a scale of 10 spaces to 20 people.) (Mark the frequency axis from 0 to 20. Use a scale of 10 spaces to a frequency of 5.)
   (b) Calculate an estimate of the mean of the numbers of people attending the church each Sunday.
   (c) In which interval does the median lie?

   (ULEAC, 1994)

6 A poultry farmer recorded the weight (w kg) of 50 chickens at the age of seven weeks. The results are shown in this table.

Weight (w kg)	Number of chickens
$1 \leq w < 1.2$	12
$1.2 \leq w < 1.4$	14
$1.4 \leq w < 1.6$	5
$1.6 \leq w < 1.8$	15
$1.8 \leq w < 2.0$	4

   (a) What is the modal class?
   (b) In which class does the median weight lie?
   (c) Calculate an estimate of the mean weight of these 50 chickens. (MEG, 1988)

7 Two groups of teenagers attended tests to join the Police Force. As part of the tests their heights were measured. The first group of 30 had a distribution of heights shown in this table.

Height, x, in centimetres	Number of teenagers
$160 \leq x < 170$	4
$170 \leq x < 180$	8
$180 \leq x < 190$	10
$190 \leq x < 200$	6
$200 \leq x < 210$	2

(a) Calculate the mean (average) height of the group.
(b) The second group consisted of 22 teenagers. The mean height of both groups taken together was 179 centimetres. Calculate the mean height of the second group alone. Give your answer correct to one decimal place.

(MEG, 1991)

P13
Linear graphs

This unit will help you to:

- draw the graph of a linear function from an equation or a relationship in words
- understand the idea of gradient
- find and use the gradient of a straight line
- interpret the gradient of a straight line graph from a practical situation.

A graph of a function

A **graph** gives you a *picture* of a **function**.

The graph of $y = x - 2$ is a single **straight line**. This shows it is the graph of a **linear function**. We call $y = x - 2$ a **linear equation**.

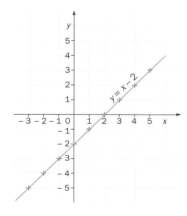

The graph of $y = x^2$ is not a single straight line. It is a **curve**. We say this is the graph of a **non-linear function**.

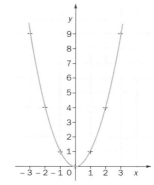

To draw the graph of a function, you can plot *many* points on it.

For a *straight line graph*, you don't have to. You really only need *two points*.

Any two points on the line will do. The straight line through them can go on and on.

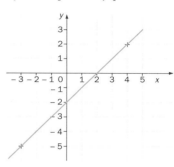

To draw a straight-line graph, we usually plot *three* points. Two points give the line. The *third point* acts as a *check* on your working.

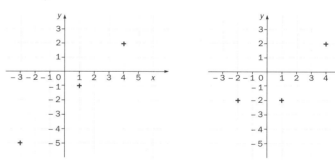

'3 points in line'
All 'probably' on the line we want.

3 'not in line'
At least one point is wrong.

Memo

When you plot points on a graph, remember:
- Use squared paper, a pencil and ruler.
- Draw the axes at right-angles to each other. Label each axis.
- Number each axis carefully. Start from 0 on each axis.
  'Right' and 'Up' are +.
  'Left' and 'Down' are −.
- Plot each point from its coordinates (x, y). Start at 0. Go across first (x-coordinate). Then go up or down (y-coordinate). Mark each point neatly with a cross **+** or **·** dot .

► *Exercise* P13.1

A student made the following tables of values for some straight line graphs.

Write down the coordinates given by each table. Plot each set of points on a separate graph. (Number the axes as given. Use the same scale on each axis).

Draw the straight line graphs if you can.

You cannot draw some of the graphs. Which ones?

What does this tell you about their table of values?

Graph 1

x	–2	0	3
y	–2	0	3

x-axis: –3 to 4
y-axis: –3 to 4

Graph 3

x	0	1	2
y	–2	1	6

x-axis: –1 to 5
y-axis: –5 to 6

Graph 2

x	–3	0	2
y	–5	0	5

x-axis: –3 to 3
y-axis: –6 to 6

Graph 4

x	5	0	–1
y	0	–5	–6

x-axis: –2 to 6
y-axis: –7 to 1

Straight lines from equations

A straight line is the graph of a linear function. You can draw this line from its equation. In mathematics equations are often given in terms of x and y.

To find the coordinates of three points on the line:

● take three values of x,

● work out the matching values of y from the equation.

You may do this by working 'in your head' or with a calculator. Take extra care with negative values.

It is a good idea to put the values in a table.

x	
y	

Question

(a) Make a table of values for $x = –1$, 0 and 4 for the function $y = 5 – 2x$

(b) Draw the graph of $y = 5 – 2x$ for values of x from –1 to 4.
Use the same scale on each axis.

Answer

(a) *Make a table of values:*

x	–1	0	4
y	7	5	–3

Working:
when $x = –1$, $y = 5 – 2(–1) = 7$
when $x = 0$, $y = 5 – 2 \times 0 = 5$
when $x = 4$, $y = 5 – 2 \times 4 = –3$

(b) *Draw graph:*
Note these key steps:

● *Draw axes*
Number x-axis from –1 to 4
(Given range of x-values.)
Number y-axis from –3 to 7
(Range of y-values from the table.)

● *Plot points from the table.*
(–1,7) (0,5) (4,–3).

● *Check they lie on a straight line.* ✓

● *Draw the straight line with a ruler. Label it with its equation.*

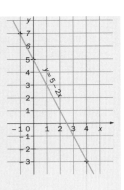

If you are *not* told which values of x to use to draw a graph, *choose three easy values.*

Here are some guidelines to help you.

● Always use $x = 0$ if you can. The 'working' is very simple.

● Don't make the points too close together.

● Look at the range of values of x you have to use. Try to use simple values of x near each end of the range. The matching y-values will show the range of values for the y-axis.

► *Exercise* P13.2

Draw the graph of each linear function.

The range of values of x is given in each case.

Find the range for y.

Use the same scale on each axis.

1   $y = 3x$. Values of x from –1 to 4.
2   $y = –2x$. Values of x from –5 to 5.
3   $y = x + 4$. Values of x from –4 to 4.
4   $y = x – 5$. Values of x from 0 to 10.
5   $y = 2x + 1$. Values of x from –3 to 3.
6   $y = 3x – 2$. Values of x from 0 to 4.
7   $y = 2 – x$. Values of x from –4 to 6.
8   $y = 2 – 3x$. Values of x from –1 to 4.

More linear equations

Some linear equations, such as $x + 3y = 6$, are not given as '$y = …$'.

Two easy points to find on such a graph are usually where $x = 0$ and $y = 0$.

These are the points where the line cuts the axes.

If you put $x = 0$ in the equation $x + 3y = 6$
                    you get: $0 + 3y = 6$
          Dividing both sides by 3: $y = 2$
This gives the point (0,2) on the line.

If you put $y = 0$ in the equation $x + 3y = 6$
                    you get: $x + 3 \times 0 = 6$
                              $x = 6$

This gives the point (6,0) on the line.

Choosing *another easy point* to find is not obvious. A simple value of x, such as 1, may not give a simple value of y.

If you put $x = 1$ in the equation $\qquad x + 3y = 6$
$\qquad\qquad\qquad$ you get: $\qquad 1 + 3y = 6$
$\qquad$ Subtract 1 from both sides: $\qquad 3y = 5$
$\qquad\qquad$ Divide both sides by 3: $\qquad y = \frac{5}{3}$ or $1\frac{2}{3}$.
This gives the point $(1, 1\frac{2}{3})$.
Plotting this point accurately is not easy.
So it is not a very good check.

In this situation it is a good idea to draw the line using the two 'easy points' first.
Then you can pick another easy point on the line to check.
You can test its x, y values to see if they 'fit' the equation.

On this graph the line
through $(0,2)$ and $(6,0)$
also passes through $(3,1)$.
At $(3,1)$, $x = 3$ and $y = 1$.
Check:
When $x = 3$ and $y = 1$,
$x + 3y = 3 + 3 \times 1 = 6$ ✓
So $(3,1)$ lies on the line
$x + 3y = 6$.

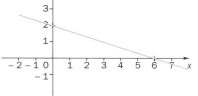

 Exercise P13.3

By finding the points where $x = 0$ and $y = 0$, draw the graph of each linear equation. (Number the axes using the given ranges of x and y).
Use a third point to check each line.
Show all your working clearly.
1 $x + y = 5$. Values of x from 0 to 5.
2 $x + y = 3$. Values of x from -2 to 4.
3 $2x + y = 4$. Values of x from 0 to 3.
4 $x + 2y = 2$. Values of x from -2 to 4.
5 $3x + 2y = 6$. Values of x from -2 to 4.

Recognising equations of linear functions

So far you have been *told* when an equation gives a straight line graph. You should also be able to *recognise* the equation of a linear function.

Discussion Exercise

Compare these two sets of equations.

Linear functions		Non-linear functions
$y = 3x$	$y = 4 - x$	$y = 5x^2$
	$y = 2x + 1$	$x^2 + y^2 = 4$
$x = y - 1$		
$x = 5$	$y = 3$	$x^3 = y$ $\qquad y = \frac{1}{x}$
$2y = 3x - 1$	$x + y = 6$	
		$y = \sqrt{x}$
$y + 2x - 1 = 0$		$\qquad y = 1 - x^2$
		$\frac{1}{x} + \frac{1}{y} = 2$
$\frac{x}{2} + \frac{y}{3} = 1$		$y = 3x^2 - x + 1$
		$\qquad y = x^3 - 5$

How are the equations of the linear functions *the same*?
How are the equations of the linear and non-linear functions *different*?
Discuss your ideas.

Discuss ways to complete this sentence.
'It looks as if the equation of a linear function has …'

Which of the following equations are for linear functions?
Explain why each of the others is not linear.
1 $y = x + 5$ $\qquad$ 7 $y = 7$
2 $x - 3 = 2y$ $\qquad$ 8 $y = x^3$
3 $x^2 + y = 25$ $\qquad$ 9 $\frac{x}{2} + y = 0$
4 $3y = 2x - 1$ $\qquad$ 10 $2y = 3x^2 + 1$
5 $y^2 = x + 3$ $\qquad$ 11 $xy = 5$
6 $2 - x = 5 + 2y$ $\qquad$ 12 $y = 1 - 2x - x^2$

Give some of your own examples of equations of linear functions.
Discuss them with other students in your group.
Make sure you all agree they are correct.

The slope of a line

These straight lines slope in *different directions*.
Some have steeper slopes than others.
We use **gradient** to describe the slope of a line.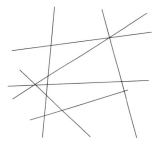

You read the words in this line from *left to right*.
We read the slope of a line in the same way.

This straight line slopes '*up*'.
It slopes from bottom left to top right.
The slope goes up at a *steady rate*.
It goes 'up 3 units for each 1 unit across'.
We say its gradient is 3.

These lines also slope 'up'.

This line goes *up 3 units* for each *2 units across*.

Its gradient is $\frac{3}{2}$.

This line goes *up 2 units* for each *3 units across*.

Its gradient is $\frac{2}{3}$.

This straight line slopes *'down'*.
It slopes from *top left* to *bottom right*.
It goes 'down 4 units
for each 1 unit across'.
We say its gradient is −4.
Remember: Up↑ is +.
            Down ↓ is −.

Each of these lines slope 'down' also.

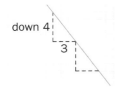

, This line goes *down 4 units* for each *3 units across*.

Its gradient is $\frac{-4}{3}$.

This line goes *down 3 units* for each *4 units across*.

Its gradient is $\frac{-3}{4}$.

This straight line is *'flat'*.
It goes neither up nor down.
It has *no slope*.
So its gradient is zero (0).

$$\text{Gradient} = \frac{\text{'vertical change'}}{\text{'horizontal change'}}$$

Always read from left to right.

Now do the same with these lines.

(d)   (e)   (f)

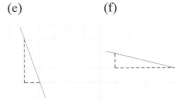

3 (a) Find the gradient of each of these three lines.
What do you notice?
What is special about these lines?
Discuss.

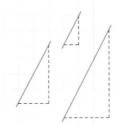

(b) Find the gradients of these lines.
Did you get the results you expected?
Discuss.

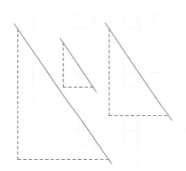

💬 ***Discussion Exercise***

1 Look at these lines.
Which have a positive gradient?
Which have a negative gradient?
Which have zero gradient?

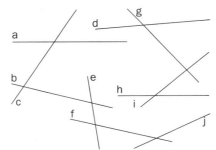

2 Look at the three lines below.
Put them in order of steepness 'by eye'.
Work out the gradient of each slope.
Comment on what you find.

(a)   (b)   (c)

4 Find the gradient of this line:
(a) from A to B
(b) from C to D
(c) from A to D
(d) from B to D.
What do you find?
What does this tell you about the gradient of the line?
Discuss.

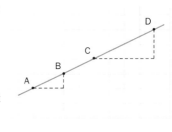

5 Find the gradient of this line:
(a) from G to H
(b) from I to J
(c) from K to L.
Were your results as you expected?
Discuss.

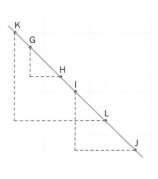

Summary

Gradient describes the slope of a line.
It measures how steeply it goes 'up'.

$$\text{Gradient} = \frac{\text{vertical change}}{\text{horizontal change}}$$

A gradient is a number.
It has a 'sign' and a 'size'.
The 'sign' shows the **direction** of the slope.

An 'up slope' has a
positive gradient.

A 'down slope' has a
negative gradient.
(Always 'read' the slope
from left to right.)

The 'size' tells you about the **steepness** of the slope.
The *steeper* the slope, the *larger* the 'size' of the *gradient*.

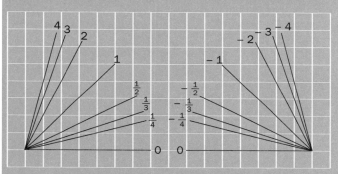

A horizontal line (that is, flat)
has no slope.
Its gradient is zero (0).

no slope
gradient 0

Lines with the same gradient
are **parallel**.
They have the same slope.

Finding gradient
The gradient of a straight
line is constant.
Every part of it has the same
slope.
You can find the gradient of a straight line from any two
points on it.
Here are the key steps to take.

- Mark two points (A and B) on the line.
  Remember: read from left to right.
  Make them a reasonable distance apart.
  Mark them where grid lines cross if you can.

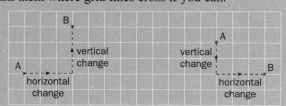

- Imagine moving from A to B.
  Find the 'vertical change' from A to B.
  Remember: Up↑ is +. Down ↓ is –.

  Find the 'horizontal change' from A to B.
  Remember: Read from left to right →.

  Mark the vertical and horizontal changes on the grid lines
  if it helps.
- Find the gradient from:

$$\text{Gradient} = \frac{\text{vertical change}}{\text{horizontal change}}$$

  Give the gradient as a whole number or a fraction.
- Check the sign makes sense for the slope of the line.
  Remember: 'Up' slopes ╱ are +.

  'Down' slopes ╲ are –.

▶ *Exercise* P13.4

1 Find the gradient of each of the lines below.

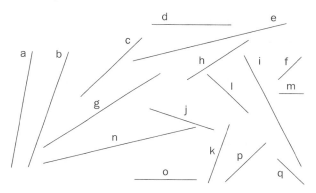

Which lines are parallel? Use the gradients to decide.
Then check with a ruler and set square.

2 Draw *x*- and *y*-axes and number them from –10 to 10.
Use the same scale on each axis.
Plot each pair of points.
Join the points in each pair with a straight line.
Find the gradient of each line.

(a) O(0,0) A(5,5) (g) I(–4,–9) J(4,–7)
(b) O(0,0) B(5,–2) (h) K(–2,9) L(–9,6)
(c) O(0,0) C(–3,6) (i) M(–2,–2) N(–10,2)
(d) O(0,0) D(–2,–6) (j) P(4,6) R(9,6)
(e) E(3,1) F(8,3) (k) S(3,4) T(2,10)
(f) G(2,–4) H(9,–9) (l) U(–2,8) V(2,4)

3 On $\frac{1}{2}$ cm squared paper draw three different lines with
these gradients.

(a) 5 (d) 4 (g) $\frac{4}{5}$
(b) –6 (e) 0 (h) 3
(c) $-\frac{1}{4}$ (f) $-\frac{3}{2}$

4 Draw the graphs of these straight lines on the same axes.
(a) $y = x$ (c) $y = \frac{1}{2}x$ (e) $y = -2x$
(b) $y = 2x$ (d) $y = -x$ (f) $y = -\frac{1}{2}x$
Find the gradient of each straight line.
Compare the gradient and equation of each line.
What do you notice?

Investigation

Gradients and straight line graphs.

- Draw the straight line graphs of these equations on the same axes. Find the gradient of each line.
  What do you notice about
  - the five equations
  - the five straight line graphs
  - the five gradients?
  Comment on what you find.

$y = 2x$
$y = 2x + 2$
$y = 2x + 5$
$y = 2x - 1$
$y = 2x - 3$

- Investigate the graphs and equations of each of these sets of functions in the same way. Comment on your results.

$y = x$	$y = \frac{1}{2}x$	$y = -\frac{1}{2}x$
$y = x + 2$	$y = \frac{1}{2}x + 2$	$y = -\frac{1}{2}x + 3$
$y = x + 5$	$y = \frac{1}{2}x + 4$	$y = -\frac{1}{2}x + 4$
$y = x - 1$	$y = \frac{1}{2}x - 2$	$y = -\frac{1}{2}x - 1$
$y = x - 3$	$y = \frac{1}{2}x - 3$	$y = -\frac{1}{2}x - 3$

$y = -x$	$y = -3x$
$y = -x + 1$	$y = -3x + 2$
$y = -x + 4$	$y = -3x + 4$
$y = -x - 1$	$y = -3x - 1$
$y = -x - 2$	$y = -3x - 3$

- Look at these linear equations.

  $y = 5x - 1, \quad y = 3 - 2x, \quad y = \frac{1}{4}x, \quad y = 2 + \frac{1}{3}x.$

  Which lines have positive gradients?
  Which have negative gradients?
  Which have the 'steepest' 'up slopes'?
  Which have the 'steepest' 'down slopes'?
  What are their gradients?
  Check by drawing the graphs on the same axes.

Straight line graphs from practical situations

We often use a graph to show the **relationship between two quantities** in a 'practical situation'.

A **steady change** in the two quantities produces a **straight line graph.** Here is an example from science.

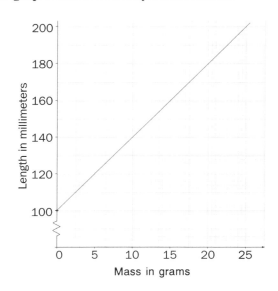

The graph shows the results of a 'stretch test' on a spring.

The straight line graph shows that the length of the spring *increases steadily* as the mass attached increases.

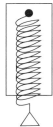

Discussion Exercise

Look at the graph in the previous column.
- How long was the spring
  (a) before any masses were hung on it
  (b) when masses of 10 g and 25 g were hung on it?
- Use the three (length, mass) values from (a) and (b) to draw the graph on 2 mm graph paper.
  Scale: On mass axis, 2 cm to 5 grams.
  On length axis, 2 cm to 20 mm.
- What is the rate of increase of length with mass?
  Give it as ' … mm per gram'.
  Discuss ways to find out.
- What is the gradient of the graph?
- Discuss what you find.

A straight line graph occurs whenever a 'steady rate' links two quantities.
This steady rate may be

a pay rate, such as £4.50 per hour
a price rate, such as £5 per square metre
an exchange rate, such as $1.5 \equiv$ £1
a conversion rate, such as 1 kg $\equiv$ 2.2 lb
a speed, such as 40 miles per hour
and so on …

You can use the 'rate' to find three points on the graph. Then you can draw the graph as before.
The *slope* of the graph corresponds to the *'rate'* used.

Question

David is paid £3 per hour.
(a) How much is he paid for
   (i) 10 hours
   (ii) 40 hours?
(b) Draw a graph showing David's pay for hours from 0 to 40. Use the values from part (a) for two points.
   Scale: On Time axis, 2 cm to 10 hours.
   On Pay axis, 2 cm to £40.
(c) Find the slope of the graph from two plotted points.
   Comment on the results.

Answer

(a) *Use rate of pay: £3 per hour*

   For 1 hour, pay is £3.
   (i) For 10 hours, pay is $3 \times 10 = £30$
   (ii) For 40 hours, pay is $3 \times 40 = £120$

(b) Part (a) gives coordinates (10,30)
(40,120)

Each gives Time (in hours) first, then Pay (in £s).

'No hours' give 'no pay', so (0,0) is a third point.
Plot points and draw graph:

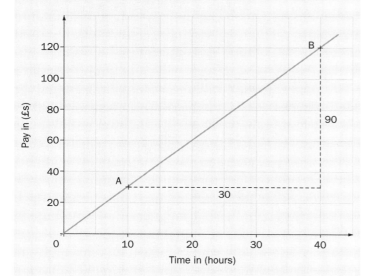

(c) Vertical change from A to B = 120 − 30 = 90
Horizontal change from A to B = 40 − 10 = 30

$$\text{Gradient} = \frac{\text{vertical change}}{\text{horizontal change}} = \frac{90}{30} = 3$$

The slope of the graph, 3, corresponds to
the rate of pay per hour for David's pay,
i.e., £3 per hour.

In the above example the straight line goes through (0,0). This
happens because 'none of one quantity' means 'none of the
other quantity'.
Sometimes the straight line *does not* go through (0,0).
This happens when one quantity is not 0 at the same time
as the other.
Here is an example of this situation.

A nurse uses his own car to
visit patients at home.

The following graph shows the
travel expenses he can
claim weekly for distances
up to 200 miles.

The graph passes through the point (0,20).
This shows that the nurse is paid £20 for travelling 0 miles.
We call this £20 his basic travel allowance.

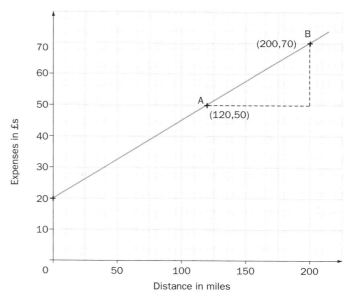

From the graph you can see that:
Vertical change from A to B = 70 − 50 = 20
Horizontal change from A to B = 200 − 120 = 80

$$\text{Gradient} = \frac{\text{vertical change}}{\text{horizontal change}} = \frac{20}{80} = \frac{1}{4}$$

The slope of the graph, $\frac{1}{4}$ (= 0.25) gives the rate per mile for his
expenses, that is, £0.25 per mile.
So the nurse's weekly travel expenses are:

basic allowance of £20 + 25 pence per mile.

Scales

For 'practical graphs' we often use *different* scales on the axes.
Take extra care when you number and use these scales.
You may need to work out what each 'small space' stands for.

On this scale, 2 cm ≡ £5.

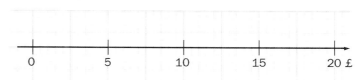

Each 'small
space' is £0.50.

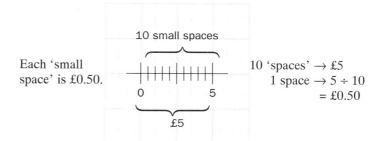

10 'spaces' → £5
1 space → 5 ÷ 10
= £0.50

A question may tell you which scales to use. You will lose
marks if you use any other scales. So read the question
carefully.
Sometimes *you* have to choose the scale for each axis.
The following Memo gives some guide lines to help you.

Memo

Choosing scales

● Look at the *range of values* (smallest – largest) for each axis. Think about the best way to fit these into the length/width of your graph paper.
   Your aim is to draw as large a graph as possible.
   (The larger the graph, the more accurate it can be.)

● Try to choose an *easy scale* to use.
   It is usually easier if the numbers go up in ...

   1's or 2's or 5's,
   10's or 20's or 50's,
   100's or 200's or 500's,
   and so on ...

   Make sure that each 'small space' is a simple value to work with. Check that you can find the position of 'in between numbers' easily.

● Number each axis in *equal steps*.
   Mark these 'equal steps' on the darker lines on the graph paper if you can. It's usually easier.

● Label each axis *clearly* with its 'description'.
   Don't forget the units if there are any.

► *Exercise* P13.5

1 For each scale below:
   (a) write the scale as '2 cm to ... units'
   (b) work out what each 'small space' stands for
   (c) find the value of each 'arrowed' point.

   Scale A
   Scale B

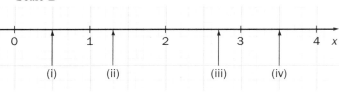

   Scale C

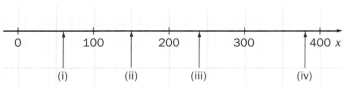

   Scale D

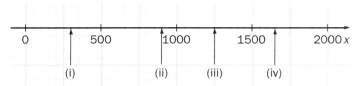

   Scale E

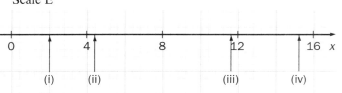

2 Betty is paid £4.50 per hour.

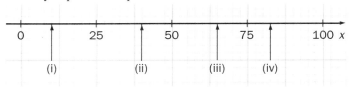

   (a) Copy and complete the table below for this rate of pay.

Time (in hours)	0	20	50
Pay (in £s)			

   (b) Draw a graph to show Betty's pay for hours from 0 to 50.
      Scale: On time axis, 2 cm to 10 hours.
             On pay axis, 2 cm to £50.
   (c) Find the slope of this graph from two of your plotted points.
      Comment on the result.
   (d) One week Betty's pay is £155.
      How many complete hours did she work?
      Find the answer from your graph.

3 The Yellow Party suggests a fixed rate of income tax of 20% on all taxable income.
   (a) Copy and complete the table below for this income tax rate.

Taxable income (in £s)	0	10 000	18 000
Income tax (in £s)			

   (b) Draw a graph of Income Tax (*T*) against Taxable Income (*I*) for *I* up to £20 000.
      Scale: On *I* axis, 2 cm to £2000
             On *T* axis, 2 cm to £1000
   (c) Find the gradient of your graph from two of your plotted points.
      Explain what this shows.
   (d) Jenny would pay £2500 tax under this system.
      Find her taxable income from your graph.

4 The cooking time for lamb is 25 minutes plus 20 minutes per pound.
   (a) Draw a graph of the cooking time, *T* minutes, against the weight, *W* pounds, for weights from 0 to 5 pounds.
      Scale: On W axis, 2 cm to 1 pound.
             On T axis, 2 cm to 25 minutes.
   (b) Find the gradient of your graph.
      Comment on what this shows.
   (c) Answer these questions from your graph.
      (i) What is the cooking time for a piece of lamb weighing $3\frac{1}{2}$ pounds?
      (ii) If a piece of lamb needs 1 hour 20 minutes cooking time, what weight is it?

5 The taxi fares charged by Rapid Cars consist of a fixed charge of 80p plus 50p per mile for the distance travelled.
   (a) Draw a graph showing the total cost £*C*, of a taxi ride of *m* miles, for any distance up to 8 miles.
      Choose your own scale for each axis.

(b) Find the gradient of your graph.
Comment on what this shows.
(c) Answer these questions from your graph.
   (i) What is the cost of a taxi ride of 3.8 miles?
   (ii) Mr Westwood paid £2.10 for a taxi ride.
      How far did he travel?

Summary

The graph of a linear function is a single straight line.
To draw a straight line graph, take these steps.

● Find the coordinates of three points on the line.
  You may find them from:
    the equation of the line
    a 'relationship' given in words.
  Choose easy values to work with if you can.
● Plot these three points.
  Check they lie in a straight line.

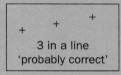
3 in a line
'probably correct'

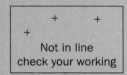
Not in line
check your working

● Draw a straight line through all three points.

Examination Questions

1 The height h cm of a candle t hours after being lit is given by the formula

$$h = 10 - 2t$$

(a) Copy and complete this table giving h for various values of t.

t (hours)	0	1	2	3	4
h (cm)					

(b) Plot the points and join them up to make a straight line.
(c) How high was the candle before it was lit?
(d) For how many hours would the candle burn?
(e) How many hours after being lit will the candle height be 3 cm?
(f) At what rate does the height of the candle change?
                             (MEG, 1989)

2   height = (1.95 × length of femur) + 28.68

The formula gives the relation between a woman's height in inches and the length, in inches, of her femur (thigh bone).
(a) A woman's femur is 18.8 inches long. Use the formula to calculate her height. Write down all the figures on your calculator display.
(b) Copy and complete the table by calculating the missing heights. Give your answers correct to the nearest whole number.

Length of woman's femur (inches)	15	16	17	18	19	20
Woman's height (inches)			62			

(c) Plot the points represented by the values in your table and join them with a straight line.
(d) Find the gradient of the line you have drawn.
(e) A woman is 63.5 inches tall. Use your graph to find the length of her femur. Give your answer correct to 1 decimal place. Make your method clear.
                             (ULEAC, 1991)

3 A plumber needed a graph to convert centimetres to inches and inches to centimetres.
(a) Using the table below, draw the conversion graph.

cm	10	20	30	40
inches	3.94	7.87	11.81	15.75

(b) Use the graph to find
   (i) the diameter in cm of a drain-pipe whose diameter is 8.5 inches
   (ii) the width in inches of a ventilator shaft whose width is 28 cm
   (ii) the area in cm^2 of a square man-hole cover of side 15 inches
   (iv) the length in metres of a 10 foot pipe
      (12 inches = 1 foot).
(c) (i) Find the gradient of the graph.
   (ii) Give, in words, a meaning for the gradient.
                           (NISEAC, 1989)

4 (a) Complete this table of values for $y = 2x - 2$.

x	0	1	2	3	4	5	6
y		0					

(b) On a grid plot the values and draw the line $y = 2x - 2$.
(c) What is the gradient of this line?
A is the point with the coordinates (2,7).
(d) Plot and label A.
The line with equation $y = 2x - 2$ is the line of symmetry of the isosceles triangle ABC, where B has coordinates (1,0).
(e) Plot and label C and write down its coordinates.
                             (ULEAC, 1989)

5 A line has the equation $4y + 3x = 12$.
(a) What are the coordinates of the point where the line
   (i) meets the x-axis
   (ii) meets the y-axis?
(b) Draw the line.
                             (SEG, 1989)

P14
In your head

This unit will help you to:

- multiply and divide, in your head, single digit multiples of any power of ten, such as 800 and 0.4
- know and use the fact that when working with positive numbers,
  - multiplying by a number less than 1 (a common or decimal fraction) gives a smaller number than you started with,
  - dividing by a number less than 1 gives a larger number than you started with
- use these mental methods in problem solving.

10 tenths make a whole one …

So 21 tenths give a decimal that has a whole number part …

Memo
Decimals in order
N10 p48

This gives … $7 \times 0.3 = 2.1$ 21 tenths

Here is another example like this: 5×0.6

To work it out, think … 5×6 tenths = 30 tenths

to get … $5 \times 0.6 = 3.0$

Multiplying by tenths

You know that 0.2 is 2 tenths.

This helps you to do multiplications like …

4×0.2

Think of the 'tenths' 'in words' …

4×2 tenths

4×0.2

Then work it out 'in your head' …

4×2 tenths = 8 tenths

4×0.2

And give the answer as a decimal …

$4 \times 0.2 = 0.8$

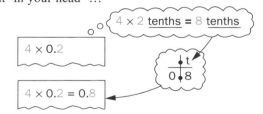

▶ *Exercise* **P14.1**

Look at this example …

1 5×0.1	**5** 3×0.3	**9** 0.4×2
2 8×0.1	**6** 2×0.3	**10** 0.2×2
3 3×0.2	**7** 0.1×6	**11** 0.2×3
4 2×0.4	**8** 0.1×9	**12** 0.3×3

Look at this example:

7×3 tenths = 21 tenths

7×0.3

▶ *Exercise* **P14.2**

Copy and complete these. Fill in the missing numbers … .
Write each as a decimal.

1 (a) 4×3 tenths = … tenths = …
   (b) 5×9 tenths = … tenths = …
   (c) 6×7 tenths = … tenths = …
   (d) 2×5 tenths = … tenths = …
   (e) 5×8 tenths = … tenths = …

2 (a) 2 tenths $\times 8$ = … tenths = …
   (b) 3 tenths $\times 5$ = … tenths = …
   (c) 9 tenths $\times 9$ = … tenths = …
   (d) 5 tenths $\times 6$ = … tenths = …
   (e) 4 tenths $\times 5$ = … tenths = …

Now try to do these 'in your head'.

3 (a) 9×0.4 **4** (a) 0.6×3
   (b) 7×0.7 (b) 0.2×6
   (c) 3×0.9 (c) 0.6×8
   (d) 6×0.5 (d) 0.8×5
   (e) 5×0.2 (e) 0.5×4

5 Look at each mental multiplication and its answer in questions **1–4**.
   Count the number of decimal places in the multiplication.
   Count the number of decimal places in the answer.
   What do you find?

You can do many other multiplications by 'tenths' in the same way. Here is an example

To work out … 400×0.2

you think … 400×2 tenths = 800 tenths

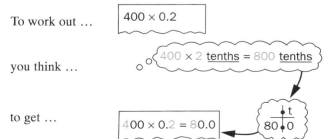

to get … $400 \times 0.2 = 80.0$

If you have forgotten how to do multiplications like 400×2, look it up.

Memo
Without a calculator
p8

Without a calculator p8

▶ *Exercise* P14.3

Copy and complete these.
Fill in the missing numbers.
Write each answer as a decimal.

1. (a) 300×2 tenths = ... tenths = ...
    (b) 8000×3 tenths = ... tenths = ...
    (c) 40×7 tenths = ... tenths = ...
    (d) $20\,000 \times 5$ tenths = ... tenths = ...
    (e) 5000×6 tenths = ... tenths = ...
2. (a) 4 tenths $\times 20$ = ... tenths = ...
    (b) 9 tenths $\times 500$ = ... tenths = ...
    (c) 7 tenths $\times 6000$ = ... tenths = ...
    (d) 5 tenths $\times 400\,000$ = ... tenths = ...
    (e) 8 tenths $\times 50\,000$ = ... tenths = ...
    Now do these 'in your head'.
3. (a) $30\,000 \times 0.6$
    (b) 7000×0.9
    (c) 500×0.3
    (d) $500\,000 \times 0.5$
    (e) $50\,000 \times 0.8$
4. (a) 0.2×80
    (b) 0.6×4000
    (c) 0.9×300
    (d) $0.5 \times 70\,000$
    (e) $0.6 \times 3\,000\,000$
5. Look at each mental multiplication and its answer in questions **1–4**.
    How many decimal places are in the multiplication?
    How many are in the answer?
    What do you notice?

A quick check

The point in a decimal must be in the correct position.
You can use 'decimal places' to check that it is.
Look at this multiplication:

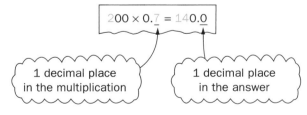

$$200 \times 0.7 = 140.0$$

1 decimal place in the multiplication

1 decimal place in the answer

See how the numbers of decimal places match.
Did you spot this in Exercise P14.2 p346 and Exercise P14.3 above?

Other decimals

To multiply by decimal fractions such as hundredths, thousandths, ... you can think it through in words as before.

Remember:
$0.01, 0.02, ...$ mean 1 hundredth, 2 hundredths, ...
$0.001, 0.002, ...$ mean 1 thousandth, 2 thousandths, ...

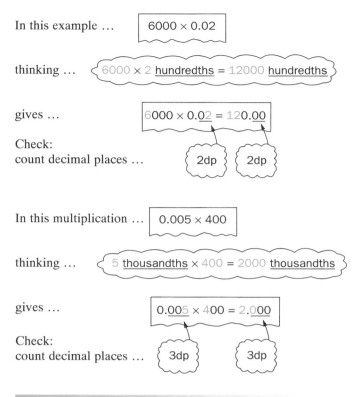

In this example ... 6000×0.02

thinking ... 6000×2 <u>hundredths</u> = 12000 <u>hundredths</u>

gives ... $6000 \times 0.02 = 120.00$

Check:
count decimal places ... 2dp 2dp

In this multiplication ... 0.005×400

thinking ... 5 <u>thousandths</u> $\times 400$ = 2000 <u>thousandths</u>

gives ... $0.005 \times 400 = 2.000$

Check:
count decimal places ... 3dp 3dp

▶ *Exercise* P14.4

Do these 'in your head' first.
Then check them with a calculator.

1. (a) 4×0.02 (e) 5×0.06 (i) 0.08×7
    (b) 7×0.05 (f) 3×0.08 (j) 0.06×8
    (c) 6×0.02 (g) 0.09×3 (k) 0.04×9
    (d) 2×0.09 (h) 0.07×4 (l) 0.05×3
2. (a) 2×0.003 (e) 8×0.002 (i) 0.007×6
    (b) 6×0.007 (f) 7×0.008 (j) 0.005×9
    (c) 3×0.006 (g) 0.009×5 (k) 0.008×8
    (d) 4×0.004 (h) 0.005×4 (l) 0.009×9
3. (a) 3000×0.02 (e) 2000×0.05 (i) 0.07×7000
    (b) 20×0.04 (f) 90×0.08 (j) 0.08×900
    (c) 500×0.07 (g) 0.04×700 (k) 0.09×6000
    (d) 600×0.06 (h) 0.03×50 (l) 0.06×90
4. (a) 300×0.003 (e) 700×0.009 (i) 0.008×5000
    (b) 2000×0.006 (f) 8000×0.006 (j) 0.004×80
    (c) 40×0.005 (g) 0.003×400 (k) 0.005×2000
    (d) 60×0.004 (h) 0.002×20 (l) 0.009×700
5. (a) $20\,000 \times 0.07$ (g) $0.03 \times 70\,000$
    (b) $0.006 \times 500\,000$ (h) $200\,000 \times 0.08$
    (c) $7\,000\,000 \times 0.02$ (i) $3\,000\,000 \times 0.009$
    (d) $900\,000 \times 0.002$ (j) $0.06 \times 300\,000$
    (e) $80\,000 \times 0.003$ (k) $0.009 \times 40\,000$
    (f) $0.004 \times 8\,000\,000$ (l) $0.05 \times 8\,000$

Decimal × decimal

Some 'all decimal' multiplications can also be done 'in your head'.
Here are some examples.

In this multiplication … 0.6×0.8

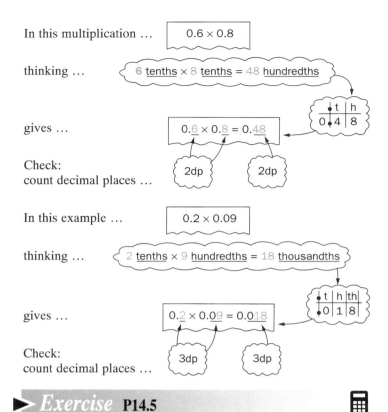

thinking …   6 tenths × 8 tenths = 48 hundredths

gives … $0.6 \times 0.8 = 0.48$

Check:
count decimal places …   2dp   2dp

In this example … 0.2×0.09

thinking …   2 tenths × 9 hundredths = 18 thousandths

gives … $0.2 \times 0.09 = 0.018$

Check:
count decimal places …   3dp   3dp

► *Exercise* P14.5

Do these in your head first.
Then check them with a calculator.

1 (a) 0.3×0.2 (c) 0.6×0.7 (e) 0.8×0.8
   (b) 0.4×0.9 (d) 0.5×0.4
2 (a) 0.7×0.03 (c) 0.02×0.4 (e) 0.05×0.02
   (b) 0.05×0.5 (d) 0.8×0.06
3 (a) 0.4×0.006 (c) 0.006×0.5 (e) 0.2×0.002
   (b) 0.007×0.008 (d) 0.009×0.003
4 (a) 0.02×0.08 (c) 0.04×0.003 (e) 0.03×0.03
   (b) 0.005×0.07 (d) 0.06×0.006
5 (a) 0.9×0.8 (c) 0.004×0.7 (e) 0.6×0.002
   (b) 0.3×0.05 (d) 0.008×0.005
6 (a) 0.02×0.007 (c) 0.9×0.6 (e) 0.004×0.04
   (b) 0.08×0.03 (d) 0.05×0.9

ACTIVITY

Decimal cards

Number some cards …
   with tenths 0.2, 0.3, …, 0.9
   with hundredths 0.02, 0.03, …, 0.09
   with thousandths 0.002, 0.003, …, 0.009
Shuffle your pack of cards.

Turn over two cards and
multiply the numbers
in your head.

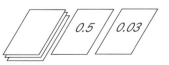

Record the multiplication and
answer. $0.5 \times 0.03 = 0.015$

Repeat this until all the cards are used up. Then check your
answers with a calculator.

Use your decimal cards to practise multiplying decimals in your
head.
Work on your own or with another student.

Dividing by tenths

Look at these 'matching divisions'.

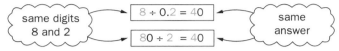

To do the division by 0.2 'in your head', you can do the
matching division by 2 instead.
It gives the same answer. But it's easier to do.
You can find the 'matching division' step-by-step like this.

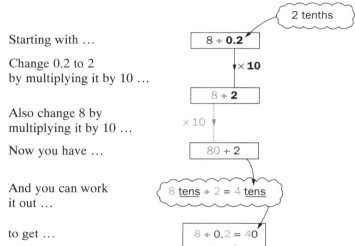

Starting with … $8 \div 0.2$ 2 tenths

Change 0.2 to 2
by multiplying it by 10 … $\times 10$

   $8 \div 2$

Also change 8 by
multiplying it by 10 … $\times 10$

Now you have … $80 \div 2$

And you can work
it out …   8 tens ÷ 2 = 4 tens

to get … $8 \div 0.2 = 40$

Check with a multiplication as usual.

   $8 \div 0.2 = 40$

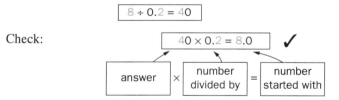

Check: $40 \times 0.2 = 8.0$ ✓

   answer × number
            divided by = number
                           started with

You can divide by other tenths such as 0.3, 0.4, … in the same way.
Remember:

> 10 tenths make a whole one.
> To change 0.1, 0.2, . . . to a whole number,
> multiply by 10.

► *Exercise* P14.6

1 For each of these divisions:
   ● write down its matching division by a single digit (1, 2, 3, …)
   ● then work it out in your head.
   (a) $6 \div 0.2$ (e) $20 \div 0.5$ (i) $300 \div 0.6$
   (b) $8 \div 0.4$ (f) $4000 \div 0.8$ (j) $90 \div 0.9$
   (c) $900 \div 0.1$ (g) $7000 \div 0.7$
   (d) $600 \div 0.3$ (h) $1000 \div 0.2$
   Check each answer with a multiplication and with a calculator.

2 Now do these 'in your head'.
Try not to write the matching division.
Just imagine it if you can.

(a) $4 \div 0.2$ (e) $400 \div 0.5$ (i) $5000 \div 0.1$
(b) $600 \div 0.6$ (f) $600 \div 0.2$ (j) $40 \div 0.8$
(c) $60 \div 0.3$ (g) $70 \div 0.7$
(d) $8000 \div 0.4$ (h) $900 \div 0.3$

Check them as before.

Dividing by other decimals

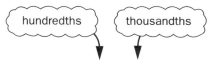

You can also divide by decimals like 0.02, 0.002, ...
'in your head'.
Simply use the matching division by a single digit that has the
same answer.
Look at this example:

$$60 \div 0.03$$

You can think it through like this ...

> 3 hundredths
> So use 100

- Decide what will change 0.03 to 3 ...

$$60 \div 0.03$$

- Multiply both numbers by this ...

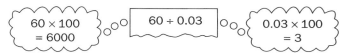

- Do the new division in your head ...

> $6\,000 \div 3 = 2\,000$

and give the answer ...

$$60 \div 0.03 = 2\,000$$

- Check it with a multiplication ...

> $2\,000 \times 0.03 = 60.00$ ✓

Remember:

> 100 hundredths make a whole one.
> To change 0.01, 0.02, . . . to a whole number,
> multiply by 100.

> 1000 thousandths make a whole one.
> To change 0.001, 0.002, . . . to a whole number,
> multiply by 1000.

Exercise P14.7

Try to do these 'in your head'.
Write down the 'matching division' if you need to.
Just imagine it if you can.

1 (a) $8 \div 0.02$ (c) $90 \div 0.03$ (e) $70 \div 0.07$
    (b) $200 \div 0.04$ (d) $300 \div 0.05$ (f) $4 \div 0.08$
2 (a) $60 \div 0.003$ (c) $400 \div 0.005$ (e) $8 \div 0.004$
    (b) $10 \div 0.002$ (d) $3 \div 0.006$ (f) $9 \div 0.009$
3 (a) $4 \div 0.002$ (d) $8 \div 0.008$ (g) $70 \div 0.007$
    (b) $20 \div 0.05$ (e) $90 \div 0.09$ (h) $800 \div 0.04$
    (c) $3 \div 0.06$ (f) $9 \div 0.003$

Comparing sizes in multiplications

Multiplying something *by 1* does *not change* its size.

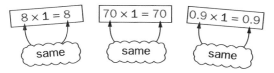

Multiplying something positive by a number *larger than 1*
makes it *larger*.

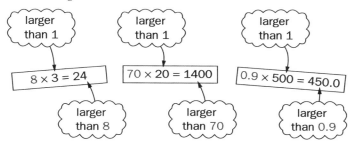

💬 *Discussion Exercise*

Does *multiplying* by a positive number *smaller than 1* have the
same effect?
What do you think?

Look at these examples:

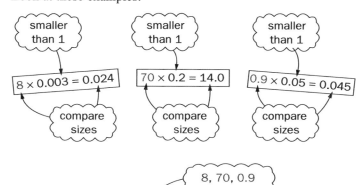

> 8, 70, 0.9

What happens to the numbers we start with?
Have they been made larger?
Or have they been made smaller?

Look at some other examples of your own ...

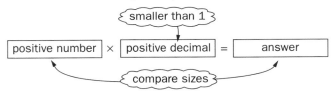

Is each answer larger or smaller than the number you start with?
Compare your findings with those of some other students.
What conclusion do you reach?

► *Exercise* P14.8

1 The missing words in each sentence are:
       'equal to'
    or 'larger than'
    or 'smaller than'.
   Look at each calculation and predict which words are missing.

   (a) 30 × 50 is 30
   (b) 800 × 1 is 800
   (c) 6 × 0.7 is 6
   (d) 0.4 × 90 is 0.4
   (e) 0.02 × 0.03 is 0.02
   (f) 1 × 40 is 40
   (g) 500 × 0.09 is 500
   (h) 500 × 0.09 is 0.09
   (i) 0.6 × 30 is 0.6
   (j) 0.6 × 30 is 30
   (k) 0.5 × 0.4 is 0.5
   (l) 0.5 × 0.4 is 0.4

   Now do the multiplications.
   Check your predictions.

2 The missing number *n* in each calculation is:
       'equal to 1'
    or 'larger than 1'
    or 'smaller than 1'.
   Use the other numbers to predict which.

   (a) 30 × n = 30
   (b) 0.2 × n = 40
   (c) 500 × n = 150.0
   (d) 4 × n = 0.24
   (e) n × 20 = 800
   (f) n × 300 = 90.0
   (g) n × 0.4 = 0.4
   (h) n × 0.2 = 0.14

Comparing sizes in divisions

When you *divide* something *by 1*, the answer is the *same* as the number you start with.

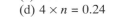

When you *divide* something *positive* by a number *larger than 1*, the answer is *smaller* than the number you start with.

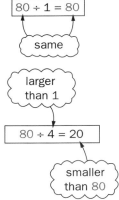

Q *Discussion Exercise*

Does *dividing* by a positive number *smaller than 1* have the same effect?
What do you think?

Here are some examples:

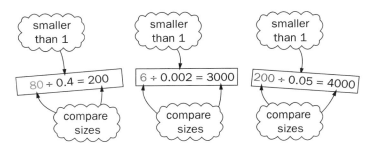

Compare each answer with the number we start with.
Is it larger or smaller?

Look at some other examples of your own.

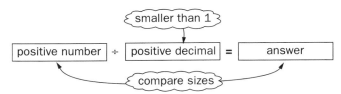

Are your answers larger or smaller than the numbers you start with?
Discuss your results with some other students.
Do they agree?

► *Exercise* P14.9

The missing words in each sentence are
    'equal to'
 or 'larger than'
 or 'smaller than'.
Without doing the division, say what they should be.
Then check with your calculator.

1   300 ÷ 60 is 300
2   600 ÷ 1 is 600
3   900 ÷ 0.3 is 900
4   8 ÷ 0.02 is 8
5   8000 ÷ 400 is 8000
6   40 ÷ 0.005 is 40

Spotting mistakes

Thinking about the *size* of numbers helps you to *spot wrong answers* to calculations.

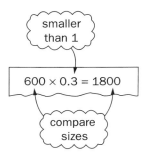

1800 must be wrong. The answer should be *smaller than 600*.

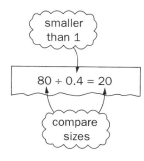

20 must be wrong. The answer should be *larger than 80*.

Exercise P14.10

Which of these answers must be wrong?
Predict first.
Then check with a calculator.

1. $80 \times 0.07 = 560$
2. $80 \div 0.002 = 40\,000$
3. $900 \times 0.4 = 360$
4. $9 \div 0.03 = 3$
5. $40 \div 0.5 = 8$
6. $5 \times 0.009 = 45$
7. $1000 \div 0.02 = 500$
8. $200 \div 0.4 = 50$
9. $6000 \times 0.6 = 3600$
10. $40 \times 0.003 = 120$

Summary

To multiply by a decimal like 0.2, 0.02, 0.002, … 'in your head':
  - Do the multiplication from your tables first.
  - Then give this result its correct place value.

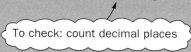

To check: count decimal places

To divide by a decimal 'in your head', use the matching division by a simple whole number.

single digit

To find this 'matching division':
  - Decide what you need (10 or 100 or 1000 or …) to change the decimal to a simple whole number.
  - Multiply both numbers by this.

decimal fraction

For positive numbers:
  - Multiplying something by a number smaller than 1 gives a smaller number than you started with.
  - Dividing something by a number smaller than 1 gives a larger number than you started with.

Exercise P14.11

Solve these problems 'in your head'.
Just write down the calculation you do for each and a sentence to answer the question.

1 Rita bought 0.8 metres of ribbon at 90p per metre.
   What was the cost in pence?
2 A designer cuts silk material into 0.6 m lengths to make scarves.
   How many can she cut from a roll of fabric 30 m long?
3 A lorry can carry a load of 20 tonnes.
   How many packing cases, each weighing 0.5 tonnes, can it carry?
4 Each kilogram of a metal alloy contains 0.2 kg of tin.
   What weight of alloy can be made from 800 kg of tin?
5 The average daily rainfall in June was 0.7 mm.
   What was the total rainfall that month?
6 A coil of electrical wire has a resistance of 0.8 ohms per centimetre of length.
   Calculate the total resistance of an 80 cm length of the wire.
7 Out of date textbooks are being sold off for £0.9 each.
   How much do they receive for the last 2000 copies sold?
8 A special day ticket at 'Parkside Centre' car park costs £0.80.
   The takings on one day were £400.
   How many motorists bought a special day ticket to park their cars?
9 A drinks company puts its orange squash in 0.3 litre cans.
   How many cans does it need for 9000 litres of orange squash?
10 A copper pipe is known to expand by about 0.009 mm for each degree Celsius (°C) rise in temperature.
   How much does it expand when the temperature rises 30°C?
11 A sheet of metal is 0.4 mm thick.
   (a) How many sheets are in a pile 20 mm thick?
   (b) How thick is a pile of 30 sheets?
12 A teabag has 0.003 kg of tea in it.
   (a) How much tea is in a box of 80 tea bags?
   (b) How many teabags can be filled from a 6 kg bag of tea?
13 An average serving of peas in a canteen weighs 0.08 kg.
   (a) How many servings should be obtained from 4 kg of peas?
   (b) What weight of peas are needed for 80 servings?
14 A factory uses 0.06 kg of metal for each can it makes.
   (a) How many cans can be made from 3000 kg of metal?
   (b) How much metal does it use to make 9000 cans?
15 Steel wire is cut into lengths of 0.02 m to make pins.
   (a) How much wire is used to make 200 pins?
   (b) How many pins can be made from 200 m of wire?

P15
Estimating probability

This unit will help you to:

- find the relative frequency of a result in an experiment

- understand relative frequency as an estimate of probability

- use random numbers to simulate the equally likely outcomes of an experiment

- understand that different outcomes may result from repeating an experiment

- use probability to predict how many times a result might occur.

Relative Frequency

Lucy's group did a travel survey at college.
This is one of the questions they asked students.

> 1. Did you go abroad last year?   Yes ☐   No ☐

Here are the results they got.

Question 1: Travel abroad			
	Lucy	Tricia	Keith
Yes	4	29	47
No	16	21	53
Number asked	20	50	100

In Lucy's survey, 'Yes' has a frequency of 4.
In Tricia's survey, 'Yes' has a frequency of 29.
In Keith's survey, 'Yes' has a frequency of 47.

   Each student asked a different number of people. So simply comparing these frequencies does not make sense. To compare their results they need to find what fraction of each number asked said Yes.

For Lucy's results,
the fraction that said Yes is $\frac{4}{20}$ ← Number saying Yes
← Total Number asked

This fraction is called the **relative frequency** of Yes in Lucy's results.
It can be given as a decimal or percentage.

Relative frequency of Yes = $\frac{4}{20}$ or 0.2 or 20%.

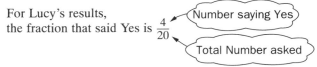

Discussion Exercise

- Look at Tricia and Keith's results.
  Find the relative frequency of Yes in each case.
  Give each as an ordinary fraction, a decimal and a percentage.
  Compare the relative frequencies from each student's results.
  Discuss what they show.

- The Student's Union wants to know about student travel abroad at Lucy's college. Which relative frequency is most likely to give the most accurate picture of this? Discuss.

- Lucy, Tricia and Keith made sure that they asked different students in their surveys. So they decided to pool their data. Find the relative frequency of Yes for their pooled data. Discuss what you find.

- Here is another question in the travel survey.

Did you use any of these means of travel last year? Tick Yes or No		Yes	No
Plane		☐	☐
Intercity train		☐	☐
Long -distance coach		☐	☐

These are the results from Lucy's group.

		Lucy	Tricia	Keith
Plane	Yes	2	32	54
	No	18	18	46
Intercity train	Yes	9	41	63
	No	11	9	37
Long-distance coach	Yes	6	17	6
	No	14	23	94

Find the relative frequency of Yes in each case. Use them to compare results.
Discuss what you find.
What happens if Lucy, Tricia and Keith pool their data?
Discuss.

Summary

The frequency of a result is the number of times that result occurs in the data.
The relative frequency of a result compares its frequency with the total number of results in the data. It is the fraction of times that result occurs in the data.
Relative frequency of a result
$= \dfrac{\text{number of times that results occurs}}{\text{total number of results}}$
or $\dfrac{\text{frequency of that result}}{\text{total of the frequencies}}$

Exercise P15.1

1 A magazine printed some statistics before the World Cup in the USA. These data are about the World Cup record of some of the qualifiers.

Country	Wins	Draws	Losses
Argentina	24	9	15
Belgium	7	4	14
Brazil	44	11	11
Germany	39	15	14
Holland	8	6	6
Italy	31	12	11
Mexico	6	6	17
Spain	13	7	12
Sweden	11	6	14
Switzerland	5	2	11

(a) How many World Cup matches had each country's team played?
(b) For each country's team, calculate the relative frequency of
(i) wins (ii) draws (iii) losses
Give each relative frequency as a decimal correct to 2 decimal places.
(c) What is the highest relative frequency of
(i) wins (ii) draws (iii) losses?
Name the country/countries with these values.
(d) What is the lowest relative frequency of
(i) wins (ii) draws (iii) losses?
Name the country/countries with these values.
(e) Find the sum of the relative frequencies for each country.
What did you expect it to be?
Explain your answers.

2 Ian writes with his left hand. He wondered how common this is. To find out, he did a survey of the classes in his school.
There are two classes, A and B, in each Year Group.
Here are Ian's data for each class.

	Year 7		Year 8		Year 9		Year 10		Year 11	
	A	B	A	B	A	B	A	B	A	B
Left	9	5	10	10	4	12	8	10	5	6
Right	21	30	15	21	25	22	25	18	21	21

(a) How many students are there in each class?
(b) Find the relative frequency of 'left-handed writers'
(i) in each class
(ii) in each Year Group
(iii) in the school.
Give each relative frequency as a decimal correct to 2 decimal places.
(c) Ian takes one student at random from each class, for a 'follow-up' interview.
In which class is that student
(i) most likely to be left-handed
(ii) least likely to be right-handed?
(d) Ian has to write a report about his survey. Based on these results what do you think he should say?

3 Mrs Sweet grows five new varieties of peas to compare their yields. She counts the number of peas inside the pods of each variety. This table gives her results. Each variety is simply labelled with a letter.

Number of peas in a pod	Number of pods				
	A	B	C	D	E
1	18	4	6	2	9
2	26	19	15	15	5
3	16	31	27	37	7
4	9	36	31	31	10
5	15	21	22	11	8
6	3	3	16	5	11

(a) How many pods of each variety did Mrs Sweet open?
(b) For each variety, find the relative frequency of
(i) only one pea in a pod
(ii) six peas in a pod
(iii) four or more peas in a pod
(iv) at most two peas in a pod.
Give each value as a decimal correct to 2 dp.
(c) On the basis of these results, Mrs Sweet has to reject two of these new varieties. Which would you advise her to reject?
Explain why.

Probability and relative frequency

A coin has two faces.
When you toss a coin, each face has an equal chance of coming up. 'Head' and 'Tail' are *equally likely outcomes*.

An ordinary dice has six faces.
When you throw a dice, each face has an equal chance of coming up.

1, 2, 3, 4, 5 and 6 are *equally likely outcomes*.
With fair coins or dice you can work out probabilities because all the possible outcomes are equally likely.

Memo

For equally likely outcomes …

probability of an event
$$= \frac{\text{number of favourable outcomes for that event}}{\text{total number of possible outcomes}}$$

For a coin:

$$P(Head) = \frac{1}{2} \qquad\qquad P(Tail) = \frac{1}{2}$$

Remember: P(Head) is a shorthand way to write:
'the probability of getting a Head'

For a dice:

$$P(four) = \frac{1}{6}$$ ← 1 four out of 6 numbers

$$P(even) = \frac{3}{6}$$ ← 3 even numbers out of 6 numbers

$$P(more\ than\ two) = \frac{4}{6}$$ ← 4 numbers 'more than two' out of 6 numbers

and so on …
You can also **do experiments** with coins and dice to **find the relative frequencies** of particular results.
Here are some experiments to try.

 Discussion Exercise

1   **Coin tossing experiment.**
   - Toss a coin 10 times.
     Record the heads (H) and tails (T) you get on a grid like this:

     The result of our first 10 tosses

     | H | T | H | H | T | T | T | H | T | T |

     Count the number of heads you get. (We got 4 heads)
   - Do this experiment at least 20 times.
     Make a table of results like this.

	Number of heads so far	Number of tosses so far	Relative frequency of heads so far (to 2 dp)
We got **4** Heads in the 1st 10 throws →	**4**	10	$\frac{4}{10} = 0.40$
We got **6** Heads in the 2nd 10 throws →	**6** + 4 = 10	20	$\frac{10}{20} = 0.50$
We got **7** Heads in the 3rd 10 throws →	**7** + 10 = 17	30	$\frac{17}{30} = 0.57$

   - Look at the **number of heads** in *each 10 tosses*.
     Did you get about the same number each time?
     Did the number vary a great deal?
     Discuss.
   - Look at the **relative frequency** of heads.
     What happened to it as more and more tosses were done?
     To get a picture of this, draw a graph.
     Plot 'Relative frequency of heads' against 'Number of tosses of a coin'.

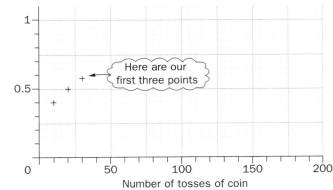

Here are our first three points

Does the graph give the picture you expected?
Discuss.
   - You know that $P(head) = \frac{1}{2}$ or 0.5.

     Compare your relative frequencies with this value.
     Did the relative frequency tend to settle down to 0.5 as the number of tosses increased?
     Discuss.
   - Compare your results with those of other students in your group.
     What happens if you 'pool' your results with theirs?
     What is the relative frequency of a head for 400, 600, 800, … tosses of a coin?
     Discuss what this shows.

2   **Dice throwing experiment.**
   - Throw a dice 300 times.
     Record the score you get each time on a grid.

     | 1 | 3 | 6 | 1 | 4 | 2 | 5 | 1 | 6 | 3 |

   - Looking at **'fours'**.
     Compare the number of 'fours' in each 10 throws.
     Comment on what you find.
     Find the relative frequency of a 'four' after 10, 20, 30, …, 300 throws of the dice.
     Give each relative frequency as a decimal correct to 3 dp.
     What do you notice?

     Draw a graph of 'Relative frequency' against 'Number of throws'.
     Discuss what this shows.

     Relative frequency of four ↑ Number of throws →

     You know that $P(four) = \frac{1}{6}$ or 0.167 (to 3 dp).

     How do your relative frequencies compare with this value?
     Is this what you expected?
     Discuss.
   - Looking at **even numbers**.
     Find the relative frequencies of an even number in your results.
     Compare these with P(even number).
     Discuss your findings.

- Looking at numbers **'more than two'**.
  Investigate the relative frequencies of 'numbers more than two' in your data.
  Discuss how they compare with P(more than two).
- Looking at **'fairness'**.
  Is your dice a fair one?
  How can you judge from your results?
  Discuss.
- Look at **the results of other students in your group**.
  Compare them with yours.
  Comment on what you find.
  What happens if you 'pool' all the results of your group?
  Discuss

Simulating results of experiments

Sometimes it is useful to **simulate the results** from repeating an experiment instead of actually doing it.
This may be because it is quicker or because it is not easy to repeat the experiment in exactly the same way each time.
To simulate the results in *random situations* you can use **random numbers**.
This is part of a table of **random numbers**.

Each digit (0 to 9) has an *equal chance* of being given in the table.
Throwing an ordinary dice is a random situation.
The six possible results, 1, 2, 3, 4, 5 and 6, are equally likely.
To simulate these results from the random numbers, simply read the digits 1, 2, 3, 4, 5, 6 in the table as scores.
From the table above,

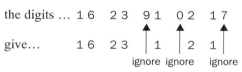

The digits 0, 7, 8 and 9 do not appear on the dice.
You can ignore them in the random numbers.
The other numbers still have an equal chance.

Tossing a fair coin is also a random situation.
The two possible results, Head and Tail, are equally likely. You can also simulate these two results from the random numbers.
You want each result to have an equal number of chances. So you let half of the ten digits 0–9 stand for Head and the other half stand for Tail.
Here is one way to do this.

  For a Head, use 'odd' numbers (1, 3, 5, 7, 9,)
  For a Tail, use 0 and even numbers (0, 2, 4, 6, 8,).
Using this system with the table above,

the digits ... 1 6   2 3   9 1   0 2   1 7

give ...   H T   T H   H H   T T   H H

You can also use these digits to *simulate the results of tossing more than one coin*.

For a 'two coin' experiment, group the digits in twos:

digits: | 16 | 23 | 91 | 02 | 17 |

'results': | HT | TH | HH | TT | HH |

For a 'three coin' experiment, group the digits in threes:

digits: | 16 2 | 3 91 | 02 1 |

'results': | HT T | H HH | TT H |

and so on …

Many **scientific calculators** have a *key* to generate random numbers.

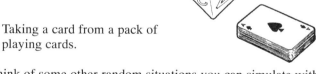

On our calculator it is marked [RAN #.]
You can also use a **computer program** to generate random numbers.
In a Logo program, you use the command RANDOM.
In a Basic program, you use RND.

Discussion Exercise

- You need a table of random numbers.
  Look at the first five lines of digits in your table.
  Discuss how to use these digits to simulate results from these random situations. Write down the results they give in each case.
    Throwing 1, 2, 3, 4, … ordinary dice.
    Tossing 1, 2, 3, 4, … fair coins.

    Throwing an octagonal dice.

    Taking a card from a pack of playing cards.

  Think of some other random situations you can simulate with these digits.
  Discuss your ideas.
- Find out how to generate random numbers with your calculator.
  Discuss how to use the numbers to simulate results as before.
- Investigate generating random numbers with a computer.
- Many software packages also have programs to simulate experiments. Find out if your school or college has any of those. Try using them if you can.

Investigation

In these experiments **the outcomes are equally likely**. Use random numbers to simulate the results in each case.

Coin tossing experiments:

Two coins
Simulate the results of tossing two coins a large number of times.
Count the number of heads each time.

Record your results in a table like this.

Number of Heads	Tally marks	Frequency
0 1 2		

Find the 'long-run' relative frequencies of getting 0 Heads, 1 Head, 2 Heads.
Comment on your results.

When you toss two coins, the possible outcomes are
    HH,   HT,   TH,   TT
Based on these equally likely outcomes, calculate P(0Heads), P(1Head) and P(2Heads).
Compare your relative frequencies and calculated probabilities.
Comment on what you find.

Three coins
For tossing three coins, the possible outcomes are:
    HHH, HHT, HTH, HTT, THH, THT, TTH, TTT
Investigate the 'long-run' relative frequencies of getting 0, 1, 2, 3 Heads.
Calculate P(0Head), P(1Head), P(2Heads), P(3Heads) based on the equally likely outcomes.
Compare your relative frequencies and probabilities.
Comment on your results.

Dice throwing experiments:

Two dice
Two dice are tossed in a game called FIFTY.
The winner is the first player to score 50 points.
A player scores only when the same number comes up on both dice.

  Double 6 scores 25 points

  Double 3 wipes out the players score so far

All other doubles score 5 points.
Simulate the results of throwing two dice a large number of times. Investigate the 'long-run' relative frequency of getting 0 points, 5 points, 25 points or 'wiped out'.
When two dice are tossed, there are 36 equally likely 'combined outcomes'.
How many of these outcomes give:
0 points, 5 points, 25 points or 'wiped out'?
Calculate the probability of getting each of these results.
Compare each relative frequency with the calculated probability using equally likely outcomes.
What do you think of the scoring system in this game? Discuss.

Memo

Combined outcomes D6 p228

Five dice
In the game CHEERIO, five dice are tossed.
Five of a kind (five 1s, five 2s and so on), scores the maximum 50 points.
Investigate the 'long-run' relative frequency of getting this maximum score.

Six dice
HEARTS is a game with six dice. The winner is the player who has scored most points after an agreed number of rounds.

Getting 1 scores 5 points.
Getting 1 and 2 scores 10 points.
Getting 1, 2 and 3 scores 15 points.
Getting 1, 2, 3 and 4 scores 20 points.
Getting 1, 2, 3, 4 and 5 scores 25 points.
Getting 1, 2, 3, 4, 5 and 6 scores 35 points.

Only one 'run' of numbers can score in each throw.
If three 1s come up, the player's total score so far is wiped out.
Investigate the 'long-run' relative frequency of getting each number of points and 'wiped out'.
How 'fair' is this scoring system?
Discuss.

Julie did the experiments on pages 354–356.
She made these comments about her results.

> - When an experiment is done many times, the relative frequency of a result tends to settle down to a steady value.
> - In experiments with equally likely outcomes, 'long-run' relative frequency ≈ calculated probability.
>   The more times the experiment is done, the closer the two values become.

Discussion Exercise

- Do Julie's comments fit the results of your experiments? Do they fit the results of other students in your group? Discuss.
- What other comments can you make about 'relative frequency' and 'calculated probability' from your results? List as many as you can.
  Compare comments with those made by other students in your group.
- How could you use this 'link' between relative frequency and probability?
  Discuss your group's ideas.

Summary

Estimating probability
You can estimate probabilities from the results of experiments.
The **relative frequency** of a result gives an **estimate of the probability** of that result occurring.

Estimated probability of a result

    = relative frequency of that result

    = number of times that result occurs
      total number of results in the data

The greater the total number of results, the better the estimate will be.

In many situations you cannot calculate probabilities exactly. However it is often possible to do an 'experiment' to find relative frequencies.
An 'experiment' for estimating probability may be an 'activity' or a 'survey'.

ACTIVITY

Experiment: Dropping a drawing pin
When you drop a drawing pin it can
land 'point up' or 'point down'.

Are these two outcomes equally likely?
Or is one more likely than the other?
What do you think is the probability of it landing 'point up'?

Discuss this with other students in your group.
Take a vote on what your group thinks about it.

Now try this experiment to see what happens.
● Drop a drawing pin 10 times on to a flat table.
  Try to do this in the same way each time.

  (Or put 10 drawing pins in a box, shake them and empty
  them on to a table.)
  Count and record how many land 'point up'.
● Do this experiment at least 20 times.
  Try to do each repeat in the same way.
  Find the relative frequency of the pin landing 'point up' after
  10, 20, 30, 40, … throws.
  Give each value correct to two decimal places.
● Show your results on a graph.
  What value do you estimate
  your relative frequency will
  settle down to in the 'long
  run'?
  If you can't decide, do the
  experiment some more times.
● Use your results to estimate the probability of your drawing
  pin landing 'point up' when dropped.
  Is this what you expected?
  Is it what most of your group expected?
  Discuss.
● Compare your results with other students in your group.
  Did you get roughly similar results?
  Discuss reasons for any differences between results.
● 'Drawing pins' are
  made in different shapes
  and sizes. What
  happens if you use a
  different type of
  drawing pin in your experiment?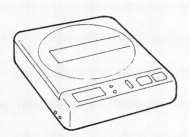

Question

A consumer magazine did
a survey about faults in
three new CD players.
These data are about faults
found before the 1 year
guarantee ran out.

(a)

Model Name	Number of CD players with faults	Number of CD players
Megabass	132	539
Hyperbass	203	927
X-bass	125	462

Estimate the probability of a fault in the first year for
each model. Give each answer as a decimal to 2 dp.
(b) Based on these data, which model is most likely to have
a fault before the 1 year guarantee runs out?
Explain your answer.

Answer

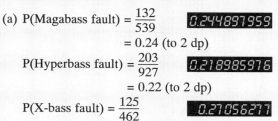

(a) P(Magabass fault) = $\frac{132}{539}$ `0.244897959`
    = 0.24 (to 2 dp)
    P(Hyperbass fault) = $\frac{203}{927}$ `0.218985976`
    = 0.22 (to 2 dp)
    P(X-bass fault) = $\frac{125}{462}$ `0.27056277`
    = 0.27 (to 2 dp)
(b) *Compare the probabilities:* 0.24, 0.22, 0.27
    P(X-bass fault) = 0.27 is the greatest probability.
    So the X-bass model is most likely to have a fault.

► **Exercise** **P15.2**

Give all estimates of probabilities in this exercise as decimals.
1 Tim Tardy has been late for college on 7 out of the last 60
  college days. Estimate the probability that he is late on his
  next college day.
2 On one day in winter, 18 of the 109 students in Year 11 of
  Heath School have 'flu. Estimate the probability of a
  student in Heath School having 'flu that day.
3 Boris has served 49 times so far
  in a tennis match. 4 of these
  serves were aces but 8 were out.
  Estimate the probability that
  Boris's next serve is
  (a) an ace
  (b) out
  (c) in.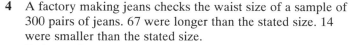
4 A factory making jeans checks the waist size of a sample of
  300 pairs of jeans. 67 were longer than the stated size. 14
  were smaller than the stated size.
  Estimate the probability that a pair of jeans made in this
  factory has a waist size
  (a) larger than the stated size
  (b) smaller than the stated size
  (c) the same as the stated size.
5 Linda was given a biased coin to test.
  She tossed it 250 times.
  Here are her results:

	Frequency
Head	197
Tail	53

  Estimate for this coin,
  the probability of
  (a) getting a Head
  (b) getting a Tail.

6 The pointer on this disc
is spun 450 times.
The results are given
in this frequency table.

Result	5	10	15	20	25	30	35	40
Frequency	42	17	49	41	118	76	81	26

The pointer is spun again.
(a) Estimate the probability of getting 35.
(b) Which number is most likely to come up?
   Estimate the probability for this.
(c) Which number is least likely to come up?
   Estimate the probability for this.
(d) Which numbers have roughly the same chance of
   coming up?
   Estimate this probability.
(e) Estimate the probability of getting a multiple of 10.

7 There are four examiners at the
local driving test centre. Each
month they record statistics about
people taking the driving test for
the first time.
Here are last month's data.

Examiner	Pass	Fail
Mr Brown	44	32
Ms White	74	62
Mrs Green	29	16
Mr Black	59	16

(a) How many people trying the test for the first time did
   each examiner test?
(b) Estimate the probability of passing the test first time, if
   tested by
   (i) Mr Brown
   (ii) Ms White
   (iii) Mrs Green
   (iv) Mr Black
(c) Estimate the probability of failing the test first time if
   tested at this driving centre.
(d) If a driver could choose the examiner for his or her test,
   who would you advise them to pick? Explain why.

ACTIVITY

Numbers and names

Your local phone book is full of numbers and names. Here are
some activities about them to try. Take pages at random for
each activity.

- **First digit**
   Look at the first digit of each
   telephone number on one page.
   Record how many times each
   digit occurs. Use a tally chart
   like this.
   Based on your results, estimate
   the probability that a telephone
   number in your local book
   begins with 0, 1, 2, ... or 9.

First Digit	Tally	Frequency
0		
1		
2		
3		
4		
5		
6		
7		
8		
9		

Is this what you expected?
Discuss.

What happens if you take a different page?
Do you expect to get the same results?
Discuss.

- **Number of digits**
   On one page, count the
   number of telephone numbers
   with 1, 2, 3, 4, ... digits.
   (The digits are in columns.
   Use this to help you to count
   them.)
   Record your results in a table.

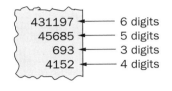

Number of digits	0	1	2	3	4	5	6	7
Frequency								

Estimate the probability that a phone number in your local
book has 0, 1, 2, 3, ... digits.
Comment on your results.
Would a different page give the same sort of result?
Discuss.

- **Initial letters**
   Names in the phone book are
   usually listed with surname
   first, then initial letter(s) of
   'first names'.
   Investigate the first initial
   letter after each surname in
   your local phone book.
   Estimate the probability that it
   is A, B, C, D, ...
   Comment on your findings.

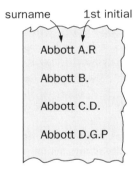

- Carry out a 'probability experiment' of your own based on
   the names or numbers in your local phone book. Write a
   short report of your results.

Investigation

Carry out an investigation of your own that involves using
relative frequency as an estimate for probability.
Here are some ideas as starting points.

- The probability that the next person at a Pelican crossing
   presses the button.
- The probability that the next person on a Zebra crossing is a
   child.
- The probability that the next vehicle to pass the
   school/college is a lorry.
- The probability that the next bus to school/college is late.
- The probability that the next student you meet was born in
   June.

Think of some other ideas yourself.
Discuss ideas with other students in your group.
Decide, with your teacher, which idea to investigate.
Write an account of your investigation and its results.

Expected number

Toss a fair coin once.
You get either a Head or a Tail.
Each has an equal chance.

The probability of getting a Head is $\frac{1}{2}$.
The probability of getting a Tail is $\frac{1}{2}$.

Toss a fair coin more than once.
You expect about $\frac{1}{2}$ of the tosses to land Heads,
    and about $\frac{1}{2}$ of the tosses to land Tails.

Toss a coin 100 times, for example.
You expect about $\frac{1}{2}$ of 100 tosses to land Heads.
    $\frac{1}{2}$ of 100 = 50 i.e., 50 Heads.

You cannot expect *exactly* 50 Heads.
You can only expect *about* 50.
However, a number very much smaller or larger than 50 will
lead you to suspect something may be wrong.
Was the coin fair?
Was it tossed properly each time?
And so on …

Summary

You can use probability to estimate the expected number of
times a result is likely to occur in some data.

   Expected number
   = probability × total number of results in the data.

Remember:
This *'expected number'* is just an estimate. It simply gives
you a rough idea of what *might* happen. The *actual* value
could be very different.

Finding 'expected numbers' in a situation can help you to look
carefully at any actual numbers you get.
They may lead you to spot **bias** in the experiment or survey.

Question

In an experiment Barry
threw three dice
1200 times.
Here are the numbers of
'twos' he got with each
dice.
How many 'two's should he expect to get from a fair dice?
Comment on his results.

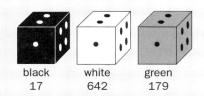

black 17   white 642   green 179

Answer

Probability of a 'two' is $\frac{1}{6}$.
Barry threw the dice 1200 times.
$\frac{1}{6}$ of 1200 = 1200 ÷ 6 = 200

So he should expect to get about 200 'twos'.
The green dice gave 179 twos. This is about 200. So I think
that the green dice is fair.
The white dice gave 642 twos. This is very much larger than
200. So I suspect that the white dice is biased.
The black dice gave only 17 twos. This is very much smaller
than 200. So I suspect that the black dice is also biased.

'Expected numbers' are used to estimate and predict numbers in
many practical and real life situations, not just games.

Question

British Rail gave the
probability of a train
leaving Trega station 'on
time' as 0.91.
63 trains leave Trega
station each day.
Estimate the number of
British Rail trains to
leave 'on time'.

Answer

Expected number = 0.91 × 63 = 57.33
So British Rail would expect 57 of the trains to leave 'on
time'.

Discussion Exercise

Think of some 'real life
situations' where probability
is used to 'predict' numbers.
Use the pictures to give you
some ideas. Make a list of as
many as you can.
Discuss your ideas with other
students in your group.
Collect examples from
newspapers, magazines, books, …
Why do people want to predict numbers in these situations?
Who uses these predictions?
Discuss.

▶ Exercise P15.3

1   Ted is football referee. He referees 138 matches each year.
    Before each match he tosses a coin. About how many times
    should he expect Heads to turn up?
2   There is a 60% chance of an April day in Triton being rainy.
    About how many rainy days would you expect in April in
    Triton?
3   The probability of guessing the correct answer in a multiple
    choice test is $\frac{1}{5}$.
    Ali guesses the answers to all 80 questions in the test. How
    many do you expect her to get correct?
4   Jason's probability of getting a double with a dart is $\frac{5}{6}$.
    In practice for a match he throws a dart 420 times. How
    many times does he expect to get a double?
5   The probability that a plane arrives late at the local airport
    is 0.15.
    2560 flights arrive there each summer. How many of these
    do you expect to be late?

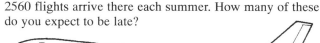

6 The probability of a runner in the local marathon getting cramp is 0.27. How many of the 1529 runners would you expect to get cramp?

7 This table gives the probabilities of getting a sunny day in Shadesville in the summer months.

Month	Probability
June	0.47
July	0.42
August	0.51
September	0.39

    (a) Calculate the number of 'sunny days' you would expect in Shadesville
      (i) in July
      (ii) in September.
    (b) How many days that are not sunny would you expect in Shadesville
      (i) in June
      (ii) in August?

8 Here are the estimated probabilities of four players winning their tennis matches.

Stefan	84%
Tod	69%
Michael	72%
Ivan	57%

    (a) How many of their next 250 matches would you expect
      (i) Stefan, (ii) Ivan, to win?
    (b) How many of their next 180 matches would you expect (i) Tod, (ii) Michael, to lose?

9 Kay spins this pointer 500 times. About how many times would you expect the pointer to stop on
    (a) black
    (b) grey
    (c) white?

10 An ordinary dice is tossed 240 times. On how many of these tosses would you expect to get
    (a) a six
    (b) an odd number
    (c) a two or three
    (d) not a four?

11 Sara tosses two coins. She records the number of times she gets these results:

two heads	exactly 1 head	at least 1 head

    (a) What is the probability of getting each result? (Remember: the equally likely outcomes are HH, HT, TH, TT.)
    (b) Sara tosses the coins 500 times. About how many times would you expect her to get each result?

Investigation

- Angela made this Wheel of Fortune Game for the primary school fete.

DOUBLE YOUR MONEY
10p A GO
Land on green and you double your money

- Do you think Angela will make 'plenty of money' with this game?
In 100 spins of the wheel, how much would you expect her to make?
Discuss.

How would you change the spinner to make more money? How much profit would you expect to make with your spinner?

- Here are some other games Angela's friends made for the fete.
Each is 10p a go.
Investigate the profit they are likely to make.

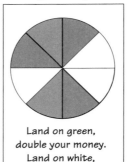

Land on green, double your money.
Land on white, get your money back.

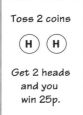

Toss 2 coins
Get 2 heads and you win 25p.

Toss 3 coins
Get 3 of a kind and you win 30p.

CUT A PACK OF CARDS
Get an ACE and you win 50p.

THROW 2 DICE
Get a double and you double your money.
Get a total of 2 or 12 and you win 40p.

- Invent some games of your own for the fete.
Find the expected profit for each game.

Examination Questions

1 Claire tossed three drawing pins together 100 times. The table below shows the results.

Result	Frequency
3 points up	7
2 points up, 1 point down	24
1 point up, 2 points down	57
3 points down	12

    (a) Use these results to estimate the probability of obtaining 3 points down.
    (b) What should Claire do to get a better estimate?

(NEAB, 1989)

2 Kim spun this pentagonal spinner 30 times and recorded the results. She drew the following diagram to illustrate them. Unfortunately she did not complete the diagram for the number 2.

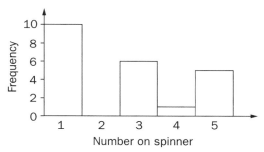

(a) Copy and complete the diagram.

(b) Use these results to suggest the probability that any given spin would result in an odd number.

(MEG, 1989)

3 A dice was rolled 200 times.
After every 20 rolls, the number of threes obtained was recorded as follows, in the order shown.

    3 5 4 4 3 3 1 4 2 2

The average number of threes obtained was plotted against the number of rolls, e.g.,

after 20 rolls, average $= \dfrac{3}{20} = 0.15$ and

after 40 rolls, average $= \dfrac{3+5}{40} = 0.20$.

The points (20,0.15) and (40,0.20) have been marked on the grid below.

(a) Copy the grid and complete the plotting of points.

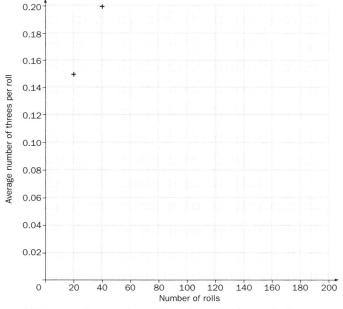

(b) Draw a line on the grid to show the theoretical probability of obtaining a 3 when a normal six-sided dice is rolled.

(NEAB, 1990)

4 John, Paul, Carl, Jean and Mary are the first names of the five members of a committee.
At the start of each meeting they decide which of them is going to wash up by selecting a name at random.
Work out the probability that the name selected will
(a) be John
(b) have an 'e' in it
(c) have an 'a' in it

(d) have 4 letters in it.
(e) In a year there are 40 meetings.
Work out how many times Paul would expect to wash up.

(ULEAC, 1991)

5 At a school fete class 1B makes a spinning wheel game.
People pay 5p to spin the pointer. If it lands on an odd number they win 25p.
(a) What is the probability that the pointer lands on an odd number?
(b) A lot of people play the game. Is the game likely to make a profit for class 1B? Give a reason for your answer.

(WJEC, 1989)

6 Three students A, B, C were each asked to toss a coin 30 times and record whether it came down heads (H) or tails (T) each time.
They said their results were as follows:
Student A:
T T T H T T H T T T H T T T H T T H T T T T H H T T T T T H T T.
Student B:
H T H T H T H T H T H T H T H T H T H T H T H T H T H T H T.
Student C:
H T H T H H H H T H T T H H H H T T H T H T T T H H T H T T.

One of the students used an unbiased coin, one used a biased coin and the remaining student did not have a coin so just made up the results.
(a) (i) Which student used a biased coin?
(ii) Estimate the probability that, the next time this coin is tossed, it will come down heads.
(b) Which student just made up the results? Give a reason for your answer.

(MEG, 1994)

7 A particular type of snail was collected from two localities: a beech wood and under hedges. Some snails had dark stripes on them ('banded'), others did not ('unbanded').
The data was recorded as a two-way table.

		Type of snail		
		Banded	Unbanded	Totals
Location	Beech wood	39	110	149
	Under hedges	46	26	72
	Totals	85	136	221

(a) Jacques found one of the snails in the beech wood. What is the probability that it was banded?
(b) All the snails collected are put in a bucket. One of them is chosen at random. Use this data to work out the probabilities (as a decimal to 2 significant figures) of choosing
(i) an unbanded snail
(ii) a banded snail from under hedges.

(MEG, 1990)

P16
Travel graphs

This unit will help you to:

- understand that a distance-time graph can show a journey
- read, use and draw simple straight line travel graphs
- find steady speeds from travel graphs
- read, use and draw travel graphs showing journeys made up of several stages
- recognise the direction of a journey from its travel graph
- interpret points where travel graphs cross.

Distance-time graphs

Nick drives home on the M6.
He takes 3 hours to drive 150 miles.
He goes at a steady speed of 50 mph.

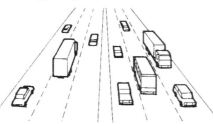

This graph is about Nick's journey.
It is a **distance-time graph**. It is also called a **travel graph**.

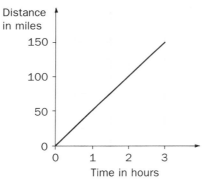

The *horizontal axis* is the Time axis.
On its scale, 2 'spaces' → 1 hour

$$1 \text{ 'space'} \rightarrow 1 \div 2 = \frac{1}{2} \text{ hour.}$$

The *vertical axis* is the Distance axis.
On its scale, 2 'spaces' → 50 miles

$$1 \text{ 'space'} \rightarrow 50 \div 2 = 25 \text{ miles.}$$

Each point on the graph represents a time and distance travelled on the journey. You can read off these values using the scales.
For example, point (2,100) is on the line. This shows that after 2 hours, Nick has gone 100 miles.

The graph is a *straight line*. This shows that the distance changes *steadily* with time.
In other words, it shows a **steady speed**.
The steady speed is given by the **gradient** (slope) of the line.

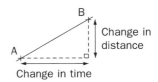

Speed between points A and B = $\dfrac{\text{change in distance}}{\text{change in time}}$

You can find the value for the speed from any two points on the line.

Here are two examples.

$$\begin{aligned} \text{speed} &= \frac{50}{1} \\ &= 50 \text{ mph} \end{aligned} \qquad \begin{aligned} \text{speed} &= \frac{75}{1\frac{1}{2}} \\ &= 50 \text{ mph} \end{aligned}$$

Remember:
Use the scales to read off the times and distances.
Make sure you use the *correct units*.
For example, for speed in *mph*, you need distance in *miles* and time in *hours*.

▶ *Exercise* **P16.1**

1 This travel graph is about a journey by motor bike. Copy the graph on to 2 mm graph paper. Answer these questions about it.

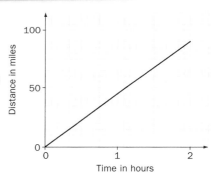

(a) What does each 'small space' on the Time axis represent?
(b) What does each 'small space' on the Distance axis represent?
(c) How long did the journey take?
(d) What was the distance travelled?
(e) Find the distance travelled in these times:
   (i)   1 hour
   (ii) 40 minutes
   (iii) $1\frac{1}{2}$ hours.
(f) Find the time taken to travel these distances:
   (i)   60 miles
   (ii) 15 miles
   (iii) 75 miles.
(g) Find the average speed of the bike on this journey.

2 This travel graph is about a journey by coach in France.

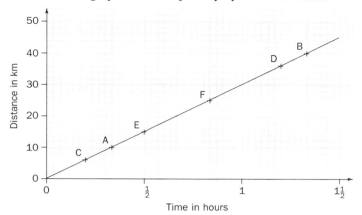

Copy the graph on to 2 mm graph paper.
Answer these questions about it.
(a) What does each 'small space' on the Time axis represent?
(b) What does each 'small space' on the Distance axis represent?
(c) How long did the coach journey take? What was the distance travelled?
(d) Give the time and distance for each lettered point on the graph.
(e) Find the speed of the journey. State the units clearly.
(f) Which points did you use to find the speed? Explain why you chose these points.

3

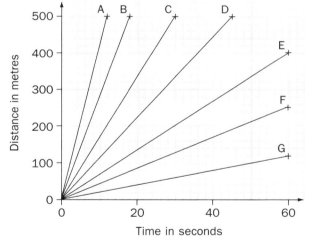

These distance-time graphs show the steady speeds of the following:
a motor bike on the motorway, a walker, a car in town, a bus, a helicopter, a car towing a caravan, and a cyclist.
(a) Match each person or vehicle to its line graph. Give reasons for your choices.
(b) Work out the speed shown by each line in metres per second. Discuss what you find.

4 (a) Draw axes for a distance-time graph on 2 mm graph paper.

Number the Time axis from 0 to 5 hours.
Use a scale of 2 cm to 1 hour.

Number the Distance axis from 0 to 80 miles.
Use a scale of 1 cm to 10 miles.

Draw travel graphs to show these journeys on your axes.
Label each line with its letter.

A 30 miles in 2 hours   D 25 miles in $4\frac{1}{2}$ hours
B 40 miles in $3\frac{1}{2}$ hours   E 80 miles in $1\frac{1}{2}$ hours
C 70 miles in 3 hours   F 15 miles in 5 hours

(b) Find the speed shown by each travel graph. Put them in order from fastest to slowest.
(c) Look at the slopes of your travel graphs. Put them in order from steepest to gentlest.
(d) Compare your answers to (b) and (c). Discuss what they show.

Using speeds

To draw a travel graph, you **plot distance against time** for a journey.
Sometimes you need to work out the distances before drawing the graph.

Memo

Distance = Speed × Time

For example,
a train travels at 45 mph for 20 minutes.

Speed: 45 mph   Time: 20 minutes $= \dfrac{20}{60}$ hours

$$\text{Distance} = 45 \times \frac{20}{60} \text{ miles} = 15 \text{ miles}$$

So when the 'time taken' is 20 minutes,
distance travelled is 15 miles.

Sometimes you need to find the time taken, before you can draw the graph.

Memo

Time = $\dfrac{\text{Distance}}{\text{Speed}}$

For example,
a train travels at 35 mph for 25 miles.

Time taken $= \dfrac{25}{35}$ hours $= \dfrac{25}{35} \times 60$ minutes

$= 43$ minutes (to the nearest minute)

So when the 'distance travelled' is 25 miles,
the 'time taken' is 43 minutes.

► *Exercise* P16.2

1 What is the distance travelled on these journeys?
(a) 20 mph for 3 hours   (d) 10 mph for 40 minutes
(b) 50 mph for 30 minutes (e) 45 mph for 15 minutes
(c) 3 mph for $2\frac{1}{2}$ hours   (f) 32 mph for 1 hour 20 minutes
Draw travel graphs to show each of these journeys.
Label each line clearly with its own letter.

2 What is the time taken on these journeys?
   (a) 48 miles at 16 mph   (d) 63 miles at 42 mph
   (b) 54 miles at 27 mph   (e) 15 miles at 20 mph
   (c) 45 miles at 36 mph   (f) 20 miles at 70 mph
   Draw travel graphs to show each journey.

Labels on axes

The axes on a travel graph are often not labelled simply 'distance' and 'time'.
Always read the labels on the axes carefully.

The 'time axis' may give the 'Time of day'.
These may be '24-hour times' or times with am and pm.

The 'distance axis' may give the 'distance from somewhere'.
It may be in kilometres, metres, …
            or miles, yards, …

These descriptions of 'time' and 'distance' help you to give an account of the journey shown.
The travel graphs below, for example, are about some journeys by train. They are on a two-track local railway between Amford and Excastle.

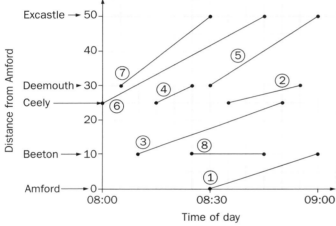

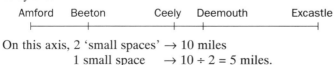

The time axis shows 'Time of day' as 24-hour times.
The times go from 08:00 to 09:00.
On this axis, 6 'small spaces' → 30 minutes
            1 'small space' → 30 ÷ 6 = 5 minutes.

The distance axis shows 'Distance from Amford in miles'.
The stations on the line are marked on the axis.
They are:

   Amford   Beeton   Ceely   Deemouth   Excastle
   |———————|——————————————|———————|————————————————|

On this axis, 2 'small spaces' → 10 miles
            1 small space → 10 ÷ 2 = 5 miles.

Each travel graph shows a journey between two stations on the Amford-Excastle line. You can work out the details of each journey from its graph.

► Exercise P16.3

1 For each travel graph on the diagram above, give
   (a) where the train journey starts and ends
   (b) the distance travelled
   (c) the departure and arrival times

   (d) the time taken on the journey
   (e) the average speed in mph.

2 Draw axes for more distance-time graphs for journeys on the Amford-Excastle railway.
   (Number the time axis from 13:00 to 15:00.
   Number the distance axis with distances from Amford.
   Use the same scales as in the graph on the left.)
   (a) On your axes, draw a travel graph for each of the following journeys. Label each line carefully.
       d means departure time.
       a means arrival time.
       A   Amford *d* 13:50, Excastle *a* 15:00
       B   Excastle *d* 14:00, Deemouth *a* 14:25
       C   Deemouth *d* 13:15, Excastle *a* 13:55
       D   Amford *d* 14:05, Ceely *a* 14:45
       E   Beeton *d* 13:05, Amford *a* 13:45
       F   Beeton *d* 13:35, Ceely a 14:20
   (b) Calculate the average speed for each journey in mph.

3 The details below are for some other journeys on the Amford-Excastle railway.
   A   16:35 from Excastle to Amford, speed 50 mph.
   B   16:15 from Amford to Beeton, speed 20 mph.
   C   16:50 from Beeton to Amford, speed 15 mph.
   D   16:00 from Deemouth to Excastle speed 48 mph.
   E   17:00 from Excastle to Beeton, speed 40 mph.
   F   16:05 from Beeton to Ceely, speed 36 mph.
       (a) Calculate the arrival time for each train.
       (b) On the same axes, draw a travel graph for each journey.
           (Number the time axis from 16:00 to 18:00.)

4 A two-track railway runs between Rymouth and Xton. These are the stations on the line:
       The details below are about journeys from Rymouth to each station.
   A   *d* 12:10 Southton *a* 12:50, speed 24 mph.
   B   *d* 12:35 Tycastle *a* 13:30, speed 38 mph.
   C   *d* 13:05 Unwin *a* 13:55, speed 49 mph.
   D   *d* 13:00 Veenor *a* 14:05, speed 51 mph.
   E   *d* 12:00 Webly *a* 13:20, speed 45 mph.
   F   *d* 12:30 Xton *a* 14:00, speed 50 mph.
       (a) Find the distance (to the nearest mile) from Rymouth to each station.
       (b) On the same axes, draw a travel graph for each journey.

```
Xton      ┬
Webly     ┼
Veenor    ┼
Unwin     ┼
Tycastle  ┼
Southton  ┼
Rymouth   ┴
```

5 The graph below shows four train journeys from Exeter St. David's station to Plymouth.

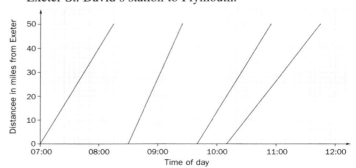

Answer these questions from the graph.
   (a) What is the distance by rail from Exeter to Plymouth?
   (b) What is the departure time for each train.

(c) Estimate, by simply looking at the graph, which train is fastest and which is slowest.

(d) What is the arrival time for each train?

(e) What is the average speed of each train?
Give your answers to the nearest 1 mph.
Were your estimates in part (c) correct?

Several stages

A journey may have several parts or stages.
A travel graph can show each part clearly.

Here is a travel graph of Alan's training session.
You can see it has three parts.
Alan runs at first.
He stops next.
Then he jogs.

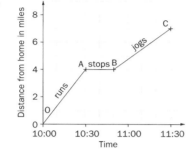

Each point on the graph links a time and distance during Alan's 'journey'.

The time is the 'time of day' in hours and minutes.
The scale on this axis gives '1 space' → 10 minutes.

The distance is the 'distance from home in miles'.
The scale on this axis gives '1 space' → 1 mile.

The *key points* on the journey have been labelled on the graph.
They are at O, A, B and C. You can use them to help you to describe Alan's 'journey'.

Point O shows the *start* of the 'journey'.
The time is 10:00. Alan is at home.

Point A shows when and where Alan *stops running*.
The time is 10:30. He is 4 miles from home.

Point B shows when and where Alan *starts jogging*.
The time is 10:50. He is 4 miles from home.

Point C shows the *end* of the 'journey'.
The time is 11:30. Alan is 7 miles from home.

The three parts of the travel graph have **different slopes**.
Each shows a **different speed**.
The *steeper* the slope, the *greater* the speed.

The *first line, OA,* is about Alan's *run*.
It is the steepest line on the graph.
This means it shows the greatest speed.
You can find the speed from the graph.

The distance he runs is 4 miles.
The time taken is 30 minutes, i.e., $\frac{1}{2}$ hour.

Alan's running speed
= 4 miles ÷ $\frac{1}{2}$ hour = 8 mph.

(Remember: For speed in *mph*, you want distance in *miles*, time in *hours*.)

The *next line, AB,* is about Alan's 'stop'.
It is parallel to the time axis.
The distance does not change, but the 'time' does.
Alan stops for 20 minutes.

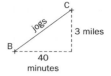

The *last line, BC,* is about Alan's *jog*.
The distance he jogs is 3 miles.
The time taken is 40 minutes.
i.e., $\frac{40}{60}$ hour.

Alan's jogging speed
= 3 miles ÷ $\frac{40}{60}$ hour = 4.5 mph.

You can also find the average speed for the 'whole journey'.
The total distance he travels is 7 miles.
The total time taken is $1\frac{1}{2}$ hours.
Average speed for the whole journey = 7 miles ÷ $1\frac{1}{2}$ hours
= 4.66 … mph
= 4.7 mph (to 1 dp).

▶ *Exercise* **P16.4**

1 Mr Parr travels from Durham to Sheffield. He catches the first afternoon train. The train stops at Darlington, York and then Sheffield.

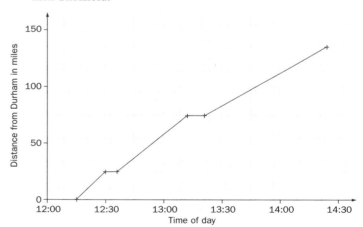

The graph above shows Mr Parr's train journey.
Use it to answer these questions.

(a) What does 1 small 'space' represent on the Distance axis?

(b) How far is each named station from Durham?

(c) How far apart are the stations?

(d) What does 1 small 'space' represent on the Time axis?

(e) How long does the train spend at Darlington and York stations?

(f) At what times does the train leave Durham?

(g) What are the arrival and departure times at Darlington and York?

(h) At what time does the train arrive in Sheffield?
(i) Calculate the average speed for these parts of the journey:
    (i)   from Durham to Darlington
    (ii) from Darlington to York
    (iii) from York to Sheffield.
(j) Calculate the average speed for the whole of the journey.

2 Whilst staying at a youth hostel, Charlie Strong decided to go on a 12 mile hike, leaving the hostel at 10:00 hours. He called at a pub for lunch, then completed his walk in time for tea. This graph shows his journey.

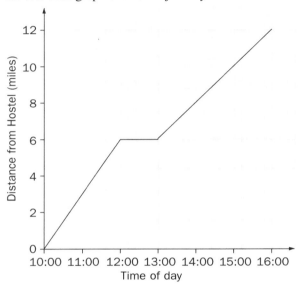

(a) How long did it take Charlie to walk to the pub?
(b) How far is the pub from the hostel?
(c) What was Charlie's walking speed on this journey to the pub?
(d) How long did Charlie spend over lunch?
(e) How long did Charlie take to complete his walk after lunch?
(f) What was Charlie's steady walking speed after leaving the pub?
(g) At what time did Charlie complete his hike?

Different directions

The *slope* of a travel graph gives the *speed* of travel.
It also tells you about its **'direction'**.

An *'up'* slope, **/**, shows travel in *one direction*.
A *'down'* slope, ****, shows travel in the *opposite direction*.
No slope, **—**, shows travel in *'no direction'*, i.e., a stop.

Always read the label on the distance axis carefully.
This tells you where distance is measured from.
For example, look at the sketch graph that follows.
Distance is measured *'from A'*.
An *'up'* slope shows travel *away from A*.
A *'down'* slope shows travel *towards A*.
'No' slope shows a *'stop'*.

opposite directions

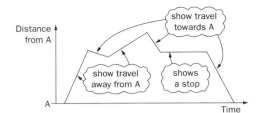

show travel towards A

show travel away from A

shows a stop

Exercise P16.5

1 A mechanic drove a car from the garage to a layby, adjusted the carburettor, then drove back to the garage. This graph shows the journey.

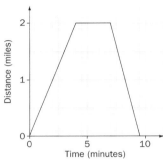

(a) How far is it from the garage to the layby?
(b) How long did the journey to the layby take?
(c) At what steady speed was the car driven to the layby?
(d) How long did it take the mechanic to adjust the carburettor?
(e) How long did the return journey take?
(f) At what steady speed was the car driven back to the garage?

2 Mr Shaw drove from his home in Norwich to a lunch-time meeting in Cambridge.
On the way back home he had a puncture.
He stopped to change the wheel.

This travel graph is about Mr Shaw's journey.

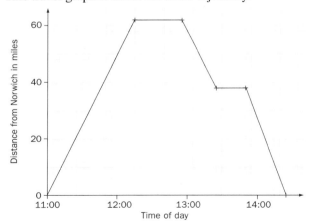

Use the graph to answer these questions.
(a) How far is it from Norwich to Cambridge?
(b) How long did Mr Shaw take to drive to Cambridge?
(c) What was his average speed on this part of the journey?
(d) How long did Mr Shaw stay in Cambridge?
(e) At what time did he stop to change the wheel?
(f) How far was he from Cambridge at this time?
(g) For how long did he 'stop' on the return journey?
(h) At what time did he get home?

(i) What was his average speed on each part of the return journey
   (i) before the stop
   (ii) after the stop?
(j) What was his average driving speed over the whole journey (excluding stops)?

 ## Discussion Exercise

One morning several students travelled between college and the town centre. The sketch graphs below are about their journeys.

d stands for 'distance from college'
t stands for 'time of day' from 9:00 to 12:00.

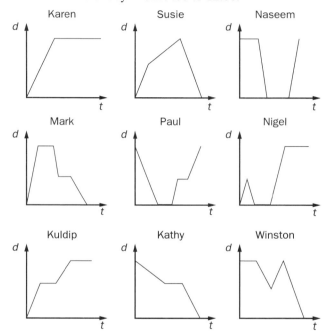

Use the travel graphs to answer these questions.
Discuss how you decided on each answer.

Who went only from college to town?
Who went only from town to college?

Who did a round trip from college to town and back again?
Who did a round trip from town to college and back again?

Who spent some time at college?
Who spent some time in the town?

Who stopped on the journey from college to town?
Who stopped on the journey from town to college?

Give a description of each journey from its travel graph.
Discuss your ideas with other students in your group.

Crossing points

The graphs of several journeys can be drawn on the *same axes*.
Sometimes the graphs *meet* or *cross* at a point.
At this point, the values for time and distance are the *same* for each 'traveller'.
If the travellers are on the same route, this means they pass each other. You can read off when and where this happens.

Here is an example.

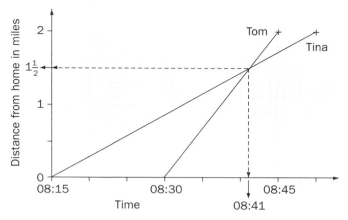

Tina and her brother Tom take the same route to school. These travel graphs show their journeys one morning.

Tina sets off at 08:15.
She walks the 2 miles to school and arrives at 08:50.
Tom sets off at 08:30.
He cycles to school and arrives at 08:45.

Tom overtakes Tina on the way to school.
The point where their travel graphs cross shows you where and when this happens.
At the crossing point, you can read off these values.
The time is 08:41.
The distance from home is $1\frac{1}{2}$ miles.

▶ *Exercise* **P16.6**

1 This travel graph represents the journeys of two trains travelling along parallel tracks.

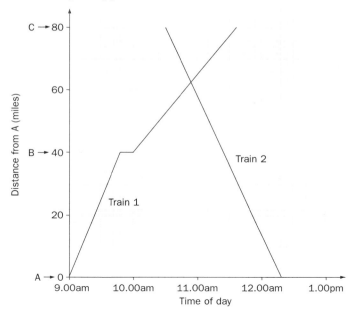

Train 1 travels from A to C but stops at B with engine trouble. Train 2 travels from C to A without stopping.

(a) At what time does Train 1 stop at B?

(b) For how long is Train 1 stopped with engine trouble?

(c) How long does Train 1 take to complete its journey from B to C?

(d) (i) For which part of its journey is Train 1 travelling most quickly?

    (ii) What is Train 1's average speed for this part of the journey?

(e) What is Train 2's average speed for its journey?

(f) At what time do the two trains pass each other?

(g) How far from A are the two trains when they pass each other?

2   This graph represents the journeys made by a car and a bus in France.

The bus went from Auray to Muzillac and back again. It made one stop at Vannes.

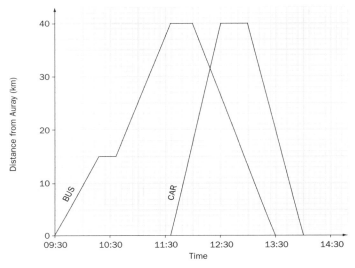

(a) What were the 'round trip' journey times for each vehicle?

(b) How long did the bus stop at (i) Vannes (ii) Muzillac?

(c) How long did the car stop at Muzillac?

(d) What were the average speeds for the bus on
    (i) each leg of its outward journey
    (ii) its return journey?

(e) What was the average speed of the car for its
    (i) outward journey
    (ii) return journey?

(f) When and where did the bus and car pass each other?

Drawing travel graphs

You draw a travel graph like any other line graph.
Use these notes to help you.

Memo
Drawing graphs p95

- A travel graph is a distance time graph.
  The 'horizontal' axis is the Time axis.
  The 'vertical' axis is the Distance axis.

Examination questions often give you these axes. Read the labels on the axes carefully. Make sure you know what 'kind' of times and distances they show.

- Check the scale on each axis.
  Work out what each 'small space' stands for if you need to.

- The information for a travel graph is usually a 'description' of the journey.
  In travel graphs you have to draw in this Unit, each part of the journey will be made at a steady speed. So each part will be shown as a straight line.

- To find the coordinates of the points to plot, read the 'story' of the journey carefully.
  Usually the journey has several parts or stages. Decide what these are. List them in 'note form' if it helps.
  Identify the key points at the start/end of each stage.
  Find the 'time' and 'distance' for each of these points.
  It often helps to put this information in a table.

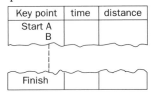

Make sure you have the kind of 'time' and 'distance' you need.
'Time' may be 'Time taken'
            or 'Time of day'.
'Distance' may be 'Distance travelled'
            or 'Distance from a place'.

- Plot the points from the 'time-distance' coordinates you have found.
  Join the Start and End points of each stage with a straight line. Use a ruler.

- Always check that your graph 'matches' the story.
  Look at the lines you have drawn.
  Does the slope of each line make sense?
  Are lines showing 'stops' parallel to the time axis?
  Is the story about a 'round trip'?
  Should the graph return to the time axis or not?
  And so on …

Question

Richard went on a sponsored walk for charity.
The walk started at college at 10.00 am and Richard reached the first Checkpoint, 5 km away at 10.45 am.
He stopped there for 15 minutes and had a drink.
From Checkpoint 1 he walked for another 7.5 km to Checkpoint 2. It took him 1 hour.
After lunch at Checkpoint 2, he started on the walk back to college at 12.30 pm.
After walking 8 km he passed Checkpoint 3, but he didn't stop.
He finished the walk at college at 2.50 pm.

Draw a travel graph for Richard's walk on the axes shown on the next page.

Answer

- *Work out the stages of the journey.*
  Walk from Start to Checkpoint 1.
  Rest at Checkpoint 1.

Walk from Checkpoint 1 to Checkpoint 2.
Lunch at Checkpoint 2.
Walk from Checkpoint 2 to Finish.

- *Find 'time' and 'distance' for key points.*
  Work out 'Time of day' and 'Distance from college'
  because the given axes are labelled in this way.

Point	Time of day	Distance from college
A Start	10.00am	0km
B Arrive Checkpoint 1	10.45am	5km
C Leave Checkpoint 1	11.00am	5km
D Arrive Checkpoint 2	12.00noon	12.5km
E Leave Checkpoint 2	12.30pm	12.5km
F Finish	2.50pm	0km

- *Work out scales on given axes.*
  'Time' axis: 12 small spaces → 1 hour (= 60 minutes)
            1 small space → 60 ÷ 12 = 5 minutes
  'Distance' axis: 10 small spaces → 5 km
            1 small space → 5 ÷ 10 = 0.5 km
- *Plot points and draw graph.*

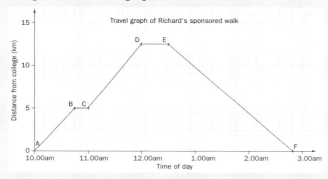

In some descriptions you may be given speeds for part of the journey.

To find the 'distance' if you know the 'time', use:

distance = speed × time

To find the 'time' if you know the 'distance', use:

time = $\dfrac{\text{distance}}{\text{speed}}$

Remember: Make sure that the units 'match'.

▶ *Exercise* **P16.7**

1 Sandie leaves home at 08:00 to go to work. She walks at a steady speed of 4 mph for $\frac{1}{4}$ hour to the bus stop where she has to wait for a bus. She waits for 15 minutes then catches the bus. The bus takes 20 minutes to travel 2 miles to the town centre where Sandie gets off. She then walks the remaining $\frac{1}{5}$ mile to work in 10 minutes.
(a) Draw a distance time graph for Sandie's journey to work. Use a scale of 6 cm to 30 minutes on the time axis and 5 cm to 1 mile on the distance axis.
(b) How far does she have to walk to the bus stop?
(c) What is the average speed of the bus journey to the town centre?
(d) How far from home is Sandie's work place?

2 Kim left home at 9:00 and drove 60 km to Cardiff, arriving there at 10:16. She stopped to buy a newspaper, then left Cardiff at 10:30 and drove 18 km to Newport. She arrived at Newport at 10:54.
(a) Draw a travel graph for Kim's journey from home to Newport.
Use a scale of 2 cm to 20 minutes on the time axis and 2 cm to 10 km on the distance axis.
(b) How far from home is Kim at 10:00?
(c) Calculate the average speed for Kim's journey from
(i) home to Cardiff
(ii) Cardiff to Newport
(iii) home to Newport.

3 On Monday morning Alec left home at 8.30 am and walked 500 m to the bus stop. It took him 6 minutes. He waited 4 minutes, then caught the bus to school, arriving there at 8.45 am. The journey from the bus stop to the school is 2500 m.
(a) Draw a travel graph showing Alec's journey from home to school on Monday.
Use a scale of 2 cm to 5 minutes on the time axis and 2 cm to 500 m on the distance axis.
(b) On which part of the journey did Alec travel fastest?
(c) Calculate the average speed for the bus journey.

4 On Wednesday, Mrs Patel travelled from her home in Winchester to Bournemouth, a distance of 60 km. She left home at 09:00 and drove for 40 minutes at an average speed of 60 km/h.
She then stopped at a garage for 10 minutes to fill up with petrol before continuing her journey to Bournemouth, arriving at 10:15.
(a) Draw a travel graph to show Mrs Patel's journey to Bournemouth.
Use a scale of 12 mm to represent 1 hour on the time axis and 2 cm to represent 10 km on the distance axis.
(b) After leaving the garage, how long did it take Mrs Patel to reach Bournemouth?
(c) What was Mrs Patel's average speed during this stage of her journey?
Mrs Patel stayed in Bournemouth for 2 hours before starting her return journey to Winchester.
(d) At what time did she leave Bournemouth?
(e) Draw a line on your travel graph to represent her stay in Bournemouth.
Mrs Patel began driving back home at an average speed of 50 km/h, but 30 minutes after starting her journey she punctured a tyre and had to stop. She took 25 minutes to change the wheel and then continued at the same average speed.
(f) Complete the travel graph to show Mrs Patel's return journey.
(g) At what time did Mrs Patel arrive home?

5 The 09:30 train from Norwich to Harwich left on time travelling at 40 mph. It stopped for 4 minutes at Ipswich, 40 miles from Norwich, before continuing on to Harwich at the same steady speed. Harwich is 35 miles from Ipswich.
(a) Draw the distance-time graph for this train.
Use a scale of 6 cm to 1 hour on the time axis and 2 cm to 10 miles on the distance axis.

(b) At what time did the train arrive at Harwich?

At 10:20 another train left Harwich and travelled directly to Norwich, arriving there at 11:38.

(c) Draw on the same grid the travel graph for the journey of this train.

(d) Calculate the average speed of this train for the journey from Harwich to Norwich.

(e) At what time did the two trains pass each other?

(f) How far from Norwich were the two trains when they passed each other?

Examination Questions

1 A boy cycles from home at an average speed of 10 miles per hour to a cycle repair shop 4 miles away. He has to wait 5 mins for service and then he walks home at an average speed of 4 miles per hour.

The graph which could represent his journey is

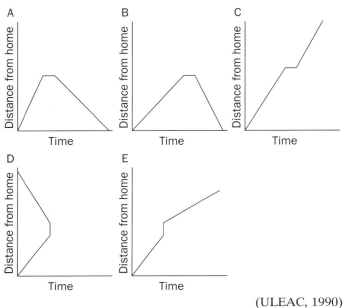

(ULEAC, 1990)

2

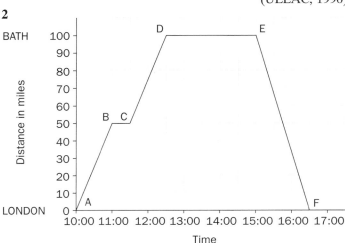

Here is a travel graph of a coach trip that Jennifer's aunt took from London to Bath, and back again.

(a) What was the coach doing between 11:00 and 11:30?

(b) At what time did the coach reach Bath?

(c) How long did Jennifer's aunt stay in Bath?

(d) (i)   How far is it from London to Bath?

(ii) How long did it take the coach to travel from Bath back to London?

(iii) Work out the average speed of the coach on the return journey.

(ULEAC, 1991)

3 Peter set off from home at 7.30 am to ride his moped 10 miles to work. After a while, he ran out of petrol and had to push his moped back along the road to a petrol station. After filling the tank with petrol, he continued his journey to work.

The travel graph below represents his journey.

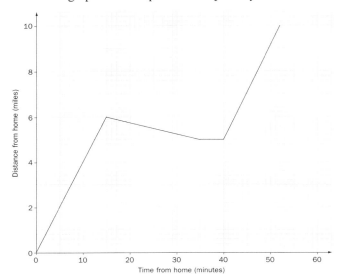

(a) At what time did Peter arrive at work?

(b) How many minutes was Peter at the petrol station?

(c) At what speed, in miles per hour, did the moped travel during the first 15 minutes of the journey?

(d) How many minutes earlier would Peter have arrived at work if his journey had not been interrupted and he had travelled at the same constant speed?

(MEG, 1990)

4 Answer the whole of this question on graph paper.

A cyclist passes the "Mortal Man" at 11.10 am, the "Kirkstone Pass Inn" at 11.50 am, and the "Brothers' Water Hotel" at 11.57 am. He goes past all of these and on to Patterdale, reaching the "White Lion" there at 12.08 pm. The distance from the Mortal Man to the Kirkstone Pass Inn is 4.5 km, from the Kirkstone Pass Inn to the Brothers' Water Hotel is 3.5 km, and from the Brothers' Water Hotel to the White Lion is 4.5 km.

(a) Draw a graph to show this journey. Assume that the cyclist travels at steady speeds. Use a scale of 6 cm to 1 hour on the horizontal axis and 1 cm to 1 km on the vertical axis.

(b) Calculate the cyclist's average speed for each of the three stages described, and for the whole journey.

(c) Suggest possible reasons for the differences between your answers in (b).

(d) The following day he plans to cycle from Patterdale to catch a train at Penrith. This is a distance of 22 km. The road is fairly hilly, but Penrith is at about the same level as Patterdale. Use your answers to suggest how long he should allow for this trip, explaining your reasons.

(MEG, 1990)

5 **The whole of this question should be answered on graph paper.**

In this question assume all speeds are constant.
Sandra and Yasmin took part in a 20 km sponsored walk.
Sandra started at 09:00. She walked the first 10 km in $1\frac{1}{2}$ hours. After stopping for a 15 minute rest she continued the walk, finishing at 13:00.

(a) On graph paper draw a distance time graph for Sandra's walk. Use a scale of 2 cm to represent 30 minutes on the horizontal axis and 2 cm to represent 2 km on the vertical axis.

Yasmin started at 09:30 and completed the walk without a rest. She walked at a speed of 6.25 km/h.

(b) At what time did Yasmin complete the walk?

(c) Add a line to your graph to represent Yasmin's journey.

(d) Use your graph to find
  (i) the time at which Yasmin passed Sandra
  (ii) the distance they had each walked at this time.

(MEG, 1991)

P17
Compound measures

This unit will help you to:

■ understand the idea of a compound measure

■ use compound measures in calculations

■ understand and use the unitary method

■ find the 'best value for money' by comparing unit prices or amounts per unit cost

■ understand and use the idea of density as a compound measure.

Looking at compound measures

Compound measures occur in many everyday situations.

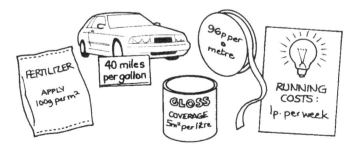

Discussion Exercise

● Compare the compound measures shown above.
  What have they got in common?
  Why are these measures called compound measures?

● Discuss what each compound measure is being used for.
  Who might use each one?
  Think of other situations in which they could be used.

● You might see '£ ... per day' in

the pay rate for
a part-time job,

the hire rate
for a car.

Look at these compound units:

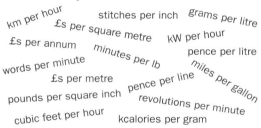

km per hour   stitches per inch   grams per litre
£s per square metre   kW per hour
£s per annum   pence per litre
words per minute   minutes per lb
£s per metre   miles per gallon
pounds per square inch   pence per line
cubic feet per hour   revolutions per minute
kcalories per gram

Discuss what each unit might measure.
Try to think of at least two examples for each.

● What other compound units do you know?
  Make a list of them.
  Think about units you have come across in your other studies, when shopping, in newspapers and magazines, in your hobbies, ...
  Discuss the examples suggested by the students in your group.

Summary

Rates such as £5 per hour, 8 m² per litre, 90 words per minute, are compound measures.

A **compound measure** links two quantities. It is about how one quantity compares or changes with another.

The quantities may be numbers, money, lengths, masses, area, volume, ...

The **unit** of a compound measure is usually given as 'somethings' per 'something'. This unit shows which two quantities are linked.

For example, grams per m² → mass linked with area.

Per means 'for each' or 'for every'. (Often shortened to p or /.)

Calculating compound measures

Speed compares *distance* and *time*.
To work out speed in *km/h*,
divide distance in *km*
by time in *hours*.
For example,
if Vicky cycles 45 km in 3 hours,
her speed is 45 ÷ 3 = 15 km/h.

Rate of pay often compares *money* and *time*.
To work out a rate of pay in *£s per hour*,
divide an amount of money in *£s*
by time in *hours*.
For example,
if Gavin is paid £20 for 4 hours work,
his rate of pay is 20 ÷ 4 = £5 per hour.

Petrol consumption
compares *distance* and
volume.
To work out petrol
consumption in *km/litre*,
divide distance in *km*
by volume of petrol in *litres*.
For example, if a car travels
600 km on 200 litres of petrol,
its petrol consumption is 600 ÷ 200 = 3 km/litre.

Summary

To calculate any compound measure, divide one quantity by another.
The unit of the compound measure tells you what to do.
For example, words/minute tells you to work out number of words ÷ number of minutes.

Remember: '/' is another way to show a division.
Write the compound unit using / to remind you what to work out.
Always make sure any units you use give the compound unit you want.
Change the unit(s) first if you need to.
Round the answer sensibly if necessary.

Question

Rick types 2500 words in an hour.
(a) What is his typing speed in words per minute (wpm)
(b) Which RSA exam could he pass?

RSA Typing
Stage 1: 25wpm
Stage 2: 35wpm
Stage 3: 50wpm

Answer

(a) *Change unit:* 1 hour = 60 minutes
    typing speed = words/minute
                 = 2500 ÷ 60 wpm
                 = 42 wpm (to nearest whole number).
(b) Rick could pass RSA stage 2 exam.

Most compound units are given 'per one unit'.
For example, 'per metre' means 'per one metre'.
Sometimes this makes the amount per unit in the rate very small.
For example, if the temperature falls 5°C when you go 1250 m up a mountain, its rate of fall is 5 ÷ 1250 = 0.004°C per metre.
We often give rates like these as 'per 100', 'per 1000', and so on …
For example, 0.004°C per metre becomes 0.4°C per 100 metres or 4°C per 1000 metres.

💬 Discussion Exercise

Think of some other examples of this kind of compound unit.
What are they used to measure?
Discuss.

▶ *Exercise* P17.1

1 James used 15 grams of salt in 75 mℓ of water to make a salt solution. What is its strength in g/mℓ?
2 Sam used 6 litres of emulsion to paint an area of 108 m². Calculate the coverage rate in m²/ℓ.
3 On a recent trip to France, Jill's car used 5 litres of oil on a journey of 1750 km. Calculate the oil consumption in kilometres per litre.
4 Pete mixed 4.5 g of plant food with 18 litres of water. The mixing instructions on the packet are given in litres per gram. What do the instructions say?
5 A fresh chicken weighing $6\frac{1}{4}$ lb costs £7.13. Calculate the price per pound for chicken.
6 A meat pie weighs 280 g and contains 1105 kcals of energy. How many kcals per 100 g is this?
7 Muriel applied 12 kg of lawn sand to her 80 m² lawn. At what rate in g/m² did she apply the sand?
8 Winston was paid £11.20 for delivering 800 copies of The Weekly Advertiser. Calculate his rate of pay per 50 copies.
9 A café charges 55 p for a piece of Cheddar cheese weighing 40 g. How much is this per kilogram?
10 Water is dripping from a leaking tap. In 3 hours, 9 litres of water dripped from the tap. At what rate is the tap leaking
    (a) in litres per hour
    (b) in mℓ per minute?

Using compound measures

The rate '£4 per hour' links money and time. You can use it to do two kinds of calculations.

If you *know time* worked, you can *find money* paid.

time → money

If you *know money* paid, you can *find time* worked.

money → time

To find 'money paid' write the rate '£4 per hour' in this order:

> For 1 hour, the pay is £4.

that is, time → money 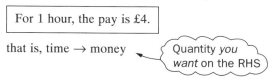 Quantity *you* want on the RHS

Now it is easy to find the pay for any number of hours.
  For 1 hour the pay is £4
  For 2 hours the pay is 4 × 2 = £8
  For 3 hours the pay is 4 × 3 = £12
  ⋮
  For $7\frac{1}{2}$ hours the pay is 4 × 7.5 = £30
  For $10\frac{1}{4}$ hours the pay is 4 × 10.25 = £41
  And so on …

To find 'time worked', write the rate '£4 per hour' in this order:

> £4 is paid for 1 hour

that is, money → time  Quantity *you* want on the RHS

For example, to find the time worked for £28:

Start with this link	£4 is paid for 1 hour
Divide by 4 to give the time for £1	£1 is paid for $\frac{1}{4}$ hour
Multiply by 28 to give the time for £28	£28 is paid for $\frac{1}{4}$ × 28 = 7 hours.

Discussion Exercise

- The method of working shown above is called the **Unitary Method**.
  Discuss why.
- Ed is paid £4 per hour.
  How much is he paid for:
  (a) 12 hours
  (b) $3\frac{1}{2}$ hours
  (c) $9\frac{1}{4}$ hours
  (d) 4 hours 20 mins?
  How long did he work for
  (a) £60
  (b) £21
  (c) £102.40
  (d) £41.67?
- Lisa is paid £5.30 per hour.
  How much is she paid for:
  (a) 16 hours?
  (b) $11\frac{1}{4}$ hours?
  (c) 6 h 45 mins?
  (d) 2 h 50 mins?
  How long did she work for:
  (a) £185.50?
  (b) £17?
  (c) £200?
  (d) £52.25?
- Martin is paid £157.70 for a basic 38-hour week.
  (a) What is his basic hourly rate of pay?
  (b) How much is he paid for $23\frac{1}{2}$ hours work?
  (c) How many hours does he work for £100 pay?

- Some employees are paid an hourly rate.
  In what other ways are employees paid?
  Discuss.

You can use the Unitary Method for calculations with any compound measure. Always make sure you write *the link* between the two quantities in the *correct way first*.

Question

The strength of a copper sulphate solution is 1.05 g per litre.
(a) How much copper sulphate is in 0.45 litres of this solution?
(b) What volume of the solution contains 0.25 g of copper sulphate?
  Give your answer in mℓ.

Answer

Rate: 1.05 g per litre links mass and volume.
(a) Known: volume 0.45ℓ *Wanted:* mass

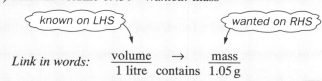

Link in words: $\dfrac{\text{volume}}{1 \text{ litre}} \rightarrow \dfrac{\text{mass}}{\text{contains } 1.05 \text{ g}}$

Multiply by 0.45: 0.45 ℓ contains 1.05 × 0.45
                = 0.4725 g
                = 0.47 g (to 2 dp)

(b) Known: mass 0.25 g *Wanted:* volume

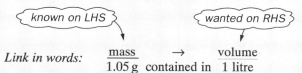

Link in words: $\dfrac{\text{mass}}{1.05 \text{ g}} \rightarrow \dfrac{\text{volume}}{\text{contained in } 1 \text{ litre}}$

Divide by 1.05, to change LHS to Unity: 1 g contained in $\dfrac{1}{1.05}$ litre

Multiply by 0.25: 0.25 g contained in $\dfrac{1}{1.05}$ × 0.25 litre

> 0.238095238 litre

Multiply by 1000, to change to mℓ

> 238.0952381 mℓ
= 238 mℓ (to nearest mℓ).

Summary

The Unitary Method can be used to solve problems with compound measures.
Take the following steps:
- Read the problem carefully.
  Sort out the facts:
  the rate,
  the value you know and the quantity you want.
- Look at the rate.
  Write the link it gives simply in words. *continued*

State any units clearly.
Remember, the order in 'your link' depends on the question:

LHS   RHS
'quantity you know' … 'quantity you want'.

- Look at the first value in your 'link'.
  If it isn't 1 (i.e., unity), you need to change it.
  Divide *both* amounts by the *same number* when you do this.
- Look at the 'value you know'.
  Change your 'unity value' to this.
  Multiply *both* parts by the *same number* when you do this.
- Check that your answer makes sense.

►*Exercise* P17.2

1 (a) Ceri puts an advert in this magazine. The advert is 14 words long. How much does it cost her?
   (b) Pete paid £8.84 to advertise his guitar for sale. How many words did Pete use in his advert?

> **MUSIC NEWS**
> Classified Ad-Rate
> 52p per word –
> minimum charge
> £6.24 (inc. VAT)

2 Ken estimates that the icicle hanging from the garage gutter is getting shorter by 1.8 cm every hour.
   At 2 pm it is 14 cm long.
   Calculate
   (a) what length it will be at 4 pm
   (b) at what time it was 23 cm long
   (c) by what time it will have melted away.

3 (a) Mr Hughes buys a 2.5 kg bag of Green Fertilizer.
       What area of the lawn will this cover?
   (b) Mrs Baxter's lawn is 140 m² in area.
       How much fertilizer does she need for it?
       How many 2.5 kg bags must she buy?
       How much fertilizer will be left over?

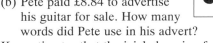

GREEN FERTILIZER
Ideal for luscious lawns
Apply: 30g per m²

4 A central heating boiler, which runs continuously, uses 5 litres of fuel every 2 hours.
   (a) At what rate, per hour, is the fuel used?
   (b) How much fuel is used in 24 hours?
   At 1 pm on Tuesday, the gauge showed that the tank contained 1012 litres of fuel.
   Calculate the number of litres of fuel
   (c) in the tank at 1 pm on the previous day
   (d) left in the tank at 1 pm on the following Saturday.

5 The price of printing advertising leaflets is £2.36 per hundred.
   (a) What is the price per leaflet?
   (b) How much does it cost to print 1500 leaflets?
   (c) Mr Gillam paid £15.34 for some leaflets.
       How many did he get?

6 (a) Sanjit bought 28 litres of unleaded petrol for £14.53.
       Find the cost of one litre of unleaded petrol, in pence correct to 1 decimal place.

At the same service station:
   (b) Sam bought 16 litres of unleaded petrol.
       How much did she pay?
   (c) Jill bought £25 worth of unleaded petrol.
       How much did she get?

7 Melanie has a Saturday job.
   Last week she was paid £9.36 for 4 hours work.
   (a) What is her rate of pay per hour?
   (b) Melanie expects to work for $5\frac{1}{2}$ hours next Saturday.
       How much should she be paid?
   (c) One Saturday last month Melanie was paid £15.21.
       How long did she work?

8 In a busy period, a multi-storey car park takes two hours to fill at the rate of 11 cars per minute.
   (a) How many cars can the car park take?
   Access is made more efficient and the car park can now fill at the rate of 12 cars per minute.
   (b) How long does it now take to fill?

9 A candle burns at a constant rate.
   It is 15 cm long at 7 pm.
   It is 13 cm long at 7.50 pm.
   (a) At what rate, per minute, is the candle burning?
   (b) At what rate, per hour, is the candle burning?
   (c) At what time is the candle 10 cm long?
   (d) How long is the candle at midnight?
   (e) At what time does the candle burn away?

10 A saline drip in a hospital releases 0.2 mℓ every 3 seconds.
    How long will it take to empty a 500 mℓ bag? ◄

Best buy

Standby Motors	
Premium Unleaded	52.9
★★★★	58.9
Diesel	53.9

Roundway Service Station	
★★★★	56.9
Premium Unleaded	50.9
Diesel	55.9

Midway Services	
Diesel	51.9
Premium Unleaded	51.9
★★★★	55.9

Southbound Garage	
Premium Unleaded	56.9
Diesel	57.9
★★★★	57.9

◯ *Discussion Exercise*

Compare the prices at the four petrol stations.
Which type of fuel is cheapest at each?
Where is ordinary ★★ petrol cheapest?
Where is unleaded petrol cheapest?
Where is diesel cheapest?
How did you find these answers?
Discuss.

Unit prices

Petrol prices are easy to compare.
They are all in *'pence per litre'*.
This shows how much is paid for each litre.
So the *smaller* the price per litre, the *less* you pay for the same amount.

> smaller price per litre → cheaper petrol.

'Pence per litre' is an example of a **unit price**.
A **unit price** gives the *price of 1 unit of something*.
The unit may be 1 item or 1 litre or 1 kilogram or 1 metre …

 ## Discussion Exercise

What sort of things are often priced
- per item
- per litre
- per kilogram
- per metre?
Look at the pictures for some ideas.
Give some examples of your own.
Discuss your group's ideas.

Other units are sometimes linked with prices. Give some examples. What sort of things are priced in those ways? Discuss.

Nowadays many things are sold pre-packed.
The price is for the amount or number of items in the pack.
But you can work out the unit price.

If the price of 2 litres of water is 68p,
the unit price is 34p per litre.

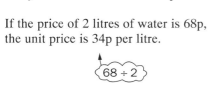

> (68 ÷ 2)

If the price of 5 oranges is 85p,
the unit price is 17p per orange.

> (85 ÷ 5)

And so on …

> **Unit price = price ÷ number of 'units'.**

Shops often sell different size packs of the same product.
The smallest size is usually the cheapest.

But it may not be the **best value for money**.
One way to compare prices is to look at the unit price of each pack.

> *smallest unit price → best value for money.*

Before you work out the unit price for each pack, check the prices and amounts.
Make sure:
- the prices are either *all in pence* or *all in £s*
- the amounts are *all in the same unit*
  (all g or all kg, all mℓ or all litres and so on …)
  Change any you need to first.
A question may tell you what kind of unit price to work out.
Make sure the prices and amounts you use give what you want.

Question

(a) Calculate the price per kg for each pack.
(b) Which size is the best buy? Why?

Answer

(a) Check units: *Work all in £s and all in kg.*
   Change units   99p = £0.99
                     400 g = 0.4 kg

   Unit price: price per kg = price ÷ number of kg
     400 g size: 0.99 ÷ 0.4 = £2.475 per kg
       2 kg size: 3.79 ÷ 2 = £1.895 per kg
     2.8 kg size: 5.39 ÷ 2.8 = £1.925 per kg.

(b) The 2 kg size is the best buy.
It costs £1.895 per kg.
This is the smallest price per kg for the three packs.

▶ Exercise **P17.3**

Calculate the unit price of these packs.

7

8

3.03 mℓ/p is larger than 2.96 mℓ/p.

So the 300 mℓ size gives more hand lotion for each penny spent.

This means that the 300mℓ size is better value for money.

Per £ or per penny

Another way to compare prices is to look at what you can buy with the same money.

For £1 I could get:

The more you get, the better the value for money.
You can work out what *£1 'buys'* in each case,
i.e., the **'amount' per £.**
For example,
if £4 buys 160 tea bags,
   £1 buys 160 ÷ 4 = 40 tea bags.

Or you can work out what
1 penny buys in each case.
i.e., the **'amount' per penny**.
For example,
if 50p buys 100 g of peanuts,
   1p buys 100 ÷ 50 = 2 g of peanuts.

To compare prices, you must work out

| **'amount' ÷ price** | for each 'pack'.

Remember:
The 'amounts' must be either *all numbers*
                    or *all in the same unit*.
The prices must be either *all in £s* or *all in pence*.
Change any first if you need to.

Summary

When you go shopping you want to find the best value for money.
Comparing prices can help you to save money.
You can compare prices in two ways.

● Compare 'unit prices'.
   Unit prices show how much you pay for the same 'amount'.
   This 'amount' may be 1 item, 1 kg, 1 ml, …
   The *smaller the unit price*, the *better the value for money*.

● Compare 'amounts' per £ or per penny.
   These show what the same money 'buys'.
   The more it buys, the better the value for money.
   Always make sure the units you use in each comparison are the same.
   Change any if you need to.

◄ *Exercise* **P17.4**

Compare 'value for money' for each product.
Find out which is the 'best buy'.
Show all your working. Explain your answer.

1 Coffee
  200 g   £2.93
  300 g   £4.25
  500 g   £7.09

2 Vegetable oil
  500 ml   42p
  1 ℓ 69p
  2 ℓ 1.29p

3 Oranges
  15p   each
  6 for   99p
  5 for   89p
  12 for   £2.49

4 Broccoli spears
  250 g   65p
  450 g   99p
  500 g   £1.12

5 Tea bags
  40 (125 g)   37p
  80 (250 g)   67p
  160 (500 g)   £1.19
  240 (750 g)   £1.79

6 Tomato soup
  290 g tin   34p
  405 g tin   41p
  425 g tin   58p

7 Salad cream
  200 g   43p
  285 g   45p
  425 g   82p

8 New potatoes
  1 lb   42p
  1.5 lb   62p
  2 lb   83p
  3 lb   £1.25

9 Washing powder
  E3 (1.2 kg) £1.79
  E10 (4 kg) £4.99

10 Crisps
  30 g bag   21p
  75 g bag   52p
  10 bags,
  each 28 g   £1.72
  5 bags,
  each 40 g   £1.26

Question

The hand lotion Terry uses is sold in these two sizes.
Which size is the better value for money?
Explain your answer.

Answer

Choose units: Work all in mℓ and all in pence.
Change units: £1.69 = 169 p
Unit price:
Millilitres per penny = number of mℓ ÷ number of pence
300 mℓ size: 300 ÷ 99 = 3.03 mℓ/p (to 2 dp)
500 mℓ size: 500 ÷ 169 = 2.96 mℓ/p (to 2 dp)

Density

Another well known example of a compound measure is **density**.
Density compares *mass* and *volume*.

$$\text{density} = \frac{\text{mass}}{\text{volume}}$$

The density of a substance is a measure of its **mass per unit volume**.

1 cubic centimetre of lead has a mass of 11.3 grams. We say the density of lead is 11.3 grams per cubic centimetre or 11.3 g/cm³.

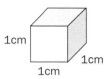

Any unit of 'mass per unit of volume' is a unit of density.
The most common units of density are:

    grams per cubic centimetre (g/cm³) and
    kilograms per cubic metre (kg/m³).

To find the density of a substance, use the formula

$$\text{density} = \frac{\text{mass}}{\text{volume}}$$

The unit of density you get from the formula depends on the unit of mass and volume you use.

$$\frac{\text{g}}{\text{cm}^3} \rightarrow \text{g/cm}^3 \qquad \frac{\text{kg}}{\text{m}^3} \rightarrow \text{kg/cm}^3$$

Always check that you have the units you want.
Change any first if you need to.

Memo

    1kg = 1000g

To change kg to g, multiply by 1000.
To change g to kg, divide by 1000.

    1m³ = 1 000 000 cm³

To change m³ to cm³, multiply by 1 000 000.
To change cm³ to m³, divide by 1 000 000.

Question

A pipe is made of 1600 cm³ of clay.
Its mass is 3.45 kg.
Find the density of the clay:
(a) in g/cm³
(b) in kg/m³.
Give each answer correct to 3 significant figures

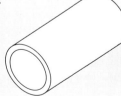

Answer

(a) *For density in g/cm³, you want:*
mass in g and volume in cm³.
mass: 3.45 kg = 3.45 × 1000 = 3450 g

volume: 1600 cm³

$$\text{Density} = \frac{\text{mass}}{\text{volume}} = \frac{3450 \text{ g}}{1600 \text{ cm}^3} \quad \text{gives g/cm}^3$$

$$= 2.15625 \text{ g/cm}^3$$
$$= 2.16 \text{ g/cm}^3 \text{ (to 3 sf)}$$

(b) *For density in kg/m³, you want:*
mass in kg and volume in m³.
mass: 3.45 kg
volume: 1600 cm³ = 1600 ÷ 1 000 000 = 0.0016 m³

$$\text{Density} = \frac{\text{mass}}{\text{volume}} = \frac{3.45 \text{ kg}}{0.016 \text{m}^3} \quad \text{gives kg/m}^3$$

$$= 2156.25 \text{ kg/m}^3$$
$$= 2160 \text{ kg/m}^3 \text{ (to 3 sf)}$$

The formula linking density, mass and volume can be written in three ways.

To find density, use … $\text{density} = \dfrac{\text{mass}}{\text{volume}}$

To find mass, use … $\text{mass} = \text{density} \times \text{volume}$

To find volume, use … $\text{volume} = \dfrac{\text{mass}}{\text{density}}$

Remember:
Make sure you use 'matching units' in each formula.

Question

A wood carving has a mass of 2.15 kg. It is made out of wood with density 0.57 g/cm³. What is its volume, to the nearest cubic centimetre?

Answer

Given density in g/cm³, you need:
mass in g to get volume in cm³.
mass: 2.15 kg = 2.15 × 1000 = 2150 g

$$\text{volume} = \frac{\text{mass}}{\text{density}} = \frac{2150}{0.57}$$

$$= 3771.929825 \text{ (calculator)}$$
$$= 3772 \text{ cm}^3 \text{ (to the nearest cm}^3\text{)}.$$

Volumes of liquids are usually given in liquid measures, such as mℓ and litres. In density calculations, you need to change them to cm³ or m³.
    1 mℓ = 1 cm³
    1 litre = 1000 cm³

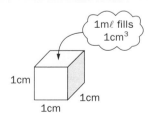

Question

The oil in this can has a density of 0.72 g/cm³.
A full can holds 1.5 litres.
What is the mass of this amount of oil?

continued

Answer

Given density in g/cm³, you need:
volume in cm³ to get mass in g.
Volume of oil: 1.5 litres = 1.5 × 1000
= 1500 cm³.

mass = density × volume
= 0.72 × 1500
= 1080 g

The oil in the can has a mass of 1080 g.

► *Exercise* P17.5

1 A 40 cm³ piece of iron has a mass of 320 g.
What is the density of iron?

2 The mass of an 800 cm³ piece of ice is 736 g.
Find the density of the ice.

3 A piece of balsa wood weighs 7 g.
Its volume is 35 cm³. What is its density?

4 The density of cork is 0.25 g/cm³.
A wine bottle cork has a mass of 3 g.
What is the volume of the cork?

5 An aluminium casting weighs 936 g.
Aluminium has a density of 2.6 g/cm³.
What is the volume of the casting?

6 The density of mercury is 13.6 g/cm³.
What is the weight of 5 mℓ of mercury?

7 Petrol has a density of 0.8 g/cm³.
What is the mass (in kg) of 45 litres of petrol?

8 The density of steel is 7.5 g/cm³ and the density of brass is 8.5 g/cm³.
A piece of steel has a mass of 850 g.
A piece of brass has a mass of 860 g.
Which piece of metal has the larger volume?

9 Water has a density of 1 g/cm³.
What is the mass of 5 ℓ of water?

10 Air has a density of 1.3 kg/m³.
A room, in the shape of a cuboid,
measures 4.5 m by 3.5 m by 3 m.
What is the mass of the air in the room?

11 The density of copper is 9 g/cm³.
The density of tin is 7.3 g/cm³.
A piece of copper and a piece of tin, each of
mass 150 grams, are melted together to form an alloy.
What is:
(a) the volume of the copper in the alloy
(b) the volume of the tin in the alloy
(c) the total volume of the alloy
(d) the total mass of the alloy
(e) the density of the alloy?

12 1.5 litres of turpentine (density 0.86 g/cm³) is mixed with
500 ml of oil (density 0.7 g/cm³) to form a mixture.
What is the density of the mixture?

Examination Questions

1

A family travelled by car from Peterborough to Exeter, a distance of 400 kilometres. For every 10 kilometres travelled, the car used 1 litre of petrol.
(a) Calculate the number of litres of petrol used on the journey.
(b) The petrol cost 45.8 pence per litre.
Calculate the cost of petrol for the journey.
(c) Calculate the cost in pence, of petrol for one kilometre travelled on this journey.

(MEG, 1991)

2 While they are sleeping, adults (male or female) use 1 calorie per hour for each kilogram that they weigh.
(a) How many calories does a woman weighing 55 kilograms use in sleeping 8 hours?
(b)

Activity	Calories used per hour
Sitting	90
Standing	100
Light work	240
Walking quickly	300
Heavy work	400

Complete the table for the total number of calories expended during 24 hours by the woman weighing 55 kilograms.

Activity	Total hours	Calories
Sleep	8	
Sitting		
Standing	3	
Light work		720
Walking quickly	3	
Heavy work		400
TOTAL	24	

(NISEAC, 1991)

3 A painter uses 3 tins of paint per day.
Each tin costs £2.90.
The painter works a five-day week.
(a) Find the total cost of the paint he uses each week.
(b) For one week there is a special offer on paint.

'5 tins for the price of 4!'

Calculate how many tins of paint the painter will actually have to pay for when he buys enough paint to last him for one working week using the special offer.

(NEAB, 1990)

4 A 375 gram packet of Nicicles costs £1.08.
(a) Calculate the cost per gram of Nicicles in this packet.
(b) At the same rate, what would a 500 gram packet of Nicicles cost?

(NEAB, 1991)

5 Shampoo is sold in three sizes.
(a) Work out the cost of 50 mℓ of shampoo for
(i) the standard size
(ii) the large size
(iii) the family size.
(b) Which size gives the best value for money?

standard size: 150ml 87p
large size: 250ml £1.30
family size: 400ml £1.76

(MEG, 1993)

6

FAST HIRE CAR RENTALS
We provide a range of vehicles for your use
Lorries (3 ton) ..... £48.95 per day
Vans (30 cwt) ...... £30.05 per day
Cars .... £28.55 per day

READY SELF-DRIVE
Transits   25p per mile
Vans   20p per mile
Cars   17p per mile
plus an additional charge of £10.50

Gary needs to hire a car for two days to make a journey of 275 miles. The charges made by two firms for hiring cars are shown above.
Calculate the cost for the two firms.
(a) Fast Hire
(b) Ready Self-Drive

(NEAB, 1988)

7   Kamal is filling the tank from a pipe which supplies water at the rate of 1.25 litres per second.
How long will it take him to fill the tank?
Give your answer to the nearest minute.

(NEAB, 1988)

8   The following information comes from the handbook in Mrs Smith's Metro City.

Economy – Petrol	In towns	At constant 56 mph	At constant 75 mph
Miles per gallon	45.7	59.7	40.2

Mrs Smith is going to drive from Warwick to Truro, a distance of 267 miles.
The journey is made up of about 20 miles in towns, about 130 miles on roads where she expects to drive at speeds between 50 and 60 mph, and the rest on a motorway at about 70 mph.
Estimate how much petrol she may expect to use according to the handbook.
Show clearly how you arrive at your answer.

(MEG, 1990)

9

A manufacturer sells weed killer in two different packs, as shown in the diagrams above.
(a) (i) In the Bargain Pack, how many grams of weed killer do you get for 1p?
   (ii) In the Value Pack, how many grams of weed killer do you get for 1p?
(b) Which of the two packs is the better value for money?

(MEG, 1991)

▶ **P18**
Inequalities

This unit will help you to:

■ use inequality symbols > and < to compare numbers and quantities

■ use a number line to compare the sizes of numbers

■ understand basic inequations and use the symbols >, <, ≥ and ≤

■ solve simple inequations

■ show the solutions of simple inequations on a number line.

Comparing quantities

Quantities are items with numerical values.
We often make statements that compare quantities.

Here are some examples:

Each statement compares *two quantities*.
It shows that they are *not equal*.
It tells you that one is *greater than* or *less than* the other.
We call statements like these **inequalities**.

💬 *Discussion Exercise*

1   Study the examples on the previous page and give another inequality about:
   (a) the price of the skirt and jeans
   (b) the speed of Tim's typing and shorthand
   (c) the temperature in the classroom and hall.

2   (a)   (b)   (c)

 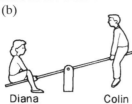 

Bob Ann   Diana   Colin   Eric Florence

   What do these pictures show you about:
   (a) the heights of Ann and Bob
   (b) the weights of Colin and Diana
   (c) the ages of Eric and Florence?
   Give two inequalities for each picture.

3   Make a list of some other phrases we use to show inequalities.
   Describe some situations in which we might use them. 💬

▶ *Exercise* P18.1

1   (a) Is 5 less than 9?   (e) Is 38 greater than 23?
   (b) Is 3 greater than 7?   (f) Is 47 less than 26?
   (c) Is 14 greater than 41? (g) Is 125 less than 800?
   (d) Is 12 less than 21?   (h) Is 299 greater than 300?

2   (a) Is $\frac{1}{2}$ greater than $\frac{1}{4}$?   (e) Is 0.9 greater than 0.7?
   (b) Is $\frac{1}{5}$ less than $\frac{3}{5}$?   (f) Is 0.3 less than 0.003?
   (c) Is $3\frac{1}{2}$ less than 3?   (g) Is 1.999 greater than 2?
   (d) Is $1\frac{2}{3}$ greater than $2\frac{1}{3}$? (h) Is 4 less than 4.0001?

3   (a) Is £1 greater than 50p?
   (b) Is 1 m less than 10 cm?
   (c) Is 1 pint less than 1mℓ?
   (d) Is 1 hour greater than 30 s?
   (e) Is 1 kg less than 1 lb?
   (f) Is 1 litre greater than 75 cℓ?
   (g) Is 1 km greater than 1 mile?
   (h) Is 1 tonne less than 5 kg?

Symbols > and <

You use **=** to show 'equal values'.
You use **>** and **<** to show inequalities.
They show how the values compare in sizes.

   > means **'is greater than'**
      or **'is more than'**

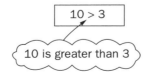

   < means **'is smaller than'**
      or **'is less than'**.

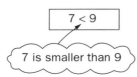

The symbol always *'points to' the smaller number.*

   | larger > smaller | | smaller < larger |

Its *'larger end'* is at the *larger* value.
Its *'smaller end'* is at the *smaller* value.

▶ *Exercise* P18.2

1   Give a sentence for each inequality for example, 1< 3 means 1 is less than 3.
   (a) 7 > 4   (c) $\frac{1}{8} < \frac{5}{8}$ (e) 0.1 < 0.7
   (b) 2 < 9   (d) $\frac{1}{3} > \frac{1}{10}$ (f) 6.0001 > 6

2   Copy each pair of numbers in the given order.
   Put the correct symbol (> or <) between them.
   (a) 3   8   (e) $\frac{1}{6}$ $\frac{5}{6}$ (i) 0.7   0.6
   (b) 7   15   (f) $\frac{1}{5}$ $\frac{1}{20}$ (j) 0.5   0.005
   (c) 5   9   (g) $1\frac{1}{2}$ 2   (k) 9.001 9
   (d) 27 13   (h) 3 $2\frac{3}{4}$ (l) 2.99 3 ◀

Comparing two numbers gives you **two inequalities**.
To compare 1 and 4,
you can say …

   | 1 is less than 4 | and | 4 is greater than 1 |

Both of these statements are true.

You can write … | 1 < 4 | and | 4 > 1 |

See how the inequality has *'turned round'* …

   same numbers, 'reverse order', symbol 'turned round'

You can give any inequality in the *'reverse order'* in this way …

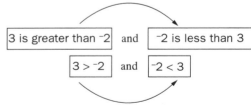

| 3 is greater than ⁻2 | and | ⁻2 is less than 3 |
| 3 > ⁻2 | and | ⁻2 < 3 |

▶ *Exercise* P18.3

1   Rewrite each inequality in another way.
   Check that it is still true.
   (a) 7 < 12   (c) $\frac{1}{4} > \frac{1}{6}$ (e) 1.8 > 0.7
   (b) 3 > 0   (d) $\frac{5}{12} < \frac{11}{12}$ (f) 3.1 < 3.8

2   Write two inequalities with each pair of numbers.
   (a) 5, 2   (c) $\frac{1}{2}, \frac{1}{6}$ (e) 0.9, 0.125
   (b) 0, 4   (d) $\frac{3}{8}, \frac{5}{8}$ (f) 1.4, 1.3

ACTIVITY

Whole number pairs

Try this on your own or take turns with another student

You need these two symbol cards …

and two sets of number cards
(each with numbers 0–9 on them).

Shuffle all the number cards together.
Turn over two cards …
Place the correct symbol card
between them …
Write down the statement you get.
Use the three cards to make
another correct statement …
Record this.

Repeat this until you have used up all the number cards.
You get a point for each correct statement you have made.

*Keep the cards you have used.
You will need them again.*

On a number line

Here is a simple **number line**:

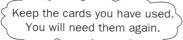

Only a few integers are marked on it.
But you know that it can go on in both directions.

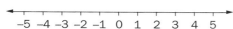

Each point on the line represents a number.

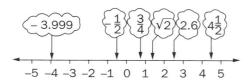

We can mark the positions of positive and negative numbers,
integers, decimals, fractions, mixed numbers, …

Discussion Exercise

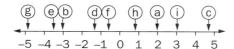

What numbers do the lettered arrows point to?
Choose from:

$\frac{7}{8}$, -3, 2, $4\frac{3}{4}$, -3.5
3.001, -4.99, $-\frac{2}{3}$, -1.3

Write the numbers in order of size, smallest first.
How did you decide on the order?

The numbers on the line are **in order of size**.

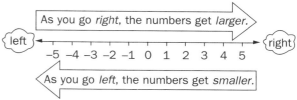

This helps you to compare them.

Look at -2 and 1 on this line.

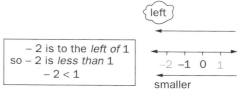

On this line, any number *to the left of* **1**
is less than **1**.

The number can be an integer, a decimal, a fraction, …
Here are some examples:

| $0 < 1$ | $-5 < 1$ | $\frac{1}{2} < 1$ |

| $0.999 < 1$ | $-2.7 < 1$ |

Discussion Exercise

Don't forget negative values.

Name some integers less than 1.
Name some decimals less than 1.
Name some common fractions less than 1.
Name some mixed numbers less than 1.

Look again at -2 and 1 on the line.

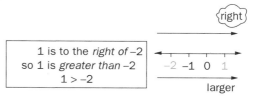

On this line,
any number *to the right of* -2
is greater than -2.

Discussion Exercise

Give some integers greater than -2.
Give some decimals greater than -2.
Give some common fractions greater than -2.
Give some mixed numbers greater than -2.
Write an inequality to show each answer.

Summary

An inequality is a statement that one quantity is greater than
or less than another.

> means 'is greater than'
< means 'is less than'.

continued

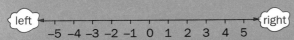

On this number line …

left ◄——————————————► right
    –5 –4 –3 –2 –1 0 1 2 3 4 5

- any number to the *left* of another number is less *than* that number
- any number to the *right* of another number is *greater than* that number.

Discussion Exercise

1 Give an integer less than:
   (a) 5   (b) – 3   (c) 0
   Write an inequality for each answer.
2 Give an integer greater than:
   (a) 0   (b) 2   (c) – 4
   Write an inequality for each answer.
3 Give a decimal less than:
   (a) 1   (b) 4   (c) – 2
   Write an inequality for each answer.
4 Give a decimal greater than:
   (a) 0   (b) 1   (c) – 1
   Write an inequality for each answer.
5 Replace each ? by a number to make a correct inequality.
   (a) $9 > ?$ (e) $12 < ?$ (i) $– 4 > ?$
   (b) $? < 4$ (f) $? > 0$ (j) $? > – 1$
   (c) $7 < ?$ (g) $– 3 < ?$ (k) $? < 2$
   (d) $? < 11$ (h) $0 > ?$ (l) $– 5 < ?$

ACTIVITY

Integer pairs

For one or two students

You need these two symbol cards …
and two sets of number cards:

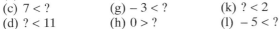

one with numbers 0–9 as before

the other with numbers 0, – 1, – 2, – 3, …, – 9.

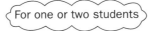
in 'Whole on p381 number pairs'

Compare number pairs as before.
But this time you have integers from – 9 to 9 to use.
Use a number line if it helps.

Keep these cards for later.

► Exercise P18.4

1 Which is smaller?
   (a) 3 or 6   (d) 0 or – 5   (g) – 8 or 7
   (b) 2 or – 3   (e) – 5 or – 2   (h) 0 or – 9
   (c) – 4 or 3   (f) 10 or 0   (i) – 7 or – 12
2 Which is larger?
   (a) 1 or 5   (d) – 4 or 0   (g) 8 or – 9
   (b) – 2 or 1   (e) – 3 or – 4   (h) – 7 or 0
   (c) 5 or – 1   (f) 0 or 9   (i) – 6 or –10

3 (a) Is 2 greater than – 6?   (d) Is – 19 greater than – 24?
   (b) Is – 3 less than 5?   (e) Is – 23 greater than 0?
   (c) Is – 9 less than – 10?   (f) Is 2 less than – 11?
4 Copy each pair of numbers in the given order.
   Place the correct symbol (> or <) between them.
   (a) – 1   1   (c) – 5   0   (e) – 1   – 4
   (b) 3   – 2   (d) 7   – 8   (f) – 10   – 3

ACTIVITY

Find the number

Try this quiz with another student. Take turns.

One person thinks of a number …

An integer between –50 and 50

… and says 'where it is on the number line'.

The other has to 'find the number'.

Is it less than 0?

The only questions allowed are …

Is it greater than…?   Is it less than…?   Is it …?

The only answers allowed are …

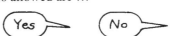
Yes   No

Don't just guess.
Use each 'try' to 'improve' the next one.
Keep a record of your 'tries' on a number line.

Score 1 point for each 'try' you need.
The winner at the end of the quiz is the person with the smaller score.

Inequations

Here are two mathematical statements:

$n > 5$ $x < 1$

n is any number greater than 5 x is any number less than 1

Each is an **inequality** and contains a **variable** i.e. a letter standing for various numbers.

We call this kind of inequality, an **inequation**.

We also use the symbols ≥ and ≤ in inequations.

≥ means 'is *greater than or equal to*'

≤ means 'is *less than or equal to*'

Here are some examples:

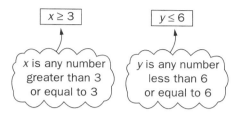

Exercise P18.5

1 Give these statements in words.
(a) $x < 4$ (c) $t \le -1$ (e) $a \le 0$ (g) $m \ge -5$
(b) $n \ge 9$ (d) $p > 0$ (f) $b > -3$ (h) $r < -2$
2 Write these statements in symbols.
(a) x is less than or equal to 8
(b) n is greater than -4
(c) m is less than 3
(d) y is greater than or equal to -2.

Making inequations

You often meet inequations in everyday life.
You can write them as mathematical statements too.

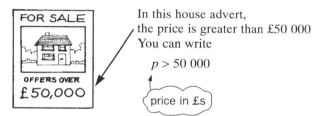

In this house advert,
the price is greater than £50 000
You can write

$$p > 50\,000$$

In this headline
the children's ages are less than 5.
You can write

$$a < 5$$

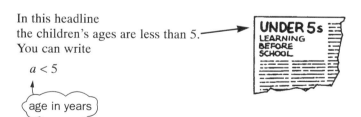

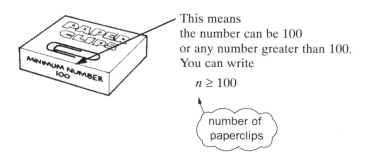

This means
the number can be 100
or any number greater than 100.
You can write

$$n \ge 100$$

This means
the speed can be 70 mph
or any speed less than 70 mph.
You can write

$$s \le 70$$

Discussion Exercise

Give an inequation for each example below.

The amount raised
is £c.

An acute angle
measures $d°$.

The price of
Ed's bike is £e.

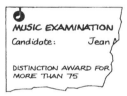

Jean gets a distinction
with m marks.

Terry has i items in
his shopping basket.

Sadie scores b points
in her first break.

Rachel is y years
old and can vote.

Jeff's lunch at 1 pm
costs £p.

Ann followed the instructions.
She cooked the turkey
h hours after defrosting it.

David's return fare
was £f with
USA TRAVEL.

Investigation

Find some other situations that give inequations.
Look for them in newspapers, magazines, books, …
or think of some yourself.
Give at least 10 different ones.

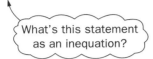
What's this statement
as an inequation?

Solving simple inequations

Testing values

Here is a simple inequation …　$\boxed{n > 3}$
The variable in it is n.

Putting 7 instead of n in $n > 3$
　　　　　gives $7 > 3$　That's true!

We say:　'7 **satisfies** $n > 3$
　　or '7 is a **solution** of $n > 3$'

Putting 1 instead of n in $n > 3$
　　　　　gives $1 > 3$.　Not true!

We say: '1 does *not satisfy* $n > 3$'
　　or '1 is *not a solution* of $n > 3$'.

▶ *Exercise* **P18.6**

1　Is $n < 5$ true when you replace n by
　(a) 7　　(b) 0　　(c) 1　　(d) -2　　(e) 5?
2　Which of these values satisfy $v > -4$?
　(a) 6　　(b) -1　　(c) -4　　(d) 0　　(e) -9
3　Which of these numbers are solutions to $x < 0$?
　(a) 2　　(b) -2　　(c) 0　　(d) 6　　(e) -5
4　Is $y \geq 0$ true when you replace y by
　(a) 3　　(b) 0　　(c) -4　　(d) -1　　(e) 2?
5　Which of these values satisfy $t \leq -1$?
　(a) -3　　(b) 0　　(c) 4　　(d) -6　　(e) -1
6　Which of these numbers are solutions to $m \geq 2$?
　(a) 2　　(b) 6　　(c) -2　　(d) 1　　(e) 0 ◀

ACTIVITY

Try this on your own
or take turns
with another student.

Is it a solution?
You need a set of inequation cards like these.

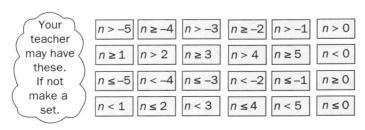

Your
teacher
may have
these.
If not
make a
set.

$n > -5$	$n \geq -4$	$n > -3$	$n \geq -2$	$n > -1$	$n > 0$
$n \geq 1$	$n > 2$	$n \geq 3$	$n > 4$	$n \geq 5$	$n < 0$
$n \leq -5$	$n < -4$	$n \leq -3$	$n < -2$	$n \leq -1$	$n \geq 0$
$n < 1$	$n \leq 2$	$n < 3$	$n \leq 4$	$n < 5$	$n \leq 0$

You also need your number cards 0–9
　　and 0–$^{-}9$　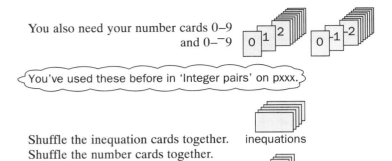

You've used these before in 'Integer pairs' on pxxx.

Shuffle the inequation cards together.　inequations
Shuffle the number cards together.
Place each pack face down.
　　　　　　　　　　　　　　numbers

Turn over an inequation　　　　　　　$\boxed{n < 5}$
card …
　　　　　　　　　inequations

and a number card …　　　　　$\boxed{-6}$　
　　　　　　　　　numbers

Is it a
solution?

If the number is a solution of the inequation …
　　- take both cards and score a point.
If it isn't …
　　- return each card to the bottom of its pack.

Turn pairs of cards as many times as you can.
Record each inequation and solution you get.

Finding solutions

Usually there are *many* numbers that *make an inequation true*.
You may be asked to give *some* of them. Or you may have to
show where they lie on a **number line graph**.

This forecast does not
give an actual
temperature. It tells you
a **range of values** the
temperature can be.
The inequation for this
is:

Temperatures
below 3°C

　$t < 3$

temperature
in °C

If t is an *integer*,
then any integer less than 3 solves the inequation.
Possible values of t are:

　2, 1, 0, -1, -2, …

The dots … show that the list goes on forever.

If t is *any kind of number*,
then you *cannot 'list'* all the possible values of t.
But you can show them on a number line graph.

This number line graph shows $t < 3$.

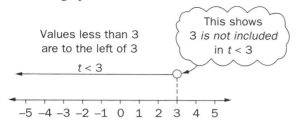

To draw this graph of $t < 3$, take these steps:
- Draw a number line.
- Find 3, the 'stated number' on the line.
  3 is *not included* in $t < 3$. So use ◯ to mark it.
- Draw a line from the ◯ over all the values included in $t < 3$.
  These values are to the left of 3.
- Use an arrowhead to show that the values go on an on … to the left.

You can give the solutions to other inequations in these ways.

▶ *Exercise* P18.7

1 Write down three possible integer values for n for each of these inequations.
    (a) $n > 0$ (b) $n < 4$ (c) $n < -3$ (d) $n > -1$

2 Illustrate the inequations in question **1** on separate number line graphs.

Use a number line like this …

Here is another temperature example.
The inequation is:

$t > 5$

If t is an *integer*,
then possible solutions of $t > 5$ are: 6, 7, 8, 9, 10, …

If t is *any kind of number,*
then possible solutions shown on this number line graph:

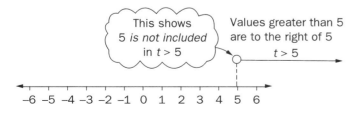

When the inequality is $\leq$ or $\geq$, the 'stated number' is *included* in the solution. Don't forget it.

Here are some more temperature examples.

In this example, the inequation is:

$t \leq 0$

If t is an *integer*,
then possible solutions of $t \leq 0$ are: 0, -1, -2, -3, …

If t is *any kind of number*
the possible solutions of $t \leq 0$ are shown on this number line graph:

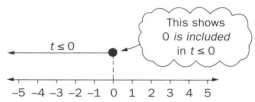

Look carefully at this number line graph of $t \leq 0$.
The end-point is at 0 (zero).
0 is included in $t \leq 0$. So it is marked with a ●.
Values less than 0 are to the left of 0.

In this example, the inequation is:

$t \geq -2$

If t is an *integer*
then possible solutions of $t \geq {}^-2$ are:
-2, -1, 0, 1, 2, …

If t is *any kind of number*
then possible solutions of $t \geq {}^-2$ are shown on this number line graph:

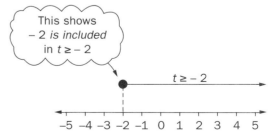

▶ *Exercise* P18.8

1 Give three possible integer values for n for each of these inequations.
    (a) $n \geq 2$ (b) $n \leq 5$ (c) $n \leq -2$ (d) $n \geq -5$

2 Show the inequations in question **1** on separate number line graphs.

3 In 'Making inequations' on page 383 you are given inequations for variables *p*, *a*, *n* and *s*.
You also wrote inequations for variables *c*, *d*, *e*, *m*, *i*, *b*, *y*, *p*, *h* and *f*.
Give three possible whole number values for each of these variables in these inequations.

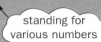

Summary

An inequation is a mathematical statement.

It has …
- an inequality symbol, < > ≤ ≥

and
- a variable.

standing for various numbers

To solve inequations you find numbers that you can put instead of the variables to give true statements.

usually shown by letters

We say these numbers **'satisfy'** the inequations. Each number is a **solution** of the inequation.
A **range of values** usually solves an inequation, not just one. You can always show these values on a number line graph. When they are integers, you can list some or all of them.
To **show the solutions on a number line graph:**
- Mark the 'stated number(s)' first.
  Use ○ when you have > or < (to show the *'number' is not included*).
  Use ● when you have ≥ or ≤ (to show the *'number' is included*).
- Draw a line from the ○ or ●
  - to the right for > or ≥ (to show 'greater than')
  - to the left for < or ≤ (to show 'less than')
- Use an arrowhead ← → on the line to show where values go on forever.

You can choose *any letter* for a variable.
But we often use *x* in examples in mathematics as in the next exercise.

► Exercise P18.9

1 Show each of the following inequalities on a separate number line graph.
Use a number line like this …

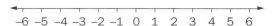

(a) $x > -1$ (e) $x > 1$ (h) $x \geq -3$
(b) $x \leq 2$ (f) $x \geq 3$ (i) $x \leq -4$
(c) $x < -4$ (g) $x < 1$ (j) $x < 0$
(d) $x \geq 0$

---

2 Give three possible integer values for *x* for each inequation in question **1**.

3 Use symbols to write the inequalities shown on these number line graphs.

(a)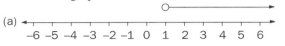

(b)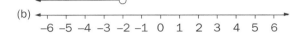

(c)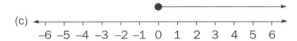

(d)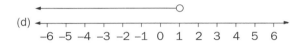

(e)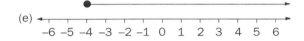

(f)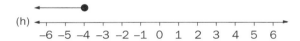

(g)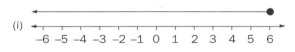

(h)

(i)

(j)

Numbers in order

You can use inequality symbols to show several numbers **in order of size**.
Look at the green numbers on this line:

They are in order, smallest first: $-1 \quad 2 \quad 4$
To show this you can write: $-1 < 2 < 4$

− 1 is less than 2   *2 is less than 4*

You can also see on the line:

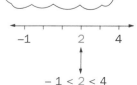

and in the inequality: $-1 < 2 < 4$

that 2 is between − 1 and 4.

Exercise P18.10

Place each set of numbers in order, smallest first.
Write them as an inequality like this:

```
... < ... < ...
```

and in a sentence like this:

```
... is between ... and ...
```

1 4, 1, 2	**5** − 1, − 3, 0	**8** − 10, − 1, − 100
2 5, 3, 0	**6** − 5, − 2, − 4	**9** 0, 50, − 50
3 0, − 1, 2	**7** 1, 100, 10	**10** − 10, − 50, 0
4 1, 4, − 2		

Ranges of values

x- and *y*- axes are number lines.
Often they show different **ranges of values**.

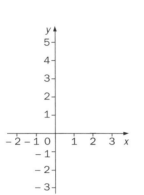

On this *x*-axis,
the numbers go from − 2 to 3.
For this range of values of *x*, you can
write this inequation ...

$$-2 \le x \le 3$$

This says that the possible values of *x* are:
$x = {}^-2$
or *x* is between $^-2$ and 3 ← greater than − 2 but less than 3
or $x = 3$
are the possible values of *x*.

Discussion Exercise

1 Which of these points could you plot on the *x*-axis above?
    (2,0),   (4,0),   (0,0),   (− 3,0),   (− 2,0),
    $(1\frac{1}{2},0)$,   (− 2.5, 0), $(3\frac{1}{4},0)$,   (0.75, 0),   (2.5,0)
    What is 'wrong' with each of the others?
2 Look at the numbers on the *y*-axis on the diagram above.
    They go from − 3 to 5.
    Give an inequation for this range of values of *y*.
3 Which of these points can be plotted on the *y*-axis above?
    Say Yes or No for each point.
    Explain each choice.
        (0,4),   (0,7),   (0,− 5),   (0,− 1),   (0,0),
        (0,6.5), $(0,\frac{1}{2})$,   (0,− 2.75), $(0,− 3\frac{1}{2})$,   (0,1.5)
4 Give inequations to show the ranges of values of *x* and *y* on these axes.
    (a)
    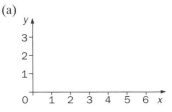

(b)
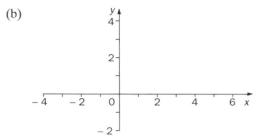

5 Draw *x*-and *y*-axes on a grid.
    Number them with $0 \le x \le 4$
                and $-1 \le y \le 6$.

You can show **ranges of other values** in the same way.

Judo Weight categories	
Men	**Women**
under 60kg	under 48kg
under 65kg	under 52kg
under 71kg	under 56kg
under 78kg	under 61kg
under 86kg	under 66kg
under 95kg	under 72kg
95kg and over	72kg and over

Ann is her Judo Club's champion in the Women's Under 56 kg category.
This means her weight *a* kg can be 52 kg but it must be *under* 56 kg.
For this range of values of *a*, you can use this inequation ...

$$52 \le a < 56$$

This says that the possible values of *a* are:
$a = 52$
or *a* between 52 and 56 ← greater than 52 but less than 56

Discussion Exercise

1 Brenda is the Judo Club's Under 72 kg champion.
    Her weight is *b* kg.
    Give an inequation for the possible values of *b*.
2 Use inequations to give the Men's Judo weight categories.
    Let *w* kg be the weight.
    Your table starts like this ...

Men (*w* kg)
w < 60

3 Use inequations to give the Women's Judo Weight categories.

Exercise P18.11

1 *n* people stayed at this Country Cottage. Write an inequation to show possible values of *n*.

SELF-CATERING
COUNTRY COTTAGE
SLEEPS 2-6 PEOPLE

2 An obtuse angle is between 90° and 180°.
A reflex angle is between 180° and 360°.
An angle of $d°$ is obtuse.
An angle of $r°$ is reflex.
Write down inequations to show the
ranges of values of d and r.

3 Tricia keeps her fridge at
the right temperature of
$t°$C. Give an inequality
statement to show this.

EXPERTS NOW AGREE THAT YOU SHOULD KEEP YOUR FRIDGE AT A TEMPERATURE BETWEEN 5°C AND 0°C

4

Letter Post

weight not over	First Class	Second Class
60g	25p	19p
100g	38p	29p
150g	47p	36p
200g	57p	43p
250g	67p	52p
300g	77p	61p
350g	88p	70p
400g	£1.00	79p
450g	£1.13	89p

This means more than 100g but less than or equal to 150g

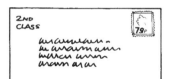

This letter weighs w grams.   This letter weighs g grams.
Write inequations to show the ranges of values for w and g.

5 For the Council Tax
each property is placed
in one of these eight
Value Bands, A–H.

Use inequations to show
these bands. Let £v be the
property value.

PROPERTY VALUE

A	up to £40,000
B	over £40,000 up to £52,000
C	over £52,000 up to £68,000
D	over £68,000 up to £88,000
E	over £88,000 up to £120,000
F	over £120,000 up to £160,000
G	over £160,000 up to £320,000
H	over £320,000

6 Mrs Clark was a
basic rate tax
payer in 1992–93.
Her taxable
income was £I.
Write an inequation to show her possible income.

Rates of pay on taxable income 1992-93

Lower rate : 20% on the first £2000
Basic rate : 25% on the next £21 700
Higher rate : 40% on income over £23 700

◉ *Investigation*

Find some other examples that give inequations like these.
Look at the different ways the ranges of values are described.
See what phrases are used …

(not over)   (between)   (from … to …)

What clues do they give to the inequality symbols to use? ◉

You can show these ranges of values on number line graphs.
In each case you have two 'stated numbers' to mark first.
Then you draw a line (or lines) to show the required ranges.

Question   Airmail

Weight (grammes) up to and including	Letters Europe £	
10g		-
20g	EC	0.25
	Non EC	0.30
40g		0.42
60g		0.54
80g		0.66
100g		0.78
120g		0.90
140g		1.02
160g		1.14

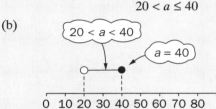

(postage)

par avion

This airmail letter
weighs a grams.

(a) Write an inequation to show the range of values of a.
(b) Illustrate this inequation on the number line below.
(c) The letter weighs a whole number of grams.
List all the possible values of a.

Answer

(a) a is more than 20 g
but a is less than or equal to 40 g

This gives:

$$20 < a \le 40$$

(b)

($20 < a < 40$)   ($a = 40$)

0 10 20 30 40 50 60 70 80

(c)   21, 22, 23, 24, 25, 26, 27, 28, 29, 30,
31, 32, 33, 34, 35, 36, 37, 38, 39, 40

▶ *Exercise* **P18.12**

1 Illustrate each inequation from Exercise P18.11 on a
separate number line graph.
For each inequality give three whole number values that
satisfy it.

2 Show the following inequations on separate number line
graphs.
List the integers included in each inequality.
(a) $-1 < x < 2$ (e) $2 < x \le 5$ (h) $-3 \le x < 0$
(b) $1 \le x < 3$ (f) $0 < x \le 4$ (i) $-6 \le x < -4$
(c) $-4 < x \le 1$ (g) $-2 < x < 5$ (j) $-1 \le x \le 1$
(d) $-5 \le x \le -3$

3 Use symbols to write the inequalities shown on these
number line graphs.
For each inequality, list the integers that satisfy it.

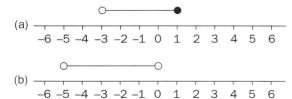

(a)
−6 −5 −4 −3 −2 −1 0 1 2 3 4 5 6

(b)
−6 −5 −4 −3 −2 −1 0 1 2 3 4 5 6

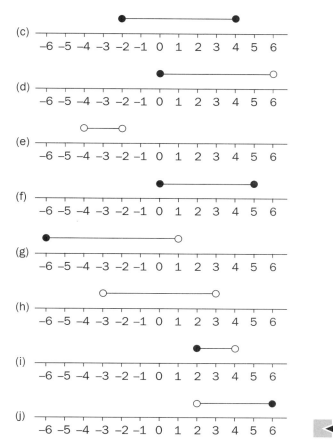

(c)

(d)

(e)

(f)

(g)

(h)

(i)

(j)

Two together

Temperatures will be below 2°C but with minimum temperatures of −3°C

This weather forecast gives *two inequations* that are true *at the same time*.

These are: $t < 2$ and $t \geq -3$

temperature in °C

You can show them on the same number line graph.

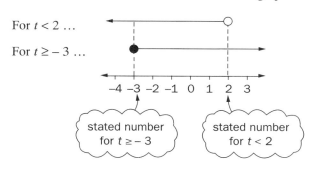

For $t < 2$ …

For $t \geq -3$ …

stated number for $t \geq -3$

stated number for $t < 2$

See how they overlap.

This 'overlap' shows the values that satisfy *both* inequations simultaneously, i.e. at the same time.

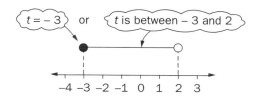

$t = -3$ or t is between −3 and 2

You can describe these values in *one* statement.

Put the 'stated numbers' in order: $\boxed{-3 \quad\quad 2}$

Write the variable between them: $\boxed{-3 \quad t \quad 2}$

Use the correct inequality symbols: $\boxed{-3 \leq t < 2}$

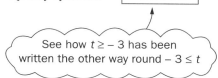

See how $t \geq -3$ has been written the other way round $-3 \leq t$

► *Exercise* **P18.13**

For each pair of inequations
(a) show them on the same number line graph
(b) write them as a single inequality statement.

1   $x > 4$ and $x < 7$
2   $x < 5$ and $x \geq 0$
3   $x \leq 1$ and $x > -2$
4   $x \geq -5$ and $x \leq -1$
5   The average maximum temperature is 30°C.
    The average minimum temperature is −10°C.

Examination Questions

1   K is a whole number such that

    $6 < K < 12$

    Give all the whole number values of K that satisfy the inequality.

                                 (ULEAC, 1994)

2   The integer n satisfies the inequality $-3 < n \leq 4$.
    List all the possible values of n.

                             (Cambridge, 1991)

3   Given that $x < 2$ and $x \geq -3$ list the possible values of x when
    (a) x is an integer
    (b) x is a natural number.

                               (SEG, 1988)

4   Triangle ABC has angle A = 75°. If $30° \leq$ angle B $\leq 90°$ find the possible range of values of angle C.

                               (SEG, 1990)

5   A piston for an engine is only passed for use if its diameter is within 0.03 cm of 12 cm. If the diameter of a usable piston is x cm, complete the inequation:

         $\ldots < x < \ldots$

                             (Cambridge, 1990)

P19
Products of primes

This unit will help you to:

■ write positive whole numbers as products of primes

■ use these to find HCFs (highest common factors) and LCMs (lowest common multiples)

■ use HCFs and LCMs to solve problems.

Products

Products are things that are made.
In mathematics **products** are made by **multiplication**.

milk products

The product of 2 and 5 is $\boxed{2 \times 5 = 10}$

The product of 3, 4 and 8 is $\boxed{3 \times 4 \times 8 = 96}$

▶ *Exercise* **P19.1**

Give the product of
1	3 and 7	**4**	2, 3 and 4	**7**	3, 3 and 11
2	4 and 8	**5**	3, 5 and 6	**8**	5, 2 and 12
3	9 and 6	**6**	2, 2 and 10	**9**	4, 5 and 30.

You can have products of many kinds of numbers:

whole numbers $\boxed{7 \times 3 = 21}$

decimals $\boxed{0.1 \times 0.5 \times 1.2 = 0.06}$

directed numbers $\boxed{+4 \times -2 = -8}$
and so on …

All the work that follows uses positive whole numbers, such as 1, 2, 3, 4, …
So the word 'numbers' in this unit means this kind of number.

Same numbers → same product

The product of 3 and 4 $\boxed{3 \times 4 = 12}$

and the product of 4 and 3 $\boxed{4 \times 3 = 12}$
are the same number.

Multiplications of the *same numbers* **in any order** give the *same product*.

▶ *Exercise* **P19.2**

Which of these multiplications give the same product? Decide by just looking at the numbers. Then check with your calculator.

1 $\boxed{7 \times 8}$ **2** $\boxed{2 \times 11 \times 4 \times 9}$ **3** $\boxed{53 \times 29}$

4 $\boxed{6 \times 12 \times 3 \times 10}$ **5** $\boxed{9 \times 4 \times 3 \times 7}$

6 $\boxed{10 \times 12 \times 6 \times 3}$ **7** $\boxed{8 \times 7}$ **8** $\boxed{4 \times 11 \times 9 \times 2}$

9 $\boxed{29 \times 53}$ **10** $\boxed{3 \times 6 \times 10 \times 12}$ **11** $\boxed{3 \times 4 \times 7 \times 9}$

Products of special numbers

All the numbers in this multiplication are special … $\boxed{2 \times 3 \times 7 = 42}$

Memo
Prime numbers
p23

2, 3 and 7 are **prime numbers**.

We say that the multiplication $2 \times 3 \times 7$ is '42 expressed as a **product of primes**'.

These multiplications all show 110 as a product of primes. They are all the same, except for the order. In answers we usually write the primes in order of size, smallest first, like this.

$\boxed{\begin{array}{l} 5 \times 2 \times 11 \\ 5 \times 11 \times 2 \\ 11 \times 2 \times 5 \\ 11 \times 5 \times 2 \\ 2 \times 11 \times 5 \\ 2 \times 5 \times 11 \end{array}}$

Remember: A prime number is divisible by exactly *two numbers*, 1 and itself.

▶ *Exercise* **P19.3**

1 Find the numbers expressed here as products of primes.
(a) 5×7		(f) 17×701
(b) 3×13		(g) $2 \times 7 \times 11$
(c) 23×29		(h) $3 \times 5 \times 23$
(d) 5×61		(i) $2 \times 3 \times 5 \times 7$
(e) 37×109		(j) $2 \times 5 \times 11 \times 17 \times 101$

2 Write down six more products of primes. Find their values.

Here is another *product of primes*:

$$\boxed{2 \times 2 \times 2 \times 3 \times 3 \times 7 = 504}$$

Some primes are *repeated* in this multiplication. You can write this more simply in index form:

$$\boxed{2^3 \times 3^2 \times 7 = 504}$$

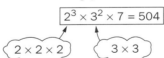

▶ *Exercise* **P19.4**

1 Write these products of primes in full.
(a) 2×5^3	(d) $5 \times 11^3 \times 23$
(b) $3^4 \times 7^2$	(e) $2^7 \times 3 \times 5^2 \times 7^4$
(c) $2^5 \times 3 \times 11^2$	(f) $2 \times 3^6 \times 13^2$

2 Give these products of primes in index form.
(a) $2 \times 2 \times 2 \times 2 \times 2 \times 2$	(d) $2 \times 5 \times 5 \times 11 \times 11 \times 11 \times 11$
(b) $3 \times 3 \times 5 \times 5 \times 5$	(e) $19 \times 19 \times 19$
(c) $7 \times 7 \times 7 \times 7 \times 7$	(f) $5 \times 7 \times 7 \times 13 \times 13 \times 13$

3 Find the numbers expressed as products of primes in questions **1** and **2**.

Investigation

Products less than 100

Find all the numbers less than 100 which can be given as a product of prime numbers.

> Share the work in this investigation with some other students

> 2, 3, 5, 7, 11, 13, …

Plan and organise your work carefully.
Be systematic.
Record you results neatly.
Show how to write each number as a product.
Use index form where possible.

Here are some possible starting points to give you some ideas.

Make products with only 2s …

$$2 \times 2 = 2^2 = 4$$
$$2 \times 2 \times 2 = 2^3 = 8$$

then only 3s,
then only 5s,
and so on…

Make products with 2s and 3s …

$$2 \times 3 = 6$$
$$2 \times 2 \times 3 = 2^2 \times 3 = 12$$
$$2 \times 2 \times 2 \times 3 = 2^3 \times 3 = 24$$

then 2s and 5s,
then 2s and 7s,
and so on…

Collect all the results together.
Check each others' work.

Make a '100 square' like this.
Ring the numbers you have found.
Write a list of the others.

1	2	3	4	5	6	7	8	9	10
11	12	13	14	15	16	17	18	19	20
21	22	23	24	25	26	27	28	29	30
31	32	33	34	35	36	37	38	39	40
41	42	43	44	45	46	47	48	49	50
51	52	53	54	55	56	57	58	59	60
61	62	63	64	65	66	67	68	69	70
71	72	73	74	75	76	77	78	79	80
81	82	83	84	85	86	87	88	89	90
91	92	93	94	95	96	97	98	99	100

Describe the numbers in your list, that is, those you have not given as a product of prime numbers.
What does this show you?
Discuss your findings and write about them.

Products of factors

Every number is a product of some of its factors.

5 is a **prime number.**
It has exactly *two factors*.
Its *only factors* are 1 and 5.
It is a product of these factors *only*.

$$1 \times 5 = 5$$

> factors

12 is a **composite number.**
It has *more than two factors*.
Its *factors* are 1, 2, 3, 4, 6 and 12.
12 is a product of 1 and 12.

$$1 \times 12 = 12$$

> factors

12 is also the product of other factors in these ways:

$$\mathbf{2} \times \mathbf{6} = 12 \qquad \mathbf{3} \times \mathbf{4} = 12 \qquad \mathbf{2} \times \mathbf{2} \times \mathbf{3} = 12$$

Look at the prime numbers in these multiplications.

Only one multiplication …

$$2 \times 2 \times 3$$

> all prime factors of 12

gives 12 as a **product of primes.**

Each of these primes is a prime factor of 12.

> index form

So we also describe

$$2 \times 2 \times 3 \quad \text{or} \quad 2^2 \times 3$$

as a **product of prime factors** of 12.

► Exercise P19.5

1. Here are some composite numbers and their factors. Write each number as a product of factors (other than 1 and itself) in as many ways as possible.
   (a) 33 has factors 1, 3, 11 and 33
   (b) 75 has factors 1, 3, 5, 15, 25 and 75
   (c) 45 has factors 1, 3, 5, 9, 15 and 45
   (d) 32 has factors 1, 2, 4, 8, 16 and 32
   (e) 169 has factors 1, 13, 169.

2. Express each number in question **1** as the product of prime factors. How many different products of primes has each number?

3. Express each of these numbers as a product of its prime factors.
   (a) 111 (b) 121 (c) 310 (d) 147 (e) 250

Finding products of primes

You can easily find the products of primes for some numbers. They are in your multiplication tables …

$$6 = 2 \times 3 \qquad 35 = 5 \times 7 \qquad 77 = 7 \times 11$$

To find other products of primes like these …

$$2592 = 2^5 \times 3^4 \qquad 1155 = 3 \times 5 \times 7 \times 11$$

… you need a systematic method.

Here are two ways to try.

Factor tree

This is a factor tree for 60.

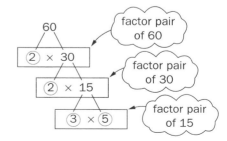

See how numbers 'branch out' to *factor pairs*.
And *branches end at prime numbers*.

This gives:

$$60 = 2 \times 2 \times 3 \times 5$$

or in index form:

$$60 = 2^2 \times 3 \times 5$$

To check,
do the multiplications

C 2 × 2 × 3 × 5 = 60.

This is also a factor tree for 60.

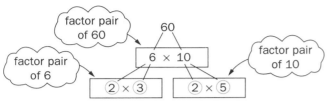

It starts with a different factor pair.
But its branches end with the same prime numbers …

2, 3, 2, and 5

These give the same product of primes:

$$60 = 2 \times 2 \times 3 \times 5$$
or in index form $60 = 2^2 \times 3 \times 5$

We usually put them in order of size

► *Exercise* P19.6

1 Make factor trees for 60 starting with:

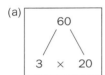 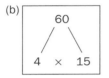

Check they give the same product of primes.

2 Make factor trees for 144 starting with:

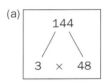 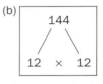

(c) Make a different factor tree for 144.
(d) Give 144 as a product of primes.

3 Copy and complete these factor trees.

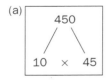 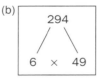 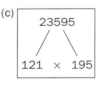

(d) Give 450, 294 and 23595 as products of primes.
(e) Make a different factor tree for each number.
Check your products of primes.

4 Make factor trees for these numbers.
Use each tree to give the number as a product of primes.

(a) 360   (e) 484   (h) 3600
(b) 1000   (f) 624   (i) 1089
(c) 648   (g) 4096   (j) 693
(d) 1250

Dividing by primes

You can also find prime factors by dividing as many times as
you can by prime numbers.

Here is 6160 factorised in this way.

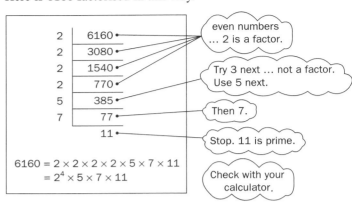

You start with the *smallest prime that divides exactly*. Divide by
it over and over again, until it no longer divides exactly.
Then try the next prime in the same way.
Then the next, … until you are left with a prime number.
You can do the divisions with a calculator.
But write down your working neatly step-by-step.
Write your prime factors as a product in full first.
Then use index form where appropriate.
Finally check the multiplication with your calculator.

Remember: The first ten prime numbers are:
2, 3, 5, 7, 11, 13, 17, 19, 23, 29

► *Exercise* P19.7

Express these numbers as products of primes.
Find them by dividing by primes.

1	90	**5**	1044	**8**	16 744
2	132	**6**	4046	**9**	6061
3	441	**7**	16 807	**10**	21 296
4	2160				

Summary

A product is the result of a multiplication.
A product of primes has only prime numbers in the
multiplication.

All numbers are products of factors.
Only composite numbers are products of prime factors.

more than two factors

Prime numbers and 1 cannot be given as a product of
primes.

A composite number can be given as a unique product of
primes.
To find this you can use:
 ● a factor tree
or ● division by primes.

Investigation

Squares, cubes and roots

144 is a perfect square.

$$144 = 2 \times 2 \times 2 \times 2 \times 3 \times 3$$
$$= 2^4 \times 3^2$$

12 is its square root.
$$12 = \sqrt{144}$$

$$12 = 2 \times 2 \times 3$$
$$= 2^2 \times 3$$

Compare their products of primes.
What do you notice?

Investigate the products of primes of other perfect squares and their square roots.
Write about what you discover.

Find the square root of each of these numbers from their products of primes.

324, 1764, 2025, 1936, 9801, 42 849,
53 361, 14 641, 8281, 7225, 20 449, 148 225

Check them with your calculator. Use $\sqrt{}$

Investigate the products of primes of perfect cubes and their cube roots.
Use what you discover to find the cube roots of these numbers from their products of primes.

343, 1728, 17 576, 9261, 21 952, 166 375, 74 088, 373 248

Highest Common Factor (HCF)

2 is a factor of both 24 and 18

$$24 \div 2 = 12$$
$$18 \div 2 = 9$$

2 divides exactly into both 24 and 18

We say: '2 is a **common factor** of 24 and 18'.

Many numbers have *more than one* common factor.
Compare the factors of 12 and 20.

Factors of 12: ①, ②, 3, 4, 6 and 12

Factors of 20: ①, ②, 4, 5, 10 and 20

There are three common factors: 1, 2 and 4.
But the largest is 4.

We say: '4 is the **highest common factor** of 12 and 20'

4 is the **largest number that divides exactly** into both 12 and 20.

$$12 \div 4 = 3$$
$$20 \div 4 = 5$$

Discussion Exercise

1   List all the common factors of:
   (a) 35 and 30   (d) 168 and 144
   (b) 63 and 42   (e) 64 and 96
   (c) 65 and 165   (f) 50, 100 and 125
Ring the highest common factor in each case.

2   Name a common factor of all numbers.
3   Write down the HCF of
   (a) 10 and 30   (c) 12, 4 and 48
   (b) 9 and 5427   (d) 18, 54 and 6
Compare the numbers and their HCF.
What do you notice?
Why does this happen?
This gives you a quick test for some HCFs.
What do you think it is?
4   Give the common factors of these prime numbers.
   (a) 3 and 7   (c) 2, 11 and 17
   (b) 5 and 13   (d) 31, 37 and 41
What do you find?
Explain why you get this result.
What does this tell you about the HCF of prime numbers?

Memo
Cancelling fractions p41

You use common factors to **cancel fractions**.

Look at this fraction: $\dfrac{18}{27}$ ← 3 is a common factor of 18 and 27

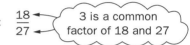

You can cancel by 3: $\dfrac{18}{27} = \dfrac{6}{9}$ ÷3 ... ÷3

Cancelling by the **highest common factor** of 'top' and 'bottom' gives the fraction's **simplest form**.

$\dfrac{18}{27}$ ← 9 is the HCF of 18 and 27

Cancelling by 9 gives: $\dfrac{18}{27} = \dfrac{2}{3}$ ÷9 ... ÷9

▶ *Exercise* **P19.8**

1   Find the HCF of :
   (a) 30 and 42   (d) 66 and 110
   (b) 45 and 60   (e) 48 and 80
   (c) 56 and 84   (f) 156 and 216
2   Reduce these fractions to their simplest forms. Use the HCFs from question **1** to help you.
   (a) $\dfrac{66}{110}$ (d) $\dfrac{156}{216}$
   (b) $\dfrac{30}{42}$ (e) $\dfrac{45}{60}$
   (c) $\dfrac{48}{80}$ (f) $\dfrac{56}{84}$

HCFs from products of primes

The HCF of 35 and 63 is 7.
This is easy to find ...
if you know your 7 times table.

$$35 \div 7 = 5$$

$$63 \div 7 = 9$$

You can also find it quickly with your calculator.
Just find the factors of 35 and 63.
And compare them.

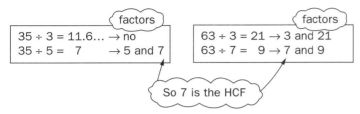

factors
```
35 ÷ 3 = 11.6... → no
35 ÷ 5 =   7     → 5 and 7
```

factors
```
63 ÷ 3 = 21 → 3 and 21
63 ÷ 7 =  9 → 7 and 9
```

So 7 is the HCF

The HCF of 440 and 858 is 22.
This is more difficult to find ...
most of us only know tables up
to 10×10.
But it is easy to see from their products of primes ...

$$440 \div 22 = 20$$

$$858 \div 22 = 39$$

$$440 = ②\times 2 \times 2 \times 5 \times \boxed{11}$$
$$858 = ②\times 3 \times \boxed{11} \times 13$$

Don't use index form

2 and 11 are common to both.
The HCF is their product:

$$2 \times 11 = 22$$

because it gives the largest number that is a factor of both.

This gives us a very neat way to find the HCF of large numbers.

Question

Find the highest common factor of 3060, 1980 and 2295.
Show your method clearly.

Answer

Work out products of primes.

2	3060		2	1980		3	2295
2	1530		2	990		3	765
3	765		3	495		3	255
3	255		3	165		5	85
5	85		5	55			17
	17			11			

Find factors that are in all of the products.

$$3060 = 2 \times 2 \times③\times\boxed{3}\times\underline{5} \times 17$$
$$1980 = 2 \times 2 \times③\times\boxed{3}\times\underline{5} \times 11$$
$$2295 = ③\times\boxed{3}\times 3 \times\underline{5} \times 17$$

Multiply these common factors together.

$$\text{HCF is } 3 \times 3 \times 5 = 45$$

► *Exercise* **P19.9**

1 Find the HCF of 168 and 180 from these:
$$168 = 2 \times 2 \times 2 \times 3 \times 7$$
$$180 = 2 \times 2 \times 3 \times 3 \times 5$$

2 Use these products of primes to find the HCF of 360, 420 and 600.
$$360 = 2 \times 2 \times 2 \times 3 \times 3 \times 5$$
$$420 = 2 \times 2 \times 3 \times 5 \times 7$$
$$600 = 2 \times 2 \times 2 \times 3 \times 5 \times 5$$

3 Use these products of primes to find the HCF of each set of numbers.
(a) $108 = 2^2 \times 3^3$
     $204 = 2^2 \times 3 \times 17$
(b) $24 = 2^3 \times 3$
     $90 = 2 \times 3^2 \times 5$
(c) $3410 = 2 \times 5 \times 11 \times 31$
     $4410 = 2 \times 3^2 \times 5 \times 7^2$
     $7260 = 2^2 \times 3 \times 5 \times 11^2$
(d) $1206 = 2 \times 3^2 \times 67$
     $648 = 2^3 \times 3^4$
     $747 = 3^2 \times 83$

4 Find the HCF of these numbers.
Use the product of primes method.
Show your working clearly.
(a) 336, 198 and 308   (d) 344, 3010 and 774
(b) 1224 and 720   (e) 84, 315 and 209
(c) 3750 and 5400   (f) 53 361 and 42 849

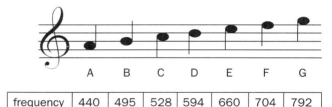

Investigation

Musical notes
Making a string on a guitar or violin vibrate produces a sound.
Musicians make it produce a musical note.
Each musical note has a **frequency**.

	A	B	C	D	E	F	G
frequency	440	495	528	594	660	704	792

This is the number of times per second that the string vibrates.
Investigate the HCFs of the frequencies of the notes shown above.

Here are some starting points to try.
● Find the HCF of all these frequencies.
● Find the HCFs of the frequencies of adjacent notes:
   A and B,   B and C,   C and D,   and so on ...
● Find the HCFs of the frequencies of:
   A and C,   B and D,   C and E,   and so on ...
What do you notice?

Continue with some ideas of your own.
Or investigate frequencies of other sets of notes.
Write about what you discover.

Lowest Common Multiple

A **multiple** of a number is made by multiplying it by any whole number like 1, 2, 3, 4, …

30 is a multiple of *both* 3 and 5.

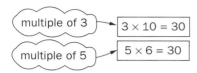

We say: 30 is a **common multiple** of 3 and 5.

Numbers can have *more than one* common multiple.
Compare these multiples of 4 and 6:

   multiples of 4: 4, 8, ⑫, 16, 20, 24̲, 28, 32, 36̲, …
   multiples of 6: 6, ⑫, 18, 24̲, 30, 36̲, 42, …

Common multiples of 4 and 6 are: 12, 24, 36, …
There are many more.
But the *smallest* is 12.
We say: '12 is the **lowest common multiple** of 4 and 6'

12 is the smallest number that
is a multiple of both 4 and 6.

$4 \times 3 = 12$
$6 \times 2 = 12$

 Discussion Exercise

1   (a) List the multiples of 4 that are less than 50.
    (b) List the multiples of 7 that are less than 50.
    (c) List the common multiples of 4 and 7 that are less than 50.
    (d) What is the LCM of 4 and 7?
2   (a) List the multiples of 9 that are less than 120.
    (b) List the multiples of 12 that are less than 120.
    (c) List the common multiples of 9 and 12 that are less than 120.
    (d) What is the LCM of 9 and 12?
3   Find the lowest common multiple of
    (a) 2 and 9   (c) 5, 10 and 25
    (b) 6 and 8   (d) 3, 7 and 9.
4   Write down the LCM of
    (a) 2 and 16   (c) 4 and 44
    (b) 5 and 40   (d) 10 and 80.
    Compare the numbers and their LCM.
    What happens in each case?
    Try to explain why.
5   Give the LCM of these prime numbers:
    (a) 3 and 7   (c) 2, 3 and 5
    (b) 2 and 17   (d) 5 and 11
    What do you notice?
    Try finding the LCM of other prime numbers.
    Are they what you expect?
    Describe a quick way to find them.
    Explain why this works if you can.

LCMs from products of primes

The LCM of large numbers can be difficult to spot.
But you can use their *products of primes* to find it.

Here are the products of primes of 120 and 198.

   $120 = 2 \times 2 \times 2 \times 3 \times 5$
   $198 = 2 \times 3 \times 3 \times 11$

Any multiple of 120 has …
in its product of primes.

Any multiple of 198 has …
in its product of primes.

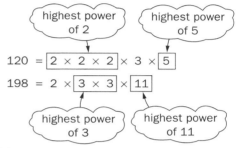

To get these prime factors in the LCM, you pick out the *highest power* of each prime that occurs in *either* number.

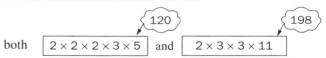

Then multiply them together …

$\boxed{2 \times 2 \times 2} \times \boxed{3 \times 3} \times \boxed{5} \times \boxed{11} = 3960$

So the LCM of 120 and 198 is 3960.

3960 is the *smallest number* that has

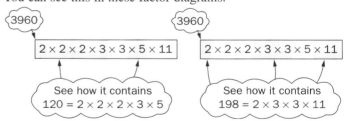

in its product of primes.
You can see this in these factor diagrams.

You can check the LCM with your calculator too.

Find the multiples of 120 up to … $120 \times 33 = 3960$

Find the multiples of 198 up to … $198 \times 20 = 3960$

Is 3960 the smallest multiple they have in common?

This product of primes method can be used to give you the LCM of *more than two* numbers.

3060 $\boxed{2 \times 2} \times 3 \times 3 \times \boxed{5} \times \boxed{17}$

1980 $2 \times 2 \times 3 \times 3 \times 5 \times \boxed{11}$

2295 $\boxed{3 \times 3 \times 3} \times 5 \times 17$

Their LCM is $2 \times 2 \times 3 \times 3 \times 3 \times 5 \times 11 \times 17 = 100\ 980$

► *Exercise* **P19.10**

Find the LCM for each set of numbers in the Discussion
Exercise on page 393.

Summary

A common factor is a factor that two or more numbers have
in common.
It divides exactly into all of them.

All numbers have a common factor of 1.
1 is the only common factor of prime numbers.

The highest common factor (HCF) of two or more numbers
is the largest of their common factors. It is the largest
number that divides exactly into all of them.

A common multiple of two or more numbers is a multiple of
each of the numbers.

The lowest common multiple (LCM) of two or more numbers
is the smallest number that is a multiple of each of them.

To find the HCF or LCM of large numbers, use a product of
primes method.
Write the numbers as products of primes in full (do not use
index form).

For the HCF:

pick out the prime factors that are common to all of the
numbers, and multiply them together.

For the LCM:

pick out the highest power of each prime that occurs in
any of the numbers, and multiply them together.

 Investigation

HCF and LCM products
The HCF of 6 and 15 is 3.
The LCM of 6 and 15 is 30.

Work out the product of 6 and 15.
Work out the product of their HCF and LCM.

What do you find?

Investigate the HCFs, LCMs and products of other pairs of
numbers.

| 20 and 50 | 8 and 48 | 12 and 35 |

| 7 and 23 | 42 and 98 |

Here are some to start with …

Choose other pairs of numbers of
your own to try.
Write about what you discover.
What conclusions do you reach?
Try to explain your findings.
What happens if you have more than two numbers?

Hint:
Look at the numbers
written as products
of primes.

Problem solving

You can use the HCF and LCM of numbers to solve some
practical problems.
The problems will not say …
'find the highest common factor'
or 'find the lowest common multiple'.
You have to decide what to do.
Look for clues in the information given.
Imagine what is happening and think it out.
In the following problem you have to
- *divide* two amounts into equal parts

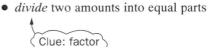
Clue: factor

- find the *largest* value that you can for *both*.

Clue: *highest common*
factor

The clues lead you to look for the HCF of the numbers.
Thinking about the problem shows you this makes sense.

Question

Ann buys two off-cuts of
ribbon in a sale. One is
117 cm long. The other is
156 cm long.
She cuts them so that she
ends up with a number of
pieces all the same length.
What is the greatest length each piece can be?

Answer

The HCF of 117 and 156 gives the wanted length.

3	117
3	39
	13

2	156
2	78
3	39
	13

117 = ③ × 3 × 13
156 = 2 × 2 × ③ × 13

HCF is 3 × 13 = 39.
Greatest length = 39 cm

In the next problem you have
- *repeating* patterns of numbers

Clue: multiples

- to find the *first* time they *match* after the start.

Clue: *lowest common*
multiple

So you use the LCM of the numbers to solve it.

Question

Gary has red, blue and green flashing lights at his disco. He switches them on together. The red light flashes every 10 seconds, the blue light every 15 seconds and the green light every 12 seconds. How many seconds after Gary switches them on will they next flash all together?

Answer

The time is the LCM of 10, 15 and 12.

10   15   12

②×⑤   ③×⑤   ②× 6

                       ②×③

$$10 = 2 \times \boxed{5}$$
$$15 = \boxed{3} \times 5$$
$$12 = \boxed{2 \times 2} \times 5$$

The LCM is $2 \times 2 \times 3 \times 5 = 60$
The lights will all flash together after 60 seconds.

► *Exercise* **P19.11**

1 Find the smallest amount of postage that can be made with an exact number of either 18 p or 24 p stamps.

2 The chairs in the college hall can be set out in 35 equal rows or in 45 equal rows or in 105 equal rows. What is the smallest possible number of chairs in the hall?

3 Brenda has a rectangular garden measuring 4.32 m by 3.36 m. She wants to divide it into square plots of equal size. What is the largest sized square she can use?

4 Time belongs to three college committees. One meets every 6 days, another meets every fortnight and the third meets every 30 days.
They all meet on the first day of the college year. How many days after this will they next all meet on the same day?

5 A farmer wants to fence a triangular field. He plans to put a fencing post in each corner and place other posts at equal distances along its sides. He wants the posts to be as far apart as possible.
The sides of the field are 603 feet, 747 feet and 648 feet long. How far apart will the posts be?

6 Mr Ferris has organised this hockey training day. He puts the players into equal sized groups for some activities during it.

> **COUNTY HOCKEY**
> **TRAINING DAY**
>
> **Maximum number:**
> **100 players**

When he puts them into 2s, he has 1 player left over.
When he puts them into 3s, he has 2 players left over.
When he puts them into 4s, he has 3 players left over.
When he puts them into 5s, he has 4 players left over.
How many players are at this training day?
Show clearly how you arrive at your answer.

Examination Questions

1 Express 360 as the product of its prime factors
(Cambridge, 1990)

2 (a) Express 960 as a product of prime numbers.
(b) Hence write down all the factors of 960 which are
(i)   prime numbers
(ii) square numbers
(iii) cubic numbers.
(NISEAC, 1990)

3 (a) Using index notation, express each of the following numbers as the product of its prime factors:
(i) 150
(ii) 252.
(b) (i) Find the largest number which is a factor of both 150 and 252.
(ii) Find the smallest number which, when divided by each of 150 and 252, leaves a remainder of 1.
(SEG, 1988)

4 (a) Express as a product of its prime factors
(i) 126
(ii) 420
(b) Find the smallest number of which 126 and 420 are factors.
(SEG, 1988)

5 Write down the prime factors of
(a) 273
(b) 2002.
Hence find the highest common factor of 273 and 2002.
(SEG, 1989)

6 (a) List the set of factors of
(i) 48
(ii) 72.
(b) List the common factors of 48 and 72.
(c) (i) List the prime factors of 48.
(ii) Express 48 as a product of primes.
(NEAB, 1988)

7 The number 24 can be expressed as follows.

$$24 = 2 \times 2 \times 2 \times 3 = 2^3 \times 3$$

(a) Write the number 36 in the form $2^p \times 3^q$, giving the values of p and q.
(b) In a French town, two church bells, rung electrically, sound every 24 and 36 seconds respectively after being switched on.
At a particular time they both sound together.
Calculate the time taken for them next to sound together.
(NEAB, 1990)

P20
Crossed lines

This unit will help you to:

■ read the coordinates of a point where two graphs cross and understand what they represent

■ solve simultaneous linear equations graphically.

Crossing points on 'practical graphs'

Ken went to town one lunch time. He cycled along the bus route from home.

Ken's mum went home for lunch that day. She caught the 12:10 bus from town.

Ken and his mum waved at each other as they passed.

The travel graph below shows the journeys of Ken and his mum.

Each point on Ken's graph gives a time and distance on his cycle ride.

Each point on his mum's graph gives a time and distance on her bus ride.

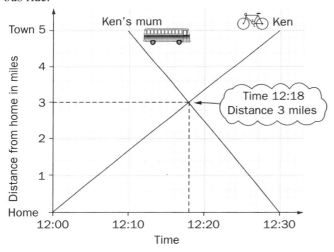

The two graphs cross.

The 'crossing point' is on *both* lines.

This shows that Ken and his mum were *at the same place at the same time*.

They reached that point of their journeys **simultaneously**.

The coordinates of the point tell you *when and where they were together*.

From the graph, the time was 12:18,
          the distance from home was 3 miles.

 Discussion Exercise

Look at the graphs drawn opposite.
Each 'crossing point' shows two things happening simultaneously.
Read its coordinates from the graph.
Discuss what they show in each case.

1   The travel graph below shows the journeys of four trains on the line between Exton and Wyeton.
The 8:30 and 9:10 trains start at Exton.
The 8:40 and 9:00 trains start at Wyeton.

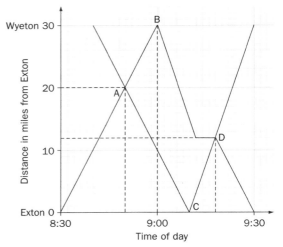

2   Three coloured liquids (red, blue and yellow) were heated, at different steady rates. The graph below shows how their temperatures rose.

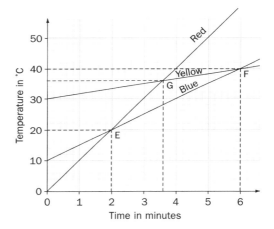

3   Kwik Hire, Rent All and Hire It hire out equipment. The graph below shows their costs for hiring the same model of maxi mower.

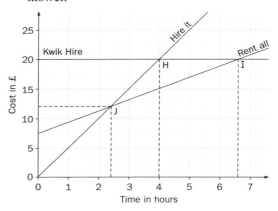

Crossing points on algebraic graphs

The graph of $x + y = 5$ is a straight line.
The coordinates of any point on this line fit the equation $x + y = 5$

(1,4), for example is a point on the line.
At (1,4), $x = 1$, $y = 4$.
For these x- and y-values,
$x + y = 1 + 4 = 5$
i.e., $x + y = 5$.

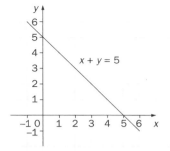

The graph of $2x - y = 1$ is also a straight line.
The coordinates of points on this line fit the equation $2x - y = 1$

(3,5), for example, is on the line.
At (3,5), $x = 3$, $y = 5$.
For these x- and y-values,
$2x - y = 2 \times 3 - 5 = 6 - 5 = 1$
i.e., $2x - y = 1$.

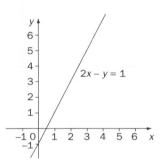

When the graphs of $x + y = 5$ and $2x - y = 1$ are drawn *on the same axes*, the two lines *cross*.
One point is on *both* lines.
Its *coordinates* must *fit both equations*.

The point of intersection is (2,3).
So $x = 2$, $y = 3$ must fit both $x + y = 5$ and $2x - y = 1$.

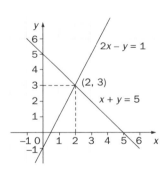

You can check this is true.
Simply use $x = 2$, $y = 3$ in each equation.
Check for $x + y = 5$:
 When $x = 2$, $y = 3$, $x + y = 2 + 3 = 5$ ✓
 i.e., $x + y = 5$
Check for $2x - y = 1$:
 When $x = 2$, $y = 3$, $2x - y = 2 \times 2 - 3 = 1$ ✓
 i.e., $2x - y = 1$
So $x = 2$, $y = 3$ make both equations *true at the same time*.
In other words, the values $x = 2$, $y = 3$ *solve* the equations $x + y = 5$ and $2x - y = 1$ *simultaneously*.

We call $x + y = 5$ and $2x - y = 1$ **simultaneous equations.**
This name shows that the equations have been *solved together*.
Each equation involves *two* unknowns, x and y. So their solution must contain *two* values, an x-value and a y-value.

Summary

Simultaneous means 'together', 'at the same time'.
When equations are solved simultaneously, they are solved together, at the same time.
Equations that have been solved together are called simultaneous equations.

Linear equations such as $x + y = 5$ and $2x - y = 1$ have two unknowns, x and y.
To solve these equations simultaneously, you have to find the value of x and value of y that make both equations true at the same time. These values may by found from the graphs of the equations.

Linear equations give straight line graphs.
The graphs of two linear equations may *cross at one point.*

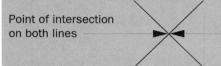

Point of intersection on both lines — x value and y value fit the equations of both graphs at the same time

The *coordinates of this point of intersection* give the *solution* of the two simultaneous equations.

The graphs of two linear equations may be *parallel*.

No point of intersection — No x and y values fit both equations at the same time

These equations have *no simultaneous solution*.
The graphs of two linear equations may be *identical*.

Every point on the line is a point of intersection — x and y values at any point on the line fit both equations together

There is an *infinite number of solutions* to their equations.

▶ *Exercise* P20.1

1 Which x- and y-value (A or B) solves the given pair of simultaneous equations? Show your 'check' clearly in each case.
 (a) $x + y = 8$ A: $x = 3$, $y = 5$ B: $x = 5$, $y = 3$
   $x - y = 2$
 (b) $y = 1 - x$ A: $x = 3$, $y = -2$ B: $x = -2$, $y = 3$
   $y = x - 5$
 (c) $x + y = 4$ A: $x = 4$, $y = 0$ B: $x = 0$, $y = 4$
   $2y = x + 8$
 (d) $y + 2 = x$ A: $x = -1$, $y = -3$ B: $x = -3$, $y = -1$
   $y + 3x + 6 = 0$
 (e) $3x + y = 13$ A: $x = 4$, $y = 3$ B: $x = 3$, $y = 4$
   $3x - 2y = 1$

2 The graphs of two simultaneous equations have been drawn on each of the six diagrams following.
 In each case, write down the two simultaneous equations and their solution.
 Check your solution by substituting in the pair of equations.

(a)

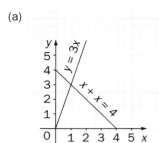

(b)

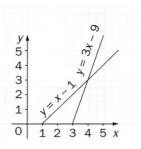

(c)

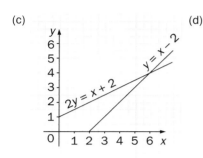

(d)

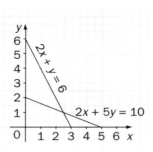

(e)

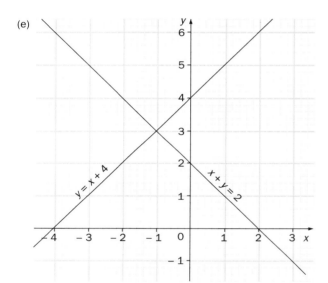

(f)

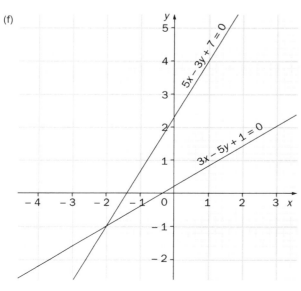

3

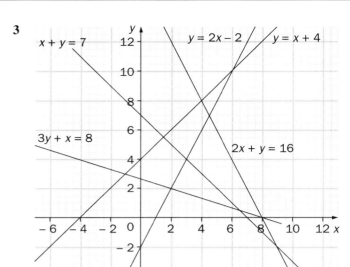

Use the above graph to find the solutions of these pairs of simultaneous equations.

(a) $y = x + 4$
   $y = 2x - 2$

(b) $3y + x = 8$
   $x + y = 7$

(c) $2x + y = 16$
   $y = x + 4$

(d) $y = 2x - 2$
   $x + y = 7$

(e) $3y + x = 8$
   $2x + y = 16$

(f) $x + y = 7$
   $y = x + 4$

Remember to check your solutions in your equations.
You can solve four other pairs of simultaneous equations using this graph. Write down these pairs of equations and their solutions.

4

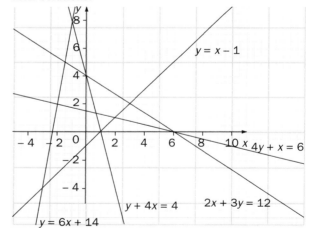

Each pair of x and y values below is the solution of two simultaneous equations. They were found from the graph above.

(a) $x = 6$, $y = 0$

(b) $x = 0$, $y = 4$

(c) $x = -2$, $y = 2$

(d) $x = 3$, $y = 2$

(e) $x = 2$, $y = 1$

(f) $x = 1$, $y = 0$

(g) $x = -1$, $y = 8$

(h) $x = -3$, $y = -4$

(i) $x = \frac{2}{3}$, $y = \frac{4}{3}$

(j) $x = -\frac{3}{2}$, $y = 5$

For each x- and y- value, use the graph to write down the pair of equations they solve. Substitute them in your chosen equations to check.

Solving simultaneous equations graphically

Summary

You may solve two simultaneous equations by drawing their graphs on the same axes.

Memo

Graphs of linear equations
P13 p337

Here are the key steps to take:
- Find the coordinates of three points on each straight line graph.
- Plot the points for each line on the same axes. Two points give each line. The third point is a check.

3 not in a line
   +   +
 +
check your working

- Draw the line through the points for each graph. Label each line with its equation.
- Read off the coordinates of the point of intersection of the graph.
  Draw dotted lines from this point to both axes if it helps.
- Write down the solution.
  Remember it needs an 'x-value' and a 'y-value'.
- Check your solution.
  Put the values into each equation. Make sure they make both equations true.

Question

Solve the simultaneous equations $y = 2 - x$ and $x = 2y + 8$ graphically.
Draw your graphs on the axes given below.

Answer

- *Tables of values and coordinates for each graph:*
  For $y = 2 - x$ For $x = 2y + 8$

x	0	2	– 2
y	2	0	4

x	0	8	10
y	– 4	0	1

(0,2) (2,0) (–2,4)   (0,–4) (8,0) (10,1)

- *Plot the points for each line.*
  Draw and label each graph.

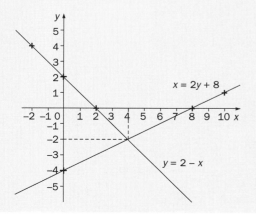

The lines cross at (4,– 2).
This means that $x = 4$, $y = - 2$ fit both equations at the same time.
So the solution of the equations is $x = 4$, $y = - 2$.
- *Check:*
  For $y = 2 - x$: when x = 4, $y = 2 - 4 = - 2$ ✓
  For $x = 2y + 8$:
  when $y = - 2$, $x = 2 \times (- 2) + 8 = - 4 + 8 = 4$ ✓

▶ *Exercise* **P20.2**

1 (a) Copy and complete these tables of values for the given equations.
     For $x + 3y = 6$ For $y = x - 2$

x	0		– 3
y		0	

x	0		9
y		0	

     (b) Draw and label x- and y-axes from – 3 to 9. Use a scale of 1 cm to 1 unit on each axis. Plot and draw the graphs of $x + 3y = 6$ and $y = x - 2$ on these axes. Label each clearly with its equation.
     (c) Find the solution of the simultaneous equations $x + 3y = 6$ and $y = x - 2$ from your graph.
     (d) Check that your solution fits both equations.

2 Solve the following pairs of simultaneous equations graphically.
A suitable range for x is given for each graph.
Use a scale of 2 cm to 1 unit on each axis.
Give your solutions as accurately as you can.

(a) $x + y = 7$
     $x - y = 3$
     (x from 0 to 8)

(b) $x = y - 1$
     $2x - 5y = 10$
     (x from – 6 to 6)

(c) $x + 3y = 12$
       $y = 2x - 10$
     (x from 0 to 12)

(d) $y + 2x = 0$
       $2y = 6 - x$
     (x from – 3 to 7)

(e) $x + y = 4$
       $y = 1 + x$
     (x from – 2 to 5)

(f) $y = x + 3$
     $y = 6x - 3$
     (x from 0 to 6)

(g) $2x + y = 3$
       $x = 2y$
     (x from 0 to 3)

(h) $5y + 2x = 0$
     $10y = 6x - 15$
     (x from 0 to 5)

ACTIVITY

Try using a graphics calculator or graphics package on a computer to solve linear simultaneous equations.
Experiment with the equations given in this unit.
Explore solving equations of your own.
Write a report on what you find.

Discussion Exercise

Try to solve these pairs of simultaneous equations graphically.

$y = 2x - 1$
$y = 2x + 3$

$y = x - 2$
$y - x = 5$

What happens in each case?

What does this tell you about each pair of equations?
Discuss.

Now try to solve these equations graphically.

$x + y = 1$		$2x + y = 3$
$3x + 3y = 3$		$8x + 4y = 12$

Describe what happens.
Look at the equations to help you explain why this occurs.
Discuss.

Examination Questions

1   From the graph find the
solutions of the
simultaneous equations
$$y = 2x - 1$$
$$x + y = 5$$

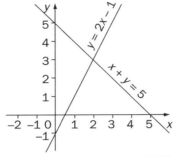

(ULEAC, 1989)

2   The diagram shows the line with equation $2x - 2y = 3$

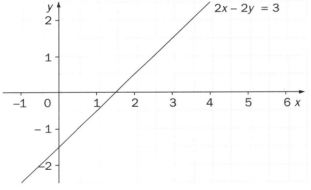

(a) Copy the diagram and draw the line with equation
$2x + 5y = 10$
(b) Solve the simultaneous equations
$2x + 5y = 10$
$2x - 2y = 3$

(MEG, 1991)

3   In this question the simultaneous equations
$$x + 2y = 8$$
$$\text{and } y = \frac{x}{2} - 1$$
are to be solved by graphical methods.
(a) Complete the table for the equation
$$x + 2y = 8$$

x	2	4	6	8
y				0

(b) Complete the table for the equation
$$y = \frac{x}{2} - 1$$

x	2	4	-6	-8
y	0			

(c) Draw the straight lines with equations
$$x + 2y = 8$$
$$\text{and } y = \frac{x}{2} - 1$$
(d) Give the solution of the equations
$$x + 2y = 8$$
$$y = \frac{x}{2} - 1$$

(ULEAC, 1990)

4   (a) On a grid, draw the graphs of the lines
(i) $2x + 3y = 9$
(ii) $4x - 3y = 0$
(b) From the graphs, find the values of x and y which satisfy
both equations simultaneously.

(NEAB, 1989)

5   (a) Draw, on a grid, the graphs of
$$y = 2x - 1$$
$$\text{and } 4x + 3y = 12.$$
(b) (i) Find the gradient of the straight line $y = 2x - 1$.
(ii) Find the gradient of the straight line $4x + 3y = 12$.
(c) Use your diagram to write down the solution of the
simultaneous equations
$$y = 2x - 1$$
$$\text{and } 4x + 3y = 12.$$

(Cambridge, 1990)

P21
Solids of uniform cross-section

This unit will help you to:

- recognise a prism and any other solid with uniform cross-section
- identify and sketch the cross-section of such a solid
- know and use the formula for the volume of any solid with uniform cross-section
- use volumes of solids with uniform cross-section to find areas and lengths
- understand the idea of surface area
- use nets of prisms to calculate their surface areas.

Looking at cross-sections

Cutting across a solid gives a cross-section.

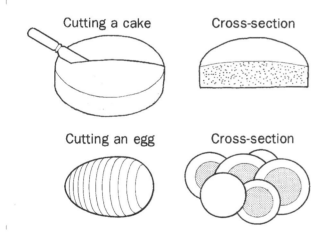

Some solids have a **uniform** cross-section. Here are some examples.

You can cut each of these solids into **parallel slices** so that each slice is exactly the same shape and size.

This solid does *not* have a uniform cross-section.

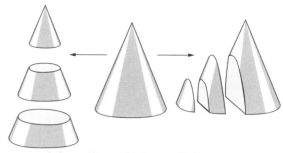

You cannot cut it into slices which are all the same shape and size.

A **solid of uniform cross-section** has two 'end-faces' that are parallel.
These *end-faces* show the *shape of the uniform cross-section*. The solid has the *same shape all the way through*.

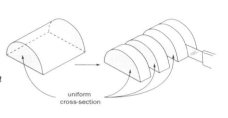

A **prism** is a special solid of uniform cross-section. The cross-section has *only straight sides*. It is a **polygon**. These are examples of prisms.

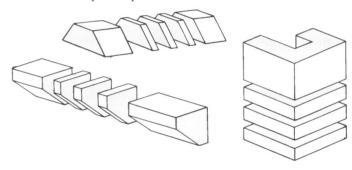

A prism often takes its name from the shape of its cross-section.

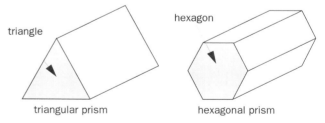

A **rectangular prism** is usually called a **cuboid.**

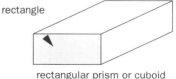

A **cylinder** is also a solid of uniform cross-section. Its cross-section is a *circle*.

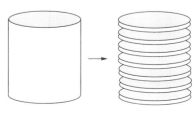

► *Exercise* P21.1

1 Which of these solids have a uniform cross-section.
Write 'Yes' or 'No' for each one.
Draw the shape of the uniform cross-section if there is one.

(a) 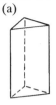 (b) 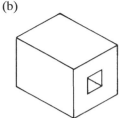 (c)

(d) 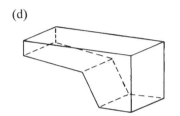 (e)

(f) 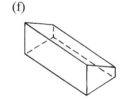 (g)   (h)

(i) 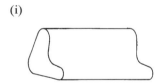 (j)

2 Which solids in question **1** are prisms?
Name the shape of the cross-section in each case.
3 Many everyday objects have a uniform cross-section.
Give some examples.
Sketch the shape of the cross-section for each example. ◄

Volume of a solid of uniform cross-section.

Memo

The amount of space an object occupies is called its **volume.**
Volume is measured in **cubic units** such as:

cubic millimetres (mm³)
cubic centimetres (cm³)
cubic metres (m³).

To find the volume of a solid made from cubes, you can count the cubes.

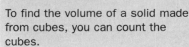

Volume: 11 cm³

◯ *Discussion Exercise*

Each of these solids has a uniform cross-section.
They are all made from centimetre cubes.
What is the volume of each solid?

1   **2**   **3**

4   **5**   **6**

7   **8**   **9**

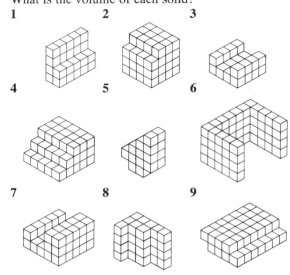

To find these volumes you do not have to count every cube.
Did you find a quick way to work out each volume?
Discuss the methods used by the students in your group.

Here are some more solids made from centimetre cubes.

In this solid, we have:
   7 cubes in a layer
   1 layer of cubes.
There are $7 \times 1 = 7$ cubes.

The area of cross-section is 7 cm².
The length of the solid is 1 cm.
The volume is 7 cm³.

1 layer
1 cm

In this solid, we have:
   7 cubes in each layer
   2 layers of cubes.
There are $7 \times 2 = 14$ cubes.

The area of cross-section is 7 cm².
The length of the solid is 2 cm.
The volume is 14 cm³.

2 layers
2 cm

In this solid, we have:
   7 cubes in each layer
   5 layers of cubes.
There are $7 \times 5 = 35$ cubes.

The area of the
cross-section is 7 cm².
The length of the
solid is 5 cm.
The volume is 35 cm³.

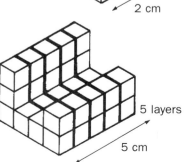

5 layers
5 cm

You can see that multiplying the area of the uniform cross-section by the length of the solid gives the volume. This gives a *formula* we can use for any solid with a uniform cross-section.

Summary

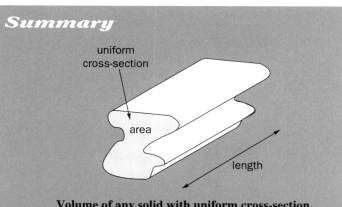

uniform cross-section

area

length

Volume of any solid with uniform cross-section = area of cross section × length

The *'length'* of the solid is always *perpendicular* to the cross-section.
It may be called the *'height'* or *'depth'* or *'thickness'* of the solid.

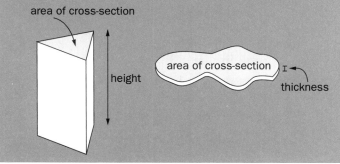

area of cross-section

height

area of cross-section

thickness

Always make sure you have 'matching' units of area, length and volume when you use this formula.

If the area is in cm^2 and the length is in cm, the volume is in cm^3.

$$cm^2 \times cm \rightarrow cm^3$$

If the area is in m^2 and the length is in m, the volume is in m^3.

$$m^2 \times m \rightarrow m^3$$

And so on …

If you need to change any unit, do it first.
Remember:

1 km = 1000 m	1 m = 100 cm 1 m = 1000 mm	1 cm = 10 mm

Question

This diagram shows a kitchen chopping block. The block is a solid with a uniform cross-section of area 546 cm² and thickness 23 mm. Calculate the volume of the block in cubic centimetres correct to the nearest cm³.

Area: 546 cm²

23 mm

Answer

For volume in cm³, use area in cm² and length in cm.

Area of cross-section = 546 cm² ← matching units

thickness (length) = 23 mm = 2.3 cm

volume of solid = area of cross-section × length
= 546 × 2.3
= 1255.8 cm³
= 1256 cm³ (to nearest cm³).

▶ Exercise P21.2

1 Calculate the volume of each of these solids with uniform cross-section in cubic centimetres.

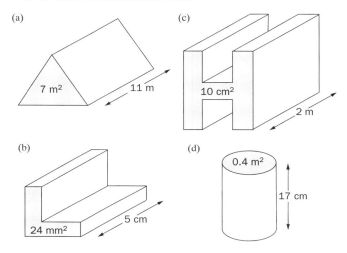

(a)

7 m²   11 m

(c)

10 cm²   2 m

(b)

24 mm²   5 cm

(d)

0.4 m²   17 cm

2 Calculate the volume of each of these metal mouldings in cubic centimetres.

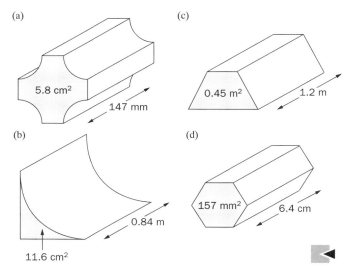

(a)

5.8 cm²   147 mm

(c)

0.45 m²   1.2 m

(b)

11.6 cm²   0.84 m

(d)

157 mm²   6.4 cm

Counting squares for cross-section area

One way to find the area of a cross-section is to use a *square grid*. You can **count the squares** covered by the cross-section.

The area of this uniform cross-section is $4\frac{1}{2}$ cm^2.

The length of the solid is 3 cm.

The volume of the solid is

$$4\frac{1}{2} \times 3 = 13\frac{1}{2} \text{ cm}^3.$$

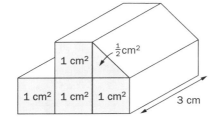

You can also use a square grid to **estimate** the area of an **irregular cross-section**.
Remember:
You count a square as 1, if $\frac{1}{2}$ or more of it is covered.
If less than $\frac{1}{2}$ of a square is covered, you do not count it.

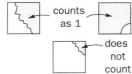

Question

A DIY catalogue gives details of decorative mouldings. This diagram shows the Quadrant moulding cross-section.
(a) Estimate the area of the cross-section of the Quadrant moulding in square centimetres.
(b) Mike Davies buys a 1.2 metre length of Quadrant moulding. Calculate its volume in cubic centimetres.

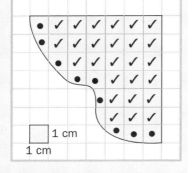

Answer

(a) Whole squares (marked ✓):   26
Other squares counted:
($\frac{1}{2}$ or more covered, marked ●)   +9
                       Total: 35
The estimated area is 35 cm^2
(b) *For volume in cm^3, use area in cm^2 and length in cm.*

Area of cross-section = 35 cm^2
length = 1.2 m = 120 cm   *matching units*

volume of moulding = area of cross-section × length
= 35 × 120
= 4200 cm^3.

► Exercise P21.3

Each of the following diagrams shows the cross-section of a decorative moulding.
For each moulding:
(a) estimate the area of the cross-section in square centimetres,
(b) calculate the volume for the length given.

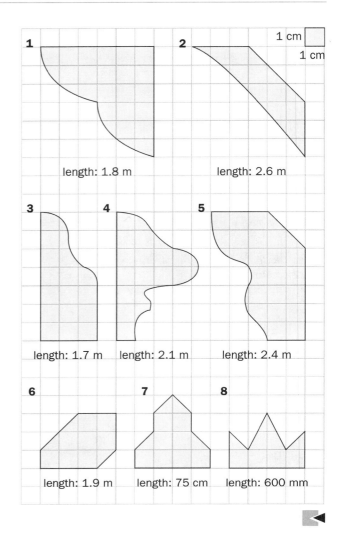

Calculating areas of cross-section

The cross-section of a prism may be a simple shape such as a triangle or parallelogram or trapezium.
You can use these *formulas* to calculate their areas.

Memo
Area of triangle = $\frac{1}{2}$ base × height
Area of parallelogram = base × height
Area of trapezium = $\frac{1}{2}$ × (sum of parallel sides) × height

Always make sure that all the lengths are in the *same unit* in the calculation. Choose the *correct unit* for the volume you want.

Question

This diagram shows a lean-to conservatory. Calculate the volume of the conservatory in cubic metres. Give your answer to the nearest cubic metre.

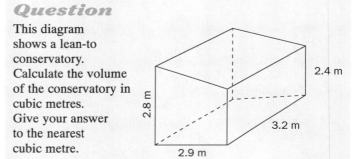

Answer

For volume in m³, all lengths must be in m.
Volume of prism

= (area of trapezium cross-section) × length

= [$\frac{1}{2}$ × (sum of parallel sides × height)] × length

= [$\frac{1}{2}$ × (2.8 + 2.4) × 2.9] × 3.2

= ($\frac{1}{2}$ × 5.2 × 2.9) × 3.2

= 24.128 m³

= 24 m³ (to the nearest m³)

You can use the *brackets* on your calculator to do the working in the example above. Here is one way to try. Find the best way on *your* calculator.

Watch the display for the result to each part.

▶ *Exercise* **P21.4**

1 Calculate the volume of each of these prisms.

(a)

(c)

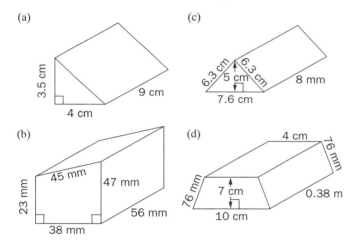

(b)

(d)

2 Calculate the volume of this swimming pool in cubic metres.
How many litres of water are needed to fill the pool?
(1 litre = 1000 cm³)

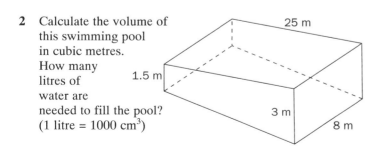

3 Find the volume of this biscuit tin. All the measurements are in centimetres.

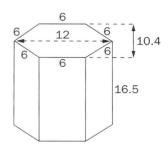

4 Find the volume of this feeding trough for chickens in cubic centimetres.

If the trough is filled with water, how many litres are needed to fill it?
Give your answer to the nearest litre.

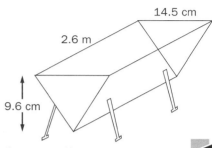

For a cylinder, the uniform cross-section is a circle.

Memo

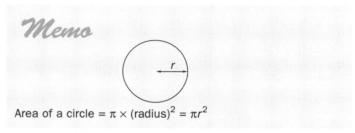

Area of a circle = π × (radius)² = πr²

This gives the following formula for the volume of a cylinder.

Summary

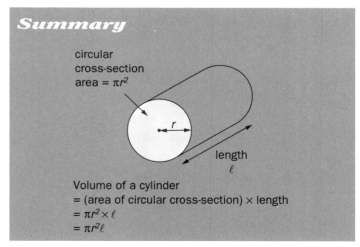

circular
cross-section
area = πr²

length
ℓ

Volume of a cylinder
= (area of circular cross-section) × length
= πr² × ℓ
= πr²ℓ

In some examples you are given the diameter of the circle. Work out the radius before you use the formula.

Remember:

| diameter = 2 × radius | radius = $\frac{1}{2}$ × diameter |

Question

A tin of Chopped Tomatoes is 12.8 cm tall and has a diameter of 74 mm. Calculate its volume to the nearest cubic centimetre.

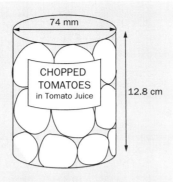

Answer

For volume in cm³, all lengths must be in cm.
To change mm to cm, divide by 10.

diameter = 74 mm
radius = 74 ÷ 2 = 37 mm = 3.7 cm

height = 12.8 cm ← *same unit*

Volume of cylindrical tin
= area of circular cross-section × height
= πr^2 × height
= $\pi \times 3.7^2 \times 12.8$
= 551 cm³ (to nearest cm³). Display: **550.5075639.**

►Exercise P21.5

1   Calculate the volume of each of these cylinders, to the nearest cubic centimetre.

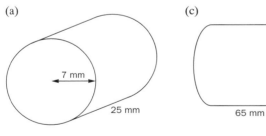

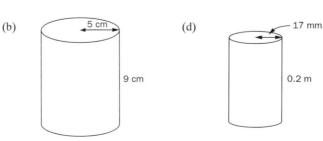

2   Measure the diameter and thickness in millimetres, to the nearest mm of these coins:
    (a) 1p   (b) 2p   (c) 5p   (d) 10p   (e) £1.
    Calculate the volume of each coin in cubic millimetres, to the nearest mm³.

3   Calculate the volume of each of these tins. Give your answers in cubic centimetres, to the nearest cm³.

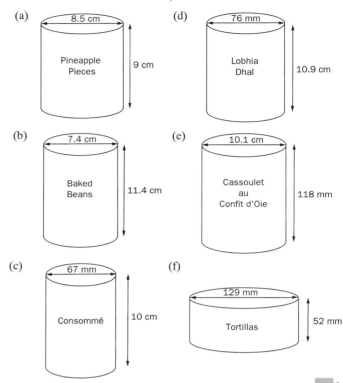

The uniform cross-section of a solid may be a **compound shape.**

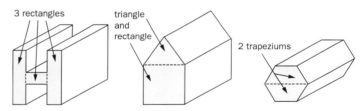

Split the compound shape into simple shapes whose areas you can calculate. Then find the total area.
A *calculator memory* is useful in these calculations.
Add all the simple areas into the memory as you work them out.
Then recall the total area to find the volume.

Question

This diagram shows an artist's sketch for the new Lesco Centre for Modern Art.

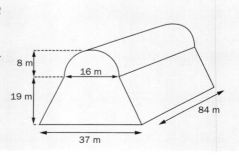

The building is 84 m long and has a uniform cross-section with the dimensions shown. Calculate the volume of the building.

Answer

The cross-section is made up of a trapezium and a semi-circle.

Trapezium: parallel sides: 16 m and 37 m
            height: 19 m
Area = $\frac{1}{2} \times$ (sum of parallel sides) $\times$ height
     = $\frac{1}{2} \times (16 + 37) \times 19$
     = 503.5 m^2

Semi-circle: radius 8 m
Area = $\frac{1}{2} \times \pi \times r^2$
     = $\frac{1}{2} \times \pi \times 8^2$
     = 100.5309649 m^2

Total area of cross-section
     = area of trapezium + area of semi-circle
     = 604.0309649 m^2

Volume of building
     = total area of cross-section $\times$ length
     = 604.0309649 $\times$ 84
     = 50738.60105 m^3
     = 50700 m^3 (to 3 sf)

Here is one way to do the working with a calculator. Try it. Then find the best way to do the working with your calculator.

Watch the display for the step-by-step results as you go along.

Some cross-section areas look like shapes with holes cut out of them.

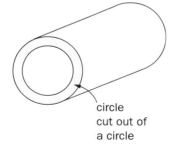

circle cut out of a circle

To find this kind of area, work out:

   area of 'whole shape' − area of 'hole'

Exercise P21.6

1 Calculate the volume of each of these shapes.

(a)   (b)

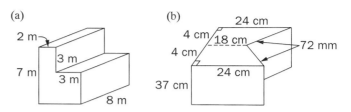

2 Calculate the volume of this barn.

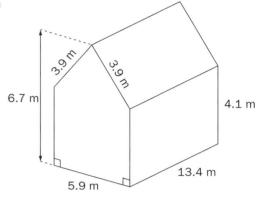

3 The diagram below represents a steel bar which has the same cross-section throughout its length. All the measurements given are in mm.

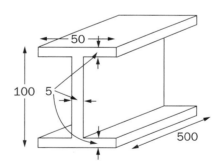

Calculate
(a) the area of the cross-section in mm^2
(b) the volume of the steel bar in cm^3.

4 This diagram shows a storage box. All dimensions are in centimetres. Calculate the volume of the box in cm^3.

5 For each of the open pipes following, calculate the volume of material needed to make the pipe in
(i) cm^3
(ii) litres.
Give your answers to a sensible degree of accuracy.

(a)

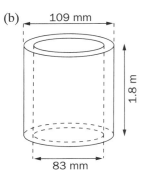

2.6 m

12.5 cm

(b)

109 mm

9.3 cm

1.8 m

83 mm

6 A factory produces plastic containers. Each container has a bottom but is open at the top.
For each container below, calculate the volume of plastic needed to make it. Give each answer to a sensible degree of accuracy.

(a)

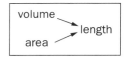

13.2 cm

6.1 cm

4.2 cm

16.2 cm

(b)

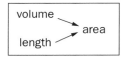

13.3 cm

17.7 cm

16.2 cm

23.3 cm

Using known volumes

Volume = Area of cross-section × length

This formula for a solid of uniform cross-section links *three measurements*.
If you know the *volume and one of the others*, you can find the *third measurement*.

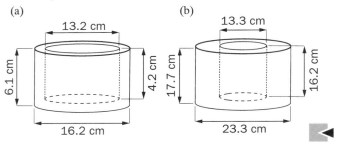

```
volume
        length
area

volume
        area
length
```

Question

This greenhouse has a volume of 50 m³. It is 8 m long. What is the area of its end-section?

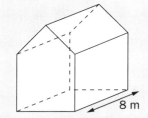

8 m

Answer

Matching units: volume 50 m³
                    length 8 m
                    'area' A m²
Formula: Volume = Area of cross-section × length
Values: 50 = A × 8
Working: 50 ÷ 8 = A
                  6.25 = A
Answer: Area of cross-section is 6.25 m²
Check: Volume ≈ 6 × 8 = 48 ✓ About the same size as 50.

The example above lists the key steps taken. Make sure you understand them.

Remember:

● Always identify the *volume*, *'area'* and *length* for the solid first. Then you can 'ignore' any other measurements you have.
● Check the measurements have *'matching units'*.
   You need … mm³, mm², mm
            or cm³, cm², cm
            or m³, m², m   and so on …
   Change units if you need to.
   Give the unit of measure clearly in your answer.
● Show your *working* step-by-step.
● *Round* your result sensibly if necessary.

Question

A child's building brick is shaped as shown in this diagram. The area of its cross-section is 68.5 cm².

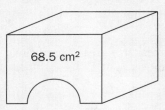

68.5 cm²

The volume of the brick is 1507 cm³. How long is the brick?

Answer

Volume of brick = area of cross-section × length
         1507 = 68.5 × length
So, length = 1507 ÷ 68.5
           = 22 cm.

► *Exercise* **P21.7**

All the solids in the questions below have uniform cross-sections.

1 A piece of guttering is shown in the diagram.
It is 135 cm long and, when full, holds 8000 cm³ of water. Calculate the area of the cross-section to the nearest square centimetre.

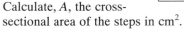

135 cm

2 Some concrete steps are in the shape of a prism as shown in the diagram.
They are 1.06 m long. The volume of concrete needed to make the steps is 91 584 cm³. Calculate, *A*, the cross-sectional area of the steps in cm².

A cm²

1.06 m

3 An oil tank has a circular base of area 12.5 square feet.
The tank holds 75 cubic feet of oil when full.
How tall is the oil tank?

OIL

4 A cast iron girder has uniform cross-section of area 650 cm². It is made from 140 000 cm³ of iron. What is the length of the girder? Give your answer to the nearest cm.

5 The diagram shows a piece of plastic guttering. When full, the guttering holds 25 litres of water. What is its area of cross-section?

6 A circular metal washer has a cross-sectional area of 1.25 cm². The volume of the metal is 0.4 cm³. How thick is the washer in millimetres?

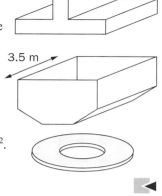

3.5 m

Working:

AC 3 5 ÷ (π × 6 • 5) = √

Don't forget to press =

Display: `1.30918918.`

Answer: radius = 1.3 cm (to 2 sf)
Check: volume ≈ 3 × 1² × 7 = 21 ✓
About the same size as 35.

In problems such as this, remember:
- Make sure you have 'matching units'.
- Replace 'area of cross-section' in the volume formula by the correct area formula. Look it up if you need to.
- Take care to do the working step-by-step. Don't try to do too much in each step.
- Plan your calculator work carefully.

The volume and length of a solid of uniform cross-section can also be used to find *another length measurement*. This measurement will be linked to the area of cross-section. It may be the length of a base or a height or a thickness or a radius …

To find this unknown measurement, write the volume formula using the correct 'area of cross-section' formula. Then put in what you know and work out what you want.

For example, the volume formula for a triangular prism is:

$$\text{volume} = (\tfrac{1}{2} \times \text{base} \times \text{height}) \times \text{length}$$

If you know the volume and length and either the base or height, you can find the unknown height or base.

The following Question/Answer shows you how to find the radius of a cylinder, given its volume and length.

Question

A machine produces steel cylinders. Each has a volume of 35 cm³ and a length of 6.5 cm. Calculate the radius of one of the cylinders. Give your answer to a sensible degree of accuracy.

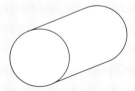

Answer

Matching units: volume: 35 cm³
length: 6.5 cm — *matching units*
radius: r cm
Formula: For a cylinder:
$$\text{volume} = (\text{area of circle}) \times \text{length}$$
$$= \pi r^2 \times \text{length}$$
Values: $35 = \pi r^2 \times 6.5$ cm
Divide by $(\pi \times 6.5)$: $35 ÷ (\pi \times 6.5) = r^2$
Take square root: $\sqrt{35 ÷ (\pi \times 6.5)} = r$

► Exercise P21.8

Each diagram shows a solid with uniform cross-section. Calculate the lengths marked with letters. Give each answer to a sensible degree of accuracy.

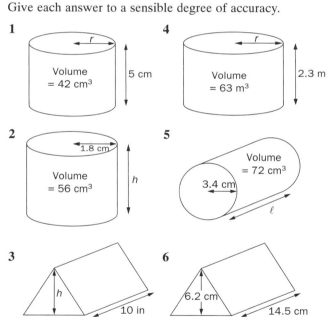

1 Volume = 42 cm³, 5 cm, r
4 Volume = 63 m³, 2.3 m, r
2 1.8 cm, Volume = 56 cm³, h
5 Volume = 72 cm³, 3.4 cm, ℓ
3 h, 3 in, 10 in, Volume = 75 cubic inches
6 6.2 cm, a, 14.5 cm, Volume = 240 cm³

7  8 mm, Volume = 750 mm³, h

Surface area

The **surface area** of a solid shape is the *total area of its surface*.
It is measured in **square units:**

    square metres (m^2)
    square centimetres (cm^2)
    square millimetres (mm^2)
    and so on …

Total surface area of an average man or
woman is about 1.5 m^2 to 2 m^2.

The **surface area of a 'mathematical solid'** is the *sum of the
areas of all its faces.*
A sketch of a solid shows some of its faces. You have to
'imagine' the others.
Look at this sketch.
It shows a solid made
from 6 centimetre cubes.
Each face on these cubes
has an area of 1 cm^2.

1 cm^2

To find the surface area of this solid, you need to be systematic.

Think about its *horizontal faces* first:
'*top* and *bottom*'.
You can see the shaded 'top faces'.
You have to imagine the 'bottom
faces'.

      Top: 4 cm^2
    Bottom: 4 cm^2

TOP
BOTTOM

Think about its *vertical faces* next:
'*front, back* and *sides*'.
You can see the shaded front and right
side faces. You have to imagine the
back and left side faces.

Front and right sides: 9 cm^2
Back and left side: 9 cm^2

Left   Back
Front   Right

The total surface area
= horizontal faces and vertical faces
= 4 + 4 + 9 + 9 = 26 cm^2

Make a model of the solid with centimetre cubes.
Count the number of square centimetres on its surface to check.

▶ *Exercise* P21.9

Each prism below is made of centimetre cubes. Find the surface
area of each solid.

1

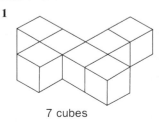
7 cubes

2

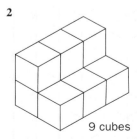
9 cubes

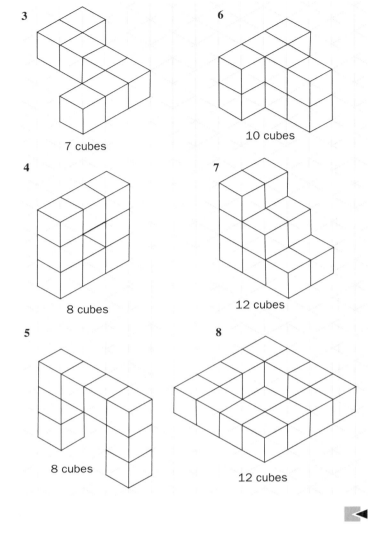

3
7 cubes

6
10 cubes

4
8 cubes

7
12 cubes

5
8 cubes

8
12 cubes

Calculating surface areas

To calculate the surface area of a solid, you may have to *find
the area of each face*.
Remember these key points:

- Identify the *number* of faces and their *shape(s)*.
  Draw a sketch and/or a net of the solid if its helps.
- Sort out the *lengths* you need to find each area.
  All lengths you use must be in the *same unit* …
      All in cm, to give areas in cm^2
      All in m, to give areas in m^2
      And so on …
  If you need to change any units, do this before calculating
  the areas.
- Try to use your *calculator efficiently*.

  Use **M+** or **SUM** to add the results of each calculation into
  the memory if it helps.
- Write down your *working* and *answer* at each stage.
- Give the correct *unit of area* in your answer.
  Round your answer sensibly if you need to.
- *Check* your answer makes sense.

The most common solids you have to deal with are cubes, cuboids and other prisms.

Cube

A cube has *six equal square faces*.

Sketch: Net:

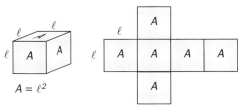

$$A = \ell^2$$

Total surface area $= 6A$
$$= 6\ell^2$$

Total surface area of a cube $= 6 \times$ area of one face
$$= 6 \times (\text{length of edge})^2$$

Question

Mrs Temple's new fridge is packed in this cube-shaped box. Calculate its surface area:
(a) in cm^2, correct to the nearest 10 cm^2
(b) in m^2, correct to the nearest 0.1 m^2.

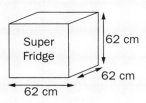

Answer

(a) *Use lengths in cm to find area in cm^2.*
Length of edge: 62 cm
Area of each square face $= (\text{length of edge})^2$
$$= 62^2 \text{ cm}^2$$
Surface area of cube $= 6 \times$ area of one face
$$= 6 \times 62^2 \text{ cm}^2$$
$$= 23064 \text{ cm}^2$$
Surface area of box is 23060 cm^2 (to nearest 10 cm^2)

(b) *Use lengths in m to find area in m^2.*
100 cm = 1 m.
So to change cm to m, divide by 100.
Length of edge: 62 cm $= 0.62$ m
Surface area of cube $= 6 \times (0.62)^2 \text{ m}^2 = 2.3064 \text{ m}^2$
Surface area of box is 2.3 m^2 (to nearest 0.1 m^2)

Cuboid

A cuboid has six rectangular faces. Opposite faces are the same shape and size. You can see this clearly from a net of the cuboid.

Sketch: Net:

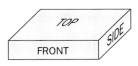

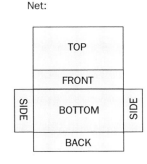

The TOP and BOTTOM are the same.
The FRONT and BACK are the same.
The two SIDES are the same.
The length, width and height of the cuboid give the edges of the faces.
You use them to find the *areas of the faces*.

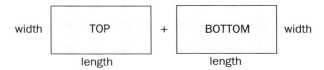

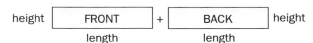

Total area of top and bottom $= 2 \times$ length $\times$ width

Total area of front and back $= 2 \times$ length $\times$ height

Total area of 2 sides $= 2 \times$ width $\times$ height

Then you *add them* together to find the *total surface area*.

Question

This sketch shows a box of paper tissues. Calculate the surface area of the box in cm^2.

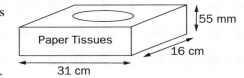

Answer

To find area in cm^2, give all lengths in cm.
Length: 31 cm
Width: 16 cm
Height: 55 mm $= 5.5$ cm
Six faces of cuboid:

Top and bottom   Two sides

Front and back

Total surface area:
Top and bottom: $2 \times (31 \times 16) = 992 \text{ cm}^2$
Front and back: $2 \times (31 \times 5.5) = 341 \text{ cm}^2$
Two sides: $2 \times (16 \times 5.5) = \underline{176 \text{ cm}^2}$
Total $= \underline{1509 \text{ cm}^2}$

You can do all this working on your calculator.
Following is one way that uses the memory. Remember to clear the memory first if you use **M+** or **SUM**

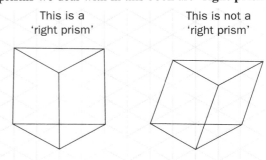

```
C  0  Min  2 × 3  1 × 1  6  =  M+   992.
          2 × 3  1 × 5 . 5  =  M+   341.
          2 × 1  6 × 5 . 5  =  M+   176.
                             MR  1509.
```

Find the 'best way' to do the working with *your* calculator.
Make a note of the keys you used.

► *Exercise* P21.10

1 Find the surface areas of cubes with these edges. Give them in mm^2, cm^2 and m^2. Say which unit is most sensible in each case.
   (a) 9 mm   (c) 6 m   (e) 43 mm
   (b) 5.1 cm   (d) 3.25 m   (f) 21.5 cm

2 Find the surface areas of cuboids with these edges. Give each answer in the most sensible unit.
   (a) 12 cm, 10 cm, 4 cm   (d) 10.5 cm, 67 mm, 12.5 cm
   (b) 2 m, 3 m, 4 m   (e) 1.3 m, 2.9 m, 60 cm
   (c) 65 mm, 25 mm, 45 mm   (f) 75 cm, 1.84 m, 35 cm

3 A giant dice is a cube with edge 75 mm long. Calculate its surface area:
   (a) in mm^2
   (b) in cm^2

4 Calculate the surface area of this matchbox:
   (a) in mm^2
   (b) in cm^2.

5 A square floor tile of edge 15 cm is 5 mm thick. Find its surface area:
   (a) in cm^2 (b) in mm^2.

6 Calculate the surface area of this brick in square inches.

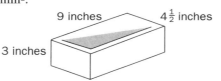

7 Mrs Brooke's kitchen units are all cuboids.
   Their inside measurements are standard sizes:
       All units are 500 mm deep.
       Wall units are 720 mm high.
       Base units are 872 mm high.
       Larder units are 2130 mm high.
   Mrs Brooke wants to paint the inside of these units:
   (i)   a base unit 1000 mm wide,
   (ii) a wall unit 1200 mm wide,
   (iii) a larder unit 600 mm wide,
   (iv) a wall unit 300 mm wide,
   (v)   a base unit 500 mm wide.
   Calculate the surface area to be painted for each unit
   (a) in cm^2 (b) in m^2.
   The paint Mrs Brooke plans to use has an expected coverage of 6 m^2 per litre.
   How much paint does she need to buy?

Prism

All the prisms we deal with in this book are **'right prisms'**.

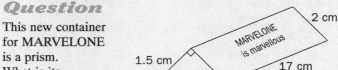

This is a 'right prism'   This is not a 'right prism'

When the *end-faces* of a right prism are *horizontal*, all its *other* faces are *vertical* and *rectangular*.
The surface area of a right prism is made up of:
   • two 'equal' end faces
   • several rectangles.
The '*length*' of the prism gives the *length of each rectangular face*.
The *sides* of the end-face give the *widths* of the rectangles.
Drawing **a net of the prism** shows this clearly.

Question

This new container for MARVELONE is a prism. What is its surface area?

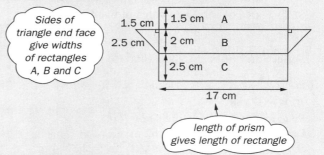

Answer

Net: 2 triangular end-faces. 3 rectangular faces.

Sides of triangle end face give widths of rectangles A, B and C

1.5 cm   A
2 cm   B
2.5 cm   C

length of prism gives length of rectangle

Use area formulas:
   Area of a triangle $= \frac{1}{2} \times$ base $\times$ height
   Area of a rectangle $=$ length $\times$ width
Total surface area:
Two triangles: $2 \times (\frac{1}{2} \times 2 \times 1.5) = $ 3 cm^2
Rectangle A : $17 \times 1.5 = $ 25.5 cm^2
Rectangle B: $17 \times 2 = $ 34.0 cm^2
Rectangle C : $17 \times 2.5 = $ 42.5 cm^2
                       Total $= $ 105.0 cm^2
The surface area of the new container is 105 cm^2.

► *Exercise* P21.11

Calculate the surface area of each prism in Exercise P21.4, p407 and in questions **1–4** in Exercise P21.6, p409.
Give your answers to a sensible degree of accuracy.

Not all faces

To solve some problems about surfaces of solids, you do *not* need the area of all the faces. Think about what makes sense in each situation. Decide which faces of the solid are involved. For example, this sketch shows the shape of a swimming pool. It is a prism. Its cross-section is a trapezium.

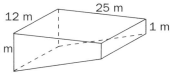

The *'inside surface'* of this pool is tiled. Common sense tells you this means the 'bottom' and 'sides' of the pool, but not the top! That's the water surface.

So don't include this face when finding the tiled area.

▶ *Exercise* **P21.12**

1 Find the tiled area for the swimming pool shown in the sketch above.

2 The sketches below show swimming and paddling pools. Each pool is a prism. The inside of each pool is tiled. Find the tiled area in each case.

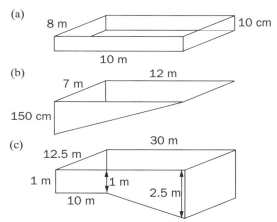

(a)

(b)

(c)

3 The objects in the sketches below are all prisms. The outside of each object needs painting. Find the area to be painted in each case.

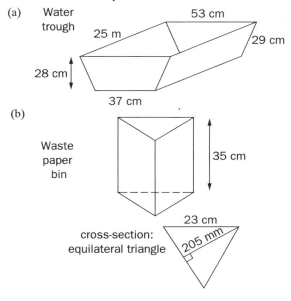

(a) Water trough

(b) Waste paper bin

cross-section: equilateral triangle

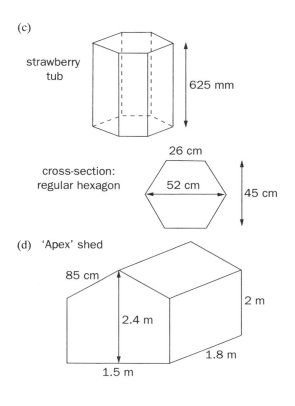

(c) strawberry tub

625 mm

cross-section: regular hexagon

26 cm

52 cm

45 cm

(d) 'Apex' shed

85 cm

2.4 m

2 m

1.5 m

1.8 m

Examination Questions

1 A cylindrical can of pineapple juice is 12.8 cm high and the radius of its base is 2.5 cm.
   Calculate the volume of the can in cm³.
   Give your answer correct to the nearest whole number.
   (ULEAC, 1991)

2 The diagram represents a triangular prism whose ends are right-angled triangles.
   (a) Write down the number of faces of the prism.
   (b) (i) Calculate the area of triangle ABC.
       (ii) Calculate the volume of the prism.
       (iii)Calculate the total surface area of the prism.
   (MEG, 1991)

3 This diagram shows a box used to hold jigsaw pieces. It is in the form of a triangular prism.
   (a) Calculate the area of each triangular end.
   (b) Calculate the volume of the box.
   (NEAB, 1994)

4 This new (not yet sharpened) pencil is a prism. The length is 18.7 cm and the area of cross-section 0.36 cm².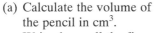

(a) Calculate the volume of the pencil in cm³.
Write down all the figures in your calculator display.

(b) Round off your answer to three significant figures.

(MEG, 1989)

5 Pete melted stolen gold and poured it into rectangular moulds as shown opposite.
He melted the gold in a large cylinder 40 cm in diameter and 60 cm high.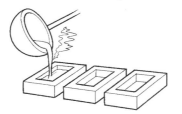

(a) Calculate the volume of this cylinder.

(b) The melted gold fills $\frac{3}{5}$ of the cylinder.
Calculate the volume of gold in the cylinder.

(c) Each rectangular mould makes a bar 6 cm by 4 cm by 15 cm.
How many of these bars can be made from the stolen gold?

(NEAB, 1991)

6 An excavator digs a hole 2 m wide.
The cross-section of the hole is shown in the sketch.
The dimensions are in metres.

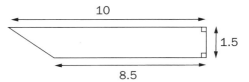

Calculate the volume of earth removed.

(MEG, 1991)

7 A plumber lags all the piping in a house using the type of lagging illustrated. The internal radius of the lagging is 7.5 mm and it is 10 mm thick.

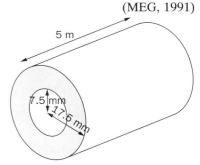

Calculate

(a) The area of the circle of radius 7.5 mm. (Give answer in square centimetres.) (You may take π = 3.14).

(b) The area of the shaded cross-section. (Give answer in square centimetres.)

(c) The lagging is sold in 5 metre lengths. Find the volume of insulating material used in each 5 metre length. (Give answer in cubic centimetres.)

(NISEAC, 1990)

P22
Simultaneous equations

This unit will help you to:

■ understand the idea of simultaneous equations

■ solve pairs of simultaneous equations with two unknowns by the following methods:
- trial and improvement
- substitution
- elimination

■ use simultaneous equations to solve problems.

Looking at problems

This 'problem' involves only **one unknown.**

The *one 'fact'* you are given about it tells you enough to find it.

> I think of a number.
> Ten times my number is 5 less than 245.
> What is the number?

 Discussion Exercise

What is the answer to the problem?
Which method did you use to find it?
Did you solve it 'by inspection',
'by trial and improvement', by algebra, ... ?
Discuss.

Here is a 'problem' involving **two unknowns.**
To find the two unknown values you have to use the *two 'facts'* that link them.

> I think of two numbers.
> They add up to 77.
> One number is ten times the other.
> What are the two numbers?

There are several ways to solve problems like this.
Here are some Discussion Exercises to explore three of them.

 Discussion Exercise

Trial and improvement

1 Tricia wants some cans of Choke and Diet Choke for a party.
She needs 50 cans altogether.

She could buy 1 Choke and 49 Diet Chokes
       or 2 Chokes and 48 Diet Chokes
       or 3 Chokes and 27 Diet Chokes
       and so on …
She decides to buy 12 more cans of Choke than Diet Choke.

Find out, by 'trial and improvement', how many cans of
each drink Tricia buys.
Discuss how you worked it out.

Use 'trial and improvement' to solve the following problems.
Discuss what you did in each case.

2   The sum of two numbers is 62.
    Their difference is 14.
    Find the numbers.
3   Jon is 13 years younger than Ian.
    Their ages add up to 37 years.
    How old are Jon and Ian?
4   Megan pays £20 for 1 Adult and 1 Child's ticket at a
    Theme Park.
    Two Adult's tickets cost the same as 3 Children's tickets.
    How much does each ticket cost?
5   Darren pays £2.50 for a piece of spicy pizza and a vanilla
    ice cream.
    Mr Saunders pays £6.80 for three pieces of spicy pizza and
    two vanilla ice creams.

    How much is a piece of spicy pizza?
    How much is a vanilla ice cream?
6   At Adkins' greengrocers, a pound of green grapes costs 35p
    more than a pound of red apples.
    Mrs Evans pays £3.70 for 2 lb of green grapes and 3 lb of
    red apples.
    What is the price per pound for
    (a) the green grapes
    (b) the red apples?
7   In a new TV quiz, Playing for Points, there are 'gold' and
    'silver' questions.

    For correct answers to 5 'gold' questions and 4 'silver'
    questions, Patrick scores 47 points.
    Sonia scores 51 points for correct answers to 3 'gold'
    questions and 10 'silver' questions.
    How many points are given for a correct answer to
    each kind of question?

 Discussion Exercise

Substitution

Use the given information to solve these puzzles.
Do *not* use a 'trial and improvement' method.
Find a way to '*think them out*'.
Explain how you found the two unknown values in each puzzle.
Discuss your method with others in your group.

1   How much does each box weigh?

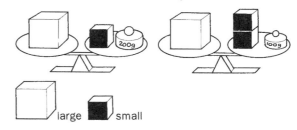

2   How much does the bottle hold?
    How much does the glass hold?

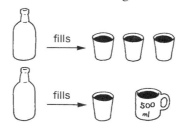

3   To get a cassette player
    from a 'vouchers'
    catalogue you can 'pay'
    … either 2 vouchers
    and £27
    … or 5 vouchers and £9.
    How many pounds is a
    'voucher' worth?
    How many pounds does the cassette player 'cost'?
4   What does each tin weigh?

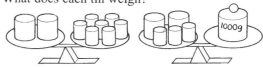

5   2 large oranges give the same calories as 3 apples.
    2 large oranges and 1 apple give 200 calories.
    How many calories does each fruit give?
6   3 pizzas cost the same as 4 hamburgers.
    3 pizzas and 2 hamburgers cost £16.20.
    How much does a hamburger cost?
    How much does a pizza cost?

Why do you think we have called this process
substitution'?
Discuss.

◯ Discussion Exercise

Elimination

A Try solving these puzzles. Do *not* use 'trial and improvement'.
Use the pictures to help you to 'think them out'.
Discuss the puzzles with the students in your group.
Compare the ways you used to solve them.
What do the 'best ways' have in common?

1 2 teas and 1 orange juice cost 55 p.
2 teas and 4 orange juices cost £1.

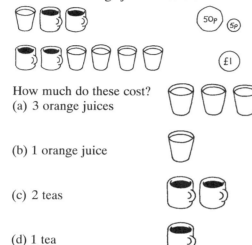

How much do these cost?
(a) 3 orange juices

(b) 1 orange juice

(c) 2 teas

(d) 1 tea

2 3 cups and 1 saucer cost £7.
1 cup and 1 saucer cost £3.

How much do these cost?
(a)   2 cups

(b)   1 cup

(c)   1 saucer

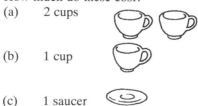

3 2 Adult and 3 Child's tickets cost £97.
1 Adult and 2 Child's tickets cost £54.

What do these tickets cost?
(a) 2 'Adult' and
4 'Child'

(b) 1 'Child'

(c) 2 'Child'

(d) 1 'Adult'

4 3 green and 2 white tokens give 34 points.
2 green and 3 white tokens give 31 points.

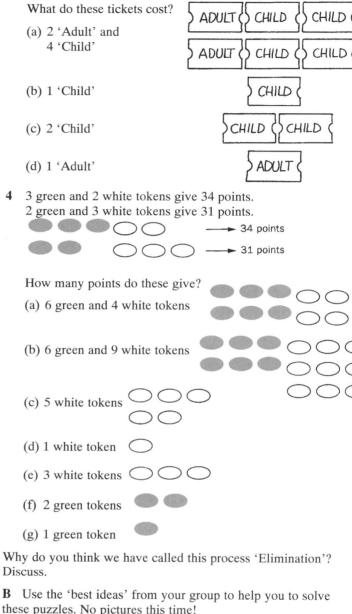

How many points do these give?

(a) 6 green and 4 white tokens

(b) 6 green and 9 white tokens

(c) 5 white tokens

(d) 1 white token

(e) 3 white tokens

(f) 2 green tokens

(g) 1 green token

Why do you think we have called this process 'Elimination'?
Discuss.

B Use the 'best ideas' from your group to help you to solve these puzzles. No pictures this time!
Discuss how you worked them out.

1 Fish and chips cost £2.
1 fish and 3 'chips' cost £3.30.
How much do these cost?
(a) 2 'chips'   (c) 1 fish
(b) 1 'chips'
2 3 large and 2 small cans hold 1850 m*l*.
1 large and 2 small cans hold 950 m*l*.
How much do these hold?
(a) 2 large cans   (c) 2 small cans
(b) 1 large can   (d) 1 small can
3 5 CDs and 2 videos cost £50.65.
3 CDs and 1 video cost £28.80.
All the CDs cost the same.
All the videos cost the same.
How much do these cost?
(a) 6 CDs and 2 videos (c) 3 CDs
(b) 1 CD   (d) 1 video

4 4 large and 3 small suitcases weigh 25.5 kg.
3 large and 2 small suitcases weigh 18.5 kg.
How much do these weigh?
(a) 8 large and 6 small suitcases
(b) 9 large and 6 small suitcases
(c) 1 large suitcase
(d) 3 large suitcases
(e) 2 small suitcases
(f) 1 small suitcase

Equations with two unknowns

An equation such as $x + 7 = 10$ has only **one unknown**.
It has only **one solution.**

$x = 3$ is the solution of $x + 7 = 10$.
This is the *only* value of x that makes the equation true.

You can *check* the solution by *putting it into* the equation.

When $x = 3$, $x + 7 = 3 + 7 = 10$ ✓ Correct.

The equation $x + y = 20$ has **two unknowns.**
A solution of this equation is a value of x and a value of y that makes the equation true.
Here are some solutions of $x + y = 20$.

$x = 1, y = 19$	because $1 + 19 = 20$
$x = 2, y = 18$	because $2 + 18 = 20$
$x = 3.5, \ y = 16.5$	because $3.5 + 16.5 = 20$
$x = 4.2, \ y = 15.8$	because $4.2 + 15.8 = 20$.

In fact, you can take *any* value for x or y and *find the 'other' value* for the solution from the equation.

For example, if $x = 12, y = 8$ because $12 + 8 = 20$
                 if $y = 4, x = 16$ because $16 + 4 = 20$.
This means there is an **infinite number of solutions.**

☐ *Discussion Exercise*

Give at least five different solutions for each of these equations.

$x + y = 100$	$y = x - 5$	$y = 2x + 1$
$x - y = 20$	$y = x + 7$	$x + 2y = 5$

Compare your solutions with those of other students in your group.
Check each others' solutions.
Discuss how you found them.

Simultaneous equations

Look at these two equations:

$x + y = 9$
$\quad y = 2x$

Each equation has two unknowns, x and y.
So each has an infinite number of solutions.

Here are some of them.

$\boxed{x + y = 9}$		$\boxed{y = 2x}$
$x = 1, y = 8$		$x = 1, y = 2$
$x = 2, y = 7$	same	$x = 2, y = 4$
$\boxed{x = 3, y = 6}$	solution	$\boxed{x = 3, y = 6}$
$x = 4, y = 5$		$x = 4, y = 8$
$x = 5, y = 4$		$x = 5, y = 10$.

There is, however, a value of x and a value of y that makes both equations true *at the same time.*

This solution is $x = 3, y = 6$.

We say that this solution solves the equations **simultaneously.**
Simultaneously means 'at the same time'.
The equations $x + y = 9$ and $y = 2x$ are called **simultaneous equations.**

> *Memo*
> Equations that are solved together are called simultaneous equations.
> The solution must make the equations true 'at the same time', that is, simultaneously.

There are several different ways to solve simultaneous equations.
In Unit P20 Crossed lines p398 they are solved *graphically*.
In this Unit the methods used are:
- trial and improvement
- substitution
- elimination

Trial and improvement is a **'numerical' method.** It involves *trying numbers* until you find the pair you want.
'Substitution' and 'elimination' are both **algebraic methods.**
They involve working with the *letters standing for the unknowns.*

Trial and improvement method

You have solved problems by 'trial and improvement' before.
The basic strategy is always the same.
Some pairs of simultaneous equations with two unknowns are simple to solve by **trial and improvement.**

Here are some guidelines to help you to use the method efficiently.
- Estimate *two simple* numbers that fit the *'easier'* equation first.
- *Try* your two numbers in the *two equations.*
  See if they fit *both* equations. (This is the **'trial'.**)

  If they do fit both, then they are the *solution.* If they don't fit both, then you choose *two 'better numbers'* for the next trial. (This is the **'improvement'.**)
  Make 'trials' and 'improvements' until you find the two numbers that fit both equations.
- Keep a neat *record* of what you try. This helps you to pick the numbers for the 'next trial'.
- Compare the results of each trial with what you want.
  Decide whether it is *'too big'* or *'too small'*.
  Use this to help you to choose 'better numbers' to try next.
- Look for trials that give *'opposite results'*, i.e., too big and too small. These 'opposite results' give you an 'extra clue'

about the numbers you want. They must be '*between*' the numbers used in these two 'trials'. So make sure you try two such numbers in your next 'trial'.

- Always *state your solution* clearly. It must be made up of two numbers. Say *which letter* stands for *which number*.

Question

Solve these simultaneous equations by trial and improvement.

$$x + y = 93$$
$$x - y = 35$$

Show your working clearly.

Answer

To solve these equations, take these steps.
- *Start with two simple numbers for x and y.*
  Make sure they add up to 93, because x + y = 93.
- *Use them to work out x − y.*
  Compare the result with 35, because x − y = 35.
- *Keep trying values for x and y, until you get*
  x + y = 93 and x − y = 35.

Try $x = 50$, $y = 43$.
  $x + y = 93$ ✓
  $x - y = 7$ ← Smaller than 35. *Try a larger number for x.*

Try $x = 60$, $y = 33$.
  $x + y = 93$ ✓
  $x - y = 27$ ← Still smaller than 35. *Try a larger number for x.*

Try $x = 70$, $y = 23$
  $x + y = 93$ ✓
  $x - y = 47$ ← Larger than 35. *Try a smaller number for x. It must be between 60 and 70.*

Try $x = 65$, $y = 28$
  $x + y = 93$ ✓
  $x - y = 37$ ← Just larger than 35. *Try a smaller number for x.*

Try $x = 64$, $y = 29$.
  $x + y = 93$ ✓
  $x - y = 35$ ✓ *That's it!*

The solution is $x = 64$, $y = 29$.

To keep track of each 'trial' and 'improvement', you can record your working in a table.

This table shows the working for the example above.

x	y	$x + y$	$x - y$	
50	43	93	7	Too small
60	33	93	27	Too small
70	23	93	47	Too big
65	28	93	37	Too big
64	29	93	35	That's it!

opposite results

See how it shows each 'trial' clearly.
It gives the two numbers in the 'trial'
and the 'results' for the two equations.

A neat record of working like this is a reminder for you. In an examination it also shows the examiner what you have tried.

▶ Exercise P22.1

Solve each pair of simultaneous equations by trial and improvement.
Keep a neat record of your working.

1	$x + y = 81$	**6**	$c - d = 36$
	$y = 2x$		$c + 3d = 180$
2	$a + b = 107$	**7**	$x + y = 12$
	$a - b = 31$		$2x + 25y = 116$
3	$p = 3q$	**8**	$3x + 2y = 5$
	$p + 2q = 30$		$5x - 6y = 27$
4	$x - y = 15$	**9**	$2x + y = 5$
	$2x - y = 97$		$3x - y = 2$
5	$7a - b = 7$	**10**	$a - 8b = 3$
	$6a = b$		$3a - 10b = 2$

🗨 Discussion Exercise

Which pairs of equations were easiest to solve by this method? Which were most difficult? Why?
What are the advantages and disadvantages of this method?
Discuss.

Trial and improvement is a quick way to solve *simple* pairs of simultaneous equations. It is not so efficient for more complicated equations. An algebraic method is usually quicker and easier in these situations.

Substitution method

Compare these two simultaneous equations:

$$y = 4x - 1$$
$$y = x + 5$$

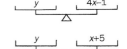

Each equation is written as
'y = something'.
This makes them easy to solve simultaneously.

When we solve the equations simultaneously, y has the *same value* in *each* equation.
So anything equal to y must *also* be equal.

We can write: $4x - 1 = x + 5$

from $y = 4x - 1$ from $y = x + 5$

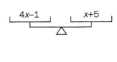

This equation has only one unknown, x.
Solving it gives us the value of x.
Here is the working, step-by-step.

Add 1 to both sides:
$$
\begin{array}{rcl}
4x - 1 &=& x + 5 \\
+1 && x + 1 \\
\hline
4x &=& x + 6
\end{array}
$$

Subtract x from both sides:
$$
\begin{array}{rcl}
-x && -x \\
\hline
3x &=& 6
\end{array}
$$

Divide both sides by 3:
$$x = 2$$

To find the value of y, we put $x = 2$ into one of the *original* equations.

When we put $x = 2$ into $y = x + 5$
we get $y = 2 + 5$
$y = 7$

The solution of the two simultaneous equations is:
$x = 2$, $y = 7$
We can check that this solution fits the *other* equation.
In $y = 4x - 1$, when $x = 2$, $y = 7$:
LHS: $y = 7$
RHS: $4x - 1 = 4 \times 2 - 1 = 8 - 1 = 7$ } LHS = RHS ✓

► *Exercise* **P22.2**

Solve these simultaneous equations.

1 $y = x + 2$
   $y = 3x - 6$

2 $x = 5y + 2$
   $x = 2y + 11$

3 $p = 2q + 4$
   $p = q + 7$

4 $r = 3s + 2$
   $r = 10 - s$

5 $u = 5v + 7$
   $u = v - 1$

6 $m = n - 4$
   $m = 5 - 2n$

Now let's consider how to solve
these simultaneous equations.

$y = x + 8$
$x + y = 20$

The value of y must be the *same* in *both* equations.
From the *first* equation we know that $y = x + 8$.
So we can **substitute** $x + 8$ for the letter y *in the second equation*.

This means that
the equation $x + y = 20$
becomes $x + (x + 8) = 20$

We now have a simple equation to solve.
It has only one unknown, x.
To find the value of x, we do this, step-by-step.

$$x + (x + 8) = 20$$
Remove the brackets: $x + x + 8 = 20$
Add x terms: $2x + 8 = 20$
Subtract 8 from both sides: $\underline{\quad -8 \quad -8}$
$2x \quad = 12$
Divide both sides by 2: $x \quad = 6$

To find the value of y,
we put $x = 6$ into *one of the original equations*.
It is easier to use $y = x + 8$.

When we put $x = 6$ into $y = x + 8$
we get $y = 6 + 8 = 14$

The solution of the two simultaneous equations is:
$x = 6$, $y = 14$.

As usual, we check the solution fits the *other* equation,
$x + y = 20$.
When $x = 6$, $y = 14$, $x + y = 6 + 14 = 20$ ✓

To solve the equations $y = x + 8$ and $x + y = 20$ simultaneously,
we **substituted** $x + 8$ for y.
So we call this the **substitution method.**

► *Exercise* **P22.3**

Solve these equations simultaneously by the substitution method.

1 $y = 5x$
   $3x + y = 8$

2 $x = 3y$
   $x - 4y = 20$

3 $x + y = 15$
   $y = x - 7$

4 $y = 2x + 3$
   $x + y = 9$

5 $x = 4 - y$
   $x - y = 2$

6 $6y - x = 12$
   $x = 2y$

When you use the substitution
method, you often have to multiply a
bracket by a number.

An example of this kind follows.

Memo
Equations with brackets
p105

Question

Solve $x = 1 - 2y$ and $3y - 2x = 5$ simultaneously.

Answer

The value of x must be the same in both equations.
From the first equation we know that $x = 1 - 2y$
So we can substitute $\boxed{1 - 2y}$ *for the letter x in the second equation.*
Put brackets round $\boxed{1 - 2y}$.
Substitute $(1 - 2y)$ for x in the second equation.

The second equation is: $3y - 2x = 5$
It becomes: $3y - 2(1 - 2y) = 5$

Multiply out brackets:
$3y - 2 + 4y = 5$
Add y terms: $7y - 2 = 5$
Add 2 to both sides: $7y = 7$
Divide both sides by 7: $y = 1$

To find the value of x,
put $y = 1$ in the first equation: $x = 1 - 2y$
$= 1 - 2(1)$
$= 1 - 2$
$= -1$

So the solution of the equations is $x = -1$, $y = 1$.
Check the solution fits the other equation, $3y - 2x = 5$.
When $x = -1$, $y = 1$,
$3y - 2x = 3(1) - 2(-1) = 3 + 2 = 5$ ✓

Summary

Solving simultaneous equations by substitution.
This method is easiest to use when one equation is written
as:

one letter = *an expression involving the other letter only*

continued

Here are the key steps to take:
- Put brackets round the 'expression':

    one letter = *(expression in other letter)*

- Substitute (expression in other letter) for the 'letter' in the other equation.
  This gives an equation with only one unknown.
- Solve this equation.
  This gives the value of one letter.
- Put this value into one of the original equations to find the value of the other letter.
- Check your solution
  Make sure your two values fit the other original equation.

▶ *Exercise* P22.4

1 Solve each pair of equations simultaneously.

(a) $y = x + 8$
  $x + y = 14$

(b) $a = b + 4$
  $2b + a = 1$

(c) $c = d + 2$
  $5d + c = 14$

(d) $m = n - 1$
  $3n - m = 7$

(e) $3p - q = 9$
  $q = 2p - 7$

(f) $r - s = 2$
  $s = 8 - r$

2 Solve these simultaneous equations.
Remember to put brackets round the expression you substitute in each case.

(a) $x = 6 - 3y$
  $3y - 2x = 6$

(b) $p = 2q - 5$
  $3q - 2p = 7$

(c) $y = 5 - 2x$
  $2x - 3y = 1$

(d) $4a = 3b - 2$
  $a = 2b - 3$

(e) $2r = 3s + 12$
  $r = 2s + 5$

(f) $p = 9 - q$
  $2p = q + 3$

Elimination method

An equation is like a balance with two scale pans.

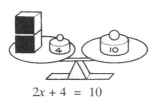

$$2x + 4 = 10$$

It stays in balance if you do the same to both sides.

Take 4 from both sides, for example, and we still have balance.

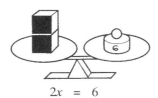

$$2x = 6$$

Divide both sides by 2, for example, and we still have balance.

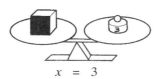

$$x = 3$$

This balance idea helps us to solve equations *with one unknown*.
We use it to 'get rid of' unwanted terms and numbers.

The same balance idea can also help us to solve simultaneous equations *with two unknowns*.
We use it to 'get rid of' one of the unknowns first.
Solving simultaneous equations in this way is often called the **elimination method.** 'Eliminate' means 'get rid of'.

Look at these pictures of two balances.
The left-hand side balances the right-hand side in each case.

We can combine the contents of the scale pans like this:

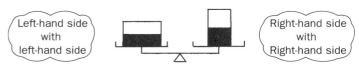

Combined LHS = Combined RHS

The two sides must *balance*.
We have *equal amounts* on each side.

Since this is true for two 'balances', it must also be true for two equations.

Here are 'balance pictures' for two simultaneous equations.

Left-hand side and right-hand sides can be combined in the same way.

Combined LHS = Combined RHS

To work out the amount on each side, we can set it out like a 'sum'.
We write one equation under the other, with = signs 'in line' and like terms 'in line'.

x's in line y's in line   numbers in line

$$\begin{aligned} x + y &= 11 \\ 2x - y &= 4 \end{aligned}$$

Now it is easy to add like terms:

$$\begin{aligned} x + y &= 11 \\ 2x - y &= 4 \\ \hline 3x &= 15 \end{aligned}$$

Adding 'gets rid of' the y term because $+y - y = 0$
It leaves: $3x = 15$
Dividing both sides by 3 gives: $x = 5$

To find the value of y, we put $x = 5$ into one of the *original equations*.

Putting $x = 5$ into $x + y = 11$
gives $5 + y = 11$
Subtracting 5 from both sides gives $y = 6$
The solution of the simultaneous equations is $x = 5$, $y = 6$.

These x- and y-values must fit both equations.

We should check that they do.
Check:
In $x + y = 11$, when $x = 5$, $y = 6$,

LHS: $x + y = 5 + 6 = 11$
RHS: 11 $\quad\rbrace$ LHS = RHS ✓

In $2x - y = 4$, when $x = 5$, $y = 6$,

LHS: $2x - y = 2 \times 5 - 6 = 10 - 6 = 4$
RHS: 4 $\quad\rbrace$ LHS = RHS ✓

The working for this method can be written out very simply.
The next example shows one way to do this.

Question

Solve the equations $-2x + 5y = 19$ and $2x + y = -1$
simultaneously.

Answer

$$
\begin{array}{r}
-2x + 5y = 19 \\
2x + y = -1 \\
\hline
+ 6y = 18
\end{array}
$$

Add equations:
Divide both sides by 6: $\quad y = 3$

To find x, put $y = 3$ in $\quad 2x + y = -1$
$\qquad\qquad\qquad\qquad 2x + 3 = -1$

Subtract 3 from both sides:
$$
\begin{array}{r}
-3 \quad -3 \\
\hline
2x \quad = -4
\end{array}
$$
Divide both sides by 2: $\quad x = -2$
The solution is $x = -2$, $y = 3$

Check in the original equations:
In $-2x + 5y = 19$, when $x = -2$, $y = 3$,
LHS:
$-2x + 5y = -2(-2) + 5 \times 3 = +4 + 15 = 19$
RHS: 19 $\quad\rbrace$ LHS = RHS ✓

In $2x + y = -1$, when $x = -2$, $y = 3$,
LHS: $2x + y = 2(-2) + 3 = -4 + 3 = -1$
RHS: -1 $\quad\rbrace$ LHS = RHS ✓

▶ *Exercise* **P22.5**

Solve these pairs of simultaneous equations. Check each
solution.

1 $x + y = 11$
   $x - y = 1$
2 $3r - s = 0$
   $2r + s = 10$
3 $9n + m = 19$
   $6n - m = 11$

4 $6m + 3n = 9$
   $m - 3n = 5$
5 $3r + 5s = 9$
   $2r - 5s = 6$
6 $4p + 3q = 7$
   $6p - 3q = 3$

◀

In examples so far you have *added* two equations. In each case
this *eliminated* (got rid of) one of the letters.
Sometimes you have to *subtract* one equation from another to
eliminate a letter. If you do the subtraction *on each side* in the
same order, then the results are equal.

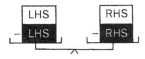

To help us to describe the working, we usually **label the
equations.**
In the example below we use the letters (A) and (B).
You may also use numbers such as (1) and (2).

Question

Solve these equations simultaneously: $2x + 3y = 7$
$\qquad\qquad\qquad\qquad\qquad\qquad\qquad\quad 2x + y = 5$

Answer

Label equations:
$$
\begin{array}{ll}
2x + 3y = 7 & \text{(A)} \\
2x + \ y = 5 & \text{(B)} \\
\hline
\end{array}
$$
Subtract equations, (A) – (B): $\quad 2y = 2$
Divide both sides by 2: $\qquad\qquad y = 1$

To find x, put $y = 1$ in
$$
\begin{array}{r}
2x + y = 5 \\
2x + 1 = 5 \\
\hline
\end{array}
$$
Subtract 1 from both sides: $\quad 2x = 4$
Divide both sides by 2: $\qquad x = 2$
The solution is $x = 2$, $y = 1$

Check in the original equations (A) and (B)
For (A), when $x = 2$, $y = 1$:
LHS: $2x + 3y = 2 \times 2 + 3 \times 1 = 4 + 3 = 7$
RHS: 7 $\quad\rbrace$ LHS = RHS ✓

For (B), when $x = 2$, $y = 1$:
LHS: $2x + y = 2 \times 2 + 1 = 4 + 1 = 5$
RHS: 5 $\quad\rbrace$ LHS = RHS ✓

In the example above, we subtracted the *second* equation from
the *first* one.
Sometimes it is easier to subtract the *first* equation from the
second.
In such examples, rewrite the equations with the second
equation 'on top'.

For example,
look at these simultaneous equations: $5x + 2y = 14$
$\qquad\qquad\qquad\qquad\qquad\qquad\qquad\qquad 7x + 2y = 22$

You can subtract them like this:
$$
\begin{array}{ll}
5x + 2y = 14 & \text{(1)} \\
7x + 2y = 22 & \text{(2)} \\
\hline
-2x \quad = -8 &
\end{array}
$$
Work out (1) – (2)

Or you can rewrite them like this:
$$
\begin{array}{ll}
7x + 2y = 22 & \text{(2)} \\
5x + 2y = 14 & \text{(1)} \\
\hline
2x \quad = 8 &
\end{array}
$$
Work out (2) – (1)

Both ways give the same value for x, that is, $x = 4$.
But the second way is easier because you get a '+' x term.
Always take extra care when '–' terms are in the subtraction.

Remember:
A subtraction involving two identical terms gives 0.

$$
\begin{array}{r}
\boxed{x} \\
- \boxed{x} \\
\hline
0
\end{array}
\ \text{and}\
\begin{array}{r}
\boxed{-x} \\
- \boxed{-x} \\
\hline
0
\end{array}
\qquad
\begin{array}{r}
\boxed{2x} \\
- \boxed{2x} \\
\hline
0
\end{array}
\ \text{and}\
\begin{array}{r}
\boxed{-2x} \\
- \boxed{-2x} \\
\hline
0
\end{array}
$$

and so on ...

Question

Solve these equations simultaneously: $2x - 5y = -4$
$x - 5y = 3$

Answer

Label equations: $2x - 5y = -4$ (A)
                                                   $x - 5y = 3$ (B)

Subtract equations, (A) – (B): $x \qquad = -7$ ⟵
                                                                        $\overbrace{-4 \; -3}$

To find y, put $x = -7$ in $x - 5y = 3$
                                               $-7 - 5y = 3$

Add 7 to both sides : $-5y = 10$
Divide both sides by –5 : $y = -2$ $\overbrace{10 \div -5}$
The solution is $x = -7$, $y = -2$.

Check solution fits both original equations, (A) and (B).
In (A), when $x = -7$, $y = -2$
LHS:
$2x - 5y = 2(-7) - 5(-2) = -14 + 10 = -4$ $\Big\}$ LHS = RHS ✓
RHS: -4

In (B), when $x = -7$, $y = -2$,
LHS: $x - 5y = -7 - 5(-2) = -7 + 10 = 3$ $\Big\}$ LHS = RHS ✓
RHS: 3

► *Exercise* P22.6

Solve these pairs of simultaneous equations.
Check each solution.

1	$3x + y = 13$	**6**	$10r - 2s = 9$
	$x + y = 7$		$7r - 2s = 6$
2	$3p + q = 1$	**7**	$2m + 3n = 4$
	$5p + q = 9$		$4m + 3n = 8$
3	$7n + m = 12$	**8**	$2x - 4y = 9$
	$2n + m = 2$		$6x - 4y = 3$
4	$7x - y = 6$	**9**	$2x + y = 3$
	$5x - y = 4$		$2x + 4y = 12$
5	$4a - b = 11$	**10**	$5r - 2s = 2$
	$a - b = 2$		$10r - 2s = 3\frac{1}{2}$

◀

ℚ *Discussion Exercise*

Add or subtract?

To eliminate a letter from a pair of equations, you have either
added or *subtracted* the equation.
So far you have been told which to do.
But you can decide *yourself* by simply *looking at the equations*.

Here are the equations we *added* in the examples on p422 & p423.

$x + \mathbf{y} = 11$	$-2\mathbf{x} + 5y = 19$
$2x - \mathbf{y} = 4$	$2\mathbf{x} + y = -1$

The letter we eliminated in each case is in bold.
What do you notice about its terms?
Why does this show us to add the equations?
Discuss.
Test your ideas also work with the equations in Exercise 22.5.

Look at the equations we *subtracted* in the examples on p423
and p424.
Again, their terms show us we should do this.
Discuss how.
Test your ideas using the equations in Exercise P22.6.

Consider each of the following pairs of equations.
Decide which to *add* and which to *subtract* to eliminate a letter.
Which letter disappears in each case?

1	$5c + 2d = 15$	**3**	$5p + 2q = 11$
	$c + 2d = 3$		$4p - 2q = 7$
2	$3a + b = 5$	**4**	$7x - 2y = 3$
	$4a - b = 2$		$7x - 3y = 1$

Now solve each pair of equations simultaneously.

Making equal amounts

Simply adding or subtracting two equations does not always
eliminate one of the letters.

Look at these equations: $3y + 2x = 4$
$y - 4x = 6$

We can add them: We can subtract them:

$3y + 2x = 4$
$y - 4x = 6$
$4y - 2x = 10$

$3y + 2x = 4$
$y - 4x = 6$
$2y + 6x = -2$

Each new equation is true.
But they do not help us to solve the original equations.
Neither x nor y has been eliminated.

To eliminate a letter by adding or subtracting, each equation
must have the *same 'number'* of that letter.

Let's look at the two equations again:
$$\mathbf{3y} + 2x = 4 \quad \text{(A)}$$
$$\mathbf{y} - 4x = 6 \quad \text{(B)}$$

Compare y terms: We have $\mathbf{3y}$ in equation (A).
                             We have $\mathbf{y}$ in equation (B).
We can make y into $3y$ by multiplying by 3.
But we must do the same to each term in equation (B) to keep
the 'balance'.

$$\underbrace{y - 4x}_{} = \underbrace{6}_{\triangle} \quad \times 3 \longrightarrow \underbrace{3y - 12x}_{} = \underbrace{18}_{\triangle}$$

The new equation, $3y - 12x = 18$, was made from equation (B).
This means it has the same x and y values as equation (B).
So instead of solving equations (A) and (B) together,
we can solve equation (A) and an equation *made from* (B).
The solution must be the same.

Let's look at the 'new' pair of equations:

Original equation (A) $\mathbf{3y} + 2x = 4$
Equation made from (B): $3 \times$ (B) $\mathbf{3y} - 12x = 18$

The two equations have the same number of 'y's, i.e., $\mathbf{3y}$.
So subtracting one from the other gets rid of y.
Then we can solve the equations as before.

Here is the working.

$$3y + 2x = 4 \quad (A)$$
$$3y - 12x = 18 \quad 3 \times (B)$$

Work out (A) $-3 \times$ (B): $\quad\overline{14x = -14}$

Divide both sides by 14: $\quad x = -1$

To find y, we put $x = -1$ into one of the original equations, (A) or (B).
We use (B) because it is easier. It has just one 'y'.

Equation (B) is: $\qquad y - 4x = 6$
Put $x = -1$: $\qquad y - 4(-1) = 6$
$$\qquad\qquad y + 4 = 6$$
Subtract 4 from both sides $\qquad y = 2$
The solution is $x = -1$, $y = 2$

As usual, we check these values fit *both* equations.
In (A): LHS $\quad 3y + 2x = 3 \times 2 + 2(-1) = 6 - 2 = 4 =$ RHS ✓
In (B): LHS $\quad y - 4x = 2 - 4(-1) = 2 + 4 = 6 =$ RHS ✓

We can also solve the *same equations*,
$3y + 2x = 4$ and $y - 4x = 6$, by *eliminating x*.
Compare their x terms: $3y + \mathbf{2x} = 4 \quad$ (A)
$$y - \mathbf{4x} = 6 \quad (B)$$

We have $+\mathbf{2x}$ in equation (A).
We have $-\mathbf{4x}$ in equation (B).
Multiplying equation (A) by 2
gives $+\mathbf{4x}$ in a new equation.

$$\boxed{3y + \mathbf{2x} = 4}$$
$$\times 2 \downarrow$$
$$\boxed{6y + \mathbf{4x} = 8}$$

This new equation has the same x and y values as (A).
We now have $+\mathbf{4x}$ in the equation *made from* (A)
and $-\mathbf{4x}$ in the original equation (B).
The '*same number*' but *opposite sign*.
So adding these equations eliminates x.
Then we can find the solution of the equations as before.

Here is one way to write down the working.

	$3y + 2x = 4 \quad$ (A)
	$y - 4x = 6 \quad$ (B)
Equation made from (A): $2 \times$ (A)	$6y + 4x = 8$
Original equation (B)	$y - 4x = 6$
Add: $2 \times$ (A) + (B)	$7y \quad\;\; = 14$
	$y \quad\;\; = 2$
To find x, put $y = 2$ in	$3y + 2x = 4$
	$3 \times 2 + 2x = 4$
	$6 + 2x = 4$
	$2x = -2$
	$x = -1$

The solution is $x = -1$, $y = 2$.

As expected, both ways give the same solution.
We have already checked it for both equations.

► *Exercise* **P22.7**

Solve each pair of simultaneous equations.
Check each solution.

1	$3x + 2y = 3$	**3**	$2p + 3q = 8$	**5**	$3x + y = 8$
	$x - y = 6$		$p + q = 3$		$2x + 3y = 10$
2	$2c + 3d = 8$	**4**	$6r + 5s = 28$	**6**	$2a + 3b = 6$
	$3c - d = 1$		$r - s = 1$		$a - 2b = 3$ ◄

Sometimes *both equations* have to be 'altered' before we can eliminate a letter.
Look at these equations: $\qquad 3x + 2y = 8 \quad$ (A)
$$4x - 5y = 3 \quad (B)$$

Let's compare x terms.
In (A) we have $3x$.
We cannot multiply $3x$ by a whole number to get $4x$.

In (B) we have $4x$.
We cannot multiply $4x$ by a whole number to get $3x$.

We cannot get the 'same number' of xs by multiplying just *one* equation by a whole number.

Let's compare y terms
In (A) we have $2y$.
We cannot multiply $2y$ by a whole number to get $5y$.

In (B) we have $-5y$.
We cannot multiply $5y$ by a whole number to get $2y$.

We cannot get the 'same number' of ys by multiplying just *one* equation by a whole number.
It looks as if we need to multiply *both* equations by numbers.

Let's look again at the x terms.
In (A) we have $3x \leftarrow$ Multiplying $3x$ by 4 gives $12x$.
In (B) we have $4x \leftarrow$ Multiplying $4x$ by 3 gives $12x$.
This gives the same number of 'x's, i.e., $12x$.
So we can eliminate x if we multiply both equations by numbers.

Here is the working to solve $3x + 2y = 8$ and $4x - 5y = 3$ in this way.

● *Label the equations:*	$3x + 2y = 8 \quad$ (A)
	$4x - 5y = 3 \quad$ (B)
● To get rid of x, make the number of 'x's the same.	
Multiply (A) by 4 (because we have $\mathbf{4x}$ in (B))	
Multiply (B) by 3 (because we have $\mathbf{3x}$ in (A))	
Equation made from (A): $4 \times$ (A)	$12x + 8y = 32$
Equation made from (B): $3 \times$ (B)	$12x - 15y = 9$
Subtract: $4 \times$ (A) $- 3 \times$ (B)	$23y = 23$
	$y = 1$
To find x, put $y = 1$ in (A) or (B).	
Put $y = 1$ in	$3x + 2y = 8 \quad$ (A)
	$3x + 2 = 8$
	$3x = 6$
	$x = 2$

The solution is $x = 2$, $y = 1$.
● *Check solution:*
In (A): LHS $= 3x + 2y = 3 \times 2 + 2 \times 1 = 6 + 2 = 8 =$ RHS ✓
In (B): LHS $= 4x - 5y = 4 \times 2 - 5 \times 1 = 8 - 5 = 3 =$ RHS ✓

Discussion Exercise

1   In the working above we eliminated x from this pair of equations:

$3x + 2y = 8$ (A)
$4x - 5y = 3$ (B)

How can you eliminate y from these equations?
Discuss.
Solve the equations by eliminating y.

2   Think about solving these equations:

$5x + 4y = 21$ (C)
$7x + 6y = 31$ (D)

(a) Discuss how you can eliminate x from these equations.
    Solve the equations by eliminating x.
(b) Discuss how to eliminate y from these equations.
    Solve the equations by eliminating y.

Exercise P22.8

Solve each pair of simultaneous equations. Check each solution.

1   $4x + 3y = 7$
    $3x - 2y = 1$
2   $5c + 2d = 7$
    $6c + 3d = 9$
3   $5r + 4s = 12$
    $2r + 3s = 9$
4   $5e - 8f = 2$
    $4e - 7f = 1$

5   $3p + 2q = 7$
    $2p + 3q = 3$
6   $2u - 3v = 5$
    $3u - 4v = 7$
7   $5n + 2m = 8$
    $4n + 3m = 5$
8   $11m - 3n = 8$
    $9m + 4n = 13$

Summary

You can use the **elimination method to solve any pair of simultaneous equations**.
Here are the basic steps you need to take.
● Label the two equations.
● Eliminate (get rid of) one of the letters first.
  (More about this below*.)
● Solve the equation you get to find the value of the letter you have left.
● Substitute this value in one of the original equations to find the value of the other letter.
  (Always use the equation that 'looks' easier.)
● Check your solution fits both original equations.

* **To decide how to eliminate one letter,** compare 'like letters' terms in the two equations.
  For example, x terms with x terms, y terms with y terms,
  Look at the number and sign in front of each letter.
● *'Same number' of one letter* in both equations.
  In this case you can *add* or *subtract* the equations, to get rid of that letter.

  Same number, *opposite* sign → *add* the equations
  (e.g., $+3x$ and $-3x$)
  Same number, *same* sign → *subtract* the equations
  (e.g., $+3x$ and $+3x$)

● *Different numbers of each letter* in both equations.
  You want the *'same* number' of *one* letter in two equations.

To get this, you may have to 'alter' one or both of the original equations.
To 'alter' the way an equation is written, multiply *each term* in that equation by the same whole number.
To choose this number, compare the numbers 'in front of' like terms.
If you have to alter *both* equations, you will have to multiply each equation by a *different number*.
When you have the 'same number of one letter', you can find the solution as before.

Exercise P22.9

Solve these pairs of simultaneous equations.
Check each solution.

1   $3x - y = 6$
    $x - y = 2$
2   $4a + 5b = 17$
    $2a - 5b = 1$
3   $3m + 2n = 16$
    $4m - n = 3$
4   $5e + 3f = 13$
    $3e + 2f = 8$

5   $6r + s = 9$
    $4r + s = 5$
6   $7e + 3f = 16$
    $2e + 9f = 29$
7   $4m - 2n = 6$
    $4m - 5n = 3$
8   $6v - 3w = 9$
    $5v - 2w = 7$

Rearranging equations

Terms in equations are not always written in the 'same order'.
For example,
in $7x - 2y = 14$, we have ⎢x-term⎢, ⎢y-term⎢ = *number*
in $3y + 5x = 10$, we have ⎢y-term⎢, ⎢x-term⎢ = *number*.

Solving equations by the elimination method is easier when the terms are in the *same order* in *both equations*. So it is sensible to rearrange them first.
The terms do not have to be in any particular order. We simply want them in 'matching places' in both equations.
We only 'move' a term if we have to.

Look again at $7x - 2y = 14$ and $3y + 5x = 10$.
The number terms are in matching places.
So we can leave them alone.
We only need to put x- and y-terms in matching places.

We can choose to have x term y term   = number
In this case …

  ● we leave $7x - 2y = 14$ as it is,
  ● we rearrange $3y + 5x = 10$

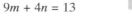

      to give $5x + 3y = 10$

Remember: A term without a sign, such as $3y$, is +.

We now have these equations to solve: $7x - 2y = 14$
$5x + 3y = 10$

We can also choose to have y term x term   = number
In this case …

  ● we rearrange $7x$ $-2y$ = 14

      to give $-2y$ $+7x$ = 14

Remember: A – sign 'belongs to' the term it is in front of.

- We leave $3y + 5x = 10$ as it is.

Now we have these equations to solve: $-2y + 7x = 14$
$$3y + 5x = 10$$

 Discussion Exercise

Discuss the two ways of rearranging the above equations.
Which do you think is easier?
Why?
Solve the pair of equations.
Use the rearrangements you find easier as the first step.

Exercise **P22.10**

Rearrange each pair of equations. Then solve them simultaneously.
Check each solution.

1 $n + 5m = 3$
   $m - 2n = 5$

2 $2x + 12 = y$
   $3x + 2y = 3$

3 $x - 2y = 10$
   $y + 3x = 2$

4 $2p - 5 = q$
   $p + 3q = 6$

5 $6s + 1 = 3r$
   $4r - 3 = 3s$

6 $3b + 4a = 9$
   $5a = 8 + 6b$

Problem solving

To solve some problems, you have to find *two values*.
You often do this by solving two simultaneous equations.
Here are the key steps you need to take.

- *Think* about the problem first.
  Read the given information carefully.
  Identify the facts you are given and what you have to find out.
  Jot them down in note form if it helps.
- Choose *two letters*, one for each unknown.
  State clearly what each stands for.
  Don't forget to include any units, such as pence, kg, …
- Look for *two 'facts'* that *link* your two unknowns.
  Work out each relationship in words.
  Then write an equation for each using your letters.
  Remember: The terms in an equation must either all stand for numbers or all stand for quantities in the same unit.
  Change any units if you need to.
- *Solve* the two simultaneous equations you have made.
  Show your working clearly.
  A question may tell you which method to use.
  If it does, then you *must* use that method.
  Don't waste your time doing it in any other way.
  (In an examination you cannot get marks for it, even if your answer is correct.)
  If it doesn't, then you can use *any* method.
  Choose the 'best method' for you and your equations.
- State your *solution to the problem*.
  Give it simply 'in words' and figures.
  Don't just write each value as 'letter = …'.
- *Check* your solution.

Make sure it fits the information in the *original* problem.
Do not simply check it fits your equations (they may be incorrect).

Question

Tim saves all the 2p and 5p coins from his change. By the end of a month he has saved 108 coins. They are worth £3.51. How many coins of each type did Tim save that month?

Answer

- *Use two letters*
  Let t be the number of 2p coins and f be the number of 5p coins.
- *Form two equations*
  Look at 'how many' 2p and 5p coins Tim has.
  Fact: 'he has saved 108 coins.'
  Relationship:
  Number of 2p coins + number of 5p coins = 108
  Equation: $t + f = 108$ ← *All terms are numbers*

Look at the value of Tim's coins.

 $t \times 2$ pence

t coins worth 2p each → $2t$ pence
f coins worth 5p each → $5f$ pence

 $f \times 5$ pence

Fact: 'They are worth £3.51'
Relationship:
Value of 2p coins + value of 5p coins = £3.51
Equation: $2t + 3f = 351$ ← *All terms in pence*

- *Solve equations*
  Label equations:

$t + f = 108$	(A)
$2t + 5f = 351$	(B)

Leave (B) as it is: $2t + 5f = 351$ (B)
Multiply (A) by 2: $2t + 2f = 216$ $2 \times$ (A)
Work out (B) $- 2 \times$ (A): $3f = 135$
Divide both sides by 3: $f = 135 \div 3$
     $f = 45$

To find t,
put f = 45 into (A): $t + f = 108$
     $t + 45 = 108$
Take 45 from both sides: $t = 63$
The solution of the equations is $f = 45$, $t = 63$.

- *Answer question:*
  Tim saved 45 five pence coins and 63 two pence coins.
- *Check:*
  Total number of coins : $45 + 63 = 108$ ✓
  Total value of coins: 45×5 pence $+ 63 \times 2$ pence
  $= 225$ pence $+ 126$ pence
  $= 351$ pence
  $= £3.51$ ✓

 Exercise P22.11

1 A college bought 30 tickets for a performance of Julius Caesar. Some were student tickets (costing £4.50 each) and some were staff tickets (costing £6.75 each). The total cost of the tickets was £148.50.

Let x be the number of student tickets and y be the number of staff tickets bought.

(a) Write down an equation in x and y for the total number of tickets bought.

(b) Write down an equation in x and y to show that the total cost of the tickets, in pence, was 14 850p.

(c) Solve your two equations simultaneously.

(d) How many tickets of each type did the college buy?

2 Catriona buys three 3-hour videos and two 4-hour videos for £16.95.

Matt buys two 3-hour videos and three 4-hour videos for £17.95.

Let x pence be the cost of a 3-hour video and y pence by the cost of a 4-hour video.

(a) Write down two equations in x and y.

(b) Solve your equations.

(c) What is the cost of

(i) a 3-hour video   (ii) a 4-hour video?

3 A bottle of Raspberry Fizz costs 20p more than a bottle of Lemonade.

Four bottles of Raspberry Fizz and five bottles of Lemonade cost £5.75.

Let x pence be the cost of a bottle of Raspberry Fizz and y pence be the cost of a bottle of Lemonade.

Find the cost of a bottle of Raspberry Fizz.

4 Joe works for Tindalls. He is paid a basic rate of £5.50 per hour. Overtime is paid at a rate of £7.40 per hour. Last week Joe worked a total of 45 hours and was paid £260.80.

How many hours overtime did Joe work?

5 Tim uses 3 jugs of lemonade and 5 glasses of lime juice to fill a 3-litre punch bowl for his party. His sister Ann uses 4 jugs of lemonade and 10 glasses of lime juice to fill a $4\frac{1}{2}$-litre bowl. How many millilitres does

(a) the jug hold   (b) the glass hold?

6 The ages of a father and his daughter add up to 56.

In two years time the father will be exactly three times as old as his daughter.

How old are they today?

Solve each problem in the Discussion Exercises on pages 416–419 by forming two simultaneous equations linking the two unknowns and solving the equations algebraically. ◀

Using known facts

A fact you use to form an equation may be stated clearly in the problem.

For example,
'The total number of boys and girls on the coach is 30.'

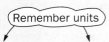

Sometimes you use a fact marked on a diagram.

For example, in this diagram, angles X and Y are marked equal.

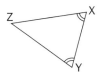

You can also use a fact you *know* about the situation. For example, you know that the angle sum of a quadrilateral is 360°. So in this quadrilateral, you know that:

$a + b + 90 + 25 = 360$

This gives $a + b = 245$

Always think about what you know about a situation, not simply what you are given.

Question

In triangle ABC, angle A is 42°.
Angle B is 30° larger than angle C.
Find the sizes of angles B and C.

Answer

- *Draw diagram*
- *Use letters for angles.*
  Let $b°$ be the size of angle B
  and $c°$ be the size of angle C.

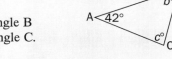

- *Form two equations*
  Given fact: 'Angle B is 30° larger than angle C'
  Equation: $b - c = 30$ ←

  〔All terms in degrees〕

  Known fact: Angle sum of a triangle $= 180°$
  Equation: $42 + b + c = 180$
  This gives: $b + c = 138$ ←

  〔All terms in degrees〕

- *Solve equations:*
  Label equations: $b - c = 30$ (A)
                               $b + c = 138$ (B)

  Add (A) and (B): $2b = 168$
  Divide both sides by 2: $b = 84$
  To find c,
  put b = 84 into (B): $b + c = 138$
                               $84 + c = 138$

  Take 84 from both sides $c = 54$
  The solution of the equations is b = 84, c = 54.

- *Answer question:*

  〔Remember units〕

  Angle B is 84°, Angle C is 54°

- *Check:*
  Compare angles B and C:
      84° is 30° more than 54° ✓
  Find angle sum:
      42° + 84° + 54° = 180° ✓

►*Exercise* P22.12

1 This diagram shows the lengths of the sides of a rectangle in centimetres.

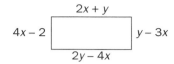

(a) What do you know about the sides of a rectangle?
(b) Use this fact to write down two equations in x and y.
(c) Solve your equations.
(d) Find the lengths of each side of the rectangle.

2 The diagram below shows the lengths of the sides of an isosceles trapezium in centimetres.

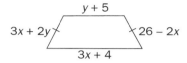

The base is twice the length of the side parallel to it.
(a) Find the size of the two equal length sides.
(b) Find the lengths of the two other sides of the trapezium.

3 The diagram below shows an isosceles triangle.

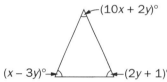

Find the size of each angle.

4 This diagram shows three parallel lines and two crossing lines (transversals).

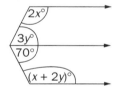

One of the marked angles is 70°. Find the sizes of the other three angles.

5 One angle is a triangle is 50°. The difference between the other two angles is 42°. What are the sizes of the other two angles?

6 Two angles in a quadrilateral are 134° and 118°. The difference between the other two angles is 52°. How big are the other two angles?

7 A straight line has the equation $y = mx + c$.
If the points $x = 3$, $y = 20$ and $x = 4$, $y = 23$ lie on this line, find the values of m and c.

For questions **8** and **9**, do **not** draw the straight lines mentioned.

8 Find the point where the straight lines with equations $2y - 3x = 3$ and $x + 2y = 7$ cross.

9 Find the point where these straight lines cross:
$4y = 3x + 7$ and $2x + 5y = 3$.

Examination Questions

1 The cost, £C, of making n articles is given by the formula
$$C = a + bn$$
where a and b are constants.
The cost of making 4 articles is £20 and the cost of making 7 articles is £29.
Write down two equations in a and b.
Solve these equations to find the values of a and b.
(ULEAC, 1988)

2 Three cans of cola and five packets of peanuts cost a total of £1.44. Five cans of cola and three packets of peanuts cost a total of £1.60. Let c pence be the cost of a can of cola and p pence the cost of a packet of peanuts.
(a) Write down two equations to represent the given data.
(b) Find the cost of a can of cola.
(MEG, 1989)

3 A farmer's young daughter surveys her father's stock of cows and hens. She counts them and notices that there are 40 altogether and that they have a total of 130 legs. Let c be the number of cows and h the number of hens and write down two simultaneous equations which follow from these data. By solving these equations, or otherwise, find the number of cows.
(MEG, 1990)

4 Given that

8 bolts and 6 nuts weigh 138 grams
and 3 bolts and 5 nuts weigh 71 grams,

work out the weight of each of the following:
(a) 4 bolts and 3 nuts   (d) 1 bolt
(b) 11 bolts and 11 nuts   (e) 1 nut
(c) 3 bolts and 3 nuts
(NEAB, 1988)

5 Mr and Mrs Stephens and their two children went with Mrs Morgan and her three children to the theatre. The cost for the Stephens family was £15.50 and that for the Morgan family was £14.25. Find the price of an adult ticket and a child ticket.
(WJEC, 1988)

6 Six pencils and seven pens cost £2.43.
Four pencils and three pens cost £1.27.
Find the cost of one pencil and of one pen.
(NISEAC, 1989)

7 A picnic is being prepared for a school outing. One drink and one pie are packed for each child.
The cans of drink each weigh 380 g and the individual pies each weigh 200 g.
They are packed into two cartons, each weighing 400 g when empty. One carton contains x drinks and y pies and the other carton contains y drinks and x pies.
The packed cartons weigh 7720 g and 7000 g respectively.
(a) Obtain the equations $19x + 10y = 366$
and $10x + 19y = 330$.
(b) Solve these equations.
(MEG, 1991)

8 A poultry keeper takes day-old chicks and ducklings to market. If the day's price of day-old chicks is 25p each and of ducklings is 30p each, she will receive £82 by selling them all. If the day's price of day-old chicks is 30p each and of ducklings is 35p each, she will receive £97 by selling them all.

(a) Let x be the number of day-old chicks and y be the number of ducklings. Write down two equations in x and y using the information above.

(b) Solve your two equations to find how many day-old chicks she took, and how many ducklings.

(MEG, 1989)

P23
Loci

This unit will help you to:

■ understand the idea of the locus of a moving object

■ sketch and describe the locus of a moving object given the rule(s) to be obeyed

■ recognise, sketch and describe some common loci

■ find a locus by experiment

■ understand that a locus may be a point, line or region

■ construct perpendiculars, bisectors and parallels accurately with ruler and compasses

■ draw loci accurately with drawing instruments

■ solve loci problems using accurate diagrams

■ use scale drawing to solve loci problems.

Paths of moving objects

Some objects leave a trail or path when they move.

Other objects move along a 'path' but do not leave a trail. You can often imagine what this path looks like.

Discussion Exercise

1 Sketch and describe the paths these objects move along. Discuss your ideas with your group.

● a basketball bounced from one player to another

● a netball thrown through the net
● a tennis ball thrown up for a serve
● a tennis ball when served
● the head of a tennis racket during a serve
● the head of a swimmer diving into a pool
● the head of a diver doing a somersault from the diving board
● the feet of a gymnast swinging round the horizontal bar
● the feet of a gymnast doing a vault over the horse
● a ball hit for six at cricket
● a horse jumping over three fences in a gymkhana
● a rugby ball scoring a goal

2 Think about some other moving objects. Sketch and describe the paths they move along. Compare your ideas with others in your group. Discuss.

Predictable paths

Here are two paths made by a moving pencil point.

Lorna simply 'doodled' when she drew the first path. She moved the point in a *random way*. The path the point moved along does *not* make a predictable pattern.

To draw the other path Lorna used a spirograph. The path the point moved along was *fixed* by the spirograph wheels used.

The moving point made a pattern you can predict. The same '*rule*' will always make the point move along the same path.

ring	$\frac{150}{105}$
wheel	60
hole	2

The spirograph pattern is an example of a **locus**.

Summary

When an object moves according to a 'rule', the path it moves along is called a **locus**. The locus is made up of all the possible positions the object can occupy.
The plural of locus is **loci**.

You can predict the shape of a locus from the rule the moving object obeys. Everywhere on the path must obey the rule.

Discussion Exercise

Think about the way some 'everyday' objects move.
Which move according to a rule?
What is the 'rule' in each case?
Discuss.
Which move along a 'fixed' path?
What 'fixes' the shape of the path?
Discuss.
What do you think the loci of these moving objects look like?
Describe or sketch the shape in each case if you can.
Discuss your ideas with your group.

Sketching loci

To find out what a locus looks like, you can *sketch a few points that fit the rule*. The pattern these points make should show what shape the path is.
Then you can *draw the locus through the points*.

In many 'everyday' situations, it is easy to work out the positions of some points on the locus.

For example,
look at this clockface. The tip of the hour hand is 2 cm from the centre of the dial. As the hour hand moves, the tip is *always* 2 cm from the centre.

The dots on this diagram show where the tip is at 1, 2, 3, 4, ... o'clock

In 12 hours, the path the tip will move along is a complete circle.
So the locus of this moving point is a circle, radius 2 cm, with its centre at the centre of the dial.

► *Exercise* P23.1

Sketch and describe the loci of these moving points. Discuss the locus in each case.
1 The tip of the minute hand of a clock over half an hour.
   (The minute hand is 28 mm long.)
2 The centre of a ball as it rolls along the ground.
   (The diameter of the ball is 8 inches.)

3 The top right-hand corner of the front cover of this book as the book is opened.
4 The bottom corner of a door as the door is opened.
   (The door is 45 cm wide.)
5 The head of a child moving down a slide.

Use your imagination to help you to 'see' loci. Imagine the way the objects move. Try to get a 'mental picture' of what happens. Then describe and sketch the paths you 'see' in your 'pictures'.

Discussion Exercise

Mike passes a motor-cycle proficiency test. He gains his certificate by completing each of the following tasks successfully.

Task 1
Ride so that you are always 1 metre to the left of the line painted on the road.

Task 2
Ride so that you are always 1 metre from this traffic cone.

Task 3
Ride so that you are always 1 metre from the line painted on the road.

Task 4
Ride so that you are always the same distance from the two lines painted on the road.

Task 5
Ride so that you are always the same distance from these two painted lines on the road.

Task 6
Ride so that you are always the same distance from each of the two traffic cones.

Each task gives Mike a 'rule' he has to obey.
What is Mike's locus in each task?
Sketch and describe what you think each locus will be.
Discuss your ideas with your group.
Explain how you worked out the shape of each path.

Summary

Common loci

Some common loci are useful to know.
Here are some loci you will meet often in questions.
For each locus we give:
* the rule the point obeys
* a description and sketch of the path.

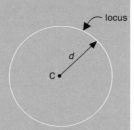

1   *Rule*: The point stays the same
distance, *d*, from a fixed point.
Locus: A circle with the fixed
point as centre and radius
the given distance, *d*.

2   *Rule*: The point stays the same distance, *d*, from an
infinite straight line.
Locus: Two parallel lines, one on each side of the line

and the given distance, *d*, from the line.

3   *Rule*: The point stays the same distance from a fixed
straight line.
Locus: Two parallel lines as above but the same length as
the line and two semicircular 'ends' with radius
the given distance, *d*.

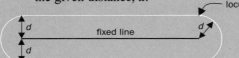

4   *Rule*: The point is the same
distance from two fixed
points.
Locus: The perpendicular
bisector of the line
joining the points.

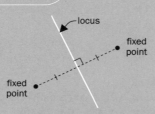

5   *Rule*: The point is the same distance from two fixed
parallel lines.
Locus: A line half-way between the two fixed lines and
parallel to them.

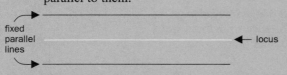

6   *Rule*: The point is the same
distance from two straight
lines meeting at a point.
Locus: The bisector of the
angle between the
lines.

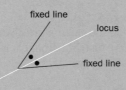

7   *Rule*: The point is the
same distance from two
straight lines that cross.
Locus: The bisectors of
the angles
between the
lines.

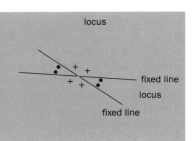

▶ *Exercise* **P23.2**

Sketch and describe each of the loci in questions **1–5**.

1   The locus of a point P which moves in such a way that it is
always 4 cm from a fixed point A.

2   The locus of a point P which moves so that its distance
from a fixed point A is equal to its distance from a fixed
point B.

3   The locus of a point Q which moves so that its distance
from line CD is always 3.5 cm.

4   The locus of a point R which moves
in such a way that its distance from
the line AB is always equal to its
distance from the line AC.

5   The locus of a point S which
moves in such a way that its
distance from line EF is
always equal to its distance
from line GH.

6   The stick AB is free to rotate about the point C.

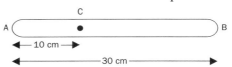

Sketch and describe the locus of
(a) the point A   (b) the point B.

7   Sketch and describe the locus of the
centre of a 10 pence coin (diameter
24 mm) as it rolls, without slipping
(a) on the inside
(b) on the outside
of a circle of radius 12 cm.

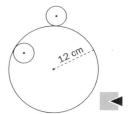

Finding a locus by experiment

To find the locus of a point, you may need to do an **experiment**.
    For the experiment, you make a 'model' of the situation.
Then you use the model to mark some points that obey the
given rule.
    You may recognise the path being moved along after marking
only a few points. Sometimes you will need to mark many
points before you get a clear idea of what the locus looks like.
    Here is an investigation that models the same situation in two
different ways.

Investigation

The rolling wheel

Imagine a bicycle being ridden along a flat road. What do you think is the locus of a point on the rim of the front wheel?

To investigate this situation you can use either an actual bicycle wheel or a circular object as a 'model' of the wheel. Try both ways if you can.
Here are some ideas about what to do.
You will need to work with a partner.

Using a bicycle

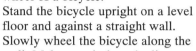

Mark a point on the rim of the front wheel of a bicycle.
Stand the bicycle upright on a level floor and against a straight wall.
Slowly wheel the bicycle along the wall. Make sure it doesn't slip.
Mark the position of the point on the wheel rim on the wall with chalk as you go along. Do this at regular intervals.
The points you get should give a picture of the locus you want.

Using a circular object

You need a circular lid, a ruler and a sheet of plain paper.

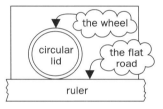

The circular lid represents the wheel.
The ruler represents the flat road.
Mark a point on the edge of the lid.
Roll the lid carefully along the edge of the ruler.
Make sure that it does not slip.
Mark the position of the point on the paper as you go along.
You should get a pattern of points like this.

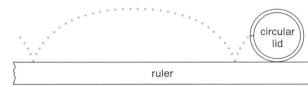

You can draw the path through the points.
The curve you get is called a **cycloid**.

Regions

A moving point may trace out an **area** rather than a line.
The locus is the **region** it covers.
For example, this 'computer picture' is a set of points that cover a region. The computer was programmed to produce a set of dots that obey a rule.

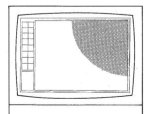

To show a locus that is a region, draw the *boundary line(s)* first.
Then you can *shade the area* that fits the rule(s).

If the boundary line is part of the locus, it is shown as a solid line ——.
If the boundary line is not included in the locus, it is shown as a dotted line - - - - -.

Question

Diane cleans the college dining room every day. This diagram shows its floor plan.
Diane's vacuum cleaner has a flex 4 m long. She plugs it into the socket S. Sketch the locus of the points she can vacuum. Describe this locus in words.

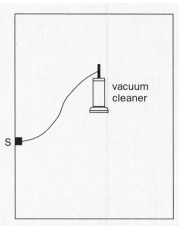

Answer

The line on this diagram shows the farthest she can vacuum. This *boundary line* is an arc of a circle, centre S, radius 4 m.
She can also vacuum *anywhere inside* this boundary line.

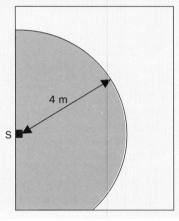

The locus of the points she can vacuum is:
- the shaded region inside the boundary line
  and
- the boundary line itself.

Exercise P23.3

Each locus in this exercise involves a region.
In each case, answer these questions before you sketch and describe the locus.
(a) Where is the boundary line?
(b) Is the boundary line included in the locus or not?
(c) Which area gives the region for the locus?

1 A point P moves in such a way that it is always less than 25 mm from a fixed point A. What is the locus of P?

2 A point Q moves so that its distance from a fixed line AB is always greater than or equal to 1.5 cm. What is the locus of Q?

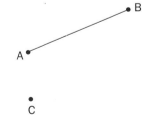

3 A point R moves in such a way that it is always closer to a fixed point C than it is to a fixed point D. What is the locus of R?

4 A point S moves such that its distance from EF is always greater than its distance from GH. What is the locus of S?

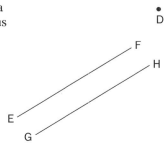

5 A point T moves in such a way that its distance from the line LM is always less than or equal to its distance from the line LN.
What is the locus of T?

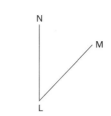

6 A goat is tied to a post in the middle of a field by a rope of length 2 m. Draw a sketch to show the area of grass the goat can reach to eat.

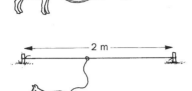

7 One end of a chain, 3 m long, is fastened to the collar of a guard dog. The other end of the chain can slide along a fixed horizontal rail 2 m long.
Sketch the region of the ground which is protected by the guard dog.

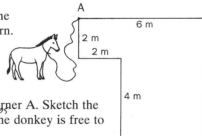

8 This diagram is the plan view of a barn. A donkey is tethered outside the barn by a rope 4 m long attached to the corner A. Sketch the region in which the donkey is free to roam.

A
6 m
2 m
2 m
4 m

9 A helicopter sets out on an air-sea rescue mission looking for a boat in distress. Its job is to fly over the area of sea, ABCD, shown in this plan.
The pilot is told by radio that the boat is within 300 m of the buoy B and nearer to D than A. Shade, on a sketch, the region in which the boat is to be found.

A   500 m   B
500 m
D   C

10 This diagram shows the plan of a new garden. P and Q are the positions of two trees.
A gardener is told to plant grass seed to make a lawn. The lawn must be at least 3 m from each tree and at least 1 m from the fence.
Sketch the plan of the garden. Shade the region to be seeded for grass.

P   Q
7 m
fence
10 m

Constructions

You may need to draw some loci *accurately*.
You have already used drawing instruments for some constructions. Here are some other drawing techniques you may need to use.

Drawing shapes
S7 p156

Remember:
A **perpendicular** is at *right angles* (90°) to another line.
A **bisector** cuts a line or angle into *two equal parts*.
Parallel lines are always the *same distance apart*.

Perpendiculars

To construct the perpendicular bisector of a line AB, take these steps.

A ——————— B

1 Open your compasses to a radius more than half AB. Keep your compasses set at this radius throughout.

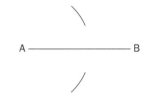

2 Put the point of your compasses on A. Draw an arc above and below the line.

3 Put the point of your compasses on B. Draw arcs to cross your first two arcs.

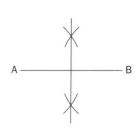

4 Draw a line through the crossing arcs.
This is the perpendicular bisector of AB.
It is at right angles (90°) to AB.
Check this with a protractor.
It crosses AB at its mid-point.
Check this with a ruler.

ACTIVITY

1 Draw a line 6 cm long. Mark the ends A and B.
Construct the perpendicular bisector.
Check with your ruler that the line AB has been cut in half.
Check with your protractor that the perpendicular is at right angles to AB.

2 Draw the perpendicular bisectors of these lines:
(a) XY = 8 cm   (c) PQ = 9.5 cm   (e) RS = 10.6 cm.
(b) CD = 12 cm   (d) MN = 11.8 cm
Check your constructions as before.

To construct a perpendicular to a line AB, from a point P, take these steps.

1 Open your compasses to a radius greater than the distance from P to AB. Keep your compasses set at this radius throughout.

2 Put the point of your compasses on P. Draw two arcs to cut the line. Call these points X and Y.

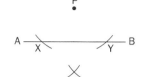

3 Put your compasses point on X and Y in turn. Draw two arcs that cross like this.

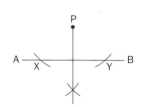

4 Draw a line from P, through the point where the arcs cross. This line is perpendicular to AB. Measure the angle between them with a protractor. Check it is 90°.

ACTIVITY

1 Draw a line 8 cm long. Mark the ends P and Q. Mark a point about 4.5 cm above the line PQ. Label the point A. Draw the perpendicular from A to the line PQ. Check with your protractor that the perpendicular is at right angles to PQ.

2 Repeat this activity for some other lines and points. Check the accuracy of your constructions with a protractor.

To construct a perpendicular to a line AB, at a point P on the line, take these steps.

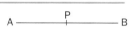

1 Put the point of your compasses on P. Draw two arcs to cut the line. Call these points X and Y.

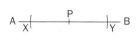

2 Open your compasses to a larger radius. Put your compasses point on X and Y in turn. Draw arcs to cut above and below the line.

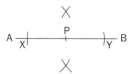

3 Draw a line through P and these crossing arcs. This line is perpendicular to the line AB at P. Check the angle with a protractor.

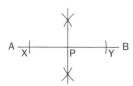

Note: If your line through the crossing arcs does *not* go through P, your construction is *not accurate*.

ACTIVITY

1 Draw a line 9.5 cm long. Mark the ends R and S. Mark a point on the line. Label it P. Draw the perpendicular at P to the line RS. Check with your protractor that the perpendicular is at right angles to RS.

2 Repeat this activity for some other lines and points labelled P. Try putting the point P at end of the line as well as between the end points of the line.

Angle bisector

To construct the bisector of any angle X, take these steps.

1 Open your compasses to a radius smaller than the length of either arm of the angle. Keep your compasses set at this radius throughout.

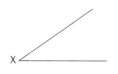

2 Put your compasses point on X, the vertex of the angle. Draw arcs to cut the arms of the angle. Call these points A and B.

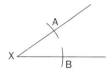

3 Put your compasses point on A and B in turn. Draw two arcs that cross like this.

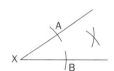

4 Draw a line through X and the point where the arcs cross. This line is the bisector of angle X. It cuts the angle in half. Use a protractor to check that you have two equal angles.

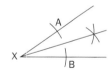

ACTIVITY

1 Draw an angle ABC equal to 70°, with each arm of the angle about 7 cm long. Draw the bisector of angle ABC. Check with your protractor that each 'half angle' is 35°.

2 Draw the bisector of these angles:
   (a) angle PQR = 80°   (d) angle LMN = 120°
   (b) angle EFG = 50°   (e) angle VWX = 146°
   (c) angle XYZ = 48°
   Check the size of each 'half angle' with your protractor.

Parallel lines, a given distance apart

To construct a line parallel to AB, a given distance *d* from it, take these steps.

1 Mark two points a reasonable distance apart on the line.

2 Draw or construct a perpendicular to the line at each of these points.

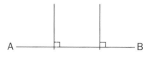

3 Mark the given distance *d*
from the line AB
along each perpendicular.

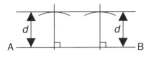

4 Draw a line through your marked
points. This line is parallel to AB
and the given distance *d* from it.
Check this with a set square and
ruler.

ACTIVITY

1 Draw a line 9 cm long. Mark the ends A and B. Draw the
perpendiculars to the line AB at the points A and B.
Mark off a distance 3.5 cm from the points A and B along
each perpendicular. Draw a line through your marked
points. Check that the line AB and the drawn line are
3.5 cm apart throughout their lengths.

2 Construct lines parallel to each of these lines at these given
distances:
(i) PQ = 7 cm, 3 cm apart
(ii) RS = 9.4 cm, 4 cm apart
(iii) TU = 8.6 cm, 5 cm apart
(iv) XY = 10 cm, 3.8 cm apart
(v) YZ = 11.2 cm, 5.3 cm apart.

In some problems you may also need
to **construct shapes** such as triangles.
The following Activity gives some
extra practice in these techniques.

Memo
Drawing triangles
p156-158

ACTIVITY

1 (a) Construct the triangle ABC with AB = 12 cm, AC = 8 cm
and angle CAB = 60°.
(b) From your triangle measure as accurately as you can
(i) the length of side BC
(ii) the size of angle ABC.
(c) Construct the perpendicular from C to meet AB at D.
Measure and write down the length of CD.
(d) Bisect angle ABC. Let this bisector meet the side AC
at E.
Measure and write down the length AE.

2 (a) Construct the triangle PQR in which QR = 8.3 cm,
RP = 5.2 cm and PQ = 6.8 cm.
(b) Draw, as accurately as you can, the perpendicular from
P to QR and measure its length.

3 (a) Construct the triangle LMN in which LM = 9 cm,
MN = 8 cm and NL = 7.5 cm.
(b) Draw the bisector of each angle in the triangle. They
should all pass through one point. Label the point O.
(c) Draw a perpendicular from point O to one side of the
triangle.
Measure and write down the length of this perpendicular.
(d) With centre point O, draw a circle inside the triangle
which just touches each side.

4 (a) Draw the triangle EFG with EF = 11.5 cm,
angle GEF = 65° and angle GFE = 45°.
(b) Draw the perpendicular bisector of each side of the

triangle. They should all pass through one point. Label
this point C.
(c) Measure and write down the lengths of CE, CF and CG.
What do you notice?
(d) With centre point C, draw a circle which passes through
E, F and G.

5 (a) Draw a line 5 cm long. Label it ST.
(b) Construct a triangle RST with ST as base,
angle RST = 60°, angle RTS = 90° and the point R
above the base ST.
Measure and write down the length of SR.
(c) Extend the line RS downwards to point M where
RSM = 13 cm.
(d) Extend the line RT downwards to point N where
RTN = 15 cm.
(e) Construct the bisectors of angle TSM and STN, and
where these lines intersect, mark the point O.
(f) From O construct a perpendicular to the line TN, and
where it meets TN, mark the point P.
(g) With centre O and radius OP draw a circle.

Solving problems

A locus problem often gives *several rules* that must be obeyed
at the same time.
To solve such a problem, draw the locus for each rule in turn on
the same diagram. Where these loci cross will obey all the
rules. The crossing places may be *points*, *lines* or *regions*.
Remember these key points:
● Always start with a *sketch* of the situation.
   Label it carefully.
● Decide on the *shape of each locus* you have to draw.
   Write down what it is, if this helps.
● Work out any values you need.
● Finally draw the diagram *as accurately as possible*.
   Remember to leave all construction lines in your answer.

ACTIVITY

1 (a) Draw a line PQ 10 cm long.
(b) Construct the locus of a point A which moves such that
PA = QA.
(c) Construct the locus of a point B which moves such that
PB = 6 cm.
(d) Mark with X and Y the two points where the two loci
meet. Measure and record the lengths of PX and PY.

2 (a) Construct the triangle ABC in which AB = 10 cm,
angle ABC = 90° and BC = 7 cm.
(b) Construct the locus of points inside the triangle which
are equidistant from AB and AC.
(c) Construct the locus of points inside the triangle which
are equidistant from points A and C.
(d) Mark the point P where the two loci intersect. Measure
and write down the length of AP.

3 (a) Draw a line AB, 8 cm long.
(b) Construct the locus of points which are equidistant from
A and B. Show this using a dotted line.
(c) Construct the locus of points which are 5 cm from
point B. Show this using a dotted line.

(d) Shade the region of your diagram within which a point must lie if it is to be within 5 cm of point B and closer to point A than point B.

4 (a) Construct the triangle PQR in which the base QR = 9 cm, angle PQR = 60° and PQ = 5.5 cm.

(b) Construct the locus of points which are equidistant from PQ and PR.

(c) Find and mark the point S which is equidistant from PQ and PR and is such that QS is parallel to PR. Measure and write down the length of PS.

5 (a) Construct the triangle ABC in which AB = 8.5 cm, angle CAB = 40° and BC = 5.5 cm.

(b) Construct the locus of points inside the triangle which are equidistant from points A and B. Show this using a dotted line.

(c) Construct the locus of points inside the triangle which are equidistant from AC and AB. Show this using a dotted line.

(d) Construct the locus of points inside the triangle which are 6 cm from point B. Show this using a dotted line.

(e) Shade the region inside the triangle that is
- within 6 cm of point B
- closer to point A than point B
- nearer to AC than AB.

Using scale drawing

Many loci problems are solved by **scale** drawing.

Memo

Scale drawing p159

Memo

Remember these key points.
● Start with a clear sketch of the situation. Sketch the loci you plan to draw.
● Use a suitable scale. Write it down. If a scale is given, you *must* use it. If you can choose your own scale, make sure it is *easy to use*.
● Change 'real lengths' to 'scale lengths' using your scale. Keep a record of your working.
● Make a neat scale drawing from your scale lengths. Label it clearly. Leave all construction lines on your drawing.
● Find the solution to the problem from your drawing.
● Explain your answer.

Question

The scale drawing in the next column shows a plan of Mr Howell's garden. It is drawn to a scale of 1 cm to 1 metre. Mr Howell wants to plant a tree in the garden.
The tree must be at least 2 m from the house wall.
It must be more than 3 m from the bird table.
It must be nearer to the fence than it is to the hedge.
Find, by construction, the region in which Mr Howell can plant the tree. Shade this region on the plan.

Answer

Draw an arc, radius 3 cm, centre the bird table.
Anywhere outside this arc is more than 3 m from the bird table.

Draw a line parallel to the house wall, 2 cm from it. Anywhere on or above this line is at least 2 m from the house wall.

Draw the bisector of the angle between the fence and hedge. Anywhere between this line and the fence is nearer to the fence than it is to the hedge.

bird table
hedge 7 m
fence 9 m
house wall   8 m

▶ *Exercise* **P23.4**

1 The sketch below shows a small area of land belonging to farmer Drabble. Farmer Drabble has agreed to allow a rambler's path to be made across his land from the gate directly to the woods, provided:
- the path is a straight line
- every point on the path is the same distance from the wall as it is from the hedge.

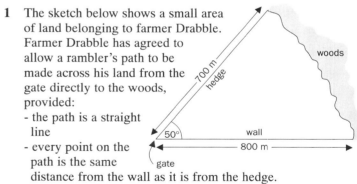

(a) Using a scale of 2 cm to 100 m, make an accurate scale drawing of the above sketch.

(b) On your diagram, draw accurately, the path which farmer Drabble has agreed to allow across his land.

2 In a type of knockout cricket match, at least six fielders must stand at or within 15 yards of the nearest point to the line joining the centre stumps of the two sets of wickets. In the diagram below, WX represents the line joining the centre stumps of the two wickets.
Using a scale of 1 cm to 4 yards, construct an accurate diagram showing the area within which the fielders must stand.

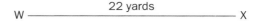

W ——————— 22 yards ——————— X

3 Binford and Corley are two villages 8 km apart. A straight road runs between them. Ansey is another village 10 km from Binford and 7 km from Corley.
   (a) Using a scale of 1 cm to 1 km construct a triangle ABC where A, B and C represent the three villages Ansey, Binford and Corley, respectively.
   (b) Ken walks along a footpath so that he is always an equal distance from Binford and Corley.
       Draw Ken's path on your diagram.
   (c) Jenny rides her pony along a track which is on the Ansey side of the road joining Binford and Corley. She is always 3 km from the road.
       Draw Jenny's track on your diagram.
   (d) Mark with the letter M, the point where Ken's path meets Jenny's track.

4 This sketch shows a plan of Mrs O'Neil's rectangular garden. It is not drawn to scale. She wants to put a clothes drier in the garden. The drier must be more than 3 m from the house. It must be an equal distance from the two pillars. It must be at least 10 m from the apple tree.
   (a) Draw an accurate scale drawing of Mrs O'Neil's garden.
   (b) Find, by construction, the possible positions for the clothes drier.

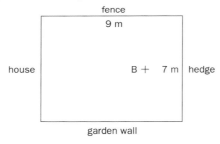

5 This sketch shows a plan of Alice's garden.
   (a) Make a scale drawing of this plan.
       Use a scale of 1 cm to 1 m.
   (b) Point B shows the position of a bird table. It is 3.5 m from the hedge and equidistant from the fence and garden wall.
       Mark point B on your diagram.
   (c) Alice's gardener Stan is going to plant a tree for her. Alice asks Stan to observe these conditions when planting the tree.
       It should be
       – at least 2.5 m from the house
       – at least 1.5 m from the hedge
       – at least 2 m from both the garden wall and the fence
       – at least 2.5 m from the bird table.
       On your diagram, shade clearly the region in which Stan may plant the tree.

Examination Questions

1 A caretaker is using a machine to polish a straight corridor 340 cm wide. The polisher is in the shape of a circle, diameter 45 cm. The caretaker moves the machine from one side to the other across the corridor at right angles to the walls.

   (a) Sketch the shape of the part of the floor that is polished in one movement.
   (b) Find the area of this polished part.
       (MEG, 1989)

2 The wheel below is rotated, without slipping, along the horizontal floor AB, then up the vertical wall BC, around the corner at C and finally along the horizontal floor CD.
   Draw the locus (path) of the centre, O, of the wheel throughout this movement.

(WJEC, 1990)

3 Two small boats set out from different points in a harbour. A bird's-eye view of the harbour is sketched below.
   One boat, called Amy, departed from point A on a bearing of 060°.
   The other boat, called Bud, departed from point B, keeping the same distance from each harbour wall AB and BC.

   (a) Using a ruler and compass only, construct on a sketch the path taken by each boat.
   (b) Label the point where their path cross with an X.
   (c) Both boats departed at the same time and almost collided with each other. Which boat was travelling the faster?
       (NEAB, 1991)

4 The diagram represents the area used for throwing a discus.
   It is a drawn to a scale of 1 cm to 10 m.
   C is the centre of the throwing circle.
   (a) Find the real length AC represents.
   (b) One competitor throws a discus which first hits the ground 15 m from AC and 33 m from BC.
       (i) Copy the diagram and find the point where the discus first hits the ground. Mark this point with a cross and label it D.
       (ii) Find the real length CD represents.
           (ULEAC, 1991)

5 The diagram shows the island of Emanon, drawn to a scale of 1 cm to represent 20 km.

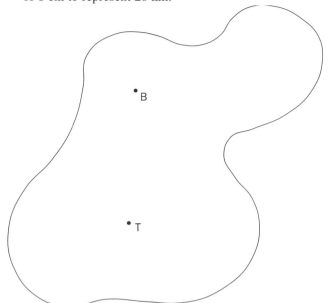

The government has built two television transmitters. The main transmitter, at T, has a range of 80 km. The transmitter at B is a 'booster' and has a range of 40 km.
(a) Copy the diagram and show accurately the part of the island in which television programmes can be received.
(b) The government intends to build a third transmitter so that television programmes can be received in all parts of the island.

(i) Will it be necessary to build a main transmitter (range 80 km) or will a booster (range 40 km) be sufficient?
(ii) On the diagram, mark with an 'X' a possible position for the third transmitter.

(MEG, 1990)

6 Martin and Dietmar are playing golf and both their golf balls are lying on the green. The balls are 5 m apart, and Martin's ball is 1 m further from the hole than Dietmar's ball.

(a) One spectator says that Martin's ball is 4 m from the hole. The diagram shows this to a scale of 1 cm to 1 m. Assuming he is right, copy the diagram, and show a possible position of Dietmar's ball on your diagram.
(b) Another spectator says that Martin's ball is 2 m from the hole. Explain why he must be wrong.

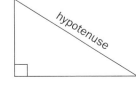

Martin's ball
•

hole
•

(MEG, 1989)

P24
Pythagoras' Theorem

This unit will help you to:

■ know and understand Pythagoras' Theorem

■ use Pythagoras' Theorem
 – to find the length of a side of a right-angled triangle
 – to check a triangle is right-angled
 – to solve practical problems.

Right-angled triangles

Pythagoras' Theorem is about **right-angled triangles**.
A right-angled triangle has *one* angle of 90° (a right angle). The longest side is *opposite* the right angle. It is called the **hypotenuse**.

Pythagoras' Theorem is also about **squares**.

Look at this diagram. The right-angled triangle has a square on each side. The square on the hypotenuse is *largest*.

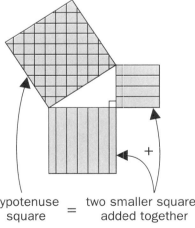

This simple rule links the three squares. ➡ hypotenuse square = two smaller squares added together

We call this rule, **Pythagoras' Theorem**.
It is often given in these words:

> **In a right-angled triangle,**
> **the square on the hypotenuse (the longest side)**
> **is equal to the sum of the squares on the other two sides.**

This diagram shows a simple example of the rule given by Pythagoras' Theorem. You can find the three areas by 'counting squares'.

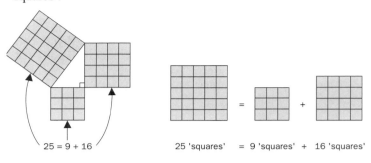

25 = 9 + 16

25 'squares' = 9 'squares' + 16 'squares'

Discussion Exercise

Here are two more diagrams.
Check that Pythagoras' Theorem works in each.
Discuss how you find out.

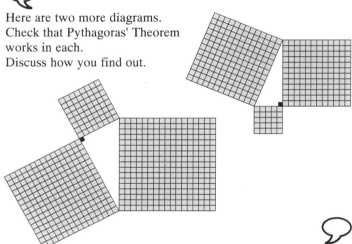

A special rule

Pythagoras' Theorem can be *proved to be true*. That's why we call it a '**theorem**'.
Pythagoras is supposed to have worked out its *first proof*.
That's why we call it his theorem.

Discussion Exercise

We don't know what Pythagoras' proof was. But it is said that a tiled floor helped him to see it. Unlike Pythagoras , most of us need more help. These shaded tiles give some clues.
How can they be used to check Pythagoras' Theorem?
Discuss.
Think of other ways to check this rule.
Discuss the ideas of the students in your group.
Try some of them if you can.

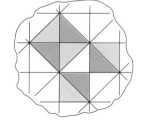

There are over 100 ways to show Pythagoras' Theorem is true.
The following puzzle gives one way.
Try it yourself.
Look up some others.

ACTIVITY

A Pythagoras puzzle

This is like a jigsaw puzzle, but you have to cut out the pieces first. These steps show you how.
You need: squared or dotty paper, scissors, glue.

1 Draw squares on the sides of a large right-angled triangle.

2 Draw lines on the middle-sized square like this.

through centre

parallel to hypotenuse

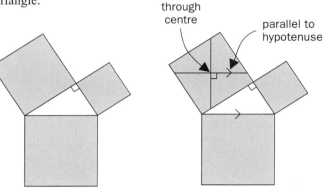

3 Cut out the two smaller squares. Cut them to give pieces 1, 2, 3, 4 and 5.

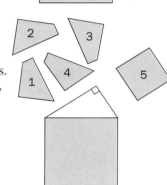

Now fit the five pieces exactly on to the largest square.
Stick them in place.
What does this puzzle tell you about the areas of the three squares?

Discussion Exercise

Find the missing area (marked ?) in each diagram.
How did you work them out?

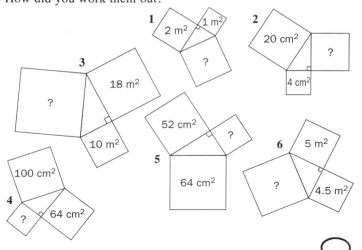

From side to area

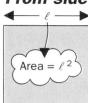

Pythagoras' Theorem is about the areas of squares.
You do not have to *draw* a square to find its area.
It is usually simpler, and quicker, to work it out.
You 'square' the length of its side.

Memo

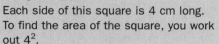

Each side of this square is 4 cm long.
To find the area of the square, you work out 4^2.

$$4^2 = 4 \times 4 = 16$$

Some squares are easy to remember:

$$1^2 = 1, \quad 2^2 = 4, \quad 3^2 = 9, \quad 4^2 = 16, \quad 5^2 = 25, \ldots$$

Use the $\boxed{x^2}$ key on your calculator for the others.
For example, for 1.7^2,

press It gives ▮ 2.89

On some calculators you need to press the 2nd Function or Inverse key before $\boxed{x^2}$.

► *Exercise* P24.1

Find the areas of squares with sides of these lengths. Don't forget the units!

1 8 mm	**3** 67 m	**5** 6.25 m	**7** 7.2 cm	**9** 11.3 m
2 21 cm	**4** 1.2 m	**6** 0.9 km	**8** 83 mm	**10** 3.5 km

From area to side

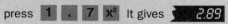

Pythagoras' Theorem gives you the area of a square. Find the square root ($\sqrt{}$) of this value and you have the length of the side of the square.

Memo

The area of this square is 16 cm^2. To find the length of its side, you work out $\sqrt{16}$

$\sqrt{16} = 4$ because $4 \times 4 = 16$.

You may know some exact square roots:

$$\sqrt{1} = 1, \quad \sqrt{4} = 2, \quad \sqrt{9} = 3, \quad \sqrt{16} = 4, \ldots$$

Use the $\boxed{\sqrt{}}$ key on your calculator for the others.

You often need to round the result to give a 'sensible answer'.
You may be told how many decimal places (dp) or significant figures (sf) to use. Or you may have to decide what to do yourself.

For example, 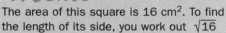 gives ▮ 3.16227766

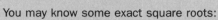

$\sqrt{10} = 3.2$ (to 1 dp). $\sqrt{10} = 3.16$ (to 3 sf).

► *Exercise* P24.2

1 Here are the areas of some squares. Find the lengths of their sides.

(a) 81 cm²	(c) 529 m²	(e) 1.96 cm²
(b) 625 mm²	(d) 1681 km²	(f) 1.44 m²

2 Find these to 1 dp and 3 sf.

(a) $\sqrt{90}$	(c) $\sqrt{43}$	(e) $\sqrt{162}$
(b) $\sqrt{175}$	(d) $\sqrt{392}$	(f) $\sqrt{280}$

Calculating lengths

Summary

Pythagoras' Theorem gives the relationship between the lengths of the sides in a right-angled triangle.
In this triangle,
r is the hypotenuse
(the longest side).
Pythagoras' Theorem gives:

$$r^2 = x^2 + y^2$$

From this we also get:

$$x^2 = r^2 - y^2$$
$$\text{and } y^2 = r^2 - x^2$$

If you know the lengths of **two sides** of a right-angled triangle, and you want the length of the **third side**, you can use Pythagoras' Theorem to find it.

The longest side (the hypotenuse)

Look at this right-angled triangle.
Its two shorter sides are 3 cm and 5 cm long.
You want to know the length of the longest side (the hypotenuse).
Follow these steps to find it.

1 Work out the areas of the smaller squares from their sides.
$$3^2 = 9 \qquad 5^2 = 25$$

2 Add these two squares to get the area of the 'hypotenuse square'.
$$h^2 = 9 + 25 = 34$$

3 Find the square root of this value to get the length of the hypotenuse.
$$h = \sqrt{34} = 5.830951895$$
$$= 5.8 \text{ cm (to 1 dp)}$$

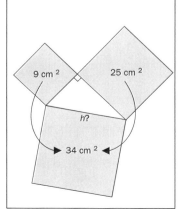

You can do all the working on a calculator.
Watch the display for each result as you press the keys.
Write them down clearly in your answer.
You will get marks for these, not just the final results.
Here is how to write down the working and do the work on
your calculator.

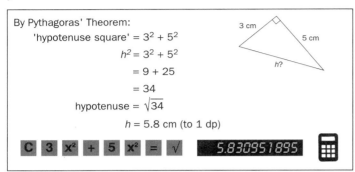

By Pythagoras' Theorem:
'hypotenuse square' $= 3^2 + 5^2$
$h^2 = 3^2 + 5^2$
$= 9 + 25$
$= 34$
hypotenuse $= \sqrt{34}$
$h = 5.8$ cm (to 1 dp)

`C 3 x² + 5 x² = √`   `5.830951895`

As usual it is a good idea to *check* that your answer isn't 'silly'.
Two facts about the triangle's sides are useful for this.
- The hypotenuse is the longest side.
- The other two sides together must be longer than the
  hypotenuse (… or they
  wouldn't make a
  triangle!).
Let's check our triangle using these facts:

5.8 cm is longest. ✓
3 cm + 5 cm = 8 cm.
That's longer than 5.8 cm. ✓
So 5.8 cm is a sensible size.

► *Exercise* **P24.3**

Calculate the length of the hypotenuse in each of these
triangles. Set out your working like the example above.
Give each length correct to 1 decimal place. Don't forget the
units!

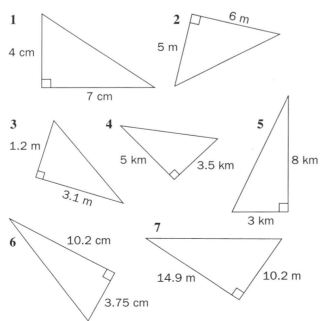

1 4 cm, 7 cm

2 6 m, 5 m

3 1.2 m, 3.1 m

4 5 km, 3.5 km

5 8 km, 3 km

6 10.2 cm, 3.75 cm

7 14.9 m, 10.2 m

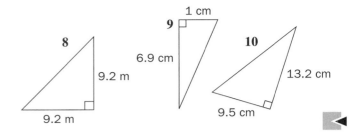

8 9.2 m, 9.2 m

9 1 cm, 6.9 cm

10 13.2 cm, 9.5 cm

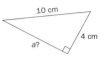

A shorter side

Here is another right-angled triangle. The
length of the hypotenuse is 10 cm. One of
the shorter sides is 4 cm long. You want the
length of the other shorter side. These steps
show you how to find it.

1 Work out the areas of the two squares from their sides.
$10^2 = 100 \qquad 4^2 = 16$

2 To find the area of the
other square, work out
$a^2 = 100 - 16 = 84$

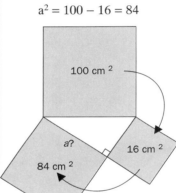

3 Find the square root of
this value to get the
side of the square.
$a = \sqrt{84} = 9.16515139$
$= 9.2$ cm (to 1 dp)

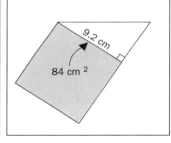

You can set out the working like this:

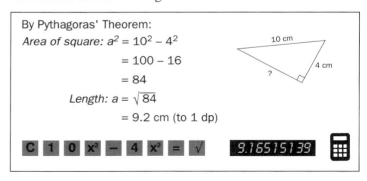

By Pythagoras' Theorem:
Area of square: $a^2 = 10^2 - 4^2$
$= 100 - 16$
$= 84$
Length: $a = \sqrt{84}$
$= 9.2$ cm (to 1 dp)

`C 1 0 x² − 4 x² = √`   `9.16515139`

Check for a 'silly' answer:

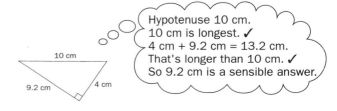

Hypotenuse 10 cm.
10 cm is longest. ✓
4 cm + 9.2 cm = 13.2 cm.
That's longer than 10 cm. ✓
So 9.2 cm is a sensible answer.

► *Exercise* **P24.4**

Calculate the unknown length in each triangle.
Give each length correct to 1 decimal place.

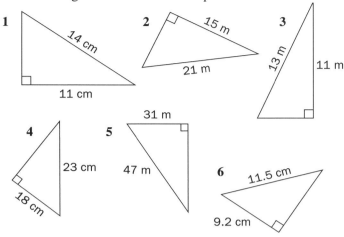

1 14 cm, 11 cm

2 15 m, 21 m

3 13 m, 11 m

4 23 cm, 18 cm

5 31 m, 47 m

6 11.5 cm, 9.2 cm

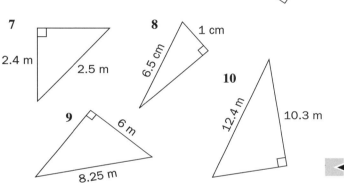

7 2.4 m, 2.5 m

8 1 cm, 6.5 cm

9 6 m, 8.25 m

10 12.4 m, 10.3 m

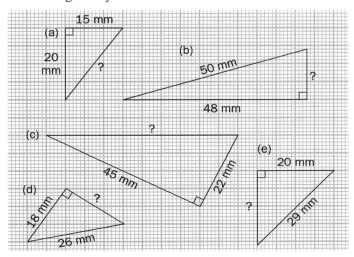

Take extra care in the next exercise. Sometimes you want the
longest side and sometimes one of the others. Look carefully to
see which you want. Then decide whether to add or subtract
squares.

► *Exercise* **P24.5**

1 Here are some right-angled triangles. Measure the side
marked ? in each. (Work to the nearest millimetre.) Then
check your answers using Pythagoras' Theorem. Show your
working clearly.

(a) 15 mm, 20 mm, ?

(b) 50 mm, 48 mm, ?

(c) ?, 45 mm

(d) 18 mm, 26 mm, ?

(e) 20 mm, 22 mm, ?, 29 mm

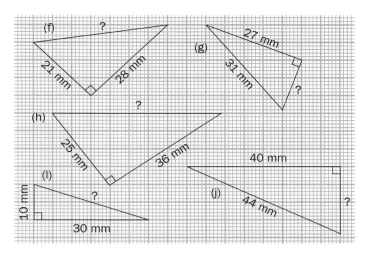

(f) ?, 21 mm, 28 mm

(g) 27 mm, 31 mm, ?

(h) ?, 25 mm, 36 mm, 40 mm

(I) 10 mm, ?, 30 mm

(j) 44 mm, ?

2 Calculate the lengths of the sides marked with letters.
You need to round some of your results to give 'sensible
answers'. Not doing this will lose you marks!

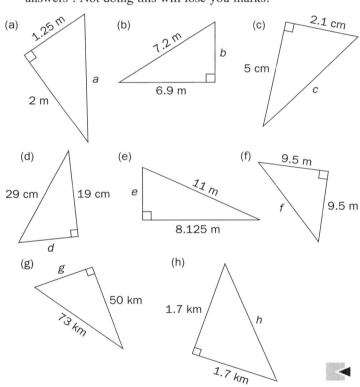

(a) 1.25 m, 2 m, *a*

(b) 7.2 m, 6.9 m, *b*

(c) 2.1 cm, 5 cm, *c*

(d) 29 cm, 19 cm, *d*

(e) *e*, 11 m, 8.125 m

(f) 9.5 m, *f*, 9.5 m

(g) *g*, 50 km, 73 km

(h) 1.7 km, *h*, 1.7 km

A special triangle

💬 *Discussion Exercise*

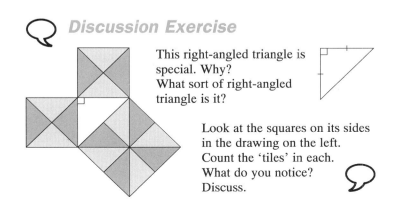

This right-angled triangle is
special. Why?
What sort of right-angled
triangle is it?

Look at the squares on its sides
in the drawing on the left.
Count the 'tiles' in each.
What do you notice?
Discuss.

Question

Calculate the missing lengths in this right-angled triangle.
Give your answer in cm correct to 1 decimal place.

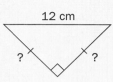

Answer

Let the missing lengths be a cm.
By Pythagoras' Theorem:

Areas:

$$a^2 + a^2 = 12^2$$
$$2a^2 = 144$$
$$a^2 = \tfrac{1}{2} \text{ of } 144 = 144 \div 2$$
$$= 72$$

Length:

$$a = \sqrt{72}$$
$$= 8.485281374 \text{ (calculator)}$$

Missing length $= 8.5$ cm (to 1 dp)

Check:

12 cm

8.5 cm　　8.5 cm

12 cm is longest ✓
8.5 cm × 8.5 cm = 17 cm
That's longer than 12 cm ✓
So 8.5 cm is a sensible answer

▶ *Exercise* **P24.6**

1　Each diagram shows a right-angled triangle with two equal length sides. Find the missing areas (marked?) in each.

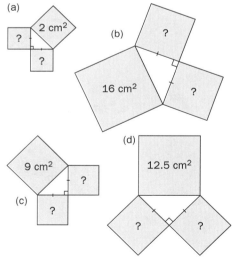

(a)

2 cm²

?

?

(b)

?

16 cm²

?

(c)

9 cm²

?

?

(d)

12.5 cm²

?　?

2　Find the lengths of sides of the triangles in question **1**.
3　Calculate the unknown lengths in these triangles.
　Look carefully to see which side you want!

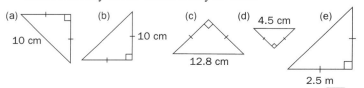

(a) 10 cm

(b) 10 cm

(c) 12.8 cm

(d) 4.5 cm

(e) 2.5 m

Problem-solving

You will need to use Pythagoras' Theorem to solve problems. Here are some key points to help you with this.

● Start with a *sketch* of the situation.
　This gives you clues about what to do.
● Find the *right-angled triangle* with the side you want.
　Draw it on its own. Put on it the lengths you know.
● Decide what you want …
　Is it the *hypotenuse* (the longest side) *or a shorter side*?
● Use *Pythagoras' Theorem* …
　Imagine the 'squares' on the diagram if it helps.
　Work out whether to add or subtract squares.
● Find the *square root* to get the length you want.
● Give a '*sensible answer*' to the problem.
　Round your result if you need to.
● Don't forget the *units*: mm, cm, m, …
● Avoid 'silly answers' … *check*.

Question

I always use a short cut across the grass from my gate to my front door. This is shown as a dotted line on the diagram. How long is my short cut?

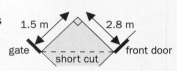

1.5 m　　2.8 m

gate　short cut　front door

Answer

Work through the key points in the answer given below:
● *sketch*
● *right-angled triangle*
● *hypotenuse wanted*
● *Pythagoras' Theorem*
● *square root*
● *Round to 1 dp (… as in given lengths)*
● *units: metres m*
● *check.*

Let the length of the shortest be h metres

1.5 m　　2.8 m
? hypotenuse

By Pythagoras' Theorem:

Areas:

$$h^2 = 1.5^2 + 2.8^2$$
$$= 2.25 + 7.84$$
$$= 10.09$$

Length:

$$h = \sqrt{10.09}$$
$$= 3.176476035 \text{ (calculator)}$$

short cut $= 3.2$ m (to 1 dp)

Check:

3.2 m is longest ✓
1.5 m × 2.8 m = 4.3 m
That's longer than 3.2 m ✓
So 8.5 cm is a sensible answer

Exercise P24.7

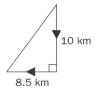

1 Here is the plan of a garden. The wall is 6 m long. The hedge is 9.5 m long. How long is the fence?

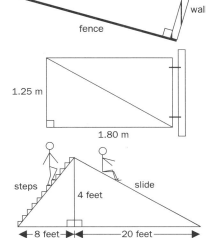

2 How long is the crossbar of this gate?

3 How long are the steps and slide in this diagram?

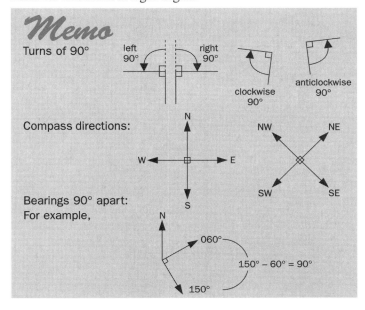

2 A boat sails 10 km due South and then 8.5 km due West. How far is it from the starting point?

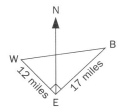

3 Wyeville (W) is 12 miles NW of Exford (E), Beeton (B) is 17 miles NE of Exford. How far apart are Wyeville and Beeton 'as the crow flies'?

4 The nearest port to oil platforms Alpha (A) and Beta (B) is Ceemouth (C). From Ceemouth, Alpha is 35 km on a bearing of 045°, Beta is 55 km on a bearing of 135°. What is the distance between Alpha and Beta?

Looking for right angles

To use Pythagoras' Theorem you need a right-angled triangle. Sometimes you are told where the right angle is. Often you have to work out where one should be.
Here are some clues to help you.

Directions

Look for directions at right angles.

Memo

Turns of 90°

Compass directions:

Bearings 90° apart:
For example,

Exercise P24.8

1 I program a computer turtle robot with these instructions.
The robot moves Forward 150 steps, turns Right 90°, then moves Forward 80 steps.
How far is it from its starting position?

```
FD   150
RT    90
FD    80
```

Horizontal and vertical

In our world many things are horizontal or vertical. You see them all around you.

Memo

Horizontal and vertical lines meet at right angles.

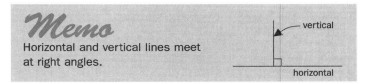

Exercise P24.9

1 A wheelchair ramp goes from a level path to the top edge of a vertical step, 20 cm high. It starts 90 cm from the bottom of the step.
How long is the ramp?

2 A ladder is 4.5 m long. Its foot is on a flat lawn, 2 m from the base of a vertical wall. How far up the wall will its top reach?

3 A vertical flagpole stands on some horizontal ground.
A 20 m long wire goes from the top of the pole to a point on the ground 15 m from the bottom of the pole.
How tall is the flagpole?

Graphs

Memo

To plot points and graphs, we use axes at right angles to each other.

x-axis is the 'horizontal axis'.
y-axis is the 'vertical axis'.

For *x*-values, go 'across'.
For *y*-values go 'up or down'.

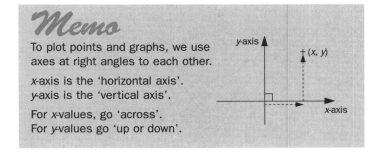

These values can help you to calculate the distance between points. Work through the next example to see how.

Question

Calculate the distance between A(1,3) and B(6,7).

Answer

- *Plot points.*
- *Join the points.*
  Draw the right-angled triangle.
- *Find shorter sides:*
  x-values → across
  y-values → up
- *Use Pythagoras' Theorem.*

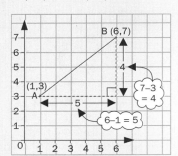

By Pythagoras' Theorem:
Areas: $AB^2 = 5^2 + 4^2$
            $= 25 + 16$
            $= 41$
Length: $AB = \sqrt{41}$
            $= 6.403124237$ (calculator)
            $AB = 6.4$ (to 1 dp)

`C` `5` `x²` `+` `4` `x²` `=` `√`   `6.403124237`

Check: 6.4 is longest ✓
          $5 + 4 = 9$
          That's longer than 6.4 ✓
          So 6.4 is a sensible answer.

▶ *Exercise* **P24.10**

Calculate the distance between each pair of points.
1 (2,6) and (8,1)   **3** (−3,2) and (4,−2)
2 (−1, 3) and (2,5)   **4** (1,−4) and (−5,1)

Facts about shapes

Right angles occur in many shapes. Here are some you have met before.

Memo

Right angles in quadrilaterals:

in 'corners' ...

'between diagonals' ...

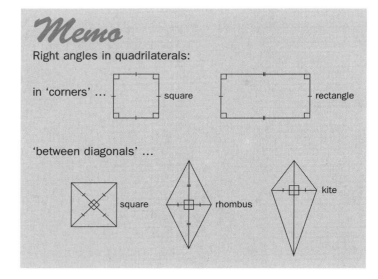

This example also uses some length facts about the shapes.

Question

The sides of this rhombus are 8 cm long. One of its diagonals measures 13 cm. How long is its other diagonal?

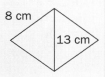

Answer

Work through these key points in the answer below.
- *Sketch rhombus and diagonals.*
- *Mark right angles.*
- *Diagonals cut each other in half.*
- *Sketch right-angled triangle.*
- *Use Pythagoras' Theorem. This gives half the diagonal.*
- *Do not round until the end of the working!*

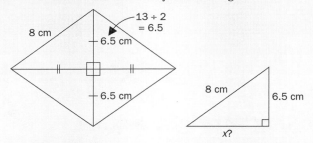

Let x cm be the missing length in this right-angled triangle.
By Pythagoras' Theorem:
Areas: $x^2 = 8^2 - 6.5^2$
            $= 64 - 42.25$
            $= 21.75$
Length: $x = \sqrt{21.75}$
            $= 4.663689527$ (calculator)
  Diagonal $= 2 \times x = 9.327379053$ (calculator)
            $= 9.3$ cm (to 1 dp)

`C` `8` `x²` `−` `6` `.` `5` `x²` `=` `√` `×` `2` `=`

Check sides of right-angled triangle
  8 cm is longest ✓
  4.7 cm + 6.5 cm = 11.2 cm
  That's longer than 8 cm ✓

▶ *Exercise* **P24.11**

1 A rugby pitch is 101.5 m long and 67.5 m wide. What is the distance between diagonally opposite corners?
2 The quadrangle in John's school is a square. Diagonal footpaths across it are 182 feet long. How long is each side of the quadrangle?
3 The diagonals of a 22" TV screen are 22 inches long. A new 22" TV screen is to be 12.5 inches high. How wide must it be?
4 The sketch shows the framework of a kite. It is made of strips of wood. What is the total length of these strips.

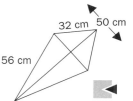

Perpendiculars

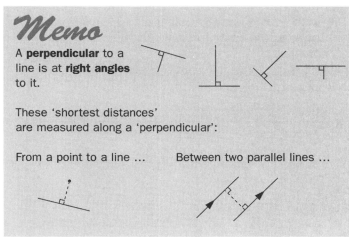

Memo

A **perpendicular** to a line is at **right angles** to it.

These 'shortest distances' are measured along a 'perpendicular':

From a point to a line ...   Between two parallel lines ...

In some problems you are *told* that there is a perpendicular. In others you may have to *find* or *draw* one yourself.

▶ *Exercise* P24.12

1 Mr James stands on level ground flying a kite using 100 m of string. Ann is 48 m from her father and the kite is directly over her head. Calculate the height of the kite above the ground. (Mr Jones is 2 m tall.)

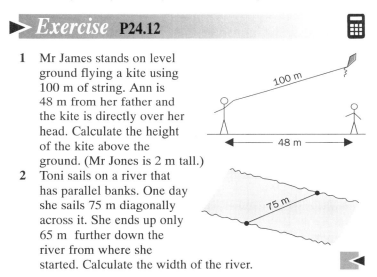

2 Toni sails on a river that has parallel banks. One day she sails 75 m diagonally across it. She ends up only 65 m further down the river from where she started. Calculate the width of the river.

Isosceles triangles

Memo

An isosceles triangle has two equal sides. The angles opposite the equal sides are also equal.

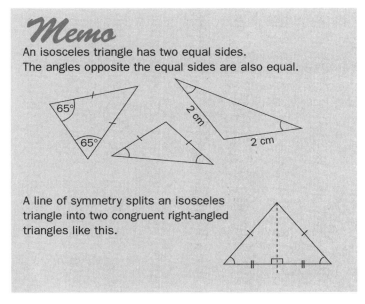

A line of symmetry splits an isosceles triangle into two congruent right-angled triangles like this.

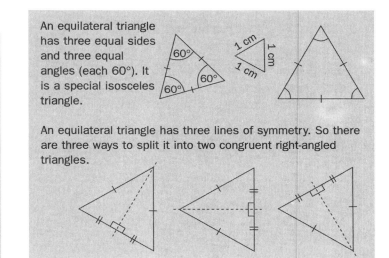

An equilateral triangle has three equal sides and three equal angles (each 60°). It is a special isosceles triangle.

An equilateral triangle has three lines of symmetry. So there are three ways to split it into two congruent right-angled triangles.

▶ *Exercise* P24.13

1 An isosceles triangle 10.8 cm high has a base 19.5 cm long. How long are its other sides?

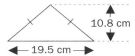

2 An equilateral triangle has sides 12 cm long. Calculate its perpendicular height.

3 The sketch shows the side view of an attic. The floor is 4 m wide. Its sloping sides are each 2.75 m long. Calculate the height of the highest point A above the floor.

4 The end-bars of this swing are each 2 m long (equilateral triangle. How far is the crossbar above the bottom bar?

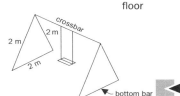

Perpendicular heights

To find the areas of some shapes you need their perpendicular heights.

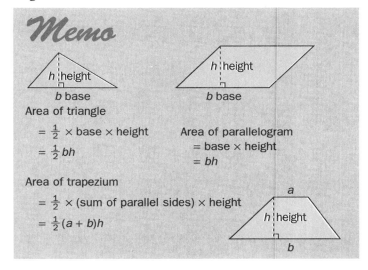

Memo

Area of triangle
$$= \tfrac{1}{2} \times \text{base} \times \text{height}$$
$$= \tfrac{1}{2} bh$$

Area of parallelogram
$$= \text{base} \times \text{height}$$
$$= bh$$

Area of trapezium
$$= \tfrac{1}{2} \times (\text{sum of parallel sides}) \times \text{height}$$
$$= \tfrac{1}{2}(a + b)h$$

Sometimes you have to use Pythagoras' Theorem to calculate these 'heights' first. Then you can find the areas.

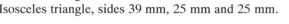 **Exercise** **P24.14**

Find the areas of these triangles.
1   Equilateral triangle, sides 15 cm long.
2   Equilateral triangle, sides 2.3 m long.
3   Equilateral triangle, sides 875 mm long.
4   Isosceles triangle, sides 7 cm, 7 cm and 9.5 cm.
5   Isosceles triangle, sides 4.8 m, 6 m and 4.8 m.
6   Isosceles triangle, sides 39 mm, 25 mm and 25 mm.

 Investigation

Other shapes
Pythagoras' Theorem links squares drawn on the sides of a right-angled triangle.
What happens if you draw other shapes on its sides instead?

What about equilateral triangles?   Or semi-circles?

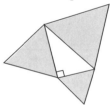

Is there a link between the three areas? If so, what is it?
Investigate other shapes if you have time.

The Converse Theorem

An ancient triangle

In Ancient Egypt, surveyors were called rope-stretchers. They stretched knotted ropes between pegs to mark and measure boundary lines.
To mark out right angles, they make triangles like this ...

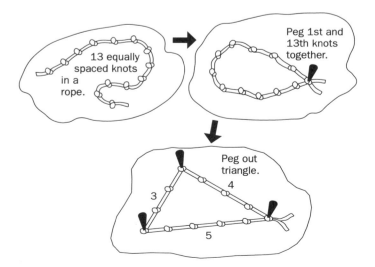

Try this yourself. Where is the right angle in it? Who still uses this method in our modern world?

The special triangle made by the rope-stretchers has sides 3, 4 and 5 units long. We call it a **3, 4, 5 triangle**.

The 3, 4, 5 triangle was known in many ancient civilisations. It was known in Ancient China, India, Babylon, Greece, ... not just in Egypt.

People in these ancient civilisations knew that the 3, 4, 5 triangle was right-angled.

You can show that they were correct.

The longest side is 5 units long.	$5^2 = 25$
The sum of the squares on the other sides	$= 3^2 + 4^2$ $= 9 + 16$ $= 25$
These two results are **equal**. Because $5^2 = 3^2 + 4^2$, the 3, 4, 5 triangle is right-angled.	

This is Pythagoras' Theorem 'the other way round'.
It is called the **Converse of Pythagoras' Theorem**.
It tells us that:

> **If the square on the longest side of a triangle is equal to the sum of the squares on the other two sides, then the triangle is a right-angled triangle.**
> **The right angle is opposite the longest side.**

Remember: Not all converses are true but this one is!

Is it right-angled?

If you know the lengths of the three sides of a triangle, you can use the converse of Pythagoras' Theorem to find out whether or not the triangle is a right-angled triangle.

Here are the steps to take:
- Square the longest side.
- Find the sum of the squares on the other two sides.
- Compare these two results.
- If they are *equal*, then the triangle is *right-angled*.
- If they are *not equal*, then the triangle is *not right-angled*.

Question

(a) This triangle 'looks' right-angled. Is it? Show your working and explain your answer.
(b) Is a triangle with sides 50 mm, 14 mm, 48 mm a right-angled triangle?

Answer

(a) The longest side is 5.7 cm. $5.7^2 = 32.49$
    The sum of the squares
    on the other two sides $= 2.7^2 + 4.5^2$
                                      $= 7.29 + 20.25$
                                      $= 27.54$
    These two results are not equal. $5.7^2 \neq 2.7^2 + 4.5^2$

    By the Converse of Pythagoras' Theorem, the triangle is not right-angled.

(b) The longest side is 50 mm. $50^2 = 2500$

The sum of the squares
on the other two sides
$$= 14^2 + 48^2$$
$$= 196 + 2304$$
$$= 2500$$

These two results are equal. $50^2 = 14^2 + 48^2$

By the Converse of Pythagoras' Theorem, the triangle is right-angled.
The right angle is opposite the 50 mm side.

▶ *Exercise* **P24.15**

Check each of these triangles for right angles. Show your working clearly. Sketch each right-angled triangle you find. Mark its right angle clearly.

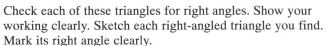

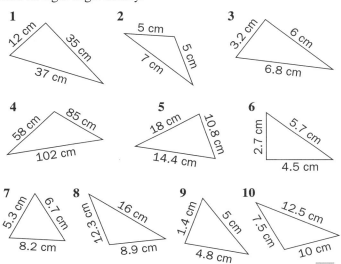

Many things in everyday life have right angles in them … or they should have.
The Converse of Pythagoras' Theorem gives us a way to check them.

▶ *Exercise* **P24.16**

1 A ladder 6.5 m long stands on a level footpath. Its top reaches 6 m up the wall and its foot is 2 m from the base of the wall.
Is the wall vertical? Explain your answer.

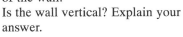

2 Tim made this picture frame, 250 mm long and 200 mm wide. To check that it is rectangular he measures its diagonal. It is 320 mm long (to the nearest mm). Is it rectangular? Explain your working.

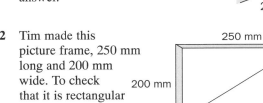

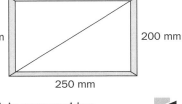

 Investigation

Pythagorean triples

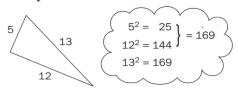

Here is a triangle with sides 5, 12 and 13 units long.
It is right-angled because $5^2 + 12^2 = 13^2$.
This gives the Pythagorean triple (5,12,13)

A **Pythagorean triple** is a set of *three whole numbers*. These numbers are the *lengths of the sides of a right-angled triangle*.

There are many Pythagorean triples.
The simplest is (3,4,5).

Find some more yourself.
Look for patterns in them.
Look for a systematic way to work them out.
    The Babylonians knew about these triples long before Pythagoras. Lists of them are on tablets from about 2000 BC.

For the computer programmer
1 Write a program to find the third side of a right-angled triangle from the lengths of the other two sides.
Run it on the computer. Test it with some questions you have done.
2 Write a program to test whether a triangle is right-angled by using its three sides.

Examination Questions

1 The diagram represents a ladder which just reaches the top of a vertical wall. The wall is 8 metres high and the base of the ladder is 2.5 metres from the foot of the wall on horizontal ground. Calculate the length of the ladder. (Give your answer in metres correct to one decimal place.)

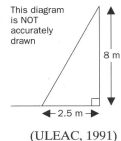

This diagram is NOT accurately drawn

8 m

2.5 m

(ULEAC, 1991)

2 A room is in the shape of a rectangle, 4.5 metres long and 3.6 metres wide. Pat plugs a vacuum cleaner into an electric point in one corner of the room and finds that the cleaner will just reach the opposite corner. Calculate the approximate length, in metres, of the flex. Give your answer correct to one decimal place.

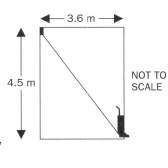

3.6 m

4.5 m

NOT TO SCALE

(MEG, 1990)

3 The diagram below shows the cross-section of a new underground railway tunnel. The cross-section is a circle of radius 4 m and O is the centre of the circle.

(a) The new tunnel will be 3 km in length. Calculate, in m^3, the volume of earth which will need to be removed.

(b) The line PQ represents the surface on which the railway track is to be placed. The angle POQ is 90°.

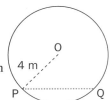

Calculate the width PQ.

(SEG, 1990)

4 The diagram shows the side view of a garden roller and the shaft for pulling or pushing it. The roller has a circular cross-section of radius 0.4 metres.

The shaft, OC, of length 1.7 metres is hinged at the centre, O, of the roller and its other end is on the level ground at C. N is the point of contact of the roller with the ground and ∠ONC = 90°.

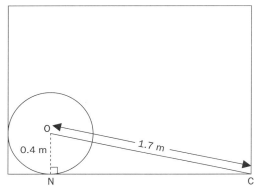

(a) Calculate NC.

(b) The surrounding rectangle is the side view of a shed. Calculate the least distance between the side walls for this to be possible.

(WJEC, 1994)

5 The sizes of television sets are determined by the length of the diagonal of the screen. The diagram shows a 20-inch television screen, which you may assume to be a rectangle.

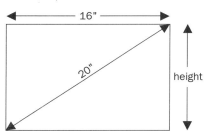

The width of the screen is 16 inches.

(a) What is the height of the screen?

A 14-inch television screen and a 20-inch screen are similar rectangles.

(b) Calculate the height and width of a 14-inch screen.

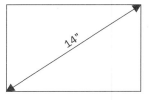

(NEAB, 1990)

6 The diagram shows a side view of a staircase going from S to T. BT is equal to AS.
The width of each step, such as PQ, is 25 centimetres.
The height of each step, such as QR, is 20 centimetres.

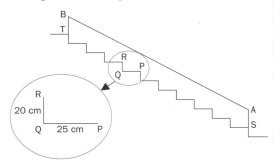

Calculate
(a) the length PR in centimetres
(b) the length of the handrail AB in metres.

(MEG, 1990)

7 This is the cross-section of a swimming pool.

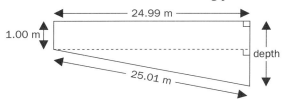

Calculate the depth at the deep end of the pool.

(NISEAC, 1990)

8 Use your knowledge of Pythagoras' Theorem to test whether this triangle is right-angled. Show your calculations and state your conclusion.

(ULEAC, 1994)

P25

Questionnaire design and hypothesis testing

This unit will help you to:

- design and use questionnaires with multiple responses to collect data
- recognise poorly written questions in questionnaires and improve them
- collate and analyse responses from questionnaires
- understand the idea of a hypothesis
- state simple hypotheses
- identify different ways to test a hypothesis
- design and use a questionnaire or experiment to test a hypothesis and collate and analyse the results.

Questionnaires

Asking people questions is a common way to collect data. This is a method often used in 'market research' and 'opinion polls'.

Different types of data can be collected by asking questions. Questions may ask for facts.

"How many GCSE subjects are you studying?"
"Which school/college do you attend?"
"Have you had a maths lesson today?"

Questions may also ask for opinions, preferences, ideas, …

"What is your favourite arts activity?"
"How would you rate your visit to this Arts Centre?"
"How could the facilities at the Centre be improved?"

In a survey the same data must be collected in the same way. To make sure everyone is asked questions in the same way, the questions are usually written down in a list. This list of questions is called a **questionnaire**.

In some surveys, an Interviewer asks the questions and records the answers.
If the question is not understood, then the interviewer may be allowed to explain it. The interviewer tries to read the questions to each person in the same way.

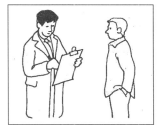

He or she must avoid showing any bias that could affect the answers.

In many surveys, the questionnaire is given or sent to people. They have to fill it in themselves without help from anyone carrying out the survey.

Questionnaire design

Whichever way a questionnaire is to be used, its **design** is important. It must be planned carefully.

When designing a questionnaire, make sure you consider these main points:

- its content
- the wording of the questions
- the way the answers are to be recorded
- the overall layout.

Content

Before you write any questions, sort out the **content** of your questionnaire.

- Think carefully about the **purpose** of your survey. Decide exactly *what* you want to know and *why*.
- Make a list of the **topics** you need to collect data about. Put them in *order of importance* for your survey. This is a useful check list when you come to write your questions. It helps you to make sure you ask questions that give the data you want. It also helps you to avoid collecting data you do not need.
- Do not try to collect too much data with your questionnaire. Try to keep the questionnaire *short* and *to the point*.

Discussion Exercise

The Board of Governors at Deacon College want a report on the College Cafeteria. The catering committee decide to do some surveys about it by questionnaire.

- The report to the governors must cover several aspects of the cafeteria and its use.

What do you think they might be interested in?
Discuss your ideas.
List the main topics you think the catering committee
should investigate.

- What data could the committee collect on each topic?
'Brainstorm' your ideas with some other students.
Compile a list of suggestions.
Discuss the ideas in your list.
Which data are the most important for the committee
to find out? Put your ideas in order of priority.
Choose the data you think they should collect on their
questionnaires.
Compare your choices with those of other
students.
Discuss what you find.

Questions and answers

The way in which questions are worded and the way answers
have to be recorded can affect the data that people give. Finding
out a person's name, for example, may seem a simple task.
Many forms simply ask for the information like this:

> Please fill in the following details:
>
> Name: ....

But look at some of the possible responses:

> Mary | Graham Norman | Mrs. Jones | J. K. Evans

None of these may in fact give the exact data you want.
If you want to know, for example, a person's 'Title', 'First
name' and 'Surname', you need to ask precisely for that.
Here is one way to do this:

> 1. What is your name?
>
> First name   Surname
> [   ]   [   ]
>
> 2. What title do you use? Tick one only.
>
> Mr ☐   Mrs ☐   Ms ☐   Miss ☐
>
> Other title ☐ Please write in [   ]

Here are some **guidelines to help you to write questions for
a questionnaire**.
The examples refer to the survey about Deacon College
Cafeteria.

- Use *simple, straightforward wording*. Make the language as
precise and concise as you can.
Avoid vague descriptions such as 'big/small'. Do not use
'technical' words that are not commonly understood.
- Write questions that have *distinct, clear-cut answers* if
possible.
Think carefully about what information you want.

Word the questions to give those data.

- When answers have to be written in, try to make them simply
a *single word* or *short phrase* or *number*.

> Which vegetarian dish would you most like to see
> on the menu? ....

Longer answers take a long time to fill in.
They are also more difficult to sort and analyse.

- Make sure that each question is *unambiguous*, (i.e. it only has
one meaning).
'When do you eat in the cafeteria?', for example, could mean
several things.
Possible answers could be:

> '12 o'clock and 3 o'clock'
> 'Tuesdays and Fridays'
> 'lunchtime and break'.

Decide which 'type' of answers you want. Write a question
specifically to get those answers.

- Phrase questions of a 'personal nature' in a *tactful* way.
Avoid questions which people may not be willing to answer.
Make sure questions are not embarrassing or offensive.
Many people do not like to give precise information about
things like age, money, ... Rephrasing a question and giving
a check list to choose from often solves this problem.
For example, if you think a simple 'How old are you?'
might be difficult, you could ask instead:

> 'What age range are you in?'
> Under 16 ☐   46–45 ☐
> 16–25 ☐   56–65 ☐
> 26–35 ☐   66 and over ☐
> 36–45 ☐

- Do not ask *leading* questions.
If a question is asking for an opinion, word it so that it is free
from bias.
Look at this question, for example.
'What do you think about the new improved menus?'
The word 'improved' may lead people to comment
favourably. They may not give their true opinion of the 'new
menus'. Removing the word 'improved' makes the question
'neutral' in approach.
- Ask questions that have *short definite answers* wherever
possible.
Give simple alternative answers to choose from.
These are easy to answer by ticking a box.
The results are also easy to analyse.

> Are you a vegetarian?   Yes ☐ No ☐

> Do they serve vegetarian meals?
> Yes ☐   No ☐   Don't know ☐

> Do you eat fish?
> Yes ☐   No ☐   Sometimes ☐

Do you eat lunch in the cafeteria when you are in college?
Always ☐   Usually ☐   Sometimes ☐   Seldom ☐   Never ☐

What do you think of the range of food available at lunchtime?
Excellent ☐   Good ☐   Fair ☐   Poor ☐   Very Poor ☐

This type of 'question' is often called a '**multiple-response**' **question**.

In 'multiple-response' questions make sure that:
- the responses match the wording in the question
- any 'positive' responses are balanced by an equal number of 'negative' responses.

● Use multiple response questions that give a *check-list* of categories where appropriate.

Allow for all possible answers in the check-list. Make sure that the categories do not overlap.

Which main course did you eat today?
Lamb Stew ☐
Nut Roast ☐
Fish Pie ☐
Curry ☐
None ☐

This lists all the main courses on that day's menus

Numerical answers may also be organised into categories. This saves having to sort out individual answers later.

How much did you spend in the cafeteria today?
Tick one box only.

Nothing	☐	£3 – £3.99	☐
Less than £1	☐	£4 – £4.99	☐
£1 – £1.99	☐	£5 – £5.99	☐
£2 – £2.99	☐	£6 and over	☐

When there are many alternative categories, list the main ones you are interested in.

End with the category: 'Other' ☐ and ask for the answer to be written in.

What did you drink in the cafeteria today?

Tick one or more boxes.

Water	☐	Tea	☐
Fruit Juice	☐	Coffee	☐
Milk	☐	Nothing	☐
Other	☐		
(Please write in ....)			

In some check lists you want *only one* response to be chosen.

Tick only ONE

In others, *several* may be selected.

Tick no more than TWO   Tick the boxes that apply to you

● To collect data or opinions, preferences, ideas, …, you can ask people to *rank a list* of responses in order.
The responses may be simply items to put in order of preference.

Which of the following do you prefer to eat with a main course?
Rank them 1 to 5 in order of preference.
(Use 1 for your first choice and 5 for your 5th choice.)
☐ Chips
☐ Mashed Potato
☐ Rice
☐ Pasta
☐ Salad

The responses can also be statements of opinion or descriptions.

Students have given the following reasons for not eating lunch in the cafeteria.
Please rank them (1 to 5) in order of importance to you.
(Use 1 for the most important and 5 for the least important.)
☐ Too expensive
☐ Prefer to go home
☐ Takes too long
☐ Too crowded
☐ Not enough choice

You may ask people to rank all the given responses or only some of them.

Which THREE of the following do you like most?
Rank these three 1 to 3 in order of preference.

Overall layout

● Try to make your questionnaire look *attractive* and *simple to understand*. The easier it is to fill in, the more likely it is to be completed.

● Write a short *introduction* to the questionnaire.
Explain why you are collecting the data.
Describe briefly what use will be made of the data.
Ask politely for the person's assistance.
Here is an example:

DEACON COLLEGE CAFETERIA SURVEY

The College governors plan to discuss the future of the cafeteria at their end-of-year meeting.
I am doing a confidential survey to find out about:

● THE PRESENT USE OF THE CAFETERIA,
● THE CHANGES STUDENTS WOULD LIKE TO SEE IN IT.

PLEASE HELP ME BY COMPLETING THIS QUESTIONNAIRE.
My survey report will be presented to the governors to help them with their decisions.
A copy will also be placed in the College reference library.
It will be available for you to read there.

● Plan the *layout* carefully
Make sure that the questions can be read easily.
Number each question and answer.

Leave a space between each question/answer and the next one.

- Give *clear instructions* on how and where you want the question answered.
  You may want them to Fill in ...

  >   or Tick ✓ and/or Cross ✗,
  >   or Ring,
  >   or Rank 1 to 5,
  >   and so on ...

- Leave *sufficient space* for answers.
  Place each space or box so that it is linked clearly to its question or statement.

- Write multiple responses such as Yes ☐   No ☐ in the *same order* each time.
  Changing the order to, for example, No ☐   Yes ☐ in some answers may give 'incorrect' data.

- At the end of the questionnaire, *thank* the person for completing it.
  Give details of how to return the questionnaire. State a date as a deadline if necessary.
  Here is an example:

> **Thank you very much for your help.**
>
> **Please put your completed questionnaire in the collection box in the College Office by the 17th November.**

Pilot Survey

Before doing a full survey, a '**pilot survey**' is often useful.

In this '**trial run**', you can try out your questionnaire on a few people to test it. This helps you to see if it is clear and gives the kind of data you want. It gives you the chance to improve it if you need to.

You can also use the results you get to test the sorting and analysing techniques you plan to use.

Discussion Exercise

Design a questionnaire for the survey about Deacon College Cafeteria. Write questions to collect facts and opinions/preferences in your survey.

Use different styles of question in your questionnaire.
Make some of them 'multiple response questions' and some statements/items that have to be ranked.

Discuss your group's questionnaires. Criticise them.
Help each other to improve them.
Make a neat copy of the final version of your questionnaire.

► Exercise P25.1

1 Write an introduction and final paragraph for questionnaires to be used in the following situations.
  (a) Trevor is doing a survey about recycling bottles, cans, newspapers, ... for an article in the College newspaper. The deadline for his copy to go to the editor is the 13th March.

  (b) For a GCSE project, Penny does a survey on the use made of the College's sports facilities.
  Her teacher wants to see and discuss her report on February 12th.
  (c) Isobel helps at Lawnstone Senior Citizens Club on a Wednesday. The committee have asked her to do a survey about public transport in their area.
  They want the report for their Annual General Meeting on 15th June.

2 Some students plan to use the following questions in their questionnaires. Criticise each question.
  Say what data you think the students want to collect in each case.
  Rewrite the questions to obtain these data. List possible responses for people to tick or order if you need to.
  (a) Do you agree that BBC 2 is the best TV channel?
  (b) How many cigarettes do you smoke?
  (c) Do you drink too much?
  (d) Where do you live?
  (e) How much do you spend on clothes?
  (f) What is your religion?

3 Criticise the way people are expected to record their answers to the following questions.
  Suggest at least one way to improve this in each case.
  Write what you think is the best version of each question, including the alternative responses you would use.

  (a) What is your annual income? £ [＿＿＿＿]
  (b) What is your marital status?
    Single ☐   Widowed ☐   Divorced/Separated ☐
  (c) How do you usually travel to work?
    Private car/ Public transport / Bus / Train / Other
  (d) Do you prefer pop or classical music? Yes ☐   No ☐
  (e) Do you hand in your college/ school assignments on time?
    Always ☐   Sometimes ☐   Seldom ☐
  (f) How important are these features of Springfield Supermarket to you?
    Wide range of fruit and vegetables   ☐
    Own brand products available   ☐
    Friendly staff   ☐
    Plenty of trolleys and baskets   ☐
    Special Offers every week   ☐

◉ Investigation

Find some people you know who have completed a questionnaire for a survey. You may have done so yourself. Ask other students in your group, relatives, teachers, other friends, ...

Find out what they remember about the survey.
  What was it about?
  Was it part of market research, an opinion poll, a government survey, ...?
  Did they fill in a questionnaire or were they asked questions?
  Where was the survey done: in the street, at home, at a college/school, ...?
  And so on ...

Discuss what they liked or disliked about completing the questionnaire.

Look for questionnaires in magazines, newspapers, mailshots, ...
Collect examples of them if you can.

Discuss the design of these questionnaires. Suggest improvements where possible.

Collating and analysing responses

After questionnaires have been filled in and returned, the data on them has to be *sorted*.

The responses to each question need to be put together in an organised way first. This is called **collating** the responses.

Responses may be collated into **lists** or on to **tables**.

A list is usually used when the responses are all *different*. They can be organised into alphabetical or numerical order.

A table is usually used when the responses are in *categories*.

The responses can be collated on to a **tally table** first. Then the data can be summarised in a **frequency table**.

Tally tables p197

Examples of collating into a list and on to a table are given below.

Jo did a survey on the use of washing powders.

The first question on her questionnaire asked each person to fill in his or her name.

First Name.........................Surname..................................

Jo listed the names in alphabetical order. She gave each person an identification number. This is part of the **data base** she made.

ID number	Surname	First name
001	Abbott	Cathy
002	Able	Alison
003	Adams	Mary
004	Andrews	Tim
005	Ayres	Alice
006	Bailey	Steve

Here is another question from Jo's questionnaire. The responses are in five categories.

Do you buy biological washing powder?
Always ☐   Usually ☐   Sometimes ☐   Seldom ☐   Never ☐

Jo collated the responses into this tally table.

Response	Tally	Frequency
Always	HH IIII	9
Usually	HH HH HH HH HH HH HH HH HH HH	57
Sometimes	HH HH HH HH HH HH HH III	38
Seldom	HH HH I	11
Never	HH	5
	Total	120

The frequencies in the table show the number of questionnaires with each response.

To compare the data, you can simply compare the frequencies.

You can see that:

'Usually' was ticked on most questionnaires ...57,
'Never' was ticked on fewest questionnaires ... 5.

Another way to compare these data is to look at what fraction of the questionnaires had each response.

57 out of 120 had 'Usually' ticked ... i.e. $\frac{57}{120}$,

5 out of 120 had 'Never' ticked ... i.e. $\frac{5}{120}$

The fraction is: $\dfrac{\text{Fraction for the response}}{\text{Total number of questionnaires}}$

A percentage is the clearest way to show such a fraction. Percentages are easy to compare. You can find the percentages with a calculator.

Response	Frequency	Percentage
Always	9	7.5 ◀
Usually	57	
Sometimes	38	
Seldom	11	
Never	5	
Total	120	

9 ÷ 120 %

Discussion Exercise

1 (a) Copy and complete the table above. Give each percentage to 1 decimal place.
   (b) The percentages in the table should add up to 100%. Explain why. The total percentage in the table above is not 100%.
   Why not? Discuss.
   In the results of a survey, percentages are often rounded so that they do add up to 100%. Discuss why and how this may be done. Is this a good idea? Discuss.

2 Here are some more questions from Jo's questionnaire.

A

Is anyone in your household allergic to biological washing powder?   Yes ☐   No ☐

B

What kind of washing machine do you use?
Automatic ☐   Twin Tub ☐   None ☐
Other ☐
Please specify..

C

How good is your present washing powder at removing stains?
Excellent ☐   Good ☐   Fair ☐   Poor ☐   Very Poor ☐

D

Tick the box which most closely matches your opinion on this statement. 'Biological powder cleans better than non-biological powder'.
Strongly agree ☐   Agree ☐   Disagree ☐
Strongly disagree ☐ Don't know ☐

These tally tables show Jo's collated results. Make a frequency table for each question's responses.
Work out a percentage for each response.

Question A

Response	Tally
YES	ⵜⵜ ⵜⵜ ⵜⵜ ⵜⵜ ⵜⵜ ⵜⵜ ⵜⵜ ⵜⵜ ⵜⵜ
NO	ⵜⵜ ⵜⵜ ⵜⵜ ⵜⵜ ⵜⵜ ⵜⵜ ⵜⵜ ⵜⵜ ⵜⵜ ⵜⵜ ⵜⵜ ⵜⵜ ⵜⵜ ⵜⵜ ⵜⵜ

Question B

Response	Tally
Automatic	ⵜⵜ ⵜⵜ ⵜⵜ ⵜⵜ ⵜⵜ ⵜⵜ ⵜⵜ ⵜⵜ ⵜⵜ ⵜⵜ ⵜⵜ ⵜⵜ ⵜⵜ ⵜⵜ I
Twin Tub	ⵜⵜ ⵜⵜ ⵜⵜ IIII
None	ⵜⵜ ⵜⵜ ⵜⵜ III
Other	ⵜⵜ ⵜⵜ II

Question C

Response	Tally
Excellent	ⵜⵜ ⵜⵜ ⵜⵜ ⵜⵜ ⵜⵜ IIII
Good	ⵜⵜ ⵜⵜ ⵜⵜ ⵜⵜ ⵜⵜ ⵜⵜ ⵜⵜ
Fair	ⵜⵜ ⵜⵜ ⵜⵜ ⵜⵜ ⵜⵜ
Poor	ⵜⵜ ⵜⵜ ⵜⵜ II
Very Poor	ⵜⵜ ⵜⵜ IIII

Question D

Response	Tally
Strongly Agree	ⵜⵜ ⵜⵜ ⵜⵜ ⵜⵜ IIII
Agree	ⵜⵜ ⵜⵜ ⵜⵜ ⵜⵜ ⵜⵜ
Disagree	ⵜⵜ ⵜⵜ ⵜⵜ ⵜⵜ ⵜⵜ ⵜⵜ ⵜⵜ
Strongly disagree	ⵜⵜ ⵜⵜ ⵜⵜ ⵜⵜ II
Don't know	ⵜⵜ ⵜⵜ IIII

3   Comment on the results for each question from Jo's survey. Write one or two sentences about each for a survey report. Discuss the sentences written by the students in your group.

4   Jo wants to use some diagrams to present her survey results. What kind of diagrams would be most suitable?

Discuss their advantages and disadvantages.

5   How could a computer be used to collate and analyse Jo's results?
Consider the computer software and facilities you have available.
Discuss how a data base, spreadsheet or any other available statistical package could be used.

Collating ranked responses

To respond to some questions you have to put a list of items in order. Here is an example of such a question from Jo's survey.

Consumers gave the following reasons for buying a particular washing powder. Please rank them 1 to 5 in order of importance to you. (Use 1 to show the most important and 5 the least important.)
☐ It gives a clean wash.
☐ It can be used for a low temperature wash.
☐ It does not produce an allergic reaction.
☐ It is good value for money.
☐ It keeps white clothes white.

Jo **collated the results** from this question in two ways.
First she listed each person's responses in a simple data base.
This is part of her data base.
Each questionnaire is identified by a number: 001, 002, …

	001	002	003	004	005
Cleanness	2	1	2	2	3
Low temperature wash	4	3	5	4	5
Non - allergic	1	5	4	5	4
Value	3	2	1	3	1
Whiteness	5	4	3	1	2

Jo also collated the results on to the following two-way tally table. The tally marks for the responses from questionnaire number 001 are shown on it in green.

Reason \ Rank	1	2	3	4	5
Cleanness	ⵜⵜ ⵜⵜ ⵜⵜ ⵜⵜ	ⵜⵜ ⵜⵜ ⵜⵜ	ⵜⵜ ⵜⵜ ⵜⵜ ⵜⵜ	ⵜⵜ ⵜⵜ ⵜⵜ ⵜⵜ	ⵜⵜ IIII
Low temperature wash	ⵜⵜ ⵜⵜ ⵜⵜ	ⵜⵜ III	ⵜⵜ ⵜⵜ ⵜⵜ ⵜⵜ	ⵜⵜ ⵜⵜ ⵜⵜ ⵜⵜ	ⵜⵜ ⵜⵜ ⵜⵜ ⵜⵜ

table continued

Rank / Reason	1	2	3	4	5
Non-allergic	卌 卌 卌 卌	卌 卌 卌 卌	卌 卌 卌	卌 卌 |||	卌	
Value	卌 卌 卌 ||||	卌 卌 卌 卌	卌 卌 卌 卌	卌 卌 卌 卌	卌 卌 卌 卌
Whiteness	卌 卌 卌 卌	卌 卌 卌 卌	卌 卌 卌 |||	卌 卌 卌 卌	卌 卌 卌 卌

To summarise the results, Jo recorded the frequency and percentage for each response in a two-way table. The start of her table is given below. It shows the figures for 'Cleanness'. The black figures are frequencies. The green figures are percentages.

Rank / Reason	1	2	3	4	5
Cleanness	34	31	22	24	9
	28.3%	25.8%	18.3%	20.0%	7.5%

As a check she works out the Totals down each column of figures. Each total should be the same as the total number of questionnaires. Jo has 120 questionnaires in her survey. So her frequencies should add up to 120.
Percentages should add up to 100% (or nearly 100%!)

 Discussion Exercise

1 (a) Make a two-way table for Jo's results.
   Copy her figures for 'Cleanness' on to it.
   (b) Fill in the other frequencies from her tally table.
   Check the totals across and down the table.
   (c) Calculate the percentages for each response.
   Give each correct to 1 decimal place.
   Write the percentages in your two-way table.
   Check the totals down the table.

2 Another question in Jo's survey is about information on washing powder packets. It asks people to rank five types of information in order of importance. Here is her data base for her pilot survey. For this she asked 20 people to try her questionnaire.

	001	002	003	004	005	006	007	008	009	010	011	012	013	014	015	016	017	018	019	020
Machine wash instructions	3	4	2	3	3	5	2	3	1	2	3	2	3	4	2	3	3	3	1	4
Handwash instructions	4	5	4	4	4	4	5	4	4	4	5	4	4	1	4	4	4	4	4	5
Handcare	5	3	5	5	5	3	4	5	5	5	2	5	5	5	5	5	5	5	5	3
Ingredients	2	2	3	2	1	1	3	2	2	3	1	3	1	3	3	2	1	2	3	2
Weight	1	1	1	1	2	2	1	1	3	1	4	1	2	2	1	1	2	1	2	1

(a) Collate Jo's pilot survey results on to a two-way tally table. Discuss the most efficient way to do this.
(b) Find the frequency and percentage for each response. Write them in a two-way table.

3 Jo used two questions with 'ranked' responses.
Discuss the responses she got to each of these questions.
Write a few sentences for Jo's survey report based on the results you have collated.
Compare the sentences written by the students in your group.
Comment on their suitability for Jo's report.

4 In what other ways could Jo present these data in her report? Which would be most suitable?
Discuss the ideas from your group.

Analysing ranked responses

Responses that rank a list of items in order can be **analysed** in several ways. Each analysis may use a different method to consider how highly each item is ranked.
Jo analysed her results in the following ways.

1st choices only
In one analysis, Jo considered 1st choices only. She looked at how many 1s there were for each item.

Reason	Number of 1s	Percentage
Cleanness	34	28.3%
Low temperature wash	15	12.5%
Non-allergic	29	24.2%
Value	19	15.8%
Whiteness	23	19.2%
Total	120	100%

1st and 2nd choices
In another analysis, Jo considered 1st and 2nd choices.

Reason	Number of 1s	Number of 2s	Total
Cleanness	34	31	65
Low temperature wash	15	8	23
Non-allergic	29	35	64
Value	19	26	45
Whiteness	23	20	43
Total	120	120	240

All choices
In her final analysis, Jo took all the rankings into account. She treated each rank (1–5) as a 'mark'.
To work out the total number of 'marks' for each item, she multiplied each rank (1, 2, 3, 4, 5) and its frequency, then added up these 'marks'.
The working for Cleanness, for example, is like this:

Rank	1	2	3	4	5	
Frequency	34	31	22	24	9	
Frequency × Rank	34×1 = 34	31×2 = 62	22×3 = 66	24×4 = 96	9×5 = 45	Total 303

Jo used her calculator memory to find each total. She cleared the memory first.
She did each multiplication and added it to the memory as she went along. She recalled the total from the memory at the end. This gave the figures in this table.

Reason	Total of 'marks'
Cleanness	303
Low temperature wash	432
Non-allergic	302
Value	377
Whiteness	386
Total	1800

This final total is a useful check.
The 'marks' given by each person (1, 2, 3, 4, 5) add up to 15.
120 people gave these 'marks'.
So the total should be: $120 \times 15 = 1800$.

In Jo's ranking, 1 is 'top' and 5 is 'bottom'. So the item with the lowest total is 'top' and the item with the highest total is 'bottom'.

Discussion Exercise

1 Look at the three tables Jo prepared for her analysis of her ranked data. Compare the rating given to the reasons in each table.
What conclusions might Jo come to based on the results in these tables?
Discuss the ideas of the students in your group.
Based on your discussion, write a brief analysis of Jo's results for this question.
Give it in a form suitable for Jo's final report.
Discuss your group's accounts.

2 Consider the ranked results you collated from Jo's pilot survey (in the Discussion Exercise on p457).
Analyse these results in Jo's three ways:
● 1st choices only
● 1st and 2nd choices
● all choices.
Write down your conclusions based on your analysis.

3 Jo chose three ways to look at her ranked data.
What other ways could be used?
Discuss.
Try some of these ways on the data from Jo's two questions.
List the main advantages and disadvantages of each method you have used (including Jo's).
Which methods do you think are best? Why?
Discuss.

4 Consider how you could use a computer to collate and/or analyse the ranked data from Jo's survey.
What use, if any, could you make of a data base, spreadsheet or other statistics software?
Discuss.
To try out your ideas, use Jo's pilot survey data (in the Discussion Exercise on p455-456).

► Exercise P25.2

1 Here are some pilot survey questions and the responses given on questionnaires numbered 001, 002, ...
The figures in the tables are the rankings.
Collate the responses for each question. Analyse them in several ways. Compare the results you get. Write some conclusions which are suitable for a survey report in each case.

(a)
> Which of these TV channels do you like best?
> Rank them in order 1 to 4.

Channel \ ID Number	001	002	003	004	005	006	007	008	009	010
BBC 1	3	2	3	1	1	2	2	4	1	4
BBC 2	2	3	1	4	2	3	4	2	2	1
ITV	4	1	4	2	4	4	1	3	3	3
Ch 4	1	4	2	3	3	1	3	1	4	2

(b)
> Students gave the following reasons for choosing a particular make of trainers.
> Rank them 1 to 5 in order of importance for you.

Reason \ ID Number	001	002	003	004	005	006	007	008	009
Good fit	3	1	3	2	1	3	5	2	4
Style	2	3	1	5	2	1	2	4	2
Designer label	1	4	2	1	3	2	1	1	1
Good value	4	5	5	3	4	5	4	3	3
Hard wearing	5	2	4	4	5	4	3	5	5

(c)
> Which three of the following activities would you most like to do on this holiday?
> Rank them in order 1 to 3.

Activity \ ID Number	001	002	003	004	005	006	007	008	009	010	011	012
Fishing	1		2		3		1	3		3		
Horse-riding		1		2		1	3		2		3	1
Canoeing	2	2	3	1		3		2	1	2	2	3
Swimming	3		1		2		2	1			1	
Orienteering		3		3	1	2			3	1		2

(d)
> Which four of the following types of TV programme do you enjoy most?
> Rank them in order 1 to 4.

Programme \ ID Number	001	002	003	004	005	006	007	008	009	010	011	012
Comedy	4	1		4	1		2	3	4	1		
Drama	3	2			2	3	1			2	1	2
Music			3		4	1				3	2	3
Quiz shows	1			3		2		2				1
Sport		3	2	2			4	1	3		4	
Films	2	4	1				3		2	4		
News			4	1	3	4		4	1		3	4

2 These tables summarise the results from 'ranking' questions in some surveys. The figures in the table give the frequencies for each response.

Analyse these data in different ways. Make comparisons between the results. Draw some conclusions from your comparisons and write a brief report in each case.

(a)
> Which of the following take-away meals do you like most?
> Rank them 1 to 5 in order of preference.

Meal \ Rank	1	2	3	4	5
Fish and chips	11	8	7	10	14
Chinese	13	9	11	9	8
Indian	9	15	8	10	8
Pizza	10	12	17	6	5
Hamburger	7	6	7	15	15

(b)
> Students on a maths course gave the following reasons for taking that College Course.
> Rank them 1 to 5 in order of importance to you.

Reason \ Rank	1	2	3	4	5
Enjoyment	6	7	17	15	10
Good at it	11	12	9	13	10
Like the teacher	15	10	8	8	14
Need it for career/job	13	14	13	8	7
Better than others available	10	12	8	11	14

(c)
> Tourists listed the following reasons for choosing their package holiday. Which three are most important to you? Rank them in order 1 to 3.

Reason \ Rank	1	2	3
Right price	14	7	13
Attractive resort	16	18	17
Suitable departures	4	9	11
High-class hotel	9	11	7
Good weather	17	15	12

(d)
> Which two of the following languages would you most like to learn?
> Rank them in order 1, 2.

Reason \ Rank	1	2
French	15	5
German	13	9
Spanish	2	5
Italian	7	12
Japanese	3	5
Russian	5	9

◀

💬 *Discussion Exercise*

Work with two or three other students. Choose one of these topics:
- school uniform
- library facilities
- provision for recycling waste materials (bottles, cans, paper, …)

● Imagine you are doing a survey related to your topic. Discuss the potential 'audiences' for the results of your survey.
Who might commission such a survey? Why?
Who else might be interested in the results? Why?
Summarise your ideas in two lists.

● You have to collect the data in your study by questionnaire. With the students in your group, 'brainstorm' at least 20 possible questions you might ask. Just note an 'outline' of the wording you could use for each.

● Discuss possible ways to word your questions for a questionnaire.
Write some questions whose answers are best given as:
    - a single word or short phrase
    - a number.
Write some questions for which these simple alternatives would be suitable answers:

> Yes ☐ No ☐

> Yes ☐ No ☐ Don't know ☐

> Yes ☐ No ☐ Sometimes ☐

> Always ☐ Usually ☐ Sometimes ☐ Seldom ☐ Never ☐

> Agree ☐   Disagree ☐   No opinion ☐

> Strongly ☐ Agree ☐ Don't ☐ Disagree ☐ Strongly ☐
> Agree   know   disagree

> Excellent ☐ Good ☐ Fair ☐ Poor ☐ Very poor ☐

Write some questions giving other check lists of possible answers.
Try to produce examples of check lists where:
    - only one category can be chosen
    - several items can be selected
    - an open category, such as
      'Other (please write in…)', is included.

● The survey must consider people's opinions and preferences related to your topic. 'Brainstorm' at least 10 statements or items you might ask people to rank on a scale of 1–5.
Discuss your ideas.
Write several questions based on these for your questionnaire.

● Design and produce a short questionnaire for your topic.
Carry out a survey using your questionnaire.
Collate your data 'by hand' and with the help of a computer if you can.
Use lists, tables, diagrams, … where appropriate.
Analyse your data.
Discuss the conclusions you reach.
Write a full survey report on your work.

Hypothesis testing

A **hypothesis** is a statement that may be **true** or **false**.
It states someone's opinion about a situation or topic.
The plural of hypothesis is **hypotheses**.

Each of these statements, for example, is a hypothesis. They are all hypotheses.

'Most people want more police on the beat'.
'This road is used mostly by lorries'.
'Wales gets more rain than East Anglia'.
'The more you feed your tomato plants, the more tomatoes you get'.

When you test a hypothesis you try to find out whether it is true or false.

To test a hypothesis you carry out a statistical investigation. These are the main steps you take.

● Collect appropriate data related to the hypothesis.
● Collate and present the data in a suitable way.
● Analyse the data.
● Decide whether the data supports or disproves the hypothesis.

Two important ways to collect data are by **survey** and by **experiment**.

In a survey you collect data from situations that occur 'naturally'. You do not try to change the situation at all. The main ways to collect data in a survey are:

● by asking questions
● by observing things
● by looking at published data.

In an experiment you set up a situation. You measure and observe the effects, if any, that result from changes in that situation. This is a standard technique you will have used in science.

Data about the hypotheses stated above can be collected in the following ways:

To test the hypothesis 'Most people want more police on the beat', you can collect data by **questionnaire**.
In a questionnaire you can collect both facts and opinions.

To find out whether the hypothesis 'This road is used mostly by lorries' is true, you can collect data by **observation**. One way to do this is to set up an observation post by the road. You can survey the vehicles passing using an observation sheet.

To support or disprove the hypothesis 'Wales gets more rain than East Anglia' you can look at **published data** about rainfall in these two areas.

To investigate the hypothesis ' The more you feed your tomato plants, the more tomatoes you get' you can set up an **experiment** with tomato plants.

Discussion Exercise

1   Consider each of the following hypotheses. Decide on the best way to collect data to test each hypothesis.
Discuss your ideas.
'Most people think the speed limit on motorways should be changed.'
'Blue is the most popular car colour.'

'Listening to Mozart helps students get better homework marks.'
'It is safer to travel facing the 'back' in a train than facing the 'front'.'
'Car accidents mostly involve drivers under the age of 25.'
'Environmental pollution retards the growth of plants.'
'On this road, most drivers break the 30 mph speed limit.'
'Diet affects intelligence.'
'Most people want seat belts fitted in all coaches.'

2   State at least two hypotheses that you could test
(a) by asking questions
(b) by observing things
(c) by using published data
(d) by experiment.
Discuss the hypotheses suggested by your group.

Coming to conclusions

Statisticians have special ways to test hypotheses that help them to **come to conclusions**. These tests involve quite difficult mathematics, so they are not included in your course.

However, as well as applying these special tests, a statistician also uses the methods you have used to analyse data. From this analysis, you can get a 'feel' about whether the hypothesis has been supported or not.

The conclusions you reach from your analysis depend upon your judgement. They also depend on many other factors. These include:

● the actual figures in your analysis
● the type of hypothesis being tested
● the reason for stating the hypothesis
● how strong a 'case' you need to put forward
● your point of view about the hypothesis, i.e. do you want it supported or disproved!

There are often no definite 'correct conclusions' from the results of hypothesis testing, However, some conclusions make more sense and are more convincing than others.

When nearly all the data appears to support (or disprove) the hypothesis, then coming to a conclusion is fairly easy.

The problem arises when the figures are not so clear cut. For example, imagine your hypothesis is 'People want the library to stay open longer'.
If 95% of the people surveyed agree with this, then your hypothesis has been very strongly supported. However, if 95% disagree with this then your hypothesis appears to have been disproved.

If only 55% agree, then the support for this hypothesis is not so strong. Other factors need to be considered in your conclusion. When coming to conclusions you have to decide what is reasonable in each case. You must consider the strength of the evidence you have and other factors involved. You must always explain why you have come to your conclusions.

Testing hypotheses by survey

Here is a check list of some important questions to think about when planning and doing a survey.
Use these as guidelines to help you to sort out your ideas.

- What do you want to *find out* in your survey? Why?
- What data will you need to *collect*? How will you decide?
- Which is the *best way* to collect the data? Why?
  Do you need any *equipment*.
- *How much* data will you need to collect?
  How will you decide?
- How *accurate* will your data have to be? Why?
  Can you *check* your data?
- How will you *record* your data? Why is this the best way?
- How will you *display* your data? Why?
- What *patterns*, if any, do your data show?
  What do they tell you?
- What *conclusions/predictions* can you make from your data?
  Can you *test* your conclusions/predictions?
- Are your results the ones you *expected*? Why?
- What kind of *report* will you present to describe what you did, your results, conclusions, …? Who is the report for?
- What *other questions* could you explore based on the results of your survey if you had time?

Discussion Exercise

- Think about the following topics for surveys.
  Discuss what hypotheses you might test as part of each survey.
  List these hypotheses for each topic.
    - The effect of pollution on the quality of life in your area.
    - The suggestion to change the UK time system (Greenwich Mean Time and British Summer Time) to keep in time with Europe.
    - The placing of a pelican/ zebra/ 'lollipop' crossing near your school/college or local shops.
    - The introduction of a four-term year and a continental 'school day' (8 am to 2 pm) to UK schools.
    - The facilities available in your area for particular groups of people:
      the very young, teenagers, disabled, elderly, …

ACTIVITY

- Choose one topic for a survey. It may be one of those given in the Discussion Exercise above or one you have chosen yourself.
  State the hypotheses you will test in your survey.
  Design a questionnaire to collect the data. Include some questions with multiple responses and statements or items for ranking.
  Discuss your group's questionnaires.
  Help each other to improve them if necessary.
- Do a pilot survey to try out your questionnaire. Rewrite any questions you need to as a result of your findings.
- Carry out a survey with the final version of your questionnaire. Write a report describing your survey methods and giving your findings.
  Use any available computer facilities in the collation and analysis of your data.

Testing hypotheses by experiment

Discussion Exercise

Here are some hypotheses that can be tested by doing an experiment.

Group A
'Students work better when listening to music.'

'The reaction times of short people are faster than those of tall people.'

'People with large hands can write faster than those with small hands.'

'Tests given in the afternoon produce better results than those given in the morning.'

'Organically grown vegetables taste better than other vegetables.'

Group B
'The more sunlight sunflower seeds get, the faster they grow.'

'The larger the bob on a pendulum, the slower it swings.'

'Biological washing powders wash better than non-biological powders.'

'The longer the wire from a battery to a light bulb, the brighter the light.'

'When a weight is dropped, the heavier the weight, the faster it falls.'

- Choose at least one hypothesis from each Group above.
  Discuss, in detail, how to test each hypothesis experimentally.
  Make sure you cover these points in your discussion:
    - What do you want to find out?
    - What data do you need to collect?
    - What variables are involved in the situation?
    - Which variables must you control and which will you vary?
    - How will you control and alter variables?
    - How will you collect and record the data?
    - How will you set up and organise the experiment?
    - How will you collate, display and analyse the data?
- Write a plan for each of your experiments. Discuss the plans written by your group. Based on this discussion, adapt your plans if you need to.

ACTIVITY

- Test a hypothesis yourself by experiment.
  It may be one you have discussed in the Discussion Exercise above or one you have made yourself.
- Write a report describing your work and giving your conclusions.

P26
More estimating

This unit will help you to:

■ use an estimate to identify that an answer may be incorrect

■ recognise that an estimate and an answer are about the same size

■ use reasonable approximations to estimate answers to calculations involving whole numbers and decimals

■ estimate and approximate to check the answers to numerical problems are 'about the right size'.

Looking at answers

Arithmetic is quick and easy to do with a calculator. If you key in a calculation correctly, then the calculator gives you the correct answer.

SORRY, WRONG NUMBER

This seems simple enough. But it is quite easy to press the wrong key or make some other mistake.

A calculator cannot tell when you have made a mistake. It simply does what you key in. You have to check that the answer it gives makes sense.

 Discussion Exercise

Three students did this calculation:

$$\frac{12 \times 31.3}{9.6}$$

Here are their 'calculator answers'.

 3.9125   39.   393.75

The answer should be about 30.

● Which answers are obviously incorrect?
  How can you tell without using a calculator?
  Discuss.
● Comment about the other answer.
  What can you say about it?
  Discuss.
● Do the calculation yourself.
  What do you find? Discuss what this shows.

 *Memo*   Estimating answers N4 p19

Estimates as checks
A rough or approximate answer to a calculation is called an **estimate**. It gives you a good idea of what size the answer should be.

Always use an estimate to *check* that your answer to a calculation is 'about the right size'.

Remember:
An estimate helps you to spot an incorrect answer. It does not show that an answer is correct.

Here is a useful routine to follow:
● Estimate the answer first. | Estimate |
                                     ↓
● Then do the calculation. | Calculate |
                                     ↓
● Check that the estimate | Check |
  and answer are 'about
  the same size'.

  Make sure the answer is *not* 10, 100, 1000, ... times too big or 10, 100, 1000, ... times too small.
● If estimate and answer are not a 'reasonable match', then do the calculation again and check again.
● If your new answer fails the check, then you need to think again:
  - your estimate may be wrong,
  - you may be working out your estimate and answer in different ways,
  and so on ...
Try to sort out what has gone wrong.

Discussion Exercise

Compare each estimate and calculator answer below.
Which answers are obviously incorrect?
Which are reasonably close to the estimate?
Discuss.
Explain your choices.

	Estimate	Calculator display
1	1500	1648.137886
2	320	296.7
3	50	643.2
4	64	7.0241798
5	100	98.75
6	0.2	0.1875
7	70 000	6363.636363
8	0.01	0.945
9	7	6.264
10	200	20.06666667

You have estimated answers before.

Memo

To estimate the answer to a calculation, you take these steps.
● Replace each number by a suitable approximation. Make sure it is easy to work with mentally.
  Remember: ≈ means 'is approximately equal to'.
● Do the calculation with these simpler numbers. Work it out in your head if you can.

Rounding the numbers in a calculation to 1 significant figure usually gives a reasonable estimate to the answer.

Memo
Significant figures
p16

Question

Tim used his calculator to work out

$$\frac{27.5 \times 41.7}{15.29 \times 4.8} = 1.5625$$

Without using a calculator show why his answer is not sensible.

Answer

Round each number to 1 significant figure.
$27.5 \approx 30, \quad 41.7 \approx 40, \quad 15.29 \approx 20, \quad 4.8 \approx 5.$
Estimate:

$$\frac{27.5 \times 41.7}{15.29 \times 4.8} \approx \frac{30 \times 40}{20 \times 5}$$

Cancel:

$$= \frac{\cancel{30}^{6} \times \cancel{40}^{2}}{\cancel{20}_{1} \times \cancel{5}_{1}} = 12$$

Tim's answer (1.5625) and this estimate (12) are not about the same size.
1.5625 is far too small.
It is about 10 times too small.
So his answer is not a sensible size.

To do the 'simpler calculation' for an estimate, you may need to multiply or divide numbers 'in your head'.
Look up how to do this if you need to.

Memo
'In your head'
p5 and P14 p346

► Exercise P26.1

1 Two answers are given for each calculation below.
One is obviously 'wrong' in each case.
By estimating answers, spot each incorrect answer.
Explain your choices.

(a) 16.5×1.4 `231.`   `23.1`
(b) 64.7×9.89 `63.9883`   `639.883`
(c) $(0.48)^2$ `2304.`   `0.2304`
(d) $\sqrt{12100}$ `34.78505426`   `110.`
(e) $25.293 - 4.678$ `20.615`   `5.406797777`
(f) $5.495 \div 3.14$ `17.2543`   `1.75`
(g) $0.0594 + 0.18$ `0.2394`   `0.010692`
(h) $\dfrac{3.85 \times 2.9}{1.75}$ `6.38`   `195.3875`

2 Choose the value nearest to the answer for each of the following calculations. Explain your choice in each case.

(a) 5.9×32
   A 1.8   B 18   C 180   D 1800
(b) 62.5×0.68
   A 0.042   B 0.42   C 4.2   D 42
(c) 2.9×0.41
   A 12   B 1.2   C 0.12   D 0.012
(d) 0.125×0.76
   A 0.8   B 0.08   C 0.008   D 0.0008
(e) $6.14 \div 2.3$
   A 0.003   B 0.03   C 0.3   D 3
(f) $0.32 \div 5.4$
   A 0.06   B 0.6   C 6   D 60
(g) $79.5 \div 0.4$
   A 2   B 20   C 200   D 2000
(h) $809 \div 0.19$
   A 4   B 40   C 400   D 4000 ◄

Using different approximations

Beth often uses different approximations in her estimates.
Here are some examples:

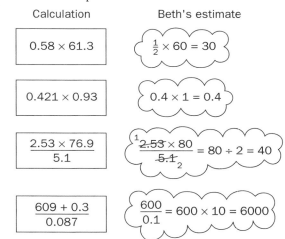

Calculation	Beth's estimate
0.58×61.3	$\frac{1}{2} \times 60 = 30$
0.421×0.93	$0.4 \times 1 = 0.4$
$\dfrac{2.53 \times 76.9}{5.1}$	$\dfrac{2.53 \times 80}{5.1} = 80 \div 2 = 40$
$\dfrac{609 + 0.3}{0.087}$	$\dfrac{600}{0.1} = 600 \times 10 = 6000$

💬 Discussion Exercise

- Discuss what Beth has done in each estimate above.
- Estimate each answer by rounding numbers to 1 significant figure.
- Compare the two methods for each example. Which do you prefer? Explain why.
- Find the actual answer to each calculation. Is each estimate reasonable? Discuss.
- Here are some other calculations.

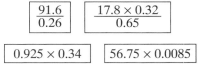

$$\frac{91.6}{0.26} \qquad \frac{17.8 \times 0.32}{0.65}$$

$$0.925 \times 0.34 \qquad 56.75 \times 0.0085$$

Estimate each answer in two different ways. Discuss the approximation used.
Compare the size of each estimate with the actual answer.
Comment on what you find.

● Think of other ways to approximate numbers.
   Discuss your ideas.
   Decide which would help you to estimate
   answers.

Approximately 1

Using the number 1 in an estimate makes it very easy to work
out.
For example,

$$\frac{1.06 \times 47.5}{0.99} \approx \frac{1 \times 50}{1} = 50$$

Rounding some decimals to 1 significant figure gives 1.
For example,   0.95 = 1 (to 1 sf)
                   0.974 = 1 (to 1 sf)
                   1.3289 = 1 (to 1 sf)
1 is also a reasonable approximation for some other decimals.
For example,   0.93 = 0.9 (to 1 sf) $\approx$ 1
                   0.781 = 0.8 (to 1 sf) $\approx$ 1
Such decimals are just less than 1.
So we can round such decimals to 1 when finding estimates.

Question

Estimate the answer to $\frac{8.75 \times 0.86}{0.948 \times 12.3}$ as a decimal.

Show the approximations you use in your working.

Answer

Approximations:
8.75 = 9 (to 1 sf)   0.86 $\approx$ 1
0.948 $\approx$ 1   12.3 = 10 (to 1 sf)
Estimate:

$$\frac{8.75 \times 0.86}{0.948 \times 12.3} \approx \frac{9 \times 1}{1 \times 10} = \frac{9}{10} = 0.9$$

► Exercise P26.2

1   Which of these decimals is it reasonable to round to 1?
   (a) 0.832   (d) 0.794   (g) 0.88
   (b) 1.832   (e) 1.16   (h) 0.0762
   (c) 0.09   (f) 1.364   (i) 1.414
2   Estimate the answer to each calculation first. Then use your
   calculator to work it out.
   (Give your answers to a sensible degree of accuracy.)
   Check that your estimate and answer are about the same
   size.
   (a) $\frac{31.6 \times 19.7}{1.24}$ (d) $\frac{0.787 \times 15.4}{3.1 + 6.87}$

   (b) $\frac{0.93 \times 48.7}{12.1 \times 1.14}$ (e) $\frac{13.4 + 7.29}{1.16 \times 1.94}$

   (c) $\frac{68.6 \times 34.9}{0.881 \times 9.7}$ (f) $\frac{(8.2)^2 \times 51.6}{0.89 \times 11.34}$

Using simple fractions

Some decimals, such as 0.5 and 0.25, are simple fractions.

$$0.5 = \frac{1}{2} \qquad 0.25 = \frac{1}{4}$$

These simple fractions are easy to work with 'in your head'.

Memo

To multiply by $\frac{1}{2}$, you divide by 2.
   For example, $\frac{1}{2} \times 300 = 300 \div 2 = 150$
To multiply by $\frac{1}{4}$, you divide by 4.
   For example, $\frac{1}{4} \times 1000 = 1000 \div 4 = 250$
And so on ...

To divide by $\frac{1}{2}$, you multiply by 2.
   For example, $700 \div \frac{1}{2} = 700 \times 2 = 1400$
To divide by $\frac{1}{4}$, you multiply by 4.
   For example, $90 \div \frac{1}{4} = 90 \times 4 = 360$
And so on ...

Look for such decimals in multiplication and division
calculations.
Replace them by simple fractions to estimate answers.

Question

Estimate the value of 186.3 ÷ 0.25
Do not use a calculator.
Show your working clearly.
Then find the answer with a calculator.
Use your estimate to check it is reasonable.

Answer

Approximations:
                    $186.3 \approx 200$ (to 1 sf)
                    $0.25 = \frac{1}{4}$
Estimate: $186.3 \div 0.25 \approx 200 \div \frac{1}{4}$
                          $= 200 \times 4$
                          $= 800$

With a calculator:
                    $186.3 \div 0.25 = 745.2$

Check:
This answer (745.2) and my estimate (800) are about the
same size. So it is reasonable.

► Exercise P26.3

Estimate the answer to each calculation. Then find the answer
with your calculator. Use your estimate to check your calculator
answer is about the right size.
1 36.4 ÷ 0.25   **3** 153.4 × 0.25   **5** 231.8 ÷ 0.25
2 92.7 × 0.5   **4** 277.9 ÷ 0.5   **6** 467.2 × 0.5

You can also approximate other decimals to simple fractions
such as $\frac{1}{2}$ and $\frac{1}{4}$.
For example,

   $0.432 \approx \frac{1}{2}$ because 0.432 is nearly 0.5
   $0.305 \approx \frac{1}{4}$ because 0.305 is just over 0.25.

Use such an approximation when it makes estimating an answer
easier.

Question

Estimate the answer to 48.36×0.527.
Show clearly the approximations made.

Answer

Approximations:
$48.36 \approx 50$ (to 1 sf) $0.527 \approx \frac{1}{2}$
Estimate: $48.36 \times 0.527 \approx 50 \times \frac{1}{2}$
$= 50 \div 2$
$= 25$

Exercise P26.4

1 Approximate these decimals to the nearest 'simple fraction'.
Choose from $\frac{1}{2}$, $\frac{1}{4}$, $\frac{1}{10}$.
(a) 0.28   (c) 0.13   (e) 0.09
(b) 0.461   (d) 0.637   (f) 0.365
2 Estimate the answer to each calculation. Then work it out
with your calculator. Check that your estimate and answer
are about the same size.
(a) 42.7×0.26 (c) $78.7 \div 0.621$ (e) $201.3 \div 0.34$
(b) 28.3×0.54 (d) 147.6×0.094 (f) $284.8 \div 0.216$

Dividing by decimal fractions

To estimate an answer you may have to divide by a decimal
fraction. The easiest decimals to divide by are 0.1, 0.01, 0.001, …
Use these as approximations if you can.
Imagine a number line if it helps to do these approximations.
Think about the size of the fractions involved.
For example,

$0.023 = \dfrac{23}{1000} \approx \dfrac{10}{1000} = 0.010$ i.e. 0.01

$0.087 = \dfrac{87}{1000} \approx \dfrac{100}{1000} = 0.100$ i.e. 0.1

Question

(a) Use a calculator to work out $\dfrac{1.9565}{0.0091}$

(b) Estimate the answer to check.
Show the working for your estimate.

Answer

(a) 215

(b) *Approximations:* $1.9565 \approx 2$ (to 1 sf)
$0.0091 \approx 0.01$

Estimate: $\dfrac{1.9565}{0.0091} \approx \dfrac{2}{0.01}$

$= 2 \div \dfrac{1}{100}$

$= 2 \times 100$
$= 200$

Check: This estimate (200) and the answer (215) are
about the same size. So the answer is reasonable.

Exercise P26.5

1 Approximate each of these decimals to 0.1 or 0.01 or 0.001.
Choose the nearest to each number.
(a) 0.034   (d) 0.0981   (g) 0.000724
(b) 0.0751   (e) 0.0008   (h) 0.0417
(c) 0.00273   (f) 0.196   (i) 0.0088
2 Estimate the answer to each calculation. Then use your
calculator to work it out.
(Give your answers to a sensible degree of accuracy.)
Check that your estimate and answer are about the same
size.
(a) $\dfrac{3.742}{0.087}$ (d) $\dfrac{0.07 \times 5.67}{0.00674}$

(b) $\dfrac{4.38 \times 2.6}{0.00793}$ (e) 23.4×0.091

(c) 14.4×0.0093 (f) $\dfrac{13.74}{0.091 \times 0.0085}$

Summary

Reasonable estimates for an answer may be different.
The result you get depends on the approximations you use.
There are no set rules about these approximations. Choose
the most suitable for each number and for you.
   Rounding all the numbers to 1 significant figure is
easy to do. This gives a reasonable estimate for an answer.
It often produces an easy calculation to work out. But not
always.
Look for other easier approximations if you need to.
Here are some ideas to help you.

Additions and subtractions
● Round all of the numbers to the same '*place value*', e.g.
   to the nearest 10, 100, … if it makes sense.

continued

Memo

$0.1 = \frac{1}{10}$. So dividing by 0.1 is the same as dividing by $\frac{1}{10}$.
   To divide by $\frac{1}{10}$, multiply by 10.
For example, $4 \div 0.1 = 4 \div \frac{1}{10} = 4 \times 10 = 40$

$0.01 = \frac{1}{100}$. So dividing by 0.01 is the same as dividing
   by $\frac{1}{100}$.
   To divide by $\frac{1}{100}$, multiply by 100.
For example, $0.7 \div 0.01 = 0.7 \div \frac{1}{100} = 0.7 \times 100 = 70$.

$0.001 = \frac{1}{1000}$. So dividing by 0.001 is the same as dividing
   by $\frac{1}{1000}$.
   To divide by $\frac{1}{1000}$, multiply by 1000.
For example, $0.6 \div 0.001 = 0.6 \div \frac{1}{1000} = 0.6 \times 1000 = 600$.

- Look for numbers that are *very small* compared to the others. They have little effect on the answer. Leave them out of your estimate.

Multiplications and divisions
- Look for decimals that *approximate to 1*.
  Replace them by 1 in the approximate calculation.
- Approximate numbers to 10, 100, 1000, ... and 0.1, 0.01, 0.001, ... where it makes sense.
- Use digits, such as 2 and 5, that are easy to work with in your head, where you can in the approximations.
- Look for decimals that are near to 0.5 ($= \frac{1}{2}$) or 0.25 ($= \frac{1}{4}$) or 0.1 ($= \frac{1}{10}$).
  Replace them by matching *simple fractions*.
- Never leave a number out of an approximate calculation, i.e., never approximate any number to 0 (zero).
  Approximate very small numbers to 0.1 or 0.01 or 0.001 ... instead.

Divisions
- Look for pairs of numbers in the calculation that are nearly multiples of each other.
  'Cancel' by the smaller number in each pair.
- Look for numbers that will cancel in the approximate calculation.
  Cancel if you can, before you work it out.
- When dividing by a decimal fraction, approximate it to a simple decimal such as 0.1, 0.01, 0.001, ... if possible.

Question

Estimate the answer to 1725 + 368 − 94.

Answer

Round each number 'to the nearest 100'.
1725 ≈ 1700,   368 ≈ 400,   94 ≈ 100.
Estimate: 1725 + 368 − 94
  ≈ 1700 + 400 − 100 = 2000

Question

Find an approximate value for $\frac{39.6 \times 0.721}{0.123}$

Answer

Spot the connection between 0.123 and 0.721:
0.721 ≈ 6 × 0.123

Cancel to get: $\frac{39.6 \times 0.721}{0.123} = \frac{39.6 \times \cancel{0.721}^{6}}{\cancel{0.123}_{1}}$

Round to 1 sf: ≈ $\frac{40 \times 6}{1} = 240$

Question

Estimate the value of $\frac{19.3 \times 82.6}{9.5 \times 0.97}$

Answer

Round to 1 sf:
19.3 ≈ 20,   82.6 ≈ 80,   9.5 ≈ 10,   0.97 ≈ 1

Estimate: $\frac{19.3 \times 82.6}{9.5 \times 0.97} \approx \frac{20 \times 80}{10 \times 1}$

Cancel to get: $= \frac{^{2}\cancel{20} \times 80}{_{1}\cancel{10} \times 1} = 160$

Exercise P26.6

1 Estimate the answer to each calculation. Show the approximations you use in each case.

(a) 6.8 × 5.32
(b) 6.9 ÷ 3.5
(c) 83.4 × 0.26
(d) 37.6 ÷ 9.1
(e) 1.694 ÷ 0.47
(f) 3.142 × (0.89)²
(g) $\frac{(5.03)^2}{4.7}$
(h) $\frac{6.73 + 3.21}{0.24}$
(i) $\frac{0.47}{586 + 3}$
(j) $\frac{29.6 \times 32.7}{4.25}$
(k) $\frac{78.31 \times \sqrt{3.97}}{0.94 \times 19.6}$
(l) $\frac{27.14 \times 958}{11.6 \times 9.26}$

2 Find the answers to the calculations in question **1** with your calculator. Round each answer sensibly. Use your estimates to check that your answers are reasonable.

3 Use your calculator to work out the following. Check that your answers are reasonable.
Round each answer sensibly where necessary.

(a) 13.2 + 18.9
(b) 94.3 − 36.4
(c) 0.37 × 11.8
(d) 162.1 ÷ 0.179
(e) 18.4 + 7.2 + 34.1
(f) 104.8 ÷ 14.7
(g) 3.14 × (0.48)² × 1.05
(h) 0.5 × (42.5 + 27.3) × 9.25
(i) $\frac{47.7 \times 8.21}{15.95}$
(j) $\frac{19.4 \times 15.8}{8.2}$
(k) $\frac{48.3 \times 17.6}{11.5 \times 6.21}$
(l) $\frac{123.6 \times 58.4}{29.28 \times 0.61}$
(m) $\frac{173 \times 49.2}{7.5}$
(n) $\frac{0.081 \times 9.2}{3.09}$

Problem solving

Usually you do calculations to solve problems. You are not given the calculations as 'sums' to do. You have to work out what calculation to do first.

The problems in the next exercise are based on work you have done already. Look up the relevant Unit(s) in this book if you want a reminder about what to do.

Exercise P26.7

For each question:
  Write down the calculation needed.
  Estimate the answer to the calculation.
  Use your calculator to work out the answer.
  (Where necessary, give the answer to a sensible degree of accuracy.)
  Check your answer is about the right size.

1 If the exchange rate is 8.84 Francs to £1, how much French money will Barry get for £320?

2 1 km is approximately 0.625 miles. One day, in Germany, Jim drove 583 km. How many miles did Jim drive?

3 Alison's new bedroom measures 4.7 m long by 3.2 m wide by 2.8 m tall. What is the volume of air in Alison's bedroom before she moves the furniture in?

4 Find the prices of the following pieces of material:
   (a) 5.6 m at £7.49 a metre
   (b) 8.2 m at £9.79 a metre
   (c) 12.8 m at £4.99 a metre.

5 1 ounce is approximately 28.4 grams. A box contains 3 kg of dishwasher powder. Approximately how many ounces is that?

6 Bev takes an average of 1.8 minutes to read a page of a detective story. How long will it take her to read the 279 pages of 'Inspector Doodle does it again'?

7 Kamal owns a clothes shop. One day he sold these items: 38 shirts at £7.95, 17 sweaters at £9.99, 23 pairs of trousers at £24.99 and 42 pairs of socks at £4.49.
   How much money did Kamal take on Saturday?

8 Lucy made a new path in her garden by laying end-to-end 34 paving slabs, each 0.47 m long. How long is Lucy's new path?

9 Fred had 9240 lb of bricks delivered. Each brick weighs 2.64 lb. How many bricks did Fred receive?

10 In Physics, the Gas Equation states:

$$\frac{P \times V}{T} = \text{constant}$$

where P is the pressure in atmospheres, V is the volume in cubic centimetres and T is the temperature in degrees K. Calculate the constant when:
   (a) $P = 2.7$ atmospheres, $V = 78$ cm^3, $T = 282$ K,
   (b) $P = 3.4$ atmospheres, $V = 113$ cm^3, $T = 297.4$ K.

Estimates in this book

Estimates are shown for many calculations in this book, but not all. To do so would take too much space.
Always make your own estimate as a check in each example.
   Questions in Exercises in other Units and Examination Questions may not remind you to estimate answers. Try to remember to do this yourself *every time*.

P27
Tangent ratio

This unit will help you to:

- 'name' the sides of a right-angled triangle
- write down the tangent ratio in a right-angled triangle
- find the tangent of an angle by calculation and with a calculator
- use a calculator to find an angle from its tangent
- use the tangent ratio to calculate angles and lengths in right-angled triangles
- solve problems with the tangent ratio.

Naming sides of a right-angled triangle

In this Unit we deal with angles and sides in **right-angled triangles**.
We use special 'names' for the sides of a right-angled triangle.
You have met '**hypotenuse**' before.
The hypotenuse is the side **opposite the right-angle**. It is the **longest side** in the triangle.

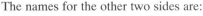

   The names for the other two sides are:

               '**opposite**' and '**adjacent**'.

These names link the sides with *another angle* in the triangle. They depend on the angle we are using.

   'Opposite' means 'opposite the angle …'
   'Adjacent' means 'adjacent to the angle …'

same angle

There are *two* 'other angles' in each right-angled triangle. We can name the sides for each angle.

Look at this triangle, for example.
The side AC is the hypotenuse.
It is opposite the right-angle.
The two 'other angles' are angles A and angle C.

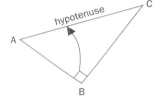

'Names' for angle A:
On this diagram, we 'name' the sides for angle A.

   The side BC is 'opposite angle A'.
   For angle A, the 'name' of BC is 'opposite'.
   The side AB is 'adjacent to angle A'.
   For angle A, the 'name' of AB is 'adjacent'.

Note: 'Adjacent to' means 'next to'.

There are two sides 'next to' angle A.
They are AC and AB.
AC already has a special 'name'.
It is the hypotenuse.
So only AB is called 'adjacent' to angle A.

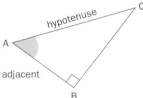

'Names' for angle C:
On this diagram, we 'name' the sides for angle C.
For angle C, AB is 'opposite',
               BC is 'adjacent'.

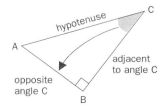

The sides in any right-angled triangle can be 'named' in this way.

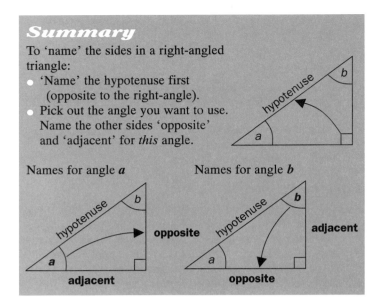

Summary

To 'name' the sides in a right-angled triangle:
- 'Name' the hypotenuse first (opposite to the right-angle).
- Pick out the angle you want to use. Name the other sides 'opposite' and 'adjacent' for *this* angle.

Names for angle *a*   Names for angle *b*

▶ *Exercise* **P27.1**

1 Copy each of these right-angled triangles.
   'Name' the sides of your triangles.
   Label the 'hypotenuse' first.
   Then label the 'opposite' and 'adjacent' sides for the marked angle.

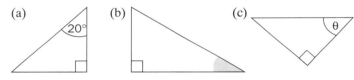

(a)   (b)   (c)

2 Copy and complete the sentences about the sides of each triangle. Use letters to identify the sides.

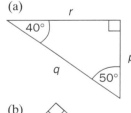

(a)
… is the hypotenuse.
For the 40° angle, …is 'opposite'
          … is 'adjacent'.
For the 50° angle, … is 'opposite'
          … is 'adjacent'.

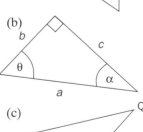

(b)
… is the hypotenuse.
For angle θ, … is 'opposite'
          … is 'adjacent'.
For angle α, … is 'opposite'
          … is 'adjacent'.

(c)
… is the hypotenuse.
For angle P, … is 'opposite',
          … is 'adjacent'.
For angle Q, … 'is 'opposite',
          … is 'adjacent'.

3 Look at the triangles in the next column.
   Use letters to name these sides:
   (a) the hypotenuse in each triangle
   (b) 'adjacent' for angle θ

(c) 'opposite' for the 70° angle
(d) 'adjacent' for angle C
(e) 'opposite' for the 20°angle

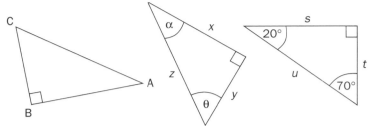

4 Look at the triangles in question **3**.
   Which angles fit these descriptions?
   (a) side *x* is 'opposite'   (c) side *t* is 'adjacent'
   (b) side AB is 'adjacent'   (d) side AB is 'opposite'

Introducing trigonometry

The word '**trigonometry**' means 'triangle measurement'.
It comes from two Greek words:

trigon … triangle
metron … measure.

We begin our study of trigonometry by measuring right-angled triangles.

👁 *Investigation*

1 These right-angled triangles are different sizes. But each has an angle of 35°.

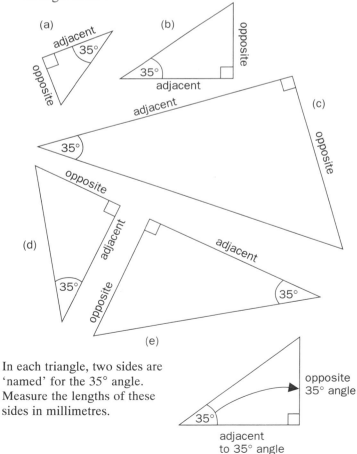

In each triangle, two sides are 'named' for the 35° angle.
Measure the lengths of these sides in millimetres.

Write your results for each triangle in a table like this.

angle	opposite	adjacent	$\dfrac{\text{opposite}}{\text{adjacent}}$
Triangle (a) 35°	14 mm		

Work out the value of $\dfrac{\text{opposite}}{\text{adjacent}}$ for each triangle.

Give each value as a decimal, correct to 1 decimal place, in your table.
What do you notice about these values?
Is this what you expected? Why?
Discuss.

Draw a different right-angled triangle with an angle of 35°.
Make it any size you like.
(Use squared paper to make it easier to draw.)

What is the value of $\dfrac{\text{opposite}}{\text{adjacent}}$ for your 35° angle?

What results do other students in your group get?
Discuss your conclusions and explanations.

2 Five right-angled triangles are in this diagram.
Each has an angle of 58° at A.

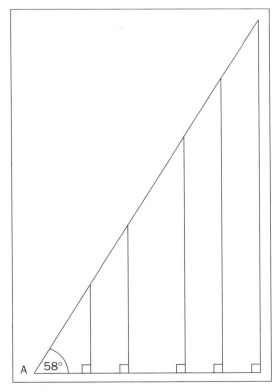

Find the value of $\dfrac{\text{opposite}}{\text{adjacent}}$ for the angle of 58° in each triangle.

What do your answers show? Discuss.
Draw some larger right-angled triangles, each with a 58° angle.

What happens when you work out $\dfrac{\text{opposite}}{\text{adjacent}}$ for your 58° angles?
Compare your results for the 58° angles and the 35° angles.
Discuss what you find.

3 Choose any acute angle you like (except 35° and 58°).
Draw five different right-angled triangles, each with this angle in it.
Find the value of $\dfrac{\text{opposite}}{\text{adjacent}}$ for your angle in each triangle.

Are the results what you expected?
Explain why.

Discuss the results of the students in your group.
What conclusions can you draw from them?
Compare the values found for different angles.
What does this show you?
Discuss your findings. Try to explain them.

4 This right-angled triangle has sides 'named' for an angle of 45°.
What kind of triangle is it?
What do you think is the

value of $\dfrac{\text{opposite}}{\text{adjacent}}$?

Explain your answer.
Measure the sides to check.

A special ratio

You can name the 'opposite' and 'adjacent' sides for an angle in a right-angled triangle.
The results from the Investigation on p468-469 show you that the ratio is special.

Here are two important things they show about it.
1 For angles of the same size, the value of

the ratio $\dfrac{\text{opposite}}{\text{adjacent}}$ *is always the same*.

The value is the same for *any* right-angled triangle with this angle in it. The size of the triangle does not matter.

For example, look at these right-angled triangles.
Each has an angle of 42° in it.

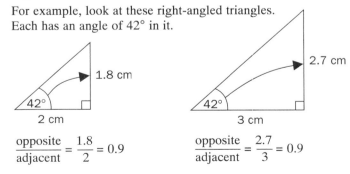

$$\dfrac{\text{opposite}}{\text{adjacent}} = \dfrac{1.8}{2} = 0.9 \qquad \dfrac{\text{opposite}}{\text{adjacent}} = \dfrac{2.7}{3} = 0.9$$

For the angle of 42°, the ratio $\dfrac{\text{opposite}}{\text{adjacent}}$ has the same value for each triangle.
In fact it is the same for an angle of 42° in any right-angled triangle.

2   The value of the ratio $\dfrac{\text{opposite}}{\text{adjacent}}$ depends on the size of the

angle. The ratio has a different value when the angle is a different size.

For example, these values are from the results of the Investigation on p468-469.

For an angle of 35°, $\dfrac{\text{opposite}}{\text{adjacent}}$ is 0.7 (to 1 dp).

For an angle of 58°, $\dfrac{\text{opposite}}{\text{adjacent}}$ is 1.6 (to 1 dp).

For an angle of 45°, $\dfrac{\text{opposite}}{\text{adjacent}}$ is 1.

This ratio $\dfrac{\textbf{opposite}}{\textbf{adjacent}}$ has a special name.

It is called the **tangent ratio**.
We often call it **tan** for short.

In the ratio, 'opposite' means opposite to an angle,
            'adjacent' means adjacent to the same angle.
The tangent ratio always refers to this angle.
We give the size of the angle or its name.

Summary

In a right-angled triangle with an angle θ in it,

the ratio $\dfrac{\text{opposite }\theta}{\text{adjacent to }\theta}$

is called the tangent of θ
or tan θ for short.

Remember: $\tan \theta = \dfrac{\text{opposite}}{\text{adjacent}}$

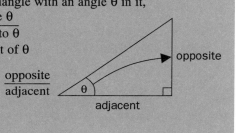

You can write down the tangent ratios for two angles in a right-angled triangle.
Using letters helps you to identify the sides in each ratio.

Question

Write the ratio of sides for
(a) tan A
(b) tan B.

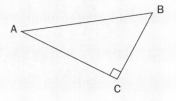

Answer

(a) For angle A,
    BC is the opposite side,
    AC is the adjacent side.

Using $\tan = \dfrac{\text{opposite}}{\text{adjacent}}$

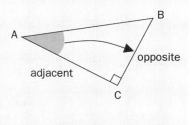

$\tan A = \dfrac{BC}{AC}$

(b) For angle B,
    AC is the opposite side,
    BC is the adjacent side.

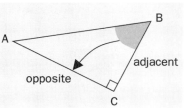

$\tan B = \dfrac{AC}{BC}$

Exercise P27.2

1   Write the ratio of sides for each tangent.

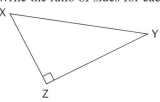
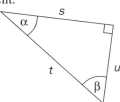

(a) tan X   (b) tan Y   (c) tan α   (d) tan β

2   Name the missing angle in each of these tangent ratios.

(a) $\dfrac{PQ}{QR} = \tan \ldots$

$\dfrac{QR}{PQ} = \tan \ldots$

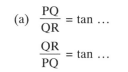

(b) $\dfrac{k}{l} = \tan \ldots$

$\dfrac{l}{k} = \tan \ldots$

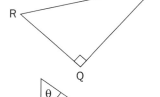

3   Write down the ratios for the tangents of these angles from the diagrams below.
(a) tan W   (c) tan N   (e) tan α   (g) tan A
(b) tan a   (d) tan c   (f) tan β   (h) tan M

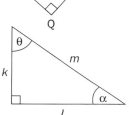

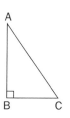

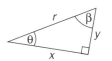
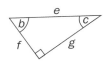

4   Name the missing angle in each of these tangent ratios from the diagrams above.

(a) $\dfrac{y}{x} = \tan \ldots$ (b) $\dfrac{UW}{UV} = \tan \ldots$

(c) $\dfrac{AB}{BC} = \tan \ldots$ (d) $\dfrac{g}{f} = \tan \ldots$

Finding tangents of angles

By calculation

You can calculate the tangent of an acute angle from the sides of a right-angled triangle.

To find the value of tan 28°, for example, you can use any right-angled triangle with an angle of 28°. You can draw the right-angled triangle *accurately* and measure its sides.

You can also use lengths *given* in a right-angled triangle to calculate tangents.
The triangle does *not* have to be drawn accurately.

Question

Calculate the value of tan 28° from this triangle.
Give your answer correct to 3 decimal places.

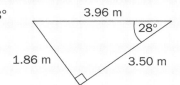

Answer

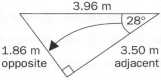

For angle 28°,
opposite = 1.86 m
adjacent = 3.50 m   (same unit)

$$\tan 28° = \frac{\text{opposite}}{\text{adjacent}} = \frac{1.86}{3.50}$$

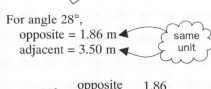

tan 28° = 0.531 (to 3 dp)

You can work out the tangents of 'unknown angles' in the same way.

Question

Calculate tan A.
Give the value of the tangent ratio as a fraction and as a decimal.

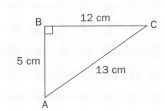

Answer

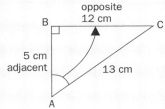

(a) For angle A
opposite: BC = 12 cm
adjacent: AB = 5 cm   (same unit)

$$\tan = \frac{\text{opposite}}{\text{adjacent}}$$

$$\tan A = \frac{12}{5} = 2.4$$

Summary

To calculate the tangent of an acute angle, you can take these steps.

- Draw a right-angle triangle.
  Mark the angle you want.
  'Name' the sides for this angle.
- Match the 'names' to lengths.
  Make sure both lengths are in the same unit.
- Write the tangent ratio: $\tan \theta = \dfrac{\text{opposite}}{\text{adjacent}}$
  Put in the correct values.
- Change the fraction to a decimal by doing the division: opposite ÷ adjacent.
- Round the decimal if asked to do so.

ACTIVITY

Tangents by drawing

1   Find the tangents of 5°, 10°, 15°, 20°, ..., 80°, 85° by drawing right-angled triangles accurately. (Use a ruler, protractor and squared paper.)
    Share this practical work with some other students in your group. Discuss the 'best way' to do it before you start.

Make a table of tangents from your results.
Give each tangent as a decimal correct to 2 decimal places.

angle	tangent of angle (to 2 dp)
5°	
10°	

2   You cannot draw a right-angled triangle with an angle of 0°. But what do you think is the value of tan 0°? Explain your answer.

3   Compare the tangents in your table. What happens to the value for tangents as the size of the angle gets larger?

4   Can you predict when the tangent of an angle will be
    (a) less than 1   (b) equal to 1   (c) more than 1?
    Explain your answers.
    How can you use this to check tangents are 'about the right size'? Discuss.

5   Compare the tangents of these pairs of angles:
    (a) 10° and 20°   (b) 25° and 50°   (c) 40° and 80°
    (d) any angle and twice that angle.
    What do you find?
    What does this show you?

What happens if you compare the tangents of
  an angle and 3 times that angle,
  an angle and 4 times that angle, and so on …?
Discuss your findings.
Write down any conclusions you reach.

► *Exercise* P27.3

1 Calculate the values of tan 67°
and tan 23° from this triangle.
Give your answers correct
to 3 decimal places.

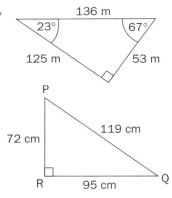

2 Calculate tan P and tan Q.
Find the value of each
tangent ratio as a fraction and
as a decimal.
Give the decimal correct
to 4 significant figures.

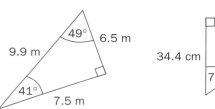

3 Using the diagrams below, calculate the values of these
tangents.
Give each answer to 2 dp.
  (a) tan 16°   (b) tan 41°   (c) tan 74°   (d) tan 49°

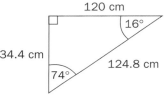

4 Calculate the value of tan θ in each of these triangles.
Give each value as a fraction and a decimal.
Round the decimal to 3 dp if necessary.
  (a)   (b)

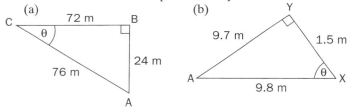

5 Calculate the value of tan A in each triangle above.
Give each tangent as a decimal correct to 4 significant
figures.

Using a calculator

A scientific calculator has a **tan key**.
You can use it to find the tangent of any
angle.
For tan 45°, you key in **4** **5** **tan**

to get

Try this on your calculator.
If you do not get 1, you may get one of these:

These show that your calculator is *not* working in **degrees**.

Angles are usually measured in degrees.
But they can also be measured in **radians** or **grades**.

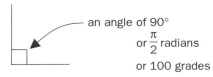

an angle of 90°
or $\frac{\pi}{2}$ radians
or 100 grades

  Most scientific calculators can be set to work in any of these
units. The display may show which unit is being used.

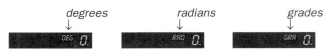

Make sure your calculator is set to work in degrees.
All of your 'angle work' in this book is in degrees.
  Some calculators work automatically in degrees. If your
calculator doesn't, then you may have to press a **DRG** key or
change it to operate in '**degree mode**'. Find out what to do
from your calculator handbook if you need to.

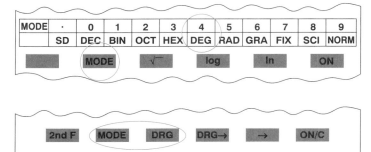

Summary

To find the tangent of an angle with a calculator, take these
steps.
● Make sure the calculator is set to work in degrees.
● Enter the angle first.
● Then press **tan** .

There is no need to press **=** .

Remember:
We *write* 'tan' first, then angle, for example, tan 45°.
We *key it in* the 'opposite way round', for example, **4** **5** **tan** .

The value given for a tangent
often has *many* digits.
You may be asked to **round it**.
Always round it to the stated
number of **significant figures (sf)**
or **decimal places (dp)**.
But *never* round the value unless
you are told to do so.

Here are some examples.

For tan 63°, key in **6** **3** **tan**

to get

Memo

Significant figures and
decimal places
N3 p 13

1.962610505 → tan 63° = 1.963 (to 4 sf)
1.962610505 → tan 63° = 1.9626 (to 4 dp).

For tan 1.5°, key in **1** **.** **5** **tan**

to get   `DEG 0.026185921`

0.026185921 → tan 1.5° = 0.0262 (to 3 sf)
0.026185921 → tan 1.5° = 0.026 (to 3 dp).

▶ *Exercise* **P27.4**

Use your calculator to find the answers in this exercise.
1   Find the values of the tangents of these angles:

5°, 10°, 15°, 20°, 25°, … 80°, 85°.

Copy each value in full
from your calculator
display and correct to 2 dp.

angle	tangent	
	from calculator	correct to 2 d p
5°		
10°		

Compare your values with the results you calculated in the
Activity 'Tangents by drawing' on p471.
2   Find the values of the following to 2 decimal places.
(a) tan 16°   (b) tan 41°   (c) tan 74°   (d) tan 49°
Compare your values with the results you found in question
3, Exercise P27.3.
3   Find the tangent of each of these angles.
Give each answer correct to 4 significant figures.
(a) 32°   (d) 76°   (g) 81°   (j) 30.9°
(b) 59°   (e) 67°   (h) 4°   (k) 63.1°
(c) 22°   (f) 13°   (i) 8.5°   (l) 87.4°
4   Find, correct to 4 dp, the values of the following:
(a) tan 18°   (c) tan 76°   (e) tan 23.8°
(b) tan 31°   (d) tan 42.5°   (f) tan 85.4°

◉ *Investigation*

Near to 90°
Investigate the tangents of angles near to 90°.
Try angles of 89°, 89.1°, 89.2°, 89.3°, …
Try angles of 89.9°, 89.99°, 89.999°, …
What happens to the tangent as the angle gets nearer and nearer
to 90°.
What does **9** **0** **tan** give?
Explain why.

Angles from tangents

With a scientific calculator, you can enter an angle and find its
tangent.
To do this you press the **tan** key.
For example,

keying in **4** **5** **tan** gives `DEG 1.`

This tells you:
the tangent of 45° is 1.
i.e. tan 45° = 1.

A scientific calculator will also do the **inverse** (opposite)
operation.
You can enter a tangent and find its angle.
To do this you press the 'inverse tangent' key or keys.

Many calculators have *just one key* for 'inverse tangent'.
It is usually marked **tan⁻¹**.

tan⁻¹ is a short way to write '**inverse tan**'.
For example,

keying in **1** **tan⁻¹** gives `DEG 45.` ← degrees

The calculator is set to work in degrees.
So this tells you:
the acute angle whose tangent is 1 is 45°.
We can write it as: tan⁻¹ 1 = 45°

On some calculators you have to press *two keys* for 'inverse
tangent'.
Here are some examples:

INV **tan**   **ARC** **tan**   **2ndF** **tan**

Find out which key or keys to use on your calculator.

We shall use **tan⁻¹** in this book.

Remember to use your 'inverse tangent' key(s) when you see
tan⁻¹ in a key code.

Question
Find the size of angle θ, if $\tan \theta = \frac{11}{15}$.

Give your answer correct to 1 decimal place and to the
nearest degree.
Answer

$\tan \theta = \dfrac{11}{15}$

$\theta = \tan^{-1} \dfrac{11}{15}$ (θ is the angle whose tangent is $\frac{11}{15}$)

• *Change* $\frac{11}{15}$ *to a decimal first.*
  Then press the 'inverse tan' key(s).

  1 **1** **÷** **1** **5** **=** **tan⁻¹** `DEG 36.25383774`

• *Round the answer.* θ = 36.3° (to 1 dp)
              θ = 36° (to the nearest degree).

Summary
To find an angle from its tangent ratio, you can use a
calculator.
Take these steps.
  • Make sure the calculator is set to work in degrees.
  • Enter the tangent ratio as a decimal.
    Change it to a decimal first if you need to.
  • Press the 'inverse tangent' key or keys.
    tan⁻¹ is short for 'inverse tan'.
  • Round the answer sensibly if necessary.
    Angles are usually given correct to the nearest degree
    or to 1 decimal place.

► *Exercise* **P27.5**

Use your calculator to do this exercise.

1   Find, to the nearest degree, the angle, whose tangent is:

(a) 0.8   (e) $\frac{3}{7}$ (g) $\frac{17}{6}$

(b) 1.79

(c) 0.283   (f) $\frac{5}{9}$ (h) $\frac{23}{4}$

(d) 2.65

2   Which angles have these tangents?
Give your answers in degrees, correct to 1 decimal place.

(a) 0.37   (e) $\frac{4}{7}$ (g) $\frac{28}{13}$

(b) 0.924

(c) 2.46   (f) $\frac{9}{4}$ (h) $\frac{43}{12}$

(d) 11.83

3   Find the size of each named angle, correct to 1 decimal place.

(a) tan θ = 2.39   (d) tan A = $\frac{16}{31}$ (f) tan P = $\frac{32}{47}$

(b) tan α = 0.7463

(c) tan β = 1.835   (e) tan X = $\frac{15}{4}$ (g) tan B = $\frac{12}{13}$

4   (a) Try   **2 9 tan tan⁻¹**   on your calculator.

What do you get?
Try it with other angles. What happens each time?
Why?

(b) Try   **. 7 tan⁻¹ tan**   on your calculator.

What happens?
Try it with other decimals.
Explain what happens each time.

Calculating angles

In a right-angled triangle the tangent ratio links an angle with its 'opposite' and 'adjacent' sides.
If you know the lengths of opposite and adjacent, you can calculate the tangent of the angle.
Then you can find the size of the angle.
This example shows the steps to take.

Memo

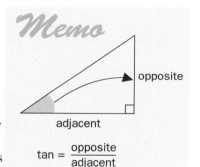

$$\tan = \frac{\text{opposite}}{\text{adjacent}}$$

Question

Find the size of angle θ.
Give your answer in degrees, correct to 1 decimal place.

Answer

● *Draw a diagram.*
● *'Name' the given sides for the wanted angle.*

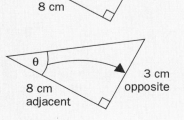

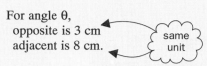

For angle θ,
opposite is 3 cm
adjacent is 8 cm.

The known lengths are 'opposite' and 'adjacent'. So use the tangent ratio.

● *Write the formula.* $\tan = \dfrac{\text{opposite}}{\text{adjacent}}$

● *Put in what you know.* $\tan θ = \dfrac{3}{8}$

$$θ = \tan^{-1}\frac{3}{8}$$

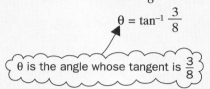

● *Find the angle.*

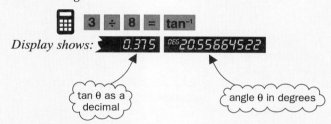

Display shows:

● *Round the answer.* θ = 20.6° (to 1 dp)
Remember the unit (°).

You now know two angles in the triangle in the last example.
Here are two ways to find the size of the third angle, α.

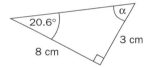

Method 1: Using the tangent ratio:

You can 'name' the given sides for angle α.
opposite α is 8 cm.
adjacent to α is 3 cm.

The formula $\tan = \dfrac{\text{opposite}}{\text{adjacent}}$

gives $\tan α = \dfrac{8}{3}$

$$α = \tan^{-1}\frac{8}{3}$$

$$α = 69.4° \text{(to 1 dp)}$$

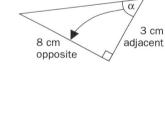

Method 2: Using the angle sum of the triangle:

Memo

The three angles of a triangle add up to 180°.
In a right-angled triangle, one angle is 90°.
So the other two angles must add up to 90°.

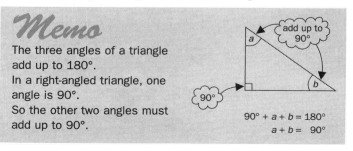

$$90° + a + b = 180°$$
$$a + b = 90°$$

In this triangle,
$$90° + 20.6° + \alpha = 180°$$
$$20.6° + \alpha = 90°$$
$$\alpha = 90° - 20.6°$$
$$\alpha = 69.4° \text{ (to 1 dp)}$$

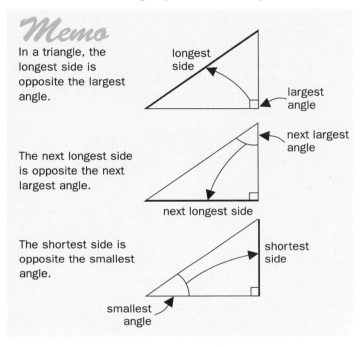

add up to 90°

Checking your answers is a good idea as usual.
Here is a fact about triangles you can use in a quick check.

Memo

In a triangle, the longest side is opposite the largest angle.

longest side

largest angle

next largest angle

The next longest side is opposite the next largest angle.

next longest side

The shortest side is opposite the smallest angle.

shortest side

smallest angle

You can use this check in the last example.

3 cm is opposite θ.

8 cm is opposite α.

3 cm is shorter than 8 cm.
So θ must be smaller than α.

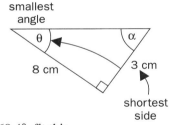

smallest angle

θ   α

8 cm   3 cm

shortest side

Our answers, θ = 20.6° and α = 69.4°, fit this.
20.6° is smaller than 69.4°.
So these sizes make sense.

Note: This check does not tell you that the answers are correct.
It simply shows that their sizes are reasonable.

▶ *Exercise* **P27.6**

1 Calculate, to the nearest degree, the angles marked with letters.

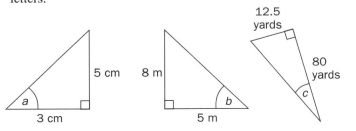

5 cm

3 cm

a

8 m

5 m

b

12.5 yards

80 yards

c

2 Find the third angle in each triangle in question **1**.
Calculate each angle in two ways
(i) using the tangent ratio
(ii) using the angle sum of the triangle.

3 Calculate the unknown angles in these right-angled triangles. Give each angle in degrees, correct to 1 decimal place.

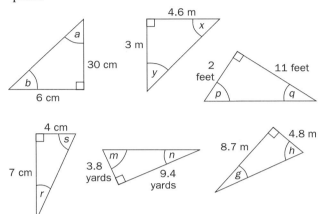

4.6 m

a

30 cm

6 cm

b

3 m

x

2 feet

y

11 feet

p

q

4 cm

s

7 cm

r

3.8 yards

m

9.4 yards

n

8.7 m

4.8 m

h

g

4 Sketch each of the following triangles.
Calculate the required angle correct to the nearest 0.1°.
(a) Triangle ABC with ∠B = 90°, AB = 3.9 cm and BC = 26 cm. Find ∠C.
(b) Triangle PQR with ∠R = 90°, PR = 3.2 m and QR = 8.8 m. Find ∠P.
(c) Triangle XYZ with ∠X = 90°, XZ = 18 mm and XY = 15 mm. Find ∠Y.
(d) Triangle DEF with ∠E = 90°, EF = 6.3 km and DE = 2.8 km. Find ∠D.

5 In each triangle below the two lengths are in different units.
Change both lengths to the same unit first. Then calculate the angles marked with letters. Give your answers correct to 1 decimal place.

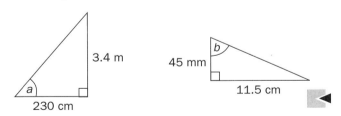

3.4 m

a

230 cm

45 mm

b

11.5 cm

◀

Calculating the length of a side

The formula for the tangent ratio links an angle and two sides in a right-angled triangle (but not the hypotenuse).

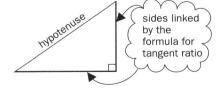

hypotenuse

sides linked by the formula for tangent ratio

You can use this formula to find the length of one of these sides.
You only need to know the length of the other side and the size of an angle (other than the right-angle).
Look carefully at the steps taken in the next example.

Question

Calculate the length of the side marked *b*.
Give your answer in kilometres, correct to 3 significant figures.

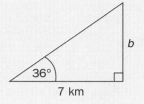

Answer

- *Draw a diagram.*
- *'Name' the wanted and known sides.*
  For angle of 36°, opposite is *b* km, adjacent is 7 km.
  The 'named' sides are opposite and adjacent. So use the tangent ratio.

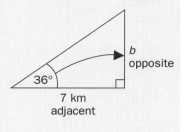

- *Write the formula.*

$$\frac{\text{opposite}}{\text{adjacent}} = \tan$$

- *Put in what you know.*

$$\frac{b}{7} = \tan 36°$$

- *Multiply both sides by 7.* $b = 7 \times \tan 36°$
- *Work it out.*

- *Round the answer.* $b = 5.09$ km (to 3 sf)
  Remember the unit (km).

It is a good idea to check that the length you find is a sensible size. Comparing the sizes of the angles and sides in the triangle helps you to do this.

Look again at the example above.
The given angle is 36°.
It is less than 45°.
So you know it is the smallest angle.
The shortest side must be opposite this angle.

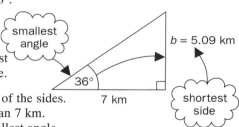

Compare the lengths of the sides.
5.09 km is shorter than 7 km.
It is opposite the smallest angle.
So it is a sensible size.

Remember:
This check does not show that the length is correct.
It just tells you that the size makes sense.

► Exercise P27.7

1 Calculate the length of the side opposite the angle of 27° in each triangle. Give your answers correct to 3 significant figures.

(a)   (b) 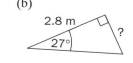   (c)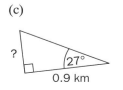

2 Calculate the length of the side opposite the angle of 35° in each triangle. Give your answers in centimetres, correct to 1 decimal place.

(a)   (b)   (c)

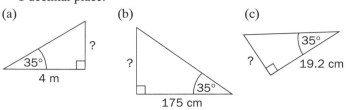

3 Calculate the lengths of the sides marked with letters in these triangles.
Give each length correct to 3 significant figures.

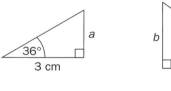   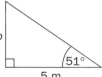

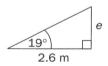   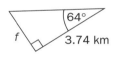

4 Sketch each of the following triangles.
Calculate the named length in each triangle.
Round your answers sensibly.
(a) Triangle ABC with ∠B = 90°, ∠A = 33° and AB = 7.2 cm. Find BC.
(b) Triangle PQR with ∠P = 90°, ∠Q = 72.5° and QP = 1.5 km. Find RP.
(c) Triangle STU with ∠S = 90°, ∠T = 59° and ST = 76.8 m. Find US.
(d) Triangle XYZ with ∠X = 90°, ∠Z = 46° and XZ = 157 cm. Find XY.   ◄

Which angle?

In this right-angled triangle, all the angles are given.
To find the length of BC, you can use either angle A or angle C.
Here are the calculations using each angle.

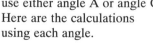

Using angle A = 25°:
BC is opposite 25°
4 cm is adjacent to 25°
This gives:

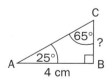

$$\frac{BC}{4} = \tan 25°$$

$$BC = 4 \times \tan 25°$$

$$BC = 1.9 \text{ cm (to 1 dp)}$$

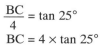

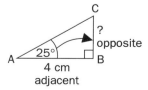

Using angle C = 65°:
4 cm is opposite 65°.
BC is adjacent to 65°.
This gives:

$$\frac{4}{BC} = \tan 65°$$

$$4 = BC \times \tan 65°$$

$$\frac{4}{\tan 65°} = BC$$

BC = 1.9 cm (to 1 dp)

Discussion Exercise

Compare the two ways shown above to find BC.
How are they the same?
How are they different?

Which way do you think is easier to use?
Explain your choice.
Discuss your ideas with students in your group.

Look at the triangles below.
The wanted side is marked with a letter on each triangle.
Which angle would you use to find this length in each case?
Explain how you chose each angle.
Discuss.

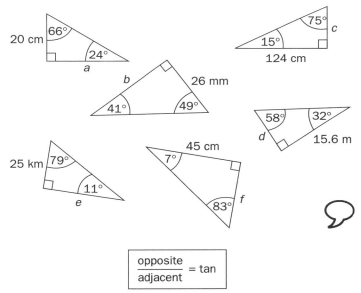

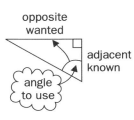

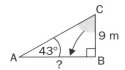

$$\boxed{\frac{\text{opposite}}{\text{adjacent}} = \tan}$$

You can use this formula to find the value of either 'opposite' or 'adjacent'.

You have seen that 'opposite' is
easier to find.
But you have to use the angle
opposite the side you want.
Sometimes this angle is not given.
To work it out, you can use the **angle sum of the triangle**.

Look at this triangle, for example.
The side you want is AB.
AB is opposite to angle C.
But the size of angle C is not given.

The three angles of the triangle add up to 180°.

$$\angle A + \angle B + \angle C = 180°$$

You know that $\angle A = 43°$ and $\angle B = 90°$.
This gives:
$$43° + 90° + \angle C = 180°$$
$$\angle C = 180° - 90° - 43°$$
$$\angle C = 47°$$
Now you can use this angle of 47° to find AB.

AB is opposite 47°.
9 m is adjacent to 47°
This gives:

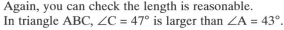

$$\frac{AB}{9} = \tan 47°$$

$$AB = 9 \times \tan 47°$$
$$AB = 9.65 \text{ m (to 2 dp)}$$

Again, you can check the length is reasonable.
In triangle ABC, $\angle C = 47°$ is larger than $\angle A = 43°$.

AB is opposite $\angle C$.
BC is opposite $\angle A$.
So AB must be longer than BC.
Our answer, AB = 9.65 m, is longer
than BC = 9 m.
So it seems reasonable.

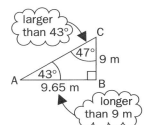

Summary

You can use the tangent ratio to calculate the length of a side
in a right-angled triangle.
The working is simpler when
you have:

$$\frac{\text{wanted side}}{\text{known side}} = \tan$$

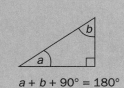

To get this ratio, use the tangent
of the angle *opposite* the side
you want.

If this angle is not given,
find it from the angle sum
of the triangle.

$$a + b + 90° = 180°$$

Always check that the length you find is a sensible size.
Compare sides and angles.
The shortest side, for example,
must be opposite the smallest
angle.

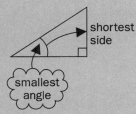

▶ *Exercise* **P27.8**

1 Calculate the named length in each triangle in the
Discussion Exercise on this page.

2 Calculate the required length in each triangle below.

(a) Find AC

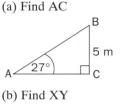

(d) Find PR

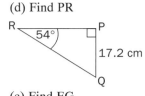

(b) Find XY

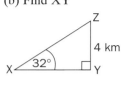

(e) Find EG

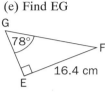

(c) Find OB

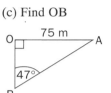

(f) Find UT

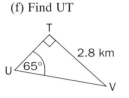

Rearranging the formula

$$\frac{\text{opposite}}{\text{adjacent}} = \tan$$

This formula is designed to find the value of 'tan'.
We say 'tan' is the *subject* of the formula.
To find the length of 'opposite', you can rearrange the formula.
Multiplying both sides of the formula by 'adjacent' gives:

$$\text{opposite} = \text{adjacent} \times \tan.$$

'Opposite' is the subject of the new formula. This makes it easy
to use to find the value for 'opposite'.
You simply put in the values for 'adjacent' and 'tan' and do
the multiplication.

Here is an example of this method to find a side.

Question

Calculate the length of the side
marked *s* in this triangle.
Give your answer correct to
3 significant figures.

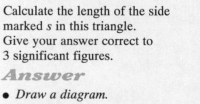

Answer

• *Draw a diagram.*
• *Name' the sides.*

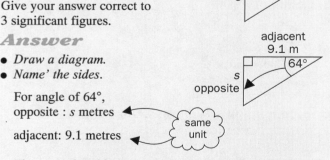

For angle of 64°,
opposite : *s* metres

adjacent: 9.1 metres

*The wanted and known sides are 'opposite' and
'adjacent'. So use the tangent ratio.*

• *Write the formula.* $\dfrac{\text{opposite}}{\text{adjacent}} = \tan$

• *Rearrange the formula.* $\text{opposite} = \text{adjacent} \times \tan$
• *Put in what you know.* $s = 9.1 \times \tan 64°$

• *Work it out.*

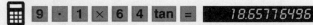

• *Round the answer.* $s = 18.7$ m (to 3 sf)
  Remember the unit (m).

Discussion Exercise

We have shown two ways you can use 'tan' to find 'opposite'
in a right-angled triangle.
In one way (example on p 476), you put values in the formula
for the tangent ratio.
In the other way (example on this page), you rearrange the
formula first.
Discuss the two methods.
How are they the same? How are they different?
Which do you think is easier? Why?
Try both ways to find some lengths. You can use triangles from
Exercise P27.7 or make up some examples of your own.
Decide which way you prefer.
Practise using this method.

Calculating lengths or angles

The next exercise contains a mixture of questions.
In some triangles you have to find a length.
In others you have to find an angle.
Think carefully about which sides and angle are linked by the
tangent ratio.
Make sure you use the correct function **tan** or **tan⁻¹** in your
calculator work.

► *Exercise* P27.9

Calculate the length marked *d* or the angle marked θ in each of
these right-angled triangles.
Give each angle in degrees correct to 1 decimal place.
Give each length correct to 3 significant figures.

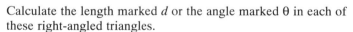

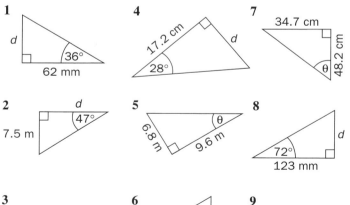

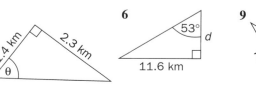

Problem solving

Many practical problems involve right-angled triangles. To solve them you can often make **scale drawings** or **use the tangent ratio**.

Using the tangent ratio is usually quicker and more accurate. Here are some hints to help you with this.

- Think about the situation in the problem.
  You may have a picture of it to look at.
  If you don't, try to imagine it and draw a sketch.
- Draw a sketch of the right-angled triangle you want to use.
  Mark the right angle clearly.
- Mark the lengths and angles you know on the triangle.
  Label what you have to find.
- 'Name' the sides of the triangle.
- Use the correct ratio to find what you want.
  Show your working clearly.
- Give a sensible answer to the problem.
  Round your result if you need to.
- Make sure you state the correct unit of measure.
  For lengths you want units such as mm, cm, m, ….
  For angles you want degrees (°).
- Check the size of your answer is reasonable.
  Try to avoid 'silly' answers.

In some problems you are shown or told where the right-angled triangle is. Sometimes you have to find it yourself. Always look for horizontal and vertical lines in a practical problem. You know that they meet at right angles. They often form two sides of a right-angled triangle.

Question

A wheelchair ramp is to be built over steps up to a college entrance. Each step has a vertical rise of 12 cm and a horizontal tread of 45 cm.
Calculate the angle the ramp makes with the horizontal.
Give your answer in degrees correct to 1 decimal place.

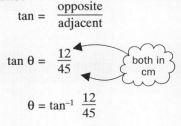

Answer

- *Sketch a diagram.*
  Vertical rise and horizontal tread are at right-angles.
  The wanted angle is given by angle θ.

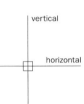
opposite 12 cm
45 cm adjacent

- *Name the sides for angle θ.*
  The known lengths are opposite and adjacent.
  So use the tangent ratio.

$$\tan = \frac{\text{opposite}}{\text{adjacent}}$$

$$\tan \theta = \frac{12}{45} \quad \text{both in cm}$$

$$\theta = \tan^{-1} \frac{12}{45}$$

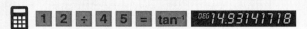

$$\theta = 14.9° \text{ (1 dp)}$$

The angle the ramp makes with the horizontal is 14.9° (to 1 dp).

▶ *Exercise* **P27.10**

1 Mr. Evans installs stair lifts.
   To make the lift safe, the angle of slope of the track on the stairs must be 58° or less.

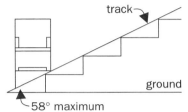

   To find the angle of slope, Mr. Evans measures the vertical rise, r, and horizontal tread, t, of the stairs.

   Calculate the angles of slope from these measurements.
   (a) $r = 12.5$ cm, $t = 14$ cm (d) $t = 2$ ft, $r = 1$ ft
   (b) $t = 8$ in, $r = 13\frac{1}{2}$ in (e) $t = 17.5$ cm, $r = 4.5$ cm
   (c) $r = 145$ mm, $t = 105$ mm (f) $r = 0.19$ m, $t = 0.32$ m
   On which of these stairs can Mr. Evans safely install a lift?

   Mr. Evans wants a ready-reckoner table as a quick check on home visits.

t in cm	10	11	12		20
maximum r in cm					

   Work out the safe maximum values for r for stairs with treads of 10 cm, 11 cm, 12 cm, … 20 cm. Copy and complete this table using your results.

2 A ladder reaches 19 feet up a wall. The foot of the ladder is 6 feet from the base of the wall. What angle does the ladder make with the ground?

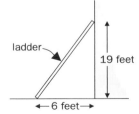

3 The foot of a ladder is 2.7 m from a wall. The ladder makes an angle of 19° with the wall. How far up the wall does the ladder reach?

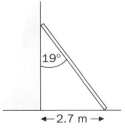

4 A ladder is leaning against a wall. It makes an angle of 70° with the ground. The foot of the ladder is 1.5 m from the wall. How high up the wall does the ladder reach?

5 Gemma tries to row straight across a river which is 46 yards wide. The current carries her downstream at an angle of 72° to the bank. How far downstream from the point she was trying to reach does she actually land?

Finding directions

You can solve many navigation problems with the tangent ratio. Compass points often give you the right-angle you need.
3-figure bearings are usually related to the angle whose tangent you use.

Memo

Compass points and Bearings S8 p161

Question

A helicopter flies 8.2 km due east from Airport A to Oil rig O. It then flies 6.5 km due south to Oil rig R.

The pilot wants to fly directly from rig R to the Airport A. What is the bearing of A from R? Give your answer to the nearest degree.

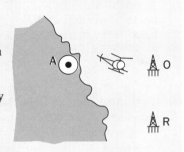

Answer

• Sketch a diagram of the situation. The angle between due east and due south is 90°.
The bearing of A from R is measured at R. It is given by angle θ.

$\theta = 360° -$ shaded angle at R.

• Name the sides for angle R. The known lengths are opposite and adjacent. So use the tangent ratio to find angle R.

$$\tan = \frac{\text{opposite}}{\text{adjacent}}$$

$$\tan R = \frac{8.2}{6.5}$$

both in km

$$R = \tan^{-1} \frac{8.2}{6.5}$$

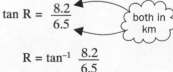

angle R = 52° (to the nearest degree)

• Find the bearing given by angle θ.
$$\theta = 360° - 52°$$
$$= 308°$$
The bearing of A from R is 308° (to the nearest degree).

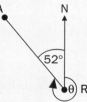

▶ *Exercise* P27.11

1 Calculate the bearing of C from A in each of these situations.
  (a) B is 5 miles due north of A.
      C is 2.3 miles due west of B.

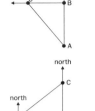

  (b) B is 30 km due east of A.
      C is 45 km due north of B.

  (c) B is 960 metres due south of A.
      C is 725 metres due east of B.
  (d) B is 1750 yards due west of A.
      C is 845 yards due south of B.
  (e) B is 7.2 km due north of A.
      C is 6.9 km due east of B.
  (f) B is 8 miles due west of A.
      C is $6\frac{1}{2}$ miles due north of B.
  (g) B is 205 km due south of A.
      C is 43 km due west of B.
  (h) B is 61 miles due east of A.
      C is 92 miles due south of B.

2 A plane flies due east from Anscombe for 300 miles to Brenton. It then turns due north and flies for 450 miles to Carnton. Calculate the bearing of Carnton from Anscombe.

3 A boat sails 37 miles due west from the Lizard in Cornwall. It then turns due south and sails for 19 miles to its fishing ground. Calculate the bearing of the Lizard from the fishing ground.

Angles of elevation and depression

Angles of elevation and depression often appear in problems you can solve by trigonometry.

Memo

An **angle of elevation** is measured *upwards* from the *horizontal*.

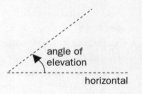

When you look *up* at an object, the angle between the horizontal and your line of sight is an angle of elevation. The angle of elevation of the plane from the man is 40°.

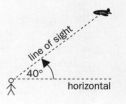

An **angle of depression** is measured *downwards* from the *horizontal*.

When you look *down* at an object, the angle between the horizontal and your line of sight is an angle of depression.
The angle of depression of the boat from the girl is 15°.

Surveyors measure angles of elevation and depression with a *theodolite*.

A simple *clinometer* can also be used to measure these angles. You can easily make one from some thick card, a protractor, a straw, a piece of string and a weight.
Try it if you can. Then use your clinometer to help you find the heights of some trees, buildings, ...

The next example shows you how to do the working.

Usually the angle measurer is mounted or held at eye-level. In some problems you have to make allowances for this in your calculations.

Question

A hedge of fast-growing cypress trees grows down one side of Jeff's garden. Local bye-laws say that hedges must not be taller than 10 metres.

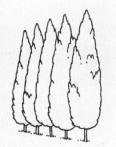

Jeff checks the height of the hedge for his mum and dad. He stands on level ground, 6 m away from the base of the hedge.
With a clinometer at eye-level he measures the angle of elevation to its top. It is 53°.

(a) Use trigonometry to calculate the height of the hedge.
(b) What should Jeff tell his parents about trimming the hedge?

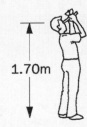

1.70m

Answer

(a) • *Sketch the diagram.*
The height of the hedge is
h + 'eye-level height'
= h + 1.70 metres

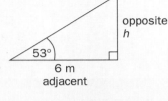

• *Name the wanted and known sides for the angle 53°.*
These are opposite and adjacent.
So use the tangent ratio to find h.

$$\frac{\text{opposite}}{\text{adjacent}} = \tan$$

$$\frac{h}{6} = \tan 53°$$

$$h = 6 \times \tan 53°$$

• *Add on the 'eye-level height' to find the height of the hedge.*
Height of hedge = h + 1.70
= $6 \times \tan 53° + 1.70$

• The height of the hedge is 9.7 m (to 1 dp)

(b) The hedge is only 0.3 m shorter than the height given in the bye-law. It will need trimming soon.

Exercise P27.12

1 Calculate the height of the hedge in the example above, when the angle of elevation is:
   (a) 46° (b) 50° (c) 35° (d) 62° (e) 71.5°
   What should Jeff tell his parents about trimming the hedge in each case?

2 The angle of elevation of the top of a flagpole, from a point on the ground 23 m from its foot, is 41°. How tall is the flagpole?

3 A tree stands 38 yards from a house. From his bedroom window Mike measures the angle of elevation of the top of the tree to be 13° and the angle of depression of the bottom to be 16°. Calculate the height of the tree.

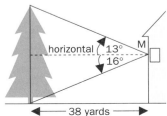

4   A flagpole in the college grounds is 4.5 m tall. Audrey measures the flagpole's shadow every hour from 10.00 to 15.00.

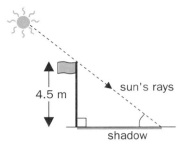
4.5 m
sun's rays
shadow

Here are her results:

time	10.00	11.00	12.00	13.00	14.00	15.00
shadow length	9.8 m	7.5 m	6.0 m	7.3 m	9.6 m	13.4 m

Calculate the angle of elevation of the sun at each of these times.
Why can't Audrey just measure each angle of elevation with a clinometer?

5   The angle of elevation of the top of the Eiffel Tower from a point on the ground 400 m away is 36.9°.
How tall is the Eiffel Tower?   ◄

An angle of elevation has an equal angle of depression and vice versa.

The angle of elevation of the top of the tower from the ship is θ.
The angle of depression of the ship from the top of the tower is θ.

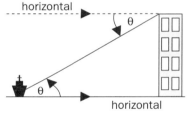
horizontal
θ
θ
horizontal

The angles are equal alternate angles because the horizontal lines are parallel.

Remember Z-angles!

You may need to use this fact in calculations.

► *Exercise* **P27.13**   ⌨

1   The angle of depression of a buoy B from T, the top of a lighthouse, is 29°.
(a) Name the angle of elevation of T from B. Write down the size of this angle.
(b) The buoy is 112 m from the foot of the lighthouse. How tall is the lighthouse?

T
horizontal
29°
B
F ← 112 m →

2   A boat is 195 m from the foot of a vertical cliff 77 m tall. What is the angle of depression of the boat measured from the top of the cliff?

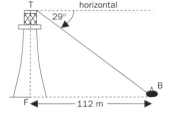
horizontal
77 m   cliff
sea level
boat
← 195 m →

3   Tim measures the angle of depression from the top of a tower T to a landmark L at ground level. It is 17°.
(a) Name the angle of depression in this diagram.
(b) Sketch triangle BLT. Mark in the size of each angle. Explain how you found each size.
(c) The top of the tower is 38 feet above ground level. How far is the landmark L from the base of the tower, B?
(d) The angle of depression from T to another landmark M is 9°. How far is M from the base of the tower?

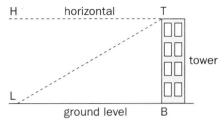
H   horizontal   T
tower
L   ground level   B

4   Kerry stands at the top of a vertical cliff, 55 m high. She finds the angle of depression to a ship at sea is 24°.
(a) How far is the ship from the base of the cliff?
The ship sails to a point 150 m from the base of the cliff.
(b) What is the angle of depression to the ship now?   ◄

👁 *Investigation*

Sloping lines

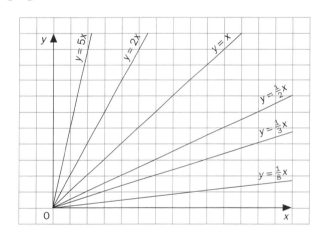

1   Six straight line graphs are drawn on the diagram above. Measure the angle, θ, between the x-axis and each line. Find the tangent of each angle. Write your results in a table like this.

y
θ
O   x

Equation	Angle θ	tan θ
y = 5x		

Look for a link between the equations and your results.
What do you find?

2   Each of these lines makes an angle with the x-axis.

$$y = 4x \quad y = 7x \quad y = 10x \quad y = \tfrac{1}{5}x \quad y = \tfrac{3}{4}x \quad y = \tfrac{7}{10}x$$

Work out what you think it is in each case.
Give each angle to the nearest degree.
To check your angles, draw the graph of each line.
How good were your predictions?

3 Each of these line graphs has a simple equation.

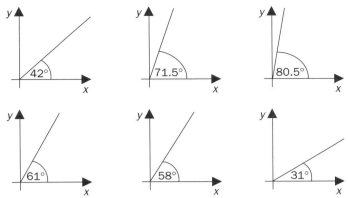

Work out what you think is the equation of each line.
Draw the graphs of your equations.
Do they give the angles in the diagram?

4 Write a short report of your findings.
Discuss your conclusions.
Try to explain the relationship between the equations
and angles.

Examination Questions

1 (a) At low tide an observer on a lighthouse sees a buoy,
120m away, at an angle of depression of 14°.
Find the height of the observer above the level of the
sea.

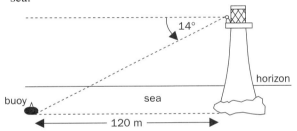

(b) At high tide, the same observer notes that the angle of
depression of the buoy is now 11°.
How much higher is the level of the sea at high tide than
it was at low tide?

(WJEC, 1990)

2 A woman is standing on horizontal ground 3 metres
away from a vertical flag pole.
She estimates that the angle of depression of the
base of the flag pole is 30°, and the angle of
elevation of the top of the flag pole is 60°.
Giving each answer to an appropriate
degree of accuracy, calculate
(a) the height of the woman's eyes
above the ground
(b) the height of the flag pole.
(NEAB, 1991)

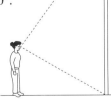

3 Salisbury Cathedral is the tallest cathedral in Great Britain.
At a distance of 20 metres horizontally from its base the
angle of elevation of the top of the spire is 80.9°.
The angle of elevation of the top of Telecom Tower is 60.0°
when measured 100 metres horizontally from the foot of the
tower.
By calculation find which of the buildings is taller and by
how much.

(NISEC 1990)

4 The diagram shows two lasers
(marked ● on the diagram) fixed
to the ceiling at a disco. They are
arranged to illuminate a spot on
the dance-floor midway between
them.
Calculate the angle A between
the laser beams.

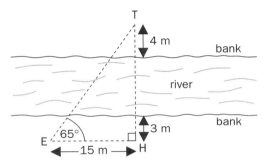

(MEG, 1989)

5 Hywel and Elaine would like to know the width of a river.

To do this Hywel (denoted by the point H) stands opposite a
tree, marked T in the diagram, which they know is 4 metres
from the edge of the river. Hywel has to stand 3 metres
away from the river's edge. Elaine walks 15 metres at right-
angles to the direction TH to the point marked E.
Angle TEH is 65°.
Calculate the width of the river to the nearest metre.

(WJEC, 1989)

P28
Calculating with fractions

This unit will help you to:

■ change improper fractions to mixed numbers and vice versa

■ add and subtract common fractions and/or mixed numbers without a calculator

■ multiply and divide common fractions and/or mixed numbers without a calculator

■ do calculations with fractions involving several operations, without a calculator

■ use fractions in formulas, without using a calculator

■ do fraction calculations with a calculator.

Common fractions

When we talk about fractions, we usually mean numbers such as

$$\frac{3}{4} \quad \frac{8}{8} \quad \frac{15}{10}$$

We write them as one number over another.

top number → numerator
top number → denominator

The **denominator** names the fraction.
It says what kind of fraction it is.
The **numerator** gives the number of these fraction parts you have.

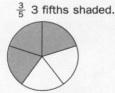

$\frac{3}{5}$ 3 fifths shaded.

3 out of 5 equal parts are shaded

A fraction such as $\frac{3}{8}$ is called a **proper fraction**.
Its top number is *smaller* than its bottom number.
It is *less than a whole one*.

A fraction such as $\frac{6}{6}$ is **equal to a whole one** (1).
Its top number is the *same* as its bottom number.

A fraction such as $\frac{11}{3}$ is called an **improper fraction** or a **'top-heavy' fraction**.
Its top number is *larger* than its bottom number.
It is *larger than a whole one*.

A number such as $2\frac{3}{10}$ is called a **mixed number**.
It is made up of a *whole number and a proper fraction*.

Discussion Exercise

- $\frac{1}{2}$ $\frac{2}{5}$ $\frac{5}{3}$ $\frac{4}{4}$ $\frac{8}{11}$ $\frac{12}{7}$ $\frac{5}{9}$

  $\frac{10}{10}$ $\frac{9}{9}$ $\frac{11}{12}$ $\frac{15}{12}$ $\frac{18}{18}$ $\frac{3}{2}$ $\frac{7}{5}$

  Which of these are proper fractions?
  Which make a whole one (1)?
  Which are improper fractions?
- Give some other examples of
  - proper fractions,
  - fractions that make a whole one,
  - improper fractions,
  - mixed numbers.

Changing improper fractions

All improper fractions are *larger than 1*.
Some improper fractions make *whole numbers*.
Some improper fractions make *mixed numbers*.

$$\frac{10}{2} = 5 \qquad \frac{15}{4} = 3\frac{3}{4} \qquad \frac{21}{3} = 7$$

$$\frac{14}{5} = 2\frac{4}{5} \qquad \frac{101}{100} = 1\frac{1}{100}$$

We usually rewrite an improper fraction using a whole number.
To do this, we find out how many whole ones it makes first.
Then we see what fraction, if any, is left over.

Discussion Exercise

Alan and Beth change $\frac{17}{6}$ to $2\frac{5}{6}$ in different ways.

Alan thinks it through like this …

> 6 sixths make 1 whole one.
> 12 sixths make 2 whole ones.
> 18 sixths make 3 whole ones.
> ◄ That's too many.
> 17 sixths make 2 whole ones and 5 sixths left over.
> So $\frac{17}{6} = 2\frac{5}{6}$

Beth changes it into a division …

> $\frac{17}{6} = 17 \div 6$
> $17 \div 6 = 2$ remainder 5
> So $\frac{17}{6} = 2\frac{5}{6}$

Discuss the two methods.

Try both ways to change these improper fractions.

$$\frac{8}{3} \qquad \frac{11}{7} \qquad \frac{57}{10} \qquad \frac{35}{12}$$

Decide which way you find easier.

Practise using this way.

► *Exercise* P28.1

1 Keith's granddad still measures things in inches and fractions of an inch.

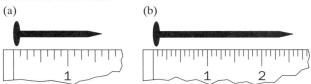

(a)   (b)

Write each length (i) as a mixed number
                  (ii) as an improper fraction.
Measure at least five small objects in inches and fractions of an inch. Write each length as a mixed number and an improper fraction.

2 Write a mixed number and an improper fraction for each of these.

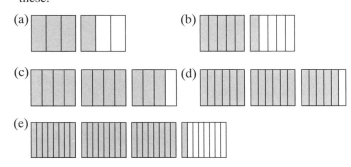

3 How many whole ones are made by these fractions?

(a) $\frac{8}{4}$ (c) $\frac{12}{3}$ (e) $\frac{9}{3}$ (g) $\frac{18}{6}$ (i) $\frac{14}{7}$

(b) $\frac{6}{2}$ (d) $\frac{15}{5}$ (f) $\frac{24}{8}$ (h) $\frac{12}{2}$ (j) $\frac{27}{9}$

4 Change these improper fractions to mixed numbers.

(a) $\frac{11}{2}$ (c) $\frac{9}{4}$ (e) $\frac{14}{6}$ (g) $\frac{23}{10}$ (i) $\frac{17}{9}$

(b) $\frac{17}{3}$ (d) $\frac{10}{4}$ (f) $\frac{15}{8}$ (h) $\frac{11}{7}$ (j) $\frac{31}{8}$

Addition and Subtraction

Same denominators.

Fractions with the *same denominator* (bottom number) are the *same kind of fraction*. The bottom number tells you what kind.
For example, $\frac{3}{8}$, $\frac{8}{8}$, $\frac{11}{8}$ are all eighths.

Fractions of the same kind are easy to add or subtract. The result is also the same kind of fraction.
Thinking of the fraction in words helps you to do the working. For example,

$$\frac{5}{9} + \frac{2}{9} = \frac{7}{9} \quad \text{or} \quad 5 \text{ ninths} + 2 \text{ ninths} = 7 \text{ ninths}.$$

$$\frac{4}{5} - \frac{1}{5} = \frac{3}{5} \quad \text{or} \quad 4 \text{ fifths} - 1 \text{ fifth} = 3 \text{ fifths}.$$

Sometimes your fraction answer is not in its simplest form.
So *cancel if you can.*
Some questions remind you to do this.
But you should do it anyway.

Memo

Dividing the top and bottom of a number by the *same number* makes an **equivalent fraction**.
This is called **cancelling**.
A fraction is in its **simplest form** when its top and bottom numbers are the smallest possible whole numbers.

$$\frac{6}{15} \xrightarrow{\div 3} \frac{2}{5}$$

$\frac{2}{5}$ is the simplest form of $\frac{6}{15}$

Question
Work out $\frac{7}{8} - \frac{3}{8}$

Answer
Think: 7 eighths – 3 eighths = 4 eighths

Write: $\frac{7}{8} - \frac{3}{8} = \frac{4}{8}$

Cancel by 4: $= \frac{\cancel{4}^{\,1}}{\cancel{8}_{\,2}}$

$= \frac{1}{2}$

The result of a calculation may be a 'top-heavy' fraction. We usually change it to a whole number or mixed number for an answer.

Question
Work out $\frac{3}{10} + \frac{9}{10}$

Answer
Think: 3 tenths + 9 tenths = 12 tenths

Write: $\frac{3}{10} + \frac{9}{10} = \frac{12}{10}$

Cancel by 2: $= \frac{\cancel{12}^{\,6}}{\cancel{10}_{\,5}}$

Write as a mixed number: $= 1\frac{1}{5}$

To subtract a fraction from a whole one (1), change the whole one to a fraction.
The fraction must be the *same kind* as the fraction you are subtracting.

Remember: $1 = \frac{2}{2} = \frac{3}{3} = \frac{4}{4} = \frac{5}{5} = \frac{6}{6} = \ldots$

For example, to work out $1 - \frac{5}{8}$, rewrite 1 as 8 eighths.

$$1 - \frac{5}{8} = \frac{8}{8} - \frac{5}{8} = \frac{3}{8}$$

To change a mixed number to an improper fraction, you have to add fractions.
You change the whole number to the kind of fraction you have.
Then add on the extra fraction.

$2\frac{3}{4}$  $\frac{11}{4}$

$$2 + \frac{3}{4} = \frac{8}{4} + \frac{3}{4} = \frac{11}{4}$$

▶ *Exercise* **P28.2**

Give each answer in its simplest form.

1 (a) $\frac{5}{9} + \frac{2}{9}$ (c) $\frac{2}{3} - \frac{1}{3}$ (e) $\frac{9}{10} - \frac{1}{10}$

(b) $\frac{6}{7} - \frac{2}{7}$ (d) $\frac{3}{8} + \frac{7}{8}$ (f) $\frac{3}{4} + \frac{1}{4}$

2 (a) $\frac{1}{4} + \frac{3}{4} + \frac{5}{4}$ (c) $\frac{4}{9} + \frac{5}{9} - \frac{1}{9}$ (e) $\frac{1}{10} + \frac{3}{10} + \frac{7}{10}$

(b) $\frac{5}{7} - \frac{3}{7} + \frac{6}{7}$ (d) $\frac{3}{8} + \frac{1}{8} + \frac{5}{8}$ (f) $\frac{7}{12} - \frac{1}{12} + \frac{5}{12}$

3 (a) $1 - \frac{2}{5}$ (c) $1 - \frac{3}{4}$ (e) $1 - \frac{7}{9}$

(b) $1 - \frac{6}{7}$ (d) $1 - \frac{3}{8}$ (f) $1 - \frac{7}{8}$

4 Change these mixed numbers to improper fractions.

(a) $3\frac{1}{2}$ (c) $1\frac{3}{5}$ (e) $3\frac{3}{8}$

(b) $2\frac{1}{4}$ (d) $4\frac{5}{6}$ (f) $2\frac{4}{5}$ ◀

Different denominators

Fractions with *different* denominators, such as $\frac{1}{2}$ and $\frac{1}{3}$, are *not* the same kind of fraction. So, you cannot add or subtract them directly. However, you can add or subtract *equivalent fractions with the same denominator*. This denominator is often called the **common denominator**.

For example, for $\frac{1}{2}$ and $\frac{1}{3}$, the common denominator is 6.

Using this common denominator gives: $\frac{1}{2} = \frac{3}{6}$ and $\frac{1}{3} = \frac{2}{6}$

So $\frac{1}{2} + \frac{1}{3} = \frac{3}{6} + \frac{2}{6} = \frac{5}{6}$

$$\frac{1}{2} - \frac{1}{3} = \frac{3}{6} - \frac{2}{6} = \frac{1}{6}$$

Memo

Multiplying the top and bottom of a fraction by the *same* number makes an **equivalent fraction**.
The 'new denominator' is a *multiple* of the old one.
A common denominator is a multiple of *each* denominator.

For example, for $\frac{1}{2}$ and $\frac{1}{3}$,

6 is a common denominator, because
6 is a multiple of 2, and 6 is a multiple of 3.

Sometimes the *largest denominator* of the fractions you *have* is a multiple of the denominators all the other fractions.
If it is, then you can use it as the common denominator.

For example, look at the denominators of $\frac{1}{4}$, $\frac{1}{8}$, $\frac{1}{16}$.

16 is its largest denominator.
$16 = 4 \times 4$, so 16 is a multiple of 4.
$16 = 2 \times 8$, so 16 is a multiple of 8.

So you can use 16 as the common denominator for $\frac{1}{4}$, $\frac{1}{8}$, $\frac{1}{16}$.

Question

Work out $\frac{5}{12} - \frac{1}{3}$

Answer

Change $\frac{1}{3}$ to twelfths, because $12 = 3 \times 4$ is a multiple of 3.
Replace $\frac{1}{3}$ by equivalent fraction $\frac{4}{12}$

$$\frac{1}{3} = \frac{4}{12} \quad (\times 4)$$

$$\frac{5}{12} - \frac{1}{3} = \frac{5}{12} - \frac{4}{12} = \frac{1}{12}$$

For some calculations you have to *change all the fractions* to equivalent fractions. To find their common denominator, you can simple multiply all the denominators together. The result will be a multiple of each of them.

For example, look at the denominators of $\frac{1}{2}$, $\frac{1}{3}$, $\frac{1}{4}$.
You can use $2 \times 3 \times 4 = 24$ as their common denominator.

Question

Work out $\frac{3}{4} - \frac{2}{5}$

Answer

Change $\frac{3}{4}$ and $\frac{2}{5}$ to twentieths because $20 = 4 \times 5$ is a multiple of 4 and 5.
Replace $\frac{3}{4}$ and $\frac{2}{5}$ by these equivalent fractions:

$$\frac{3}{4} = \frac{15}{20} \quad (\times 5) \qquad \frac{2}{5} = \frac{8}{20} \quad (\times 4)$$

$$\frac{3}{4} + \frac{2}{5} = \frac{15}{20} + \frac{8}{20} = \frac{23}{20} = 1\frac{3}{20}$$

To keep the numbers as small as possible, we often use the LCM (lowest common multiple) of the bottom numbers as the common denominator. This number is called the **lowest common denominator.**

For example, for $\frac{1}{2}$, $\frac{1}{3}$ and $\frac{1}{4}$ the lowest common denominator is 12.

To find this, we can think of multiples of 4, the largest denominator, first.
We 'test' each one to see whether it is also a multiple of 2 and 3.

   4...No, 8...No, 12...Yes

We stop when we reach 12. It is the smallest multiple of 4 that is also a multiple of 2 and 3.
However, don't worry if you do not spot the lowest common denominator.
You can simply cancel the answer at the end.

Using LCD	Using other denominator
$\frac{1}{2} + \frac{1}{3} + \frac{1}{4} = \frac{6}{12} + \frac{4}{12} + \frac{3}{12}$	$\frac{1}{2} + \frac{1}{3} + \frac{1}{4} = \frac{12}{24} + \frac{8}{24} + \frac{6}{24}$
$= \frac{13}{12} = 1\frac{1}{12}$	$= \frac{26}{24}^{13}_{12} = 1\frac{1}{12}$

▶ *Exercise* P28.3

1 Give the lowest common denominator for the fractions in each calculation.

(a) $\frac{3}{4} + \frac{1}{12}$ (d) $\frac{7}{20} + \frac{2}{5}$ (g) $\frac{11}{12} + \frac{5}{6} + \frac{1}{3}$

(b) $\frac{5}{8} - \frac{1}{4}$ (e) $\frac{5}{6} - \frac{2}{3}$ (h) $\frac{7}{10} - \frac{2}{5} + \frac{1}{10}$

(c) $\frac{7}{9} - \frac{2}{3}$ (f) $\frac{1}{2} + \frac{3}{4} - \frac{5}{8}$ (i) $\frac{5}{12} + \frac{3}{4} - \frac{1}{2}$

2 Work out the calculations in question **1**.

3 Calculate:

(a) $\frac{1}{3} + \frac{2}{5}$ (d) $\frac{6}{7} + \frac{3}{4}$ (g) $\frac{1}{2} + \frac{2}{3} + \frac{3}{4}$

(b) $\frac{3}{7} + \frac{1}{5}$ (e) $\frac{7}{9} - \frac{1}{5}$ (h) $\frac{1}{5} + \frac{3}{10} + \frac{2}{15}$

(c) $\frac{5}{8} - \frac{1}{3}$ (f) $\frac{5}{6} - \frac{2}{5}$ (i) $\frac{4}{9} - \frac{1}{4} + \frac{1}{2}$

Mixed numbers

To add or subtract mixed numbers, you deal with the whole numbers first and then the fractions.

Question

Work out $2\frac{4}{5} + 1\frac{2}{3}$

Answer

$$2\frac{4}{5} + 1\frac{2}{3}$$

Add whole numbers: $= 3\frac{4}{5} + \frac{2}{3}$

Use equivalent fractions: $= 3\frac{12}{15} + \frac{10}{15}$

Add fractions: $= 3\frac{22}{15}$

Change improper fraction: $= 3 + 1\frac{7}{15}$

Answer: $= 4\frac{7}{15}$

▶ *Exercise* P28.4

Work out these:

1 (a) $1\frac{1}{4} + 2\frac{3}{4}$ (c) $2\frac{5}{6} - 1\frac{1}{6}$ (e) $1\frac{2}{9} + 2\frac{5}{9} - 2\frac{4}{9}$

(b) $2\frac{1}{5} + 1\frac{2}{5}$ (d) $5\frac{1}{8} - 3\frac{1}{8}$ (f) $5\frac{2}{3} + 1\frac{1}{3} + 3\frac{2}{3}$

2 (a) $3\frac{3}{4} + 1\frac{5}{8}$ (c) $5\frac{1}{5} - 2\frac{1}{10}$ (e) $4\frac{4}{5} - 3\frac{1}{4}$

(b) $2\frac{1}{2} + 3\frac{1}{4}$ (d) $3\frac{3}{4} - 1\frac{1}{3}$ (f) $6\frac{2}{3} - 4\frac{3}{5}$

◯ *Discussion Exercise*

Some 'mixed number subtractions are more awkward to do than others.

Look at this example:

$$5\frac{1}{6} - 1\frac{3}{4}$$

What makes it 'awkward'?
How would you deal with this problem?
Here are three methods to consider.

Ann's method:	$5\frac{1}{6} - 1\frac{3}{4} = \frac{31}{6} - \frac{7}{4}$
	$= \frac{62}{12} - \frac{21}{12}$
	$= \frac{41}{12}$
	$= 3\frac{5}{12}$

Brian's method:	$5\frac{1}{6} - 1\frac{3}{4} = 4\frac{1}{6} - \frac{3}{4}$
	$= 4\frac{2}{12} - \frac{9}{12}$
	$= 4 - \frac{7}{12}$
	$= 3\frac{5}{12}$

Carol's method:	$5\frac{1}{6} - 1\frac{3}{4} = 4\frac{1}{6} - \frac{3}{4}$
	$= 4\frac{2}{12} - \frac{9}{12}$
	$= 3 + 1\frac{2}{12} - \frac{9}{12}$
	$= 3 + \frac{14}{12} - \frac{9}{12}$
	$= 3 + \frac{5}{12}$
	$= 3\frac{5}{12}$

Work through each method step-by-step.
Explain what each student has done.

Use all three methods to do these subtractions.

| $4\frac{1}{3} - \frac{1}{2}$ | $3 - 1\frac{1}{6}$ | $3\frac{1}{4} - 1\frac{7}{10}$ | $8\frac{5}{9} - 3\frac{11}{12}$ | $16\frac{1}{5} - 3\frac{7}{8}$ |

What are the advantages and disadvantages of each method?
Which do you think is easiest?
Give reasons for your choice.

Do other students in your group agree with you?
Discuss what they think.

▶ *Exercise* P28.5

Calculate:

1 $2\frac{1}{5} - 1\frac{1}{4}$ **3** $4\frac{2}{3} - 2\frac{4}{5}$ **5** $8\frac{2}{3} - 5\frac{5}{7}$

2 $5\frac{3}{7} - 2\frac{2}{3}$ **4** $7\frac{1}{6} - 3\frac{5}{12}$ **6** $3\frac{1}{8} - 1\frac{2}{5}$

Summary

To add or subtract numbers involving fractions, take these steps.

● Deal with any whole numbers first.
● Write all fractions with the same denominator. Use all equivalent fractions if you need to.
● Deal with the fractions next.
● Give your answer in its simplest form. Cancel if you can.
Change any improper fractions to whole numbers or mixed numbers.

► *Exercise* **P28.6**

1 In a case of fruit juices, $\frac{3}{8}$ of the bottles contain orange juice, $\frac{1}{3}$ contains grapefruit juice and the rest contain lime juice. What fraction of the case contains lime juice?

2 Mrs Webster's petrol tank was $\frac{5}{8}$ full when she left home. She used $\frac{2}{5}$ of a tank driving to Honiton. What fraction of a tank did she have left? Did she have enough petrol left to get home again?

3 A regional council stated that $\frac{1}{4}$ of its employees were teachers, $\frac{3}{8}$ were manual workers and $\frac{1}{4}$ were professional, clerical and technical staff. The rest were a mixture of police officers and firemen. What fraction of the employees were a mixture of police officers and firemen?

4 From a 30 m roll of carpet, lengths of $5\frac{1}{2}$ m, $6\frac{1}{4}$ m and 4 m are removed. What length remains?

5 A class survey showed that $\frac{1}{16}$ of the students come to school by train, $\frac{1}{4}$ walk, $\frac{3}{8}$ come by bus and the rest come by car. What fraction of the students travel to school by car?

6 Rod joins two pieces of wood together using a $1\frac{3}{4}$" screw, as shown.
   (a) Calculate the total thickness of wood.
   (b) Calculate the distance marked *a*.

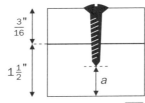

Multiplication

Mr Green has a rectangular garden. It is covered with grass. He marks out the whole garden into fifths with string and pegs like this …

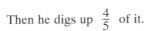

Then he digs up $\frac{4}{5}$ of it.

Next he marks the whole garden into thirds like this …

He plants vegetables in $\frac{2}{3}$ of the dug up patch. And he covers this area with netting.

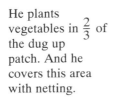
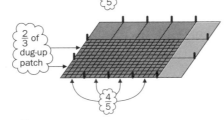

The picture shows that $\frac{8}{15}$ of the whole garden has netting over it.

So, $\frac{2}{3}$ of $\frac{4}{5} = \frac{2}{3} \times \frac{4}{5} = \frac{8}{15}$.

► *Exercise* **P28.7**

Do this exercise on centimetre squared paper.
1 (a) Draw a rectangle 7 cm by 2 cm.
   (b) Rule down into sevenths. Faintly shade $\frac{5}{7}$.
   (c) Rule across into halves. Heavily shade $\frac{1}{2}$ of $\frac{5}{7}$.
   (d) What fraction of the whole rectangle is heavily shaded?
   (e) Copy and complete: $\frac{1}{2} \times \frac{5}{7} =$

2 (a) Draw a rectangle 8 cm by 5 cm.
   (b) Rule down into eighths. Faintly shade $\frac{3}{8}$.
   (c) Rule across into fifths. Heavily shade $\frac{2}{5}$ of $\frac{3}{8}$.
   (d) What fraction of the whole rectangle is heavily shaded?
   (e) Copy and complete: $\frac{2}{5} \times \frac{3}{8} =$

3 Draw a rectangle 3 cm by 10 cm.
   Use it to work out $\frac{2}{3} \times \frac{1}{10}$.

4 Draw a rectangle 6 cm by 9 cm.
   Use it to work out $\frac{5}{6} \times \frac{4}{9}$.

You may have spotted a quick way to multiply fractions.
Multiply the top numbers.
Multiply the bottom numbers.
For example,

$$\frac{2}{3} \times \frac{4}{5} = \frac{2 \times 4}{3 \times 5} = \frac{8}{15}.$$

Check this way works for all the questions in Exercise P28.7.

You can often simplify fraction multiplications by **cancelling**. Look at this multiplication.

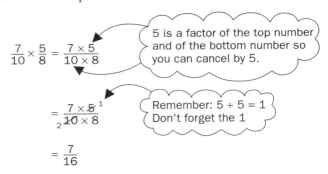

$$\frac{7}{10} \times \frac{5}{8} = \frac{7 \times 5}{10 \times 8}$$

5 is a factor of the top number and of the bottom number so you can cancel by 5.

$$= \frac{7 \times \cancel{5}^{1}}{{}_{2}\cancel{10} \times 8}$$

Remember: 5 ÷ 5 = 1
Don't forget the 1

$$= \frac{7}{16}$$

We usually write the working like this:

$$\frac{7}{10} \times \frac{5}{8} = \frac{7}{{}_{2}\cancel{10}} \times \frac{\cancel{5}^{1}}{8} = \frac{7}{16}$$

Cancelling *before* you do the multiplication makes the working much simpler. But if you forget, you can cancel the answer.

$$\frac{7}{10} \times \frac{5}{8} = \frac{\cancel{35}^{7}}{\cancel{80}_{16}} = \frac{7}{16}$$

So always *check your answer* is in its *simplest form*.

In some multiplications you can *cancel by more than one number*.
Always compare each top number with each bottom number in turn. This helps you to spot all the numbers to cancel by.

For example, look at $\frac{14}{45} \times \frac{12}{35}$.

Compare 14 with 45 → no common factor
Compare 14 with 35 → 7 is a common factor.

You can divide 14 and 35 by 7.

Dividing by 7 gives: $\dfrac{^{2}\cancel{14}}{45} \times \dfrac{12}{\cancel{35}_{5}}$

Compare 12 with 45 → 3 is a common factor.
          You can divide 12 and 45 by 3.
Compare 12 with 35 → no common factor.
Dividing by 3 gives: $\dfrac{^{2}\cancel{14}}{_{15}\cancel{45}} \times \dfrac{\cancel{12}^{4}}{\cancel{35}_{5}}$

Now you can work it out …

$$\dfrac{14}{45} \times \dfrac{12}{35} = \dfrac{^{2}\cancel{14}}{_{15}\cancel{45}} \times \dfrac{\cancel{12}^{4}}{\cancel{35}_{5}} = \dfrac{8}{75}$$

► Exercise P28.8

1 Calculate:
  (a) $\frac{1}{2} \times \frac{5}{8}$ (c) $\frac{3}{5} \times \frac{4}{7}$ (e) $\frac{3}{4} \times \frac{1}{5}$
  (b) $\frac{2}{3} \times \frac{4}{9}$ (d) $\frac{5}{8} \times \frac{7}{9}$ (f) $\frac{2}{5} \times \frac{3}{7}$

2 Do these. Cancel if you can.
  (a) $\frac{2}{3} \times \frac{5}{8}$ (c) $\frac{2}{7} \times \frac{3}{4}$ (e) $\frac{7}{8} \times \frac{2}{3}$
  (b) $\frac{1}{4} \times \frac{2}{5}$ (d) $\frac{3}{5} \times \frac{1}{9}$ (f) $\frac{3}{7} \times \frac{8}{9}$

3 In the Exleigh half-marathon, $\frac{3}{8}$ of the runners were over the age of 35. $\frac{2}{5}$ of the 'over 35's' were women. What fraction of the runners were women over 35?

4 Two-thirds of a magazine consists of adverts. Three-quarters of the adverts are for cars. What fraction of the magazine consists of car adverts?

5 Jim saves one-fifth of his pocket money each week. He puts five-eighths of his savings each week into a building society. What fraction of Jim's pocket money goes into the building society each week?

6 Sarah travelled the first $\frac{5}{12}$ of her journey by car and the rest by train. Half the car journey was made at 70 mph. For what fraction of her journey did Sarah travel at 70 mph by car? ◄

Mixed numbers

A **mixed number** is made up of two parts:

          a whole number and a fraction.

In mixed number calculations, you must make sure you use the 'total amount' for each number.
For example, $1\frac{4}{5} \times 2\frac{1}{3}$ means

     (all of 1 and $\frac{4}{5}$) multiplied by (all of 2 and $\frac{1}{3}$).

Discussion Exercise

Compare the methods used by David and Kate to work out:
$$1\frac{4}{5} \times 2\frac{1}{3}$$

David's method: $1\frac{4}{5} \times 2\frac{1}{3} = \left(1 + \frac{4}{5}\right) \times \left(2 + \frac{1}{3}\right)$

×	2	$\frac{1}{3}$
1	2	$\frac{1}{3}$
$\frac{4}{5}$	$\frac{8}{5}$	$\frac{4}{15}$

$2 + \frac{1}{3} + \frac{8}{5} + \frac{4}{15}$
$= 2 + \frac{5}{15} + \frac{24}{15} + \frac{4}{15}$
$= 2 + \frac{33}{15}$
$= 2 + 2\frac{3}{15}$
$= 4\frac{1}{5}$

Kate's method: $1\frac{4}{5} \times 2\frac{1}{3} = \frac{9}{5} \times \frac{7}{3}$

$$= \dfrac{^{3}\cancel{9}}{5} \times \dfrac{7}{\cancel{3}_{1}} = \dfrac{21}{5} = 4\frac{1}{5}$$

Make sure you understand both methods. Explain what each student has done step-by-step.

Do these multiplications both ways.

$\boxed{\frac{7}{8} \times 2\frac{1}{4}}$ $\boxed{1\frac{1}{2} \times 2\frac{1}{2}}$ $\boxed{2\frac{5}{8} \times 2\frac{2}{3}}$ $\boxed{1\frac{5}{6} \times 2\frac{3}{7}}$

Which method do you prefer?
Explain why.
Discuss what other students in your group think about them.

► Exercise P28.9

1 Calculate:
  (a) $\frac{2}{3} \times 3\frac{1}{4}$ (c) $\frac{3}{5} \times 2\frac{1}{3}$ (e) $\frac{4}{5} \times 2\frac{1}{2}$
  (b) $2\frac{1}{2} \times \frac{4}{5}$ (d) $\frac{4}{11} \times 2\frac{3}{4}$ (f) $\frac{6}{7} \times 5\frac{1}{4}$

2 Work out:
  (a) $1\frac{1}{3} \times 1\frac{4}{5}$ (c) $1\frac{3}{5} \times 1\frac{1}{2}$ (e) $4\frac{1}{8} \times 5\frac{1}{3}$
  (b) $2\frac{2}{5} \times 3\frac{1}{3}$ (d) $1\frac{5}{8} \times 2\frac{2}{7}$ (f) $3\frac{2}{9} \times 4\frac{1}{5}$

Summary

To multiply by numbers involving fractions, you can take these steps.
 ● Write whole numbers or mixed numbers as improper fractions (that is, 'top-heavy' fractions).
 ● Cancel if you can.
   Remember: You can cancel by dividing any numerator and   any denominator. But you must divide them both by the   same number.
 ● Multiply the top numbers (numerators).
 ● Multiply the bottom numbers (denominators).
 ● Make sure your answer is in its simplest form.
 ● Change an improper fraction to a whole number or mixed

► Exercise P28.10

1 Paul bought $3\frac{1}{2}$ pounds of potatoes. He used $\frac{3}{7}$ for chips and boiled the rest. What weight of potatoes did Paul use to:
  (a) make chips
  (b) make boiled potatoes?

2 $4\frac{1}{4}$ litres of emulsion was used to paint a hall. One-fifth was needed for the ceiling and the rest for the walls. How much paint was needed to paint
  (a) the ceiling
  (b) the walls?

3 Simon bought $3\frac{1}{2}$ metres of cable to rewire a porch light. He only used $\frac{7}{8}$ of the cable bought. What length of cable did Simon use?

4 Helen bought a $2\frac{1}{4}$ metre piece of wood. She used $\frac{3}{4}$ of the wood for shelving and $\frac{1}{8}$ for a book stand.
  How much wood did Helen use for
  (a) the shelving   (b) the book stand?

5 When Warren hired a car, the tank was $\frac{3}{4}$ full of petrol. He used $\frac{2}{5}$ of the petrol to visit his mother and $\frac{1}{6}$ to travel to the supermarket.

What fraction of a full tank of petrol was used by Warren to
(a) visit his mother
(b) travel to the supermarket?

6 Two-fifths of the weight of an orange is peel. What weight of peel is there in a $4\frac{1}{2}$ pound bag of oranges?

Division

$\boxed{3 \div \frac{1}{6}}$ means 'How many sixths in 3 whole ones?'

 3 whole ones  18 sixths

The picture shows 18 sixths in 3 whole ones.

So $3 \div \frac{1}{6} = 18$

You can also work it out like this:

    1 whole = 6 sixths
    3 wholes = 3 × 6 sixths = 18 sixths.

So $\boxed{3 \div \frac{1}{6}}$ and $\boxed{3 \times 6}$ give the same answer.

Compare the two calculations.
Note: ÷ and × are *inverse operations*.
    $\frac{1}{6}$ and 6 are *inverses* (called *reciprocals*).

$\boxed{4 \div \frac{2}{3}}$ means 'How many two-thirds in 4 whole ones?'

To answer this you can find out how many thirds in 4 first.

Then you can put these thirds into groups of two.

The diagram shows 6 'two-thirds' in 4.
    So $4 \div \frac{2}{3} = 6$

You can work it out in the same way.
Find thirds first.
Then divide by 2 to get the number of two-thirds.

    4 wholes = 4 × 3 thirds
             = 4 × 3 ÷ 2 two-thirds
             = 6 two-thirds

We can write $\boxed{4 \times 3 \div 2}$ as $\boxed{4 \times \frac{3}{2}}$

So $\boxed{4 \div \frac{2}{3}}$ and $\boxed{4 \times \frac{3}{2}}$ give the same answer.

Compare the two calculations.
Note: ÷ and × are *inverse operations*.

$\frac{2}{3}$ and $\frac{3}{2}$ are *inverses* (*called reciprocals*).

For any division by a fraction, you can write a 'matching' multiplication by its reciprocal.
The two calculations give the same answer.
For example,

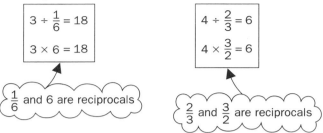

$3 \div \frac{1}{6} = 18$

$3 \times 6 = 18$

$4 \div \frac{2}{3} = 6$

$4 \times \frac{3}{2} = 6$

$\frac{1}{6}$ and 6 are reciprocals

$\frac{2}{3}$ and $\frac{3}{2}$ are reciprocals

We use this fact to change division calculations into multiplications. These are easier to do.

Summary

To divide by a fraction, you *multiply by its reciprocal.*
Remember:
To find the reciprocal of a fraction, you *invert* the fraction (i.e. *turn it upside-down*).

To divide by $\frac{1}{n}$, you multiply by $\frac{n}{1}$.

To divide by $\frac{n}{1}$, you multiply by $\frac{1}{n}$.

To divide by $\frac{a}{b}$, you multiply by $\frac{b}{a}$.

Question

Work out :
(a) $\frac{1}{12} \div \frac{1}{7}$ (b) $\frac{5}{6} \div \frac{10}{11}$

Answer

(a) $\frac{1}{12} \div \frac{1}{7}$

Change $\div \frac{1}{7}$ *to* $\times \frac{7}{1}$: $= \frac{1}{12} \times \frac{7}{1}$

Multiply top:
Multiply bottom: $= \frac{7}{12}$

(b) $\frac{5}{6} \div \frac{10}{11}$

Change $\div \frac{10}{11}$ *to* $\times \frac{11}{10}$: $= \frac{5}{6} \times \frac{11}{10}$

Cancel by 5: $= \frac{{}^1\cancel{5}}{6} \times \frac{11}{\cancel{10}_2}$

Multiply top:
Multiply bottom: $= \frac{11}{12}$

▶ *Exercise* **P28.11**

1 Give the reciprocals of each of these numbers.

(a) $\frac{1}{4}$ (c) $\frac{1}{7}$ (e) $\frac{2}{3}$ (g) $\frac{7}{8}$

(b) $\frac{1}{5}$ (d) $\frac{1}{10}$ (f) $\frac{6}{7}$ (h) $\frac{3}{10}$

2 Work out

(a) $7 \div \frac{1}{4}$ (c) $\frac{1}{4} \div \frac{1}{7}$ (e) $\frac{10}{9} \div \frac{2}{3}$ (g) $\frac{1}{16} \div \frac{7}{8}$

(b) $\frac{2}{3} \div \frac{1}{5}$ (d) $\frac{3}{5} \div \frac{1}{10}$ (f) $\frac{3}{5} \div \frac{6}{7}$ (h) $\frac{2}{5} \div \frac{3}{10}$

3 Calculate

(a) $\frac{1}{3} \div \frac{1}{4}$ (c) $\frac{4}{5} \div \frac{3}{4}$ (e) $\frac{3}{4} \div \frac{6}{5}$

(b) $\frac{1}{2} \div \frac{2}{3}$ (d) $\frac{2}{3} \div \frac{4}{3}$ (f) $\frac{3}{4} \div \frac{5}{2}$

4 How many $\frac{1}{10} \ell$ measures can be poured from a $\frac{1}{2} \ell$ bottle of cordial?

5 A scoopful of tea weighs $\frac{1}{64}$ lb. How many scoopfuls can be taken from a $\frac{1}{4}$ lb packet of tea?

6 A recipe for risotto needs $\frac{1}{4}$ lb of rice. How many risottos could be made from a 5 lb bag of rice? ◄

Always *change* any whole numbers or mixed numbers in a division *to improper fractions* first.

Question

Calculate:

(a) $\frac{2}{5} \div 8$ (b) $4\frac{1}{6} \div 1\frac{2}{3}$

Answer

(a) $\frac{2}{5} \div 8$

$= \frac{2}{5} \div \frac{8}{1}$

$= \frac{2}{5} \times \frac{1}{8}$

$= \frac{{}^1\cancel{2}}{5} \times \frac{1}{\cancel{8}_4}$

$= \frac{1}{20}$

(b) $4\frac{1}{6} \div 1\frac{2}{3}$

$= \frac{25}{6} \div \frac{5}{3}$

$= \frac{25}{6} \times \frac{3}{5}$

$= \frac{{}^5\cancel{25}}{{}_2\cancel{6}} \times \frac{\cancel{3}^1}{\cancel{5}_1}$

$= \frac{5}{2}$

$= 2\frac{1}{2}$

1 Change these to improper fractions.

(a) 3   (c) 2   (e) $2\frac{2}{9}$ (g) $4\frac{2}{3}$

(b) 5   (d) $6\frac{1}{4}$ (f) $1\frac{1}{10}$ (h) $1\frac{5}{7}$

2 Give the reciprocal of each answer to question **1**.

3 Calculate

(a) $1\frac{1}{2} \div 3$ (c) $1\frac{1}{2} \div 2$ (e) $1\frac{2}{3} \div 2\frac{2}{9}$ (g) $3\frac{1}{2} \div 4\frac{2}{3}$

(b) $\frac{5}{9} \div 5$ (d) $5 \div 6\frac{1}{4}$ (f) $4\frac{2}{5} \div 1\frac{1}{10}$ (h) $2\frac{4}{7} \div 1\frac{5}{7}$

4 Find the answers to these.

(a) $\frac{1}{9} \div 4$ (c) $2\frac{2}{9} \div 1\frac{2}{3}$ (e) $\frac{7}{8} \div 4\frac{2}{3}$

(b) $\frac{6}{11} \div 12$ (d) $5\frac{1}{2} \div 4\frac{1}{3}$ (f) $6\frac{3}{4} \div 1\frac{1}{7}$

5 How many $\frac{1}{4}$ m lengths of pipe can be cut from a $2\frac{1}{2}$ m length of piping?

6 $\frac{7}{8}$ m of braid is needed to trim a cushion. How many cushions can be trimmed from $10\frac{1}{2}$ m of braid? ◄

Order of operations

Sometimes a calculation involves *more than one operation*. Doing the operations in the correct order is important.

Fractions and mixed numbers obey the same 'order' rules as whole numbers.
Remember: Brackets first, $\times$ and $\div$ next, then $+$ and $-$.

Question

Calculate:

(a) $1\frac{1}{6} \div \left(\frac{5}{12} + \frac{1}{4}\right)$ (b) $1\frac{1}{6} \div \frac{5}{12} + \frac{1}{4}$

Answer

(a) *Brackets first, then division.*

$1\frac{1}{6} \div \left(\frac{5}{12} + \frac{1}{4}\right)$

$= 1\frac{1}{6} \div \left(\frac{5}{12} + \frac{3}{12}\right)$

$= 1\frac{1}{6} \div \left(\frac{8}{12}\right)$

$= \frac{7}{6} \div \frac{8}{12}$

$= \frac{7}{\cancel{6}_1} \times \frac{\cancel{12}^{2\,1}}{\cancel{8}_4}$

$= \frac{7}{4}$

$= 1\frac{3}{4}$

(b) *Division first, then addition.*

$1\frac{1}{6} \div \frac{5}{12} + \frac{1}{4}$

$= \frac{7}{6} \div \frac{5}{12} + \frac{1}{4}$

$= \frac{7}{\cancel{6}_1} \times \frac{\cancel{12}^2}{5} + \frac{1}{4}$

$= \frac{14}{5} + \frac{1}{4}$

$= \frac{56}{20} + \frac{5}{20}$

$= \frac{61}{20}$

$= 3\frac{1}{20}$

Work out these:

1 $\left(2\frac{1}{4} \div \frac{5}{6}\right) \times 3\frac{1}{3}$ **4** $1\frac{1}{5} - \left(\frac{3}{5} \div 2\frac{1}{4}\right)$

2 $\left(2\frac{3}{4} + 2\frac{2}{3}\right) \times \frac{2}{5}$ **5** $\left(\frac{1}{2} + \frac{2}{5}\right) \div \left(2\frac{1}{5} - 1\frac{3}{10}\right)$. ◄

3 $\frac{3}{4} \div \left(\frac{3}{8} + 1\frac{1}{4}\right)$

Fractions in formulas

Some formulas contain simple fractions.

For example, $F = \frac{9}{5}C + 32$.

We often change such fractions to decimals.

Remember: $\frac{a}{b} = a \div b$

e.g. $\frac{9}{5} = 9 \div 5$

Then we can do the working with a calculator. For example, when you put $C = 11$ into $F = \frac{9}{5}C + 32$

you get $F = \frac{9}{5} \times 11 + 32$.

You can key in:

   9 ÷ 5 × 1 1 + 3 2 =

This gives the answer F = 51.8
Sometimes the working is easier and quicker to do *without a calculator*.

For example,

when you put $C = 10$ into $F = \frac{9}{5}C + 32$

you get $F = \frac{9}{5} \times 10 + 32$.

You can cancel by 5 and work it out.

$$F = \frac{9}{\cancel{5}_1} \times \cancel{10}^2 + 32$$

$$= 18 + 32$$

$$= 50$$

Often you can do such working in your head.

In some situations you have to substitute fractions and/or mixed numbers into a formula.

Always put in the values first. Then do the working step-by-step.

Do not try to do too much in each step. It's easy to make mistakes.

Finally make sure you answer the question asked.

Question

A cylinder has a radius of 9 inches and a height of 7 inches.

(a) Write these measurements as fractions of a foot.
(12 inches = 1 foot)
Give your answers in their simplest form.

(b) Find the volume of this cylinder in cubic feet.
(use $V = \pi r^2 h$ and $\pi = 3\frac{1}{7}$).

Do not use a calculator in this question. Show all your working clearly.

Answer

(a) radius 9 inches = $\frac{9}{12}$ foot = $\frac{3}{4}$ foot

height 7 inches = $\frac{7}{12}$ foot

(b) *Formula*: $V = \pi r^2 h$

Put in values: $= 3\frac{1}{7} \times \left(\frac{3}{4}\right)^2 \times \frac{7}{12}$

$= \frac{11\cancel{22}}{1\cancel{7}} \times \frac{3}{\cancel{4}_2} \times \frac{\cancel{3}^1}{4} \times \frac{\cancel{7}^1}{\cancel{12}_4}$

$= \frac{33}{32}$

$= 1\frac{1}{32}$

Answer: The volume is $1\frac{1}{32}$ cubic feet.

Always read the wording in examination questions carefully. Questions are often designed to test whether you can do the working in a particular way. Make sure you do what it says. If you don't you will gain *no marks* for that working.

► *Exercise* P28.14

Use the fractions given in this exercise. Do not change them to decimals to do the calculations.

1 Use the formula
$$C = \frac{5}{9}(F - 32)$$
to change these Fahrenheit temperatures (F) to Celsius temperatures (C) when:
(a) $F = 77$ (b) $F = 54\frac{1}{2}$.

2 The mean average (A) of three numbers a, b and c is given by
$$A = \frac{1}{3}(a + b + c)$$
Find the mean average of:
(a) $a = \frac{1}{2}$, $b = \frac{1}{3}$, $c = \frac{1}{6}$ (b) $a = 1\frac{1}{2}$, $b = 1\frac{1}{4}$, $c = 2\frac{1}{8}$

3 Use the formula $v = u + at$ to find v when:
(a) $u = 3$, $a = 1\frac{1}{2}$, $t = 2\frac{1}{4}$ (b) $u = 4\frac{1}{2}$, $a = 2\frac{1}{8}$, $t = 1\frac{3}{5}$

4 For this rectangle

perimeter = $2(l + b)$
area = lb.

Find its perimeter and area when
(a) $l = 2\frac{3}{4}$ m, $b = 1\frac{2}{3}$ m   (b) $l = 7\frac{5}{12}$ feet, $b = 2\frac{1}{6}$ feet.

5 Use the formula
$$I = \frac{PTR}{100}$$
to find I when
(a) $P = 500$, $T = 2$, $R = 3\frac{4}{5}$ (b) $P = 2500$, $T = 3$, $R = 5\frac{1}{4}$.

6 For this triangle,
Area = $\frac{1}{2}bh$.

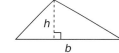

Find its area when
(a) $b = 3\frac{1}{3}$ yards, $h = 1\frac{1}{2}$ yards (b) $b = 6\frac{2}{5}$ cm, $h = 3\frac{3}{4}$ cm.

7 The surface area of this ball is given by the formula

surface area = πd^2

Calculate the surface area when $\pi = 3\frac{1}{7}$ and
(a) r = 7 cm   (b) r = $24\frac{1}{2}$ cm.

8 The resistance, R, in an electrical circuit when two resistances P and Q are connected in parallel is given by the formula
$$R = \frac{PQ}{(P + Q)}$$
Use the formula to find R when
(a) $P = 3$, $Q = 5\frac{1}{4}$,   (b) $P = 3\frac{1}{3}$, $Q = 2\frac{1}{2}$.

9 The area of the trapezium is given by the formula
Area = $(a + b)h$.

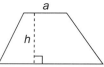

Find the area of the trapezium in which
(a) $a = 1$ yard, $b = 2\frac{1}{2}$ yards, $h = 2\frac{2}{3}$ yards,
(b) $a = 2\frac{3}{5}$ m, $b = 3\frac{3}{4}$ m, $h = 5$ m.

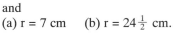

► *Exercise* **P28.15**

1 A straight road runs from the village to the beach.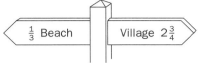
The signpost shows the distance, in miles, to the two places.
How far is it from the village to the beach?

2 Saeed filled the petrol tank in his car with 9 gallons of petrol. He used $2\frac{1}{4}$" gallons of petrol driving to Coventry. How much petrol did he have left in the tank when he arrived in Coventry?

3 Carl needs to drill a hole in a piece of timber $2\frac{3}{8}$" thick.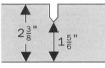
The bottom of the hole must be $1\frac{5}{16}$" from the opposite face of the timber, as shown.
How deep is the hole?

4 In a by-election $\frac{3}{10}$ of the voters voted for Miss Wright and $\frac{2}{5}$ voted for Mr Able. The rest voted for Mrs Bright.
(a) What fraction of the voters voted for Mrs Bright?
(b) Who won the election? Explain your answer.

5 A piece of blockboard is made from a $1\frac{5}{16}$ inch centre core sandwiched between two pieces of plywood each $\frac{1}{8}$ inch thick.
(a) What is the total thickness of this blockboard?
(b) Some customers want their blockboard veneered. A layer of veneer, $\frac{1}{32}$ inch thick, is glued to the top face only of the blockboard. What is the total thickness of this veneered blockboard?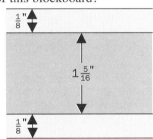

6 Sid works in a garage. It takes him $2\frac{1}{2}$ minutes to check the tyre pressures on a car. How many cars could Sid check in 30 minutes?

7 The diagram shows an L-shaped worktop and some of its dimensions in yards.
(The drawing is not to scale.)
(a) Work out the length labelled x.
(b) Calculate the area of the worktop.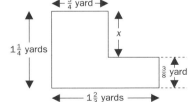

8 Roger has a $2\frac{1}{4}$ metre length of copper piping.
(a) He uses $\frac{2}{3}$ of this for a job. What length of pipe is left?
(b) For another job, Roger needs $\frac{1}{8}$ of a metre of piping. He cuts this length from the pipe left over from his first job. How much of the original pipe is now left?
(c) For the final job. Roger cuts the remaining piece of pipe in half. What length are these two pieces?

9 Lisa brews her own beer in a $45\frac{1}{2}$ litre tub. She puts it into bottles that hold $\frac{9}{20}$ of a litre.
How many bottles can be filled from a full tub of beer?

10 A rainwater barrel was $\frac{2}{3}$ full of water. After 60 litres of water were used from the barrel it was $\frac{5}{12}$ full. How much water does the barrel hold when full?

11 In Mrs Steen's garden, $\frac{1}{6}$ of the area is used for vegetables, $\frac{1}{4}$ for fruit, $\frac{5}{12}$ is lawn and the remainder is a flower bed.
(a) $\frac{2}{3}$ of the fruit patch is used for strawberries. What fraction of the garden is used for growing strawberries?
(b) Mrs Steen uses $\frac{3}{5}$ of the vegetable plot for potatoes. What fraction of the garden is used for growing potatoes?
(c) $\frac{3}{4}$ of the lawn is covered in weeds. No other part of the garden contains weeds. What fraction of the garden contains weeds?
(d) (i) What fraction of the garden is a flowerbed?
(ii) $\frac{3}{4}$ of the flower bed is used for growing roses. What fraction of the garden is used for roses?

12 Electrical engineers use the formula

$$\frac{1}{R} = \frac{1}{R_1} + \frac{1}{R_2}$$

to calculate the combined resistance R ohms when two separate resistances of R_1 ohms and R_2 ohms are connected in parallel in a circuit.
Calculate the combined resistance when two separate resistances of 5 ohms and 7 ohms are connected in parallel.

👁 **Investigation**

Fraction key
Many modern calculators have a **fraction key**.
It is usually labelled $a\,^b/_c$ or $a/_b$
If your calculator has such a key, investigate how to use it.
Here are some things to try.
We describe how to use the fraction key on *our* calculator.
Find out how to get the same results with *yours*.
Check what the calculator display shows.

● **Enter a fraction**
We key in

Can you key in any number of digits for the numerator and denominator?

Try entering $\frac{1}{7}$, $\frac{12}{7}$, $\frac{123}{7}$, $\frac{1234}{7}$, …

Try entering $\frac{5}{9}$, $\frac{5}{99}$, $\frac{5}{999}$, …

What happens?

● **Enter a mixed number.**
We key in

Is there a limit to how many digits you can key in for each part?

● **Simplify a fraction.**
We press = to simplify whatever fraction is on the display.
This process cancels a proper fraction to its simplest form.
The same process also changes an improper fraction to a mixed number in its simplest form.
Try entering and simplifying some proper and improper fractions.
See if you can predict the result first in each case.
Use your calculator to check your answers to question **4** on p485.

- **Change a mixed number to an improper fraction.**

  We enter the mixed number, then key in SHIFT $a\,^{b}/_{c}$
  The result is an improper fraction in its simplest form.
  Check your answers to question **4** on p486 with your calculator.
  Try changing some mixed numbers to improper fractions.
  Predict the answers first as extra practice.

- **Do fraction calculations**

  For a calculation using fractions, we simply key in the numbers and operations in the correct order.
  Pressing = gives the answer in its simplest form.
  It will either be a proper fraction or a mixed number.
  Try some fraction calculations of your own.
  Check your answers to the Exercises in this Unit.

- **Find out what else your fraction key will do.**

  Can you change fractions to decimals with it?
  Can you change decimals to fractions with it?

Note:
Even if your calculator has a fraction key, make sure you can do all of your fraction work *without* it. You need the skills for your work in algebra.

Also, in written exams a question may tell you to show working done without a calculator. If it does, then simply writing down the answer from your calculator will gain you no marks.

However you can *check* your answer with your calculator.

In Aural Tests, calculators are often banned altogether.

Examination Questions

1 $\frac{1}{3}$ of a rectangular garden is grass and $\frac{3}{5}$ is a vegetable plot. The remainder is a path. What fraction of the garden is the path?

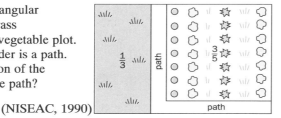

(NISEAC, 1990)

2 It takes $1\frac{5}{8}$ yards of material to make a pair of trousers. Tracey bought a remnant of material $2\frac{1}{4}$ yards long at the market and made a pair of trousers. How much material did she have left over?

(ULEAC, 1991)

3 The following instructions are given for finding out how long a curtain rod must be.

   "Measure the width of the window and add $4\frac{3}{8}$ inches at each end."

Bob measures his window. It is $86\frac{1}{2}$ inches wide.
How long must his curtain rod be?

(WJEC, 1990)

4 A metal rivet fits into a hole as shown.
The diameter of the rivet is $\frac{3}{5}$".
The diameter of the hole is $\frac{7}{8}$".
Calculate the distance *a*, which you should express as
(a) a fraction of an inch,
(b) a decimal.

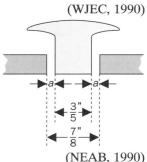

(NEAB, 1990)

5 A quarter of the World's population is Chinese.
One fifth of the rest is Indian.
What percentage of the World's population is Indian?

(NEAB, 1991)

6 When Philip had completed $2\frac{1}{4}$ miles of a 6-mile sponsored walk, he twisted his ankle.
He kept going for another $1\frac{2}{3}$ miles, but then had to stop.
(a) How many miles had he covered before he had to stop?
(b) How many miles remained to finish the walk?
He then had his ankle bandaged and was able to walk $\frac{2}{5}$ of the remaining distance.
(c) How many miles did he complete altogether?
(d) What fraction of the sponsored walk did he complete?

(NISEAC, 1990)

7 Joan divides her pocket money into three parts.
She spends $\frac{1}{3}$ of it on makeup. She spends $\frac{3}{5}$ of it on magazines.
The rest is saved.
(a) What fraction of her pocket money is saved?
(b) If she saves 6p each week, how much pocket money does she receive?

(SEG, 1988)

▷ P29
Inequations

This unit will help you to:

- ■ know and understand the rules of inequalities
- ■ use these rules to solve inequations
- ■ make inequations from 'real life' situations and solve them.

Balanced or unbalanced?

An **equality** is like a '*balanced*' pair of scales. It shows that two quantities are **equal**.

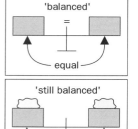

Like scales, an equality still balances if you do *exactly the same to both sides*. The new quantities are equal too.

An **inequality** is like *'unbalanced'* scales.
It shows one quantity is *greater than* or *less than* another.

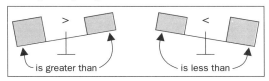

Let's see if doing the same to both sides changes these situations.

ACTIVITY

> Try this on your own or with another student

Same or different?

You need an inequality symbol card …
and two packs of number cards …

> You used these in Integer pairs p 382

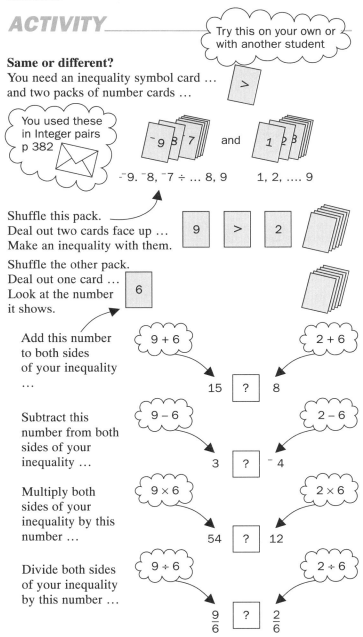

Shuffle this pack.
Deal out two cards face up …
Make an inequality with them.

Shuffle the other pack.
Deal out one card …
Look at the number it shows.

Add this number to both sides of your inequality …

Subtract this number from both sides of your inequality …

Multiply both sides of your inequality by this number …

Divide both sides of your inequality by this number …

Record your results. Put the correct inequality symbol between the two numbers each time.
Compare this with the symbol on the card.
Is it the same or different?
Repeat this several times.
Deal the numbers from your pack of cards each time.

What do your results show you about inequalities?

Compare your ideas with others in your group.
Write down your conclusions.

Looking at negatives

So far all the numbers to add, subtract, multiply or divide by have been positive?
What happens if they are negative?
Write negative signs on the numbers in the smaller pack …

… and repeat the activity to find out.

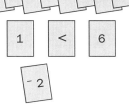

Are your 'general results' the same as before?
Discuss your conclusions with your group.
Try to generalise what you have found out.

💬 Discussion Exercise

Here are some inequalities:

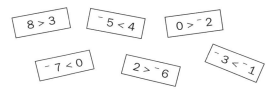

(a) Do this to each inequality:
   • add 5 to both sides
   • subtract 5 from both sides
   • multiply both sides by 5
   • divide both sides by 5
   Record your results.
   Say whether each is TRUE or FALSE.
   What do you notice?
Now repeat (a) for each of these numbers …
(b) 2   (c) 7   (d) ⁻1   (e) ⁻2   (f) ⁻5

Is the inequality you get always true?
If not, when is it false?
Are the 'general results' you found earlier still true?
If you didn't do so before, try to generalise what you have found out now.

Solving inequations

Here are some simple inequations:

$$x > 1 \qquad t \geq {}^{-}4 \qquad n \leq 0 \qquad y < {}^{-}2$$

Each inequation has a variable shown by a letter.
Finding values for this variable is called **solving the inequation**.
When you replace the variable by a solution, the inequality is true.

Memo
Solving simple inequations p384

$x > 1$ 5 is a solution because 5 > 1

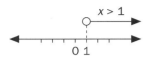 0 is a solution because 0 = 0

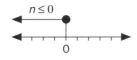 ⁻3 is a solution because ⁻3 > ⁻4

$y < ^-2$ ⁻5 is a solution because ⁻5 < ⁻2

You can show *all* the solutions on a **number line graph**:

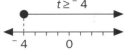 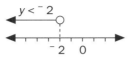

When the solutions are integers you can *list some or all* of them.

▶ *Exercise* **P29.1**

Give five integer solutions of:
1 $x > 1$　　　2 $n \le 0$　　　3 $t \ge ^-4$　　　4 $y < ^-2$　◀

Simplify and solve

A '**simple inequation**' compares a *variable* and a *number*.
The variable is *on its own* on one side.
The number is *on its own* on the other.
Not all inequations are like this.
Here are examples of some others.

$\boxed{x + 5 > 2}$　　$\boxed{y - 1 \le 0}$　　$\boxed{2n \ge ^-8}$　　$\boxed{\frac{a}{3} < 2}$

These 'look' more complicated.
But each can be made into a 'simple inequation'.

$\boxed{x + 5 > 2}$　　$\boxed{y - 1 \le 0}$　　$\boxed{2n \ge ^-8}$　　$\boxed{\frac{a}{3} < 2}$

This gives the *range of values* that solves the inequation.
You can show these values on a number line graph as before.

▶ *Exercise* **P29.2**

1 Show the solutions of these inequations on number lines.
　(a) $x + 5 > 2$　(b) $y - 1 \le 0$　(c) $2n \ge ^-8$　(d) $\frac{a}{3} < 2$
2 (a) Give three integer solutions of $x > ^-3$.
　　Check each is also a solution of $x + 5 > 2$.
　(b) Give three integer solutions of $y \le 1$.
　　Check each is also a solution of $y - 1 \le 0$.
　(c) Give three integer solutions of $n \ge ^-4$.
　　Check each is also a solution of $2n \ge ^-8$.
　(d) Give three integer solutions of $a < 6$.
　　Check each is also a solution of $\frac{a}{3} < 2$.　◀

To make inequations simpler, you may need to 'get rid of'
numbers you don't want.
You want to end up with …
　● the variable on its own on one side
　● the number on its own on the other.
You use the rules of inequalities to achieve this.

These are the rules you investigated on p495.

Summary
Rules for inequalities
An inequality is *still true*, if you
　● add the same number to both sides
　● subtract the same number from both sides
　● multiply both sides by the same *positive* number
　● divide both sides by the same *positive* number.
The 'direction' of the symbol does not change.

An inequality *changes*, if you
　● multiply both sides by the same *negative* number
　● divide both sides by the same *negative* number.
The 'direction' of the symbol changes:
> changes to <　　　　$\ge$ changes to $\le$
< changes to >　　　　$\le$ changes to $\ge$

In some inequations an 'unwanted number' is *added to the variable*.
The opposite of $\boxed{+}$ is $\boxed{-}$.
To 'get rid of' an unwanted $\boxed{+}$ number,
　　　　　　　use $\boxed{-}$ this number.
Do the same to both sides.

Question
Solve x + 3 > 9 and show the solution on a number line graph.

Answer
To get rid of +3, use –3　　　　　$x + 3 > 9$

–3 from both sides　　　　　$x + 3 - 3 > 9 - 3$
　　　　　　　　　　　　　　　　$x > 6$

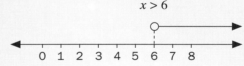

In other inequations an 'unwanted number' is *subtracted from the variable*.
The opposite of $\boxed{-}$ is $\boxed{+}$.
To 'get rid of ' an unwanted $\boxed{-}$ number,
　　　　　　　use $\boxed{+}$ this number.
Do the same to both sides.

Question
Solve $x - 5 \le 3$ and show the solution on a number line graph.

Answer
To get rid of –5, use +5　　　　　$x - 5 \le 3$

+5 to both sides　　　　　$x - 5 + 5 \le 3 + 5$
　　　　　　　　　　　　　　$x \le 8$

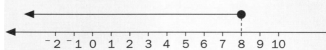

▶ *Exercise* P29.3

1 Solve each of these inequations.
Show each answer on a number line graph.
(a) $x + 2 > 5$ (c) $3 + y < 7$ (e) $x + 3 < 2$
(b) $x - 4 \leq 2$ (d) $y - 2 \geq {}^-1$ (f) $y - 9 \leq 0$

2 For each inequation in question **1**, give three integer
solutions.

You may find an unwanted *positive* number *multiplying the
variable*.
The opposite of $\boxed{\times}$ is $\boxed{\div}$.
To 'get rid of' an unwanted $\boxed{\times}$ by a positive number,
use $\boxed{\div}$ by this number.
Do the same to both sides.

Question

Solve $4n \geq 20$ and show the solution on a number line graph.

Answer

4n means n × 4.
To get rid of × 4, use ÷ 4. $4n \geq 20$

Divide both sides by 4 $4n \div 4 \geq 20 \div 4$
                     $n \geq 5$

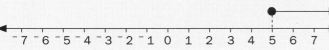

The *variable may be divided* by an unwanted *positive* number.
The opposite of $\boxed{\div}$ is $\boxed{\times}$.
To 'get rid of' an unwanted $\boxed{\div}$ by a positive number,
use $\boxed{\times}$ by this number.
Do the same to both sides.

Question

Solve $\frac{n}{2} < 1$ and show the solution on a number line graph.

Answer

$\frac{n}{2}$ *means n ÷ 2*

To get rid of ÷ 2, we use × 2. $\frac{n}{2} < 1$

Multiply both sides by 2 $\frac{n}{2} \times 2 < 1 \times 2$
                       $n < 2$

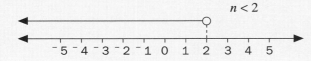

▶ *Exercise* P29.4

1 Solve each of these inequations.
Represent each answer on a number line graph.
(a) $2x \geq 4$ (c) $\frac{x}{2} \leq 1$ (e) $\frac{x}{7} > 0$
(b) $3x < 6$ (d) $10 \geq 5x$ (f) $\frac{x}{4} > 3$

2 For each inequation in question **1**, write down three integer
solutions.

Watch out for negatives

So far solving inequations has been like solving equations.
But it isn't always!
Multiplying or dividing by a negative number is different.
It **changes the inequality symbol**.
The rules of inequalities tell you this.
To 'get rid of' an unwanted $\boxed{\times}$ by a negative number,

     • $\boxed{\div}$ both sides by this number,
and • change the inequality symbol.
       The 'direction' of the symbol changes:
     $>$ to $<$ $\geq$ to $\leq$ $<$ to $>$ $\leq$ to $\geq$

Question

Solve $-n < 2$ and show the solution on a number line graph.

Answer

$-n$ *means n ×* $^-1$

To get rid of × $^-1$*, use ÷* $^-1$ $-n < 2$

Divide both sides by −1 and change < to > $\frac{-n}{-1} > \frac{2}{-1}$

                                    $n > -2$

To 'get rid of' an unwanted $\boxed{\div}$ by a negative number,

     • $\boxed{\times}$ both sides by this number,
and • change the inequality symbol.
       The 'direction' of the symbol changes:
     $>$ to $<$ $\geq$ to $\leq$ $<$ to $>$ $\leq$ to $\geq$

Question

Solve $\frac{-n}{4} \geq 3$ and show the solution on a number line graph.

Answer

$\frac{-n}{4}$ *means n ÷* $^-4$

To get rid of ÷ $^-4$*, use ×* $^-4$ $\frac{-n}{4} \geq 3$

Multiply both sides by $^-4$
and change ≥ to ≤ $\frac{-n}{4} \times {}^-4 \leq 3 \times {}^-4$

                              $n \leq {}^-12$

▶ *Exercise* P29.5

1 Find the range of values of x for which each of these
inequalities is true.
Show the answer to each inequation on a number line graph.
(a) $^-3x \geq 9$ (c) $-\frac{x}{6} < 1$ (e) $18 > -6x$
(b) $-\frac{x}{3} \leq 2$ (d) $-4x < 20$ (f) $-\frac{x}{5} \geq 0$

2 For each inequation in question **1**, write down three
whole number solutions.

Take extra care in the following 'Mixed Exercise'.
You have to decide whether to add, subtract, multiply or divide
to solve the inequation.

▶ *Exercise* P29.6

1 Find the solution of each of these inequations. Represent
   each solution on a number line graph.
   (a) $y - 7 > 1$ (d) $-3x \geq 12$ (g) $9 + m < 8$
   (b) $n + 5 \leq 0$ (e) $p - 3 \leq -4$ (h) $-5y \geq 20$
   (c) $\frac{x}{2} > -1$ (f) $-\frac{y}{7} < 1$ (i) $r - 4 \geq 0$

2 For each inequation in question 1, write down three
   integer solutions.

ACTIVITY

Think of a number
Look at this puzzle.

> I think of a number.
> Add 4.
> The result is less than 10.

It gives an inequation like this ...

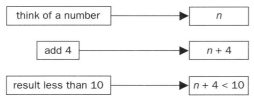

Now you can solve it...   (Subtract 4 from both sides) $n < 6$

The number must have been less than 6.
Make an inequation for each of these puzzles and solve them.

> Think of a number.
> Subtract 7.
> The result is less than 4.

> Think of a number.
> Add it to 11.
> The result is more than 20.

> Think of a number.
> Multiply it by 4.
> The result is more than 12.

> Think of a number.
> Divide it by 5.
> The result is less than 2.

> Think of a number.
> Subtract it from 10.
> The result is more than 6.

> Think of a number.
> Divide it into 15.
> The result is less than 3.

Invent five of your own puzzles like these.   (Make sure you can do them yourself!)
Give them to another student to solve.

More than one operation

Solving an inequation may take more than one operation.
Always get rid of unwanted numbers by $\boxed{+}$ or $\boxed{-}$ first,
then by $\boxed{\times}$ or $\boxed{\div}$ next.
Write out each step in full. It's safer.

Question
Solve the inequations
(a) $3x - 1 \leq 5$ (b) $7 - \frac{x}{2} > 1$

Answer
(a)
$$3x - 1 \leq 5$$
Add 1 to both sides $$3x - 1 + 1 \leq 5 + 1$$
$$3x \leq 6$$
Divide both sides by 3 $$3x \div 3 \leq 6 \div 3$$
$$x \leq 2$$

(b)
$$7 - \frac{x}{2} > 1$$
Subtract 7 from both sides $$7 - 7 - \frac{x}{2} > 1 - 7$$
$$-\frac{x}{2} > {}^-6$$
Multiply both sides by $^-2$. $$-\frac{x}{2} \times {}^-2 < {}^-6 \times {}^-2$$
and change > to <
$$x < 12$$

Inequations with brackets

To get rid of a number multiplying the brackets, use
multiplication or division as before, if you can. Then you can
remove the brackets.
If not, remove the brackets first.

Question
Solve $4(x - 1) < 8$.

Answer
$$4(x - 1) < 8$$
Divide both sides by 4 $$\frac{4}{4}(x - 1) < \frac{8}{4}$$
$$(x - 1) < 2$$
Remove brackets $$x - 1 < 2$$
Add 1 to both sides $$x - 1 + 1 < 2 + 1$$
$$x < 3$$

▶ *Exercise* P29.7

Solve these inequations
1 $2x + 5 < 13$ 5 $5n + 1 > 31$ 9 $5(y - 1) > 10$
2 $3y - 2 \geq 7$ 6 $8 - n \geq 7$ 10 $\frac{1}{2}(2n + 3) \leq 2$
3 $4p + 3 \leq 9$ 7 $2(3x + 1) \geq 14$
4 $5x + 3 <$ 8 $3(2p - 1) < 15$

ACTIVITY

More number puzzles
Make an inequation for each of these puzzles and solve them.

> Think of a number.
> Double it and add 1.
> The result is more than 14.

> Think of a number.
> Multiply it by 4.
> Subtract 2.
> The result is less than 18.

Think of a number. Double it and subtract from 10. The result is more than 3.	Think of a number. Add 5 and then multiply by 2. The result is less than 24.
Think of a number. Subtract it from 9 and then multiply by 3. The result is less than 30.	Think of a number. Double it and subtract 7. Then multiply by 3. The result is more than 18.

Invent some number puzzles like these.
See if you and your group can solve them.

Variable on both sides

Sometimes the variable is on *both sides* of the inequation.
You want it on one side only.
'Get rid of it' from the 'other side'.
Then simplify the inequation as before.

Question

Solve $5x - 7 < 3x - 1$

Answer

'x term' on both sides
Get rid of it from one side.

To get rid of $3x$, subtract $3x$ from both sides	$5x - 7 < 3x - 1$ $5x - 3x - 7 < 3x - 3x - 1$
	$2x - 7 < -1$
Add 7 to both sides	$2x - 7 + 7 < -1 + 7$ $2x < 6$
Divide both sides by 2	$2x \div 2 < 6 \div 2$ $x < 3$

Usually we leave the variable on the left hand side.
Sometimes it is easier to get rid of it from this side.
With practice you will be able to spot which side to choose.

Question

Solve $9 - 2x \geq 7x$

Answer

It's easier to 'get rid of' $2x$ here.
This leaves a number on one side
and the x term on the other side.

	$9 - 2x \geq 7x$
Add $2x$ to both sides	$9 - 2x + 2x \geq 7x + 2x$
Divide both sides by 9	$9 \geq 9x$ $1 \geq x$
Turn inequation 'round' to give x on LHS	or $x \leq 1$

In simple inequations the variable is usually on the left hand
side. If it ends up on the right hand side, you can easily 'turn it
round'. But make sure the inequality stays true.

► **Exercise** P29.8

Solve these inequations

1 $4x + 2 > x + 7$	**6** $5 - 3p \leq 6 - 4p$
2 $2x - 1 < x + 9$	**7** $6 - 3m \geq 3m$
3 $8x - 5 \geq 3x + 15$	**8** $3y < y - 2$
4 $3n - 2 \leq n$	**9** $4(x - 3) \leq 3(x - 2)$
5 $8 - 3x > x$	**10** $y + 2 < 6(2 + y)$

◄

Two inequations

You may have to solve **two inequations 'simultaneously'** i.e. 'at
the same time'. You want the range of values that satisfy *both*.

You may be given the inequations separately. Just make each
into a simple inequation as before. Then give their combined
solution. It often helps to use a number line.

Question

Given $5x > 2$ and $\frac{1}{2}x \leq 4$, list all the possible integral
values of x.

Answer

Solve $5x > 2$ on its own.   *Solve $\frac{1}{2}x \leq 4$ on its own.*

$$5x > 2$$
$$\frac{5x}{5} > \frac{2}{5}$$
$$x > \frac{2}{5}$$

$$\frac{1}{2}x \leq 4$$
$$\frac{1}{2}x \times 2 \leq 4 \times 2$$
$$x \leq 8$$

Show the overlap of $x > \frac{2}{5}$ and $x \leq 8$ on a number
line graph.
Mark the integer solutions on the number line.

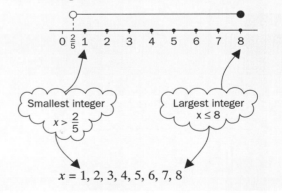

Exercise P29.9

Given that x is an integer, solve the following pairs of inequations.

1 $2x \leq 6$ and $x > 1$	**6** $\frac{x}{2} > -1$ and $x + 1 \leq 3$
2 $x \geq 0$ and $3x < 6$	**7** $0 < x + 1$ and $5x \leq 0$
3 $x + 1 > 3$ and $x < 5$	**8** $2x > -2$ and $2 > x + 1$
4 $\frac{x}{2} \leq 5$ and $2x > 16$	**9** $3x \geq -2$ and $2(x - 1) \leq 0$
5 $2x \geq -6$ and $x + 3 < 4$	**10** $2(x + 3) < 12$ and $\frac{x}{3} > -1$

The two inequations to be solved together may be together in *one statement*.

Look at the 'middle part' of the statement. It will have the variable in it.

Decide what to do to 'get rid of' unwanted numbers in this *middle part*.

Then do this to *all three 'parts'* of the statement.

Question

Solve the inequation $3 \le y + 4 < 7$.
Show your solution on a number line graph.

Answer

$y + 4$ is in the 'middle' of $3 \le y + 4 < 7$.
You want to get rid of $+ 4$.
To get rid of $+ 4$, use $- 4$

$$3 \le y + 4 < 7$$

Subtract 4 from each part $$3 - 4 \le y + 4 - 4 < 7 - 4$$
$$-1 \le y < 3$$

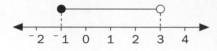

You may need to use more than one operation to get the variable on its own in the 'middle part' of the statement.

Question

Solve the inequation $-1 < 5n - 6 \le 4$ and give its whole number solutions.

Answer

$5n - 6$ is in the 'middle' of $-1 < 5n - 6 \le 4$.
You want to get of $- 6$ first,
  then get rid of $\times 5$ next.

$$-1 < 5n - 6 \le 4$$

To get rid of $- 6$, add 6 $$-1 + 6 < 5n - 6 + 6 \le 4 + 6$$
to each part

$$5 < 5n \le 10$$

To get rid of $\times 5$, $$\frac{5}{5} < \frac{5n}{5} \le \frac{10}{5}$$
divide each part by 5

$$1 < n \le 2$$

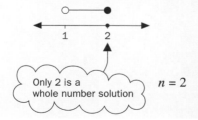

Only 2 is a whole number solution $n = 2$

▶ Exercise P29.10

1 $2 \le 2n < 8$ **6** $5 < 2y + 3 < 11$
2 $6 < x + 7 \le 13$ **7** $0 < 3m + 6 \le 15$
3 $-2 < y - 1 < 2$ **8** $10 < 3p + 4 \le 30$
4 $-1 \le \frac{m}{3} \le 5$ **9** $-1 \le 5n - 11 < 9$
5 $7 < 3x + 1 \le 16$ **10** $1 < 5 - n \le 4$

Problem solving

A problem is usually described in words, not algebraic symbols. But translating it from words into algebra can often help you to solve it.

You need to give the 'unknown' a letter. Then you use the given information to 'make **expressions**' with it.

Making expressions p78

The unknown may be a quantity with a unit such as cm, hours, ...

Don't forget to take this into account. Make sure you give all expressions in the same unit. Change any if you need to.

Some problems give you two equal quantities. You can make them into an **equation**. Then solve it.

Making and solving equations A7 p107

Other problems give you an inequality. You can make an **inequation** from this. Then solve it too.

Always **check** your answer makes sense.
Try it out with the information in the original problem.
Don't use the inequation you made to check it ... just in case!

Question

Carol visits schools for the local authority. She claims £3 a day for lunch and 35p per mile for car expenses. Carol travels x miles for work each day.
(a) Write down, in terms of x, an expression for the amount in pence
   (i) Carol claims for car expenses each day
   (ii) Carol claims altogether each day.
(b) Carol always claims less than £20 each day. Express this as an inequation in x.
(c) Carol can only claim for a whole number of miles. What is the maximum number of miles she could claim each day?

Answer

(a) (i) For 1 mile Carol claims 35 pence.
       For x miles Carol claims $35x$ pence.

    (ii) Carol claims Car expenses + lunch.
        Car expenses = $35x$ pence.
        Lunch = £3 = 300 pence.
        Total claim for a day: $35x + 300$ pence.

(b) Daily claim is less than £20;
         i.e. less than 2000 pence.

So $35x + 300 < 2000$

(c)
$$35x + 300 < 2000$$

Subtract 300 from both sides $35x + 300 - 300 < 2000 - 300$

$$35x < 1700$$

Divide both sides by 35 $\dfrac{35x}{35} < \dfrac{1700}{35}$

$$x < 48.57\ldots$$

48 is the largest whole number less than 48.57…
Maximum: 48 miles

To check this answer, work out Carol's expenses for 48 miles.

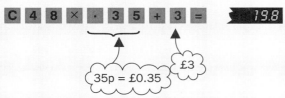

| C | 4 | 8 | × | . | 3 | 5 | + | 3 | = | | 19.8 |

35p = £0.35   £3

£19.80 is less than £20 … that's alright.
But another 35p makes it more than £20.
So 48 miles is the maximum.

Exercise P29.11

1. A lift weighs 750 kg.
   It is designed to carry p people of average weight 80 kg.
   (a) Write down, in terms of p, the total weight in kilograms of the lift and its passengers.
   (b) The maximum weight the lift cable can hold is 1650 kg.
   Express this as an inequation in p.
   (c) Give the possible numbers of people the lift can carry safely.

2. The floor of Ann's living room is a rectangle, w metres wide.
   (a) The floor is 1.5 metres longer than it is wide.
   Write down an expression, in terms of w, for its length.
   (b) Ann wants some carpet gripper to go round the perimeter of the room.
   Write down, in terms of w, the length of carpet gripper she needs.
   (c) Ann finds she needs less than 25 m of carpet gripper.
   Use this to make an inequation in w and solve it.

3. Neil buys s 24p stamps and the same number of 18p stamps.
   He pays with a £5 note and gets some change.
   (a) Express this as an inequation in s and solve it.
   (b) What is the maximum number of stamps Neil could buy?

4. Wayne wants to take a trolley with n packing cases in this service lift.
   Each case weighs 36 kg.
   The trolley weighs 85 kg.

Wayne weighs 73 kg.
(a) Form an inequation for n from this information and solve it.
(b) List the possible numbers of cases he can load on his trolley to take safely in the lift.

SERVICE LIFT
Load must not exceed 500 kg

5. The car park of a new supermarket can occupy an area up to 8000 m². 950 m² of the car park must be left for driveways and turning areas. Each car parking space must be 20 m². Make an inequation from this information and solve it to find how many cars the new car park will hold.

NEW SUPERMARKET
TO OPEN
ON THIS SITE

EARLY NEXT YEAR

6. A vegetable garden is a rectangle l metres long and 3 metres wide.
   (a) Write down an expression in l for the area of the garden in square metres.
   (b) The garden has an area of between 15 m² and 24 m². Write this as an inequation in l and solve it.
   (c) Each side of the garden is a whole number of metres. Give its possible dimensions.

Investigation

Triangle inequality
A triangle has three sides.
You can draw it if you know their lengths.
Draw a triangle with sides
5 cm, 2 cm, and 4 cm.

Memo
Drawing triangles
p156–157

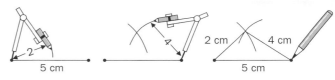

Try to draw a triangle with sides 5 cm, 1 cm, 4 cm.
What happens? Why?

Now try to draw a triangle with sides 5 cm, 1 cm, 2 cm.
What do you find this time?

Can you draw triangles with the following sides?
Explain how you decided.
(a) 6 cm, 3 cm, 4 cm
(b) 13 cm, 4 cm, 6 cm
(c) 10 cm, 2 cm, 8 cm
(d) 1 cm, 5 cm, 12 cm
(e) 4 cm, 9 cm, 4 cm
(f) 2 cm, 8 cm, 7 cm
(g) 12 cm, 12 cm, 13 cm
(h) 5 cm, 9 cm, 4 cm
(i) 10 cm, 20 cm, 12 cm
(j) 3 cm, 10 cm, 2 cm

Hint:
Compare the longest length with the sum of the other two.

What does this tell you about the longest side of a triangle?
Give your answer as an inequality.

Now use this inequality to solve these puzzles.

A The longest side of a triangle is 10 cm long.
One of the other sides is x cm long.
The other side is 1 cm longer than this.
Make an inequation in x and solve it.

B One side of a triangle is c cm long.
Another is twice as long as this.
The third is 45 cm.
Find the possible ranges of values for c.
There are two ranges. Can you find them both?

Other inequations

Here is another inequation.
This time you have the square
of the variable x, not just x.
To solve it, you have to find the values of x that satisfy it.

$$x^2 \geq 25$$

You know two solutions already.
$5^2 = 25$ so $x = 5$ is a solution of $x^2 \geq 25$,
and $(^-5)^2 = 25$, so $x = ^-5$ is also a solution.

Let's see what others you can find.

Discussion Exercise

The two solutions you know
are $x = ^-5$ and $x = 5$.
The other solutions must
be associated with $x = ^-5$
and $x = 5$.

Try squaring numbers
between $^-5$ and 5.
Try whole numbers and
decimals.
Do they satisfy $x^2 \geq 25$?

Try squaring numbers
greater than 5. Do they
satisfy $x^2 \geq 25$?

Try squaring numbers less
than $^-5$.
Do they satisfy $x^2 \geq 25$?

Now give the range(s) of values of x that satisfy $x^2 \geq 25$.
Show the solution on a number line graph.

What happens if the inequation is $x^2 > 25$?
How does it affect the solution?

Exercise P29.12

Solve these inequations in the same way.
Show each solution on a separate number line graph.

(a) $x^2 \leq 9$ (c) $x^2 \leq 1$ (e) $x^2 > 4$
(b) $x^2 \geq 16$ (d) $x^2 < 81$ (f) $x^2 \geq 0.01$

Investigation

Cubes

| $x^3 \leq 64$ | $x^3 \geq 125$ | $x^3 > 8$ | $x^3 < 1000$ |

These inequations have cubes of the variable x. See if you can
solve them. Don't forget to try different numbers.
Try positive and negative numbers and zero.
Try whole numbers, decimals,…
Use your calculator and a number line to help.

Roots

| $\sqrt{x} \leq 2$ | $\sqrt{x} \geq 1$ | $\sqrt{x} < 10$ | $\sqrt{x} > ^-4$ |

| $\sqrt[3]{x} \geq 3$ | $\sqrt[3]{x} \leq 1$ | $\sqrt[3]{x} < 2$ | $\sqrt[3]{x} > ^-2$ |

Now try to solve these inequations. They have square roots or
cube roots of the variable.

Describe how you solved these 'cube' and 'root' inequations.
Compare your method with others in your group.

Mixtures
Investigate solving inequations like these:

Comment on what you find.

Examination Questions

1 Find the whole numbers y such that $-7 \leq 2y < 4$.
(MEG, 1994)

2 Given that $3x > 2$ and $\frac{1}{2}x \leq 1\frac{1}{2}$, list the possible integral
values of x.
(SEG, 1989)

3 What can you say about x if $17 - 5x$ is less than 7?
(MEG, 1994)

4 (a) The temperature, $x°C$, inside a freezer is between $-15°C$
and $-20°C$. Write this statement as an inequality.
(b) Solve the inequality $3x + 7 \geq 1$.
Represent your answer on this number line.

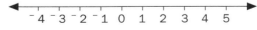

(MEG, 1990)

5 (a) Indicate, by thickening the appropriate parts of number
lines drawn from -2 to 5, the solution sets of each of the
following inequalities.
(i) $3x - 2 \leq x + 4$
(ii) $6 < 4x + 2$
(b) Write down the whole number values of x which satisfy
both of these inequalities simultaneously.
(NEAB, 1989)

6 After a hockey match the captain goes to the local shop to buy cans of lemonade and shandy for the players. She buys x cans of lemonade and y cans of shandy. Express each of the following instructions as inequalities.
(a) Buy at least 4 cans of shandy.
(b) Buy more shandy than lemonade.
(c) Buy at least 11 cans altogether, including some cans of lemonade and some of shandy.
(d) Do not spend more than £5. (Lemonade costs 28p per can and shandy costs 34p per can.)
(NEAB, 1991)

7 A craftsman can be paid in one of two ways:
Method A A down payment of £300, then £4 an hour.
Method B £9 an hour.
(a) He works for n hours. Write down, in terms of n, an expression for his earnings using
(i) Method A
(ii) Method B.
(b) Write down an inequality that will be true if his earnings by Method B are greater than his earnings by Method A.
(c) Solve your inequality for n.
(MEG, 1989)

8 Find the range of values of n for which $n > 2 - n$.
(SEG, 1990)

9 Given that x is an integer and that
$$x - 3 \leq 6 \text{ and } \frac{x}{2} > 3,$$
find all the values of x which satisfy both these inequalities.
(Cambridge, 1990)

10 (a) Find the set of values of x for which
$$2x - 1 > -3$$
(b) Copy this number line and show on it the values of x which satisfy $2x - 1 > -3$

```
   ‾4    ‾2    0    2    4
```
(SEG, 1990)

11 A rectangle is $(3x - 4)$ cm long and $(2x + 5)$ cm wide.
(a) In terms of x, by how much is the length greater than the width?
(b) Find the value of x for which the figure is a square.
(c) For what values of x is the width of the rectangle less than its length?
(NISEAC, 1990)

12 Some pupils were making up number puzzles. One pupil's number puzzle was written like this:
$$2(3x - 1) < 18$$
What is the largest whole number that this pupil could have thought of?
(NEAB, 1994)

13 Prakash discovers that for some numbers the square root is larger than the number itself. For what numbers is this true?
(SEG, 1990)

14 Given that $-6 \leq x \leq 3$ and $-4 \leq y \leq 5$, find
(a) the largest possible value of x^2
(b) the smallest possible value of xy
(c) the value of x if $x^2 = 25$.
(NEAB, 1989)

P30
Mutually exclusive events

This unit will help you to:

■ calculate the probability that one event or another happens

■ recognise mutually exclusive events

■ understand that the addition law for probabilities only works for mutually exclusive events

■ know and use the addition law for probabilities.

One thing or another

Tim is playing Scrabble.
It is his turn to take a tile.
If he gets a T or an E, he can make a word.

You can work out the probability of this event happening.

Memo

Probability of an event

$$= \frac{\text{Number of favourable outcomes for that event}}{\text{Total number of possible outcomes}}$$

These are the tiles in the bag:

The letters on the tiles are all the possible outcomes.
The total number of possible outcomes is 25.

Tim wants either a T or an E.
Here are the favourable outcomes for this event:

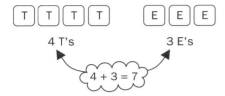

The number of favourable outcomes is 4 + 3 = 7
The probability of getting T or E = $\frac{7}{25}$
You can write this in shorthand as

$$P(T \text{ or } E) = \frac{7}{25}$$

You can also work out the same probability in a different way.

For the event, 'get a T',
there are 4 favourable outcomes:
The total number of possible outcomes is 25.

$$P(T) = \frac{4}{25}$$

For the event, 'get an E',
there are 3 favourable outcomes:
The total number of possible outcomes is 25.

$$P(E) = \frac{3}{25}$$

Look at the result of adding these fractions
$$\frac{4}{25} + \frac{3}{25} = \frac{7}{25}$$

It gives: P(T) + P(E) = P(T or E)

Adding the probabilities of the two separate events gives the probability of *one event or the other happening*.
This is an example of the **addition law for probabilities**.

We get this result because the two events, 'get a T', 'get an E' are special. Tim takes *one tile* from the bag. Each tile has *only one letter* on it. The tile he takes could have *a T or an E* on it. It *cannot* have *both* letters on it.

If he gets a T, he cannot get an E.

If he gets an E, he cannot get a T.

The two events ('get a T', 'get an E') are called **mutually exclusive events**.
If one of them happens, it *excludes* the other. The two events cannot happen at the same time.

Discussion Exercise

1   In another game of Scrabble, these tiles are in the bag.

It is Zoe's turn to take a tile.
(a) How many tiles are in the bag?
(b) How many tiles have B or S on them?
(c) What is the probability that Zoe takes a B or S?
    P(B or S) = ?
(d) Work out P(B).
    Work out P(S).
(e) Work out P(B) + P(S).
(f) Compare your answers to (c) and (e).
    Is the result what you expected?
    Discuss.
(g) What is the probability that Zoe takes an A or E or S?
        P(A or E or S) = ?
(h) Work out P(A), P(E), P(S).
    Add your three answers.
(i) Compare the results from (g) and (h).
    Discuss what you find.
(j) What is the probability that Zoe takes an A or B?
    Work out P(A or B) in two different ways.
    Discuss your two methods.

2   Nerissa bought a packet of fruit sweets. There were 5 black, 4 green, 5 red, 6 orange and 4 yellow sweets in it. Nerissa's friend Matt takes one sweet out of the packet without looking at the colour.
(a) How many sweets were in the packet?
(b) How many sweets in the packet were green or yellow?
(c) What is the probability that Matt takes a green or yellow sweet?
        P(green or yellow) = ?
(d) Work out P(green).
    Work out P(yellow).
    Add your two answers.
(e) Compare your results from (c) and (d).
    Do they give you what you expect? Discuss.
(f) What is the probability that Matt takes a black or yellow sweet?
        P(black or yellow) = ?
(g) Which two probabilities added together do you think give the same result as (f)?
    Work them out to check.
(h) What is the probability that Matt takes a black or red or orange sweet?
        P(black or red or orange) = ?
(i) Which three probabilities added together do you think will give the same result as (h)?
    Work them out to check.
(j) Find the probability that Matt takes a red or orange sweet.
    Work it out in two different ways. Discuss.

3   Lisa is dealt this hand of thirteen cards.

She takes a card at random from her hand.

(a) In Lisa's hand, these cards are Aces or Clubs. What is the probability that she takes an Ace or Club from her hand?
P(Ace or Club) = ?

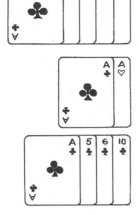

(b) These are the Aces in Lisa's hand. What is the probability that she takes an Ace from her hand?
P(Ace) = ?

(c) These are the Clubs in Lisa's hand.
What is the probability she takes a Club from her hand?
P(Club) = ?

(d) Work out P(Ace) + P(Club).
Compare the answer with P(Ace or Club).
What do you find?
Is it what you expected? Discuss.
Why did you get this result?
What does this show about the addition law of probabilities?

Mutually exclusive events

The *addition law* for probabilities only works for **mutually exclusive** events. To use this law, you need to be able to identify whether events are mutually exclusive or not.

> ### *Summary*
> Events that cannot happen at the same time are called mutually exclusive events. If one of them happens, it excludes the other(s).

Ted takes a card at random from this hand.
In this situation, the events 'get a 5', 'get a 6' are *mutually exclusive*.
The card Ted takes could have a 5 or 6 on it. It cannot have both numbers on it.
If he gets a 5, he cannot get a 6.
If he gets a 6, he cannot get a 5.

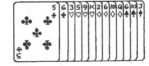

Not *all* events in this situation are mutually exclusive.
If Ted gets a 5, he can also get a Heart.
If Ted gets a Heart, he can also get a 5.
The card Ted takes could be the 5 of Hearts.
This shows that the events 'get a 5', 'get a Heart' *are not mutually exclusive*. They *can* happen at the same time.

Discussion Exercise

For each activity, say whether or not the two events are mutually exclusive. Explain your choice in each case.

1 Activity: Pat goes for the bus.
Event A: She catches the bus.
Event B: She misses the bus.

2 Activity: Darren goes for a walk on Tuesday.
Event A: It is raining.
Event B: The sun is shining.

3 Activity: Ceri goes to the disco.
Event A: Ceri goes with Pete.
Event B: Ceri goes with Sue.

4 Activity: Tom takes a sock at random from a drawer.
Event A: He gets a green sock.
Event B: He gets a long sock.

5 Activity: Charlotte enters the raffle for a turkey.
Event A: She wins the turkey.
Event B: She does not win the turkey.

6 Activity: Mick takes a shape from a box containing cubes and blue shapes.
Event A: He takes a blue shape.
Event B: He takes a cube.

7 Activity: Throw a dice.
(a) Event A: Get an even number.
Event B: Get an odd number.
(b) Event A: Get an even number.
Event B: Get a prime number.

8 Activity: Toss two coins.
(a) Event A: Get two tails.
Event B: Get one head and one tail.
(b) Event A: Get two tails.
Event B: Get at least one tail.

9 Activity: Take a card at random from a full pack.
(a) Event A: Get a club.
Event B: Get a spade.
(b) Event A: Get a king.
Event B: Get a heart.

Addition law for probabilities

> ### *Summary*
> The **addition law** for probabilities only applies to **mutually exclusive events**. These are events that cannot happen at the same time.
> The addition law is often called the **'or law'**. It gives the probability that one event **or** another happens.
>
> To find this combined probability you *add* the probabilities for the two separate events.
> If event A and event B are mutually exclusive, then:
>
> $$P(A \text{ or } B) = P(A) + P(B).$$
>
> This addition law also works for *more than two* mutually exclusive events.
> If A, B, C, … are mutually exclusive events, then the law gives:
>
> $$P(A \text{ or } B \text{ or } C \text{ or } …) = P(A) + P(B) + P(C) + …$$

Probabilities are often written as common fractions. We usually cancel them to their *simplest form*.
When using the addition law, do not do any cancelling *until the very end* of the working. It is easier to add common fractions with the *same* denominator.

Question

Dean has only these 12 coins in his pocket.

He takes a coin at random from his pocket.
What is the probability that it is
(a) either a 1p or 10p coin
(b) a 1p or 2p or 5p or 10p or £1 coin?
Explain your answer to (b).

Answer

When Dean takes a coin from his pocket, getting one type of coin excludes getting any other type. He cannot get a coin of two different types at the same time. This means the events 'get a 1p coin', 'get a 2p coin', and so on … are mutually exclusive. So we can use the addition law to combine the probabilities of these events.

(a) $P(\text{1p coin}) = \frac{2}{12}$, $P(\text{10p coin}) = \frac{3}{12}$

$P(\text{1p or 10p coin}) = P(\text{1p coin}) + P(\text{10p coin})$

$$= \frac{2}{12} \quad + \frac{3}{12}$$

$$= \frac{5}{12}$$

(b) $P(\text{1p coin}) = \frac{2}{12}$, $P(\text{2p coin}) = \frac{1}{12}$

$P(\text{5p coin}) = \frac{4}{12}$, $P(\text{10p coin}) = \frac{3}{12}$, $P(\text{£1 coin}) = \frac{2}{12}$

$P(\text{1p or 2p or 5p or 10p or £1 coin})$
$$= P(\text{1p}) + P(\text{2p}) + P(\text{5p}) + P(\text{10p}) + P(\text{£1})$$

$$= \frac{2}{12} \quad + \frac{1}{12} + \frac{4}{12} \quad + \frac{3}{12} \quad + \frac{2}{12}$$

$$= \frac{12}{12}$$

$$= 1.$$

1 is the probability of a certainty. So this answer shows that Dean is certain to get a 1p or 2p or 5p or 10p or £1 coin when he takes one coin from his pocket. This makes sense because Dean has only got 1p, 2p, 5p, 10p and £1 coins in his pocket. So the coin he takes is certain to be one of these.

▶ Exercise P30.1

For each question in this exercise
● explain why the events are mutually exclusive
● use the addition law for probabilities to answer it.

1   A tin contains buttons all the same shape and size. In the tin there are 16 white buttons, 12 blue buttons and 10 grey buttons. Andrea takes a button at random from the tin to sew on her blouse. What is the probability that Andrea picked a button which was
(a) white or blue
(b) blue or grey?

2   A bag contains eight toffees, five caramels and seven chocolates. Paul takes a sweet from the bag without looking. What is the probability that he takes
(a) a toffee or a caramel
(b) a toffee or a chocolate?

3   In a Bingo game, numbers are chosen at random from the numbers 1 to 50 inclusive. What is the probability that the first number chosen is
(a) a multiple of 7 or a multiple of 11
(b) an odd number or a multiple of 2?

4   These 'Scrabble letters' make up the word MATHEMATICS.

All of these letters are placed in a bag. One letter is taken at random from the bag. What is the probability that the letter taken will be:
(a) an A or an E
(b) a vowel
(c) a consonant?

5   When 50 sixth form students were asked which football team they supported, 15 replied Manchester United, 14 said Manchester City and the rest said they supported Liverpool. If one of these sixth formers is chosen at random, what is the probability that he/she will be a supporter of
(a) Manchester United or Liverpool
(b) a Manchester team?

6   Kent and Pete went camping together one weekend. They took 3 cans of tomato soup, 2 cans of vegetable soup, one can of onion soup and 4 cans of chicken soup. In the dark, Pete opened one of the cans at random. What is the probability that the can opened contained
(a) tomato or onion soup
(b) vegetable or tomato soup
(c) vegetable or onion or chicken soup?

7   A crate contains 8 bottles of orange juice, 11 bottles of pineapple juice and 5 bottles of grapefruit juice. The bottles are all identical in size and colour.
Ben picks a bottle at random from the crate. What is the probability that the bottle contains
(a) orange or pineapple juice
(b) pineapple or grapefruit juice
(c) orange or pineapple or grapefruit juice?
Comment on your answer to (c).

8   A jar contains 10 mints, 9 fruitdrops, 4 eclairs and 8 chews. Dapinder takes one sweet at random from the jar. What is the probability that he gets
(a) a mint or a chew
(b) a fruitdrop or a mint
(c) a mint or an eclair or a chew
(d) a mint or a fruitdrop or an eclair or a chew?
Explain your answer to (d).

In some situations you *know* the probabilities for some events. These may be given as common fractions, decimal fractions or percentages. If these events are mutually exclusive, you can use the addition law to find probabilities of other events from them. The probabilities in the next Exercise are given in one of these ways.

► *Exercise* P30.2

1 Jeff follows Ringland Rovers.
   Here are his estimates of the probabilities of the results of their next match.
   What is the probability that the result of the next match is

Win	Draw	Lose
0.5	0.3	0.2

   (a) win or draw
   (b) lose or draw?

2 Becky did a survey of makes of car in her local car park. She classified $\frac{1}{5}$ of the cars as British, $\frac{1}{3}$ as Japanese, $\frac{1}{4}$ as German, $\frac{1}{6}$ as Italian and $\frac{1}{20}$ as American.
   What is the probability that the first car to leave the car park is
   (a) German or Italian
   (b) not European (i.e. Japanese or American)?

3 Kate got a big box of sugared almonds for Christmas. 35% of the sweets are pink, 40% are blue, 15 % are white and 10% are green. Kate takes one sweet out of the box without looking.
   What is the probability that it is
   (a) white or green
   (b) white or blue
   (c) pink or green?

4 Richard makes a biased dice.
   On this dice the probabilities of throwing 1, 2, 3, 4, 5, 6, are $\frac{1}{12}, \frac{1}{24}, \frac{1}{8}, \frac{1}{6}, \frac{1}{3}, \frac{1}{4}$, respectively.
   Richard throws his biased dice once. What is the probability that the score is
   (a) 1 or 5
   (b) a multiple of 3
   (c) an even number
   (d) a prime number?

5 Sid bought a packet of wine gums and found that there were 7 red, 6 green, 5 orange and 2 black gums.
   He let his friend pick one of the gums at random. What is the probability that the chosen gum was
   (a) orange or red
   (b) orange or black
   (c) red, green or black?

6 A supermarket freezer contains a large number of tubs of ice-cream. $\frac{3}{10}$ of the tubs are vanilla, $\frac{1}{5}$ are strawberry, $\frac{1}{4}$ are blackcurrant, $\frac{1}{10}$ are hazelnut and $\frac{3}{20}$ are chocolate. When shopping one day, Mrs Saunders is in a hurry and takes one of the tubs at random from the freezer. What is the probability that the ice-cream is
   (a) vanilla or hazelnut
   (b) strawberry or blackcurrant
   (c) vanilla, chocolate or hazelnut?

7 Isobel did a football supporters survey at college. This table shows her results.

Team supported	Percentage
Manchester United	34
Manchester City	13
Sheffield United	22
Sheffield Wednesday	12
Leeds United	19

   A student is chosen at random from the survey. What is the probability that the student supports
   (a) a Manchester team (i.e. United or City)
   (b) a Sheffield team (i.e. United or Wednesday)
   (c) a Yorkshire team (i.e. from Sheffield or Leeds)?

8 Kirsty bought a packet of flower seeds. The information on the packet gave the percentages for the different coloured flowers expected.

red	yellow	white	pink
33%	27%	18%	22%

   If a seed is taken at random from the packet and planted, what is the probability that the seed will produce
   (a) a red or pink flower
   (b) a yellow or white flower
   (c) a yellow, white or pink flower?

9 A machine outside a shop contains red, green, blue and black Gob-stoppers. Each Gob-stopper is all one colour. When a 5p coin is put into the machine, one Gob-stopper is dispensed at random. The probability of getting each colour is given in this table:

Colour	red	green	blue	black
Probability	$\frac{3}{10}$	$\frac{4}{25}$	$\frac{1}{5}$	$\frac{17}{50}$

   Kamran puts a 5p coin into the machine. What is the probability that the Gob-stopper he gets is
   (a) red or black
   (b) green or red
   (c) red or green or blue?
   Give each probability as a fraction in its simplest form.

P31
Standard form

This unit will help you to:

- recognise and write numbers given in 'calculator shorthand' in standard form
- understand that the place values of the figures in a number are powers of ten
- write place values as powers of ten in index form
- multiply numbers by positive and negative integer powers of ten without a calculator
- re-write numbers in standard form as ordinary numbers
- re-write ordinary numbers in standard form
- change any number multiplied by a power of ten into standard form
- compare and order numbers in standard form
- calculate with numbers in standard form with and without a calculator
- recognise when numbers need to be changed to standard form when using a calculator
- use standard form to solve problems with and without a calculator.

Number shorthand

Scientific calculators have a *shorthand* way to display *very large numbers*.
Try this multiplication on your calculator.

$$5\ 000\ 000 \times 7\ 000\ 000$$

The answer is 35 000 000 000 000.
This number has 14 digits.
There are too many digits to fit on most calculator displays.
   To display this answer most calculators show:

The 13 on the right is called the exponent. (This is another word for index.)
It tells you that the 3.5 is multiplied by 10^{13}.
We write it as: 3.5×10^{13}.
   We say: 'three point five times ten to the thirteen'.
This way of writing a number is called **standard form**.
It is also called **standard index form** and **scientific notation**.

Compare the 'calculator shorthand' ...   3.5 ¹³

with the written standard form ... 3.5×10^{13}.
See how the display shows the 3.5 and the 13.

It does not show the × 10. Do not forget these when you write down an answer.
   Scientific calculators also use this *shorthand* for *very small numbers*.
Multiply these very small numbers with your calculator.

$$0.000\ 000\ 3 \times 0.000\ 06$$

The answer is 0.000 000 000 018.
A scientific calculator usually gives this as:

We write it in standard form as 1.8×10^{-11}.

Discussion Exercise

- Each answer below is shown on a calculator display.
  Write each in standard form.

- Compare the numbers you have written in standard form.
  What is 'standard' about their form?
  What common features do they all have?
- Which of the numbers below are in standard form?
  Say what is 'wrong' with each of the others.

2×10^{7}	6×9^{2}	11×10^{4}
$5.3 \div 10^{9}$	$1.7 + 10^{6}$	1.2×10^{-3}
3.5×2^{10}	4.31×10^{12}	125×10^{11}
0.56×10^{15}	$1.4 \times 10^{3.5}$	2.006×10
$7 \times 10^{0.2}$	3.05×10^{-7}	1×10^{8}

- Describe, in your own words, what a number in standard form 'looks like'.
  Compare your description with others from your group.
  Write the best, short description from your group's ideas.
  Discuss.

Powers of 10

In standard form we use powers of 10 such as 10^4 and 10^{-4}.
These are in index form.
You have met this number shorthand before.

Remember:

10^4 means
$10 \times 10 \times 10 \times 10 = 10\ 000$

Memo
Index notation
P1 p236

10^{-4} means $\dfrac{1}{10^4}$ = $\dfrac{1}{10 \times 10 \times 10 \times 10}$ = $\dfrac{1}{10000}$ or 0.0001

Here are some more reminders:

10^6 = 1 000 000 1 million
10^5 = 100 000 1 hundred thousand
10^4 = 10 000 1 ten thousand
10^3 = 1000 1 thousand
10^2 = 100 1 hundred
10^1 = 10 1 ten
10^0 = 1 1 unit $\frac{1}{10}$
10^{-1} = 0.1 1 tenth or $\frac{1}{100}$
10^{-2} = 0.01 1 hundredth or $\frac{1}{1000}$
10^{-3} = 0.001 1 thousandth or
and so on …

Powers of ten are used in standard form because our number system is based on 'ten'.
Each figure's place in a number shows what it is worth.
Each place value is a power of 10.

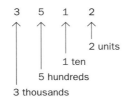

3 thousands
5 hundreds
1 ten
2 units

In this place value table we show the names and index form of the powers of 10.

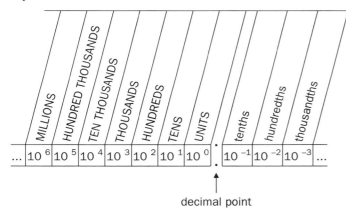

decimal point

We can use the index form to write the values of numbers.

10^6	10^5	10^4	10^3	10^2	10^1	U	
7	0	0	0	0	0	0	

The number 7 000 000 has the 7 in the 10^6 column.
It is 7 lots of 10^6 or 7×10^6.
So 7 000 000 = 7×10^6.

U	10^{-1}	10^{-2}	10^{-3}	10^{-4}
0	0	0	0	2

The number 0.0002 has the 2 in the 10^{-4} column.
It is 2 lots of 10^{-4} or 2×10^{-4}.
So 0.0002 = 2×10^{-4}

► *Exercise* P31.1

1 Work out:
(a) 10^3 (b) 10^5 (c) 10^7 (d) 10^9 (e) 10^{12}

2 Write as a power of ten in index form:
(a) 10 000 (d) 1 million
(b) 100 000 000 (e) a hundred million
(c) 10 (f) a billion

3 Write as an ordinary decimal:
(a) 10^{-1} (b) 10^{-4} (c) 10^0 (d) 10^{-7} (e) 10^{-5}

4 Write as a power of ten in index form:
(a) 0.01 (c) 0.001 (e) 1 millionth
(b) 0.000 001 (d) 1 tenth (f) 1 billionth

5 Write each number in this table in the form: $\boxed{\text{Figure} \times 10^?}$

	10^{12}	10^{11}	10^{10}	10^9	10^8	10^7	10^6	10^5	10^4	10^3	10^2	10^1	U	
(a)								2	0	0	0	0	0	
(b)				7	0	0	0	0	0	0	0	0	0	
(c)			3	0	0	0	0	0	0	0	0	0	0	
(d)									5	0	0	0	0	
(e)					6	0	0	0	0	0	0	0	0	
(f)						9	0	0	0	0	0	0	0	
(g)	4	0	0	0	0	0	0	0	0	0	0	0	0	
(h)		8	0	0	0	0	0	0	0	0	0	0	0	

6 Write each number in this table in the form: $\boxed{\text{Figure} \times 10^?}$

	U	10^{-1}	10^{-2}	10^{-3}	10^{-4}	10^{-5}	10^{-6}	10^{-7}	10^{-8}	10^{-9}
(a)	0	0	7							
(b)	0	0	0	0	0	2				
(c)	0	0	0	9						
(d)	0	6								
(e)	0	0	0	0	3					
(f)	0	0	0	0	0	0	0	4		
(g)	0	0	0	0	0	0	0	0	0	8
(h)	0	0	0	0	0	0	5			

7 Copy and complete these:
(a) 6000 = $6 \times 10^?$
(b) 2 000 000 = $2 \times 10^?$
(c) 70 = $7 \times 10^?$
(d) 900 000 = $9 \times 10^?$
(e) 0.04 = $4 \times 10^?$
(f) 30 000 = $3 \times 10^?$
(g) 0.009 = $9 \times 10^?$
(h) 0.5 = $5 \times 10^?$
(i) 400 000 000 = $4 \times 10^?$
(j) 0.000 08 = $8 \times 10^?$ ◄

Multiplying by powers of 10

To understand and use standard form you need to be able to multiply by powers of 10.

Positive powers of 10
10 is a positive power of 10. It is 10^1. Let's see what happens when you multiply a number by 10 over and over again.
Try this on your calculator to check.

Start with 7.5…							7	5
multiply by 10…						7	5	
and by 10 again…					7	5	0	
and by 10 again…				7	5	0	0	
and by 10 again…			7	5	0	0	0	
and by 10 again.		7	5	0	0	0	0	
and so on…								

10 is *larger than 1*.
So multiplying by 10 makes a number *larger*.
Each time you multiply by 10, the figures move *up 1 place in value*. Any empty spaces *up to the decimal point* are filled with 0s (zeros). This keeps the place value of each figure correct.
The pattern you can see in the last table helps us to multiply by positive powers of 10.

Remember: $10^1 = 10$.
So $\boxed{\times 10^1}$ means *'multiply by 10 once'*.
This moves the figures *up 1 place*.

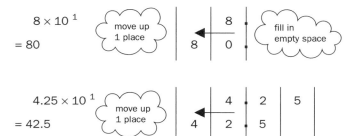

8×10^1
$= 80$

4.25×10^1
$= 42.5$

Remember: $10^2 = 10 \times 10$.
So $\boxed{\times 10^2}$ means *'multiply by 10 twice'*.
This moves the figures *up 2 places*.

9×10^2
$= 900$

Remember: $10^3 = 10 \times 10 \times 10$.
So $\boxed{\times 10^3}$ means *'multiply by 10 three times'*.
This moves the figures *up 3 places*.

8.2×10^3
$= 8200$

And so on …

Negative powers of 10
10^{-1} is a negative power of 10. It is $\frac{1}{10}$.
Let's see what happens when you multiply a number by $\frac{1}{10}$ over and over again.
Remember: *Multiplying by $\frac{1}{10}$ is the same as dividing by 10*.

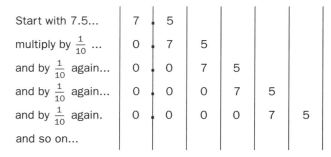

Start with 7.5...	7	5				
multiply by $\frac{1}{10}$ ...	0	7	5			
and by $\frac{1}{10}$ again...	0	0	7	5		
and by $\frac{1}{10}$ again...	0	0	0	7	5	
and by $\frac{1}{10}$ again.	0	0	0	0	7	5
and so on...						

$\frac{1}{10}$ is a proper fraction. It is *smaller than 1*. So multiplying by $\frac{1}{10}$ makes a number *smaller*.

Each time you multiply by $\frac{1}{10}$, the figures move *down 1 place in value*. Any empty 'places' *up to the decimal point* are filled with 0s. This keeps the place value of each figure correct. This pattern helps us to multiply by negative powers of 10.

Remember: $10^{-1} = \frac{1}{10}$

So $\boxed{\times 10^{-1}}$ means *'multiply by $\frac{1}{10}$ once'*.
This moves the figures *down 1 place*.

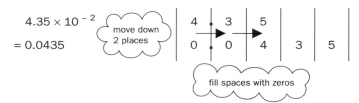

6×10^{-1}
$= 0.6$

4.3×10^{-1}
$= 0.43$

Remember: $10^{-2} = \frac{1}{10^2} = \frac{1}{10 \times 10} = \frac{1}{10} \times \frac{1}{10}$.

So $\boxed{\times 10^{-2}}$ means *'multiply by $\frac{1}{10}$ twice'*.
This moves the figures *down 2 places*.

4.35×10^{-2}
$= 0.0435$

Remember: $10^{-3} = \frac{1}{10^3} = \frac{1}{10 \times 10 \times 10} = \frac{1}{10} \times \frac{1}{10} \times \frac{1}{10}$.

So $\boxed{\times 10^{-3}}$ means *'multiply by $\frac{1}{10}$ three times'*.
This moves the figures *down 3 places*.

7.9×10^{-3}
$= 0.0079$

Multiplying by 10^0
We have multiplied by positive and negative powers of 10.
Now let's see what happens when you multiply a number by 10^0.
Try this on your calculator.

Enter: **7 . 5**
then key in **× 1 0 x^y 0 =** → **7.5**
and again **× 1 0 x^y 0 =** → **7.5**

And so on …
Multiplying by 10^0 does not change the number.
Remember: $10^0 = 1$.
So multiplying by 10^0 is the same as multiplying by 1.

Summary
When you multiply by a power of 10 such as 10^n, use the value of the index n to help you.
The index shows how many places to move the figures and which way.

Positive n in $\boxed{\times 10^n}$:
Move figures 'up n places' in value, i.e. to the left ($\leftarrow$), e.g. $2.7 \times 10^5 = 270\,000$ (move figures up 5 places).

Negative *n* in $\boxed{\times 10^n}$.
Move figures 'down *n* places' in value i.e. to the right (→),
e.g. $8.6 \times 10^{-4} = 0.000\ 86$ (move figures down 4 places)

$\boxed{\times 10^0}$ is the same as $\boxed{\times 1}$.
Multiplying by 1 does not change the size of a number,
e.g. $9.4 \times 10^0 = 9.4 \times 1 = 9.4$.

▶ *Exercise* P31.2

1 Predict the answers to these. Write them down first. Then
check them with your calculator.
Use the power key $\boxed{x^y}$ or $\boxed{y^x}$ to key in the power of 10.

(a) 4×10^3 (f) 5.3×10^0
(b) 1.7×10^2 (g) 6.072×10^1
(c) 9.162×10^5 (h) 1.29×10^4
(d) 8.06×10^7 (i) 4.1×10^6
(e) 4.7×10^3 (j) 6×10^8

Find the place value of the first figure in each answer.
Write them in index form.
What do you notice?

2 Work out the answers to the following. What happens when
you try to check them with your calculator?

(a) 3×10^{-2} (f) 5.017×10^{-1}
(b) 2.8×10^{-3} (g) 7.61×10^0
(c) 1.74×10^{-1} (h) 4.47×10^{-3}
(d) 6.09×10^{-4} (i) 9×10^{-5}
(e) 8.42×10^{-6} (j) 3.016×10^{-4}

Find the place value of the first figure that is not zero (0) in
each answer. Write them in index form.
Comment on what you find.

3 Now do these.
Look carefully at the sign of each index.

(a) 1.6×10^4 (f) 7.063×10^{-4}
(b) 5.07×10^{-2} (g) 4.101×10^0
(c) 2.31×10^{-3} (h) 6.205×10^{-2}
(d) 8.04×10^5 (i) 8.74×10^{-6}
(e) 3.19×10^1 (j) 9.909×10^8

Standard form
→ ordinary number

An answer given in **standard form** can also be written as an
ordinary number.

Here are two examples we gave earlier.

Calculator shorthand:

Standard form: $\boxed{3.5 \times 10^{13}}$ $\boxed{1.8 \times 10^{-11}}$

Ordinary number: $\boxed{35\ 000\ 000\ 000\ 000}$ $\boxed{0.000\ 000\ 000\ 018}$

Standard form has **two parts multiplied together:**

$$\boxed{\text{number part}} \times \boxed{\text{power of 10}}$$

To change standard form to an ordinary number, simply do
the multiplication. This will move the figures in the number
part into the correct places in the ordinary number.
Look at the index of the power of 10 to find out how to move
the figures.

Question

Allan got these answers on his calculator display.

(a) $\boxed{6.73\ ^{12}}$ (b) $\boxed{5.\ ^{-09}}$

Write each in standard form and as an ordinary number.

Answer

(a) Standard form: 6.73×10^{12}
Index 12: move up 12 places.

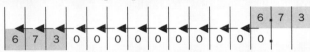

fill empty spaces with zeros

Ordinary form: 6 730 000 000 000

(b) Standard form: 5.1×10^{-9}
Index –9: move down 9 places.

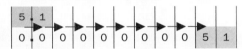

fill empty spaces with zeros

Ordinary form: 0.000 000 0051

Here are some useful **checks** you can use.

- **With a place value table**
Find the *place value* of the first *non–zero digit* in your
'ordinary number'. It must be the *same as the power of 10*
in the standard form.
Look at the examples in the tables below.

	10^{12}	10^{11}	10^{10}	10^9	10^8	10^7	10^6	10^5	10^4	10^3	10^2	10^1	U
$6.73 \times 10^{12} =$	6	7	3	0	0	0	0	0	0	0	0	0	0

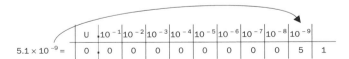

	U	10^{-1}	10^{-2}	10^{-3}	10^{-4}	10^{-5}	10^{-6}	10^{-7}	10^{-8}	10^{-9}
$5.1 \times 10^{-9} =$	0	0	0	0	0	0	0	0	5	1

Remember:
The *first* place value to the *left* of the decimal
point is for Units (U).

- **Checking number size**
You can check that the *size* of the ordinary number makes
sense for the power of 10 in the standard form.

A *positive power of 10*, such as 10^{12}, is *larger than 1*.
Multiplying by a number *larger than 1* makes a number
larger.
For example, 6.73×10^{12} must be larger than 6.73.
So 6 730 000 000 000 makes 'sense' as an 'ordinary
number' for it.

A *negative power of 10*, such as 10^{-9}, is a *decimal
fraction*. It is *smaller than 1*. *Multiplying* by a number
smaller than 1 makes a number *smaller*.
For example, 5.1×10^{-9} must be smaller than 5.1.
So 0.000 000 0051 makes 'sense' as an 'ordinary number'
for it.

10^0 *is equal to 1.*
Multiplying by 1 does not change the size of a number.
For example, 3.4×10^0 must be equal to 3.4×1.
So $3.4 \times 10^0 = 3.4$

- **Counting places**
  Compare the 'old' and 'new' positions of the decimal point
  on the 'ordinary number'. Count the *number of places*
  between them.
  Remember: the decimal point always comes at the *end* of
  the whole number.

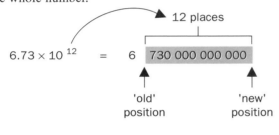

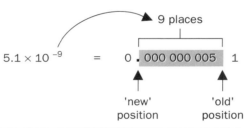

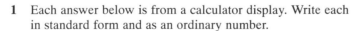

3 Change these to ordinary numbers.
  (a) 2.7×10^2 (c) 1.67×10^5 (e) 7.2×10^6
  (b) 4.93×10^4 (d) 8.34×10^1 (f) 5.04×10^3

4 Write these numbers, given in standard form, as ordinary
  numbers.
  (a) 6.8×10^{-2} (c) 8.76×10^{-1} (e) 1.59×10^{-3}
  (b) 3.6×10^{-4} (d) 4.02×10^{-6} (f) 2.8×10^{-5}

5 Rewrite these as ordinary numbers.
  (a) 3.6×10^2 (c) 8.6×10^{-3} (e) 9.004×10^{-2}
  (b) 7.31×10^{-2} (d) 5.92×10^4 (f) 4.801×10^{-6}

6 Write the numbers in these statements as ordinary numbers.
  (a) The diameter of the Sun is about 1.39×10^6 m.
  (b) The depth of the Reseau du Foillis cave in France is
      about 1.46×10^3 m.
  (c) The wavelength of visible light is about 5×10^{-5} cm.
  (d) The mass of a grain of sand is about 1.1×10^{-7} kg.
  (e) The distance to the nearest star is about 4.6×10^{13} km.
  (f) The mass of an electron is about 9.1×10^{-31} kg.
  (g) The half-life of uranium is about 1.4×10^{17} seconds.
  (h) The mass of the earth is about 5.97×10^{24} kg.

Discussion Exercise

Look at the multiplications in question **2** of Exercise P31.3.
(a) Which have answers less than 1?
    Compare their answers in standard form.
    What do you notice?
(b) Which have answers greater than 1?
    Compare their answers in standard form.
    What do you find?
(c) Comment on your answers to parts (a) and (b).
    What do they tell you about numbers in standard form?
(d) Look at these numbers in standard form.
      5×10^4 7.2×10^{-3} 6.09×10^{12}
      9×10^{-1} 4.3×10^6 2.08×10^{-9}
    Which do you think are less than 1?
    Which do you think are greater than 1?
    Explain your answers.
    Write each number as an ordinary number to check.

Exercise P31.3

1 Each answer below is from a calculator display. Write each
  in standard form and as an ordinary number.

2 Do these multiplications with a calculator.
  Write each answer in standard form and as an ordinary
  number.
  (a) $300 \times 80\,000\,000$
  (b) $560\,000 \times 200\,000$
  (c) $0.000\,04 \times 0.000\,007$
  (d) $0.000\,052 \times 0.000\,003\,9$
  (e) $9\,900\,000 \times 125\,000$
  (f) $0.000\,000\,95 \times 0.000\,000\,73$

Ordinary number
→ standard form

Very large and very small numbers can be awkward to read and
write in full.
For example,

  the mass of the earth is approximately
  5 978 000 000 000 000 000 000 000 kg
  the mass of an electron is approximately
  0.000 000 000 000 000 000 000 000 000 000 911 kg

Standard form is a concise way to give such numbers.
For example,

  in standard form the earth's mass $\approx 5.978 \times 10^{24}$ kg
  an electron's mass $\approx 9.11 \times 10^{-31}$ kg.

Summary

A number in standard form has two parts, multiplied together:

$$\boxed{\text{number part}} \times \boxed{\text{power of 10}}$$

The $\boxed{\text{number part}}$ must be either 1 or between 1 and 10.
This means it has just one digit (not zero) before the decimal point.
The $\boxed{\text{power of 10}}$ is in index form.
The index must be a positive or negative whole number or zero (0).

These numbers are in standard form:

$$3.21 \times 10^7, \quad 6.9 \times 10^0, \quad 5.27 \times 10^{-2}$$

These numbers are *not* in standard form:

$$0.321 \times 10^8, \quad 6.9, \quad 52.7 \times 10^{-3}$$

You will also find standard form described in this way:
A number in the form: $a \times 10^n$
where $1 \le a < 10$ and n is an integer.

Any 'ordinary number' can be given in standard form.
Here are some examples:

$$350 = 3.5 \times 10^2$$
$$17.6 = 1.76 \times 10^1$$
$$9 = 9 \times 10^0$$
$$0.74 = 7.4 \times 10^{-1}$$
$$0.0306 = 3.06 \times 10^{-2}$$

Summary

To change an ordinary number to standard form, take these steps.
- Write down the $\boxed{\text{number part}}$ first.
  This starts with the first non–zero figure in the ordinary number.
  It has a decimal point after this first figure.
- Work out $\boxed{\text{power of 10}}$ next.
  To do this, imagine moving the figures in the $\boxed{\text{number part}}$ into their original places. Count how many places and which way you have to move them. This tells you the $\boxed{\text{power of 10}}$ you need to multiply by to give the figures their full values.
- Write the standard form in the correct way.

$$\boxed{\text{number part}} \times \boxed{\text{power of 10}}$$

Don't forget the × sign and the 10.

Follow these steps in the examples below.
In the standard form of **8**30 000, the *number part* is **8**.3.
Imagine moving the figures in 8.3 into their original places.
This table shows the moves:

up five places

The figures have to *move up 5 places*.

To produce this you have to multiply by 10^5.
This gives the standard form: 8.3×10^5

$$\boxed{830\ 000 = 8.3 \times 10^5}$$

In the standard form of 0.000 7**61**, the *number part is* **7**.61.
Imagine moving the figures in 7.61 into their original places.
Look at the moves in this table:

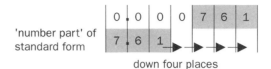

down four places

The figures have to *move down 4 places*.
You have to multiply by 10^{-4} to produce this move.
This gives the standard form: 7.61×10^{-4}

$$\boxed{0.000\ 761 = 7.61 \times 10^{-4}}$$

In the standard form of **4**.05, the *number part* is **4**.05.
Compare these two numbers.
The figures are in the *same* places,
i.e. a *move of 0 places*.
So the power of 10 is 10^0.
This gives the standard form: 4.05×10^0

$$\boxed{4.05 = 4.05 \times 10^0}$$

As usual, it is a good idea to **check your answers.**
Here are some checks you can use.

- **With a place value table**
  Find the *place value* of the *first non–zero digit* in the ordinary number. The *power of 10* in your standard form must have the *same value*.
  Look at the examples in the tables below.

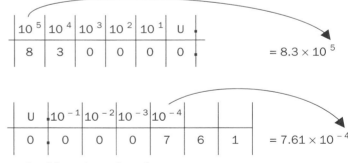

- **Looking at number size**
  To check your *power of 10* makes sense, look at the *size* of the ordinary number.

Ordinary number:		Index:
10 or more	$\longrightarrow$	positive index
proper fraction	$\longrightarrow$	negative index
1 or between 1 and 10	$\longrightarrow$	zero index

  Here are some examples of these checks.

$$\boxed{830\ 000 \ = \ 8.3 \times 10^5}$$

Check: 830 000 is *larger than 10*.
Its *power of 10* must have a *positive index*.
So 8.3×10^5 makes 'sense' for its standard form.

$$0.000\,761 = 7.61 \times 10^{-4}$$

Check: 0.000 761 is a *proper fraction*.
Its *power of 10* must have a *negative index*.
So 7.61×10^{-4} makes 'sense' for its standard form.

$$4.05 = 4.05 \times 10^{0}$$

Check: 4.05 is *between 1 and 10*.
Its *power of 10* must have *zero index*.
So 4.05×10^{0} makes 'sense'.

- **Counting places**
Count the number of places between the 'old' and 'new' positions of the decimal point.

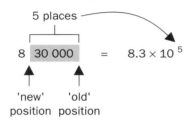

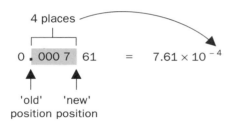

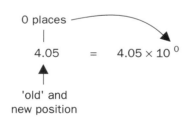

▶ *Exercise* P31.4

1 Write these numbers in standard form.
(a) 150   (e) 825   (i) 500 000
(b) 34 000   (f) 4 600 000   (j) 72 000 000 000
(c) 275 000   (g) 64 500
(d) 16 000 000   (h) 2100

2 Write these numbers in standard form.
(a) 0.03   (e) 0.000 012   (i) 0.000 000 08
(b) 0.0047   (f) 0.0508   (j) 0.000 000 902
(c) 0.0005   (g) 0.000 0036
(d) 0.006 34   (h) 0.000 000 74

3 Write these numbers in standard form.
(a) 63 000   (e) 51 400   (i) 70
(b) 242 000   (f) 0.000 58   (j) 0.000 000 1
(c) 0.024   (g) 47 000 000
(d) 0.003 21   (h) 0.000 001 3

4 Write the numbers in these statements in standard form.
(a) The height of Mount Everest is about 29 000 feet.
(b) The thickness of a 1p coin is about 0.0018 m
(c) The radius of the Moon is about 1 700 000 m.
(d) The distance from the Earth to the Moon is about 400 000 km.
(e) The period of the AC mains is about 0.02 seconds.
(f) The length of the Yangtze river is about 3430 miles.
(g) The diameter of a blood corpuscle is about 0.000 75 cm.

Number × power of 10

Look at these numbers:

$$296 \times 10^{3} \qquad 0.74 \times 10^{9}$$

Each has a $\boxed{\text{number part}} \times \boxed{\text{power of 10}}$.

But they are *not* in standard form.
The '*number parts*', 296 and 0.74, are *not* correct for standard form.
They should be 1 or between 1 and 10. Numbers such as these are easy to write in standard form.
You change the 'number part' into standard form first. Then you multiply the powers of 10, by adding the indices.

Remember:
$$10^{m} \times 10^{n} = 10^{m+n}$$

Here is the working for the numbers given above.
Look carefully at it step-by-step.

$$296 \times 10^{3}$$
$$= \boxed{2.96 \times 10^{2}} \times 10^{3}$$
$$= 2.96 \times 10^{2+3}$$
$$= 2.96 \times 10^{5}$$

$$0.74 \times 10^{9}$$
$$= \boxed{7.4 \times 10^{-1}} \times 10^{9}$$
$$= 7.4 \times 10^{-1+9}$$
$$= 7.4 \times 10^{8}$$

With practice, you may do this working in your head.
You can always write it down step-by-step if you want to.

▶ *Exercise* P31.5

1 Copy and complete the following:
(a) $24.7 \times 10^{4} = 2.47 \times 10^{?} \times 10^{4} =$
(b) $56 \times 10^{7} = 5.6 \times 10^{?} \times 10^{7} =$
(c) $0.72 \times 10^{3} = 7.2 \times 10^{?} \times 10^{3} =$
(d) $632 \times 10^{-4} = 6.32 \times 10^{?} \times 10^{-4} =$
(e) $0.395 \times 10^{-2} = 3.95 \times 10^{?} \times 10^{-2} =$

2 Find the missing index.
(a) $832 \times 10^{5} = 8.23 \times 10^{?}$
(b) $17.8 \times 10^{-5} = 1.78 \times 10^{?}$
(c) $4231 \times 10^{8} = 4.231 \times 10^{?}$
(d) $0.468 \times 10^{-4} = 4.68 \times 10^{?}$
(e) $0.000\,701 \times 10^{6} = 7.01 \times 10^{?}$

3 Write these in standard form
(a) 245×10^3 (e) 0.57×10^9 (i) 0.48×10^{-6}
(b) 56×10^7 (f) 0.027×10^{12} (j) 0.0031×10^{-4}
(c) 87.4×10^6 (g) 14×10^{-7}
(d) 0.7×10^8 (h) 734×10^{-10}

Discussion Exercise

5.9×10^6 is a number in standard form.
Here are some other ways to write the same number.

59×10^5 5900×10^3 $59\,000\,000 \times 10^{-1}$

0.59×10^7 $0.000\,59 \times 10^{10}$

Show that each way gives 5.9×10^6.
Compare how these numbers are written.
How are they the same?
How are they different?
Discuss.
Each number is written in this form:

number $\times$ power of 10

Find different ways to write 5.9×10^6 in this form.
Describe how you found each new way.
Compare your ideas with others in your group.
These numbers are all in standard form.

5×10^7 2.6×10^4 3.97×10^{11}

6×10^{-3} 7.2×10^{-1} 4.05×10^{-6}

Find at least three different ways to write each number in the form:

number $\times$ power of 10

Compare answers within your group. Discuss how to work out each new form of a number.
Decide on the 'key steps' you have to take.
Test your 'steps' on some other numbers.

Exercise P31.6

Find the missing number in each of these.
1 $2.6 \times 10^5 = ? \times 10^3$ **6** $8.3 \times 10^4 = ? \times 10^3$
2 $7.35 \times 10^7 = ? \times 10^4$ **7** $4.7 \times 10^3 = ? \times 10^1$
3 $6.0 \times 10^8 = ? \times 10^6$ **8** $2.76 \times 10^{-2} = ? \times 10^{-3}$
4 $1.93 \times 10^6 = ? \times 10^2$ **9** $5.01 \times 10^{-6} = ? \times 10^{-4}$
5 $6.04 \times 10^{10} = ? \times 10^7$ **10** $1.304 \times 10^{-8} = ? \times 10^{-5}$

Comparing numbers

Standard form gives a number in two simple parts.

number part $\times$ power of 10

This makes it easy to compare numbers.
You can *look at each part in turn*.

The $\boxed{\text{power of 10}}$ tells us the *highest place value* of the number.

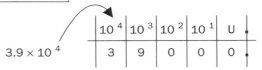

3.9×10^4

10^4	10^3	10^2	10^1	U
3	9	0	0	0

This gives us a good idea of the 'size' of the number.
    The *bigger the power of 10*, the *bigger the number*.
    The *smaller the power of 10*, the *smaller the number*.
    Numbers with the *same power of 10* are about the *same size*.

Look at these numbers, for example.
    1×10^7 5×10^7 8×10^7 3×10^7 4×10^7
They all have the *same power of 10*. So they are 'about the *same size*'.
The *number parts* show how they differ. Putting these *number parts in order*, puts the *numbers in order*.
You can see this when we write them in full.

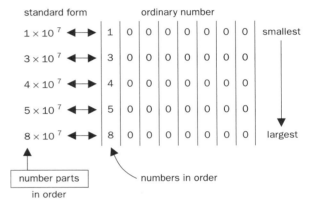

Comparing the *number parts* is easy. They all start with a 'units' figure. So you put these in order first.
Then you order the *decimal places* in turn.

Memo
Decimals in order
N10 p48

Compare these numbers, for example.
8.012×10^3 1.2×10^3 8.91×10^3
9.6×10^3 8.5×10^3 4.09×10^3

The smallest number is 1.2×10^3.
The next number is 4.09×10^3.
Three numbers starting **8.** come next.
In order of size, they are: 8.012×10^3
                  8.5×10^3
                  8.91×10^3
The largest number is 9.6×10^3.
You can see this when they are given in full.

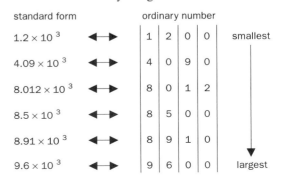

► *Exercise* P31.7

1 Which number is larger in each pair?

(a) 7×10^4, 2×10^4 (f) 5.34×10^8, 5.321×10^8

(b) 8×10^{-2}, 9×10^{-2} (g) 1.812×10^{-4}, 1.817×10^{-4}

(c) 3.1×10^7, 8.5×10^7 (h) 7.4×10^5, 7.39×10^5

(d) 2.9×10^{-1}, 2.0×10^{-1} (i) 4.009×10^1, 4.031×10^1

(e) 6.05×10^{-3}, 6.02×10^{-3} (j) 9.037×10^2, 8.096×10^2

2 Put each list of numbers in order of size, smallest first.

(a) 5.3×10^{-3}	(b) 3.12×10^5	(c) 1.092×10^6
4.7×10^{-3}	3.25×10^5	3.298×10^6
4.2×10^{-3}	3.28×10^5	3.157×10^6
5.2×10^{-3}	3.53×10^5	1.503×10^6
2.1×10^{-3}	3.19×10^5	1.521×10^6

Numbers in standard form with *different powers of ten* are obviously different sizes.
Look at these numbers, for example.

$$3.5 \times 10^4 \qquad 3.5 \times 10^2$$
$$3.5 \times 10^5 \qquad 3.5 \times 10^3 \qquad 3.5 \times 10^7$$

The *number part* is the *same* in each.
But the *powers of 10* are *different*.
So the numbers must be different sizes.
Let's see how they compare in a place value table.

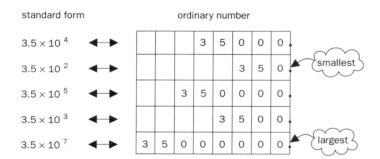

The smallest number, 350, has the smallest power of 10, i.e. 10^2.
The largest number, 35 000 000, has the largest power of 10, i.e. 10^7.
Putting the powers of 10 in order of size, puts the numbers in order.

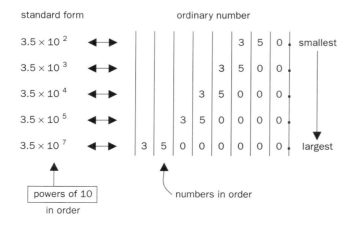

To put numbers in order, you may have to compare positive and negative powers.
Take care with the signs.
Think of their order on a number line if it helps.

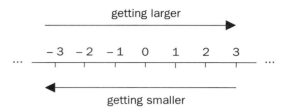

Question

Each length in this list is given in metres and in another unit.

| $2 \, mm = 2 \times 10^{-3} \, m$ |
| $5 \, cm = 5 \times 10^{-2} \, m$ |
| $8 \, \mu m = 8 \times 10^{-6} \, m$ |
| $4 \, km = 4 \times 10^3 \, m$ |
| $7 \, nm = 7 \times 10^{-9} \, m$ |
| $3 \, hm = 3 \times 10^1 \, m$ |

Put them in order of size, largest first.

Answer

Put powers of 10 in order, largest first.

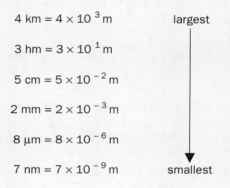

$4 \, km = 4 \times 10^3 \, m$	largest
$3 \, hm = 3 \times 10^1 \, m$	
$5 \, cm = 5 \times 10^{-2} \, m$	
$2 \, mm = 2 \times 10^{-3} \, m$	
$8 \, \mu m = 8 \times 10^{-6} \, m$	
$7 \, nm = 7 \times 10^{-9} \, m$	smallest

Summary

To compare numbers in standard form, take these steps.

- Compare their ⬚ powers of 10 ⬚ first.
  Put them in order:
  smallest power ↔ smallest number
  largest power ↔ largest number
- For numbers with the same ⬚ power of 10 ⬚, put the ⬚ number parts ⬚ in order of size.

Question

Put these numbers in order of size, largest first.

| 3.21×10^5 | 8.9×10^{-3} | 9.65×10^4 |
| 6.3×10^9 | 3.5×10^4 | 7.62×10^{-1} |

Answer

The order is:

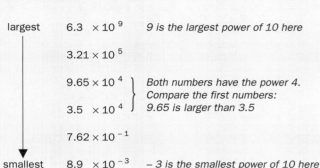

largest	6.3×10^9	*9 is the largest power of 10 here*
	3.21×10^5	
	9.65×10^4	*Both numbers have the power 4.*
	3.5×10^4	*Compare the first numbers:* *9.65 is larger than 3.5*
	7.62×10^{-1}	
smallest	8.9×10^{-3}	*−3 is the smallest power of 10 here*

► *Exercise* **P31.8**

1 Which is the larger number in each pair?
 (a) 3×10^5 or 3×10^9
 (b) 2.7×10^{-8} or 2.7×10^{-2}
 (c) 7×10^{-11} or 8×10^6
 (d) 1.23×10^9 or 2.1×10^{-13}
 (e) 5.2×10^3 or 4.9×10^7
 (f) 3.051×10^{-6} or 9.352×10^{-5}
 (g) 6.7×10^{-21} or 8×10^{19}
 (h) 7.000×10^{-12} or 1.999×10^{-8}

2 Put each list in order of size, smallest first.
 (a) 7×10^1 (b) 2.9×10^{-14} (c) 4.31×10^{21}
   7×10^8 5.8×10^{-12} 8.05×10^{19}
   7×10^{11} 8.4×10^{-7} 8.75×10^{-9}
   7×10^{20} 4.7×10^{-10} 6.52×10^{-14}
   7×10^{15} 9.5×10^{-6} 5.29×10^{-23}

Write the numbers in place value tables to check.

3 (a) Which of these stars is furthest from Earth?
 (b) Which star is nearest to Earth?
 (c) Rewrite this list of stars using distance from the Earth.
   Start with the nearest.

Brightest stars	Distance from Earth
Sirius	8.18×10^{13} km
Canopus	1.89×10^{15} km
α Centauri	4.14×10^{13} km
Arcturus	3.41×10^{14} km
Vega	2.46×10^{14} km
Capella	3.97×10^{14} km

4 Which is the larger number in each pair?
 (a) 3×10^5 or 700 (e) 0.0058 or 6.9×10^{-2}
 (b) 8500 or 8.3×10^{-4} (f) 3.9×10^{-5} or $0.000\,17$
 (c) 61×10^3 or $61\,000$ (g) $0.000\,86$ or 1.2×10^{-3}
 (d) $150\,000\,000$ or 9.2×10^7 (h) 2.7×10^{-6} or $0.000\,000\,72$

5 (a) Which of these countries has the smallest area?
 (b) Which has the largest area?
 (c) Rewrite this list of countries in order of land area.
   Start with the smallest.

Country	Area (km^2)
Greenland	2.18×10^6
Borneo	$726\,000$
China	1.04×10^9
USA	$239\,000\,000$
India	7.62×10^8
New Guinea	$777\,000$
Indonesia	$170\,000\,000$
Sumatra	4.74×10^5

Calculating with numbers in standard form

Numbers in standard form can be used in calculations.
The working can be done with and without a calculator.

Without a calculator

Multiplication and division

To multiply or divide numbers in standard form without a calculator, you use the **laws of indices**.

Memo
Laws of indices
p240

You take these steps.
● Rearrange the working first.
 Each number in standard form has a 'number part' and a 'power of 10'.
 Put the 'number parts' together.
 Put the 'powers of 10' together.
● Do the working (× or ÷) with the 'number parts', then with the powers of 10.
 Remember:
 To multiply powers of 10, add the indices. $\boxed{10^m \times 10^n = 10^{m+n}}$
 To divide powers of 10, subtract the indices. $\boxed{10^m \div 10^n = 10^{m-n}}$
 10 means 10^1.
● Write the answer in the form you want.
 Give it either in standard form or as an ordinary number.
● Round the answer to a sensible number of significant figures if you need to.

All the working, step-by-step, is shown in the following example.
With practice you may be able to do some steps in your head.
It is a good idea, however, to write down all the steps at first.

Question

Do these calculations without a calculator.
Give the answers in standard form.
(a) $(6.1 \times 10^8) \times (3.0 \times 10^4)$
(b) $(3.2 \times 10^6) \div (4.0 \times 10^2)$

Answer

(a)
$$(6.1 \times 10^8) \times (3.0 \times 10^4)$$

- *Rearrange working* $= 6.1 \times \boxed{10^8} \times \boxed{3.0} \times 10^4$

  Group 'number parts' $= 6.1 \times 3.0 \times 10^8 \times 10^4$
  and group powers of 10. $= (6.1 \times 3.0) \times (10^8 \times 10^4)$

- *Multiply number parts* $=\quad 18.3 \quad \times \quad 10^{8+4}$
  Multiply powers of 10
  (Use the laws of indices) $=\quad 18.3 \quad \times \quad 10^{12}$

- *Put the answer into* $= (1.83 \times 10^1) \times \quad 10^{12}$
  standard form $= 1.83 \times 10^{1+12}$

    $= 1.83 \times 10^{13}$

(b)
$$(3.2 \times 10^6) \div (4.0 \times 10^2)$$

- *Write division* $= \dfrac{3.2 \times 10^6}{4.0 \times 10^2}$
  as a fraction

- *Group number parts* $= \dfrac{3.2}{4.0} \times \dfrac{10^6}{10^2}$
  and group powers of 10.

- *Do 'number' division.* $=\quad 0.8 \quad \times \quad 10^{6-2}$
  Do power of 10 division
  (Use laws of indices) $=\quad 0.8 \quad \times \quad 10^4$

- *Put the answer into* $= (8 \times 10^{-1}) \times 10^4$
  standard form $= 8 \times 10^{-1+4}$
    $= 8 \times 10^3.$

Always take extra care when the powers of 10 have *negative* indices. Make sure that you add or subtract these indices correctly. Think carefully about the size of the numbers you are using.

Memo

Directed numbers
N7 p31

Question

Work out the following without a calculator. Give the answers in standard form.

(a) $\dfrac{6 \times 10^{-8}}{4 \times 10}$

(b) $(3 \times 10^{-5}) \times (7 \times 10^9)$

Answer

(a)
$$\dfrac{6 \times 10^{-8}}{4 \times 10^1}$$

- *Rearrange working* $= \dfrac{6}{4} \times \dfrac{10^{-8}}{10^1}$

- *Do 'number' division* $= 1.5 \times 10^{-8-1}$
  Do 'power of 10 division'
  (Use laws of indices) $= 1.5 \times 10^{-9}.$

(b)
$$(3 \times 10^{-5}) \times (7 \times 10^9)$$

- *Rearrange working* $= 3 \times \boxed{10^{-5}} \times \boxed{7} \times 10^9$

  Group 'number parts' $= 3 \times 7 \times 10^{-5} \times 10^9$
  and group powers of 10 $= (3 \times 7) \times (10^{-5} \times 10^9)$

- *Multiply 'numbers'.* $= 21 \times 10^{-5+9}$
  Multiply powers of 10
  (Use the laws of indices) $= 21 \times 10^4$

- *Put the answer into* $= (2.1 \times 10) \times 10^4$
  standard form $= 2.1 \times 10^{1+4}$
    $= 2.1 \times 10^5.$

▶ *Exercise* P31.9

Calculate the following without using a calculator. Give your answers in standard form.

1 (a) $(3 \times 10^2) \times (3 \times 10^3)$ (d) $(1.9 \times 10^2) \times (2 \times 10^3)$
  (b) $(6 \times 10^4) \div (2 \times 10^2)$ (e) $(4.7 \times 10^5) \times (3.1 \times 10^1)$
  (c) $(2.5 \times 10^4) \div (5 \times 10^3)$ (f) $(5.6 \times 10^5) \div (2 \times 10^2)$

2 (a) $(4 \times 10^{-2}) \times (2 \times 10^{-1})$ (d) $(1.0 \times 10^{-2}) \times (2.4 \times 10^{-3})$
  (b) $(8 \times 10^{-3}) \div (4 \times 10^{-4})$ (e) $(6.1 \times 10^{-4}) \times (5 \times 10^{-2})$
  (c) $(6.2 \times 10^{-1}) \div (3.1 \times 10^{-2})$ (f) $(7.5 \times 10^{-3}) \div (2.5 \times 10^{-6})$

3 (a) $(4.7 \times 10^2) \times (2 \times 10^{-1})$ (e) $(9.3 \times 10^5) \div (3.1 \times 10^4)$
  (b) $(7.6 \times 10^4) \div (3.8 \times 10^2)$ (f) $(8.1 \times 10^{-4}) \times (3.0 \times 10^2)$
  (c) $(2.1 \times 10^{-1}) \times (3.0 \times 10^4)$ (g) $(4 \times 10^{-3}) \times (1.7 \times 10^{-2})$
  (d) $(9 \times 10^3) \div (2 \times 10^{-2})$ (h) $(1.2 \times 10^{-3}) \div (4.0 \times 10^1)$

Addition and subtraction

Numbers in standard form can be added or subtracted without a calculator.
The method you use depends on whether the numbers have the same or different powers of 10.

Same power of 10
Numbers with the same power of 10 in standard form are the same 'type'.

$\boxed{\blacksquare} \times 10^1$	is always a number of 'tens' … $10^1 = 10$
$\boxed{\blacksquare} \times 10^2$	is always a number of 'hundreds' … $10^2 = 100$
$\boxed{\blacksquare} \times 10^3$	is always a number of 'thousands' … $10^3 = 1000$ and so on …

This means they are easy to add or subtract. Look at these numbers, for example.

$$5 \times 10^6 \qquad 3 \times 10^6$$

10^6 is 1 000 000 or 1 million.
So both 5×10^6 and 3×10^6 are numbers of millions.
Thinking of them 'in words' helps you to add and subtract them.

Addition: $\boxed{5 \times 10^6} + \boxed{3 \times 10^6}$

    means   5 million +   3 million
The answer is $(5 + 3)$ million
        $= 8$ million or 8×10^6

Subtraction: $\boxed{5 \times 10^6} - \boxed{3 \times 10^6}$

    means   5 million $-$ 3 million
The answer is $(5 - 3)$ million
        $= 2$ million or 2×10^6

To do this working you do not need to work out what 'type' of number they are. You can think of them simply as several 'lots of the same thing'.
You can write down the working and think it through like this.

    Written working: Thinking:

$$\begin{array}{r} 5 \times 10^6 \\ + \, 3 \times 10^6 \\ \hline 8 \times 10^6 \end{array}$$

                5 'lots of 10^6'
                add 3 'lots of 10^6'
                gives 8 'lots of 10^6'

    Written working: Thinking:

$$\begin{array}{r} 5 \times 10^6 \\ - \, 3 \times 10^6 \\ \hline 2 \times 10^6 \end{array}$$

                5 'lots of 10^6'
                take away 3 'lots of 10^6'
                leaves 2 'lots of 10^6'

Sometimes the result is not in standard form.
You can change it into standard form if you need to.

Question

If $x = 7.2 \times 10^{-3}$ and $y = 6.4 \times 10^{-3}$, find the value of:
(a) $x + y$ (b) $x - y$
Give your answers in standard form.

Answer

(a)   *Addition:*   *Thinking:*

$$\begin{array}{r} 7.2 \times 10^{-3} \\ + \, 6.4 \times 10^{-3} \\ \hline 13.6 \times 10^{-3} \end{array}$$

            7.2 'lots of 10^{-3}'
          add   6.4 'lots of 10^{-3}'
         gives 13.6 'lots of 10^{-3}'

     Change to standard form:
$$13.6 \times 10^{-3} = (1.36 \times 10^1) \times 10^{-3}$$
$$= 1.36 \times 10^{1 + -3}$$
$$= 1.36 \times 10^{-2}$$

(b)   *Subtraction:*   *Thinking:*

$$\begin{array}{r} 7.2 \times 10^{-3} \\ - \, 6.4 \times 10^{-3} \\ \hline 0.8 \times 10^{-3} \end{array}$$

            7.2 'lots of 10^{-3}'
       take away 6.4 'lots of 10^{-3}'
         leaves 0.8 'lots of 10^{-3}'

     Change to standard form:
$$0.8 \times 10^{-3} = (8 \times 10^{-1}) \times 10^{-3}$$
$$= 8 \times 10^{-1 + -3}$$
$$= 8 \times 10^{-4}$$

Summary

To add or subtract numbers **with the same power of 10**, you take these steps.
- Add or subtract the 'number parts'
- Multiply by the given power of 10.

Think it through in words to help you. Put the answer into standard form if you need to.

Different powers of 10.
To add or subtract numbers with different powers of 10, it is often easier if you *change them into 'ordinary numbers'* first.
Then you can do the working as usual.
Remember:
Keep the figures in the correct columns in your working.
Put in extra 'zeros' if you need to.

Question

Calculate: (a) $(7 \times 10^5) + (4 \times 10^3)$
            (b) $(4.3 \times 10^{-1}) - (9.2 \times 10^{-3})$
Give the answers in standard form.

Answer

(a) *Change to ordinary* $7 \times 10^5 \rightarrow$ 700 000
    form and add: $4 \times 10^3 \rightarrow +$ 4 000
                                $\overline{704\ 000}$

    Change to
    standard form: $704\ 000 = 7.04 \times 10^5$

(b) *Change to ordinary* $4.3 \times 10^{-1} \rightarrow$ 0.4300
    form and subtract: $9.2 \times 10^{-3} \rightarrow -$ 0.0092
                                  $\overline{0.4208}$

Add extra zeros to do the working

    Change to
    standard form: $0.4208 = 4.208 \times 10^{-1}$

You can also add or subtract numbers with different powers of 10 if you rewrite them with the *same power of 10* first. Work in the *smallest* power of 10.
This usually makes the working easier to do.
Remember: All the numbers will *not* be in standard form.
         Change the answer into standard form if you
         need to.

Question

Find, in standard form, the value of:
(a) $(6.7 \times 10^{18}) + (4.1 \times 10^{20})$
(b) $(5.4 \times 10^{-8}) - (1.6 \times 10^{-9})$.

Answer

(a) The powers of 10 in the numbers are 10^{18} and 10^{20}.
10^{18} is smaller than 10^{20}
So rewrite 4.1×10^{20} using 10^{18}.

$4.1 \times 10^{20} = 4.1 \times 10^{2+18}$
$\qquad\qquad = 4.1 \times 10^2 \times 10^{18}$
$\qquad\qquad = 410 \times 10^{18}$

Work out addition:
$\qquad 6.7 \times 10^{18} \rightarrow \qquad 6.7 \times 10^{18}$
$\qquad 4.1 \times 10^{20} \rightarrow + 410 \quad \times 10^{18}$
$\qquad\qquad\qquad\qquad\overline{\quad 416.7 \times 10^{18}}$

Change to standard form:
$\qquad 416.7 \times 10^{18} = (4.167 \times 10^2) \times 10^{18}$
$\qquad\qquad\qquad\quad = 4.167 \times 10^{2+18}$
$\qquad\qquad\qquad\quad = 4.167 \times 10^{20}$

(b) The powers of 10 in the numbers are 10^{-8} and 10^{-9}.
10^{-9} is smaller than 10^{-8}
So rewrite 5.4×10^{-8} using 10^{-9}.

$5.4 \times 10^{-8} = 5.4 \times 10^{1+-9}$
$\qquad\qquad = 5.4 \times 10^1 \times 10^{-9}$
$\qquad\qquad = 54 \times 10^{-9}$

Work out subtraction:
$\qquad 5.4 \times 10^{-8} \rightarrow \quad 54 \quad \times 10^{-9}$
$\qquad 1.6 \times 10^{-9} \rightarrow - 1.6 \times 10^{-9}$
$\qquad\qquad\qquad\qquad\overline{\quad 52.4 \times 10^{-9}}$

Change to standard form:
$\qquad 52.4 \times 10^{-9} = (5.24 \times 10^1) \times 10^{-9}$
$\qquad\qquad\qquad\quad = 5.24 \times 10^{1+-9}$
$\qquad\qquad\qquad\quad = 5.24 \times 10^{-8}$

▶ *Exercise* P31.10

Calculate the following without using a calculator. Give your answers in standard form.

1. (a) $2 \times 10^2 + 3 \times 10^2$
   (b) $5 \times 10^3 - 2 \times 10^3$
   (c) $5 \times 10^{-2} + 8 \times 10^{-2}$
   (d) $8 \times 10^{-3} - 6 \times 10^{-3}$
   (e) $7 \times 10^{-4} + 4.5 \times 10^{-4}$
   (f) $9.6 \times 10^8 - 5.9 \times 10^8$

2. (a) $3 \times 10^2 + 2 \times 10^3$
   (b) $9 \times 10^5 - 4 \times 10^2$
   (c) $7.2 \times 10^3 - 3.4 \times 10$
   (d) $5.3 \times 10^{-2} + 2.1 \times 10^{-3}$
   (e) $9.0 \times 10^4 - 4.7 \times 10^2$
   (f) $6.8 \times 10^{-1} + 1.5 \times 10^{-4}$

3. (a) $6 \times 10^2 + 3 \times 10^2$
   (b) $8 \times 10^3 - 4 \times 10$
   (c) $5.7 \times 10^4 + 6.0 \times 10^4$
   (d) $5.3 \times 10^{-3} + 6.8 \times 10^{-3}$
   (e) $1.9 \times 10^{-1} - 9.1 \times 10^{-2}$
   (f) $1.4 \times 10^4 - 2.0 \times 10^{-1}$
   (g) $3.4 \times 10^4 + 7.2 \times 10^3$
   (h) $2.9 \times 10^2 - 1.7 \times 10^{-2}$

With a calculator

Numbers in standard form can also be keyed into your calculator.

To enter a number in standard form, you can use an **exponent key.**
It is usually marked **EXP** or **EE** or **E**

Find the exponent key on your calculator. Use it whenever we use **EXP** in a key code.
To key in the standard form of a number, you take these steps.
- Key in the '*number part*' first.
- Press the *exponent key* next.
- Then key in the *index* of the power of 10.

To enter 2.7×10^5, for example, you key in

2 . 7 EXP 5

Watch the display carefully to see what it shows.

2 . 7 $\rightarrow$ [2.7]
then **EXP** $\rightarrow$ [2.7 00]
then **5** $\rightarrow$ [2.7 05]

To enter a *negative index* for the power of 10, you use the change sign key **+/-**.
To enter 3.1×10^{-2}, for example, you key in

3 . 1 EXP 2 +/-

The display shows:

[3.1] $\rightarrow$ [3.1 00] $\rightarrow$ [3.1 02] $\rightarrow$ [3.1 -02]

When doing **calculations with a calculator,** you can enter numbers in standard form. You simply key in the numbers, operations, ... in the *correct order* for the working.
Remember: Press **=** at the end if you need to.
Estimate the answer to check as usual.

To work out $\dfrac{5.225 \times 10^7}{1.9 \times 10^{-4}}$, for example, we key in ...

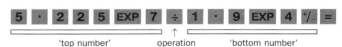

5 . 2 2 5 EXP 7 ÷ 1 . 9 EXP 4 +/- =
   '*top number*'   *operation*   '*bottom number*'

The display shows: [2.75 11]
In standard form, this is 2.75×10^{11}.
As an 'ordinary number', it is 275 000 000 000.
Estimate to check:

$\dfrac{5.225 \times 10^7}{1.9 \times 10^{-4}} \approx \dfrac{5 \times 10^7}{2 \times 10^{-4}} = \dfrac{5}{2} \times \dfrac{10^7}{10^{-4}}$

$\qquad\qquad\qquad\qquad = 2.5 \times 10^{7-(-4)}$
$\qquad\qquad\qquad\qquad = 2.5 \times 10^{11}$

(About the same size as 2.75×10^{11})

The answer to a calculation may be displayed in 'calculator standard form' or as an ordinary number.
Make sure you give it in the form you want.
Round it to a sensible number of significant figures if necessary.

Question

Use a calculator to work out:

$(6.08 \times 10^{-2}) \times (7.5 \times 10^8)$

Write down the key sequence you used. Give your answer
(a) as shown on the calculator display,
(b) in standard form, correct to 2 significant figures.

Answer

Key sequence:

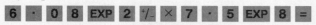

(a) *The display shows:* `45600000.`

(b) *In standard form this is* 4.56×10^7
$= 4.6 \times 10^7$ (to 2 sf)

Exercise P31.11

Use a calculator to find answers to questions **1–3**.
Write down the key sequences you use for each. Give your answer as shown on the calculator display and in standard form. Round answers sensibly.
Estimate the answer to each question without using a calculator. This acts as a check.

1
(a) $7.4 \times 10^3 + 1.5 \times 10^2$
(b) $3.7 \times 10^4 - 6.8 \times 10^3$
(c) $5.02 \times 10^2 + 4.3 \times 10^1$
(d) $7.28 \times 10^6 - 4.81 \times 10^4$
(e) $3.69 \times 10^{-2} + 5.04 \times 10^2$
(f) $9.67 \times 10^{-3} - 1.08 \times 10^{-4}$

2
(a) $(8.4 \times 10^5) \times (2.07 \times 10^2)$
(b) $(3.08 \times 10^{-4}) \div (1.5 \times 10^2)$
(c) $(4.6 \times 10^4) \div (3.68 \times 10^3)$
(d) $(7.36 \times 10^{-3}) \times (3.3 \times 10^5)$
(e) $(1.67 \times 10^{-4}) \times (2.4 \times 10^4)$
(f) $(5.7 \times 10^{-7}) \div (2.08 \times 10^{-5})$

3
(a) $7.3 \times 10^2 + 2.7 \times 10^3$
(b) $(8.9 \times 10^{-1}) \times (1.7 \times 10^3)$
(c) $(9.07 \times 10^4) \div (8.2 \times 10^{-1})$
(d) $1.81 \times 10^1 - 7.3 \times 10^{-3}$
(e) $4.731 \times 10^0 + 5.64 \times 10^2$
(f) $(6.71 \times 10^{-2}) \div (2.34 \times 10^{-6})$
(g) $9.47 \times 10^2 - 3.35 \times 10^{-1}$
(h) $(4.72 \times 10^{-4}) \times (1.63 \times 10^3)$

Do the questions in Exercise P31.9 on p518 and Exercise P31.10 on p520 with a calculator.
Compare your answers with those you found without a calculator.

Too many digits

To enter ordinary numbers into a calculator, you usually key in each digit.
To enter 517 000, for example, you key in

The display shows `517000.`

Some very large and very small numbers cannot be entered in this way.
See what happens when you try to key in these numbers:

25 370 000 000 000   `2537000000.`

0.000 000 000 0426   `0.000000000`

Each number has *too many digits* to fit into the display.
You cannot key them all in directly.
You can, however, key in these numbers in standard form.

To enter 25 370 000 000 000,
you change it to standard form: 2.537×10^{13}

then key it in:

To enter 0.000 000 000 0426,
you change it to standard form: 4.26×10^{-11}

then key it in: **4** **.** **2** **6** **EXP** **1** **1** **⁺/₋**

This means you can do *calculations* with such numbers on a calculator.
To work out:
25 370 000 000 000 × 0.000 000 000 0426

you key in:

2 **.** **5** **3** **7** **EXP** **1** **3** **×**

4 **.** **2** **6** **EXP** **1** **1** **⁺/₋** **=**

The display shows: `1080.762`

It is sensible to round this to 3 significant figures, (because there are just 3 sf in one of the numbers multiplied).
1080.762 = 1080 (to 3 sf)
This gives:
25 370 000 000 000 × 0.000 000 000 0426 = 1080 (to 3 sf)

Summary

A scientific calculator works with numbers in 'ordinary form' and in standard form. You can key in numbers in both forms in the same calculation.
Enter numbers by keying in the digits if you can.
If there are too many digits to key in, change the number to standard form. Then key in the standard form.

Question

Use your calculator to work out:
3 749 000 000 000 × 0.000 516.

Write down the key sequence you used and the answer given on the display. Give your answer correct to 3 significant figures:
(a) as an ordinary number   (b) in standard form.

Answer

3 749 000 000 000 = 3.749×10^{12}
Key sequence:

3 **.** **7** **4** **9** **EXP** **1** **2** **×**

First number in standard form

. **0** **0** **0** **5** **1** **6** **=**

Second number in ordinary form

Display shows: `1934484000.`

(a) 1 930 000 000 (to 3 sf)   (b) 1.93×10^9 (to 3 sf)

Exercise P31.12

1 How many digits can your calculator display?
2 Look at the numbers in the calculations below. Decide how you have to key in each number into your calculator.
Write 'ordinary form' or 'standard form' for each number.
Give the standard forms you would use.
(a) 36 000 000 000 × 241 000
(b) 2 300 000 000 000 × 41 600 000 000
(c) 0.000 673 × 0.000 000 000 017
(d) 364 000 000 000 ÷ 126 000 000

(e) 0.000 000 000 074 ÷ 0.000 000 27
(f) 0.000 000 005 48 ÷ 0.000 000 000 244
(g) 872 400 000 000 ÷ 9 836 000
(h) 0.000 000 000 218 × 0.000 000 043
(i) 83 000 000 000 000 × 571 300 000 000
(j) 0.000 000 769 ÷ 0.000 000 188

3 Use your calculator to do the calculations in question **2**.
Round your answers to a suitable degree of accuracy.

 Investigation 🖩

Scientific mode on a calculator

Many scientific calculators have a special **scientific mode.**
In this mode the calculator works in standard form.
It also displays all answers in 'calculator' standard form.

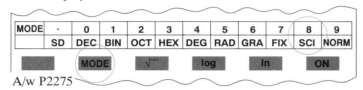

A/w P2275

Find out whether your calculator has this facility.
If it does, investigate how to use it. Write a short report on what
you discover.
Give examples of key sequences for calculations you can do in
this scientific mode.
Describe the advantages/disadvantages of having this facility on
your calculator. ◉

Problem solving

To solve some problems you use numbers in standard form.
As usual try to be systematic.
Remember the key steps to take:

> • Think • Plan • Calculate • Answer • Check

If a problem seems difficult, try this strategy.
- Imagine the same problem with easy numbers.
- Plan how to solve it with these easy numbers.
- Take the same steps with the 'harder' numbers.

A question may ask you to do the working without a calculator.
Make sure you show your method clearly.
A correct answer without the working will get no marks.
You can always *check* your answer with your calculator.

Question

The Earth is 1.49×10^8 km from the Sun. Uranus is
2.87×10^9 km from the Sun.
Find, without using a calculator, the distance between the
Earth and Uranus when all three bodies are in line, with the
Earth and Uranus on
(a) opposite sides of the Sun
(b) the same side of the Sun.
Give your answers in standard form.

Answer

(a)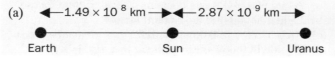

Change powers of ten to 10^8.
Sun to Uranus: $2.87 \times 10^9 = 28.7 \times 10^8$

From Earth to Sun:	1.49×10^8
From Sun to Uranus:	$28.7\ \times 10^8$
Total distance:	$\overline{30.19 \times 10^8}$

Change to standard form:
$$= 3.019 \times 10^1 \times 10^8$$
$$= 3.019 \times 10^9$$

Total distance is approximately 3.02×10^9 km (to 3 sf)

(b)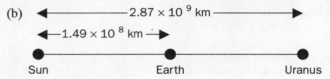

From Sun to Uranus:	$28.7\ \times 10^8$ *(see part (a))*
From Earth to Uranus:	1.49×10^8
Distance apart:	$\overline{27.21 \times 10^8}$

Change to standard form:
$$= 2.721 \times 10^1 \times 10^8$$
$$= 2.721 \times 10^9$$

Distance apart is approximately 2.72×10^9 km (to 3 sf)

When a question does not tell you the method to use, you can
do the working with a calculator.
You can *estimate* the answer, without using a calculator, as a
check.

Question

In astronomy very large distances are measured in light
years. A light year is the distance travelled by light in 1 year
($365\frac{1}{4}$ days).
(a) The speed of light is approximately 2.998×10^8 metres
per second. Work out the approximate length of a light
year in metres (to 4 sf). Give your answer in standard
form.
(b) The Earth is approximately 1.496×10^{11} metres from the
Sun. How many light years is this? Use your
approximate length of a light year to work it out to 4 sf.
Give your answer as an ordinary number.

Answer

(a) Distance travelled by light: 🖩
in 1 second $\approx 2.998 \times 10^8$ m
in 60 seconds $\approx 2.998 \times 10^8 \times 60$ m
in 60 minutes $\approx 2.998 \times 10^8 \times 60 \times 60$ m
in 24 hours $\approx 2.998 \times 10^8 \times 60 \times 60 \times 24$ m
in $365\frac{1}{4}$ days $\approx 2.998 \times 10^8 \times 60 \times 60 \times 24 \times 365.25$ m
So 1 light year $\approx 9.461 \times 10^{15}$ m (to 4 sf)

`9.4609684` ¹⁵

(b) Distance from Earth to Sun:
$\approx 1.496 \times 10^{11}$ metres
$\approx (1.496 \times 10^{11}) \div (9.461 \times 10^{15})$ light years
$\approx 1.581 \times 10^{-5}$ light years (to 4 sf)
$\approx 0.000\ 015\ 81$ light years (to 4 sf)

`1.5812334` ⁻⁰⁵

Exercise P31.13

Estimate answers to the questions in this exercise without using a calculator. Use a calculator to work out the actual answers.

1 The mass of a house mouse is about 1.5×10^{-2} kg. The mass of a molecule of water is 3×10^{-26} kg. How many molecules of water have the same mass as a house mouse?

2 The diameter of a mumps virus is 2.25×10^{-4} mm whilst that of a flu virus is 5×10^{-5} mm. How many times greater is the diameter of a mumps virus than a flu virus?

3 In 1989, the amount of money spent on women's clothing in the UK was about £1.57×10^{9}. Of this, about £3.54×10^{8} was spent on dresses.
How much was spent on other clothing?

4 The atomic mass of gold is approximately 3.27×10^{-25} kg and the atomic mass of potassium is about 6.49×10^{-26} kg. Approximately how many times greater is the atomic mass of gold than the atomic mass of potassium?

5 The amount of money spent on TV advertising in the UK rose from about £7.22×10^{8} in 1980 to about £2.28×10^{9} in 1990. How much more was spent on TV advertising in 1990 than in 1980?

6 A hydrogen atom is about 1.67×10^{-24} grams. What is the mass of 15 000 hydrogen atoms?
Give your answer to 2 sf.

7 A sheet of paper measures 2.12×10^{2} mm by 3.0×10^{2} mm.
What is the area of the sheet of paper?
Give your answer in mm^2 correct to 2 sf.

8 The distance from Earth to Venus is about 2.5×10^{7} miles and from Earth to Neptune is about 2.68×10^{9} miles. How many times greater is the distance from Earth to Neptune than the distance from Earth to Venus? Give your answer correct to 3 sf.

9 The half-life of radium is about 1.6×10^{3} years. Approximately how many seconds is this? Give your answer correct to 2 sf.

10 The areas, in square miles, of three continents are given in this table.

Land area (square miles)	
Asia	1.7×10^{7}
North America	9.42×10^{6}
South America	6.87×10^{6}

Calculate:
(a) the combined areas of North and South America
(b) the difference in area between Asia and the combined areas of North and South America.

11 The nearest star to Earth, Proxima Centauri, is about 40 207 000 000 000 km away.
In a year, light travels about 9.46×10^{12} km. Approximately how many light years from Earth is Proxima Centauri?

12 The Wright brothers' aircraft 'Flyer 1' weighed just 2.75×10^{2} kg.
A Boeing 747 'Jumbo Jet' weighs 3.18×10^{5} kg.
How many times heavier is a Boeing 747 than 'Flyer 1'? Give your answer correct to 2 sf.

13 Mars is 1.42×10^{8} miles from the Sun. Pluto is 3.67×10^{9} miles from the Sun. Calculate the distance between Mars and Pluto when all three bodies are in line, with
(a) Mars and Pluto on opposite sides of the Sun
(b) Mars and Pluto on the same side of the Sun.

14 The area of England is about 1.3×10^{5} km^2 and the area of Wales is about 2.08×10^{4} km^2.
(a) Calculate the total area of England and Wales. Give your answer in standard form.
(b) How much greater is the area of England than the area of Wales? Give your answer in standard form.
(c) Approximately how many times greater is the area of England than the area of Wales? Give your answer correct to 2 sf.

15 In 1990 the population of Britain was about 56 million people and the world's population was about 4.5×10^{9} people.
(a) Approximately how many people lived outside Britain in 1990?
(b) Approximately how many times greater was the number of people living outside Britain than the British population in 1990?

Examination Questions

1 A Rubik Cube has 43 252 003 274 489 856 856 000 possible combinations. Express this number correct to 3 significant figures. Give your answer in standard form.
(ULEAC, 1990)

2 The wavelength of blue light is 0.000 000 72 m. Write this number in standard form.
(MEG, 1990)

3 (a) The diameter of the Sun, correct to two significant figures, is 140 000 000 km. Express the diameter of the Sun in standard form.
(b) The diameter of the smallest hole ever bored is 0.000 000 002 mm. Express the diameter of the hole in standard form.
(NISEAC, 1990)

4 Jim had been taught about standard form. 'The Eiffel Tower is 2.95×10^{5} millimetres high!' he said. Write down the height of the Eiffel Tower in metres.
(MEG, 1990)

5 Write the following numbers in order of size, smallest first:
3.25×10^{4} 2.35×10^{5} 9.21×10^{-6} 5.32×10^{3}.
(SEG, 1989)

6 Dinosaurs died out about 66 million years ago. They first appeared on Earth 280 million years ago. For roughly how many years did they exist? Give your answer in standard index form.
(MEG, 1991)

7 (a) A large locust swarm contains 40 000 million locusts. Write this number in standard form.
(b) Each locust needs to eat about 2 g of food a day. How much will the whole swarm eat in a day, in kg?

(c) In Africa farmers grow about 1000 kg of maize to the acre. If a swarm of locusts invades an area growing maize, how many acres of this crop would be destroyed in a day?

(MEG, 1988)

8 Before there were calculators with a π key, books used various approximations. Here are two:
What is the difference between these two values?
Give your answer:
(a) as a decimal correct to 4 decimal places,
(b) in standard index form correct to 2 significant figures.

$\pi = 3.1416$

TAKE THE VALUE OF π AS $\frac{22}{7}$

(MEG, 1991)

9 The human heart beats at an average rate of 70 beats per minute. Estimate the number of beats it makes in a lifetime of 80 years. Give your answer in standard form correct to 2 significant figures.

(MEG, 1991)

10 This table shows how quickly some radioactive substances decay.
What is the ratio of the half-life of Radiothorium to that of Thoron?
Show all the steps of your working.
Write the ratio as n to 1. Give n in standard form to two significant figures.

Substance	Half-life
Uranium$_{238}$	4.51×10^9 years
Radiothorium	1.90 years
Thoron	54.5 seconds

(MEG, 1990)

11 (a) In a nuclear experiment, a proton moves at a speed of 2.8×10^8 metres per second.
How far will it travel in 7.1×10^{-5} seconds. Give your answer in standard form.
(b) The mass of a proton is 1.627×10^{-27} kg. How many protons are needed to make up a mass of 100 g? Give your answer, correct to two significant figures, in standard form.

(MEG, 1994)

12 The distance, in kilometres, of five planets from the Sun are as follows:

Planet A	1.43×10^9
Planet B	5.97×10^7
Planet C	7.78×10^8
Planet D	2.87×10^9
Planet E	1.50×10^8

(a) Which of these planets is nearest to the Sun?
(b) Which of these planets is about 20 times as far away from the Sun as Planet E?
(c) Find the ratio of the distance of Planet D from the Sun to the distance of Planet B from the Sun. Give your answer in the form k:1.
(d) Light travels at a speed of 3.00×10^5 km/s. Calculate the time, correct to the nearest minute, that light takes to travel from the Sun to Planet C.

(MEG, 1994)

▶▶▶ **P32**

Sine and cosine

This unit will help you to:

■ write down the sine and cosine ratios for a right-angled triangle

■ find the sine and cosine of an angle by calculation and with a calculator

■ use a calculator to find an angle from its sine or cosine

■ use the sine and cosine ratios to calculate angles and lengths in right-angled triangles

■ solve problems with the sine and cosine ratios.

Naming sides

Memo

We give special names to the sides of a right-angled triangle:
hypotenuse, opposite and adjacent.

You have met these names already (see p467).
Each name links the side with an angle.

Hypotenuse is always the side opposite the right angle.
Opposite is the side opposite another chosen angle.
Adjacent is the side adjacent to the same chosen angle.
Here are the two ways to name the sides of triangle ABC.

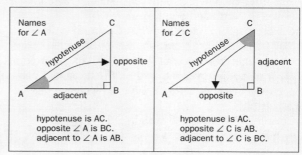

Names for ∠ A
hypotenuse
opposite
A   adjacent   B
C

hypotenuse is AC.
opposite ∠ A is BC.
adjacent to ∠ A is AB.

Names for ∠ C
hypotenuse
adjacent
A   opposite   B
C

hypotenuse is AC.
opposite ∠ C is AB.
adjacent to ∠ C is BC.

Ratios of sides

A ratio of two sides of a right-angled triangle is called a **trigonometrical ratio.**
We usually call it a **trig. ratio** for short.
The three basic trig. ratios are called **tangent**, **sine** and **cosine**.
The tangent ratio is introduced in Unit P27.
The other two basic ratios are introduced in this unit.

Each trig. ratio links two sides with an angle in a right-angled triangle.

The ratio $\dfrac{\text{opposite}}{\text{hypotenuse}}$ is called the **sine** of the angle.

The ratio $\dfrac{\text{adjacent}}{\text{hypotenuse}}$ is called the **cosine** of the angle.

Sin is short for **sine**.
We say sine and sin like 'sign'.

Cos is short for **cosine**.
We say cosine like 'co-sign'. We say cos like 'coz'.

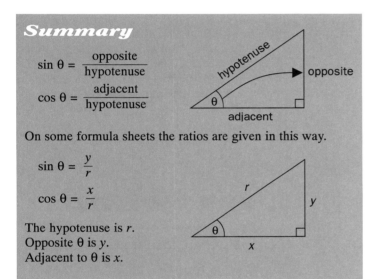

Summary

$\sin \theta = \dfrac{\text{opposite}}{\text{hypotenuse}}$

$\cos \theta = \dfrac{\text{adjacent}}{\text{hypotenuse}}$

On some formula sheets the ratios are given in this way.

$\sin \theta = \dfrac{y}{r}$

$\cos \theta = \dfrac{x}{r}$

The hypotenuse is r.
Opposite θ is y.
Adjacent to θ is x.

You can write down trig. ratios for *two angles* in a right-angled triangle.
Always state clearly which angle you are using.
Name the sides of the triangle for the chosen angle. Then write down the correct ratio of sides for the trig. ratio you want.

Question

Write down the ratio of sides for:
(a) sin α and cos α
(b) sin β and cos β
What do you notice about your results?

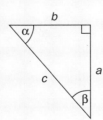

Answer

Use these trig. ratios:

$\sin = \dfrac{\text{opposite}}{\text{hypotenuse}}$ $\cos = \dfrac{\text{adjacent}}{\text{hypotenuse}}$

(a) *For sin α and cos α, name the sides for angle α.*
The hypotenuse is c.
Opposite α is a.
Adjacent to α is b.

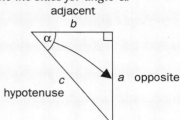

$\sin \alpha = \dfrac{a}{c}$

$\cos \alpha = \dfrac{b}{c}$

(b) *For sin β and cos β, name the sides for angle β.*
The hypotenuse is c.
Opposite β is b.
Adjacent to β is a.

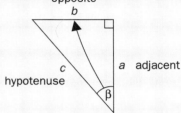

$\sin \beta = \dfrac{b}{c}$

$\cos \beta = \dfrac{a}{c}$

The ratio $\dfrac{a}{c}$ gives sin α and cos β.

$$\sin \alpha = \cos \beta = \dfrac{a}{c}$$

The ratio $\dfrac{b}{c}$ gives cos α and sin β.

$$\cos \alpha = \sin \beta = \dfrac{b}{c}$$

▶ *Exercise* **P32.1**

1   Copy these right-angled triangles.
For each of your triangles, name the sides for the shaded angle.
Write the ratio of sides for each trig. ratio.

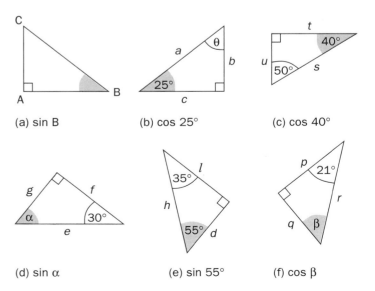

(a) sin B   (b) cos 25°   (c) cos 40°

(d) sin α (e) sin 55°   (f) cos β

2 Write the ratio of sides for each sine and cosine:
(a) sin θ, cos θ   (b) sin A, cos A
    sin α, cos α   sin B, cos B

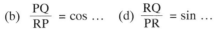

3 Name the missing angle in each of the following.

(a) $\dfrac{PQ}{RP}$ = sin ...   (c) $\dfrac{RQ}{PR}$ = cos ...

(b) $\dfrac{PQ}{RP}$ = cos ...   (d) $\dfrac{RQ}{PR}$ = sin ...

4 Which name (sin or cos) is missing in each of these?

(a) $\dfrac{a}{h}$ = ... α   (c) $\dfrac{b}{h}$ = ... θ

(b) $\dfrac{a}{h}$ = ... θ   (d) $\dfrac{b}{h}$ = ... α

5 These ratios of sides are for the triangles in question **1**.
What is each ratio called?
(Remember: There are two answers for each.
            Each answer must name an angle.)

(a) $\dfrac{t}{s}$ (b) $\dfrac{d}{h}$ (c) $\dfrac{p}{r}$ (d) $\dfrac{AB}{BC}$ (e) $\dfrac{f}{e}$ (f) $\dfrac{b}{a}$ ◄

Finding sines and cosines of angles

By calculation
To find the sine and cosine of an angle in a right-angled triangle
you can use the lengths of its sides.
The right-angled triangle below has an angle of 42° in it.
You can use its sides to
find sin 42° and cos 42°.

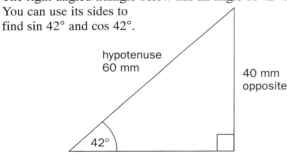

You name the sides of the angle of 42° first.

The hypotenuse is 60 mm.
Opposite 42° is 40 mm.
Adjacent to 42° is 44.5 mm.
Then you work out the ratios you want.

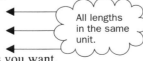
All lengths in the same unit.

$$\sin 42° = \frac{\text{opposite}}{\text{hypotenuse}} = \frac{40}{60}$$

This gives: sin 42° = 0.67 (to 2 dp)

$$\cos 42° = \frac{\text{adjacent}}{\text{hypotenuse}} = \frac{44.5}{60}$$

This gives: cos 42° = 0.74 (to 2 dp)

You can calculate the sine or cosine of an *unknown* angle in a
right-angled triangle in the same way. The angle is usually
named by using a letter.

Question

Find the values of sin θ and cos θ in
this right-angled triangle.
Give each answer as a fraction and as
a decimal.
Round the decimals to 4 significant
figures.

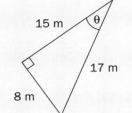

Answer
Name the sides for angle θ.
For angle θ,

opposite is 8 m,
adjacent is 15 m,
hypotenuse is 17 m.

All the same unit.

$$\sin = \frac{\text{opposite}}{\text{hypotenuse}}$$

$$\sin θ = \frac{8}{17} = 0.4706 \text{ (to 4 sf)}$$

$$\cos = \frac{\text{adjacent}}{\text{hypotenuse}}$$

$$\cos θ = \frac{15}{17} = 0.8824 \text{ (to 4 sf)}$$

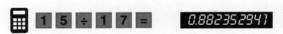

👁 Investigation

Measuring right-angled triangles.
1 These right-angled triangles are of different sizes. But one
angle in each triangle is 30°.

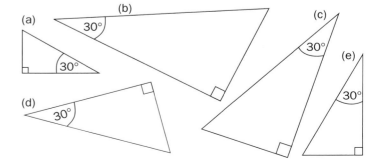

Measure the lengths of the sides of each triangle in millimetres.
Write your results in a table like this.

Angle θ	Opposite angle θ	Adjacent to angle θ	Hypotenuse
(a) 30°			

Work out the ratios $\dfrac{\text{opposite}}{\text{hypotenuse}}$ and $\dfrac{\text{adjacent}}{\text{hypotenuse}}$ for each triangle.
Give each value as a decimal correct to 2 decimal places.
What do you find? Is this what you expected? Why?

Draw a different right-angled triangle with an angle of 30° in it.
What are the values of $\dfrac{\text{opposite}}{\text{hypotenuse}}$ and $\dfrac{\text{adjacent}}{\text{hypotenuse}}$ for your angle of 30°?
Explain what your results show about the values of sin 30° and cos 30°.

2 Measure the sides of these triangles.

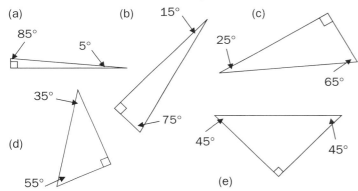

(a) 85° 35° (b) 15° 5° 75° (c) 25° 65° (d) 55° (e) 45° 45°

Work out the values of the ratios $\dfrac{\text{opposite}}{\text{hypotenuse}}$ and $\dfrac{\text{adjacent}}{\text{hypotenuse}}$

for angles 5°, 15°, 25°, …, 85°. Discuss your findings.
What conclusions can you come to from your results?

3

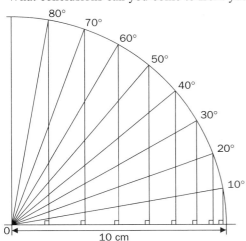

80° 70° 60° 50° 40° 30° 20° 10° O 10 cm

Draw a full-size diagram of the sketch shown above.
Use 1 mm squared paper.
To draw this diagram, take these steps:

- Draw a horizontal 'baseline' through O.
- Draw an arc of a circle, centre O, radius 10 cm.
- Draw radii at angles of 10°, 20°, …, 80°, 90° to the horizontal base line.
- Draw perpendiculars from the ends of the radii to the horizontal base line.

You now have 8 right-angled triangles, each with a hypotenuse of 10 cm.
Take measurements from your diagram to work out the sines and cosines of 10°, 20°, …, 80°.
Copy and complete this table using your results. Give the values of sine and cosine as decimals correct to 2 decimal places.

Angle	hypotenuse	opposite	adjacent	sine	cosine
10°	10 cm				
20°	10 cm				

4 You cannot draw a right-angled triangle with an angle of 0° in it.
What do you think are the values of sin 0° and cos 0°?
How did you decide what they might be?

5 You cannot draw a right–angled triangle with another angle of 90° in it.
What do you think are the values of sin 90° and cos 90°?
Explain how you chose your answers.

► *Exercise* **P32.2**

1 Calculate the values of sin α and cos α in each triangle.
Give each answer as a decimal correct to 4 significant figures.

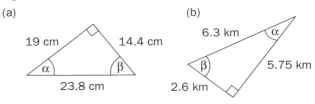

(a) 19 cm 14.4 cm α β 23.8 cm   (b) 6.3 km α β 2.6 km 5.75 km

2 Calculate the values of sin β and cos β in each triangle in question **1**.
Give each answer as a decimal correct to 4 significant figures.

3 (a) Calculate the value of each trig. ratio as a decimal correct to 3 decimal places.

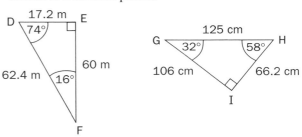

D 17.2 m E 74° 62.4 m 16° 60 m F   G 125 cm 32° 58° H 106 cm 66.2 cm I

sin 16° and cos 16°   sin 32° and cos 32°
sin 74° and cos 74°   sin 58° and cos 58°

(b) Compare the four answers for each triangle in part (a).
Write about what you notice.

(c) Compare your answers for angles α and β in questions
1 and **2**.
What do you find? Is this what you expected? Why?

Using a calculator

A scientific calculator has **sin** and **cos** keys.
You find the sines and cosines of angles with these keys.
You use them in the same way as the **tan** key.
Take these steps:

● Make sure the calculator is set to work in degrees (see p 472)
● Enter the angle first.
● Then press **sin** or **cos** .

There is no need to press **=**

Remember: We write the sin or cos first, then the angle.
We key in the opposite way round.

Here are some examples.

For sin 46°, key in **4** **6** **sin**

to get **0.7193398**

For cos 60°, key in **6** **0** **cos**

to get **0.5**

You may be asked to round the value
given. Round it to the stated number
of significant figures (sf) or decimal
places (dp). But never round the value
unless you are told to do so.

> ### Memo
> Significant figures
> and decimal places
> N3 p13

Question

Use a calculator to find the value of each trig. ratio. Give
each answer as shown on your calculator display and to the
stated degree of accuracy.

(a) sin 30° (to 1 dp)   (c) sin 64.5° (to 3 sf)
(b) cos 73° (to 3 dp)   (d) cos 85.9° (to 3 sf)

Answer

(a) **3** **0** **sin**   sin 30° = 0.5 (calculator)
= 0.5 (to 1 dp)

(b) **7** **3** **cos**   cos 73° = 0.292371704 (calculator)
= 0.292 (to 3 dp)

(c) **6** **4** **.** **5** **sin** sin 64.5° = 0.902585284 (calculator)
= 0.903 (to 3 sf)

(d) **8** **5** **.** **9** **cos** cos 85.9° = 0.071497444 (calculator)
= 0.0715 (to 3 sf)

▶ *Exercise* **P32.3**

1 Use your calculator to find the values of (a) the sines,
(b) the cosines of:
0°, 10°, 20°, 30°, ..., 90° and 5°, 15°, 25°, ..., 85°.

Copy each value in full from your calculator display and
correct it to 2 decimal places.
Write your results in a table.
Compare your answers with the results you got in the
Investigation on p526-527.

2 What do you notice about
(a) the value of sin θ as angle θ increases from 0° to 90°
(b) the value of cos θ as angle θ increases from 0° to 90°?
Write about what you find.

3 Find, correct to 4 significant figures, the value of:
(a) sin 32°   (e) cos 47.5°   (i) sin 46°
(b) sin 74.9°   (f) cos 65.7°   (j) cos 29°
(c) sin 81°   (g) cos 4°   (k) sin 51.4°
(d) sin 17°   (h) cos 53°   (l) cos 83.2°

Angles from trig. ratios

To find an angle from its tangent ratio, you can use the
'inverse tangent' key(s) on a calculator.

tan⁻¹ is short for 'inverse tan'.

A scientific calculator also has '**inverse sine**' and
'**inverse cosine**' keys.
Using these keys you can find an angle from its sine or cosine
ratio.

On many calculators these inverse keys are marked like this:

sin⁻¹ ← short for 'inverse sin'

cos⁻¹ ← short for 'inverse cos'

On some calculators you have to press two keys for each
inverse.

You press **INV** or **ARC** or **2nd F** first,

then **sin** or **cos** .

So for 'inverse sine', you press:

INV **sin** or **ARC** **sin** or **2nd F** **sin**

We use **sin⁻¹** and **cos⁻¹** in key codes in this book. Make sure
you use the correct inverse key(s) for *your* calculator in your
working.

**Starting with a sine, you use the 'inverse sine' key(s) to find
its angle.**
For example,
to find the angle whose sine is 0.5,
key in **.** **5** **sin⁻¹** to get **30.** ⟨ degrees ⟩
The calculator is set to work in degrees.
So this tells you: the acute angle whose sine is 0.5 is 30°.
We can write it as: sin⁻¹ 0.5 = 30°.

**Starting with a cosine, you use the 'inverse cosine' key(s) to
find its angle.**
For example,
to find angle θ, if cos θ = $\frac{3}{11}$, change $\frac{3}{11}$ to a decimal first:

3 **÷** **1** **1** **=** **0.272727272** ⟨ cos θ as a decimal ⟩

then press the inverse cosine key:

  angle θ in degrees

Rounding the answer gives:
   θ = 74.2° (to 1 dp)
or θ = 74° (to the nearest degree).

Summary

To find an angle from its sine or cosine ratio, you can use a calculator.
Take these steps.
• Make sure the calculator is set to work in degrees.
• Enter the sine or cosine ratio as a decimal.
  Change it to a decimal first if you need to.
• Press the correct 'inverse' key or keys.
        $\sin^{-1}$ is short for 'inverse sin'
        $\cos^{-1}$ is short for 'inverse cos'.
• Round the answer sensibly if necessary.
  Angles are usually rounded to 1 decimal place or to the nearest degree.

▶ Exercise P32.4

Use your calculator to do this exercise.
1 Find, to the nearest degree, the angle whose sine is:
   (a) 0.9   (b) 0.68   (c) 0.327   (d) 0.5628
   (e) $\frac{2}{5}$ (f) $\frac{5}{8}$ (g) $\frac{12}{20}$ (h) $\frac{15}{23}$

2 Find, to the nearest degree, the angle whose cosine is:
   (a) 0.4   (b) 0.75   (c) 0.547   (d) 0.8341
   (e) $\frac{3}{5}$ (f) $\frac{9}{13}$ (g) $\frac{17}{23}$ (h) $\frac{74}{163}$

3 Which angles have these sines?
   Give your answers in degrees, correct to 1 decimal place.
   (a) 0.52   (b) 0.638   (c) 0.137   (d) 0.3285
   (e) $\frac{4}{7}$ (f) $\frac{5}{9}$ (g) $\frac{12}{17}$ (h) $\frac{32}{55}$

4 Which angles have these cosines?
   Give your answers in degrees, correct to 1 decimal place.
   (a) 0.64   (b) 0.194   (c) 0.523   (d) 0.8741
   (e) $\frac{5}{7}$ (f) $\frac{11}{15}$ (g) $\frac{23}{36}$ (h) $\frac{94}{125}$

5 Find the size of each named angle correct to the nearest degree.
   (a) sin θ = 0.735   (b) cos α = 0.328   (c) cos A = 0.4621
   (d) sin B = 0.1936   (e) sin W = 0.4677   (f) cos ν = 0.9232
   (g) sin T = $\frac{13}{17}$ (h) cos β = $\frac{84}{130}$
   (i) cos x = $\frac{63}{88}$ (j) sin S = $\frac{124}{219}$

6 (a) Try 3 8 sin sin⁻¹ on your calculator.
      What do you get?
      Try it with other angles. What happens each time?

Is this what you expected? Why?
   (b) Try . 4 sin⁻¹ sin on your calculator.
      What happens?
      Try it with other decimals.
      Explain what happens each time.
7 Repeat question **6** but use cos and cos⁻¹ instead of sin and sin⁻¹.
   Discuss your findings.

Calculating angles

You can find the size of an angle in a right-angled triangle if you know the lengths of two of its sides.
Here are the steps to take.
• Draw a sketch of the right-angled triangle.
  Mark on it the lengths you know and the angle you want.
• 'Name' the sides for the angle you want.
• Choose the trig. ratio that links the angle you want, and the two lengths you know.
  Write down the formula for that trig. ratio.

If you know the lengths of the opposite side and the hypotenuse, you choose the sine ratio.

$\sin = \dfrac{\text{opposite}}{\text{hypotenuse}}$

If you know the lengths of the adjacent side and the hypotenuse, you choose the cosine ratio.

$\cos = \dfrac{\text{adjacent}}{\text{hypotenuse}}$

• Put the lengths you know in the formula you use.
  Make sure these lengths are in the same unit.
• Work out the value of this trig. ratio as a decimal.
• Use the correct 'inverse' trig. key(s) on your calculator to find the angle.
• Round the answer sensibly if you need to.

The working in this example follows these steps.

Question

Find the size of angle C in this right-angled triangle.
Give your answer in degrees, correct to 1 dp.

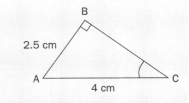

Answer
• *Name the sides for angle C.*
  For angle C,
  opposite: 2.5 cm
  hypotenuse: 4 cm

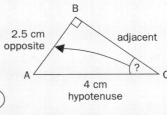

The sides you know are opposite and hypotenuse.
So use the sine ratio.

continued

- *Write the formula:* $\sin = \dfrac{\text{opposite}}{\text{hypotenuse}}$

- *Put in what you know:* $\sin C = \dfrac{2.5}{4}$
- *Find the angle:*

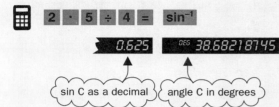

sin C as a decimal   angle C in degrees

- *Round the answer:*
  Angle C = 38.7° (to 1 dp)

Discussion Exercise

You now know two angles in
triangle ABC in the last
example.

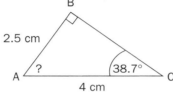

You can calculate the third angle, A, in two ways:
(a) by trigonometry,
(b) by using the angle sum of the triangle.
Try both ways.
Discuss the advantages and disadvantages of each way.
Which do you think is better? Why?
As usual it is a good idea to check the answers found for angles
C and A make sense.
How can you do this?
Discuss the ways suggested by your group.

Exercise P32.5

1 Calculate, to the nearest degree, the angles marked with
   letters.

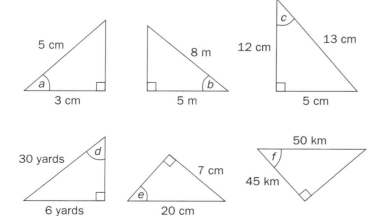

2 Find the third angle in each triangle in question **1**.
   Calculate each angle by trigonometry and by using the angle
   sum of the triangle.

3 Calculate the unknown angles in these right-angled
   triangles. Give each angle in degrees, correct to 1 decimal
   place.

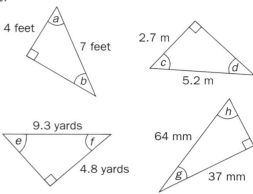

4 Sketch each of these triangles.
   Calculate the size of each named angle, correct to the
   nearest 0.1°.
   (a) Triangle ABC with ∠B = 90°, AB = 4 cm and
       AC = 6 cm. Find ∠A.
   (b) Triangle MNO with ∠N = 90°, NO = 2 km and
       OM = 4.5 km. Find ∠O.
   (c) Triangle STU with ∠T = 90°, ST = 5.4 m and
       US = 7.8 m. Find ∠U.
   (d) Triangle XYZ with ∠Z = 90°, XY = 3.8 cm and
       ZY = 1.8 cm. Find ∠X.

5 Use the sine or cosine ratio to solve
   these problems.
   Round your answers sensibly.
   (a) The top of a ladder, 17 feet long,
       is placed against a window sill
       15 feet from the ground. What
       angle does the ladder make with
       the wall?

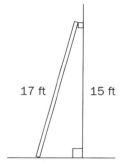

   (b)
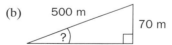

   A straight section of road has a uniform slope. The road
   rises a vertical distance of 70 m when the distance
   measured along the road is 500 m.
   Calculate the angle the section of road makes with the
   horizontal.
   (c) A wooden door, 75 cm wide, has a
       bracing spar lying across a diagonal,
       The length of the spar is 185 cm.
       What angle does the spar make with
       the vertical?

   (d) This diagram shows a lorry tipping a
       load of sand. What angle
       does the lorry's hold
       make with the
       horizontal
       when
       tipping?

Calculating the length of a side

To find the length of a side in a right-angled triangle you can use a trig. ratio. You only need to know *one angle* (other than the right-angle) *and a side*.

You can use the sine or cosine ratio to calculate a side when the *known side or the wanted side is the hypotenuse.*

Some questions tell you which trig. ratio to use.
Usually you have to decide yourself.
Here are some hints to help you.

- Draw the right-angled triangle.
  Mark on it what you know and what you want.
- Find an angle you know (other than the right-angle).
  'Name' the sides for this angle.
- Look at the 'names' for the side you want and a side you know.
  If these sides are 'opposite' and 'hypotenuse', you use the sine ratio.

$$\frac{\text{opposite}}{\text{hypotenuse}} = \sin$$

If these sides are 'adjacent' and 'hypotenuse' you use the cosine ratio.

$$\frac{\text{adjacent}}{\text{hypotenuse}} = \cos$$

- Write down the formula for the trig. ratio you decide to use.
- Put in what you know.
- Solve the equation you get to find the unknown value.
- Round the answer sensibly if you need to.
  Don't forget to give the correct unit of length.
- Check the length you find is a sensible size.
  Use the fact that the hypotenuse is the longest side. The other sides must be shorter.

Given the hypotenuse

In these examples the length of the hypotenuse is given. Look carefully at the steps taken to find another side.

Question

Calculate the lengths of sides *a* and *b* in these triangles.

Give your answers correct to 2 significant figures.

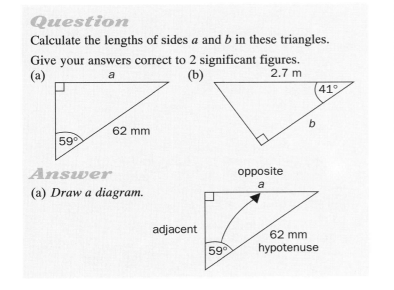

Answer

(a) *Draw a diagram.*

- 'Name' the sides for the given angle.
  For angle of 59°, opposite is *a* mm,
  hypotenuse is 62 mm.   *same unit*

  The wanted and known sides are 'opposite' and hypotenuse. So use the sine ratio.

- *Write the formula.* $\dfrac{\text{opposite}}{\text{hypotenuse}} = \sin$

- *Put in what you know.* $\dfrac{a}{62} = \sin 59°$

- *Multiply both sides by 62.* $a = 62 \times \sin 59°$
- *Work it out.*

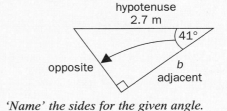

- *Round the answer.*
  Remember the unit (mm). $a = 53$ mm (to 2 sf)
- *Check size.*
  The length found
  (*a* = 53 mm) is shorter than
  the hypotenuse (62 mm).

  This is a sensible answer.

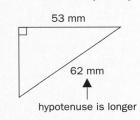

(b)   *Draw a diagram.*

- 'Name' the sides for the given angle.
  For angle of 41°, adjacent is *b* metres,
  hypotenuse is 2.7 metres.   *same unit*

  The wanted and known sides are adjacent and hypotenuse. So use the cosine ratio.

- *Write the formula.* $\dfrac{\text{adjacent}}{\text{hypotenuse}} = \cos$

- *Put in what you know.* $\dfrac{b}{2.7} = \cos 41°$

- *Multiply both sides by 2.7.* $b = 2.7 \times \cos 41°$
- *Work it out.*

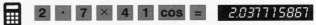

- *Round the answer.* $b = 2.0$ metres (to 2 sf)
  Remember the unit (metres).
- *Check size.*
  $b = 2.0$ m is shorter than the hypotenuse, 2.7 m.
  So this answer
  seems reasonable.   2.7 m   This side is longer than this.

  b = 2.0 m

▶ *Exercise* **P32.6**

1 Find the length of the side marked with a letter in each of these triangles. Give each answer to a sensible degree of accuracy.

(a)
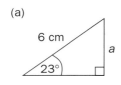
6 cm   a   23°

(b)
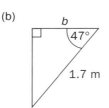
b   47°   1.7 m

(c)
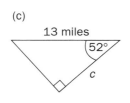
13 miles   52°   c

(d)
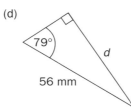
79°   d   56 mm

2 Sketch each of these triangles. Use trigonometry to calculate the named lengths. Give each answer correct to 3 significant figures.
  (a) Triangle ABC with ∠B = 90°, ∠A = 20°, AC = 4 cm. Find AB and BC.
  (b) Triangle FGH with ∠H = 90°, ∠G = 48.5°, FG = 9 m. Find GH and FH.
  (c) Triangle XYZ with ∠X = 90°, ∠Z = 53.5°, YZ = 10.5 km. Find XZ and XY.
  (d) Triangle STU with ∠T = 90°, ∠U = 36.7°, US = 4.9 m. Find ST and TU.

3 Calculate the lengths marked with letters in these triangles. Round your answers sensibly.

(a)
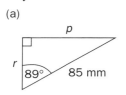
p   r   89°   85 mm

(b)
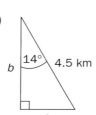
14°   4.5 km   b   e

(c)
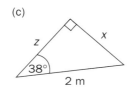
z   x   38°   2 m

(d)
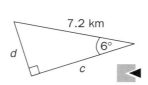
7.2 km   d   6°   c   ◀

Rearranging formulas

These trig. ratio formulas are 'designed' to find the values of sine and cosine.

$$\frac{\text{opposite}}{\text{hypotenuse}} = \sin \qquad \frac{\text{adjacent}}{\text{hypotenuse}} = \cos$$

To use them to find the values of 'opposite' or 'adjacent' sides you can rearrange the formulas.

You can multiply both sides of each formula by 'hypotenuse'. This gives these 'length formulas'.

$$\text{opposite} = \text{hypotenuse} \times \sin$$

$$\text{adjacent} = \text{hypotenuse} \times \cos$$

 Discussion Exercise

Try using these 'length formulas' to calculate some lengths in right-angled triangles in Exercise P32.6.

Compare your calculations using the 'ratio formulas' and the 'length formulas'.
How are they the same?
How are they different?
Which way do you think is easier? Why?
Discuss.

Finding the length of the hypotenuse

In a right-angled triangle, the sine ratio and cosine ratio both involve the hypotenuse.
You can use one of these ratios to find its length, if you know another angle and a side.

If you know an *angle* and its 'opposite' side, the *sine* ratio gives the length of the *hypotenuse*.

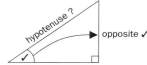
hypotenuse ?   opposite ✓

$$\sin ✓ = \frac{\text{opposite} ✓}{\text{hypotenuse} ?}$$

If you know an angle and its 'adjacent' side, the cosine ratio gives the length of the hypotenuse.

hypotenuse ?   adjacent ✓

$$\cos ✓ = \frac{\text{adjacent} ✓}{\text{hypotenuse} ?}$$

The length you want (the hypotenuse) is on the 'bottom' of each of these ratios. This means you need to take several steps to find its value. Here are the main steps to take.
  ● Write down the formula for the trig. ratio you decide to use.
  ● Put in what you know.
  ● Rearrange the equation you get to give:

    hypotenuse = ...

  Do this rearranging in two steps:
  (1) Multiply both sides by the hypotenuse.
  (2) Divide both sides by the trig. ratio (sin or cos).
  ● Do the working with a calculator.
  ● Round the answer sensibly if you need to.

The working in the next example follows these steps.
Work through them step-by-step.
Do not try to do too many steps at a time. It is easy to make mistakes.

Question

Find the length of the side marked *h* in this triangle. Give your answer in cm, correct to 3 significant figures.

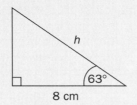

Answer

Draw a diagram.

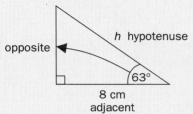

'Name' the sides. For the angle of 63°,
adjacent : 8 cm,
hypotenuse: *h* cm.

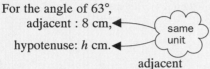

same unit

Choose the trig. ratio.
$$\cos = \frac{\text{adjacent}}{\text{hypotenuse}}$$

Put in what you know.
$$\cos 63° = \frac{8}{h}$$

Multiply both sides by h.
$$h \times \cos 63° = 8$$

Divide both sides by cos 63°.
$$h = \frac{8}{\cos 63°}$$

Work it out.

 | 8 | ÷ | 6 | 3 | cos | = | 17.62151412

Round the answer.
$$h = 17.6 \text{ cm (to 3 sf)}$$

Check size.
The answer for the hypotenuse (17.6 cm) is longer than the given side (8 cm). So this is a reasonable answer.

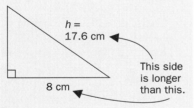

h = 17.6 cm

This side is longer than this.

Exercise P32.7

1 Find the length of the hypotenuse, marked *h*, in each of these triangles. Round your answers sensibly.

(a)
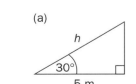

(b)
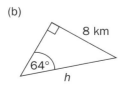

(c)

(d)
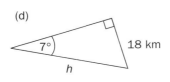

2 Find the length of the side marked with a letter in each of these triangles. Give each answer to a sensible degree of accuracy.

(a)
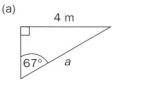

(b)
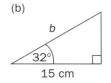

(c)
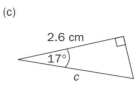

(d)
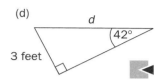

Exercise P32.8

This exercise has a mixture of length questions in it.
In some of them the given length is the hypotenuse.
In the others, the hypotenuse is wanted.

1 Find the length of the side marked with a letter in each of these triangles.

(a)
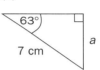

(b)
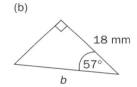

(c)
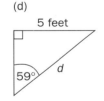

(d)
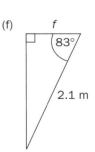

(e)
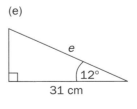

(f)

2 A ladder, 3.7 m long stands against a wall. The ladder makes an angle of 68° with the ground.
(a) How far up the wall does the ladder reach?
(b) How far is the bottom of the ladder from the wall?

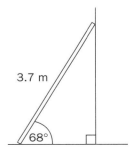

3 Tom cat is lying on the ground, 16 feet from the foot of a tree.
Sam sparrow is sitting in the tree.
The angle of elevation of Sam from Tom is 39°.
What is the distance from Tom to Sam?

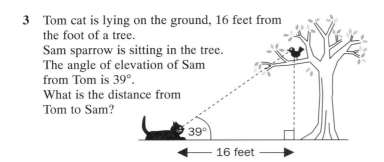

4 An aircraft takes off and climbs at an angle of 7°. How high is the aircraft when it has travelled 20 km from its take-off point?

5 A ship sails from Lowestoft on a bearing of 043° for 27 km to a buoy B.
How far is the buoy
(a) east of Lowestoft
(b) north of Lowestoft?

6 A wire stay, 26 feet long, is fixed to the top of a flagpole and makes an angle of 62° with the ground.
How tall is the flagpole?

7 A plank is leaning against a wall. It makes an angle of 75° with the ground. The foot of the plank is 1 metre from the wall. How long is the plank?

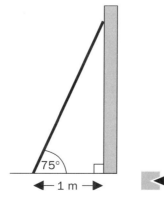

Calculating angles or lengths

The next exercise contains a mixture of problems.
In some of them you have to find an angle.
In others you have to find a length.
Think carefully about which ratio to use. Make sure you use the correct function **sin** , **cos** , **sin⁻¹** , **cos⁻¹** on your calculator.

▶ *Exercise* **P32.9**

1 A boat sails from a port P to a wreck W, 17 km away. When the boat reaches the wreck it is 11 km east of P.
On what bearing did the boat sail to the wreck?

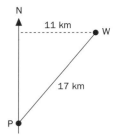

2 Jim is flying a kite. The string is 95 m long.
The angle between the string and the horizontal is 58°.
If Jim is holding the string 1.2 m above the ground, how high is the kite above the ground?

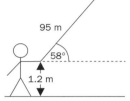

3 Sita stands at the top of a cliff 55 m high. She finds the angle of depression to a ship is 24°.
How far is Sita from the ship?

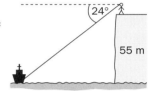

4 Ali and Pam are on the see-saw.
Calculate the angle between the see-saw and the ground when B touches the ground.

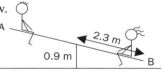

5 A ladder, 10 m long, rests against a wall. The angle between the wall and the ladder is 25°.
How far up the wall does the ladder reach?

6 A model aircraft attached to the end of a wire 18 m long, is flying in a horizontal circle of radius 9 m.
What angle does the wire make with the vertical?

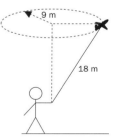

7 ABCD is the end face of a garden shed. The roof, AB, slopes at 18° to the horizontal. Calculate the height of B above the ground.

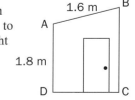

8 Kamal is standing at the top of a cliff 46 m high, looking out to sea, when he sees a swimmer 70 m away from him.
Calculate the angle of depression of the swimmer from Kamal.

9 The diagram shows a footbridge, AB, of length 24 m, spanning a railway cutting. Use the dimensions shown in the diagram to calculate the angle AB makes with the horizontal.

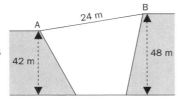

10 The angle of elevation of the top of a tower from a point on the ground is 41°. The distance between the top of the tower and the point on the ground is 40 m. How tall is the tower?

11 Jack puts his 23 ft ladder against a wall. The foot of the ladder is 8 ft from the base of the wall. Calculate the angle the ladder makes with the ground.

12 A pendulum, 1.4 m long, swings through an angle of 8° on each side of the vertical. What is the greatest height reached by the 'bob, above the lowest point of its swing?

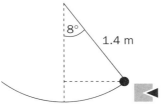

Examination Questions

1 Colin needs to fix a new gutter to a porch. His DIY manual says:
Ideally, the slope of the gutter should give a drop of 1 inch for every 40 inches of gutter.
Calculate the ideal angle of a gutter to the horizontal, giving your answer to the nearest tenth of a degree.

(MEG, 1990)

2 Beckthorpe House (B) is 25 km from Appletree Inn (A) on a bearing of 150°.
(a) What is the bearing of Appletree Inn from Beckthorpe House?
(b) Calculate how far, in km correct to three significant figures, Beckthorpe House is south of Appletree Inn.

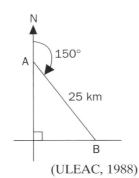

(ULEAC, 1988)

3 A ramp has to be fitted to allow access to the local Community Centre by people in wheelchairs. The entrance is 0.65 metres above the ground and the ramp must make an angle of 17° with the horizontal. Calculate the length of the ramp correct to 2 decimal places.

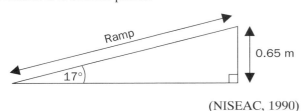

(NISEAC, 1990)

4 The leaning Tower of Pisa is 54.56 m tall. At present, in 1991, it is leaning 5.03 metres away from the vertical.

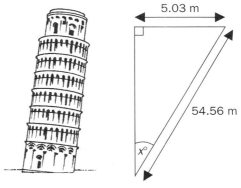

(a) Calculate the angle of tilt marked $x°$ in the diagram above.
(b) Calculate the distance that the tower would lean away from the vertical when the angle of tilt is 5.5°. This is distance y on the diagram opposite.
(c) Experts believe that if the angle of tilt is more than 5.5° then the tower will collapse. The distance from the vertical increases by 1 mm per year. If nothing is done to stop it, when will the tower collapse?

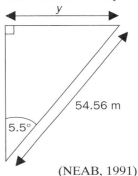

(NEAB, 1991)

5 This is Tower Bridge in London. The span between the towers is 76 m.

This is a simplified drawing of the bridge showing the two halves raised to 35°. How wide is the gap?

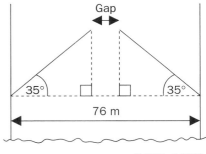

(MEG, 1988)

6 Simon is flying his kite and the 50 m ball of string is fully extended. He thinks the kite is about 30 m above the level of his hand holding the string.
His sister Alyson is trying to estimate angles. She thinks the string makes an angle of about 40° with the horizontal.
Are their estimates in agreement?
Show all the calculations needed to support your answer.

(WJEC, 1990)

P33

More calculations with negative numbers

This unit will help you to:

■ do calculations with more than two directed numbers

■ use negative numbers in algebraic expressions

■ use negative numbers in formulas

■ decide when substituting a negative number into a formula has a 'real' meaning.

Looking back ...

Memo

Directed numbers
N7 p31

Memo

Negative numbers

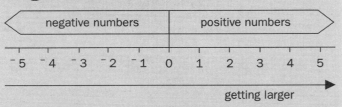

| negative numbers | positive numbers |

getting larger

getting smaller

Negative numbers are *smaller than 0.*
Positive numbers are *larger than 0.*
Imagine a number line, such as a temperature scale, if it helps to understand them.
A **negative number** must have a – sign, for example, ⁻7.
A **positive number** does not need a + sign.
A number without a sign is positive, for example, 8 is ⁺8.

Addition and subtraction

Use a number line to add and subtract directed numbers if it helps.
Adding a positive number makes a number larger (like adding hot air makes something hotter).
For example, ⁻5 + 2 = ⁻3 ⟵ 2 *larger* than ⁻5.
Adding a negative number makes a number smaller (like adding cold air makes something colder).
For example, ⁻5 + ⁻2 = ⁻7 ⟵ 2 *smaller* than ⁻5.

Subtracting a positive number makes a number smaller (like taking away hot air makes something colder).
For example, ⁻5 –2 = ⁻7 ⟵ 2 *smaller* than ⁻5.
Subtracting a negative number makes a number larger (like taking away cold air makes something hotter).
For example, ⁻5 – ⁻2 = ⁻3 ⟵ 2 *larger* than ⁻5.

Multiplication and division

Deal with the 'figures' and signs separately.
Multiply or divide the 'figures' first. Then put in the sign for the answer.
Use this rule:
   2 '*like* signs' give a *positive* result.
   2 '*different* signs' give a *negative* result.
For example, both ⁻ ...   ⁻2 × ⁻3 = 6   ... ⁺answer
                                  ⁻8 ÷ ⁻2 = 4
         ⁺ and ⁻ ...   ⁻4 × 5 = ⁻20   ... ⁻answer
                                  18 ÷ ⁻6 = ⁻3

On a calculator

To enter a negative number,
key in the 'figures' first, then press key.

▶ *Exercise* P33.1

Do these without a calculator first.

1	(a) 3 + ⁻2 =	(e) ⁻7 – 3 =	(i) ⁻11 – 7 =
	(b) 7 + ⁻4 =	(f) ⁻12 + 5 =	(j) ⁻15 + 9 =
	(c) ⁻6 + 1 =	(g) 4 – ⁻1 =	
	(d) 8 – ⁻2 =	(h) ⁻3 – 8 =	
2	(a) 6 × ⁻2 =	(e) 7 × ⁻3 =	(i) 23 × ⁻2 =
	(b) ⁻5 × 4 =	(f) ⁻27 ÷ 9 =	(j) 25 ÷ ⁻5 =
	(c) 10 ÷ ⁻2 =	(g) 18 ÷ ⁻6 =	
	(d) ⁻12 ÷ 3 =	(h) ⁻9 × 4 =	
3	(a) 8 + ⁻7 =	(e) 48 ÷ ⁻8 =	(i) ⁻36 ÷ 4 =
	(b) 0 – ⁻3 =	(f) ⁻12 × 3 =	(j) 28 + ⁻7 =
	(c) ⁻8 × 6 =	(g) 7 × ⁻9 =	
	(d) ⁻14 – 9 =	(h) 17 – ⁻5 =	

Now check them with a calculator.
Any mistakes? Make sure you understand what went wrong.

Several operations (+, −, ×, ÷)

In some calculations with negative numbers there is more than one operation (+, −, ×, ÷).
For example, ⁻3 + 2 × ⁻5 has two operations (+ and ×).
The order in which you do these operations is important.

Memo
Order of operations

Negative numbers obey the same 'order rules' as positive numbers.
Only + and/or − ... do in the order given.
Only × and/or ÷ ... do in the order given.
A mixture of + and/or − with × and/or ÷ ... do multiplication and division first, then addition and subtraction.

You can do a calculation such as $^-3 + 2 \times {}^-5$ **with a calculator**.

You simply key it in step-by-step as given.

`AC 3 ⁺/₋ + 2 × 5 ⁺/₋ =` **-13.**

Your calculator does the operations in the correct order automatically for you.

You can also do the same calculation **without a calculator**. But don't forget that you have to do it in the correct order:

$$^-3 + 2 \times {}^-5$$

multiplication first …

$$= {}^-3 + {}^-10$$

then the addition …

$$= {}^-13$$

Combine the numbers 'two at a time' in the correct order. Do the working 'step-by-step. But don't try to do more than one 'step' at a time. This will help you to avoid mistakes.

► *Exercise* P33.2

Do these without a calculator first. Show your working clearly. Then check with a calculator.

1 Calculate:
 (a) $^-2 + 4 + {}^-1$ (c) $5 - 4 + {}^-2$ (e) $^-1 - {}^-1 + 1$
 (b) $^-3 + 1 - {}^-2$ (d) $8 - {}^-2 + 3$ (f) $5 - 2 + {}^-4$

2 Evaluate:
 (a) $2 \times {}^-3 \times 3$ (d) $10 \times {}^-2 \div {}^-5$ (f) $\dfrac{{}^-3 \times {}^-5}{{}^-2}$
 (b) $^-2 \times 3 \div {}^-3$ (e) $\dfrac{4 \times {}^-6}{{}^-3}$
 (c) $4 \times {}^-3 \div 6$

3 Work out:
 (a) $2 + {}^-3 \times 4$ (c) $5 \times {}^-2 + 7$ (e) $^-3 \times {}^-5 - 6$
 (b) $12 - 2 \times {}^-3$ (d) $^-8 \div 4 + 9$ (f) $^-12 \div {}^-3 - 5$

4 Evaluate:
 (a) $^-2 \times {}^-3 + 5 \times {}^-1$ (c) $^-5 \times {}^-6 - 2 \times {}^-3$ (d) $\dfrac{{}^-2 + 2 \times {}^-5}{4}$
 (b) $^-3 + {}^-2 \times {}^-5 - 1$

Indices

Negative number calculations may also involve **indices** such as squares and square roots.

For example, $5 - ({}^-3)^2$ and $\dfrac{{}^-6}{\sqrt{9}}$

Remember: *You cannot find the square root of a negative number.*

Indices are worked out before $+, -, \times, \div$.

Your calculator uses this order in its working.

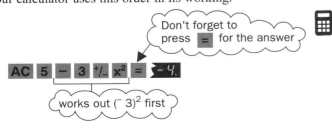

Don't forget to press `=` for the answer

`AC 5 - 3 ⁺/₋ x² =` **-4.**

works out $({}^-3)^2$ first

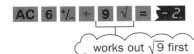

`AC 6 ⁺/₋ ÷ 9 √ =` **-2.**

works out $\sqrt{9}$ first

Here is the same working without a calculator.

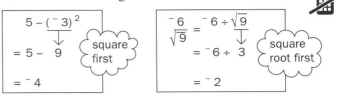

$$5 - ({}^-3)^2$$
$$= 5 - \quad 9 \qquad \text{(square first)}$$
$$= {}^-4$$

$$\frac{{}^-6}{\sqrt{9}} = \frac{{}^-6 \div \sqrt{9}}{}$$
$$= {}^-6 \div 3 \qquad \text{(square root first)}$$
$$= {}^-2$$

► *Exercise* P33.3

Do these with and without a calculator.
Show your working clearly.
Check you get the same answer each way.

1 $({}^-2)^2 + 1$ **5** $\dfrac{{}^-10}{\sqrt{25}}$ **8** $({}^-4)^2 - \dfrac{6}{\sqrt{9}}$
2 $3 - ({}^-1)^2$ **6** $\dfrac{\sqrt{36}}{{}^-4}$ **9** $\dfrac{({}^-2)^2}{\sqrt{16}}$
3 $7 + ({}^-4)^2$
4 $({}^-5)^2 - 8$ **7** $\dfrac{({}^-3)^2}{2}$ **10** $\dfrac{\sqrt{81}}{({}^-3)^2}$

Brackets

Brackets may also appear in negative number calculations.
For example, in $^-4(5 + {}^-2)$.
Working inside brackets is always done first.

The brackets facility on your calculator does this for you.
Simply key in the brackets as given.

Here is the working for
   $^-4(5 + {}^-2)$:

Memo
Calculator brackets
p279

You may need to put × between number and bracket

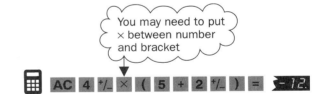

`AC 4 ⁺/₋ × ( 5 + 2 ⁺/₋ ) =` **-12.**

Don't forget to do the working in the brackets first *yourself* when working without a calculator.
Here is the same working without a calculator.

$$^-4(5 + {}^-2)$$

Put in × sign: $= {}^-4 \times (5 + {}^-2)$

'Inside brackets' first: $= {}^-4 \times \quad 3$

Then multiply: $= {}^-12$

You may need to put in *extra brackets* to make the order of working clear.

A 'fraction line', used for division, acts as a bracket.
For example,

$\dfrac{{}^-8}{{}^-3 + 1}$ means work out $^-3 + 1$ first,

then divide $^-8$ by the answer.

To remind you to do this, put in the bracket …

$$\frac{{}^-8}{({}^-3 + 1)} = {}^-8 \div ({}^-3 + 1)$$

Now you can do the working with or without a calculator.

Display shows: **-2. 4.**

Watch the display carefully. Note the results step-by-step.

$$-8 \div (-3 + 1)$$

'Inside brackets' first:  $-8 \div \quad -2$

Then divide: $\quad 4$

A 'square root line' acts as a bracket.
For example, $\sqrt{-3 + 7} = \sqrt{(-3 + 7)}$

Display shows: **4. 2.**

$$\sqrt{-3 + 7} = \sqrt{(-3 + 7)} = \sqrt{4} = 2$$

▶ *Exercise* **P33.4**

1 Evaluate:
  (a) $2(9 + {}^-4)$ (c) ${}^-4(8 + {}^-5)$ (e) ${}^-5({}^-3 - 9)$
  (b) $3({}^-6 + 2)$ (d) ${}^-2({}^-7 + 6)$ (f) ${}^-6(2 - {}^-7)$

2 Work out:
  (a) $\dfrac{{}^-12}{4 - {}^-8}$ (c) ${}^-18 \div (3 - {}^-6)$ (e) $\dfrac{13 - 7}{{}^-2}$
  (b) $\dfrac{{}^-10}{1 + {}^-4}$ (d) $21 \div ({}^-5 - 2)$ (f) $\dfrac{{}^-10 - 6}{8}$

3 Calculate:
  (a) $\sqrt{{}^-3 + 12}$ (c) $3\sqrt{({}^-12 + 37)}$ (e) $\dfrac{{}^-81}{\sqrt{5 - {}^-4}}$
  (b) $\sqrt{70 + {}^-6}$ (d) $5\sqrt{(50 + {}^-1)}$

         (f) $\dfrac{{}^-42}{\sqrt{25 - {}^-24}}$

👁 Investigation

Take three numbers

These three numbers are combined in each calculation below.
$\boxed{2} \quad \boxed{{}^-4} \quad \boxed{{}^-8}$

 $\boxed{} + \boxed{} - \boxed{} = 6$

 $\boxed{} \div \boxed{} \times \boxed{} = 1$

 $\boxed{} - \boxed{} \times \boxed{} = 0$

 $\boxed{} \div \boxed{} - \boxed{} = {}^-10$

Put the numbers in the boxes to make these true.

Explore other ways of combining these three numbers with the operations $+, -, \times, \div$. You may use each operation more than once.
Write down each calculation you make and its answer.
Comment on your results.
What happens if …
● the numbers are $\boxed{{}^-2} \quad \boxed{{}^-4} \quad \boxed{{}^-8}$

● you use squares of numbers
● you use brackets
● you take four numbers?

In algebraic expressions

> ### *Memo*
>
> An algebraic **expression** is a calculation written using letters.
> For example, $3x + 5y$ is an expression.
> You can replace the letters by numbers. This is called **substitution**.
> It gives a calculation using numbers. You can work out the 'number calculation' as usual. This is called **evaluation**. It gives a numerical value for the expression.

The numbers you **substitute** into an expression can be *positive* or *negative* or *zero*.
For example, $x - 2$ is a simple expression.

    If $x = 3$, $x - 2 = 3 - 2 = 1$
    If $x = {}^-3$, $x - 2 = {}^-3 - 2 = {}^-5$
    If $x = 0$, $x - 2 = 0 - 2 = {}^-2$

Before substituting numbers into an expression, think carefully about *what it means*.

Remember, $\times$ and $\div$ signs are usually not used. You have to decide where you must multiply or divide.
For example, $5ab^2$ means $5 \times a \times b^2$

     $\dfrac{a}{4}$ means $a \div 4$

Take great care when working with negative numbers. Don't forget to deal with the signs correctly.

▶ *Exercise* **P33.5**

Do these in your head if you can.

1 If $x = {}^-6$, find the value of:
  (a) $x + 1$ (c) $x - 5$ (e) $1 - x$
  (b) $x + 7$ (d) $7 - x$ (f) ${}^-3 - x$

2 Given $y = {}^-2$, calculate the value of:
  (a) $3y$ (c) $(3y)^2$ (e) ${}^-5y^2$
  (b) $3y^2$ (d) ${}^-5y$ (f) $({}^-5y)^2$

3 When $r = {}^-30$ evaluate:
  (a) $\dfrac{r}{5}$ (b) $\dfrac{r}{3}$ (c) $\dfrac{60}{r}$ (d) $\dfrac{{}^-30}{r}$

4 If $m = 4$ and $n = {}^-3$, find the values of:
  (a) $m + n$ (e) $4mn$ (h) $(mn)^2$ (k) $\dfrac{m}{n}$
  (b) $m - n$ (f) ${}^-5mn$ (i) $3mn^2$ (l) $\dfrac{n}{m}$
  (c) $n - m$ (g) mn^2 (j) $3m^2n$
  (d) mn

5 Find the values of the expressions in question **4** when $m = {}^-8$ and $n = {}^-10$. Check your answers with a calculator. Don't forget to use the ▨ key to enter negative numbers.
  Any mistakes? Find out why they are wrong.

Many expressions involve several different operations. It often helps to write down what such an expression means.
For example, $u + at$ means $u + a \times t$.

Insert brackets if necessary to keep the working in the correct order. For example, $\frac{x}{a+b}$ means x divided by the sum $a + b$.

i.e. $\frac{x}{a+b} = x \div (a + b)$

Remember the order of operations:

> Inside **B**rackets first.
> **I**ndices next.
> **D**ivision and **M**ultiplication in order.
> **A**ddition and **S**ubtraction in order.

You should be able to evaluate an expression *with and without a calculator*. In the example below, both ways are shown. See how each has the same key steps. They are given in this Memo.

- You write down the *expression*.
- You work out its *meaning*.
- Then you *substitute* the numbers into it.
- You do the *working* next, step-by-step.
- And finally you give the *answer*.

It is a good idea to put brackets round negative numbers, for example ($^-$3), in your written working. This makes them stand out clearly.

Question

If $a = 2$, $b = ^-3$ and $c = ^-5$, find the value of $b^2 - 4ac$.

Answer

With a calculator:

Expression	$b^2 - 4ac$
Meaning	$= b^2 - 4 \times a \times c$
Substitution	$= (^-3)^2 - 4 \times 2 \times (^-5)$

Working `AC 3 +/- x² − 4 × 2 × 5 +/- =`

Answer $= 49$

Without a calculator:

Expression	$b^2 - 4ac$
Meaning	$= b^2 - 4 \times a \times c$
Substitution	$= (^-3)^2 - 4 \times 2 \times (^-5)$
Working	$= 9 \quad - (^-40)$
Answer	$= 49$

When working with a calculator, try to use it *efficiently*. *Plan* how to key in the working as usual.

Use brackets and/or the memory if it helps.

Calculator brackets and memory
P7 p278

When working without a calculator, don't try to do too much in each step. It's easy to make mistakes.

Question

Find the value of $x - (2y - 6)$ when $x = ^-9$ and $y = ^-4$.

Answer

Without a calculator:

Expression	$x - (2y - 6)$
Meaning	$= x - (2 \times y - 6)$
Substitution	$= (^-9) - (2 \times (^-4) - 6)$
Working: brackets first	$= (^-9) - (^-8 - 6)$
	$= (^-9) - (^-14)$
Answer	$= 5$

With a calculator:
Key in the working like this:

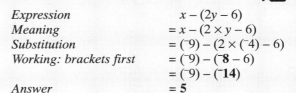

The display shows these step-by-step results:

▶ Exercise P33.6

1 Find the value of $3x - (4y - 1)$ if
   (a) $x = 4$ and $y = ^-1$ (c) $x = ^-1$ and $y = \frac{1}{2}$
   (b) $x = ^-2$ and $y = ^-3$ (d) $x = ^-3$ and $y = -\frac{1}{4}$.

2 If $a = ^-3$ and $b = ^-2$, find the value of:
   (a) a^2b^2 (c) $a - 3b$ (e) $3a - 2b$
   (b) $a^2 - b^2$ (d) $a^2 - 3b^2$ (f) $ab - 5b$

3 If $p = ^-3$ and $q = 2$, find the value of:
   (a) $\frac{4p}{q}$ (c) $\frac{p}{q-5}$ (e) $(q - p)^2$
   (b) $\frac{3q}{p}$ (d) $\frac{p-q}{10}$ (f) $\frac{(p-q)^2}{5}$

4 Find the value of each of these expressions. Use the values given for each letter.
   (a) $u + at$ when $u = 60$, $a = ^-10$ and $t = 4$
   (b) $b^2 - 4ac$ when $a = 3$, $b = ^-2$ and $c = ^-1$
   (c) $4x^2 - 5y^2$ when $x = \frac{1}{2}$ and $y = ^-3$
   (d) $x^3 - x + 1$ when:
      (i) $x = ^-2$ (ii) $x = ^-3$ (iii) $x = ^-5$.

In formulas

We often have algebraic expressions in **formulas**.

For example, the expression $\frac{9}{5}C + 32$

is in the formula $F = \frac{9}{5}C + 32$

(This formula is used to change temperatures in degrees Celsius (C) into degrees Fahrenheit (F).)
The letters in such expressions may stand for negative numbers. For example, temperatures in °C can be negative.
To use the formulas in such situations, you substitute the negative numbers as before.
For example, to change $^-88.3$°C to °F, you take these steps:

> $^-88.3$°C is the coldest temperature recorded on earth in Vostock, Antarctica.

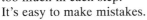

Write down the formula

$$F = \frac{9}{5}C + 32$$

Say what the expression means

$$= 9 \times C \div 5 + 32$$

Substitute $C = {}^-88.3$

$$= 9 \times ({}^-88.3) \div 5 + 32$$

Do the working

The result is

$$-126.94$$

Round it sensibly to give the answer

$${}^-88.3°C = {}^-126.9°F \text{ (to 1 dp)}$$

(We give it to 1 dp because $^-88.3$ has 1 dp.)

► *Exercise* P33.7

1   Use the formula $F = \frac{9}{5}C + 32$ to change these temperatures in °C to temperatures in °F.
    (a) $^-8°C$ (b) $^-20°C$ (c) $^-12°C$

2   The formula $v = u + at$ is used in science to work out the speed, v, of an object which starts with speed, u, has an acceleration, a, and moves for a time t. Use this formula to find v if
    (a) $u = 3$, $t = 2$ and $a = {}^-2$
    (b) $u = {}^-4$, $t = 3$ and $a = 5$
    (c) $u = {}^-5$, $t = 4$ and $a = {}^-3$
    (d) $u = 16$, $t = 3.5$ and $a = {}^-4$.

3   The formula $S = \frac{n}{2}[12 + (n - 1)d]$

    can be used to work out the sum, S, of the first n terms of a sequence which begins 6, 1, $^-4$, …
    Use this formula with $d = {}^-5$, to find the first
    (a) 10 terms   (b) 14 terms   (c) 27 terms.

4   The formula $s = \frac{(u + v)t}{2}$ is used in science to find the

    distance, s, an object travels when it moves for time, t.
    Use the formula to calculate s when
    (a) u = $^-2$, v = 3 and t = 6
    (b) u = $^-3$, v = $^-2$ and t = 2
    (c) u = 7, v = $^-4$ and t = 1.5

Does it make sense?

Here is a formula you have met before.
    p = 2 (*l* + w)
It gives the perimeter of a rectangle.

You could replace the letters

by negative numbers …

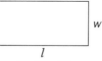

and work out an answer …
but this doesn't make sense. *l* and w are lengths on a rectangle. They cannot be negative.

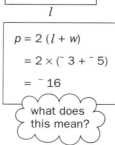

what does this mean?

◯ *Discussion Exercise*

1   The coldest possible temperature is called 'absolute zero'.
    On the Kelvin scale it is 'zero K'.
    The formula $C = K - 273$ changes K to °C.

Pete uses $K = {}^-20$ in this formula. What does this mean? Does it make sense? Discuss.

°C	$^-273$		0	100

K   0   273   373
    Absolute   Freezing   Boiling
    zero   point of   point of
                      water   water

2   Ann stands on a station platform. It is on a straight railway line running from south to north. A train on the line moves steadily north at v metres/second.
    At 12 noon its front reaches Ann. At t seconds after 12 noon, the train is d metres due north of Ann.
    This distance is given by $d = vt$.
    • $v = 15$ means the train moves north at 15 m/s.
       $t = 3$ means the time is 3 seconds after noon.
       What do $v = {}^-15$ and $t = {}^-3$ mean?
       Discuss.
    • Find the value of d if
       (a) $v = 12$, $t = 10$ (c) $v = {}^-24$, $t = 5$
       (b) $v = 30$, $t = {}^-4$ (d) $v = {}^-20$, $t = {}^-7$
       Look carefully at the signs for v, t and d.
       Discuss what is happening to the train in each case.

3   Look at the formulas in Exercise P33.7.
    Which letters could stand for negative numbers?
    Discuss.
    Explain what the negative values mean in each case.

Summary

You can substitute a negative number into any formula. But this may not have a 'real meaning'.
Always consider what the formula is about. Look at what each letter stands for. Then decide whether using a negative number for that letter makes real sense.

◯ *Discussion Exercise*

• Look up other formulas you have met in your studies.
  List some where substituting negative numbers has real meaning.
  List others where it does not.

Yes	No
$F = ma$	$A = lw$
Newton's Second law	Area of a rectangle

Compare your lists with other students in your group.
Discuss your choices.

• Who might need to substitute negative numbers in a formula in their jobs?
  Discuss your ideas.

P34

Independent and combined events

This unit will help you to:

■ calculate the probability that one event and another happens

■ recognise independent events

■ understand that the multiplication law for probabilities only works for independent events

■ know and use the multiplication law for probabilities

■ use probability tables and tree diagrams to calculate the probabilities of combined events.

One thing and another

This is a game at the Summer Fair.

Toss the coin.
Throw the dice.

Only 10p a go!

Get a head and a three.

- You win 50p!

You can work out the probability of winning on each 'go'.
At each go you toss the coin and throw the dice. Whether you win depends on the combined outcome you get.

To find all the possible combined outcomes you can make a list, a table or a tree diagram.

Memo

Combined outcomes
D6 p228

This table shows all the possible outcomes.

The coin and the dice are *fair*. They are *not biased*.
So each of these outcomes is *equally likely*.
The total number of possible outcomes is 12.
To win, you have to get (H) and [⫶]
There is only *1 favourable outcome* for this 'combined event'.

So, the probability of 'getting (H) and [⫶]' = $\frac{1}{12}$.

In shorthand, we write P((H) and [⫶]) = $\frac{1}{12}$.

You can also work out the probability for the same combined event in a different way.
Work out the probabilities of the two separate events:

'get a (H)'

Possible outcomes
on coin:

(H) (T)

P ((H)) = $\frac{1}{2}$

'get a [⫶]'

Possible outcomes
on dice:

P ([⫶]) = $\frac{1}{6}$

Look at what multiplying these fractions gives:

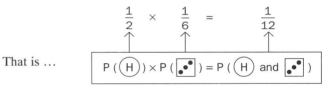

$$\frac{1}{2} \times \frac{1}{6} = \frac{1}{12}$$

That is …   P ((H)) × P ([⫶]) = P ((H) and [⫶])

Multiplying the probabilities of the two separate events gives the probability of *both events happening*.
This is an example of **the multiplication law for probabilities**.
  We get this because the two events 'get a (H)' and 'get a [⫶]' are **independent**. If one of these events happens, it has *no effect* on whether the other happens.

Imagine you toss the coin first.
You could 'get a (H)'
Whether this event does or does not happen has *no effect* on whether you 'get a [⫶]' when you throw the dice.
The probability of 'get a [⫶]' will still be $\frac{1}{6}$.

Imagine you throw the dice first.
You could 'get a [⫶]'
Whether this event does or does not happen has *no effect* on whether you 'get a (H)' when you toss the coin.
The probability of 'get a (H)' will still be $\frac{1}{2}$.

The probabilities of 'get a (H)' and 'get a [⫶]' are independent of each other.
These events are said to be **independent events**.

Discussion Exercise

1   Look again at the 12 possible outcomes for the coin and dice game.

(a) Pick out the favourable outcomes for the combined event 'get a tail and an even number'?
What is the probability for this combined event?
P(tail and even) = ?

(b) Work out P(tail) from the coin.
Work out P(even) from the dice.

(c) Work out P(tail) × P(even).
Compare your answer with P(tail and even) from (a).
Is the result what you expected?
Discuss.

(d) What is the probability for the combined event 'get a head and a multiple of 3'?
P(head and multiple of 3) = ?

(e) Work out P(head) × P(multiple of 3).
Compare your answer with (d).
Discuss what you find.

(f) What is the probability for the combined event 'get a tail and an odd number'?
Work out P(tail and odd) in two different ways.
Discuss your two methods.

2   Kirsten spins these two spinners for another game at the Fair.

Investigate all the possible outcomes when she spins them together.
Find out whether the multiplication law for probabilities works for combined events in this situation.
Discuss your results.

3   Ben spins this spinner and throws an ordinary dice.

What is P(green and 4)?
Is P(green and 4) less than, equal to or more than
(a) P(green)
(b) P(4)?
Is this answer what you expected?
Discuss.

Would you expect the *same* answer when you combine *any two independent events*?
Discuss your ideas.
As part of your discussion, compare these probabilities:
*   P(colour and 4) with P(colour), P(4).
*   P(red and number less than 7) with P(red), P(number less than 7).
*   P(green and 10) with P(green), P(10).
*   P(colour and number less than 7) with P(colour), P(number less than 7).
*   P(red and 10) with P(red), P(10).
What conclusions do you come to?

Discuss ways to complete this sentence:
'When the probabilities of two independent events happening are *both fractions*, then the probability of *both events happening* is …'

What can you say about the probability of combined events if:
*   one of the events is certain to happen
*   one of the events is impossible?
Discuss.

Multiplication law for probabilities

Summary

The **multiplication law** for probability only applies to **independent events.** Two events are independent if one event happening (or not happening) has *no effect* on whether the other happens. The probabilities of the two events are independent of each other.
The multiplication law is often called the '**and law**'. It gives the probability that one event **and** another happens.
To find the probability of this combined event, you *multiply* the probabilities for the two separate events.
If A and B are independent events, then

$$P(A \text{ and } B) = P(A) \times P(B).$$

This multiplication law can be used for *more than two* independent events.
If A, B, C, … are independent events, then:

$$P(A \text{ and } B \text{ and } C \text{ and } …) = P(A) \times P(B) \times P(C) \times …$$

When the probabilities used in the multiplication law are *all fractions* (i.e. not 0 or 1), the answer must be *smaller than* any of these fractions. (Multiplying any number by a fraction makes it smaller.)
This fact acts as a useful check when working out probabilities for combined events.

The multiplication law is a quick way to find the probability that one event *and* another happens. It saves you having to list all the possible combined results for the two activities and picking out the favourable results for a combined event.
However, before you use it, make sure the events to be combined are independent.

Different activities

When two events result from *two completely separate and different activities* it is clear that they must be independent. Here are some examples of such 'different activities'.

Tossing a coin
and taking a card …

Throwing a dice
and spinning a spinner …

Choosing a main course and choosing a sweet from a menu …

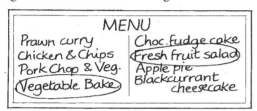

MENU
Prawn curry   Choc. fudge cake
Chicken & Chips   Fresh fruit salad
Pork Chop & Veg.   Apple pie
Vegetable Bake   Blackcurrant cheesecake

Another example is given in the next question.

Question

Terry takes a card at random from a full pack. He also spins an arrow on this 'Lucky Wheel'.
What is the probability that Terry gets
(a) an Ace and white on the wheel.
(b) a Club and grey on the wheel,
(c) black on both card and wheel?

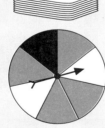

Answer

The two activities 'taking a card' and 'spinning the arrow' are completely separate and different.
An event resulting from one of these activities must be independent of an event resulting from the other.
This means that we can use the multiplication law to combine the probabilities of such events.

(a) $P(\text{Ace}) = \frac{4}{52}$

$P(\text{white}) = \frac{2}{7}$

$P(\text{Ace and white}) = P(\text{Ace}) \times P(\text{white})$

$$= \frac{4}{52} \times \frac{2}{7}$$

$$= {}_{13}\frac{{}^1 4}{52} \times \frac{2}{7}$$

$$= \frac{2}{91}$$

(b) $P(\text{Club}) = \frac{13}{52}$, $P(\text{grey}) = \frac{4}{7}$

$P(\text{Club and grey}) = P(\text{Club}) \times P(\text{grey})$

$$= \frac{13}{52} \times \frac{4}{7}$$

$$= {}_{{}_1 4}\frac{{}^1 13}{52} \times \frac{4}{7}{}^1$$

$$= \frac{1}{7}$$

(c) *For P(both black), we want P(black and black).*
For the cards: $P(\text{black}) = \frac{26}{52}$

For the wheel: $P(\text{black}) = \frac{1}{7}$

$P(\text{black and black}) = P(\text{black}) \times P(\text{black})$

$$= {}_2\frac{{}^1 26}{52} \times \frac{1}{7}$$

$$= \frac{1}{14}$$

▶ *Exercise* **P34.1**

1   At the summer fete, to win a prize on 'Rolaspin' you need to get an 'orange' on the spinner, and a 5 with one throw of an unbiased dice. The probability of getting an 'orange' with one spin of the spinner is $\frac{3}{8}$.
Andrea spins the spinner and throws the dice. What is the probability that Andrea wins a prize at her first attempt?

2   'Sure delivery' deliver 95% of the parcels it agrees to carry within 24 hours. Brian sent two parcels by 'Sure delivery' at 11 am on Monday. What is the probability that both parcels will be delivered by 11 am the next day?

3   The probability that a five-year-old car, tested at random, passes the MOT test is 0.2. What is the probability that two five-year-old cars, tested at random, will both
(a) pass the MOT test
(b) fail the MOT test?

4   On any day during the month of September 1990 the probability that it did not rain was $\frac{2}{3}$.
(a) Calculate the probability that any two days, chosen at random during September 1990, were fine.
(b) Calculate the probability that any three days chosen at random during September 1990 were all wet. ◀

Repeated activity

Repeating an activity in exactly the same way and circumstances results in independent events.
Tossing a coin twice …
or tossing two coins …
give independent events.

Throwing a dice several times …
or throwing several dice …
give independent events.

The next question gives another example like this.

Question

Colin is a keen darts player. The
probability that he scores treble 20
with any dart he throws is $\frac{2}{5}$.
What is the probability that when
Colin throws three darts he gets
(a) three treble 20s
(b) no treble 20
(c) a treble 20 with his first dart only?

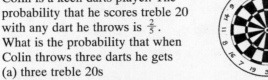

Answer

*The separate events in each part of this question are
independent. So we can use the multiplication laws to
combine their probabilities.*

(a) *For P(three treble 20s), we want*
   P(treble 20 and treble 20 and treble 20)

   P(treble 20) = $\frac{2}{5}$

   So P(three treble 20s) $= \frac{2}{5} \times \frac{2}{5} \times \frac{2}{5}$

   $= \frac{8}{125}$

(b) *For P(no treble 20), we want*
   P('not treble 20' and 'not treble 20' and 'not treble 20')

   P(treble 20) = $\frac{2}{5}$

   P(not treble 20) = 1 – P(treble 20)

   $= 1 - \frac{2}{5}$

   $= \frac{3}{5}$

   P(no treble 20) $= \frac{3}{5} \times \frac{3}{5} \times \frac{3}{5}$

   $= \frac{27}{125}$

(c) *'A treble 20 with his first dart only' means the other two
   throws must give 'not treble 20'.
   For this probability, we find:*
   P(treble 20 and 'not treble 20' and 'not treble 20')

   $= \frac{2}{5} \times \frac{3}{5} \times \frac{3}{5}$

   $= \frac{18}{125}$

▶ Exercise P34.2

1 Mr and Mrs Miller have two children. Given that the
probability of having a boy is 0.4 calculate the probability that:

(a) both children are boys
(b) both children are girls.

2 In a game of cricket, the probability that any single delivery
by 'demon bowler' Mo is a bouncer is $\frac{1}{8}$
. What is the probability that any two deliveries by Mo, chosen
at random, will both be:
(a) bouncers
(b) not bouncers.

3 The probability that a broad bean seed will germinate is $\frac{19}{20}$.
Calculate the probability that 3 broad bean seeds will
germinate.

With replacement

In some situations, the activity involves taking an item *at
random* from a group of items.
For example,
   taking a card from a full pack,
   taking a bead from a bag,
   taking a pen from a box.
To repeat such an activity in exactly the same way, the item
taken must be *replaced* first.
For example,
imagine you take a card at random
from a full pack. This leaves 51
cards in the pack.
To repeat the activity exactly, you
have to *replace the card you took
first*.
By replacing the card, you have the *same 52 cards* to draw from
the second time.
   In situations like this look for words such as '**replaced**' or
'**with replacement**'. These show you that *independent events*
are involved.

Question

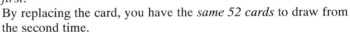

There are 10 cups on the shelf in Mrs Sharp's kitchen
cupboard.
Each cup is a single colour.
1 is black, 2 are green, 3 are grey and the rest are white.
Mrs Sharp takes a cup at random from the shelf for her
morning cup of coffee. After washing it she replaces it on
the shelf.
Later, she takes another cup at random for her afternoon cup
of tea.
Find the probability that Mrs Sharp takes
(a) a green cup for her coffee and a white cup for her tea,
(b) a white cup for her coffee and a green cup for her tea,
(c) a grey cup for coffee and for tea,
(d) not a green cup for both drinks.

Answer

*In this situation, the first cup is replaced before the second
cup is taken. So each part of the question involves
independent events.
This means we can use the multiplication law to combine
their probabilities.*

(a) P(green) = $\frac{2}{10}$

Number of white cups = 10 − (1 + 2 + 3)

= 10 − 6 = 4

P(white) = $\frac{4}{10}$

P(green and white) = $\frac{2}{10} \times \frac{4}{10}$

= $\frac{1\cancel{2}}{\cancel{10}_5} \times \frac{\cancel{4}^2}{\cancel{10}_5}$

= $\frac{2}{25}$

(b) P(white and green) = $\frac{4}{10} \times \frac{2}{10}$

= $\frac{2}{25}$

(c) P(grey) = $\frac{3}{10}$

P(grey and grey) = $\frac{3}{10} \times \frac{3}{10}$

= $\frac{9}{100}$

(d) P(not green) = 1 − P(green)

= 1 − $\frac{2}{10}$ = $\frac{8}{10}$

P(not green and not green) = $\frac{8}{10} \times \frac{8}{10}$

= $\frac{4\cancel{8}}{\cancel{10}_5} \times \frac{\cancel{8}^4}{\cancel{10}_5}$

= $\frac{16}{25}$

► *Exercise* **P34.3**

1 Rod has a collection of 20 compact discs. His favourite disc is 'On fire'. On Monday he takes a disc at random, plays it and then puts it back into his collection. On Tuesday he again takes a disc at random from his full collection to play. Calculate the probability that Rod
(a) played his favourite disc on both days
(b) did not play his favourite disc on Monday or Tuesday.

2 Andrea has six pencils in her case: 3 blue, 2 red and 1 black. She takes a pencil from her case, without looking, uses it to write a note and replaces it. She again takes a pencil, at random, from her case to make a shopping list. Calculate the probability that Andrea
(a) wrote the note and made her shopping list using the black pencil
(b) used a red pencil on both occasions.

3 Gordon has three full bottles of fruit juice in his fridge on Saturday morning: apple, orange and grapefruit. He takes a bottle, at random, pours a glass of juice for breakfast and returns the bottle to the fridge. He does the same on Sunday morning. Calculate the probability that on Saturday and Sunday mornings, Gordon has
(a) orange juice each time   (b) not apple juice each time. ◄

More combined events

To combine the probabilities of *independent events*, you have used the *multiplication law*.

To combine the probabilities of *mutually exclusive events*, you have used the *addition law*.

Addition law.
p505

If A, B, C, … are mutually exclusive events,
P(A or B or C or …) = P(A) + P(B) + P(C) + …

To find probabilities for some combined events, you have to use **both the multiplication law and the addition law**.
An example of this is given in the next Question/Answer.

Question

April takes a card at random from a full pack.
The card is replaced and the pack is shuffled.
Then April again takes a card at random from the pack.
What is the probability that she takes
(a) a king *then* a 'number card',
(b) a 'number card' *then* a king,
(c) a king *and* a 'number card'.

Answer

In this situation, the first card is replaced before the second card is taken. So we are dealing with independent events. We can use the multiplication law for these independent events.
In a pack of cards,
*   there are 4 kings (1 in each of the 4 suits)*
*   and 36 number cards (9 in each of the 4 suits).*

P(king) = $\frac{4}{52}$

P(number card) = $\frac{36}{52}$

(a) *When we say 'take a king then a number card' we mean 'take a king and a number card in that order'.*
These are different ways to describe the same combined event.
P(king then number) = P(king) × P(number)

= $\frac{4}{52} \times \frac{36}{52}$

= $\frac{1\cancel{4}}{\cancel{52}_{13}} \times \frac{\cancel{36}^9}{\cancel{52}_{13}}$

= $\frac{9}{169}$

(b) *When we say 'take a number card then a king' we mean 'take a number card and a king in that order'.*
P(number then king) = P(number) × P(king)

= $\frac{36}{52} \times \frac{4}{52}$

= $\frac{9}{169}$

continued

(c) *When we say 'take a king and a number card', we mean the two cards can be taken in either order.*
There are two ways to do this:
   'take a king then a number card'
OR
   'take a number card then a king'.
These two combined events are mutually exclusive. They cannot happen at the same time. So we can use the addition law to combine their probabilities.

P(king and number in either order)
= P(king then number or number then king)
= P(king then number) + P(number then king)
= $\frac{9}{169}$ + $\frac{9}{169}$
= $\frac{18}{169}$

► *Exercise* P34.4

For each question in this exercise, explain *clearly* why the events are independent *before* calculating probabilities.

1   In a game of darts, the probabilities of two players, Ben and Kirstin, scoring a double with their first dart are $\frac{2}{3}$ and $\frac{4}{5}$ respectively.
    Ben and Kirstin each throw one dart. Calculate the probability that
    (a) both players score a double
    (b) neither player scores a double
    (c) only one player scores a double.

2   Three unbiased coins are tossed.
    What is the probability that
    (a) they all show tails
    (b) at least two show heads
    (c) only one shows heads?

3   To be in time for school, Nick and Sue need to catch the 8.10 bus. The probability that on any morning Nick will catch the bus is 0.8 and Sue will catch the bus is 0.95. Calculate the probability that
    (a) Nick and Sue will both catch the bus on Tuesday morning
    (b) neither Nick nor Sue will catch the bus on Wednesday morning
    (c) only one of them will catch the bus on Friday morning.

4   The probability that Mr Weston's car starts without needing a push on any morning is 0.8. If it needs a push it will start. What is the probability that Mr Weston's car
    (a) starts without needing a push on both Tuesday and Wednesday mornings
    (b) needs to be pushed to get it started on both Thursday and Friday mornings
    (c) needs to be pushed on only one morning at the weekend?

5   Lawrence has a collection of sixty paperback books. Forty-two are fiction and the rest are non-fiction. On Wednesday, Lawrence takes a book at random from his collection, reads it, and puts it back.

On Thursday, Lawrence takes a book from his collection without looking, quickly checks its contents and returns it to his shelf. Calculate the probability that Lawrence
   (a) picked a fiction book on both evenings
   (b) picked a non-fiction book on both evenings
   (c) picked a fiction book on only one evening.

6   The probability that a 'Supaglow' electric light bulb will last at least 800 hours is 0.7. The bulbs are sold in packs of two and in packs of three. Calculate the probability that
   (a) each bulb in a pack of 3 will last at least 800 hours
   (b) neither bulb in a pack of two will last 800 hours
   (c) only one bulb in a pack of two will last at least 800 hours
   (d) at least two bulbs in a pack of three will last at least 800 hours.

Table of probabilities

Memo
Combined outcomes
p228

The results of combining two activities can be shown in a table.
You write the results for one activity down the side of the table.
You write the results for the other activity along the top.
A combined result from the two activities goes in each square in the table.

   For example, in a football match a team can win, draw or lose. One Saturday United and City play matches against other teams.

		City	
	W	D	L
United w	wW	wD	wL
d	dW	dD	dL
ℓ	ℓW	ℓD	ℓL

In this table:
The possible results for United's match are down the side.
The possible results for City's match are across the top.
The possible combined results from the two matches are given in the table.

(wD means a win for United and a DRAW for City).

For independent events you can also use a table like this **to find the probabilities of two combined events.**
The probability for each separate event goes on the 'outside' of the table.
Then you use the multiplication law to combine these probabilities. You write the answers '*inside*' the table.

   For example, Jurgen estimates, for next Saturday's match, the probability that

United wins is $\frac{7}{10}$,   draws is $\frac{1}{5}$,   loses is $\frac{1}{10}$;

City WINS is $\frac{1}{2}$,   DRAWS is $\frac{1}{6}$,   LOSES is $\frac{1}{3}$.

This table shows these probabilities and the probability of each combined event.

		City		
		P (W) = $\frac{1}{2}$	P (D) = $\frac{1}{6}$	P (L) = $\frac{1}{3}$
United	P (w) = $\frac{7}{10}$	P (wW) $\frac{7}{10} \times \frac{1}{2} = \frac{7}{20}$	P (wD) $\frac{7}{10} \times \frac{1}{6} = \frac{7}{60}$	P (wL) $\frac{7}{10} \times \frac{1}{3} = \frac{7}{30}$
	P (d) = $\frac{1}{5}$	P (dW) $\frac{1}{5} \times \frac{1}{2} = \frac{1}{10}$	P (dD) $\frac{1}{5} \times \frac{1}{6} = \frac{1}{30}$	P (dL) $\frac{1}{5} \times \frac{1}{3} = \frac{1}{15}$
	P (ℓ) = $\frac{1}{10}$	P (ℓW) $\frac{1}{10} \times \frac{1}{2} = \frac{1}{20}$	P (ℓD) $\frac{1}{10} \times \frac{1}{6} = \frac{1}{60}$	P (ℓL) $\frac{1}{10} \times \frac{1}{3} = \frac{1}{30}$

You can **read the probabilities of some combined events directly from this table.**

Here are some examples.
The probability that United wins and City WINS is given by
$P(wW) = \frac{7}{20}$.
The probability that United loses and City DRAWS is given by
$P(\ell D) = \frac{1}{60}$.

The **probabilities of other combined events can also be calculated** from the table. The combined results in the table are all for mutually exclusive events. So you can use the addition law to do these calculations. These examples show how to work them out. See how we write all fractions with a *common denominator* before adding them. Then we *cancel* at the end if we can.

For P(only one team wins), you look for all the combined results that show *only one win*.
These are: wD, wL, dW, ℓW.
So P(only one team wins) = P(wD or wL or dW or ℓW)

$$= P(wD) + P(wL) + P(dW) + P(\ell W)$$
$$= \frac{7}{60} + \frac{7}{30} + \frac{1}{10} + \frac{1}{20}$$
$$= \frac{7}{60} + \frac{14}{60} + \frac{6}{60} + \frac{3}{60}$$
$$= \frac{30}{60} = \frac{1}{2}.$$

For P(same result), you look for all the combined results that have the same two letters.
These are: wW, dD, ℓL.
So P(same result) = P(wW or dD or ℓL)

$$= P(wW) + P(dD) + P(\ell L)$$
$$= \frac{7}{20} + \frac{1}{30} + \frac{1}{30}$$
$$= \frac{21}{60} + \frac{2}{60} + \frac{2}{60}$$
$$= \frac{25}{60} = \frac{5}{12}.$$

For P(different results), you can do the working in two different ways.

Method 1: The combined results that show *two different results* are: wD, wL, dW, dL, ℓW, ℓD.
So P(different results)

$$= P(wD \text{ or } wL \text{ or } dW \text{ or } dL \text{ or } \ell W \text{ or } \ell D)$$
$$= P(wD) + P(wL) + P(dW) + P(dL) + P(\ell W) + P(\ell D)$$
$$= \frac{7}{60} + \frac{7}{30} + \frac{1}{10} + \frac{1}{15} + \frac{1}{20} + \frac{1}{60}$$
$$= \frac{7}{60} + \frac{14}{60} + \frac{6}{60} + \frac{4}{60} + \frac{3}{60} + \frac{1}{60}$$
$$= \frac{35}{60} = \frac{7}{12}.$$

Method 2: It is *certain* that the results of the two matches are *either the same or different*.
So P(same result) + P(different results) = 1
i.e. P(different results) = 1 − P(same result)
$$= 1 - \frac{5}{12}$$
$$= \frac{7}{12}.$$

Both methods give the same probability.

Use the football probability table on p546 for this exercise.

Discussion Exercise

1 Find the probability that
 (a) United win and City LOSE
 (b) United draw and City WIN
 (c) United lose and City WIN
 (d) both teams draw
 (e) both teams lose.

2 Calculate the probabilities for these combined events:
 (a) only one team loses,
 (b) only one team draws.

3 (a) Work out the sum of the probabilities given down the 'side' of the table.
$$P(w) + P(d) + P(\ell) = ?$$
Explain the result you get.
Discuss.

 (b) Work out the sum of the probabilities given at the 'top' of the table.
$$P(W) + P(D) + P(L) = ?$$
Comment on the results you get.

 (c) What do you expect the total of all the probabilities 'inside' the table to be?
Explain your answer.
Find the actual total of these probabilities.
Was your prediction correct?
Discuss.

 (d) Will the results you have found in (a), (b) and (c) be the same for all probability tables for combined events?
Discuss your ideas.

► *Exercise* P34.5

1 Beryl takes two cards, without looking, from a full pack. She replaces the first card before taking the second.
 (a) Calculate the probability that the first card taken is
 (i) red (R)
 (ii) black (B).
 (b) Calculate the probability that the second card taken is
 (i) a number card (N)
 (ii) is not a number card (N̸).
   (Assume that an Ace is not a number card.)
 (c) Copy and complete this probability table.

Second card

	P (N) =	P (N̸) =
P (R) =	P (RN)	
P (B) =		P (BN̸)

(First card)

 (d) Use your table to find the probability that Beryl takes
 (i) first a red card and then a number card
 (ii) first a black card and then not a number card.

2 Pete enters both the 100 m sprint and the long jump in the school sports.
The probability that he wins the 100 m sprint is 0.4. The probability that he wins the long jump is 0.7. The two events are independent.

(a) What is the probability that Pete
  (i) does not win the 100 m sprint
  (ii) does not win the long jump?
(b) Copy and complete this probability table

Long jump

Sprint	P (W) = 0.7	P (L) =
P (w) = 0.4	P (wW)	
P (ℓ) =		

(ℓ means Pete does not win the sprint,
L means Pete does not win the long jump.)
(c) Use your table to find the probability that Pete
  (i) wins both competitions
  (ii) wins the 100 m sprint but does not win the long jump
  (iii) does not win either competition
  (iv) wins only one of the competitions.

3 A fair red dice has its faces marked with the numbers 1, 1, 2, 2, 2, 3.

A fair blue dice has its faces marked 2, 2, 2, 2, 3, 3.
The two dice are thrown together.
(a) Copy and complete this probability table for this situation.

Red dice

Blue dice	P (1) =	P (2) =	P (3) =
P (2) =	P (2, 1)		
P (3) =			

(b) Use your table to find the probability of getting
  (i) 2 on the blue dice and 1 on the red dice
  (ii) 3 on the blue dice and 2 on the red dice
  (iii) 'double 2'
  (iv) 'double 3'
  (v) exactly one 2
  (vi) exactly one 3.

4 Ranjit tosses two coins once. Make a table showing the probabilities of all the possible outcomes.
What is the probability that Ranjit gets
(a) two heads
(b) two tails?

5 The probability that Gwen wins the 100 m hurdles race is $\frac{2}{3}$. The probability that Rick wins the 200 m sprint is $\frac{7}{15}$.
(a) What is the probability that
  (i) Gwen does not win her race
  (ii) Rick does not win his race?
(b) Make a probability table for the combined results of the two races. Use your table to find the probability that
  (i) both Gwen and Pete win their races
  (ii) neither Gwen nor Pete wins their race
  (iii) only one of these competitors wins a race.

6 Each morning Jim and Jo have to catch the 8 am bus, otherwise they are late for work.
The probability that Jim catches the bus is 0.8.

The probability that Jo catches the bus is 0.9. (The two events are independent.)
(a) What is the probability that, on any one morning
  (i) Jim does not catch the bus
  (ii) Jo does not catch the bus?
(b) Make a table showing the probabilities of all possible outcomes for this situation.
(c) Use your table to find the probability that, on a given morning
  (i) both Jim and Jo catch the bus
  (ii) Jim catches the bus but Jo does not
  (iii) they both miss the bus
  (iv) only one of these two people catch the bus
  (v) at least one of them catches the bus.

7 A spinner has the shape of a regular pentagon. The five sections of the spinner are numbered 2, 2, 3, 5, 5. When the spinner is used, it is equally likely to stop on any one of its five edges.
In a game, a player spins the spinner twice and notes the results.
  Make a probability table showing the probabilities of all possible results for two spins.
Use your table to calculate the probability that, with two spins, a player gets
(a) 2 followed by 2   (e) exactly one 2
(b) 2 followed by 5   (f) exactly one 3
(c) 3 followed by 3   (g) at least one 5.
(d) a 'double'

Probability tree diagrams

A **tree diagram** is another way to work out the possible results of two or more activities.

Memo

Tree diagrams
p229-231

Memo

In a tree diagram you show each activity by a 'stage' in the diagram.

A tree diagram for 2 activities has 2 stages.
A tree diagram for 3 activities has 3 stages.

At each stage you draw branches from a point to show the results for that activity. You write the results at the ends of the branches.
  Each route from left to right along the branches leads to a combined result. You write the combined result at the end of the route.

For example,
two friends Sam and Jill take the driving test on the same day. The possible combined results of the two tests are shown on the tree diagram overleaf. The first stage shows the possible results for Sam's test. The second stage is about Jill's test.

The possible combined results are at the ends of the branches.
pF means a pass for Sam and a Fail for Jill.

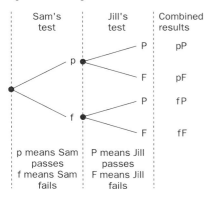

The probabilities of results can also be shown on a tree diagram.
You write the probability of each separate result for each stage
on its branch.
For example, the driving school estimates
the probability that Sam will pass is 0.7,
the probability that Jill will pass is 0.6.
   So the probability that Sam will fail is 1 − 0.7 = 0.3,
   and the probability that Jill will fail is 1 − 0.6 = 0.4.
We can write these probabilities on the branches of the tree
diagram.
   The probabilities on all branches from each dot • must add
up to 1. The results at the ends of these branches cover all
possible outcomes.

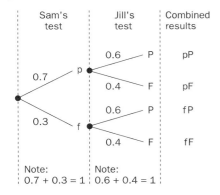

To work out the probability of each combined result, follow
the route along the branches that lead to that result.
You *multiply* the probabilities on each branch you go along.

Sam's test	Jill's test	Combined results	Probability
0.7 → p	0.6 → P	pP	0.7 × 0.6 = 0.42
	0.4 → F	pF	0.7 × 0.4 = 0.28
0.3 → f	0.6 → P	fP	0.3 × 0.6 = 0.18
	0.4 → F	fF	0.3 × 0.4 = 0.12

The four combined results cover all possible outcomes.
So their probabilities must add up to 1:
$$0.42 + 0.28 + 0.18 + 0.12 = 1.$$
This is a useful check.

You can **read the probabilities of some combined events
directly from the tree diagram.**
Here are some examples.
   The probability that Sam passes and Jill fails is given by
   P(pF) = 0.28.
   The probability that both girls pass is given by P(pP) = 0.42.

The **probabilities of other combined events can also be
calculated** from the diagram.
The combined results on the diagram are all for mutually
exclusive events. So you can use the addition law to do these
calculations. These examples show you how to work them out.

For P(only one girl passes), you look for all the combined
results that show *only one pass*.
These are: pF, fP.
So P(only one girl passes) = P(pF or fP)
$$= P(pF) + P(fP)$$
$$= 0.28 + 0.18$$
$$= 0.46.$$
For P(at least one girl passes), you can do the working in two
different ways.
Method 1: The combined results that show 'at least one girl
          passes' are: pP, pF, fP.
          So P(at least one girl passes) = P(pP or pF or fP)
$$= P(pP) + P(pF) + P(fP)$$
$$= 0.42 + 0.28 + 0.18$$
$$= 0.88.$$
Method 2: It is *certain* that *either* 'at least one girl passes' or
          'both girls fail'.
          So P(at least one girl passes) + P(both girls fail) = 1
          i.e. P(at least one girl passes) = 1 − P(both girls fail)
$$= 1 − 0.12$$
$$= 0.88.$$

Both methods give the same answer.

▶ *Exercise* **P34.6**

1   A card is taken from a full pack and its colour (red or black)
   is noted. After replacing it and shuffling the pack, a second
   card is taken.
   Copy and complete this probability tree diagram.

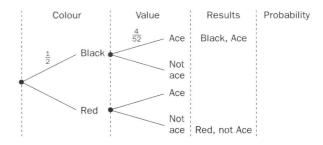

   Use your tree diagram to find the probability that the two
   cards chosen are
   (a) a black card and an ace
   (b) a red card and not an ace
   (c) a red card and an ace.
2   Two bags contain coloured marbles.
   Bag X contains 4 red and 6 green marbles.
   Bag Y contains 5 red and 7 yellow marbles.

One marble is chosen at random from bag X followed by one marble chosen at random from bag Y.

Draw a probability tree diagram to show all possible combined results and probabilities. Calculate the probability that:

(a) a green marble is chosen from bag X and a yellow marble is chosen from bag Y

(b) two red marbles are chosen

(c) two green marbles are chosen.

3   On his route to work, Stan goes through one set of traffic lights at roadworks, and a level crossing. The probability that when he arrives at the traffic lights they are green is $\frac{1}{4}$. The probability that when he reaches the level crossing the barrier is down is $\frac{1}{10}$.

Draw a probability tree diagram for this situation. Use it to calculate the probability that on Stan's route to work he finds

(a) the light is green and the barrier is not down

(b) the light is not green and the barrier is down

(c) the light is green and the barrier is down.

4   On average, Karen travels to school by bus on 4 days out of 5. Otherwise she walks. Richard cycles to school, on average, 3 days out of 5. Otherwise he travels by bus.

Copy and complete this probability tree diagram for this situation.

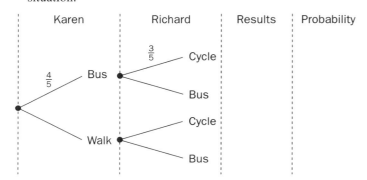

Calculate the probability that on a certain school day:

(a) both Karen and Richard travel to school by bus

(b) only one of them travels to school by bus

(c) neither Karen nor Richard travel to school by bus.

5   Leaflets for the local Council elections are printed in two colours, black and blue. Each leaflet passes through two parts of the printing press. The first part contains the black ink and the second part the blue ink. It is possible that one or both of the colours fails to get printed. The probability that the 'black' fails to get printed is 0.1. The probability that the 'blue' fails to get printed is 0.2.

Draw a probability tree diagram for this situation and use it to calculate the probability that for a leaflet passing through the press

(a) both colours are printed

(b) only one colour is printed.

Sometimes you do *not* need to calculate the probabilities of all the combined results to solve a problem. However, it is still a good idea to list all these results. This makes sure you do not miss any. You may find it helpful to highlight the combined results you are interested in. Then you can easily spot the probabilities you need to find.

▶ *Exercise* P34.7

1   Sam is about to choose two subjects to study at A-level. She will choose one modern language: French, German or Spanish; and one performing Arts subject: either Drama or Music. The probability that Sam chooses French is 0.4 and the probability that she chooses German is 0.3. The probability that she will choose Music is 0.6. Sam's choice of a Modern language in no way affects her choice of a performing Arts subject.

Copy and complete as required this probability tree diagram showing the possible combined results and probabilities for Sam's choice of subjects.

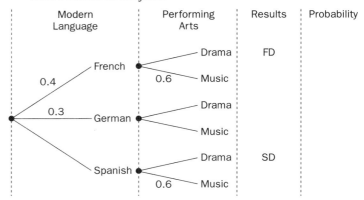

Use your completed tree diagram to calculate the probability that Sam chooses

(a) French and Drama

(b) German and Music

(c) Spanish and not Drama.

2   Sandra Ferguson always travels to work by bus or train. The probability that she travels by train being $\frac{1}{4}$. When she comes home from work she either walks, with probability $\frac{1}{10}$, or travels by bus, with probability $\frac{1}{2}$, or catches the train. The way she chooses to travel home is not affected by the way she travelled to work in the morning.

Copy and complete this probability tree diagram to show the combined results for Sandra's outward and home journeys.

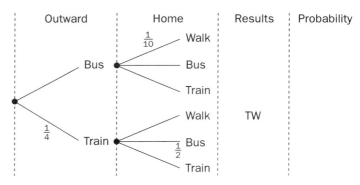

(TW means Train outward and Walk home)

What is the probability that Sandra

(a) catches the train to work and walks home

(b) catches the bus to work and the train home

(c) travels to work and back by bus

(d) travels to work and back by train?

3 Southwood school allows its students to wear a white or grey or blue shirt to come to school. The probability that Kevin chooses a white shirt is $\frac{1}{5}$. The probability that he chooses a grey shirt is $\frac{3}{10}$.

The probability that Kevin's friend Matthew wears a white shirt is $\frac{1}{2}$ and the probability that he wears a blue shirt is $\frac{2}{5}$.

Draw a probability tree diagram and use it to calculate the probability that on Wednesday morning

(a) Kevin and Matthew both arrive at school wearing white shirts

(b) Kevin is wearing a blue shirt and Matthew is wearing a grey shirt

(c) Kevin is wearing a grey shirt and Matthew is wearing a blue shirt

(d) Kevin and Matthew both wear grey shirts.

4 24 counters are placed in two bags labelled A and B.

Bag A contains 15 counters: 4 red, 6 blue and 5 green.

Bag B contains 10 counters: 6 green and 4 red.

A bag is chosen at random, then a counter is chosen at random from that bag. Copy and complete this probability tree diagram to show all possible results.

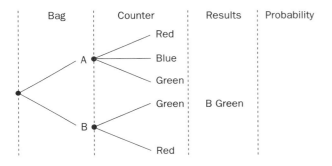

Use the completed tree diagram to calculate the probability that the chosen counter will be

(a) red, and come from bag A   (c) red

(b) green, and come from bag B   (d) green.

5 At the annual county sports day Brenda is running for her local club in both the 100 m and 200 m races. The probability that she will break the club's record for the 100 m race is $\frac{1}{10}$. The probability that she will break the club's record for the 200 m race is $\frac{1}{30}$.

(The two events may be assumed to be independent.)

Draw a probability tree diagram for this situation. Use your tree diagram to calculate the probability that

(a) Brenda breaks both the club's 100 m and 200 m records

(b) Brenda breaks just one of the club's records.

A probability tree diagram can be used to solve problems when *more than two* activities are involved. The method used is basically the same as that for two activities.

▶ *Exercise* **P34.8**

1 A drinks machine dispenses either tea or coffee. The customer obtaining a drink from the machine may choose to have it with or without sugar and with or without milk. The proprietor of the machine knows that, for a customer taken

at random, the probability that he/she will choose: tea is 0.4, milk is 0.6 and sugar is 0.3. Copy and complete this probability tree diagram.

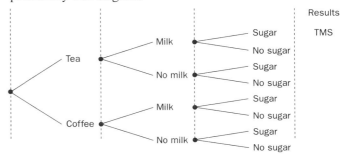

(TMS means: Tea with Milk and Sugar.)

Use your tree diagram to calculate the probability that the next customer to use the machine will choose

(a) tea with milk but no sugar

(b) coffee without both milk and sugar

(c) a drink containing both milk and sugar.

2 The probability that Wayne obtains grade C or above is: $\frac{5}{8}$ in mathematics, $\frac{3}{5}$ in science and $\frac{1}{2}$ in English. (His performance in one subject does not affect his performance in any other subject.) Draw a probability tree diagram which relates to Wayne's performance in these three subjects. Use C^+ for 'gets C or above' and C^- for 'gets lower than C'. Calculate the probability that Wayne will obtain results which are:

(a) grade C or above in all three subjects

(b) lower than grade C in all three subjects

(c) grade C or above in just two subjects.

3 In a local darts match, Damien aims to score 'treble 20' with each of his three darts. The probability that he gets 'treble 20' with any one dart is $\frac{3}{4}$. (Each score obtained by a single dart is independent of the score obtained by any previous dart thrown.)

By drawing a tree diagram, or otherwise, calculate the probability that, with his next three darts, Damien scores

(a) at least one 'treble 20'

(b) no more than two 'treble 20s'

(c) at most one 'treble 20'.

Examination Questions

1 The Post Office estimates that 46% of all letters are posted first class and 54 % are posted second class. It claims that 88.5% of all first class letters and 94.4% of all second class letters are delivered by the delivery target. The delivery target for first class mail is the next working day after collection, and for second class mail the third working day after collection.

(a) Fill in the missing probabilities on the tree diagram.

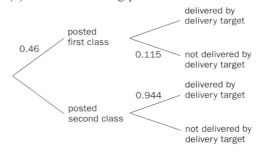

(b) What percentage of all letters, whether posted first or second class, are delivered by their delivery target?

(NEAB, 1989)

2   In a game of snakes and ladders, Josie's counter needs to move two squares to reach the bottom of a ladder.

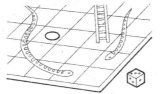

For each turn a die is thrown and the counter is moved the number of squares shown. What is the probability that Josie's counter will land on the bottom of this ladder

(a) in one turn   (b) in two turns?

(MEG, 1990)

3   The figure shows the wheel of a 'Wheel of Fortune' game used at a School Fair. The letter in the sector by the arrow is the one selected by a spin of the wheel. After a spin of the wheel, each of the twelve sectors is equally likely to stop by the arrow.

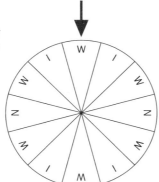

(a) Calculate the probability that after one spin the selected letter will be
(i) W   (ii) N

One 'go' of the game consists of two spins.

(b) Calculate the probability of spinning W followed by W.

A prize is won by spinning two letters that are the same.

(c) Calculate the probability of winning a prize in one 'go'.

(ULEAC, 1990)

4   Natasha and Simon are both taking a driving test. The probability that Natasha will pass is $\frac{13}{16}$ and the probability that Simon will pass is $\frac{4}{5}$.

(a) Which of Natasha and Simon is the more likely to pass the test? (Show your working.)

(b) What is the probability that Natasha will not pass the test?

(c) Calculate, as a fraction in its lowest terms, the probability that
(i) both Natasha and Simon will pass the test
(ii) just one of them will pass the test.

(d) Julie is also taking a driving test. The probability that she will pass is $\frac{3}{4}$. Using a tree diagram, or otherwise, calculate the probability that at least one of Julie, Natasha and Simon will pass the test.

(MEG, 1994)

5   A *biased* coin is tossed twice. The partly completed tree diagram for this shows that the probability of obtaining two heads is $\frac{1}{9}$.

Calculate the probability of obtaining

(a) two tails
(b) one head and one tail.

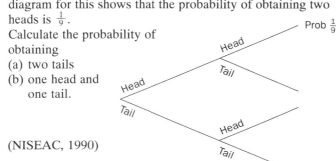

(NISEAC, 1990)

6   Complete the results column to show all the eight equally likely results when three coins are tossed together.

1st coin	2nd coin	3rd coin	Results
	H	H	HHH
		T	HHT
H		H	....
	T	T	....
		H	....
	H	T	....
T		H	....
	T	T	....

When three coins are tossed together, what is the probability
(a) that the result contains three heads
(b) that the result contains exactly two heads
(c) that the result contains one or more heads?
(d) What are the fair odds for obtaining the result TTT?

(NEAB, 1989)

7   In a game of darts, the probabilities of three players Ann, Brian and Chetan scoring a double are $\frac{1}{2}$, $\frac{3}{4}$ and $\frac{2}{5}$ respectively.

Each of the players throws one dart.

Calculate the probability that
(a) all three players will score a double
(b) only Ann will score a double
(c) only one of the three players will score a double.

(ULEAC, 1989)

P35
Cumulative frequency

This unit will help you to:

- find the median, lower quartile, upper quartile and interquartile range of a set of raw data and ungrouped data in a frequency table

- construct a cumulative frequency table and use it

- draw a cumulative frequency graph for grouped data and use it to solve problems

- find the median, lower quartile, upper quartile and interquartile range for grouped data from a cumulative frequency graph

- use cumulative frequency tables and graphs to describe and compare frequency distributions.

Looking at data

To describe and **compare sets of data**, you can use these two simple statistics.

- average (mean, median or mode)

and ● range.

Look at these two groups and their heights, for example.

Girls' heights	Boys' heights
149 cm, 147 cm, 148 cm,	149 cm, 146 cm, 143 cm,
134 cm, 146 cm, 160 cm,	152 cm, 147 cm, 146 cm,
172 cm, 147 cm, 147 cm,	144 cm, 142 cm, 147 cm,
112 cm, 136 cm, 147 cm,	150 cm, 147 cm, 145 cm,
149 cm, 150 cm, 161 cm.	149 cm, 150 cm, 148 cm.

The average height of the girls and of the boys is the same. The **mean**, **median** and **mode** of each group's heights is 147 cm.

It is obvious, however, that in the girls' group the heights *vary more* than in the boys' group.

To describe how spread out these heights are you can use the range.

Range = largest value – smallest value.

Range: 172 cm – 112 cm	Range: 152 cm – 142 cm
= 60 cm	= 10 cm

The range for the girls' heights is very large. This gives the impression that the heights vary a great deal.

Looking at the girls' heights in order of size shows that, in general, this is not true.

The range gives a misleading picture of how spread out *most* of the heights are.

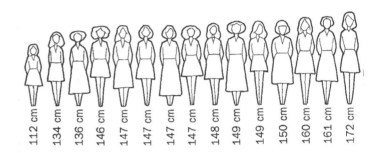

Most of the girls' heights are about the same.
The heights that give the range are exceptional.
The shortest girl is much shorter than most of the group.
The tallest girl is much taller than most of the group.
Simply comparing these two extreme heights distorts the picture we get of the whole group.

One way to overcome this problem is to look at the *range of the 'middle half'* of the ordered data.

To do this we divide the ordered data into *four equal parts*. We divide the data into *two equal parts first*.

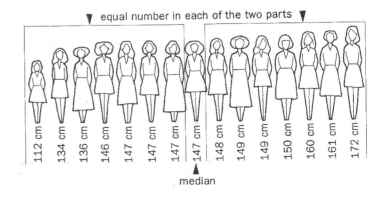

The value at this 'mid-point' is called the **median**.
For these girls' heights, the median is 147 cm.

Then we divide each 'part' into *two equal parts*.

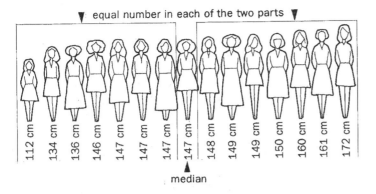

The value at the mid-point of the 'lower part' is called the **lower quartile**.

The value at the mid-point of the 'upper part' is called the **upper quartile**.

For these girls' heights, the lower quartile is 146 cm
the upper quartile is 150 cm.

The range between these two quartiles is called the **interquartile range**.

interquartile range = upper quartile − lower quartile.

For the girls' heights,
the interquartile range = 150 cm − 146 cm
= 4 cm

 Discussion Exercise

1   Look at the heights in the boys' group.
Discuss how to find the lower and upper quartiles for these data. Describe what to do step-by-step.
What is the interquartile range for the boys' heights?

2   Make a list of statistics you know about the heights in the girls' and boys' groups.
Use them to compare the two sets of data.
Discuss what they show.

3   A student has eight lists of data to analyse.
Here are the numbers of values in each list:
- 13 Maths marks
- 9 English marks
- 14 heights
- 16 ages
- 20 weights
- 22 speeds
- 17 days
- 23 times

Discuss how to find the position of the median, lower quartile and upper quartile in each list.

4   Jane uses this 'rule' to help her to work out the positions of the median and quartiles.

> If there are *n* values listed in order, from smallest to largest, then …
> - to find the median, look for the $\dfrac{n+1}{2}$ th value,
> - to find the lower quartile, look for the $\dfrac{n+1}{4}$ th value,
> - to find the upper quartile, look for the $\dfrac{3(n+1)}{4}$ th value.

Try this rule with different numbers for *n*.
Discuss what you find.

Question

Find the median, lower quartile, upper quartile and interquartile range for each set of data.
(a) 5.1, 6.8, 7.9, 3.2, 7.0, 4.7, 6.3
(b) 20, 15, 19, 12, 21, 21, 14, 19, 15, 14
(c) 31, 18, 27, 30, 17, 30, 20, 28, 30, 29, 26, 27.

Answer

(a) *Put the values in order of size first.*

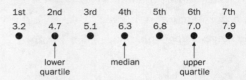

There are 7 values in the list.
The 4th value is at the 'middle point'. $\dfrac{7+1}{2}=\dfrac{8}{2}=4$
   median = 6.3
3 values are below the median.
The 2nd value is in the middle of these. $\dfrac{3+1}{2}=\dfrac{4}{2}=2$
   lower quartile = 4.7
3 values are above the median.
The 6th value is in the middle of these.
   upper quartile = 7.0
interquartile range = upper quartile − lower quartile
= 7.0 − 4.7
= 2.3

(b) *Put the values in order of size first.*

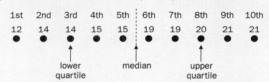

There are 10 values in the list.
The 'middle point' is between the 5th and 6th values. $\dfrac{10+1}{2}=\dfrac{11}{2}=5.5$
   median = $\dfrac{15+19}{2}=\dfrac{34}{2}=17$

5 values are below the median.
The 3rd value is in the middle of these. $\dfrac{5+1}{2}=\dfrac{6}{2}=3$
   lower quartile = 14
5 values are above the median.
The 8th value is in the middle of these.
   upper quartile = 20
interquartile range = upper quartile − lower quartile
= 20 − 14
= 6

(c) *Put the values in order of size first.*

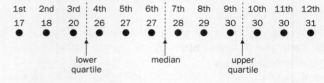

There are 12 values in the list.
The 'middle point' is between the 6th and 7th values. $\dfrac{12+1}{2}=\dfrac{13}{2}=6.5$

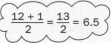

$$\text{median} = \frac{27 + 28}{2} = \frac{55}{2} = 27.5$$

6 values are below the median.
The middle of these is between the
3rd and 4th values.

$$\frac{6 + 1}{2} = \frac{7}{2} = 3.5$$

$$\text{lower quartile} = \frac{20 + 26}{2} = \frac{46}{2} = 23$$

6 values are above the median.
The middle of these is between the 9th and 10th values.

$$\text{upper quartile} = \frac{30 + 30}{2} = \frac{60}{2} = 30$$

$$\text{interquartile range} = \text{upper quartile} - \text{lower quartile}$$
$$= 30 - 23$$
$$= 7$$

Summary

Median and quartiles
To find the median and quartiles of a set of data, take these steps.
- Put the data in order of size, smallest first.
- Find the 'points' that divide the ordered data into four equal parts.
  The values at these points are (in order):
  the lower quartile, the median, the upper quartile

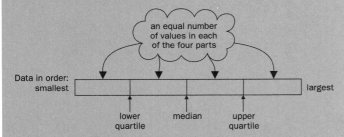

To find the **median**, look at the 'middle point' of the list of data. It has the same number of values above it as below it.

To find the **lower quartile**, look at the 'middle point' of the 'lower part' of the data, i.e. below the median.

To find the **upper quartile**, look at the 'middle point' of the 'upper part' of the data, i.e. above the median.

Remember:
To find the 'middle point' of *n* values, count along to the $\frac{1}{2}(n + 1)$th position in the list.

If the 'middle point' is half-way between two values, the value you want is their mean.

Measures of dispersion (spread)
The dispersion of a set of data is how spread out the data are. The simplest measures of dispersion are the **range** and **interquartile range**.

$$\text{range} = \text{largest value} - \text{smallest value}$$
$$\text{interquartile range} = \text{upper quartile} - \text{lower quartile}$$

The range is not a good measure of dispersion. It depends on the two 'extreme' values and these may be exceptional.

The interquartile range is a slightly better measure of dispersion. It is not affected by 'extreme' values. It is based on the 'middle half' of the data.
It is the range between the upper and lower quartiles.

▶ *Exercise* P35.1

1 Find the median, lower quartile, upper quartile and the interquartile range for each of these sets of data.
   (a) 8   11   11   13   15   21   23
   (b) 6   6   7   8   10   11   12   14   15   15
   (c) 10   14   15   16   18   18   21   23
   (d) 22s   17s   28s   19s   23s   32s   18s   25s   29s   19s   29s
   (e) 18m   15m   21m   16m   13m   15m   14m   18m
   (f) 12g   7g   1g   3g   2g   12g   2g   9g   14g   5g   6g   5g

2 A scientist checked the weights of a sample of eggs from hens fed with a new type of food. These are what he found the weight (in grams) to be:
   35g   39g   40g   34g   39g   37g   41g   39g   41g   47g
   44g   47g   51g   43g   27g   29g   29g   35g   39g   43g.
   Find the median, range, lower and upper quartiles and interquartile range for these weights.

3 (a) Find the median, range and lower and upper quartiles and interquartile range for the second hand car prices in this advert.
   (b) Find the same statistics for the ages of the cars given in the advert.

SANDBY MOTORS	
QUALITY USED VEHICLES	
94 (L) Renault Clio 1.9 RT, blue, 1 owner	£8695
94 (L) Metro CD, 5 door, white	£7250
92 (K) Rover Metro 1.1S, red, 1 owner	£6395
90 (G) Escort 1.3 Bonus, blue, radio	£4795
90 (G) Volvo 340GL, 5 door, red	£4795
89 (G) Renault Espace 2000i, alarm, silver	£3395
89 (F) Volvo 340DL 1.4 Hatchback, grey	£3375
89 (G) Sierra Sapphire 1.8L, blue	£3995
89 (F) Cavalier 1.6L, blue, sunroof	£4250
88 (G) Montego 1.6L Auto, blue	£2595
MARKET PLACE GARAGE	
Essex Street Telephone: 728888	

4 These data are the marks (out of 20) obtained by twelve students for tests in number and algebra.
   Number: 13   11   16   12   12   15   16   12   13   16   14   13
   Algebra: 18   8   20   6   15   12   16   7   7   20   8   16
   (a) Find the median, range, lower quartile, upper quartile and interquartile range for each test.
   (b) Comment on the students' performance in the two tests.

Using frequency tables

Mr Hart gave his class a maths test.
Here are the 18 marks listed in order, smallest to largest.
By dividing the list into four equal parts, you can find:
   lower quartile = 3
   median   = 4.5
   upper quartile = 6

	1
	2
	2
	2
lower quartile →	3 *5th mark*
	3
	4
	4
median 4.5 →	4 *9th mark*
	5 *10th mark*
	5
	6
	6
upper quartile →	6 *14th mark*
	6
	7
	8
	8

The median and quartiles can also be found from this **frequency table** of the data.

Mark	Frequency
1	1
2	3
3	2
4	3
5	2
6	4
7	1
8	2

The values of the median and quartiles depend on their *position* in the ordered data.

The marks in the table are *in order*, smallest first.

The frequencies show how many of each mark we have.

So we can work out which marks are in the 1st, 2nd, 3rd, 4th, …, 18th positions from the frequencies.

To help us to do this, we **cumulate** (add up) the frequencies. We add each frequency to the total of the previous frequencies in the table.

These cumulative frequencies are written in an extra column next to the table below.

Note: The final cumulative frequency is equal to the total frequency. This is because all the values have been counted.

Mark	Frequency	Cumulative Frequency	'Positions' in ordered data
1	1	1	1st mark on this line
2	3	4	2nd–4th marks on this line
3	2	6	5th and 6th marks on this line
4	3	9	7th–9th marks on this line
5	2	11	10th and 11th marks on this line
6	4	15	12th–15th marks on this line
7	1	16	16th mark on this line
8	2	18	17th and 18th marks on this line
Total	18		

The cumulative frequencies show us which marks are in the 1st, 2nd, … 18th positions in the data.

We have written these positions at the side of the table above.

Look carefully to see how we have worked them out.

Now we can find the median and quartiles from the table.

For the median of 18 values, we look for the 9th and 10th values.

$$\frac{18 + 1}{2} = \frac{19}{2} = 9\tfrac{1}{2}$$

The cumulative frequencies show that:
 4 is the 9th mark
 5 is the 10th mark

So median mark $= \frac{4 + 5}{2} = \frac{9}{2} = 4.5$

For the lower quartile of 18 values, we look for the 5th value.

$$\frac{18 + 1}{4} = \frac{19}{4} = 4\tfrac{3}{4} \approx 5$$

The cumulative frequencies show that:
 3 is the 5th mark, so lower quartile = 3

For the upper quartile of 18 values, we look for the 14th value.

$$\frac{3(18 + 1)}{4} = \frac{3(19)}{4} = 14\tfrac{1}{4} \approx 14$$

The cumulative frequencies show that:
 6 is the 14th mark, so upper quartile = 6

The interquartile range is the difference between the upper and lower quartiles.

For these data, the interquartile range = 6 − 3 = 3

Summary

You can find the median and quartiles from a frequency table of ungrouped data.

Here are the steps to take.

- Add each frequency to the total of the previous frequencies in the table.
  Write these cumulative frequencies in an extra column at the side of the table.
- Work out the positions of the median, lower quartile and upper quartile from the total frequency.
- Look down the cumulative frequency column to see where each of these positions lies.
  Read the value for each position from the 'value' column.

▶ *Exercise* **P35.2**

1 Each frequency table below gives some data from a survey. Find the median, lower quartile, upper quartile and interquartile range for the data in each table.

(a) Survey: marks gained by students in a test.

Mark	Frequency
0	0
1	2
2	3
3	5
4	7
5	7
6	4
7	0
8	1
9	1
10	0

(b) Survey: trusses grown on tomato plants.

Number of trusses per plant	Frequency
0	1
1	1
2	2
3	4
4	5
5	7
6	9
7	12
8	6
9	3

(c) Survey: visits to the doctor last year.

Number of visits	Frequency
0	9
1	12
2	8
3	5
4	3
5	2
6	1

(d) Survey: visits to the cinema last month.

Number of visits	Frequency
0	8
1	9
2	6
3	3
4	3
5	2
6	1
7	0

2 Penny is doing a project on people's shopping habits. She has gathered these data on the number of times families from two different neighbourhoods had shopped at the new shopping mall since its opening.

Cranford Terrace residents

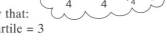

Number of visits	0	1	2	3	4	5	6	7	8
Frequency	3	13	12	6	7	2	1	0	1

St. Stephen's Close residents

Number of visits	0	1	2	3	4	5	6	7	8	9	10	11	12
Frequency	0	2	4	6	9	0	8	0	7	3	0	0	1

Penny wants to compare the data from the shoppers living on the two streets.
Write a short report·for Penny based on these data.
Include in it, comments on these statistics for the data: the medians, ranges, lower and upper quartiles and the interquartile ranges.

Cumulative frequency tables
Ungrouped data

Here again are the frequency and cumulative frequencies for Mr Hart's maths test results.

Mark	Frequency	Cumulative Frequency	Comments
1	1	1	← 1 student got *a mark of 1*
2	3	4	← 4 students got *marks of 2 or less*
3	2	6	← 6 students got *marks of 3 or less*
4	3	9	← 9 students got *marks of 4 or less*
5	2	11	← 11 students got *marks of 5 or less*
6	4	15	← 15 students got *marks of 6 or less*
7	1	16	← 16 students got *marks of 7 or less*
8	2	18	← 18 students got *marks of 8 or less*

The **frequency** for each mark tells us *how many students got that mark*.
For example, 4 students got *a mark of 6*.

The **cumulative frequency** tells us *how many students got that mark or less*.
For example, 15 students got *marks of 6 or less*.

The comments at the side of the table above describe the marks for each cumulative frequency. The same information is given in a separate **cumulative frequency table** below.
This table shows it more clearly.

Frequency table

Mark	Frequency
1	1
2	3
3	2
4	3
5	2
6	4
7	1
8	2

Cumulative Frequency table

Mark	Cumulative Frequency
1 or less	1
2 or less	4
3 or less	6
4 or less	9
5 or less	11
6 or less	15
7 or less	16
8 or less	18

Look at the wording for the 'marks' for each cumulative frequency.

'1 or less' means '0 and 1'
'2 or less' means '0, 1 and 2'
'3 or less' means '0, 1, 2 and 3'
and so on …

The same marks can be described in other ways. Here are some examples.

Marks
up to and including 1
up to and including 2
up to and including 3

Marks
≤ 1
≤ 2
≤ 3

Marks
0–1
0–2
0–3

In many statistical investigations, you want to answer questions such as:

'How many are less than or equal to …?'
'How many are less than …?'
'How many are more than …?'
'How many are more than or equal to…?'

Looking at a cumulative frequency table is often a quick way to do this.

The following questions are about Mr Hart's maths results.
See how each answer comes from the cumulative frequency table.

How many students got *7 marks or less*?
Answer: 16 because 16 scored *7 or less*.

How many students got *less than 5*?
Answer: 9 because 9 scored *4 or less*.

How many students got *more than 3*?
Answer: 18 – 6 = 12 because 6 scored *3 or less*.

How many students got *6 marks or more*?
Answer: 18 – 11 = 7 because 11 scored *5 or less*.

⬭ *Discussion Exercise*

- Discuss the four questions and answers above.
  Which 'values' does each question ask about?
  Explain how these are related to the 'values' in the cumulative frequency table.
- Answer these questions from the same table.
  How many students got 5 marks or less?
  How many got less than 7?
  How many got more than 6?
  How many got 4 marks or more?
  How many got less than 4?
  How many got more than 5?
  How many got 2 marks or more?
  Explain how you found each answer.
  Discuss.

▶ *Exercise* **P35.3**

Use the frequency tables in question **1**, Exercise P35.2 on p556 for this exercise.
Copy and complete each cumulative frequency table. Answer the questions from your table.

1 Survey: marks gained by students in a test.
How many students scored
(a) 7 marks or less
(b) less than 6
(c) more than 4
(d) 3 marks or more?

Mark	Cumulative frequency
0	0
1 or less	2
2 or less	5

2 Survey: trusses grown on tomato plants.
How many plants had
(a) 4 trusses or less
(b) 2 trusses or more
(c) more than 3 trusses
(d) less than 7 trusses?

Number of trusses per plant	Cumulative frequency
0	1
0–1	2
0–2	4

3 Survey: visits to the doctor last year.
How many people visited the doctor
(a) 5 times or less
(b) more than twice
(c) 4 times or more
(d) less than 3 times?

Number of visits	Cumulative frequency
0	
up to and including 1	
up to and including 2	

4 Survey: visits to the cinema last month.
How many people visited the cinema
(a) 3 times or less
(b) more than once
(c) less than 5 times
(d) 3 times or more?

Number of visits	Cumulative frequency
0	
≤ 1	
≤ 2	

Grouped data

A cumulative frequency table can also be made from a **frequency table of grouped data**.

Discrete data
The tables below are for the marks of Deacon College GCSE students in an English examination.
These data are *discrete*.
Each mark is a *whole number*.

Frequency table

Mark	Number of students
1–10	0
11–20	2
21–30	6
31–40	7
41–50	14
51–60	20
61–70	35
71–80	29
81–90	6
91–100	21
total	120

Cumulative frequency table

Mark	Cumulative frequency	
≤ 10	0	
≤ 20	2	+2
≤ 30	8	+6
≤ 40	15	+7
≤ 50	29	+14
≤ 60	49	+20
≤ 70	84	+35
≤ 80	113	+29
≤ 90	119	+6
≤ 100	120	+1

Check: The final cumulative frequency is the same as the total number of students. This is a useful check.

The **frequency for each class interval** tells us *how many data values are in that class*.
For example, 29 students' marks are in the class 71–80.
Each frequency is added to the total of the previous frequencies to get the cumulative frequencies.
The **cumulative frequency** tells us *how many data values are in that class and all lower classes*.
For example, 113 students' marks are *80 or less*.
In the table, we describe *80 or less* as '≤ 80'.
Other ways to write the same thing are:

'0 – 80'
'up to and including 80'

We call the cumulative frequency table for these marks a **'less than or equal to' table** or '≤' **table**.

Marks are discrete data.
The cumulative frequencies are the number of data values that are *'less than or equal to' the greatest possible value* in each group.
This fact helps us to answer some questions about the data from the cumulative frequency table.
Some examples are given in the Question/Answer below.
To answer each of these questions, we take these steps.
- Think about the values the question asks about.
- Decide which 'description of values' in the table they are related to.
- Read its cumulative frequency from the table.
- Then use the cumulative frequency to answer the question.

Question

The Head of English at Deacon College tells the GCSE students about their exam results.
'If you get 40 marks or less, you have to resit the exam.
If you get less than 51, you have to write an extra essay.
If you get more than 70, you get an A grade.
If you get 81 or more, you get an A*.'
How many students: (a) have to resit the exam
(b) have to write an extra essay
(c) get an A grade
(d) get an A* grade?

Answer

(a) '40 marks or less' is the same as '≤ 40'.
   From the table, '≤ 40 marks' ↔ 15 students.
   So 15 students have to resit the exam.
(b) 'less than 51' is the same as '50 or less', i.e. ≤ 50.
   From the table, '≤ 50 marks' ↔ 29 students.
   So 29 students have to write an extra essay.
(c) 'more than 70' gives an A grade.
   So '70 or less', i.e. ≤ 70 does not give an A.
   From the table, '≤ 70 marks' ↔ 84 students.
   So 84 students do not get an A
   and 120 − 84 = 36 students do get an A.

(d) '81 or more' gives an A* grade.
So '80 or less', i.e. '≤ 80' does not give an A*.
From the table, '≤ 80 marks' ↔ 113 students.
So 113 students to do not get an A*
and 120 − 113 = 7 students do get an A*.

Continuous data

Cumulative frequency tables are also made for **grouped continuous data.**
For continuous data, the upper class boundaries are at the 'ends' of the class intervals.

Memo

Class boundaries
p309

We use these upper boundaries to describe the values in cumulative frequency tables.

This frequency table shows the distribution of times in a Fun Run for charity. Times are continuous data.

Time (*t* minutes)	Number of runners
25 < t ≤ 30	1
30 < t ≤ 35	3
35 < t ≤ 40	14
40 < t ≤ 45	38
45 < t ≤ 50	28
50 < t ≤ 55	11
55 < t ≤ 60	3
60 < t ≤ 65	2
Total	100

The times are measured in 'completed minutes'.
The upper class boundaries are clearly:

30, 35, 40, …, 65.

In this table, *each upper class boundary is included in the class interval*. For example, the first class interval is 25 < t ≤ 30. The upper class boundary, 30, is in the class.
The *cumulative frequencies* will be the *number of data values that are '**less than or equal to**' these upper boundaries*.

Here is the start of a cumulative frequency table for this time distribution.
Note the extra first row in the table. It is often useful to have a cumulative frequency of 0 at the beginning.
In this table it shows that:
'0 runners took 25 minutes or less'.

Time (*t* minutes)	Cumulative frequency
t ≤ 25	0
t ≤ 30	1
t ≤ 35	4
t ≤ 40	18

+3
+14

Cumulative frequency tables for continuous data may be '**less than' tables.**

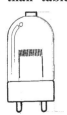

This frequency table shows the distribution of the working life of 200 projector bulbs.
The lifetimes were measured in complete hours.

Working life (*x* hours)	Number of bulbs
10 to under 20	4
20 to under 30	2
30 to under 40	8
40 to under 50	13
50 to under 60	18
60 to under 70	44
70 to under 80	68
80 to under 90	24
90 to under 100	19
Total	200

The upper class boundaries are:

20, 30, 40, …, 90, 100.

In this table, *each class interval does not include its upper class boundary*.

For example, the first class interval is '10 to under 20'.
The upper class boundary, 20, is not in the class.
The *cumulative frequencies* will be the *number of data values that are 'less than' the upper class boundaries*.

Look at the start of the cumulative frequency table for this distribution.
This first row shows that '0 bulbs lasted less than 10 hours'.

Working life (*x* hours)	Cumulative frequency
less than 10	0
less than 20	4
less than 30	6
less than 40	14

+2
+8

The class intervals used for these bulb 'lifetimes' could be described in different ways in a frequency table.
Instead of

'10 to under 20'	'20 to under 30'	'30 to under 40'	…

you may find

10 ≤ x < 20	20 ≤ x < 30	30 ≤ x < 40	…

or

10–20	20–30	30–40	…

or

10–	20–	30–	…

and so on …
Each way has the *same upper class boundaries*.
Each class interval does *not* include the upper boundary.
So these class intervals all give the same cumulative frequency table.

When data are measured 'to the nearest…' you have to work out the upper boundaries from the class intervals.

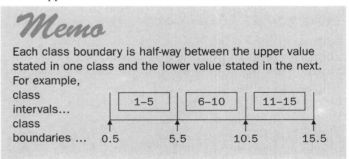

Memo

Each class boundary is half-way between the upper value stated in one class and the lower value stated in the next.
For example,
class intervals…
class boundaries …

1–5	6–10	11–15

0.5   5.5   10.5   15.5

The heights of 180 girls were measured in a medical survey.
This frequency table shows the results.
The measurements are 'to the nearest cm'. So the upper class boundaries are:

144.5,
149.5,
154.5, and so on …

Each upper class boundary does *not* belong to its class interval. It is the smallest value in the next class. So heights in each class interval are '*less than*' the upper class boundary.

Height in cm to the nearest cm	Number of girls
140–144	3
145–149	25
150–154	51
155–159	36
160–164	25
165–169	14
170–174	5
175–179	1

For example,
the upper class boundary of 140–144 is 144.5 cm.
Since 144.5 cm = 145 cm (to the nearest cm),
144.5 cm is not in the class 140–144.
It is the smallest height in the next class (145–149).
So every height in the class 140–144 is 'less than 144.5 cm'.

A cumulative frequency table for these data shows how many
heights were 'less than' the
upper boundary of each class.
Since '0 girls were less than
139.5 cm', we start the table
with this row.
The other cumulative
frequencies are found from the
frequency table as before.

Height in cm to nearest cm	Cumulative frequency
< 139.5	0
< 144.5	3
< 149.5	28
< 154.5	79

+25
+51

Summary

A **cumulative frequency** shows the number of results that
are 'less than'(<) or 'less than or equal to' (≤) a stated value
in a set of data.

Data are often grouped into class intervals. The frequency
for a class interval shows the number of results in that class.
Its cumulative frequency gives the number of results in that
class and all lower classes.

You can make a cumulative frequency table from a
frequency table of grouped data.

Use these notes to help you.
● We usually write the table in columns like these.

'Less than' table

Values	Cumulative frequency
< ……	0

'Less than or equal to' table

Values	Cumulative frequency
≤ ……	0

● To find the cumulative frequencies, add up the frequencies
as you go down the frequency table.
Write each 'running total' in your table.
Remember:
The last cumulative frequency = total frequency.
This is a useful check of your addition.
● To describe the 'Values' in your table, look at how each
class interval is given.

For discrete data:
Identify the greatest possible value in each class.
All the values for a class are 'less than or equal to' (≤) its
greatest possible value.

For continuous data:
Identify the upper class boundary of each class.
Decide whether the upper class boundary is in the class
or not.
If it is, then all the values for a class are
'less than or equal to' (≤) its upper class boundary.
If it is not, then all the values for a class are
'less than' (<) its upper class boundary.

▶ *Exercise* **P35.4**

1 Gerry did a survey of the
'copper coins' in the pockets
of 160 students. Their values
are shown in this frequency
distribution table.
Make a cumulative frequency
table for these data. Start with
a cumulative frequency of 0.
How many students had
copper coins worth
(a) 19 p or less
(b) less than 40 p
(c) more than 34 p
(d) 15 p or more?

Value of coins in pence	Number of students
5–9	2
10–14	3
15–19	22
20–24	30
25–29	40
30–34	26
35–39	22
40–44	10
45–49	5

2 Copy and complete the cumulative frequency table for the
times in a charity Fun Run given on p559.
How many runners took
(a) 45 minutes or less   (b) more than 40 minutes?

3 Use the frequency distribution of projector bulb lifetimes
given on p559 to make a cumulative frequency table.
It is started for you on that page.
How many bulbs lasted:
(a) less than 60 hours   (b) 70 hours or more?

4 Construct a cumulative frequency table for the distribution
of girls' heights given on p559.
How many girls heights were given as
(a) 154 cm or under   (b) more than 159 cm?

5 A sample of 90 eggs were
weighed 'to the nearest gram'.
This frequency table shows the
results.
Construct a cumulative
frequency table for these data.
Start with a cumulative
frequency of 0.
How many eggs were
recorded as
(a) 60 g or less   (b) 51 g or more?

Mass in g to the nearest g	Frequency
41–45	5
46–50	9
51–55	19
56–60	31
61–65	20
66–70	6

Note: Keep neat copies of your tables. You will use
them in Exercise P35.5, p563.

Cumulative frequency graphs

The information in a cumulative frequency table can be shown
on a graph.
The **cumulative frequency curve** shown opposite was drawn
from Deacon College's English marks on p558.
The Marks are on the horizontal axis.
The Cumulative frequency is on the vertical axis.

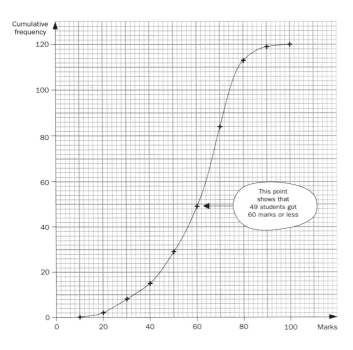

The cumulative frequency curve is a characteristic leaning S-shape.
It is called an **ogive**.
This name comes from a term in architecture for this shape.

Compare the entries in this cumulative frequency table with the plotted points on the cumulative frequency graph above.
Each *cumulative frequency* is plotted over the 'end' of its group.
This makes sure that all the values in the group have been included.

Marks	Cumulative frequency	Plotted points
≤ 10	0	(10, 0)
≤ 20	2	(20, 2)
≤ 30	8	(30, 8)
≤ 40	15	(40, 15)
≤ 50	29	(50, 29)
≤ 60	49	(60, 49)
≤ 70	84	(70, 84)
≤ 80	113	(80, 113)
≤ 90	119	(90, 119)
≤ 100	120	(100, 120)

Marks are discrete data.
So, for the 'end' of each group, we use the *greatest possible value* in that group.
   We call the graph drawn from these points, a **'less than or equal to' graph.**
Each plotted point shows *how many data values are 'less than or equal to' a value x.*
You can use the graph to estimate this number for any value *x* and vica versa.

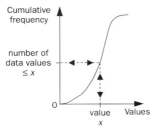

Some examples are given opposite.
Always draw lines on your graph to show how you get each answer.
In an examination you will get marks for using the correct method.
Remember: Find the 'number' on the Cumulative frequency axis.
      Read the 'value' from the Value axis.

Question

Use the cumulative frequency curve for Deacon College's English marks to find the following estimates.
Show how you obtained each estimate on the graph.
(a) Estimate the number of students who got 25 marks or less.
(b) Estimate the number of students who got more than 65 marks.
(c) If 20 students must fail the examination, estimate what the pass mark should be.
(d) If the top 20 students will be given book prizes, estimate the marks they must obtain.

Answer

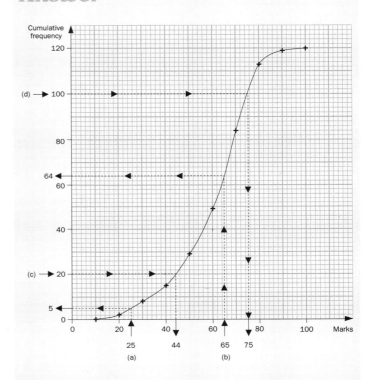

(a) From the curve,
   25 marks ↔ 5 c.f.
   5 students got
   25 marks or less.

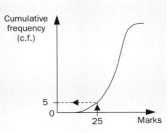

(b) 'More than 65 marks' is related to '65 marks or less'.
   From the curve,
   65 marks ↔ 64 c.f.
   64 students got
   65 marks or less.
   This gives:
   120 − 64 = 56 students got more than 65 marks.

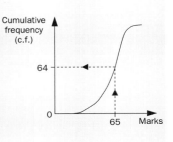

continued

(c) From the curve,
20 c.f.↔ 44 marks.
20 students got
44 marks or less, i.e. those
who fail get 44 marks or
less.
So the students who pass
got more than 44 marks,
i.e. the pass mark must be 45.

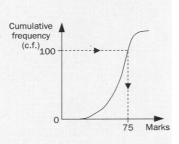

(d) The top 20 get book prizes.
This means that
120 − 20 = 100 will not.
From the curve,
100 c.f.↔ 75 marks.
100 students got
75 marks or less.
i.e. students with 75 marks
or less do not get prizes.
So students with more than 75 marks get book prizes.

◯ **Discussion Exercise**

Draw the cumulative frequency graph for the English
marks on 2 mm graph paper.
Use these scales:
　　Marks axis: 1 cm to 10 marks
　　Cumulative frequency axis: 1 cm to 10 students.
Use your graph to estimate the answers to the questions above.
Your answers may not be exactly the same as ours. Why?

Estimate the answers to these questions from your graph.
(a) How many students got 36 marks or less?
(b) How many students got 58 marks?
(c) 35 students got a certain mark or less.
　　What was that mark?
(d) 5 students got more than a certain mark.
　　What was that mark?

Discuss how you obtained each answer.
Suggest other questions you could answer from this graph.
Find the answers from your graph.
Compare your answers with those of other students in
your group.

Cumulative frequency graphs are also drawn for **grouped
continuous data**.
For these graphs, we plot *cumulative frequency* against the
upper class boundary of each class interval.

Question

Pupils in the same Year
Group in four schools had a
medical examination.

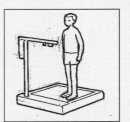

Mass in kg to the nearest kg	Number of pupils
26–30	15
31–35	42
36–40	65
41–45	92
46–50	75
51–55	67
56–60	37
61–65	7
Total	400

The distribution of their
masses is shown in this frequency table.
(a) Construct a cumulative frequency table for these data.
(b) Draw the cumulative frequency curve from your table.

Answer

(a) *The masses are measured 'to the nearest kg.' So the
upper boundaries of the class intervals are:*

　　30.5, 35.5, 40.5, ... 65.5.

*Each group in the cumulative frequency table is given as
'less than' its upper class boundary.*
*Since '0 pupils were less than 25.5 kg', we start the
cumulative frequency table with this row. This gives a
graph that starts on the horizontal axis.*

Mass	Cumulative frequency	Points to plot
less than 25.5 kg	0	(25.5, 0)
less than 30.5 kg	15	(30.5, 15)
less than 35.5 kg	57 +42	(35.5, 57)
less than 40.5 kg	122 +65	(40.5, 122)
less than 45.5 kg	214 +92	(45.5, 214)
less than 50.5 kg	289 +75	(50.5, 289)
less than 55.5 kg	356 +67	(55.5, 356)
less than 60.5 kg	393 +37	(60.5, 393)
less than 65.5 kg	400 +7	(65.5, 400)

Check: Total number of pupils is 400. ✓

(b) *The points to plot are shown above, beside the table.*
The horizontal axis is the Mass axis.
Number it from 25 to 70.
The vertical axis is the Cumulative frequency axis.
Number it from 0 to 400.
Plot the points given above.
Draw a smooth curve through the plotted points.

The cumulative frequency graph is shown here.

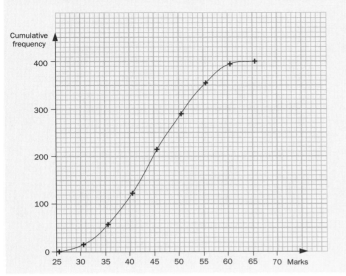

Discussion Exercise

Draw your own copy of the cumulative frequency graph shown above.
Use 2 mm graph paper and these scales.

> Mass axis: 2 cm to 10 kg
> Cumulative frequency axis: 2 cm to 100 pupils.

Use your graph to estimate answers to these questions.

(a) How many pupils weighed less than 42 kg?
(b) How many weighed 54 kg or more?
(c) 70 pupils were thought to be 'underweight'.
    What mass were they all less than?
(d) 50 pupils were thought to be 'overweight'.
    What was thought to be the largest 'suitable' mass for this Year Group?

Discuss how to find each answer.
Suggest other questions you could answer from this graph.
Find the answers from your graph.
Compare answers with your group.

Summary

To draw a **cumulative frequency graph** for **grouped data**, take these steps.

● Make a cumulative frequency table from the frequency table.
  Always start your table with a cumulative frequency of 0.
  (Note: This may result in your table having one row more than the frequency table.)

● Draw two axes at right angles.
  The vertical axis is always the Cumulative frequency axis.
  Number the scale from 0 up to the total frequency, *n*.
  The horizontal axis is the 'Values' axis. Number the scale to cover the full range of values in the data.

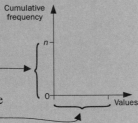

● Work out the points to plot from the cumulative frequency table.
  The coordinates to plot are:
      ('end value' of class interval, cumulative frequency)
  For *discrete data*, we use the greatest possible value in a class as its 'end value'.
  For *continuous data*, we use the upper class boundary of a class as its 'end value'.

● Plot the points neatly with a cross or dot.

● To draw a **cumulative frequency curve**, draw a *smooth curve* through the plotted points.
  Remember: The graph always starts on the horizontal axis, i.e. where the cumulative frequency is 0.
  The shape of the curve is usually a leaning S-shape or ogive.
  If you obtain any other shape, then you may have made a mistake.
  Check that your axes are the 'correct way round'.
  Make sure that you have plotted the points correctly.

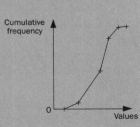

● To draw a **cumulative frequency polygon**, join the plotted points with *straight lines*.
  Straight lines are usually used only when they give a graph that is 'nearly a curve'.
  In an examination, however, you must draw the graph the question asks for.

► Exercise P35.5

Questions **1–5**.
Use your cumulative frequency tables from questions **1–5**, Exercise P35.4, p560.
Draw a cumulative frequency curve for each distribution.
Here are the scales to use on 2 mm graph paper.

Question **1**: Value axis: 1 cm to 5 pence.
           Cumulative frequency axis: 1 cm to 10 students.
Question **2**: Time axis: 2 cm to 5 minutes.
           Cumulative frequency axis: 2 cm to 10 runners.
Question **3**: Working life axis: 2 cm to 10 hours.
           Cumulative frequency axis: 2 cm to 20 bulbs
Question **4**: Height axis: 2 cm to 5 cm.
           Cumulative frequency axis: 2 cm to 20 girls.
Question **5**: Mass axis: 2 cm to 5 g.
           Cumulative frequency axis: 2 cm to 10 eggs.

> Note: Keep neat copies of your graphs. You will use them in the Discussion Exercise on p565.

Median and quartiles for grouped data.

The age distribution in this table is from a survey of 500 people. From this table you can say which *groups* contain the median and the lower and upper quartiles of the data.

Age in years	Frequency	Cumulative frequency
0–9	11	11 +51
10–19	51	62 +130
20–29	130	192 +90
30–39	90	282 +55
40–49	55	337 +52
50–59	52	389 +40
60–69	40	429 +30
70–79	30	459 +21
80–89	21	480 +20
90–99	20	500

For the **median**, we look for the 'mid-point' of the 500 values.
This lies between the 250th and 251st values.
The cumulative frequencies show that these two values are in the class 30–39.
So the median lies in the class 30–39.

For the **lower quartile**, we look for the 'mid–point' of the '*lower 250 values*'.
This lies between the 125th and 126th values.
These two values are in the class 20–29. So the lower quartile lies in the 20–29 class.

For the **upper quartile**, we look for the mid–point of the '*upper 250 values*'.
This lies between the 375th and 376th values.
These two values are in the class 50–59.
So the upper quartile lies in the 50–59 class.

You cannot find the *actual values* for the median and quartiles from this table. But you can find estimates for them from a cumulative frequency graph.

Median and quartiles from a cumulative frequency graph.

A cumulative frequency graph shows the data in order, from smallest to largest.
Each point on the graph gives an *estimate* of a value in a particular 'position' in the data.
For example, to estimate the 100th value, you find the point on the graph with cumulative frequency 100. You read off the value from the Value axis.

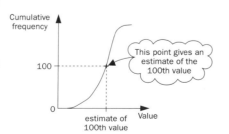

Remember:
Find the 'position' on the Cumulative frequency axis.
Read the 'value' from the Value axis.

The median and quartiles of a distribution depend on their 'position' in the ordered data.
So points on a cumulative frequency graph give estimates for their values.

Question

Draw a cumulative frequency curve for the age distribution given in the table on the left.
Use the cumulative frequency curve to estimate:
(a) the median age
(b) the lower and upper quartiles
(c) the interquartile range.

Answer

To draw the cumulative frequency curve, we plot each cumulative frequency against its upper class boundary. The table gives these points:

(10, 11), (20, 62), (30, 192), (40, 282), (50, 337),
(60, 389), (70, 429), (80, 459), (90, 480), (100, 500).

The graph must start on the horizontal axis. So we also plot (0,0) because '0 people' were 'under 0 years old' in the survey.
The cumulative frequency curve is shown here.

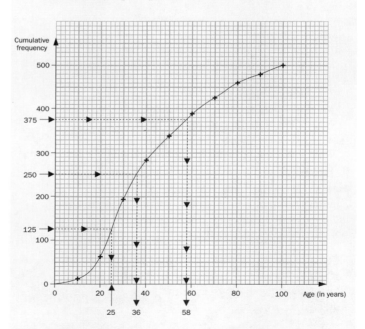

(a) There are 500 values in the distribution.
The median is the $\left(\dfrac{500+1}{2}\right)$th value.
Since the number of values is large (500), there is very little difference between the $\left(\dfrac{500+1}{2}\right)$th and $\left(\dfrac{500}{2}\right)$th values.
So, we use the $\left(\dfrac{500}{2}\right)$th value for the median,
i.e. 250th value → median

From the graph,
250 c.f. → 36 years.
This gives:
median ≈ 36 years.

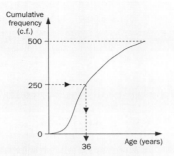

(b) The lower quartile is the $\left(\dfrac{500+1}{4}\right)$ th value.

The upper quartile is the $3\left(\dfrac{500+1}{4}\right)$ th value.

Because we have a large number of data (500),

we use the $\dfrac{500}{4}$ th value for the lower quartile,

i.e. 125th value → lower quartile.

We use the $\dfrac{3(500)}{4}$ th value for the upper quartile,

i.e. 375th value → upper quartile.

From the graph,
125 c.f. → 25 years
375 c.f. → 58 years
This gives:
lower quartile ≈ 25 years
upper quartile ≈ 58 years.

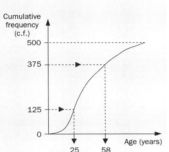

(c) Interquartile range = upper quartile − lower quartile
= 58 − 25
= 33 years.

Summary

The median, lower quartile and upper quartile of grouped data can be estimated from a cumulative frequency graph.

To estimate the median, take these steps.
- Work out the 'position' of the median.
  For n values, the median is the $\dfrac{(n+1)}{2}$ th value.

  If n is large, we use the $\dfrac{n}{2}$ th value.

- Mark this 'position' on the cumulative frequency axis.
- From this number, go across to the graph, then down to the Values axis. Draw lines to show what you have done.
- Read off the estimate of the median from the Value axis.

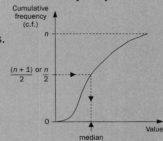

To estimate the lower and upper quartiles, take these steps.
- Work out their 'positions' first.
  For n values, lower quartile → $\dfrac{(n+1)}{4}$ th value

  upper quartile → $\dfrac{3(n+1)}{4}$ th value.

  If n is large, we use:
  lower quartile → $\dfrac{n}{4}$ th value

  upper quartile → $\dfrac{3n}{4}$ th value.

- Mark each 'position' on the cumulative frequency axis.
- Read off the value for each number from the graph. Draw in the lines to show how you get each value.

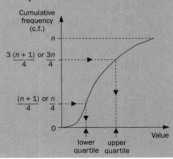

Discussion Exercise

1 Draw your own copy of the cumulative frequency graph for the age distribution.
Use these scales:
Age axis: 2 cm to 20 years
Cumulative frequency axis: 2 cm to 100 people.
Estimate the median, lower quartile and upper quartile from your graph.
Your values may not be exactly the same as ours.
Explain why.
Find the interquartile range from your values.

Questions **2 – 6**.
Use your cumulative frequency graphs from
Exercise P35.5, p563. Estimate the median, lower quartile and upper quartile for each distribution.
Discuss how you found each value.
Find the interquartile range for each distribution.

Exercise P35.6

1 This cumulative frequency graph shows the frame scores made by 60 players in the first round of a snooker knockout competition.

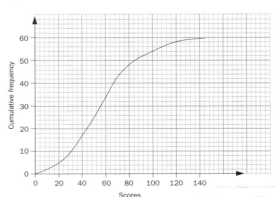

Use the graph to answer these questions.
(a) What is the median score?
(b) What is the interquartile range?
(c) How many players scored less than 20?
(d) How many players scored 100 or more?
(e) Two-thirds of the players made less than a certain score. What is that score?

2   The speeds of 50 cars travelling in a built-up area were recorded by the police last Sunday.
The graph below shows this information as a cumulative frequency curve.

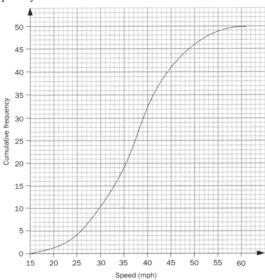

(a) How many of these cars were travelling at a legal speed, that is, at 30 mph or less?
(b) What percentage of cars were travelling at over 40 mph?
(c) What was the median speed?

3   This grouped frequency table shows the distribution of batsmen's scores in a cricket league.

Number of runs	Frequency
0– 20	9
21– 40	25
41– 60	38
61– 80	48
81–100	29
101–120	9
121–140	2

(a) Make a cumulative frequency table for these scores.
(b) Draw the resulting cumulative frequency curve.
Use your graph to answer (c) to (f).
(c) What was the median number of runs scored?
(d) What is the interquartile range?
(e) Estimate the number of times a score of 35 or under was made.
(f) The batsmen making the five best scores in the league are given medals. What is the lowest score to qualify for a medal?

4   100 athletes take part in a high jump competition. The information in this grouped frequency table shows the height of their best jumps.

Height (cm)	Number of athletes
<131	0
131–135	4
136–140	6
141–145	9
145–150	15
151–155	21
155–160	23
161–165	14
166–170	5
171–175	2
176–180	1

(a) Make a cumulative frequency table for this information.
(b) Represent the data on a cumulative frequency graph.
Use a scale of 2 cm to 10 cm on the Height axis and 2 cm to 20 athletes on the Cumulative frequency axis.

(c) From your graph estimate
    (i) the median height achieved in the competition
    (ii) the interquartile range.
(d) Certificates are awarded to athletes who jump at least 168 cm. How many certificates will be needed?

5   Ninety players entered a golf competition. Their scores are shown in this grouped frequency table.

Score	Number of golfers
65–69	5
70–74	9
75–79	19
80–84	31
85–89	20
90–94	6

(a) Construct a cumulative frequency table for these data.
(b) Draw the cumulative frequency graph. Use a scale of
    2 cm to 5 units on the Score axis
    2 cm to 10 golfers on the Cumulative frequency axis.

Use your graph to estimate
(c) the median
(d) the upper and lower quartiles
(e) the interquartile range
(f) the number of golfers scoring less than par (72).
(g) The ten players with the highest scores received wooden spoons. What was the lowest score to qualify for a wooden spoon?

6   The distribution of points scored by 50 teams in a Basketball League is shown in this grouped frequency table.

Points	Number of teams
0–4	4
5–9	6
10–14	6
15–19	14
20–24	12
25–29	8

(a) Make a cumulative frequency table for these data.
(b) Draw the cumulative frequency curve. Use a scale of
    2 cm to 4 points on the Points axis,
    2 cm to 5 teams on the Cumulative frequency axis.

Use your curve to estimate
(c) the median number of points scored
(d) the lower quartile
(e) the upper quartile
(f) the interquartile range
(g) the number of teams scoring 12 points or fewer.

7   Two hundred runners took part in a race. This grouped frequency table shows their finishing times.

Time (t mins)	Number of runners
t ≤ 25	0
25 < t ≤ 30	4
30 < t ≤ 35	8
35 < t ≤ 40	16
40 < t ≤ 45	24
45 < t ≤ 50	32
50 < t ≤ 55	40
55 < t ≤ 60	32
60 < t ≤ 65	24
65 < t ≤ 70	16
70 < t ≤ 75	4

(a) Use the given data to make a cumulative frequency table.
(b) Draw the cumulative frequency curve. Use a scale of
    2 cm to 10 minutes on the Time axis,
    2 cm to 20 runners on the Cumulative frequency axis.

From your graph estimate
(c) the median time
(d) the interquartile range
(e) the number of runners who finished the race in under 62 minutes.
(f) Medals will be awarded to the fastest 10% of the runners. What is the qualifying time for a medal?

8 The contents of a sample of 80 packets of E10 washing powder were weighed to the nearest 10 g. The results are given in the table.
(a) Make a cumulative frequency table for these data.
(b) Draw a cumulative frequency diagram. Use a scale of
   2 cm to 100 g on the Weight axis,
   2 cm to 20 packets on the Cumulative frequency axis.
Use your graph to estimate
(c) the median weight
(d) the interquartile range
(e) the number of packets containing less than the stated weight of 4 kg
(f) the number of packets with contents weighing between 3960 g and 4120 g.

Weight (g)	Frequency
≤3840	0
3850–3890	4
3900–3940	6
3950–3990	9
4000–4040	11
4050–4090	19
4100–4140	13
4250–4190	9
4200–4240	6
4250–4290	3

9 The distribution of marks obtained by 184 Year 11 students in an examination is given in this grouped frequency table.
(a) Construct a cumulative frequency table.
(b) Draw the cumulative frequency curve. Use a scale of
   2 cm to represent 20 marks on the Marks axis,
   2 cm to represent 20 students on the Cumulative frequency axis.
Use your graph to estimate
(c) the median mark
(d) the interquartile range
(e) the number of students who obtained a mark of less than 45 (the passmark),
(f) the minimum mark required to be awarded a distinction if 20 students gained distinctions.
Last year's Year 11 students took a similar examination. This frequency table shows their results.
(g) Repeat parts (a) – (f) for last year's results.
(h) Write a short report comparing the exam results for the Year 11 students in the two years. In your comparison, use the graphs you have drawn and the statistics you have found.

Mark	Frequency
1–10	1
11–20	3
21–30	13
31–40	45
41–50	42
51–60	33
61–70	24
71–80	12
81–90	7
91–100	4

Mark	Frequency
1–10	2
11–20	9
21–30	28
31–40	59
41–50	47
51–60	21
61–70	13
71–80	4
81–90	1
91–100	0

10 A survey of the age distribution of 100 shoppers in a supermarket was made last month. This table shows the results.
(a) Make a cumulative frequency table for these data.
(b) Draw a cumulative frequency diagram to represent this distribution.
   Use a scale of
   2 cm to 10 years on the Age axis,
   2 cm to 10 people on the Cumulative frequency axis.

Age (x years)	Number of shoppers
0 ≤ x < 15	0
15 ≤ x < 30	22
30 ≤ x < 45	34
45 ≤ x < 60	30
60 ≤ x < 75	14

From your graph estimate
(c) the median age of shoppers
(d) the interquartile range
(e) the number of shoppers under the age of 50.
Free samples of biscuits were given to all people aged 65 or over who took part in the survey.
(f) How many people received free biscuits?
When a similar survey was carried out during the same month last year, the results were as in this table:

Age (x years)	Number of shoppers
0 ≤ x < 15	0
15 ≤ x < 30	12
30 ≤ x < 45	27
45 ≤ x < 60	46
60 ≤ x < 75	15

(g) Repeat parts (a)–(f) for last year's data.
(h) Write a short report comparing the results of these two surveys. Include in your report, comments on the graphs and statistics you have obtained.

Examination Questions

1 The lighting in a concert hall is provided by 500 lamps. When the lamps need to be replaced a tall tower has to be brought in and erected. So all the lamps are changed at the same time.
The manager obtains this graph from the makers of the lamps.

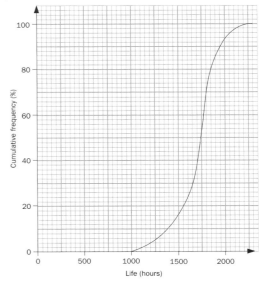

This cumulative frequency graph shows the life of the lamps.
(a) What percentage of lamps have failed after 1500 hours?
(b) In the concert hall, how many lamps are expected still to be working after 1800 hours?
(c) Safety regulations state that at least 70% of the lamps in the concert hall should be working.
   After how many hours of use should the manager arrange for all the lamps to be changed?
(MEG, 1989)

2 The time interval (measured in seconds) between the passing of cars at a particular point on a road through a village was measured and a cumulative frequency table drawn up as shown on the next page.

(a) Draw a cumulative frequency polygon. Use a scale of
   2 cm to 40 seconds on the Time axis,
   2 cm to 20 cars on the Cumulative frequency axis.
(b) Find the interquartile range and show your construction lines.
(c) The Parish Council was asked to install traffic lights on the road in order to allow villagers to cross in safety. The road was 10 metres wide. Use your graph, or the information in the table, to decide whether you think the installation of traffic lights was necessary. Give your reasons.

(NEAB, 1989)

Time interval (in seconds)	Cumulative frequency
Less than 30	0
Less than 40	4
Less than 50	12
Less than 60	24
Less than 70	40
Less than 80	54
Less than 90	68
Less than 100	76
Less than 110	83
Less than 120	91
Less than 130	95
Less than 140	98
Less than 150	100

3 Kew Gardens keeps a record of the damage caused by oak tree roots.
The 293 cases recorded are in the table given, showing the distance from the tree at which damage occurred.

(a) Complete the cumulative frequency table.

Distance from tree (m)	Number of incidents	Cumulative number of incidents
0–5	44	
5–10	111	
10–15	79	
15–20	30	
20–25	14	
25–30	15	

(b) Show this information as a cumulative frequency graph. Use a scale of
   2 cm to 5 m on the Distance axis,
   2 cm to 50 incidents on the Cumulative frequency axis.
(c) Use your graph to find
   (i) the median distance at which an oak tree caused damage
   (ii) the percentage of oak trees which caused damage at over 22 m distance.

(MEG, 1990)

4 A farmer reared 250 turkeys for Christmas. He weighed each to the nearest one tenth of a pound. His results are shown in the table.

Number of pounds	Number of turkeys
0–3.9	0
4–7.9	10
8–11.9	77
12–15.9	96
16–19.9	44
20–23.9	23

(a) Complete the cumulative frequency table.

Number of pounds less than	Cumulative frequency
4	
8	
12	
16	
20	
24	

(b) Using a scale of 2 cm for 4 pounds on the horizontal axis and 2 cm for 25 turkeys on the vertical axis, draw the cumulative curve.
(c) Find from the graph
   (i) the median
   (ii) the interquartile range.
(d) A small supermarket ordered 100 of these turkeys with a median weight of 12.8 pounds and a minimum range of weights. Between what weights did these turkeys lie?

(NISEAC, 1990)

5 A pupil working on a GCSE project investigates the distance travelled by day-trippers visiting Blackpool by coach. She obtains the following information from 130 coach drivers.

Distance travelled d (miles)	$0 < d \leqslant 30$	$30 < d \leqslant 60$	$60 < d \leqslant 90$	$90 < d \leqslant 120$	$120 < d \leqslant 160$
Number of coaches	7	45	32	24	22

(a) On graph paper draw a cumulative frequency diagram to represent this information.
(b) Find the median distance and the upper and lower quartiles.
(c) Estimate the percentage of coaches that have travelled more than 100 miles to get to Blackpool.

(NEAB, 1989)

P36
Similarity

This unit will help you to:

■ understand that similar shapes are mathematical enlargements of each other
■ recognise similar shapes
■ identify matching angles and matching lengths in similar shapes
■ check whether shapes are similar are not
■ use the idea of similarity to find lengths
■ use similarity to solve practical problems.

Recognising similar shapes

We often call things 'similar' in everyday life.

KEN AND SUE DRIVE SIMILAR CARS   KEN AND SUE LIVE IN SIMILAR HOUSES   KEN AND SUE HAVE SIMILAR DOGS

 Discussion Exercise

How are the things in these pictures similar?
Think of some other examples of similar things.
What do we mean by similar?

In mathematics the word **similar** has a very precise meaning.
Similar shapes *look alike*. They are the *same 'shape'* but they
may be *different sizes*.
These shapes are similar.

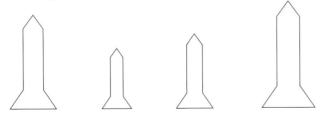

Each shape is a **mathematical enlargement** of the others.
The shapes are still similar if we turn them round or flip them
over.

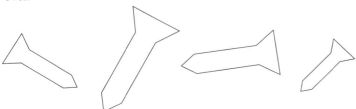

These shapes are *not* all similar.

You can easily spot that Natasha is the odd one out.
Natasha is *not* a mathematical enlargement of the others.

▶ *Exercise* **P36.1**

1   Look for the odd one out in these pictures. Which shapes
are similar?
(a)

(b)

(c)

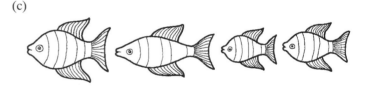

(d)

(e)

(f)

2   Name the similar shapes below.
Trace them if it helps to compare them.

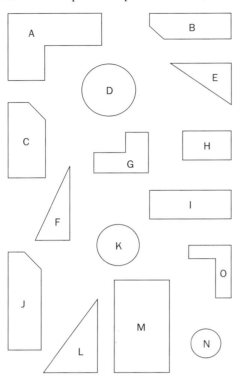

Comparing angles

Shapes ABCD and WXYZ are similar.
Each is an '**enlargement**' of the other.
The rays on the diagram show
matching points.
A ↔ W   B ↔ X
C ↔ Y   D ↔ Z

centre of
enlargement

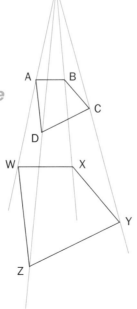

 Discussion Exercise

• Trace this diagram carefully.
Use it to answer these questions.

• Compare matching angles in the
two similar shapes ABCD and
WXYZ.
Are the matching angles:
- always different sizes
- sometimes different sizes
- always the same size?

• Draw some other similar polygons
by enlarging shapes. Use the ray
method. Compare matching angles in
your similar shapes.
Discuss what you find with other
students in your group.

• Write a statement about
matching angles in
similar shapes.

Memo
Drawing enlargements
S11 p190

Exercise P36.2

The diagrams in this exercise have all been drawn accurately.
1   These shapes are all similar.

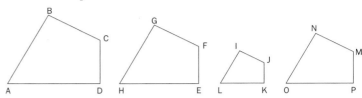

(a) Which points match point C?
What can you say about the angles at these points?
(b) Which angles are equal to the angle at G?
(c) In shape IJKL, angle L = 60°.
Which angles in the other shapes are 60°?
Can you say without measuring?
(d) What other equal angles can you name in these shapes?

2   These two shapes are similar.

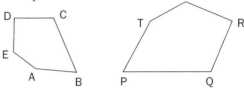

Name their matching points and angles.

A ↔ ?   B ↔ ?   C ↔ ?   D ↔ ?   E ↔ ?

It may help to trace one. Then you can turn it round to
'match' the other.

3   Compare these similar shapes.

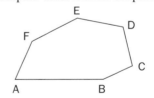 

Name their matching points and angles.
Trace one shape if it helps.
You can flip it over to 'match' the other.

Comparing lengths

The shapes ABCDE and LMNOP are similar.

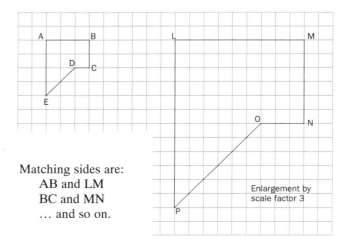

Matching sides are:
AB and LM
BC and MN
… and so on.

Enlargement by
scale factor 3

● Compare matching sides of ABCDE and LMNOP on the previous page.
Work out the ratios:
$\dfrac{\text{LM}}{\text{AB}}$, $\dfrac{\text{MN}}{\text{BC}}$, and so on …

What did you find?
● Copy and enlarge each of these shapes. Use squared paper and the given scale factors.

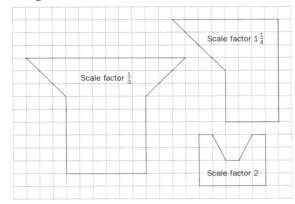

Compare matching sides of each pair of similar shapes.

Work out the ratio $\dfrac{\text{enlarged length}}{\text{original length}}$ in each case.

Discuss your results.
Were they what you expected?
Explain why.
● Discuss how to complete this sentence.
'When two shapes are similar, the ratio of matching sides …'

Summary

When two shapes are similar, these facts about them are true.
● Each is a mathematical enlargement of the other.
● 'Matching' angles are equal.
● 'Matching' lengths are in the same ratio.
   The value of this ratio is the **scale factor** of the enlargement.

The word 'corresponding' is often used instead of 'matching'.
   corresponding angles ↔ matching angles
   corresponding lengths ↔ matching lengths.

Finding scale factors

You can find the scale factor of an enlargement from just two 'matching lengths'.

$$\text{scale factor} = \dfrac{\text{length on enlargement}}{\text{matching length on original}}$$

The lengths must be in the same unit.

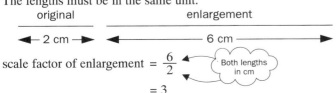

scale factor of enlargement $= \dfrac{6}{2}$ (Both lengths in cm)

$= 3$

You can measure 'matching lengths' on accurate diagrams.

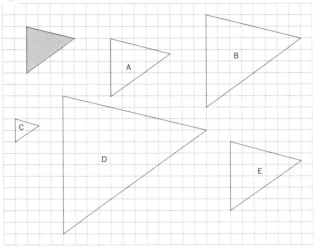

The shaded triangle has been enlarged to make each of the other triangles.
Find the scale factor of the enlargement in each case.
Which lengths did you use to find them?
Explain why.

Not all diagrams of similar shapes are drawn to scale.
But you can often use lengths you know to find scale factors.

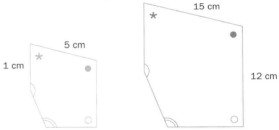

These two shapes, for example, are not drawn accurately.
But they are similar.
To find 'matching lengths', we look for *lengths 'between' matching equal angles.*
   The 5 cm length is 'between' angles ✱ and ●.
   The 15 cm length is 'between' angles ✱ and ●.
   So these are 'matching lengths' on the two shapes.
If the *grey shape* is the 'enlargement',
then the scale factor is given by:

$$\dfrac{\text{length on } grey\ shape}{\text{matching length on green shape}} = \dfrac{15}{5} = 3$$

If the *green shape* is the 'enlargement',
then the scale factor is given by:

$$\dfrac{\text{length on } green\ shape}{\text{matching length on grey shape}} = \dfrac{5}{15} = \dfrac{1}{3}$$

Remember: The lengths must be in the same unit.
            Change one of them if you need to.

The following diagrams are not drawn to scale. Each pair of shapes is similar. In each case find the scale factor used
(a) to enlarge the grey shape to make the green shape
(b) to enlarge the green shape to make the grey shape.

1

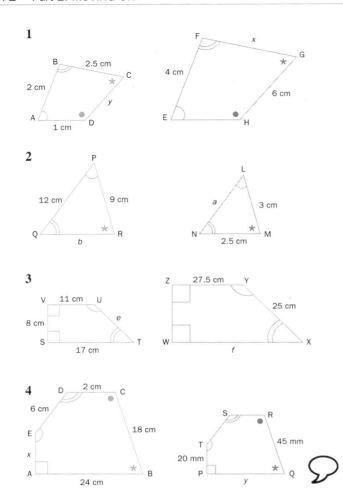

2

3

4

Similar shapes are not always drawn the 'same way up' or to scale. When this happens you have to take extra care to spot 'matching lengths'. 'Matching lengths' are always 'between' matching pairs of equal angles. So you can use this fact to help you.

Here are two similar quadrilaterals.

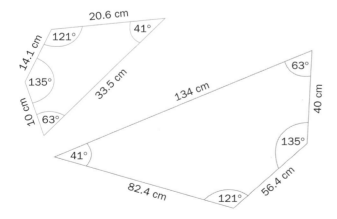

You can work out their 'matching lengths' in this way.

Matching lengths	Green shape	Grey shape
'Between' 121° and 41°	20.6 cm	82.4 cm
'Between' 41° and 63°	33.5 cm	134 cm
'Between' 63° and 135°	10 cm	40 cm
'Between' 135° and 121°	14.1 cm	56.4 cm

If the *grey shape* is the 'enlargement', the scale factor is given by:

$$\frac{82.4}{20.6} \text{ or } \frac{134}{33.5} \text{ or } \frac{40}{10} \text{ or } \frac{56.4}{14.1} \text{ ... all equal to 4.}$$

If the *green shape* is the 'enlargement', the scale factor is given by:

$$\frac{20.6}{82.4} \text{ or } \frac{33.5}{134} \text{ or } \frac{10}{40} \text{ or } \frac{14.1}{56.4} \text{ ... all equal to } \frac{1}{4}.$$

▶ *Exercise* P36.3

Find the matching lengths on these pairs of similar shapes. Use them to find the scale factor:
(a) if the grey shape is the enlargement
(b) if the green shape is the enlargement.

1

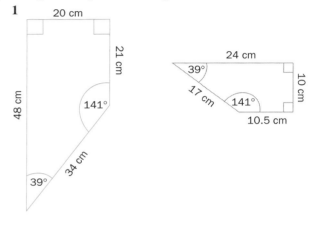

2

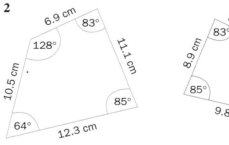

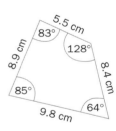

3

Checking for similarity

A shape and a true enlargement are similar.

Matching angles are equal.

The ratio of each pair of matching sides gives the same scale factor.

You use these two facts to check whether two shapes are similar.

Take these steps:
- Compare the angles of the two shapes. If the shapes do not have the same angles, they are not similar.
- Find the ratios of matching sides. If any two ratios are different, then the shapes are not similar.

Question

Sid took a photograph of the Eiffel tower when he was on holiday. The photograph is 7.4 cm wide and 11.6 cm high. Could a poster of the Eiffel tower measuring 22.8 cm wide by 39.7 cm high be a true enlargement of Sid's photograph? Give a reason for your answer.

Answer

- The photo and poster are both rectangles. So they have the same angles.
- *Compare matching lengths on the poster and photo.*

  Ratio of heights = $\frac{39.7}{11.6}$

  = 3.422413793

  Ratio of widths = $\frac{22.8}{7.4}$

  = 3.081081081

These ratios are not the same. So the poster and photo are not similar. The poster is not a true enlargement of the photo.

▶ *Exercise* **P36.4**

Give a reason for your answer to each question.

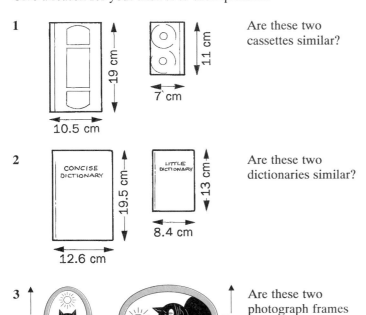

1 Are these two cassettes similar?

2 Are these two dictionaries similar?

3 Are these two photograph frames similar?

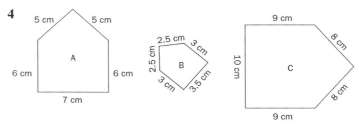

4

(a) Two of these diagrams are the plans for the end section of the same house. Which ones are they?
(b) Plan A is used to build a house. The scale factor of the enlargement being 100.
What is the width of the end section of the real house?

Finding lengths

When a shape is enlarged, each length is enlarged *by the same scale factor*.

   Length on enlargement
      = scale factor × matching length on original.

You can use this to find unknown lengths on similar shapes. Make sure you work with 'matching lengths'.

Question

The measurements of a standard size can of Huxters soup are given in this picture.
Huxters new size cans are similar to their standard size can.
What is the diameter of their new small size can? Give your answer in centimetres.

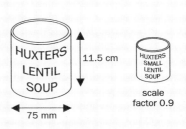

Answer

Standard size: diameter 75 mm = 7.5 cm ◄ *change to cm*
Small size: scale factor 0.9
small diameter = 0.9 × standard diameter
   = 0.9 × 7.5
   = 6.75 cm

To solve some problems you have to find the scale factor first. Then you can use it to calculate some unknown lengths.

Question

June wants to have an enlarged print made from this holiday slide.
(a) Measure the width and height of the slide in millimetres.

continued

(b) June wants a Deluxe enlargement with a width of 19.8 cm. What scale factor will be used?

(c) How high will the Deluxe enlargement be?

(d) What will be the height in centimetres of the Deluxe enlargement?

Answer

(a) width: 36 mm   height: 24 mm.

(b) *Known 'matching lengths' are the widths*
enlarged width: 19.8 cm = 198 mm ◄───

original width: 36 mm ◄───

make units the same

$$\text{scale factor} = \frac{\text{enlarged width}}{\text{original width}}$$

$$= \frac{198}{36}$$

$$= 5.5$$

(c) Enlarged height = scale factor × original height
$$= 5.5 \times 24 \text{ mm}$$
$$= 132 \text{ mm}$$
$$= 13.2 \text{ cm}$$
The height of the Deluxe enlargement is 13.2 cm.

► *Exercise* P36.5

Questions **1–5**:
Calculate the lengths of the lines marked with small letters in the Discussion Exercise on p571 and 572.
Use the scale factors you found in that Exercise.

6 Bradburys have produced a similar 'New Size' bar of chocolate.

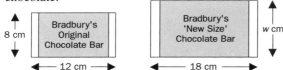

(a) What is the scale factor?   (b) Calculate w.

7 The inside of this picture frame is similar to the outside. Calculate *h*.

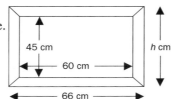

8 The Keen Kite Company make these two similar models. What is the length, *l* cm, of the smaller kite?

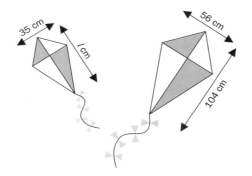

9 KWIK KLEEN is sold in standard size tins like this.
A new jumbo size tin is to be introduced which is mathematically similar to the standard size. Its diameter will be 9 cm.
How tall will the jumbo size tin be?

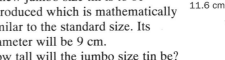

10 The two sails on this model boat are similar.
(a) What is the scale factor if you:
    (i) enlarge the smaller sail to make the larger one
    (ii) enlarge the larger sail to make the smaller one?
(b) Calculate, using the results found in (a):
    (i) *x*   (ii) *y*.

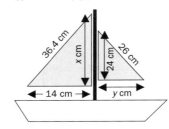

11 Kong Cones use cones and chocolate bars for their ice creams. They want to make a new King Kong cone and chocolate bar similar to those in the Big Kong 88.

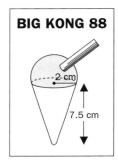

BIG KONG 88

(a) The new larger cone will have a radius of 2.8 cm.
    What is the scale factor of the enlargement?

(b) The Big Kong uses a cone 7.5 cm tall.
    How tall will the King Kong cone be?

(c) Their new ice cream will have a chocolate bar 9.8 cm long in it.
    How long is the chocolate bar in a Big Kong 88?

Looking at shadows

Beth is 1.40 m tall.

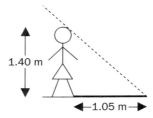

Alan is 1.68 m tall.

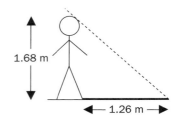

On a sunny day they measure their shadows at the same time.

The ratio $\dfrac{\text{Alan's height}}{\text{Beth's height}} = \dfrac{1.68}{1.40} = 1.2$

So Alan's height is 1.2 × Beth's height.

The ratio $\dfrac{\text{Alan's shadow length}}{\text{Beth's shadow length}} = \dfrac{1.26}{1.05} = 1.2$

So Alan's shadow length is 1.2 × Beth's shadow length.

Discussion Exercise

Later on the same day, Alan and Beth measure their shadows again.

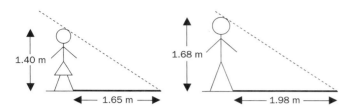

Work out the ratio of their shadow lengths again.
What do you find?

Again on the same day, Beth measures her shadow.

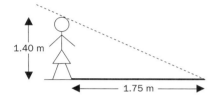

Predict how long Alan's shadow should be at the same time.
Explain your answer.
Beth, Chris and Dave's shadows are measured at the same time.

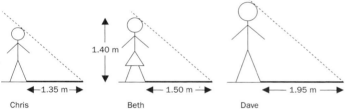

Discuss how to work out the heights of Dave and Chris.

ACTIVITY

Work with another student.
Measure each other's shadow lengths at different times of the day.
Work out the ratio of these lengths at each time.
Comment on your results.
Measure your height or your partner's height. Use your results to work out the height you don't know. Then measure it to check.

Using Shadows

You can **find the height of an object** from the length of its shadow.
You need to know the height of another object and the length of its shadow at the same time.
You can work out the ratio of matching 'shadow lengths'. Then use this 'scale factor' to find the unknown height.
Make sure that all the lengths used are in the same unit. Change any if you need to.

Question

On a sunny day, Sam found the height of a tree by measuring the lengths of shadows.

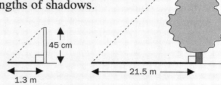

A stick of height 45 cm cast a shadow 1.3 m long. At the same time a tree cast a shadow 21.5 m long.
Calculate the height of the tree.

Answer

Facts: tree's shadow length = 21.5 m
           stick's shadow length = 1.3 m
           stick's height = 45 cm = 0.45 m

Scale factor $= \dfrac{\text{tree's shadow length}}{\text{stick's shadow length}}$

$= \dfrac{21.5}{1.3}$

Height of tree = scale factor × height of stick

$= \dfrac{21.5}{1.3} \times 0.45$

$= 7.442307692$

$= 7.4$ m (to 1 dp)

ACTIVITY

Use the 'shadow method' to find the heights of some trees or other tall objects.
Write a report on your work and findings. Comment on the advantages and disadvantages of finding heights by this method.

▶ Exercise P36.6

1   Ruth measured Mike's shadow to be 2.45 m. Mike is 1.72 m tall. At the same time, a building cast a shadow 21.4 m long.
    Ruth used these facts to calculate the height of the building to be 30 m (to the nearest m). Was she right? Show all your working to support your answer.

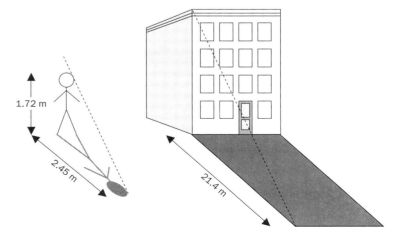

2 A tree of height 9.5 m casts a shadow 17 m long. Find the length of Helen's shadow at the same time. Helen is 1.66 m tall.

3 A house of height 8.6 m casts a shadow 16 m long. At the same time, the house next door casts a shadow 17.5 m long. How tall is this house?

Examination Questions

1 Six triangles are drawn on the grid below.

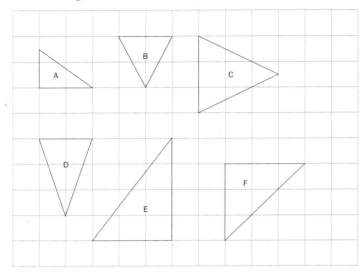

(a) Which triangle is similar to triangle B?
(b) Triangle E is an enlargement of triangle A.
   What is the scale factor for this enlargement?
(c) Triangle F is both isosceles and right-angled.
   Write down the sizes of the three angles in this triangle.
                                              (NEAB, 1989)

2 A pole of height 2 m casts a shadow 3 m long. At the same time a tree casts a shadow 18 m long.
Calculate the height of the tree.

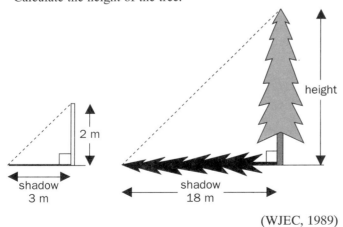

                                              (WJEC, 1989)

3 An Art Gallery sells two different postcard copies of a famous painting.

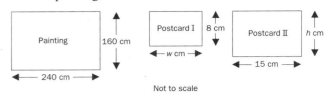

Not to scale

(a) Calculate the width, w cm, of postcard I.
(b) Calculate the height, h cm, of postcard II.
                                              (MEG, 1990)

4 Jane wants to have a photo of Bill enlarged to poster size.
The photo is 14 cm long and 11 cm wide.
The poster will be 36 cm wide.
How long will it be?
                                              (MEG, 1990)

5 A page of a book is 169 mm wide and 238 mm long. When reduced on a photocopier, the copy is 119 mm wide. Find the length of the copy, to the nearest millimetre.
                                              (MEG, 1991)

6

This diagram is not to scale

Sonya goes to the cinema to see a new film and has a lady wearing a large hat sitting in front of her so that she cannot see the screen. The lady sits 0.5 m in front of Sonya and the top of her hat is 0.3 m above the back of the seat. Sonya is in a row 20 m from the screen. Calculate
(a) the scale factor which would enlarge the lady's head, shoulders and hat to reach the top of the screen,
(b) the value of h.
                                              (ULEAC, 1994)

7 This is a picture frame. The largest picture it can take measures 62.5 cm by 45 cm.

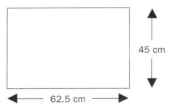

This photo measures 12.5 cm by 9 cm.
Will an enlargement of this photo fit exactly into the picture frame?
Give a reason for your answer.
                                              (MEG, 1990)

Selected Answers

NUMBER

N1.1
1 215 **2** 59 **3** 45 **4** 114 **5** 59
6 31 **7** 262p or £2.62 **8** 26927

N1.2
1 (a) 16.146 788 99 (b) 59.61
(c) 6395.03 (d) 2295.415
(e) 606.68
2 (a) 52.871 (b) 3648.44
(c) 7.961 627 907 (d) 458.89
(e) 150 564.5

N1.3
1 450 Obviously wrong
2 80
3 3 Obviously wrong
4 14 Obviously wrong
5 180 Obviously wrong
6 40 Obviously wrong
7 3.75
8 5 Obviously wrong

N1.4
1 (a) Correct (b) Wrong 413
(c) Correct (d) Wrong 1978
2 (a) Correct (b) Wrong 729
(c) Wrong 2119 (d) Correct
3 (a) Correct (b) Correct
(c) Wrong 78546 (d) Correct
4 (a) Correct (b) Correct
(c) Wrong 64 (d) Wrong 58

N1.5
Wrong answers 1, 2, 3, 4, 6, 8

N1.6
1 60 mℓ **2** 2 feet **3** 80 g
4 7.95 metres **5** 1.7°C

N2.1
1 (a) 3 (b) 9 (c) 5 (d) 8 (e) 4
2 (a) 5 (b) 3 (c) 9 (d) 6 (e) 8
3 (a) 7 (b) 4 (c) 9 (d) 6 (e) 7
(f) 8
4 (a) 8 (b) 7 (c) 9 (d) 9 (e) 8
(f) 7 (g) 4 (h) 6 (i) 5 (j) 6
(k) 6 (l) 7
5 (a) 9r1 (b) 7r4 (c) 9r2 (d) 8r7
(e) 9r4 (f) 6r4
6 (a) 2 (b) 1 (c) 4 (d) 4 (e) 1
(f) 3

N2.2
1 (a) (i) 80 (ii) 800 (iii) 8000
(b) (i) 130 (ii) 1300 (iii) 13 000
(c) (i) 70 (ii) 700 (iii) 7000
(d) (i) 240 (ii) 2400 (iii) 24 000
(e) (i) 190 (ii) 1900 (iii) 19 000
(f) (i) 720 (ii) 7200 (iii) 72 000
(g) (i) 1540 (ii) 15400 (iii) 154 000
(h) (i) 2790 (ii) 27900 (iii) 279 000
(i) (i) 3600 (ii) 36000 (iii) 360 000
(j) (i) 42 160 (ii) 421 600 (iii) 4 216 000
(k) (i) 4 (ii) 40 (iii) 400
(l) (i) 26 (ii) 260 (iii) 2600
(m) (i) 0.7 (ii) 7 (iii) 70
(n) (i) 229 (ii) 2290 (iii) 22 900
(o) (i) 582 (ii) 5820 (iii) 58 200
(p) (i) 0.08 (ii) 0.8 (iii) 8
(q) (i) 1274 (ii) 12 740 (iii) 127 400
(r) (i) 193.6 (ii) 1936 (iii) 19 360
(s) (i) 0.1 (ii) 1 (iii) 10
(t) (i) 5279.6 (ii) 52 796 (iii) 527 960
2 (a) (i) 0.8 (ii) 0.08 (iii) 0.008
(b) (i) 1.3 (ii) 0.13 (iii) 0.013
(c) (i) 0.7 (ii) 0.07 (iii) 0.007
(d) (i) 2.4 (ii) 0.24 (iii) 0.024
(e) (i) 1.9 (ii) 0.19 (iii) 0.019
(f) (i) 7.2 (ii) 0.72 (iii) 0.072
(g) (i) 15.4 (ii) 1.54 (iii) 0.154
(h) (i) 27.9 (ii) 2.79 (iii) 0.279
(i) (i) 36 (ii) 3.6 (iii) 0.36
(j) (i) 421.6 (ii) 42.16 (iii) 4.216
(k) (i) 0.04 (ii) 0.004 (iii) 0.0004
(l) (i) 0.26 (ii) 0.026 (iii) 0.0026
(m) (i) 0.007 (ii) 0.0007 (iii) 0.000 07
(n) (i) 2.29 (ii) 0.229 (iii) 0.0229
(o) (i) 5.82 (ii) 0.582 (iii) 0.0582
(p) (i) 0.0008 (ii) 0.000 08
(iii) 0.000 008
(q) (i) 12.74 (ii) 1.274 (iii) 0.1274
(r) (i) 1.936 (ii) 0.1936 (iii) 0.01936
(s) (i) 0.001 (ii) 0.0001 (iii) 0.000 01
(t) (i) 52.796 (ii) 5.2796 (iii) 0.52796
3 (a) 5600 (b) 94.3 (c) 0.078
(d) 4300 (e) 905 000 (f) 6.5
(g) 39 000 (h) 0.062 (i) 0.27
(j) 53 000
4 (a) 0.64 (b) 0.0925 (c) 17 (d) 10.5
(e) 800 (f) 0.0059 (g) 0.0678
(h) 0.086 (i) 2500 (j) 90

N2.4
1 (a) 200 (b) 2000 (c) 300 000
(d) 10 000 (e) 30
2 (a) 7000 (b) 600 (c) 80
(d) 40 000 (e) 300 000
3 (a) 5000 (b) 80 (c) 50 000
(d) 200 (e) 500 000
4 (a) 4 (b) 40 (c) 40 (d) 40
(e) 4000
5 (a) 70 (b) 7 (c) 700 (d) 700
(e) 7
6 (a) 60 (b) 600 (c) 6 (d) 600
(e) 60
7 (a) 3000 (b) 3 (c) 20 (d) 100 000
(e) 200
8 (a) 80 (b) 400 (c) 500 (d) 500
(e) 5
9 (a) 80 (b) 400 (c) 70 000 (d) 50
(e) 50
10 (a) 90 (b) 30 (c) 20 000 (d) 30
(e) 5

N2.5
1 (a) 774 (b) 1653 (c) 2664
(d) 5915 (e) 1066 (f) 3102
2 (a) 12008 (b) 4929 (c) 17192
(d) 56280 (e) 29632 (f) 29638

N2.6
1 120 **2** 690 **3** 1380 **4** 850
5 2500 **6** 41500 **7** 216 **8** 1233
9 5184 **10** 1782 **11** 14454
12 35046

N2.7
1 1084.2 **2** 490.2 **3** 1.911
4 29.736 **5** 291.92 **6** 84.6
7 103.88 **8** 29.882

N2.8
1 (a) 3 (b) 5 (c) 4 (d) 2 (e) 7
(f) 3
2 (a) 8 remainder 5
(b) 6 remainder 8
(c) 3 remainder 3
(d) 3 remainder 2
(e) 4 remainder 4
(f) 6 remainder 10
3 (a) 9 remainder 2
(b) 15 remainder 3
(c) 10 remainder 17
(d) 12 remainder 20
(e) 15 remainder 26
(f) 16 remainder 14

N2.9
1 40 **2** 9 **3** 12 **4** 710 **5** 7 **6** 28
7 900 **8** 50 **9** 70 **10** 8 **11** 14
12 10

N2.10
1 (a) 3600 eggs (b) 20 000 people
(c) 150 mm (d) £50 000
(e) 630 000 pages (f) 50 minutes
2 (a) 1620 biscuits (b) 3072 sheets
(c) 4 balloons (d) 8 films
(e) 35 720 words
(f) 18 packs, 6 envelopes left over

N3.1
1 (a) 3.7 (b) 11.7 (c) 9.8 (d) 27.3
(e) 0.4 (f) 33.0 (g) 52.0
(h) 64.8
2 (a) (i) 15.4 (ii) 15.42 (iii) 15.421
(b) (i) 5.8 (ii) 5.83 (iii) 5.826
(c) (i) 9.5 (ii) 9.53 (iii) 9.529
(d) (i) 6.5 (ii) 6.49 (iii) 6.492
(e) (i) 0.3 (ii) 0.32 (iii) 0.321
(f) (i) 2.9 (ii) 2.90 (iii) 2.903

N3.2
1 (a) 7.5 kg (b) 7.48 kg
(c) 7.483 kg
2 (a) 10.1 m (b) 10.07 m
(c) 10 074 m
3 (a) 2.5 km (b) 2.55 km
(c) 2.549 km
4 (a) 17.4 miles (b) 17.36 miles
(c) 17.358 miles
5 (a) 1.7 hours (b) 1.67 hours
(c) 1.675 hours
6 (a) 0.0 m (b) 0.03 m (c) 0.026 m

N3.3
1 2.651 km (to the nearest m)
2 3.475 kg (to the nearest g)
3 1.69 m (to the nearest cm)
4 15.892 kg (to the nearest g)
5 12080 m (to the nearest mm)

N3.4
1 (a) 2 (b) 1 (c) 3 (d) 6 (e) 5
(f) 2
2 (a) 4 (b) 6 (c) 2 (d) 8 (e) 0
(f) 4

N3.5
1 (a) 10 (b) 15 (c) 14.7
2 (a) 6 (b) 5.8 (c) 5.83
3 (a) 8 (b) 8.3 (c) 8.25
4 (a) 200 (b) 160 (c) 164
5 (a) 0.3 (b) 0.32 (c) 0.322
6 (a) 2000 (b) 2400 (c) 2380
7 (a) 0.06 (b) 0.061 (c) 0.0615
8 (a) 0.0008 (b) 0.000 85
(c) 0.000 847
9 (a) 0.04 (b) 0.037 (c) 0.0368
10 (a) 0.01 (b) 0.0095 (c) 0.009 52

N3.6
1 (a) 200 000 (b) 190 000
(c) 187 000 (d) 186 500
2 (a) 400 000 (b) 370 000
(c) 375 000 (d) 374 900
3 (a) 500 000 (b) 490 000
(c) 493 000 (d) 492 800
4 (a) 50 000 000 (b) 52 000 000
(c) 51 800 000 (d) 51 810 000
5 (a) 30 000 000 (b) 30 000 000
(c) 29 500 000 (d) 29 500 000
6 (a) 100 000 000 (b) 100 000 000
(c) 99 500 000 (d) 99 540 000

N3.7
1 0.048 **2** 0.066 **3** 0.0036
4 0.0090 **5** 0.10

N3.8
1 (a) 6000°C (b) 5700°C
2 (a) 9 light years (b) 8.7 light years
3 (a) 100 000 square miles
(b) 140 000 square miles
4 (a) 100 000 mph (b) 150 000 mph
5 (a) 0.0001 kg (b) 0.000 11 kg

N3.9
1 33.3 cm **2** 0.38 g **3** 67 mℓ
4 0.12 lb or 1.8 oz **5** 1.7 m

N4.1
1 (a) £21 (b) £89 (c) £38 (d) £4
2 14 bags of crisps **3** 10 peaches
4 9000 bottles **5** 2250 tickets

N4.2
1 (a) Estimate 450 Actual 435
(b) Estimate 1000 Actual 816
(c) Estimate 3 Actual 3.315 789 474
(d) Estimate 3 Actual 2.967 741 935
(e) Estimate 4500 Actual 4558
(f) Estimate 5 Actual 4.34 375
(g) Estimate 300 000 Actual 316 317
(h) Estimate 200 Actual 184.5 757 576
2 £3 **3** 20 cm **4** 6000 miles
5 150 boxes

N4.3
1 1800 **2** 15 **3** 1.4
4 400 **5** 600

N4.4
1 (b), 1 (f), 2, 3, 5 are obviously wrong

N5.1
1 Yes **2** Yes **3** No **4** No **5** Yes
6 No **7** Yes **8** No **9** Yes **10** No

N5.2
1 1, 2, 3, 5, 6, 10, 15, 30
2 1, 2, 3, 4, 6, 9, 12, 18, 36
3 1, 2, 3, 6, 7, 14, 21, 42
4 1, 2, 3, 4, 5, 6, 10, 12, 15, 20, 30, 60
5 1, 2, 4, 19, 38, 76
6 1, 2, 3, 5, 6, 9, 10, 15, 18, 30, 45, 90
7 1, 2, 5, 10, 13, 26, 65, 130
8 1, 2, 3, 4, 6, 8, 9, 12, 18, 24, 27, 36,
54, 72, 108, 216

N5.3
1 1×4, 2×2
2 1×10, 2×5
3 1×13
4 1×35, 5×7
5 1×52, 2×26, 4×13
6 1×72, 2×36, 3×24, 4×18,
6×12, 8×9
7 1×88, 2×44, 4×22, 8×11
8 1×130, 2×65, 5×26, 10×13

N5.4
1 1,3 **2** 1 **3** 1,5 **4** 1 **5** 1, 2
6 1, 3, 9 **7** 1, 2 **8** 1, 5

N5.5
1 42, 91, 105 **2** 112, 210
3 68, 102, 221 **4** 92, 184, 529
5 94, 282, 423

N5.6
1 24 **2** 60 **3** 80 **4** 60 **5** 90 **6** 48

N5.7
1 (a), (f), (g), (h), (i), (j), (l) all have
2 as a factor

(c) has 5 as a factor

(b), (k) have 3 as a factor

(d), (e) are prime

2 The first 10 prime numbers larger than 200 and not mentioned in either 1 or 3 are;
223, 227, 229, 241, 251, 263, 269, 271, 277, 281

3 (d), (f), (h), (j) all have 2 as a factor

(a) has 5 as a factor

(e) has 3 as a factor

(g) has 7 as a factor

(k) has 11 as a factor

(b), (c), (i), (l) are prime each having only two factors, 1 and itself

N5.8

1 (a) 2,5　(b) 3　(c) 2, 3, 11　(d) 2, 5　(e) 2, 17

2 (a) 2, 3　(b) 2, 23　(c) 2, 23　(d) 3, 5　(e) 2, 3　(f) 2　(g) 3　(h) 2, 5　(i) 2, 3, 11　(j) 2, 3, 13

N6.1

1 (a) 5　(b) 64　(c) 49　(d) 9

2 (a) 2　(b) 2　(c) 10　(d) 3

3 (a) 144　(b) 225　(c) 400　(d) 289　(e) 37.21　(f) 1444　(g) 84.64　(h) 116.64

4 (a) 0.25　(b) 0.09　(c) 0.81　(d) 0.49　(e) 0.0441　(f) 0.2209　(g) 0.7396　(h) 0.3969

The squared number is smaller than the original number.

N6.2

1 (a) 9 cm^2　(b) 20.25 cm^2　(c) 1225 mm^2　(d) 81 m^2　(e) 4.41 km^2　(f) 153.76 mm^2

2 (a) 24.01 m^2　(b) 6.76 m^2　(c) 30.77 m^2

N6.3

1 (a) 2.24　(b) 2.45　(c) 3.16　(d) 4.69　(e) 1.67　(f) 4.87　(g) 7.48　(h) 6.01

2 (a) 0.837　(b) 0.447　(c) 0.949　(d) 0.202　(e) 0.583　(f) 0.245

The square roots are larger than the original number.

N6.4

1 15.7 cm (to the nearest mm)

2 19.1 cm (to the nearest mm)

3 2.59 m (to the nearest cm)

4 2.90 m (to the nearest cm)

5 4.14 km (to 3 sf)

6 22.8 km (to 3 sf)

N6.5

1 8　**2** 125　**3** 512　**4** 216　**5** 343　**6** 729　**7** 1728　**8** 12167　**9** 15.625　**10** 389.017　**11** 1685.159　**12** 50 120.9637

N6.6

1 2.20 m^3　**2** 3375 cm^3　**3** 1 331 000 mm^3　**4** 439 cm^3　**5** 50 653 mm^3

N6.7

1 5　**2** 14　**3** 2.5　**4** 9　**5** 6　**6** 0.5　**7** 1.8　**8** 3.1

N6.8

1 16.8 cm　**2** 24.3 cm　**3** 1.6 m　**4** 27.0 mm　**5** 1.97 m　**6** 48.0 cm

N6.9

1 23　**2** 27　**3** 47　**4** 6　**5** 14　**6** 61

N6.10

1 2.24　**2** 3.48　**3** 10.82　**4** 7.07　**5** 12.65　**6** 8.11

N7.1

1 (a) 4°C　(b) 1°C　(c) –6°C　(d) 0°C　(e) –21°C　(f) 1°C

2 (a) –3°C　(b) –15°C　(c) –11°C　(d) –10°C　(e) 0°C　(f) 0°C

3 (a) –6°C, –1°C, 0°C, 1°C, 5°C
(b) –10°C, –4°C, –1°C, 4°C, 9°C
(c) –3°C, –2°C, 0°C, 4°C, 10°C
(d) –7°C, –2°C, –1°C, 3°C, 9°C
(e) –95°C, –70°C, –11°C, 43°C, 100°C

N7.2

1 (a) Wrong　(b) Right　(c) Right　(d) Wrong　(e) Right　(f) Right　(g) Wrong　(h) Right　(i) Wrong　(j) Right

2 (a) 2 > 1　(b) –3 < 4　(c) 1 > 0　(d) –2 > –5　(e) 2 > –3　(f) –7 < 7　(g) 12 > –5　(h) –13 < 0　(i) –10 > –17　(j) 8 > –9

N7.3

1 (a) 7 down　(b) 9 up　(c) 16　(d) 8 up　(e) 20　(f) 4 up　(g) –5　(h) 7

2 (a) 4°C　(b) 7°C　(c) –1°C　(d) 3°C　(e) –3°C

N7.4

1 –1　**2** 3　**3** –9　**4** –1　**5** 3　**6** 6　**7** 8　**8** –8　**9** 13　**10** –1　**11** 21　**12** –15　**13** –5　**14** 7　**15** 0

N7.5

1 –7　**2** –3　**3** 1　**4** 1　**5** 6　**6** –7　**7** –3　**8** 0　**9** 0　**10** 0

N7.6

1 –15　**2** –12　**3** –6　**4** 6　**5** –8　**6** –9　**7** 6　**8** –6　**9** –35　**10** 72

N7.7

1 –24　**2** 72　**3** 30　**4** 6　**5** 48　**6** 504　**7** 24　**8** –864　**9** 2880　**10** 0

N7.8

1 –5　**2** 4　**3** –3　**4** 4　**5** 2　**6** –8　**7** –2　**8** –5　**9** 9　**10** –7

N7.9

1 –2　**2** –5　**3** 14　**4** –8　**5** 12　**6** –16　**7** –18　**8** 48　**9** –3　**10** 1

N7.10

1 3　**2** 12　**3** –5　**4** 8　**5** –6　**6** –30　**7** 16　**8** 10　**9** –4　**10** 4　**11** –5　**12** –36

N7.11

1 +£200　**2** +£250　**3** –£75　**4** –£35　**5** £50

N8.1

1 Common　**2** Decimal　**3** Percentage　**4** Decimal　**5** Common　**6** Percentage

N8.2

1 (a) $\frac{5}{6}$　(b) $\frac{1}{4}$　(c) $\frac{7}{18}$　(d) $\frac{5}{9}$　(e) $\frac{3}{8}$　(f) $\frac{4}{12}$

2 (a) $\frac{1}{4}$ litre　(b) $\frac{3}{5}$ litre　(c) $\frac{1}{3}$ litre　(d) $\frac{5}{8}$ litre

N8.3

1 (a) 840.3　(b) 32.54　(c) 0.637　(d) 902.05　(e) 4006.1

2 (a) 6 units 2 tenths 9 hundredths
(b) 1 ten 7 units (0 tenths) 3 hundredths 4 thousandths
(c) (0 units) 4 tenths 7 hundredths
(d) 8 units 7 tenths 0 hundredths 5 thousandths
(e) (0 units 0 tenths 0 hundredths) 6 thousandths

N8.4

1 (a) $\frac{10}{100}$　(b) $\frac{50}{100}$　(c) $\frac{75}{100}$　(d) $\frac{25}{100}$　(e) $\frac{5}{100}$　(f) $\frac{28}{100}$　(g) $\frac{54}{100}$　(h) $\frac{95}{100}$

2 (a) 20%　(b) 30%　(c) 16%　(d) 8%　(e) 1%　(f) 100%

3 23%　**4** 64%　**5** 5%

N8.5

1 40%　**2** 15%　**3** 48% 35%　**4** 11%

5 They total 105% which is greater than 100%. Therefore some of the figures must be wrong.

N9.1

1 (a) False　(b) True　(c) True　(d) True　(e) False　(f) False　(g) True　(h) False

2 (a) 8　(b) 8　(c) 1　(d) 6　(e) 12　(f) 8　(g) 10　(h) 4

N9.2

1 (a) 4　(b) 8　**2** (a) 4　(b) 12　**3** (a) 3　(b) 15　**4** (a) 4　(b) 12　**5** (a) 2　(b) 9　**6** (a) 3　(b) 15　**7** (a) 3　(b) 9　**8** (a) 5　(b) 25　**9** (a) 10　(b) 7　**10** (a) 5　(b) 20　**11** (a) 7　(b) 35　**12** (a) 3　(b) 15

N9.3

1 (a) $\frac{2}{3}, \frac{4}{6}, \frac{6}{9}, \frac{8}{12}, \frac{10}{15}$　(b) $\frac{3}{4}, \frac{6}{8}, \frac{9}{12}, \frac{12}{16}, \frac{15}{20}$　(c) $\frac{4}{5}, \frac{8}{10}, \frac{12}{15}, \frac{16}{20}, \frac{20}{25}$　(d) $\frac{5}{8}, \frac{10}{16}, \frac{15}{24}, \frac{20}{32}, \frac{25}{40}$

2 (a) $\frac{10}{12}$　(b) $\frac{15}{18}$　(c) $\frac{25}{30}$　(d) $\frac{35}{42}$　(e) $\frac{50}{60}$

3 (a) 6, 21, 28, 15
(b) 18, 15, 20, 45
(c) 6, 30, 12, 15

4 (a) No　(b) No　(c) Yes　(d) No　(e) Yes　(f) No

N9.4

1 (a) $\frac{3}{5}$　(b) $\frac{1}{4}$　(c) $\frac{2}{3}$　(d) $\frac{4}{5}$　(e) $\frac{3}{7}$　(f) $\frac{1}{3}$

2 (a) 6, 1　(b) 3, 9　(c) 3, 7　(d) 6, 18　(e) 10, 60　(f) 7, 4　(g) 5, 45　(h) 7, 2　(i) 7, 5　(j) 6, 6　(k) 5, 15　(l) 2, 8

N9.5

1 $\frac{3}{5}$　**2** $\frac{3}{4}$　**3** $\frac{1}{2}$　**4** $\frac{2}{5}$　**5** $\frac{2}{5}$　**6** $\frac{1}{5}$　**7** $\frac{9}{10}$　**8** $\frac{3}{4}$　**9** $\frac{7}{15}$　**10** $\frac{9}{16}$　**11** $\frac{4}{5}$　**12** $\frac{8}{13}$

N9.6

1 0.6　**2** 0.375　**3** 0.875　**4** 0.35　**5** 0.26　**6** 0.72　**7** 0.75　**8** 0.4

N9.7

1 (a) 0.$\dot{1}$　(b) 0.$\dot{4}$　(c) 0.1$\dot{6}$　(d) 0.4$\dot{5}$　(e) 0.$\dot{4}$6153$\dot{8}$　(f) 0.08$\dot{3}$　(g) 0.5$\dot{1}$$\dot{8}$　(h) 0.$\dot{3}$5$\dot{1}$

2 (a) 0.$\dot{1}$42857　(b) 0.$\dot{2}$85714　(c) 0.$\dot{4}$28571　(d) 0.$\dot{5}$71428　(e) 0.$\dot{7}$14285　(f) 0.$\dot{8}$57142

The repeating digits in all the answers are in the same order, the only difference being the initial digit.

N9.8

1 (a) 26%　(b) 45%　(c) 8%　(d) 17%　(e) 53%　(f) 67%　(g) 77%　(h) 94%

2 (a) 14, 14　(b) 70, 70　(c) 24, 24　(d) 45, 45　(e) 74, 74　(f) 85, 85

N9.9

1 40%　**2** 50%　**3** 28.5%　**4** 75%　**5** 25%　**6** 37.5%　**7** 65%　**8** 68%　**9** 87.5%　**10** 24%　**11** 18.75%　**12** 57.5%

N9.10

1 71.4%　**2** 54.5%　**3** 41.2%　**4** 69.2%　**5** 77.8%　**6** 16.7%　**7** 21.1%　**8** 9.5%　**9** 18.5%

N9.11

1 $\frac{3}{10}$　**2** $\frac{5}{10}$　**3** $\frac{26}{100}$　**4** $\frac{7}{1000}$　**5** $\frac{13}{1000}$　**6** $\frac{106}{1000}$　**7** $\frac{318}{1000}$　**8** $\frac{41}{100}$　**9** $\frac{73}{1000}$　**10** $\frac{205}{1000}$　**11** $\frac{85}{100}$　**12** $\frac{27}{1000}$

N9.12

1 30%　**2** 76%　**3** 8%　**4** 37%　**5** 1%　**6** 0.5%　**7** 24%　**8** 3.5%　**9** 75%　**10** 68%　**11** 6.5%　**12** 30.5%

N9.13

1 $\frac{17}{100}$　**2** $\frac{20}{100} = \frac{1}{5}$　**3** $\frac{5}{100} = \frac{1}{20}$　**4** $\frac{30}{100} = \frac{3}{10}$　**5** $\frac{40}{100} = \frac{2}{5}$　**6** $\frac{66}{100} = \frac{33}{50}$　**7** $\frac{80}{100} = \frac{4}{5}$　**8** $\frac{95}{100} = \frac{19}{20}$　**9** $\frac{2}{100} = \frac{1}{50}$　**10** $\frac{12}{100} = \frac{3}{25}$　**11** $\frac{60}{100} = \frac{3}{5}$　**12** $\frac{38}{100} = \frac{19}{50}$

N9.14

1 0.17　**2** 0.26　**3** 0.3　**4** 0.65　**5** 0.8　**6** 0.99　**7** 0.03　**8** 0.09　**9** 0.64　**10** 0.73　**11** 0.48　**12** 0.88

N9.15

1 (a) $\frac{5}{7}$　(b) $\frac{9}{10}$　(c) $\frac{16}{32}$　(d) $\frac{15}{21}$　(e) $\frac{7}{40}$

2 $\frac{9}{11}, \frac{5}{6}, \frac{1}{2}, \frac{1}{11}$　**3** $\frac{3}{20}, \frac{8}{20}, \frac{12}{20}, \frac{16}{20}, \frac{19}{20}$

N9.16

1 $\frac{5}{16}, \frac{8}{16}, \frac{13}{16}, \frac{4}{16}, \frac{6}{16}$　**2** $\frac{1}{2}, \frac{8}{16}, \frac{1}{2}$　

2 $\frac{9}{10}, \frac{4}{10}, \frac{8}{10}, \frac{1}{10}, \frac{5}{10}, \frac{7}{10}, \frac{9}{10}$

3 $\frac{1}{6}, \frac{1}{4}, \frac{1}{3}, \frac{7}{12}, \frac{7}{12}, \frac{3}{4}$

4 $\frac{1}{2}$", $\frac{1}{3}$", $\frac{7}{15}$", $\frac{5}{7}$", $\frac{1}{10}$", $\frac{1}{1}$"

5 $\frac{7}{10}$", $\frac{1}{5}$", $\frac{7}{20}$", $\frac{1}{7}$", $\frac{7}{4}$", $\frac{4}{5}$"

N9.17

1 (a) 12, $\frac{8}{12}, \frac{2}{12}, \frac{9}{12}$
(b) 30, $\frac{15}{30}, \frac{18}{30}, \frac{4}{30}$
(c) 24, $\frac{9}{24}, \frac{10}{24}, \frac{4}{24}$
(d) 42, $\frac{14}{42}, \frac{6}{42}, \frac{7}{42}$
(e) 60, $\frac{6}{60}, \frac{16}{60}, \frac{21}{60}$
(f) 24, $\frac{8}{24}, \frac{18}{24}, \frac{15}{24}$

2 The group who disliked the powder.

N9.18

1 (a) 13%, 40%, 50%
(b) 25%, 37.5%, 70%
(c) 50%, 62.5%, 75%
(d) 26%, 35%, 80%, 90%
(e) 55%, 62%, 71%, 87.5%
(f) 66%, 73%, 77%, 83%
(g) 42%, 50%, 58%, 85%
(h) 60%, 85%, 93%, 94%

2 (a) Design and technology
(b) English
(c) Maths and Geography

3 (a) Tina 62% Pete 65% Alison 38% Charlotte 90% Nick 48% Jim 80%
(b) Charlotte
(c) Alison
(d) $\frac{19}{50}, \frac{21}{25}, \frac{31}{50}, \frac{13}{20}, \frac{4}{5}, \frac{9}{10}$

N10.1

1 (a) 0.537　(b) 0.0953　(c) 0.281　(d) 0.036 14　(e) 0.006 13　(f) 0.008 67

2 (a) 0.17 < 0.3　(b) 0.2101 > 0.1947　(c) 0.0237 < 0.024　(d) 0.013 42 < 0.0135　(e) 0.0264 > 0.026 04　(f) 0.003 71 > 0.007 309

N10.2

1 (a) 0.9 largest 0.06 smallest
(b) 0.06 < 0.207 < 0.27 < 0.6 < 0.83 < 0.9

2 (a) 0.094, 0.13, 0.131, 0.756
(b) 0.0742, 0.2047, 0.4072, 0.7042
(c) 0.064, 0.21, 0.397, 0.6
(d) 0.005, 0.0051, 0.0512, 0.4
(e) 0.0037, 0.003 74, 0.0038, 0.003 808

N10.3

1 1.98 m, 2.17 m, 3.02 m, 3.2 m, 4.35 m, 4.5 m

2 4.2 kg, 4.02 kg, 3.15 kg, 2.85 kg, 2.14 kg, 0.93 kg

3 (a) 2.31 m
(b) 2.31 m > 2.08 m > 1.87 m > 1.64 m > 1.27 m > 1.07 m > 0.34 m

N11.1

1 (a) $\frac{2}{10}$ (b) $\frac{8}{10}$ **2** (a) $\frac{3}{8}$ (b) $\frac{5}{8}$

3 (a) $\frac{28}{30}$ (b) $\frac{2}{30}$ **4** (a) $\frac{9}{100}$ (b) $\frac{91}{100}$

5 (a) $\frac{177}{200}$ (b) $\frac{23}{200}$

N11.2

1 (a) $\frac{7}{20}$ (b) $\frac{2}{5}$ (c) $\frac{3}{20}$ (d) $\frac{1}{10}$

2 (a) $\frac{3}{8}$ (b) $\frac{6}{25}$ (c) $\frac{31}{200}$ (d) $\frac{23}{100}$

3 (a) $\frac{3}{10}$ (b) $\frac{7}{20}$ (c) $\frac{3}{20}$ (d) $\frac{1}{5}$

4 (a) $\frac{1}{5}$ (b) $\frac{1}{3}$ (c) $\frac{7}{15}$

5 (a) $\frac{5}{12}$ (b) $\frac{1}{3}$ (c) $\frac{1}{4}$

N11.3

1 (a) $\frac{5}{50} = \frac{1}{10}$ (b) $\frac{10}{40} = \frac{1}{4}$ (c) $\frac{8}{64} = \frac{1}{8}$
(d) $\frac{12}{60} = \frac{1}{5}$ (e) $\frac{6}{30} = \frac{1}{5}$ (f) $\frac{20}{80} = \frac{1}{4}$
(g) $\frac{2}{12} = \frac{1}{6}$ (h) $\frac{500}{2000} = \frac{1}{4}$ (i) $\frac{2}{6} = \frac{1}{3}$
(j) $\frac{750}{2000} = \frac{3}{8}$ (k) $\frac{20}{60} = \frac{1}{3}$ (l) $\frac{30}{500} = \frac{3}{50}$

2 $\frac{11}{40}$

3 (a) $\frac{5}{12}$ (b) $\frac{5}{24}$ (c) $\frac{3}{8}$

4 (a) $\frac{3}{8}$ (b) $\frac{5}{16}$ (c) $\frac{5}{16}$

5 (a) 40 cm (b) $\frac{4}{5}$ (c) $\frac{1}{5}$

N11.4

1 (a) 0.25 (b) 0.2 (c) 0.6 (d) 0.25
(e) 0.2 (f) 0.3 (g) 0.2333
(h) 0.3333 (i) 0.4375 (j) 0.2727

2 (a) 0.025 (b) 0.0385 (c) 0.05
(d) 0.2083 (e) 0.0083 (f) 0.15
(g) 0.5714 (h) 0.16

N11.5

1 (a) 25% (b) 20% (c) 5% (d) 20%
(e) 12.5% (f) 5% (g) 40%
(h) 15% (i) 17% (j) 23%

2 (a) 65% (b) 35%

3 (a) 80% (b) 20%

4 (a) 95% (b) 5%

5 (a) 84% (b) 16%

N11.6

1 The bag with 25 apples **2** Science

3 Weakling Wanderers

4 The bag of 25 sweets

5 Sid's allotment

N11.7

1 (a) 25% (b) 10% (c) 14.5%
(d) 2% (e) 5% (f) 19%

2 20% **3** 6% **4** 8% **5** 6%

N11.8

1 (a) 20% increase (b) 50% decrease
(c) 13% decrease (d) 12% decrease
(e) 5.3% decrease (f) 13% decrease

2 (a) 11% increase (b) 4% increase
(c) 6% increase (d) 20% decrease
(e) 4% increase

3 7% reduction **4** 8% increase

5 15% loss **6** 13% increase

7 5% increase **8** 10% loss

9 52% profit

10 43% profit on the fire
16% loss on the cooker

N12.1

1 (a) (i) 15 m (ii) 30 m
(b) (i) £14 (ii) £70
(c) (i) 7.5 kg (ii) 22.5 kg
(d) (i) 60 cm (ii) 180 cm
(e) (i) 44 mℓ (ii) 748 mℓ

2 (a) (i) 2400 (ii) 2100
(b) (i) 3200 (ii) 2000

(c) (i) 99 (ii) 66
(d) (i) 40 (ii) 32
(e) (i) 117 (ii) 65

N12.2

1 420 apples **2** 100 biscuits

3 250 books **4** 120 cars

5 4200 trees

N12.3

1 (a) of £40 (b) of 49 kg
(c) of 80ℓ (d) of 60 m
(e) of 2.5 km (f) of 4.6 kg

2 David, £1 more **3** Ann, 20 g more

N12.4

1 £24 **2** 15 kg **3** £20 **4** 1 m

5 £2.55 **6** 1.5 g

N12.5

1 (a) 3.6 (b) 5.4 (c) 8.4

2 (a) 3 (b) 6.75 (c) 8.25

3 (a) 10.4 (b) 16.9 (c) 23.4

4 (a) 9.5 (b) 24.7 (c) 30.4

5 (a) 22.2 (b) 62.9 (c) 88.8

N12.6

1 (a) £3.64 (b) £61.20 (c) 4.65ℓ
(d) 3.64 kg (e) 2.24 m
(f) 45.6 km

2 (a) (i) £42.30 (ii) £14.10
(iii) £11.75 (b) £166.85

N12.7

1 (a) £10 (b) £5 (c) £2 (d) £3
(e) £0.60 (f) £60 (g) £16.50
(h) £8.25

2 (a) £7 (b) £10.50 (c) £15.75

N12.8

1 (a) 345 (b) 138 (c) 46 (d) 575
(e) 97.75 (f) 124.2

2 (a) £21.20 (b) £16.96 (c) £50.88
(d) £127.20 (e) £13.78 (f) £44.52

3 4947 **4** 540 sheep **5** £376.20

6 £274.95

N12.9

1 (a) £4.00 (b) £35.99

2 (a) £26.88 (b) £197.12

3 (a) £750.40 (b) £1125.60

4 (a) £3.65 (b) £69.30

5 (a) £455.92 (b) £5243.08

N12.10

1 £132.60 **2** £662.23 **3** £72.08

4 £28.34 **5** £56135

N12.11

1 38 p **2** 395.25 kg **3** 240 people

4 £57.35 **5** £161

N12.12

1 (a) £40 (b) £64 (c) £25 (d) £50
(e) £50

2 £24 for the trousers
£20 for the shirts

N12.13

1 (a) 56.25 (b) 75 (c) 131.25
(d) 37.5 (e) 33.75 (f) 67.5

2 768 members

N13.1

1 (a) 2:1 (b) 3:1 (c) 1:7
(d) 1:1000 (e) 2:3 (f) 5:4

2 (a) $\frac{5}{8}$ (b) $\frac{3}{7}$ (c) $\frac{4}{9}$ (d) $\frac{2}{5}$ (e) $\frac{5}{7}$
(f) $\frac{9}{16}$

3 3:2 **4** (a) $\frac{10}{3}$ (b) $\frac{3}{10}$

5 (a) 12:5 (b) 5:12

N13.3

1 (a) 10:6 (b) 1:5 (c) 12:7 (d) 8:3
(e) 8:3 (f) 1:2

2 (a) 15:4 (b) 4:15

3 (a) 5:2 (b) 2:5

4 (a) 5:2 (b) 1:8 (c) 50:9 (d) 1:2
(e) 35:16 (f) 1:28

5 (a) 3:10 (b) 10:3

N13.4

1 7:3 **2** 7:3 **3** 2:3 **4** 5:23

5 12:5

N13.5

1 (a) 10:16 (b) 25:40 (c) 35:56
(d) 40:64

2 (a) 21:9 (b) 28:12 (c) 63:27
(d) 84:36

3 The first 5 examples are;
6:4 multiple 2 9:6 multiple 3
12:8 multiple 4 15:10 multiple 5
18:12 multiple 6

N13.6

1 (a) × 5, 20 (b) × 6, 12
(c) × 12, 36 (d) × 11, 66

2 £28 **3** 9 lb **4** 10 000 **5** (a) 80 cm
(b) 260 cm

N13.7

1 (a) 3, 1, 5 (b) 1, 4, 24 (c) 2, 3, 8
(d) 5, 4, 20 (e) 3, 5, 45
(f) 2, 5, 70

2 (a) 15 (b) 15 (c) 35 (d) 35

3 £60

N13.8

3 (a) 6 fl. oz egg white, 100 fl. oz
orange juice, 10 fl. oz lemon juice,
30 fl. oz soda water
(b) 180 mℓ grenadine, 270 mℓ egg
white, 4500 ml (4.5ℓ) orange juice,
1350 ml (1.35ℓ) soda water
(c) 1 cup of grenadine, 25 cups of
orange juice, $2\frac{1}{2}$ cups of lemon juice,
$7\frac{1}{2}$ cups of soda water
(d) 10 cℓ grenadine, 15 cℓ egg
white, 250 cℓ (2.5ℓ) orange juice,
25 cℓ lemon juice
(e) 0.04ℓ (40 mℓ) grenadine, 0.06l
(60 mℓ) egg white, 0.1 ℓ (100 mℓ)
lemon juice, 0.3ℓ (300 mℓ) soda
water

N13.9

1 The first quantity is $\frac{3}{5}$ of the second quantity

2 The first quantity is $\frac{2}{7}$ of the second quantity

3 The first quantity is $\frac{5}{4}$ of the second quantity

4 The first quantity is $\frac{5}{8}$ of the second quantity

5 The first quantity is $\frac{3}{1}$ of the second quantity

6 The first quantity is $\frac{1}{6}$ of the second quantity

N13.10

1 1:6 **2** 1:4 **3** 3:4 **4** 7:10

5 11:16 **6** 3:4 **7** 2:3 **8** 3:7

N13.11

1 55% **2** 1:4 **3** 2:5 **4** 7:10

5 38% **6** 25%

N13.12

1 (a) £13.00 (b) £19.50 (c) £52.00
(d) £260.00

2 (a) £1.30 (b) £3.25 (c) £13

3 (a) 42 miles (b) 100.8 miles
(c) 378 miles

4 (a) 13 cm (b) 22.75 (c) 48.75

5 (a) £76 (b) £114 (c) £19
(d) £76 (e) £228

N13.13

1 £22.50 **2** £2.88 **3** 125 washes

4 £2.25 **5** 75 miles

6 1600 washers

N13.14

1 (a) Baps 15 mℓ, 15 mℓ, 0.5 mℓ,
2.5 g, 1 g, 45 g, 0.5 mℓ, 5 g
Soup 75 g, 5 g, 12.5 g, 0.25ℓ
(b) Baps 240 mℓ, 240 mℓ, 8 mℓ
40 g, 16 g, 720 g, 8 mℓ
Soup 1200 g, 80 g, 200 g, 24ℓ

2 (a) Casserole 1080 g, 540 g, 60 g,
150 g, 120 g, 60 g, 990 mℓ, 18 mℓ
Oranges 150 g, 240 mℓ, 6 oranges,
30 mℓ
Rice salad 300 g, 360 g, 24 g, 42 g,
72 mℓ
(b) Casserole 1800 g, 900 g, 100 g,
250 g, 200 g, 100 g, 1650 mℓ, 30 mℓ
Oranges 250 g, 400 mℓ, 10 oranges,
50 mℓ
Salad 500 g, 600 g, 40 g, 70 g,
120 mℓ
(c) Casserole 3780 g, 1890 g, 210 g,
525 g, 420 g, 210 g, 3465 mℓ, 63 mℓ
Oranges 525 g, 840 mℓ, 21 oranges
105 mℓ
Salad 1050 g, 1260 g, 84 g, 147 g,
252 mℓ

N14.1

1 (a) £12 and £8
(b) £55 and £33
(c) £210 and £150
(d) 1.5 kg and 3.5 kg
(e) 35 minutes and 10 minutes
(f) 270 mℓ and 60 mℓ
(g) 15 m and 20 m
(h) 90 g and 110 g

2 Sam Tom
(a) 4 pies 2 pies (b) £5 £45
(c) £1.00 £0.25 (d) 30 mℓ 270 mℓ

3 bran oats rye sultanas
(a) 0.3 kg 1.2 kg 0.6 kg 0.9 kg
(b) 0.5 kg 2 kg 1 kg 1.5 kg
(c) 1.8 kg 7.2 kg 3.6 kg 5.4 kg

4 1950 £20 prizes, 3250 £10 prizes,
4550 £5 prizes

5 2.4ℓ pineapple, 0.4ℓ grapefruit,
1.2ℓ passion fruit, 6ℓ lemonade

N14.2

1 (a) 3:5 (b) Ann has 18 sweets,
Brenda has 30

2 (a) 11:7 (b) Jean gets £6600, Sue
gets £4200

3 £15 000, £7500, £22 500, £30 000

4 (a) Bill got £2.25, Ben got £2.75
(b)

Bill	Ben
£2.73	£3.27
£3.21	£3.79
£3.69	£4.31
£4.18	£4.82
£4.67	£5.33
£5.16	£5.84
£5.65	£6.35

N15.1

1 1 to 15, 1:15

2 1 cm represents 24 cm, , 1:24

3 1 cm represents 10 cm, 1 to 10, 1:10
4 1 cm represents 75 cm, 1 to 75,
5 (a) Lengths on the object are 30 times larger than those on the model
(b) Lengths on the model are 30 times smaller than those on the real object

N15.2
1 (a) (i) 40 cm (ii) 120 cm
(iii) 400 cm (iv) 640 cm
(b) (i) 1 cm (ii) 2 cm (iii) 4 cm
(iv) 2.5 cm
2 (a) 435 cm (b) 270 cm
(c) 105 cm (d) 60 cm
(e) 30 cm (f) 75 cm
(g) 33 cm (h) 45 cm
(i) 78 cm (j) 4
3 (a) 60 cm (b) 12 cm (c) 14 cm
(d) 11 cm (e) 50 cm (f) 52 cm
(g) 9 cm (h) 6 cm (i) 5 cm
(j) 5.5 cm

N15.3
1 (a) 270 km (b) 67.5 km
(c) 210 km (d) 300 km
(e) 142.5 km (f) 420 km
2 (a) 50 m (b) 31 cm (c) 7.6 m
(d) 4.5 cm (e) 0.8 cm (f) 0.8 m
(g) 78 m (h) 2.6 m (i) 0.5 cm
(j) 144

N15.4
1 1:1000 2 1:300 3 1:5000
4 1:40 5 1:250

N15.5
1 1 cm represents 2 km
2 1 cm represents 0.3 km
3 1 cm represents 0.25 km
4 1 cm represents 0.5 km
5 1 cm represents 6.25 km

N15.6
1 (a) 1:32 (b) 1:32 (c) 1:48
(d) 1:72 (e) 1:720
2 (a) 1:50000 (b) 1:21120
(c) 1:1000000 (d) 1:250000
(e) 1:5000000

BASIC ALGEBRA
A1.1
1 (a) $7 \times x$ or
$x + x + x + x + x + x + x$
(b) $c \div 5$ or $\frac{1}{5}$ of c
(c) $y \times y \times y \times y$
(d) $3 \times p \times p \times q$
(e) $-4 \times 3p \times 3p$ or
$-4 \times 3 \times p \times 3 \times p$
(f) $\sqrt{c}$
(g) $5ab \times 5ab \times c$ or
$5 \times a \times b \times 5 \times a \times b \times c$
(h) $5 \times abc \times abc$ or
$5 \times a \times b \times c \times a \times b \times c$
2 (a) x^4 (b) $2x$ (c) $\frac{x}{4}$ (d) $7r^2$
(e) $-2pq$ (f) $(2q)^3$ (g) $2q^3$ (h) $9r^2s$

A1.3
1 (a) $2ab$, $2ab$, yes
(b) x^2y, xy^2, no
(c) pqr, pqr, yes
(d) $5acd$, $5acd$, yes
(e) $3rst^2$, $3r^2st$, no
(f) $2p^2q$, $7p^2q$, yes
(g) $9e^2fg$, $2efg^2$, no
(h) $-3x^2y^2$, $6x^2y^2$, yes
(i) $-2r^3s^2$, $5r^3s^2$, yes
(j) $2pqs^2$, $-9p^2qs$, no
2 (a) False (b) True (c) False

(d) False (e) False

A1.4
1 $5a$ 2 $8p$ 3 $10m$ 4 $7r$ 5 $8x$
6 $11p$ 7 $-q$ 8 $6x^2$ 9 $5a$ 10 pq
11 $6xy^2$ 12 $8ab^2$ 13 $4r^2st$
14 $8xy^2z^3$

A1.5
1 $3p + 5q$ 2 $2r + 3s$ 3 $6m + n$
4 $3x + y + 2z$ 5 $5p + 4q$ 6 $x - y$
7 $9xy - 7yz$ 8 $7rs - 2r^2$
9 $9a^2b - 3ab^2$ 10 $5pq^2 - 9p^2q$

A1.6
1 $8p$ 2 $15ab$ 3 $3x$ 4 $2p$ 5 $2pqr$
6 $40c^2d$ 7 $5pq$ 8 $6a^2b^3$ 9 $15x^2y^3$
10 $3a^2b^3$ 11 $30p^2qr^3$ 12 $\frac{5}{3}x^2y$

A1.7
1 (a) 20 (b) 28 (c) 17 (d) 27
(e) 47 (f) 30 (g) 2 (h) 12 (i) 2
(j) 23
2 (a) 7 (b) 3 (c) 9 (d) 12 (e) 7
(f) 12 (g) $\frac{5}{2}$ or 2.5 (h) $\frac{75}{8}$ or 9.375
3 (a) 30 (b) 10 (c) 29 (d) 18
(e) 96 (f) 66 (g) 84 (h) 653
4 (a) 9.6 (b) 23.6 (c) 6.2 (d) 30.8
(e) 20.04
5 (a) 7 (b) 9.8 (c) 30.8 (d) 41.72
(e) –5.28

A1.8
1 (a) £10.64 (b) £14.00 (c) £25.20
2 (a) 125 minutes (b) 95 minutes
(c) 205 minutes (d) 250 minutes
3 (a) 1.8 secs (b) 1.9 secs
(c) 2.0 secs (d) 2.6 secs
4 (a) 315 cm³ (b) 191.4 cm³
(c) 400.7 cm³ (d) 87.4 cm³

A2.1
1 Rectangular (a), (d), (e), (f), (g), (h)
2 (a) 63, 45, 30, 18, 9, 3, 0
(b) 28 (c) 55

A2.2
1 Square numbers (b), (d), (e), (h)
2 (a) 1, 4, 9, 16, 25
   4, 12, 24, 40, 60
(b) 84 matches
3 (b) 1, 2, 3, 4, 5
   1, 5, 9, 13, 17
4 (a) 1 (b) 8
(d) The 2nd and 4th rows are both made up of square numbers. The 3rd row is the multiples of 4.

A2.3
1 1 + 2 + 3 + 4 + 5 + 6 + 7 + 8 + 9 + 10 = 55
2 10th and 9th triangular numbers
3 (a) The third square number and four of the second triangular number.
(c) You need the sixth square number (36) and on each side you need the fifth triangular number (15) that is, 36 + (4 × 15) = 96
4 (a) (i) 13 (ii) 16 (iii) 19
(b) Add 3 on to the number of seats in the previous rows.
5 (c) 21 matches, 12 matches
(d) 48 triangles

A2.4
1 1, 8, 27, 64, 125, 216, 343, 512, 729, 1000
2 Pattern A (c) 25; Pattern B (c) 153

A3.1
1 35, 42, 49 2 100, 144, 196
3 729, 1331, 2197 4 81, 243, 729

5 1000, 1728, 2744 6 121, 169, 289
7 55, 66, 77 8 225, 441, 784
9 24, 39, 63 10 –5, –8, –13

A3.2
1 18, 22, 26 2 180, 175, 170
3 256, 1024, 4096 4 9, 3, 1
5 52, 77, 10 6 600, 3600, 25200
7 –11, –20, –31 8 80, 70, 58
9 56, 70, 84
10 1.25, 0.625, 0.3125

A3.3
1 18, 27, 38 2 23, 33, 45
3 28, 39, 52 4 40, 35, 29
5 40, 30, 18 6 45, 65, 89
7 58, 83, 113 8 48, 33, 15

A3.4
1 74, 107 2 78, 107 3 71, 104
4 39, 52 5 97, 144 6 122, 201

A3.5
1 511, 728
2 42, 68 'Fibonacci type'
3 109, 142
4 63, 102 'Fibonacci type'
5 105, 170 'Fibonacci type'

A3.6
1 2, 11, 20, 29, …
2 5, 20, 80, 320, …
3 16, 13, 10, 7, …
4 64, 32, 16, 8, …
5 7, 22, 67, 202, …
6 10, 24, 66, 192, …
7 1, 9, 121, 15129
8 1, 3, 11, 123, …
9 2, 2, 2, 2, …
10 3, 5, 9, 17, …

A3.7
1 1, 2, 6, 16, 44, …
2 2, 5, 11, 56, 617, …
3 2, 1, 4, 8, 64, …
4 2, 4, 36, 1600, 2 676 496, …
5 3, 5, 4, 1, 9, …

A3.8
1 Each term is obtained by adding 2 to the term before it.
2 Each term is obtained by adding 4 to the term before it.
3 Each term is obtained by multiplying the term before by 2.
4 Each term is obtained by subtracting 3 from the term before it.
5 Each term is obtained by dividing the term nefore it by 2.
6 Each term is obtained by doubling the term before it and adding 1.

A3.9
Listed below are 3 possible solutions to each question
1 (i) 16, 32, 64, … previous term × 2
(ii) 14, 22, 32, … 1st difference + 2
(iii) 92, 256, 8192, … previous 2 terms multiplied by 2.
2 (i) 18, 108, 1944, … previous 2 terms multiplied together
(ii) 11, 18, 27, … 1st difference + 2
(iii) 13, 29, 62, … (2 × 1st difference) + 1
3 (i) 17, 23, 30, … 1st difference + 1
(ii) 19, 30, 48, … previous 2 terms added –1
(iii) 19, 30, 48 previous 2 1st differences added together
4 (i) 4, 5, 6, … previous term + 1

(ii) 5, 8, 13, … previous 2 terms added together
(iii) 5, 16, 191, … (1st previous term)² – (2nd previous term)²
5 (i) 27, 47, 79, … previous 2 terms added together + 5
(ii) 27, 43, 63, … 1st difference + 4
(iii) 28, 47, 73, … 2nd difference +1

A4.2
2 (a) Rectangle (b) Parallelogram
(c) Kite (d) Square
(e) Trapezium

A4.3
1 First 2 Second 3 First 4 Fourth
5 Fourth 6 Between third and fourth
7 Third 8 Second 9 Fourth
10 Third

A4.4
1 y-coordinate always 3
2 y-coordinate always 8
3 y-coordinate = -x-coordinate
4 y-coordinate half the x-coordinate
5 y-coordinate double the x-coordinate
6 y-coordinate 3 times the x-coordinate
7 y-coordinate + x-coordinate = 10
8 y-coordinate = x-coordinate – 2

A5.1
1 (a) (i) 14 cm (ii) 15.2 cm
(iii) 17.6 cm (iv) 19.8 cm
(b) (i) 20 g (ii) 2.5 g (iii) 18 g
(iv) 6g
2 (a) 13°C max 5°C min (b) Day 1
(c) Day 4 (d) 10°C, day 5
(e) 8°C, day 2 (f) Day 4, 15°C
(g) Day 2, 6°C
3 (a) (i) 500 feet (ii) 240 feet
(iii) 80 feet
(b) (i) 50 mph (ii) 80 mph
(iii) 20 mph
(c) 240 feet

A5.2
1 (d) (i) –8°C (ii) 3°C (e) 7°C, July
(f) January, –10°C
(g) September, 3°C or March, –8°C
(h) No
2 (d) (i) 5.0 ohms (ii) 5.6 ohms
(iii) 4.64 ohms (iv) 6.12 ohms
(e) (i) 20°C (ii) 35°C (iii) 47.5°C
3 (d) (i) 10.09 a.m., 310 ℓ
(ii) Tank B, 130 ℓ

A6.1
1 $x = 7$ 2 $x = 8$ 3 $x = 8$ 4 $x = 6$
5 $x = 11$ 6 $x = 8$ 7 $x = 3$ 8 $x = 5$
9 $x = 18$

A6.2
1 $x = 14$ 2 $x = 16$ 3 $x = 33$
4 $x = 23$ 5 $x = 17$ 6 $x = 27$
7 $x = 16$ 8 $x = 21$ 9 $x = 19$
10 $x = 13$

A6.3
1 3.7 2 2.8 3 1.1 4 2.3 5 1.4
6 1.9

A6.4
1 (a) $x = 7$ (b) $x = 2$ (c) $y = 3$
(d) $p = 4$ (e) $r = 8$ (f) $s = 3$
(g) $w = 5$ (h) $d = 0$
2 (a) $x = 12$ (b) $y = 16$ (c) $m = 10$
(d) $a = 30$ (e) $p = 42$ (f) r = 20
(g) $z = 31$ (h) q = 25
3 (a) $x = 13$ (b) $m = 19$ (c) $n = 38$
(d) $m = 51$ (e) $n = 13$ (f) $a = 36$
(g) $s = 54$ (h) a = 1

A6.5
1 (a) $n = 4$ (b) $x = 8$ (c) $p = 3$
(d) $r = 9$ (e) $w = 9$ (f) $s = 5$
(g) $m = 7$ (h) $q = 9$
2 (a) $x = 6$ (b) $y = 15$ (c) $a = 36$
(d) $b = 24$ (e) $m = 91$ (f) $p = 10$
(g) $c = 45$ (h) $r = 24$
3 (a) $m = 3$ (b) $y = 99$ (c) $a = 2.5$
(d) $b = 32$ (e) $s = 3$ (f) $p = 3.5$
(g) $w = 1.5$ (h) $t = 27$

A6.6
1 $x = 2$ 2 $y = 7$ 3 $a = 3$ 4 $r = 3$
5 $x = 2$ 6 $b = -1$ 7 $n = 4$ 8 $p = 6$
9 $q = 3.5$ 10 $m = -2$

A6.7
1 $x = 2$ 2 $y = 2$ 3 $c = 2$ 4 $n = 12$
5 $r = 3$ 6 $s = 1$ 7 $p = 4$ 8 $m = 4$
9 $d = -2$ 10 $z = -8$

A6.8
1 $x = 2$ 2 $r = 5$ 3 $m = 12$ 4 $y = 7$
5 $p = 4$ 6 $r = 6.5$ 7 $z = 0.5$
8 $m = -0.5$ 9 $s = 1$ 10 $q = 0$

A6.9
1 $x = 2$ 2 $n = 3$ 3 $w = 8$ 4 $x = 2$
5 $a = 7$ 6 $x = 1$ 7 $n = 1$ 8 $r = 3$
9 $b = 2$ 10 $c = 3$ 11 $a = 14$
12 $y = 11$ 13 $p = 3$ 14 $x = 3$
15 $r = -10$ 16 $s = 22$ 17 $b = 0$
18 $m = \frac{7}{6}$ 19 $x = \frac{9}{2}$ 20 $z = \frac{1}{2}$

A6.10
1 (a) $x = 7.5$ (b) $a = 7.5$ (c) $n = 8$
(d) $p = 4$
2 (a) $x = 5$ (b) $d = 12$ (c) $c = 15$
(d) $y = 8$
3 (a) $n = 10.5$ (b) $r = 4$ (c) $m = 1.5$
(d) $p = 4$

A6.11
1 $a = 2$ 2 $x = 1.5$ 3 $p = 3$
4 $y = -1$ 5 $x = 7.5$ 6 $x = 5$
7 $x = 4$ 8 $c = 4.5$ 9 $m = 3$
10 $x = 5$

A7.1
1 (a) (i) $x + 55$ (ii) $5x$ (iii) $3x + 165$
(b) $8x + 165 = 405$ (c) $x = 30$p
(d) (i) 30p (ii) 85p
2 (a) $n + 24, 2n$ (b) $n + 24 = 2n$
(c) $n = 24$ (d) (i) 24 years old
(ii) 48 years old
3 5 5p coins and 10 10p coins
4 (a) $2x$ (b) $x + 5$ (c) $4x + 5 = 73$
(d) 17 (e) 34, 17 and 22
respectively
5 (a) $x + 3$ (b) $2x + 3$
(c) $4x + 6 = 26$ (d) $x = 5$
(e) Wayne = £5, Sue = £8, Pat = £13

A7.2
1 (a) $2x + 1 = 3x - 6$, $x = 7$, 15 cm
(b) $5x + 3 = 2x + 9$, $x = 2$, 13 cm
(c) $7x - 11 = 4x + 1$, $x = 4$, 17 cm
(d) $5x - 4 = x + 8$, $x = 3$, 11 cm
2 (a) $5x - 1 = 14$ (b) $x = 3$
(c) 3 cm, 3 cm, 8 cm
3 (a) $3x - 15 = 90$ (i) $x = 35$
(ii) 70° and 20°
(b) (i) $7x + 19 = 180$ (ii) $x = 23$
(iii) 115° and 65°
(c) (i) $5x - 17 = 4x + 11$ (ii) $x = 28$
(iii) 123° and 123°
(d) (i) $6x - 7 = 4x + 31$ (ii) $x = 19$
(iii) 107° and 107°
4 (a) $x + 3$ metres
(b) $4x + 6 = 36$, $x = 7.5$ metres

(c) 10.5 metres
5 (a) $30 - 2x$ (b) $20 - 2x$
(c) $100 - 8x$ (d) $8x = 20$
(e) $x = 2.5$ cm

A7.3
1 (a) 70 (b) 114
(c) $n, n +1, n + 4, n +5$ (d) $4n + 10$
(e) $4n + 10 = 126$, $n = 29$
(f) (i) 63 is not divisible by 4
(ii) 76 is not divisible by 4
2 (b) $5x + 147 = 377$ (c) $x = 46$
(d) 46 tickets at the Ravers,
92 tickets at the Stompers
(e) 128 tickets at the Ravers,
111 tickets at the Stompers

MEASURES

M1.1
1 (a) centimetre cm (b) millimetre mm
(c) metre m (d) kilometre km
(e) centimetre cm (f) metre m
(g) kilometre km (h) millimetre mm
2 (a) gram g (b) kilogram kg
(c) kilogram kg (d) tonne t
(e) gram g (f) tonne t
(g) gram g (h) kilogram kg
3 (a) litre ℓ (b) millilitre mℓ
(c) millilitre mℓ (d) litre ℓ
(e) litre ℓ (f) millilitre mℓ
4 (a) (iii) 10 m (b) (iv) 4 m
(c) (ii) 5 mℓ (d) (iii) 200 mℓ
(e) (iv) 65 kg (f) (ii) 180 g

M1.2
1 kilogram 2 litre 3 kilometre
4 tonne 5 centimetre

M1.3
1 (a) 5000 (b) 51.6 (c) 4000
(d) 0.429 (e) 3 (f) 6310 (g) 200
(h) 0.36 (i) 8 (j) 500 (k) 7
(l) 0.276 (m) 856 (n) 28
2 (a) 5000 (b) 1500 (c) 2540
(d) 2000 (e) 4800 (f) 0.75
(g) 4 (h) 3.75 (i) 0.45
(j) 8.5 (k) 6.85 (l) 100 000
3 (a) 5000 (b) 1500 (c) 5650
(d) 8000 (e) 6.72 (f) 0.15 (g) 6
(h) 0.75 (i) 2750 (j) 5.5
(k) 4500 (l) 0.005

M1.4
1 6ℓ 2 (a) 3.75 ℓ (b) 4 jugs
3 (a) 20 cakes (b) 17.5 kg
4 (a) 9.6 kg (b) 25 bags
5 160 lengths 6 300 g 7 4.04 kg
8 (a) 700 mℓ (b) 0.7ℓ
9 (a) 143 cm (b) 1.43 m
10 (a) 1500 boxes (b) 1.125 t
(c) 1700 boxes (d) 1.842 t

M1.5
1 (a) (i) 3.25 m (ii) 4.14 m
(iii) 10.06 m (iv) 7.02 m
(b) (i) 325 cm (ii) 414 cm
(iii) 1006 cm (iv) 702 cm
2 (a) (i) 2.7 cm (ii) 5.2 cm
(iii) 6.0 cm (iv) 5.1 cm
(b) (i) 27 mm (ii) 52 mm
(iii) 60 mm (iv) 51 mm
3 (a) (i) 1.8 kg (ii) 2.72 kg
(iii) 5.078 kg (iv) 3.009 kg
(b) (i) 1800 g (ii) 2720 g
(iii) 5078 g (iv) 3009 g
4 (a) (i) 2.90ℓ (ii) 3.25ℓ (iii) 5.084ℓ
(iv) 1.008ℓ
(b) (i) 2900 mℓ (ii) 3250 mℓ

(iii) 5084 mℓ (iv) 1008 ml
5 (a) (i) 1.8ℓ (ii) 2.67ℓ (iii) 5.5ℓ
(iv) 3.07ℓ
(b) (i) 180 cℓ (ii) 267 cℓ (iii) 550 cℓ
(iv) 307 cℓ
6 (a) (i) 1.96 t (ii) 2.3 t (iii) 3.072 t
(iv) 4.009 t
(b) (i) 1960 kg (ii) 2300 kg
(iii) 3072 kg (iv) 4009 kg
7 1.253 m 8 2.6031
9 (a) 13 people (b) 38 kg
10 (a) 53.8 cm (b) 538 mm

M2.1
1 (a) 16 (b) 5280 (c) 80 (d) 64
(e) 24 (f) 2 (g) 2, 4 (h) 11, 11
(i) 4, 5 (j) 9, 1
2 (a) 11 st. 12 lb. by 1 lb.
(b) 15 yards 2 feet by 4 feet
(c) 46 pints by 7 pints
(d) 3 miles 27 yards by 112 yards
(e) 6 pints 13 fl. oz. by 2 fl. oz.

M2.2
1 15 2 10 3 50 4 90 5 5
6 2 7 4 8 40 9 5 10 3

M2.3
1 (a) $2\frac{1}{2}$ kg (b) $1\frac{1}{2}$ kg (c) 125 g
(d) $\frac{1}{2}$ l (e) 30 g (f) 1 m
2 (a) 2 ft (b) 2 lb (c) $\frac{1}{2}$ lb
(d) 6 pt (e) 3 yd (f) $12\frac{1}{2}$ lb

M2.4
1 1.35 kg oranges 1 lemon
3.08ℓ water 2.25 kg sugar
2 340 g onion 110 g potato
30 g butter 560 mℓ milk
280 mℓ stock 1 bay leaf
salt and pepper
3 140 mℓ water 60 g butter
110 g flour 2 eggs
4 120 g pasta 180 g pepper
60 g olives 15 g parsley
56 mℓ dressing 1 garlic clove
salt and pepper

M2.5
1 (a) 1170 (b) 256 800 (c) 30 360
(d) 2412 (e) 1320 (f) 210
(g) 344.4 (h) 1650
2 (a) 243.75 Francs (b) 1475 Francs
(c) 20.25 Pounds (d) 172.5 Markka
(e) 7625 Drachmas (f) 27 Punts
(g) 73.75 Dollars (h) 61.5 Francs

M2.6
1 £2.99 2 £1.64 3 £2.46 4 £2.16
5 £2.90 6 £2.36 7 £1.27 8 £2.23

M2.7
1 £19.08 2 £48.23 3 £37.44
4 £41.67 5 £47.10 6 £25.45
7 £40.72 8 £34.40

M3.1
1 66 m 5 46 m² 6 198 m²

M3.2
1 (a) Tennis 70 m, Netball 90 m
Hockey 294 m, Rugby 440 m
Basketball 80 m, Soccer 420 m
(b) Soccer 10800 m², Rugby 10500 m²
Hockey 5060 m², Netball 450 m²
Basketball 364 m², Tennis 264 m²
2 (a) 50 cm (b) 156.25 cm²
3 (a) 2260 cm (b) 31.5 m²
4 (a) 288 mm (b) 51.84 cm²
5 (a) 8000 m (b) 3.36 km²

M3.3
1 18 cm 2 19 mm 3 11 cm

4 1.25 m, 6.5 m 5 94.1 m, 358.2 m
6 6 ft 6 in, 55.25 square ft
7 (a) 34.8 cm (b) 947 cm²
8 (a) 73 ft (b) 343 ft

M3.4
1 1 km², 1 000 000 m²,
1 000 000 m² in 1 km²
2 10 000 cm² in 1 m²
3 1 000 000 mm² in 1 m²
4 5 000 000 m²
5 80 000 cm²
6 10 000 mm²

M3.5
1 (a) 12 m, 6 m²
(b) 30 m, 30 m²
(c) 19.2 m, 17.5 m²
(d) 31.7 m, 47.5 m²
2 (a) 312 mm, 40.8 cm²
(b) 167 mm, 13 cm²
(c) 175 mm, 6 cm²
(d) 170 mm, 6.3 cm²

M4.1
1 dinner plate (a) 817 mm
(b) 81.7 cm
compact disc (a) 377 mm
(b) 37.7 cm
metal washer (a) 69 mm
(b) 6.9 cm
coat button (a) 60 mm
(b) 6.0 cm
model car tyre (a) 41 mm
(b) 4.1 cm
2 1p 63 mm 6.3 cm
2p 79 mm 7.9 cm
5p 53 mm 5.3 cm
10p 75 mm 7.5 cm
£1 69 mm 6.9 cm
3 (a) 43.98 m (b) 15.71 m
(c) 11.94 cm (d) 30.16 cm
4 1.88 m 5 314.16 m

M4.2
1 clock face 41 548 mm², 415.48 cm²
glass coaster 7238 mm², 72.38 cm²
saucer 15 393 mm², 153.93 cm²
container lid 9852 mm², 98.52 cm²
badge 962 mm², 9.62 cm²
2 1p 314 mm² 2p 491 mm²
5p 227 mm² 10p 452 mm²
£1 380 mm²
3 (a) 12.57 m² (b) 254.47 m²
(c) 9.62 m² (d) 506.71 cm²
(e) 624.58 cm²
4 (a) 5541.77 cm² (b) 0.005 54 m²
5 (a) 3.80 m² (b) 3 801 327 cm²

M4.3
1 21.96 cm 2 21.01 cm
3 18.54 cm 4 1.99 cm
5 8.368 m 6 3.34 cm

M5.1
1 32 m² 2 80.34 cm² 3 45.6 cm²
4 53.75 cm² 5 25.6 m² 6 508 mm²

M5.2
1 4418.95 cm 2 20.31 m²
3 14 611 mm

M5.3
1 (a) 550 mm² (b) 74 cm²
2 164 cm² 3 1671.33 mm²
4 157.08 cm² 5 67.04 cm²

M6.1
1 (a) 37 259 mm³ (b) 37.259 cm³
2 (a) 7500 mm³ (b) 7.5 cm³
3 614.125 cm³ 4 6.9 m³ 5 138.012 m³

M6.2

1 1 000 000 cm^3 = 1 m^3

2 1 000 000 000 mm^3 =1 m^3

3 1 000 000 000 m^3 =1 km^3

4 (a) 4000 mm^3 (b) 0.75 cm^3

  (c) 800 000 cm^3 (d) 0.005 175 m^3

  (e) 6 000 000 mm^3

  (f) 0.000 2761 m^3 (g) 7000 m^3

  (h) 0.002 km^3

5 (a) 250 000 cm^3 (b) 0.45 cm^3

  (c) 0.0675 cm^3 (d) 7900 cm^3

6 (a) 350 000 000 mm^3 (b) 620 mm^3

  (c) 4100 mm^3 (d) 800 000 mm^3

7 (a) 0.00098 m^3 (b) 200 000 m^3

  (c) 0.000 008 951 m^3

  (d) 12 500 000 m^3

M6.3

1 (a) 7 cm^3 (b) 590 cm^3

  (c) 9000 cm^3 (d) 300 cm^3

2 (a) 4 ℓ (b) 1.502 ℓ (c) 0.709 ℓ

  (d) 0.006 ℓ

3 (a) 5 mℓ (b) 93 mℓ (c) 275 mℓ

  (d) 6000 mℓ

4 2.15ℓ

5 No, since 960 cm^3 is less than 1ℓ.

6 843 750 cm^3. It can hold 843.75ℓ

SHAPE AND SPACE

S1.3

1 (a) acute 50° (b) acute 73°

  (c) obtuse 127° (d) reflex 340°

  (e) reflex 255°

S2.1

1 a = 130° **2** b = 18° **3** c = 225°

4 d = 51° **5** e = 118° **6** x = 40°

S2.2

1 a = 85°, b = 95°, c = 95°

2 d = 140°, e = 140°, f = 40°

3 g = 142°, h = 38°, i = 142°

4 x = 153°, y = 27°, z = 27°

S2.3

1 a = 50°, b = 130°

2 c = 120°, d = 60°

3 e = 35°, f = 48°, g = 97°

4 x = 85°, y = 95°

S2.4

1 x = 66°, y = 114°

2 n = 133°, m = 47°

3 r = 42°, s = 138°

4 a = 25°, b = 155°

S2.5

1 a = 130°, b = 50°, c = 130°,

  d = 130°, e = 50°, f = 130°,

  g = 50°

2 a = 125°, b = 55°, c = 125°,

  d = 55°, p = 55°, q = 125°, r = 55°

3 p = 38°, q = 142°, r = 38°, s = 142°,

  t = 142°, u = 142°, v = 38°

S3.1

1 (a) 51° (b) 107° (c) 36° (d) 67°

  (e) 61° (f) 38°

2 (a) 165° (b) 93° (c) 82° (d) 91°

  (e) 43° (f) 127°

S3.2

1 180°, 55° **2** 360°, 74°

3 540°, 149° **4** 540°, 79°

5 720°, 81° **6** 900°, 145°

S3.3

1 (a) 60° (b) 90° (c) 108° (d) 120°

2 20 sides

S3.4

(a) 108° (b) 120° (c) 135° (d) 140°

(e) 144°

S3.5

1 (a) 90° (b) 60° (c) 36°

2 24 sides

3 36 sides

S3.6

1 a and e **2** g and h **3** l and n

4 g

S3.7

1 a = 30°, b = 90°, c = 60°

2 a = 90°, b = 26°, c = 26°

3 x = 64°, y = 64°, z = 52°

4 p = 45°, q = 90°, r = 45°, s = 45°

5 m = 74°, n = 16°, p = 90°

6 x = 74°, y = 18°, z = 81°

S4.4

1 I O X

2 a, c and e have both

  (a) 4 lines, order 4 (b) 1 line

  (c) 4 lines, order 4 (d) order 4

  (e) 3 lines, order 3 (f) 1 line

S5.1

1 Rectangle AEFK Kite LDPY

  Trapezium JZWU Square HOSM

  Trapezium TRZV

  Parallelogram TRXV

S5.3

1 Rectangle, square

2 Kite, rhombus, square

3 Parallelogram, rectangle, rhombus, square

4 Trapezium

5 Parallelogram, rectangle, rhombus, square

6 Rhombus, square

7 Kite

8 Rectangle, square

S5.4

1 (a) x = 60°, y = 30°, z = 120°

  (b) AB = 8 cm

2 (a) x = 42°, y = 42°, z = 42°

  (b) BD = 5 cm, CD = 5 cm

3 (a) p = 60°, q = 60°, r = 35°,

  x = 55°, y = 30°, z = 35°

  (b) AB = 5 cm, CD = 8 cm

4 (a) m = 140°, n = 140°, x = 20°,

  y = 20°, z = 20°

  (b) AB = 12 cm, CD = 12 cm,

  DA = 12 cm

S6.1

1 (a) Parallelogram, rectangle, rhombus

  (b) Rectangle, rhombus

  (c) Kite, trapezium, irregular quadrilateral

  (d) Square

  (e) Parallelogram

  (f) Kite, isosceles trapezium

S6.2

1 5 lines of symmetry, order 5 rotational symmetry

2 8 lines of symmetry, order 8 rotational symmetry

3 10 lines of symmetry, order 10 rotational symmetry

4 12 lines of symmetry, order 12 rotational symmetry

S6.3

1 (a) x = 72°, y = 18°, z = 18°

  (b) No additional lengths can be found.

2 (a) x = 70°, y = 110°, z = 110°

  (b) AQ = 5 cm, SP = 8 cm

3 (a) w = 54°, x = 36°, y = 54°,

  z = 90° (b) PQ = 6 cm

4 (a) x = 44°, y = 78° (b) AB = 7 cm

S6.4

1 (a) 4 (b) 4 (c) 9 (d) 4

2 (a) 1 (b) 2 (c) 4

S7.3

2 (a) angle L = 57° (b) angle V = 42°

  (c) angle R = 116°

S7.4

1 5.2 cm

  ABCD is a trapezium

3 11.6 cm, 116°

4 108°, 13.4 cm

5 68 mm, 50°

6 DE = 5.6 cm, EA = 3.5 cm

S7.5

1 (b) 5.12 m (c) 4.81 m

2 (b) A = 34°, B = 96°, C = 50°

  (c) 29.6 m

3 (b) 3.3m (c) 9° **4** (b) 12.1 m

S8.1

1 (a) N 43° E (b) N 30° W

  (c) S 52° E (d) S 15° W

2 (a) N 28° E (b) S 52° W

  (c) S 73° E (d) N 14° W

S8.2

1 Derby 030° Nottingham 45°

  Leicester 065° Warwick 110°

  London Heathrow 145°

  Southampton 170°

  Gloucester 195° Bristol 210°

  Cardiff 235° Shrewsbury 310°

  Edinburgh 340° Newcastle 355°

2 (a) 189°, H; 108°, C; 214°, Q; 332°,

  P; 317°, D; 081°, M; 017°, A;

  136°, I

  (b) B, 223°; E, 044°; F, 279°;

  G, 156°; J, 343°; K, 028°; L, 251°;

  O, 171°

S8.3

1 Pen–y–Afr 013°

  Bronze age burial mound 042°

  Foel Feddau 102°

  Worm's Head 136°

  Rosebush Quarries 148°

  Lundy Island 174°

  Woodstock TV mast 206°

  St. Anne's Head 222°

  Ramsey Island 249°

  Fishguard Harbour 294°

  Dinas Head 321°

  Cam Ingli 348°

3 (a) Catterick 005° Hamble 150°

  Linton-on-Ouse 012°

  Portland 193° Finningley 020°

  Plymouth 225° Cranwell 036°

  Culdrose 233° Marham 058°

  Fairwood Common 266°

  Lakenheath 066° Brawdy 275°

  Bentwaters 076° Aberporth 285°

  Halton 085° Mona 318°

  Manston 098° Shawbury 342°

  Farnborough 117°

  Burtonwood 349°

  (b) (i) 073° (ii) 308° (iii) 095°

  (iv) 216° (v) 036°

1 (a) 236° (b) 311° (c) 096°

  (d) 060° (e) 249° (f) 000°

2 A 340°, B 043°, C 252°, D 149°,

  E 115°, F 000°, G 270°, H 090°,

  I 180°

S8.5

1 (a) (i) 062° (ii) 242°

  (b) (i) 113° (ii) 293°

  (c) (i) 328° (ii) 148°

  (d) (i) 233° (ii) 053°

  (e) (i) 042° (ii) 222°

  (f) (i) 214° (ii) 034°

2 Axle: 145° Baker: 275°

  Congress: 009° Defiant: 124°

  Esquire: 043° Federal: 312°

S8.6

4 (b) 281°

S8.8

1 6 miles. The yacht needs to sail back at a bearing of 59°

2 The plane is 73 km from Home Airfield. The pilot should fly back on a bearing of 121°.

3 The ship is 9.8 km from Lowestoft. The ship must sail on a bearing of 282°.

4 Richard is 405 m away from his starting point.

  He needs to travel on a bearing of 284°.

5 4.55 km

  Bearing of B from S: 27°

S9.1

2 (a) Sphere (b) Cone (c) Cuboid

  (d) Cylinder (e) Cube

  (f) Triangular prism

S9.2

1 cube (a) (i) 6 (ii) 0

  (b) (i) 12 (ii) 0

  (c) 8

  cuboid (a) (i) 6 (ii) 0

  (b) (i) 12 (ii) 0

  (c) 8

  cylinder (a) (i) 2 (ii) 1

  (b) (i) 0 (ii) 2

  (c) 0

  triangular prism (a) (i) 5 (ii) 0

  (b) (i) 9 (ii) 0 (c) 6

  cone (a) (i) 1 (ii) 1

  (b) (i) 0 (ii) 1 (c) 1

  square based pyramid (a) (i) 5 (ii) 0

  (b) (i) 8 (ii) 0 (c) 5

  tetrahedron (a) (i) 4 (ii) 0

  (b) (i) 6 (ii) 0 (c) 4

  sphere (a) (i) 0 (ii) 1

  (b) (i) 0 (ii) 0 (c) 0

2 (a) cube, cuboid, triangular prism, square based pyramid, tetrahedron

  (b) Euler's theorem E = F + V − 2

S9.5

3 (a) Triangular prism

  (b) Square based pyramid

  (c) Tetrahedron

S10.1

3 (b) (4,6), (−7,2), (0,8), (5 −3), (0,−7), (3,0), (−9,−4), (−6,0)

  The coordinates of each image are equal to the value of the translation.

S10.4

1 (a) 2 and 6

  (b) 1 D +180° (−180°)

  3 A +180° (−180°)

  4 D +270° (−90°)

  5 E +180° (−180°)

  7 F +90° (−270°)

  8 B +270° (−90°)

9 C +90° (−270°)

10 F +180° (−180°)

2 A (0,1) +270°　B (0,0) +270°

C (2,0) +180°　D (1,0.5) +180°

E (−2,0) +90°　F (1,2) +180°

G (1,2) +90°　H (−1,0) +180°

I (2,2) +90°　J (0.5,−2.5) +90°

K (−1,0) +270°　L (1,−2) +270°

S10.7

1 (a) A′(1,−2), B′(2,0), C′(3,4), D′(0,3), E′(−3,2), F′(−1,−3)

(b) A′(−1,2), B′(−2,0), C′(−3,−4), D′(0,−3), E′(3,−2), F′(1,3)

(c) A′(1,2), B′(0,0), C′(−1,−4), D′(2,−3), E′(5,−2), F′(3,3)

(d) A′(1,−6), B′(2,−4), C′(3,0), D′(0,−1), E′(−3,−2), F′(−1,−7)

(e) A′(2,1), B′(0,2), C′(−4,3), D′(−3,0), E′(−2,−3), F′(3,−1)

(f) A′(−2,−1), B′(0,−2), C′(4,−3), D′(3,0), E′(2,3), F′(−3,1)

S10.8

1 C, F, H, J

A – wrong shape

B, E, I are rotations

D, K, L are translations

G is an enlargement

2 (a) B　(b) D　(c) C　(d) A　(e) A

(f) D　(g) H　(h) F

S11.4

1 (a) A′(12,6), B′(18,12), C′(9,18)

(b) A′(4,2), B′(8,6), C′(2,10)

(c) A′(0,−2), B′(10,8), C′(−5,18)

(d) A′(4,−4), B′(12,4), C′(0,12)

(e) A′(−2,−6), B′(4,0), C′(−5,6)

2 (a) W′(8,6), X′(16,6), Y′(16,10), Z′(8,10)

(b) W′(0,1), X′(12,1), Y′(12,7), Z′(0,7)

(c) W′(−2,−9), X′(14,−9), Y′(14,−1), Z′(−2,−1)

(d) W′(0,1), X′(8,1), Y′(8,5), Z′(0,5)

(e) W′(−2,3), X′(10,3), Y′(10,9), Z′(−2,9)

3 (a) A′(6,4), B′(6,10), C′(2,10)

(b) D′(−4,−2), E′(−4,−6), F′(−10,−6), G′(−10,−2)

(c) O′(0,0), P′(4,0), Q′(8,−4), R′(8,−6), S′(0,−8)

(d) T′(−4,4), U′(−2,4), V′(−2,2), W′(−6,2), X′(−6,4), Y′(−4,6)

Each coordinate of the image is twice the coordinate of the object.

S11.5

(a) 2　(b) 4　(c) 3　(d) 3

HANDLING DATA

D1.1

1 (b) Raspberry　(c) 2　2 (b) 0

D1.2

1 (a) Location and times observing could be added. A tally column could be added to ease the recording of data. Motorbike could be added to the vehicle column.

(c) To assess the need for a ringroad around the town centre.

2 (a) Location, brand and weight of packet. Space to list other flavours.

(c) Consumer survey on price differences between shops and/or brands.

3 (a) Date and time columns switched around, the tally column added. Drinks listed.

(c) Improving the availability of the drinks on sale.

4 (a) Date and times added. Space given for titles of programmes watched.

(c) TV ratings

D1.3

2 (a) £1 000 000

(b) Donations £5 000 000

Interest £3 000 000

Legacies £2 500 000

D1.5

1 Scale distorted, squashed up initially then spreads further out

2 Our bran's bar is wider than bran X's

3 No scale

4 The scale starts at 15

D2.1

1 Fair 120 students

Brown 60 students

Black 30 students

Other 30 students

2 Cottage pie 80 students

Fish and chips 160 students

Vegetarian bake 160 students

Sausage and chips 80 students

D2.2

1 (a) 110°, 80°, 60°, 50°, 40°, 20°

(b) Maths 33 students

P.E. 24 students

English 18 students

History 15 students

Biology 12 students

Art 6 students

2 (i) 150°, 150 pupils

(ii) 20°, 5 vehicles

(iii) 10°, 5 pupils

D2.3

1 (a) 5%

(b) Cricket 65 students

Tennis 65 students

Rugby 39 students

Football 78 students

Netball 13 students

2 (a) 5%　(b) £15.00

(c) (i) £6.00　(ii) £3.00　(iii) £4.50

D2.4

2 (a) 30°

3 6° represents one person

4 2° represents 1 student

D3.1

1 (a) (i) 3.6 kg　(ii) 27 kg　(iii) 1 kg

(iv) 2.25 kg

(b) (i) 4.4 lb　(ii) 70 lb　(iii) 2 lb

(iv) 0.55 lb

2 (a) (i) 850 FF　(ii) 250 FF

(iii) 635 FF　(iv) 550 FF

8.5 FF for every £1.00

(b) (i) £47　(ii) £59

(iii) £88　(iv) £27.10

D3.2

1 (b) (i) 55 Fl

(ii) 192 Fl　(iii) 242 Fl　(iv) 151 Fl

(c) (i) £36　(ii) £80　(iii) £18

(iv) £48

2 (a) (i) 48 km　(ii) 16 km

(iii) 112 km　(iv) 72 km

(b) (i) 16 miles　(ii) 40 miles

(iii) 66 miles　(iv) 6 miles

D4.1

1 (a) £1.30　(b) 6 g　(c) 9 m

(d) 42 kg　(e) £4.10

2 £87.70　3 13°C　4 £1.45

5 3.9 mm

D4.2

1 64　2 (a) 44 miles　(b) 11 miles

3 (a) 54.6 kg　(b) 63 kg

4 290 000 entries

5 (a) 9397　(b) 11 140 people

D4.3

1 (a) (i) 6 cm, 11 cm, 12 cm, 14 cm, 15 cm (ii) 12 cm

(b) (i) 4 kg, 8 kg, 9 kg, 12 kg, 13 kg, 14 kg, 15 kg (ii) 12 kg

(c) (i) 14 s, 15 s, 18 s, 19 s, 20 s, 22 s, 24 s (ii) 19 s

(d) (i) 36, 37, 37, 41, 43, 47, 54, 67, 68 (ii) 43

(e) (i) 3 m, 5 m, 5 m, 7 m, 7 m, 9 m, 10 m, 12 m, 13 m, 13 m, 15 m (ii) 9 m

2 (a) 10 kg　(b) £6.50　(c) 7h

(d) 179 cm　(e) 7　(f) 16.5 m

(g) 6.7　(h) 8.1

3 26.5°C

D4.4

1 (a) 4　(b) £5.50　(c) 9 cm

(d) 15 kg　(e) 1

2 (a) 9p　(b) 19　(c) 6 m

(d) 10.4 kg　(e) £3.01

3 Size 7

D4.5

1 (a) 9 cm　(b) 11 kg　(c) 10 s

(d) 32　(e) 12 m

2 (a) 6 kg　(b) £8　(c) 6 h　(d) 23 cm

(e) 4　(f) 9 m　(g) 9.9　(h) 7.2

3 11°C　4 6 goals　5 35

D5.1

1 No chance, no way, very unlikely, poor chance, possibly evens, fifty = fifty, likely, good chance, highly likely, probably, sure, certain, dead cert.

2 (a) Very unlikely　(b) Certain

(c) Possibly　(d) Probably

(e) Evens　(f) No chance

D5.2

1 (a) E　(b) D　(c) F　(d) A　(e) C

(f) B

3 (a) (i) Molton Street junction

(ii) Monument Square

(b) Monument Square, Renton Avenue, Highcliff roundabout, Molton Street junction.

4 (a) (i) Blackheaded gull (ii) Snipe

(b) Snipe, avocet, oystercatcher, redshank, blackheaded gull

5 (a) (i) Coffee (ii) Soup

(b) Coffee, tea, chocolate, soup

D5.3

1 1, 2, 3, 4, 5, 6　Event D 2

Event E 1, 3, 5　Event F 5, 6

2 1p, 2p, 5p, 10p, 20p, 50p, £1

Event A £1

Event B 5p, 10p, 20p, 50p

Event C 1p, 2p, 5p, 10p, 20p

3 P, R, O, B, A, I, L, T, Y

Event A R

Event B O, A, I

Event C P, R, B, L, T, Y

4 7C, 7H, QH, QS, KC

Event A 7H, 7C

Event B No chance

Event C H, S, C

D5.4

1 Event D $\frac{1}{6}$

Event E $\frac{1}{2}$

Event F $\frac{1}{2}$

2 Event A $\frac{1}{7}$

Event B $\frac{4}{7}$

Event C $\frac{5}{7}$

3 Event A $\frac{1}{11}$

Event B $\frac{4}{11}$

Event C $\frac{7}{11}$

4 Event A $\frac{2}{5}$

Event B 0

Event C $\frac{3}{5}$

5 (a) $\frac{1}{8}$　(b) $\frac{1}{2}$　(c) $\frac{1}{2}$　(d) $\frac{5}{8}$　(e) $\frac{1}{4}$

6 (a) $\frac{1}{5}$　(b) $\frac{2}{5}$　(c) $\frac{3}{5}$　(d) 0

7 (a) $\frac{1}{6}$

8 (a) $\frac{1}{10}$　(b) $\frac{1}{5}$　(c) $\frac{3}{5}$　(d) $\frac{2}{5}$　(e) $\frac{1}{2}$

(f) $\frac{2}{5}$

D5.5

1 (a) $\frac{1}{5}$　(b) $\frac{3}{5}$　(c) $\frac{4}{5}$

2 (a) $\frac{1}{3}$　(b) $\frac{1}{2}$　(c) $\frac{1}{3}$　(d) $\frac{1}{3}$

3 (a) $\frac{2}{7}$　(b) $\frac{1}{3}$　(c) $\frac{8}{21}$

4 (a) $\frac{1}{6}$　(b) $\frac{1}{2}$　(c) $\frac{1}{2}$

5 (a) $\frac{18}{29}$　(b) $\frac{11}{29}$

6 (a) $\frac{9}{240}$　(b) $\frac{7}{240}$

7 (a) $\frac{1}{90}$　(b) $\frac{1}{10}$　(c) $\frac{1}{9}$

8 (a) $\frac{9}{34}$　(b) $\frac{13}{34}$

9 (a) $\frac{1}{52}$　(b) $\frac{1}{13}$　(c) 1　(d) $\frac{1}{4}$　(e) $\frac{3}{13}$

10 (a) $\frac{1}{2}$　(b) $\frac{2}{13}$

D5.6

1 (a) $\frac{1}{50}$　(b) $\frac{49}{50}$

2 (a) $\frac{17}{30}$　(b) $\frac{13}{30}$

3 (a) $\frac{2}{7}$　(b) $\frac{5}{7}$　(c) $\frac{3}{14}$　(d) $\frac{11}{14}$

4 (a) $\frac{2}{3}$　(b) $\frac{1}{3}$　(c) $\frac{13}{18}$　(d) $\frac{17}{18}$

5 (a) $\frac{1}{3}$　(b) $\frac{7}{12}$　(c) $\frac{3}{4}$　(d) $\frac{1}{4}$

D6.1

5 2 3 4 3 4 5

2 3 5 3 4 6

2 3 6 3 4 7

2 3 7 3 5 6

2 4 5 3 5 7

2 4 6 3 6 7

2 4 7 4 5 6

2 5 6 4 5 7

2 5 7 4 6 7

2 6 7 5 6 7

6 (b) Al Ben　Al Colin　Al Sally

Al Tracy　Ben Colin　Ben Sally

Ben Tracy　Colin Sally

Colin Tracy　Sally Tracy

D6.2

1 (a) 12　(b) 2　(c) (i) $\frac{1}{6}$　(ii) $\frac{1}{12}$

(iii) $\frac{1}{2}$　(iv) $\frac{1}{4}$

2 (a) 12　(b) (i) $\frac{1}{2}$　(ii) $\frac{1}{3}$

(iii) $\frac{1}{4}$　(iv) $\frac{1}{6}$　(v) $\frac{1}{12}$

3 (a) 9　(b) $\frac{1}{3}$　(c) $\frac{1}{3}$　(d) $\frac{1}{9}$　(e) $\frac{1}{3}$

(f) $\frac{1}{3}$

4 (a) (i) $\frac{1}{6}$　(ii) $\frac{1}{36}$　(iii) $\frac{1}{6}$　(iv) $\frac{1}{12}$　(v) $\frac{7}{36}$

(vi) $\frac{5}{12}$

(b) (i) $\frac{1}{18}$　(ii) $\frac{25}{36}$　(iii) 0　(iv) $\frac{2}{9}$　(v) $\frac{1}{6}$

(c) (i) $\frac{1}{6}$　(ii) 0　(iii) $\frac{2}{3}$　(iv) $\frac{1}{18}$　(v) $\frac{4}{9}$

5 (a) $\frac{1}{2}$　(b) $\frac{1}{2}$　(c) $\frac{3}{20}$　(d) $\frac{1}{2}$　(e) $\frac{1}{20}$

6 (a) (i) $\frac{1}{2}$　(ii) $\frac{1}{3}$　(iii) $\frac{1}{6}$　(b) (i) $\frac{1}{10}$　(ii) $\frac{3}{10}$

P1.1

(a) 3^2　(b) 2^4　(c) 8^3　(d) 7^2　(e) 6^5

(f) 5^7　(g) 10^6　(h) 9^6

2 (a) $10 \times 10 \times 10 \times 10 \times 10 \times 10 \times 10 \times 10 = 100\,000\,000$

(b) $2 \times 2 \times 2 \times 2 \times 2 \times 2 \times 2 \times 2 \times 2 \times 2 = 1024$

(c) $7\times7\times7\times7\times7\times7 =117\,649$
(d) $4\times4\times4\times4\times4\times4\times4\times4 = 65\,536$
(e) $5\times5\times5 = 125$
(f) $3\times3\times3\times3\times3\times3\times3\times3\times3 = 19\,683$
(g) $6\times6\times6\times6\times6\times6 = 279\,936$
(h) $8\times8\times8\times8 = 4096$

3 (a) $7^5 = 7\times7\times7\times7\times7$
(b) $4^9 = 4\times4\times4\times4\times4\times4\times4\times4\times4$
(c) $10^4 = 10\times10\times10\times10$
(d) $2^7 = 2\times2\times2\times2\times2\times2\times2$
(e) $4^6 = 4\times4\times4\times4\times4\times4$
(f) $9^5 = 9\times9\times9\times9\times9$
(g) $6^4 = 6\times6\times6\times6$
(h) $5^{10} = 5\times5\times5\times5\times5\times5\times5\times5\times5\times5$

4 (a) 6^3, $6\times6\times6$ (b) 4^2, 4×4
(c) 10^2, 10×10 (d) 8^3, $8\times8\times8$
(e) 9^3, $9\times9\times9$ (f) 5^2, 5×5

P1.2

1 (a) $a\times a\times a$
(b) $x\times x\times x\times x\times x\times x\times x$
(c) $y\times y\times y\times y\times y$
(d) $m\times m\times m\times m$
(e) $n\times n\times n\times n\times n\times n\times n\times n$
(f) $p\times p\times p\times p\times p\times p$
(g) $u\times u$
(h) $v\times v\times v\times v\times v\times v\times v\times v\times v\times v$

2 (a) x^3 (b) n^4 (c) p^6 (d) m^2
(e) a^5 (f) s^7 (g) b^2 (h) r^8

3 (a) $x^4 = x\times x\times x\times x$
(b) $y^5 = y\times y\times y\times y\times y$
(c) $p^2 = p\times p$
(d) $r^6 = r\times r\times r\times r\times r\times r$
(e) $n^7 = n\times n\times n\times n\times n\times n\times n$
(f) $m^2 = m\times m$
(g) $y^3 = y\times y\times y$
(h) $a^6 = a\times a\times a\times a\times a\times a$

4 (a) $2\times x\times x\times x$
(b) $4\times p\times p\times p\times p\times p\times p$
(c) $3\times x\times y\times y$
(d) $5\times n\times n\times m$
(e) $6\times a\times a\times b\times b\times b$
(f) $4\times u\times u\times v\times v\times v\times v\times v\times v$
(g) $8\times r\times r\times r\times r\times s\times s\times s$
(h) $9\times a\times b\times c\times c\times c$
(i) $10\times u\times u\times v\times w\times w\times w\times w\times w$

5 (a) $4a^3$ (b) $7b^2$ (c) $3u^2v^2$
(d) $4m^2n^3$ (e) $7x^3y$ (f) $2p^2q^4$
(g) $8rs^5$ (h) $6b^3c^2$ (i) $12p^2q^3$
(j) $20m^2n^4$

P1.3

1 (a) 729 (b) 46 656 (c) 2401
(d) 759 375 (e) 10 000 000
(f) 6561 (g) 2 097 152
(h) 20 736

2 (a) 512 (b) 262 144 (c) 177 147
(d) 390 625 (e) 1024
(f) 60 466 176 (g) 6561 (h) 13 824

3 (a) 3^2 (b) 2^{10} (c) 3^4 (d) 7^1
(e) 5^8 (f) 6^9

4 (a) 4000 (b) 4 000 000 (c) 3969
(d) 2500 (e) 1 (f) 8 (g) 59 049
(h) 128 (i) 10 000

P1.4

1 3^5 2 2^6 3 7^4 4 10^7 5 9^3 6 5^9

P1.5

1 3 2 3 3 5 4 5^4 5 12^5 6 20^3

P1.6

1 (a) 2^8 (b) 3^6 (c) 3^4 (d) 5^7
(e) 7^6 (f) 6^8 (g) 8^7 (h) 3^{13} (i) $9''$
2 (a) a^7 (b) b^6 (c) x^7 (d) y^{10}
(e) a^9 (f) p^5 (g) x^{10} (h) n^9
(i) m^6
3 (a) $6x^3$ (b) $6x^7$ (c) $8b^7$ (d) $6y^6$
(e) $12p^5$ (f) $6q^{10}$ (g) $18p^6$
(h) $5x^8$ (i) $63a^{16}$

P1.7

1 (a) 3^4 (b) 5^6 (c) 4^7 (d) 2^2
(e) 6^2 (f) 7^1 (g) 9^2 (h) 8^2
(i) 10^2
2 (a) a^2 (b) b^2 (c) x^2 (d) p^4
(e) n^3 (f) y^3
3 (a) x^5 (b) p^1 (c) a^3 (d) n^4
(e) m^5 (f) c^1 (g) y^3 (h) k^5
(i) w^3
4 (a) $3a$ (b) $3b$ (c) $2m^3$ (d) $3p^5$
(e) $2t^5$ (f) b (g) $6s^2$ (h) $4m^4$
(i) $\frac{7}{2}x$
5 (a) 1 (b) 1 (c) 1 (d) 3 (e) 4
(f) $3\frac{1}{2}$ (g) 2 (h) $2\frac{1}{2}$ (i) $\frac{3}{4}$

P1.8

1 5^6 2 7^4 3 x^7 4 m^5 5 $2n^3$
6 $7m^{11}$ 7 1 8 $3x^5$ 9 $15r^3$ 10 $\frac{5}{4}$
11 $3x^7$ 12 2 13 $4p^2$ 14 $10d^5$
15 $4u^3$ 16 $2m$ 17 $5n^6$ 18 $14a^5$ 19 4
10 $18n^8$

P1.9

1 (a) 0.03125 (b) 0.1 (c) 0.015 625
(d) 0.04 (e) 0.012 345 679
(f) 0.027 777 777 (g) 1
(h) 0.012 345 679 (i) 0.01 (j) 1
2 (a) $\frac{1}{4^2}$ (b) $\frac{1}{6}$ (c) $\frac{1}{8^3}$ (d) $\frac{1}{2^6}$ (e) $\frac{1}{10^4}$
(f) $\frac{1}{a^7}$ (g) $\frac{1}{x^3}$ (h) $\frac{1}{y^2}$ (i) $\frac{1}{b^8}$ (j) $\frac{1}{c}$
3 (a) 10^{-2} (b) 4^{-7} (c) 3^{-5}
(d) 2^{-9} (e) 9^{-1} (f) x^{-3}
(g) a^{-4} (h) y^{-1} (i) c^{-6} (j) b^{-8}
4 (a) 4^3 (b) 7^0 (c) 6^1 (d) 10^4
(e) 3^{-2} (f) 5^1

P2.1

1 Outputs 10, 9, 8, 7, 6, 5
2 Outputs $-15, -10, -5, 0, 5, 10, 15$
3 Outputs $-1, 2, 4, 8, 11, 14$
4 Outputs $7, 5, 3, 1, -1$
5 Outputs $14, 11, 8, 5, 2, -1$

P2.2

1 (b) $(-5,-2), (-4,-1), (-3,0), (-2,1), (-1,2), (0,3)$ $(1,4), (2,5), (3,6), (4,7), (5,8)$
2 (b) $(-3,-5),(-2,-3), (-1,-1), (0,1), (1,3), (2,5), (3,7)$
(e) $y = 10$, $y = 6$, $y = -2$, $y = -6$

P2.3

1 (i) $y = 1$, $y = 7.5$ (ii) $x = 3$, $x = 0.5$
2 (i) $y = -5.5$, $y = -1.5$
(ii) $x = -3$, $x = 3$
3 (i) $y = -1$, $y = 6$
(ii) $x = -2.5$, $x = 4.5$
4 (i) $y = 9$, $y = -7$ (ii) $x = 3$, $x = -3$
5 (i) $y = 5$, $y = -8.5$
(ii) $x = -0.5$, $x = -3$

P2.4

1 (a) £59 (b) $3\frac{1}{4}$ m
2 (a) 37 m/s (b) 2.8 s
3 (a) 1050 people (b) 1978
4 (a) 56 km (b) 45 miles

P2.5

1 (b) $(-3,4.5), (-2,2), (-1,0.5), (0,0), (1,0.5), (2,2), (3,4.5)$
(f) 2.9, 1.4, 0.4, 4.2

(g) 2.8 and -2.8, 1.2 and -1.2, 1.9 and -1.9, 2.6 and -2.6
2 (c) (i) $y = 6.8$, $y = 4.2$ (ii) $y = 3.8$, $y = 1.2$ (iii) $y = -5.76$, $y = -3.24$
(iv) $y = 4.2$, $y = 6.8$
(d) (i) $x = 2.8$ (ii) 3.3
(e) (iii) $x = \pm3$ (iv) $x = \pm4.4$
3 (c) (i) 0.8 (ii) 12.8 (iii) 6.1
(d) (i) 0.8 (ii) 1.4 (iii) 1.9

P3.2

1 (a) A(6,6), B(10,5), C(10,4), D(6,2)
(b) A(1,5.5), B(5,4.5), C(5,3.5), D(1,1.5)
(c) A(2,11), B(6,10), C(6,9), D(2,7)
(d) A(4,9), B(8,8), C(8,7), D(4,5)
2 (a) J(9,6), K(7,6), L(7,9), M(9,9), N(8,7)
(b) J(3,2), K(1,2), L(1,5), M(3,5), N(2,3)
(c) J(5,6), K(3,6), L(3,9), M(5,9), N(4,7)
(d) J(11,8), K(9,8), L(9,11), M(11,11), N(10,9)
3 (a) A(2,6), B(3,3), C(4,6)
(b) D(5,5), E(7,4), F(8,5), G(6,9)
(c) H(1,0), I(1,1), J(0,1), K(-1,0)
(d) L(1,-3), M(1,2), N(0,-2), P(0,-1), Q(-1,-1), R(-1,-3)
(e) S(-8,-2), T(-7,-2), U(-7,-3)

P3.3

1 Centre (5,7) scale factor $\frac{1}{3}$
2 (a) Centre (1,1) scale factor $\frac{1}{3}$
(b) Centre (1,1) scale factor $\frac{1}{4}$
(c) Centre (2,2) scale factor $\frac{1}{3}$
(d) Centre (0,0) scale factor $\frac{1}{3}$
(e) Centre (0,4) scale factor $\frac{1}{4}$

P3.4

1 (a) A(9,9), B(14,9), C(14,14), D(19,14), E(11.5, 24), F(4,14), G(9,14)
(b) A(10,10), B(15,10), C(15,15), D(20,15), E(12.5, 25), F(5,15), G(10,15)
(c) A(8,8), B(13,8), C(13,13), D(18,13), E(10.5, 23), F(3,13), G(8,13)
(d) A(7.5,5), B(12.5,5), C(12.5,10), D(17.5,10), E(10, 20), F(2.5,10), G(7.5,10)
2 (a) A(-2,16), B(10,13), C(10,10), D(-2,4)
(b) A(3,16.5), B(15,13.5), C(15,10.5), D(3,4.5)
(c) A(2,11), B(14,8), C(14,5), D(2,-1)
(d) A(0,13), B(12,10), C(12,7), D(0,1)
3 (a) J(6,0), K(-2,0), L(-2,12), M(6,12), N(2,4)
(b) J(9,2), K(1,2), L(1,14), M(9,14), N(5,6)
(c) J(8,0), K(0,0), L(0,12), M(8,12), N(4,4)
(d) J(5,-1), K(-3,-1), L(-3,11), M(5,11), N(1,3)
4 (a) A(5,21), B(9,9), C(13,21)
(b) D(-3,-1), E(3,-4), F(6,-1), G(0,11)
(c) H(6,0), I(6,6), J(0,6), K(-6,0)
(d) L(5,1), M(5,6), N(0,6), P(0,11), Q(-5,11), R(-5,1)
(e) S(-2,4), T(5,4), U(5,-3)

5 (a) Centre (0,-2) scale factor 1
(b) Centre (2,-1) scale factor 1
6 (a) Centre (2,1) scale factor 2
(b) Centre (5,2) scale factor 1
(c) Centre (2,4) scale factor 1

P4.1

1 (a) 4(4 + 1), 5(5 + 1), 6(6 + 1)
(b) 10(10 + 1), 100(100 + 1)
(c) $n(n + 1)$
2 (a) 4(4 - 1), 5(5 - 1), 6(6 - 1)
(b) 10(10 - 1), 100(100 - 1)
(c) $n(n - 1)$
3 (a) 4(2 × 4 + 1), 5(2 × 5 + 1), 6(2 × 6 + 1)
(b) 10(2 × 10 + 1), 100(2 × 100 + 1)
(c) $n(2 \times n + 1)$ $n(2n + 1)$
4 (a) 4(3 × 4 - 1), 5(3 × 5 - 1), 6(3 × 6 - 1)
(b) 10(3 × 10 - 1), 100(3 × 100 - 1)
(c) $n(3 \times n - 1)$ $n(3n - 1)$
5 (a) (2 × 4 - 1)(4 + 1), (2 × 5 - 1)(5 + 1), (2 × 6 - 1)(6 + 1)
(b) (2 × 10 - 1)(10 + 1), (2 × 100 - 1)(100 + 1)
(c) $(2n - 1)(n + 1)$

P4.2

1 (a) 2, 3, 4, 5, 6, 21
(b) 0, 1, 2, 3, 4, 19
(c) 7, 9, 11, 13, 15, 45
(d) 2, 5, 8, 11, 14, 59
(e) $-1, -4, -7, -10, -13, -58$
(f) 1, 7, 13, 19, 25, 115
(g) $\frac{1}{2}$, 1, $1\frac{1}{2}$, 2, $2\frac{1}{2}$, 10
(h) $\frac{2}{3}$, 1, $1\frac{1}{3}$, $1\frac{2}{3}$, 2, 7
(i) 5, $2\frac{1}{2}$, $1\frac{2}{3}$, $1\frac{1}{4}$, 1, $\frac{1}{4}$
(j) 1, 3, 6, 10, 15, 210
(k) 4, 15, 30, 49, 72, 897
(l) 2, $\frac{3}{4}$, $\frac{2}{5}$, $\frac{1}{4}$, $\frac{6}{35}$, $\frac{3}{220}$
2 (a) 3, 5, 7, 51
(b) 10, 17, 24, 31, 87
(c) 4, $-1, -6, -11, -16, -41$
(d) 4, 6, 6, 4, -546
(e) 4, 15, 32, 260
(f) 0, 1, 3, 6, 10, 15, 1225
(g) $2\frac{2}{3}$, $9\frac{1}{3}$, 20, 460

P4.3

1 10th term 2 8th term 3 10th term
4 23rd term 5 6th term

P4.4

1 (a) 27 (b) 13 (c) 33
2 (a) -21 (b) -24 (c) -60
3 (a) -38 (b) -143 (c) -73
4 (a) 143 (b) 296 (c) 503
5 (a) 159 (b) 564 (c) 1380

P4.5

1 $n + 2$ 2 $4n$ 3 n^2 4 $-n$ 5 $n - 6$
6 $10 - n$ 7 $n - 3$ 8 $\frac{n}{10}$ 9 $-3n$
10 $\frac{n}{2}$

P4.6

1 (a) 20, 24, 28, $4n$
(b) 9, 11, 13, $2n - 1$
(c) $-7, -9, -11, 3 - 2n$
(d) 27, 32, 37, $5n + 2$
(e) $-9, -12, -15, 6 - 3n$
2 (a) $U_n = 5n - 4$ (b) $U_n = 5 - 2n$
(c) $U_n = 6n + 2$ (d) $U_n = 1 - n$
(e) $U_n = 2n - 7$
3 $U_n = 3n + 3$ 4 $U_n = 10 - 6n$

P4.7

1 (a) $\frac{1}{10}$, $\frac{1}{12}$ (b) $U_n = \frac{1}{2n}$
2 (a) $\frac{5}{6}$, $\frac{6}{7}$ (b) $U_n = \frac{n}{n+1}$
3 (a) $\frac{7}{9}$, $\frac{8}{10}$ (b) $U_n = \frac{n+2}{n+4}$

4 (a) $\frac{9}{25}, \frac{11}{30}$ (b) $U_n = \frac{2n-1}{5n}$

5 (a) $\frac{25}{11}, \frac{36}{13}$ (b) $U_n = \frac{n^2}{2n+1}$

6 (a) $\frac{4}{5}, \frac{5}{6}$ (b) $U_n = \frac{n-1}{n}$

7 (a) $\frac{32}{13}, \frac{64}{15}$ (b) $U_n = \frac{2^n}{2n+3}$

8 (a) $\frac{9}{35}, \frac{11}{42}$ (b) $U_n = \frac{2n-1}{7n}$

P4.8

1 $U_n = n^2 + 1$ **2** $U_n = 2n^2 - 1$
3 $U_n = n^2 - 3$ **4** $U_n = n^2 - 4$
5 $U_n = n^2 + n$ **6** $U_n = n^2 - n$
7 $U_n = 3n^2$ **8** $U_n = 2n^2 + 5$
9 $U_n = 5(2n^2 - 1)$ **10** $U_n = 4n^2 - 1$

P4.9

1 Sequence 1
(b) (i) 13 (ii) 31 (iii) $3n + 1$
Sequence 2 (a)
(b) (i) 22 (ii) 52 (iii) $5n + 2$
2 Sequence 1 (a) 10 (b) 15 (c) 78
(d) $\frac{n(n+1)}{2}$
Sequence 2 (a) 10 (b) 13 (c) 34
(d) $3(n-1) + 1$
3 (a) (i) 20 (ii) 24 (iii) 64
(iv) $4(n+1)$ (b) 29th shape
4 (b) $U_n = 2n + 1$ (c) 375 triangles
(d) There would be one left over as each shape uses an odd number of matches
5 (a) (i) 30 m (ii) 34 m (iii) 38 m
(iv) 66 m (v) 186 m
(vi) $4(n-1) + 30$
(b) (i) 21st tree (ii) 33rd tree
6 (a) The fourth year
(b) (i) £5800 (ii) £10300
(iii) £14800
(iv) $U_n = 900(n-1) - 2300$
7 (a) (i) 6.3°C (ii) 4.6°C (iii) –0.5°C
(iv) –26°C (v) –41.3°C
(vi) $U_n = 8 - 1.7n$
(b) (i) 15 000 ft (ii) 22 000 ft
8 (a) 12 m and 17 m
(b) $U_n = \frac{n^2 - n}{2} + 2$ (c) 9s
9 (a) £9100 (ii) £12300
(iii) $U_n = 7500 + 800(n - 1)$
(b) Her 13th year

P5.3

1 Negative correlation
2 Positive correlation
3 No correlation
4 Negative correlation
5 Negative correlation

P5.4

2 (a) Mean rainfall 8.4 mm Mean sunshine 3.8 hours

P5.5

1 (a) (i) 3.5 hours (ii) 2.5 hours
(iii) 1.9 hours
(b) (i) 15.5 mm (ii) 12.5 mm
(iii) 4.5 mm
2 (a) (i) 55 (ii) 52.5 (iii) 48.5
(b) (i) 65 (ii) 45.5 (iii) 77
3 (a) (i) 43 mg/ℓ (ii) 47.4 mg/ℓ
(iii) 50 mg/ℓ
(b) (i) 23.9 mg/ℓ (ii) 30 .6 mg/ℓ
(iii) 32.9 mg/ℓ
4 (a) (i) 24.5 mpg (ii) 44 mpg
(iii) 37 mpg
(b) (i) 1.4ℓ (ii) 3.3ℓ (iii) 3.65ℓ
5 (a) (i) 45 (ii) 56 (iii) 42.5
(b) (i) 10.8°C (ii) 5.8°C
(iii) 18.5°C
6 (c) (i) 175 cm (ii) 83 kg
7 (c) 46 marks (d) 53 marks

P6.1

1 (a) 0.5 kg (b) 67.5 kg, 68.5 kg
(c) 67.5 kg ≤ w < 68.5 kg
2 (a) 0.5 m (b) 11 m, 12.5 ,
(c) 11.5 m ≤ l < 12.5 m
3 (a) 0.5° (b) 16.5°, 17.5°
(c) 16.5° ≤ a < 17.5°
4 (a) 0.5 min (b) 8.5 min, 9.5 min
(c) 8.5 min ≤ t < 9.5 min
5 (a) 0.5°C (b) 30.5°C, 31.5°C
(c) 30.5°C ≤ t < 31.5°C
6 (a) 0.5 cm²
(b) 241.5 cm², 242.5 cm²
(c) 241.5 cm² ≤ a < 242.5 cm²
7 (a) 0.5 ft³ (b) 890.5 ft³, 891.5 ft³
(c) 890.5 ft³ ≤ v < 891.5 ft³
8 (a) 0.5 m³ (b) 9.5 m³, 10.5 m³
(c) 9.5 m³ ≤ v < 10.5 m³
9 (a) 0.5 g (b) 29.5 g, 30.5 g
(c) 29.5 g ≤ w < 30.5 g
10 (a) 0.5 cℓ (b) 74.5 cℓ, 75.5 cℓ
(c) 74.5 cℓ ≤ v < 75.5 cℓ

P7.2

1 (a) 91 (b) 9 (c) 55 (d) 11 (e) 4
(f) 3 (g) 2 (h) 2 (i) 4 (j) 6
2 (a) 16.61 (b) 74.9 (c) 1253
(d) 270.48 (e) 9 (f) 183.48
(g) 2284.5 (h) 4.6 (i) 8.224
(j) 64.94
3 (a) 419.58, 420
(b) 5.523 809 524, 5.52
(c) 42.91, 42.9
(d) 2.299 122 807, 2.30
(e) 7.278 325 123, 7.28
(f) 55.738, 55.7
(g) 151.524, 152
(h) 2.192 095 588, 2.19
(i) 66.15, 66.2
(j) 3.185 803 758, 3.19
4 (a) 14.9, 14.9
(b) 40.48, 40.5
(c) 5.132 051 661, 5.13
(d) 11 139.7 376, 1140
(e) 6.4516, 6.45
(f) 0.467 508 2581, 0.468
(g) 1198.089 997, 1200
(h) 48.689 1643, 48.7
(i) 0.398 873 2186, 0.399
(j) 6.954 116 319, 6.95

P7.3

1 (a) 3 (b) 3 (c) 3 (d) 5 (e) 3
(f) 4 (g) 3 (h) 1 (i) 7
2 (a) 32 (b) 6 (c) 7 (d) 6 (e) 2
(f) 3 (g) 3 (h) 4 (i) 2
3 (a) 4.809 523 81, 4.81
(b) 1.191 780 822, 1.19
(c) 1.450 847 458, 1.45
(d) 4.296 918 768, 4.30
(e) 2.742 038 217, 2.74
(f) 12.990 270 27, 13.0
(g) 1.170 852 018, 1.17
(h) 3.124 067 797, 3.12
4 (a) 3.627 639 744, 3.63
(b) 0.418 201 028, 0.418
(c) 1.984 057 971, 1.98
(d) 2.385 757 741, 2.39
(e) 0.876 736 1111, 0.877
(f) 0.773 005 5785, 0.773
(g) 1.298 748 239, 1.30
(h) 3.873 461 463, 3.87

P7.4

1 (a) 54 (b) 243 (c) 972 (d) 3
(e) 3 (f) 6 (g) 1944 (h) 2754
(i) 810 (j) 1620
2 (a) 151 (b) 25.2 (c) 18.7
(d) 13.9 (e) 5.62 (f) 8.19
(g) 28.5 (h) 8.73 (i) 403
(j) 7.26
3 (a) 1.20 (b) 3.12 (c) 0.538
(d) 2.41 (e) 0.231 (f) 7.95
(g) 10.3 (h) 5.42 (i) 0.896

P7.5

1 (a) 997.5 mm² (b) 7.83 cm²
2 (a) 34 557.5 mm³ (b) 2597.5 cm³
3 (a) 51 779.7 mm² (b) 349.5 cm²
4 (a) 15°C (b) 60°C (c) 37.8°C
5 (a) 16 m (b) 69 m (c) 290.5 m
6 (a) 4.5 m (b) 25 m (c) 30.4 m
7 (a) (i) 4.31 m/s² (ii) 4.29 m/s²
(b) (i) 21.3 newton
(ii) 8.04 newtons

P7.6

1 (a) 625.82, 550.82, 851.62, 5588.82, 1347
(b) 101.24, 53.24, 291.14, 167.28, –15.41
(c) 136.5, 300.3, 507.78, 4149.6, 5834.01
(d) 2.03, 2.52, 3.34, 0.077, 0.637
2 (a) 17, 34, 51, 68, 85, 102, 119, 136, 153, 170
(b) 41, 82, 123, 164, 205, 246, 287, 328, 369, 410
(c) 53, 106, 159, 212, 265, 318, 371, 424, 479, 530
(d) 79, 158, 237, 316, 395, 474, 553, 632, 711, 790
3 (a) 1, 2, 3, 6, 7, 11, 14, 21, 22, 33, 42, 66, 77, 154, 231, 462
(b) 1, 2, 4, 5, 7, 8, 10, 14, 20, 28, 35, 40, 56, 70, 140, 280
(c) 1, 3, 7, 11, 13, 21, 33, 39, 77, 91, 143, 231, 273, 429, 1001, 3003
(d) 1, 2, 3, 4, 5, 6, 7, 10, 12, 14, 15, 20, 21, 25, 28, 30, 35, 42, 50, 60, 70, 75, 84, 100, 105, 140, 150, 175, 210, 300, 350, 420, 525, 700, 1050, 2100
4 (a) £94.42 (b) £114.67
(c) £288.69 (d) £629.98
5 (i) £2.86 (ii) £4.46 (iii) £5.93
(iv) £8.92 (v) £4.81 (vi) £0.57
(vii) £1.14 (viii) £15.56
6 (a) 4.57 m, 12.796 m, 20.108 m, 51.641 m
(b) 7.659 yd, 25.164 yd, 55.799 yd, 83.151 yd, 109.409 yd
7 (i) £5.10, (ii) £6.38, (iii) £5.09, (iv) £13.50, (v) £6.80, (vi) £10.46, (vii) £9.77, (viii) £22.94
8 (a) £89.91 (b) £104.97
(c) £68.47 (d) £110.07
(e) £121.03 (f) £154.15

P7.7

1 (a) 171 (b) 21.36 (c) 2.01
2 (a) 628 (b) 55.12 (c) 70.1152
3 (a) –188 (b) –1.61 (c) 4.76
4 (a) –671 (b) 1.6 (c) 1.6875
5 (a) 3120 (b) 212.48 (c) 34.92
6 (a) –2607 (b) –68.25
(c) –184.146
7 (a) –1100 (b) –1.36 (c) 0.84
8 (a) 976.89 (b) –4.88 (c) 319.99
9 (a) 3525 (b) 159.624 (c) 3.048

P7.9

2 1917 miles
3 (a) £60.70 (b) 35.488 cm
(c) 55.044 kg
4 341.04
5 £16.92, £87.36, £5.88
6 1, 2, 4, 7, 14

P8.1

1 (a) same base
(b) same height
4 (a) 8 squares (b) 2 squares
(c) 15 squares (d) 8 squares
(e) 12 squares (f) 12 squares
(g) 4 squares (h) 8 squares

P8.2

1 (a) 22 cm (b) 24.12 cm²
2 (a) 14.4 cm (b) 8.1 cm²
3 (a) 13.4 cm (b) 10.325 cm²
4 (a) 12.4 cm (b) 7.14 cm²
5 (a) 14.4 cm (b) 12.2 cm²

P8.3

1 (a) 30 m (b) 40 m²
2 (a) 70 mm (b) 228.mm²
3 (a) 14.7 km (b) 4.25 km²
4 (a) 254 mm (b) 2940 mm²
5 (a) 6.7 m (b) 1.7 m²
6 (a) 20.2 cm (b) 22.5 cm²
7 (a) 5 km (b) 0.75 km²
8 (a) 15.4 m (b) 19.5 m²

P8.4

1 (a) 16.2 cm (b) 13.8 cm²
2 (a) 15.6 cm (b) 13 cm²
3 (a) 13.5 cm (b) 10.3 cm²
4 (a) 17.9 cm (b) 16.3 cm²
5 (a) 14 cm (b) 11.2 cm²

P8.5

1 (a) 26.46 m (b) 39.6 m²
2 (a) 23.3 m (b) 29.58 m²
3 (a) 37 cm (b) 81 cm²
4 (a) 67.5 mm (b) 266.5 mm²
5 (a) 11.2 m (b) 6.12 m²
6 (a) 3.25 km (b) 0.44 km²
7 (a) 53.1 cm (b) 63.9 cm²
8 (a) 32.1 cm (b) 52.85 cm²

P8.6

1 (a) 2.79 m² (b) 8.08 m
2 5813.0 cm²
3 (a) 34.81 m² (b) 56.1 m
4 (a) 14.89 m² (b) 18.75 m

P8.7

1 (a) ha, acres
(b) km², miles²
(c) are, chain² or yd²
(d) km², miles²
(e) ha, acres
(f) are, chain² or yd²
2 (a) 752.5 a 7.525 ha
(b) 42000 a 420 ha
(c) 69 a 0.69 ha
(d) 3500 a 35 ha
3 (a) 9500 m² 0.0095 km²
(b) 1800 000 m² 1.8 km²
(c) 609 200 m² 0.6092 km²
(d) 50 000 000 m² 50 km²
4 (a) 1.86 acres (b) 2560 acres
(c) 0.74 acres (d) 480 acres
5 (a) 14 520 yd² 0.0047 miles²
(b) 2807 200 yd² 0.91 miles²
(c) 140 360 yd², 0.045 miles²
(d) 3 388 000 yd², 1.09 miles²
6 (a) 58 hectares (b) 3.6 hectares
(c) 0.33 hectares (d) 128 hectares

7 (a) 17.5 acres   (b) 1.125 acres
   (c) 16.25 acres   (d) 1.8 acres
8 Kite park 25.925 acres
   0.25925 hectares 0.648 acres
   Parallelogram park 3625 ares
   36.25 hectares 90.625 acres

P8.8
1 718.64 m² 7.19 a
2 2131.85 m² 21.3 a

P8.9
1 3.1 cm   **2** 1.5 cm   **3** 51 mm
4 9.2 cm

P8.10
1 8 cm   **2** 24 m   **3** 6.4 cm   **4** 8.4 m

P9.1
1 (a) 45   **2** (a) 60
3 (a) Renstone   Snaresbrook

P9.2
1 (a) 25 marks
2 (a) 10 marks
   (b) 10 class intervals 11–20, 21–30,
   31–40, 41–50, 51–60, 61–70, 71–80,
   81–90, 91–100
3 (a) 5

P9.3
1 (a) 45 students

P9.4
1 (a) 80 tomatoes
   (b) Class boundaries 60, 65, 70, 75,
   80, 85
   Class width 5
2 (b) Class boundaries 5, 10, 15, 20,
   25, 30, 35, 40, 45
   Class width 5
3 (b) Class boundaries 30, 40, 50, 60,
   70, 80, 90, 100
   Class width 10
4 (b) Class boundaries 0, 5, 10, 15, 20,
   25, 30
   Class width 5

P9.5
1 (a) 125 eggs

P9.7
1 (a) 10, 11, 12, 13, 14, 15, 16, 17, 18, 19
   (b) Class width = 10
   midpoint = 14.5
   (c) 14.5, 24.5, 34.5, 44.5, 54.5, 64.5
2 (a) Class boundaries 0.5, 5.5
   Class width 5 Mid-point 3
   (b) 3, 8, 13, 18, 23, 28

P10.1
1 63 mph   **2** 26 m/s   **3** 9 mm/s
4 37 km/h   **5** 79 mph   **6** 80 km/h
7 8 m/s   **8** 80 km/h   **9** 55 yd/minute
10 52 ft/s   **11** 24.6 mph
12 126.5 mph
13 312.5 miles per day
14 27.6 m/s   **15** 188.6 ft/s
16 1.1 mm/s   **17** 8.2 mph
18 1833.3 km/h   **19** 4.5 m/minute
20 18.1 yd/s

P10.2
1 (a) 3 km   (b) 5.5 km   (c) 27.8 km
   (d) 0.785 km
2 (a) 4000 m   (b) 3800 m   (c) 4.5 m
   (d) 0.66 m
3 (a) 300 s   (b) 7200 s   (c) 8400 s
4 (a) 120 h   (b) 149 h   (c) 336 h
   (d) 240 h
5 (a) 31.3 km/h   (b) 4.7 km/h
   (c) 5.9 km/h   (d) 53 571.4 km/h
   (e) 45 km/h

6 (a) 13.9 m/s   (b) 7.1 m/s
   (c) 8.6 km/s   (d) 12.2 m/s
   (e) 0.003 m/s

P10.3
1 (a) 46 mph   (b) 42 mph
   (c) 39 mph   (d) 42 mph
   (e) 49 mph
2 (a) 54 mph   (b) 81 mph
   (c) 52 mph   (d) 54 mph
   (e) 91 mph

P10.4
1 22 km   **2** 399 km   **3** 42 m
4 13 500 m   **5** 4165 ft   **6** 55.5 miles

P10.5
1 (a) (i) 120 miles (ii) 260 miles
   (iii) 45 miles (iv) 205 miles
   (b) (i) 45 miles (ii) 30 miles
   (iii) 101.25 miles (iv) 82.5 miles
   (c) (i) 64 miles (ii) 29 miles
   (iii) 48 miles (iv) 69 miles
   (d) (i) 16 miles (ii) 36 miles
   (iii) 6 miles (iv) 40 miles
2 (a) 0.48 km   (b) 7.2 km
   (c) 153.6 km   (d) 691.2 km
3 (a) 810 000 km   (b) 18 000 000 km
   (c) 2100 km   (d) 7500 km
4 (a) 17.5 km   (b) 5.8 km
   (c) 0.7 km   (d) 0.49 km

P10.6
1 7 hours   **2** 2 hours   **3** 3.5 hours
4 2.5 hours   **5** 40 s

P10.7
1 (a) 15 minutes
   (b) 1 hour 16 minutes
   (c) 2 hours 35 minutes
   (d) 3 hours 42 minutes
   (e) 4 hours 51 minutes
   (f) 7 hours 4 minutes
2 (a) 4 minutes 3 seconds, 4 minutes
   (b) 8 minutes 47 seconds, 9 minutes
   (c) 24 minutes 42 seconds,
   25 minutes
   (d) 2 hours 40 minutes 51 seconds,
   2 hours 41 minutes
   (e) 3 hours 32 minutes 13 seconds,
   3 hours 32 minutes
   (f) 4 hours 49 minutes 54 seconds,
   4 hours 50 minutes
3 (a) 2 hours 33 minutes
   (b) 1 hour 42 minutes
   (c) 7 hours 29 minutes
   (d) 10 minutes
   (e) 27 minutes

P10.8
1 (a) 115 miles, 51 mph
   (b) 200 miles, 62 mph
   (c) 45 miles, 60 mph
   (d) 119 miles, 43 mph
   (e) 281 miles, 51 mph
2 1133
3 (a) (i) 380 km (ii) 142.5 km
   (iii) 253.3 km (iv) 324.6 km
   (b) (i) 96 km (ii) 132 km
   (iii) 36 km (iv) 76 km
   (c) (i) 17.5 km (ii) 23.3 km
   (iii) 40.8 km (iv) 84.6 km
   (d) (i) 12.7 km (ii) 14.25 km
   (iii) 26.9 km (iv) 34.8 km
   (e) 230.5 km
4 (a) 100 m 8.3 m/s, 200 m 7.7 m/s,
   400 m 6.2 m/s, 800 m 5.5 m/s,
   1000 m 4.4 m/s, 1500 m 4.3 m/s

5 (a) 2 hours 42 minutes   (b) 1.57 pm
6 8 minutes 20 seconds
7 (a) E180 262.4 m E240 349.9 m
   E210 306.2 m
   (b) Tom and Jerry 7.3 m Neighbours
   36.5 m
8 4 hours 46 minutes
9 15 km, 18.1 km/h, 20 km,
   17.9 km/h, 25 km, 16.3 km/h,
   30 km, 16.8 km/h, 50 km, 13.8 km/h
10 9.6 seconds

P10.9
1 (a) 44 km/h   (b) 37.5 mph
   (c) 48 mph   (d) 83.4 km/h
   (e) 6.6 m/s
2 22.1 km/h
3 43.8 mph
4 Monday 53.0 mph
   Tuesday 39.6 mph
   Wednesday 42.9 mph
   Thursday 36.3 mph

P10.10
1 (a) 50 mph   (b) 22.5 mph
   (c) 37.5 mph   (d) 62.5 mph
   (e) 234.4 mph   (f) 750 mph
2 (a) 112 km/h   (b) 72 km/h
   (c) 160 km/h   (d) 384 km/h
   (e) 1120 km/h   (f) 1600 km/h
3 (a) 0.15 m/s   (b) 0.68 m/s
   (c) 0.25 m/s   (d) 0.867 m/s
   (e) 0.065 m/s   (f) 0.007 m/s
4 (a) 10 m/s   (b) 25 m/s
   (c) 19.4 m/s   (d) 23.6 m/s
   (e) 33.3 m/s   (f) 97.2 m/s
5 (a) 72 km/h   (b) 126 km/h
   (c) 25.2 km/h   (d) 306 km/h
   (e) 381.6 km/h   (f) 828 km/h
6 (a) 44 feet/s   (b) 2.9 feet/s
   (c) 85.1 feet/s   (d) 132 feet/s
   (e) 180.4 feet/s   (f) 366.7 feet/s

P11.1
B: 3 cm × 5 cm × 5 cm
C: 5 cm × 12 cm × 12 cm
D: 2 cm × 15 cm × 15 cm
E: 8 cm × 7.5 cm × 7.5 cm

P11.2
II $x = 17 : \frac{1}{4}'' \times 17'' \times 17''$
III $x = 11 : 1'' \times 11'' \times 11''$
IV $x = 12 : 1'' \times 12'' \times 24''$
V $x = 6 : 1'' \times 6'' \times 18''$
VI $x = 8 : \frac{1}{2}'' \times 8'' \times 8''$
VII $x = 3 : \frac{1}{2}'' \times 3'' \times 12''$

P11.3
1 $x = 3.1$ **2** $x = 2.8$ **3** $x = 0.6$
4 $x = 5.3$ **5** $x = 3.2$ **6** $x = 5.7$
7 $x = 6.1$ **8** $x = 0.9$ **9** $x = 4.5$
10 $x = 8.8$

P11.4
1 (a) 2.7 or –3.7   (b) 3.2 or –2.2
   (c) 3.8 or –1.3   (d) 2.1 or –3.6
2 (a) 2.70 or – 3.70   (b) 3.19 or –2.19
   (c) 3.81 or – 1.31
   (d) 2.09 or – 3.59
3 (a) 5   (b) 4   (c) 9   (d) 3
4 (a) 1.4   (b) 2.5   (c) 2.8   (d) 4.3
5 (a) 1.38   (b) 2.54   (c) 2.84
   (d) 4.26

P11.5
1 (b) 9 and 10
   (c) 9.35
2 (a) 11 and 12   (b) 11.48
3 (a) 3.41 or –4.41   (b) 6.39 or –9.39

   (c) 3.81 or –1.31   (d) 6.05
4 (c) 5.56 and 1.44
5 (a) 0.6 and 3.4   (b) 0.6 and 5.4
   (c) 1.0 and 0.8   (d) 0.3 and 1.7

P11.6
1 60p   **2** 24 mm   **3** 1.33 m
4 0.8 s   **5** 85 mph

P12.1
1 100 students took the test. Mean 6.48
   marks Median 7 marks Mode 7 marks
   Range 9 marks
2 60 drivers were surveyed. Mean 1.52
   accidents Median 1.5 accidents Mode
   2 accidents Range 6 accidents
3 51 classes surveyed. Mean 29.92
   students Median 30 students Mode 32
   students Range 5 students
4 25 shops surveyed. Mean 54.88 pence
   Median 55 pence Mode 57 pence
   Range 6 pence
5 Mean 3.93 letters Median 3 letters
   Mode 2 letters Range 9 letters
   (e) Total number of 200 letters
6 Mean 17.89 passengers Median 18
   passengers Mode 18 passengers Range
   5 passengers
   (e) 92 days recorded

P12.2
1 (a) 250 plants
   (b) Range 7 flowers Mode 2 flowers
   Median 3 flowers Mean 3.56 flowers
2 (a) 59 baskets
   (b) Range 7 items Mode 6 items
   Median 5 items Mean 4.51 items
3 Range 4 fillings Mode 1 filling
   Median 1 filling Mean 1.51 fillings
4 Range 7 accidents Mode 3 accidents
   Median 2.5 accidents Mean 2.2
   accidents
5 Ranstone Range 5 residents Mode 2
   residents
   Median 3 residents Mean 3.06
   residents
   Snaresbrook Range 4 residents
   Mode 1 resident
   Median 1 resident Mean 1.8
   residents

P12.3
1 (a) 36 batsmen   (b) 49 runs
   (c) 10–19 runs   (d) 10–19 runs
   (e) 19.8 runs
2 (a) 12 cars   (b) 32.6 cars
   (c) 30–34 cars   (d) 30–34 cars
   (e) 39
3 (a) Mean 62.7 marks Median 67
   marks Mode No one modal value
   Range 90 marks
   (b) Modal class 61–80 marks
   Median class 61–80 marks
   Estimated mean 62.5 marks
   (c) (i) Modal class 51–75 and
   76–100 marks
   Median class 51–75 marks
   Estimated mean 63 marks
   (ii) Modal classes 61–70 and 81–90
   marks
   Median class 61–70 marks
   Estimated mean 62.17 marks
   (iii) Modal class 81–85 marks
   Median class 66–70 marks
   Estimated mean 61.83 marks
4 Modal class 16–20 students Median

class 16–20 students
Estimated mean 16.67 students
5 Modal class £40.01–£50.00
Median class £30.01–£40.00
Estimated mean £35.405

P12.4
1 (a) 3, 8, 13, 18, 23, 28
(b) 18.18 hours (c) 11–15 hours
(d) 16–20 hours (e) 29 hours
2 (a) 152, 157, 162, 167, 172, 177, 182
(b) 167.25 cm (c) 160–164 cm
(d) 165–169 cm (e) 34 cm
3 (a) 18, 23, 28, 33, 38, 43
(b) 27.62 years (c) 21–25 years
(d) 26–30 years (e) 29 years
4 Estimated mean 71.94 g
Modal group 70–75 g
Median class 70–75 g
5 Estimated mean 19.83°C
Modal group 20–25°C
Median class 20–25°C
6 Estimated mean 69.33 mm
Modal group 70–80 mm
Median class 70–80 mm
7 Estimated mean 15.31 minutes
Modal group 15–20 minutes
Median class 15–20 minutes
8 Estimated mean 58.64 g
Modal group 60–64 g
Median class 55–59 g
9 Estimated mean 35.1 seconds
Modal group 31–40 seconds
Median class 31–40 seconds
10 Estimated mean 18.92 years
Modal group 0–9 years
Median class 10–19 years

P12.5
1 Algebra test Estimated mean 43.62 marks
Modal group 30–39 marks
Median class 30–39 marks
Arithmetic test Estimated mean 45.86 marks
Modal group 40–49 marks
Median class 40–49 marks
2 Abbeyvale Estimated mean 14.63 hours
Modal group 11–15 hours
Median class 11–15 hours
Newton Estimated mean 9.25 hours
Modal group 6–10 hours
Median class 6–10 hours
3 Cheapo Food Estimated mean 9.05 years
Modal group 9–11 years
Median class 9–11 years
Upmark Delifood Estimated mean 4.31 years
Modal group 3–5 years
Median class 3–5 years
4 Female Estimated mean 155.7 cm
Modal group 155–160 cm
Median class 155–160 cm
Male Estimated mean 160.57 cm
Modal group 160–165 cm
Median class 160–165 cm

P13.4
1 (a) 6 (b) 3 (c) 1 (d) 0 (e) $\frac{1}{4}$
(f) 1 (g) $\frac{2}{3}$ (h) $\frac{2}{3}$ (i) -2 (j) $-\frac{1}{3}$
(k) 3 (l) -1 (m) 0 (n) $\frac{1}{4}$
(o) 0 (p) 1 (q) -1

b and k c, f and p d, m and o
e and n g and h l and q
2 (a) 1 (b) $-\frac{2}{5}$ (c) -2 (d) 3
(e) $\frac{2}{5}$ (f) $-\frac{5}{7}$ (g) $\frac{1}{4}$ (h) $\frac{3}{7}$
(i) $-\frac{1}{2}$ (j) 0 (k) -6 (l) -1
4 (a) 1 (b) 2 (c) $\frac{1}{2}$ (d) -1 (e) -2
(f) $-\frac{1}{2}$

P13.5
1 Scale A (a) 2 cm to 1 unit
(b) 0.1 (c) (i) 0.5 (ii) 1.3 (iii) 2.7
(iv) 3.5
Scale B (a) 2 cm to 100 units
(b) 10 (c) (i) 60 (ii) 150 (iii) 240
(iv) 380
Scale C (a) 2 cm to 500 units
(b) 50 (c) (i) 300 (ii) 900 (iii) 1250
(iv) 1650
Scale D (a) 2 cm to 4 units
(b) 0.4 (c) (i) 2 (ii) 4.4 (iii) 11.6
(iv) 15.2
Scale E (a) 2 cm to 25 units
(b) 2.5 (c) (i) 10 (ii) 40 (ii) 65
(iv) 82.5
2 (c) 4.5 (d) 34 hours
3 (c) $\frac{1}{5}$ (d) 12500
4 (b) 20 (c) (i) 95 min (ii) 4.75 lb
5 (b) $\frac{1}{2}$ (c) (i) £2.70 (ii) 2.6 miles

P14.1
1 0.5 **2** 0.8 **3** 0.6 **4** 0.8 **5** 0.9
6 0.6 **7** 0.6 **8** 0.9 **9** 0.8 **10** 0.4 **11** 0.6 **12** 0.9

P14.2
1 (a) 12, 1.2 (b) 45, 4.5 (c) 42, 4.2
(d) 10, 1.0 (e) 40, 4.0
2 (a) 16, 1.6 (b) 15, 1.5 (c) 81, 8.1
(d) 30, 3.0 (e) 20, 2.0
3 (a) 3.6 (b) 4.9 (c) 2.7 (d) 3.0
(e) 1.0
4 (a) 1.8 (b) 1.2 (c) 4.8 (d) 4.0
(e) 2.0

P14.3
1 (a) 600, 60.0 (b) 24000, 2400.0
(c) 280, 28.0 (d) 100 000, 10 000.0
(e) 30 000, 3000.0
2 (a) 40, 4.0 (b) 4500, 450.0
(c) 42000, 4200.0
(d) 2000 000, 200 000.0
(e) 400 000, 40 000.0
3 (a) 18 000 (b) 6300 (c) 150
(d) 250 000 (e) 40 000
4 (a) 16 (b) 2400 (c) 270
(d) 35 000 (e) 1800 000

P14.4
1 (a) 0.08 (b) 0.35 (c) 0.12
(d) 0.18 (e) 0.30 (f) 0.24
(g) 0.27 (h) 0.28 (i) 0.56
(j) 0.48 (k) 0.36 (l) 0.15
2 (a) 0.006 (b) 0.042 (c) 0.018
(d) 0.016 (e) 0.016 (f) 0.056
(g) 0.045 (h) 0.020 (i) 0.042
(j) 0.045 (k) 0.064 (l) 0.081
3 (a) 60 (b) 0.8 (c) 3.5 (d) 3.6
(e) 100 (f) 0.72 (g) 2.8
(h) 1.5 (i) 490 (j) 72 (k) 540
(l) 5.4
4 (a) 0.9 (b) 12.0 (c) 0.2 (d) 0.24
(e) 6.3 (f) 48.0 (g) 1.2 (h) 0.04
(i) 40.0 (j) 0.32 (k) 10.0 (l) 6.3
5 (a) 1400 (b) 3000 (c) 140 000
(d) 1800 (e) 240 (f) 32 000
(g) 2100 (h) 16 000 (i) 27 000
(j) 18 000 (k) 3600 (l) 400

P14.5
1 (a) 0.06 (b) 0.36 (c) 0.42
(d) 0.2 (e) 0.64
2 (a) 0.021 (b) 0.025 (c) 0.008
(d) 0.048 (e) 0.001
3 (a) 0.0024 (b) 0.000 056
(c) 0.003 (d) 0.000 027
(e) 0.0004
4 (a) 0.0016 (b) 0.000 35
(c) 0.000 12 (d) 0.000 36
(e) 0.0009
5 (a) 0.72 (b) 0.015 (c) 0.0028
(d) 0.000 04 (e) 0.0012
6 (a) 0.000 14 (b) 0.0024 (c) 0.54
(d) 0.045 (e) 0.000 16

P14.6
1 (a) 60 ÷ 2 = 30 (b) 80 ÷ 4 = 20
(c) 9000 ÷ 1 = 9000
(d) 6000 ÷ 3 = 2000
(e) 200 ÷ 5 = 40
(f) 40 000 ÷ 8 = 5000
(g) 70 000 ÷ 7 = 10 000
(h) 10 000 ÷ 2 = 5000
(i) 3000 ÷ 6 = 500
(j) 900 ÷ 9 = 100
2 (a) 20 (b) 1000 (c) 200
(d) 20 000 (e) 800 (f) 3000
(g) 100 (h) 3000 (i) 50 000
(j) 50

P14.7
1 (a) 400 (b) 5000 (c) 3000
(d) 6000 (e) 1000 (f) 50
2 (a) 20 000 (b) 5000 (c) 80 000
(d) 500 (e) 2000 (f) 1000
3 (a) 2000 (b) 400 (c) 50
(d) 1000 (e) 1000 (f) 3000
(g) 10 000 (h) 20 000

P14.8
1 (a) larger, 1500
(b) equal to, 800
(c) smaller than, 4.2
(d) larger than, 36
(e) smaller than, 0.0006
(f) equal to, 40
(g) smaller than, 45
(h) larger than, 45
(i) larger than, 18
(j) smaller than, 18
(k) smaller than, 0.2
(l) smaller than, 0.2
2 (a) equal to 1 (b) larger than 1
(c) smaller than 1 (d) smaller than 1
(e) larger than 1 (f) smaller than 1
(g) equal to 1 (h) smaller than 1

P14.9
1 smaller than **2** equal to
3 larger than **4** larger than
5 smaller than **6** larger than

P14.10
1, 4, 5, 6, 7, 8, 10 are wrong

P14.11
1 72 p **2** 50 scarves **3** 40 cases
4 4000 kg **5** 21 mm **6** 64 ohms
7 £1800 **8** 500 motorists **9** 30 000
10 0.27 mm
11 (a) 50 sheets (b) 12 mm
12 (a) 0.24 kg (b) 2000 tea bags
13 (a) 50 servings (b) 6.4 kg
14 (a) 50 000 cans (b) 540 kg
15 (a) 4 m (b) 10 000 pins

P15.1
1 Argentine (a) 48 (b) (i) 0.50

(ii) 0.19 (iii) 0.31 (e) 1.00
Belgium (a) 25 (b) (i) 0.28
(ii) 0.16 (iii) 0.56 (e) 1.00
Brazil (a) 66 (b) (i) 0.67
(ii) 0.17 (iii) 0.17 (e) 1.01
Germany (a) 68 (b) (i) 0.57
(ii) 0.22 (iii) 0.21 (e) 1.00
Holland (a) 20 (b) (i) 0.40
(ii) 0.30 (iii) 0.30 (e) 1.00
Italy (a) 54 (b) (i) 0.57 (ii) 0.22
(iii) 0.20 (e) 0.99
Mexico (a) 29 (b) (i) 0.21 (ii) 0.21
(iii) 0.59 (e) 1.01
Spain (a) 32 (b) (i) 0.41 (ii) 0.22
(iii) 0.38 (e) 1.01
Sweden (a) 31 (b) (i) 0.35
(ii) 0.19 (iii) 0.45 (e) 0.99
(c) (i) Brazil (ii) Holland
(iii) Switzerland (d) (i) Mexico
(ii) Switzerland (iii) Brazil
2 Year 7 A (a) 30 (b) (i) 0.30
(ii) 0.22 (iii) 0.27
B (a) 35 (b) (i) 0.14
Year 8 A (a) 25 (b) (i) 0.40
(ii) 0.36
B (a) 31 (b) (i) 0.32
Year 9 A (a) 29 (b) (i) 0.14
(ii) 0.25
B (a) 34 (b) (i) 0.35
Year 10 A (a) 33 (b) (i) 0.24
(ii) 0.3
B (a) 28 (b) (i) 0.36
Year 11 A (a) 26 (b) (i) 0.19
(ii) 0.21
B (a) 27 (b) (i) 0.22 (c) (i) 8A
(ii) 8A
3 A (a) 87 (b) (i) 0.21 (ii) 0.03
(iii) 0.31 (iv) 0.51
B (a) 114 (b) (i) 0.04 (ii) 0.03
(iii) 0.53 (iv) 0.20
C (a) 117 (b) (i) 0.05 (ii) 0.14
(iii) 0.59 (iv) 0.18
D (a) 101 (b) (i) 0.02 (ii) 0.05
(iii) 0.47 (iv) 0.17
E (a) 50 (b) (i) 0.18 (ii) 0.22
(iii) 0.58 (iv) 0.28

P15.2
1 0.12 **2** 0.17
3 (a) 0.08 (b) 0.16 (c) 0.84
4 (a) 0.22 (b) 0.05 (c) 0.73
5 (a) 0.79 (b) 0.21
6 (a) 0.18 (b) 25, 0.26 (c) 10, 0.04
(d) 5 and 20 0.09 (e) 0.36
7 Mr. Brown (a) 76 (b) 0.58
Ms. White (a) 136 (b) 0.54
Mrs. Green (a) 45 (b) 0.64
Mr. Black (a) 75 (b) 0.79
(c) 0.38 (d) Mr. Black

P15.3
1 69 times **2** 20 days **3** 16 answers
4 350 **5** 384 flights **6** 413 runners
7 (a) (i) 13 days (ii) 12 days
(b) (i) 16 days (ii) 15 days
8 (a) Stefan 210 matches, Ivan 143 matches
(b) Tod 56 matches, Michael 50 matches
9 (i) 63 times (ii) 188 times
(iii) 250 times
10 (i) 40 times (ii) 120 times
(iii) 80 times (iv) 200 times
11 (a) two heads 0.25, exactly 1 head

0.50, at least 1 head 0.75

(b) two heads 125 times, exactly 1 head 250 times, at least 1 head 375 times

P16.1

1 (a) 5 minutes   (b) 5 miles
(c) 2 hours   (d) 90 miles
(e) (i) 45 miles (ii) 30 miles
(iii) 67.5 miles
(f) (i) 1 hour 20 minutes (ii) 20 minutes (iii) 1 hour 40 minutes
(g) 45 mph

2 (a) 2 minutes   (b) 2 miles
(c) Time $1\frac{1}{2}$ hour Distance 45 km
(d) A 20 mins, 10 km
  B 1 hr 20 mins, 40 km
  C 12 mins, 6 km
  D 1 hr 12 mins, 36 km
  E 30 mins, 15 km
  F 50 mins, 25 km
(e) 30 km/h

3 (a) A a helicopter, B a motorbike on the motorway, C a car towing a caravan, D a car in town, E a bus, F a cyclist, G a walker
(b) A 41.7 m/s B 27.8 m/s
C 16.7 m/s D 11.1 m/s E 6.7 m/s
F 4.2 m/s G 2 m/s

4 (b) E 53.3 mph C 23.3 mph
A 15 mph B 11.4 mph D 4.4 mph
F 3 mph
(c) E C A B D F
(d) The order is identical

P16.2

1 (a) 60 miles   (b) 25 miles
(c) $7\frac{1}{2}$ miles   (d) $6\frac{2}{3}$ miles
(e) $11\frac{1}{4}$ miles (f) $42\frac{2}{3}$ miles

2 (a) 3 hours   (b) 2 hours
(c) $1\frac{1}{4}$ hour   (d) $1\frac{1}{2}$ hour
(e) $\frac{3}{4}$ hour   (f) $\frac{2}{7}$ hour

P16.3

1 (1) (a) Amford, Beeton
(b) 10 miles   (c) 08:30, 09:00
(d) 30 minutes   (e) 20 mph
(2) (a) Ceely, Deemouth
(b) 5 miles   (c) 08:35, 08:55
(d) 20 minutes
(e) 15 mph
(3) (a) Beeton, Ceely   (b) 15 miles
(c) 08:10, 08:50   (d) 40 minutes
(e) 23 mph (to nearest mph)
(4) (a) Ceely, Deemouth
(b) 5 miles   (c) 08:15, 08:25
(d) 10 minutes   (e) 30 mph
(5) (a) Deemouth, Excastle
(b) 20 miles   (c) 08:30, 09:00
(d) 30 minutes   (e) 40 mph
(6) (a) Ceely, Excastle   (b) 25 miles
(c) 08:00, 08:45   (d) 45 minutes
(e) 33 mph (to nearest mph)
(7) (a) Deemouth, Excastle
(b) 20 miles   (c) 08:05, 08:30
(d) 25 minutes   (e) 48 mph
(8) (a) Beeton, Beeton   (b) 0 miles
(c) 08:25, 08:45   (d) 20 minutes
(e) 0 mph

2 (b) (A) 43 mph (to nearest mph)
(B) 48 mph   (C) 30 mph
(D) 38 mph (to nearest mph)
(E) 15 mph   (F) 20 mph

3 (a) (A) 17:35   (B) 16:45
(C) 17:30   (D) 16:25   (E) 18:00

(F) 16:30

4 (a) Southton 16 miles, Tycastle 35 miles, Unwin 41 miles, Veenor 55 miles, Webly 60 miles, Xton 75 miles

5 (a) 50 miles
(b) 7:00, 8:30, 9:40, 10:10
(c) Fastest 8:30 Slowest 10:10
(d) 8:15, 9:25, 10:55, 11:45
(e) 40 mph, 55 mph, 40 mph, 32 mph

P16.4

1 (a) 5 miles
(b) Darlington 25 miles, York 75 miles, Sheffield 135 miles
(c) Durham – Darlington 25 miles, Darlington – York 50 miles, York – Sheffield 60 miles
(d) 3 minutes
(e) Darlington 6 minutes, York 9 minutes
(f) 12:15
(g) Darlington A 12:30 D 12:36 York A 13:12 D 13:21
(h) 14:24
(i) (i) 100 mph   (ii) 83.3mph (1 dp)
(iii) 57.1 mph (1 dp)
(j) 62.8 mph (1 dp)

2 (a) 2 hours   (b) 6 miles   (c) 3 mph
(d) 1 hour   (e) 3 hours   (f) 2 mph
(g) 16:00

P16.5

1 (a) 2 miles   (b) 4 minutes
(c) 30 mph   (d) 3 minutes
(e) 2 minutes   (f) 48 mph

2 (a) 62 miles   (b) $1\frac{1}{4}$ hour
(c) 49.6 mph   (d) 40 minutes
(e) 13:25   (f) 24 miles
(g) 25 minutes   (h) 14:25
(i) (i) 48 mph (ii) 65.1 mph (1 dp)
(j) 41.3 mph (1 dp)

P16.6

1 (a) 9.48 am   (b) 12 minutes
(c) 1 hour 36 minutes
(d) (i) A to B (ii) 50 mph
(e) 45.7 mph (1 dp)   (f) 10.56 am
(g) 62 miles

3 (a) bus 4 hours
  car 1 hour 54 minutes
(b) (i) 18 minutes (ii) 24 minutes
(c) 30 minutes
(d) (i) 18.75 km/h, 25 km/h
(ii) 26.67 km/h (2 dp)
(e) (i) 44.44 km/h (2 dp)
(ii) 40 km/h
(f) 12.18   33 km from Auray

P16.7

1 (b) 1 mile   (c) 6 mph   (d) $3\frac{1}{5}$ miles

2 (b) 47 km/h   (c) (i) 47.4 km/h (1 dp)
(ii) 45 km/h (iii) 41.1 km/h (1 dp)

3 (b) The bus ride   (c) 30 km/h

4 (b) 25 minutes   (c) 48 km/h
(d) 1215   (g) 1350

5 (b) 1124   (d) 57.7 mph (1 dp)
(e) 1047   (f) 59 miles

P17.1

1 0.2 g/mℓ **2** 18 m²/ℓ **3** 350 km/ℓ

4 4 ℓ/g   **5** £1.1408 per lb

6 394.6 kcals per 100 g   **7** 150 g/m²

8 £0.70 per 50 copies

9 £13.75 per kg

10 (a) 3 litres per hour
(b) 150 mℓ per minute

P17.2

1 (a) £7.28   (b) 17 words

2 (a) 10.4 cm   (b) 9 a m   (c) 9.47 p m

3 (a) 83 m²
(b) 4.2 kg, 2 bags, 0.8 kg left over

4 (a) 2.5ℓ per hour   (b) 60ℓ
(c) 1072ℓ (d) 772ℓ

5 (i) 2.36 pence per leaflet
(b) £35.40   (c) 650 leaflets

6 (a) 51.9 p   (b) £8.30   (c) 48.2ℓ

7 (a) £2.34 per hour   (b) £12.87
(c) $6\frac{1}{2}$ hours

8 (a) 1320 cars
(b) 1 hour 50 minutes

9 (a) 0.04 cm per minute
(b) 2.4 cm per hour   (c) 9.05 p m
(d) 3 cm   (e) 1.15 a.m.

10 (a) 2 hours 5 minutes

P17.3

1 £0.1625 per bun   **2** £4.72 per litre

3 £0.081 per oz   **4** £0.43 per litre

5 £0.332 per roll   **6** £4.975 per kg

7 £0.563 per kg   **8** £1.38 per litre

P17.4

1 (a) 300 g £4.25   **2** 2 £1.29

3 15 p each   **4** 450 g 99p

5 160 (500 g) £1.19   **6** 405 g tin 41p

7 285 g 45p   **8** 1.5 lb 62p

9 E10 (4 kg) £4.99

10 10 bags, 28 g each £1.72

P17.5

1 8 g/cm³   **2** 0.92 g/cm³   **3** 0.2 g/cm³

4 12 cm³   **5** 360 cm³   **6** 68 g

7 36 kg   **8** Steel   **9** 5 kg

10 61.425 kg

11 (a) 16.7 cm³   (b) 20.5 cm³
(c) 37.2 cm³   (d) 300 g
(e) 8.1 g/cm³

12 0.82 g/cm³

P18.1

1 (a), (d), (e), (g) yes (b), (c), (f), (h) no

2 (a), (b), (e), (h) yes (c), (d), (f), (g) no

3 (a), (d), (f) yes (b), (c), (e), (g), (h) no

P18.2

1 (a) 7 is greater than 4
(b) 2 is less than 9
(c) $\frac{1}{8}$ is less than $\frac{5}{8}$
(d) $\frac{1}{3}$ is greater than $\frac{1}{10}$
(e) 0.1 is less than 0.7
(f) 6.00001 is greater than 6

2 (a) 3 < 8   (b) 7 < 15   (c) 5 < 9
(d) 27 > 13   (e) $\frac{1}{6} < \frac{5}{6}$ (f) $\frac{1}{5} > \frac{1}{20}$
(g) $1\frac{1}{2} < 2$ (h) 3 > $2\frac{3}{4}$ (i) 0.7 > 0.6
(j) 0.5 > 0.005   (k) 9.001 > 9
(l) 2.99 < 3

P18.3

1 (a) 12 > 7   (b) 0 < 3   (c) $\frac{1}{6} < \frac{1}{4}$
(d) $\frac{11}{12} > \frac{5}{12}$ (e) 0.7 < 1.8
(f) 3.8 > 3.1

2 (a) 5 > 2, 2 < 5   (b) 0 < 4, 4 > 0
(c) $\frac{1}{2} > \frac{1}{6}, \frac{1}{6} < \frac{1}{2}$ (d) $\frac{3}{8} < \frac{5}{8}, \frac{5}{8} > \frac{3}{8}$
(e) 0.9 > 0.125, 0.125 < 0.9
(f) 1.4 > 1.3, 1.3 < 1.4

P18.4

1 (a) 3   (b) –3   (c) –4   (d) –5   (e) –5
(f) 0   (g) –8   (h) –9   (i) –12

2 (a) 5   (b) 1   (c) 5   (d) 0
(e) –3   (f) 9   (g) 8   (h) 0   (i) –6

3 (a), (b), (d) yes (c), (e) (f) no

4 (a) –1 < 1   (b) 3 > –2   (c) –5 < 0
(d) 7 > –8   (e) –1 > –4
(f) –10 < –3

P18.5

1 (a) x is less than 4
(b) n is greater than or equal to 9
(c) t is less than or equal to –1
(d) p is greater than 0

2 (a) $x \le 8$ (b) $n > -4$ (c) $m < 3$
(d) $y \ge -2$

P18.6

1 (b), (c), (d) yes (a), (e) no

2 (a), (b), (d)   **3** (b), (e)

4 (a), (b), (e) yes (c), (d) no

5 (a), (d), (e)   **6** (a), (b)

P18.7

1 Possible values are:
(a) 1, 2, 3, 4, …
(b) 3, 2, 1, 0, –1, …
(c) –4, –5, –6, –7, …
(d) 0, 1, 2, 3, …

P18.8

1 Possible values
(a) 2, 3, 4, 5, …
(b) 5, 4, 3, 2, …
(c) –2, –3, –4, –5, …
(d) –5, –4, –3, –2, …

3 Possible values
p 50 001, 50 002, 50 003, …
a 4, 3, 2, 1, 0, …
n 100, 101, 102, …
c 2001, 2002, 2003, …
d 89, 88, 87, …
e 9, 8, 7, …1
m 76, 77, 78, …
i 8, 7, 6, …, 1
b 1, 3, 4, 5, …147 (2 is not a possible break as red ball worth 1 point must be followed by one of the coloured balls worth at least 2 points)
y 18, 19, 20, …, 120
l 4, 5, 6, …
h 0, 1, 2, …, 24
f 199, 200, 201, …

P18.9

2 Possible values
(a) 0, 1, 2, …   (b) 2, 1, 0, …
(c) –5, –6, –7, …   (d) 0, 1, 2, …
(e) 2, 3, 4, …   (f) 3, 4, 5, …
(g) 0, –1, –2, …   (h) –3, –2, –1, …
(i) –4, –5, –6, …   (j) 0, –1, –2, …

3 (a) $x > 1$ (b) $x < -2$ (c) $x \ge 0$
(d) $x < 1$ (e) $x \ge -4$ (f) $x \ge 5$
(g) $x < 0$ (h) $x \le -4$ (i) $x \ge 6$
(j) $x > -3$

P18.10

1 1 < 2 < 4   2 is between 1 and 4

2 0 < 3 < 5   3 is between 0 and 5

3 –1 < 0 < 2   0 is between –1 and 2

4 –2 < 1 < 4   1 is between –2 and 4

5 –3 < –1 < 0   –1 is between –3 and 0

6 –5 < –4 < –2   –4 is between –5 and –2

7 1 < 10 < 100   10 is between 1 and 100

8 –100 < –10 < –1   –10 is between –100 and –1

9 –50 < 0 < 50   0 is between –50 and 50

10 –50 < –10 < 0   –10 is between –50 and 0

P18.11

1 $2 \le n \le 6$

2 $90 < d < 180$ $180 < r < 360$

3 $0 < t < 5$

4 $100 < w \le 150$ $350 < g \le 400$

5 A $v \le 40\,000$

B $40\,000 < v \le 52\,000$

C $52\,000 < v \le 68\,000$

D $68\,000 < v \le 88\,000$

E $88\,000 < v \le 120\,000$

F $120\,000 < v \le 160\,000$

G $160\,000 < v \le 320\,000$

H $320\,000 < v$

6 $2000 < 1 \le 23\,700$

P18.12

3 (a) $-3 < x \le 1$ (b) $-5 < x < 0$
(c) $-2 \le x \le 4$ (d) $0 \le x < 6$
(e) $-4 < x < -2$ (f) $0 \le x \le 5$
(g) $-6 \le x < 1$ (h) $-3 < x < 3$
(i) $2 \le x < 4$ (j) $2 < x \le 6$

P18.13

1 (b) $4 < x < 7$ **2** (b) $0 \le x < 5$

3 (b) $-2 < x \le 1$ **4** (b) $-5 \le x \le -1$

5 (b) $-10 \le x \le 30$

P19.1

1 21 **2** 32 **3** 54 **4** 24 **5** 90

6 40 **7** 99 **8** 120 **9** 600

P19.2

1 and 7 **2** and 8 **3** and 9

4, 6 and 10 **5** and 11

P19.3

1 (a) 35 (b) 39 (c) 667 (d) 305
(e) 4033 (f) 11 917 (g) 154
(h) 345 (i) 210 (j) 188 870

P19.4

1 (a) $2 \times 5 \times 5 \times 5$
(b) $3 \times 3 \times 3 \times 3 \times 7 \times 7$
(c) $2 \times 2 \times 2 \times 2 \times 2 \times 3 \times 11 \times 11$
(d) $5 \times 11 \times 11 \times 11 \times 23$
(e) $2 \times 2 \times 2 \times 2 \times 2 \times 2 \times 3 \times 5 \times 5 \times 7 \times 7 \times 7 \times 7$
(f) $2 \times 3 \times 3 \times 3 \times 3 \times 3 \times 3 \times 13 \times 13$

2 (a) 2^6 (b) $3^2 \times 5^3$ (c) 7^5
(d) $2 \times 5^2 \times 11^4$ (e) 19^3
(f) $5 \times 7^2 \times 13^3$

3 (a) 250 (b) 3969 (c) 11 616
(d) 153 065 (e) 23 049 600
(f) 246 402

4 (a) 64 (b) 1125 (c) 16 807
(d) 732 050 (e) 6859 (f) 538 265

P19.5

1 (a) 3×11
(b) $3 \times 25, 3 \times 5^2, 5 \times 15$
(c) $3 \times 15, 3^2 \times 5, 5 \times 9$
(d) $2 \times 16, 2^2 \times 8, 2^3 \times 4, 2^4 \times 2,$
$2^5, 4 \times 8, 4^2 \times 2$
(e) 13^2

2 (a) 3×11 (b) 3×5^2 (c) $3^2 \times 5$
(d) 2^5 (e) 13^2 .One

3 (a) 3×37 (b) 11^2 (c) $2 \times 5 \times 31$
(d) 3×7^2 (e) 2×5^3

P19.6

2 (d) $2^4 \times 3^2$

3 (d) $2 \times 3^2 \times 5^2, 2 \times 3 \times 7^2, 3 \times 5 \times 11^2 \times 13$

4 (a) $2^3 \times 3^2 \times 5$ (b) $2^3 \times 5^3$
(c) $2^3 \times 3^4$ (d) 2×5^4
(e) $2^2 \times 11^2$ (f) $2^4 \times 3 \times 13$
(g) 2^{12} (h) $2^4 \times 3^2 \times 5^2$
(i) $3^2 \times 11^2$ (j) $3^2 \times 7 \times 11$

P19.7

1 $2 \times 3^2 \times 5$ **2** $2^2 \times 3 \times 11$

3 $3^2 \times 7^2$ **4** $2^2 \times 3^3 \times 5$

5 $2^2 \times 3^2 \times 29$ **6** $2 \times 7 \times 17^2$

7 7^5 **8** $2^3 \times 7 \times 13 \times 23$

9 $11 \times 19 \times 29$ **10** $2^4 \times 11^3$

P19.8

1 (a) 6 (b) 15 (c) 28 (d) 22
(e) 16 (f) 12

2 (a) $\frac{3}{5}$ (b) $\frac{5}{7}$ (c) $\frac{3}{5}$ (d) $\frac{13}{18}$ (e) $\frac{3}{4}$
(f) $\frac{2}{3}$

P19.9

1 12 **2** 60 **3** (a) 12 (b) 6 (e) 10
(f) 9

4 (a) 2 (b) 72 (c) 150 (d) 86
(e) 1 (f) 9

P19.10

1 (a) 210 (b) 126 (c) 2145
(d) 1008 (e) 192 (f) 500

2 (a) 30 (b) 5427 (c) 48 (d) 54

4 (a) 21 (b) 65 (c) 374 (d) 47 027

P19.11

1 72p **2** 315 chairs **3** 0.48 m length

4 210 days **5** 9 feet **6** 59 players

P20.1

1 (a) B (b) A (c) B (d) A (e) B

2 (a) $y = 3x, x + y = 4,$
$x = 1$ $y = 3$
(b) $y = x - 1, y = 3x - 9, x = 4$ $y = 3$
(c) $2y = x + 2, y = x - 2, x = 6$ $y = 4$
(d) $2x + y = 6, 2x + 5y = 10,$
$x = 2.5$ $y = 1$
(e) $y = x + 4, x + y = 2, x = -1$ $y = 3$
(f) $5x - 3y + 7 = 0, 3x - 5y + 1 = 0,$
$x = -2$ $y = -1$

3 (a) $x = 6$ $y = 10$ (b) $x = 6.5$ $y = 0.5$
(c) $x = 4$ $y = 8$ (d) $x = 3$ $y = 4$
(e) $x = 8$ $y = 0$ (f) $x = 1.5$ $y = 5.5$
$y = x + 4, 3y + x = 8, x = -1$ $y = 3$
$y = 2x - 2, 2x + y = 16, x = 4.5$ $y = 7$
$x + y = 7, 2x + y = 16, x = 9$ $y = -2$

4 (a) $4y + x = 6, 2x + 3y = 12$
(b) $y + 4x = 4, 2x + 3y = 12$
(c) $y = 6x + 14, 4y + x = 6$
(d) $y = x - 1, 2x + 3y = 12$
(e) $y = x - 1, 4y + x = 6$
(f) $y = x - 1, y + 4x = 4$
(g) $y = 6x + 14, y + 4x = 4$
(h) $y = 6x + 14, y = x - 1$
(i) $y + 4x = 4, 4y + x = 6$
(j) $y = 6x + 14, 2x + 3y = 12$

P20.2

1 (c) $x = 3, y = 1$

2 (a) $x = 5, y = 2$
(b) $x = -5, y = -4$
(c) $x = 6, y = 2$
(d) $x = -2$ $y = 4$
(e) $x = 1.5, y = 2.5$
(f) $x = 1.2, y = 4.2$
(g) $x = 1.2, y = 0.6$
(h) $x = 1.5, y = -0.6$

P21.2

1 (a) 77 000 000 cm³ (b) 1.2 cm³
(c) 2000 cm³ (d) 68 000 cm³

2 (a) 85.26 cm³ (b) 974.4 cm³
(c) 540 000 cm3 (d) 10.048 cm3

P21.3

1 (a) 22 cm² (b) 3960 cm³

2 (a) 12 cm² (b) 3120 cm³

3 (a) 16 cm² (b) 2720 cm³

4 (a) 15 cm² (b) 3150 cm³

5 (a) 24 cm² (b) 5760 cm³

6 (a) 9.5 cm² (b) 1805 cm³

7 (a) 10 cm² (b) 750 cm³

8 (a) 7 cm² (b) 420 cm³

P21.4

1 (a) 63 cm³ (b) 74 480 mm³
(c) 15.2 cm³ (d) 1862 cm³

2 450 m³, 450 000 litres

3 1544 cm³ (to nearest cm³)

4 18 096 cm³, 18 litres (to nearest litre)

P21.5

1 (a) 4 cm³ (b) 707 cm³
(c) 327 cm³ (d) 182 cm³

2 (a) 314 mm³ (b) 1062 mm³
(c) 201 mm³ (d) 905 mm²
(e) 1140 mm³

3 (a) 511 cm³ (b) 490 cm³
(c) 353 cm³ (d) 494 cm³
(e) 945 cm³ (f) 680 cm3

P21.6

1 (a) 208 m³ (b) 6216 cm³

2 426.924 m³

3 (a) 950 mm² (b) 475 cm³

4 16 960 cm³

5 (a) (i) 14 245 cm³ (to nearest cm³)
(ii) 14.2 litres (1 dp)
(b) (i) 7057 (to nearest cm³)
(ii) 7.1 litres (1 dp)

6 (a) 682.6 cm³ (1 dp) (b) 5296.4 cm³

P21.7

1 59 cm² **2** 864 cm² **3** 6 foot

4 215 cm **5** 71.4 cm² (1 dp)

6 3.2 mm

P21.8

1 r = 1.6 cm (1 dp)

2 h = 5.5 cm (1 dp)

3 h = 5 inches

4 r = 3.0 m (1 dp)

5 l = 2.0 cm (1 dp)

6 a = 5.3 cm (1 dp)

7 h = 3.7 mm (1 dp)

P21.9

1 30 cm² **2** 30 cm² **3** 30 cm²

4 32 cm² **5** 34 cm² **6** 34 cm²

7 36 cm² **8** 48 cm²

P21.10

1 (a) 486 mm² 4.86 cm²
0.000 486 m², cm²
(b) 15 606 mm² 156.06 cm²
0.015 606 m², cm²
(c) 216 000 000 mm² 2160 000 cm²
216 m², m²
(d) 63 375 000 mm² 633 750 cm²
63.375 m², m²
(e) 11 094 mm² 110.94 cm²
0.011 094 m², cm²
(f) 277 350 mm² 2773.5 cm²
0.277 35 m², cm²

2 (a) 416 cm² (b) 52 m²
(c) 113.5 cm² (d) 570.7 cm²
(e) 12.58 m² (f) 4.573 m²

3 (a) 33 750 mm² (b) 337.5 cm²

4 (a) 7342 mm² (b) 73.42 cm²

5 (a) 480 cm² (b) 48 000 mm²

6 162 square inches

7 (i) (a) 36 160 cm² (b) 3.616 m²
(ii) (a) 36 480 cm² (b) 3.648 m²
(iii) (a) 52 860 cm² (b) 5.286 m²
(iv) (a) 14 520 cm² (b) 1.452 m²
(v) (a) 22 440 cm² (b) 2.244 m²
3 litres

P21.11

1 (a) 129.2 cm² (b) 112.28 cm²
(c) 54.16 cm² (d) 1207.6 cm²

2 548.5 m² **3** 781.2 cm² (1 dp)

4 239.46 cm²

P21.12

1 468 m² (to nearest m²)

2 (a) 83.6 m² (b) 113.15 m (2 dp)
(c) 509.5 m² (1 dp)

3 (a) 2.63 m² (2 dp) (b) 2650.75 cm²
(c) 11 505 cm²

P22.1

1 $x = 27$ $y = 54$ **2** $a = 69$ $b = 38$

3 $p = 18$ $q = 6$ **4** $x = 82$ $y = 67$

5 $a = 7$ $b = 42$ **6** $c = 72$ $d = 36$

7 $x = 8$ $y = 4$ **8** $x = 3$ $y = -2$

9 $x = 1\frac{2}{5}$ $y = 2\frac{1}{5}$ **10** $a = -1$ $b = -\frac{1}{2}$

P22.2

1 $x = 4$ $y = 6$ **2** $x = 17$ $y = 3$

3 $p = 10$ $q = 3$ **4** $r = 8$ $s = 2$

5 $u = -3$ $v = -2$ **6** $m = -1$ $n = 3$

P22.3

1 $x = 1$ $y = 5$ **2** $x = -60$ $y = -20$

3 $x = 11$ $y = 4$ **4** $x = 2$ $y = 7$

5 $x = 3$ $y = 1$ **6** $x = 6$ $y = 3$

P22.4

1 (a) $x = 3$ $y = 11$ (b) $a = 3$ $b = -1$
(c) $c = 4$ $d = 2$ (d) $m = 2$ $n = 3$
(e) $p = 2$ $q = -3$ (f) $r = 5$ $s = 3$

2 (a) $x = 0$ $y = 2$ (b) $p = 1$ $q = 3$
(c) $x = 2$ $y = 1$ (d) $a = 1$ $b = 2$
(e) $r = 9$ $s = 2$ (f) $p = 4$ $q = 5$

P22.5

1 $x = 6$ $y = 5$ **2** $r = 2$ $s = 6$

3 $n = 2$ $m = 1$ **4** $m = 2$ $n = -1$

5 $r = 3$ $s = 0$ **6** $p = 1$ $q = 1$

P22.6

1 $x = 3$ $y = 4$ **2** $p = 4$ $q = -11$

3 $n = 2$ $m = -2$ **4** $x = 1$ $y = 1$

5 $a = 3$ $b = 1$ **6** $r = 1$ $s = \frac{1}{2}$

7 $m = 2$ $n = 0$ **8** $x = -1\frac{1}{2}$ $y = -3$

9 $x = 0$ $y = 3$ **10** $r = \frac{3}{10}$ $s = -\frac{1}{4}$

P22.7

1 $x = 3$ $y = -3$ **2** $c = 1$ $d = 2$

3 $p = 1$ $q = 2$ **4** $r = 3$ $s = 2$

5 $x = 2$ $y = 2$ **6** $a = 3$ $b = 0$

P22.8

1 $x = 1$ $y = 1$ **2** $c = 1$ $d = 1$

3 $r = 0$ $s = 3$ **4** $e = 2$ $f = 1$

5 $p = 3$ $q = -1$ **6** $u = 1$ $v = -1$

7 $n = 2$ $m = -1$ **8** $m = 1$ $n = 1$

P22.9

1 $x = 2$ $y = 0$ **2** $a = 3$ $b = 1$

3 $m = 2$ $n = 5$ **4** $e = 2$ $f = 1$

5 $r = 2$ $s = -3$ **6** $e = 1$ $f = 3$

7 $m = 2$ $n = 1$ **8** $v = 1$ $w = -1$

P22.10

1 $m = 1$ $n = -2$ **2** $x = -3$ $y = 6$

3 $x = 2$ $y = -4$ **4** $p = 3$ $q = 1$

5 $r = 1$ $s = \frac{1}{3}$ **6** $a = 2$ $b = \frac{1}{3}$

P22.11

1 (a) $x + y = 30$
(b) $450x + 675y = 14\,850$
(c) $x = 24$ $y = 6$
(d) 24 student tickets and 6 staff tickets

2 (a) $3x + 2y = 1695$ $2x + 3y = 1795$
(b) $x = 299$ $y = 399$
(c) (i) £2.99 (ii) £3.99

3 75 pence

4 7 hours

5 (a) 750 mℓ (b) 150 mℓ

6 43 years old and 13 years old

7 31 Choke and 19 Diet Choke

8 38 and 24

9 John 12; Ian 25

10 Child £8; Adult £12

11 Pizza £1.80; Ice 70 p

12 (a) 95p (b) 60p

13 Silver 3; Gold 7

14 Economy 5; Kingsize 9

P22.12

1 (a) Opposite sides of equal length
(b) $6x = y$ $7x = y + 2$
(c) $x = 2$ $y = 12$ (d) 16 cm by 6 cm

2 (a) 18 cm (b) 8 cm and 16 cm

3 166°, 7° and 7°

4 60°, 120° and 110° **5** 86° and 44°

6 80° and 28° **7** (a) $m = 3$ $c = 11$

8 (1,3) **9** (−1, 1)

P23.1

1 Semi circle radius 28 mm

2 Straight line parallel to the ground 4 inches above the ground.

3 Semi circle, radius = page width

4 Arc 45 cm in radius

5 Curved line parallel to the slope of the slide

P23.2

1 A circle centre A radius 4 cm

2 The perpendicular bisector of AB

3 Two parallel lines, one on each side of CD 3.5 cm from CD and two semi–circular ends radius 3.5 cm.

4 The bisector of the angle between AB and AC

5 A line halfway between EF and GH and parallel to them

6 (a) Circle radius 10 cm centre C
(b) Circle radius 20 cm centre C

7 (a) A circle radius 10.8 cm centre A
(b) A circle radius 13.2 cm centre A

P23.3

1 (a) A circle centre A radius 25 mm
(b) No
(c) The area inside the boundary line

2 (a) 2 parallel lines one either side 1.5 cm away and 2 semi circles
$r = 1.5$ cm
(b) Yes
(c) The area outside and including the boundary line.

3 (a) The perpendicular bisector of CD
(b) No (c) The region with C in it.

4 (a) A line halfway between EF and GH, parallel to them (b) No
(c) The side in which GH lies.

5 (a) The bisector of the angle between LM and LN (b) Yes
(c) The region with M in it.

6 (a) A circle centre at the post radius 2 m (b) Yes
(c) The area inside the boundary.

7 (a) 2 parallel lines 3 m from the rail 2 m long and a semicircle radius 3 m at each end (b) yes
(c) The area inside the boundary.

8 (a) A circle 4 m in radius centre A
(b) Yes
(c) The area outside the barn and inside the circle.

9 (a) A 300 m arc from centre B and the perpendicular bisector of AD
(b) No
(c) Within the arc and on the D side of the bisector.

10 (a) Two arcs centres P and Q 3 m

in radius and a line parallel to the fence 1 m in distance (b) No
(c) The region outside the arcs and the tree side of the parallel line.

P24.1

1 64 mm² **2** 441 cm² **3** 4489 m²

4 1.44 m² **5** 39.0625 m² **6** 0.81 km²

7 51.84 cm² **8** 6889 mm²

9 127.69 m² **10** 12.25 k²

P24.2

1 (a) 9 cm (b) 25 mm (c) 23 m
(d) 41 km (e) 1.4 cm (f) 1.2 m

2 (a) 9.5, 9.49 (b) 13.2, 13.2
(c) 6.6, 6.56 (d) 19.8, 19.8
(e) 12.7, 12.7 (f) 16.7, 16.7

P24.3

1 8.1 cm **2** 7.8 m **3** 3.3 m²

4 6.1 km **5** 8.5 km **6** 10.9 cm

7 18.1 m **8** 13.0 m **9** 7.0 cm

10 16.3 cm

P24.4

1 8.7 cm **2** 14.7 m **3** 6.9 m

4 14.3 cm **5** 35.3 m **6** 6.9 cm

7 0.7 m **8** 6.4 cm **9** 5.7 m

10 6.9 m

P24.5

1 (a) 25 mm (b) 14 mm (c) 50 mm
(d) 19 mm (e) 21 mm (f) 35 mm
(g) 15 mm (h) 44 mm (i) 32 mm
(j) 18 mm

2 (a) 2.36 m (b) 2.1 m (c) 5.4 m
(d) 22 cm² (e) 7.415 m
(f) 13.4 m (g) 53 km (h) 2.4 km

P24.6

1 (a) 1 cm² (b) 8 cm²
(c) 4.5 cm² (d) 6.25 cm²

2 (a) 1 cm (b) 2.83 cm
(c) 2.12 cm (d) 2.5 cm

3 (a) 7.07 cm (b) 14.14 cm
(c) 9.05 cm (d) 3.18 cm
(e) 3.54 cm

P24.7

1 7.4 m **2** 2.19 m

3 Steps 9 feet, slide 20 feet

P24.8

1 170 steps **2** 13.1 km **3** 21 miles

4 65 km

P24.9

1 92 cm **2** 4 m **3** 13 m

P24.10

1 7.8 **2** 3.6 **3** 8.1 **4** 7.8

P24.11

1 121.9 m **2** 129 feet **3** 18.1 inches

4 296 cm

P24.12

1 89.7 m **2** 37.4 m

P24.13

1 14.55 cm **2** 10.4 cm (1 dp)

3 1.89 m (2 dp) **4** 1.7 m (1 dp)

P24.14

1 48.7 cm² (1 dp) **2** 1.15 m² (2 dp)

3 165 763 mm² (nearest mm²)

4 12.21 cm² (2 dp) **5** 5.62 m² (2 dp)

6 152.5 mm² (1 dp)

P24.15

Right angled triangles are: 1, 3, 5, 9, 10

P24.16

1 No. For the wall to be vertical 6.5^2 must equal $6^2 + 2^2$; $6.5^2 = 42.25$ and $6^2 + 2^2 = 40$

2 Yes, since $320^2 = 220^2 + 250^2$ the triangle is right angled.

1 Incorrect answers listed
(a) 231 (b) 63.9883 (c) 2304
(d) 34.780 5426 (e) 5.406 797 777
(f) 17.2543 (g) 0.010 692
(h) 195.3875

2 (a) C 180 (b) D 42 (c) B 1.2
(d) B 0.08 (e) D 3 (f) A 0.06
(g) C 200 (h) D 4000

P26.2

1 (a), (d), (e), (f), (g), (i)

2 (a) 600, 502 (b) 5, 3.28
(c) 210, 280 (d) 2, 1.22
(e) 10, 9.2 (f) 320, 344

P26.3

1 145.6 **2** 46.35 **3** 38.35 **4** 555.8

5 927.2 **6** 233.6

P26.4

1 (a) $\frac{3}{10}$ (b) $\frac{1}{2}$ (c) $\frac{1}{10}$ (d) $\frac{6}{10}$ (e) $\frac{1}{10}$
(f) $\frac{4}{10}$

2 (a) 10, 11.102 (b) 15, 15.282
(c) 133, 126.731 (d) 10, 13.8744
(e) 667, 592.059
(f) 1500, 1318.519

P26.5

1 (a) 0.01 (b) 0.1 (c) 0.001
(d) 0.1 (e) 0.001 (f) 0.1
(g) 0.001 (h) 0.01 (i) 0.01

2 (a) 30, 43.011 (b) 1200, 1436.066
(c) 0.1, 0.134 (d) 50, 58.887
(e) 2, 2.129 (f) 10 000, 17763.413

P26.6

1 (a) $7 \times 5 = 35$ (b) $7 \div 4 = 1.75$
(c) $80 \times 0.3 = 24$ (d) $40 \div 9 = 4.44$
(e) $2 \div 0.5 = 4$ (f) $3 \times (1)^2 = 3$
(g) $\frac{5^2}{5} = 5$ (h) $\frac{7+3}{0.2} = 50$
(i) $\frac{0.5}{600} = 0.0008$ (j) $\frac{30 \times 30}{4} = 225$
(k) $\frac{80 \times \sqrt{4}}{1 \times 20} = 8$ (l) $\frac{30 \times 1000}{10 \times 10} = 300$

2 (a) 36.18 (b) 1.971 (c) 21.68
(d) 4.132 (e) 3.604 (f) 2.489
(g) 5.383 (h) 41.42 (i) 0.000 7980
(j) 227.7 (k) 8.469 (l) 242.1

3 (a) 32.1 (b) 57.9 (c) 4.366
(d) 905.6 (e) 59.7 (f) 7.129
(g) 11.90 (h) 404.1 (i) 1135
(j) 0.024 12 (k) 0.7596 (l) 322.8
(m) 24.55 (n) 37.38

P26.7

1 320×8.84, 2700, 2828.8 FF

2 583×0.625, 360, 364.4 miles

3 $4.7 \times 3.2 \times 2.8$, 45, 42.1 m³

4 (a) 5.6×7.49, 42, £41.94
(b) 8.2×9.79, 80, £80.28
(c) 12.8×4.99, 65, £63.87

5 $3000 \div 28.4$, 100, 105.6 ounces

6 279×1.8, 600, 502.2 minutes

7 $38 \times 7.95 + 17 \times 9.99 + 23 \times 24.99 + 42 \times 4.49$, 1080, £1235.28

8 34×0.47, 15, 15.98 m

P27.1

2 (a) q is the hypotenuse. For the 40° angle, p is 'opposite', r is 'adjacent'. For the 50° angle, r is 'opposite', p is 'adjacent'.
(b) a is the hypotenuse. For angle θ, c is 'opposite', b is 'adjacent'. For angle α, b is 'opposite', c is 'adjacent'.
(c) PQ is the hypotenuse. For angle P, QR is 'opposite', PR is 'adjacent'. For angle Q, PR is 'opposite', QR is 'adjacent'.

3 (a) AC, z, u (b) y (c) s (d) BC
(e) t

P27.2

1 (a) $\frac{YZ}{XZ}$ (b) $\frac{XZ}{YZ}$ (c) $\frac{u}{s}$ (d) $\frac{s}{u}$

2 (a) R, P (b) α, θ

3 (a) $\frac{UV}{UW}$ (b) $\frac{d}{q}$ (c) $\frac{MO}{NO}$ (d) $\frac{f}{g}$
(e) $\frac{q}{d}$ (f) $\frac{v}{u}$ (h) $\frac{BC}{AB}$ (i) $\frac{NO}{MO}$

4 (a) θ (b) V (c) C (d) b

P27.3

1 Tan 67° = 2.358 (3 dp)
tan 23° = 0.424

2 tan P = $\frac{95}{72}$ = 1.319 (4 sf)
tan q = $\frac{72}{95}$ = 0.7579 (4 sf)

3 (a) 0.29 (2 dp) (b) 0.87 (2 dp)
(c) 3.49 (2 dp) (d) 1.15 (2 dp)

4 (a) 0.333 (3 dp) (b) 6.467 (3 dp)

5 (a) 3 (b) 0.1546 (4 sf)

P27.4

2 (a) 0.29 (2 dp) (b) 0.87 (2 dp)
(c) 3.49 (2 dp) (d) 1.15 (2 dp)

3 (a) 0.6249 (b) 1.664 (c) 0.4040
(d) 4.011 (e) 2.356 (f) 0.2309
(g) 6.314 (h) 0.069 93 (i) 0.1495
(j) 0.5985 (k) 1.971 (l) 22.02

4 (a) 0.3249 (b) 0.6009 (c) 4.011
(d) 0.9163 (e) 0.4411 (f) 12.43

P27.5

1 (a) 39° (b) 61° (c) 16° (d) 69°
(e) 23° (f) 29° (g) 71° (h) 80°

2 (a) 20.3° (b) 42.7° (c) 67.9°
(d) 85.2° (e) 29.7° (f) 66.0°
(g) 65.1° (h) 74.4°

3 (a) $\theta = 67.3°$ (b) $\alpha = 36.7°$
(c) $\beta = 61.4°$ (d) A = 27.3°
(e) X = 75.1° (f) P = 34.2°
(g) B = 42.7°

4 (a) 29 (b) 0.7

P27.6

1 q = 59° b = 58° c = 9

2 (a) (i) 31° (ii) 31°
(b) (i) 32° (ii) 32°
(c) (i) 81° (ii) 81°

3 $a = 11.3°$ $b = 78.7°$ $x = 33.1°$
$y = 56.9°$ $p = 79.7°$ $q = 10.3°$
$r = 29.7°$ $s = 60.3°$ $m = 68.0°$
$n = 22.0°$ $g = 28.9°$ $h = 61.1°$

4 (a) $\angle$C = 8.5° (b) $\angle$P = 70.0°
(c) $\angle$Y = 50.2° (d) $\angle$D = 66.0°

5 a = 55.9° b = 68.6°

P27.7

1 (a) 1.53 m (b) 1.43 m
(c) 0.459 km

2 (a) 280.1 cm (b) 122.5 cm
(c) 13.4 cm

3 $a = 2.18$ cm $b = 6.17$ m
$c = 4.05$ cm $d = 38.4$ mm
$e = 0.895$ m $f = 7.67$ km

4 (a) BC = 4.68 cm (2 dp)
(b) RP = 4.76 km (2 dp)
(c) US = 127.82 m (2 dp)
(d) XY = 162.58 cm (2 dp)

P27.8

1 $a = 44.92$ cm $b = 29.9$ mm
$c = 33.23$ cm $d = 9.75$ m
$e = 128.61$ km $f = 5.53$ cm

2 (a) AC = 9.81 m
(b) XY = 6.40 km
(c) OB = 69.94 m
(d) PR = 12.50 cm
(e) EG = 3.49 cm
(f) UT = 1.31 km

P27.9
1 d = 45.0 mm 2 d = 6.99 m
3 θ = 58.7° 4 d = 9.15 cm
5 θ = 35.3° 6 d = 8.74 km
7 θ = 35.8° 8 d = 379 mm
9 θ = 36.7°

P27.10
1 (a) 41.8° (b) 59.3° (c) 545.1°
(d) 26.6° (e) 14.4° (f) 30.7°
A stair lift can be safely installed on the following sets of stairs; (a), (c), (d), (e), (f)
2 72.5 (1 dp) 3 7.84 m (2 dp)
4 4.12 m (2 dp) 5 141.6 yards (1 dp)

P27.11
1 (a) 335° (to nearest °)
(b) 34° (to nearest °)
(c) 143° (to nearest °)
(d) 244° (to nearest °)
(e) 44° (to nearest °)
(f) 309° (to nearest °)
(g) 192° (to nearest °)
(h) 146° (to nearest °)
2 33.7° (1 dp) 3 242.8° (1 dp)

P27.12
1 (a) 7.91 m does not need trimming
(b) 8.85 m does not need trimming
(c) 5.90 m does not need trimming
(d) 12.98 m needs to be trimmed 3 m
(e) 19.63 m needs to be trimmed 10 m
2 20.0 m (1 dp) 3 19.7 yards (1 dp)
4 24.7°, 31.0°, 36.9°, 31.7°, 25.1°, 18.6°
It is dangerous to stare directly into the sun.
5 300 m (to nearest m)

P27.13
1 (a) $\angle$FBT 29° (b) 62.1 m (1 dp)
2 21.5° (1 dp) 3 (a) $\angle$HTL
(c) 124.3 feet (1 dp)
(d) 239.9 feet (1 dp)
4 (a) 123.5 m (b) 20.1° (1 dp)

P28.1
1 (a) (i) $1\frac{5}{8}$" (ii) $\frac{13}{8}$"
(b) (i) $2\frac{7}{12}$" (ii) $\frac{31}{12}$"
2 (a) $= 1\frac{1}{3}" = \frac{4}{3}"$ (b) $= 1\frac{1}{2}" = \frac{6}{3}"$
(c) $= 2\frac{3}{4}" = \frac{11}{4}"$ (d) $= 2\frac{5}{6}" = \frac{17}{6}"$
(e) $= 3\frac{1}{8}" = \frac{25}{8}"$
3 (a) 2 (b) 3 (c) 4 (d) 3 (e) 3
(f) 3 (g) 3 (h) 6 (i) 2 (j) 3
4 (a) $5\frac{1}{2}$ (b) $5\frac{2}{3}$ (c) $2\frac{1}{4}$ (d) $2\frac{1}{2}$ (e) $2\frac{1}{3}$
(f) $1\frac{7}{8}$ (g) $2\frac{3}{10}$ (h) $1\frac{4}{7}$ (i) $1\frac{8}{9}$
(j) $3\frac{7}{8}$

P28.2
1 (a) $\frac{7}{9}$ (b) $\frac{4}{7}$ (c) $\frac{1}{3}$ (d) $\frac{5}{4}$ (e) $\frac{4}{5}$
(f) 1
2 (a) $2\frac{1}{4}$ (b) $1\frac{7}{9}$ (c) $\frac{8}{9}$ (d) $1\frac{1}{8}$
(e) $1\frac{1}{10}$ (f) $\frac{11}{12}$
3 (a) $\frac{3}{5}$ (b) $\frac{1}{7}$ (c) $\frac{1}{4}$ (d) $\frac{5}{8}$ (e) $\frac{2}{9}$
(f) $\frac{1}{8}$
4 (a) $\frac{7}{2}$ (b) $\frac{9}{4}$ (c) $\frac{8}{5}$ (d) $\frac{29}{6}$ (e) $\frac{27}{8}$
(f) $\frac{14}{5}$

P28.3
1 (a) 12 (b) 8 (c) 9 (d) 20 (e) 6
(f) 8 (g) 12 (h) 10 (i) 12
2 (a) $\frac{5}{6}$ (b) $\frac{3}{8}$ (c) $\frac{1}{9}$ (d) $\frac{3}{4}$ (e) $\frac{1}{6}$
(f) $\frac{5}{8}$ (g) $\frac{5}{12}$ (h) $\frac{5}{2}$ (i) $\frac{2}{3}$
3 (a) $\frac{11}{15}$ (b) $\frac{22}{35}$ (c) $\frac{7}{24}$ (d) $1\frac{17}{28}$
(e) $\frac{26}{45}$ (f) $\frac{13}{30}$ (g) $1\frac{11}{12}$ (h) $\frac{19}{30}$
(i) $\frac{25}{36}$

P28.4
1 (a) 4 (b) $3\frac{3}{5}$ (c) $1\frac{2}{3}$ (d) 2
(e) $1\frac{1}{3}$ (f) $10\frac{2}{3}$
2 (a) $5\frac{3}{8}$ (b) $5\frac{3}{4}$ (c) $3\frac{1}{10}$ (d) $2\frac{5}{12}$
(e) $1\frac{11}{20}$ (f) $2\frac{1}{15}$

P28.5
1 $\frac{19}{24}$ 2 $2\frac{16}{21}$ 3 $1\frac{13}{15}$ 4 $3\frac{3}{4}$ 5 $2\frac{20}{21}$ 6 $1\frac{29}{40}$

P28.6
1 $\frac{7}{24}$ 2 $\frac{9}{40}$, no 3 $1\frac{1}{8}$ 4 $14\frac{1}{4}$ m
5 $\frac{5}{16}$ 6 (a) $2\frac{5}{16}$" (b) $\frac{9}{16}$"

P28.7
1 (d) $\frac{5}{14}$ (e) $\frac{1}{2} \times \frac{5}{7} = \frac{5}{14}$
2 (d) $\frac{3}{20}$ (e) $\frac{2}{3} \times \frac{3}{8} = \frac{3}{20}$
3 $1\frac{1}{15}$ 4 $\frac{10}{27}$

P28.8
1 (a) $\frac{5}{16}$ (b) $\frac{8}{27}$ (c) $\frac{12}{35}$ (d) $\frac{35}{72}$ (e) $\frac{3}{20}$
(f) $\frac{6}{35}$
2 (a) $\frac{5}{12}$ (b) $\frac{1}{10}$ (c) $\frac{3}{14}$ (d) $\frac{1}{15}$ (e) $\frac{7}{12}$
(f) $\frac{8}{21}$
3 $\frac{3}{20}$ 4 $\frac{1}{8}$ 5 $\frac{1}{8}$ 6 $\frac{5}{24}$

P28.9
1 (a) $2\frac{1}{6}$ (b) 2 (c) $1\frac{2}{5}$ (d) 1 (e) 2
(f) $4\frac{1}{2}$
2 (a) $2\frac{2}{5}$ (b) 8 (c) $2\frac{2}{5}$ (d) $3\frac{5}{7}$
(e) 22 (f) $13\frac{8}{15}$

P28.10
1 (a) $1\frac{1}{2}$ lb (b) 2 lb
2 (a) $\frac{17}{20}$ ℓ (b) $3\frac{2}{5}$ ℓ 3 $3\frac{1}{16}$ m
4 (a) $1\frac{11}{16}$ m (b) $\frac{9}{32}$ m 5 (a) $\frac{3}{10}$ (b) $\frac{1}{8}$
6 $1\frac{4}{5}$ lb

P28.11
1 (a) 4 (b) 5 (c) 7 (d) 10 (e) $\frac{3}{2}$
(f) $\frac{7}{6}$ (g) $\frac{8}{7}$ (h) $\frac{10}{3}$
2 (a) 28 (b) $3\frac{1}{3}$ (c) $1\frac{3}{4}$ (d) 6
(e) $1\frac{2}{3}$ (f) $\frac{7}{14}$ (g) $1\frac{3}{14}$ (h) $1\frac{1}{3}$
3 (a) $1\frac{1}{3}$ (b) $\frac{3}{4}$ (c) $1\frac{1}{15}$ (d) $\frac{1}{2}$ (e) $\frac{5}{8}$
(f) $\frac{3}{10}$
4 5 measures 5 16 scoopfuls
6 20 risottos

P28.12
1 (a) $\frac{3}{1}$ (b) $\frac{5}{1}$ (c) $\frac{2}{1}$ (d) $\frac{25}{4}$ (e) $\frac{20}{9}$
(f) $\frac{11}{10}$ (g) $\frac{14}{3}$ (h) $\frac{12}{7}$
2 (a) $\frac{1}{3}$ (b) $\frac{1}{5}$ (c) $\frac{1}{2}$ (d) $\frac{4}{25}$
(e) $\frac{9}{20}$ (f) $\frac{10}{11}$ (g) $\frac{3}{14}$ (h) $\frac{7}{12}$
3 (a) $\frac{1}{2}$ (b) $\frac{1}{2}$ (c) $\frac{3}{4}$ (d) $\frac{4}{5}$ (e) $\frac{3}{4}$
(f) 4 (g) $\frac{3}{4}$ (h) $1\frac{1}{2}$
4 (a) $\frac{1}{36}$ (b) $\frac{1}{22}$ (c) $1\frac{1}{5}$ (d) $1\frac{7}{26}$
(e) $\frac{3}{16}$ (f) $5\frac{29}{32}$
5 10
6 12

P28.13
1 9 2 $2\frac{1}{6}$ 3 $2\frac{1}{2}$ 4 $\frac{14}{15}$ 5 1

P28.14
1 (a) 25°C (b) 12.5°C
2 (a) $\frac{1}{3}$ (b) $1\frac{5}{6}$
3 (a) $6\frac{3}{8}$ (b) $7\frac{9}{10}$
4 (a) Perimeter $8\frac{5}{6}$ m Area $4\frac{7}{12}$ m²
(b) Perimeter $19\frac{1}{6}$ feet Area $16\frac{5}{72}$ square feet
5 (a) 38 (b) $393\frac{3}{4}$
6 (a) $2\frac{1}{2}$ square yards (b) 12 cm²
7 (a) 154 cm² (b) 7546 cm²
8 (a) $1\frac{30}{33}$ (b) $1\frac{3}{7}$
9 (a) $9\frac{1}{3}$ square yards (b) $31\frac{3}{4}$ m²

P28.15
1 $3\frac{1}{2}$ 2 $6\frac{3}{4}$ gallons 3 $\frac{13}{24}$"
4 (a) $\frac{3}{10}$ (b) Mr. Able
5 (a) $1\frac{9}{16}$ inch (b) $1\frac{19}{32}$ inch
6 12 cars
7 (a) $\frac{7}{24}$ yard (b) $1\frac{9}{24}$ square yards
8 (a) $\frac{3}{4}$ metre (b) $\frac{5}{8}$ metre (c) $\frac{5}{16}$ metre
9 101 bottles 10 240 litres

11 (a) $\frac{1}{6}$ (b) $\frac{1}{10}$ (c) $\frac{5}{16}$ (d) (i) $\frac{1}{6}$ (ii) $\frac{1}{8}$
12 $\frac{12}{35}$ ohms

P29.1
1 2, 3, 4, 5, …
2 0, –1, –2, –3, …
3 –4, –3, –2, –1, …
4 –3, –4, –5, –6, …

P29.2
2 (a) –2, –1, 0, … Yes
(b) 1, 0, –1, … Yes
(c) –4, –3, –2, … Yes
(d) 5, 4, 3, … Yes

P29.3
1 (a) $x > 3$ (b) $x \leq 6$ (c) $y < 1$
(d) $y \geq 1$ (e) $x < -1$ (f) $y \leq 9$
2 (a) 4, 5, 6, … (b) 6, 5, 4, …
(c) 3, 2, 1, … (d) 1, 2, 3, …
(e) –2, –3, –4, … (f) 9, 8, 7, …

P29.4
1 (a) $x \geq 2$ (b) $x < 2$ (c) $x \leq 2$
(d) $2 \geq x$ (e) $x > 0$ (f) $x > 12$
2 (a) 2, 3, 4, … (b) 1, 0, –1, …
(c) 2, 1, 0, … (d) 2, 1, 0, …
(e) 1, 2, 3, … (f) 13, 14, 15, …

P29.5
1 (a) $x \leq -3$ (b) > -6 (c) $x > -6$
(d) $x > -5$ (e) $-3 < x$ (f) $x \leq 0$
2 (a) –3, –4, –5, …
(b) –6, –5, –4, …
(c) –5, –4, –3, …
(d) –4, –3, –2, …
(e) –2, –1, 0, …
(f) 0 –1, –2, …

P29.6
1 (a) $y > 8$ (b) $n \leq -5$ (c) $x > -2$
(d) $x \leq -4$ (e) $p \leq -1$ (f) $y > -7$
(g) $m < -1$ (h) $y \leq -4$ (i) $r \geq 4$
2 (a) 9, 10, 11, … (b) –5, –6, –7, …
(c) –1, 0, 1, … (d) –4, –5, –6, …
(e) –1, –2, –3, … (f) –6, –5, –4, …
(g) –2, –3, –4, …
(h) –4, –5, –6, … (i) 4, 5, 6, …

P29.7
1 $x < 4$ 2 $y \geq 3$ 3 $p \leq 1\frac{1}{2}$ 4 $x < \frac{4}{5}$
5 $n > 6$ 6 $n \leq 1$ 7 $x \geq 2$ 8 $p < 3$
9 $y > 3$ 10 $n \leq \frac{1}{2}$

P29.8
1 $x > 1\frac{2}{3}$ 2 $x < 10$ 3 $x \geq 4$ 4 $n \leq 1$
5 $x < 2$ 6 $p \leq 1$ 7 $m \leq 1$
8 $y < -1$ 9 $x \leq 6$ 10 $y > -2$

P29.9
1 $x = 2,3$ 2 $x = 0,1$ 3 $x = 3,4$
4 $x = 9,10$ 5 $x = -3,-2,-1,0$
6 $x = 0,1,2$ 7 $x = 0$ 8 $x = 0$
9 $x = 0,1$ 10 $x = -2,-1,0,1,2$

P29.10
1 $1 \leq n < 4$ 2 $-1 < x \leq 6$
3 $-1 < y < 3$ 4 $-3 \leq 15$ 5 $2 < x \leq 5$
6 $1 < y < 4$ 7 $-2 < m \leq 3$
8 $2 < p \leq 8\frac{2}{3}$ 9 $2 \leq n < 4$
10 $1 \leq n < 4$

P29.11
1 (a) $80p + 750$ kg
(b) $80p + 750 \leq 1650$
(c) p = 1, 2, 3, 4, 5, 6, 7, 8, 9, 10, 11
2 (a) $w + 1.5$ metres
(b) $4w + 3$ metres
(c) $4w + 3 < 25$, $w < 5\frac{1}{2}$
3 (a) $(24 + 18)s < 500$
(b) 22 stamps (11 of each)
4 (a) $36n + 85 + 73 \leq 500$, $n \leq 9\frac{1}{2}$
(b) n = 1, 2, 3, 4, 5, 6, 7, 8, 9

5 $20c + 950 \leq 8000$, $c \leq 352$ cars
6 (a) 3ℓ m² (b) $15 \leq 3\ell \leq 24$
(c) $5 \leq \ell \leq 8$
(d) 3 m by 5 m, 3 m by 6 m, 3 m by 7 m, 3 m by 8 m

P29.12
(a) $-3 \leq x \leq 3$ (b) $x \geq 4$, $x \leq -4$
(c) $-1 \leq x \leq 1$ (d) $-9 < x < 9$
(e) $x > 2$, $x < -2$
(f) $x \geq 0.1$, $x \leq -0.1$

P30.1
1 (a) $\frac{14}{19}$ (b) $\frac{11}{19}$ 2 (a) $\frac{13}{20}$ (b) $\frac{3}{4}$
3 (a) $\frac{11}{50}$ (b) 1
4 (a) $\frac{3}{11}$ (b) $\frac{4}{11}$ (c) $\frac{7}{11}$ 5 (a) $\frac{18}{25}$ (b) $\frac{29}{50}$
6 (a) $\frac{2}{5}$ (b) $\frac{1}{2}$ (c) $\frac{7}{10}$
7 (a) $\frac{19}{24}$ (b) $\frac{2}{3}$ (c) 1
8 (a) $\frac{18}{31}$ (b) $\frac{19}{31}$ (c) $\frac{22}{31}$ (d) 1

P30.2
1 (a) 0.8 (b) 0.5 2 (a) $\frac{5}{12}$ (b) $\frac{23}{60}$
3 (a) 25% (b) 55% (c) 45%
4 (a) $\frac{5}{12}$ (b) $\frac{3}{8}$ (c) $\frac{11}{12}$ (d) $\frac{1}{2}$
5 (a) $\frac{3}{5}$ (b) $\frac{7}{20}$ (c) $\frac{3}{4}$
6 (a) $\frac{2}{5}$ (b) $\frac{9}{20}$ (c) $\frac{11}{20}$
7 (a) 47% (b) 34% (c) 53%
8 (a) 55% (b) 45% (c) 67%
9 (a) $\frac{16}{25}$ (b) $\frac{23}{50}$ (c) $\frac{33}{37}$

P31.1
1 (a) 1000 (b) 100 000
(c) 10 000 000 (d) 1000 000 000
(e) 1 000 000 000 000
2 (a) 10^4 (b) 10^8 (c) 10^1 (d) 10^6
(e) 10^8 (f) 10^9
3 (a) 0.1 (b) 0.0001 (c) 1
(d) 0.000 0001 (e) 0.000 01
4 (a) 10^{-2} (b) 10^{-6} (c) 10^{-3}
(d) 10^{-1} (e) 10^{-6} (f) 10^{-9}
5 (a) 2×10^5 (b) 7×10^9
(c) 3×10^{11} (d) 5×10^4
(e) 6×10^8 (f) 9×10^6
(g) 4×10^{12} (h) 8×10^{10}
6 (a) 7×10^{-2} (b) 2×10^{-5}
(c) 9×10^{-3} (d) 6×10^{-1}
(e) 3×10^{-4} (f) 4×10^{-7}
(g) 8×10^{-9} (h) 5×10^{-6}
8 (a) $6000 = 6 \times 10^3$
(b) $2\,000\,000 = 2 \times 10^6$
(c) $70 = 7 \times 10^1$
(d) $900\,000 = 9 \times 10^5$
(e) $0.04 = 4 \times 10^{-2}$
(f) $30\,000 = 3 \times 10^4$
(g) $0.009 = 9 \times 10^{-3}$
(h) $0.5 = 5 \times 10^{-1}$
(i) $400\,000\,000 = 4 \times 10^8$
(j) $0.00008 = 8 \times 10^{-5}$

P31.2
1 (a) 4000, 10^3 (b) 170, 10^2
(c) 916 200, 10^5
(d) 80 600 000, 10^7 (e) 4700, 10^3
(f) 5.3, 10^0 (g) 60.72, 10^1
(h) 12 900, 10^4 (i) 4 100 000, 10^6
(j) 600 000 000, 10^8
The place value is the same as the exponent.
2 (a) 0.03, 10^{-2} (b) 0.0028, 10^{-3}
(c) 0.174, 10^{-1} (d) 0.000 609, 10^{-4}
(e) 0.000 008 42, 10^{-6}
(f) 0.5017, 10^{-1} (g) 7.61, 10^0
(h) 0.004 47, 10^{-3} (i) 0.000 09, 10^{-5}
(j) 0.000 3016, 10^{-4}
The place value is the same as the exponent.

3 (a) 16 000   (b) 0.0507
   (c) 0.00231   (d) 804 000
   (e) 31.9   (f) 0.000 7063   (g) 4.101
   (h) 0.062 05   (i) 0.000 008 74
   (j) 990 900 000

P31.3
1 (a) 3×10^8, 300 000 000
   (b) 2×10^{-3}, 0.002
   (c) 6.5×10^9, 6 500 000 000
   (d) 7.1×10^{-5}, 0.000 071
   (e) 8.94×10^{-6}, 0.000 00894
   (f) 4.02×10^{11}, 402 000 000 000
   (g) 5.009×10^{14}, 500 900 000 000 000
   (h) 9.333×10^{-4}, 0.000 9333
   (i) 1.2345×10^{12}, 1 234 500 000 000
2 (a) 2.4×10^{10}, 24 000 000 000
   (b) 1.12×10^{11}, 112 000 000 000
   (c) 2.8×10^{-10} 0.000 000 000 28
   (d) 2.028×10^{-10}, 0.000 000 000 2028
   (e) 1.2375×10^{12} 1 237 500 000 000
   (f) 6.935×10^{-13} 0.000 000 000 000 000
   6935
3 (a) 270   (b) 49 300   (c) 167 000
   (d) 83.4   (e) 7 200 000   (f) 5040
4 (a) 0.068   (b) 0.000 36   (c) 0.876
   (d) 0.000 004 02   (e) 0.001 59
   (f) 0.000 028
5 (a) 360   (b) 0.0731   (c) 0.0086
   (d) 59 200   (e) 0.09004
   (f) 0.000 004 801
6 (a) 1390 000   (b) 1460
   (c) 0.000 05   (d) 0.000 000 11
   (e) 46 000 000 000
   (f) 0.000 000 000 000 000 000 000
   000 000 000 91
   (g) 140 000 000 000 000 000
   (h) 5970 000 000 000 000 000 000
   000

P31.4
1 (a) 1.5×10^2 (b) 3.4×10^4
   (c) 2.75×10^5 (d) 1.6×10^7
   (e) 8.25×10^2 (f) 4.6×10^6
   (g) 6.45×10^4 (h) 2.1×10^3
   (i) 5×10^5 (j) 7.2×10^{10}
2 (a) 3×10^{-2} (b) 4.7×10^{-3}
   (c) 5×10^{-4} (d) 6.34×10^{-3}
   (e) 1.2×10^{-5} (f) 5.08×10^{-2}
   (g) 3.6×10^{-6} (h) 7.4×10^{-7}
   (i) 8×10^{-8} (j) 9.02×10^{-7}
3 (a) 6.3×10^4 (b) 2.42×10^5
   (c) 2.4×10^{-2} (d) 3.21×10^{-3}
   (e) 5.14×10^4 (f) 5.8×10^{-4}
   (g) 4.7×10^7 (h) 1.3×10^{-6}
   (i) 7×10^1 (j) 1×10^{-7}
4 (a) 2.9×10^4 (b) 1.8×10^{-3}
   (c) 1.7×10^6 (d) 4×10^5
   (e) 2×10^{-2} (f) 3.43×10^3
   (g) 7.5×10^4

P31.5
1 (a) $24.7 \times 10^4 = 2.47 \times 10^1 \times 10^4 =$
   2.47×10^5
   (b) $56 \times 10^7 = 5.6 \times 10^1 \times 10^7 =$
   5.6×10^8
   (c) $0.72 \times 10^3 = 7.2 \times 10^{-1} \times 10^3 =$
   7.2×10^2
   (d) $632 \times 10^{-4} = 6.32 \times 10^2 \times 10^{-4} =$
   6.32×10^{-2}
   (e) $0.395 \times 10^{-2} = 3.95 \times 10^{-1} \times$
   $10^{-2} = 3.95 \times 10^{-3}$
2 (a) 7   (b) −4   (c) 11   (d) −5   (e) 2
3 (a) 2.45×10^5 (b) 5.6×10^8
   (c) 8.74×10^7 (d) 7×10^7

(e) 5.7×10^8 (f) 2.7×10^{10}
   (g) 1.4×10^{-6} (h) 7.34×10^{-8}
   (i) 4.8×10^{-7} (j) 3.1×10^{-7}

P31.6
1 260   **2** 7350   **3** 600   **4** 19300
5 6040   **6** 83   **7** 470   **8** 27.6
9 0.0501   **10** 0.001304

P31.7
1 (a) 7×10^4 (b) 9×10^{-2}
   (c) 8.5×10^7 (d) 2.9×10^{-1}
   (e) 6.05×10^{-3} (f) 5.34×10^8
   (g) 1.817×10^4 (h) 7.4×10^5
   (i) 4.031×10^1 (j) 9.037×10^2
2 (a) 2.1×10^{-3} 4.2×10^{-3}
   4.7×10^{-3} 5.2×10^{-3} 5.3×10^{-3}
   (b) 3.12×10^5 3.19×10^5
   3.25×10^5 3.28×10^5 3.53×10^5
   (c) 1.092×10^6 1.503×10^6
   1.521×10^6 3.157×10^6
   3.298×10^6

P31.8
1 (a) 3×10^9 (b) 2.7×10^{-2}
   (c) 8×10^6 (d) 1.23×10^9
   (e) 4.9×10^7 (f) 9.352×10^{-5}
   (g) 8×10^{19} (h) 1.999×10^{-8}
2 (a) 7×10^1 7×10^8 7×10^{11}
   7×10^{15} 7×10^{20}
   (b) 2.9×10^{-14} 5.8×10^{-12}
   4.7×10^{-10} 8.4×10^{-7}
   9.5×10^{-6}
   (c) 5.29×10^{-23} 6.52×10^{-14}
   8.75×10^{-9} 8.05×10^{19}
   4.31×10^{21}
3 (a) Canopus   (b) Centauri
   (c) Centauri, Sirius, Vega, Arcturus,
   Capella, Canopus
4 (a) 3×10^5 (b) 8500
   (c) 61 000   (d) 150 000 000
   (e) 6.9×10^{-2} (f) 0.00017
   (g) 1.2×10^{-3} (h) 2.7×10^{-6}
5 (a) Sumatra   (b) China
   (c) Sumatra, Borneo, New Guinea,
   Greenland, Indonesia, USA, India,
   China

P31.9
1 (a) 9×10^5 (b) 3×10^2
   (c) 5×10^0 (d) 3.8×10^5
   (e) 1.457×10^7 (f) 2.8×10^3
2 (a) 8×10^{-3} (b) 2×10^1
   (c) 2×10^1 (d) 2.4×10^{-5}
   (e) 3.05×10^{-5} (f) 3×10^3
3 (a) 9.4×10^1 (b) 2×10^2
   (c) 6.3×10^3 (d) 4.5×10^5
   (e) 3×10^1 (f) 2.43×10^{-1}
   (g) 6.8×10^{-5} (h) 3×10^{-5}

P31.10
1 (a) 5×10^2 (b) 3×10^3
   (c) 1.3×10^{-1} (d) 2×10^{-3}
   (e) 1.15×10^{-3} (f) 3.7×10^8
2 (a) 2.3×10^3 (b) 8.996×10^5
   (c) 7.166×10^3 (d) 5.51×10^{-2}
   (e) 8.953×10^4 (f) 6.8015×10^{-1}
3 (a) 9×10^2 (b) 7.96×10^3
   (c) 1.17×10^5 (d) 1.21×10^{-2}
   (e) 9.9×10^{-2} (f) $1.399 98 \times 10^4$
   (g) 4.12×10^4 (h) $2.899 83 \times 10^2$

P31.11
1 (a) 7550, 7.55×10^3
   (b) 30200, 3.02×10^4
   (c) 545, 5.45×10^2
   (d) 7231 900, 7.23×10^6 (3 sf)
   (e) 504.0369, 5.04×10^2 (3 sf)

(f) 0.009562, 9.56×10^{-3} (3 sf)
2 (a) 173 880 000, 1.74×10^8 (3 sf)
   (b) $2.05333333 \times 10^{-6}$, 2.05×10^{-6}
   (3 sf)
   (c) 12.5, 1.25×10^1
   (d) 2428.8, 2.43×10^3 (3 sf)
   (e) 4.008×10^0
   (f) 0.027 403 846 15, 2.74×10^{-2}
3 (a) 3430, 3.43×10^3
   (b) 1513, 1.51×10^3 (3 sf)
   (c) 110 609.7561, 1.11×10^5 (3 sf)
   (d) 18.0927, 1.81×10^1 (3 sf)
   (e) 568.731, 5.69×10^2 (3 sf)
   (f) 28 675.213 68, 2.87×10^4 (3 sf)
   (g) 946.665, 9.47×10^2 (3 sf)
   (h) 0.769 36, 7.69×10^{-1} (3 sf)

P31.12
2 Standard forms for each question
   given
   (a) 1.2874×10^{11} (b) 2.3×10^{-7}
   (c) 7.305×10^6 (d) 9.48×10^8
   (e) 5.2×10^{-10} (f) 4.28×10^{10}
   (g) 9×10^{-6} (h) 9.4762×10^{10}
   (i) $2.516 84 \times 10^{-7}$
   (j) $8.374 64 \times 10^{11}$
3 (a) 8.676×10^{15} (b) 9.568×10^{22}
   (c) 1.144×10^{-14}
   (d) 2.889×10^3 (4 sf)
   (e) 2.471×10^{-4} (4 sf)
   (f) 2.246×10^1 (4 sf)
   (g) 8.869×10^4 (4 sf)
   (h) 9.374×10^{-18}
   (i) 4.742×10^{25} (4 sf)
   (j) 4.090×10^0 (4 sf)

P31.13
1 5×10^{23} **2** 4.5   **3** £1.22 × 10^9 (3 sf)
4 5.03 (3 sf)   **5** £1.56 × 10^9 (3 sf)
6 2.5×10^{-20} grams (2 sf)
7 6.4×10^4 mm^2 (2 sf)   **8** 1.07×10^2
9 5.0×10^{10} seconds (2 sf)
10 (a) 1.63×10^7 (3 sf)   (b) 7.1×10^5
11 4.25 light years   **12** 1.2×10^3
13 (a) 3.81×10^9 miles (3 sf)
   (b) 3.53×10^9 miles (3 sf)
14 (a) 1.51×10^5 km^2
   (b) 1.09×10^5 km^2 (c) 6.3×10^0
15 (a) 4.44×10^9 (b) 7.93×10^1 (3 sf)

P32.1
2 (a) $\sin \theta = \frac{y}{r}$, $\cos \theta = \frac{x}{r}$, $\sin \alpha = \frac{x}{r}$,
   $\cos \alpha = \frac{y}{r}$
   (b) $\sin A = \frac{BC}{AB}$, $\cos A = \frac{CA}{AB}$,
   $\sin B = \frac{CA}{AB}$, $\cos B = \frac{BC}{AB}$
3 (a) R   (b) P   (c) R   (d) P
4 (a) cos   (b) sin   (c) cos   (d) sin
5 (a) sin 50°, cos 40°
   (b) sin 35°, cos 55°
   (c) sin β, cos 21°
   (d) sin C, cos B
   (e) sin α, cos 30°
   (f) sin 25°, cos θ

P32.2
1 (a) sin α = 0.6050, cos α = 0.7983
   (b) sin α = 0.4127, cos α = 0.9127
2 (a) sin β = 0.7983, cos β = 0.6050
   (b) sin β = 0.9127, cos β = 0.4127
3 (a) sin 16° = 0.276, cos 16° = 0.961
   sin 74° = 0.961, cos 74° = 0.276
   sin 32° = 0.530, cos 32° = 0.848
   sin 58° = 0.848, cos 58° = 0.530

P32.3
2 (a) The value of sin θ increases as θ
   increases

The rate of increase lessens as θ gets
larger.
   (b) The value of cos θ decreases as
θ increases
   The rate of decrease lessens as θ
gets larger.
3 (a) 0.5299   (b) 0.9655   (c) 0.9877
   (d) 0.2924   (e) 0.6756   (f) 0.4115
   (g) 0.9976   (h) 0.6018   (i) 0.7193
   (j) 0.8746   (k) 0.7815   (l) 0.1184

P32.4
1 (a) 64°   (b) 43°   (c) 19°   (d) 34°
   (e) 24°   (f) 39°   (g) 37°   (h) 41°
2 (a) 66°   (b) 41°   (c) 57°   (d) 33°
   (e) 53°   (f) 46°   (g) 42°   (h) 63°
3 (a) 31.3°   (b) 39.6°   (c) 7.9°
   (d) 19.2°   (e) 34.8°   (f) 33.7°
   (g) 44.9°   (h) 35.6°
4 (a) 50.2°   (b) 78.8°   (c) 58.5°
   (d) 29.1°   (e) 44.4°   (f) 42.8°
   (g) 50.3°   (h) 41.2°
5 (a) θ = 47°   (b) α = 71°   (c) A = 62°
   (d) B = 11°   (e) W = 28°   (f) V = 23°
   (g) T = 50°   (h) β = 50°   (i) x = 44°
   (j) s = 34°

P32.5
1 (a) 53   (b) 51   (c) 23   (d) 12
   (e) 20   (f) 26
2 (a) 37   (b) 39   (c) 67   (d) 78
   (e) 70   (f) 64
3 a = 55.2°, b = 34.8°, c = 58.7°,
   d = 31.3°, e = 31.1°, f = 58.9°,
   g = 35.3°, h = 54.7°
4 ∠A = 48.2°   (b) ∠O = 63.6°
   (c) ∠U = 43.8°   (d) ∠X = 28.3°
5 (a) 28.1° (1 dp)   (b) 8.05° (2 dp)
   (c) 23.9° (1 dp)   (d) 35.7° (1 dp)

P32.6
1 (a) a = 2.34 cm   (b) b = 1.16 m
   (c) 8 miles   (d) 54.97 mm
2 (a) AB = 3.76 cm   BC = 1.37 cm
   (b) GH = 5.96 m   FH = 6.74 m
   (c) XZ = 6.25 km   XY = 8.44 km
   (d) ST = 2.93 m   TU = 3.93 m
3 (a) p = 84.99 mm   r = 1.48 mm
   (b) b = 4.37 km   e = 1.09 km
   (c) x = 1.23 m   z = 1.58 m
   (d) c = 7.16 km   d = 0.75 km

P32.7
1 (a) h = 5.77 m   (b) h = 8.90 km
   (c) h = 11.13 cm   (d) h = 147.70 km
2 (a) a = 4.35 m   (b) b = 17.69 cm
   (c) c = 2.72 cm   (d) d = 4.48 feet

P32.8
1 (a) a = 6.24 cm   (b) b = 33.05 mm
   (c) c = 3.62 miles   (d) d = 5.83 feet
   (e) e = 31.69 cm   (f) f = 0.26 m
2 (a) 3.43 m   (b) 1.39 m
3 20.59 feet   **4** 2.44 km
5 (a) 18.41 km   (b) 19.75 km
6 22.96 feet   **7** 3.86 m

P32.9
1 40.3 (3 sf)   **2** 81.76 m (2 dp)
3 135.22 m (2 dp)   **4** 23.0 (3 sf)
5 9.06 m (2 dp)   **6** 30.0 (3 sf)
7 2.29 m (2 dp)   **8** 41.1 (3 sf)
9 14.5 m (3 sf)   **10** 26.24 m (2 dp)
11 69.6 ft (3 sf)   **12** 0.014 m (2 sf)

P33.1
1 (a) 1   (b) 3   (c) −5   (d) 10
   (e) −10   (f) −7   (g) 5   (h) −11
   (i) −18   (j) −6

2 (a) –12 (b) –20 (c) –5 (d) –4 (e) –21 (f) –3 (g) –3 (h) –36 (i) –46 (j) –5
3 (a) 1 (b) 3 (c) –48 (d) –23 (e) –6 (f) –36 (g) –63 (h) 22 (i) –9 (j) 21

P33.2

1 (a) 1 (b) 0 (c) –1 (d) 13 (e) 1 (f) –1
2 (a) –18 (b) 2 (c) –2 (d) 4 (e) 8 (f) –7.5
3 (a) –10 (b) 18 (c) –3 (d) 7 (e) 9 (f) –1
4 (a) 1 (b) 6 (c) 36 (d) –3

P33.3

1 5 **2** 2 **3** 23 **4** 17 **5** –2
6 –1.5 **7** 4.5 **8** 14 **9** 1
10 1

P33.4

1 (a) 10 (b) –12 (c) –12 (d) 2 (e) 60 (f) –54
2 (a) –1 (b) 2 (c) –2 (d) –3 (e) –3 (f) –2
3 (a) 3 (b) 8 (c) 15 (d) 35 (e) –27 (f) –6

P33.5

1 (a) –5 (b) 1 (c) –11 (d) 13 (e) 7 (f) 3
2 (a) –6 (b) 12 (c) 36 (d) 10 (e) –20 (f) 100
3 (a) –6 (b) 10 (c) –2 (d) 1
4 (a) 1 (b) 7 (c) –7 (d) –12 (e) –48 (f) 60 (g) 36 (h) 144 (i) 108 (j) –144 (k) $-1\frac{1}{3}$ (l) $-\frac{3}{4}$
5 (a) –18 (b) 2 (c) –2 (d) 80 (e) 320 (f) –400 (g) –800 (h) 6400 (i) –2400 (j) –1920 (k) $\frac{4}{5}$ (l) $1\frac{1}{4}$

P33.6

1 (a) 17 (b) 7 (c) –4 (d) –7
2 (a) 36 (b) 5 (c) 3 (d) –3 (e) –5 (f) 16
3 (a) –6 (b) –2 (c) 1 (d) $-\frac{1}{2}$ (e) 25 (f) 5
4 (a) 20 (b) 16 (c) –44 (d) (i) –5 (ii) –23 (iii) –119

P33.7

1 (a) 17.6°F (b) –4°F (c) 10.4°F
2 (a) –1 (b) 11 (c) –17 (d) 2
3 (a) –165 (b) –371 (c) –1593
4 (a) 3 (b) –5 (c) 2.25

P34.1

1 $\frac{1}{16}$ **2** 90.25% **3** (a) 0.04 (b) 0.64
4 (a) $\frac{4}{9}$ (b) $\frac{1}{27}$

P34.2

1 (a) 0.16 (b) 0.36 **2** (a) $\frac{1}{64}$ (b) $\frac{49}{64}$
3 $\frac{6859}{8000}$

P34.3

1 (a) $\frac{1}{400}$ (b) $\frac{361}{400}$ **2** (a) $\frac{1}{36}$ (b) $\frac{1}{9}$
3 (a) $\frac{1}{9}$ (b) $\frac{4}{9}$

P34.4

1 (a) $\frac{8}{15}$ (b) $\frac{1}{25}$ (c) $\frac{2}{5}$
2 (a) $\frac{1}{8}$ (b) $\frac{1}{2}$ (c) $\frac{3}{8}$
3 (a) 0.76 (b) 0.01 (c) 0.23
4 (a) 0.64 (b) 0.04 (c) 0.32
5 (a) $\frac{49}{100}$ (b) $\frac{9}{100}$ (c) $\frac{21}{50}$
6 (a) 0.343 (b) 0.09 (c) 0.42 (d) 0.784

P34.5

1 (a) (i) $\frac{1}{2}$ (ii) $\frac{1}{2}$
(b) (i) $\frac{4}{13}$ (ii) $\frac{9}{13}$
(d) (i) $\frac{9}{26}$ (ii) $\frac{2}{13}$
2 (a) (i) 0.6 (ii) 0.3
(c) (i) 0.28 (ii) 0.12 (iii) 0.18 (iv) 0.54
3 (b) (i) $\frac{2}{9}$ (ii) $\frac{1}{6}$ (iii) $\frac{1}{3}$ (iv) $\frac{1}{18}$
4 (a) $\frac{1}{4}$ (b) $\frac{1}{4}$
5 (a) (i) $\frac{1}{3}$ (ii) $\frac{8}{15}$
(b) (i) $\frac{14}{45}$ (ii) $\frac{8}{45}$ (iii) $\frac{23}{45}$
6 (a) (i) 0.2 (ii) 0.1
(c) (i) 0.72 (ii) 0.08 (iii) 0.02 (iv) 0.26 (v) 0.98
7 (a) $\frac{4}{25}$ (b) $\frac{4}{25}$ (c) $\frac{1}{25}$ (d) $\frac{8}{25}$ (e) $\frac{4}{25}$

P34.6

1 (a) $\frac{2}{52}$ (b) $\frac{24}{52}$ (c) $\frac{2}{52}$
2 (a) $\frac{7}{20}$ (b) $\frac{1}{6}$ (c) 0
3 (a) $\frac{9}{40}$ (b) $\frac{3}{40}$ (c) $\frac{1}{40}$
4 (a) $\frac{8}{25}$ (b) $\frac{2}{5}$ (c) $\frac{3}{25}$
5 (a) 0.72 (b) 0.26

P34.7

(a) 0.16 (b) 0.18 (c) 0.18
2 (a) $\frac{1}{40}$ (b) $\frac{3}{10}$ (c) $\frac{3}{8}$ (d) $\frac{1}{10}$
3 (a) $\frac{1}{10}$ (b) $\frac{1}{20}$ (c) $\frac{3}{25}$ (d) $\frac{3}{100}$
4 (a) $\frac{2}{15}$ (b) $\frac{3}{10}$ (c) $\frac{1}{3}$ (d) $\frac{7}{15}$
5 (a) $\frac{1}{300}$ (b) $\frac{19}{150}$

P34.8

1 (a) 0.168 (b) 0.168 (c) 0.180
2 (a) $\frac{3}{16}$ (b) $\frac{3}{40}$ (c) $\frac{17}{40}$
3 (a) $\frac{63}{64}$ (b) $\frac{37}{64}$ (c) $\frac{5}{32}$

P35.1

1 (a) 13, 11, 21, 10
(b) 10.5, 7, 14, 7
(c) 17, 14.5, 19.5, 5
(d) 23 s, 19 s, 29 s, 10 s
(e) 15.5 m, 14.5 m, 18 m, 3.5 m
(f) 5.5 g, 2.5 g, 10.5 g, 8 g
2 Median 39 g, range 24 g, lower quartile 35 g, upper quartile 43 g, interquartile range 8 g
3 (a) Median £4522.5, range £6100, lower quartile £3395, upper quartile £6395, interquartile range £3000
(b) Median 89.5, range 6, lower quartile 89, upper quartile 92, interquartile range 3
4 (a) Number 13, 5, 12, 15.5, 3.5
Algebra 13.5, 14, 7.5, 17, 9.5

P35.2

1 (a) Median 4, lower quartile 3, upper quartile 5, interquartile range 2
(b) Median 6, lower quartile 4, upper quartile 7, interquartile range 3
(c) Median 1, lower quartile 1, upper quartile 3, interquartile range 2
(d) Median 1, lower quartile 0.5, upper quartile 3, interquartile range 2.5
2 Cranford Tr. Median 2, lower quartile 1, upper quartile 3.5, interquartile range 2.5
St. Stephens Cl. Median 4, lower quartile 3, upper quartile 8, interquartile range 5

P35.3

1 (a) 28 students (b) 24 students (c) 13 students (d) 25 students
2 (a) 13 plants (b) 48 plants (c) 42 plants (d) 29 plants
3 (a) 39 people (b) 11 people (c) 6 people (d) 29 people
4 (a) 26 people (b) 15 people (c) 29 people (d) 9 people

P35.4

1 (a) 27 students (b) 145 students (c) 37 students (d) 155 students
2 (a) 56 runners (b) 82 runners
3 (a) 45 bulbs (b) 43 bulbs
4 (a) 79 girls (b) 45 girls
5 (a) 64 eggs (b) 76 eggs

P35.6

1 (a) 56 points (b) 38 points (c) 4 players (d) 6 players (e) 66 points
2 (a) 10 cars (b) 36% (c) 37.5 mph
3 (c) 63 runs (d) 36 runs (e) 26 times (f) 110 runs
4 (c) (i) 154 cm (ii) 12 cm (d) 2 certificates
5 (c) 81 (d) 84.5, 77 (e) 7.5 (f) 10 golfers (g) 87
6 (c) 17.5 points (d) 11.5 points (e) 22 points (f) 10.5 points (g) 13 teams
7 (c) 52 mins (d) 14.5 mins (e) 168 runners (f) 38 mins
8 (c) 4075 g (d) 135 g (e) 20 packets (f) 44 packets
9 (c) 46 marks (d) 22 marks (e) 86 students (f) 72 marks
39 marks, 16 marks, 130 students, 59 marks
10 (c) 43 years old (d) 21 years (e) 69 shoppers (f) 8 biscuits
47 years, 16 years, 61 shoppers, 9 biscuits

P36.1

1 (a) iii (b) iv (c) ii (d) ii (e) iii (f) i
2 A and G D, K and N E and L H and M B and J

P36.2

1 (a) F, J and M (b) B, I and N
(c) A, H and O
(d) D, E, K and P
2 A ↔ T, B ↔ P, C ↔ Q, D ↔ R, E ↔ S
3 A ↔ O, B ↔ N, C ↔ M, D ↔ L, E ↔ Q, F ↔ P

P36.3

1 (a) 2 (b) $\frac{1}{2}$
2 (a) 1.25 (b) 0.8
3 (a) 2.74 (b) 0.36

P36.4

1 No **2** yes **3** No
4 (a) A and B (b) 7 m

P36.5

1 x = 5 cm y = 3 cm
2 a = 4 cm b = 7.5 cm
3 c = 3 cm d = 19.5 cm
4 e = 10 cm f = 42.5 cm
5 x = 8 cm y = 60 mm
6 (a) 1.5 (b) 12 cm
7 49.5 cm **8** 65 cm **9** 14.5 cm
10 (a) (i) 1.4 (ii) 0.714
(b) (i) 33.6 cm (ii) 10 cm
11 (a) 1.4 (b) 10.5 cm (c) 7 cm

P36.6

1 No. Building 15 m tall (to nearest m)
2 2.97 m
3 9.4 m

Index